HISTORY
and
PROPHECY

THE ANCHOR BIBLE REFERENCE LIBRARY is designed to be a third major component of the Anchor Bible group, which includes the Anchor Bible commentaries on the books of the Old Testament, the New Testament, and the Apocrypha, and the Anchor Bible Dictionary. While the Anchor Bible commentaries and the Anchor Bible Dictionary are structurally defined by their subject matter, the Anchor Bible Reference Library serves as a supplement on the cutting edge of the most recent scholarship. The series is open-ended; its scope and reach are nothing less than the biblical world in its totality, and its methods and techniques the most up-to-date available or devisable. Separate volumes will deal with one or more of the following topics relating to the Bible: anthropology, archaeology, ecology, economy, geography, history, languages and literatures, philosophy, religion(s), theology.

As with the Anchor Bible commentaries and the Anchor Bible Dictionary, the philosophy underlying the Anchor Bible Reference Library finds expression in the following: the approach is scholarly, the perspective is balanced and fair-minded, the methods are scientific, and the goal is to inform and enlighten. Contributors are chosen on the basis of their scholarly skills and achievements, and they come from a variety of religious backgrounds and communities. The books in the Anchor Bible Reference Library are intended for the broadest possible readership, ranging from world-class scholars, whose qualifications match those of the authors, to general readers, who may not have special training or skill in studying the Bible but are as enthusiastic as any dedicated professional in expanding their knowledge of the Bible and its world.

David Noel Freedman
GENERAL EDITOR

THE ANCHOR BIBLE REFERENCE LIBRARY

HISTORY
and
PROPHECY

THE DEVELOPMENT OF LATE JUDEAN
LITERARY TRADITIONS

Brian Peckham

Doubleday

NEW YORK LONDON TORONTO SYDNEY AUCKLAND

THE ANCHOR BIBLE REFERENCE LIBRARY

PUBLISHED BY DOUBLEDAY
a division of Bantam Doubleday
Dell Publishing Group, Inc., 666 Fifth Avenue, New York,
New York 10103

THE ANCHOR BIBLE REFERENCE LIBRARY, DOUBLEDAY,
and the portrayal of an anchor with the letters ABRL are trademarks of Doubleday, a division of
Bantam Doubleday Dell Publishing Group, Inc.

Portions of this book appeared originally as "The Composition of Hosea" in *Hebrew Annual Review*,
"The Vision of Habakkuk" in *The Catholic Biblical Quarterly* and in *Law in Its Social Setting in the
Ancient Mediterranean*, edited by Baruch Halpern and Deborah W. Hobson, copyright © 1991 by
Sheffield Academic Press; reprinted by permission.

Book design by Patrice Fodero

Library of Congress Cataloging-in-Publication Data
Peckham, Brian, 1934–
History and prophecy : the development of late Judean literary
traditions / Brian Peckham. — 1st ed.
p.   cm. — (The Anchor Bible reference library)
Includes bibliographical references and indexes.
1. Bible.   O.T. — Criticism, interpretation, etc.   2. Bible as
literature.   I. Title.   II. Series.
BS1171.2.P37   1993
221.6'6 — dc20   92-11671
CIP

ISBN 0-385-42348-9

1   3   5   7   9   10   8   6   4   2

April 1993

Contents

Preface

History and Prophecy was written to reconstruct the history of Israel as it was understood and interpreted by the writers of the Bible. It starts at the beginning, pays attention to how and why they wrote, pursues the order and discovers the relationship of their writings, uncovers their sources and explains their interpretations, and articulates the cumulative and progressive contribution of the works to an ongoing, developing tradition. History is the product of historiography, and *History and Prophecy* examines how in biblical days it was done.

The Bible is treated as literature, as the production of a literate society, the creation of people who knew how to read and write for an audience that read and listened and understood them. It is often attributed to an oral culture, "oral" sometimes as if untutored, or "oral" as the unfettered phase before things took shape and words were committed to tablets, time, and permanence. Such a primitive or pristine time sometimes is mentioned and might be imagined but has left no trace in the text. The evidence is, on the contrary, that the text at first was written; that from the beginning it was read and provoked written response; that it was quoted and alluded to in later writings; that what was first composed became a source for the next; that what seemed right or evident to one writer was disputed, corrected, and reinterpreted by another; that nothing of significance in the process was erased or omitted but was inscribed with the rest for all time.

The absence of orality is odd and almost disconcerting. It might be thought that the Bible is coterminous with Israel, that here and there, through design or oversight, something from the most distant past had survived, something unoriginate that would reveal the sources of its life and beliefs. It has, in fact, been thought that the text is a pathetic declension from the realities that once occurred and were celebrated in rituals and worship and handed down from generation to generation until they were written and excerpted, fragmented and sometimes distorted, and inevitably drained of their life. The prophets, in particular, who surely embodied the spirit of their time, have been seen as the victims of time and of editors who meant well but who were not nearly so inspired and who rummaged through their oracles but misremembered their meaning and rearranged them in a lesser mold. But orality is missing, and the Bible, far from being the mirror of a parallel and unwitting reality, or the concomitant of Israel's pilgrimage through the ages, is a product of the late Judean period when a people reflected and took responsibility for its destiny.

Orality has seemed to be the clue to historicity and in its train has fostered a slew of methodologies to match. In tracing the development of late Judean literary traditions, however, it has become clear that history is not something that happened but is the product of research and reflection, the creation of people who understood, arranged, and interpreted their past, and who made choices to find a place for themselves in the future. The critical methods, in turn, have to be altered to appreciate these facts.

The text is read and not rewritten. There are difficult places, some that seem nonsensical, and plenty of chances to go with another version and reduce the idiosyncrasies of the Hebrew text to common sense; but although nothing historical is perfect, it was not fabricated and cannot be undone. The text is read as a whole, from the start, as continuous, meaningful, and complete, with distinctive genres and forms. Its basic units are not critical pieces, with formal and typical structures, that can be detached from their context and assigned to various times and occasions and places, but they are elements of the language—sentences and stanzas and paragraphs that are susceptible to grammar and syntax and that conform to oral and literate norms. Whole texts have parts and were composed with design and acumen by authors with training and skill who meant what they said. They were read and redone by others who knew what they said but meant something different. Together, in sequence and in dependence, they created the traditions that did not exist without their thoughtfulness and determination, the traditions that were not just their heritage from the past but a form of the future they envisioned.

History and Prophecy, like the history that it unfolds, is the product of a literate tradition. It assembles the influences of students, colleagues, and scholarly disciplines under the dominant inspiration of great teachers whose insight and relentlessly free spirit gave the book its impetus and essential form. It depends on what has been written, quotes some of it and alludes to the rest, and waits to be read, corrected, and redone. It is a lot of the past and hopefully a form of the future.

Joyce Rilett Wood discussed the biblical text with me and helped in the preparation of the manuscript. David Noel Freedman was my magnanimous mentor, creative editor, and arbiter of insight and good taste. The bright upbeat people at Doubleday made it all seem easy. To these and many more I am indebted and grateful.

Figures

Abbreviations

AB	Anchor Bible
ANET	*Ancient Near Eastern Texts Relating to the Old Testament*, ed. J. B. Pritchard, 2nd ed. with Suppl. Princeton: Princeton University Press, 1954, 1969
ASTI	*Annual of the Swedish Theological Institute*
BETL	Bibliotheca ephemeridum theologicarum lovaniensium
Bib	*Biblica*
BKAT	Biblischer Kommentar — Altes Testament
BZ	*Biblische Zeitschrift*
BZAW	Beihefte zur Zeitschrift für die alttestamentliche Wissenschaft
CBQ	*Catholic Biblical Quarterly*
ETL	*Ephemerides Theologicae Lovanienses*
HAR	*Hebrew Annual Review*
HSM	Harvard Semitic Monographs
HSS	Harvard Semitic Studies
HTR	*Harvard Theological Review*
HUCA	*Hebrew Union College Annual*
ICC	International Critical Commentary
JAOS	*Journal of the American Oriental Society*
JBL	*Journal of Biblical Literature*
JCS	*Journal of Cuneiform Studies*
JJS	*Journal of Jewish Studies*
JNES	*Journal of Near Eastern Studies*
JQR	*Jewish Quarterly Review*

JSOT	*Journal for the Study of the Old Testament*
JSOTSS	Journal for the Study of the Old Testament Supplement Series
LXX	Septuagint
MT	Masoretic Text
Or	*Orientalia*
OTL	Old Testament Library
OTS	Oudtestamentische Studiën
RB	*Revue biblique*
SBL	Society of Biblical Literature
UF	*Ugarit Forschungen*
VT	*Vetus Testamentum*
VTSup	Vetus Testamentum Supplements
WMANT	Wissenschaftliche Monographien zum Alten und Neuen Testament
ZAW	*Zeitschrift für die alttestamentliche Wissenschaft*
ZTK	*Zeitschrift für Theologie und Kirche*

Introduction

The literature of the northern kingdom of Israel did not survive the Assyrian invasions and the incorporation of Samaria into the Assyrian provincial system. What remains in the Bible is the literature of Judah that was preserved in the libraries of Jerusalem and that survived the sack of the city and became the theoretical basis of its reconstruction. It comprises historical and prophetic works inspired by the fall of the northern kingdom and the prose and poetic works that took their place as the country was reclaimed and the practical problems of restoration were resolved (fig. 1).

History and prophecy were correlative. History was a literate prose tradition, prophecy a schooled poetic tradition. Each was written with a view toward the other, history revealing the reasonable bases of life over time, and prophecy injecting the gathering past with a sense of futurity, willingness, and change. History could be pleasing, instructive, and impersonal. Prophecy was particular, adamant, and demanding. Together they gradually produced a weave of conflicting interpretations that achieved a sensible balance only when prophecy succumbed to the pressure of historical theory, framed by the Deuteronomist and apotheosized in the law, and when history was reduced to programs and practical details.

Symptoms of the reciprocity of prophecy and history can be found in all the writings of the Bible. They know about each other, acknowledge each other as alternative traditions, refer to each other, adopt the other style or mannerism, become what the other might have been. In the gradual development of late Judean literature, the striking individ-

FIGURE 1

The Development of Late Judean Literary Traditions

| | Poetry | | History | Drama |
	Lyric	Elegiac	Prose	Verse
700			Epic	
690	Isaiah			
680			Sequel	
670		Amos		
660			Priestly Writer	
650			Elohist	
640				Hosea
630	Micah			
620				Jeremiah
610		Nahum		
600	Habakkuk			
590		Zephaniah		
570			Ezekiel	
560			Deuteronomist	
550				Job
540	II Isaiah			
535		Joel		
				Obadiah
			II Amos	
530			II Jeremiah	
			Jonah	
			II Ezekiel	
525	II Micah			II Hosea
		II Joel		II Job
520	III Isaiah			
	II Habakkuk	II Zephaniah	II Nahum	
				Song of Songs
		Lamentations	Proverbs	
515			Haggai	
			Zechariah	
	Psalms			II Song of Songs
				II Jonah
500			Chronicler and P$_S$	
				Malachi
			Ruth	
	II Psalms		II Proverbs	
450			Ezra	
			II Malachi	
420			Nehemiah	
			II Haggai-Zechariah	
				Qohelet
			Esther	
300			Daniel	
150			II Daniel	

Figure 1. Dates are relative and approximate.

uality of the traditions gives way to uniformity; conflicting perspectives and expectations are riddled and sifted into sameness; and reciprocity slowly cedes to imitation.

The Sequence of Late Judean Literature

The earliest work is the prose epic narrating the origins of the nation and its adherence to Yahweh. This Yahwist work does not refer to any other Judean literature, but it is indebted to Greek, Babylonian, and Canaanite sources, to late Assyrian political institutions, and to the Transjordanian literary legends of Balaam. It is a history and not simply a story. It has a point—about heroic adventures, Joseph in jeopardy, and the journey to the promised land—and makes it with reference to literary evidence that was familiar and available to independent scrutiny. But it ends in poetry and prophecy, neither of them indigenous to Judah, and in a vision of history unfolding again as it did from the start.[1]

The earliest prophecy is Isaiah's. It is written in poetry but in the same episodic manner as the epic. Its point is that what happened to Israel will certainly happen to Judah, and its prediction worried all its successors. Its historical evidence is much more specific and concrete than the legendary transformation transcribed by the epic, and it disagrees with the epic's wishful thinking. It describes an Assyrian invasion of Judah and a siege of Jerusalem that no one in the city took seriously because they relied on their covenant with Yahweh. It derides this confidence and portrays the epic source that encouraged it as the work of fabulators and storytellers who would be appalled at the outcome of the story.[2] It ends by replacing the epic version of history with its own prediction, which it commits to writing for some later generation to understand (Isa 30:8).[3]

This prompted another historian to write a sequel to the epic, an *Odyssey* to the epic's *Iliad*, that proved the truth of its basic assumptions. This Deuteronomistic sequel defends the treaty and points out that one of its clauses assured the special status of Jerusalem as the place where the people would assemble to worship Yahweh.[4] Then it traces the subsequent history of the kings of Judah to show how this happened. The sequel ends with the Assyrian invasion that Isaiah mentioned, but it describes the miraculous deliverance of Jerusalem at that time to prove that the treaty really worked. It rejects the contrary lesson that Isaiah drew from the fall of the northern kingdom by explaining that

Samaria was captured simply because it had not observed the covenant and had not worshiped in Jerusalem but had gone to Bethel instead.

Amos was next, writing poetry like Isaiah but somber and elegiac and without his lyricism, exploring like Isaiah and the sequel to the epic the reasons for the fall of Samaria and the lesson to be learned to Zion. Amos concedes the sequel's point that it was wrong to worship in Bethel as they did, but he hardly agrees with its confidence in Jerusalem's treaty with Yahweh. He points out that what was wrong with worship in Bethel was that it was financed by oppression of the poor. The place of worship was irrelevant, and the same criticism could apply to Gilgal and Beersheba and Zion. Amos concludes that Isaiah was right and the sequel was wrong, since the covenant is no security and the end is coming on Judah and Jerusalem as it had on Israel and the city of Samaria.[5]

The Priestly writer tried to take account of these prophetic criticisms and added stories and documentation to the histories that drove a middle road between the grandiose vision of the epic and the parochial interests of the sequel. It eliminated the epic covenant and replaced it with a normal created order and with the promise to Abraham concerning posterity, possession of the land, and the peaceful coexistence of nations and kings. It recognized the ancient prerogatives of Bethel but eliminated the pretension of a sacred place and fixed the worship of Yahweh in a movable tent. It recognized the ritual excesses condemned by the prophets and in their place prescribed simpler observances such as the sabbath and the familial celebration of Passover. It gave prominence to the people and emphasized the flaws of their leaders like Pharaoh and Moses and Aaron. But it did not believe with Amos that the end was really coming or with Isaiah that what was written would inevitably happen, since the end had come in the great flood and would never be again, and since other things happen freely at the creative instigation of God.[6]

The problem with the Priestly interpretation, apart from its cosmopolitan and tolerant outlook, was that it omitted reference to Joseph and to the subjugation of the northern kingdom and also failed to deal with prophetic concern for injustice and crime. This lack was supplied by the Elohist history, which retouched the epic from a North Israelite, legal, and prophetic point of view. Joseph was included among the patriarchs, and their stories were changed to include critical circumstances — such as deportation and the possibility of death — that clarified the constant operation of divine providence. Worship at Bethel was legitimized by association with the story of Jacob, and the golden calves of the northern kingdom were traced to the original will of the people and the honest inspiration of Aaron. Instead of the covenant on Sinai there was the law, and instead of secure possession of the land there was the promise of angelic presence and continual guidance. The local and national pretensions of the epic and its sequel were snubbed. In the Elohist version God is so named, and not Yahweh, and speaks to Moses in person and to other leaders in dreams. Reuben, not Judah, is the spokesman for the brothers, and Ephraim and Manasseh are preeminent among peers. Mount Moriah in Judah becomes notorious for the sacrifice of children, and its Passover is replaced by Massot, but Shechem and Bethel remain for the Elohist famous centers of worship endowed with the presence of God.

Hosea was also sympathetic to the northern heritage but could not quite agree with the Elohist's optimism or with plain historical sense. He views history as a ritual performance that is gradually abstracted from the rites of Baal to be enacted by Yahweh and the traditional personifications of Israel. The scene is set with the marriage of Yahweh to the land of Israel and with the birth of unwanted children from the land's insinuations with Baal. With this the epic covenant is abolished and replaced, in accordance with the perspective of the Priestly version, by the covenant of created cycles. These cycles are represented in the rituals of death and resurrection, correspond to the seasons, and are illustrated in the history of Israel and in the stories of Jacob and Ephraim. In Hosea's interpretation, Ephraim has died and Judah is subject to the same fate, but Ephraim is destined to return, and eventually historical fact is bound to yield to ritual expectation.

Micah, on the contrary, was interested in the historical realities confronting Judah and Jerusalem and was concerned to defend the insights advanced by Isaiah and Amos. He transformed the enemy invasion and siege of the city that Isaiah saw into a belligerent manifestation of Yahweh against Zion and the people of Jerusalem. He blamed it, as Amos did, on greed. He insisted, against the sequel to the epic and common belief, that Jerusalem was neither privileged nor secure. He summarized the epic and its sequel and drew contrary conclusions from the history that he retold. He followed Hosea's lead in inserting himself into his text, but he disagreed with Hosea in taking no solace from the seasons and took what comfort he could as a witness to the truth.

Jeremiah tried to reconcile the conflicting opinions of the prophets and the perennial optimism of the historians. He chose a dramatic format with competing and discordant voices and a plot that moved from scene to scene until it reached a sudden climax and a final denouement. He starts with the history of Israel as Hosea and the histories had described it and attributes the fall of Ephraim to the faults of a stubborn child who is now learning his lesson in exile. He applies the lesson to Judah and Jerusalem by repeating Isaiah's vision of enemy invasion and siege of the city, and by taking the end of the world that Amos described and tempering it with the worldly realism of the Priestly writer into a moderate and meaningful discipline. He imitates Micah by making himself the paradigm of prophecy and shows himself an advocate of the Elohist law against those who relied on the covenant. The drama that he presents reaches a sudden climax in the weeping and wailing and sadness of the city, and the plot is resolved in the return of the child Ephraim to his mother Rachel in Zion. The boldness of this dramatic presentation, the sweep of its original synthesis, its triumphant amalgam of prophecy and history, the reconciliation that he envisaged and that did not take place, all made Jeremiah a pivot of tradition and a controversial figure for some time to come.[7]

Nahum soon rose to the challenge with a witty and chilling riposte. The centerpiece of his prophecy is a brilliant little poem on the fall of Nineveh, completely unobjectionable in theory and in fact to any self-satisfied Judean of the late seventh century. However, he prefaced it with a traditional ditty that took the covenant seriously but turned it against its admirers and subtly contradicted Jeremiah's sanguine view of an impending but manageable catastrophe. Not to be too subtle, he concluded with a ballad warning Jerusalem that it was next now that the capitals of Egypt and Assyria had succumbed to the onslaught of Yahweh's wrath.

Habakkuk agreed with Nahum when he saw that the Chaldeans were coming. He reiterated Isaiah's vision of invasion and defeat and accepted the inevitability of what was written. But he was also influenced by Jeremiah's confidence in the stability of the created order, and he composed the kind of lament that Jeremiah had prescribed. In the end he recalled the original victory of Yahweh in the battle of creation and, despite the gloom and his grim prediction, took comfort in the thought.

Zephaniah also agreed with Nahum but appealed to the sayings of Amos. He thought, as Amos predicted, that the end of the world was coming. But he thought it would be the end of all creation and he could hardly share Habakkuk's hope. The only chance that he saw was in the country's conversion and willingness to do what was right. But since the government and agencies of change were corrupt, and since the people had not learned anything from the recent destruction of Philistia and Assyria, Zephaniah did not believe the end would be averted.

The first big change in the literature came with Ezekiel. Jerusalem had been captured; he was in Babylon; and dire warnings about impending doom, no matter how cleverly put, seemed pretty tasteless. But the weight of tradition impelled him and he wrote as others dictated. He wrote prophecy, however, as if it were history, in prose. He began at the end, in the thirtieth year of his exile, with a vision that made sense of what had happened. Then he went through the last days of Judah and Jerusalem, explaining the earlier historical accounts and showing bit by bit what the earlier prophecies meant, until he came full circle to the complementary vision of a new beginning. His work was a vast imagining with local, national, international, and cosmic dimensions, blocked at either end with a sense of divine immanence, unraveling as it went the mysteries of death and resurrection. It was comprehensive, but it was too much to digest and it marked the beginning of the end of prophetic inspiration.

A more reasonable and convincing alternative as provided by the writer of the universal Deuteronomistic History. This person was impressed by the prophetic tradition, less by the specific things that it said than by its persistence in saying them, more by its proof that history was rational and predictable than by the personality and individuality of its bearers. The History, then, set out to establish once and for all the cause of the fall of Jerusalem and the necessary principles of the nation's survival. It began at the beginning, collating and expanding the earlier histories to situate Israel and Judah in the history of the world. Its high point was the book of Deuteronomy and the Mosaic promulgation of the law in which it presented both a systematic reworking of the Elohist code and a typological abstraction of Jeremiah's involvement in its promulgation. It ended with the reform of Josiah, which illustrated the boundaries and inadequacies of the epic covenant, and with the fall of Jerusalem, which proved to the contrary the truth and limitless application of the law. In the Deuteronomist's history the law is its own justification. It is the drift of history and the message of the prophets and sin is its surd. Its observance is life. Its neglect invariably is punished by death.

It was a splendid synthesis of historical and prophetic tradition. Suddenly everything fit and made sense. Or almost. The Deuteronomistic system worked only by conflating, homogenizing, submerging, changing, and generalizing sources and traditions. Not everyone could agree, but everyone had to take a position with respect to it, and almost immediately an array of more or less talented scholars began to bring the literature into line with its vision.

The most famous reply came from Job. It was written in prose and poetry. The prose mimics the historical mannerisms of the Deuterono-

mist with its patriarchal, archetypal, and cosmological elements combined in an interesting, instructive, and moralizing story. The poetry
takes up where prophecy left off and follows the story in dramatic acts
and sequences. As the Deuteronomist theory goes, sin is punished and
punishment is a symptom of sin. Job disputes it, but everybody else
believes it—except God, who scolds Job for even considering it, and
who simply assumes that among the many amazing things that occur
and are worth knowing bad things happen for no reason at all. The
reply is clever, but it had little effect, and later someone revised the
book to agree with the Deuteronomist's position and put Job in his
place.

The next writer to take a position was the author of II Isaiah. This
update emphasized points of disagreement between Isaiah and the
Deuteronomist concerning history and the prophetic tradition. In the
Deuteronomistic interpretation the nations were Israel's natural adversaries and were inimical to the proper worship of God, but in the
opinion of Isaiah and II Isaiah the nations did what God wanted them
to do and in better times would even worship in Zion. In the History,
law was the basic motive and meaning of events, but the Isaiahs thought
that it was truth and justice that made the world go round. Isaiah was
the only true-to-life prophet mentioned in the History and the Deuteronomist had misquoted him mainly to show that the sequel to the epic
was wrong in its glowing opinion of Hezekiah. II Isaiah quoted the
whole story of Hezekiah but rewrote it first in oracular form to prove
that the sequel was right, that Hezekiah was the paradigm of the future
Davidic king, and that the original Isaiah was in basic agreement with
it.[8] The Deuteronomist was disdainful of the individual prophets whose
writings are preserved. The History told an unflattering story about
Amos, dramatized Micah's conflict with the prophets but associated
him with the court of Ahab, tinged the itinerant prophets of the North
with Ezekiel's madness, and included a snide allusion to Jeremiah in
the guise of Huldah the prophet, who encouraged Josiah to think that
all would be well with his reform and ultimately misled him.[9] In
response, II Isaiah repeated what Jeremiah had said about prophecy
falling on deaf ears and made Jeremiah's troublesome prediction of the
reunion of Rachel and Ephraim the model of his own account of the
reunion of Jacob and Sion and of universal harmony.

The librarian who revised Micah's prophecy used the occasion to
quote and correct II Isaiah toward agreement with the Deuteronomistic
viewpoint. The Isaian irenics are replaced by antagonism toward the
nations, who have to be punished before they become acceptable to
Yahweh. The future Davidic king will fulfill II Isaiah's expectations,

but he will be a humble viceroy of Yahweh. The universal reprieve that II Isaiah described is partial in this version, and only a remnant will be spared to return from exile. Apparently this librarian or archivist was convinced that there was too much at stake in the Deuteronomistic position to be undone by faith or hope or inspired writing.

Different approaches to the Deuteronomistic History were taken by Joel, Obadiah, and Jonah. Joel treats the fall of Jerusalem as a natural disaster, a plague of locusts, that the people can overcome by prayer and penance. There is not a hint of sin or guilt or historical necessity as God responds to their lament by driving the locusts out of the land and bringing the gentle rains that make up for the crops that they lost in the bad years. Obadiah, on the other hand, simply ignores the historical theory imposed by the Deuteronomist, deals with the facts, and blames the Edomites for their part in the siege of the city. Jonah parodies the Deuteronomistic claim that the fall of Jerusalem was the inevitable result of the sin of Manasseh and of disdain for the message of the prophets. It begins with a story of the prophet who was sent to help but, being unwilling to go, brought evil on a totally innocent people, who could be saved only by killing him. It ends with the other side of the story, in which the prophet reluctantly goes to Nineveh, where everyone, from the king to the cattle, repents and is saved simply because God is merciful and mightily impressed by the size of the city. Nineveh, in Nahum and Zephaniah, was the symbol and antitype of Jerusalem, and Jonah's point could hardly be missed.

In time this wit and wisdom wore thin. Jonah was written in prose but a later edition added a poetic prayer that made him submit to the Deuteronomistic point of view.[10] Obadiah acquired a context and a kind of orthodoxy by incorporation into the book of Jeremiah (see Jer 49:7–22). Joel was turned into a typically prophetic diatribe against the nations and was adjusted further to suit the moral and religious outlook of the now-standard history.[11]

Some of their successors were impressed by the History and others took a more critical view. The writer who redid Amos, for instance, was a total adherent of the Deuteronomistic system and revised his prophecy to include the law and the curses attending its neglect, prosaic stories and stereotypes about the prophets, historical summaries and signs of divine transcendence, and the Deuteronomistic theory of punishment for sin and its corollary of innocent survivors. Jeremiah's poetic drama, on the other hand, was saved in a history of the last days of Judah and Jerusalem that copied and mimicked the Deuteronomistic History but also dealt with its disdain for the prophet and with its completely incredible ending.[12] This history shows that Jeremiah was

not one of the lying prophets, since his misdated predictions eventually
came true. It associates him with Josiah and blames the fall of the city
on the ignorant policies pursued by Zedekiah. It assimilates the prophet
to Moses and gives the word of Yahweh priority over the law. It
includes a reference to the sin of Manasseh, but it replaces the
Deuteronomistic idea of inevitable punishment for sin with the fact
that the kings and the country consistently refused to listen to the
words of Jeremiah until finally he became exasperated and was unable
to intercede.

The scholar who undertook Ezekiel was far more favorably disposed to the History, if not for its theory, at least for its amazing
collection of facts. This version undermined the originality and idiosyncrasies of the prophet's vision by adding touches that made him seem
personally bizarre, and it undid the mystique of his speculation with
common knowledge and comforting thoughts. Ezekiel saw visions of
God in the sky that the new edition explained by analogy with the
Deuteronomist's conception of the appearance of God in the temple
enthroned upon the cherubim. Ezekiel recited history as prophecy and
the revision, inspired by the revision of Jeremiah, dotted it with
biographical notes on the prophet. Ezekiel wrote from a Babylonian
perspective, but the new edition of his work was written from a
Jerusalem point of view. He explained the prophetic tradition in Israel,
but his editor was interested in conventional topics such as kings and
institutions, historical paradigms and primordial events, the surrounding nations, the justification of God and the law, and the relations
between Israel and Judah. Ezekiel described a new beginning, but the
scholar who redid his work assimilated it to the ancient order that had
been described by the Deuteronomist.

The revisers of the prophetic works, especially after the book of
Jeremiah had argued that prophecy had preeminence over the law,
were anxious to establish a uniform prophetic tradition to balance the
growing consensus being forged between prophecy and the Deuteronomistic History. Hosea's artistry, for instance, was fitted out with
pseudo-historical references that brought his interpretation into line
with the theory of the Deuteronomist, but it was also adorned posthu-
mously with typically prophetic devices, including the now standard
apologies for punishment and predictions of popular conversion and
divine restoration. Nahum's vision, similarly, was dotted with ideas
and attitudes mirroring the Deuteronomist's ideology and, since it
seemed to have nothing prophetic about it, was pointed with prophetic
jargon, with a blatant quotation from II Isaiah, and with obvious
allusions to Joel. The writer who redid Zephaniah's prophecy made it

clear that, in accordance with the law, only the guilty had been punished, but also indulged in the now common prophetic reviling of the neighboring nations, and took part in the current debate on the relative merits of the remnant that had remained in Judah or was returning from Babylon. Some elements in the revision of Habakkuk turned it into a more or less typical prophecy; others adapted the Deuteronomistic theory of retribution to prove that people in Jerusalem had suffered unjustly, and the remaining hymnic parts that did not fit either concern or the developing perception of prophecy were put into an appendix. The whole process of revision came to a climax in the work of the third Isaiah, who recapitulated the prophetic spirit and set history on the road to apocalyptic.

The effect of the Deuteronomistic synthesis was to bring prophecy and history to a close. When the spate of revisions was finished, poetry was used for prayers, lamentations, aphorisms, and songs. Prophecy soon became an interpretation of recent history written in prose and eventually gave way to stories and legends. History acquired characteristics of prophecy and was rewritten as biographical record or projected as apocalyptic onto a future world of fantasy. The law had been promulgated and sealed in the History, but it underwent expansions and amendments authorized by the prophetic revisions and it was corroborated by the wisdom of the ages.[13] The literary renaissance abated, but the debate with the Deuteronomistic system continued to the end.

Sometime after III Isaiah, Lamentations redid history and prophecy as a prayer.[14] The contemporary Song of Songs is lyrical about life and explicit about the physical expression of love to which Isaiah, Hosea, and Ezekiel had alluded, and it illustrates a nonprophetic use of the poetic and dramatic traditions familiar in their works and in the writings of the other prophets.[15] In the same milieu Haggai authorized the rebuilding of the temple by appealing both to the chronology of the book of Jeremiah and to the religious significance of the seasons and the agricultural calendar.[16] Zechariah was a younger contemporary who thought that the temple should not be rebuilt until the people settled their differences and Yahweh returned to his place. At about the same time the Chronicler rewrote the Deuteronomistic History, starting with Adam, as the Deuteronomist did, but reinstating the Judean and monarchic values of the sequel, eliminating the History's conflict with Isaiah and its slight to Jeremiah, tracing the idea and institutions of the temple to the time of David and keeping the prophets alive as singers of liturgical songs. In keeping with this mood the book of Ruth revived the hope of a Davidic restoration, the Song of Songs was associated with Solomon, the book of Proverbs was linked to him and to Hezekiah, and there was a first edition of the Psalms from which Jonah could improvise in the belly of the whale.

Later in the Persian period Ezra gave an account of the building of the temple and of the revival of Judean nationalism. The book of Nehemiah ignored Ruth's appeal for tolerance but also went over Ezra's account to correct it and elaborate on the political structure and the religious expectations of the restored community.[17] In response to their exclusive outlook and to their neglect of the promise to the house of David—but in agreement with the perspective of Haggai, Zechariah, and the Chronicler—a later writer undertook a revision of these works to designate Zerubbabel the legitimate successor of David and to make Joshua the appointed priest. The same writer composed the second part of Zechariah's prophecy in an apocalyptic mode by projecting a deliberately garbled version of past events into the future in order to express the current ideal of independence from Persia. Esther was an excellent tale in the same vein, and the first version of the book of Daniel looked forward to a revival of national pride in the bright new Hellenistic age.[18]

The Chronology of Late Judean Literature

The literature is late and local and mostly undated, but it can be aligned in a relative typological sequence and attached at a few discrete points to absolute chronological tables. Its date and provenance frustrate Near Eastern analogies and disappoint the antiquarian expectations created by the Deuteronomistic Historian. In effect, late Judean literature is coterminous with early Greek literary traditions and is a product not of national origins and early enthusiasm but of Judah's final independence from the kingdom of Israel. The contrary expectation—that the literary traditions are contemporary reflections of historical origins, organization, and expansion—is due in part to Israel's intermediate position among ancient and erudite nations, and in part to the impression created by the Deuteronomistic theory of history, according to which Judah flourished in the beginning, in the time of David and Solomon, and then gradually and inevitably declined.

The epic is the earliest composition, because subsequent works suppose it and it presupposes none of them. But the only evidence for its date is its position at the head of the sequence and the date of its sources. Its priority places it sometime before 701 B.C.E. since the events of this year are ignored by it but are described and disputed by

Isaiah and the epic sequel. Its main Babylonian sources, *Enuma elish*, *Gilgamesh*, and *Atrahasis*, are not useful in deciding its date, since the edition it used cannot be determined. Its Assyrian sources are the theory and practice of vassal treaties, but since they are not specifically literary, and since the policy they represent flourished in the Neo-Assyrian period but can be traced to Middle Assyrian times, they are a prime analogy for the epic but do not fix its date. Its Israelite or indigenous source is the legend of Adonis, which underlies the story of Joseph, but it too has neither literary nor chronological substance. However, its sources that can be dated give it a literary context in the latter part of the eighth century. Its Greek source is the tradition of the demigods and heroes who were destined to die in the Trojan War, which it knew from Hesiod's account and adapted for its own story of the sons of God and the daughters of men and the primordial heroes whose presumption precipitated the flood.[19] Its Transjordanian source is the story of Balaam that is known from a late eighth century inscription from Deir 'Alla (ca. 750–700).[20] These sources give the epic an air of alienation and antiquity, but it is clearly a historical work about earlier times to which it certainly does not belong.

The prophecy of Isaiah is built around the invasion of Judah and siege of Jerusalem by Sennacherib in 701 B.C.E. The prophecy does not mention the Assyrian king by name, but its description of the events generally corresponds to other accounts, and more than a hundred years later II Isaiah used the Deuteronomistic version of the same campaign to comment on it (see 2 Kings 18–19; Isaiah 36–37). Its interpretation, besides, and its affront to the epic covenant were challenged almost immediately by the sequel in a different and more detailed account of the invasion and its political implications. Isaiah's prophecy, consequently, is later than 701 B.C.E. and earlier than 681/680 B.C.E., the year of Esarhaddon's accession to the throne of Assyria and the last date mentioned in the sequel. It is clear from Isaiah's response and the prompt reply by the sequel that the epic was not a literary exercise or an ancient document but a novel composition with contemporary implications.

The sequel to the epic ended with the reign of Hezekiah in Judah (ca. 715–687 B.C.E.) and with the death of Sennacherib in Assyria (681/680 B.C.E.). It provoked or influenced a series of works composed before the end of the seventh century and must have been written during the reign of Manasseh (687–642 B.C.E.), a vassal of Esarhaddon and contemporary of Asshurbanipal of Assyria (669–627 B.C.E.). The lowest limit of this series is defined by the work of Jeremiah, which the book of Jeremiah, with its flair for accurate chronology, dates around

627 in the thirteenth year of Josiah (640–609 B.C.E.). This means that seven Judean classics were composed in a period of about sixty years — the sequel to the epic, Amos, the Priestly commentary, the Elohist version of the epic, Hosea, Micah, and Jeremiah — and during a corresponding period of literary ferment in Assyria. There is no other evidence to support the chronology of these works, but it does assemble in one place and in one regime all the elements that prompted the reform of Josiah and forced the Deuteronomist's interpretation of his reign.

The contrary evidence is the traditional chronology of these works, which is suggested in part by hypothesis and in part by the texts themselves. There are alternative dates for the epic sequel, but these have no justification apart from the different literary and historical reconstructions on which they depend. An earlier date for Amos is also just a matter of interpretation: it is based either on the edited text, which brought his work into line with Deuteronomistic opinion by pitting him against a composite and typical Jeroboam, or on the failure to perceive that prophecy addressed the future in terms of the past, or on the supposition that Amos predicted the fall of Samaria rather than the fate of Jacob and Zion.[21] There is no good evidence either for the date of the Priestly document apart from its relative position in the series, but a late date is based on attributing to it material that belongs to the Deuteronomist or to the later pentateuchal supplement.[22] The Elohist is often thought to have been an early northern variant to the epic, when in fact it merely touched up the epic to take issue with Judean parochialism.[23] Hosea was familiar with all the earlier literature, but it was his editor who made him a contemporary of Isaiah and Amos in the eighth century.[24] Micah redid Isaiah and gave urgency to his prophecy, and his editor naturally thought of him as a younger contemporary of Isaiah.[25] For all these authors, in fact, there is not any evidence to contradict or outweigh their place in the development of Judean literary traditions.

Nahum wrote after the Assyrians captured and plundered Memphis (671 B.C.E.);[26] after the fall of Nineveh to the Babylonians (612 B.C.E.), Habakkuk alluded to Nebuchadnezzar's western campaigns (Hab 1:5–11)[27] and Zephaniah referred to the fall of Nineveh, to the battle of Carchemish (605 B.C.E.), and to Babylonian campaigns against Philistia and Egypt (604–601 B.C.E.) (Zeph 2:4–5, 12–15). Their relative dates are determined by the literary evidence.

Ezekiel dated his prophetic history between the sixth year and the thirtieth of the imprisonment of Jehoiachin in exile (592–567 B.C.E.). The Deuteronomistic History was slightly later and was written sometime after Jehoiachin's release from prison in the thirty-seventh year of his exile and in the first year of the reign of Amel-Marduk, king of Babylon (562–560 B.C.E.).[28] There is no independent evidence for the date of Job. II Isaiah mentioned the accession of Cyrus and the fall of Babylon (539 B.C.E.). Joel wrote after the temple in Jerusalem had been plundered and took sides with Job and II Isaiah against the Deuteronomist. Obadiah described the fall of Jerusalem and was known to the editors of Amos and Jeremiah. The revision of Jeremiah traces the history of Judah to the middle of the sixth century, perhaps as late as the seventieth year after the exile of Jehoiachin (527 B.C.E.), but is dated more certainly only in relation to the literature that it cites.[29] Jonah can be dated by the literature it quotes; the later prophetic revisions can be arranged in relative order; and the early poetic writings such as the Song of Songs, the book of Lamentations, and Proverbs can be set in a typological sequence.

Haggai and Zechariah wrote in the last quarter of the sixth century, after the second year of Darius I (521–486 B.C.E.) but before the rebuilding or restoration of the temple had been completed. The prophet Malachi was slightly later and critical of the rituals that were being performed in the temple. The first edition of the Psalms is presupposed by the revision of Jonah and by the work of the Chronicler. They have no absolute date but they, along with the second edition of the Psalms and the revision of Proverbs precede the composition of Ezra and Nehemiah in the latter half of the fifth century. The book of Ruth takes a position with respect to the Chronicler's reticence on the restoration of the Davidic monarchy. Malachi was revised to agree with the perspective of Ezra and to seal the law and the prophets. The writer who redid Haggai and Zechariah witnessed the decline of the Persian empire and brought their works into line with the monarchic bias of the Chronicler's history and earlier messianic expectations. Qohelet was less optimistic. Esther and Daniel presuppose the Greek revival and the advent of Hellenistic civilization. Daniel was redone in the second century to deal with the hopes that had been dashed. History was finished, and in their own way the prophecies had been fulfilled.

The Characteristics of Late Judean Literature

Although the literature is locally and temporally restricted and sometimes partial or intolerant, its predominant tendency is to inclusion, comprehension, and universality. It is an obvious characteristic of the late Judean mentality manifested in these works to aspire to centrality and eminence in an ongoing and enveloping world. This could lead to fear of assimilation or to denunciations of arrogance among later politicians and scribes, but the spirit showed itself in imitation and innovation, and in the development of standards of excellence in schools devoted to literature, history, geography, music, law, mathematics, and international relations. It was this thorough intrusion into its world that in time turned Judean literary traditions into a traditional literature of the world.

The epic related the journey of the ancestors of Jacob and the sons of Israel from the four corners of the world to the land of Canaan. In its temporal sequence Abraham came from the east after the great flood and as part of the universal migrations that occurred when an original common language was reduced to incomprehensible dialects. His son Isaac, born many years later, lived among the Philistines who had settled in the south. His grandson Jacob was affiliated to the Arameans in Assyria, and most of his children were originally from Mesopotamia. Israel, the ideal and destiny of Jacob, is associated only with the land of Canaan, but the children of Israel — Judah and Simeon and Joseph and Benjamin and their brothers — grew up in cosmopolitan Egypt and were subjects of the Pharaoh. Under the leadership of Moses, a son of Levi and a naturalized Egyptian, the sons of Israel became the people of Yahweh and acquired the land of Canaan. In their triumphal march they were resisted by the border countries, Edom, Moab, and Ammon, but they received from Balaam the blessing of the nations. Israel, in the epic's perspective, is the residue and distillation of the civilized world that gradually disentangled itself from other people and lived apart from them in the land that belonged to Yahweh.

This provided the basic outline of the history of Israel for subsequent poets and historians. The epic was a marvelous amalgam of fact and fiction in a narrative that other writers were eager to embellish or correct. It had assumptions and implications that did not correspond to traditional teaching, belief, living memory, or common sense and that contemporary scholars were not willing to ignore. But it was an idea of what the country was and ought to be, and over the years it was debated and edited and gradually assimilated to what everybody thought and believed.

The sequel overlaps the epic and continues its process of dissimilation beyond the conquest of Canaan and through the wars of the kings to the eventual and irreparable separation of Judah from Israel. It gives details on the subjection of indigenous nations, which the epic had merely suggested, and has a different version of early Israelite relations with the Ammonites and the Philistines. It begins in the heroic and episodic mood of the epic but quickly confines its interest to Judah and Jerusalem and in the end becomes an annalistic account of their relations with Egypt, the Arameans, and Assyria.

The Priestly version corrected the epic's chronology. The epic combined different opinions and incongruous information on the origin and development of Israel into a coherent story with a simple, linear, and abbreviated temporal sequence. The Priestly writer depended on cosmology, genealogy, geography, and chronology to transpose the origins of Israel from the unruly past into the defined and measurable realms of scientific history. Creation took place in time. The flood occurred after a certain number of generations whose duration was regular and calculated.[30] The descendants of Noah were related genealogically and distributed geographically in Greece and the Mediterranean countries, in Egypt, South Arabia, and Africa, and in Syria, Assyria and Babylonia. Abraham was a descendant of the eastern group and the important stages of his life and the time of his death could be dated precisely. All of his descendants had manageable lifetimes and decent burials, and the irrational elements in their story — the conflicts between Isaac and Ishmael, Israel and Judah, Jacob and Esau — are explained in oracles or directly by God. The children of Israel are listed and counted; the amount of time that they spent in Egypt is recorded exactly; and the stages in their journey to Canaan are noted and described. In the end all the heroes are dead, and the mystery surrounding Moses and Aaron is dispelled by an account of their foibles. The Priestly writer took Israel out of the magical web of international relations that the epic describes and enshrined it in an ordered succession of nations and governments.

The Elohist restored the inclusiveness and appreciation of antiquity that the sequel to the epic had relinquished. From the beginning it is interested in people and places and institutions in Samaria, and it ends with the promulgation of traditional laws that reflect the rural and tribal constitution of the northern kingdom. It associates Jacob with Shechem and Bethel, and gives preeminence to Ephraim and Manasseh among the tribes. It includes customs and practices associated with the northern shrines and provides local agricultural alternatives to the pilgrim festivals favored by the epic and its sequel. It establishes the connection between prophecy and government — the antithesis of the conflict between the sequel and its prophetic contemporaries — and defends the inspired and charismatic leaders who are guided by dreams and divine providence. It includes respect for such persons among its legal prescriptions and codifies laws and customs that inculcate com-

mon decency and elementary justice and provide for an ultimate appeal
to God.

On the basis of such precedents and independent research the
Deuteronomist endeavored to incorporate the epic and the sequel into
a universal history. Its focus was Judah and Jerusalem and the Davidic
dynasty, but its interest radiated from them to the northern kingdom
and the relationship of greater Israel to every epoch, culture, nation,
land, and capital of the world. The Priestly writer had lengthened and
measured the time that the epic and its sequel telescoped and contemporized, but the History extended it further and divided it into separate
eras. According to this scheme, which corresponds in general to the
division of the biblical books, history is a series of natural new
beginnings and of artificial prolepses and recapitulations. Genesis, in
this version, is devoted to the primordial creation and to the now-
primeval patriarchs, to the origin of nations, cities, customs, worship,
livelihoods, and trades, to the birth of the tribal league in Israel and its
relations with the principal powers of the world—until the era ends
with a poetic summary of tribal characteristics and a privileged glimpse
of time to come. Exodus and parts of Leviticus establish the origin and
constituents of Israel's civil and religious laws and institutions, and the
Sinai era ends with their enactment and performance. Numbers defines
the tribal structure of society and government, and the era of the
wilderness wanderings ends with a summary of the journey that they
took and an anticipation of the borders they will inherit. Deuteronomy
explains the new covenant in the land of Moab, and the Mosaic era
ends with tribal songs and with dire predictions of uncommon crimes
and a common fate. The book of Joshua covers the era of national
conquest and tribal partition of the land and ends with a summary of
the preceding eras and still another warning. The book of Judges is
about tribal settlement in the land and the era ends in ruins and in
anticipation of the monarchy to come. The book of Samuel tells the
story of the house of David, and the era ends with songs and summaries
and a prelude to the building of the temple. The book of Kings
describes the requirements of right worship and the conflicts that these
engendered between Israel and Judah until both kingdoms were
destroyed, and the era of the monarchy ends with a recapitulation of
the covenant, of the conquest and the era of the judges, and with an
inkling of another era still to come. The History's chronology and
geography are global; its perspective is universal; its sources are ancient
and modern and made for the occasion; its information is gathered
from lore and libraries; and its monumental scope overwhelms any
particular bias of the materials that it absorbed. Its adoption of the

antecedent histories, its detailing and distribution into eras, makes it seem more like a product of the ages than the acme of local and learned traditions.

The later histories had limited resources and restricted interests but continued to insist on the centrality of Judah in world or cosmic history. The Chronicler reviewed the history of Judah and Jerusalem from the creation of the world to the edict of Cyrus. The climax of the history is the building of the Solomonic temple, but the point of the review is that it was founded and accoutred by David and was destined to be rebuilt according to the same plans. In the course of this privileged history the Chronicler surveys all the nations and kings who threatened or contributed to the stability of the Davidic dynasty and the realization of Jerusalem as the pinnacle of creation. The book of Ezra continues the history and records the contribution of the Persian kings to the rebuilding of the temple despite the stubborn resistance of local and regional officials. Its primary inspiration, however, is not Chronicles but the Deuteronomistic notions of the law and the promise to David and the dangers of mingling with the nations. Nehemiah is a later interpretation that admits Ezra as a minor official and retrieves the ideal of the Jerusalem covenant from the Chronicler and the sequel to the epic. These works are unfettered by historical theory and deal mainly with practical problems and programs, but they agree with the earlier works in carving a niche for the people of Judah in the real world of encompassing nations.

The prophetic literature transcends national boundaries to deal with Israel and Judah and the principles of universal order and government. It views history as the concomitance or conflict between natural and divine decrees and the policies and practices of nations. In preexilic times prophets saw Judah abandon its heritage and succumb to the pressure of international politics. During and after the exile the scholars who redid their work were divided between extricating the nation from its predicament and integrating it into a new world order.

Isaiah opposed the Jerusalem covenant because it neglected the principles of fundamental justice and ignored the influence of God in changing world affairs. Amos described the injustice in detail and linked it to a misunderstanding of God especially by the new class of merchants and financiers. Hosea mentioned the injustice and attributed it to serious confusion about the written law's relation to basic issues of life and death. Micah repeated the point and connected current injustice in Jerusalem to a misunderstanding of history. Jeremiah was appalled at the contemporary ignorance of God and contempt for traditional ways and blamed it on refusal to listen to the prophets or

observe the law that just recently was codified. Nahum compared
Jerusalem to the capitals of Egypt and Assyria and saw the capture
and looting of the city as the inevitable outcome of its unscrupulous
pursuit of wealth. Habakkuk spoke of violence that would be punished
by the Babylonian invasion. Zephaniah saw the end of the world as a
just solution to universal injustice. For all these prophets Judah was
special but not unique and would not be exempted from punishment
for flouting the law and tradition.

Ezekiel described the fall of Jerusalem as the collapse of the
civilized world and saw Israel alone rising from the embers. II Isaiah
foresaw a new era of justice in which all the nations of the world would
worship with Judah in Jerusalem. II Micah added to this the extermination of the forces that opposed God in Zion. Joel saw Judah
recovering from a plague of locusts and once again enjoying the seasons
and the fruit of its labor. The book of Jeremiah erased the former
regimes and looked forward to the return of the exiles dispersed among
the nations. III Isaiah was content with a humble new beginning by
the returning exiles who had extricated themselves from the nations
and by the few who had survived in Jerusalem and were purified of
their contamination with foreigners. It was not always clear to individual writers or conceded by the schools who was the true Judean or
how the country would be organized, only that Judah and Jerusalem
would survive. It was this matter of survival that hurried the written
traditions to a close.

Late Judean Literary Traditions

Late Judean traditions were literate and eclectic. The epic was stately,
with long, involved sentences in self-enclosed episodes, and easy to
read. Isaiah quoted songs and conversations and wrote poetry to be
sung or declaimed. The sequel had charming stories and official records
that had to be read and considered. Amos had ponderous, almost
prosaic cadences suitably chanted; the Priestly writer wrote in regular
repetitive prose that could be recited and remembered; Hosea composed intricate texts with changes of mood and perspective that invited
impersonation, and Jeremiah had to be acted to be understood. Some
of the authors were from the city and talked about its walls, streets,
and houses; its people, markets, and spectacles; its architecture, rituals,
mores, and scandals. Some were interested in war and the clatter of
arms, the panoply and the commotion and the bravery of the troops.
Some were familiar with the country, the seasons, the animals that

grazed, the crops that were planted and harvested, and some of them saw the city from the outside with a little apprehension and disdain. Some were familiar with officialdom and institutions, and others had observed people and could describe their behavior and personalities. Some were dreamers; others had observed the stars; some were artists who knew nothing except literature and life. The Deuteronomist in particular indulged in every style and genre and mannerism and gathered material from multiple sources, but saw everything from an abstract, synthetic, or transcendent point of view. The sources that the authors used were cited or mentioned or paraphrased or reconstructed from research, legend, hearsay, or recollection, but they were not preserved. What was written and what is left is literature, not excerpts or fragments, but a few related books, edited and arranged in a collection that was stored and studied until there was nothing more to add and the books were closed.

The literary traditions were active and incremental. They grew under the inspiration of writers from Jerusalem and other parts of the country who had the same education and similar training but different backgrounds, occupations, and interests. They learned the traditions, belonged to them, contributed to them, shaped them, and gave them existence in readable and memorable writings. Each author depended on all or parts of what preceded, and some, like Jeremiah, Ezekiel, and the Deuteronomist, had a comprehensive grasp of it. Their libraries, or others like them, became the core and basis of subsequent collections. Later scribes and scholars arranged their texts, put them in standard form, determined their true historical reference, and gave them contemporary relevance, and even assigned their authors a time and place and personality. They were not responsible, however, for writing or selecting the texts that they annotated but only for homogenizing the traditions and making them exclusive and complete. More literature was written and added to the collection later, but it was always complementary or supplementary and just filled out the lines and the categories that had been determined over time.

The traditions, like the collection, began as literature. They can be attributed to authors who composed them according to the rules of grammar and syntax and prosody and rhetoric and with the language, style, and structure of a written text. They were edited by other writers who recognized the rules and organization of the texts and added comments, commentaries, and interpretations that imitated or adapted their language and style and appealed to parallel texts. They were collected by others who put them into an order that the texts themselves and the development of the literary traditions suggested. The collections were reworked for translation into the language and literary canons of the Hellenistic world. The entire process of composition, editing, transmission, and translation took place in a sophisticated and studied world of faith.

The beginning of the literary traditions is easier to trace than their origin. From the epic onward genres and traditions are mixed, but there is no earlier evidence for literary history and no anterior independent control on the opinions and information they provide. Historiography was the product of an official and learned profession, but extant annals and chronicles and epics are distant analogies that do not explain the instant perfection of the Judean exemplars. Prophecy was the heir of a popular oral tradition, but it was written; and although it is poetry, drama, and oratory composed in direct discourse, all the signs of oral composition and transmission and the clues to an oral society are missing. The traditions appeared at once alive and fully formed. Their beginning is obviously not their origin but is relatively late in a literate world.

Although the literature of the prophets and historians who wrote before the exile was not unoriginate, it was a departure and a new beginning that suddenly exploded and then evolved rapidly over the century or two that it flourished. Isaiah, for instance, still wrote in the episodic style of the epic, but he wrote poetry and introduced the characters, action, and quoted speech that became fully developed in Jeremiah's dramatic presentation. Hosea also contributed to the structure of drama and the development of characterization, but his work reflects a rare georgic or bucolic tradition that reoccurs raucously in the Song of Songs and in a refined and subdued form in Haggai and Joel. Amos still declaimed in long elegiac periods, but when Zephaniah took up his banner and tried to do the same, his own poetry turned out to be pithy and staccato. Micah and Habakkuk redid Isaiah but they are different from him and from each other, and still more unlike the lyrical artistry of II Isaiah. Nahum transposed parts of the prose epic into song and composed an accompanying ode and ballad that by later standards were hardly prophetic at all. Ezekiel wrote elegant poetry and repetitive magical prose, which led the editor of his book to think of him as a minstrel. The author of the book of Jeremiah could distinguish all the styles and meters and mannerisms and included imitations of each. The historians, it seems, were teachers, and the prophets were the dramatists, entertainers, and commentators of their time. They rose one after the other to the occasion of national crisis and created a common literature that was to be read and heard and understood and that changed easily to suit the mood of the time and the constant turn of events.

Literary excellence continued beyond the exile, but the new prophets and historians lacked the themes and exaltation of their predecessors. The intermediate editors took up a challenge, which required a great deal of reflection and sometimes made their work artificial or contrived. The book of Psalms, for instance, and the Deuteronomistic History included songs from other times and places, but the authors treated them like texts to be molded to their frame and demonstrated little interest in their originality or difference. In the same spirit, the marvelous scenes described by Hosea became occasions for puzzling historical references and snide political remarks. III Isaiah, similarly, could match the lyricism of II Isaiah but often added commentaries on the earlier works that were dense, turgid, and almost unintelligible. Literary genius survived, but literary canons were ignored and the function of the literary artist became redundant in the aphoristic world of administrators and pedants. Haggai, Zechariah, and Malachi were critics who wrote trenchant, allusive, and entertaining prophecy, but by their time prophets had become singers in the temple and all they could do was write their prophecy in prose speeches and in the guise of historical records. Ezra and Nehemiah took up where they left off and gave the background and sequel to their works. The writer who rounded off the story and rewrote Zechariah rewrote history as poetry and apocalyptic. Literary traditions had come to a reflective resolution, and tradition was maintained, as it has been originally, in the life and learning of the people.

Tradition was an articulation of life, and the literature was its expression. The tradition did not exist in isolation and was not unchanging but was manifested in its images, analogies, and variants. Literary traditions did not reflect or mimic life but by reflection on themselves became surrogates and arbiters of life. Late Judean literary traditions were manifold, intricate in their expression and transmission, profound in their creative consequences. They can be unraveled in part and appreciated as they were composed. The unraveling consists in recognizing and undoing the editing and in extricating the original work from its comparable sources of composition. It is a form of attention to the text and, in relation to other texts, generates literary sense and historical meaning. The residue of the unraveling is the literature itself, which is left to be read and repeated.

The traditions include both their matter and their manner and the way they were received and retrieved. The matter of the traditions is what is said: it is not a fact, or data, or a real event but an interpretation from which the evidence for such things might be reconstructed. The manner is how it is said: this does not reveal the attitude of the writer or the intention of the writer's milieu but consists in the language, style, form, genre, and context of the text from which these and similar things might be gathered. The reception of the tradition is not a personal or contemporary response to what is heard or read but is the precise and literal means that the editor used to frame and reformulate the matter and the manner of the tradition. The retrieval of the tradition is not its use and repercussions but the changes that the text underwent in becoming a source. All in all, a tradition is grasped only as it grew. It is not a vague antecedent of what is already known or an imagined beginning of the obvious, but a literate transformation of the origins, the realizations, and the renewals of life.

The following examination of the development of late Judean literary traditions is an attempt to recreate the composition of individual historical and prophetic texts, to explain their cumulative order and sequence, and to describe the editorial policies that changed the texts and transformed the traditions. It is a literary endeavor with urgent historical implications. It takes the texts seriously, supposing that the authors of the texts had something to say and, from them and the sources that they used, reconstructing what they meant. It recognizes that what they said and meant was understood, adapted, appreciated, and applied by the writers of their time and later. It observes that what was said acquired different meanings when the literature was edited and gathered in libraries and read at different times and under changing circumstances. It attempts to gather from the cumulative evidence the relationship between late Judean literary and historical traditions and their actual significance for those who believed in them.

NOTES

[1] The epic, usually known as the "Yahwist" or, from the German spelling, "J" is in prose but relies on poetic originals as its sources and models. These sources and models are still extant, but the principles and techniques, memory and information, tradition and milieu that produced their transformation into a national epic have to be reconstructed.

[2] Isaiah derides the covenant as a pact with death and Sheol (Isa 28:15, 18) and refers to those who invoke it as ʾanšê lāṣôn and mōšĕlê hāʿām hazzeh (Isa 28:14). The whole context (Isa 28:9–19) has to do with speaking the truth, telling lies, hearing what is said or listening to gibberish. Those who promote the covenant are repudiated as fast talkers, liars, people who are good with

words and images, riddlers, jokers, or some such, who mistakenly think that they will escape the Assyrian menace.

3 The reasons that Isaiah gives for preserving the prophecy are the reasons that prompted its initial delivery (Isa 30:9; cf. Isa 1:2–3, 4–6), namely, that no one listened or was willing to believe or, as his detractors might say, that what he said was unbelievable. What he committed to writing, as a matter of fact, was the prophecy he composed.

4 The sequel to the epic begins in Deuteronomy and precedes and determines the course of the Deuteronomistic History and, in this sense, is aptly named "Deuteronomistic." But since it is, in fact, a small part of the History and bears no resemblance to the finished product, the designation is barely suitable.

5 Most of the basic clues to Amos are assembled in H. W. Wolff, *Dodekapropheton, 2: Joel und Amos*, BKAT 14/2 (Neukirchen-Vluyn: Neukirchener Verlag, 1969). The prophecy, however, is taken as the product of transmission and redaction rather than as a literary composition with consequences for its own time and interest for later writers.

6 The text traditionally ascribed to the Priestly document is listed and evaluated in M. Noth, *Überlieferungsgeschichte des Pentateuch* (Stuttgart: W. Kohlhammer, 1948); K. Elliger, "Sinn und Ursprung der priesterlichen Geschichtserzählung," *ZTK* 49 (1952) 121–43 (= *Kleine Schriften zum Alten Testament* [Munich: Chr. Kaiser, 1966] 174–98); N. Lohfink, "Die Priesterschrift und die Geschichte," in *Congress Volume: Göttingen 1977* (VTSup 29; Leiden: Brill, 1977) 189–225.

7 The main task of Jeremiah's editor was to show how the predicted reconciliation of Ephraim and Judah took place. The solution was to repeat the words of Jeremiah and distribute them in a chronological and pseudo-historical sequence so that his prediction came after the Babylonian invasion and the capture of Jerusalem and referred to the eventual return of the exiles. The procedure embedded and obscured the original prophecy, but it can be recognized by its apologetic, repetitive, chronological, and historical characteristics.

8 The quotation is in Isaiah 36–39, the rewriting in Isaiah 6°–9° (the asterisks indicate that this rewriting was revised again by III Isaiah).

9 These stories of Amos, Micah, Ezekiel, and Jeremiah are in 1 Kings 13; 22; and 2 Kings 1–13; 22. The stories are not fictions but true, if irreverent, interpretations of the prophets. The disdain that the Historian felt for the prophets was systematic and had to do with the transcendence of the law over the word of God and with the Deuteronomistic notion that the prophets were supposed to be teachers and transmitters of the Torah. It was precisely on this point that the book of Jeremiah took issue with the History.

10 The revision (Jonah 2:2–10), characteristically, emphasizes the bio-

graphical aspects of prophecy. It is a concatenation of quotes from the Psalms and is easier to analyze apart from the satirical stories it repoints.

[11] The revision (Joel 3:1-4:21) is a duplicate and reworking of the original. It gives the prophecy an entirely different drift.

[12] The last part of the Deuteronomistic History builds up to the reform of Josiah and then, apparently inexplicably, negates its effect by an arbitrary and literarily jarring appeal to the sin of Manasseh. The ending, however, is typical of Deuteronomistic books, and is essential to the story that began at the beginning in Genesis. All the books have a finish and a finale: the story line comes to an end (Genesis 48; Exodus 32-34; Numbers 31; Deuteronomy 30; Joshua 22; Judges 16; 2 Samuel 21; 2 Kings 23), but there is always a sort of appendix that summarizes the point and makes a transition to the next book (Genesis 49-50; Exodus 35-40; Numbers 32-36; Deuteronomy 31-34; Joshua 23-24; 2 Samuel 22-24; 2 Kings 23-25). The second part of the History describes the inadequacy of the notion of covenant, but the whole History, from the beginning of creation, explains the effects of sin.

[13] The supplement to the Pentateuch (P_S) in Leviticus 1-7; 12-27 depends on the Deuteronomistic code in Deuteronomy, but many of its departures from this source are influenced by the book of Ezekiel, as is evident in their common language.

[14] The date of Lamentations is not known. The Chronicler refers to a lament that Jeremiah composed for Josiah (2 Chr 35:25) and might have meant some (e.g., Lamentations 3) or all of the book available at that time. See D. R. Hillers, *Lamentations* (AB 7A; Garden City, N.Y.: Doubleday & Company, 1972) 61-64.

[15] The date of the Song of Songs is determined only by its position in the typological sequence. The evidence of its late, informal language and expression suggests that colloquialisms crept into the otherwise conservative literary language of Judah first in poetry and texts done in direct discourse.

[16] The two arguments are juxtaposed in Hag 1:2-4, 5-6. The first concerns the appropriate or predetermined time for building the temple and is related implicitly to chronological speculation in the book of Jeremiah. The second argument has to do with life and fertility and the presence of God and is related to the religious values described most fully by Hosea.

[17] Nehemiah contains the sequel to Ezra but also quotes from it (e.g., Nehemiah 7 = Ezra 2) and gives a different impression of Ezra's personal contribution to restoration politics. It was attached to the book of Ezra just as this attached itself to Chronicles to create a continuous history from the beginning of time to the fourth century.

[18] The first edition of Daniel (essentially Daniel 1-6) redoes history as legend to describe the triumph of Israel and its God in the Persian period. The

second edition purportedly deals with the same period but is filled with the secretiveness, distortion, and fantastic transpositions of contemporary occurrences, which are characteristic of apocalyptic.

[19] R. S. Hendel, "Of Demigods and the Deluge: Toward an Interpretation of Genesis 6:1–4," *JBL* 106 (1987) 13–26; J. Van Seters, "The Primeval Histories of Greece and Israel Compared," *ZAW* 100 (1988) 1–22.

[20] J. Hoftijzer and G. Van Der Kooij, *Aramaic Texts from Deir 'Alla* (Leiden: Brill, 1976).

[21] After the Babylonian invasion and the capture of Jerusalem, when all the dreadful prophecies had come true, it became evident that prophecy involved prediction and that true prophecy was what happened. The idea, of course, was expressed most insistently by the Deuteronomistic Historian, in dogmatic (Deut 13:1–5; 18:15–22), narrative (Josh 6:26 and 1 Kgs 16:34; 1 Kgs 14:1–20), and dramatic terms (1 Kgs 22:1–40). However, there was a correlative tendency among the scholars who revised the prophetic works to suppose that what happened had been predicted. The scholar who redid Amos was interested in limiting the effect of his prophecy to those who had worshiped in Bethel and to like-minded sinners and naturally dated his prophecy before the fact: it was located two years before the earthquake that ruined the temple in Bethel (Amos 1:1; 9:1) and in the days of Jeroboam II (Amos 1:1; 7:10–17). Apart from this sort of scholarship and speculation it is evident that Amos's text moves beyond the destruction of Samaria and the ruin of Joseph (Amos 1–5°) to predict the fate of Zion and Jacob (Amos 6–8°). His prophecy took the past as a paradigm of the future and expressed it all as an urgent possibility, and the fact that his prophecy came true obviously justified his editor in taking all of his text as prediction.

[22] The linguistic evidence for the dating of the Priestly document depends on what texts are attributed to it and on the relative order that is assigned to the comparative material.

[23] There is considerable diversity of opinion concerning the date, provenance, extent, and existence of the Elohist version. See M. Noth, *Überlieferungsgeschichte des Pentateuch*; A. W. Jenks, *The Elohist and North Israelite Traditions* (SBL Monograph Series 22; Missoula, Mont.: Scholars Press, 1977).

[24] Contemporaneity is indicated in the superscription (Hos 1:1) that dates his prophecy, like Amos's, to the reigns of Uzziah and Jeroboam (Amos 1:1) and, like Isaiah's, to the reigns of Uzziah, Jotham, Ahaz, and Hezekiah (Isa 1:1). The editor also added oblique references to earlier incidents recounted in the Deuteronomistic History, and these, on the assumption that prophecy is a reflex of its occasion, have been used to establish an eighth-century date for Hosea.

[25] The superscription (Mic 1:1) simply omits Uzziah, the first of the kings of Judah mentioned in the superscription to Isaiah (Isa 1:1). The book of

Jeremiah knows Micah in its revised version, but when it quotes an original saying it ascribes it to the reign of Hezekiah (Jer 26:18). On this basis, and on the assumption that prophetic interpretations of history are always predictions, Micah usually is dated in the eighth century (see H. W. Wolff, *Dodekapropheton: Micah* [BKAT 14/14; Neukirchen-Vluyn: Neukirchener Verlag, 1982]), but some see his work as an element of living tradition (D. R. Hillers, *Micah: A Commentary on the Book of the Prophet Micah* [Hermeneia; Philadelphia: Fortress, 1984]).

26 A. Spalinger, "Esarhaddon and Egypt: An Analysis of the First Invasion of Egypt," *Or* 43 (1974) 295–326; W. G. Lambert, "Booty from Egypt?" *JJS* 33 (1982) 61–70.

27 The description of these campaigns is stereotyped and mostly dependent on Isaiah, Micah, and Jeremiah. The mention of the Chaldaeans (1:6) makes ca. 626 the earliest date for the composition of the prophecy, and it is only the supposition that the description refers to Chaldean, rather than Assyrian or just typical, campaigns that suggests a more accurate chronology. But this calendar reckoning, combined with Habakkuk's relative place in the sequence of Judean literature, suggests a date around 600 B.C.E. for his prophecy.

28 E. F. Weidner, "Jojachin, König von Juda, in babylonischen Keilschrifttexten," in *Mélanges syriens offerts à M. René Dussaud* (Paris: Paul Geuthner, 1939) 2:33–46.

29 The book of Jeremiah refers twice to the seventy years of Babylonian servitude (Jer 25:11–12; 29:10). The prediction is ascribed to Jeremiah once in a speech from the fourth year of Jehoiakim (605 B.C.E.; cf. Jer 25:1) but with reference to the invasion of Nebuchadnezzar (597 or 587 B.C.E.), and once in a speech from the beginning of the reign of Zedekiah (597 B.C.E.) referring to the exile of Jehoiachin (Jer 29:1–2). In the Chronicler's interpretation the period ended in the first year of Cyrus with the proclamation that ended the exile (539/538 B.C.E.)—the period being calculated from the date of the speech rather than from its contents, and according to the sixty-five-year period mentioned by II Isaiah (Isa 7:8). In the book of Jeremiah the later date may have been meant (527 B.C.E.). Both Haggai and Zechariah attest that the date was disputed (Hag 1:1–4; Zech 7:1–7). Ezra and Nehemiah associate it with the return of the temple vessels, but on this point the book of Jeremiah is deliberately vague (Jer 27:22). The alternative dates may correspond to the return under Sheshbazzar or under Zerubbabel which was at the center of the dispute.

30 See D. W. Young, "A Mathematical Approach to Certain Dynastic Spans in the Sumerian King List," *JNES* 47 (1988) 123–29; idem, "On the Application of Numbers from Babylonian Mathematics to Biblical Life Spans and Epochs," *ZAW* 100 (1988) 331–61.

The Foundations of Belief

*T*he epic and its sequel outlined the history of Israel from the beginning of the civilized world to the emergence of Judah as a world power. Their scheme was hasty and cribbed but brilliant and intriguing, and it informed every other attempt to describe the meaning of Israel and every theory that rationalized its relations with God. Their brilliance lay in their transformation of familiar stories into episodes in the history of the nation, and their interest derived from their original interpretation of the elemental and traditional foundations of belief.

The text of the histories can be retrieved from the mass of queries, refinements, and conflicting information that was built around them. They dealt with things that mattered, proposed theories that made a difference, and made real demands on their adherents. But opinions varied, practice changed, and theories were revised, and in time their texts were annotated and became the subject of commentary and interpretation. Annotations marked the points of disagreement; commentaries were added in adjacent contexts to explain what was meant; and interpretations, either anticipatory or resumptive, presented the alternatives that the comments and annotations implied. The primary texts, therefore, can be retrieved by undoing the editorial process, recognizing the variant interpretations, isolating the commentaries that made them fit, and bracketing the annotations that marked their place.

The primary texts were fundamental to the editorial process and were preserved intact so that their wording, order, and organization were maintained while their elements were dispersed in new and original texts. These revised texts, conversely, were whole and coherent compositions that subsumed the primary sources in different structures and interpretations. The epic, over the years, was subjected to a series of such revisions that repeated the same process and produced a complex and cumulative history. The sequel, in turn, was overwhelmed by a mass of commentary and interpretation that related it to the various stages in the development of the epic. The primary histories, consequently, can be retrieved by undoing the editorial process, by following the construction of the subsequent editions, and by disentangling from one another the conglomerate sequence of meanings.

The Editorial Process and the Construction of Texts

The epic and its sequel were written in episodes narrating the achievements of ancient heroes and famous kings. The episodes in their turn were composed of incidents highlighting particular occasions and circumstances in the hero's life. The compositional process used by the commentators, therefore, consisted in adding other episodes to the narrative or other incidents to the episodes and in modifying existing incidents to accommodate the changes.

The editorial process that made this possible consisted in repetition and cross-reference. Repetition is the use of words from the primary or original text in a transferred sense, in a different order, or in an opposite context. Cross-reference consists in the insertion of one or more words that are odd or inconsequential in their context but appropriate to a preceding or following editorial context. Repetition usually occurs at the beginning or at the end of the intrusive text: when it occurs at some other point it is harmonizing and is related to sequential commentary or to continuous and developing interpretation. The additions that the editors made in rewriting the text were composed to blend with the original and can be distinguished from it mainly by their sense and direction. The editorial process, by contrast, was formal and artificial and deliberately evident.

These editorial and compositional techniques can be verified in any particular episode or incident since the original text was left to be read with the texts that circumscribe and expand it. The procedures are partial and piecemeal, but their divergence from the original becomes clear in the sequence of episodes and incidents.

The Yahwist Epic (fig. 2)

THE FIRST EPISODE

The first episode is about Man and Woman and their natural affinity with God. It begins with the story of heaven and earth, the making of man, and the garden that was planted for his sake. In the second incident Man is forbidden under pain of death to eat the fruit of the tree of knowledge of good and evil. In the third incident the birds and the animals are created to keep him company, and in the fourth Woman becomes his companion. In the end when they have eaten the forbidden fruit and have become like God and might live forever, they are sent out of the garden to till the land from which they were taken.

The episode was reinterpreted by prefixing another version of creation and by appending genealogies that both eliminated the divine aspirations of Man and Woman and reduced their affinity with God to mere likeness. The epic text, consequently, was annotated and fitted with comments that made it consistent with these revised perspectives.[1]

According to the epic, Yahweh formed Man from the soil and breathed into him the breath of life. This is portentous and becomes crucial in the narrative of Man's quest for everlasting life. The Priestly writer, however, did not believe that Man was destined to live forever and reserved the title "living being" for the other creatures that God made. The epic version, therefore, was harmonized with the Priestly account by adding, redundantly, that Man became a living being. The addition was made by repeating two key words from the immediate context—"Man" and "life"—but in a sense that did not agree either with the context, since it put Man in a cosmological category, or with the Priestly writer, since it classified Man among the animals.[2]

In the epic version, before there was any rain or vegetation and when the earth was watered from below, Yahweh put Man in the Garden of Eden, planted trees for his enjoyment, and instructed him not to eat the fruit of the tree of knowledge of good and evil. But there is another version, inserted between the actions and the instructions of Yahweh, that gives a different impression of the garden and a different explanation of how the earth was watered.[3] The intrusiveness of this version can be recognized by the editorial procedure that fitted it into a developing and overarching interpretation. The intrusive text ends by repeating, in a different sense, the text that preceded it, so that instead of enjoying the garden Man is supposed to cultivate and take care of it.[4] The intrusion also situates the garden in the world of the patriarchs and kings. In this version the garden is watered by a river that has four

F I G U R E　2

The Yahwist Epic (J)

Episode I

1　Genesis 2:4b–7a, 8–9
2　2:16–17
3　2:18, 19aA, 20b
4　2:21–23a, 25
5　3:1–13, 22–23

Episode II

1　Genesis 6:1–2, 4aBb
2　6:5–6, 7aAb, 8
3　7:1a, 4, 7
4　7:10, 17, 23a°b
5　8:6, 8–12

Episode III

1　Genesis 11:1, 4–7, 8b, 9b
2　12:1, 2a, 3a, 4a, 5bB, 6a, 8a, 9
3　13:2, 5–6a, 7a, 8–10a, 11
4　13:12, 18a
5　18:1b–6
6　18:7–8a
7　18:8b–10a
8　18:10b–16
9　19:1aBb–3
10　19:4–6
11　19:7–8, 9aAb, 10
12　19:12–14
13　19:24a, 25, 27, 28
14　21:1a, 2a, 3

Episode IV

1　Genesis 26:1aAb, 7
2　26:8–9, 11–14, 16–17
3　26:26–31
4　27:1–4
5　27:5–16
6　27:17–29
7　27:30–35, 26b–40
8　27:41–44
9　29:1–3
10　29:4–8
11　29:9–12
12　29:13–15
13　29:16–22

continued

FIGURE 2 (*cont*)

14 29:23, 25–28, 30
15 30:25–36
16 30:37–42
17 30:43; 31:1–3; 32:4–7
18 32:14a, 25b, 26aA, 27–30, 32a
19 33:1a, 4, 12–15
20 33:16–17a

Episode V

1 Genesis 37:3a, 4, 12–18, 25–27, 28aBb
2 39:1–6a
3 41:56a, 57
4 42:1–4
5 42:5, 7, 9b–18a, 19–20, 24, 29–34, 36, 38
6 43:1–11, 13, 14b, 15aAb–16, 23b–29a, 30–31, 34b
7 44:18–34
8 45:1–3
9 45:16–21a, 25–28
10 46:28–34a; 47:1–6

Episode VI

1 Exodus 1:8–12a
2 1:22; 2:1–6abA, 7aAb, 8–10
3 2:11–12, 15
4 2:16–22
5 2:23aA; 3:2–4a, 7–8; 4:19–20a
6 4:24–26a
7 12:37–38; 13:20–22
8 14:5a, 6
9 14:9aA, 19b–20
10 14:24, 27b, 30–31
11 19:1b, 2b, 9a, 10aBb–11, 14b–15a
12 19:16aA, 20; 34:6–7, 10–12, 14, 19, 20b–22, 24, 27, 28abA
13 34:29aA; Numbers 10:29–33a; 13:1–2a, 17–20
14 Numbers 13:22a, 23, 25a, 27–28, 30–31
15 14:11abA, 12–19a, 20–21, 23–24
16 16:12–14, 25a, 27b–32a, 33a, 34
17 20:14–16aAb, 17–21; 21:21–24abA
18 22:4b–6, 7b–21aAb, 36–40
19 22:41; 23:1–10
20 23:11–24
21 23:25–30; 24:1–6, 8–9
22 24:10–13, 25

Figure 2. The incidents in each episode are numbered.
°An asterisk in a biblical reference indicates an edited text.

tributaries delimiting the territories of Egypt and Assyria and of the land of Canaan, which lies between them (Gen 2:10–14). This geography is developed in the ensuing genealogies and becomes crucial in the Deuteronomistic History from the time of Abraham to the fall of Jerusalem.[5]

In the epic version Yahweh looked for a suitable companion for Man and, not finding any among the animals, made Woman. Since the Priestly writer had a different version of creation, according to which Man and Woman had dominion over the animals, the epic was changed to agree with it and to lessen its own mythological and legendary allure. In this edition Yahweh does not make the animals as potential companions for Man but brings them to Man to be named. The editing is done, typically, by ending the addition as the prior context had ended: the epic narrated that God formed all the beasts of the field and the birds in the sky, and the new version mentions them again in the opposite order—the birds in the sky and all the beasts of the field—and with an allusion to the other animals the Priestly writer mentioned.[6] The change is obvious in its immediate context, but it is unobtrusive in the total rewriting of the epic as a history of the world concerned with such contemporary scientific matters as the names and origins of things.[7] This particular interest, besides, is immediately reinforced in the etiology of marriage that is attached to the epic by a pun on the word for "woman" and by a paraphrase of what the epic had just narrated (Gen 2:23b–24).[8]

The most extensive change in the epic version was the curse that the Deuteronomistic version invoked on the earth and on the serpent that crawled upon it. The curse was added to the text by repeating words from the beginning of the narrative it replaced, and since this is the standard introduction to direct discourse—"And Yahweh God said"—the editing is fairly unobtrusive. But this curse becomes a major theme of the Deuteronomistic History, illustrates the History's usual interest in the origin and reason for things, and is cited and developed in what follows (Gen 3:14–21).[9]

The last change in this episode occurs at the very end. In the epic version Yahweh sent Man out of the garden so that he might till the land and not have access to the tree of life. In the revised version the same things are repeated in a different way. Man is banished, not sent away. The garden is guarded by the cherubim. The tree of life is protected by a flaming sword. It is a fairly obvious duplicate, and the elements of it that are not taken up immediately in the story of Cain and Abel become central in the construction of the ark of the covenant and the temple.[10]

The editorial changes are plain and are supposed to be noticed. All the changes, however, produce a completely different text, whose meaning is complex and compacted. The original episode is simple and straightforward. The Deuteronomistic version means the same things and also the things that it adds, and the whole history into which they are integrated.

THE SECOND EPISODE

The second episode is the story of Noah and the flood. The first incident tells of the demigods who were born to the sons of God and the daughters of Man. The second recalls their raving ambition, which induced Yahweh to destroy them but exempts Noah from their fate. The third, fourth, and fifth incidents describe the flood and explain how Noah and his family escaped. The story was revised by the Priestly writer and by the Deuteronomistic Historian to eliminate its legendary and mythological elements and to harmonize it with their ideas of creation and historical sequence.

The first incident was changed by the Deuteronomistic Historian to temper its notion of demigods. This was done simply by identifying them with the giants who were supposed to have lived in Canaan in ancient times and by assigning them manageable life spans (Gen 6:3–4aA).[11] The change consists of sentences inserted between the marriage of the Gods and the birth of their children. The insertion is marked by ending it as the preceding sentence in the epic had ended and, conversely, is made less obtrusive by cross-reference to earlier and later texts.[12]

The second incident was left unchanged but was matched in the Priestly version by a different reason for Noah's exemption. The epic had said that Noah found favor in the sight of Yahweh, but the Priestly writer explained that he was the only just man in a violent and corrupt generation. The paragraph is filled with formulaic expressions and with references to preceding texts and ends like the beginning of the paragraph that it reduplicates (Gen 6:9–12).[13]

In the third incident Yahweh told Noah to enter the ark because within a week it would begin to rain for forty days and nights, and the incident ends with Noah doing as he was told. The Priestly writer, to take the flood out of the primordial past and situate it in measurable time, added that Noah was six hundred years old at the time: the addition is made by repeating, in an odd and redundant manner, exactly what the epic said about the flood.[14] The Deuteronomistic History, with its usual interest in matters of worship, prepares for the sacrifice Noah will offer by having him distinguish between the clean and the unclean animals that he brings on board. This version is inserted into the epic between the command that Yahweh gave Noah and the reason, and between the reason and the fact that he did what he was told (Gen 7:1b–3, 5).[15] It is inserted, as usual, by repeating parts of its context and by cross-reference to other editorial contexts. The first part of the insertion begins with another reason and repeats one word from the epic. The second part simply comments on the fact that in the epic version Noah did exactly what he was told.[16] The editorializing is evident because it modifies and seems to contradict the preceding Priestly text, but it is fitted into its context by cross-references that assimilate the epic to the Priestly version and completely reorganize the story to suit the Deuteronomist's perspective.[17]

The fourth incident says that within a week the flood came and lasted for forty days and that the ark floated high above the earth while everything else was destroyed. The Priestly writer added two extended comments to record the precise date of the beginning of the flood and its exact duration and a detailed list of what was destroyed and what survived (Gen 7:11, 13–16a, 18–21). The first comment fits in by specifying the day of the week on which the flood occurred, and consists in repeating a great deal of the preceding text to show that Noah did exactly what he was told (Gen 7:11, 13–16a).[18] The second comment is a list of the creatures that perished, and it is fitted into the epic version by repeating how high the water was and by referring to the preceding text.[19] The Deuteronomistic History merely added a couple of annotations to smooth the connection between the two versions and thereby created a text whose only rough and really noticeable features made its own ideas predominate.[20]

The final incident describes the release of the doves and the realization that the flood was finished. The Deuteronomistic Historian inserted a prior reference to the release of a raven: it was inserted by anticipating the first words of the epic text, and it makes sense by resuming the Deuteronomistic interest in clean and unclean animals and by assimilating the epic version of the floodwaters seeping away to the Priestly version, where they simply dry up (Gen 8:7).[21] The Priestly writer added an alternative ending to the flood that established its exact date and brought creation back to normal.[22] The Deuteronomistic Historian noted that the ark had a protective cover that, by anticipation, assimilated it to the tabernacle and the tent of meeting (Gen 8:13b).[23]

The Deuteronomistic version situated the flood in recurrent historical and ritual patterns and gave it a moral and religious cast. The

Priestly writer had simply tried to place it in time and gave it political and agricultural significance. In the epic it was just part of the great adventure that separated people from God and ended with the covenant binding Israel and Yahweh. In the process of redaction and composition the epic became a little remote and arcane, and the perspectives of the later two writers predominated. But it was the epic version that set the pace, and it is only in relation to the epic and each other that their editions make sense.

THE THIRD EPISODE

The third episode tells the story of Abraham and is composed of fourteen incidents. The first and second explain that he came to the land of Canaan on the authority of Yahweh during the great migrations from the East. The third and fourth describe his separation from Lot and settlement in the land. The next four narrate his encounter with Yahweh and the promise of a son for Sarah. The next five illustrate Yahweh's authority over the land in the destruction of Sodom and Gomorrah. The episode ends with the birth of Isaac.

The episode was revised by the Priestly writer, the Elohist, and the Deuteronomistic Historian to remove it from the realm of unabashed conversation with God to the arenas of historical and theological speculation. The Priestly writer determined the geographical and chronological boundaries of the story and put the birth of Isaac under the tutelage of a covenant with Abraham and all his descendants.[24] The Elohist considered the birth of Isaac a manifestation of divine providence.[25] The Deuteronomist situated Abraham in world history and explained that this history unfolds according to the plan and prevision of God.[26] The episode became ever more complicated as the text of the epic receded into obscurity.

The first incident separates Abraham from the postdiluvian nations descended from Noah and was changed by the Deuteronomist into the familiar story of the Tower of Babel. In the epic version Yahweh frustrates the pretensions of the first city dwellers by confounding their speech. The Historian identified the city as Babylon by the usual process of repetition and cross-reference. The first addition hangs by one word, but it binds the episode to the geography and genealogy that the History has already established (Gen 11:2–3).[27] The second addition repeats key words from the beginning and end of the episode and gives the etiology of the city's name.[28] The changes in the text are minor, but they are exceedingly important for the Deuteronomistic contention that Abraham foresaw and embodied the history of the nation.[29]

The second incident tells of Abraham's journey to the land of Canaan with the blessing of Yahweh and lists the stops that he made at Shechem and Bethel on his way to the Negeb. The Priestly writer added a chronological and genealogical note (Gen 12:4b–5abA).[30] The History gave the journey historical verisimilitude and related it to its own historical theory. The first addition in this version insists on the blessing in order to make Abraham the focus of world history (Gen 12:2b, 3b).[31] The second addition corrects the impression that the land was empty and that Abraham could simply walk in and take possession of it (Gen 12:6b–7).[32] The third addition anticipates the conquest of Ai under the leadership of Joshua (Gen 12:8b; cf. Joshua 7–8).[33] Instead of following naturally on the first incident, Abraham's journey now takes place much later, in a political context, and as part of a world history.

The third and fourth incidents describe the conflict between Abraham and Lot, their separation, and Abraham's sole possession of the land of Canaan. The Deuteronomistic Historian, meanwhile, had recounted Abraham's sojourn in Egypt, and was about to record his decisive victory over a coalition of Mesopotamian kings. The epic incidents were trivial by comparison and were changed to suit the Deuteronomistic point of view and still maintain the drift of the epic.

The additions to the third incident return to the edited version of Abraham's journey that preceded his sojourn in Egypt but also anticipate the following story of Sodom and Gomorrah.[34] The revision of the fourth incident returns to the promises that Abraham received on that journey and holds the story of Sodom and Gomorrah in abeyance.[35] The editorializing is a little bizarre and confusing, but the rewriting homogenizes the text, fits it into the overall plan of the Deuteronomistic History, and makes it read like an original composition.

The following incidents narrate the different destinies of Abraham and Lot. The fifth, sixth, seventh, and eighth incidents take place in Hebron, where Abraham had settled after separating from Lot. The ninth to thirteenth incidents end the story of Lot with the destruction of Sodom and Gomorrah. Together they show that Yahweh owned the land where Abraham lived and took eminent care of his protégé.

The opening incidents tell the tale of three travelers on their way to Sodom who spent an afternoon with Abraham under the oak of Mamre and how Sarah laughed when one of them promised to return the next year when she would give birth to a son. The tale was not changed but was put into an editorial framework that related it to the Deuteronomistic Historian's belief that Abraham played a major role in world affairs and in the subsequent history of Israel.[36]

The next five incidents underwent slight modification to harmonize them with the preceding changes and to allow for the inclusion of archaeological and ethnographic information. In the framework that was added to the preceding incidents a distinction was made between Yahweh, who stayed to talk to Abraham, and the other travelers, who went on to Sodom. Consequently, the first of these five incidents begins by saying that, after Yahweh finished talking to Abraham and left, the other two messengers arrived at Sodom in the evening: the editorial link consists in repeating the name of the city; the compositional procedure is logical and arithmetic and consists in subtracting one God from three men and in calculating how long it would take the travelers to stop for a noon meal with Abraham in Hebron and still arrive at Sodom on the same day.[37] In the third of these incidents Lot tries to persuade the Sodomites not to molest the travelers, and the Deuteronomistic Historian, in whose version Lot survives the destruction of Sodom to become the father of Moab and Ammon, adds a clause to suggest that Lot was an upright person: the editorial link consists in repeating the verb that began the preceding clause; the compositional process consists in a vague allusion to the preceding discussion between Abraham and Yahweh.[38]

In the last of the five incidents the epic describes the ruin of the cities of Sodom and Gomorrah, and the Deuteronomistic History adds cross-references to its own interpretation. In the epic version Yahweh rains fire and brimstone on the cities, and the revision makes it clear that Yahweh has left and is back in heaven when the disaster occurs (Gen 19:24b).[39] In the revised version Lot and his family had escaped to Zoʻar and had been warned not to look back toward the city, and that incident is integrated into the main plot with the remark that Lot's wife did look back and became a pillar of salt.[40] In the epic version Abraham woke up the next morning and, looking in the direction of Sodom and Gomorrah, saw thick smoke rising, but in the revised version it was thanks to him that Lot managed to escape (Gen 19:29; cf. 19:13, 25).

The final incident in this episode records the birth of Isaac. It was a crucial event in the Priestly revision of the epic, and so the incident was changed to note that the child was born in fulfillment of God's covenant with Abraham. The changes are made, as usual, by repetition and cross-reference and relate the original story to a larger and more complicated context (Gen 21:1b, 2b, 4–5).[41]

THE FOURTH EPISODE

The fourth episode is the story of Jacob. It begins with Isaac's migration to Gerar where he acquired unexpected wealth and sudden ascendancy over the Philistines. It tells how Jacob, with his mother's connivance, managed to oust his brother Esau and accede to the status of firstborn. It describes Jacob's flight to Haran to escape his brother's wrath and dwells on the deceptions surrounding his marriages with Laban's daughters and his unscrupulous acquisition of Laban's wealth. The story ends with his return to Canaan, his struggle with God at the crossing of the Jabbok, and, after he overcame God and men, his apotheosis as Israel.

The episode was revised by the Priestly writer, the Elohist, and the Deuteronomistic Historian. The Priestly writer inserted chronological and genealogical remarks and added other comments that downplayed Jacob's cleverness and made him the heir of the promise to Abraham.[42] The Elohist put Jacob's journey to Haran under the aegis of the God of Bethel and described the divine providence that constantly attended him in exile and until he returned to fulfill his vow at Bethel.[43] The Deuteronomistic Historian added incidents and comments that related the story to the history of the twelve tribes of Israel, their settlement in the land, and their relationship with neighboring peoples.[44]

The beginning of the story was changed to agree with the Deuteronomistic revision of the life of Abraham. The change took place, as usual, through repetition and cross-reference: the epic begins by saying that Isaac went to Gerar because there was a famine in the land, and the revision repeats that he went to Gerar to note that the famine was not the one that occurred in the time of Abraham. The epic goes on to tell about all the blessings that accrued to Isaac, and the revision transfers to Isaac the blessing of Abraham.[45] The change was not absolutely necessary, but it took cognizance of the material that had been added between this episode and the last and made the story part of a different history.

The second incident begins the theme of deception that characterizes the Jacob cycle with the story of Isaac fooling the Philistines about his wife Rebekah and thereby gaining immunity among them and becoming so powerful that they asked him to leave. In the Deuteronomistic version of the Pentateuch the story had already been told twice about Abraham, once in Egypt and once in Gerar, and it sufficed to relate it to the second of these by adding two remarks. The first addition is made by repeating one word and its connection with the preceding version consists in exonerating the Philistines and in stating explicitly that the chastity of the patriarch's wife had not been violated (Gen 12:10–20; 20:1–18).[46] The second remark—that the Philistines filled up the wells Abraham had dug—was inserted by referring to an editorial comment in the preceding incident.[47] The changes add substance to the story of Isaac and give the impression that his life followed the model and course set by Abraham.

The third incident emphasizes Isaac's significance in the region by narrating his agreement to a nonaggression pact with the Philistines. The Deuteronomistic Historian added concluding remarks, some to situate Isaac in Beersheba, where Abraham had lived, and others to anticipate the story of Jacob's flight to Haran (Gen 26:32–35).[48]

The following incidents in which Jacob steals his brother's birthright and has to flee eastward to Haran were changed by the juxtaposition of variant interpretations and by the insertion of four notes that relate the incidents to the general thrust of the Deuteronomistic History. The interpretations are coherent blocks of material that do not affect the epic text. The annotations are barely noticeable in the overall reworking of the Pentateuch.[49]

The last four incidents narrate Jacob's return to Canaan, his wrestling with God, and his final deception of Esau, and these became the subject of serious disagreement. The encounter with God was especially troublesome, and, whereas the Priestly writer was content to replace it with a divine revelation, the Elohist rewrote the whole story to emphasize his encounter with Esau. The epic still supplied the narrative outline for the Deuteronomist, but its point became lost in the maze of conflicting interests.

In the first of these incidents Yahweh tells Jacob to return to the land of his birth; Jacob notifies Esau that he has become very wealthy during his sojourn in Haran and is about to return; and Esau comes to meet him with four hundred men. In between Yahweh's advice and Jacob's compliance the Elohist inserted another version of Jacob's sojourn in Haran, a lengthy account of his return journey, and an alternative meeting with angels. The passages are connected to the original by initial and final repetition, but their detail takes the epic out of its marvelous mode into a human and political world governed by providence.[50]

The second incident is the narrative of the crossing of the Jabbok and the wrestling ordeal in which Jacob was victorious and received the name Israel because he had overcome God and men. It made God seem human and accessible, and the Elohist absorbed it into a different story, according to which Jacob found God at Bethel and it was Esau that he encountered on his journey.[51] The Deuteronomist, in turn, had

Jacob recite a humble prayer before the match and then overloaded the incident with etiologies that made his survival an act of God.[52]

In the third incident the meeting between Jacob and Esau takes place peaceably, Esau supposing that Jacob was surrendering to him all the possessions that he had acquired in Haran, but Jacob deceives him and, instead of following him to Seir, travels to Succoth and Shechem. The Priestly document brought him to Bethel, where he became the heir of the promise to Abraham. The Elohist narrated his amicable meeting with Esau and brought him to the same place. The Deuteronomistic Historian added the story of Dinah, recounted the birth of Benjamin and the death of Rachel, and concluded with the genealogy of the twelve sons of Jacob. All in all the story of Jacob is blended into the history of Israel.[53]

THE FIFTH EPISODE

The fifth episode is the story of Joseph. Joseph was Israel's favorite son, and when his brothers tried to kill him Judah persuaded them to sell him to some Ishmaelites who were passing by on their way to Egypt. In Egypt he became the servant of an officer of the court and, because Yahweh was with him and blessed the Egyptian's house, eventually was put in charge of the royal estates. In this capacity he distributed supplies during the famine that soon overtook the whole world. When his brothers came to Egypt to buy grain, he sold it to them on the condition that they bring Benjamin when they returned. Although Joseph took Simeon hostage, Israel at first refused to let Benjamin go with his brothers but when the famine became severe, and when Judah went ransom for the boy, he sent them back. At the feast that was prepared for them on their return Judah retold the whole story to Joseph, dwelling especially on Israel's grief at the loss of his favorite son, and Joseph, being unable to contain himself any longer, revealed his identity and sent them back to Canaan to get their father and families. The story ends with the reunion of Israel and Joseph and with the settlement of the children of Israel in Egypt.

The Priestly document left the epic unchanged and merely incorporated the story into its chronological and genealogical scheme.[54] The Elohist made Joseph a dreamer and an instrument of divine providence by adding the subplot of his imprisonment and gradual accession to a position of authority in Egypt and among his brothers.[55] The Deuteronomistic Historian added theological, geographical, ethnographic, and genealogical comments, the story of Judah and Tamar, and the other subplot about the money that was returned to the brothers or used to acquire all the land of Egypt for the Pharaoh.[56]

The first incident describes Israel's love for Joseph, the jealousy that this caused among his brothers, his journey from Hebron to Shechem and Dothan where they were pasturing their sheep, their decision to kill him, and Judah's attempt to save him by having him sold to Ishmaelites on their way from Gilead to Egypt. The Elohist added the part about his dreams and his coat of many colors, had him sold to Midianites, and made Reuben his protector. All the additions are linked to the original by simple repetition. Together they emphasize the legendary character of the incident and introduce the theme of Joseph's supremacy among his brothers, which dominates the Elohist account.[57]

In the second incident the epic relates that Joseph was successful in Egypt because Yahweh was with him and blessed his Egyptian owner. The Elohist added the story of Potiphar's wife to emphasize Joseph's innocence and to begin the story of his unjust imprisonment and providential rise to power. The Deuteronomistic Historian made the Elohist version more integral to the epic by repeating that Yahweh was with Joseph in prison.[58]

The third incident simply recounts that the whole world was beset by famine and came to Egypt to buy grain. The Elohist includes Pharaoh's dreams and Joseph's prediction of the famine, and this part of the story ends repeating the first part of the epic text. The Deuteronomistic Historian extended the famine to the land of Egypt by repeating the Elohist and epic texts about the famine and Joseph's preparations for it. The edited text is somewhat cumbersome, but in it all the plots mesh.[59]

The fourth and fifth incidents tell how the brothers journeyed to Egypt to buy grain but were accused of being spies and had to leave Simeon behind as hostage while they went back to Canaan to fetch Benjamin. The Elohist narrative was maintained by adding cross-references to Joseph's dreams and to Reuben's pleas on his behalf. The Deuteronomistic Historian began to weave the subplot of Joseph's cunning and financial wizardry into the earlier versions by adding the story of the money that was put into their sacks of grain.[60]

In the sixth incident Judah assumes responsibility for Benjamin and persuades Israel to send him with them when they return to Egypt. The Deuteronomistic History continued the subplot by explaining how the money got to be in their grain sacks, alluded to its earlier lists of the twelve tribes of Israel, and explained the eating habits of the

Egyptians.[61] The additions are done in imitation of the Elohist[62] and give the History the appearance of a unified and original piece of work.

In the seventh incident Judah tries to persuade Joseph not to keep Benjamin in Egypt by telling him of Israel's reaction to his purported death and disappearance. The incident was not revised, but the Deuteronomistic Historian prefixed another incident in the subplot concerning the money that, to the brothers' dismay on their journey home, kept reappearing in their sacks (Gen 44:1–17).[63]

In the eighth and ninth incidents Joseph reveals his identity to his brothers and sends them back to Canaan to get their father and their families. The Elohist added a speech in which Joseph explained to his brothers the working of divine providence. The Deuteronomist continued the subplot but, instead of putting their money back in their bags to terrify them on the way home, gave them presents and told them not to be dismayed.[64]

The last incident describes the reunion of Joseph and Israel and the settlement of the people, under the authority of Pharaoh, in the land of Goshen. The Elohist prefaced Jacob's descent into Egypt with a vision assuring him that he would come out of Egypt and appended to their settlement in the land a blessing of Jacob and a final discourse by Joseph (Gen 46:1–5; 48:1–2, 8–21; 50:1–8, 14–26). The Deuteronomistic Historian ended the epic subplot by describing how Pharaoh bought all the land and enslaved his own people, and added genealogies and the Blessing of Jacob to the other versions (Gen 46:8–27, 34b; 47:7–26; 48:3–7, 22; 49:1–33a; 50:9–11).

In its epic version the story of Joseph had legendary, historical, and symbolic significance. The Priestly writer was interested in its historicity and added chronological notices. The Elohist was interested in its symbolic significance and incorporated its theme of life and death into the general scheme of divine providence. The Deuteronomist gave substance to its legendary basis by including its hero in a history of tribal origins. The first two editors were content to let their ideas compete with the text they embellished. The last edition smoothed out their differences but gave prominence to its own perspective. The epic can be recovered, as a result, only by abstracting from the final and familiar text.

THE SIXTH EPISODE

The sixth episode is the story of Moses. He was born during the oppression of the people of Israel in Egypt and was raised in the Pharaoh's household. He went into exile in Midian to escape death for having murdered one of the Egyptian overseers. There he encountered Yahweh, who promised to lead the people out of Egypt to the land of Canaan. When Moses had returned to Egypt, Yahweh went before them from Rameses to Succoth, defeated the pursuing Egyptians at the Sea, and brought them to Sinai, where they agreed to worship him as their God in the land to which he was leading them. But when they had reconnoitered the land they were afraid to go up and take it, and, for their lack of faith, their whole generation was deprived of the land and their leaders were condemned to Sheol. And there the story ends, with Israel in the land of Moab looking forward to the day when, in accordance with the covenant and the word of Yahweh to Balaam, the land would be theirs.

The story was allusive and suggestive and underwent serious revision in all the subsequent writings. The sequel brought Israel into the land under the leadership of Joshua and followed the plan of the covenant and the word of God down to the time of Hezekiah. The Priestly writer had a different version of almost everything and added many details: in this version God revealed himself to Moses in Egypt, not in Midian, and with many plagues and wonders brought Israel out of Egypt into the wilderness, where they rebelled against him time and again; on Mount Sinai God did not make a covenant with them but revealed to Moses the design of the tabernacle where he would dwell with them; on their journey to the land that had been promised to Abraham, Isaac, and Jacob, Moses and Aaron rebelled against God, died in the wilderness, and were succeeded by Joshua and Eleazar. The Elohist left most of this story untouched but replaced the covenant on Sinai and the gift of the land with the revelation of the law and the assurance of divine guidance. The Deuteronomistic Historian corrected, expanded, and blended all these versions and then completely rewrote the story as the history and theory of Israel's legal, religious, and social constitution. The epic, by default, was left as the simplest motive and construction of them all.

The first incident recounts the enslavement of the people of Israel by a Pharaoh who did not know about Joseph, when they had become too powerful and threatened Egypt's internal security. The Priestly writer gave the incident a genealogical and theological context by prefixing a list of the sons of Israel and a reference to the fulfillment of the promise to Abraham. The Deuteronomistic History incorporated the incident into its own perspective.[65] But no writer challenged the veracity of the epic account.

The next three incidents tell the story of the birth of Moses, his abandonment by the Nile in accordance with Pharaoh's decree, his adoption by Pharaoh's daughter, his flight to Midian, his marriage to Zipporah the daughter of Reuel, and the birth of their son. The Priestly writer left the story unchanged but introduced it with a reference to the enslavement of the people that becomes crucial as this version develops. The Historian added another introduction to the birth narrative to extol the courage of the Hebrew women and inserted a different conclusion to the rest of the story to emphasize its salient points. The changes do not affect the flow of the epic text but prepare it for incorporation into another version of the exodus from Egypt.[66]

The next two incidents[67] recount Moses' meetings with Yahweh, once at the burning bush, when Yahweh promised to free the people and bring them to a land flowing with milk and honey, and once on his journey back to Egypt when Yahweh tried to kill him. The Priestly writer introduced the first incident with a cross-reference to the enslavement of the people and to the covenant with Abraham, Isaac, and Jacob.[68] The Elohist added another introduction to the first meeting to situate it on Mount Horeb and to include the vocation of Moses and the correct name of his father-in-law.[69] The Deuteronomistic Historian rewrote the text as the introduction to the story of the plagues.[70] The epic had described the initiation of Moses as a rite of circumcision, but all the subsequent writers found this either embarrassing or bizarre or irrelevant and tried to circumvent it. The Priestly writer had made circumcision the sign of the covenant with Abraham and therefore tried to ignore the epic by spanning its text.[71] In the Elohist version God simply assigned Moses a task. The Deuteronomistic Historian converted the entire sequence of texts into a test of Israel's faith.

The next four incidents[72] are the account of the exodus and the defeat of the Egyptians at the Sea. It is terribly jejune but was filled out by the Priestly writer and by the Deuteronomistic Historian and was redone by the Elohist to suit their individual purposes.[73] The Elohist described the defeat of the Egyptians by Israelite forces in a land battle near the Reed Sea.[74] The Priestly writer made the miraculous crossing of the Reed Sea the last in a series of plagues and manifestations of God's power.[75] The Deuteronomistic Historian rewrote the sources on the model of a lamentation liturgy culminating in a song of praise.[76] The epic was content to narrate the events that brought the people to believe in Yahweh and Moses. The later versions gave the story force by listing the things to be believed.

The next six incidents[77] describe the covenant ceremony on Sinai, the immediate reconnoitering of the promised land, and the punishment of the spies who dissuaded the people from entering it. The Priestly writer surrounded the covenant text with the plan and construction of the tabernacle and added incidents and comments that fitted the spy narrative into a chronological, geographical, and theological mold.[78] The Elohist reshaped the covenant with the revelation of the law and with the construction of the golden calf.[79] The Deuteronomistic Historian, besides adding comments and extended interpretations to each of the versions, created a separate wilderness era in which Israel acquired its spiritual, social, legal, and political identity.[80] The first two revisions took issue with the covenant but left the epic sequence almost intact. The last version followed another route and introduced numerous theories and practices that left its sources scattered and inconsequential.

The last six incidents[81] follow Israel's route past Edom to the conquest of the Amorites and the resistance of the Ammonites and Moabites, and merely mark time until the faithless generation is past. The Priestly writer surrounded them with two incidents concerning the unfaithfulness of Moses and Aaron and the appointment of Joshua and Eleazar as their successors.[82] The Deuteronomistic Historian elaborated on the itinerary that they followed and on the battles that they fought and added prophecies to fill out the time.[83]

The epic combined diverse traditions in a sequential and symbolic narrative, of interest to the historian and applicable to its own time. Later writers appreciated the history and its applications but saw them from different perspectives and rewrote them accordingly. The epic discussed the history of faith and disbelief. The later writers tried to incorporate it into the visions and realities of their own times.

The Sequel to the Epic (fig. 3)

The sequel to the epic, like the epic itself, was composed in episodes or parts revolving around the life and times of a leader or king. The episodes, similarly, comprise incidents or sections each of which was constructed of matching segments or parallel paragraphs. The Deuteronomistic revision, as usual, consisted in rewriting the paragraphs, incidents, and episodes and in adding many others that were more or less like them.

The sequel is more doctrinaire than the epic, and the personalities of its heroes are less carefully drawn; but its reliance on the text of the epic covenant is constant and clear. Its revision by the Deuteronomistic Historian was extensive and dependent, analogously, on the revised version of the epic. Both editions consequently suppose, cite, elaborate, and extend their antecedent histories, and neither can be read or understood without them.

The Deuteronomistic History integrated the sequel into its own version of the Pentateuch through persistent and detailed revisions. Its editorial principles, as usual, were repetition and cross-reference. Its repetitions of the immediate context were signaled by using one or more words from the original in a different order, conflicting context, or contradictory sense. Its cross-references to a remote or proximate context were either direct, that is, marked by deictics[84] and formulaic expressions,[85] or indirect, that is, consisting of quotations and allusions. Its deictic references included particles (e.g., "then") and phrases (e.g., "at that time") that summarized or implied the entire ambient context rather than particular parts of it. Formulaic references included clichés and stereotypical phrases in successive and cumulative contexts. Allusions were essentially paraphrases of a prior or subsequent text. Quotations were texts that were copied from or modeled on a remote context and that were indicated either by quotation marks (e.g., "as Yahweh your God commanded you") or by verbatim repetition from the text they mimicked or replaced.

The Deuteronomist, besides editing and rewriting the sequel, incorporated it into a massive and systematic history. The sequel became completely assimilated to its enveloping context and can be retrieved, consequently, only by undoing the compositional and editorial process. This undoing, however, is complicated by the extent of the revision and reorganization and by the History's reliance on other real or purported sources that it enters into its text by deploying the same editorial features. However, the sequel gave the History its basic thrust and, though minimal and restricted by comparison, it is most easily identified as the non-repetitive, non-referential, and relatively uncomplicated structure of the narrative.

EPISODE I: MOSES — COVENANT AND CENTRALIZATION (FIG. 3)

The first episode contains the speech that Moses made to the people in Transjordan concerning the covenant concluded at Horeb. Its first section recalls Yahweh's gift of the land (1a) and the first generation's refusal to accept it (1b). The second section repeats the stipulations of the epic covenant for the present generation (2a) and traces the legislative authority of Moses to the will of the people at that time (2b). The third reformulates the stipulations of the covenant in terms of personal devotion (3a) and defines the legal principles to be observed

FIGURE 3

The Sequel to the Epic
The First Edition of the Deuteronomistic History

I. MOSES—Covenant and Centralization

Deuteronomy

1	a	1:1a, 6–8;
	b	1:19°, 20–30, 32–34, 35aAb, 36
2	a	5:1aA, 2–4, 6–7, 9–11
	b	5:23aA, 24a, 25, 27
3	a	6:4–9
	b	6:10–13, 14a, 15a
4	a	7:1–2a, 2bB
	b	7:17–18, 21, 23–24
5	a	8:1, 7–10
	b	8:11a, 12–14, 17–18a
6	a	9:1–3
	b	10:12, 14, 17–18, 20
7	a	11:8–12
	b	11:13–15
8	a	11:18–21
	b	11:22–25
9	a	12:13–14, 17, 18aAb
	b	12:20, 26
10	a	14:4–5, 11–12
	b	14:22, 25–26
11	a	15:19–20
	b	16:1–2a, 3aA, 7, 16aAb
12	a	29:1a, 9a, 11, 13–14
	b	31:1, 2a, 3a, 6

II. JOSHUA—Covenant and Conquest

Joshua

1	a	1:1–2°, 3–5
	b	2:1–9a, 12–16, 22–24a
2	a	3:1aAb, 5, 10b, 16b
	b	6:1aAb, 2–3, 4aB, 5aBb, 7a, 10aBb, 14–15a, 16aAb, 20a, 22–23aA, 25aAb

continued

FIGURE 3 (*cont*)

3 a 8:1–2aAb, 3–5a, 6aAb, 7, 9aA, 10a, 11a, 14–16, 18–19a, 21aAb
 b 9:1–6a, 8–9abA, 11–13, 15a

4 a 10:1°, 2–10a
 b 11:1–3, 5–6a, 7–8a, 23aAb

III. SAUL—Covenant and Kingship

1 Samuel

1 a 1:1–3a, 4–9aA, 11abA, 18b–19
 b 1:20abA, 21, 22, 23aAb, 24aAb

2 a 9:1–2aA, 3–6aAb, 10
 b 9:11–14, 18–20a, 22a, 24b–26; 10:10aA, 14–16

3 a 11:1–5, 7
 b 11:9–11, 12aAG, 14a, 15aAb; 14:52

4 a 17:1aA, 2–4aA, 7b–9, 11
 b 17:12a, 13aB, 17, 18b–23aAb, 24–25aAb, 32–33, 37, 40–41, 49, 51

5 a 17:55–58; 18:2, 5, 20, 27b
 b 31:1a, 2–3, 4b–6

IV. DAVID—Covenant and Dynastic Promise

2 Samuel

1 a 5:1abA, 2a, 3b
 b 5:4, 6abA, 7

2 a 7:4–5a, 12, 14a, 15a, 16a, 17aAb
 b 11:1–3, 14–20, 21b–27aA; 12:24b–25

3 a 13:1–2aAb, 3–12aA, 14–15, 19aAb, 20
 b 13:23–29

4 a 15:1–6
 b 15:7, 9–10, 12b–13, 17, 18a

5 a 18:1–6a, 8–16, 17aAb, 19–32
 b 19:1–5, 6abA, 7–9abA

V. SOLOMON—Covenant and Conspiracy

1 Kings

1 a 1:1a, 5, 7–10, 32–35a, 38–40, 41abB, 42–45a, 49
 b 2:10–11a, 46b

2 a 11:26, 40–43
 b 12:1, 3b–4, 6–11, 13–14, 16aAb, 17, 18b–20, 25–29

continued

FIGURE   3   *(cont)*

3   a   14:21a, 25, 26a, 29–31
     b   15:2, 7–8, 10, 17–24

4   a   22:42, 45, 46, 48–51

     2 Kings

     b   8:17, 20–22a, 23–24, 26, 28–29

VI. HEZEKIAH—Covenant and History

1   a   9:14a, 16–20, 21abA, 22abA, 23–24, 27–28
     b   11:1–4a, 12–14, 17aA, 19–20

2   a   12:1, 2aBb, 18–22
     b   14:2, 5, 18–21aAb

3   a   15:2, 5–7, 33, 36, 38
     b   16:2a, 5, 7–9, 20

4   a   18:2, 5, 7, 9aAb, 10aBbB, 11–13, 17abA, 18–32a, 36
     b   19:8–9a, 36–37

Figure 3. Incidents are numbered. Letters denote matching segments or parallel paragraphs.

in the land to which Yahweh is bringing them (3b). The fourth section previews the conquest (4a) and the victory of Yahweh (4b). The fifth describes the land (5a) and introduces the commandments of Moses that are to be observed in it (5b). The sixth anticipates the crossing of the Jordan under the command of Yahweh (6a) and the recognition of Yahweh's dominion over the Gods of the land (6b). The seventh associates obedience to the commandments of Moses (7a) with the fertility of this land (7b). The eighth concludes the preamble by repeating the reformulation of the epic covenant from the third section (8a) and by relating it to the occupation of the land as it was described in the first section (8b). The ninth contains the law of centralization promulgated by Moses (9a) and situates the central sanctuary at the center of the promised land (9b). The tenth lists the kinds of meat that can be eaten in the celebrations at the central sanctuary (10a) and prescribes tithes for the purchase of food and beverages at the festivals (10b). The eleventh regulates the offering of the firstborn sheep and cattle (11a) and the presentation of these animals at Passover (11b). The last section concludes with the oath of the covenant (12a) and Moses' farewell (12b). The entire speech of Moses is designed to

reaffirm the covenant and justify the inclusion of the law of centralization.

The Deuteronomist incorporated the speech into a survey of past
and future history, subordinated the covenant to the law and the
decalogue, and converted the central sanctuary into a symbol of order
and divine transcendence and a bulwark against indigenous cults. The
survey of past history was added to the first section of the speech and
covered the wilderness wanderings and the conquest of Transjordan
(Deuteronomy 1–3). The preview of future history was built around
the farewell of Moses and predicted the fall of the nation and the
survival of its tribal constituents (Deuteronomy 31–34*).[86] The intermediate sections of his speech, which reformulated the epic covenant,
were modified to give prominence to the law and the decalogue and to
the curses attendant on their neglect (Deuteronomy 1–11*; 26–30*).
The legislation of the central sanctuary became the heart of the speech
and was expanded to include the centralization of judicial, religious,
and political authority and the extirpation of alien practices (Deuteronomy 12–18*; 19–25). The speech, in effect, through a series of
matching introductions and conclusions became the book of the law of
Moses.[87]

The first paragraph in the first section was edited by the Priestly
writer and by the Deuteronomist and was separated by the latter from
its continuation in the second paragraph. According to the Priestly
writer, Israel spent forty years in the wilderness, and therefore the
final speech by Moses before the conquest is dated to the eleventh
month of the fortieth year (Deut 1:3; cf. Exod 16:35*; Num 14:31).[88]
Similarly, in the Deuteronomistic version of the Pentateuch, Moses
addressed the people first in the wilderness and later, after their journey
from Egypt and their defeat of Sihon and Og, in the plains of Moab.
The literary location of this final speech, therefore, is in the wilderness,
in the plains of Moab, along the route from Egypt, and after the defeat
of Sihon and Og (Deut 1:1b–2, 4–5).[89] In this version, as well, since
the speech of Moses became the law of Moses, it was natural enough
to separate the two original paragraphs with an excursus on the
establishment of the courts (Deut 1:9–18).[90] In the original version the
two paragraphs recounted the journey from Horeb, the reconnoitering
of the land, and the unwillingness of the people to invade it.[91] In the
Deuteronomistic version the same two paragraphs were subsumed in a
story of the succession from Moses to Joshua and the judges.[92]

The second section of the speech conveys the covenant to the

°An asterisk in a biblical text reference indicates an edited text.

postwilderness generation. The first paragraph is essentially a para-phrase of the preamble to the epic covenant,[93] and the second explains how, as the epic simply assumed, Moses came to represent the people before Yahweh.[94] The Deuteronomistic Historian revised the first par-agraph to turn the covenant into the decalogue,[95] and changed the second paragraph to refute the sequel's idea that Yahweh spoke to the people face to face and that they actually saw the glory of God.[96] In the editorial process Moses became a prophet and the repository of oral tradition.[97]

The third section of the speech expresses the attitude that the people must adopt toward Yahweh in the land that he is about to give them under the terms of the covenant.[98] The Deuteronomist incorpo-rated the section into the book of the law by associating the proposed attitude with more general stipulations and with the curses attendant on their neglect.[99]

The fourth section describes the conquest of the land and prohibits covenants with any of the seven nations that inhabit it.[100] The Deuter-onomistic Historian modified both paragraphs by adding a repudiation of the nations and their Gods, and separated one paragraph from the other by inserting a eulogy of Israel and its God.[101]

The fifth section describes the land that Yahweh is giving them and includes obedience to the commandments of Moses among the norms of fidelity to the covenant.[102] The Deuteronomist added a contrast between the promised land and the wilderness and subsumed the laws of Moses under the divine stipulations that were regulated by blessings and curses.[103]

The sixth section is composed of two paragraphs each of which was elaborated by the Deuteronomistic Historian. The first paragraph assures Israel, poised at the Jordan, that Yahweh will lead the invasion and quickly rout the enemy.[104] The Deuteronomist notes first that the victory is due to the fidelity of Yahweh and is not deserved by Israel and then reviews the history of their rebellions, beginning at Horeb and all through the wilderness, to emphasize their unworthiness (Deut 9:4–6, 7–29; 10:1–11).[105] The second paragraph urges Israel to follow Yahweh since he is not only their God but the God of all Gods and the Lord of heaven and earth.[106] The Deuteronomistic Historian interprets the following of Yahweh both metaphorically, as adherence to his laws, precepts, and commandments, and literally, as their journey through the wilderness with him.[107]

The seventh and eighth sections of the speech return to the com-mands of Moses and relate the occupation and the enjoyment of the land to their observance.[108] The Deuteronomistic Historian was content to subsume these commands and promises of Moses under the blessings and curses regulating the law.[109]

The ninth section follows on the eighth and stipulates that Yahweh is not to be worshiped at just any place they conquer but only at the place that Yahweh will choose.[110] The Deuteronomist includes eating meat among the elements of worship and insists that all the pagan sanctuaries and symbols be destroyed.[111]

The tenth section lists the types of meat that can be eaten at home or at the festivals and allows tithes to be paid to the central sanctuary instead of offerings in kind.[112] The History completed the dietary list, limited the payment of tithes to cases of extreme distance from the temple, and legislated triennial tithes in kind that were to be donated to the widows, orphans, aliens, and Levites in their local communities.[113]

The eleventh section of the speech legislates the offering of firstborn lambs and calves and the sacrifice of these animals at Passover.[114] The Deuteronomistic History subordinated Passover to the feast of Unleavened Bread and included both celebrations in a complete festal calendar (Deut 16:2b, 3aBb–6, 8, 9–15, 16aB).[115]

In the last section the people are bound by the oath of the covenant and Moses bids them farewell.[116] The Deuteronomistic Historian foresaw the decay of the covenant and extended the farewell to include a blessing on each of the tribes.[117]

In its original version the speech of Moses takes place beyond the Jordan and makes the conquest and possession of the land contingent on the covenant. It differs from the epic in many details but chiefly in making the centralization of worship a stipulation of the covenant and a matter of belief. The revised version remained aloof from the central sanctuary and distrustful of the covenant and had Moses speak from the perspective of their ruin and disuse. In their place it put the law, the word of God, and fate. In the original version it was possible to understand why Judah survived and why Israel perished for refusing to worship at the place that Yahweh had chosen. In the revised version it was clear that Judah, like the nations before it who had not observed the law, was bound to be destroyed. Nations might come and go, but the law and the promise went on forever.

EPISODE II: JOSHUA—COVENANT AND CONQUEST

In the second episode the sequel relates how the covenant took effect under Joshua. In the first section Joshua assumes command and, heralding a reversal of fortune, the scouts that he sends to prepare for the invasion report that the land is theirs. The second and third sections describe the conquest of the border lands in the battles of Jericho and Ai and through negotiation with the people of Gibeon. The fourth section describes Joshua's defeat of a coalition of southern kings and a stunning victory over Hazor and its dependencies, which gave Israel control of the entire land ceded to it in the covenant between Yahweh and Moses.

The Deuteronomistic History has a different view of Israel's gradual occupation of the land, which it will propound in the book of Judges. Its revision of the conquest, therefore, consists in limiting its effect and in making Joshua less a military leader than a politician and partitioner of the land. In its view the conquest was slow and partial and, because many nations were left in the land, burdened with disastrous consequences. It was Joshua's lasting achievement, on the other hand, to assign the tribes their hereditary lands and to unite all Israel under God.

In the first incident Joshua is named the successor of Moses and at once begins the invasion with diplomatic preparations for an attack against Jericho. In the Deuteronomistic version, being the successor of Moses means being charged with the law and redoing the typical things that he did. The attack, consequently, is orchestrated by the Transjordanian tribes; the crossing of the river is assimilated to the crossing of the Sea; and the invasion of the land is typified in the defeat of Sihon and Og.[118]

In the second incident Joshua refers to the original epic formulation of the covenant to encourage the people and, when they attack, the walls of Jericho tumble down to reveal the wonders of Yahweh. The text is completely absorbed into a totally different version, marked by solemn processions, rituals, visions, and the celebration of Passover, in which the era of wilderness wanderings, begun in the book of Exodus, finally comes to an end and the sanctification of the land begins.[119]

The third incident includes the battle of Ai and describes the great impression that it made on the Gibeonites. In the Deuteronomistic version, however, the battle of Ai was preceded by a sinful and unsuccessful attempt to take the city,[120] and the treaty with the Gibeonites was considered a violation of the laws of war from which Joshua had to be absolved.[121]

The final incident in the story of the conquest recounts the defeat of the southern and northern coalitions aligned with Hazor and Jerusalem and the complete accomplishment of the word of God to Moses. The Deuteronomistic Historian modified the two accounts to illustrate the performance of the ban and then added detailed reports of other battles to indicate the duration and serious limitations of the conquest.[122]

The sequel's version is partial and determined by the ideology of the covenant. It supposes that Israel took control of the land through diplomacy, through force of arms, and with the collusion of the native population, but nevertheless insists that the entire country was turned over to Israel in accordance with the terms of the covenant. The Deuteronomistic History was intent on introducing the law into the land and on determining the norms and boundaries that would be applied to its inheritance. The first act of conquest under Joshua was partial and prolonged and mainly symbolic of Israel's tribal organization. The real conquest was a process that occurred within the country and continued through the period of the judges and the early monarchy until it was achieved in the promise to David and the accession of Solomon.

EPISODE III: SAUL—COVENANT AND KINGSHIP

The third episode is the story of Saul. It moves quickly from the account of his birth to how he met Samuel and happened to be king. It tells of his war with the Ammonites and of his chance meeting with David in a clash with the Philistines. It ends with his death and with David in command of his troops.

The Deuteronomist made it into a history and theory of political institutions. There is a story of Samuel and of the origins of prophecy in Israel. The story of Saul is ensconced in a debate on the merits of kingship. The succession of David is laden with political and priestly intrigue. In this version the simple and original truth becomes complex and memorable in the concrete unraveling of the nation's history.

The story begins with the birth of Samuel. In the original version it has to do with the celebration of the annual festivals at the central sanctuary and in particular with the performance of vows. The sanctuary at this time is at Shiloh and is dedicated to Yahweh of Hosts. Hannah, who is childless, promises to dedicate her firstborn son to Yahweh and as pledge of her piety gives birth to Samuel and presents him in the temple. The Deuteronomistic Historian fitted the story into its ongoing saga of the era of the judges by assimilating Samuel to Samson, by referring to the vintage festival at Shiloh, and by bringing Hannah into contact with Eli, who was the priest at Shiloh who judged Israel at that time.[123]

The next segment follows precipitously with the story of Saul searching for his father's asses and stumbling instead on Samuel and on the prospect of becoming king. The Deuteronomist fitted it into a theory of kingship and charism and into the legend of Saul's wild inspiration, which made him seem like a fool or a charlatan and eventually led to his ruin.[124]

The third segment tells how Saul was made king at Gilgal after he had led the people to victory at the battle of Jabesh-gilead.[125] The Deuteronomistic Historian attributed the victory to Yahweh and reduced the celebration at Gilgal to a renewal of the choice that had been made earlier at Mizpah.[126]

The following segment tells the story of David and Goliath and, like the others in this episode that tell of chance occurrences, describes how Saul and David happened to meet. The Deuteronomist left nothing to chance but prefaced the narrative with the story of David's anointing and turned his single combat with Goliath into a holy war and a great victory for Israel and Judah.[127]

The fifth segment tells how David rose to preeminence among Saul's warriors, and the sixth recounts the tragic death of Saul and his sons in another battle with the Philistines. They were both included by the Deuteronomist in the story of the rivalry between Saul and David, which ended in David's accession to the throne and Saul's demented death.[128]

In the sequel's version Saul was a great warrior and David a hero and faithful friend of the king. The Deuteronomist developed the basic narrative thread into a history of Israel and Judah by describing the growing hostility between them. The sequel supposed a unified Israel and tranquil succession from Saul to David. In the revised version, on the contrary, David's rise to power at the expense of Saul coincided with the emergence of Judah and foreshadowed the eclipse of the northern tribes.

EPISODE IV: DAVID — COVENANT AND DYNASTIC PROMISE

The fourth episode is the story of David. The first incident relates his coronation in Hebron and his installation in the former Jebusite fortress on Zion. The second is an account of the dynastic promise and its immediate fulfillment in the birth of Solomon. In the third incident the dynasty is threatened by the death of Amnon and in the fourth by the rebellion of Absalom and the northern tribes, but in the fifth the promise takes effect and the kingdom of Israel is finally confirmed in David's hands.

The Deuteronomistic History explained David's accession to the

throne of Israel as the result of crime and callous intrigue. He was king
of Judah first and became king of Israel because the legitimate heir to
the throne was killed. His coronation was in accordance with his prior
selection as the viceroy of Yahweh but took place only because Abner
manipulated events in the North. The promise of a perpetual kingdom
was revised to keep David humble and was fitted with riders to deal
with the recalcitrant kings who would succeed him. His whole family
was beset by sin and he himself almost brought ruin on the land. For
the Deuteronomistic Historian the promise to David was true, but it
was meant for the people of Israel.

In the original version of the first incident all the tribes of Israel
come to Hebron, acknowledge David as military leader, and anoint
him as king, and then he and his men capture Zion from the Jebusites
and make it his capital. In the revised version it is the elders with
whom Abner had negotiated who come to Hebron, accept David as an
equal, and make a treaty with him, and his capital is envisaged not
only as the city of David but as the prospective site of the temple.[129]

According to the sequel the word of Yahweh came to Nathan the
prophet that same night, assuring David that his son would succeed
him on the throne as the vassal of Yahweh and that his kingdom and
dynasty would endure forever. The Deuteronomist gave the prophecy
a prior and posterior historical context. In this version the dynasty is
linked to the temple, the house of David with the house of Yahweh,
and the promise is applied specifically to Solomon. The word of God to
Nathan is situated in the history of God's dealings with Israel, from the
exodus and the period of the judges into the distant future and forever.
The promise to David becomes, in effect, a reaffirmation of the ancient
word to Israel.[130]

In the sequel the promise to David is verified immediately in the
birth of Solomon, the child whom Yahweh loved, and the story is set,
like Saul's accession to the throne, in the context of an Ammonite war.
In the Deuteronomistic version, in accordance with the principles set
out in the decalogue, David's liaison with Bathsheba is condemned and
the illegitimate child of their union is destroyed. The story is pursued
both for its historical and its theological interest and becomes an
occasion to subject the monarchy to the scrutiny of the prophets.[131]

The story of Absalom follows abruptly. It begins with the rape of
his sister Tamar, on which the Deuteronomist makes a few critical
comments, and with Absalom's murder of Amnon, to which the Deuteronomist appends Absalom's flight to Geshur.[132] What had seemed
like simple retaliation for the humiliation of his sister soon emerges in
the sequel as a full-scale revolt.[133] In typical fashion, the Deuterono-

mistic Historian has David respond to the threat by fleeing the city in solemn procession and, when Absalom has been defeated, lets him return to Jerusalem in the same orderly fashion.[134]

The sequel narrates a simple family history in all its squalid and pathetic details. The Deuteronomist fills it with intrigue and rewrites it as the history of Israel and Judah. The sequel invented the story-line. The History made it memorable.

EPISODE V: SOLOMON — COVENANT AND CONSPIRACY

The fifth episode is the story of the succession of Solomon and of the wars of secession with the northern kingdom after the revolt of Jeroboam. The Deuteronomistic Historian developed this story of dynastic succession in Jerusalem into a synchronistic history of Israel and Judah and a condemnation of the syncretism that riddled both regimes.

The first incident covers the succession of Solomon during the last days of David, but the Deuteronomistic History revised it to suit its general pattern of palace intrigue.[135] The second is about the revolt of Jeroboam, which the Deuteronomistic Historian took as the model of religious apostasy. The third incident spans the reigns of Rehoboam, Abijam, and Asa and the invasion of Shishak and the wars with the North, which threatened Jerusalem. It was taken up by the Deuteronomist into the story of Elijah and Ahab. The fourth covers reconciliation with the North in the time of Jehoshaphat and military alliance with the house of Ahab in the time of Ahaziah, and it was subsumed by the Deuteronomist in the story of Elisha.

In the first incident Adonijah meant to be king, but David named Solomon his successor; Nathan the prophet and Zadok the priest and David's bodyguard performed the anointing and royal rituals; and the people acclaimed Solomon as king. According to the Deuteronomistic version David was old and incompetent and impelled to his decisions by Nathan and Bathsheba but had enough composure to advise Solomon how to retaliate against his enemies and to remind him that the effectiveness of the dynastic promise depended on his fidelity to the law.[136]

The second incident recounts the revolt of Jeroboam and the secession of the northern tribes. In the Deuteronomistic version this is preceded by a full account of Solomon's reign, which begins with his skillful organization of the kingdom and with his lavish accoutrement of the temple, and ends with his defection from God and the law. The revolt, consequently, was ordained by Yahweh and predicted by the prophet Ahijah, but when Jeroboam in his turn transgressed the law and established an alien cult at Bethel, he too was roundly condemned.[137]

The third incident covers the reigns of Rehoboam, Abijam, and Asa and includes the invasion of Shishak and wars with the northern kingdom. The Deuteronomistic History synchronized their reigns with the reigns of the northern kings, traced the crimes of all the kings to the sins of their fathers but attributed the virtues of the Judean kings to their imitation of David, noted cultic innovations and reforms in the South, and followed the line of the kings of Israel to the reigns of Omri and Ahab. The original is a rapid survey of Judean affairs and of political events as they impinged on Jerusalem. The revised version was a reasoned history of Israel and Judah written from the perspective of their royal houses and their fidelity to the requirements of the law and the covenant.[138]

The fourth incident is a chronicle of events in the reigns of Jehoshaphat and his successors. It notes that Jehoshaphat made peace with the northern kingdom but did not allow Ahab to take advantage of Judah's overseas trade, that his son Jehoram tried unsuccessfully to put down a rebellion affecting their seaports in Edom, and that his grandson Ahaziah was an ally of the house of Ahab against the Arameans in Gilead. The Deuteronomistic Historian antedated the alliance against the Arameans to the reigns of Ahab and Jehoshaphat and to the parallel prophetic time of Elijah and Elisha. The original reported the reconciliation with the North without comment. The Deuteronomist emphasized the extent and duration of the alliance but kept Jehoshaphat clear of any contamination with the reprobate house of Ahab.[139]

The first version had limited interests and a restricted viewpoint. It was interested in Jerusalem and in the succession of Davidic kings and in affairs of the North that might affect the prestige or stability of one or the other. The Deuteronomist was concerned with the history of both kingdoms, with the basic flaws and the cumulative mistakes that led to their downfall, with the persistent efforts of the prophets to turn aside their fate, and with the institutions of their survival.

EPISODE VI: HEZEKIAH— COVENANT AND HISTORY

The sixth episode covers a period of crisis for the Davidic dynasty. The first incident tells of the death of Ahaziah and the interregnum under Athaliah. The second mentions the Aramean threat to Jerusalem in the time of Jehoash and the assassination of his son Amaziah. The third mentions the coregency of Jotham and Azariah and explains Ahaz's alliance with Assyria against the combined attack of Israel and Damascus. The last describes the Assyrian invasion of Judah and siege of Jerusalem and the miraculous deliverance of the city. The dynastic crisis, in this view, is finally overcome by complete fidelity to the covenant and the law of centralization.

The Deuteronomist is more concerned with the crisis in the history of Israel. The first incident is incorporated into the story of Elisha and the ongoing struggle against the worship of Baal.[140] The second is taken up into an account of foreign wars and internal strife.[141] The third ends with the destruction of the northern kingdom and with the certainty that the same fate is awaiting Judah.[142] The fourth incident ends with a prediction of the Babylonian exile. One other incident was added in this edition to prove the ineffectiveness of the covenant in the reign of Josiah and to emphasize the inevitability of punishment for sin in the time of his successors (2 Kings 21–25).[143]

The sequel is deeply embedded in an encompassing historical work but can be reconstructed by observing the editorial and compositional features of the text into which it was subsumed. It supposes the epic covenant and illustrates the effectiveness of fidelity to the covenant and to the law of Moses in the history of Judah and Jerusalem and the house of David. Although it provided the structure and motive of the Deuteronomistic revision it is also clearly distinguished from the History by its original form and substance.

The Composition of the Primary Texts

The texts of the epic and its sequel that are retrieved from the revised versions of the Pentateuch and the Deuteronomistic History are continuous narratives composed of distinct episodes and incidents. These episodes and incidents were constructed deliberately and artistically and can be distinguished from their surroundings both by their recognized structure and by their characteristic language and style.

STRUCTURE

Episodes

In the epic each episode is distinguished by an introductory text that is anomalous and undeveloped but thematically proleptic to the following episode. Each episode, further, begins with some reference to the preceding episode and narrates a complete story whose conclusion reflects the way it began. The sequel to the epic omits the epic's use of anomalous introductory texts but otherwise follows the same pattern of separation and connection in the episodes.

The first episode in the epic is the story of a Man and a Woman. It begins with a sort of preterition that alludes to the creation of heaven and earth without developing it or integrating it into the plot. The allusions, however, have to do mostly with the lack of rain and anticipate the rain that becomes thematic in the following story of the flood. The episode itself begins with Man, who is formed from the earth and put into a garden with the tree of life and the tree of the knowledge of good and evil. It ends, with literal references to the beginning of the story, when Man has eaten the fruit of the tree of knowledge and must be kept from the tree of life and is expelled from the garden to till the earth from which he was formed. Subsequent revisions recognized the significance of the episode and enclosed it with alternative theories of creation and the origin of evil.[144]

The second episode is introduced by the story of the marriage of the sons of God and the daughters of Man, which ostensibly motivates the flood but nevertheless seems to have nothing to do with what follows. The children born of these marriages were the ancient heroes and men of renown, and the third episode follows its lead by introducing Abraham into the postdiluvian era and promising him great renown. The episode itself begins with the decision to annihilate everyone who was created in the first episode, except Noah and those who were with him in the ark that he built, and it ends satisfactorily with the literal execution of the plan. Later writers recognized the unit, remodeled it, and surrounded it with genealogies.[145]

The third episode is introduced by the story of the tower and city built by the children of Man. It leads into the account of Abraham's migration to Canaan and the destruction of Sodom, but it is the antithesis of his own nomadic and pastoral way of life. It is anticipatory, however, of the next episode, in which Isaac gives up his nomadic way of life to live in Gerar as a client of the king. The episode is complex and narratively complete. In it Abraham travels to Canaan and takes possession of the land but abandons Sodom and Gomorrah to Lot. Sarah laughs at the news that she will have a son the next year. Yahweh destroys Sodom and Gomorrah to prove that nothing is too wonderful for him, and in fact Sarah gives birth to a son. The plan of the episode was obvious to the Priestly writer, who enveloped it in geographical, genealogical, and ethnographic accounts and then interrupted the story to convert the promise to Sarah into a covenant with Abraham.[146]

The fourth episode begins with the story of Isaac among the

Philistines. It is an obvious link between the narratives of Abraham and Jacob and continues the theme of blessing that is crucial to the epic. Its introductory incidents, however, in which Isaac is afraid that he might be killed because of Rebekah and claims that she is his sister and not his wife, are odd and anomalous in the family history. But their theme of life and death, emphasized in the king's warning that whoever harms them will be executed, is basic to the following story of Joseph. The episode itself is consistent in illustrating the theme of deceit and is encased between two circumambient incidents in which an adversary travels to meet the hero of the story and seeks reconciliation. The Priestly writer recognized the structure of the episode and gave it a new introduction, a pivot, and a new conclusion. The Deuteronomist enclosed it in genealogical lists.[147]

The fifth episode is introduced by the story of conflict between Joseph and his brothers, which led to his enslavement in Egypt. In the rest of the episode he is in charge of the royal domains, but the theme of enslavement appears again in the next and final episode. The episode itself begins and ends with the brothers shepherding their flocks, at first in Canaan and later in Egypt, and it is related to the previous episode by its insistence on the appellation of Jacob as Israel. The Priestly writer surrounded the story with genealogical and chronological notices, and the Deuteronomistic Historian made the episode even more isolated with initial and final embellishments.[148]

The last episode begins with an incident that relates it to the story of Joseph. It is introduced by the legend of the birth of Moses and his adoption by the daughter of Pharaoh, which has no further repercussions in the episode. In the end Balaam recalls all the main points of the episode and the pervasive themes of the epic. The structure of the whole was clearly recognized by the Priestly writer, who incorporated it into the life of Moses and manipulated all of its parts. The Deuteronomistic Historian, on the basis of the Elohist predilection for the law, expanded it bit by bit into a theory of Israel's constitution.[149]

The first episode in the sequel supposes the epic and quotes and embellishes its final episode. It is a speech of Moses with an introduction, an argument, and a conclusion that ends where it began. The writer recognized its boundaries and enclosed it in chronological and genealogical notices. The Deuteronomist enclosed it between historical and theological introductions and conclusions.[150]

The second episode begins by referring to the conclusion of the first.[151] It is the story of the conquest, illustrates a simple program, and ends with an indication of its completion.[152] In the Deuteronomistic History the beginning of the episode is marked by a further link to what precedes; the end of the episode is also marked by another summary, and the whole story is reduplicated in another version of the occupation of the land.[153]

The third episode begins with a brief allusion to the second and recounts the political antecedents of the Davidic dynasty.[154] It builds up through the story of Samuel to the coronation of Saul and declines through the ascendancy of David to the death of the king. The Deuteronomistic Historian turned the story of Saul into an analysis of the monarchy and linked it backward to the period of the judges and forward to the supremacy of Judah.[155]

The fourth episode begins with a brief allusion to the third and narrates the vicissitudes of David.[156] It moves from the choice of David by the tribes of Israel to the choice of his successor by Yahweh and reaches a climax in the death of Amnon and the ruin at the heart of his regime. It ends with the revolt and the death of Absalom and, as it began, with the people submitting to David as leader, sole commander and king. The Deuteronomistic Historian encased the episode in poems relating to the preceding and to the following episodes.[157]

The fifth episode is the story of Solomon and his successors and the secession of the North. It begins with an allusion to the preceding episode and ends in the mood of its beginning with the restoration of peace between the North and the South.[158] The Deuteronomist turned it into a chronicle of the apostasy of the northern kingdom and surrounded it with stories of prophetic intrigue in affairs of state and at the investiture of kings.[159]

The last episode begins as the preceding episode ends and tells the story of Judah through the crises that threatened the Davidic dynasty.[160] Its conclusion refers to the very beginning of the entire composition, and the Deuteronomistic History used the occasion to append a reference to the changes that it had made at that point.[161]

The episodes are part of a continuous composition, and their separation is relative and contributory to the development of the plot. Both the epic and the sequel supposed that the stories they told were already known. They mentioned well-known people without any introduction, they omitted background information, left gaps, telescoped sequences; and, instead of developing logical detailed arguments, they juxtaposed interpretations and let the argument accumulate through easy and artificial transitions. The authors who rewrote and revised them, consequently, filled in the blanks and created a progressively more logical and persuasive form of argumentation. The Deuteronomist marked the culmination of this process in a history that meant to be comprehensive, completely reflective, and totally convincing. The episodes in the epic and the sequel, by comparison, leave much to be imagined and desired.

Incidents

In the epic, incidents are grammatically, syntactically, and topically distinct paragraphs. In the sequel they are composed of parallel paragraphs arranged serially or combined in matching segments.[162] In the epic the incidents are linked by repetition and narrative development. In the sequel they are juxtaposed more or less abruptly, and their connection in the episode is either cumulative or allusive. Paragraphs are revised according to the grammar and syntax of the original and by introducing different topics or subtopics that are developed in separate paragraphs, incidents, or episodes.

The first episode in the epic, for instance, is composed of five paragraphs. The first is filled with asides and subordinate clauses concerning the creation of the world. Its main-clause narrative sequence is about the creation of Man but it ends with an ominous afterthought on the tree of life and the tree of good and evil. The topic of the paragraph is indicated by the words that it keeps repeating in new combinations. The second paragraph is linked to it by mentioning the two trees: these become its main topic, and this topic too is marked by repeating a few words in contrasting commands. The third paragraph is linked to the second by its interest in what is good, and it begins and ends with the same expression, "a companion like himself." The fourth paragraph is linked to the third by the repetition of the statement "and he brought . . . to the Man," and its topic is evident in its insistence on Man and Woman. The last paragraph is linked to the fourth by a pun and brings all the topics to a close in a conversation filled with repetition.

The fourth paragraph was changed by the Deuteronomistic Historian to include a reference to marriage and family life: the addition follows the narrative syntax of the original, but it anticipates the dialogue pattern of the next paragraph; the subtopic of marriage and family life becomes the main topic of another paragraph that the Historian added just before the end of the episode to describe the strained relationships between wives and their husbands and their children (Gen 3:14–21).[163] The fifth paragraph was changed by the addition of another sentence with the right syntax but with a different perception of the Garden of Eden: its notion that Man was driven off to the east is latent until the story of the Tower of Babel, when people start to migrate from the east (Gen 3:24; cf. 11:2–3). The two paragraphs that the Deuteronomist added to the episode fit in like the original paragraphs by repeating their context, and the geographical and theological issues that they introduce are pursued in later incidents and episodes.[164]

In the second episode the five paragraphs follow a simple story line and are linked by obvious verbal repetitions. The first says that people became numerous. The second says that their faults were numerous and introduces Noah. The third is a conversation with Noah mentioning among other things the rains that are to begin in seven days. The fourth begins seven days later and ends after the flood, when no one is left except Noah and those who were with him in the ark. The last dwells on Noah in the ark. All of the paragraphs were changed, and many others were added.

The paragraphs in the third episode were written in the standard narrative mode and were linked to each other in sequence by literal repetitions. Many of them were left intact, but some were changed by adding more narrative elements and others were modified by parentheses or asides.

The first paragraph tells of the famous men of primordial times, and the second promises Abraham great fame. The second mentions Lot in passing, and the third includes him as its main topic. In the third paragraph Lot chooses the Jordan Valley, and in the fourth, since Lot chose the Jordan Valley, Abraham took Canaan and pitched his tent at Mamre. In the fifth he is sitting at the entrance to his tent when visitors arrive but he rises to greet them and asks Sarah to hurry and prepare bread for them. In the sixth he asks his servant to hurry and prepare meat for them and then he places it before them. In the seventh he stands by them as they eat and their conversation makes Sarah laugh, but in the eighth she says that she did not laugh; they insist that she did and then depart for Sodom. In the ninth they arrive at Sodom and enter Lot's house, but in the tenth the people of the city surround Lot's house and he goes out to speak to them and locks the door. In the next paragraph they threaten to harm him, but his guests pull him inside the house and lock the door. These guests tell Lot in the twelfth paragraph that they are going to destroy the city and the region, and in the thirteenth paragraph Sodom and Gomorrah are destroyed. The last paragraph refers to the conversation that made Sarah laugh and brings the narrative to a close.

Most of the paragraphs were revised by the Deuteronomistic Historian, and only the second and last were edited by the Priestly writer. The changes in the first preserve the narrative sequence of the original and situate the city and the tower in Babylon (Gen 11:2–3, 8a,

9a). In the second paragraph the Priestly writer added a chronological note and a cross-reference to earlier genealogies in a sentence that begins parenthetically but continues in the original narrative sequence (Gen 12:4b–5abA). The Deuteronomistic Historian followed the same grammatical pattern to modify the promise to Abraham and to include cross-references to an earlier discussion of world geography.[165] The third paragraph has the same mixture of sequence (developing the main plot) and parenthesis (introducing subtopics).[166] In the fourth paragraph the changes are introduced between the opening and closing sentences and follow the consecutive and disjunctive pattern of the epic text. The fifth to tenth paragraphs were unchanged, and the eleventh was expanded with further dialogue in the original sequence.[167] The twelfth was not edited, but the thirteenth was revised in sequence and by the addition of a parenthetical phrase that related it to the Deuteronomistic story line.[168] The last was edited by the Priestly writer with sequential and parenthetical remarks that related the birth of Isaac to the preceding covenant with Abraham (Gen 21:1b, 2b, 4–5; cf. chap. 17).

The fourth episode displays in various incidents how the blessing and renown promised to Abraham took effect in the lives of Isaac and Jacob. The early part of the narrative was changed by the Deuteronomist to relate it to incidents and ideas in the History, and the sequence of the final paragraphs was obscured by the insertion of many varying viewpoints.[169]

In the fifth episode the original paragraphing is obscured by extensive rewriting. The additions, as usual, are narrative or disjunctive, but the rewriting, besides adding a mass of material, often required the redistribution of original elements over two or more paragraphs.

The last episode was edited, elaborated in added incidents, episodes, and parts, and included in a series of interpretations that left it barely perceptible as the outline of the narrative. Its paragraphs, however, are left untouched, or modified in the usual consecutive and disjunctive ways, or redistributed by their rewriting over two or more paragraphs.

The doctrinaire attitude of the sequel is evident in the arrangement of its paragraphs and segments in parallel, matching, and mutually reinforcing sets. This arrangement is suitable to narrative development but also contributes to the development of an argument as one text reflects on another.

The first episode is composed of parallel paragraphs that gradually effect a transition from the epic covenant concerning the land to the covenant with the present generation concerning its religious and political capital in Jerusalem. The paragraphs are composed in the standard consecutive mode and distinguished from each other by disjunctions. They deal mostly with the norms of future behavior rather than with the pattern of past events.

The second episode is also composed of a series of parallel paragraphs that narrate the conquest and at the same time prove that the covenant with Moses and the present generation is valid. In the first paragraph Joshua is commissioned to cross the Jordan and undertake the conquest of the land that Yahweh is giving to the people, and in the second spies cross the Jordan and report that Yahweh has given them the land. In the next pair the marvels that Yahweh has said he would perform for them are illustrated in the effortless capture of Jericho. Its connection with the first pair is abrupt and consists in the actual crossing of the Jordan. The third pair describes the capture of Ai and the effect that this had on the people of Gibeon. It is related to the preceding pair by recalling what had happened to Jericho. The last pair recounts similar campaigns against northern and southern alliances. It has the same sort of explicit reference to the preceding pair and ends with a cross-reference to the assurance that Yahweh gave at the very beginning of the episode.

The third episode is composed of five incidents that are loosely connected and illustrate in their construction the theme of chance encounter that they narrate. The incidents themselves are composed of matching segments, each of these in turn made up of parallel paragraphs.

The fourth episode is the story of David's reign written in parallel paragraphs and in incidents only incidentally connected. The first incident balances the anointing of David as king, and the foundation of his royal capital. The second relates Nathan's oracle and the promise of a son chosen by Yahweh to succeed him with the story of David and Bathsheba and the birth of Solomon, whom Yahweh loved. The third incident recounts the rape of Tamar and Absalom's revenge. The fourth explains how by kindness and then by cunning Absalom stole the hearts of the people. The last incident recounts the death of Absalom and how David overcame his sorrow in order to keep his kingdom intact.

The fifth and sixth episodes relate the history of the monarchy from David to Hezekiah. They are composed in the same abrupt and cumulative, narrative and argumentative manner. The reigns of Solomon and Rehoboam in the fifth episode and of Joash and Hezekiah in the sixth are related in some detail, but the others are reported in brief annalistic fashion. The incidents in which these occur, therefore, are composed of paragraphs that list and compare successive reigns and mark the passage of time.

The epic and its sequel share many features and differ mainly in their ultimate purpose. They view history as a family affair revolving around the lives of heroes and kings. They like to tell of journeys, marvelous occurrences, conflicts and reconciliations. They are interested in divine laws and commands, in prophecies and promises that positively shape the course of events. They have an ethereal perception of time that lets events converge and coalesce and that has nothing to do with chronology and accurate dating. They let their stories end in their own time and with reference to world affairs. They differ mainly in their use of argument and persuasion, rare in the epic, predominant and built into the structure of the sequel. The epic, consequently, was a national heritage worth updating, while its sequel became a source of conflict and contention.

LANGUAGE AND STYLE

The Epic

The epic strings together in a single narrative a series of more or less unrelated episodes in the history of one family. The narrative traces the circumstances that separated Abraham and his descendants from the rest of the world and follows the roundabout journey that would bring the children of Israel to the land of Canaan. Each of the episodes describes a marvelous occurrence, the resolution of some conflict, and a particular facet in the continuing relationship between members of the family and Yahweh. In almost all of the incidents dialogue, monologue, soliloquy, or response predominates and contributes to the development of the action, and the few paragraphs that do not contain any form of address describe transitions that are crucial in the development of the plot.[170]

The first episode begins with a crucial non-verbal paragraph that sets the stage for the episode and the entire epic, but it continues with paragraphs that are dominated by direct discourse, soliloquy, and dialogue. These paragraphs contain consecutive narrative, but they emphasize developments in the plot, usually in disjunctive clauses, at the points that separate them from each other: the first paragraph ends with a disjunctive reference to the trees of life and knowledge; the second ends with a reference to the tree of knowledge and death; the third ends with the remark that there was no companion for the Man among the animals; the fourth observes at the end that the Man and the Woman were naked and unashamed, and the fifth notes at the beginning that the serpent was a bare-faced liar. In almost every paragraph the action is explained or motivated. The reason for planting the garden was that there was no vegetation, and the reason for that was that there was no rain. The command not to eat the fruit of the tree of knowledge was accompanied by the threat of death. God tried to find a true companion for the Man because he said to himself that it was not good for Man to be alone. The serpent had arguments to persuade the Woman, and God had good reasons for sending the Man and the Woman out of the garden. Throughout the episode both the narration and the action are accompanied by words. In the second paragraph the narration introduces Yahweh, and the entire action is his command. In the third paragraph there is a perfect balance between the soliloquy, in which God decides to find a companion for Man, and the action of creating the animals, in which he does not. In the fourth paragraph the magical creation of Woman makes Man exclaim. In the fifth paragraph the conversation between the serpent and the Woman is reflected exactly both in its immediate consequences and in the conversation with God and the soliloquy that explains them.

The second episode begins, as usual, with an anomalous paragraph that sets the stage for what follows but does not enter into the plot (Gen 6:1–2, 4aBb).[171] In the epic version there is no direct discourse in the paragraph, but all its elements are balanced and repeated. In the revised version the Deuteronomist introduced a subplot, in imitation of the epic style, by inserting a divine soliloquy and a reason for the action, but then went on to add an extraneous historical comment (Gen 6:3–4aA). The second paragraph balances the narrative of God's regret for having made Man against a soliloquy in which he decides to annihilate Man, and ends disjunctively excluding Noah from the plan. In the third paragraph there is God's command and the reason for it, which are matched by the narrative of Noah's prompt obedience. The fourth paragraph describes the flood, and, as is usual when narrative elements cannot be spoken, represented, or performed,[172] it substitutes literal repetition for the regular balance between speech and action. The last paragraph, similarly, describes the flight of the doves and the gradual receding of the waters in a series of repetitive and climactic sentences.

The language and style of the episode contrast sharply with the comments and interpretation of the Priestly writer.[173] In this version there are statements and matching direct discourse, in imitation of the epic, but either there is no action or the action is reported and analyzed to no effect. The first paragraph in the Priestly text is a duplicate of the first paragraph in the epic, but it omits God's soliloquy and the reason for the flood and merely lists facts as if they were events in a consecutive series (Gen 6:9–12).[174] In the second paragraph God speaks, repeats some of the facts from the first paragraph, and tells Noah to build an ark; but most of the text is taken up with building specifications and other instructions and nothing happens—although at the end of the next paragraph the writer notes that Noah did what he was told (Gen 6:13–16; cf. 6:22). In the third paragraph God announces what will happen later in the Priestly version and gives Noah further instructions, but nothing happens until later (Gen 6:17–22).[175] In the actual story of the flood this version reports that Noah and his family and the animals went on board the ark, but it says the same thing over and over again instead of narrating a sequence of actions (Gen 7:13–16a).

The dramatic quality of the epic is particularly evident in the third episode. The first paragraph has some narration at the beginning and at the end, but all the action takes place in reported speech and soliloquy. The opening narration sets the scene for the building of a city with a tower reaching the sky, but all the action takes place in the conversation where the plans and the reasons are discussed. Yahweh comes down to see the project, but the confusion of tongues takes place in his soliloquy and is not narrated.[176] In the second paragraph the meeting between Yahweh and Abraham is not narrated but takes place in the promise that Yahweh makes to him, and the narrative of his journey to Canaan simply reproduces in fact the things that were said. The action in the third paragraph pivots on Abraham's conversation with Lot, and the surrounding narrative is composed of repetitive and precisely balanced statements.[177] The fourth paragraph is transitional to Abraham's encounter with the three men at Mamre and therefore is composed of matching descriptions without direct discourse. The fifth opens and closes with the circumstances surrounding the conversation that Abraham had with the three men. In the sixth the feast is prepared: it is merely transitional to the promise to Sarah that is made during the feast and, since the slaughtering and preparation of the animal took place without a word, no time is spent on it. The seventh and eighth paragraphs, except for rubrics noting how old Abraham and Sarah were and where they stood during the meal, are dramatic dialogues, and nothing is narrated except the transition to the next scene. In this scene, similarly, the stage is set by narration but the action takes place in the conversation between Lot and the men. In what follows as well the word is the thing until in the last two paragraphs the fulfillment of the word, to Lot and to Sarah, is described.

In editing this text the Deuteronomist tended to imitate its language and style but then abandoned the pretense in composing a different and more comprehensive interpretation. The story of Abraham and Sarah, for instance, was revised by adding a serious discussion between Abraham and Yahweh on the reasons for the destruction of Sodom and Gomorrah (Gen 18:17–33). This began with two divine soliloquies more or less in the style of the epic, but they were filled, in Deuteronomistic fashion, with explanatory clauses and with cross-references to earlier texts.[178] The discussion itself follows the epic pattern of giving a reason or motive for everything, but elaborate repetitions and careful modulation make it more like a debate than a real conversation. The story of Abraham's battle with the kings of the East, on the other hand, is done in annalistic fashion and bears no literary resemblance whatever to the epic mode (Genesis 14).

The fourth episode differs from the preceding mainly in its depiction of shifting scenes and in the extent and elaboration of its dramatic dialogue. Only one incident is completely narrative and without direct discourse, but, although it is crucial in the development of the plot, it is anecdotal and technical and does not contain human characters or events that could be depicted or dramatized (Gen 30:37–42).[179]

The first scene is set in Gerar, in the palace of the king of the Philistines, in the immediate countryside, and finally at Isaac's home. Each of the paragraphs contains a narrative of events and a dialogue or monologue that provides their motive or explanation. Important information that later writers narrated explicitly is noted by the way, such as the fact that Isaac was married and that his wife's name was Rebekah, or that he had two boys and that Esau was a hunter, or that her family was from Haran. The narrative in each paragraph provides the staging, but the speeches and dialogue reflect all the action and motivation and develop the plot in which the blessing bestowed on Isaac is transmitted to Jacob. Nothing was added in the later versions except cross-references to earlier events and to the developing historical argument.[180]

The second scene takes place in Haran at Laban's home and in the adjacent countryside. The narration provides the setting. The dialogue is extended into full-scale negotiations and agreements. The point of the drama, that Jacob became Israel in overcoming God and humans, is withheld until the end of the episode, and there it is revealed in dialogue and is not narrated.

The characteristics of the epic's language and style are evident in contrast to the Elohist incidents that surround this scene. The introductory passage, like the epic, is composed of consecutive narrative and direct discourse, but, unlike the epic, all the action occurs in the narrative and the direct discourse merely interprets it. It is in the narrative that Jacob journeys to Haran, stops for the night, puts a stone under his head, sleeps and dreams, wakens, sets the stone upright and anoints it, and calls the place Bethel. It is his exclamation that explains that Bethel is the house of God and gate of heaven, and it is his vow that interprets the real significance of his journey (Gen 28:10–12, 17–18, 20–21a, 22).[181] In the concluding passage, where Jacob and his wives set out from Haran for Bethel, there is the same preponderance of narrative action over spoken interpretation (Gen 31:4–16, 19a, 20–27, 29, 36b, 38–42, 51–54).[182] The contrast, in effect, emphasizes the dramatic quality of the epic as compared to the clever storytelling of the Elohist.

The third scene shifts to Jacob's homeward journey. The narrative elements, as usual, link sections of direct discourse in which the plot takes shape and is interpreted. The Elohist, as before, uses narrative to tell the story and direct discourse to explain it. The Deuteronomist, as might be expected, imitates the earlier versions but adds a prayer to the dialogue and monologue and inserts explanations in the narratives and fills all the new text with cross-references to the old.

The fifth episode has a simple story line with significant narrative elements that explain its contribution to the epic plot, and with extensive dialogue that reflects on the drama and reveals the personality of its principal characters. In the first paragraph there is a narrative segment about Israel loving Joseph more than his other sons, but there are also three dialogues that represent Israel as a solicitous father, reveal Joseph as an innocent and obedient youngster, and portray Judah as a clever and thoughtful brother among a pack of ruffians. The second paragraph is entirely narrative, contains no action, relays the general epic theme of divine presence and blessing, and like all such paragraphs is characterized by strict repetition. The third paragraph, similarly, introduces the famine that leads to the denouement, but it is disjunctive rather than narrative and moves the story forward without prescribing any action. The fourth paragraph repeats the point of the third but adds a speech in which Jacob tries to motivate his lethargic sons, as well as musings in which he reveals his affection for Benjamin. In the fifth paragraph the brothers speak to Joseph and retell part of the story. He in turn speaks to them and anticipates the next part of the story, and they return to Jacob and repeat the conversations. The dialogue reveals the aloofness of Joseph and callousness of the brothers, who not only sold him into slavery but were ready to give up Benjamin in order to save their own lives. In the sixth paragraph Judah repeats part of the story, Jacob replies, the brothers return to Egypt, and Joseph prepares a feast for his brothers. But the effect of the conversations and descriptions is dramatic characterization rather than narrative progression. In the next paragraph Judah uses the occasion of the feast to retell the whole story up to this point, but in a version that reveals Jacob's affection for Joseph as well as his own integrity and concern for his brother. In the next paragraphs the dialogue portrays Joseph as a gentle character after all, Pharaoh as the soul of generosity, and Jacob as the affectionate father, while the narrative presents Judah as a singularly good and reliable type among otherwise nondescript brothers.

The last episode is essentially the same as the others and differs mainly in introducing Yahweh directly into the drama and in extending the use of soliloquy to include poetic compositions. Moses is portrayed in typical terms and Yahweh, though marvelous and mysterious, succumbs to dramatic characterization. The drama unfolds, as usual, in direct speech, and events that are critical in the development of the plot but that cannot be dramatized are simply narrated.

The Sequel to the Epic

The sequel is like the epic but lacks its dramatic quality. The action does not take place in direct discourse—in monologue, dialogue, or soliloquy—but is narrated. The motives and reasons for the action are given in conversation, as in the epic, but in the sequel talk is also programmatic and a clue to the structure of things to come.[183]

The sequel also differs from the epic in its use of parallel paragraphs and balanced segments. Narrative and discourse are set against each other to further the plot and the argument. Event follows on event in a narrative sequence, or a narrated event is explained in a complementary discourse, or words once spoken are illustrated in the record of historical events. What is said and not narrated is typical and doable but did not happen.

In the sequel each episode deals with different issues and is written in a different genre. The first episode, Deuteronomy, is law and covenant in a speech that narrates their historical origin and application, and in speeches within the speech that explain the circumstances and motives of their amendment. The second episode, the book of Joshua, is composed of legends of the conquest, narratives of great battles accompanied by marvels, which illustrate the truth of the law and the covenant. The third episode, 1 Samuel, the saga of King Saul, is composed of tales in which important persons stand out from their general pastoral and agricultural setting in ritual or cultic occurrences. The fourth episode, 2 Samuel, is the history of the family of David written from an urban perspective and composed of narratives with political and administrative interests. The fifth episode, the first book of Kings, is a chronicle of Solomon and the successors of David, and the last, 2 Kings, is a narrative excerpted from the annals of the kings of Judah. The episodes are linked in logical and chronological order and develop the sequel's theory of the covenant in the narration of historical facts.

The first episode subsumes narrative and direct discourse into a speech by Moses. The action and events occur in narration and are anticipated and explained in conversation, but the speech itself, being spoken and not narrated, is less factual than programmatic.[184] This distinction between narrative and direct discourse was not maintained by the Priestly writer, who included the speech in historical time,[185] or by the Deuteronomist, who explained past and future events in song and narrative.

The first two paragraphs match a quotation from the address of Yahweh at Horeb against a narrative of the non-accomplishment of the things that Yahweh commanded at that time. The narrative is patched with matching quotations from the discussions between Moses and the people and with words that have no corresponding narrative occurrence but have a literary or ideological effect.[186] The second incident interprets the covenant on Mount Horeb in two paragraphs: the first narrates that Yahweh concluded a covenant with the people and confirms it by quoting the words that were used; the second quotes the people's agreement to do what they are told but, since the agreement is programmatic, it does not narrate that they did.[187] The third set of paragraphs states the law in all its ramifications and then matches the law against a narrative anticipation of its observance in the land. The rest of the preamble and the sections on the law of centralization are also composed of parallel paragraphs that combine narrated action and explanatory discourse. The episode ends with a discourse on the covenant ceremony, which is not narrated but typical and takes place with every present generation, and with another discourse previewing the conquest under the aegis of Yahweh.

The Deuteronomistic History edited the sequel by observing its mannerisms but added its own interpretation in a different style. The covenant on Horeb, for instance, is fitted out in this version with more narrative and more direct discourse in the same pattern of occurrence and explanation.[188] The rephrasing of the law follows the sequel's penchant for details by adding a number of other ramifications.[189] But in other places the Historian steps out of the speech-of-Moses mode to state facts or violates the rules of word and deed by treating narrative as explanatory and discourse as event.[190]

The second episode is marked by speeches and dialogue that set the pattern for occurrences. In the first incident Yahweh speaks to Joshua about the conquest and the story of the spies is narrated to confirm his words. The story of the spies itself is composed of programmatic speech and narrative action and, as is particularly evident in the lie that Rahab told to the king of Jericho, things that are said but not narrated do not occur.[191] In the second incident Joshua announces the wonders of Yahweh, and the story of the battle of Jericho illustrates them. The battle of Ai is introduced by Yahweh's assurance of its capture and the battle takes place exactly according to plan. The treaty with the Gibeonites is plotted and then executed in narrative style, and their conversation contains no action but merely reflects on its rationale in the stipulations of the covenant. The wars with the northern and southern coalitions finally illustrate the truth of the covenant by narrating how the whole land was captured and by explaining that this fulfilled the words of Yahweh to Moses.

The separate vignettes in the third episode contain fairly detailed narrative along with direct discourse that either repeats and explains the narrated events or refers to programs, ideologies, and expectations. The Deuteronomistic Historian either followed suit or added narrative interpretations.

The story of the birth of Samuel begins with a narrative paragraph that lists Elkanah's genealogy and the names of his wives, introduces the issue of childlessness, and mentions the annual pilgrimage to Shiloh. The second paragraph describes a typical pilgrimage, narrating and explaining its essential points but using direct discourse to supply motives for the action. The ritual and the family strife are narrated and repeated in part in Elkanah's words, but the motive for Hannah's vow is Elkanah saying "Why are you crying? . . . Am I not better than ten sons?" The vow would have been just words except that its fulfillment was narrated in the next two paragraphs. The Deuteronomistic Historian added narrative asides to introduce the story of the Elide priesthood at Shiloh and added conversations between Hannah and Eli that, besides transforming Samuel into a nazirite, related the ritual backward to the vintage festival at Shiloh and forward to the story of Saul, which the history of Eli was about to delay.[192]

The story of Saul is either narrative or narrative that is reproduced and explained in direct discourse. In the first segment Saul and his servant travel through the land and finally, because of his servant's suggestion, arrive at the town where Samuel lived: the servant's suggestion motivates the action, but the course of action that he proposes is repeated and takes place in the narrative. In the second segment they meet girls who tell them what is going to happen; narratively it does; and then they meet Samuel. He invites them to come to the high place and eat with him, and this happens. He tells them that the donkeys have been found, but the fact is not narrated and has no importance in the story. He speaks with Saul on the roof about the kingship, but the conversation is narrated and not recorded and therefore no reason is given for the discussion; and in the next incident the same idea occurs unprompted to the people. In the third and fourth segments each paragraph contains direct discourse either as a motive for the action contained in the subsequent narrative or as empty words flung against the enemy with rhetorical rather than historical effect.[193] In the first paragraph the king of the Ammonites utters an idle threat, but the proposal by the people of Jabesh-gilead to send messengers throughout Israel takes immediate effect in the embassy that they send to Gibeah of Saul. In the second paragraph Saul threatens to butcher the oxen of anyone refusing to join the militia, and according to the story no one refused. In the third paragraph the messengers report to Jabesh-gilead that there will be a battle the following day, which occurs in the next paragraph exactly as it was announced. In the fourth paragraph the people propose making Saul king; Samuel suggests going to Gilgal; and Saul in fact is made king at Gilgal. The Deuteronomistic Historian followed the sequel's pattern by adding narrative statements that supposedly reflected historical reality, as well as elements of direct discourse that merely related the original narrative to the preceding story of the choice of Saul at Mizpah.[194]

The story of David's single combat with the Philistine champion begins with a narrative paragraph in which the armies of the Philistines draw up for battle against Saul and troops from Israel. The Deuteronomist added a few notes on the location of the battle that repeated the language and imitated the style of the original.[195] The second paragraph combines narrative and direct discourse to introduce the champion and his challenge: the challenge in part reflects the actual situation of the opposing forces, but in part reflects Philistine boasting that does not produce any results in the narrative (1 Sam 17:3–4aA, 7b–9). The third paragraph also illustrates the various uses of narrative and direct discourse. It quotes the command given to David and narrates his ensuing trip to the battlefield. It mentions that he became engaged in conversations and heard the Philistine challenge, but it does not quote

or record them. It quotes Saul's offer of romance, freedom, and fortune
to whoever would accept the Philistine challenge. These become David's motive for entering the fray, but the offer was only hearsay and
has little narrative effect (1 Sam 17:25b).[196] The fourth paragraph,
conversely, is mostly narrative, and the little direct discourse that it
contains does not further the action but just reveals its motives and
meaning.[197]

The final incident is composed mostly of narrative elements. At the
beginning there is a conversation between Saul and Abner and David
in which nothing happens and the king and his general merely discover
what the narrative recounted earlier about David. The conversation,
however, motivates Saul's choice of David to be commander of his
troops and offers an explanation of the bond between them that made
David the natural choice as his successor. The Deuteronomist, of
course, introduced other similar material to lead into the story of the
growing hostility between them.[198]

In the story of David in the fourth episode all of the incidents
illustrate the standard uses of direct discourse to explain events,
motivate actions, and direct history. The first incident recounts the
anointing of David and the capture of the citadel of Jerusalem. The
anointing is explained by quoting the tribes as saying that, even when
Saul was king, David led them in battle. The capture of Zion is
motivated by a quotation from the Jebusites that was aimed at keeping
him out of the city. The next incident begins with the prophecy of
Nathan, which is immediately fulfilled in the story of the birth of
Solomon and which remains programmatic for the rest of the history.
In the third incident, recounting Amnon's rape of Tamar, every phase
of the narrative is accompanied by explanatory or modulating conversation. Amnon's pretense of being sick was suggested by his cousin.
Tamar's visit was suggested by his cousin, repeated to his father, and
impelled by a command from David. They were left alone at his
command; she went into his bedroom at his suggestion; he raped her
despite her pleas; she left when he dismissed her; and her brother tried
to express the meaning of her silent tears. In the revolt of Absalom
there is the same sense that what is spoken is nothing unless or until it
happens. Absalom, for instance, asks permission to go to Hebron,
receives it, and goes. From there he sent messengers to urge his co-
conspirators to proclaim "Absalom is king in Hebron," but it is never
reported that they did and, narratively, his kingship is held in abeyance.
David lamented when his son Absalom was killed, but Joab remarked
aptly that his words were useless and contrary to the facts.

The power of words reflects the rationality of history. In the account of the succession of Solomon in the fifth episode, the sequel points the narrative with statements that explain and direct events. Adonijah's revolt was not motivated by paternal restrictions but began with his declaration "I want to be king." It ended when David declared otherwise and Solomon was anointed because the king's instructions were carried out to the letter. In the sequel's account of the revolt of the northern kingdom the bad advice that Rehoboam received did not take effect, but the smart decision of Jeroboam to build sanctuaries at Bethel and Dan was carried out immediately in the narrative.[199] In the rest of the episode, apart from a treaty with the Arameans (1 Kgs 15:19), no words are spoken, and therefore it is just the facts that are recorded without reason or comment.

The last episode has brief annalistic accounts enclosed between a narrative introduction and conclusion. In both of these incidents what happens is narrated and interpreted in direct speech, while what is said and not represented does not occur. In the first incident a messenger intervenes and the relationship between speech and action becomes exceedingly complicated. In the last incident everything revolves around a speech by the Assyrian administrator and the total silence of the Judeans who listened to him. None of the things that the Assyrian says are narrated. All of them are programmatic and spoken in response to criticisms of the sequel's theology in the contemporary prophecy of Isaiah.

Sources and Interpretation

The epic had no Judean literary sources but relied on the classics of Greek, Assyrian, Babylonian, and Canaanite literature for the outline of its episodes and its basic themes.[200] It had other information and demonstrates familiarity with diverse historical traditions,[201] but it fitted them into its genre of travelogue and heroic adventure and there is no evidence that they were either formalized records or literary compositions rather than hearsay, folklore, legend, rituals, or the residue of oral tradition and common knowledge. The epic's construction of a history from literary tradition was novel, but it was not entirely without precedent[202] and certainly was recognized by the later writers, who generally used the same sources to revise and update it.

The sequel's principal source was the epic, which it quoted constantly, and its own rendition of the epic, which it reused in many of the stories it told. It differs from the epic in its toying with traditional wisdom and in its preoccupation with the court, the administration of treaties, the conduct of war, and the organization of households. Its peculiar bias prompted the Deuteronomistic Historian to give a more sophisticated account of the same affairs.

THE EPIC

The epic did not copy its sources but used them to construct an original history of Israel. The elements in each episode that do not have literary antecedents can be traced to the epic genre, to the author's education and habitual interests, or to available sources of information. It was this skillful recreation of almost universal traditions that made the epic delightful, acceptable to a cosmopolitan Judean audience, and an expression of its belief.

The first episode supposes the Mesopotamian myths embodied in *Atrahasis* and the *Enuma elish*, the epic of *Gilgamesh*, and the story of *Adapa*.[203] The Priestly and Deuteronomistic revisions of the text rely in part on the same sources and indirectly confirm the influence of this literature on the original work.

The preterition in the first paragraph combines an allusion to the creation of heaven and earth at the beginning of the *Enuma elish* with an allusion to the toil of the Gods at the beginning of *Atrahasis* (Gen 2:4b–5).[204] In their revisions of the epic the Priestly writer elaborated the allusions into an alternative account of creation, and the Deuteronomistic History added notes that insinuated its familiarity with the same texts.[205] The creation of Man from earth and the spirit of God has analogies in *Atrahasis* (Gen 2:7).[206] The garden that God planted for him in Eden has no basis in the tradition and may just betray the epic's awareness of urban and courtly life,[207] but the tree of life and the tree of knowledge are local transformations of perennial and legendary hopes.[208] In the beginning Man, like Enkidu in the epic of *Gilgamesh*, associated with birds and animals, and, as with Enkidu, it was not until his association with Woman that he became wise and like God.[209] The Deuteronomist, in reliance on *Atrahasis*, took the creation of Woman as an occasion to delve into the mysteries of marriage.[210] The snake that deluded the Man and Woman into being like God but at the same time prevented them from attaining eternal life is modeled in part on the serpent in the epic of *Gilgamesh*, who stole from him the plant that would keep him young forever,[211] although the clever conversation in which this occurs is totally a creation of the epic. The epic, like *Atrahasis*, began when God and Man were barely distinguishable.[212] It differed from its sources in believing that Yahweh was God and the creator of the world, and it followed, in this episode and the rest, the process of gradual separation of Man from God and the journey that finally brought them together again as Israel and Yahweh in the land of Canaan.

The second episode depends on *Atrahasis* and on *Gilgamesh* for the flood story, and on the Hesiodic *Catalogue of Women* for the story of the sons of God and the daughters of Man that leads into it. Nearly every element in the narrative is taken from its literary antecedents, and almost every correction by the Priestly writer and the Deuteronomist depends on different editions of the same works.

The plot and the details of the flood are similar or the same in the epic and in its Mesopotamian exemplars. When humanity had *increased* and had begun to make too much noise for the Gods, the Gods decided to annihilate the humans. In the Babylonian version the noise that humans made was associated with a conspiracy and an unwillingness to serve the Gods.[213] In the epic's version the *increase* of humanity led to the birth of beautiful women, to their marriages with the sons of God, and to the birth of their children, the heroes of old, whose evil schemes brought on the flood.[214] In both versions there is a divine decision to destroy humanity and a divine exemption of one particular person.[215] In both versions this one person, Atrahasis or Noah, escapes the decree of destruction by building a boat for himself and his family.[216] In both the survivor has seven days to prepare his escape.[217] In both the flood is brought on by rain.[218] In both the end of the destruction is signaled by the release of birds who at first returned because they could find no footing and in the end found a place to rest and did not return.[219]

The epic combined selected elements of its sources to create an original story, and the writers who revised the epic relied on the complete versions of the same sources to correct it. The Priestly writer, on the model of Mesopotamian originals, fitted the flood into a genea-logical scheme[220] and blamed it on the commotion that filled the earth and bothered God.[221] The epic had merely mentioned the ark, but the Priestly writer described its construction and its use with details taken from *Gilgamesh* and *Atrahasis*.[222] In the Priestly version, as in *Gilgamesh*, the ark ended up on top of a mountain in Urartu, east of the Tigris.[223] In the epic, Noah sent out three doves, and in the Deuteronomistic version, anomalously but in dependence on *Gilgamesh*, he also sent out a raven.[224] In the Deuteronomistic version, as well as in *Gilgamesh* and in *Atrahasis*, the hero of the flood, called Noah, Utnapistim, or Atra-hasis, offered a sacrifice to the Gods when the flood had subsided.[225] In the Priestly document, finally, as in *Gilgamesh*, the hero of the flood was rewarded with an eternal covenant, if not with eternal life.[226]

The third episode begins in the same mythical mode but soon moves to the more practical world of politics. According to the *Enuma elish*, after the defeat of the stormy Sea, the Gods of the earth built Babylon and the temple Esagila for Marduk and named him king of the Gods.[227] The epic transposed the story to the populated world after the flood, but the city and the temple tower that people proposed to build still symbolized the choice of some other God and led Yahweh to frustrate their plans.[228] The story's Mesopotamian derivation clearly was known to the Deuteronomistic Historian, who added details from the same source and supplied an etiology of the city's name.[229] The story seems isolated, but its underlying theme of devotion to a single God is developed in the rest of the epic episode.

The following incidents in the third episode introduce the conceptions and themes and suppose the sort of negotiations that were typical of treaties and oaths of fidelity. Abraham's journey to the land of Canaan is the result of the confusion of tongues and the dispersal of nations, but the promise of blessing that he received was derived from treaty assurances and, in the Priestly version of the epic, was formalized in a covenant.[230] Abraham's negotiations with Lot to settle their dispute over grazing rights supposed the bond of brotherhood and respect for boundaries, which were standard topics of treaties and contracts.[231] His hospitality toward the three travelers and the assurance they gave that Sarah would have a son are based on legendary motifs, but they also reflect the proper attitude of a devoted subject toward the messengers of the suzerain and the extension of treaty agreements from one generation to the next.[232] It was, in fact, the improper reception of the messengers in the following incident that led to Yahweh's destruction of Sodom and Gomorrah.

The fourth episode is a family saga that interweaves the epic cycle of blessing and fertility with the ideology of law and covenant. The opening scene took place in the palace at Gerar, where from his window the king of the Philistines observed the amusement of Isaac and Rebekah in the garden and knew that she was his wife. The pretense that she was his sister was a legal fiction reflecting her social status but also made their marriage an imitation of pairing in the divine realm. The instructions that the king gave his people not to touch the couple under pain of death repeat those that God gave in the Garden of Eden concerning the tree of knowledge. Their dalliance in the garden preceded, and maybe mirrored, the planting of seed in the ground and the hundredfold yield of the crops that Isaac harvested that same year. As Yahweh sent the Man and the Woman out of the garden when they had eaten the fruit of the tree of knowledge and risked living forever like God, so the king of the Philistines sent Isaac and Rebekah away from Gerar when with the blessing of God they became potential rivals. As Yahweh had promised Abraham the blessings and effects of an alliance, so the Philistines sought a treaty with Isaac because Yahweh was with him and blessed him. The form of the narrative, in effect, is transposed from myths and rituals of fertility, and its facts, though historical, are few and far between. The later versions recognized this bold connivance of history, myth, and ritual, and sorted the narrative into its separate legal, religious, and historical elements.[233]

The second scene, in which Isaac blesses Jacob instead of Esau, continues the same themes of fertility and depicts the blessing not in its personal but in its agricultural and historical effects (Gen 27:26–29).[234] The third scene, similarly, narrates Jacob's marriage to Rachel and Leah but does not narrate the birth of their children, as the Deuteronomist eventually did (Gen 29:24, 29, 31–35; 30:1–24), and instead parlays the blessing into the fertility of their surrogate flocks.[235] In the last scene Jacob receives the great name that was promised to Abraham and, by overcoming God and men as Adam and the sons of God and the descendants of Noah could not, enters once and for all into the world of legend (Gen 32:27–30; cf. 12:2a).

The fifth episode was modeled on the Canaanite legend of Daniel and on its refraction in the myth of Adonis. The epic is faithful to the broad contours of the legend in fleshing out the age-old tradition of Israel's Egyptian or African origins, and in symbolizing the expected return of Joseph, eponym of the northern kingdom, from exile and death in Assyria. Both the Elohist and the Deuteronomist recognized its sources and appealed to them in making their revisions.[236]

In the epic version Israel loved his youngest son Joseph more than his brothers and they became jealous and decided to kill him. The love and the jealousy seem hardly commensurable and a fragile motive for murder, but they acquire singular force as a narrative transposition of Anat's love for Daniel's son, or of the love of Aphrodite for Adonis, which aroused the jealousy of Artemis or one of the Gods and led to the violent death of the young hero. The transposition is creative and does not have an exact literary parallel, but the motifs are found separately and are reinforced in a number of ways in the Deuteronomist and Elohist versions.[237] The Elohist dream sequence includes the wheat harvest, presaging the motif of famine and infertility at the death of the boy, and the vision of cosmic obeisance that suggests the astral association of the jealous Goddess. In this version, furthermore, the young hero is said to have been killed by a wild animal, as Adonis was killed hunting for wild boar. Finally, Potiphar's wife, like Anat, for instance, in the epic of Aqhat, attempts to seduce Joseph and when rebuffed plots his destruction. The Deuteronomistic tale of Judah and Tamar fills out the legend by rewriting as history the story of the birth of Adonis from the incestuous union of lord Kinyras and his daughter Myrrha.

According to the legend, Adonis descends into Sheol and is sorely lamented. In the epic this descent into Sheol is replaced by a descent into Egypt, but the original motif is represented by the theme of life and death and more accurately by Israel's fear that he must descend into Sheol after his sons.[238] In the Elohist version Joseph's descent into Sheol is explicit and is filled out with the traditional lamentation for the departed son and darling boy (Gen 37:29–36).

According to the legend, the return of the God who died is preceded by a search for his remains and is marked by the end of the drought or famine and a celebration of the renewed fertility of the land at a festival in the royal palace. In some versions this is followed by a ritual conquest of the land, and in others the issue is settled by taking revenge on the murderer of the young hero. In the epic it is Israel or Judah who instigates the search; Joseph is found alive; the brothers are entertained at his table; and the Pharaoh himself provides for them. The Elohist deals in great detail with the years of drought and of plenty, emphasizes that Joseph is the source of life and blessing and daily sustenance, and explicitly rejects the revenge that the brothers fear (see Genesis 40–41; 45:4–15; 50:14–21). The Deuteronomist replaces the ritual conquest with Pharaoh's acquisition of all the land of Egypt, except what belonged to the priests (see Gen 47:7–26).

The literary use of legend to interpret historical tradition is equally obvious in the sixth and final episode. The birth of Moses incorporates typical features of folklore and may have been modeled on the *Legend of Sargon*.[239] His flight to Midian and meeting with the daughters of Reuel redoes the themes of Jacob's flight to Haran and meeting with the daughters of Laban. The manifestation of Yahweh in the burning bush, in pillars of cloud and fire, and in the flames that descended on Mount Sinai deploys immemorial images of West Semitic religion.[240] The defeat of the Egyptians at the Sea, as the Deuteronomist made absolutely clear, is a reflex of Canaanite cosmogony and the primordial victory of God.[241] The covenant on Mount Sinai and the determination of the boundaries of the land in the scout narrative reflect the imperial policy of contemporary Assyria, but the cataclysmic punishment of the spies who rejected the covenant combines the effect of treaty curses with indigenous depictions of the dead who died ignominiously in battle.

The epic ends with the oracles of Balaam, which situate Israel in history and prophecy and have verbatim links to contemporary Transjordanian literary legend.[242]

The epic used and modified these sources to interpret the historical traditions of Israel. They were not specific to Israel or Judah but took on their local color in the process of being fitted together into a single interpretation of Israel's origin and destiny. The sources were familiar, reliable, indubitable, and the interpretation supposed a common readiness to believe. The sources were literary, the interpretation original. None of the writers who followed impugned the authenticity of the epic but all felt obliged to elaborate, update, comment or explain.

THE SEQUEL

The sequel continued the epic past its prophetic conclusion to the firm and final acquisition of the land under Hezekiah. It supposed a knowledge of the epic, specifically of its final episode, and in particular of the covenant on Sinai, its prelude in the victory at the Sea, its actual wording, and its consequences in the incident of the spies. Its real meaning, consequently, consists in the interplay of familiar quotations and original applications.

The sequel does not refer directly to the victory at the Sea but, in association with other events, to its implications. In redoing the incident of the spies, for instance, the sequel has Moses encourage the people by assuring them that Yahweh, who went before them on their way out of Egypt, will fight for them now.[243] The people refuse his encouragement, and Moses refers to the end of the Sea incident by remarking that this refusal is really lack of faith in Yahweh their God (Deut 1:32; cf. Exod 14:31b). This connection between accepting the word of Moses and believing in God is crucial to the sequel's legislation on a single place of worship, but it is based on the same incident in the epic, when the people believed in God and in Moses his servant.

The spy narrative is the basis of the sequel's insistence on the obligation of the present generation to observe the covenant. The first time the story is told it follows the sequence and some of the wording of the epic version and differs mainly in shifting the emphasis from Yahweh to Moses and the people.[244] There is another allusion to the story in the following exhortation, which repeats the report of the spies almost verbatim and combines it with elements of the incident at the Sea and with allusions to the covenant on Sinai.[245] The story is retold at the beginning of the narratives of the conquest, but the plot is reversed, little of the original text is repeated, and the story is combined with more allusions to the covenant on Sinai.[246] The military stratagem that was the downfall of the people who witnessed the covenant on Sinai and still did not believe became the victory signal for the next generation, to whom Moses spoke beyond the Jordan.

In his speech Moses quotes and interprets every important element of the epic covenant on Sinai. He says that Yahweh made a covenant with them, as Yahweh himself said at the time, and that Yahweh spoke to them face to face, as the epic recalled later, and he ends by quoting its exact words.[247] He exhorts the people to remember the words and write them down just as Yahweh had told him on Sinai to inscribe the words of the covenant.[248] He assures them of victory by combining a paraphrase of the epic covenant with a summary of the exodus and with allusions to the story of creation.[249] He surrounds the law of centralization with allusions to the festivals described in the epic[250] and ends his speech by recalling the basic assurances contained in the covenant.[251]

The second episode treats the covenant as the program for the conquest and refers to its original or amended form wherever possible. The first paragraph gives the credentials that Moses acquired at the Sea and quotes from the assurances that he gave beyond the Jordan.[252] In the second paragraph the spies confirm that the land has been given to the people in accordance with the covenant (Josh 2:9a, 24a; cf. Deut 1:8). The third paragraph quotes the words of Yahweh on Sinai ceding the land to Israel (Josh 3:10b = Exod 34:11). The fourth and fifth quote the words of Moses to the same effect (Josh 6:2; 8:1; cf. Deut 7:23–24). The sixth paragraph illustrates the covenant stipulation prohibiting treaties with the inhabitants of the land (Josh 9:8–9abA; cf. Exod 34:12). The seventh quotes the words of Moses and the eighth confirms that all the words of the covenant were fulfilled (Josh 10:8; cf. Deut 7:23; Josh 11:23aA; cf. Exodus 34).

In the third episode the narratives are lightly threaded with allusions to the covenant and the conquest of the land. The story of the birth and dedication of Samuel supposes provisions of the covenant concerning festivals, the fulfillment of vows, and the offering of first-born male children to Yahweh.[253] The story of Saul's meeting with Samuel revolves around the sacrificial meal on the high place and supposes the law permitting meat to be eaten apart from the central sanctuary in any town (1 Samuel 9; cf. Deut 12:20). The story of the Ammonite war supposes that centralization had not taken effect and that Yahweh was worshiped not only at Shiloh but at Gilgal as well (1 Sam 11:14a, 15aAb).[254] In the story of his combat with the Philistine David is implicitly compared to Moses and Joshua.[255] It is only the death of Saul that does not in any way exemplify the law and the covenant.

The fourth episode has similar allusions to the covenant and the conquest. It begins, on the model of annual pilgrimage to the central sanctuary, with all the tribes of Israel coming to anoint David in the presence of Yahweh at Hebron (2 Sam 5:1abA, 2a, 3b).[256] David's capture of the Jebusite fortress in Zion fulfills the covenant concerning the land (2 Sam 5:6abA, 7).[257] The model for the covenant with David was the Sinai covenant between Yahweh and Moses and Israel.[258] The conquest of the Ammonites completes the sweep of Transjordan that Israel did not accomplish under Moses, and the battle for Rabbah is like the battle at Ai (2 Samuel 11).[259] The revolt of Absalom put the covenant with David in jeopardy.[260] The stories are new, but the ideology is the same.

The fifth and sixth episodes treat the covenant mainly from the perspective of the choice of David and of Jerusalem. The accession of Solomon fulfills the promise to David (see 2 Sam 7:12; 1 Kgs 2:46b). The revolt of the North succeeded because the construction of sanctuaries at Bethel and Dan discouraged the people from going to the temple of Yahweh in Jerusalem (1 Kings 12). The few events of importance in subsequent reigns are those that affect Jerusalem and the Davidic dynasty.[261] Ahaz's submission to Tiglath-pileser violated the terms of the covenant between Yahweh and David.[262] Hezekiah's rebellion against Assyria restored the Davidic covenant and finally implemented the covenant on Horeb by centralizing worship in Jerusalem (2 Kgs 18:7, 22).

The sequel was a history of Israel from Moses to Hezekiah. It was completely indebted to the epic and like the epic adopted an ever more restrictive viewpoint, which gradually led it to focus on Judah and Jerusalem and the house of David. It was also like the epic in the interesting traditions that it transmitted and in the economy and charm of the stories that it told. It was too critical to ignore, but it was too narrow, too partisan, too prejudiced to escape correction by later historians such as the Priestly writer, the Elohist, and the Deuteronomist, who thought that it did the literary and historical traditions of Israel a disservice.[263]

Conclusion

Although the texts of the epic and the sequel have to be retrieved and reconstructed, it is evident from the complicated process of edition and

composition preserving and transmitting them that they were considered to be the basis of Israel's self-consciousness and belief. The edition
was meticulous, and each successive version carefully preserved its
antecedents and clearly marked its own contributions as it rewrote the
text. The compositions were bold restructurings of the original works
that distributed their elements in new contexts and subsumed their
meanings in more accurate and complicated interpretations. There was
much to supplement and correct, but nothing was rejected or lost; and
for successive generations of writers the original text was the main and
constant inspiration.

The epic was the most creative composition. It is filled with
knowledge and information for which there are no discernible sources,
and with themes and motifs and sequences that belong to the classics
of world literature. It was the first of Judean writings, sprung like the
Iliad or the *Odyssey* whole and entire from the genius of the time. It
arrayed in narrative sequence all the local and regional traditions
germane to the origins and differentiation of Israel. It created heroes
that everyone knew and told familiar stories that everyone was ready
to believe. It was learned and charming and, in the right hands,
inspiring and totally and perpetually harmless.

It fell right away into the hands of political liberals. The sequel
extracted its essence as an antidote to Assyrian hegemony. The North
had fallen to the invaders. The South after a reckless moment of glory
had submitted and survived. The Sinai covenant, with provisions for
the centrality and grandeur of Jerusalem, was a clue to better times
but, in times of political restriction, could not be bruited abroad. It was
established, therefore, in the sequel as a declaration from the past
meant for the present and recurring generation. Its truth and validity
were traced from the beginning through the defeat of kings and critical
times in the kingdom to the reigns of Hezekiah, Esarhaddon, and
Tirhaqah. At every turn the promises proved true and, one had to
believe, Assyria's turn was due.

It was, indeed, but there was more to come and the sequel's theory
of history did not wear well. Contemporaries were appalled at its
simplicity and neglect of tradition. Later generations had to reconcile
it with catastrophe and collapse and the fate of the pathetic remnant in
Judah and Jerusalem. It was not until the Chronicler's time that
anyone dared to dream and believe so much.

NOTES

[1] The Priestly writer prefixed the alternative story of creation (Gen 1:1–
2:4a) and added the chronological and genealogical sequence (5:1–29abA,

30–32). The Deuteronomistic Historian inserted an etiological genealogy (4:1–26) and made changes in the epic text that harmonized it with P (2:7b, 19aBb–20a, 23–24) and redirected it to the etiology (2:10–15; 3:14–21).

² The epic text (Gen 2:7a) has the expression *nišmat ḥayyîm*. The Priestly writer uses the expression *nepeš ḥayyâ* (1:20, 24, 30). The harmonization uses the Priestly expression (2:7b) and is to be attributed to the Deuteronomistic Historian, who uses the same expression later in the text to explain Man's dominion over the animals (2:19aBb–20a).

³ The differences are generally recognized, but there is no agreement on their interpretation (see C. Westermann, *Genesis* [BKAT 1/1; Neukirchen-Vluyn: Neukirchener Verlag, 1974] 229–302).

⁴ The epic version places Man in the garden and mentions the trees that are in the middle of it (Gen 2:8–9). The alternate version (Gen 2:10–15) reproduces the same material sequence: it ends with Man again being placed in the garden (2:15) and leads back into the original instructions not to eat the fruit of the forbidden tree (2:16–17). The final repetition, therefore, is a way of returning to the original context so that the epic might continue naturally.

⁵ The territories are described in the Deuteronomistic version of the genealogy of the sons of Noah (Genesis 10). In this History, as well, Abraham spends some time in Egypt (Gen 12:10–20) and fights the kings of Mesopotamia (Genesis 14). Canaan is the land to which Abraham traveled in the epic (12:5bB) and becomes the land of Israel. Havilah is mentioned in the genealogies and in the stories of Abraham and Saul (Gen 10:7, 29; 25:18; 1 Sam 15:7), and the gold for which it is famous helps to explain how Abraham became so wealthy (Gen 13:2). The Gihon is the river in Jerusalem where Solomon was anointed king (1 Kgs 1:33). It seems clear that the geography of the garden is artificial and meant to be allusive and proleptic (cf. Gen 25:18) as well as a demurral on the epic's fondness for primordial times.

⁶ The addition (Gen 2:19aBb–20a) ends (2:20a) the way the last sentence of the epic ended (2:19aA) and so allows the narrative to resume smoothly. The word "animals" (*bĕhēmâ*) is not used in the epic but is used by the Priestly writer in the expression of Man's dominion over them (1:26).

⁷ Names are important, for instance, in the geography of the Garden of Eden (Gen 2:10–14), in the etiology of "woman" and "wife" (Gen 2:23b–24), and in the story of Cain and Abel (Genesis 4). The origins that interest the Deuteronomistic Historian are not so much the things that were created as the elements of culture and civilization—the professions, for instance, of Cain and Abel, marriage, the origins of sin and worship, the beginning of world empires, and the like.

⁸ The epic tells the story of woman (*ʾiššâ*) fashioned from a rib and flesh (*bāśār*), and the Deuteronomistic Historian explains that this is why a man

clings to a woman (*ʾiššâ*) so that they become one flesh (*bāśār*). This interest in the institution of marriage is alien to the epic but regularly recurs in the Deuteronomistic History—for instance, in the stories of Abraham, Jacob, and David.

⁹ A reference to the curse was inserted into the introduction to the flood story (Gen 5:29bB). The ambivalence in the relations between men and women (3:16bA) is the ambivalence that makes sin possible (4:7b). The conflict between the woman and the serpent is like the conflict between a horse and a snake on its path (3:15b; 49:17). In the epic, blessing and curse are introduced in the stories of Abraham and Jacob and their recurrence marks the end of the narrative (Genesis 12; 27; Numbers 22–24°). In the Deuteronomistic version they are introduced in the story of creation (Genesis 3) and become crucial in the promises to the patriarchs and in the covenant texts that subsume and replace them.

¹⁰ Cain is driven out east of Eden (Gen 4:14, *grš*; 4:16, *qiḏmat ʿēden*) as Man was driven out (Gen 3:24, *grš*) and the cherubim were stationed east of Eden (3:24, *miqqeḏem lěgan ʿēden*). Fire and sword are the ministers of Yahweh (cf. Num 22:31; Josh 5:13). The cherubim are associated with the ark of the covenant (1 Sam 4:4) and with the temple (e.g., 1 Kgs 8:7).

¹¹ The demigods are identified with the Nephilim, who roamed the land when Israel migrated from Egypt (Num 13:33). They are reduced to flesh-and-blood creatures who receive the breath of life from God, and their attraction to the daughters of men is construed as a crime that is punished by a normal and, in contrast to the antediluvian generations, mundane life span.

¹² The preceding sentence in the epic mentioned the marriages (Gen 6:2b, *wayyiqěḥû lāhem nāšîm*) between the sons of God and the daughters of Man (6:2a, *běnê hāʾělōhîm ʾet běnôt hāʾāḏām*), and the revision repeats the same thing in opposite order, replacing marriage with sexual intercourse, or rape (6:4aA, *ʾǎšer yābōʾû běnê hāʾělōhîm ʾel běnôt hāʾāḏām*). The reference to the sons of God as flesh (6:3, *bāśār*) and spirit (6:3, *rûḥî*) is taken from the story of creation and its editorial additions (Gen 1:2; 2:21, 23b–24) and from the Priestly and Deuteronomistic versions of the flood (Gen 6:12, 13, *kol bāśār*; Gen 6:17; 7:15, *rûaḥ ḥayyîm*). The ambition to live forever reflects the story of the Garden of Eden (*lěʿōlām*, Gen 3:22; 6:3). The life span of the giants is expressed in the terms that the Priestly writer used in the preceding genealogy (6:3b, *wěhāyû yāmāyw*; cf. Gen 5:5, 8, 11, 14, 17, 20, 27, 31, *wayyihyû kol yěmê-X*). The cross-references make the edited text seem original, but the editorial process is also marked by the use of a strange word and an odd alliterative expression (6:3, *lōʾ yāḏôn rûḥî bāʾāḏām lěʿōlām běšaggam* . . .). It seems clear that the reader is supposed to notice the change without being jarred from the flow of the text.

¹³ The formula "These are the generations of . . ." (Gen 6:9) is typical of the Priestly version and was used in the transition from its story of creation to the epic story of Man and Woman (Gen 2:4a). The fact that Noah walked with God recalls a similar saying about Enoch (Gen 6:9b; cf. 5:22a). The

statement that Noah had three sons repeats a recurring expression from the preceding genealogies (6:10, *wayyôled*; cf. 5:3, 6; etc.). The epic incident had begun with Yahweh seeing the great evil in the world (6:5aA, *wayyar' yhwh*), and the last sentence in the matching Priestly paragraph begins the same way (6:12, *wayyar' 'ĕlōhîm*).

[14] According to the epic, Noah and his family entered the ark to escape the waters of the flood (Gen 7:7b, *mippĕnê mê hammabbûl*) and in the Priestly version Noah was six hundred when the flood occurred (7:11). The epic refers to "flood waters" (*mê hammabbûl*, Gen 7:10) or the "flood" (7:17, *hammabbûl*) or "waters" (*mayim*, 8:8–12). The Priestly writer refers to the "flood" (*mabbûl*) in genealogical texts (9:28; 10:1, 32; 11:10) but in the narrative parts uses one or another of the epic expressions ("waters" [*hammayim*], 7:18–20; 8:3, 5; "flood waters" [*mê hammabbûl*], 6:17; 9:11, 15). The Deuteronomistic editor (7:6b), blending both versions, combines both their lexicons in the remarkable expression "Noah was six hundred years old when the flood (*hammabbûl*) became water (*mayim*) on the earth." Noah's age is part of the ongoing calendrical and chronological scheme devised by the Priestly writer (cf. Gen 2:1–4a; 5:1–32*; 7:11; 8:13a, 14; 9:28–29).

[15] See Westermann, *Genesis* 1:572–77.

[16] The insertion begins in Gen 7:1b (*kî* . . .) and repeats the beginning of the clause it displaces (7:4, *kî* . . .). In the epic Yahweh tells Noah to take his family and enter the ark (7:1aB, *bō' 'attâ wĕkol bêtĕkā 'el hattēbâ*), and Noah does exactly that (7:7a, *wayyābō' nōaḥ ûbānāyw wĕ'ištô ûnĕšê bānāyw 'ittô 'el hattēbâ*). The Deuteronomistic History simply reflects on the fact (7:5, *wayya'aś nōaḥ kĕkol 'ăšer ṣiwwāhû yhwh*) in a literal quotation from an earlier statement in the Priestly version (6:22, *wayya'aś nōaḥ kĕkol 'ăšer ṣiwwâ 'otô 'ĕlōhîm kēn 'āśâ*): this quotation is taken from the text in which God instructs Noah to take a pair of each species into the ark, and it is precisely this text that the Deuteronomist manipulates in order to distinguish between clean and unclean animals (7:1b–3).

[17] The reorganization consists essentially in giving the story of the flood a beginning and an end focused on the sacrifice of clean animals (Gen 7:1–5; 8:20–22): the focus is maintained by an intermediate reference to the unclean animals (7:8–9), by including among the birds that Noah sent out not only the clean doves that the epic mentioned but an unclean raven (Gen 8:7; Lev 11:15; Deut 14:14 [cf. Cassuto quoted in Westermann, *Genesis* 1:600]), and by interrupting the concluding covenant with Noah to discuss sacrifice (Gen 9:2–8). The cross-references are to surrounding Priestly texts: Yahweh sees that Noah alone is innocent among his contemporaries (Gen 7:1b, *kî 'ōtĕkā rā'îtî ṣaddîq lĕpānay baddôr hazzeh*) just as in the Priestly version Noah is just (6:9, *nōaḥ 'îš ṣaddîq tāmîm hāyâ bĕdōrōtāyw*) and God sees that the world is ruined (6:12, *wayyar' 'ĕlōhîm* . . .). In the Priestly version God instructs Noah to take two of everything into the ark, male and female, birds and animals, in order to keep them alive (6:19–20), and the Deuteronomistic version repeats the same elements in a different order—animals and birds, male and female, to keep seed alive on the earth (7:2–3)—and distinguishes between clean

animals that enter the ark in groups of seven and unclean animals that go on board in pairs. The purpose of keeping seed alive on the earth (7:3b) is an indirect reference to plant life (Gen 1:11–12), which is not mentioned otherwise in the Priestly version of the flood; the insertion ends by quoting the ending of the Priestly version (Gen 7:5 = 6:22).

¹⁸ In the epic the flood occurred on the seventh day after Yahweh had warned Noah (Gen 7:10), and the Priestly writer is at pains to insist that it was exactly on the seventeenth day of the second month that it occurred (*bayyôm hazzeh*, 7:11) and precisely on that day that they all got into the ark (*bĕ˓eṣem hayyôm hazzeh*, 7:13). Most of the comment repeats God's instructions to Noah earlier in the story (Gen 6:19–22).

¹⁹ The epic mentions that the depth of the water increased (Gen 7:17, *˓al hā˒āreṣ / wayyirbû hammayim*). The Priestly version insisted on the force of the water (Gen 7:18, 24, *wayyigbĕrû hammayim*; 7:19, 20, *wĕhammayim gābĕrû*), but it also included an initial and redundant reference to the depth of the water that repeats the epic text in an opposite order (7:18, *wayyirbû mĕ˒ōd ˓al hā˒āreṣ*), as well as a paraphrase of the epic depiction of the ark floating on the waters (7:18b = 7:17b). The rest of the text repeats elements from Yahweh's instructions to Noah (6:17) and—in order to suggest that even the fish perished in the flood—from the Priestly version of creation (1:21), and prepares for the landing of the ark on the mountains of Ararat by noting several times that the water was higher than the mountains (7:19–20; 8:4).

²⁰ The epic attributed the flood to incessant rain (Gen 7:4, *mṭr*), and the Priestly writer traced it to inundation by the cosmic waters above the sky and below the earth (Gen 7:11). Since the epic did not mention the rain when the flood actually occurred (7:10), the first annotation includes a reference to the rain that was appropriate to the season mentioned by the Priestly writer (7:12, *gešem*): it is inserted by repeating elements of the epic text in the opposite order (7:10, 12, *wayhî . . . ˓al hā˒āreṣ*; 7:4, 12, *˒arbā˓îm yôm wĕ˒arbā˓îm lāylâ*). The epic says that everything was destroyed except Noah and those who were with him in the ark (Gen 7:23°). The Priestly writer says that all flesh perished (7:21), and the second annotation makes it clear that all of creation, including plant life, was undone: it is inserted by the usual repetition of its context (Gen 7:22, *kol ˒ăšer*; cf. 7:21, *kol . . . kol*; 7:23, *kol . . . ˒ăšer*) and consists of a cross-reference to the epic story of the creation of Man combined with some Priestly terminology (7:22, *kol ˒ăšer nišmat rûaḥ ḥayyîm bĕ˒appāyw*; cf. 2:7aB, *wayyipaḥ bĕ˒appāyw nišmat ḥayyîm*; 7:15bB, *˒ăšer bô rûaḥ ḥayyim*), and of another cross-reference to the Priestly story of the creation of dry land where plants grew (7:22, *ḥārābâ*; cf. 1:9–12, [*yābāšâ*]). The last annotation (7:23, "including man and beast and creeping things and even birds in the sky, they were wiped off the face of the earth") adjusts the epic text to the list in the Priestly revision and is added by repeating at the end the expression that the epic used in the beginning (7:23, *wayyimaḥ / wayyimmāḥû*). This sort of harmonization, with repetitions and cross-references that imitate and combine the versions, allowed the Deuteronomistic Historian to construct a single consistent text with hardly visible seams and sutures that was sown

with Deuteronomistic ideologies and subtly changed to emphasize the Deuteronomistic point of view.

21 See Westermann, *Genesis* 1:600. The insertion begins like the epic text it displaces (*wayšallaḥ ʾet*; cf. Gen 8:8). The last part of the sentence (8:7bB, *ʿaᵭ yĕbōšet hammayim mēʿal hāʾareṣ*) anticipates the Priestly version (8:13aB, *ḥārĕbû hammayim mēʿal hāʾareṣ*; 8:14b, *yābĕšâ hāʾareṣ*).

22 The new ending (Gen 8:13a, 14–19) is appended by repeating a key expression from the end of the epic version (*hammayim mēʿal hāʾareṣ*, 8:11bB, 13aB). The dating of the flood indicates that it did not disrupt the chronology of creation, and the final command to increase and multiply shows that it had no impact on the world order established in the beginning (8:17bB; cf. 1:28).

23 The note is added by repeating part of the Priestly text that precedes it and combining it with elements from the parallel epic text (8:13b, *wayyarʾ wĕhinnēh ḥārĕbû pĕnê hāʾăᵭāmâ*; cf. 8:13a, *ḥārĕbû hammayim mēʿal hāʾareṣ*; and 8:8b, *lirʾôt hăqallû hammayim mēʿal pĕnê hāʾăᵭāmâ*). Both the epic (Gen 8:6) and the Priestly writer (Gen 6:16) suppose that the ark had a door and a window. The Deuteronomistic Historian furnishes it with a tarpaulin or an awning (Gen 8:13bA, *wayyāsar nōaḥ ʾet miksēh hattēbâ*) that is like the covering of the tent of meeting (*miksēh*, Exod 26:14) except that it is not made of any specific material. The assimilation is bold and surprising, but it is compatible with the Historian's persistent interest in cultic matters and with the specific interest of the Deuteronomist's version of the flood story in the rules of acceptable sacrifice.

24 The Priestly text includes geographical (Gen 10:1–7, 20, 22–23, 31–32), genealogical (11:10–28, 31–32), chronological (12:4b–5abA), ethnographic (16:1, 3, 15–16), theological (17:1–27; 21:1b, 2b, 4–5), and historical material (23:1–20). It follows the epic and corrects it and can be read with it or separately in sequence.

25 The Elohist text was intruded before and after the birth of Isaac (Gen 20:1aAb, 2–3, 8, 10–11, 14–16; 21:6–24, 27, 34); 22:1–14, 19). It was complicated by its incorporation into the Deuteronomistic History.

26 The Deuteronomistic History brought Abraham into remote or direct contact with Egypt and Assyria (Gen 10:8–19, 21, 24–30; 11:2–3, 8a, 9a; 12:9–20; 14:1–24; 24:1–67) and with neighboring nations (16:2, 4–14; 19:15–23, 24b, 26, 29–38; 22:20–24), and outlined a theory of prevenient history determined by the word of God (12:2b, 3b, 6b, 7, 8b; 13:14–17; 15:1–21; 18:17–33; 20:4–7, 9, 12–13, 17–18; 22:15–18). It also added annotations and comments to make its version adhere to its sources and produce a smooth and continuous text (Gen 11:29–30; 13:1, 3–4, 6b, 7b, 10b, 13, 18b; 18:1a; 19:1aA, 9a°, 11; 20:1aB; 21:28–33).

27 The key words are *wayhi* and *wayyōʾmĕrû*, which introduce the original and the intrusive text (11:1, 2). The first addition (11:2) refers to the

preceding genealogy of Nimrod and situates the incident in Mesopotamia (cf. Gen 10:10). It is constructed from earlier references to the East (Gen 2:8; 3:24) and later references to migrations (Gen 12:8b; 13:3, 11), and the familiar language makes it seem to fit. The second addition (11:3) follows on it and illustrates the Deuteronomistic Historian's knowledge of Mesopotamian literature and interest in the origins of culture and civilization.

[28] Gen 11:8a repeats 11:9b in opposite order, and 11:9a includes a cross-reference to the beginning of the incident (11:9a, *śĕpat kol hā'āreṣ* = 11:1, *kol hā'āreṣ śāpâ* . . .). The etiology is a pun, but it brings Abraham into contact with Babylon and the great powers of the world (cf. Genesis 14) and situates the original story with reference to ancient history (Gen 10:10) and contemporary events.

[29] Abraham's implication in the history of the nation is expressed in the Deuteronomistic program and the promises (Gen 12:2b, 3b, 7; 13:14–17), in texts that have him anticipate the sojourn in Egypt (12:10–20) and the Babylonian invasion (Genesis 14), in the covenant that anticipates the vicissitudes of the people (Genesis 15), and in those texts that make him a prophet (Gen 18:17–19; 20:4–7, 17–18) or prototypical subject of the law (26:2–5).

[30] The insertion is made by repeating words from the beginning and the end of the original text (12:5bA, *wayyēṣĕ'û lāleket 'arṣâ kĕna'an* = 12:4a *wayyēlek*, and 12:5bB *wayyābō'û 'arṣâ kĕna'an*) and by cross-reference to the preceding genealogy (Gen 11:31–32).

[31] See A. K. Jenkins, "A Great Name: Genesis 12:2 and the Editing of the Pentateuch," *JSOT* 10 (1978) 41–57. The addition is made by repeating a word from the epic text (12:2a, 3a, *wa'ăbārekĕkā*) in two variant forms (12:2b, *bĕrākâ*; 12:3b, *wĕnibrĕkû*). The addition makes sense and fits into the total context by anticipating the Priestly covenant with Abraham (Genesis 17) and resuming the earlier genealogies (*mišpĕḥôt*; cf. 10:31–32). In the epic the notion of blessing and curse becomes a leitmotif of the history of Jacob and Israel (Gen 12:3a = 27:29b = Num 24:9b). The revised version becomes important in the Deuteronomistic History (Gen 12:2b, 3b; cf. Gen 18:17–18; 22:17–18).

[32] The correction is made by repeating one word (*hā'āreṣ*, Gen 12:6a, 6b) and by cross-references to earlier and later texts: the Canaanites were inserted into the earlier genealogies by the Deuteronomistic Historian (Gen 12:6b; cf. 10:15–19); the custom of building altars began with Noah (12:7b; cf. 8:20); the apparition to Abraham anticipates the covenant with Abraham in the Priestly document (12:7aA; cf. 17:1a; 18:1a). The point of the addition is to make it clear that Abraham might have traveled through the land, but secure possession of the land was reserved for his descendants.

[33] The addition is made by repeating the word *bêt 'ēl* (Gen 12:8a, 8b) and by having Abraham build another altar like the first (Gen 12:8b; cf. 12:7b).

[34] Most of the additions (Gen 13:1, 3–4, 6b, 7b, 10b) were made by

repeating the preceding incident in its edited form and in opposite order. The first addition (13:1) brings Abraham out of Egypt and back to the Negeb, where the epic incident transpires: it is inserted by repeating one word from the original text (*hannegbâ*, 12:9; 13:1); it is composed by paraphrasing the Priestly text in the preceding incident (13:1, *hû³ wĕ³iśtô wĕkol ³ăśer lô wĕlôṭ ʿimmô*; cf. 12:5, *³et śāray ³iśtô wĕ³et lôṭ ben ³āḥîw wĕ³et kol rĕkûśām . . .*). The second addition (13:3–4) was inserted by repeating the same word and the words that occurred before it in the original (13:3a, *wayyēlek lĕmassā³āyw minnegeb*; cf. 12:9, *hālôk wĕnāsôʿ hannegbâ*): it was composed by paraphrasing the preceding part of the edited text (12:8b). The third addition (13:6b) was inserted by verbatim repetition of an expression from the original (*laśśebet yaḥdāw* = 13:6a) and was composed by citing the Priestly text in the preceding incident (*kî hāyâ rĕkûśām rāb*; cf. 12:5aA). The fourth addition (13:7b) was added by repeating a different part of the same text in opposite order (*yōśēb bā³āreṣ*; cf. 13:6a, *hā³āreṣ laśśebet*) and was composed by varying an editorial comment in the preceding incident ("the Canaanites and Perizzites then lived in the land"; cf. 12:6b, "the Canaanites were then in the land"). The fifth addition (13:10b) was inserted by repeating a preposition ("like Egypt"; cf. "like the garden of Yahweh") and consists of proleptic references to the destruction of Sodom and Gomorrah (cf. Gen 19:13, 20, 22, 24) and of a resumptive reference to Abraham's sojourn in Egypt. The purpose of the additions is to make this sojourn look like part of the original text: the editorializing, as usual, is obvious; the rewritten text, on the other hand, fits smoothly into the Deuteronomistic version of the life of Abraham (Genesis 10–24) and has links to many of its important moments.

35 The first addition (Gen 13:13) is linked to the adjacent text by repeating one of its words ("Sodom" = 13:12) and was composed by cross-reference to the sin and the evil of Sodom, which are the topics of two later texts (18:20 [sin]; 19:17 [evil]). The second addition (Gen 13:14–17, 18b) was linked by direct reference to the immediately preceding text (13:14, *³aḥărê hippāred lôṭ mēʿimmô*; cf. 13:11b) and was composed of cross-references to the second incident in its edited form (13:15b, 17, 18b; cf. 12:4, 6, 7, 8b), and of anticipatory references to the stories of Balaam and Moses (13:14–15; cf. Num 23:9–10; Deuteronomy 34). The purpose of the new edition is to emphasize ideas of special interest and to make Abraham typical or paradigmatic in the history of Israel.

36 The framework consists of a single clause at the beginning (Gen 18:1a) and an extended discussion between Abraham and Yahweh at the end (Gen 18:17–33). Gen 18:1a reconnects the tale to its epic antecedents after all the material that the Priestly writer and the Deuteronomistic Historian had inserted³ (Genesis 14–17). The first part of the clause (18:1aA, *wayyērā³ ³ēlāyw yhwh*) is a quotation, in opposite order, from the beginning of the Priestly covenant with Abraham (17:1b, *wayyērā³ yhwh ³el ³abrām*). The second part (18:1aB, *bĕ³ēlōnê mamrē³*) repeats two words from the last sentence in the preceding epic incident (= Gen 13:18a). Gen 18:17–33 relates the tale to the program and promises that were made to Abraham in the Deuteronomistic version of the same incident (18:18–19; cf. 12:2b, 3b, 7; 13:14–17) and develops the notion that the Sodomites were terrible sinners (18:20–33; cf.

13:13). The addition is made by repeating one word of the original at the beginning and end of the discussion (18:18, 33b, wĕᵓabrāhām = 18:16b) and is composed in part on the basis of cross-references to earlier material: for instance, the discussion distinguishes between the innocent and the guilty (ṣaddîq / rāšāᶜ, 18:23 etc.) and supposes the prior declaration of Abraham's innocence (Gen 15:6, "And he believed in Yahweh and he considered it his justification [ṣĕdāqâ]").

[37] The editorial link (Gen 19:1aA) repeats the name sĕdōm from the end of the preceding section (18:16a) and the beginning of the new section (19:1aB). The editor also ended the discussion between Abraham and Yahweh by repeating in opposite order the ending of the Priestly covenant with Abraham (18:33a, "And Yahweh went on his way when he finished speaking to Abraham"; cf. 17:22, "and he finished speaking to him and God went up away from Abraham"). It was no longer possible to speak of the travelers as the epic continued to do (Gen 19:5, 10, 12), but it was natural enough to refer to them as messengers, like the angel who had accosted Hagar (16:7–14).

[38] In the epic the Sodomites speak to Lot and tell him to get away from the door (Gen 19:9aA, wayyōᵓmĕrû): in the addition they immediately speak to him again (19:9aB, wayyōᵓmĕrû). In the epic Lot begged them not to do this evil thing (19:7b), and in the addition they threaten to do even worse to him (19:9aB). In his discussion with Yahweh, Abraham had argued that Yahweh the Judge of the whole world surely knew the distinction between the innocent and the guilty, and the addition maintains the forensic motif and also insinuates that Lot was upright by having the Sodomites accuse him of trying to be a judge (Gen 18;25; 19:9aB). The Deuteronomistic Historian could not accept the implication in the epic that Lot had died in the destruction of the city and emphasized his distinction from the Sodomites by referring to him as an alien and an immigrant (19:9aB, lāgûr).

[39] The text is added by repeating the name Yahweh from the original (19:24a). Yahweh left after talking to Abraham (Gen 18:33) and the Deuteronomistic Historian, who generally thinks of Yahweh as residing in heaven (Exod 20:22; 1 Kgs 8:23, 27), uses the occasion to insist that the three travelers were not three men, as the epic said, but Yahweh and two messengers (cf. also Gen 19:15).

[40] The addition (Gen 19:26) contains a reference to the story of their escape (Gen 19:17).

[41] The Elohist additions (Gen 21:6–24, 27, 34) are attached by the same sort of artificial repetition and systematic cross-reference.

[42] The Priestly writer records the death and burial of Abraham (Gen 25:7–10) and Isaac (Gen 35:27–29), the genealogy of Abraham and Isaac (Gen 25:12–17, 19–20), the providential conception and birth of Jacob and his early adolescence (Gen 25:21–34), the real reason for his flight from Esau (Gen 28:1–5), and his inheritance, as Israel, of the promise to Abraham (Gen 35:9–15).

43 The Elohist records Jacob's vow and its fulfillment (Gen 28:10–12, 17–18, 20–21a, 22; 35:1–4, 6aAb–7) and the providence that saved him from Laban (31:4–16, 19a, 20–27, 29, 36b, 38–42, 51–54) and from Esau (32:1–3, 8–9, 14b–22; 33:3, 8–11).

44 These include genealogies (Gen 25:1–6; 29:24, 29, 31–35; 30:1–24; 35:16–26), etiologies (26:32–35; 32:26aBb, 31, 32b–33), geographical notes (25:11, 18; 31:43–50), items of theological (26:10; 28:13–16, 21b) and ethnographic (31:19b, 30–36a, 37) interest, and cross-references that smooth out the text and relate it to the History's comprehensive context (Gen 26:1aB, 2–5, 15, 18–25; 27:36a, 45–46; 28:6–9; 32:10–13, 23aB, 24a, 25a; 33:18b–20; 35:5b, 8).

45 The addition (Gen 26:1aB, 2–6), in general if not in detail, is recognized in any analysis of the text: see, for instance, Westermann, *Genesis* 2:516–18. It begins (26:1aB) by repeating the word famine (*rāʿāb*; cf. 26:1aA) and ends repeating that Isaac lived in Gerar (26:6, *bigrār*; cf. 26:1b, *gĕrārâ*). All of its elements are taken from Deuteronomistic texts in the Abraham cycle: the apparition of Yahweh (26:2; cf. 12:7; 18:1a), the command not to go down to Egypt but to remain in the land that Yahweh promised to Abraham and to the multitude of his descendants (26:2–4a; 12:7; 13:14–17), the blessing that extends from Abraham to all the nations (26:4b; 12:3b), and the fact that Abraham was considered to be a faithful adherent of the law (26:5; cf. 15:6; 18:19).

46 The disclaimer (Gen 26:10) begins by repeating *wayyōʾmer* (cf. 26:9). In the preceding story, before the birth of Isaac, it is crucial to ascertain that Abimelech, who had taken Sarah as his wife, had not slept with her (20:4a), and therefore God claims to have protected her (20:6) and Abimelech protests his innocence (20:4b–5) and makes the same disclaimer (20:9). In this story the question of paternity is not in doubt since Rebekah has already given birth to Jacob and Esau, and the addition serves only to make a seamless narrative and homogenize the history.

47 Gen 26:15 repeats *bîmê ʾabrāhām* from the opening editorial comment (26:1aB) and refers to the incidents reported in the Elohist version of Abraham's sojourn in Gerar (21:22–24, 27, 34) and revised by the Deuteronomistic Historian (21:25–26, 28–33). Once this insertion was made, the Historian could refer to it and add other material that confirmed the transferral of the blessing of Abraham to Isaac (26:18-25).

48 The first comment (26:32–33) is added by repeating the name Isaac and the temporal reference in the preceding sentence (26:31, *babbōqer . . . yiṣḥāq*; 26:32, *bayyôm hahûʾ . . . yiṣḥāq*) and consists in referring once again to the wells that he dug and in giving still another etiology for the name Beersheba (cf. Gen 21:25–26, 28–33; 26:15, 18–25). The second comment (26:34–35) is usually attributed to the Priestly writer, but its list conflicts with the Priestly genealogy of Esau (cf. Gen 36:1–3), it includes a typical Deuteronomistic pun (one of his wives is the daughter of *bĕʾērî*; cf. *bĕʾēr*, 26:15, 18, 19, 20, 21, 22, 23, 32, 33), and it is part of the genealogical thrust that the Deuteronomistic

Historian gave to the episode (cf. 25:1–6; 27:46; 28:6–9; 29:24, 29, 31–35; 30:1–24).

49 The Priestly (Gen 28:1–5; 35:9–15, 27–29) and Elohist texts do not disturb the flow of the epic but fit in between and explain its stages. In the Priestly version Isaac sends Jacob on his way; God receives him on his return; and he and Esau bury their father when he dies. In the Elohist version God accompanies him on all the stages of his journey. The first Deuteronomistic annotation (Gen 27:36a) is fitted in by anticipatory repetition (*wayyŏ'mer* = 27:36b) and relates the epic story to the preceding Priestly version of how Jacob obtained the right of the firstborn (cf. 25:26, 33). The second (27:45) repeats a phrase about Esau's anger (27:44b) and relates the conflict between the brothers to the stories of Cain and Abel and Joseph: Rebekah's fear of losing the two boys on one day supposes that Esau would be banished or put to death for killing Jacob (cf. Gen 4:10–15; 9:4–6) and anticipates Jacob's fear of losing Benjamin as well as Joseph (Gen 42:36, 38). The third and fourth annotations (29:24, 29) are fitted in with the usual repetitions and prepare for the birth narratives that follow (29:31–35; 30:1–24).

50 Gen 31:4–16, 19a, 20–27, 29, 36b, 38–42, 51–54; 32:1–3; see Westermann, *Genesis* 2:599–617. The insertion begins with the same words as the epic text that it displaced (31:4, *wayyišlaḥ ya'ăqōb* = 32:4, *wayyišlaḥ ya'ăqōb*) and with a quotation from the epic text that immediately precedes it (31:5a = 31:2; 31:5b = 31:3b). The following version of Jacob's sojourn in Haran is mostly a rewriting of the earlier epic text (31:6–16; cf. 30:25–42) and attributes Jacob's success to God rather than to his own craftiness. The account of his journey follows naturally on it but was modified by the Deuteronomistic Historian to include information on the worship of household Gods (Gen 31:19b, 30–36a, 37) and on the rituals associated with boundary stones (Gen 31:43–50) as well as etiologies of the names Gilead and Mizpah. The transition to the epic incident (Gen 32:1–3) uses one of its words (32:2, *mal'ăkê*; cf. 32:4, *mal'ākîm*) and introduces the theme of two camps that will be basic in the Elohist revision of Jacob's encounter with Esau (cf. Gen 32:8–9, 14b–22).

51 The Elohist insertion (Gen 32:14b–22, 23aAb, 24b) depends on the repetition of the last words of the epic text preceding it (32:14a, *wayyālen šām ballaylâ hahû'*; cf. 32:22, *wĕhû' lān ballaylâ hahû' bammaḥăneh*) and on cross-references to its own remarks on the preceding incident (32:8–9). In the epic version Jacob travels past Penuel (32:32a), whose etiology in the History is "Because I have seen God face to face" (*pānîm 'el pānîm*, 32:31), and the Elohist uses the name to insist that it was Esau's face that Jacob saw (*lĕpānay*, 32:17; *lĕpānêkā*, 32:18; *pānāyw . . . lĕpānay . . . pānāyw . . . pānay . . . pānāyw*, 32:21–22; *lipnêhem*, 33:3), and finally has Jacob say that seeing Esau's face is like seeing the face of God (Gen 33:10). But in fact it was at Bethel that God revealed himself to Jacob (Gen 35;1–7°).

52 Gen 32:10–13, 23a°, 24a, 25a, 26aBb, 31, 32b–33. The prayer is inserted by repeating a word from the preceding Elohist text (32:10, *wayyŏ'mer*; cf. 32:9) and by quoting the earlier command of Yahweh in the epic

text (32:10b = 31:3aB). It is made up of cross-references to the immediate context and to the promises that Yahweh made to the patriarchs. The etiologies make it clear that God won by noting that Jacob was hurt (32:26aBb, 32b–33) and barely survived (32:31). The rest of the Deuteronomistic text was added to smooth the connection between the revised epic and the revised Elohist text.

53 The Priestly writer added Gen 35:9–15, 27–29 at the end of the episode. The Elohist finished the story of their meeting (Gen 33:3, 8–11, 18a) and brought him from Shechem to Bethel (35:1–5a, 6aAb, 7). The Deuteronomistic History added an etiology of Succoth (Gen 33:17b) and a transition to its story of Dinah (33:18b–20) by repeating words from the immediate context. The concluding story of the birth of Benjamin (Gen 35:16–20) is affixed by initial literal repetition (*bêt 'el*, 35:16 = 35:15), and the following item on Reuben is added in the same way (*wayyissaʿ yiśrāʾēl* in 35:21 takes up the first word of 35:16 and itself is taken up in 35:22a). The genealogy (35:22b–26) begins by repeating in opposite order the last words of the Priestly text (35:22b, *wayihyû bĕnê yaʿăqōb*; cf. 35:29, *yaʿăqōb bānāyw*).

54 The Priestly writer added the genealogy of Esau in Seir (Gen 36:1–8) and of Jacob in Canaan (37:1–2aA°), the statement that Jacob and his entire family went down to Egypt (46:6–7), and a note on the length of time that he lived there and his age when he died (47:27–31; 49:33b) but had no particular interest in the story of Joseph. The genealogies are inserted (Gen 36:1, *ʿēśāw* = 35:29b) and related to each other (36:8, *wayyēśeb ʿēśāw bĕhar śēʿîr*; 37:1, *wayyēśeb yaʿăqōb . . . bĕʾereṣ kĕnāʿan*) by verbatim repetition. The statement is linked to the preceding epic text by repeating some of it (46:6; cf. 45:18a, 25b). The chronological notes, similarly, are attached by literal repetition (47:27, *wayyēśeb . . . bĕʾereṣ gōśen* = 47:6bA).

55 The Elohist added blocks of material (Gen 37:5–11, 19–24, 29–36; 39:6b–20; 40:1–23; 41:1–54; 45:4–15; 46:1–5; 48:1–2, 8–21; 50:1–8, 14–26) and the few sutures that were required to fit the subplot smoothly into the epic (37:2aBb, 3b, 28aAb; 42:6, 8–9a, 18b, 21–23).

56 The Deuteronomist redid the history by modifying all the previous versions. Genealogical notes were added to the Priestly version (Gen 36:9–43; 37:2aG; 46:8–27) and were supplemented by the story of Tamar and by a genealogical poem (chap. 38; 48:22; 49:1–33a). Ethnographic notes were included in the subplot that extended the famine to Egypt itself (41:55, 56b), turned Joseph into a crafty financier (42:25–28, 35, 37; 43:12, 14a, 15aB, 17–23a, 29aB, 32–34a; 44:1–17) and eventually gave him control of the country (47:7–26). Theological and geographical comments were inserted into the Elohist text by cross-reference to the epic (39:21–23) or to the Priestly version (48:3–7; 50:9–11).

57 The epic begins with Israel's love for Joseph and the jealousy of his brothers (Gen 37:3a, 4), and the Elohist adds that he was seventeen years old at the time, a shepherd like his brothers, but spoiled and a tattletale (37:2aBb, 3b) by repeating its key words "Joseph," "his brothers," and "their father."

The part about his dreams (37:5–11) was inserted by repeating a phrase from the epic and a pun on the name Joseph (37:5b, *wayyôsīpû 'ôd śĕnō' 'ōtô*; cf. 37:4aB, *wayyiśnĕ'û 'ōtô*). Reuben's attempt to save him (37:19–24) was added by cross-reference to the dream sequence and by anticipating what the brothers did and, in an opposite sense, what Judah said (37:20, 22; cf. 37:26). The smearing of the coat of many colors in blood and the reactions of Reuben and his father (37:28aAb, 29–36) were inserted into the text by initial and final repetitions. At the beginning, in anticipation of the next incident in the epic, Joseph is brought to Egypt by Midianites (37:28aAb, 36; cf. 39:1a). At the end, both resuming the preceding (37:28aB, "sell") and anticipating the following text in the epic (39:1b, Potiphar), the Midianites sell him to Potiphar. The epic incident is modeled on the legend of Adonis, and the Elohist additions enhance the basic resemblance: Joseph is a youth and a shepherd; his dreams reflect the summer festival of Adonis and the cult of Astarte; he is lamented; it is supposed that he was killed by a wild animal; his father is resigned to following him into Sheol. In the tale of Tamar, the Deuteronomistic Historian added a witty and scurrilous touch to this legendary background. See Jacqueline Isaac, "The Composition of the Joseph Story" (M.A. thesis, University of Toronto, 1986).

[58] The Elohist text (Gen 39:6b–20) is introduced by another mention of Joseph (39:6b), by a deictic reference to the epic incident (39:7aA, "Now it happened *after this* . . ."), and by having Joseph repeat the epic's final clause to Potiphar's wife (39:8aB, "My master has no cares whatever in his household" = 39:6aA). The Deuteronomistic addition (39:21–23) repeats the last clause of the Elohist version (39:21, *wayhî . . . bêt hassōhar* = 39:20b, *wayhî śām bĕbêt hassōhar*) and phrases from the epic (39:23aBb = 39:2a).

[59] The epic text (Gen 41:56a, 57) begins disjunctively and with the definite article to introduce a particular but still to be defined and therefore indefinite thing (*wĕhārā'āb hāyâ 'al kol pĕnê hā'āreṣ*, "Now there was *a* famine over the whole face of the earth"). The preceding Elohist text ends with a consecutive clause that repeats the same information (41:54bA, *wayhî rā'āb bĕkol hā'ărāṣôt*) but explicitly exempts Egypt from the effects of the famine (41:54bB, *ûbĕkol 'ereṣ miṣrayim hāyâ lāhem*). The Deuteronomistic text (41:55, 56b) begins by repeating and contradicting the Elohist text (41:55, *wattir'ab kol 'ereṣ miṣrayim*), ends by quoting and reapplying the epic text (41:56b, *wayyehĕzaq hārā'āb bĕ'ereṣ miṣrayim*; cf. 41:57b, *kî hāzaq hārā'āb bĕkol hā'āreṣ*), and in between refers obliquely to the store cities that Joseph had established in the different regions (41:56b, *'et kol 'ăśer bāhem*; cf. 41:35, 48). The editing is obvious and disconcerting but marks the point where the three interpretations meet. In the Elohist version Joseph provided food for Egypt and the whole world, and the famine that he predicted for Egypt is merely recalled in passing (41:54), but did not occur, and is not narrated. The Deuteronomistic Historian began to narrate the famine in Egypt at this point (41:55) and kept the story alive in the subplot about moneybags until the point of the subplot could be made (47:7–26). Both writers were filling the void left by the epic's nonchalant omission of Egypt from the famine that ravaged the whole world.

[60] The Elohist's references to Joseph's dreams (Gen 42:6b, 8–9a) are

added by repeating the epic text: the epic narrates that the sons of Israel came to Egypt to buy grain (42:5, *wayyābō'û*), and the Elohist repeats that they came (42:6bA, *wayyābō'û*) and, with reference to Joseph's dreams, adds that they bowed down before him (42:6bB = 37:7, 9–10); the epic narrates that Joseph recognized them but they did not recognize him (42:7a, *nkr*), and the Elohist repeats it (42:8) in order to add that Joseph understood their obeisance as a fulfillment of his dreams (42:9a). The reference to Reuben's pleas (42:21–23) is inserted by repeated use of deictic pronouns referring to the preceding context. The first Deuteronomistic addition (42:25–28) was made by repeating a clause from the original (42:25, *wayya'aś lāhem kēn*; cf. 42:20b, *wayya'aśû kēn*; cf. also 42:28bB, *māh zō't 'āśâ 'ĕlōhîm lānû*) and by repeating a phrase from the beginning of the Elohist addition (42:28bB, *'iš 'el 'āḥîw* = 42:21a). The second addition is a sentence that ends with words from the beginning of the sentence that it displaced (42:35, *hēmmâ wa'ăbîhem*; cf. 42:36, *'ălêhem . . . 'ăbîhem*) and that refers back to the first addition. In the third addition (42:37) Reuben anticipates Judah's offer to guarantee Benjamin's safety (cf. 43:9): it interrupts Jacob's reply and then returns to it, and is inserted by repeating the first word of the preceding sentence (*wayyō'mer*; cf. 42:36).

61 Gen 43:12, 14a, 15aB, 17–23a, 29b, 32–34a. The first begins and ends like the sentence it displaces (43:12, *qēḥû . . . tāšîbû*; cf. 43:13, *we'et 'aḥîkem qāḥû wĕqûmû šûbû 'el hā'iš*). The second repeats two other key words from the same sentence (43:14a, *'aḥîkem, hā'iš*). The third repeats its context and the preceding insertions in an opposite order (43:15aB, *ûmišneh kesep lāqĕḥû bĕyādām*; cf. 43:12, *wĕkesep mišneh qĕḥû*; 43:15aA, *wayyiqĕḥû . . . 'et hamminḥâ*). The fourth begins by referring to the epic text before it (43:17a, "And the man did as Joseph said"; cf. 43:16b) and by quoting the beginning of the epic text that it displaced (43:17b, "And the man brought the men to the house of Joseph" = 43:24a). The fifth and sixth begin by repeating their contexts (43:29b, *wayyō'mer*; cf. 43:29a; 43:32, *wayyāśîmû . . . lāhem* = 43:31b, *śîmû lāhem*).

62 The main similarity to the Elohist is the insistence on divine providence (Gen 43:14a, 23a, 29b) and the use of the expression "the God of your father" (43:23a). These texts, however, also refer to the attributes of God that the epic was the first to record (43:14a, 29b, *rḥm, ḥnn*; cf. Exod 34:6).

63 The incident ends on the same note as the original incident in the epic (44:17, *we'attem 'ălû lĕšālôm 'el 'ăbîkem*; cf. 44:34, *kî 'êk 'e'ĕleh 'el 'ābî*). It fits into the total reworking of the story by repeating elements of the epic (e.g., the role of Judah) and of the Elohist version (e.g., the role of divine providence) in combination with its own special interests (e.g., money and sin). The result is a coherent but different story in which all the characters, except God, are wrong or slightly foolish.

64 The Elohist's addition (Gen 45:4–15) begins by citing the beginning of the preceding sentence in the epic (45:4, *wayyō'mer yôsēp 'el 'eḥāyw* = 45:3) and ends by paraphrasing it and the one before it (45:15, he cried and they spoke to him; cf. 45:2–3, he cried and spoke to them and they could not

answer). The History added its material (45:21b–24) by repeating the last verb in the epic version (45:21b, *wayyittēn* = 45:21aB). It anticipates a theme in the later story of the exodus by supplying them with food and clothing for their journey out of Egypt (cf. Deut 8:2–5; 29:4–5). The addition is devoted entirely to this journey (*ðerek*), and Joseph's exhortation not to be troubled on their journey (45:24bB, *ʾal tirgĕzû baððerek*) recalls their distress on all the preceding occasions when they discovered the money in their grain bags (Gen 42:28; 43:18).

65 The Priestly text (Exod 1:1–4, 5b–7) is linked to the original (1:8–12a) by the repetition of key words (*bĕnê yiśrāʾēl*, 1:1, 7, 9, 12; *yôsēp*, 1:5b, 8; °*rbh*, 1:7, 9; *bāʾāreṣ*, 1:7, 10). It fits into the Priestly version by reference to its earlier texts on the blessings of creation, the covenant with Abraham, and the descent of Israel into Egypt (cf. Gen 1:28; 17:6, 20; 46:6–7). The genealogy was anticipated and corrected by the Deuteronomistic Historian (Gen 46:8–27) and the Priestly text has been embellished with a cross-reference to the earlier complete form (Exod 1:5a).

66 The Priestly text (Exod 1:13–14) begins with one expression from the beginning of the preceding epic incident (*bĕnê yiśrāʾēl*, 1:13; cf. 1:9). The same term constitutes a cross-reference to the earlier Priestly text (1:7). These two texts (1:1–4, 5b–7; 1:13–14) belong together, bracket the epic incident (1:8–12a), and illustrate the Priestly writer's habit of composing a text that both fits its context and also follows consecutively and independently of the text it corrects. The enslavement of the people (*ʿbð*, 1:13–14 [five times]) is taken up at the start of the next incident (2:23aBb). The Deuteronomistic introduction (1:15–21; 2:6bB, 7aB) begins by repeating items from the beginning of the epic incident in opposite order (1:15, *wayyōʾmer melek miṣrayim*; cf. 1:8–9, *wayyāqom melek . . . ʿal miṣrāyim . . . wayyōʾmer*) and ends by anticipating one word from the next epic incident (1:21, *wayyaʿaś lāhem bāttîm*; cf. 2:1, *wayyēlek ʾîš mibbêt lēwî*). The Deuteronomist also added a second altercation (2:13–14) in order to insinuate that Moses was a judge: the insertion begins like the original text (*wayyēṣēʾ*, 2:11, 13) and refers to it, and ends like the beginning of the next text (*haððābār*, 2:14, 15).

67 Incidents ## 5–6: Exod 2:23aA; 3:2–4a, 7–8; 4:19–20a, 24–26a.

68 The Priestly text (Exod 2:23aBb–25) is composed of cross-references to texts in the previous incidents (cf. 1:7, 14) and of anticipations of the epic text to follow (2:24a, *wayyišmaʿ ʾĕlōhîm ʾet naʾăqātām* = 3:7bA, *wĕʾet ṣaʿăqātām šāmaʿtî*; 2:25a, *wayyarʾ ʾĕlōhîm ʾet bĕnê yiśrāʾēl* = 3:7a, *rāʾōh rāʾîtî ʾet ʿŏnî ʿammî*; 2:25b, *wayyēðaʿ ʾĕlōhîm* = 3:7bB, *kî yāðaʿtî ʾet makʾōbāyw*).

69 The Elohist text (Exod 3:1, 4b–6, 9–14; 4:18) was fitted into and around the epic version. Its introduction (3:1) paraphrases and interprets the previous epic incident: in the epic Moses performed a shepherd's chores (2:19), and here he is a shepherd; in the epic he married the daughter of the priest of Midian, and here the priest of Midian is his father-in-law. The other changes repeat their context (3:4b; cf. 3:3, 7) or are linked to it by key word (3:6, *wayyōʾmer*; cf. 3:7; 3:9).

70 The Deuteronomistic History corrected the Elohist explanation of the name of God (3:14) by repeating most of the Elohist sentence (3:15, *wayyōᵓmer ῾ôd ᵓĕlōhîm ᵓel mōšeh . . . kōh tōᵓmar ᵓel bĕnê yiśrāᵓēl* = 3:14aAbA). It added a synthesis of the exodus story (3:16–22) by repeating itself (3:16; cf. 3:15), the Elohist (3:16, *ᵓĕlōhê ᵓăbōtêkem* = 3:13), and the epic (3:17 = 3:8) at the beginning of its addition. The commissioning of Moses (4:1–17) follows naturally on this addition, and revisions of the second encounter between Moses and Yahweh (4:20b–23, 26b–31) are made by referring to it and by repeating the immediate context (4:20b, *wayyiqqaḥ mōšeh* = 4:20a; 4:20b, *ᵓet maṭṭēh hāᵓĕlōhîm bĕyādô* = 4:17; 4:21, 27, *wayyōᵓmer yhwh* = 4:19; 4:26b = 4:25b).

71 The Priestly writer surrounded the epic text (Exod 2:23aA; 3:2–4a, 7–8; 4:19–20a) with matching texts on God's resolve to free the people from Egypt (Exod 3:23aBb–25; 6:2–9). They fit their individual contexts but belong together sequentially and, in mass and meaning, overshadow the significance of the original that they enclose.

72 Incidents ## 7–10: Exod 12:37–38; 13:20–22; 14:5°–31°.

73 In the epic version the exodus and defeat of the Egyptians are wonders accomplished by Yahweh for his people, on behalf of Moses and as a prelude to the covenant. The epic does not dwell on them.

74 The Elohist begins (Exod 13:17–19) in imitation of the epic (13:20–22), with reference to earlier incidents in its own version (cf. Gen 50:25), in dependence on the Priestly version (Exod 13:17, *šlḥ*; cf. 7:2, etc.), and in preparation for the battle that is to follow (13:18b). The victory at the Sea is changed into a land battle by having the Pharaoh regret that he let the people go (14:5b); muster his chariotry (14:7) against the Israelites, who bore only light arms (14:8b); set out along the route that they followed (14:10abA); and finally run up against the angel of God, who moved from the vanguard to the rearguard (14:19a) and bent the wheels of Pharaoh's chariots so that they moved slowly (14:25a). The changes are made, as usual, by repetition of their immediate context and by cross-reference to the continuing Elohist story.

75 The Priestly writer began by redoing the meeting between Moses and Yahweh as a declaration of Yahweh to Moses (Exod 6:2–12; cf. 3:2–4a, 7–8). The plagues and Passover and prelude to the crossing of the Sea follow naturally (7:1–13, 19–20, 21b–22; 8:1–3, 9b–15; 9:8–12; 11:9–10; 12:1–6, 8–11, 28, 40–42). The crossing of the Sea itself (14:1–4, 8a, 9aBb, 10bB, 15–18, 21–23, 25b–27a, 28, 29) is affixed to the epic text and embellished by the concluding Song of Miriam (15:20–21).

76 The Deuteronomist included plagues that separated Israel from the Egyptians and demonstrated the intercessory role of Moses (Exod 7:14–18, 21a, 23–29; 8:4–9a, 16–28; 9:1–7, 13–35; 10:1–29; 11:1–8), ritual texts (12:7, 12–27, 29–36, 39, 43–51; 13:1–16; 15:1–19), disputes between Moses and the people (5:1–23; 14:11–14), and genealogies (6:1, 13–30). The mate-

rial is arranged according to the model of lamentation liturgies by describing the distress at great length to produce a greater sense of relief at the end.

77 Incidents ## 11–16: Exodus 19°; 34°; Numbers 10°; 13°; 14°; 16°.

78 According to the epic, Israel arrived in the wilderness of Sinai and encamped at the foot of the mountain on the same day that Yahweh defeated the Egyptians at the Sea (Exod 19:1b, 2b). The Priestly writer disagrees and rephrases the epic text to situate the day in the third month after the exodus (19:1a) and to put the wilderness of Sinai on the route past Rephidim (19:2a; cf. Exod 17:1abA). In the epic version Moses ascended the mountain (19:20, wayyaʿal mōšeh), where Yahweh revealed his identity and concluded the covenant with him and with Israel (Exodus 34°). The Priestly writer inserts the revelation of the plans for the tabernacle (25:1–5, 8; 26:1–30; 29:43, 45–46; 31:13–18) by repeating that Moses ascended the mountain (24:15, wayyaʿal mōšeh), where the glory of Yahweh was revealed (24:15–18). The epic covenant was concluded with Moses and Israel according to the words that Yahweh spoke (34:27, haddĕbārîm hāʾēlleh), and the Priestly writer inserts the construction of the tabernacle (35:1–7, 20–29; 36:2–38; 40:16–19, 35b–37) by having Moses repeat these words to the people of Israel (35:1, ʾēlleh haddĕbārîm). The spy account is put into a specific itinerary (Num 12:16b; 13:3, 21, 26a), included among the repeated rebellions in the wilderness (Num 13:32, 33b; 14:1a, 2–4, 26–32), and related to the eventual succession of Joshua (Num 14:36–38) by the same sort of literal links and periphrastic cross-references.

79 The Elohist prepares for the revelation of the law by describing the judicial process of the time (Exod 18:1a, 2a, 3–5, 12–27): the incident is attached to its surroundings by resuming the previous and anticipating the following epic text (18:1a, ʾet kol ʾăšer ʿāšâ ʾĕlōhîm lĕmōšeh ûlĕyiśrāʾēl; cf. Exod 14:31; 18:5b, ʾel hammidbār ʾăšer hûʾ ḥōneh šām har hāʾĕlōhîm; cf. 19:1b, 2b). The revelation of the law is fitted into the epic's theophany by repeating adjacent texts and referring to other key texts (Exod 19:3a, 16aBb–17, 18bB–19), and it is introduced by anticipating the words that conclude the epic covenant (Exod 20:1, waydabbēr ʾĕlōhîm ʾet kol haddĕbārîm hāʾēlleh; cf. Exod 34:27). The story of the golden calf (Exod 32:1–6, 15–19a, 21a, 22–25) is attached to the Priestly version of Moses' sojourn on the mountain (Exod 31:18). The conclusion of the Elohist text (Exod 34:29aBb–32a, 33) is affixed to the end of the covenant text by literal repetition (34:29aB, ûšĕnê lūḥōt hāʿēdût bĕyad mōšeh bĕridtô min hāhār = 34:28bA + 29aA, ḥallūḥōt . . . wayhî bĕredet mōšeh).

80 The Deuteronomist changed the epic version by replacing the covenant with the ten commandments, the Priestly version by changing the itinerary and turning the tabernacle into a tent of meeting, and the Elohist version by assimilation to the epic (Exodus 16–40°). The connection between the covenant and the decision to take possession of the land is immediate in the epic version (Exod 34:29aA + Num 10:29–33a + 13:1–2a), almost unchanged by the additions in the Elohist version (Exod 34:29aBb–32a, 33), and delayed almost a year by the construction of the tabernacle in the Priestly version (Exodus 35°–36°, 40°), but it is completely lost in the Deuterono-

mistic History by the inclusion of the tent of meeting and the establishment of the wilderness camp (Lev 8:1–11:45; Num 1:1–10:10, 13–28, 33b–36; 11:1–12:16a).

81 Incidents ## 17–22: Numbers 20°–24°.

82 Num 20:1–5, 7–13, 22–25, 27, 28aBb, 29; 27:12–23. The first is attached to the epic text by its association with Qadesh (Num 20:1, 14). The second is attached by imitating the locale of Balaam's last discourse (Num 23:25–30; 24:1–9) and is composed by cross-reference to the first. The Priestly writer did not correct the sequel to the epic but added a reference to the death of Moses at the end of its first part (Num 22:1; Deut 32:48–50, 51b–52; 34:1–5°, 7–9).

83 The Deuteronomistic History corrected the Priestly texts (Num 20:6, 26, 28aA; 27:1–11), added material on Israel's dealings with the Canaanites, Midianites, and Moabites (Num 21:1–20, 25–35; 22:7a; 25:1–19), and completely reworked the sequel to the epic, so that the conclusion of the Priestly document seems impossibly remote in the present arrangement. It added a transition from its own material to the oracles of Balaam (Num 22:2–4a) and inserted (Num 22:21aB, 22–35) or appended (Num 24:14–24) prophecies and related discussions.

84 See M. Fishbane, *Biblical Interpretation in Ancient Israel* (Oxford: Clarendon, 1985) 44–55.

85 See M. Weinfeld, *Deuteronomy and the Deuteronomic School* (Oxford: Clarendon, 1971) Appendix A: Deuteronomic Phraseology (pp. 320–65). The formulas are often broken and combined and have a cumulative referential effect in the composition of the Deuteronomistic History.

86 The preview includes the commissioning of Joshua, the anticipation of Israel's defection from Yahweh and the Song of Moses that encapsulates it, and the blessing of Moses on the individual tribes. It modifies the last section in the sequel's version, redistributes the Priestly materials (Deut 32:48–50, 51b–52; 34:1°, 2–5, 7–9), and incudes an array of cross-references to texts in the Deuteronomistic version of the epic.

87 The book of Deuteronomy has a historical introduction (chaps. 1–3) and conclusion (chaps. 31–34), a theological preface (chaps 4–11) and epilogue (chaps. 26–30), and a section on legal theory (chaps. 12–18) and practice (chaps. 19-25). The laws are mostly traditional or borrowed from the Elohist code but were composed by the Deuteronomistic Historian for their literary context. See C. M. Carmichael, *The Laws of Deuteronomy* (Ithaca, N.Y.: Cornell University Press, 1974); idem, *Women, Law and the Genesis Traditions* (Edinburgh: Edinburgh University Press, 1979); idem, *Law and Narrative in the Bible: The Evidence of the Deuteronomic Laws and the Decalogue* (Ithaca, N.Y.: Cornell University Press, 1985). Since the book balances theory or synthesis (Deuteronomy 1–18) against practice or analysis (chaps. 19–34), the arrange-

ment of the decalogue corresponds to the general arrangement of the laws (see S. A. Kaufman, "The Structure of the Deuteronomic Law," *Maarav* 1/2 [1978–79] 105–58).

[88] The text is inserted by repeating and paraphrasing (*ðibbēr mōšeh 'el bĕnê yiśrā'ēl*) part of the original (1:1, *'ăšer ðibber mōšeh 'el kol yiśrā'ēl*). With the account of the death of Moses at the end of the speech (Deut 32:48–50, 51b–52; 34:1–9°) it constitutes a typical Priestly frame to existing material and does not entail further editing.

[89] The insertion ends (1:5, *bĕ'ēber hayyarðēn . . . hô'îl mōšeh bē'ēr 'et hattôrâ hazzō't*) repeating the text of the sequel in the opposite order (1:1a, *ðibber mōšeh . . . bĕ'ēber hayyarðēn*). The cross-references to the speeches (in the plains of Moab—Num 33:50; 36:13; Deut 1:5; 28:69; in the wilderness—Num 1:1), to the itinerary (Numbers 33) and to the defeat of Sihon and Og (Numbers 21) relate the sequel to the Deuteronomistic version of the book of Numbers. The difficulty involved in a literal interpretation was explained by S. R. Driver (*Deuteronomy* [ICC; 3rd. ed.; Edinburgh: T. & T. Clark, 1901) 1–5.

[90] The paragraph was inserted by deictics ("at that time," 1:9, 18) and began (1:9, *wā'ōmar 'ălêkem*) like the sentence it displaced (1:20, *wā'ōmar 'ălêkem*).

[91] The sequel paraphrases and embellishes the epic version. The first paragraph (Deut 1:1a, 6–8) takes up a key phrase from the Sinai covenant (*'ēlleh haððĕbārîm*; cf. Exod 34:27), recalls that Moses and the people had spent a long time at the mountain (cf. Exod 34:28a), supposes the covenant's gift of the land (Exod 34:11, 24a) that had been promised to the fathers (Num 14:23), and substitutes a geographical description for the covenant's list of nations (cf. Exod 34:11). The second paragraph (Deut 1:19–36°) is based on the epic's spy account (Numbers 13–14°) and on its version of Yahweh's leadership in a pillar of cloud and fire (Exod 13:20–22).

[92] This version inserted a reference to the wilderness wanderings (1:19, "that vast and terrible wilderness which you saw") with the help of a deictic particle (*'et*) and a deictic clause ("which you saw"), and another reference to the same time (1:31) by repeating a small part of the immediate context (1:30–31, "*in* Egypt, and *in* the wilderness") and a significant part of the first reference (1:19, 31, "the wilderness . . . which you saw"). It also added the repudiation of Moses (Deut 1:37–38) by paraphrasing the original (1:37aA; cf. 1:34b) and by marking the paraphrase with deictic particles (1:37, *gam, šām*). Its text is based on the Priestly version of the spy narrative (cf. Num 14:26–32, 36–38).

[93] Deut 5:1 (*wayyiqrā' mōšeh 'el kol yiśrā'ēl wayyō'mer 'ălêhem*), 2–4, 6–7, 9–11 repeats the epic text, with additions and variations, in an opposite order (Exod 34:6, 7, 10, 14). This paragraph supposes the preceding section in which the wilderness generation was repudiated by insisting that the covenant was made with those present.

[94] Deut 5:23aA, 24a, 25, 27; cf. Exod 34:27, where the covenant is made with Moses and with Israel; Num 14:12, where Moses is treated as surrogate people; and Num 16:13, 28, where Yahweh's prior choice of Moses is articulated. The sequel, on the other hand, insists that the people were the original party to the covenant and that they chose him as their leader.

[95] This reworking of the covenant into the decalogue was an explicit project of the Deuteronomistic Historian (Exod 34:28bB; Deut 4:13), and it was accomplished by direct and indirect references to preceding texts. The commandment against idols (5:8) is fitted in by repeating one word (*lōʾ*; cf. 5:7, 9) and by paraphrasing a text from the preceding chapter (4:16–18, 23). The sabbath and submission commandments (5:12–15, 16) are taken from the Sinai pericope (Exod 20:8–11, 12) by direct quotation ("as Yahweh your God commanded you," 5:12, 16; see D. E. Skweres, *Die Rückverweise im Buch Deuteronomium* [Analecta Biblica 79; Rome: Biblical Institute Press, 1979] 182–84). The commandments against murder, adultery, theft, and jealousy (5:17-21) follow naturally from the same source and fit in to their new context by repetition of the same one word (*lōʾ*). The conclusion (5:22) to the decalogue repeats the caption from the beginning of the speech (*ʾet haddĕbārîm hāʾēlleh* = 1:1a = Exod 34:27) and modifies the sequel's text (*bāḥar mittôk hāʾēš* = 5:4) by reference to a paraphrase of this text in the preceding chapter (4:11–12).

[96] Both of these points are made explicitly and emphatically in a separate preface to the covenant composed by the Deuteronomist (Deut 4:1–49): this chapter begins like the revised version of the chapter it displaces (4:1 = 5:1aB), and ends (4:44–49), after all the intervening material, like the revised version of the first paragraph in the sequel (1:1–8). The mediation of Moses is interposed at the very beginning (5:5): the sentence contradicts the preceding verse but repeats some of its elements (*ʾdbr yhwh, ʾēš, har*) and the first word of the sentence it replaced (5:6, *ʾānōkî*), and it is inserted by a deictic reference ("at that time"). The people stand at a distance during the revelation of the decalogue, and only their leaders approach Moses when Yahweh has finished speaking (5:23b). The complete text (5:22 + 23b) is derived from the preceding chapter in an opposite order (4:11) and, in an opposite sense, from the earlier appointment of legal secretaries (5:23b = 1:15, 17). The sense that the people had seen Yahweh's glory (5:24a) is diminished by insistence on the fact that they heard the voice of Yahweh (5:26) and had *seen* (that is, "perceived") only that they could hear the voice without dying (5:24b).

[97] The History added another section on the mediation of Moses (5:28–33) according to which Yahweh revealed to him alone the commandments, laws, and precepts that the people had to know. The section is added by repeating all the key words of the preceding paragraph (*šmʿ* 5:28 [twice]; *qôl* 5:28 [twice]; *ʾdbr* 5:28 [five times].

[98] The preceding section ended with the people agreeing to listen and do as they were told (Deut 5:27, *wĕšāmaʿnû wĕʿāšînû*), and this section begins with the command to listen (6:4, *šĕmaʿ*) and continues with a list of the things they are to do. The idea that Yahweh is One is taken up later in the command to

worship Yahweh in the place that he will choose in one of their tribes (Deut 12:14). The sequel supposes that Yahweh is not indigenous to the land of Canaan but is about to take possession of it and give it to his people, and therefore Moses exhorts the people not to forget once they are in the land that Yahweh is the God who brought them out of Egypt.

99 The section begins by repeating in opposite order the end of the preceding chapter (6:1–3; cf. 5:31–33; see N. Lohfink, *Das Hauptgebot: Eine Untersuchung literarischer Einleitungsfragen zu Dtn 5–11* [Analecta Biblica 20; Rome: Biblical Institute Press, 1963] 149–50). This introduction also repeats the opening words of the text it introduces (6:3, *wĕšāmaʿtā yiśrāʾēl* = 6:4a, *šĕmaʿ yiśrāʾēl*) and the key words of the text that once preceded it (6:3aA, *wĕšāmaʿtā . . . laʿăśôt*; cf. 5:27, *wĕšāmaʿnû wĕʿāśînû*). The original warning against apostasy was modified by the addition of geographical precision (6:14b) and by a threat (6:15b). The threat was added by repeating parts of the immediate context (6:15b, *yhwh ʾĕlōhêkā bāk*; cf. 6:15a, *yhwh ʾĕlōhêkā bĕqirbekā*). The precision focuses on the neighboring nations and was added in the same way (6:14b, *mēʾĕlōhê hāʿammîm*; cf. 6:14a, *ʾĕlōhîm ʾăhērîm*). The rest of the chapter was affixed by adding another warning (6:16) and consists largely of stylized expressions familiar from Deuteronomy and earlier books of the Pentateuch.

100 This section is related to the preceding by the motif of entry into the land (7:1aA; cf. 6:10aA). It is constructed of quotations from the epic covenant (7:1aB, 1bA, 2bB, cf. Exod 34:24, 11b, 12a; Deut 7:18b, cf. Exod 14:31aA) and of material specific to the sequel.

101 Deut 7:2bA injects the Deuteronomistic notion of the ban (*ḥrm*) by adding a deictic pronoun ("You shall devote them [*ʾôtām*] to the ban"). The prohibition of foreign marriages and the command to destroy the cultic paraphernalia of the nations (7:3–5) are appended by the repetition of one word (*wĕlōʾ*) and by cross-reference to earlier stories (Gen 34:8–9; Num 25:1–5) and laws (Exod 34:13, 15–16). The exhortation to be brave and remember what Yahweh did to Egypt (Deut 7:17–18) is expanded by a reference to the plagues in Egypt (7:19), which is attached to the original by the deictic definite article. The sequel's assurance that Yahweh will defeat the indigenous nations is changed into an assurance that they will be eliminated gradually (7:20, 22) by repeating some of the context (7:20, 22, *mippānêkā*; cf. 7:1–2a, 23–24, *mippānêkā / lĕpānêkā / bĕpānêkā*) and by quoting from the Elohist code (cf. Exod 23:28a, 30a). The end of the chapter (7:25–26) is added by cross-reference to the ending of its first paragraph (7:25a = 7:5bB).

102 The sequel refers to the commandments of Moses (*miṣwâ*, 8:1; 11:8, 22; *miṣwōt-*, 11:13), but the Deuteronomistic Historian includes them among the commandments, laws, and prescriptions of Yahweh (*miṣwōt, ḥuqqîm, miš-pāṭîm*, e.g., 6:2; 7:11; 8:11b; 11:1). Variations in singular and plural address (e.g., 8:1) are part of the compositional and editorial process. The plural is normal in narrative and descriptive texts, and the singular is usual in quoted speech or direct discourse. Change from one to the other in the same text marks quotations or cross-references to texts that are already known from the

antecedent context and may be the work of the author, or of the editor, or, in the case of repeated change, of both.

103 The first addition (8:2–6) begins like the last sentence in the sequel's version (8:2, *wĕzākartā* = 8:18a) and ends resuming the opening sentence and anticipating the sentence it displaced (8:6a, *wĕšāmartā ʾet miṣwōt yhwh ʾĕlōhêkā*; cf. 8:1a, *kol hammiṣwâ . . . tišmĕrûn*; 8:7, *yhwh ʾĕlōhêkā*). The second addition (8:11b) refers to the first, in which the commandment of Moses was interpreted as the command of Yahweh, and is indicated by quotation marks ("which I command you today"). The third (8:15–16) is marked by the deictic definite article and resumes the wilderness theme of the first addition. The last addition (8:18b–20) repeats the first words of the second paragraph in the sequel (8:19; cf. 8:11a).

104 Deut 9:1–3 combines earlier elements of the speech (cf. 1:1a, 28; 5:4, 24a, 25; 7:1) but also adds that Yahweh is about to cross the Jordan with Israel, that it is Yahweh who will win the war, and that the land will be conquered quickly—all of them statements that will be verified in the time of Joshua.

105 The initial dispute (Deut 9:4–6) begins and ends like the sentence to which it is attached: in the sequel Yahweh subdues the enemy before them (9:3aB), and in the addition he drives them out before them (9:4a). In the sequel the people are to realize that Yahweh goes before them as a raging fire, and in the revised version they are to realize that they are unworthy (9:3a, 6a, *wĕyāḏaʿtā*).

106 The paragraph (10:12, 14, 17–18, 20) begins and ends with elements from the third section of the speech (cf. 6:5, 13). The central affirmations situate Yahweh in the hierarchy of creation.

107 The paragraph is revised (10:13, 15–16, 19, 21–22) and expanded (11:1–7). The first revision (10:13) is inserted by repetition of the preposition *l-* and with the help of a deictic clause ("which I am commanding you today"). The second revision (10:15–16) takes up elements from its context in an opposite sense: in the sequel they are to love Yahweh with all their heart, but in the revised version it was Yahweh who loved their fathers, and they are to circumcise their hearts. The third (10:19) also repeats its context ("love the immigrant"; cf. 10:18) and the fourth, introduced by deictic pronouns (10:20, "*He* is your praise, *he* is your God . . ."), is related both to it (10:19, 22, "Egypt") and to the second revision (10:15, 22, "your fathers"). The expansion begins (11:1) by copying the beginning of the revised paragraph (10:12–13) in an opposite order.

108 Deut 11:8–12 relates observance of the command of Moses (11:8, *miṣwâ*) to the possession of the land that Yahweh tends from the beginning to the end of the year. Deut 11:13–15 relates observance of the commands (11:13, *miṣwōtay*) of Moses to the fertility of the land. Deut 11:18–21 rephrases the basic covenant stipulation (Deut 6:4–9) and replaces the traditional reference to the words of Yahweh (6:6, *haddĕbārîm hāʾēlleh*) with a reference to

the words of Moses (11:18, *děbāray*). Deut 11:22–25 relates Yahweh's conquest of the land to the observance of the command of Moses (11:22, *miṣwâ*).

109 The Deuteronomist added a threat of destruction (11:16–17) by repeating bits of the original context in opposite order (11:17a, *šāmayim . . . māṭār*, cf. 11:11, *limṭar haššāmayim*; *lōʾ tittēn*, cf. 11:14, 15, *wěnātattî*). The concluding section (11:26–32) changes the commandments of Moses into the commands of Yahweh (11:27, 28) and regulates their observance with blessings and curses.

110 Deut 12:13–14, 17–18aAb forbids the offering of oblations (*ʿōlōt*) at just any place they see (*běkol māqôm ʾăšer tirʾeh*) and is directly related to the preceding section in which the people are given secure possession of every place their feet touch (11:24, *kol māqôm*). Distance from the central sanctuary required the desacralization of the eating of meat, but the exemption was based on a condition in the epic covenant (12:20, *kî yarḥîb yhwh ʾělōhêkā ʾet gěbûlěkā kaʾăšer ðibber lāk* = Exod 34:24aB, *wěhirḥabtî ʾet gěbûlekā*; see Skweres, *Die Rückverweise*, 171).

111 The sequel did not consider the eating of meat a sacral event (12:20, 26). The Deuteronomistic History, on the contrary, associated the eating of meat with sacrifice (*zebaḥ*, 12:21) and included sacrifice among the elements of worship to be performed at the central sanctuary (12:6, 11), but also allowed the eating of meat in any other place as long as the sacrificial ritual was observed (12:15–16, 21–25). The changes in the legislation are emphasized (12:1–7, 8–11) and are made by repeating its essential parts (12:5–7 and 12:11–12 = 12:13–14, 17–18*). The chapter is attached to the end of the preceding chapter (12:1 = 11:32), and its various elements are added by repetition and cross-reference.

112 The list of animals and birds (Deut 14:4–5, 11–12) follows naturally enough on the desacralization of slaughter and the provision for eating meat to their hearts' content (Deut 12:20, 26).

113 The Deuteronomistic History leads into the list with a general prohibition against eating anything that might defile the holy people of Yahweh (14:1–3). Most of the changes in the list are made with reference to its own list in the book of Leviticus (see W. L. Moran, "The Literary Connection between Lv 11, 13–19 and Dt 14, 12–18," *CBQ* 28 [1966] 271–77). All of them are made by literal and deictic repetition of the original.

114 The legislation concerning the firstborn (Deut 15:19–20) depends on similar legislation in the epic covenant (Exod 34:19). The feast of Passover (16:1–2a, 3aA, 7) may be a development of the related offering of firstborn children (Exod 34:20b). The harvest festivals (Exod 34:22), it appears, were replaced by the legislation concerning tithes (Deut 14:22, 25–26).

115 The basic change in the legislation is made by extending the prohibition against eating leaven (Deut 16:3aA, *lōʾ tōʾkal ʿālāyw ḥāmēṣ*) into a command to

eat unleavened bread for seven days (16:3aB, *tōʾkal ʿālāyw maṣṣôt*) before Passover (16:4), and for another six days afterward, with a solemn assembly on the seventh day (16:8). The change is fitted into the legislation by repetitions: the sequel situates the Passover sacrifice in the central sanctuary at night in memory of the exodus from Egypt (16:1, 2a, 7a), and the revision inserts its own rules by repeating all of these circumstances at least twice (16:2b, 5–6). The other festivals are added in sequences of seven and in the language peculiar to the law of centralization. The list of festivals at the end (16:16aB) omits Passover altogether and puts Massot in its place.

116 The conclusion to the covenant (Deut 29:1a, 9a, 11, 13–14) corresponds to its introduction (cf. 5:1aA, 2–4), and the final words of Moses (31:1–2a, 3a, 6) are reminiscent of the very beginning of the speech (1:1a) and of the first exhortations to enter and take the land (1:29; 9:3).

117 Since the Deuteronomistic History has a different version of the covenant, which subordinates it to the law (Deut 26:16–19), it includes the sequel's covenant ceremony in a speech in which Moses reviews the events of the exodus, wilderness, and conquest (Deut 29:1b–8, 9b–10, 12) and predicts the utter failure of the covenant (29:15–28). The farewell, similarly, is assimilated to the beginning of the book and to the earlier Priestly material in which the succession of Joshua was assured by decree of Yahweh (Deut 31:2b, 3b–5, 7–23; cf. Num 27:12–23; Deut 1:37–38; 3:23–29).

118 The additions to the first paragraph (Josh 1:6–9) are made, as usual, by repeating at their beginning and end elements from the beginning and end of the original (cf. 1:2 and 1:6; 1:5 and 1:9). The changes to the second paragraph (Josh 2:9b, 17–21, 24b) are made by minimal repetitions of the same kind. The first depends on the repetition of one word (2:9b, *wĕkî* [twice]; cf. 2:9a, *kî*). The second (2:17–21) ends resuming the conversation with Rahab that preceded its intrusion (2:21, *wattōʾmer* = 2:16) and anticipating the original continuation of the story (2:21, *wayyēlēkû* = 2:22). The last is like the first and is added by repeating and paraphrasing its immediate context (2:24b, *kol yōšĕbê hāʾāreṣ* = 2:24a *kol hāʾāreṣ*). The Transjordanian tribes, living outside the land of Yahweh, are a constant preoccupation of the Deuteronomistic Historian and get a foothold in the land as the vanguard of the invading armies (Num 27:1–11; 32:1–42; 36:1–12; Deut 3:12–22; Josh 1:12–18; 4:12–13; 13:1–33; 17:1–6; 22:1–34).

119 The original text of the first paragraph (Josh 3:1aAb, 5, 10b, 16b) alludes to Jacob's crossing of the Jabbok (Gen 32:14a) and cites the text of the epic covenant in which the people prepare themselves (3:5, *hitqaddāšû*; cf. Exod 19:10, 14, *°qiddēš*) for the wonders Yahweh will perform in driving out the nations who inhabit the land (Exod 34:10–11). The revised version absorbed the text with repetition and deictic references. The original begins with Joshua and the people marching to the Jordan, where they spend the night before crossing (3:1aAb), and the revision refers to him and to them (3:1aB, *hûʾ wĕkol bĕnê yiśrāʾēl*) and to the field marshals crossing through the camp (3:2). In the sequel Joshua addresses the people (3:5a, *wayyōʾmer yĕhôšûaʿ*), and in the revised version he does so again and again (3:6, 9, 10).

In the sequel Joshua tells the people that Yahweh will do wonders in their midst by driving out the inhabitants of the land (3:5b, 10b), and in the revised version he tells them that Yahweh is in their midst (3:10a). In the sequel the people cross at Jericho (3:16b, *wĕhāʿām ʿābĕrû negeᵭ yĕrîḫô*), but in the Deuteronomistic version the crossing of the Jordan (3:14a, *hāʿām . . . laʿăbōr ʾet hayyarᵭēn*) is shrouded in ceremony (3:14–17). The text of the second paragraph was changed chiefly by including references to the priests, the ark of the covenant, and the dedication of the city. In Yahweh's address (6:1–5), apart from the standard reference to the people of Israel (6:1aB), the changes are made by repeating the words "seven" and "trumpets" (6:4aAb, 5aA). In Joshua's address (6:6–10*) the changes are introduced by repeating the word *ʾmr* (6:6, 8, 10aA), once in a totally incongruous manner (6:8aA). A whole section (6:11–13) is added by anticipating the sentence it displaces (6:11, cf. 6:14). In the account of the battle the changes are made mainly by cross-reference, repetition of the word "city" (*hāʿîr*, 6:16bB, 17–20a), and resumption of a preceding clause (6:20bA = 6:20a). In the conclusion a text is inserted by repeating the verb "bring out" (6:23aBb–24, 25aB).

120 The Deuteronomistic Historian added the unsuccessful attack on Ai (Joshua 7) between its actual destruction and the capture of Jericho (chaps. 6, 8) by describing how Achan's violation of the ban brought guilt on the whole nation. The actual battle, therefore, is revised to ensure that the ban is observed: the ban is inserted at the beginning of the story by repeating the deictic elements of the context (8:2aB, the pronominal suffix -*āh*; cf. 8:2aA); the earlier defeat is recalled (8:6aB) by repeating one word of the original (*nāᵭîm*; cf. 8:6b, *wĕnaᵭnû*); the ban is reinforced (8:8) by repeating one word from the context (*hāʿîr*; cf. 8:7) and by marking the addition with a deictic clause (8:8b, "Do as Yahweh says, see, I am commanding you"); the original violation of the ban is associated, typically but incongruously, with Bethel (8:9aB, 10b, 11b–13, 17) with the help of deictics (8:10b, *hûʾ*) and repetitions of the immediate contexts; the carrying out of the ban (8:19b–20, 21aB, 22) is inserted the same way (8:19b, *wayĕmahărû* = 8:19a, *mĕhērâ*; 8:21aB, *wĕkî* = 8:21aA, *kî*; 8:22, *wĕʾelleh . . . wayyakkû* = 8:21b, *wayyakkû*) and is carried out to the letter at the end of the story (8:23–29).

121 The treaty with the Gibeonites violated the Deuteronomistic rules for the conduct of war (Deuteronomy 20) and therefore the History is obliged to shift the blame from Joshua to the people and their leaders (Josh 9:6b–7, 9bB–10, 14, 15b) and then to exonerate them by appeal to a legal fiction (Josh 9:16–27; cf. Deut 29:10). The first insertion (9:6b–7) begins like the sentence it displaced (*wayyōʾmĕrû*; cf. 9:8), the second (9:9bB–10) is introduced by deictics (*wĕʾet*), and the last contain deictic cross-references to the revised version (9:14, *hāʾănāᵭîm*; cf. 9:6b, 7, *ʾîᵭ yiᵭrāʾēl*) and repetition of the near context (9:15b, *lāhem*; cf. 9:15a).

122 The war against the southern coalition includes a reference to the imposition of the ban on Ai (Josh 10:1, *wayyahărîmāh*; cf. the deictic -*āh* in *lĕmalkāh*) and is embellished by many other battles illustrating the same practice (Josh 10:10b–43): these reports are appended by repeating the last

word of the original and the phrase that was added to it in the revised version (10:10bB–11, *wayyakkēm . . . bêt ḥôrōn*; cf. 10:10aB + 10:10bA, *wayyakkēm . . . bêt ḥôrōn*). The war against the northern coalition applies the ban to the horses and chariots (11:6b, 8b–9): the additions are made by deictics (11:6b, *'et*; 11:9, *ka'ăšer 'āmar lô yhwh*; *'et*) and by repetitions (11:8b, *wayyakkûm*; cf. 11:8aA).

[123] The Deuteronomist added references to Eli and his sons (1 Sam 1:3b, 9aBb, 12–18a, 24aB, 25–26), to the nazirite vow that was required of Samson's mother (1 Sam 1:11bB; cf. Judg 13:5), and—since its intrusions will break the connection—to the following story of Samuel and Saul (1 Sam 1:17, 20bB, 23aB, 27–28). The changes are made by repetitions and deictic references. The first mention of Eli and his sons begins with a reference to the place that was just mentioned (1:3b, *wěšām*) and ends like the clause to which it is attached (1:3b, *layhwy*; cf. 1:3a, *layhwh ṣěbā'ôt běšīlōh*). The second reference (1:9aBb–10) repeats and contradicts its immediate context (Hannah cries as the sequel said [1:10b, cf. 1:8a], but eats and drinks as it said she would not [1:9aB; cf. 1:8a]) and refers to it explicitly (1:10, *wěhî'*; cf. 1:9 [Hannah]). The reference to the nazirite vow supposes the ongoing literary context, fits into a passage that enumerates many bodily parts (1:10, 11bB–18a, *nepeš, rŏ'šô, pîhā, libbāh, rûaḥ, 'ênêkā, pānêhā*), and contains a pun on the name Eli (1:11bB, *ya'ăleh*; cf. 1:12, *wě'ēlî*). A similar pun accounts for the allusion to Saul (1:20bB). The allusion to Samuel's prophetic role is marked by a deictic particle (1:23aB, *'ak*), and the concluding rites are added by repeating a word from the original (1:24aB–28 *gml*; cf. 1:23b).

[124] The Deuteronomistic History was critical of the institution of kingship but recognized individual kings who were chosen by Yahweh and designated by the prophets as his subalterns. The story of Saul's chance meeting with Samuel the man of God, therefore, is changed into a providential meeting with Samuel the prophet, who privately anoints him *nāgîd* and publicly supervises his selection by lot (1 Sam 9:2aBb, 6aB, 7–9, 15–17, 20b–21, 22b–24a, 27; 10:1–9, 10aBb–13, 17–27). The link between the public and private ceremonies is anticipated at the beginning (9:2aBb; cf. 10:23–24): the editorial remark is added by repeating the key word of the original text on which it is a comment (*ṭôb*, 9:2aA and 2aB). The transformation of Samuel the man of God into Samuel the prophet begins in a conversation between Saul and his servant (9:6aB, 7–8) and with an explicit narrative statement to that effect (9:9): the change is made with the help of a deictic repetition (9:6aB, *wěhā'îš*; cf. 9:6aA, *'îš*), by beginning the insertion like the sentence that it displaced (9:7, *wayyō'mer šā'ûl lěna'ărô* = 9:10), and by a pun on the word for prophet (*nābî'*, 9:7, 9). The transformation continues with an account of the revelation that Samuel had received from Yahweh before Saul arrived (9:15–17): the insertion begins and ends with a reference to Samuel and Saul, reversing the order in which they were mentioned in the original but displaced sentence (9:18). The choice of Saul by lot at Mizpah is anticipated again (9:20b–21): it is affixed by repeating a deictic pronoun that contrasts the losing of the donkeys and the finding of a kingdom (*lěkā*, 9:20a, 20b). The anointing of Saul (9:27–10:9) is inserted with an opening deictic (9:27 *bēmmâ*) and by

ending the insertion as the original continuation began (10:9b, *wayyābō'û* = 10:10aA).

125 The story supposes the meeting between Saul and Samuel and their journey together to Gibeah (11:7; cf. 9:26; 10:10aA).

126 1 Sam 11:6, 8, 12aBb (*mî hā'ōmēr . . . těnû hā'ănāšîm ûněmîtēm*), 13, 15aB. The first addition is made with the help of a deictic phrase ("these words," referring to 11:5). The second is made by repeating a word (11:8, *wě'îš*; cf. 11:7, *kě'îš*). The third (11:12aBb–13) contains a cross-reference to the preceding story (10:27). The last repeats its immediate context (11:15, *šām lipnê yhwh*).

127 The Deuteronomistic Historian added the geographical notices (1 Sam 17:1aBb, 52–54), the name of the Philistine and a description of his armor (17:4aBb–7a), the challenge to all Israel (17:10, 25aB, 34–36, 42–48), and references to the story of David's anointing and rivalry with his brothers (17:12b, 13aAb, 14–16, 26–31; cf. chap. 16).

128 The first additions in the revised version (1 Sam 18:1, 3–4) are made by referring in general to the preceding conversation between Saul and David (18:1; cf. 17:58) and by anticipating in Jonathan's love for David the love that Michal had for him (18:1b, cf. 18:20a). The second addition (18:6–19) repeats a previous clause from the sequel (18:6aA = 17:57aA). The third (18:21–27a) begins like the sentence that it replaces (18:21, *wayyō'mer šā'ûl 'ettěnennā lô* = 18:27b, *wayyitten lô šā'ûl*). The story of David's rise to power follows naturally up to the death of Saul. In this last segment the Deuteronomist was concerned once more to turn the struggle of heroic warriors into a war between armies massed for battle (1 Sam 31:1b, 4a, 7–13).

129 The defeat of the Jebusites in the original version is in partial fulfillment of the covenant on Horeb (cf. Exod 34:11; Deut 7:1). The Deuteronomistic History made its changes with deictic pronouns (2 Sam 5:1bB, *hiněnû . . . 'ănāḥnû*; 5:2b, *'attâ*; cf. 5:2a), deictic phrases (5:8, *bayyôm hahû'*), and repetitions (5:3a; cf. 5:1; 5:5, *mālak*; cf. 5:4; 5:6bB, *lē'mōr lō' yābō' dāwid hēnnâ*; cf. 5:6bA, *lēdāwid lē'mōr lō' tābō' hēnnâ*). In this version David was made king of Judah by the people of Judah (2:4; 5:5) and king of Israel by the elders of Israel (3:17; 5:3a, 5). The text of the capture of Jerusalem is changed in bits and pieces and becomes convoluted, but it allows for a connection between the temple in Zion (5:8, *bayit*) and the house of David (5:11, *bayit*) that becomes crucial in the account of the dynastic promise. The change begins with the intrusion of the lame and the blind (5:6bB). After the capture of the city it is noted (5:8) that David had given orders to enter the city via the water conduit, thereby showing his contempt for the lame and the blind who would have prevented him from entering. And therefore, since David despised them, it is said that the lame and the blind will not enter the temple (5:8; cf. Deut 15:21).

130 The original promise to David begins and ends with a reference to the word of Yahweh to Nathan (7:4, 17aAb) and assures David that his kingdom

will endure (7:12, 16a) and that his sons will rule after him under the protection of Yahweh (7:14a, 15a). The revised version (7:1–3, 5b–11, 13, 14b, 15b, 16b, 17aB, 18–29) adds another introduction and conclusion. The introduction links the dynasty and the temple: the beginning (7:1–3) harks back to the original context of the oracle—interrupted by the insertion of the ark narrative in 2 Samuel 6—in which David had just taken possession of Zion as his capital (5:6–12). The link between the original prophetic formula (7:5a) and the message (7:12) is broken by two speeches that develop the introductory topic, the first introduced by a deictic pronoun (*'attâ*, 7:5b–7), the second introduced by repeating the prophetic formula (7:8–11a). The transition between these additional speeches and the original oracle (7:11b; cf. 7:16a) again focuses on the secondary pun on the word "house." The interest in the relation between house (= dynasty) and house (= temple) persists in another insertion, also made with the help of a deictic pronoun (7:13, *hû'*). The assertion that the king will be the son of Yahweh is toned down with the remark that he will be treated as any human (7:14b), and the modification is signaled by deictic pronominal suffixes. The relation between David and Saul is recalled by repeating one word from the original oracle in an opposite sense (7:15a, *lō' yāsûr*, but 7:15b, *hăsîrōtî* [twice]). The permanence of David's house and kingdom is given the more abstract significance of permanent power, without reference to land or offspring, by referring to the throne of David (7:16b; cf. 7:16a). The prayer of David (7:18–29) reorganizes and refocuses all the concepts of the revised version.

131 The Deuteronomistic additions (2 Sam 11:4–13, 21a, 27aBb; 12:1–24a) are made with the help of deictics (11:4aB, *wĕhî'*) and by repeating displaced texts. David's attempt to disclaim paternity (11:6–13) begins with the letter that he sent to Joab (11:6aA) and anticipates the letter that he sent to Joab with Uriah (11:14a). The birth of the first child (11:27aB, *wattēled lô bēn*) replaces the birth of Solomon (12:24b, *wattēled bēn*). A cross-reference to the story of Abimelech in the book of Judges (11:21a) repeats, in opposite order, the sentence to which it is appended (11:21a, *mē'al hahômâ . . . lāmmâ niggaštem 'el hahômâ*; cf. 11:20, *maddûa' niggaštem . . . mē'al hahômâ*).

132 The Deuteronomist situates the rape in the legal traditions of Israel. The additions (2 Sam 13:2aB, 12aB–13, 16–18, 19aB, 21–22, 30–39) are made with the help of deictic pronouns (2 Sam 13:2aB [*hî'*], 12Bb–13 [*hazz'ōt*], 30 [*hēmmâ*]) and phrases (13:21–22 [*kol haddĕbārîm hā'ēlleh*]).

133 The Deuteronomist relates the story of Absalom's revolt (15:1–7, 9–10, 12b–13, 17, 18a) to his earlier flight to Geshur (15:8) and to the theme of wisdom and providence that governs both stories (15:11–12a). The additions are made by repetition. The flight to Geshur is inserted by repeating the mention of Absalom's vow (15:8, cf. 15:7). Ahitophel is introduced by referring to the people who went with Absalom (*'et 'abšālôm*, 15:11; cf. 15:12b). The announcement of David's flight from Jerusalem (15:14–16) ends like the sentence it displaced (15:16, *wayyēṣe' hammelek wĕkol* = 15:17); a cross-reference to David's sojourn in Gath depends on the repetition of one word from the preceding context (15:18b, *wĕkol*; cf. 15:18a).

134 See D. M. Gunn, "From Jerusalem to the Jordan and Back: Symmetry in 2 Samuel 15–20," *VT* 30 (1980) 109–13. In the original version David never left the city, and the battle is fought by his lieutenants (18:1a ["And David organized the people who were with him"] follows naturally on 15:17–18a ["And the king and all the people in his train went out and stood at the gate house . . ."]). The Deuteronomist changed the battle account to agree with its own version of conflict between Israel and Judah (18:6b–7, added by anticipating 18:8 in 18:6b), and added a reference to Absalom's funerary stele (18:17aB, 18) and a cross-reference to the story of David's concubines (19:6bB).

135 The Deuteronomist has the better story, but it tends to downgrade the effectiveness of the dynastic promise to David by linking the succession to craft and intrigue (1 Kgs 1:1b–4, 11–31, 35b–37, 41bA, 45b–48, 50–53; 2:1– 9, 11b–46a).

136 The Deuteronomistic version is full of intriguing details that were fitted in by deictic references and by repetition. The first indication that David is incompetent (1 Kgs 1:1b–4) is fitted in by deictic pronouns (1:1b, *waykaṣṣūhû*, *lô*), constantly refers to "the king" (1:2 [three times], 3 [once], 4 [twice]; cf. 1:1a) and ends as the original began (1:4bB, *wĕhammelek* = 1:1a). Adonijah's revolt (1:5–10) is related to that of Absalom both explicitly by referring to Absalom and by remarking that he too was handsome (1:6b), and the addition is made with the help of a deictic pronoun (1:6b, *wĕgam hû*). The intrigue between Nathan and Bathsheba (1:11–31) tends to obscure the validity of the dynastic promise, and it is inserted by having Nathan repeat the beginning of the original story in opposite order (1:11, *mālak ʾădōniyyāhû* = 1:5, *ʾădōniyyāh . . . ʾemlōk*). The succession of Solomon is related to the Deuteronomistic notion that the Davidic kings were meant to be Yahweh's viceroys (*nāgîd*) in a passage (1:35b–37) that begins with a deictic pronoun (1:35b, *wĕʾōtô*) and that ends insisting on the terms preceding the intrusion (1:35a, *kiʾî*; cf. 1:37, *kiʾô mikkissēʾ*). A further reference to the age and illness of the king (1:45b–48) is introduced with a deictic reference to the beginning of the scene (*hûʾ haqqōl*; cf. 1:41bB). Before being murdered Adonijah takes refuge at the altar (1:50– 53), and the scene is enacted with the help of repetition (1:50, *ʾădōniyyāhû . . . wayyāqom wayyēlek*; cf. 1:49, *wayyāqūmû . . . laʾădōniyyāhû wayyēlĕkû*). The original ending of the story (2:10–11a, 46b) is deferred to allow time for retaliation against David's enemies, and the delay is marked by repetition (1:11b, *malak* = 1:11a; 1:12 = 1:46b).

137 The prophetic legitimation of Jeroboam's revolt (1 Kgs 11:27–39) was added to the text and was indicated as such by a deictic phrase (11:27, *wĕzeh haddābār*). This foreknowledge of Jeroboam's destiny required that he be present at the Shechem convention from the beginning (1 Kgs 12:2–3a), even though this created problems in the narrative (1 Kgs 12:5, 12). His presence is signaled by a deictic pronoun (12:2, *wĕhûʾ ʿōdennû*), cross-reference to the preceding text (cf. 11:40), and repetition of the original (12:3a, *wayyābōʾ*; cf. 12:1, *bāʾ*). His active participation at the meeting is noted by having the assembly withdraw and return with him (12:5, 12), and the additions are

related to each other and anticipate the king's original address to the people (12:5, 12, *hāʿām*; cf. 12:13, *hāʿām*). Another reference to the prophetic legitimation of the revolt (12:15) begins by citing the text it replaced (*wĕlōʾ šāmaʿ hammelek ʾel hāʿām*; cf. 12:16, *kî lōʾ šāmaʿ hammelek ʾălêhem*). The revolt itself is accompanied by a familiar ditty (12:16aB) that ends like the following text (cf. 12:16b). A cross-reference to the forced labor that caused the strife (12:18a; cf. 1 Kgs 5:28) is introduced like the sentence it displaced (*hammelek rĕhabʿām*; cf. 12:18b). Rehoboam's abortive attempt to force the submission of the northern tribes (12:21–24) uses key words of the preceding context in a different order and meaning (*šēbeṭ* and *bêt*). The extension of the schism to include apostasy and an illegitimate priesthood (12:30–33) is introduced by a deictic clause (12:30a, *wayhî haddābār hazzeh lĕhaṭṭaʾt*) and by an awkward repetition of the preceding phrase (12:30b, *wayyēlĕkû hāʿām lipnê hāʾehad ʿad dān*; cf. 12:29, *wĕʾet hāʾehād nātan bĕdān*).

138 The synchronisms illustrate the principle of repetition: in the original version Rehoboam dies and is succeeded by Abijam (1 Kgs 14:31), but in the Deuteronomistic version the accession of Abijam is computed according to the reign of Jeroboam simply by repeating that Abijam succeeded his father (14:31b, *wayyimlōk ʾăbiyyām*; cf. 15:1, *mālak ʾăbiyyām*); similarly, Asa reigned after Abijam, but the history dates his accession according to the reign of Jeroboam by repeating that he reigned after Abijam (15:8, 9). The evaluations of the kings are added by repetition and by cross-reference. The evaluation of Rehoboam (1 Kgs 14:21b–24) begins with items from the original that precedes it (14:21b, *bĕmolkô . . . mālak*; cf. 14:21a, *mālak*) and follows it (14:21b, *wĕšēm ʾimmô naʿămâ hāʿammōnît* = 14:31aB), and it is filled with clichés and stereotypes. The evaluation of Abijam (15:3–6) anticipates the text it preempted (15:6 = 15:7b). The evaluation of Asa (15:11–16) in the same way anticipates the text that follows it (15:15–16; cf. 15:17–18). The other changes are introduced by repetitions and deictic references: Shishak's raid, in the original version, ruined the palace and temple finances (14:26a), but the History inserted references to the accoutrements of the Solomonic temple (14:26b–28) by repeating the key words (14:26b, *wayyiqqah ʾet kol* = 14:26a, *wĕʾet hakkol lāqah*). The additional reigns in the northern kingdom are noted by synchronism with the reign of Asa (15:25, 33; 16:8).

139 The Deuteronomist separated the original notices on the reigns of Jehoshaphat (1 Kgs 15:24 and 22:42 etc.) and Jehoram (1 Kgs 22:51 and 2 Kgs 8:17 etc.) by describing the political and social role of prophets in the northern kingdom. The synchronisms (1 Kgs 22:41; 2 Kgs 8:16, 25) are added by repetition and cross-reference (cf. 1 Kgs 22:40; 2 Kgs 8:17, 26). The evaluation of Jehoshaphat (1 Kgs 22:43–44, 47) is entered by reference to the edited text (cf. 22:41) and by repeating a key word from the end of the original (22:47, *wĕyeter* = 22:46). The evaluation of Jehoram (2 Kgs 8:18–19), similarly, begins with reference to the preceding synchronism (cf. 8:16) and ends with reference to the following report (8:19, *kol hayyāmîm*; cf. 8:20, *bĕyāmāyw*), and a note on the revolt of Libnah during his reign (2 Kgs 8:22b) is inserted via repetitions and deictics (*tipšaʿ*; cf. 8:22a, *wayyipšaʿ*; *ʾaz . . . bāʿēt hahîʾ*). The evaluation of Ahaziah (2 Kgs 8:27) begins with the first word of the sentence it displaced (*wayyēlek* = 8:28).

140 In the original version Jehu is a usurper whose actions threaten the stability of the Davidic dynasty, but in the revised version he is a hero who cleanses the dynasty and both kingdoms of the cult of Baal. All the additions relate the story of the assassination of the kings to the earlier stories of Ahab and Jezebel (2 Kgs 9:15b, 21bB, 22bB, 25–26, 29–37) or to the subsequent story of the renovation of the temple (2 Kgs 10:1–36; 11:4b–11, 15–16, 17aBb–18).

141 The changes (2 Kgs 12:2aA, 3–17; 13:1–25; 14:1, 3–4, 6–17, 21aB, 22–29) are made by repetition and deictic cross-references and incorporate the little that the original narrated about Judah into an account of the much more serious situation that was developing in Israel. The synchronism between Jehu and Jehoash (12:2aA) repeats items from the surrounding text (cf. 12:1, 2aB). The account of the reparations of the temple (12:3–17) is affixed via the stereotyped evaluation (12:3) and repetition of the name of the king. The evaluation of Amaziah (14:3–4) repeats part of the edited text (14:1). The war between Israel and Judah (14:7–17) belongs to an account of the reign of Joash of Israel, and it is inserted by repetition (14:6; cf. 14:5) and by use of the deictic pronoun (14:7, *hû'*). The addition of Azariah's age at his accession (14:21aB = 15:2) anticipates the original account and allows for the insertion of further material concerning the northern kingdom (14:22–29).

142 The synchronisms and evaluations of the kings are added, as usual, by repetition of their near and remote contexts (2 Kgs 15:1, 3–4, 8–32, 34–35; 16:1, 2b–4). Other additions are made by deictic references (15:37; 16:6) or by repetition of key words (16:10–19; cf. 16:9). The explanation of the fall of the northern kingdom presupposes the history of the kings from Jeroboam I on as well as the interpretation of the covenant that the Deuteronomistic Historian supplied in the book of Deuteronomy.

143 The reform of Josiah is the culmination of the covenant as this was narrated by the sequel and described by the Deuteronomist in the book of Deuteronomy. The fall of Jerusalem, on the other hand, is the result of the sin of Manasseh and the conclusion of the theory of history that the Deuteronomist developed beginning in the book of Genesis. Law and covenant coincide in the abstract since the Deuteronomist identified the covenant with the decalogue. But literarily and historically they hardly mesh since, as the Historian interpreted it, the ideology of covenant reached its logical but absurd conclusion in Josiah's useless reform and covenant renewal but did nothing to prevent the continuation of the determined history of sin.

144 The Priestly writer prefixed a version of creation (Gen 1:1–2:4a) suggested by the preterition at the beginning of the epic version (Gen 2:5–6). The Deuteronomist appended the story of Cain and Abel (Genesis 4) that brought sin and violence into the world.

145 The epic version was revised (Genesis 6–8) and bracketed by the Priestly writer (Gen 5:1–29abA, 30–32; Gen 9:1, 9–17, 28–29) and by the Deuteronomist (Gen 5:29bB, 32; 9:2–8, 18–27).

[146] The Priestly writer prefixed a geography (Gen 10:1–7, 20, 22–23, 31–32) and an ethnographic genealogy (Gen 11:10–28, 31–32) that completely isolated the beginning of the epic version (Gen 11:1, 4–7, 8b, 9b), and appended an ethnographic narrative (Genesis 23) to conclude the story of Abraham and Sarah. The original was split by the Priestly covenant with Abraham (Gen 16:1, 3, 15–16; 17:1–27) and was modified at the beginning and the end by chronological and theological remarks (Gen 12:4b–5abA; 21:1b, 2b, 4-5).

[147] The Priestly writer wrote at the beginning (Gen 25:7–10, 12–17, 19–34), in the middle (Gen 28:1–5), and at the end (Gen 35:9–15, 28–29). The Deuteronomistic Historian added genealogical lists at the beginning (Gen 25:1–6) and at the end (Gen 35:22–26).

[148] The Priestly writer included genealogical and chronological information on Jacob and Esau at the beginning (Gen 36:1–8; 37:1, 2aA) and chronological notes on Jacob at the end (Gen 46:6–7; 47:27–31; 49:33b). The Deuteronomist, besides rewriting the story of Joseph, added more genealogical references at the beginning and the end (Gen 36:9–43; 49:1–33a).

[149] The Priestly writer redid the epic by modifying its preface (Exod 1:1–4, 5b–7, 13–14; 2:23aBb–25), its description of the exodus (Exodus 6–15°), its interpretation of the revelation on Sinai (Exodus 16–40°), its spy narrative (Numbers 12–14°), and its evaluation of Moses (Numbers 20°; 27°), and by including all these events as incidents in the life of Moses. The Elohist also changed the introduction (Exodus 3–4°), the account of the exodus (Exodus 13–14°) and the interpretation of Sinai (Exodus 18–34°). The Deuteronomist rewrote the epic; the Priestly writer and the Elohist added extensive information on the ideal organization of Israel (Leviticus 8–11; Numbers 1–36°).

[150] The Priestly writer enclosed the episode between chronological notices pertaining to the life of Moses (Deut 1:3; 32:48–50, 51b–52; 34:1°, 2–5, 7–9). The Deuteronomist added a historical introduction and conclusion (Deuteronomy 1–3°; 31–34°), a theological preface and epilogue (Deuteronomy 4–11°; 26–30°), and detailed stipulations (Deuteronomy 19–25) to match and deemphasize the laws of centralization (Deuteronomy 12–18°).

[151] Josh 1:1–5, besides recounting the death of Moses, which is imminent at the end of the preceding episode (Deut 31:2), refers to what Moses said at that time (Josh 1:5; cf. Deut 31:6). This introductory segment, besides, is constructed of sayings that are familiar from the preceding speech of Moses (Deut 1:8; 7:24; 9:1; 11:24).

[152] Josh 11:23° refers to the statement in Josh 1:3 and recognizes that it was said the first time to Moses (Deut 11:24).

[153] Josh 1:6–9 refers to Deut 31:7–8 and to its immediate context concerning the book of the law which Moses wrote (Deut 31:9–13, 24–29). The book

is summarized in Joshua 23, and Joshua 24 is a transition to the following books. The account of the conquest is brought to a close by a summary that limits it to thirty-one towns and dominions (Joshua 12), and it is matched by a variant account in which the land is assigned to the tribes rather than conquered (Joshua 13–22).

154 The last battles in the second episode take place in the hill country around Mizpah (Josh 11:2–3, 8a), and the third episode begins in the hill country of Zuph (1 Sam 1:1). The Deuteronomist inserted the period of the judges between Joshua and Samuel, but the sequel separated them by no more than four generations (1 Sam 1:1).

155 The first section of the Deuteronomistic book (1 Samuel 1–7) is related thematically to the concluding section of the book of Judges (Judges 17–21) and brings the period of the judges to a close. The reign of Saul is subsumed in an evaluation of the monarchy in general and of his reign in particular (1 Samuel 8–15). The rest of the book anticipates the succession of David (1 Samuel 16–31) and describes, in the conflict between Saul and David, the eclipse of the northern kingdom and the ascendancy of Judah.

156 When all the tribes assembled before David in Hebron, they recalled that Saul had put him in charge of the armies of Israel (2 Sam 5:2a; cf. 1 Sam 18:5).

157 The episode begins with a variant interpretation of the death of Saul recounted at the end of the preceding episode (2 Samuel 1; cf. 1 Samuel 31). The episode ends with poems and lists (2 Samuel 22–23) that summarize and situate the preceding account and also introduce the issue of the survival of the Davidic dynasty, which surfaces sporadically in the following books.

158 The revolt of Adonijah (1 Kgs 1:1a, 5, 7–10) begins like the revolt of Absalom (2 Sam 15:1) and includes a Deuteronomistic reference to him (1 Kgs 1:6).

159 Nathan the prophet is predominant at the beginning of the book (1 Kings 1), and Elijah and Elisha dominate its conclusion (1 Kings 17– 2 Kings 8). The intervening material is governed by the earlier prophecy of Nathan (1 Kings 3–11; cf. 2 Samuel 7) and by the prophecy of Ahijah (1 Kings 12–16; cf. 1 Kings 11).

160 At the beginning of Jehu's revolt there is a reference to the end of the preceding episode (2 Kgs 9:16; cf. 2 Kgs 8:28–29). In the Deuteronomistic version the transition is even more marked, since Elisha legitimates the coup (2 Kgs 9:1–13), and the entire ending of the preceding episode is repeated (2 Kgs 9:14b–15 = 2 Kgs 8:28–29).

161 The sequel explains that Samaria was captured by the Assyrians because it had violated the law of centralization and the covenant as these were narrated in the first episode (2 Kgs 18:12): that is, they had not listened

to Yahweh (cf. Deut 5:23; 6:4; 9:1); they had reneged on the covenant (cf. Deut 5:2–3; 29:11, 13–14); they had not done what Moses the servant of Yahweh commanded them (cf. Deut 8:1; 11:8, 13, 22; 12:14); and they had not listened and obeyed (= Deut 5:27). Hezekiah, on the contrary, had removed the high places and had centralized worship in Jerusalem (2 Kgs 18:22; cf. Deut 12:13–14, 17, 18aAb, 20, 26) and, in accordance with the prohibition of alliances with inhabitants of the land, had broken Judah's alliance with the Assyrians (2 Kgs 18:7). The Deuteronomist surrounded this incident with a theological summary that insisted on the inevitability of punishment for sin (2 Kings 17) and with a fable that applied the theology to Judah. In its version of the reform of Josiah it illustrated how even perfect adherence to the covenant was of no use (2 Kings 22–23) if sin had corrupted the foundations of life (2 Kings 21; 24–25).

162 See fig. 3. The exposition of the covenant and the law of centralization in the first episode is achieved in incidents composed of two paragraphs that balance and match each other. In other less discursive episodes, such as the history of Saul, the incidents are composed of matching segments, each of which has a pair of parallel paragraphs.

163 This issue is developed in the story of Cain and his descendants (Genesis 4).

164 The paragraph on the river that flowed out of Eden and became four rivers (Gen 2:10–15) situates the story of creation in a world dominated by Egypt, Assyria, Babylonia, and Jerusalem. The same perspective on world history accounts for the idea that Abraham went to Egypt (Genesis 12), defeated the kings of Mesopotamia (Genesis 14), and was honored by the king of Salem, the erstwhile Jerusalem (Genesis 14).

165 The Deuteronomistic History added Gen 12:2b, 3b, 7 to make the promise to Abraham more suited to his posterity. It also added a reference to the Canaanites (Gen 12:6b) and to the actual location of Bethel (Gen 12:8b) that, in view of the later defection of his posterity, introduced an ominous note into the narrative.

166 The sequential elements (Gen 13:1, 3–4, 6b) corroborate the epic version in part but are meant mostly to integrate the epic version into the continuous narrative of Abraham's journey from Mesopotamia to Egypt. The disjunctive elements (Gen 13:7b, 10b) situate the narrative in world history and in relation to the following story of Sodom and Gomorrah, since there is a great deal of secondary intervening material (Genesis 14–17) that obscures the relationship.

167 The Deuteronomist added Gen 19:9aB to separate Lot from the local inhabitants and to suggest that he was innocent and deserved, as it happened, to escape the destruction of the city.

168 The parenthesis (Gen 19:24b) relates the story of Lot to the preceding

story, in which Abraham stood with Yahweh and talked about justice and the punishment of the guilty before Yahweh left and returned to heaven. The sequential addition (Gen 19:26) fits the epic version into the Deuteronomistic version, according to which Lot escaped from Sodom and, through incestuous unions with his daughters, became the father of Moab and Ammon.

169 The first two paragraphs suffered Deuteronomistic additions (Gen 26:1aB, 2–6, 10, 15) and supplements (Gen 26:18–25) that linked the story of Isaac to the theological interpretation of the story of Abraham. The episode was broken in the middle by Priestly, Elohist, and Deuteronomistic additions (Genesis 28). The later paragraphs were modified by the Deuteronomistic genealogy of the sons of Israel (fig. 2, ## 14–16) and by the Priestly, Elohist, and Deuteronomistic interpretations of Jacob's encounter with God (## 17–20).

170 In similar scenes in the Deuteronomistic History direct discourse functions mainly as a commentary on the narrative. In the Priestly document speeches, directives, and sayings abound, but the words either contain the action or mark the stages in the development of the argument.

171 The epic implies, but does not say, that Noah was one of the ancient heroes born to the sons of God and the daughters of Man.

172 Although there is no evidence that the epic was composed orally, it may be supposed, at least by analogy with contemporary Green compositions, that it was read, recited, or dramatized. It follows, then, that things that could not be indicated by tone or gesture or representation might be emphasized by repetition.

173 The Deuteronomist adds remarks in the style of the original, but they tend to be listlike and pedantic. The distinction between clean and unclean animals is inserted into the epic speech as direct discourse (Gen 7:1b–3) and into its narration as narrative (Gen 7:8–9): the pedantry is subordinate modifiers that explain everything; the catalog quality is produced by asyndesis and juxtaposition.

174 The paragraph follows the repetitive pattern of epic paragraphs that do not contain direct discourse, but there is no action and it is essentially a commentary on the epic version.

175 God announces the flood, which will be described in what follows, and the covenant with Noah, which will occur at the end of the episode (Genesis 9). His instructions concerning the food and animals that are to be taken on board the ark are observed in theory (6:22), but they are not carried out in fact.

176 Although the epic narrates that Yahweh came down to see the city and the tower (Gen 11:5, *wayyēreḏ*), the descent also takes place in the soliloquy (11:7, *hābâ nērĕḏâ*). The Deuteronomist, on the other hand, does narrate the

confusion of tongues (11:8a, 9a) in order to insert an etiology reflecting on the epic action.

177 The paragraph says that Abraham had wealth and possessions and that Lot too had many possessions (Gen 13:2, 5), that Lot saw the Jordan Valley and chose the Jordan Valley (Gen 13:10a, 11a). The actions that are narrated—that the country was too small for both of them, that there were disputes between their shepherds, and that they separated from each other—are merely reflections of Abraham's speech (Gen 13:8–9).

178 The soliloquies are set apart in a separate paragraph (Gen 18:17–21) and relay the general argument of the Deuteronomistic Historian rather than contribute to the current action.

179 As usual, the absence of direct discourse is compensated for by careful repetition.

180 In the Deuteronomistic version of Genesis 26–27 the action is narrated (Gen 26:18–25, 32–33) and interpreted by etiologies (26:20, 22, 32) or by a literary *deus ex machina* (Gen 26:2–6, 24) or even by a narrative aside (Gen 26:15).

181 Since the point of the story is to justify Israel's worship at Bethel, there is also an aside in which it is explained that the place used to be called Luz but that it became the house of God through the providence of God and the persistent belief of Jacob.

182 Much of the interpretation, besides, is a reflection on the epic text rather than on events narrated by the Elohist. The Elohist also gives fewer reasons and motives, and these often occur from the outside, in divine intervention, rather than in conversation between the main characters.

183 The distinction and relationship between spoken words and narrated deeds are suggested by the Assyrian taunt to Hezekiah: "You think that a spoken word is a plan and preparation for battle" (2 Kgs 18:20a).

184 The original version of Deuteronomy illustrates the sequel's theory that history unfolds according to plans that are worked out in dialogue with God or in rational discourse. The basic form of such mutual understanding is treaty and covenant. The proof of the theory is that it actually worked in the history of Judah. The Deuteronomist lived at another time—when the theory could not be sustained, when despite the covenant Judah had not survived—and found a better justification for universal history in the fateful interplay of law, sin, and punishment.

185 The Priestly writer made the speech just another event in the life of Moses, which was of little practical consequence for him because he had already been excluded from the promised land (Deut 1:3; 32:48–50, 51b–52; 34:1–5, 7–9).

[186] The most obvious instance of matching occurs at the beginning of the paragraph, where Moses recounts the journey from Horeb to the hill country of the Amorites (Deut 1:19°) and immediately, in a quoted speech to the people, declares that they have completed the journey to the hill country of the Amorites (1:20). The promise to Caleb, on the other hand, is spoken but not narrated and is a literary link to the epic version of the story (1:35–36; cf. Num 14:30).

[187] The agreement to listen and do (Deut 5:27, *wěšama'nû wě'āśînû*) is taken up in various ways in Deuteronomy (e.g., 6:4; 8:1; 9:1; 12:14; 16:1), and at the end of the sequel the fall of Samaria is attributed to the North's failure to live up to the agreement (2 Kgs 18:12b, *lō' šāmě'û wělō' 'āśû*).

[188] The History added another paragraph (Deut 5:28–33), in which Moses gained access to all the revealed tradition that had not been disclosed publicly on Sinai. It narrates that Yahweh heard the people agree to the decalogue (5:28a) and then has Yahweh say that he heard (5:28b). The other things that Yahweh says are not narrated and do not occur but express hopes and expectations.

[189] In the sequel Moses summarized the covenant (Deut 6:4–9). The Deuteronomist did not change the summary but added stipulations and warnings (Deut 6:14b, 15b, 16–18) that observe the essentials of the sequel's style.

[190] Facts include the list of cities of refuge (Deut 4:41–43). Explanation takes place in a narrative of historical events (e.g., Deut 7:6–11; 8:2–6; 9:7–10:11), and history takes place in a song (Deuteronomy 32).

[191] It is typical of the sequel to narrate that the spies came to Jericho (Josh 2:1) and then have the king say that they came (2:3), or to have Rahab urge the king's men to pursue the Israelites (2:5b) and then narrate that they did (2:7). Other things, such as the fact that Yahweh has given Israel the land (2:9a, 24a), are said but not narrated and suggest the point or structure of succeeding narratives. Rahab's lie (2:5a—that the spies left before the gates were shut) is just words and did not happen.

[192] The narrative aside (1 Sam 1:3b) and the conversations (1:12–17, 25–28) follow the rules of occurrence and interpretation established by the sequel. The main difference between the two versions is their literary scope and historical sequence: in the sequel Samuel is the fifth generation after the conquest; in the Deuteronomistic History Eli is the last of the judges.

[193] The paragraphs are 1 Sam 11:1–4; 11:5, 7, 9–10; 11:11, 12aA ("The people said to Samuel: 'Let Saul be King over us' "), 14a, 15aAb; 14:52.

[194] The narrative additions (1 Sam 11:6, 8, 15aB) include things that suit the Deuteronomist's interests and ideologies but that supposedly were done. The added dialogue (11:12aBb, 13, 14b) does not result in action but refers to Deuteronomistic revisions in the preceding incident (cf. 1 Sam 10:1, 27).

195 In the original paragraph (1 Sam 17:1aA, 2) Saul is the leader of Israel. The Deuteronomistic addition (1 Sam 17:1aBb) follows the narrative pattern and plays with the same words but it distinguishes "Israel" from Judah. This distinction becomes crucial as the History proceeds.

196 The reported promise of manumission matches the Philistine's offer (17:9). The prospect of wealth is illusory and is not narrated. The fairy-tale marriage to the daughter of Saul was narrated by the sequel (1 Sam 18:27b) but is integrated into the plot by the Deuteronomist (1 Sam 19:11–17; 25:44; 2 Sam 3:12–16; 6:20–23).

197 The original (1 Sam 17:23*, 24–25aAb, 32–33, 37, 40–41, 49, 51) was expanded with a conversation between David and one of his brothers (17:26–30) that supposes and develops the earlier story of the choice of David from among his brothers (1 Samuel 16), and by another conversation between David and Saul (17:34–36) in which the Deuteronomist interprets the Philistine challenge as an affront to God. Neither element of direct discourse adds to the action, but both suggest some other motive for David's acceptance of the challenge besides the courage and ambition that the sequel ascribed to him.

198 In the sequel's version, Saul had made up his mind to recruit David even before his victory over the Philistine champion (1 Sam 17:55, "When Saul saw David going out to meet the Philistine . . ."). In the Deuteronomistic version the bond is established between Jonathan and David (1 Sam 18:1, 3–4), and the relationship between Saul and David is troubled from the very start (1 Sam 18:6–9).

199 The Deuteronomistic Historian attributed this turn of events to words spoken by Yahweh to the prophet Ahijah (1 Kgs 12:15, etc.).

200 There does not seem to have been much Egyptian influence on Judean literary traditions until sometime after the fall of the Assyrian empire. The term "Canaanite" refers to the literature indigenous to the land of Canaan rather than to an ethnic and presumably non-Israelite literature.

201 Its information is restricted, but its understanding of historical traditions is impressive. It has a vague acquaintance with farming, animal husbandry, transhumance, and stylized features of nomadic existence. It can typify female, subservient, and courtly characters and has a good grasp of conflict and reconciliation. It knows about laws and rituals and the marvels of divine manifestation. It also seems to have known all the local and regional traditions concerning the origins of Israel and the stages of its settlement in the land of Canaan. Some of them were unreliable; others were elided in the interest of the story; and all were corrected by the Deuteronomistic Historian.

202 The updating of myths and reorganization of mythical themes in Babylonian and Assyrian literature is somewhat analogous (see W. von Soden, *Reflektierte und Konstruierte Mythen in Babylonien und Assyrien* [Helsinki: The

Finnish Oriental Society, 1984] 149–57). In contemporary literature there is an analogous use of tradition as the organizing principle of personal history (see J. Cruikshank, "Myth and Tradition as Narrative Framework: Oral Histories from Northern Canada," *International Journal of Oral History* 9 [1988] 198–214).

203 Although individual mythical themes were known across the ancient world from time immemorial, the peculiar distribution and combination of entire works in the epic suggest that the author of the epic knew them as literature. But it is not possible to determine the edition or wording of the works that were available to the author at that time in the libraries of Jerusalem, or to establish literal references or verbatim quotations.

204 The epic's opening statement (*běyôm 'ǎśôt yhwh 'ělōhîm 'ereṣ wěśāmayim*) resembles the beginning of the *Enuma elish* ("When [*inūma*] on high heaven had not been named, the earth below had not been called by name"), and its inversion of the original word order may mark a literal quotation. Similarly, the epic refers to the absence of grass and shrubbery and refers to the waters that seeped up and watered the earth, and the *Enuma elish* refers to the absence of pastureland and reed marshes and to the mingling of sweet and salt water (see A. Heidel, *The Babylonian Genesis* [Chicago: University of Chicago Press, 1963] p. 18, tablet 1, lines 3–6). The story of *Atrahasis* begins before Man was made to do the labor of the Gods when the Gods had to do the work themselves (W. G. Lambert and A. R. Millard, *Atra-ḫasis: The Babylonian Story of the Flood* [Oxford: Clarendon Press, 1969] tablet I:1, 1–2, 190–191). The epic mentions that there was no Man to do the work (Gen 2:5), deals with the toil of the Gods only indirectly in relating that Yahweh God planted a garden in Eden (Gen 2:8), and makes labor the destiny of Man and Woman because they became like God but failed to attain everlasting life (Gen 3:22–23).

205 In Genesis 1 the Priestly writer demonstrates familiarity with the *Enuma elish* and Canaanite myths of fertility and world order but shows the same sort of artistic freedom from its subject that the epic exercised (see C. Westermann, *Genesis* 1:111–244 passim). Later in the first episode the Deuteronomistic History seems to allude to the *Enuma elish*'s interest in the names of things (Gen 2:19aBb–20a; see Heidel, *The Babylonian Genesis*, p. 18, tablet 1, lines 1–10). When it returns from its digression on the world rivers that issued from the Garden of Eden (Gen 2:10–14) it repeats the epic text from which it was diverged (2:15 = 2:8) but changes it to agree with *Atrahasis*. In the epic, Man was formed and placed in the garden (2:8); in the Deuteronomistic version Man was formed to work in the garden (2:15; cf. *Atrahasis*, I:5, 228–43).

206 In *Atrahasis* (I:2, 189–247) mankind is composed of clay, made from the flesh and blood of a God, and spirit, from the spit of the heavenly Gods.

207 See D. J. Wiseman, "Mesopotamian Gardens," *Anatolian Studies* 33 (1983) 137–44. In commenting on this passage the Deuteronomist added that there was a river that came out of Eden and became four streams (Gen 2:10–15). One of these was Gihon, a river in Jerusalem, perhaps associated with

the palace and royal gardens, where Solomon was anointed and proclaimed king (1 Kgs 1:33, 38).

[208] The tree of life (Gen 2:9) was ultimately beyond the reach of Man (Gen 3:22), as the plant of life was beyond the reach of Gilgamesh (see Westermann, *Genesis* 1:288–92). Its contrast with the tree of knowledge resembles the contrast between wisdom and life in the story of *Adapa* (Westermann, *Genesis* 1:335). In the epic the tree of knowledge, or the two trees together, may represent the groves on high places where Israel worshiped. These were associated with wisdom and knowledge and natural cycles (Hos 4:6a, 12–13a) and, as later polemic reveals, were incorporated into temples as shrines or symbolized as ornate pillars representing the Goddess Asherah. In the history of Isaac (Genesis 26) most of the basic themes of the Eden story come alive, and this symbolism is maintained by literal repetition. Isaac claims that Rebekah is his sister, not his wife, related to him by natural bonds and not by marriage (26:7, 9; cf. 2:23a and 2:23b) because he is afraid of dying (26:9; cf. 2:17). The truth is recognized in his physical relationship with Rebekah (26:8–9; cf. 3:4–13). The Philistines speak to him about good and evil (26:29; cf. 2:9, 17). Rebekah is as lovely to look at as the tree of the knowledge of good and evil (26:7; cf. 3:6), and the command not to touch it on pain of death refers to her (26:11; cf. 2:17; 3:3).

[209] See *ANET*, 75; W. L. Moran, "Ovid's *Blanda Voluptas* and the Humanization of Enkidu," *JNES* 50 (1991) 121–27. Enkidu wore no clothing, and when the woman from Uruk seduced him she was naked and not ashamed (Gen 2:25).

[210] Gen 2:23b–24; cf. *Atrahasis* I:6, 299ff.

[211] See *ANET*, 96.

[212] *Atrahasis* begins "When Gods were Man . . ." (*inūma ilū awīlum*). The epic is slightly more nuanced but supposes that Man had the spirit of God and became like God.

[213] *Atrahasis*, I:7–8, 352–415; see W. L. Moran, "Some Considerations of Form and Interpretation in *Atra-Hasis*," in *Language, Literature and History: Philological and Historical Studies Presented to Erica Reiner*, ed. F. Rochberg-Halton (New Haven: American Oriental Society, 1987) 245–55.

[214] Gen 6:1–2, 4aBb and 6:5–6, 7aAb, 8. The epic combines the Mesopotamian version of murmuring and conspiracy with the more specific and equally reprehensible divine aspirations of primordial, or pre–Trojan War, Man and Woman in Greek tradition. The epic's Greek source is an eighth-century text traditionally, but perhaps erroneously, attributed to Hesiod (see M. L. West, *The Hesiodic Catalogue of Women: Its Nature, Structure and Origins* [Oxford: Clarendon Press, 1985]; R. S. Hendel, "Of Demigods and the Deluge: Toward an Interpretation of Genesis 6:1–4," *JBL* 106 [1987] 13–26).

[215] Gen 6:5–6, 7aAb, 8; *Atrahasis* II:8, 34–35; III:i, 1–26.

[216] Gen 7:1a, 4, 7; *Atraḫasis* III:i, 22–50; III:ii, 10–43.

[217] Cf. Gen 7:4, 10; *ANET*, 93–94.

[218] Gen 7:4; *ANET*, 94; *Atraḫasis* III:2, 50–55.

[219] Gen 8:6, 8–12; ANET, 94–95.

[220] Gen 5:1–29abA, 30–32, 6:9–10; 9:28–29; see T. Jacobsen, "The Eridu Genesis," *JBL* 100 (1981) 513–29; P. D. Miller, Jr., "Eridu, Dunnu, and Babel: A Study in Comparative Mythology," *HAR* 9 (1985) 227–51; R. S. Hess, "The Genealogies of Genesis 1–11 and Comparative Literature," *Bib* 70 (1989) 241–54.

[221] Gen 6:11–13; see Westermann, *Genesis* 1:558–60. In the Priestly version God declared an end (*qēṣ*; cf. Amos 8:2) to all flesh because he saw that the earth was full of violence (*ḥāmās*) and in ruins (*°šḥt*). The terms have a moral connotation—the state of the world is contrasted with the innocence of Noah (Gen 6:9; cf. 7:1, *ṣaddîq*)—but otherwise correspond to the "noise" (*rigmu*) and "commotion" (*ḫuburu*) that disturbed the Gods and motivated the flood in the epic of *Atraḫasis*.

[222] Gen 6:13–22; cf. *ANET*, 93; *Atraḫasis* III:i–ii. In this version the ark had a door (6:16), and the Deuteronomist made sure that it was closed (Gen 7:16b, *wayyisgōr yhwh baʿādô*; cf. *Atraḫasis* III:ii, 52). The Deuteronomist also referred to the fact that the ark was covered (Gen 8:13b; cf. *Atraḫasis* III:i, 29). The epic supposed that Noah and his household went on board the ark, but the Priestly writer and the Historian followed the ancient sources more closely in supplying provisions for the duration of the flood and in providing for the survival of all sorts of animals (Gen 6:17-22; 7:1b-3, 8-9, 14-16; cf. *Gilgamesh* XI [*ANET*, 93–94]; *Atraḫasis*, III:ii, 30–43).

[223] Gen 8:4; cf. Westermann, *Genesis* 1:594–96.

[224] Gen 8:7; cf. *ANET*, 95.

[225] Gen 8:20–22; *ANET*, 95.

[226] Gen 9:1, 9–17; *ANET*, 95.

[227] *ANET*, 68–69.

[228] Gen 11:1, 4–7, 8b, 9b. The epic combined the story with another and with its own theme of Israel's gradual separation from the world and distinction from God. According to this other story people once spoke the same language and worshiped the same God, but some other God confused their speech and subverted their devotion (see S. N. Kramer, "The 'Babel of Tongues': A Sumerian Version," *JAOS* 88 [1968] 108–11).

[229] Gen 11:2–3, 8a, 9a. An important part of the construction of the city

and the temple tower is the preparation of the bricks (Gen 11:2–3; cf. *ANET*, 68; D. O. Edzard, "Deep-Rooted Skyscrapers and Bricks: Ancient Mesopotamian Architecture and its Imagery," in *Figurative Language in the Ancient Near East*, ed. M. Mindlin, M. J. Geller, and J. E. Wansbrough [London: University of London, 1987] 13–24).

230 Gen 12:1, 2a, 3a; cf. Gen 17. The promise to make Abraham a great nation establishes the basic condition for the treaty. The promise to magnify his name is the opposite of the standard treaty curse concerning the obliteration of an offender's name and seed. The commitment to blessing those who bless Abraham and cursing those who curse him is a summary and variation on the usual mutual assistance pacts. Curses are the most developed feature of Neo-Assyrian treaties. Blessings are not expressed in Assyrian treaties, but in the negotiations between Sennacherib and Hezekiah the sequel referred to the treaty that the Assyrians proposed as a "blessing" (2 Kgs 18:31).

231 Gen 13:2, 5–6a, 7a, 8–10a, 11, 12, 18a. The Deuteronomist expanded the territorial considerations by inserting a divine grant of the land to Abraham (Gen 13:14–17).

232 It is generally the vassal who must profess loyalty to the suzerain's successor (cf. the vassal treaties of Esarhaddon; S. Parpola and K. Watanabe, *Neo-Assyrian Treaties and Loyalty Oaths* [State Archives of Assyria 2; Helsinki: Helsinki University, 1988] # 6), but in the biblical tradition the order is reversed.

233 The Deuteronomist made sure that Isaac and Rebekah were married before this incident at Gerar (see Genesis 24) and, in an addition to the Elohist variant of the story, noted that Abraham and Sarah really were brother and sister (Gen 20:12). This version also replaced the implicit fertility rituals with divine promises (Gen 26:2–6, 23–25), moved Isaac away from Gerar to Beersheba, and explained the fertility of the soil by reference to the wells that were dug (Gen 26:15, 18–22, 32–33). The Priestly writer had mentioned their marriage, had described the miraculous birth of Jacob and Esau, and had established Jacob's right to primogeniture before the epic version could begin (Gen 25:19–34°).

234 The blessing paraphrases the blessing that was promised to Abraham and transmitted to Isaac (Gen 27:29; cf. Gen 12:2a, 3a; 26:12–14, 28–29) but compares Jacob to a fertile field (Gen 27:27) and the blessing to the benefits of heaven and earth.

235 The names of Jacob's wives are homographs of "ewe" (*rāḥēl*) and "heifer" (*lēʾâ*). The epic describes how Jacob acquired large flocks (Gen 30:37–43) and when he sends messengers to Esau mentions that he has cattle, pack animals, sheep, and servants, but does not mention his children (Gen 32:6; cf. 33:13). In the Elohist version, on the other hand, the children are mentioned (Gen 32:1), and in the Deuteronomistic version they are of paramount importance (Gen 31:43–50; 33:1b–2, 5–7).

236 The following analysis is indebted to J. Isaac, "The Composition of the Joseph Story" (M.A. thesis, University of Toronto, 1986). Elements of the legend were incorporated into the epic of *Gilgamesh* (tablet VI: *ANET*, 83–85).

237 The shepherd motif, although characteristic of the epic's evaluation of the ancestors of Israel, is proper to the story of Tammuz. See T. Jacobsen, "The Name Dumuzi," *JQR* 76 (1985) 41–45.

238 Israel's descent into Sheol is mentioned in Gen 42:38 and 44:31. The theme of life and death (Gen 42:2; 43:8) is taken up in the Elohist version (Gen 45:5). One of the products brought by the Ishmaelite merchants to Egypt, and later sent by Israel as a gift to Joseph, was myrrh or balsam—that is, resin of the tree that, in the Greek legend, gave birth to Adonis (cf. Gen 37:25; 43:11). The products were used in embalming and symbolize the death and ritual burial of the God.

239 *ANET*, 119; T. Longman III, *Fictional Akkadian Autobiography: A Generic and Comparative Study* (Winona Lake, Ind.: Eisenbrauns, 1991) 53–60.

240 See P. D. Miller, Jr., "Fire in the Mythology of Canaan and Israel," *CBQ* 27 (1965) 256–61; W. G. Lambert, "Old Testament Mythology in its Ancient Near Eastern Context," in *Congress Volume: Salamanca 1984*, ed. J. A. Emerton (VTSup 36; Leiden: Brill, 1985) 132.

241 See F. M. Cross, "The Song of the Sea and Canaanite Myth," *Canaanite Myth and Hebrew Epic: Essays in the History of the Religion of Israel* (Cambridge, Mass.: Harvard University Press, 1973) chap. 6, pp. 112–44. The epic version of the defeat of the Egyptians is part of the journey to the promised land, but the poetic version composed by the Deuteronomist (Exodus 15) presents all the mythic features in a song that is sung in praise of Yahweh.

242 See Jo Ann Hackett, *The Balaam Text from Deir 'Alla* (Chico, Calif.: Scholars Press, 1980). Both the epic and the Deir 'Alla texts know the seer's full name and his association with a group called "his kin" (*'mw* / *'mh*). In both the consultation of the seer is occasioned by an ominous darkness (Num 22:5, 11; Deir 'Alla I, 6–7). In both the seer meets God at night and delivers his oracle in the morning, is deprived of honor, and is inspired by God or El or Shadday, but not by Yahweh. In the Deir 'Alla texts the Gods speak to Balaam about the "hereafter," and he summons the people to see "the works of God" or "what the Shadday have done." In the epic text Balaam prays that his "hereafter" might be like Jacob's (Num 23:10) and, with a literal reference to the Deir 'Alla texts, proclaims "Now it has been said to Jacob and Israel 'What has God done!' " (Num 23:23).

243 Deut 1:30aA, *yhwh 'ĕlōhêkem hahōlēk lipnêkem*; cf. Exod 13:21.

244 The sequel's version of the spy narrative (Deut 1:19°, 20–30, 32–35aAb, 36) quotes part of the original (Num 13:1–2a, 23a, 25a, 27, 28, 31;

14:11, 21, 23), combines it with references to related texts (Deut 1:19*, 20; cf. Num 20:14, 16; 21:21), and fills it out with material from the exhortations that follow (Deut 1:21–27, 29).

245 Deut 9:1–3 quotes Num 13:22a, 28 in an opposite order and combines the quotation with references to the covenant (Exod 34:11, 24) and to the exodus (Exod 13:22).

246 Josh 2:1–9a, 12–16, 22–24a; 3:1aAb, 5, 10b, 16b. This story quotes the original spy narrative at the beginning (2:1–2; cf. Num 13:17–18, 22a) and at the end (2:23–24a; cf. Num 13:27) and combines it with ample references to the covenant on Sinai (3:5; cf. Exod 19:10 [°qdš] and 34:10 [niplā'ôt]; 3:10b cf. Exod 34:11).

247 Deut 5:2–4; cf. Exod 34:10; Num 14:14b. Deut 5:6–7, 9–11 quotes Exod 34:6–7, 14 in a different order and combines it with an allusion to the intercession of Moses at the time of the rebellion in the wilderness (cf. Num 14:13). The response of the people (Deut 5:23aA, 24a, 25, 27) deals mostly with the sequel's interest in the fire that enveloped the mountain, but it also refers to the oath that Yahweh took concerning the generation that refused to believe in him (Deut 5:24a; cf. Num 14:21).

248 Deut 6:4–9; cf. Exod 34:27–28abA. The beginning of this exhortation (6:4, *yhwh 'ĕlōhênû yhwh 'eḥāḏ*) seems to reflect Yahweh's opening words on Sinai: "And Yahweh came face to face with him and proclaimed: *yhwh yhwh* . . ." The matching paragraph (Deut 6:10–13, 14a, 15a) is mostly a paraphrase of the sequel's version of the covenant (Deut 5:6–7, 9–11) but also contains a quotation from the epic text and an allusion to the intercession of Moses in the wilderness (6:15a; cf. Exod 34:14b + Num 14:14).

249 Deut 7:1, 2*, 17–18, 21, 23–24; 10:12, 14, 17–18, 20; cf. Exod 34:11–12; 14:30–31; Gen 2:4b; 7:23.

250 Some of the allusions are explicit: Deut 12:14b = Exod 34:11a; Deut 12:20a = Exod 34:24; Deut 16:16aAb = Exod 34:20b, 24b. The sequel legislates tithes (Deut 14:22, 25–26) in place of the epic's harvest festivals (Exod 34:21–22), the offering of firstborn cattle and sheep (Deut 15:19-20) as the epic prescribed (Exod 34:19), and Passover (Deut 16:1–2a, 3aA, 7) instead of the dedication of firstborn children (Exod 34:20b).

251 Deut 31:1, 2a, 3a, 6; cf. Exod 34:11; Num 14:14.

252 Josh 1:1–2a; cf. Exod 14:31; Josh 1:3 = Deut 11:24.

253 Shiloh is a precursor of the central sanctuary and is distinguished from the place that Yahweh will choose by its dedication to Yahweh of Hosts. The annual pilgrimages (1 Sam 1:3, *miyyāmîm yāmîmâ*; 1:7, *šānâ bĕšānâ*; 1:20, *tĕqūpôt hayyāmîm*) are prescribed in the covenants on Sinai (Exod 34:22b) and Horeb (Deut 14:22). According to Deuteronomy the festivals are times to eat

and drink and be happy (Deut 12:18aAb), but at Shiloh Hannah wept and refused to eat or drink (1 Sam 1:7–8). Firstborn males belong to Yahweh (Exod 34:19, 20b; 1 Sam 1:11). Vows are to be paid at the central sanctuary (1 Sam 1:11, 21; Deut 12:17, 26). Elkanah and Hannah clearly recognize the obligation of appearing before Yahweh three times a year (1 Sam 1:22–24°; Exod 34:20b, 24; Deut 16:16aAb).

254 Saul is anointed in the presence of Yahweh (*lipnê yhwh*) and the people rejoice (*śmḥ*) as the law of centralization prescribed (Deut 12:18).

255 1 Sam 17:37 ("And Saul said to David: 'Go and may Yahweh be with you' "); cf. Josh 1:5 ("I will be with you as I was with Moses").

256 In the narrative development of the sequel, the central sanctuary seems at first to be Shiloh, then Gilgal, and then Hebron. It is only at the end of the history in the reign of Hezekiah that it becomes certain, although still not explicit, that Jerusalem is the place that Yahweh chose.

257 Cf. Exod 34:11; Deut 7:1; Josh 9:1.

258 David, like Moses, is the servant of Yahweh (2 Sam 7:5a; cf. Exod 14:31; Josh 1:1–2a). The promise to David uses the words that summarized the covenant on Sinai (*haddĕbārîm hāʾēlleh*, Exod 34:27; Deut 1:1a; 2 Sam 7:17aAb).

259 Cf. Num 21:24; Joshua 8°.

260 It is clear before the events that led up to the revolt of Absalom that Solomon is the successor of David chosen by Yahweh (cf. 2 Sam 12:24b–25). It is clear after the revolt of Absalom that David was willing to risk his alliance with the northern tribes (cf. 2 Sam 19:6–9°) to protect his son.

261 Cf. 1 Kgs 14:25–26a; 15:17–24; 2 Kings 9°; 11°; 12:18–19; 14:19.

262 Compare 2 Sam 7:14 ("I will be a father to him and he will be a son to me") with Ahaz's declaration to Tiglath-pileser (2 Kgs 16:7, "I am your servant and your son").

263 Apart from its interpretation of the epic, the sequel held no interest for the Priestly writer and the Elohist; they therefore confined their criticisms of it to their own commentaries on the epic.

CHAPTER 2

The Prophetic Paradigms

*T*he first prophets who recorded their oracles in writing were Isaiah, Amos, and Hosea. They spoke, as the authors of the epic and the sequel had written, about the fall of Samaria and its repercussions for Judah. They spoke not only about the facts as they saw them but about the interpretations that the events had received in the histories that were published before them. They addressed, in particular, the covenant bias of the epic and the sequel and in their oracles attempted to adjust these foundations of belief to agree with the faith of their ancestors.

Their works, above all the prophecy of Isaiah, became the literary models and historical paradigms for all the prophets who followed them. Isaiah dealt with the political illusions and realities that exercised the government and people of Jerusalem. Amos described the religious and social activities of the elite that had lured Samarians to their fate and continued to be in vogue in Judah. Hosea drew the analogy between natural cycles and historical recurrence that explained the inexorable tug on the destiny of Jacob. Together they saw, Isaiah more boldly than the rest, that tradition would outlast innovation and that the new political, social, and spiritual orders were doomed. They all composed poetic texts—texts that could be recited, chanted, or performed—in lyric, elegiac, and dramatic forms that remained popular until prophecy ceased. Isaiah was imitated by Micah and Habakkuk, among others, and lived on in the masterful revisions of his work. Amos's images and intonation were taken up in Zephaniah and Joel and Obadiah. Hosea influenced the form and function of Jeremiah, and the analogy that he drew between ritual and history became basic to the magical visions of Ezekiel. Isaiah, Amos, and Hosea were the orators and entertainers of their time, and it was in their words and rhythms that the spirit of prophecy took shape and became a living tradition.

The order and sequence of their writings can be gathered from their mutual acquaintance and from the books they had read. Isaiah knew the national epic and imitated its episodic form but rejected its implication that, according to the covenant between Yahweh and Israel, worship was right and nothing else mattered. He did not refer to Amos or Hosea but they knew his prophecy; and, like the author of the sequel, they made a point of quoting and adapting his words. Amos also knew the sequel to the epic, and, in turn, his best-known saying was quoted by the Priestly writer. Hosea used some of Amos's liturgical material and was acquainted with Isaiah and the earlier historians.

They all postdate, in absolute chronological terms, the fall of Samaria and flourished in the reigns of Hezekiah and Manasseh. Isaiah, as his prophecy intimates and as his critics and editors attest, was aware of Judah's deals with Assyria and drew lessons for Jerusalem from the recent invasion of Sennacherib. Amos used the Assyrian suppression of rebellion in Aram, Philistia, Samaria, and Transjordan as the model of the day of Yahweh, when the revolt of Israel would be brought to an end. Hosea described Israelite and Judean alliances with the great powers as a death from which there would be no resurrection. Their editors considered them to be near contemporaries and dated their careers, according to the subject matter of their prophecies, to the critical periods of Assyrian intervention in the West.[1]

The skills and literary artistry of these prophets are remarkably individualized but share the elementary features of a common poetic tradition. The essence of this poetic tradition is its composition in direct discourse, in cadenced speech, and in a tense and mood that evoke response. The discourse is colored by frequent change of person and address. The tense is generally future, the mood often interrogative, optative, and subjunctive. The cadence is marked by the brief stanzaic structure of the speech and by the formal and artificial linkage of the language so enclosed. The cadence varies from stanza to stanza and stanzas coalesce in strophe and antistrophe. Isaiah's poetry is narrative and recitative; Amos gesticulates and is declamatory; Hosea lets the characters speak for themselves. Together their compositions reveal the range, repertory, and traditional characterizations of an educated, inspired, and theatrical milieu.

Isaiah

The aspects of Isaiah's prophecy that his commentators found most intriguing were his recognition that he had failed to convince his audience and his determination to commit his words to writing for a later time when he was sure that they would come true. In the time of his commentators, of course, his words had come true, and the problem was to describe what hope remained after Yahweh's seemingly reckless chastisement of Israel. Their explanations, naturally, were that Judah and Jerusalem had fallen to the invaders because neither the people nor their leaders had listened to Isaiah, or that such a thing would not happen again because everything that had been written had been accomplished, or that Judah and Jerusalem would become, as Isaiah thought they were meant to be, the pure and spiritual center of a new world.

The task of reinterpretation was urgent and gigantic and ended by inflating Isaiah's text beyond every due proportion. His prophecy had proceeded step by step, describing the situation, searching for its causes, and demanding resolutions. The writers who redid his work followed its progress, annotating his sayings, interspersing them with commentary, proofs, and illustrations, and supplementing them with comprehensive alternative perspectives. He had challenged the common sense and confidence of the nation, and they, bit by bit, rebuilt the trust that was destroyed (fig. 4).

STRUCTURE AND ORGANIZATION (FIG. 4A)

Isaiah's vision comprised six scenes arranged in two parts and composed of stanzas and strophes in alternating or matching order. The revision of his work consisted in adding lines to stanzas, or stanzas to strophes, or strophes to scenes, or scenes and whole parts to the complete work.[2]

Parts

The vision builds to a climax in the first part and returns, revolving on itself in the second part, to the place where it began. In the first scene the people of Israel are called stubborn children, and Zion, under siege in a ravaged country, is compared to a shed in an open field. The last scene corresponds to it by describing the children in similar terms and by comparing the isolation of Zion to a flag fluttering on a hill.[3] The second scene is filled with songs and occasions of senseless rejoicing,

FIGURE 4

The Book of Isaiah

Isaiah	II Isaiah	III Isaiah
1:1aA, 2–7abA, 8, 18–20	1:1aBb, 16–17, 21–26	1:7bB, 9–15, 27–31
	2:1–5	2:6–22
	3:13–15	3:1–12, 16–26
		4:1–6
5:1–2, 4–5, 11–12, 18–19 26–29	5:3, 6–10, 13, 20–24	5:14–17, 25, 30
	6:1–11	6:12–13
	7:1–3aAb, 4–15	7:3aB, 16–25
	8:1–15, 23°	8:16–23°
	9:1–6abA	9:6bB–20
10:5–7, 13–14, 28–32	10:15–19, 24–27, 33–34	10:1–4, 8–12, 20–23
	11:1–10	11:11–16
	12:1–6	
		13:1–22
	14:1–21	14:22–32
	15:1–6	15:7–9
	16:1–5	16:6–14
		17:1–14
	18:1–7	
		19:1–25
		20:1–6
	21:1–10	21:11–17
	22:1–24	22:25
	23:1–12	23:13–18
		24:1–23
		25:1–12
		26:1–21
		27:1–13
28:9–19	28:20–29	28:1–8
29:1–4, 9–14	29:5–8, 15–24	
30:1–5, 8–17	30:6–7	30:18–33
		31:1–9
		32:1–20
		33:1–24
		34:1–17
		35:1–10
	36:1–22	
	37:1–38	
	38:1–22	
	39:1–8	
	40:1–11	40:12–31
	41:1–6, 8–20	41:7, 21–29

continued

FIGURE 4 (*cont*)

Isaiah	II Isaiah	III Isaiah
	42:1-7, 10-16°	42:8-9, 16°-25
	43:1-21	43:22-28
		44:1-28
	45:1-13	45:14-25
		46:1-13
	47:1-11	47:12-15
		48:1-22
	49:1-26	
	50:1-11	
	51:1-23	
	52:7-15	52:1-6
	53:1-12	
	54:1-17	
	55:1-13	
		56:1-12
		57:1-21
		58:1-14
		59:1-22
		60:1-22
		61:1-11
		62:1-12
		63:1-19
		64:1-11
		65:1-25
		66:1-24

but in the fifth scene these festivals are converted to lamentations and empty words give way to ghastly silence.[4] In the third scene Yahweh dispatches the Assyrians against his own people, and in the fourth scene it is these babbling aliens who teach Judah and Jerusalem the lesson they refused to learn from God.[5] The two parts of Isaiah's vision, in effect, are mirror writings bound together in a closed book.[6]

The coherence of Isaiah's vision was obscured by comments and interpretations that disrupted the sequence of the scenes but that attempted, nevertheless, to maintain the correspondence between the parts (fig. 4). In II Isaiah's version of the first scene Zion's splendid isolation was compared to a high mountain toward which the whole world would converge (2:1-5),[7] while III Isaiah differed from both of his predecessors by envisaging Zion as a modest pavilion where the

FIGURE 4A

Isaiah

Isaiah			II Isaiah			III Isaiah		
Scene I								
A		1:1a	A	1	1:1b	A	1	
	1	1:2		2			2	
	2	1:3		3			3	
B	1	1:4	B	1		B	1	
	2	1:5		2			2	
	3	1:6		3			3	
C	1	1:7abA	C	1		C	1	1:7bB
	2	1:8		2			2	
							3	1:9
						D	1	1:10
							2	1:11
						E	1	1:12
							2	1:13
						F	1	1:14
							2	1:15
			D	1	1:16–17	G	1	
D	1	1:18–19		2			2	
	2	1:20		3			3	
			E	1	1:21	H	1	
				2	1:22–23aA		2	
				3	1:23aBb		3	
			F	1	1:24–26a	I	1	
				2	1:26b		2	
						J	1	1:27–28
							2	1:29–30
							3	1:31
Scene II								
A	1	5:1a	A	1		A	1	
	2	5:1b–2a		2			2	
	3	5:2b		3			3	
			B	1	5:3	B	1	
B	1	5:4		2			2	
	2	5:5		3			3	
				4	5:6		4	
				5	5:7		5	
			C	1	5:8	C	1	
				2	5:9–10		2	

continued

FIGURE 4 A (*cont*)

Isaiah			II Isaiah			III Isaiah		
C	1	5:11–12	D	1		D	1	
				2	5:13		2	
						E	1	5:14
							2	5:15
							3	5:16–17
	2	5:18–19	E	1		F	1	
				2	5:20–23		2	
				3	5:24			
						G	1	5:25a
							2	5:25b
D	1	5:26	F	1		H	1	
	2	5:27		2			2	
	3	5:28		3			3	
	4	5:29		4			4	
							5	5:30

Scene III

Isaiah			II Isaiah			III Isaiah		
						A	1	10:1–2
							2	10:3–4a
							3	10:4b
A	1	10:5–6	A	1		B	1	
	2	10:7		2			2	
						C	1	10:8–9
							2	10:10–12
B	1	10:13	B	1		D	1	
	2	10:14		2			2	
			C	1	10:15	E	1	
				2	10:16–17		2	
				3	10:18–19		3	
							4	10:20–21
							5	10:22–23
			D	1	10:24–25	F	1	
				2	10:26		2	
				3	10:27		3	
C	1	10:28	E	1		G	1	
	2	10:29		2			2	
D	1	10:30	F	1		H	1	
	2	10:31–32		2			2	
				3	10:33–34			

continued

F I G U R E   4 A *(cont)*

Isaiah			II Isaiah			III Isaiah		
Scene IV								
						A	1	28:1–2
							2	28:3–4
						B	1	28:5–6
							2	28:7–8
A	1	28:9–10	A	1		C	1	
	2	28:11–12		2			2	
	3	28:13		3			3	
B	1	28:14	B	1		D	1	
	2	28:15		2			2	
	3	28:16		3			3	
	4	28:17–18		4			4	
	5	28:19		5			5	
			C	1	28:20	E	1	
				2	28:21		2	
				3	28:22		3	
			D	1	28:23–26	F	1	
				2	28:27–28		2	
				3	28:29		3	
Scene V								
A	1	29:1	A	1		A	1	
	2	29:2–3		2			2	
	3	29:4		3			3	
			B	1	29:5–6	B	1	
				2	29:7		2	
				3	29:8		3	
B	1	29:9–10	C	1		C	1	
	2	29:11–12		2			2	
	3	29:13–14		3			3	
			D	1	29:15	D	1	
				2	29:16		2	
			E	1	29:17	E	1	
				2	29:18–19		2	
				3	29:20–21		3	
			F	1	29:22	F	1	
				2	29:23–24		2	
Scene VI								
A	1	30:1–2	A	1		A	1	
	2	30:3–5		2			2	
			B	1	30:6abA	B	1	

continued

FIGURE 4 A (*cont*)

Isaiah			II Isaiah			III Isaiah		
				2	30:6bB		2	
				3	30:7		3	
B	1	30:8	C	1		C	1	
	2	30:9–11		2			2	
C	1	30:12–14	D	1		D	1	
	2	30:15–17		2			2	
						E	1	30:18
							2	30:19–22
							3	30:23–26
						F	1	30:27–28
							2	30:29–30
							3	30:31–33

Figure 4a. Letters indicate strophes. Numbers denote stanzas.

purified remnant of Yahweh's purge of Judah and Jerusalem would assemble (4:2–6).[8] In II Isaiah's version of the second scene the time of senseless rejoicing was contrasted with a time of rejoicing at the birth of a Davidic king who would free the people from the burden of Assyria,[9] but in III Isaiah's version the king was ignored and the effects of the prior purge were extended to Ephraim in prolonged and exaggerated detail.[10] In II Isaiah's version of the third scene the defeat of Assyria and the universal effects of the coming reign were described, but in III Isaiah's version the effects of this new era were limited to the return of a remnant and to the resolution of the perennial conflicts between Ephraim and Judah.[11] II Isaiah's version of the fourth scene corresponded to his interpretation of the third scene by confirming the defeat of Assyria and the dawn of a new age (cf. 28:20–29 and 10:24–27), and III Isaiah, similarly, referred to the comments that were made at the end of the first part by mentioning Ephraim and the return of a purified remnant (cf. 28:1–8 and 10:1–4, 8–12, 20–23).[12] In the fifth scene II Isaiah repeated themes from the second (29:5–8, 15–24; cf. 5:20–24), and in the sixth he matched Isaiah's vision of the siege of Jerusalem with a quotation from the Deuteronomistic History according to which Zion was saved from the siege of Sennacherib (Isaiah 36–39; 2 Kings 18–20). III Isaiah did not comment on the fifth or sixth scene but instead appended an analysis of the whole second part and added an alternative interpretation of the entire vision (Isa 30:18–33; 31–35). The sequence of the scenes, obscured by these comments, became still more tenuous when the two parts were separated by oracles against Judah and other nations that were peripheral to Isaiah's vision but essential to the view of world history adopted in later time by his disciples (Isaiah 13–27; see fig. 4).

Scenes

Scenes have either the same sort of rounded coherence as the vision or are distinguished by their gradual and cumulative consistency (fig. 4a). The first scene, like the vision itself, begins and ends the same way, with an apostrophe to heaven and earth and with an appeal to the nation, both of them explicitly identified as the word of Yahweh (1:2–3, 18–20). The fourth scene, similarly, begins with a question about the message to be understood and ends with the answer.[13] The second scene, however, does not have obvious external boundaries but moves in gradual thematic accumulation from a song about a vineyard to a taunt against those who drink wine and do not see what Yahweh is doing, and from a challenge to Yahweh to do quickly what he is doing to a vision of a distant nation summoned by Yahweh and advancing quickly.[14] The third scene, similarly, moves from a summons to Assyria to a description of its arrogance and from a narrative of its advance against Jerusalem to a further demonstration of its arrogance.[15] The fifth scene is slightly different and merely accumulates expressions of the puzzlement of those who know how to read and write but cannot grasp the meaning of the literal and mysterious actions of Yahweh.[16] The sixth scene is also slightly different and gradually over three strophes establishes the irreconcilable intentions of Yahweh, the Holy One of Israel, and of his children, who refused to listen.[17]

The scenes in the revised versions are distinguished by a similar use of inclusion and thematic consistency (fig. 4a). The first scene, in II Isaiah's version, was modified at the beginning to refer to Judah and Jerusalem in the reigns of Uzziah, Jotham, Ahaz, and Hezekiah, and then was expanded at the end by ascribing the ruin of the city to the injustice of its rulers and by attributing its eventual reconstruction to the restoration of the judges.[18] In III Isaiah's version the focus shifts from injustice to ritual wrongs, but there is a deliberate effort to have the scene end as it originally began.[19] The second scene, in II Isaiah's version, maintained its original structure but was converted into a courtroom scene by adding a series of comments condemning injustice in Israel and Judah.[20] III Isaiah added a few touches, partly in the same vein, that related the scene to its own ongoing and circumambient interpretation but otherwise left it unchanged.[21] II Isaiah redid the middle of the third scene and lessened the impact of the Assyrian invasion envisaged by Isaiah by predicting the ultimate defeat of Assyria. III Isaiah, on the other hand, added matching statements to Isaiah's text to emphasize the disastrous results of the invasion and to insist that only a remnant of Jacob would survive.[22] In the fourth scene II Isaiah added a commentary on the conclusion of Isaiah's text, and III Isaiah added a preface that both redid the body of Isaiah's text and provided an introduction to the whole second part, with the result that there is an accumulation of themes without any inclusion or formal coherence.[23] III Isaiah did not comment on the fifth scene, but II Isaiah added a comment on each of its strophes and a different interpretation of the whole that extended the episode without altering its basic structure.[24] In the last scene, in the same manner, II Isaiah added a matching strophe that did not disrupt the sequence, and III Isaiah added a concluding analysis of the entire triptych.[25]

Strophes and Stanzas

Strophes and stanzas follow grammatical and syntactic rules, are distinguished from one another by their various topical and imaginative interests, and are defined by their adherence to prosodic conventions. The second and third editions of the vision are distinguished from Isaiah's work by their different topics and interests and by their technical use of repetition and cross-reference.

Isaiah's work usually combines imagery and allegory with conceptualization and explanatory discourse (fig. 4a). II and III Isaiah attempt to maintain the same pattern in commenting on his work but tend to be more compact and discursive.

The first scene in Isaiah's vision has four strophes. The second and third strophes combine a metaphor of wounds that will not heal with an elaborate image of Zion isolated in a devastated land. But the framing strophes develop an encompassing theme. The first strophe calls heaven and earth as witnesses and tells them the allegory of Israel as willful children who are more stubborn than domestic animals. The last strophe calls the children to their own defense and explains that their wounds and devastation will continue if they refuse to do what they are told.[26]

In II Isaiah's version the vision is given a specific and a symbolic historical context. The specific context is the sequence of reigns of Judean kings that was added to the title to date the vision and redirect it to Judah and Jerusalem.[27] The typical or symbolic context is the future time of just and more pliable rulers like the judges of old. This was added at the end of the scene by changing Isaiah's summons to the children into an apostrophe to the city and by including proleptic references to the changes.[28] The specific context was given in a factual and prosaic manner. The typical context links the image of cleansing with the reality of doing what is right and just,[29] and combines a whole series of symbols and their interpretations. The city is compared to a harlot, and this is explained by saying that justice used to be her delight but now murderers spend the night with her. The city is compared to stained silver and to wine mixed with water, and this means that the princes are rebels and unjust. The result is that Yahweh will vent his anger on the city, and this is portrayed first as smelting the silver and then as restoring the order of premonarchical judges.

Whereas Isaiah enclosed images within an allegory, and II Isaiah composed a text that oscillated between symbols and their interpretations, III Isaiah wrote a text cluttered with words, images, cliches, and changing perspectives. Isaiah had invoked heaven and earth, and II Isaiah had composed an apostrophe to Zion, but III Isaiah repeated key words from the original texts to change the message and redirect it to the leaders of Jerusalem. Isaiah was concerned with the ignorance and ill will that left Zion alone and without resources, but III Isaiah condemned the prayers and rituals that had not helped and that left a tiny remnant in the city. The evil of the city and the notion that only a few people had escaped the conflagration that destroyed it suggested a comparison with Sodom and Gomorrah, but the comparison was trite and became lost in a list of cultic offenses.[30] II Isaiah was concerned with the injustice sponsored by the royal court, but III Isaiah was interested in ridding the city of the evildoers who worshiped Adonis instead of Yahweh. The shift in perspective was fitted in by combining snippets of the original texts with a raft of vaguely related images (1:27–31).[31]

In the second scene Isaiah combined an allegory and its imaginative development with the response to the allegory and matching images. The allegory is a song about a vineyard that was carefully tended but produced sour grapes. The development describes how the exasperated owner decided to turn the vineyard back into pastureland. Those who responded to the song were those who drank the wine but did not understand the owner's frustration, and for them the story is retold in the imagery of an enemy army advancing rapidly to invade the land.[32]

II Isaiah was eager to interpret the allegory and comment on the response. In this version the singer of the song is Yahweh, the vineyard is Israel and Judah, the hearers are the inhabitants of Jerusalem, the sour grapes are evil and injustice, and the response betrayed the ignorance and pretense that led to the exile. The changes were made, as usual, by repeating some of the original context and referring to the ongoing interpretation. II Isaiah made a break between the allegory and its development to give the song a forensic context by presenting the case against the vineyard before the tribunal of Judah and Jerusalem (5:3).[33] The identification of the vineyard and of the sour grapes was added after the original development (5:6–7)[34] and was illustrated in the usual combination of metaphor and meaning. The planting of the vineyard was interpreted discretely so that the vineyard could be identified as the house of Israel and the plantings as the people of Judah. The hope of a good vintage was explained as an expectation of justice and decency, and the corresponding frustration of the owner was expressed in images that exactly matched these ideas.[35] The comments on the response imitated its form and content and were constructed from similar mixtures of images and reality.[36] Specific crimes of oppression and unjust foreclosure are mentioned, but in the end they are assimilated to the song of the vineyard (5:8–10). General ignorance and ill will are condemned, but in the end they meld into the drinking parties that Isaiah mentioned or into specific acts of injustice that II Isaiah had already condemned (5:20–24). The penalty exacted of those who rejected the law of Yahweh is described as a fire that burns their roots to cinders and their fruit into dense smoke (5:24).

III Isaiah, as usual, complicated an already dense mixture with a massive cluttering of ideas and images. The consequences that II Isaiah mentioned are matched by further consequence in which the exile is described as a descent into Sheol, the descent is understood as a humiliation of the proud and an exaltation of Yahweh, and Jerusalem so depopulated is viewed as a ruin overrun by sacrificial animals (5:14–17).[37] Similarly, the punishment that Yahweh exacted of those who rejected the law is matched by depictions of cosmic repercussions and rotting corpses and is attributed twice in the same terms to the power and anger of Yahweh (5:25).[38] At the end of his description of the Assyrian invasion Isaiah noted how lions growl as they devour their prey. III Isaiah was interested in the effects of this invasion on Ephraim and Manasseh and contrived a set of cross-references that by their obscurity and awkwardness point to obvious connections in the text.[39] He began by comparing the growls to the roaring of the sea, then dated the invasion to an ill-fated day, and then described it as a day when the earth would be covered with an oppressive darkness and the light in the sky would be darkened by clouds. It barely fits in its present position but succeeds in giving the original texts a different and more encompassing context.

In the third scene Isaiah juxtaposed two sets of strophes. The first set contrasts Yahweh's purpose in sending the Assyrians to punish his people with the intentions of the Assyrians as they set out to conquer the world. The second set describes the armies advancing through Israel and the reaction of the villages as they move on toward Jerusalem. In each set one strophe is imaginative discourse and the other is predominantly narrative.[40]

II Isaiah commented on both sets of strophes by combining an imaginative description of a fever that consumed the Assyrian army besieging Jerusalem, with a literal and historical version of Yahweh's defeat of the Assyrians.[41] III Isaiah also commented on both strophes and on II Isaiah's text as well. The commentary on the siege of Jerusalem is put first: it mimics the beginning of Isaiah's text, quotes II Isaiah but disagrees with II Isaiah's version in seeing the siege as successful, and is characterized by its ornateness and comprehensiveness (10:1–4).[42] The commentary on the first set of strophes also mimics Isaiah's text, but it has the verbosity and jumbling of perspectives that are typical of III Isaiah's commentaries (10:8–12).[43] The commentary on the text of II Isaiah is inserted between his imaginative and literal descriptions, and it is marked by III Isaiah's predilection for repetition and conceptual clarity.[44]

In the fourth scene Isaiah reflected, in two strophes, on the ineffectiveness of divine discipline up to this point and on what would be done about it (Isa 28:9–19). The opening strophe contains three stanzas that develop and explain the single metaphor of learning. In the first stanza Isaiah muses that babies and infants might understand the message from Yahweh if it were put in baby talk, and the stanza asks a question and answers it and mimics the talk (28:9–10).[45] In the second stanza he says that since Yahweh spoke to them directly and they refused to listen it would be the turn of foreigners to talk to them in a stammer. In the third stanza the stammer turns out to be like the baby talk, and the effect of the message is described as panic and total discomfiture. The second strophe has five stanzas and gives the message an allegorical form (28:14–19). The first stanza, curiously enough, is addressed to the interpreters of foreign languages in Jerusalem who speak to the people in allegories.[46] The second stanza quotes them as saying that they have a covenant with Death and Sheol and have taken refuge in lies.[47] The third and fourth stanzas counter with the allegory of the foundation laid in Zion, which will remain when their refuge of lies has been swept away in a storm and when their covenant with Death and Sheol no longer stands.[48] The last stanza explains that this is the message, that it can be heard night and day, day after day, and that it will be sheer terror finally to understand it.

The allegories are striking but not easily rationalized—Isaiah had to explain parts of them in the following scenes—and II and III Isaiah did not comment so much on their content as on their allegorical form. II Isaiah added one strophe to situate the allegories in historical perspective and another to suggest that there was a more benign form of divine discipline. The first adds a metaphor of sleeplessness along with a historical simile and an allusion to captivity before explaining that the vision of destruction will affect the whole world (28:20–22).[49] The second strophe gives examples from agriculture to suggest, despite what Isaiah said, that destructive storms do not last forever and that divine discipline is generally positive and beneficent (28:23–29). III Isaiah wrote a preface to the second part of Isaiah's vision and commented briefly on the first two episodes (28:1–8).[50] The first strophe takes the destructive storm out of its narrow Judean context and applies it to Ephraim as well by mixing Isaiah's images with a clutter of images and ideas expressing III Isaiah's attitude toward human pride (28:1–4).[51] The second strophe alludes to the siege of Jerusalem and to the sodden stupefaction of the prophets that Isaiah described in the second scene, but amidst the bombast and verbosity III Isaiah also reintroduces the familiar notion of the remnant (28:5–8; cf. 29:1–4, 9–10). The allegories, in effect, are not explained, and their difficulty is compounded in a surge of imagery and conflicting ideas.

In the fifth scene Isaiah juxtaposed an allegory and a parable and their interpretations. The first strophe contains the allegory of Ariel. The first stanza depicts the yearly festivals in Ariel, the city of David; the second portrays the siege of the city in which it truly becomes an Ariel; and the third explains the meaning of Ariel by describing ghostly voices ascending out of the ground. The second strophe is the parable of the book. The first stanza depicts the stupefaction of a people whose prophets cannot see and whose seers cannot understand. The second stanza, conversely, compares Isaiah's vision to a sealed book that cannot be read and to an open book that cannot be understood. The third stanza explains the incomprehensibility of the vision by saying explicitly that Yahweh will again perform wonders that will ruin conventional wisdom.

The juxtaposition of images, as Isaiah said, was not easy to understand, and the interpretations were as allusive as their subjects. II Isaiah commented on the first strophe by describing the sudden lifting of the siege and by comparing Isaiah's vision to a bad dream (29:5–8).[52] He commented on the second strophe by changing Isaiah's criticism of conventional wisdom into a tirade against skeptics,[53] by replacing the parable of the book with a book that even the blind and the deaf would understand (29:17–21),[54] and by envisaging a time when those who went astray would be amazed at the wonders of Yahweh (29:22–24). The commentary leaves Isaiah's vision substantially intact and complements and contradicts its more obvious elements instead of giving it a subtler nuance.

The last scene in Isaiah's vision is composed of three strophes. The first strophe retrieves themes from the beginning of the vision and combines an imaginative description of reliance on Egypt with an outright condemnation of the fact (30:1–5). II Isaiah added a strophe that changed the historical reference and the quality of the condemnation by referring to the Egypt of the exodus (30:6–7; cf. 51:9–11). The second strophe resembles the first in its retrieval of earlier themes, but it is an explicit and almost prosaic account of Jerusalem's unwillingness to pay attention to the teaching of Yahweh and to the visions of the prophets. The last strophe describes, in the metaphor of a bulging wall that all at once collapses, and in a factual account of defeat in battle, how by getting its own way Jerusalem got just the opposite of what it wanted.

The vision of Isaiah had intricate internal consistency based on the constant interplay of images, transformations, and interpretations. The editors of his work composed running commentaries, each with its own overall coherence, that ran parallel and even counter to his vision. The result is an enormously dense and multidimensional work that extends beyond the boundaries that he envisaged through the history and the literature of Judah's most creative centuries.

SOURCES AND INTERPRETATION

The significance of Isaiah's work can be judged against the background of the history and belief that it supposes and through the reflections it cast on contemporary prophets and historians. What it meant to II and to III Isaiah in their time can be discerned, in the same way, by comparing their understanding of his vision with the perceptions of their predecessors and contemporaries.

Isaiah was familiar with the system of beliefs enshrined in the epic covenant, and he opposed it because it ignored matters of justice and divine sovereignty that he thought were more sacred and more fundamental. In its simplest and most startling form this opposition was declared by Yahweh himself in summoning the Assyrians against his own people. In more subtle ways it was manifested in Isaiah's opposition to the festivals celebrated in Jerusalem, to the city's reliance on arms instead of believing in Yahweh, and to their resistance to himself and to the prophets. It is clear from his insistence that what was at stake was not just the issue of the moment but principles of interpretation and their long-range effects on the minds of the people.

Apart from his reliance on the epic, obvious in quotations and frequent allusions,[55] Isaiah does not display familiarity with any other written source. He was sophisticated, however, and is clearly dependent on literary genres and artistic conventions. The genres have determinable forms and are constructed from traditional material and common presuppositions that are attested in later works, but they have no literary precedent that is earlier than Isaiah. Isaiah's genius is evident in the influence that he had on contemporaries and on his disciples but it is also apparent in his free use of convention and in his deviation from expected forms and structures.

II Isaiah differed from his mentor in principle and in fact. By the time he wrote, Isaiah's prophecies had been fulfilled and justice had become enshrined in the Book of the Law codified and verified in the Deuteronomistic History. His task was not to condemn the past but to forecast and influence the reconstruction of a Judean state reconciling those who remained in Jerusalem with those who had gone into exile. He therefore redid Isaiah as history and as prophecy. By relying on the opposing perspectives of Jeremiah and Ezekiel he described the return of Yahweh and his servant to Zion, and by sophisticating the opposing ideologies of the sequel and of its revision in the Deuteronomistic History, he could trace the fall of Jerusalem to the machinations of Ahaz and base the future era of world peace and justice on the restoration of the Davidic monarchy in Zion.

III Isaiah tried to restore Isaiah's point of view against the changes that II Isaiah had engineered. His work signaled the end of prophecy, and he could draw on most of the prophetic works in their finished forms; but he depended especially on the theory of history that had been worked out by the author of the book of Jeremiah to establish Judah as a theocratic state. In this view the dominant issues were the elimination of those who worshiped other Gods, the purification of the remnant of Judah that had remained in Jerusalem and of the remnant of Israel that had been exiled, and the inauguration of right worship in Zion.

Scene I (fig. 4a)

In the first scene Isaiah uses the analogy of a lawsuit to press his point. In the first strophe he summons heaven and earth as witnesses and cites Yahweh's charge of rebellion, stupidity, and stubbornness against his people. In the second strophe the rebellion is defined as sin and wrongdoing, inveterate evil and perversion, abandonment of Yahweh, rejection of the Holy One of Israel, and total alienation. The evidence for their stupidity and stubbornness is that they continue to be beaten and are covered with sores and, in the third strophe, the irony of their alienation is that aliens have destroyed their land and are besieging Zion. In the last strophe judgment is rendered and Yahweh leaves the people the option of submitting to him and eating the fruit of the land or of persisting in their rebellion and being devoured by the sword.

The basis of the dispute is the presumed parent–child relationship between Yahweh and Israel, but the forensic setting suggests a legal obligation. The specific charges that are laid allude to the violation of the epic covenant.[56] It was the covenant that assured Israel of its quiet possession of the land, and it is precisely this which is at stake in the first scene.[57] In the epic text the covenant consists in the words that Yahweh speaks, and Isaiah, similarly, insists that it is Yahweh who is speaking.[58] In the epic Yahweh declared that he would forgive the wrongdoing, rebellion, and sin of the covenant people, but that he would not absolve the guilty and would punish them and their children to the third and fourth generation. In Isaiah's text this is reflected in inverse order in the charge that the nation is sinful and burdened with wrongdoing, offspring of evildoers, children who have rebelled and are being punished for their crimes.[59] In the only instance of rebellion recorded in the epic, it is described as a rejection of Yahweh that is punishable by physical blows and by the disbanding of the people and the creation of another nation in its place. In Isaiah's version the culprits are the people and the nation, and their rejection of Yahweh has already resulted in painful physical blows.[60]

The elements of the scene that cannot be traced to the covenant source or the lawsuit genre are literary conventions or favorite themes of Isaiah. His imagery is georgic, bucolic, and military.[61] His major topic is education and instruction.[62] His language suggests familiarity with Assyrian foreign policy and historical propaganda.[63] The scene as a whole has no adequate parallel in Judean literature, but all of its parts reveal his learning and acquaintance with artistic and skilled traditions.[64]

II and III Isaiah simply expanded the genre by appealing to different sources and traditions. II Isaiah modified the charge to include basic injustice and laid it specifically against the government of Jerusalem. He knew the king lists (1:16),[65] the legal terminology,[66] the decalogue,[67] and the theory of government of the Deuteronomistic

History (1:26).[68] He knew Ezekiel's vision of Israel as tarnished metal refined in the fires of Jerusalem (Isa 1:22a, 25; cf. Ezek 24:9–12, 13–14). He knew Nahum's vision of Yahweh arriving in judgment against the city that had become a whore.[69] He put them together in a gathering vision of Zion as the source of justice and peace for the whole world.[70] III Isaiah, on the other hand, redirected the charge to the entire population of Jerusalem and made it include every form of parasitical prayer and worship practiced in the city. His main source was the Deuteronomistic History and its obsession with the ritual causes of the country's defeat, and his intention was to secure the city for the few pious people who remained.[71]

Scene II (fig. 4a)

The second scene revolves around a drinking song, the feast where it might have been performed, and the dulling effect of strong drink on those who were supposed to be alert to what was happening. The first two strophes contain the song of the vineyard, a song of disappointed love and tragic abandonment. The third strophe chides the merrymakers, who seem to appreciate the song but do not see what it means,[72] and they in turn reply that before they can know they must wait and see what will happen. The fourth strophe tells them that they will see the distant nation that was summoned by Yahweh advancing against them and taking them captive.

The imagery, as usual, is georgic, bucolic, and military, but the conceptualizations in the poem are associated with seeing and doing and are derived from the epic. When Yahweh defeated the Egyptians the people saw what a great thing he had done and they believed in him.[73] Later, in making the covenant with Israel Yahweh explained to Moses that he was doing a wonderful thing that had never been done before for any nation and that the people would see what a marvelous thing he was doing.[74] At the end of the epic, in the oracles of Balaam, the occupation of the land is ascribed to a people that, like a lioness, devours its prey; and the victory of the nation is described as what God has done.[75] Isaiah uses the ideas in an opposite sense to portray the Assyrian invasion as Yahweh's doing, which the people neither see nor understand.[76] In effect, the covenant did not work; Yahweh destroyed his vineyard;[77] and the Assyrians were the wild animals that trampled it and the lions that carried it away (Isa 5:29; Num 23:24).

II Isaiah changed the genre and the setting. In this version the first part of the scene becomes an indictment of the elders and princes who have despised the law,[78] and the Assyrian invasion in the second part is associated with events in Judah from the Syro-Ephraimite war to the reign of Hezekiah.[79] III Isaiah accepted these specifications but tempered their Judean and dynastic bias by concentrating on events surrounding the fall of Samaria. II Isaiah made the changes with the help of Jeremiah, Ezekiel, and the Deuteronomistic History.[80] III Isaiah knew the same sources but came back to Isaiah's point of view mainly by paraphrasing his work.[81]

Scene III (fig. 4a)

The third scene is a dramatic piece, with Yahweh as the protagonist, Assyria as the antagonist, and the prophet as the narrator or messenger. It begins with two soliloquies juxtaposing the intentions of Yahweh and of the Assyrian invaders and ends with a matching narration in which the messenger announces the invasion and reports that the Assyrians are advancing on Jerusalem. II Isaiah followed the same pattern, adding another soliloquy to comment on the Assyrian boasting, and another report to explain the intentions of Yahweh. III Isaiah did the same, commenting first on Yahweh's soliloquy and attributing another soliloquy, with its own commentary, to the king of Assyria.

Isaiah's imagery, as usual, is bucolic, georgic, and militaristic, and some of the themes are familiar from the earlier scenes.[82] What is new is the choice of Assyria as the instrument of Yahweh's anger toward his own people.[83] What makes it particularly alarming is that it contradicts the expectation, founded in the epic presentation of Israel's history, that Yahweh had blessed his people and would not renounce them.[84]

II Isaiah's alarm is evident in the constant reworking of Yahweh's choice of Assyria, until the wrath of God is turned away from his people and against their oppressors. This version begins with the Assyrian boastfulness and, by turning it into blasphemy, provokes Yahweh to destroy all but a remnant of them. The sources of this interpretation, besides Isaiah, are Yahweh's primordial defeat of the Sea as it was recounted in the Priestly version of the exodus, and the defeat of Midian and of Assyria as described in the Deuteronomistic History (10:15–19, 24–27).[85] III Isaiah, however, says explicitly that the wrath of Yahweh did not turn away and that only a remnant of Israel remained. He refers to Isaiah's text but contradicts II Isaiah and bases his revision on other material in the Deuteronomistic History. (Isa 10:1–4, 8–12, 20–23).[86]

Scene IV (fig. 4a)

In the fourth scene there are two speeches, one by Isaiah summarizing the present situation, the other by Yahweh announcing the coming predicament. Both contain riddles about listening and learning.[87] In Isaiah's speech the riddle concerns the learning of the alphabet: if children refuse to learn the elements of their own language—that is, God telling them to rest and be at peace—they will be absolutely dismayed to learn it from the babbling of foreigners. In Yahweh's speech the two parts of the riddle, about listening and learning, are translated into a dispute with the leaders of Jerusalem. In this version the choice is between listening to Yahweh, who explains the riddle of faith and a firm foundation in Zion, or listening to the lies of their leaders, who tell them a riddle about taking refuge in a covenant with Death and Sheol. In both speeches the lesson is the same: if they listen to nonsense they will learn defeat in battle, but if they listen to Yahweh they will understand that they are safe in the city.

The scene combines elements familiar from school days and story-telling—listening and learning—with elements of war and diplomacy. The military themes are taken from descriptions of the Assyrian invasions in the preceding scenes. Among the Assyrian invaders none was weary or stumbled, but among the defenders the weary do not seek rest in Jerusalem and the others stumble.[88] As the Assyrian army passed through specific towns in its advance on Jerusalem, so it will continue indefinitely to pass through the land and terrorize the population.[89] Assyria was sent by Yahweh to trample on his people, and so it will.[90] Jerusalem challenged Yahweh to hurry and do what he was doing, and he told them to believe and not be in a hurry.[91] The whip that ripples and snaps is like the rod that was used in earlier scenes to discipline children or beat animals.[92] The fortification of Zion is the antithesis of the temporary shelter that, according to the first episode, the Assyrians had besieged (cf. 1:8 and 28:16). The diplomatic themes, on the other hand, reverse the covenant ideals of the epic. In the epic Yahweh made a covenant with the leaders and the people. It was based on faith, gave them possession of the land, and excluded treaties with the inhabitants of the land. But they refused to believe and take possession of the land, and the instigators of the rebellion were swallowed alive into Death and Sheol.[93] In Isaiah's view, on the contrary, this was a lie. Their covenant was with Death and Sheol. It excluded faith. It was a trap based on covenants with foreigners that ultimately would deprive them of the land.[94] Isaiah's alternative to the covenant was to listen to Yahweh and take refuge in the Zion that he had built on the foundation of faith and fortified with truth and justice.

This prophetic repudiation of the epic interpretation of history was troublesome, and II Isaiah added an appendix to mitigate it. It began by identifying the repudiated covenant as the treaty that, according to the final scene, Jerusalem made with Egypt, by associating Yahweh's use of foreigners against his own people with other strange and unusual things recorded in the Deuteronomistic History, and finally by turning the whole scene into a sort of lesson for doubters.[95] Once this new course had been established, II Isaiah could let the appendix drift in this new direction by likening the Assyrian invasion to the ordinary lessons of common sense and moderation taught by Yahweh. The first lesson is about plowing, harrowing and planting and argues that these are seasonal jobs, that they take place in a certain order and follow set routines, and that the people who do them know the correct procedures because they are instructed by Yahweh. The second lesson is about harvesting and threshing and argues that the people who do these things know, because they get it from God, that these tasks have to be done in moderation and with the right equipment. The lessons are obtrusive appendages to the vision of Isaiah, and their obvious point is that, despite what Isaiah said about invaders sweeping incessantly through the land, Yahweh would discipline his people for a limited time and only in due measure (28:23–26, 27–29; cf. 10:5; 28:9, 17).

Scene V (fig. 4a)

In the fifth scene Isaiah begins with the siege of Ariel, the city of David, that was instigated by Yahweh, continues with descriptions of the drowsiness, stupidity, and stupefaction that have overcome the city, and ends ascribing the city's ignorance and immobility to its reliance on the covenant. He admits that the people have been faithful to the covenant, but he insists that the covenant is wrong. They think of it as worship of Yahweh, but he says it is merely adherence to human commands (cf. Isa 29:13b; Exod 14:31; 34:11). These have nothing to do with justice or common decency but just prescribe the annual festivals that the people can observe while totally ignoring Yahweh (29:1b; cf. Exod 34:22, 24). But, Isaiah insists, the time for ignorance is over and the wonderful things that the people keep expecting from the covenant will turn out to be the amazing things that Yahweh does to punish them (cf. 29:14; Exod 34:10).

In II Isaiah's version, on the contrary, the siege will be unsuccessful, ignorance will be resolved in the joy of a new creation, and the return of the exiles will satisfy the need for knowledge. This version's disagreement with Isaiah is based on other texts that reflect more ancient and more traditional beliefs. It does not accept Isaiah's statement that Yahweh laid siege to Jerusalem but attributes the siege to aliens and, relying on the visions of Nahum and Ezekiel, describes a sudden manifestation of divine power that will disperse them (29:5–8; cf. 29:1–4).[96] The self-satisfaction of those who thought it was smart to rely on the covenant becomes, in II Isaiah's view, the vanity of those who dare to contend with their maker (29:15–16; cf. 45:7, 9). The illiteracy of those who could not read the book of Isaiah's vision, and the stupidity of those who would not listen to him, is removed in II Isaiah's version when Yahweh gives sight to the blind and hearing to the deaf (29:17–21). The amazing thing that Yahweh will do, in this version, is the return of the children of Jacob (29:22–24).[97] The horrifying future that Isaiah predicted becomes, in II Isaiah's view, the future magnification of God by the people whom he created and who finally understand what he has done.

Scene VI (fig. 4a)

In the last scene Isaiah describes Judah's alliance with Egypt in the image of ambassadors sprawled under the pitiful shade of the Pharaoh, and depicts the fate of Jerusalem in the image of a bulging wall that suddenly collapses. The alliance is an example of the shortcomings of the covenant, an unreliable support, a perversion of fundamental justice, and a source of wrongdoing that is to be replaced by the teaching of Yahweh that Isaiah has announced and, in imitation of the Sinai covenant, is committing to writing.[98] The fall of Jerusalem illustrates the point because the city could have relied on Yahweh instead of making a military alliance with Egypt. Since it did not, it will be defeated in battle and left, as it was in the beginning, like a flag on a mountain or a signal on a hill.[99]

It is evident, therefore, that Isaiah knew the epic version of the covenant at Sinai and rejected it. Elements of the epic covenant are quoted consistently in a contradictory sense. The epic transferred the covenant from the parents to their children for a thousand generations, but in Isaiah's view the children who are heirs to the covenant, far from enjoying its benefits, are being punished for their transgressions. In the epic version the festivals are supposed to be a celebration of what Yahweh has done for them, but in Isaiah's opinion they are celebrations that dull them to what Yahweh is actually doing. The covenant that was supposed to give them security condemns them to death. The words of the covenant were written down but the book is closed and no one can read them. In their place are the words of Isaiah written for a later generation to read and understand.

His words caused an instant furor, and the sequel to the epic set out to refute them. The author of this history shows that the covenant is the basic structure and motive of historical events and in its final episode, when Hezekiah is confronted with the Assyrian siege of Jerusalem, takes specific issue with the things Isaiah had said. His words are put into the mouth of the enemy and are refuted one by one as the Assyrian legates, and with them Isaiah, undermine their own argument and make progressively worse fools of themselves (fig. 3). In the end, when the siege is lifted, Isaiah and the ambassadors are wrong and Hezekiah and the sequel are proved right.[100]

The Assyrian ambassadors begin by challenging Hezekiah's reliance on Egypt while supposedly trusting in Yahweh. They ask whether Hezekiah thinks that words are sufficient planning and preparation for war, but their argument is taken from the text of Isaiah, who had accused those who relied on the covenant of flattering Yahweh with words, of making plans and relying on Egypt without consulting Yahweh, and of rejecting the trust in Yahweh that would have been the right preparation for war.[101] They use the language of Isaiah to ridicule Hezekiah for relying on Egypt, but in the same breath they contradict what Isaiah said by admitting that Hezekiah really did trust in Yahweh (2 Kgs 18:19, 22, 30).[102]

The speech continues to present Isaiah's arguments in the words of the Assyrian ambassadors and at the same time subtly suggest their refutation. Isaiah said that Yahweh had sent the Assyrians against his own people, and the ambassadors quote the command that Yahweh supposedly gave to Sennacherib (Isa 10:5-7, 13-14; 2 Kgs 18:25). The point, however, is prefaced by its own refutation. Isaiah said that the people refused to be quiet and trust in Yahweh and had insisted on riding their horses and chariots and therefore would ride to defeat, a thousand of them fleeing before a single foe, all of them fleeing before five of the enemy. The ambassadors, on the contrary, say that Hezekiah relies on the Egyptians and does not have his own army, and they use Isaiah's language to refute him, betting if Sennacherib gave Hezekiah two thousand horses that he would not be able to find riders for them and, if he could, that they would not be able to repulse even one measly lieutenant in the Assyrian army (Isa 30:15-17; 2 Kgs 18:23-24). Isaiah thought that Yahweh turned against his own people because they refused to believe in him. The sequel thought this was Assyrian boasting.[103]

The next part of the ambassadors' speech deals specifically with Isaiah's charge that the people have been deceived by their leaders. Isaiah castigates those who rely on the covenant and refuse to listen to Yahweh, and he warns them that Yahweh will speak to the people through aliens stuttering and stammering and that it will be sheer terror to hear what they have to say. This is refuted diplomatically in the sequel's version, where the aliens speak perfect Judean Hebrew and the leaders of Jerusalem hear them without fear, merely suggesting that they speak Aramaic so that the people will not hear or understand (Isa 28:9–19; 2 Kgs 18:26). Isaiah also blamed the people for not wanting to listen to the hard words spoken by the prophets, and he compared their fate to the sudden collapse of a bulging wall, but in the sequel's version the people sit quietly on the wall listening to every word, including the crude description of their fate, spoken by the Assyrians (Isa 30:8–14; 2 Kgs 18:27).

The last part of the speech deals with Isaiah's rejection of the covenant. In his address to the leaders of Jerusalem, Isaiah introduced what he was about to say as the word of God, quoted their own words against them, and ridiculed their covenant as a pact with Death and Sheol. The ambassadors, in the same way, begin their summation by introducing it as the word of the king of Assyria, and quote the words of Hezekiah (cf. Isa 28:14–16 and 2 Kgs 18:28–29) but instead of ridiculing their covenant with Yahweh offer them another covenant just like it. The king of Assyria invites them to surrender and make a treaty. The treaty is called a blessing because, instead of proposing the terms of the treaty, the king simply describes its benefits. The benefits, however, are precisely those that Judah now enjoys under its covenant with Yahweh, and since the treaty, consequently, is of no interest to the people, they ignore it and are completely silent as Hezekiah advised.[104] Isaiah had accused Jerusalem of making a covenant with Death and Sheol. The sequel puts his words in the mouth of the Assyrian embassy and proves, on the contrary, that Jerusalem is secure in its covenant with Yahweh and Life.

This conflict between Isaiah and the author of the sequel was resolved in different and unexpected ways by II Isaiah and III Isaiah, by the Deuteronomistic Historian and the Chronicler. The Deuteronomist agreed with Isaiah but replaced his simple traditional faith with a theory of history governed by the law, sin, and divine retribution (2 Kings 18–20).[105] II Isaiah agreed with the sequel but downplayed the covenant and concentrated on the crucial role that the Davidic dynasty and the likes of Hezekiah would play in the postexilic restoration.[106] III Isaiah agreed with Isaiah in having Jerusalem punished for its crimes and sided with the Deuteronomist in identifying these crimes as alien forms of worship. But he disagreed with the exclusive interest in Judah and in the permanence of the Davidic dynasty that governed the sequel and the work of II Isaiah, and described a glorious new era in Zion when those who had been purified by punishment would live under the direct hegemony of Yahweh. The Chronicler, finally, synthesized the divergent viewpoints by making Hezekiah the culmination of the line of David who instituted right worship and attempted to reconcile Israel and Judah in the celebration of Passover in Jerusalem (2 Chronicles 29–32).[107]

Isaiah, by his own admission, had little effect on the Judah and Jerusalem of his time. But his influence over the centuries can be calculated in the impetus he gave to prophecy and history and in the depth of the revisions of his work. He was the model of the urbane critic, of the shrewd and severe singer of tales, of the seer who predicted the future. Micah was like him; Nahum and Habakkuk followed in his train; and it was impressed upon all who came after them that what he had said came true. But, in his own time, there was room to maneuver, and other perspectives and opinions had the stamp of prophetic approval.

Amos

Isaiah challenged beliefs current in the Jerusalem of his time, but Amos criticized traditional religious practice and the normal expectations of a devout people. All their crimes hinged, he said, on their observance of times and seasons and assemblies and the festivals at Bethel and Gilgal. Their mistake was naïve reliance on God and hoping that he would protect them for their piety. The real error of their ways was indulgence in prayer and sacrifice along with a concomitant disdain for common sense, the rules of daily existence, and the motives of social subsistence.

Isaiah's work was lyrical and recitative, neatly sculpted in segments easily sung, evenly distributed in discrete scenes. Amos wrote a long narrative poem filled with repeated forms, refrains, catalogs, and listlike chants and declamations. Each part of the poem is a collection of rhetorically similar sayings, a canto with its own rhythm and beat building in a crescendo of insistent sound. Each canto covers the same ground as the others, and all together converge in detailing facets and characteristics of the great and chilling day to come.

As Isaiah took issue with the national epic, Amos confronted the confidence of its historical sequel. The sequel based its hope on the worship of Yahweh in Jerusalem and took comfort from the fate that befell Samaria for worshiping at Bethel and Dan. Amos parodied this simplistic view in diatribes against Bethel and Gilgal but undermined the sequel's position by rejecting all forms of worship at the central sanctuary and insisting on ordinary justice. He wrote in the future tense, ostensibly, about Samaria and the house of Jeroboam, but he insinuated or even said that Samaria was a foil for all Israel, the children of Israel, for Jacob and the people of Zion.

The revision of his poem is literarily and historically straightforward (fig. 5). Literarily, it is added at strategic points, at the beginning and the end of the book, at the end of cantos, or between the lays that compose them. Historically, it brings the prophecy up to date by including the fall of Judah and Jerusalem; it interprets Amos's blanket condemnation of Israel to include strict retribution against those who actually sinned and pardon for the innocent remnant; and it reduces the inevitability of times and seasons and the inexorable day of doom to the cosmic control exercised by Yahweh the Lord of Hosts.[108]

STRUCTURE AND ORGANIZATION (FIG. 5A)

Cantos are distinguished by their topics and genres and by the forms and refrains that they repeat. In the original version the end of a canto is signaled by changing or abandoning the established patterns in the final stanzas and strophes. In the revised version the cantos became separated from each other by the intrusion of commentary and interpretation, and the restored connection between the rewritten parts was marked by anticipating in each the dominant image or idea of the next.

The first canto, after the heading identifying Amos as the author of the work, contains a series of four oracles with the same form and

FIGURE 5

The Book of Amos

Amos		Book of Amos	
CANTO		PART	
I	1:1a, 3–8, 13–15	I	1:1b–2, 9–12
	2:1–3, 6–8, 13–16		2:4–5, 9–12
II	3:1–6, 9–12	II	3:7–8, 13–15
	4:1–5	III	4:6–13
	5:1–2, 4–7	IV	5:3, 8–9
III	5:10–12, 18–24	V	5:13–17, 25–27
	6:1–7, 12–13	VI	6:8–11, 14
IV	7:1–9	VII	7:10–17
	8:1–3a, 4–6, 9–10	VIII	8:3b, 7–8, 11–14
		IX	9:1–15

FIGURE 5A

Amos

	Amos				*Book of Amos*	
CANTO I				**PART I**		
		1:1a			1	1:1b
					2	1:2
A	1	1:3–5a		A	1	
	2	1:5b			2	
B	1	1:6–8a		B	1	
	2	1:8b			2	
				C	1	1:9
					2	1:10
				D	1	1:11
					2	1:12
C	1	1:13–14		E	1	
	2	1:15			2	
D	1	2:1–2		F	1	
	2	2:3			2	
				G	1	2:4
					2	2:5
E	1	2:6		H	1	
	2	2:7–8			2	
				I	1	2:9
					2	2:10–11a
					3	2:11b–12
F	1	2:13		J	1	
	2	2:14–16			2	
CANTO II				**PART II**		
A	1	3:1		A	1	
	2	3:2			2	
B	1	3:3–4a		B	1	
	2	3:4b–5a			2	
	3	3:5b–6			3	
				C	1	3:7
					2	3:8
C	1	3:9		D	1	
	2	3:10			2	
D	1	3:11		E	1	
	2	3:12			2	
					3	3:13–15

continued

FIGURE 5 A (*cont*)

	Amos				Book of Amos		
				PART III			
E	1	4:1		A	1		
	2	4:2–3			2		
F	1	4:4		B	1		
	2	4:5			2		
				C	1	4:6	
					2	4:7	
					3	4:8	
				D	1	4:9a	
					2	4:9b	
				E	1	4:10	
					2	4:11	
				F	1	4:12	
					2	4:13	
				PART IV			
G	1	5:1		A	1		
	1	5:2			2		
					3	5:3	
H	1	5:4–5		B	1		
	2	5:6–7			2		
				C	1	5:8	
					2	5:9	
CANTO III				**PART V**			
A	1	5:10–11		A	1		
	2	5:12			2		
				B	1	5:13	
					2	5:14	
				C	1	5:15	
					2	5:16–17	
B	1	5:18		D	1		
	2	5:19			2		
	3	5:20			3		
C	1	5:21–22		E	1		
	2	5:23–24			2		
				F	1	5:25	
					2	5:26–27	

continued

FIGURE 5 A *(cont)*

		Amos			Book of Amos	
				PART VI		
D	1	6:1		A	1	
	2	6:2			2	
E	1	6:3–4		B	1	
	2	6:5–7			2	
				C	1	6:8
					2	6:9–10
					3	6:11
F	1	6:12		D	1	
	2	6:13			2	
					3	6:14
CANTO IV				**PART VII**		
A	1	7:1		A	1	
	2	7:2			2	
	3	7:3			3	
B	1	7:4		B	1	
	2	7:5			2	
	3	7:6			3	
C	1	7:7		C	1	
	2	7:8–9			2	
				D	1	7:10
					2	7:11
				E	1	7:12–13
					2	7:14–15
				F	1	7:16
					2	7:17
				PART VIII		
D	1	8:1–2abA		A	1	
	2	8:2bB–3a			2	8:3b
E	1	8:4–5a		B	1	
	2	8:5b–6			2	
				C	1	8:7
					2	8:8
F	1	8:9–10aA		D	1	
	2	8:10aBb			2	
				E	1	8:11
					2	8:12
					3	8:13–14

continued

FIGURE 5A *(cont)*

Amos	Book of Amos		
	PART IX		
	A	1	9:1a
		2	9:1b–4
	B	1	9:5
		2	9:6
		3	9:7
	C	1	9:8
		2	9:9
		3	9:10
	D	1	9:11–12
		2	9:13–15

Figure 5a. Letters indicate strophes. Numbers denote stanzas.

refrains, and a fifth that begins in the expected manner but then abandons the established pattern. The first four oracles are paired,[109] but the last is composed of matching strophes directed against Israel. All the oracles are about war, and all except the last mention the people, the land, the leaders, and the capital city of the nation concerned. All of them refer in formulaic terms to the crimes of the nation, mentioning one in particular, but the last lists the criminals and catalogs their specific crimes. All describe, at least in general and typical terms, the assault on the capital cities of the nations and the immediate effect of their capture, but the final oracle against Israel lists the different contingents in the army and describes their gradual disorder and defeat.

In the revised version the heading was expanded to indicate the date and content of the book; the oracles against the nations were elaborated to include a different sort of malefactor; and another strophe was inserted to lead into the next canto and to introduce some of the principal ongoing themes of the prophecy. The oracles against Tyre and Edom were added as a pair,[110] and the oracle against Judah was matched with the existing oracle against Israel.[111] But although they maintained the form of the original sayings and repeated their formulas, they omitted the closing formula and replaced their original interest in land and leaders and war with a concern for law and covenant. The new heading distinguished between Israel and Judah and included a motto that gave the prophecy a narrow Judean bias and at the same time anticipated one of the major themes of the second canto.[112] The additional strophe, like the strophe with which it was matched, completely abandoned the form and genre and repetitive patterns of the oracles. However it introduced the theme of repudiated prophets, which becomes crucial in the book's justification of Yahweh's catastrophic intervention in the history of the nation, and it included a proleptic quotation that linked the canto, in its new lopsided version, with the original canto that followed.

The second canto is addressed to the people, land, leaders, and capital city of Israel and is composed of proclamations in various genres addressed to progressively more specific groups.[113] The first proclamation is addressed to the people of Israel and contains a sort of riddle, in which occurrences common in the countryside are the clue that something dreadful is about to befall the city.[114] It is continued in a kind of judicial process, which identifies the city as Samaria, summons Ashdod and Egypt to witness the dishonesty, oppression, and violence stored within its walls, and announces the invasion of the land and the destruction of the city in battle.[115] The second proclamation taunts the lords and ladies of Samaria who used to traipse to Bethel and Gilgal to worship and do wrong but now will scurry into exile through the breaches in the wall.[116] The third proclamation is a lament over the house of Israel as a young woman who has fallen in battle and will not rise (5:1–2).[117] The canto ends by abandoning the proclamation of cumulative and encroaching doom and appeals instead to the house of Israel to seek Yahweh and live.[118]

The revised version commented on each of the proclamations and converted them into distinctive parts of the prophecy with artificial and obvious links to each other. One part encloses the first proclamation. It begins by emphasizing that Yahweh had declared in advance through the prophets that something dreadful would befall the city. It closes with a matching proclamation that both summarizes the argument up to this point and leads into the following warnings about worship in Bethel.[119] The next part includes the second proclamation but, instead of commenting on it, merely continues its own argument about prophecy by affixing numerous examples of dreadful natural occurrences to prove that the people had adequate warning and did not repent. It ends, however, by referring to the punishment decreed in the original proclamation and by attempting to assimilate it to the natural cycles that Yahweh controls.[120] The next part comments on the third proclamation and ends with the sort of hymnic element that concluded the preceding part.[121] By breaking up the sequence of proclamations and creating secondary links between them, the revision was able to introduce key points in its argument and set about establishing the connection between them.

The third canto alternates legal wranglings with warnings about religious feasts and festivals and ends anomalously with a proverb and its application. The first legal section describes popular contempt for ordinary justice in the court at the city gate and condemns to futility and hopelessness those who commit such crimes. The second legal section matches it by describing Yahweh's total contempt for their festivities and religious rites and by condemning them to futile worship for their injustice.[122] The warnings, similarly, correspond to each other by describing in general the expectation of the day of Yahweh and in detail what transpired on that day to make it unacceptable to Yahweh.[123] The concluding proverb illustrates the basic futility, and its application illustrates in crazy contradictions the reversals and inevitability implicated in the day of Yahweh (6:12–13).

The revised version added comments that regrouped the warnings and disputations into two parts and inserted other comments that reconnected the parts and related them to earlier and later material. The first of these parts incorporated both of the legal disputations and the first warning about the day of Yahweh into an exhortation addressed to the northern kingdom.[124] The second part included the second warning to Samaria and Zion in a vague and allusive description of the downfall of North and South.[125] In both parts the comments do not contribute directly to an understanding of the original context, but rather bolster and develop the ongoing argument of the revised version.[126]

The fourth canto is a series of four visions, grouped like the opening oracles in pairs, with concluding strophes that do not follow the pattern but provide a summary of the prophecy. The first two visions have the same subject, form, and formulas and differ only in the agent and extent of the destruction that they envisage. In the first locusts eat all the grass in the land, and in the second fire engulfs the land and the waters of the world.[127] The second pair of visions shares the same variants, including a question for Amos and his failure to intercede with Yahweh, but it deflects divine judgment away from the natural order to the people of Israel and their places of worship.[128] The first of the concluding strophes repeats the charges and specifies the crimes of injustice that were mentioned in the opening oracle against Israel (cf. 8:4–6 and 2:6b–7a). The final strophe concludes the theme of the day of Yahweh that was introduced in the same oracle and then gradually developed in the second and third cantos (Amos 8:9–10; cf. 2:16b; 4:2; 5:18, 20, 21, 23; 6:3). The canto confirms the judgment against the house of Jeroboam but insinuates that the same judgment, deflected for the moment by the intervention of Amos, awaits the house of David.[129]

In the revised version the canto was divided into two parts by intruding the encounter between Amos and Amaziah between the third and fourth visions, and by appending concluding remarks on the role of the prophet to the conclusion of the fourth vision. In addition, a final part was added to the book by constructing a fifth vision, whose interpretation brought the argument of the book to a close. The encounter between Amos and Amaziah confirms the theory of the book that Yahweh did nothing, such as the ruin of the northern kingdom and the extirpation of its priesthood, without first revealing it to his servants the prophets. The end of the fourth vision reflects on the natural catastrophes that were supposed to warn Israel to repent and describes Israel's terrible predicament when prophecy, repeatedly repudiated, finally ceased. The concluding vision restricts Yahweh's judgment to the temple and altar at Bethel and to the sinners who worshiped there, and looks forward to the restoration of the kingdom of Judah and the return of the faithful from exile.

The prophecy composed by Amos is compact and difficult but has rhetorical and thematic consistency and a rounded development from beginning to end. The revision is often allusive and, even when carefully fitted into the original text, often out of harmony with its context. Its difficulty is greatly magnified, however, by its ongoing and cumulative interpretation and by its development of an independent and sometimes contradictory line of argument.

LANGUAGE AND STYLE

The four cantos in the original version share a similar use of language but differ in the grammatical choices and style that they display. The revised version was inserted into the original by the usual process of repetition and cross-reference and, especially where it does not deliberately imitate the original, differs from it in its choice of words and in its construction of stanzas and strophes.

The Editorial Process

The revision of the first canto consists of additional stanzas or strophes inserted by simple repetition when they imitate the original and by means of deictics when they break with the original patterns.

The heading was expanded to situate Amos chronologically and historically by repeating the relative pronoun that identified him in order to identify the subject of his prophecy. Once this comment had been added it was possible to continue, without any further indication of the editorial process, by interpreting his words as spoken under the impulse of Yahweh who dwelt in Zion. The insertion fulfills the requirements of cross-reference by anticipating later statements concerning Judah and Jerusalem and the necessity of prophesying.[130]

The oracles against Tyre and Edom were inserted by copying the preceding oracle against the Philistines. The oracle against Tyre, apart from a clause copied from the oracle against Gaza and one original clause, is composed entirely of formulas.[131] The oracle against Edom, although it does not need to be marked as an editorial addition, actually elaborates on the single clause that was peculiar to the oracle against Tyre and thereby satisfies the requirement of cross-reference.[132]

The oracle against Judah copies the formulas of the surrounding oracles. In conjunction with the following oracle against Israel it constitutes a cross-reference to the revision's preferred distinction of greater Israel, contrary to the drift of the original prophecy, into the kingdoms of Israel and Judah.[133]

The additional strophe inserted into the oracle against Israel does not follow any established pattern. It was added with the help of deictic pronouns that establish a stark contrast between Yahweh and his people Israel, between what he did and how they responded to his initiative. The addition itself, however, has nothing to do with its immediate context but continues the revision's preoccupation with the role of prophecy and forges an artificial link with the following canto.[134]

In the second canto the revisions are made by copying the immediate context or by bold and irrelevant deictic references. The revisions themselves are either continuations of the preceding argument or anticipations of its further stages.

The riddle in Amos's version was an attempt to explain the startling statement that Yahweh punished the children of Israel because they were the only family that he recognized. The editor simply copied its concluding words in order to argue that the extraordinary situation had been revealed to the prophets, that the punishment had been announced in advance, and that the people had sufficient warning. The argument is clinched by referring to the motto at the beginning of the book.[135]

This part of the canto is separated from its natural sequel by a concluding strophe that reinterprets the punishment of the children of Israel in terms of the physical destruction of the temple at Bethel and the pretentious royal buildings in Samaria. The strophe was added by repeating the formula that Amos used in the preceding strophe, by anticipating the opening words of the following proclamation, and by paraphrasing parts of the preceding text. The editor's fixation on the altar at Bethel becomes thematic toward the end of the book, and the destruction of houses and public buildings is symbolic of the ruin of the kingdoms.[136]

Later additions in the canto, after the proclamation to the lords and ladies of Samaria, were inserted by emphasizing deictic pronouns and adverbs. The catalog of catastrophes that should have alerted Israel but had no effect on their behavior is added to the proclamation, as were the nontypical elements in the first canto, by emphasizing the contrast between Yahweh and the people. The very abruptness of the addition prompted the editor to add an artificial summary at the end of the list that referred explicitly but obliquely to the point of the original text. The catalog develops the editor's theory of prophetic forewarning and anticipates later discussions of prophecy, ruination, and the remnant.[137]

The last proclamation in the second canto was modified by anticipating and repeating the circumambient context. The lament that Amos composed for the death of the woman Israel was applied to those who died in battle but not to the few that survived.[138] The canto ended with an appeal to the nation to seek Yahweh and live, but in the revision the canto has been divided into separate parts and the ending is repeated to allow for a cross-reference to the ongoing eulogy of Yahweh's cosmic control.[139] In the original version Amos appealed to Israel to consider and avert the fate of Joseph, but in the revised version their fate is sealed and the implicit appeal is to consider the astronomical manifestations of Yahweh's power.

The third canto, with its interlocking sequence of warnings and disputations, was divided into two parts and criss-crossed by exhortations and condemnations. Changes that contribute to the ongoing argument but are irrelevant to their context are marked by deictics, while those that comment on their context are marked by literal repetitions.

The first disputation describes the contempt that the people of Samaria displayed for due process, and it outlines, in typical terms, the futility of amassing wealth at the expense of the poor and defenseless. The first part of the commentary refers vaguely, in general deictic terms, to the original text but consists in an exhortation to submit and to repent, which repeats and continues the themes of earlier texts.[140] The second part of the commentary flows naturally from the first, but it repeats key words from the original and reintroduces the theory of a remnant.[141] The third part of the commentary anticipates, but in an opposite sense, the original sequel to the disputation.[142]

In the second disputation Amos rejected Israel's effort to conceal its contempt for justice by multiplying its festivals and religious devotions. The commentary is attached by repeating and paraphrasing the original. It fits into the revised version's ongoing interpretation by recalling the precedents of Israel's time in the wilderness and by pitting Yahweh's cosmic authority against the nation's pitiful worship of the heavens.[143]

The rest of the canto, with its final warnings to those who live in Samaria and Zion, was amplified with condemnations that applied specifically to the southern kingdom. It has little to do with the original description of worshipers eating and drinking and lolling about but is attached to it by deictics that refer in explicit but general terms to the place of worship. It fits into the ongoing argument by applying to this place the destructive symbolism of the oracles against the nations and by developing in poignant detail the earlier image of lamentation for the dead.[144]

The fourth canto, with the visions and concluding summary of the original prophecy, was also divided into two parts and fitted with its own concluding summary in a separate part. The first three visions are separated from the last by the story of Amos's meeting with Amaziah of Bethel. The story was added by repeating the last part of the third vision and was inserted to conclude the argument that Yahweh had given Israel fair warning through the spirit of prophecy manifested in Amos.[145] The last vision was changed to make the day of Yahweh seem like a normal cyclic occurrence and to confirm the preceding argument by making this day coincide with the end of prophecy. Both of these changes were irrelevant to the original context and were inserted with the help of deictics.[146] The concluding part was presented as a separate vision, and it collected in one place all the important themes of the revision—the destruction of the sanctuary at Bethel, the cosmic and universal dominion of Yahweh of Hosts, the limitation of punishment to the sinful kingdom of Israel and to all sinners whether they remained in the land or went into exile, the reconstruction of Judah under David, and the restoration of a holy remnant.[147]

Apart from the editorial insertions, there is a clear order and sequence in the cantos and from one canto to the next until the entire prophecy is resumed in a concluding summary. However, the editorial insertions are clearly marked and were meant to be noticed without totally disrupting the intelligibility and flow of the original. As far as possible, therefore, they repeat and imitate and fit into their context without being wholly absorbed into their environment. This is evident, for instance, in the motto of the book, which seems to summarize its themes so well but still is uniquely phrased to stand out from its context. The added oracles against the nations, similarly, could have been indistinguishable from the oracles composed by Amos if the editor had simply added all the requisite formulaic expressions, and the omission of these, when everything else is so carefully copied and imitated, must betray craft and deliberation. But there were also points of disagreement that had to be emphasized and made plain. These points were not minor but concerned the outlook and interpretation of the writer and consequently stood out from the text that surrounded them and revealed an ongoing argument and developing subtext. The most important of these points was Amos's cavalier announcement of the destruction of Israel, with almost no compunction and with hardly a hint that their doom could be averted. The editor, on the contrary, made it plain that Amos was one of the many prophets who had been sent by Yahweh and silenced by the people who, no matter how urgently they had been warned, generally refused to repent. However, a minority, a remnant, did repent, and not all were guilty of the sins of Bethel. Unlike Amos, who was indiscriminate in his announcement of punishment, the editor was at pains to exclude these few from the dreaded day of Yahweh. The day of Yahweh, consequently, had to be interpreted not simply as an apocalyptic reversal of every reasonable hope and expectation but as one of those terribly unlucky days that occurs in the cyclic order of things. The total editorial effect is quite marvelous and disconcerting, but it gives the prophecy a density and a historical relevance that independently it never had.

The Compositional Process

All of Amos's interests are directed to juridical, military, economic, and liturgical practices. He writes about nations and kingdoms and their capitals, about cities and markets and the process of law. He knows about war and can describe battle scenes and the panic of defeat. He is familiar with worship and rituals and the lavish feasts of the urban elite and, despite his ostensible small-town origins and rustic occupation, knows little about life outside the city walls. His editor, on the other hand, was familiar with rural life and had observed the motives and emotions of common folk, was steeped in cosmological lore, and trained in historical and legal traditions. Amos is concrete and clear in his descriptions; his editor is imaginative, reflective, complex, and logical.

Amos composed his prophecy in poetic stanzas and strophes with prosodic variations from canto to canto.[148] His editor wrote poetry at times but usually indulged in more prosaic sentences and paragraphs. Amos's poetry is narrative, sometimes elegiac, but rarely melodic. The editor's poetry tends to be more lyrical, the prose periodic and persuasive.

The First Canto   The heading in Amos's version is brief and to the point and illustrates at once this canto's preference for the alternation of long and short lines (1:1a). The revised heading, in the same way, reveals the editor's preference for periodicity, subordination, and balanced clauses (1:1b).

The oracles against the nations, in Amos's version, note their crimes, narrate their punishment, and conclude with some specific reference to the people or their rulers. The notation of their crimes is done by alternating long and short lines (1:3; see also 1:6a, 13; 2:1, 6). The narrative of their punishment is composed of consecutive clauses that are repetitive and listlike (1:4–5a, 7, 14; 2:2). The concluding couplet or triplet returns, with slight variation, to the alternation of long and short lines (1:5b, 8b, 15; 2:3).

The oracles against the nations in the revised version follow the same general pattern but expand the notation of their crimes and omit the narrative of their punishment. The notation is expanded, not unnaturally, by imitating the narrative pattern that Amos followed in listing their punishments, even though it clashes with the grammar of the opening statement. The oracle against Tyre adds one such awkward clause. The oracle against Edom adds a series of them that are marked, however, with the balance typical of this edition. In the oracle against Judah the combination of grammatically odd and rigidly balanced clauses is complicated by an additional subordinate clause.[149]

In the original version the canto comes to a close with stanzas and strophes that do not fit the pattern of the oracles against the nations. However, the stanzas are constructed in the same manner of alternating long and short lines or of narrative chains of consecutive and disjunctive clauses.[150] In the revised version, similarly, the stanzas are composed mostly of balanced and subordinate clauses.[151]

The text composed by Amos is narrative and descriptive and almost completely unadorned by imagination. What it does have is resonance and intricate patterns of similar sounds—rhyme, assonance, and alliteration in clauses with a similar cadence.[152] The second edition, on the other hand, relies on repetition and imagination to make its point.[153]

Amos describes acts of aggression, battles, the siege and capture of cities, the deposition of rulers, the exile of whole populations, and, in the case of Israel, the ritual crimes of the people. His editor is interested in emotions and motives. Tyre's crime was not remembering. Edom's crime was anger, vengeance, and lack of pity. Judah's crime was following in the footsteps of their ancestors. Israel's crime was ignoring what Yahweh did for them. In this version even the ground reacted in anguish when Yahweh roared.

The Second Canto   The second canto is a series of proclamations and differs from the first in substituting vocatives and imperatives for descriptive discourse. Stanzas generally include some alternation of long and short lines, but even narrative lines, in general, are succinct and less rambling than in the first canto. Cadence is marked by rhyme and by interlinear assonance and alliteration.

The second edition tends to copy poetic features from the original but usually is distinguished from it by the length and lack of cadence in its lines and by the absence of vocatives and imperatives. The riddle, for instance, was modified by long and prosaic subordinate clauses introducing a stanza that imitated the sharp caesura of the original but that lacked its alternation of long and short lines and its direct address to the reader (3:7–8). The concluding announcement imitated the sequential style of its context but was written in the narrative mode of the first canto, and with the balance and repetition that the editor enjoyed (3:13–15; cf. 1:3–5). The catalog of natural catastrophes that was added to the second proclamation imitates its dominant rhyme but omits its assonance and alliteration and is composed in a narrative, repetitive, and prosaic style.[154] The comments on the third proclamation copy its words but clash with its rhythm and poetic cadence (5:3, 8–9).

The canto, in Amos's version, was about the city Samaria, the injustice that it stored up, and the punishment that was exacted on it. War recedes into the background, and the legal and ritual fabric of the city is laid bare. The riddle contrasts events that took place in the city with everyday occurrences in the country. The summons to Philistia and Egypt has them witness the life-style of Samaria's inhabitants, which was to be punished by the siege of the city and its utter destruction. The appeal to the lords and ladies of Samaria describes the breaching of the city walls and ironically compares their flight from the city with their former sorties to Bethel and Gilgal. The lament over the house of Israel supposes the fall of the city and the death of its inhabitants and leads into the exhortation to seek Yahweh and live.

The revised version comments briefly on the destruction but mentions cities in general rather than Samaria in particular and is interested in the random effect of natural phenomena rather than in war and injustice. It notes that there was a famine that affected every city but that the drought was more devastating for some cities than for others.

It mentions plagues that ruined their vines and fruit trees, and diseases that destroyed their camps, but it also compares Israel to Sodom and Gomorrah, where some escaped, and it notes that cities would be decimated in wartime but that some of their troops would survive. Controlling these occurrences, however, and bringing order to their seemingly random effects, is Yahweh, who created the world, who strides the earth and turns day into night, and who is responsible for rain and ruin. The destruction of Samaria, in this version, is not the bitter end of Israel but is comparable to a natural disaster and consistent with astrological observation and cosmic design.

The Third Canto The third canto combines the narrative style of the first canto with the vocative and hortatory style of the second. Its interest is in the city and the temple and in the liturgies that were financed by injustice. The revised version imitates the style but is absorbed in lamentations for those who died in the siege and capture of the city.

The opening disputation narrates the crime and punishment of the people and formulates the basic charge against them. It is like the earlier cantos in its use of initial and final rhyme, but differs from them in its use of parallel or subordinate phrases and clauses. The revised version makes a general comment on it and adds an exhortation to reform and it constructs both, in imitation of Amos in the preceding cantos, of alternating long and short lines (5:10–11, 12, 13–14).

The first warning begins and ends with rhetorical questions that enclose the analogy of the inevitability of the day of Yahweh. The questions are marked by literal repetition, and the enclosure is emphasized by alliteration and rhyme (5:18, 19, 20). In the commentary one stanza has two balanced lines and a final line that does not fit, and the other stanza is composed in the same way of balanced lines but with an initial and a final line that do not fit.[155]

The second disputation is composed of two stanzas held together by rhyme, and the commentary imitates the original (5:21–24).[156] The second warning, similarly, is marked mainly by rhyme, but the commentary follows a completely different pattern.[157]

The Fourth Canto The visions in the fourth canto contain description and dialogue, while the concluding strophes are marked by listlike or consecutive narrative. The descriptive sections are characterized by rhyme, alliteration, and literal repetition (7:1, 4, 7; 8:1–2), and the ensuing dialogues by the sequence of longer and shorter lines and some of the same features (7:2–3, 5–6, 8–9; 8:3a). The listlike narrative is set apart by the repetition of words and grammatical forms, while the consecutive narrative displays the usual preference for rhyme, alliteration, and assonance.[158]

The commentary begins with a pseudo-historical narrative mostly in prose but with some admixture of direct discourse and oracular material that approximates poetic style (7:10–17). The comment on the listlike narrative is hymnic and marked by parallelism, but the comment on the consecutive narrative imitates the style of the original. The concluding part, as it summarizes the point of the revision, is a conglomerate of all its styles.[159]

The two versions are characterized by variety and internal consistency. The four cantos composed by Amos differ from one another in the issues they cover and in the grammar and style that they adopt, but resemble one another in their literary and syntactic preferences. The work of the editor stands out from its context as more lyrical in some instances and as more prosaic in others. It betrays different interests, a logical and imaginative cast, and a concern to establish homogeneous strands that guide the reader through the complexity of text and commentary, beyond the original conclusion to the ultimate meaning of the book.

SOURCES AND INTERPRETATION

Amos composed his prophecy after the fall of Samaria as a lesson for the people in Judah and Jerusalem. He had the detailed information available to an educated person of the time but also was familiar with earlier interpretations of the event and wrote with them in mind. The most important of these was the historical sequel to the epic. It had argued, naïvely and with considerable hauteur, that Samaria fell because from the time of Jeroboam I it had worshiped in Bethel and Dan rather than in Jerusalem. Amos treated the explanation subtly and sarcastically. He chastised Samaria for its treks to Bethel and for its faithful observance of the rituals that the sequel wanted to centralize in Jerusalem. But he went further and condemned the faithful observance of any ritual, insinuating that the centralization of worship in any place was a vain and useless exercise. The basis of this critique was Isaiah's prophecy, which had covered some of the same ground but risked being quashed by the clever historical interpretation in the sequel. Isaiah had recorded his prophecy for a later day when Jerusalem would be defeated and left like a signal on a hill, and Amos transformed that day into a day of battle when all of Israel's hopes would be dashed. Isaiah had repudiated the covenant because it encouraged worship but ignored oppression and injustice, and Amos described in great detail how the worship that the covenant prescribed was in inverse proportion to the misery of the poor.

The revision of the prophecy was a scholarly work indebted to the establishment of a prophetic tradition and to advances in historical research. It was most indebted, of course, to the work of the Deuteronomistic Historian and transposed into prophecy and poetry many of its more memorable texts. It knew Isaiah too, and Ezekiel and Obadiah and Joel, and relied on them to take issue with the Historian's sense that the sin of Jeroboam was final and led to an inexorable finish. The day Amos predicted was past, another day was dawning with much to be done, and prophecy had to be remolded into history to suit the times to come.

Of the many differences between Amos and the editor of his book none is so startling as the things that they meant. Amos wrote in a vibrant time when people listened but criticism barely dented the surface of life. He said smart things that he thought were true and like Isaiah saw strange things in the distance. The editor of his book wrote in a timid time when all the things had come true and life seemed to hang in the balance. Amos was harsh when hope was alive. His editor had to defend him by putting his words into historical perspective. Amos meant what he said. The editor meant what tradition allowed.

The First Canto

The first canto threatens people who at various times had invaded Israel. All of them are known from historical accounts in the epic sequel, and all of them are threatened equally with the inevitable day of Yahweh. The irony, of course, is that Israel is included in the list and identified as the real culprit.[160]

The invasion of Gilead by Hazael was a critical time in the history of Israel. It provoked a coup in the northern kingdom and sparked a revolution in Judah that threatened the Davidic dynasty and eventually led to Assyrian intervention in Israel's internal affairs. It was a turning point in the sequel's interpretation of the history of Israel,[161] the climax of the Deuteronomistic theory of prophetic tradition (1 Kings 17–2 Kings 13), the initial inspiration for Hosea's prophecy (Hos 1:4), and the first illustration chosen by Amos. His oracle against the Arameans refers to it explicitly but, in agreement with the sequel's interpretation, associates the war in Gilead with the Syro-Ephraimite war and the combined attack under Rezin and Pekah the son of Remaliah.[162]

The oracle against the Philistines contains information that is not confirmed in any other source and that is designed in part to connect it with the preceding oracle against the Arameans.[163] The Philistines were early enemies of Israel and could have been included in the catalog on that account. But the allusion to their Pentapolis, the reference to their remnant, the omission of Gath in this oracle, and a later reference to its destruction suggest that the connection with the oracle against the Arameans is an oblique reference to Hazael's capture of Gath recounted by the sequel to the epic.[164]

The Ammonites and Moabites, like the Philistines, were ancient enemies of Israel. According to the epic the Ammonites were not conquered by Israel because their borders were too well defended (Num 21:24b). According to the sequel they tried to annex Gilead and were defeated by Saul but persisted in challenging Israel and were defeated again by David in the battle of Rabbah (1 Samuel 11°; 2 Samuel 11). The epic ends with the oracles of Balaam, who had been summoned by the king and princes of Moab to curse Israel but who instead predicted the victory of Yahweh and Israel over their enemies. The oracles against Ammon and Moab, therefore, in a temporal and historical crasis that suits their stereotyped and formulaic spirit, quote a key word from the epic oracles[165] and surround it with references to these ancient wars.[166]

The oracle against Israel is the ironic conclusion of the catalog of nations and has no basis in the historical sources. Most of the crimes that Amos condemns, however, are included in felonies in later legal codes.[167] The punishment for their crimes, not surprisingly, is defeat in battle at the hands of Yahweh, and Amos describes the anguish of that day in terms that Isaiah used to portray Jerusalem's reliance on arms instead of trusting in Yahweh.[168]

The catalog of nations rehearses, in a mumbo jumbo that might have lulled the listener into complacency, the vile but ancient and familiar crimes of traditional enemies. The surprise is the list of current and specific charges against Israel. Amos spends the rest of his time detailing the charges and explaining the punishment of Israel on the dreadful day of Yahweh. But the revised version adds other nations and other crimes and relies on later historians and prophets to justify its changes.

The expanded title of the prophetic book depends on the synchronism established by the Deuteronomistic History between the reigns of Uzziah king of Judah and Jeroboam son of Joash king of Israel.[169] Its reference to this source is confirmed by a later quotation from the same passage that describes the devastation of the land from Lebo Hamath to the brook of the Arabah.[170]

The motto that the book added after the title uses the metaphor of a lion roaring to portray Yahweh speaking from Zion so that pasture-lands mourn and the tip of Carmel withers. The metaphor is borrowed from the riddle in the second canto but the effect of the lion's roar is taken from the prophecy of Joel. The reference to Zion and Jerusalem, besides betraying the editor's peculiar point of view, also reflects the original context of the quotation from Joel.[171] The motto effectively introduces the editor's interpretation of the original prophecy and situates it in an exilic and Judean context.

The same context is maintained in the oracles against the nations that were added in this edition. The oracle against Tyre refers to the friendly relations between the city and Israel in the time of Solomon as these were recorded in the Deuteronomistic History,[172] but it describes the city's crime and punishment in terms taken from a speech by Ezekiel (Ezek 26:2, 9, 10, 12). The oracle against Edom, similarly, combines elements from the epic, the Deuteronomist, and Obadiah to condemn it for its role in the siege and capture of Jerusalem.[173] The oracle against Judah, in the same way, combines prophetic and histo-riographic cliches to summarize the reasons for the fall of Jerusalem.[174] The sources were popular and the references would have been apparent to the editor's readers and contemporaries, who would have appreciated them and comments like them, for giving the original prophecy an immediate and useful significance.[175]

The commentary on the oracle against Israel begins by comparing the Israelites to the Amorites whom Yahweh destroyed. The comparison is temporally out of place—the conquest of the Amorites is mentioned again in the next stanza in its proper place after the exodus—but alludes to the Deuteronomistic statement that Israel's apostasy and worship of other Gods made it worse than the Amorites. The destruc-tion of the Amorites, similarly, is expressed both in the terms that the Deuteronomist used for the extermination of indigenous peoples and kings and in the metaphorical terms that Ezekiel devised to describe the execution of the king of Judah for having violated his oath of allegiance to Yahweh.[176] This choice of sources reflects the revised edition's current concern for the violation of treaties and covenants and its ongoing interpretation of Israel's sin, typified by the cult at Bethel, as the worship of other Gods.

The commentary on the Israel oracle continues with a recital of the standard Deuteronomistic history of salvation.[177] It also appends a reference to the origins of the prophetic tradition and to its own version of the Deuteronomistic theory that the people consistently refused to listen to the prophets. The total effect of the commentary is to divert attention from the injustice that Amos condemned to the general apostasy that Amos and the prophets tried unsuccessfully to combat.[178] This change in emphasis helped explain why the day of Yahweh was inevitable and for its time was much more satisfactory than the original explanation that Yahweh had simply refused to listen to the supplication of his people.

The Second Canto

In the second canto Amos refers to the assumptions of the epic covenant, to the basic beliefs of the sequel, and to their radical rejection in the prophecy of Isaiah. The revised version continues its reflection on prophecy and, with the help of items from the Deuteronomistic History, prepares for its final defense of the prophet's hopeless mission.

Amos alludes to the covenant by combining elements of its preamble and its conclusion. The preamble to the epic covenant declares Yahweh's attributes and ends with the statement that Yahweh punishes the crimes of the fathers and their children to the third and fourth generations. The conclusion to the covenant insists on the importance of the words that Yahweh has spoken. Amos combines both elements in a striking contradictory sense by subverting the words of Yahweh and by making the punishment of Israel the consequence of its privileged position.[179]

The crimes that Israel committed and that Amos invites the nations to observe are tumult and oppression, which he defines more specifically as harm and violence and the inability to do what is right. The expression "harm and violence" was coined by Amos and is quoted by Jeremiah and Habakkuk and later writers.[180] Tumult, according to the sequel's military program, is the thing that destroys a city.[181] Oppression and the inability to do what is right were defined by Isaiah as the crimes that would be the downfall of the city and the correlative of its refusal to accept prophetic reproof.[182]

The invasion, siege, and capture of Samaria that Amos sees as the punishment for these crimes were already foreseen by Isaiah as the punishment for the sins of Jerusalem. In separate oracles he had described the advance of the enemy and the capture of the city, portraying one in the metaphor of lions seizing and roaring over their prey, and the other in the visible act of looting or in the imaginative act of a bull deposing the ruler of the city. Amos, similarly, identifies Yahweh as a lion and describes an enemy that will overrun the land, depose the city's mighty ruler, and loot its fortifications.[183]

The borrowing of images, ideas, and assumptions that were native to Jerusalem and pertinent to the Assyrian siege of the city in the time of Sennacherib gives Amos's elegy on Samaria a subtle rhetorical twist. Things that Amos says of Samaria become things that are equally or primarily applicable to Jerusalem, and the lesson for Judah lies in reciting the familiar judgment on past events in an ominous future tense.

The editor, on the contrary, although admitting that the prophecy was pertinent to Judah, insisted that Amos had spoken in advance of the fall of Samaria. In reliance on the prophetic tradition propounded by the Deuteronomistic Historian, the editor insists that Yahweh does nothing without revealing it first to his servants the prophets. With specific reference to the story of a Judean prophet who went to Bethel in the time of Jeroboam I and prophesied against it, the editor includes a prediction that the altars of Bethel will be destroyed. The new proclamation was addressed to the house of Jacob, but it was meant for the likes of Ahab and the sinful kingdom of the North.[184]

In the second proclamation Amos, like Isaiah, criticized the festivals that blinded the people to the seriousness of their situation and, like the author of the sequel, supposed that the festivals were celebrated at the central sanctuary. Both Isaiah and Amos saw their festivals as drinking bouts; both likened the faithful participants to cattle; both referred to the offense they caused Yahweh the Holy One of Israel; and both pictured as Yahweh's response an enemy attack that left the walls of the city in ruins.[185] The sequel, however, promoted the festivals at the central sanctuary, where the people ate and drank to their hearts' content, and Amos alludes to its legislation in an ironic summons to celebrate and be unfaithful at Bethel and Gilgal.[186]

The editor affixed a catalog of hardships that, apart from its opening reference to lack of food and drink, has nothing to do with the content of the original but comments on its form and assumptions. Amos's ironic invitation to Bethel ruined Samaria's hopes of escaping the day of Yahweh by excluding recourse to prayer and sacrifice. But the catalog of calamities, on the contrary, was taken from the prayer of Solomon at the dedication of the temple in Jerusalem, where the invitation is honest and where precisely the opposite effect is envisaged. In this Deuteronomistic prayer, as in the editor's text, it is assumed that calamity is a punishment for sin. In both texts—explicitly in the prayer, obliquely in the commentary—the calamities are the occasion for repentance and for supplications addressed to God in the central sanctuary. In both, God is not restricted to the perimeters of the temple but fills and indeed transcends the universe. In the Deuteronomist's view prayer and repentance would be effective even in exile, but in the editor's view, despite the prompting of Amos, they had not taken place.[187]

The first calamity is famine and is reflected both in the prayer of Solomon and in the curses consequent on neglect of the law.[188] The second calamity is drought and has parallels in the prayer, in Jeremiah, and in the drought that the Deuteronomist describes in the time of Ahab.[189] The third calamity is plague and blight, and it is described in terms taken from the prayer of Solomon and from the testimony of Joel (4:9; 1 Kgs 8:37–40; Joel 1:4, 7, 11, 12). The fourth calamity is pestilence, and it is elaborated with reference to the history of Israel according to the Deuteronomist and Joel (4:10; 1 Kgs 8:37; Exod 15:26; Deut 28:27, 60; Joel 2:20). The final calamity is a catastrophe like the primordial overthrow of Sodom and Gomorrah: it is not mentioned in the prayer of Solomon but is the Deuteronomistic model for the destruction of Jerusalem (4:11; Gen 19:25; Deut 29:22).

The original canto ends with its proper interpretation. The harsh indictment, condemnation, and sentence on Samaria are summed up in a lament for the dead daughter of Israel. But the ironic undercurrent of the canto, expressed in quotations and allusions to texts that once applied just as well to Judah and Jerusalem, is redeemed in the closing appeal to the house of Israel to seek Yahweh and live. This appeal offers a choice between living and being engulfed by the fires spreading from the house of Joseph, and it turns out in the end to be addressed quite openly to those in Zion who disdain justice and the due process of law.[190]

The revised version of the canto resisted this undercurrent, which made the canto a subtle lesson for Judah. The author of this version was particularly interested in making it a true prophecy, about Bethel and the northern kingdom, that pronounced punishment on all those who worshiped at Bethel but made allowances for an innocent remnant. This edition makes it clear that Amos is a true prophet and gives numerous examples of a popular unwillingness to repent. It turns original judgments against Samaria into general warnings against cities and their sanctuaries, especially Bethel, but it allows for the survival of some in the overall decimation of the country. It ruins the implicit analogy between the local sanctuaries at Bethel and Jerusalem by eulogizing the universal and transcendent attributes of Yahweh. It continues, in effect, its interpretation of the first canto, which situated Amos in a historical past and in the venerable succession of prophets and nazirites whose message the people had disdained.

The Third Canto

In the third canto Amos describes, in increasingly detailed strophes, how the people of Samaria and Zion look forward to the feasts and festivals, where they can indulge themselves and pay no attention to the misery that surrounds them or to the sorry fate of the house of Joseph. The undercurrent of the preceding cantos enters into the mainstream of this song; the illusion of Samaria as sole antagonist is dispelled; the day of defeat in battle emerges as the day of Yahweh, an amalgam of evil, the antithesis of every hope, the day on which Jerusalem will go into exile.

The editor did not try to dispel the pall that fell over the entire nation but shifted emphases and left room for hope. A remnant of Joseph might escape the evil time, and some will be left to mourn those who have died. In Jerusalem destruction will be total, and the few who remain will not dare to invoke the name of Yahweh over the ruins. The country will be overrun by an enemy nation, but the ruin has specific causes and can be corrected.

Amos demonstrates his usual familiarity with the epic, the sequel, and the prophecy of Isaiah but composes long descriptive passages that cannot be attributed to any source. The first strophe, for instance, may allude to the sequel's appreciation of the promised land and to the epic's definition of infidelity, but it describes a court in session at the city gate, the charge, the evidence, and the judgment against the accused, and does not have an adequate parallel in the literature.[191] The third and fifth strophes, in the say way, reflect Isaiah's descriptions of the festivities in Jerusalem and the sequel's interest in centralized worship, but are filled with independent observations (Amos 5:21–24; 6:3–7; cf. Deut 12:13–14; Isa 5:11–12; 29:1). The other strophes demonstrate even greater originality, and some were copied by later historians and prophets.[192]

The editor's work is indebted mainly to the Deuteronomistic History and the prophets, but it also contains original elements. Jeremiah and the History were useful sources in describing the Babylonian siege and capture of Jerusalem.[193] The prophecies of Micah were an apt commentary on the situation confronting a city under siege.[194] Lamentations for the dead were common occurrences, but they had been prepared by Micah and Jeremiah to be recited at the siege of Jerusalem (Amos 5:16–17; Mic 1:8; 2:4; Jer 5:1; 6:26). What is most original in the editor's version is its attribution of the fall of the city to its worship of astral divinities in defiance of Yahweh the God of the Hosts of Heaven.[195]

The Fourth Canto

The visions of Amos in the fourth canto, like the oracles in the first, are stylized and allusive. Unlike the strophes at the end of the canto, which summarize and synthesize the entire cycle in a clear conceptual manner, the visions return to the beginning of the cycle to present a more personal and idealized portrait of Israel and to unravel the undercurrent of the prophet's thought.

The visions describe the progress of the seasons from the mowing of the hay, through the summer heat and dry spells, to the harvesting of the fall crops.[196] In step with this agricultural calendar, and in dependence on the epic, the visions move through the personal history of Jacob to his destiny as Israel.[197]

In the oracles against the nations the irrevocability of the day of Yahweh was expressed by alluding to the oracles of Balaam, and Amos ends his poem by returning to the same source in his visions. In both texts the prophet is given a perspective on the history and the destiny of the nation, and in both the nation is named Jacob and Israel.[198] Within this framework, the history begins with an allusion to creation and to Jacob as the younger son of Isaac, but in a perverse and opposite sense, with creation devoured by locusts, and Jacob threatened with death.[199] The history moves quickly to the covenant on Sinai, but again the visions contradict the original, with Yahweh manifested in a devouring fire to declare that he will never again pass by his people.[200] In the oracles of Balaam, Yahweh, through the covenant and the blessings bestowed on Jacob, was on Israel's side against its enemies. In the visions of Amos, after all the criticisms of the covenant for not assuring ordinary justice, Yahweh changed his mind.[201]

The editor recognized the political and cosmic ramifications of these words but commented less on their content than on their authoritative prophetic form.[202] The sequence of Amos's visions was interrupted to include an encounter between Amos and Amaziah. The encounter itself presupposes the Deuteronomistic History's condemnation of the cult and altar and priesthood of Bethel and is based on its legend of the Judean prophet who went to Bethel in the reign of Jeroboam I to foretell its destruction in the reign of Josiah.[203] The point of the encounter is to confirm the prophetic authority of Amos and to limit the disaster that he foretold to those who rejected the words of the prophets and persisted in the worship of other Gods. The first point is illustrated at the end of the canto in the miserable death, by hunger and thirst for the word of Yahweh, that overtakes the devotees of alien Gods from Dan to Beersheba.[204] The second point is illustrated in a vision that the editor added to describe the demise of the kingdom of Israel and the survival of Jacob in the restored kingdom of Judah.[205]

CONCLUSION

The cycle of poems that Amos composed revolves around the single issue of the survival of Israel. There is only one point, when Amos calls on his hearers to seek Yahweh and live, at which this seems at all likely. The fate of Samaria is clearly sealed, and there is no hope that fidelity, devotion, or sacrifice will be of any help to Zion. What matters is justice, but it is denied to the ignorant masses and ignored by those who believe that Yahweh is with them. In the end, on the day of battle when they need him most, he will appear not as they expected but only to judge them.

The editor had a different notion of Israel and a different understanding of prophecy and history. Israel included Israel and Judah and was not a family with a common destiny. It was not, as Amos said, that Yahweh had abandoned a pious and unsuspecting people with a good conscience and a poor sense of justice. In fact, Israel sinned by worshiping other Gods at Bethel despite the instruction of the law and the warning of the prophets. Its punishment was not, as Amos predicted, fateful and inevitable and final. It was administered by Yahweh, who transcended fate and destiny and the cycles of necessity, and by the universal Lord of Hosts, who, being unconfined by location or historical tradition, was constantly and visibly accessible. The Israel that Amos knew did come to an end. Another that the editor understood survived.

Hosea

Hosea was more nuanced than Amos in his critique of the kingdoms and more imaginative in proposing a solution to the problem of Israel's perennial infidelity. Amos said that their worship was senseless, but Hosea thought it was mistaken. Amos thought that the people were devoid of common sense and incapable of justice and therefore doomed, but Hosea thought that they were devious and disobedient and determined to die. Amos argued from traditional examples and by analogy with the liturgical and agricultural calendars that the history of Israel was coming to an inevitable end. Hosea imagined that the fate of Israel was bound by affection to Yahweh and that its history was designed to continue and repeat itself like every living thing.

Hosea's work was revised by an editor with a totally different view of history. History, for this writer, was not analogous to nature and romance. It was factual rather than emotional and rational rather than cyclic. The trouble with Israel, therefore, was not some suspicious trait it had inherited from Jacob, which kept coloring its behavior, but some specific and documented things that it did at various times and in various places, which affected Israel and Judah in quite different ways. The people were mistaken, as Hosea said, but it was because they were misled by the priests. They were headed for disaster, but that was because their kings relied on intrigue and the force of arms. It was not Israel that was finished but its evil institutions.

STRUCTURE AND THEMES

Hosea composed a dramatic work, written, by analogy with the writing boards on which it might have been inscribed, in a series of triptychs and tableaux. The revision of his work consisted in remodeling the tableaux by adding lines to stanzas and stanzas to strophes, and in spoiling the connection between the triptychs by giving a separate interpretation to each. Hosea's work was filled with abrupt transitions and was not easy to follow. The rewriting introduced conceptual clarity but ruined the dramatic flow of the original (fig. 6).[206]

Tableaux generally coincide with chapters in the printed Bible and are simply graphic or dramatic collections of images, ideas, and individuals in a single scene. Triptychs, literally sets of three writing boards bound by hinges, are sets of three tableaux bound by patterns of repetition. The evidence for this sort of deliberate and systematic composition is most obvious in the first three chapters, and it is clear that they were written as a preface and paradigm for the rest of the work.

The first triptych comprises Hosea's prophecy and its later interpretation. Each has a different structure and organization, but it is clear that the revised version recognized the original arrangement and deliberately changed it (fig. 6a). In Hosea's version the first tableau narrates Yahweh's marriage with the land; the second explains their divorce; and the third portrays their reconciliation. The editor added a different conclusion to both the first and the third tableaux, inserted the antecedent adjustments these required, and smoothed the transition from the revised first tableau to the second. This version concentrates on the children of the marriage and anticipates their return to the land and the establishment of a theocracy. It substitutes logical progression

FIGURE 6

The Book of Hosea

Hosea		Book of Hosea	
	First Triptych		
A	1:2–4, 6, 8–9	A	1:1, 5, 7
B	2:4–15	B	2:1–3
C	2:16–17aAb, 18–20a, 21–25	C	2:17aB, 20b; 3:1–5
	Second Triptych		
A	4:1–2aAb, 3, 6a, 7–8, 10, 12–13a, 16–19	A	4:2aB, 4–5, 6b, 9, 11, 13b–15
B	5:3–4, 6–7, 11–15	B	5:1–2, 5, 8–10
C	6:1–6	C	6:7–11
	Third Triptych		
A	7:1a, 2, 8–9, 11–14 8:1–3, 7–9, 11–13abA	A	7:1b, 3–7, 10, 15–16 8:4–6, 10, 13bB, 14
B	9:1–8, 10a, 11–14, 16–17	B	9:9, 10b, 15
C	10:1–2, 4–6, 8aBb, 11–12	C	10:3, 7–8aA, 9–10, 13–15
	Fourth Triptych		
A	11:1–5	A	11:6–11
B	12:1–5, 8–11, 13–15	B	12:6–7, 12
C	13:1–2aAb, 3–8, 12–14	C	13:2aB, 9–11, 15 14:1–10

Figure 6. Letters denote tableaux.

for the original dramatic development and reiteration for symbolic transformation.

Tableaux in both versions are composed in a narrative, descriptive, or explanatory order.[207] In Hosea's version the first and third tableaux are composed in a narrative order, each with two strophes that complement each other and that combine to tell a continuous story in proper chronological and dramatic sequence. The first tableau moves from Yahweh's marriage with the land to the birth of their children in a crescendo that obliterates first the house of Jehu, then the northern kingdom, and finally the entire people. The third tableau recounts Yahweh's reconciliation with the land and their joyful reunion with their children. The second tableau, however, is composed in an explanatory order that begins with the case against the land and continues in inverse order with an explanation of the facts and their consequences. The case opens with an accusation of adultery against the land, cites her trysts and the birth of her illegitimate children as evidence, and

FIGURE 6 A

Hosea

First Triptych

Tableau 1		*Tableau 2*		*Tableau 3*	
Hosea	*Book of Hosea*	*Hosea*	*Book of Hosea*	*Hosea*	*Book of Hosea*
1:2	1:1	2:4 2:5	2:3	2:20a 2:21–22	2:20b
1:3–4	1:5	2:6–7a 2:7b		2:23–24 2:25	
1:6	1:7	2:8 2:9			3:1 3:2–3
1:8–9	2:1 2:2	2:10 2:11			3:4 3:5
		2:12–13 2:14–15			
		2:16–17aAb 2:18–19	2:17aB		

Second Triptych

Tableau 1		*Tableau 2*		*Tableau 3*	
Hosea	*Book of Hosea*	*Hosea*	*Book of Hosea*	*Hosea*	*Book of Hosea*
4:1 4:2aAb–3	4:2aB		5:1a 5:1b–2	5:11–12 5:13a 5:13b–14a	
4:6a	4:4–5 4:6b	5:3 5:4		5:14b–15 6:1–2	
4:7–8	4:9	5:6a 5:6b–7	5:5	6:3	
4:10				6:4 6:5–6	
4:12 4:13a	4:11 4:13b		5:8 5:9 5:10		6:7–8 6:9 6:10–11
	4:14 4:15				
4:16 4:17–19					

continued

FIGURE 6 A (*cont*)

Third Triptych

Tableau 1		Tableau 2		Tableau 3	
Hosea	*Book of Hosea*	*Hosea*	*Book of Hosea*	*Hosea*	*Book of Hosea*
7:1a		9:1		10:1	
	7:1b				
7:2		9:2–3		10:2	
	7:3–4	9:4			10:3
	7:5–6	9:5–6		10:4	
	7:7			10:5	
		9:7a			
7:8–9		9:7b–8		10:6	
	7:10		9:9		10:7–8aA
7:11–12				10:8aBb	
		9:10a	9:10b		
7:13		9:11–12			10:9
7:14					10:10
		9:13			
	7:15	9:14		10:11	
	7:16			10:12	
			9:15		
8:1		9:16			10:13
8:2–3		9:17			10:14
	8:4				10:15
	8:5				
	8:6				
8:7					
8:8–9					
	8:10				
8:11–12					
8:13abA	8:13bB				
	8:14				

continued

F I G U R E   6 A *(cont)*

Fourth Triptych

Tableau 1		*Tableau 2*		*Tableau 3*	
Hosea	*Book of Hosea*	*Hosea*	*Book of Hosea*	*Hosea*	*Book of Hosea*
11:1–2		12:1		13:1	
11:3		12:2		13:2aAb	13:2aB
		12:3			
11:4				13:3	
11:5		12:4–5		13:4	
			12:6–7		
		12:8–9			
11:6		12:10		13:5–6	
11:7		12:11		13:7–8	
			12:12		
11:8					13:9
11:9		12:13–14			13:10
		12:15			13:11
11:10					
11:11				13:12–13	
				13:14	
					13:15
					14:1
					14:2–3a
					14:3b
					14:4
					14:5
					14:6–7
					14:8
					14:9
					14:10

Figure 6a. Stanzas are on separate lines. Strophes are composed of two or three stanzas separated by horizontal lines.

ends with the idea of keeping her from her trysts in the hope of reconciliation. The review argues that deprivation will bring the land to its senses, make her repulsive to her lovers, and eventually effect a reconciliation.

The revised version is concerned with issues of war and government.[208] Its argument is perfectly clear, but it is extraneous to Hosea's metaphor and tends to confuse or contradict it. In the first tableau the additions dissolved the original narrative development and produced an explanatory order.[209] The first strophe was changed to include a duplicate introduction that mentioned Israel and Judah and their ruling houses, and a final strophe was added to correspond to it by mentioning them again reunited under one rule. The second strophe was modified to include the breaking of Israel's weapons, and the third matches it by commenting that Yahweh will save Judah without weapons. The second tableau was unchanged except for the addition of two lines that repeat and contradict elements from the original text in order to ease the transition from the editor's intervening remarks.[210] The third tableau was modified to agree with the editor's perspective on war and was changed into the descriptive pattern by appending two strophes that duplicate and interpret Hosea's strophes and effectively suppress the original metaphor of Yahweh's marriage with the land.[211]

Tableaux are distinguished by their subject matter. They have beginnings and ends, and the boundaries between them consist in the exhaustion of one subject and the transition to the next. But the beginnings and ends and the different phases in tableaux are also clearly marked by different types of repetition. The first tableau in Hosea's version, for instance, is composed of two strophes that are pretty well formal duplicates (cf. 1:2–4 and 1:6, 8–9). Most of the clauses are consecutive; the stanzas have exactly the same pattern of main and subordinate clauses; and the strophes both end with the birth of a son and two consecutive reasons for his symbolic name. The last tableau, similarly, has two strophes that begin with the same temporal formula and share the same interest in heaven and earth and natural cycles.[212] The central tableau has a different pattern, in which all the matching strophes are linked by thematic and verbatim repetition. The first and last contrast the land with the wilderness and repeat the marriage formula, "You are my husband and I am your wife" (cf. 2:4–5 and 2:16–17*, 18–19). The second and second to last mention the land and her lovers and explain the motives of her infidelity (cf. 2:6–7 and 2:12–15). In the middle strophes the land decides to come back to Yahweh, and Yahweh decides to take back the good things he gave her (cf. 2:8–9 and 2:10–11).

Triptychs resolve particular issues and, like tableaux, are distinguished by the correspondences between their introductions and their conclusions. In the first triptych this is most obvious in the revised version, which ends with another wedding like the first,[213] and with a repeated and more explicit understanding of the reunification of Israel and Judah (cf. 2:1–2 and 3:4–5). But it is also clear in the original version, where the land is restored as the bride of Yahweh (1:2 and

2:21–22; cf. 2:4 and 2:18–19), and they and their children are reunited (1:6, 8–9; 2:23–25). The issues in each version are different, and in each they are resolved in a different way. Hosea dramatizes Yahweh's involvement in the life of the people; the book describes the institutions of its survival.

The second triptych has analogous interlocking structures (fig. 6a). It is differentiated from the first by its internal design and by the issue that it raises and resolves, but it is also distinguished from the first triptych by an introductory summary that restates its principal relevant points.[214] In the first triptych Yahweh spoke to Hosea, and in the second Hosea reports to the people what Yahweh said.[215] The first recorded Yahweh's dispute with the land, and the summary introduces his dispute with the inhabitants of the land.[216] The first looked forward to a time of fidelity and truth and knowledge of God, and the introduction complains that all of these are presently missing.[217] The first triptych mentioned the beasts of the field and the birds of the air and the reptiles, and the transition mentions some of these and the fish in the sea.[218] The first attributed the end of the dynasty of Jehu to his murderous coup, and the summary associates murder with the lack of the knowledge of God.[219] The first described the failure of the crops and the abandonment of the land, and the introductory summary repeats that the land is desolate (cf. 2:5, 11, 14b and 4:3). There are only two elements in the whole introduction that do not resume elements from the first triptych, and these have a specific proleptic function. Hosea notes that oaths and lies abound and both of these anticipate developments in the third triptych (see 4:2 and 7:1, 13; 9:2; 10:4). The book identified lack of knowledge of God with ignorance of the decalogue and with the proliferation of murder, theft, and adultery, and all of these are crimes that are attributed to the priests in this triptych and the next (see 4:2aB and 4:6b, 13b–14; 6:7–11; 7:15).

In Hosea's version the issue is the repentance of the people and its failure to divert the impending calamity. The triptych's boundaries are marked by referring to Hosea's prophetic mission at the beginning and the end, and by repeating at the end all the accusations that were made at the beginning concerning the lack of truth and knowledge.[220] In the revised version the issue is the responsibility of the priesthood in misleading the people, in supporting the monarchy, and in promoting violence. Its boundaries are deliberately marked by mentioning the priests' involvement in murder at the beginning, where it might be considered pertinent, and at the end, where it is artificial and totally incongruous.[221]

The first tableau in Hosea's version is composed of four strophes in a narrative order that relates the various effects of ignorance and sin. In the first strophe ignorance of God is said to affect the birds, the fish, the animals, and the inhabitants of the world. In the second strophe ignorance leads the people to abandon Yahweh and feed on sin without being satisfied. In the third strophe, led astray by the breeze, they abandon Yahweh to inquire of their idols and to worship in shady groves. In the last they are stubborn animals caught up in the wings of the wind that has deceived them.[222] The second tableau narrates successive stages in a pilgrimage. It has two matching strophes that portray an unclean people, ignorant of Yahweh and truly unrepentant, pretending to repent and being abandoned by Yahweh to their own devices.[223] The third tableau has an explanatory structure that describes the military situation in which Israel should have repented instead of entering into an alliance with Assyria, the pilgrimage and halfhearted repentance that they performed, and Yahweh's distress at their unwillingness and lack of knowledge.[224] Together the tableaux describe a sinful people that repented for the wrong reasons, in the wrong way, to the wrong God.

The revision took place by adding words, lines, stanzas, and strophes that reorganized the tableaux and changed the structure of the triptych. They interrupt the thematic flow of Hosea's work by combining clever allusions to the first triptych with jarring comments on their present context. Together they shift the blame from the people to the institutions that the editor was eager to reform.

In the first tableau strophes were modified, and two others were added in the same relative position in order to preserve the narrative structure while diverting attention from the ignorance of the people to the crimes of the priest and his family.[225] A few words were added to the first strophe to include crimes that the editor thought were typical of the priests.[226] The second strophe was added to introduce one of these priests and to interpret the wicked woman of the first triptych as his mother.[227] In the third strophe a stanza was added to shift the blame from the people to the priest.[228] A few lines were added in the fourth strophe to accuse this priest of ignorance and infidelity and to identify his daughters-in-law with the symbolic unfaithful wife of the opening triptych.[229] The fifth strophe resumes these themes and finally identifies the typical priest as the officiant at Bethel and Gilgal and Beersheba.[230]

In the second tableau the original was enclosed between two symmetrical strophes dealing with different issues. The first strophe implicated the priests and the kings in Hosea's critique by alluding to ancient crimes that they committed in particular places.[231] The second strophe changed original musings on Ephraim into an alarm summoning all the tribes to battle, and it required a corresponding change in the original complaint.[232] The effect of these changes was to shift attention from religious to historical issues, and from the failings of Ephraim, one of the children, to the crimes and punishment of all the children of Israel.[233]

The third tableau was changed by adding a final strophe that maintained and complemented the original structure.[234] The strophe interprets the expected pilgrimage and repentance of Ephraim as a pilgrimage by both Israel and Judah to Shechem under the guidance of unscrupulous priests. It has a tenuous connection with its context, but it continues and develops the revised edition's interest in providing a historical explanation of the downfall of Israel and Judah.

The third triptych (fig. 6a) also begins with a resumptive introduction. In Hosea's version this first strophe summarizes the basic point of the preceding triptych by recalling Yahweh's attempt to heal Israel and the incessant crimes that kept Israel from turning to him (Hos 7:1a, 2).[235] It also introduces, as the issue to be discussed in the rest of the triptych, the lies and deceitfulness of Samaria that Yahweh has uncovered. In the revised version the resumptive cross-reference consists in recalling the thievery of the priests, and the introduction is the extended metaphor of the mad baker, told to ridicule the kings and to begin this version's incessant diatribe against the monarchy.[236]

The first tableau in Hosea's version explains that Israel's alliances, despite their protestations to the contrary, violated their covenant with Yahweh. Its six strophes are arranged in the standard argumentative pattern, which outlines a situation and then analyzes it.[237] The first part argues that although the people lie and think that Yahweh will not find out or remember, Yahweh has found out about their alliances with Egypt and Assyria and does not believe them when they appeal to him. The second part responds to their appeal, accuses them of violating the covenant and taking the nations as lovers, and concludes that Yahweh will remember the wrongs they have done. The revised version preserved and enlarged the original argumentative pattern, but it argued a totally different point.[238] The lies that Hosea condemned are equated with palace intrigue (7:1b, 3–7). Foreign alliances are taken as the work of princes of the royal house (7:15–16). The only real fault of the people was choosing kings who established an idolatrous cult and engaged in disastrous wars (8:4–6, 14).[239]

In the second tableau Hosea described Israel's desperation when everything it did to avoid disaster brought it closer to its doom. The first part of the description traces their misfortune from the failure of their crops, through the lapsing of their rituals, to their final inability to cope with the day of Yahweh. In the second part, Israel itself is the crop that fails and falls and is finally destroyed.[240] The revised version added a few historical touches for the consistency of its argument, but it generally left the triptych unchanged. The effect is puzzling, but the rewriting managed to keep attention fixed on the editor's thesis that all of Israel's troubles could be traced to the dual evil of idolatry and kingship.[241]

The third tableau in Hosea's version follows the same descriptive pattern as the second. Israel is the produce of the land, whose altars and rituals flourished as the nation did, but its alliances with Assyria and its devotion to the calves of Samaria are weeds. When these symbolic calves have been taken as booty to Assyria, thorns and thistles will grow up over their altars, and Judah and Ephraim literally will be calves who once were spared but now will have to plow and harrow, sow the seed of justice and reap the harvest of fidelity, till the soil and wait for Yahweh's rain of pardon.[242] The revised version maintained the descriptive pattern but added stanzas and strophes to change the emphasis. It simply abandoned Hosea's image of a productive land gone to ruin for explicit and convoluted condemnations of kings and cults.[243]

The last triptych (fig. 6a) has the usual introductory summary that links it to what precedes and sets the tone for what is to follow. In Hosea's version the summary repeats that Yahweh might have healed Israel except that Israel was involved in offering sacrifice and persisted in making alliances with Egypt and Assyria.[244] The introduction is the story of Israel from infancy to maturity, which becomes a paradigm for the following stories of Jacob and Ephraim from their birth to their death.[245] In the revised version there is an added cross-reference to Israel's defeat in battle and to its reliance on useless idols, but the new introduction consists in foretelling Israel's return from exile.[246] The two have opposite perspectives, with Hosea insisting that Israel will not go back to Egypt but will suffer exile and die in Assyria, and the author of the book protesting that Israel will survive and return to Yahweh.

In the first tableau there are two strophes narrating the story of Israel. The first returns to Israel's childhood in Egypt and traces its history from the exodus to apostasy in the land. The second is like it in affirming the parent–child relationship between Yahweh and Israel, but it adds details on the journey through the wilderness and concludes that Israel will not return to Egypt but will be subject to Assyria.[247] The revised version simply pursued the story to its happy conclusion. It added a historical reason for the exile to refute Hosea's suggestion that Yahweh was Israel's natural parent and had simply abandoned it.

It added another strophe that made the same point by affirming that Yahweh would not abandon Israel because he is God and not human, and it appended a final strophe that confirmed that fact by describing Israel's return from exile in Egypt and Assyria.[248]

The second tableau is composed of four strophes that tell the story of Jacob and explain its repercussions both in Judah and in the troubled career of Ephraim.[249] The first strophe describes Ephraim's deceitful alliances with Egypt and Assyria and refers to Judah's independence and persistence in the unruly ways of Jacob. The second strophe explains Judah's character through anecdotes about Jacob and God, but attributes Ephraim's bad habits to the kind of life he led in the land of Canaan. The third strophe compares Ephraim's life in the land with living in tents in the wilderness, and contrasts the God who spoke to Jacob at Bethel with Yahweh, who brought Israel and Judah out of Egypt and spoke through the prophets. The last strophe contrasts Jacob, who took care of sheep to win a wife, and Yahweh, who took care of Israel through the prophets, with Ephraim, who did not care and was doomed to die. The natural history of Jacob, in this version, is an allegory of Judah's deceitfulness, while his metamorphosis as Israel is a metaphor of Ephraim's brilliant and disastrous career. In the revised version the tableau was left alone except for additions that removed Yahweh from the trauma of this family history and traced Ephraim's rejection to documented historical events.[250]

The third tableau is composed of four strophes that explain why Ephraim died. The first strophe attributes his death to the sin of worshiping Baal and sacrificing to the calves at Bethel. The second strophe blames his death on ignoring Yahweh, who brought him out of Egypt. The third says he was consumed because he grew fat, lazy, and forgetful in the land. The last traces his death to his lack of understanding and his unwillingness to count on Yahweh to be saved. In the first strophe Ephraim is a son of Israel; in the second he is vanity and emptiness; in the third he is a frisky calf that became a dumb ox; and in the fourth he is a child again without enough sense to be born. In the first his death was decreed; in the second he dissipates and disappears; in the third he is devoured by wild animals; and in the last he is a prisoner of Death and Sheol. With the death of Ephraim, and with the hope of resurrection on the third day, which Ephraim professed in the second triptych, the drama comes to an end.

The revised version attempted to suppress this dramatic effect by explaining the historical causes of the fall of the northern kingdom and by prescribing a more routine ritual that would remedy it.[251] The editor does not suppose that Ephraim died for his sins but thinks that Samaria was captured because Israel abandoned Yahweh and relied on its kings. The fall of the North cannot be resolved by relying on natural rites but through prayer and repentance. History, in the final analysis, is not like the cycles of nature.

The four triptychs are distinct and self-contained, related to each other in sequence by their introductory summaries, and arranged together in a comprehensive argumentative pattern. In both versions the first triptych is paradigmatic, covers the entire story from beginning to end, and introduces all the elements to be developed in the sequel. Hosea begins with Yahweh, the land, and their children, spends the second and third triptychs exploring the rituals associated with fertility and the loss of the land, and ends with the parent–child relationship between Yahweh and Israel. The book begins with the return from exile and the creation of a theocratic state, spends the second and third triptychs eliminating rival priestly and monarchic forms of government, and ends with the nation's return from exile and total allegiance to Yahweh.

LANGUAGE AND STYLE

Hosea's language is personal and concrete; his style is vivid and dramatic; and both vary from triptych to triptych. The revised edition attempts to imitate his work and inserts its comments by redoing his lines, but its language is more stilted and abstract, its sense of drama often overwhelmed by bombast.

In the first triptych the characters are Yahweh and Hosea, his wife and the children. In the first tableau Yahweh speaks to Hosea, who narrates the story and mimes the action. In the second tableau Yahweh speaks to the children about his wife, about his wife and children to Hosea, to his wife directly and indirectly and with a quotation of her response, and then in a monologue about his wife in past, present, and future tense.[252] In the third tableau Yahweh speaks to the woman, first in personal terms, and then in the discourse of heaven and earth (2:20a, 21–22 and 2:23–25). The action takes place in three different times: in the beginning in the first tableau, in the present in the second, and in the future in the third.[253] The stanzas are held together mainly by the repetition of words in the first tableau,[254] by rhyme in the second tableau,[255] and by rhyme and repetition in the third tableau.[256] The words are taken from the realm of family relationships, agriculture, ritual, and judicial procedure, and signify mainly physical and personal activities. The entire triptych unfolds the single lavish metaphor of marriage from its symbolic past to its final consummation.

The revised version made its changes by catchword and cross-reference.[257] The new introduction to the book begins with a formula that repeats in abstract terms the fact that Yahweh spoke to Hosea, but it substitutes the two kingdoms of Israel and Judah for the land that Yahweh married, and a precise chronology for the primordial past that Hosea presents.[258] The first time this edition talks about war it repeats Hosea's references to Israel and Jezreel, but it omits his mention of Jehu and the northern kingdom and refers more specifically to the valley of Jezreel. The second time, it contradicts Hosea's immediate claim that Yahweh will not have mercy and adds a cross-reference to its own inclusion of Judah. The third time, it simply summarizes the others.[259] Its prediction of the return from exile contradicts the immediate context, includes a cross-reference to the kingdoms of Israel and Judah, and becomes plausible in the context only by an incongruous attempt to identify the two kingdoms with the three children of the land.[260] The contrast between the ancient debacle in the *valley* of Achor and hope for the future has no basis in the immediate context but rather depends on a cross-reference to the earlier mention of the *valley* of Jezreel (2:17aB and 1:5).[261] The duplicate marriage returns to the beginning of the first tableau, where Yahweh spoke to Hosea, but it describes the sort of dickering that went on in dealing with prostitutes.[262] The editorializing is artificial and obvious, but it gives the finished text consistency and, by sheer insistence, makes contrary statements seem right.

The additions usually mimic the original dialogue sequence, but they tend to be vague, abstract, and reflective interruptions that contribute little to the dramatic action. The introduction uses substantives and cliches instead of the concrete and direct diction favored by Hosea. Hosea refers to the imminent punishment of specific crimes of Jehu but the editor is vague about the time and omits the specific culprit and the crime.[263] The interpolation that exempts Judah from the original merciless verdict against Israel maintains the dialogue pattern by continuing as a speech of Yahweh, but it is not addressed to Hosea or to anyone in particular, refers to Yahweh in the third person and interrupts the cycle of births to list the implements of war.[264] The first decree of restoration is expressed mostly in the passive voice and reflects on the drama without contributing to it (2:1–2). The abrupt reference to the valley of Achor creates a hiatus between Yahweh wooing the land and the land's response, and interrupts a physical relationship with talk of history and hope (2:17).[265] The duplicate marriage contains a mixture of concrete detail and theological speculation, but it comes at the end of the action and just summarizes the points made by the revision (3:1–5).

The revised edition is sparing in its use of repetition and rhyme[266] and favors compound or complex clauses with little or no adornment. Most of its interpolations contain subordinate clauses or compound listlike phrases and clauses.[267] Its preferred poetic features are assonance and alliteration, but it is often prosaic and plain.[268] The obvious divergences of this edition from Hosea's style are exaggerated by the editor's equally evident ability to copy the rhythm of the original.[269]

Hosea continues his dramatic style in the second triptych but abandons the narrative mode for dialogue and soliloquy. The revised version recognized the pattern but changed the plot and neglected the drama.

The opening strophe sets the scene and introduces the dramatic characters. Hosea speaks and describes the cosmic courtroom in which Yahweh is about to present his case against the people of Israel.[270] What follows in the first tableau is a series of interchanges between Yahweh and Hosea, with Yahweh speaking first and Hosea musing on what he says.[271] In the second strophe Yahweh complains that his people are perishing because they are like dumb animals grazing on sin, and Hosea reflects that they will never get their fill because they have abandoned Yahweh (4:6a, 7–8, 10). In the third strophe Yahweh bemoans their infidelity and their rituals in shady groves (4:12–13a), and in the fourth Hosea reflects that Israel is like a worshiper of the wind or like a stubborn heifer that refuses to graze in Yahweh's pasture (4:16–19). The second tableau is composed mostly of soliloquies in which Yahweh and Hosea consider Ephraim's useless and reprobate rituals.[272] Hosea does not appear in the third tableau, but in one soliloquy Yahweh muses about what to do with Ephraim; in another Yahweh decides what to do and Ephraim rehearses the rituals on which it relies; and in a concluding strophe Yahweh speaks to Ephraim about its inconsistency, and to the audience about Hosea and the prophets.[273]

The editor wrote threatening speeches for Yahweh and Hosea, but ignored or suppressed the dynamic interplay between them. In the first tableau Yahweh harangues the priest and his family, and Hosea is left to utter an editorial aside.[274] Hosea makes typical prophetic proclamations at the beginning and the end of the second tableau, and Yahweh admonishes or rebukes.[275] In the third tableau Hosea does not appear, as in the original, but Yahweh does not interact with Ephraim and instead goes over the history of Israel and issues a final warning (6:7–11). There are no musings and interpretations; the speeches are direct and argumentative; the measured dramatic interchange is replaced by stentorian briefs.

Hosea's text has rhyme and some literal repetition, but it relies mainly on interlinear assonance and alliteration.[276] This affects only two or three lines at a time and in any stanza can be combined with lines that are unique or blank.[277] Analogously, and unlike the first triptych, where narrative and consecutive clauses predominated, most of the original stanzas are composed of asyndetic clauses.[278] The revision, however, continues to use consecution and relies as before on compound clauses and complex sentences.[279] Since the editor can also imitate the style of the original, these differences are clearly deliberate and alert the reader to points in the ongoing interlinear argument.[280]

In the third triptych in Hosea's version the prophet himself assumes a leading role, most notably when he defends his mission and intervenes to demand redress.[281] His stanzas acquire their artistic cohesion less from assonance and alliteration and rhyme than from syllogistic reasoning and the constant deployment of proper names, personal pronouns, and pronominal suffixes. Proper names accumulate or are repeated in the same stanza (7:1a, 8–9, 11–12; 8:2–3; 9:13; 10:6, 11). Verbal clauses have pleonastic pronominal subjects (7:8–9, 13; 8:9; 10:2, 11), and lines are related and images are reinforced by repeated pronominal suffixes (7:2, 12, 13, 14; 8:11, 13abA; 9:11–12, 14; 10:1, 2). The syllogistic reasoning is a sort of sorites or inference drawn from a concatenation of images and events.[282] It is directed to proving that nothing is as it appears and, in fact, all of Hosea's text in this triptych has to do with lies and deception in worship and politics, in agriculture and human relations.

The revised version carefully imitated these mannerisms,[283] but it tried to show that all these evils could be traced to the kings who inaugurated and encouraged the worship of the calves at Bethel. It is interested not in the covenant or fertility but in the official cult and its promoters. At first it keeps to Hosea's sense that things are not what they should be, but it leaves his idyllic realm of natural commonplace occurrence for urban courtly existence and the world of institutions. Soon, however, it drops the pretense and inserts clear and incisive commentaries.

There are lines added to stanzas, or stanzas inserted in strophes, or entire strophes interpolated into tableaux,[284] and in each case they are justified by repetition or cross-reference. The repetitions are literal and contrary. Yahweh remembered the evil of Samaria, but this version refers to the evil of the priests.[285] Although Israel claimed to know Yahweh, it rejected the good, but in this version Yahweh claims not to know the kings and rejects the idols of Samaria.[286] Ephraim hired lovers, but this version dismisses the point.[287] Israel was punished for its rituals, but the book recalls what happened at Gibeah.[288] Hosea envisaged the nation with its hand to the plow looking forward to a new crop of righteousness, but the revised version uses the same words to condemn them for their reliance on arms.[289] The cross-references are intrusive and recall the book's general line of argument. The crimes of Samaria are glossed by reference to the crimes of the priests.[290] Foreign alliances are nothing compared to the pretensions of the monarchy.[291] The halfhearted repentance of the people is not as bad as the pretension and deceit of the court.[292] Israel made idols and forgot the God who made it.[293] All their evil began at Gilgal, and in the end they reject the king they tried to please.[294] All the new material is fitted in carefully as the book hammers home its point.

The drama reaches a climax when Hosea is rejected by the people, and he applauds as Yahweh describes to him the punishment that has been reserved for Ephraim. The first tableau begins with divine monologues that portray the nation calling to Yahweh for help but actually relying on Egypt and Assyria. The revised edition kept the focus on Yahweh but could not resist adding a prophetic disquisition and an editorial comment.[295] In the second part of the tableau Hosea quotes the prayer of the people that Yahweh rejected and contrasts their pretended trust in Yahweh with their actual reliance on the nations. The revised version added monologues in which Yahweh contradicted Hosea and put the blame on the kings and the royal cult.[296] In the second tableau Hosea announces the day of Yahweh, defends himself against the mockery of the people, and applauds as Yahweh explains to him what the day involves. The editor maintains the speech patterns of the original but blames the day of Yahweh on the kings and their cult.[297] In the last tableau Hosea describes the effects of the day of Yahweh; Yahweh intervenes with a lament of Ephraim, Judah, and Jacob; and Hosea concludes with a plea to the people to seek Yahweh. The editor generally follows the dramatic sequence but has Yahweh intervene to berate the monarchy.[298]

In the final triptych Hosea returns to the narrative mode of the first. The plot does not hinge on careful and detailed argumentation but is stated openly and revolves around stories about famous people in the past. The characters are Yahweh, Hosea, and the children. The topics are mostly those that have already been introduced in the earlier triptychs. The techniques include repetition and rhyme, assonance and alliteration, and pleonastic pronouns. The entire triptych is designed to resume the others and bring the prophecy to a successful conclusion.

In the first tableau Yahweh reminisces about Israel and Ephraim whom he loved and brought up and reluctantly lèt go. In the second tableau Yahweh bemoans the infidelity of Ephraim, and Hosea explains it with the story of Jacob. Yahweh recalls the exodus from Egypt, and Hosea compares it with Jacob's sojourn in Aram. In the last tableau Hosea recounts Ephraim's sin and exile, and Yahweh wonders how they could have abandoned him. Hosea compares them to a stupid child, and Yahweh thinks about saving them.

The revision added extended commentaries to the first and last tableaux and inserted other incidental remarks for the sake of the consistency of its argument.[299] It sets in with a barrage of cross-references to its argument about kings and idolatry, but instead of dealing only with the story at hand attempts to refute the entire drift of Hosea's prophecy. The story treats Yahweh as Israel's parent, but the revision insists that Yahweh is God and not human. Hosea described Yahweh as a lion lurking on the way to devour Ephraim, but the revision sees Yahweh as a lion roaring to summon Ephraim home. Hosea saw Ephraim as a silly dove flying from the country to Assyria, but the revision sees Ephraim as a dove returning from Egypt and Assyria to nestle in houses. The final commentary is just as incongruous in its effort to emphasize the point of the book. Ephraim is not a stupid child, as Hosea said, but just one brother among many. His death is not literal but refers to the casualties in Samaria. His redemption from Death and Sheol is a figure of repentance and resettlement in the land. The contradictions are obvious but justify the ways of God, and the reader will understand.

The revision appreciated Hosea's work, completely changed it, and was careful to make its revisions both obvious and compatible with the original. Hosea's prophecy was vivid, dramatic, and soon out-of-date. The revision was clear and authentic and seemed to ring true. Their movement *pari passu* is the meaning of the book.

SOURCES AND INTERPRETATION

The different language, style, structure, and organization in the two versions can be traced not only to different times and writers but also to different inspirations. The book treats Hosea's prophecy with respect and cites authorities to justify the radical changes that it makes. It demonstrates a certain familiarity with Amos and Ezekiel, but it is compacted mainly of quotations from Deuteronomy and the Deuteronomistic History. Hosea, similarly, created an original literary work but quoted contemporary historians, the authors of the epic and the sequel, the Priestly writer, and the Elohist, to develop his argument, and alluded to Isaiah and Amos to give his prophecy substance and credibility.

The first triptych in Hosea's version was composed with reference to historical texts on the covenant, the wilderness wanderings, and the occupation of the land. The revised version used some of the same texts but introduced notions derived from Deuteronomistic legal and patriarchal traditions.

In the first tableau, where quotations stand out as being anomalous in their context, the anomaly is in the names of the children, which are interpreted symbolically and, in contrast to the names of their mother and father, are filled with foreboding. They are all taken from other narrative contexts to which Hosea alludes later and in which they have a literal meaning that explains their symbolism in the present context. Jezreel, the name of the first child, is the place where Jehu assassinated Joram and Ahaziah. In the sequel's version of this story, Jehu was a usurper whose coup destroyed the alliance between Israel and Judah. This led to the wars between them, which were settled at first by foreign alliances but ended with the fall of Samaria and the Assyrian siege of Jerusalem.[300] Hosea understood it in the same way, as the beginning of the end for the kingdom of Israel and as a timely warning to Judah.[301] He gave the name Jezreel a negative connotation that it did not have in the source, but he returned to it later to explain its original positive symbolic sense.[302] The name "Unpitied," given to the second child, is taken from the prologue to the epic covenant on Sinai, where Yahweh declares that he is the God of pity. Hosea immediately quotes again from the same text, in which Yahweh also declared that he is forgiving, to insist that Yahweh will not forgive the northern kingdom.[303] These quotations contradict the source text, but they are confirmed by Hosea's repeated allusions to the epic covenant of mercy and fidelity[304] as well as to the crimes that undermine it[305] and to the threats of punishment that safeguard it.[306] The name of the last child, "Not My People," and its corollary that Yahweh is not their *Ehyeh*, is a quotation from the Elohist commentary on the same text. In the original epic version Yahweh declared that his name was "Yahweh, Yahweh," but in the Elohist version Moses tells the people that they are the people of God whose name is "Ehyeh . . . Ehyeh." The quotation contradicts the source, but it is confirmed by other quotations and allusions to the same text.[307]

The names of the three children signify the end of the northern kingdom and the abrogation of the covenant with Yahweh. In the third tableau, consequently, when Hosea describes the eventual restoration of Israel, he has to appeal to a different covenant. He continues to draw on the language of the epic,[308] but he takes the terms of the restored covenant from the Priestly version of the covenant with Noah. This is the eternal covenant that God made with Noah and his descendants, with the birds and the animals, and with all living things on the earth.[309] However, not only is it anomalous in the present context of courtship and marriage, but the quotation follows the order and terminology of the epic rather than the language and arrangement of the Priestly writer in describing them.[310] The quotation is confirmed at the beginning of the second triptych when Hosea repeats part of the list of creatures but also includes the fish of the sea, which the Priestly writer mentions and the epic ignores.[311] It is also supported in Hosea's opening words, which allude to the Priestly account of creation, and in the next strophe when Hosea refers to the Priestly order of created things.[312]

The second tableau alludes to the combined epic and Priestly stories of rebellion in the wilderness. The wife is mother earth, who thought that it was her lovers who gave her food and water to drink. In fact it was Yahweh, and in exasperation he has brought her into the wilderness to kill her with thirst. In every instance of rebellion in the wilderness the people fear that they will die in the wilderness, but in the epic version Dathan and Abiram accuse Moses of bringing them into the wilderness to kill them.[313] The allusion to this incident is supported by quotations from the same sources later in Hosea's text. The reconciliation between Yahweh and his wife takes place on a journey through the wilderness, and it includes, oddly enough, giving her "vineyards from there," contradicting Dathan and Abiram's complaint in the wilderness that Moses had not given them vineyards.[314] A constant theme in the Priestly story of the manna is having enough to eat, and later in the fourth triptych Hosea again refers to the time in the wilderness when Yahweh fed the people and they had enough to eat (Hos 13:5–6 and Exod 16:3, 8, 12).

In the same tableau Hosea mentions the clothing that Yahweh gave his wife, the oil that she needed, and the silver and gold that she used for Baal (2:7b, 10b, 11b). But he also includes the "grain, the wine, and the oil" and the vines and olive trees that she thought were gifts from her lovers (2:10, 14; see also 2:11; 7:14; 9:1–2). These are not particularly appropriate gifts for a woman, but they are the typical produce of a fertile land. They are an allusion to the sequel's decree of centralization according to which the tithes of "grain, wine, and oil" or their value in silver was to be offered to Yahweh in Jerusalem.[315] Hosea quotes from the same decree later, when he criticizes the people for eating meat and maintaining their local festivals instead of worshiping Yahweh in Jerusalem.[316]

The revised version alludes to some of the same texts but expresses itself in Deuteronomistic phraseology. When Hosea mentions Jehu in Jezreel, this author mentions the bow that Jehu used on that occasion but quotes the Deuteronomistic expression *"valley* of Jezreel."[317] When Hosea quotes from the early history of Moses in Midian, the revised version quotes a saying of Pharaoh from the same story, but instead of citing what Pharaoh also said in the same place about the large number of Israelites, it alludes to the typical patriarchal promises formulated by the Deuteronomist.[318] In other instances this edition simply relies on its system of cross-referencing to inject illustrations, such as the crime of Achan, or historical information, such as the synchronism of the kings, that it knew from the Deuteronomistic History.[319]

Its quotations are signaled in the usual way, but its language is typically Deuteronomistic. At the end of the first tableau, for instance, the revised version quotes from the book of Ezekiel to describe the restoration and reunification of Israel under one king. The quotation is anomalous in a text that predicts the destruction of the nation. It includes Judah and Israel in a context dealing with Israel; it inverts the order of the original text; and it rephrases Ezekiel in the official Deuteronomistic terminology for the installation of kings.[320] Toward the end of the third tableau the revised version quotes the decalogue's stipulations against adultery and covetousness. It is anomalous since it is quoted as part of a divine command; it is quoted as usual in opposite order; its Deuteronomistic derivation is confirmed both immediately, by a typically Deuteronomistic reference to the worship of other Gods, and at the beginning of the next triptych when other commandments of the decalogue are quoted.[321] The triptych ends with another quotation from the Deuteronomistic Historian. The editor and the source both suppose that Israel is in exile, but there the Deuteronomist depicts them enslaved in idolatry, while the author of the book imagines them finally removed from its occasion; there both agree, but in differing order, that they will seek Yahweh and eventually will return to Yahweh and serve him.[322] The quotation is confirmed by an allusion later in the book, where the author notes that, in spite of everything, Israel did not return to Yahweh or even seek him (7:10b; cf. Deut 4:29–30).

The second triptych in Hosea's version describes Ephraim's fascination with ritual, but it occasionally conceptualizes the problem in language original to Isaiah. The references are slight but clear and cumulative in their effect. The most obvious is Hosea's charge that Ephraim has gone after nonsense. The anomaly is its unintelligibility, although he explains in the next stanza that it means going to Assyria. It is an obvious reference to Isaiah's description of the Assyrians trying to learn Hebrew and speaking nonsense, and it quotes snippets of the text in opposite order. It is confirmed by Hosea's later references to the lies that Isaiah denounced in the same text, by his present allusion to the judgment with which Yahweh counters these lies, and by his final allusion to the dreadful covenant with Death and Sheol that Isaiah foresaw.[323] The triptych actually begins with another quotation from the same text where Isaiah summons the people to hear the word of Yahweh.[324] It is the only time that either prophet issues the summons, and it is one of the few times that Hosea steps out of his dramatic persona to speak directly to the people.[325] He differs from Isaiah in addressing the people and not their leaders, but his reliance on Isaiah's text is confirmed by an enigmatic saying at the end of the tableau, which seems to allude to the gist of Isaiah's message.[326]

Later in the first tableau Hosea abandons his description of the people's rituals to explain that their frustration is due to the fact that they have abandoned Yahweh. This is a quotation from Isaiah's opening discourse, in the usual opposite order, and it is confirmed by several allusions to the same discourse.[327] Isaiah refers to Israel as the children of Yahweh who have become estranged from him, and Hosea refers to the estranged children born to Ephraim.[328] Isaiah complains that Israel does not know Yahweh, and Hosea insists on the same topic.[329] Isaiah calls them sinful and burdened with guilt, and Hosea portrays them feeding on sin and guilt.[330] Isaiah describes their military defeat as a sickness or wound that has not been tended and will not heal, and Hosea refers to Ephraim's sickness and unhealed wounds.[331] Isaiah sees the Assyrians devouring their land, and later Hosea adapts the same image to Ephraim's alliances.[332] The triptych, finally, borrows an image from Isaiah's description of the Assyrian invaders and applies it directly to Yahweh, and the borrowing is confirmed by another allusion to the same passage later in the same triptych.[333]

The revised version adds another slight reference to the text of Isaiah[334] but depends mostly on the book of Amos and the Deuteronomistic History for its additions. The book of Amos is the basis of the editor's condemnation of the northern shrines and the priesthood at Bethel. The references in the revised version to the Deuteronomistic History are mainly to the end of the book of Judges and the beginning of the books of Samuel.[335] The most obvious reference to Amos is the exhortation to stay away from Gilgal and Bethel and to avoid swearing by the life of Yahweh.[336] The references to the Deuteronomistic History are found in the editor's pseudo-historical allusions to places associated with judges and kings. Mizpah and Tabor are mentioned in a warning to the kings and the priests. Gibeah, Ramah, and Bethel are listed in a proclamation to Judah, Benjamin, and Israel, but the references are vague and elusive. However, these are important places in the story of the Levite from Ephraim who traveled from Judah to Ramah and Gibeah in Benjamin and from there, after the assault on his wife, to the shrines at Bethel and Mizpah—a story that the Deuteronomistic Historian told as a balance and counterpoise to the story of Samuel and Saul and the origins of the monarchy.[337] The road to Shechem, where the priests robbed and murdered the unwary, is mentioned only in this edition and in the same Deuteronomistic story.[338] Gilead is not a city, as the editor seems to imply; but Jabesh-gilead was a city notorious for the atrocities that were committed against it, and it is crucial both in the story of the Levite and in the life of Saul.[339] Benjamin is the culprit in that story, and a slogan from the Song of Deborah is quoted by the editor to recall this fact.[340] Adam is the city associated with the crossing of the Jordan, but the book, with its penchant for tracing things to their origins, takes it as the place where they contravened the covenant.[341]

In the third triptych Hosea continues to cite Isaiah but also refers to Amos and the usual narrative sources. The revised version, similarly, mentions some of the same sources and refers to the book of Ezekiel but mainly persists in its reliance on the Deuteronomistic History.[342]

Hosea's quotations from Isaiah are from the same texts that appeared in the second triptych.[343] An obvious quotation from Amos is the strange contempt that Hosea expresses for justice because it flourishes like weeds in the furrows of the fields. However, the image occurs in his rebuke to those who worship at Bethel and, by its oddity, refers the reader to a precedent in Amos.[344] A no less obvious quotation is his reference to the day of Yahweh. It is the day of assembly or the day dedicated to Yahweh, which, as Amos said, unexpectedly becomes a day of punishment or like a day of mourning for a child who has died. Amos described it as the antithesis of every ritual expectation, and Hosea typically sees it as the day the crops failed and the rituals finally ceased.[345]

In the third tableau Hosea uses an unusual idiom, "to display fruit," which he explains by saying that as Israel multiplied its fruit so it multiplied its altars and embellished its memorial stones. The whole passage is a quotation from the Priestly version of Yahweh's apparition at Bethel, where Jacob received the standard blessing "Be fruitful and multiply" and then proceeded to erect a memorial stone.[346] It is marked by the usual reversal of word order and is confirmed in the following triptych where Hosea quotes the Priestly statement that God spoke to Jacob at Bethel but takes it to mean that the God Bethel spoke to Jacob there.[347]

In the fourth triptych Hosea returns to the narrative sources and interweaves them with quotations from the prophets[348] to interpret the stories of Israel, Ephraim, and Jacob. In the story of Jacob in particular it is evident that Hosea could distinguish the Pentateuchal sources but was familiar with them in their combined form.[349] The revised version refers to some of the same sources but depends mainly on the Deuteronomistic History.[350]

Hosea was not alone in trying to understand why the North had fallen or what hope was left. The historians all had different solutions. The epic considered the history of Israel a marvelous journey filled with dangers and calamities. The Elohist was convinced of divine providence. The Priestly writer relied on the original promises to the patriarchs. The author of the sequel clung tenaciously to Jerusalem and the Davidic covenant. But the prophets were not convinced by these interpretations and were determined to draw the lesson for Judah. Isaiah was critical of the kings and filled with foreboding. Amos demanded legislative and social reform. But Hosea relived the drama of Israel as a family history, and his bold assumption that Yahweh was physically involved in the destiny of his people needed all the support it could get from tradition. In the end, however, it found none from the editor who revised his work and for whom all the issues had been resolved, less by the events than by their ready interpretation in the Deuteronomistic History.

Conclusion

Isaiah, Amos, and Hosea shaped the prophetic response to history. They were the models of prophetic form and became the heroes of the prophetic age. Isaiah was the poet who wrote prophecy that told a story and could be sung. Amos was the orator, the prophet who chanted, whose periodic declamations circled and recircled the vision to be cleared. Hosea was the dramatist who more than the others was engaged in his work. Together they had confronted the wisdom of their time and of historical tradition and had prevailed.

Their vision expanded outward from the narrow Judean point of view to include Israel and the world. The epic had an opposite focus and from God and creation and endless time concentrated on Yahweh and Israel in the immediate past. The sequel went further in its partiality and gloried in the greatness of Yahweh recently revealed to Judah and Jerusalem. Isaiah saw that Yahweh, despite his familial bond with Israel, despite the histories and what had happened, was not bound by their belief but would do the unheard of and astonishing truth. Everything that he saw took real shape in Amos, where Yahweh was revealed in worldwide reversals and where all that stood fixed was fate. But Hosea gave destiny a human face, his own and that of God, and fixed the dreadful day that Isaiah and Amos had predicted among the seasons of life and death and regeneration.

History goes on, but the prophets made their mark when what they said came true. Isaiah complained that no one was listening and wrote for a later time; Amos hoped that David and Zion would react; and Hosea envisioned the time when Israel and the good land would respond. Their mark was to be made for a time in the age of reform.

NOTES

[1] This progressive historicization of the prophetic tradition was recognized by H. Barth, who followed the example of the ancient editors in dating some of the material in Isaiah according to its subject matter rather than according to its relative position in the sequence of Judean literature (*Die Jesaja-Worte in der Josiazeit: Israel und Assur als Thema einer produktiven Neuinterpretation der Jesajaüberlieferung* [Neukirchen-Vluyn: Neukirchener Verlag, 1977]).

[2] Some of the material in this chapter appeared in *Law and Ideology in Monarchic Israel*, ed. B. Halpern and D. W. Hobson (JSOTSS 124; Sheffield: JSOT Press, 1991) 108–46, and is reused with the permission of the copyright holder, Sheffield Academic Press.

[3] The correspondence is marked by repetition of key words: 1:2 (*bānîm*); 1:4 (*bānîm mašḥîtîm*) and 30:1 (*bānîm sôrĕrîm*); 30:9 (*bānîm kĕḥāšîm / bānîm lōʾ ʾābû šĕmôaʿ tôrat yhwh*); also 1:8 (*wĕnôtĕrâ bat ṣiyyôn*) and 30:17 (*ʿad ʾim nôtartem*). Since the triptychs mirror each other there are also significant parallels between the first episodes in each part: cf. *ydʿ* (1:3; 28:9), *dbr* (1:3, 20; 28:11); *ʾbh šmʿ* (1:19; 28:12).

[4] The correspondences include Yahweh's labors on the vineyard and the city of David (Isa 5:1–2, 4–5; 29:1–4); feasts (5:11–12) and festivals (29:1); noise (5:11–12) and stupefaction (29:4, 9). The more obvious correspondences are marked by key words: *hôy* (5:11, 18; 29:1); *yyn* and *škr* (5:11; 29:9); *ʾmr* (5:19; 29:4).

[5] The literal correspondences between the two episodes include the approach of the enemy toward Jerusalem (10:28, 29, 32, *ʿbr . . . yĕrûšālayim*) and the warning to Jerusalem that an overwhelming scourge is approaching (28:14, 15, 18, *yĕrûšālayim . . . ʿbr*).

⁶ The analogy of writing-boards and books is suggested by Isaiah's text. His vision, in his own words, was written on tablets, in a book, for a later time (Isa 30:8) and was like a sealed book that no one could read or understand (Isa 29:11–12).

⁷ This text is presented as an alternative to the original vision of Isaiah (compare 1:1 and 2:1).

⁸ This text supposes the scouring and purification of the land that is described in 2:6–4:1 and is a correction and alternative to Isa 2:1–5. The lofty mountain that II Isaiah described is countered by the humiliation of everything that is lofty (cf. 2:1–3 and 2:9, 11, 12, 14). II Isaiah described Zion as a source of justice, but III Isaiah described the abolition of the judges and common decency (compare 2:3–4 and 3:1–5). II Isaiah called on the house of Jacob to walk in the ways of Yahweh (2:5), and III Isaiah said that Yahweh had rejected the house of Jacob (2:6). II Isaiah envisaged Zion as the center of the world (2:1–5), but III Isaiah reserved it for the purified remnant of Israel (4:2–6).

⁹ II Isaiah turned the episode into a formal indictment of the government of Judah and Jerusalem (3:13–15; 5:3, 6–10, 13, 20–24) and then described the historical context to which it seemed to belong and the birth of the king who would usher in the new era (6:1–11; 7:1–15; 8:1–15, 23°; 9:1–6abA).

¹⁰ Each time that II Isaiah said that warfare and desolation were a prelude to the restoration of the Davidic monarchy, III Isaiah countered with a reference to the purified remnant: Isa 6:12–13; 7:16–25; 8:16–23°; 9:7–20.

¹¹ The defeat of Assyria (II Isaiah: 10:15–19, 24–27, 33–34; III Isaiah: 10:8–12) is interpreted later as the overthrow of Babylon (II Isaiah: 14:1–21; III Isaiah: 14:22–27). II Isaiah is particularly concerned at this point with the restoration of the Davidic monarchy in Zion (11:1–10; 12:1–6), but III Isaiah is concerned more generally with the restoration of both kingdoms of Israel (10:1–4, 8–12, 20–23; 11:11–16). The conflict between Israel and Judah came to a climax in the Syro-Ephraimite war: it was mentioned by II Isaiah (7:1–15; 8:1–15, 23°), but was critical for III Isaiah (7:16–25; 8:16–23°; 9:7–20; 10:8–12; 28:1–8).

¹² Symptomatic of the editors' recognition of the relationship between the triptychs is III Isaiah's quotation (Isa 10:23) of II Isaiah's interpretation (Isa 28:22b) of Isaiah's judgment against Judah and Jerusalem (Isa 28:14–19).

¹³ Compare Isa 28:9 (*wĕ'et mî yābîn šĕmûʿâ*) and 28:19 (*hābîn šĕmû ʿâ*). The strophes are bound by repetition: 28:9–13 repeats part of the alphabet at the beginning and the end; 28:14–19 has *šmʿ* and a description of the covenant at the beginning and the end.

¹⁴ The accumulation of themes is marked by repetition of key words, for instance, from what Yahweh did for his vineyard (Isa 5:4, *ʿśh*) to what Yahweh

is doing (5:12, *ʿśh*), from "woe" to "woe" (5:11, 18), from doing quickly (5:19, *mhr*) to advancing quickly (5:26, *mhr*).

15 The accumulation of themes is marked by repetition of key words (Assyria's arrogance is manifested in its use of power [*yād*, Isa 10:5, 13, 14, 32]; Yahweh sent them against a nation and a people, but they set out to destroy many nations and peoples [10:6, 7, 13, 14]), or by correspondence of topics (sending and going, 10:6, 28), or by contrast (there was not a peep out of the nations [10:14], but the towns on the route of the Assyrian advance cry out [10:30]).

16 The episode begins and ends with the same key word (*yśp*, 29:1, 14) and with concrete and abstract descriptions of what Yahweh will do (29:2–3, 14). The first strophe mentions their voices and speech (29:4), and the second mentions reading (29:11–12) and mumbling (29:13).

17 The episode describes Jerusalem's reliance on Egypt instead of trusting in Yahweh. The first and last strophes (30:1–5, 8–17) deal with the military alliance, and the middle strophe deals with the effects of not listening to Yahweh and the prophet. All the strophes are bound by key-word links: cf. *bānîm śôrĕrîm* (30:1) and *bānîm kĕḥāśîm / bānîm lōʾ ʾābû śĕmôaʿ tôrat yhwh* (30:9); also *qĕdôś yiśrāʾēl* (30:11, 12, 15) and *lōʾ ʾăbîtem* (30:15).

18 The major changes at the beginning and the end of the episode (1:1aBb, 21–26) were facilitated by an added stanza in which Yahweh called on Judah and Jerusalem to learn the difference between right and wrong (1:16–17).

19 The additions (Isa 1:10–15) are made by adapting Isaiah's image of Zion's isolation (1:8, *wĕnôtĕrâ*) to III Isaiah's interest in the remnant (1:9, *hôtîr lānû*) and by calling on Sodom and Gomorrah as the archetypal evil cities from which Lot and no one else escaped. The new conclusion of the episode (1:27–31) takes up some key terms from the original beginning: cf. 1:28 (*pōśĕʿîm wĕḥaṭṭāʾîm . . . wĕʿōzĕbê yhwh*) and 1:2, 4 (*pāśĕʿû, gôy ḥōṭēʾ, ʿāzĕbû ʾet yhwh*).

20 The comments, obvious from their forensic interest, were added discretely and did not alter the original drift of the episode. They were prepared, as well, by inserting introductory strophes (2:1–5; 3:13–15) that established a juridical and forensic context for Isaiah's vision.

21 The III Isaiah texts ostensibly share II Isaiah's legal and forensic interests but in fact relate the episode to the preceding purge of Judah and Jerusalem (5:14–17; cf. 2:6–4:1, esp. 2:9, 11) and to the following decimation of Ephraim and Manasseh (5:25; cf. 9:7–10:4).

22 Isaiah's warning to Judah and Jerusalem (10:5–7) was anticipated in this version by another warning to Jacob (10:1–4), and his quotation of an Assyrian boast (10:13–14) was anticipated by another boast, which implicated Jerusalem in the wrong worship of Samaria (10:8–12). III Isaiah's theory of

the remnant (10:20–23) was inserted between the two parts of II Isaiah's vision of the destruction of Assyria (10:15–19, 24–27). The additions gave a different weight, complexity and literary context to the episode but did not change its overall narrative flow.

23 The conclusion deals with the terrible scourge announced by Isaiah by extending it to the whole world (28:20–22) and with the lesson that Isaiah tried to teach by including other lessons that suggested moderation in all things (28:23–29). III Isaiah did not deal with this conclusion but commented on the tempest that Isaiah announced (28:1–4; cf. 28:15, 17, 18) and on the foundation of faith and justice on which Zion would be built (28:5–6; cf. 28:16). The preface ends with an allusion to the stupefaction of the prophets (28:7–8) that Isaiah noted in the next episode.

24 The comments contradict (29:5–8; cf. 29:1–4; 29:17–21; cf. 29:11–12;) or modify the original (29:15–16, 22–24; cf. 29:9–14).

25 II Isaiah added another oracle against Egypt (30:6–7), which repeats the original and anticipates a later description of the primordial defeat of Egypt (cf. 51:9). III Isaiah added an analysis of the whole triptych (30:18–33), which contradicts the immediate context (cf. 30:17 and 30:18) but leads into the radical interpretation that follows (chaps. 31–35).

26 The strophes are arranged in an argumentative pattern in which the issue is presented (A = 1:2–3), argued (B = 1:4–6), explained (B' = 1:7abA, 8) and recapitulated (A' = 1:18–20).

27 The original title was 1:1a "The vision (ḥāzôn) of Isaiah the son of Amoz." II Isaiah specified the date and content of the vision by repeating that it was a vision (1:1b, "which he saw . . ." ['ăšer ḥāzâ . . .]).

28 Isaiah's summons began with an imperative and optative sequence (1:18, lĕkû nāʾ wĕniwwākĕḥâ) and described the cleansing of the people from sin. II Isaiah imitated the imperative with a sequence of nine imperatives (1:16–17) and spoke expressly of washing and scouring (1:16). This sequence of imperatives ended with the command to be a recourse for orphans and an advocate for widows (1:17), and the first strophe condemning the leaders ends with the fact that they did neither of these things (1:23).

29 The stanza (1:16–17) begins imaginatively and becomes gradually more discursive.

30 The shift in perspective and content is made by repeating parts of Isaiah's text. Isaiah said that the countryside was in ruins and that aliens had devoured it (1:7abA, šĕmāmâ . . . zārîm) and III Isaiah repeated the words and added another that alluded to the destruction of Sodom and Gomorrah (1:7bB, kĕmahpēkat). Isaiah said that Zion was left isolated (1:8, wĕnôtĕrâ), and III Isaiah said that if Yahweh had not left (1:9, hôtîr) a remnant the nation would have been like Sodom and Gomorrah. With these intrusions into the text III

Isaiah could proceed to imitate Isaiah's invocation (1:10; cf. 1:2) and redirect it to the leaders of Sodom and Gomorrah (1:10). But the list of rituals and festivals is hackneyed and, in this context, has nothing to do with the image that introduces it.

31 The addition begins by repeating part of II Isaiah's text (1:27, *mišpāṭ . . . ṣĕdāqâ*; cf. 1:21, 26) and part of Isaiah's text (1:28, *šeber pōšĕ'îm wĕḥaṭṭā'îm yaḥdāw wĕ'ōzĕbê yhwh yiklû*; cf. 1:2, 4, 6), although neither text is really germane to the interpretation in III Isaiah. The addition proceeds with a concatenation of images: there is a condemnation of terebinths and gardens (1:29), a comparison of the people with terebinths that wither or with gardens that have no water (1:30), and the image of an unquenchable fire destroying the tinder and the dried shoots (1:31).

32 The strophes are arranged in a narrative order. The song (A = 5:1–2) and its interpretation (A' = 5:4–5) supposedly take place at the festivals that are condemned (B = 5:11–12, 18–19) because these dull those who hear the song to its literal and imaginative meaning (B' = 5:26–29).

33 The text is inserted by deictics (proper nouns) and by repeating the word *karmî* (see 5:4).

34 The addition is made by using a deictic pronominal suffix (5:6, *wa'ăšî-tēhû*) and by repeating key words from the original (5:7; cf. 5:1b, *kerem*; 5:2, *nṭ'*; 5:2, *wayĕqaw*) and from the ongoing interpretation (5:7, *mišpāṭ, ṣĕdāqâ*; cf. 1:21–26; 2:3b–4a; 3:13–15).

35 In one instance (5:7a, the vineyard and the plantings) the imaginative usage is explained by a concept, and in the other (5:7b, *mišpāḥ* instead of *mišpāṭ*, and *ṣĕ'āqâ* instead of *ṣĕdāqâ*) the concept is explained by an imaginative pun.

36 II Isaiah lists specific examples of injustice (5:8–10): the passage begins like the passage it displaces (5:8, *hôy* = 5:11) and ends with the image of the vineyard that preceded it. A reference to the exile (5:13) supposes the preceding interpretation of the vineyard (5:13, "my people"; cf. 5:7, Israel and Judah; 5:13, "hunger and thirst"; cf. 5:10, one measure of wine, one measure of grain) but is added by anticipating the ignorance mentioned in the next stanza (5:13, *mibbĕlî da'at*; cf. 5:19, *wĕnēdā'â*). The final repudiation of the leaders of Judah and Jerusalem (5:20–24) imitates the form of the original (5:20, 21, 22, *hôy* = 5:18) and refers both to the original (5:22; cf. 5:11) and to the ongoing interpretation (5:23; cf. 5:7; 5:24, cf. 2:3).

37 The addition is made by repeating the first word of II Isaiah's explanation (5:14, *lākēn* = 5:13). Typical of the cluttering effect is the repetition of redundant concepts (e.g., 5:14, "and its important people and its crowds and its throngs and its dignitaries who are in it"), the concatenation of concepts (e.g., 5:15b–16a, "and the eyes of the high and mighty were brought low, and Yahweh of Hosts was high and mighty in judgment"), and the juxtaposition of

concepts and incongruous images (e.g., 5:16b–17, "and the holy God was holy in justice, and lambs grazed as in a pasture").

38 The passage is affixed to the original texts by repeating a variant (5:25, ʿal kēn) of the conjunction that began the last stanza in II Isaiah's text (5:24, lākēn). The reference to the anger and might of Yahweh (5:25a) becomes a refrain (5:25b) that marks stages in III Isaiah's text (cf. 9:11, 16, 20; 10:4).

39 The addition at this point (5:30) anticipates an addition to the biography of Isaiah (8:20–23°; cf. esp. 8:22) that minimizes the importance of the Davidic monarch (cf. 9:1–6) and keeps the mood of gloom and destruction alive. A similar function can be attributed to the refrain on the anger of Yahweh (5:25; 9:11, 16, 20; 10:4).

40 The strophes are arranged in a narrative sequence (A-A'-B-B') that portrays the situation from the time that the Assyrians are summoned until the day that they stand at the gates of Jerusalem. In each pair (10:5–7, 13–14; 10:28–29, 30–32) it is primarily the second strophe that abounds in images while the first sets the tone and explains the situation.

41 The first strophe (10:15–19) is attached to Isaiah's text by repeating its key terms (10:15b, ḥanîp, šēbeṭ, maṭṭeh; compare 10:5, šēbeṭ, maṭṭeh; 10:32, yĕnōpēp). It combines the image of a woodsman chopping down trees (10:15, 19) with the image of a fever (10:16a, 18) sent by Yahweh to devour the army (10:16b–17). The second strophe (10:24–27) uses some of the same key terms to explain that Yahweh's anger (10:25, zaʿam wĕʾappî; cf. 10:5) will turn against the Assyrians and destroy them as he used to destroy his enemies in the good old days.

42 This strophe begins like the beginning of Isaiah's text (10:1, hoy = 10:5) and includes two of its key terms (10:2, ʾll, bzz; cf. 10:6). The first stanza (10:1–2) gathers instances of injustice that are more typical of II Isaiah (cf., for instance, 1:16–17), seems to parody a later expression of Isaiah's (10:1, ḥqq and ktb; cf. Isa 30:8), and justifies the fall of the city to the Assyrians. The second stanza describes the desperate outcome of the siege (10:3–4a), and the third (10:4b) is the refrain that binds this episode to the preceding commentary.

43 The strophe begins (10:8, kî yōʾmar) like the beginning of the strophe it displaced (10:13, kî ʾāmar) and uses some of the same terms (10:10, kaʾăšer māṣĕʾâ yādî lĕ . . .; cf. 10:14, wattimṣāʾ kaqqēn yādî lĕ . . .; 10:11, ʿăšîtî; cf. 10:13, ʿăšîtî). It lists the places that the Assyrians boasted of having captured and compares them to Jerusalem and Samaria, and then compares Jerusalem and its fetishes to Samaria and its idols. It ends, rather incongruously but in imitation of the commentary in II Isaiah (cf. 10:15–19), with Yahweh humbling the pride of the Assyrians (10:12).

44 This commentary (10:20–23) was added with the help of a deictic clause (10:20, wĕhāyâ bayyôm hahûʾ) and by repeating a word from II Isaiah's text in an opposite context (10:19, šĕʾār = 10:20, 21, 22).

⁴⁵ The talk (28:10) is made up of words that amount to gibberish, but it has four consonants in their proper order (*ṣ* + *q* + *r* + *š*) and, by its repetitive and mnemonic form, might be an apt means of teaching the alphabet (see W. W. Hallo, "Isaiah 29:9–13 and the Ugaritic Abecedaries," *JBL* 77 [1958] 324–38).

⁴⁶ The addressees (28:14) are *'anšê lāṣôn* (= "interpreters" [cf. Gen 42:23] or "satirists") and *mōšělê hā'ām hazzeh* (= "allegorists," from *mšl* II, "proverb, parable, allegory"). In the context of foreigners speaking gibberish to them (28:11) it is fair to suggest that the interpreters speak in riddles.

⁴⁷ The fifth scene associates their pact with Sheol (28:15, *ḥōzeh*; 28:18, *ḥāzûtĕkem*) with visionaries (cf. 29:10, *ḥōzîm*) who cannot comprehend the prophecy (29:11, *ḥāzût*). The sixth scene relates it to their reliance on Egypt (cf. 30:2, they "go down" to Egypt and do not inquire [*š'l*] of Yahweh; they take shelter in the shade of Egypt as they took shelter in a lie [*ḥsh*]).

⁴⁸ The allegory is interpreted in the sixth scene. II Isaiah's interpretation of it was introduced into the first part (cf. Isa 8:14–15).

⁴⁹ The strophe is linked to the original by repeating its introductory conjunction (*kî*, 28:19, 20) and a variant of one of its terms (28:22, *'al titlôṣāṣû*; cf. 28:14, *'ānšê lāṣôn*). It begins by interpreting Isaiah's reference to morning, evening, and nighttime (28:19) in terms of fitful sleep on a bed that is too short with coverlets that are too narrow (28:20). This is joined without comment to a reference to battles recorded in the Deuteronomistic History (28:21; cf. Josh 10:12–13; 2 Sam 5:17–21) and to an allusion to captivity (28:22a). The images are explained by saying that God is doing strange things (28:21b; cf. 28:11) and that God has decreed destruction upon the whole world (28:22b).

⁵⁰ The passage is linked to the original by a pun on its key terms (28:8, *qî' ṣō'â* = 28:10, 13 *ṣāw . . . qāw* in opposite order); this link is recognized and interpreted differently by B. Halpern, " 'The Excremental Vision': The Doomed Priests of Doom in Isaiah 28," *HAR* 10 (1986) 109–21.

⁵¹ Isaiah's storm imagery is taken up by repeating some of its words (28:2, *brd*, *mym*, *štp*; cf. 28:15, 17, 18). The clutter of images and ideas results from combining this image of a storm with allusions to the first part of Isaiah's vision and with the description of Ephraim both as a drunken person and as a fertile valley in the wine-growing district. It is extremely clever but clearly too much for the language to bear.

⁵² The lifting of the siege is concretely a visitation from Yahweh and imaginatively a storm blowing away chaff (29:5–6). The siege, similarly, is a fact and like a nightmare (29:7–8). The strophe was added to the original by repeating the beginning of its last clause (*wĕhāyâ kĕ*, 29:4, 5).

⁵³ The strophe (29:15–16) was added by repeating the last word of the original text in a different form and meaning (29:14, *tistattār*; 29:15, *lastîr*).

54 The strophe follows naturally on II Isaiah's first strophe and comments on Isaiah's text by repeating some of its words (ḏibrê ṣēper, 29:18, cf. 29:11; ʿênê, 29:18, cf. 29:10) and by transposing some of its themes (darkness, 29:10, 18; people who should instruct and who in fact mislead, 29:10–11, 20–21).

55 Quotations are a form of repetition and consist of words that (1) are unusual or anomalous in their present context, and that (2) are repeated in an opposite order or contrary sense from another text which (a) explains both the words and the present context, and (b) is quoted again or alluded to elsewhere in the present context. Allusions are a form of cross-reference and comprise groups of words that are distributed in their present context but that are peculiar to another context where they are combined and explained.

56 The references to the people as children (1:2, bānîm) may mean as children of Israel (cf. 1:4, zeraʿ mĕrēʿîm // bānîm maṣḥîtîm). However, the father–son relationship also expresses political dependence (2 Sam 7:14; 2 Kgs 16:7), and the contrast between Israel and domestic animals who know their masters may imply such a treaty relationship between Israel and Yahweh.

57 According to the epic covenant, Yahweh will drive out the inhabitants of the land and no one will have designs on it when they celebrate the annual festivals before Yahweh (Exod 34:11, 24). In Isaiah's text the land and countryside — once a garden and vineyard — are devastated (1:7abA), and the people will continue to enjoy its produce only if they stop their rebellion and begin to listen (1:18–19).

58 Isaiah notes "Yahweh is speaking" (1:2, kî yhwh ḏibbēr), "says Yahweh" (1:18, yōʾmar yhwh), and "for the mouth of Yahweh is speaking" (1:20, kî pî yhwh ḏibbēr); and the epic covenant concludes (Exod 34:27) with Yahweh speaking to Moses (wayyōʾmer yhwh) and instructing him: "Write these words (ʾet haddĕbārîm hāʾēlleh) for yourself because according to the letter of these words (kî ʿal pî haddĕbārîm hāʾēlleh) I have made a covenant with you and with Israel." This qualifies as a quotation since it repeats the same words in an opposite order and in a contrasting context, as an agreement in the epic, as a dispute in Isaiah.

59 Cf. Exod 34:7, ʿāwōn, peṣaʿ, ḥaṭṭāʾâ; and Isa 1:2, 4, pṣʿ, ḥṭʾ, ʿwn).

60 The rebellion is a violation of the covenant (Num 14:13–19). It consists in not believing in Yahweh and in rejecting him (Num 14:11, nʾṣ) and, as a result, Yahweh proposes to strike (nkh) the people (ʿām) with a plague and make Moses a nation (gôy) in their place (Num 14:12). In Isaiah's text the charge is that the nation (gôy), or the people (ʿām), has rejected (nʾṣ) Yahweh, and the result is that they have been struck (nkh) and are afflicted with running sores (1:4–6).

61 Military imagery is found in all the episodes: reference to wounds (1:5–6), siege (1:7; 29:1–3), and the sword (1:20); a description of an advancing army (5:26–29), the reaction of the towns in its path (10:28–32; 28:15, 18),

and of a defeated army in disarray (30:15–17). The bucolic imagery includes a comparison between children and domestic animals (1:3), between the burden of sin and laden oxcarts (5:18), the vineyard that is trampled by cattle (5:5), the conqueror as a bull or a scavenger who steals eggs from abandoned nests (10:13–14). The georgic imagery includes an interest in vineyards and gardens (1:8, 19; 5:1–2).

[62] In the first episode Isaiah refers to the education of children (1:2), to their lack of understanding (1:3), and to the uses of argumentation (1:18). The second episode has an explicit question-and-answer lesson (5:4–5) and makes the connection between observation and catching on (5:11–12, 18–19). The third episode describes the thinking of the king of Assyria (10:7, 13–14). The fourth episode reflects on the educational process (28:9–13); the fifth refers to the ability to read and write (29:11–12) and to the rules learned in school (29:13–14); and the sixth records the vision in a book because the people have refused instruction (30:8–9).

[63] Isaiah's text demonstrates familiarity with topics and themes of Assyrian literature. As in Assyrian treaties, the covenant is made in the presence of heaven and earth (Isa 1:2); violation of the covenant is a sin (1:4); halfhearted service is a crime (29:13); incurable wounds are an effect of covenant curses (1:5–6); children bear the brunt of their elders' sins (1:4) (see S. Parpola and K. Watanabe, *Neo-Assyrian Treaties and Loyalty Oaths* [State Archives of Assyria 2; Helsinki: Helsinki University, 1988] passim). The description of the country ravaged by an invader, on the other hand, is indebted to Assyrian annalistic writing (see P. Machinist, "Assyria and its Image in the First Isaiah," *JAOS* 103 [1983] 719–37).

[64] The description of untended wounds suggests a physician's skills (1:5–6), and Yahweh's argument with the people is based on knowledge of the fuller's trade (1:18). He describes the music at a typical festival (5:11–12), the construction and collapse of a wall (28:16–17; 30:13–14), and the art of the necromancer (29:4).

[65] II Isaiah agrees with the sequel in listing only the Judean kings and omitting synchronisms with the kings of Israel (cf. 2 Kgs 14:21; 15:7, 38; 16:20), but he knows the Deuteronomistic History's form of the list (including Uzziah [2 Kgs 15:32, 34] instead of Azariah [2 Kgs 14:21; 15:7]).

[66] The Deuteronomist has a special interest in orphans and widows among the nations dispossessed (e.g., Deut 14:29; 16:11, 14; 24:19; 26:12, 13) and, like II Isaiah, talks about their rights (*špṭ*, Isa 1:17; Deut 24:17 [cf. Exod 22:21]; 27:19). The Deuteronomist attributed Israel's abandonment of Yahweh to their evil ways (Deut 28:20, *rōaʿ maʿălālêkā ʾăšer ʿăzabtānî*), and II Isaiah comments on their abandonment of Yahweh as the evil of their ways (Isa 1:16, *rōaʿ maʿalêlêkem*).

[67] The list of crimes in Isa 1:21–23 (*znh, rṣḥ, gnb, šḥd*) corresponds to the list of crimes in the latter part of the decalogue (Deut 5:17–20, *rṣḥ, nʾp, gnb, ʿēd šawʾ*).

68 In the Deuteronomistic History judges were the ideal leaders under the monarchic rule of God (cf. 1 Samuel 8), and the era of the judges foreshadowed the postmonarchic period.

69 Isa 1:21a, *zônâ*; Nah 3:4, *zônâ*. Isa 1:24b (*hôy 'ennāḥēm miṣṣāray / wĕ'innāqĕmâ mēʾôyĕbay*) repeats Nah 1:2 (*nōqēm yhwh lĕṣārāyw / wĕnôṭēr hûʾ lĕʾōyĕbāyw*) in a partially opposite order.

70 The themes are presented synthetically at first (Isa 1:21–26; 2:1–5; 11:1–10) and in their separate elements later in the work of II Isaiah, where the servant, returning to Zion from exile, becomes in the manner of David the source of justice and peace for all the nations of the world: cf. Isa 42:1–4; 49:1–18; 51:1–11; 52:13–53:12; 55:1–5.

71 The comparison of Zion with Sodom and Gomorrah (1:7, 9–10) is taken from the Deuteronomistic prediction of the result of worshiping other Gods (Deut 29:22–27). The idea of the remnant is taken from the Deuteronomistic description of the effects of disobedience (Isa 1:9, *hôtîr lānû śārîd kim'āṭ*; cf. Deut 28:62, *wĕniśʾartem bimtê mĕʾāṭ*). The reference to the rulers of Sodom and Gomorrah (Isa 1:10, *śimʿû dĕbar yhwh qĕṣînê sĕdōm*) is from Micah (Mic 3:1, *śimʿû nāʾ . . . qĕṣînê bêt yiśrāʾēl*). Both texts introduce a list of sacrificial practices, and each concludes with Yahweh's declaration that he will hide himself and not answer their prayers (cf. Isa 1:10–15; Mic 3:1–4). The list of festivals and offerings (Isa 1:10–15) corresponds to the Deuteronomistic list in Numbers (Chaps. 7; 28–29), and the negative attitude toward them has precedents in Amos (5:21) and Micah (6:6–8). III Isaiah's condemnation of the gardens of Adonis (Isa 1:29; 65:3; 66:17) and of worship under the oaks (1:29; 57:5; 61:3) and the comparison with an oak that is used for ritual purposes and then burned (Isa 1:30; 2:13; 6:13; 44:14) are typical of his interest in purifying the cult and eliminating all of its alien elements.

72 In the last scene Isaiah quotes his hearers as saying that they enjoy such light entertainment but cannot stand reproof (Isa 30:10).

73 Exod 14:31 mentions seeing (*rʾh*) and doing (*ʿśh*).

74 Exod 34:10 mentions seeing (*rʾh*) and doing (*ʿśh* [three times]).

75 Balaam is a visionary (Num 24:3–4), and there is considerable concentration on what he saw (*rāʾâ*, Num 23:9, 21; 24:2; *nbṭ*, 23:21). The image of the lioness is applied to the people (Num 23:24) and to Yahweh (Num 24:9). The deeds of Yahweh (Num 23:23 *pʿl*) cannot be undone.

76 The scene insists on seeing and doing and knowing. In the song of the vineyard the singer wonders what more could have been done for the vineyard (Isa 5:4–5 has "do" [*ʿśh*] five times). The revelers are reproved for hearing the song but not perceiving (*nbṭ*) the deeds (*pʿl*) of Yahweh (5:12) or noticing (*rʾh*) what he is doing (5:12, *ʿśh*). They reply that Yahweh should hurry up and act (*ʿśh*) so that they can see it (5:19, *rʾh*).

77 The vineyard is Israel, the northern kingdom. The Assyrian threat to Jerusalem begins at the end of the scene (5:26–29) and is the topic of the third scene. The metaphor was understood in this sense by II Isaiah but was applied to Judah (5:7). III Isaiah understood it in its original reference to the North (7:17; 9:7–20).

78 The genre is changed antecedently by establishing Zion as a court (Isa 2:1–5) and Yahweh as judge in the case against the elders and princes who have ruined the vineyard (3:13–15). It is changed in the episode itself by appealing to the people of Judah and Jerusalem as witnesses (5:3) and by identifying the culprits and their crimes in general (5:6–7, 20–24) and in particular (5:8–10).

79 II Isaiah added Isa 6:1–11; 7:1–3aAb, 4–15; 8:1–15, 23°; 9:1–6abA, which trace events from the time of Uzziah to the time of the successor of Ahaz, presently unnamed but eventually identified as Hezekiah (Isaiah 36–39), who is the model of the Davidic kings.

80 II Isaiah's main source was Isaiah and a considerable amount of the revised text is a paraphrase of Isaiah's fourth scene (for example, compare Isa 8:5–15 and 28:13, 14–19). The temple vision (Isa 6:1–11) owes a lot to Ezekiel's vision (Ezekiel 1°) and to the vision of Micaiah ben Imlah in the Deuteronomistic History (1 Kings 22). The fact that the people did not notice what was happening and did not listen was emphasized by Isaiah, but this version (Isa 6:10) depends on a saying in Jeremiah (Jer 5:21). II Isaiah also quotes from the original and Deuteronomistic introductions to the Syro-Ephraimite war (Isa 7:1 = 2 Kgs 15:37; 16:1, 5) but conflates it with circumstances of the Assyrian invasion in the time of Hezekiah (Isa 7:3b = 2 Kgs 18:17b = Isa 36:2b).

81 Every time that II Isaiah insinuates or says that the Davidic dynasty will be restored (Isa 2:1–5; Chaps. 6°–9°; 11:1–10) III Isaiah counters with the notion of a remnant (2:6–4:6; 6:12–13; 7:16–25; 8:16–23°; 9:7–20). One of the sources of this notion is the Deuteronomistic interpretation of the siege of Jerusalem by Sennacherib, which concludes with the promise of a remnant (2 Kgs 19:29–31), and III Isaiah counters the Immanuel oracle (Isa 9:1–6abA) by quoting from it (9:6bB, *qinʾat yhwh ṣĕbāʾôt taʿăśeh zōʾt* = 2 Kgs 19:31b).

82 This scene, like the second, refers to the trampling of the country (*mirmās*, 5:5; 10:6), describes the advance of the enemy forces (5:26–29; 10:28–32), and refers to the actions of its principal characters (ʿśh, 5:4–5, 12, 19; 10:13) and, like the first, refers to the gift of understanding (*byn*, 1:3; 10:13).

83 Esarhaddon's annalists had the same idea when they attributed Sennacherib's despoliation of Babylon to the anger of Marduk (see J. A. Brinkman, "Through a Glass Darkly: Esarhaddon's Retrospects on the Downfall of Babylon," *JAOS* 103 ([1983] 35–42).

84 Isaiah says that Assyria is the rod of Yahweh's anger and that the stick

of his renunciation (*z^cm*) is in their hands (Isa 10:5). In the first of Balaam's oracles the epic has him say that he cannot renounce what Yahweh has not renounced (Num 23:7–8, *z^cm* [three times]).

[85] II Isaiah repeats the words "rod" and "staff" from the immediate context (10:15b, 24, 26; cf. 10:5) and says explicitly that Yahweh's anger and renunciation will come to an end (10:25; cf. 10:5). This version also refers to the song of the vineyard as Isaiah wrote it (5:1, *šāmen*; cf. 10:16, *mišmannāyw*; 10:27, *mippĕnê šāmen*) and as it was revised (*šîtô ûšĕmîrô*, 5:6; 10:17 [opposite order]), and to a key term that Isaiah used in the next episode (*šôṭ*, 10:26; cf. 28:15, 18). The reference to the Priestly writer is the mention of the staff that will be lifted up against the Sea in the manner of Egypt (Isa 10:26b), which repeats the key exercise of the parting and surging of the waters during the exodus (Exod 14:16, 26). There is an explicit reference to the Deuteronomistic story of Gideon (Isa 10:26 = Judg 7:25) and an allusion to the boasting of Sennacherib during the battle of Jerusalem. In this version (2 Kgs 19:21–28) the boasting is taken as blasphemy (19:22) but also includes Sennacherib's claim that he went up to Lebanon and destroyed its forests (2 Kgs 19:23, *ya^car karmillô*); II Isaiah compares Assyrian boasting to an axe or a saw vaunting itself over the one who wields it, refers to the destruction of the Assyrian forest (Isa 10:18, 19, *ya^crô wĕkarmillô* . . . *^cĕṣ ya^crô*), and to the heights of Lebanon (Isa 10:33–34; cf. 2 Kgs 19:23), and contrasts the ruin of this forest with the sprout from the stump of Jesse (Isa 11:1).

[86] The references to Isaiah are slight (e.g., 10:2b = 10:6b). He counters II Isaiah's reference to Gideon with another from the Song of Deborah quoted in an opposite sense (10:1, *hôy haḥōqĕqîm ḥiqĕqê 'āwen*; cf. Judg 5:9, 15, *ḥōqĕqê* . . . *ḥiqĕqê*). He reapplies words of II Isaiah from Assyria to Israel: II Isaiah described the writing of the name "Booty-and-Spoil" to indicate the imminent defeat of Damascus and Samaria (Isa 8:1–4) but III Isaiah refers to the those who wrote the name as the ones who took spoil and booty from the unsuspecting (10:1–2). II Isaiah referred to the glory of the Assyrian invaders (10:18), and III Isaiah refers to the glory of Israel (10:3). II Isaiah referred to the remnant of the Assyrian forest (10:19), and III Isaiah refers to the remnant of Jacob (10:20–22). II Isaiah referred to the blows from an Assyrian enemy (10:24b), and III Isaiah refers to the Assyrians as allies (10:20b). II Isaiah gave the expected Davidic king the title of Divine Warrior (*'ēl gibbôr*, Isa 9:5), but III Isaiah reserves the title for God (Isa 10:21; cf. Deut 10:17). II Isaiah mentioned the destruction of the whole world, but III Isaiah made it a complete destruction of part of the world (Isa 10:23 = Isa 28:22b). These changes were made with the help of literary and historical tradition. II Isaiah used Assyrian boasting during the battle of Jerusalem to predict Yahweh's defeat of the Assyrians, and III Isaiah used a text from Micah and another version of their boasting during this battle to convict Jerusalem of idolatry (Isa 10:9–11 = Mic 1:7 + 2 Kgs 18:33–35; cf. Isa 36:18–20). In reply to this boasting the Deuteronomist had given God's assurance that survivors and a remnant would remain in Judah and Jerusalem (2 Kgs 19:30–31), and III Isaiah refers to the same assurance (Isa 10:20). Isaiah had seen the Assyrians coming against the land to take booty (10:6b), but III Isaiah, relying on Amos

and Jeremiah, described the local government taking booty from the poor and unfortunate (Isa 10:2; cf. Amos 2:7; Jer 5:28).

[87] Isaiah's speech (28:9–13) has to do with learning (*yrh*), knowing (*yd*ʿ), understanding (*byn*), listening (*šmʿ*), speaking (*dbr*) and saying (*'mr*). Two lines of gibberish—that is, seeming meaning in rapid repetitive nonsense—are repeated near the beginning and the end (28:10, 13a), and the only parts that make sense are the lesson that Yahweh taught (28:9a, 12a) and the penalty for not listening (28:11, 13b). Yahweh's speech (28:14–19) has to do with speaking (*dbr*), saying (*'mr*), listening (*šmʿ*) and understanding (*byn*). It contrasts the riddle going the rounds in Jerusalem with the solution that Yahweh proposes: the riddle is told near the start (28:15), solved in the middle (28:16–17), and rejected at the end (28:18).

[88] Cf. *ʿāyēp* and °*kšl* in Isa 5:27 and 28:12, 13. Other military terms from Isa 5:26–28 (*nws*, *sûs*, *qāl*) are taken up in the last scene to describe the impending defeat (cf. Isa 30:16).

[89] Cf. *ʿbr* in Isa 10:28–29 and 28:15, 18–19.

[90] Cf. *mirmās* in Isa 5:5; 10:6; 28:18.

[91] Cf. *ḥwš* in Isa 5:19 and 28:16.

[92] Isaiah compares the children to domestic animals (1:2–3), describes the beating they have received (*nkh*, 1:4–6), and refers to Assyria as a staff, a stick (*šēbeṭ*, *maṭṭeh*, 10:5) and a whip (*šôṭ*, 28:15, 18). II Isaiah ascribed the beating to the staff (10:24, *šēbeṭ*, *nkh*) and associated the stick with the whip (10:26, "Yahweh will wield a whip [*šôṭ*], as when he beat [*nkh*] Midian at the Rock of Oreb, and his stick [*maṭṭēhû*] will be over the sea . . ."). III Isaiah, in the context of I and II Isaiah's manipulation of these weapons, refers to the beating (*nkh*, 10:20) that Israel had received.

[93] Exod 14:31; 34:10–12, 14; Num 14:11; 16:29–30, 33a.

[94] The covenant was made according to the word of Yahweh (Exod 34:27), but Isaiah proposes another word of Yahweh (Isa 28:11, 13, 14) and refers to their covenant as taking refuge or hiding in a lie (Isa 28:15, 17, *kzb*, *šqr*). They are not only beaten in battle but trapped (°*yqš*, Isa 28:13; Exod 34:12b). Faith is not a basis of the covenant but its antithesis (Isa 28:16). Their reliance on a covenant with Death is a claim to its indissolubility, but in fact Isaiah sees it dissolved (Isa 28:18a). The loss of the land to aliens (Isa 28:11, 13b, 18b) is a repudiation of the covenant that assured them peaceful possession of the land (Exod 34:24).

[95] The saying "The bed is too short to stretch out, and the coverlet (*wĕhammassēkâ*) too tight a wrapping" (Isa 28:20) contains a pun on the intrigues with Egypt that Isaiah condemned (30:1, *linsōk massēkâ*). The battles at Mount Perazim (Isa 28:21; 2 Sam 5:17–21) and at Gibeon (Isa 28:21; Josh

10:6–14) were won by Yahweh's amazing use of meteorological phenomena, the first involving water (*māyim*, 2 Sam 5:20; Isa 28:17), the second deploying rocks or hailstones (*'ăbānîm*, *'abnê bārād*, Josh 10:11; cf. *'eben*, *bārād*, Isa 28:16–17). The activity of Yahweh (*'śh*, Isa 28:21b) is a theme of the first part of Isaiah (5:4–5, 12, 19). The aliens (28:21, *zār*, *nokriyyâh*) were responsible for the destruction of the land in the first episode (1:7). The scoffers or doubters (28:22, *'al titlôṣāṣû*) are modeled on the diplomats of Jerusalem who told lies (28:14, *'anśê lāṣôn*), and the instruction they receive (28:22, *môsrêkem*) is another lesson from Yahweh (28:9, *yôreh*). The destruction that has been decreed against the whole world (28:22b) removes the emphasis that Isaiah had put on the ruin of Jerusalem.

96 In commenting on Isaiah's vision of approaching disaster (28:15, 18, *śôṭ śôṭēp kî ya'ăbōr*; cf. Nah 1:8, *ûbĕśeṭep 'ōbēr*), Nahum described a theophany in which Yahweh would come against his enemies in natural phenomena, in a tempest and storm (Nah 1:3, *bĕsûpâ ûbiś'ārâ darkô*; cf. Isa 29:6 *sûpâ ûsĕ'ārâ*), with dust under his feet (Nah 1:3, *'ăbaq*; cf. Isa 29:5), ravaging the world with earthquake and fire (Nah 1:5–6, *r'ś's*; cf. Isa 29:6). Ezekiel also described the appearance of God in the sound of a mighty rumbling (Ezek 3:12, *qôl ra'aś gādôl*; cf. Isa 29:6, *ûbĕra'aś wĕqôl gādôl*).

97 The same theme is developed in Isa 49:19–23.

98 The alliance is described in Isa 30:1–5 and explained in 30:9–11. Isaiah's decision to write down his vision (Isa 30:8 is like Yahweh's command to write down the words of the covenant (Exod 34:27–28abA).

99 The collapse of the wall (30:12–14) is explained in terms of the failure of Jerusalem's mutual assistance pact with Egypt (30:15–17).

100 The Deuteronomistic Historian, of course, took the opposite tack. This version introduces Isaiah explicitly into the debate (2 Kings 18–20), associates the lifting of the siege with his intervention, and makes Hezekiah antecedently responsible for the fall of the city to the Babylonians.

101 The ambassadors say that Hezekiah thinks that a word on the lips is sufficient planning and preparation for war (2 Kgs 18:20a, *'āmartā 'ak dĕbar śĕpātayim 'eṣâ ûgĕbûrâ lammilḥāmâ*). Isaiah had said that the people in Jerusalem relied on words and lip service (Isa 29:13a, *bĕpîw ûbiśpātāyw kibbĕdûnî*), that they made plans that were not Yahweh's (30:1a, *la'ăśôt 'eṣâ wĕlō' minnî*), and that they rejected trust in Yahweh as a preparation for war (30:15a, *bĕhaśqēṭ ûbĕbiṭḥâ tihyeh gĕbûratĕkem*).

102 Isaiah used the words "trust" and "reliance" (30:12, *wattibṭĕḥû . . . wattiśśā'ānû*), and the ambassadors say that the king trusted in Egypt even though it was unreliable (2 Kgs 18:21, *bāṭaḥtā lĕkā 'al miś'enet haqqāneh . . . 'al miṣrāyim*). The sequel, in its own right, refers to Tirhaqah as "king" (2 Kgs 19:9, *tirhāqâ melek kûś*), but puts Isaiah's words about "Pharaoh" into the mouth of the ambassadors (2 Kgs 18:21, *par'ōh melek miṣrāyim*; Isa 30:2–3, *mā'ôz par'ōh / ṣēl miṣrāyim*).

103 II Isaiah agrees with the sequel (see Isa 10:15–19; 29:15–16). The Deuteronomistic Historian turned the boasting into blasphemy (2 Kings 18–19), and III Isaiah followed suit (Isa 10:8–12; 30:18–33).

104 The covenant is called a blessing (2 Kgs 18:31, *bĕrākâ*). Its benefits are those described in Deuteronomy as the benefits of the covenant with Yahweh: vineyards and olive trees and cisterns (2 Kgs 18:31b; cf. Deut 6:11; 8:8); a land like their own (2 Kgs 18:32a; cf. Deut 11:10); a land of grain and wine, of oil and honey (2 Kgs 18:32; cf. Deut 8:8–9; 11:9, 14); a land that gives life (2 Kgs 18:32; Deut 8:1). Isaiah said the leaders refused to trust and be still and accept Yahweh's assurance of victory, but the Assyrians say that Hezekiah has repeated the assurance to the people and has encouraged them to trust and be quiet (Isa 30:15; 2 Kgs 18:30, 36).

105 Hezekiah's submission to Assyria in this version (2 Kgs 18:14–16) negates his purported confidence in the covenant, and the terms of his submission (2 Kgs 18:14a "I have sinned," *ḥāṭāʾtî*), reflect his recognition of the treaty that Ahaz had made with Assyria and suggest that Isaiah was correct in his judgment of the leaders (*ḥṭʾ*, Isa 1:4, 18; 5:18). Isaiah wrote his prophecy so that it would serve a later generation (Isa 30:8, 13), and the Deuteronomist did not hesitate to identify this time with the Babyonian exile (2 Kgs 20:17–19). The sequel put words in the mouth of the Assyrian ambassadors to ridicule Isaiah's position. The Deuteronomistic version introduced Isaiah into the episode and, by duplicating the embassy and giving him a major role in responding to their threats (2 Kgs 19:1–7, 9b–35), let him bring his own prophecy up to date. The Deuteronomist agreed with Isaiah on the importance of justice, but identified it with observance of the law (2 Kgs 18:4, 6), the extirpation of the worship of foreign Gods (2 Kgs 18:32b–35), and the worship of a transcendent God (2 Kgs 19:14–19). Consequently, it was for his observance of the law and not, as the sequel thought, for his defense of the covenant, that Hezekiah was famous (2 Kgs 18:6; 20:1–3).

106 II Isaiah made Isaiah and the Deuteronomist both seem right by composing a biography of the prophet and a new interpretation of history. This predated Isaiah's antagonism toward the monarchy to the reign of Ahaz and made him instrumental in foretelling the reign of Hezekiah (Isa 7:1–15; 8:1–15; 8:23°–9:6abA). Among the oracles to the nations II Isaiah also included a vision of the fall of Jerusalem that exonerated Hezekiah by blaming Shebna, the Judean secretary of state at the time of Sennacherib's siege of Jerusalem (2 Kgs 18:18, 26), for the official arrogance that Isaiah had blamed (Isa 22:1–24; cf. Isa 28:14–19). II Isaiah quoted the Deuteronomistic version of the Assyrian invasion (Isa 36–39 = 2 Kgs 18–20), but eased its conflict with the sequel by omitting its synchronisms, its exaltation of the law, its story of Hezekiah's capitulation, and anything that might mar the image of Hezekiah as the most faithful king in the line of David. This reconciliation of their views allows II Isaiah to praise Hezekiah and express continued confidence in the Davidic dynasty as the guarantors of fundamental justice without neglecting either Isaiah's vision and interpretation of history, or the synthesis of history, law, and prophecy that had recently been published by the Deuteronomistic Historian.

107 The Chronicler tried to combine the best of both historians, recording Hezekiah's building projects and cultic reforms as the Deuteronomist had done, but still insisting on the covenant and its festivals, ignoring his capitulation to Assyria, and omitting his confrontation with Isaiah, as the sequel had done.

108 See Joyce Rilett Wood, "Amos: Prophecy as a Performing Art and its Transformation in Book Culture" (Ph.D. thesis, University of Toronto, 1992).

109 There is a marked similarity between the oracles against the Arameans (1:3–5) and the oracle against the Philistines (1:6–8), and between the oracle against Ammon (1:13–15) and the oracle against Moab (2:1–3).

110 The connection between the oracle against Tyre (1:9–10) and the oracle against Edom (1:11–12) is marked by their concern for brotherhood (°ʾḥ, 1:9, 11) and by their common omissions.

111 The connection between the oracle against Judah (2:4–5) and the first part of the oracle against Israel (2:6–8) depends on the pairing of Israel and Judah in the superscription (1:1b). The oracle against Judah, however, unlike the oracle against Israel, maintains the basic form of the oracles.

112 Amos addressed Israel and Judah together as Israel, the people of Israel, and Jacob and, unlike his editor, did not refer to them separately as the kingdoms of Israel and Judah (1:1b; cf. 2:4–5 / 6–8). The motto (1:2) takes up the motif of the lion, which is the basis of the riddle in the second canto (3:3–6, 12) and is recalled in the description of the day of Yahweh (5:19) in the third canto.

113 The proclamations begin with the imperative of the verb ʃmʿ (3:1; 4:1; 5:1), are developed in different ways (3:1–2; 4:1–3; 5:1), and introduce different sorts of material (3:3–6, 9–12; 4:4–5; 5:2, 4–7).

114 The proclamation (3:1, ʃmʿ) is addressed to the children, or family, of Israel whom Yahweh brought out of Egypt (3:1), and it makes the puzzling announcement (3:2) that the riddle is meant to resolve. The riddle (3:3–6) points out that things do not go together unless they belong together (3:3), illustrates the point with rustic examples of cause and effect (3:4–5), and concludes by analogy that the punishment that befalls a city must be from Yahweh (3:6).

115 The summons to Ashdod and Egypt is followed by an accusation (3:10), a sentence (3:11), and an interpretation that relates it to the preceding riddle (3:12; cf. 3:3–6). Egypt is the place of Israel's origin (3:1) and is called to witness its obliteration. Ashdod (ʾaʃdôd) is a cipher for the violence of which Israel has been accused (3:10, ʃod) and for the devastation (°ʃādôd) decreed against it. Similar etymological puns on place-names include the association of Gilgal with exile (5:5, kî haggilgāl gālōh yigleh) and of Bethel, the "house of divinity," with vanity (5:5, ûbêt ʾēl yihyeh lěʾāwen), and the insinuation of a

commercial link between Samaria and Damascus (3:12). The devastation was accomplished by Assyria, and the cipher has been understood in this way (see F. I. Andersen and D. N. Freedman, *Amos* [AB 24A; Garden City, N.Y.: Doubleday, 1989] 402–6).

116 The proclamation (4:1, *šmᶜ*) is addressed to the women of Samaria and repeats against them in particular the charges that were laid against the city in general (4:1; cf. 3:9b, 10). Their punishment is exile (4:2–3) and supposes the capture and looting of the city that were described in the preceding proclamation (cf. 3:11, 12). The taunt includes the women and their husbands and the children of Israel and makes the usual connection between their wrongdoing and their worship (4:4–5; cf. 2:6, 8).

117 The first canto mentions men, women, and children. The second canto addresses the family of Israel, refers to the sons of Israel, chides the wives and husbands of Samaria, and identifies northern Israel either as a girl or as the boy Joseph. The third canto concentrates on David and the men in Zion who, like the women of Samaria, will be the first to go into exile (cf. 4:3 and 6:7) and, like the cows of Bashan, fancy themselves as bulls (cf. 4:1 and 6:12–13). The last canto also ignores the women to deal with famous male figures of the past—Isaac, Jacob, Israel, Jeroboam—and with the calamitous loss of an only son.

118 This final appeal (5:4–7) repeats the basic charge against the people and takes up the point of the earlier taunt (cf. 4:4–5) in a more positive way.

119 Amos said that Yahweh did the evil that befell the city (3:6), and the revised version said that Yahweh did nothing without revealing it first to the prophets (3:7–8). Instead of referring to the family of Israel (3:1) it mentions the house of Jacob (3:13), but it repeats the original decree of punishment (3:14a, *pqd*; cf. 3:2).

120 The catalog of dreadful occurrences includes only natural calamities (4:6–10) and culminates in the traditional example of Sodom and Gomorrah (4:11). It begins abruptly and has no apparent relationship to the preceding proclamation (4:1–5). At the end of the catalog, however, there is a statement on what Yahweh has done and is liable to do once more (4:12) that seems to refer to the decree of destruction in the original version (4:2), and there is also a warning to be prepared to meet Yahweh (4:12), which seems to replace the taunt about going to Bethel (4:4). The punishment is not described, however, but is merely attributed to Yahweh, who is portrayed as the creator and controller of natural cycles (4:13).

121 The commentary (5:3) introduces the notion of remnant, which becomes crucial in the revision's argument that Yahweh punished only the sinners and not the whole nation indiscriminately. The concluding hymnic element (5:8–9) has literal links with the preceding hymnic element (4:13) and like it prepares the reader to understand the day of Yahweh, which Amos considered the end of Israel, as one day in a continuous cycle.

122 The two sections (5:10–12, 21–24) begin with the same word for contempt (5:10, 21, *śn'*) and evince the same interest in uprightness (5:12, 24, *ṣaddîq, ṣĕdāqâ*) and legal procedure (due process is mentioned in the second section [5:24, *mišpāṭ*] and is described in detail in the first section [5:10, 12b]). Futility is exemplified in the first section by building a house and not living in it, or planting a vineyard and not drinking its wine (5:11), and in the second section by making the proper offerings and not having them accepted (5:22). The topics and themes of both sections are taken up in the concluding proverb (Amos 6:12).

123 The two sections (5:18–20; 6:1–7) share an introductory particle (*hôy*), the same grammatical construction, and an interest in advancing or retarding the day (cf. 5:18, 20; 6:3). The warnings are addressed to the house of Israel, including the capital cities Samaria and Zion, and distinguish between "Israel," which is inclusive, and "Joseph" which refers to the North.

124 This part, the fifth in the completed book, was changed by adding a strophe to match each of the original strophes. The opening disputation (5:10–12) is matched by a strophe (5:13–14) that refers to it in general terms (5:13) but mainly establishes a link with the preceding part (5:14; cf. 5:6). The warning about the day of Yahweh (5:18–20) is preceded by a strophe (5:15–17) that urges repentance (5:15) and describes the desired lamentation liturgy (5:16–17). The correction of the second disputation tempers Amos's rejection of sacrifice (5:21–24) by noting that Israel did not offer sacrifice in the wilderness (an exemplary period [Amos 2:10]) and that it was sent into exile not for any twist in its devotion to Yahweh but for its devotion to astral Gods and Goddesses (5:25–27).

125 In this part, the sixth in the completed book, the warning to Zion in the original version (6:1) leads to a repudiation of the city (6:8). The lament for the dead begun in the preceding part (5:16–17) continues with details on the burial services (6:9–10), and the earlier saying about the obliteration of houses (3:15; cf. 5:11) is elaborated (6:11). The part ends (6:14) with the prediction of an enemy invasion that will overrun the whole land.

126 The homogeneity of the revision is evident in recurrent themes. There is a constant insistence on the name Yahweh of Hosts (e.g., 5:14–15). There is the conviction that only the sinners were punished and that there was a righteous remnant (e.g., 5:15). The universal bitter end that Amos predicted is replaced by the death of many in battle (e.g., 5:16–17; 6:9–10). The phenomenal and astronomical dominion of Yahweh is opposed to the worship of planets and stars (e.g., 5:26). The proper response to divine judgment is silence (e.g., 5:13; 6:10; 8:3).

127 In the two visions (7:1–3; 7:4–6) most of the text is identical and only a few clauses differ, but even these are partial variants of each other.

128 The two visions (7:7–9; 8:1–3a) have the same form and interests and share in particular Yahweh's determination to abandon his people (7:8bB = 8:2bB). Judgment is passed on the high places (7:9a, *bāmôt*) and sanctuaries

(7:9a, *miqdĕšê*) in the kingdom of Jeroboam and, in the grouping and balancing of the visions, on the royal temple in the South (8:3a).

129 In the prophecy of Amos "the house of Jeroboam" refers to the kingdom of Jeroboam I with its capital in Samaria, and contrasts with the kingdom founded by David with its capital in Zion. The revision was at pains to situate Amos in the reign of Jeroboam II (1:1) but recognized the original reference and, in describing his encounter with the priest at Bethel, used the Deuteronomist's description of the encounter of a Judean prophet with Jeroboam I (7:10–17; cf. 1 Kings 13).

130 The repetition (1:1b, *ʾăšer ḥāzâ* . . .) mimics the original (1:1a, *ʾăšer hāyâ*) but, unlike the original relative clause, refers not to Amos but to his words (1:1b, "The words of Amos . . . which he saw"; cf. Isa 2:1, "The word which Isaiah saw . . ." [*haddābār ʾăšer ḥāzâ yĕšaʿyāhû*]; see Andersen and Freedman, *Amos*, 188–89). The motto (1:2) refers again to the words of Amos, which, as will become clear (cf. 3:7–8), the editor attributes to divine inspiration and revelation. Judah and Jerusalem are also mentioned in one of the additional oracles (2:4–5), and the distinction between the northern and southern kingdoms, foreign to Amos, who assimilates one to the other and includes both in the designation Israel, becomes characteristic of this version.

131 The use of formulaic expressions is evident in comparing 1:9a + 10 with, for example, 1:6a + 7. The copied clause (1:9bA = 1:6b) is taken from the same context. The only nontypical clause (1:9bB) begins the concern for law and covenant that is peculiar to the revision (cf. 1:11; 2:4).

132 The violation of Tyre's covenant of brotherhood (1:9bB) finds resonance in Edom's pursuit of his brother with the sword (1:11b). The covenant bond is explicit in the oracle against Tyre and implied in the reference to mercy in the oracle against Edom (see M. Fishbane, "The Treaty Background of Amos 1:11 and Related Matters," *JBL* 89 [1970] 313–18; idem, "Additional Remarks on *rḥmyw* [Amos 1:11]," *JBL* 91 [1972] 391–93).

133 The oracle against Judah (2:4–5) also agrees with the opening motto (1:2) in mentioning Jerusalem and in alluding to the words or instructions that Yahweh uttered from Zion.

134 The addition (2:9–12) contrasts Yahweh (2:9, 10, "And I . . ." [*wĕʾānōkî*]) and Israel (2:9, "from before *them*"; 2:10, "you"; 2:11, "your") and is an explicit but general reference to the preceding context in which Israel acted improperly in the temple of *their* God (2:8, *bêt ʾĕlōhêhem*). The stanzas in the strophe (2:9, 10–11a, 11b–12) are linked to each other by verbatim repetitions. The reference to the exodus anticipates the words of Amos in the next canto (2:10a + 11b; cf. 3:1). The attempt to silence the prophets is an important undercurrent of the revision that finally surfaces in the encounter between Amos and Amaziah at Bethel (2:10–12; cf. 7:10–17).

135 The addition (3:7–8) begins (*kî lōʾ yaʿăśeh ʾădōnāy yhwh dābār*) by

paraphrasing the end of Amos's text (3:6b, *wayhwh lōʾ ʿāśâ*). The prophets to whom the revelation is made were noted at the end of the preceding part (3:7b; cf. 2:11–12). The reference to the lion roaring and Yahweh speaking (3:8) echoes the riddle (cf. 3:4) but refers explicitly to the motto at the head of the book (1:2). The fact that the people were warned well in advance of the catastrophe is emphasized in the catalog of plagues in the third part (4:6–13) and is implicit in those passages which suppose that a remnant actually survived.

136 The additional strophe (3:13–15) begins like the other proclamations (*šimʿû*, 3:1, 13; 4:1; 5:1). Its reference to the punishment of Israel (3:14, *pqd*) is taken from the enigmatic statement at the beginning of the canto (3:2). Its summons to witness (3:13a, *wĕhāʿîdû*) and its use of the prophetic formula (3:13, *nĕʾum*) paraphrase the preceding context, where Egypt and Ashdod are summoned to witness practices in Samaria (3:9) and where the same formula is used (3:10). The elaboration of the formula with the title Yahweh God of Hosts (3:13b) anticipates the common parlance of the second edition and its interest in Yahweh's cosmic attributes (cf. 4:13; 5:8–9, 13–14, 15–17, 25–27; 6:14; 8:7; 9:1b–4, 5–7). The reference to the altars at Bethel (3:14b) becomes thematic in this version's rejection of sacrifice (5:25), in its contempt for the Bethel priesthood (7:10–17), and in its description of the collapse of the temple on the heads of its devotees (9:1a, 1b–4). The stanza's reference to the house of Jacob (3:13) anticipates later texts where the house of Jacob is spared the fate of Bethel (e.g., 9:8). Its reference to the ruin of great houses (3:15) is reflected later in its sense of doom lurking in houses (6:9), in its rejection of lavish structures (6:8), in its depiction of the destruction of houses great and small (6:11), and in its vision of a restoration without houses (9:14–15; cf. 5:11).

137 The catalog (4:6–11) begins with a contrast between Yahweh ("And I . . . ," 4:6, 7) and Israel ("you," "your," 4:6) that corresponds to the contrast or conflict established by Amos in the preceding proclamation (4:5b). The summary is convoluted (4:12, "Indeed so I will do to you, Israel / since this I have done to you / be prepared to meet your God, Israel") and seems to refer both to the catalog and to the initial proclamation of exile (4:2–3). The famine becomes a longing for the word of Yahweh (4:6; cf. 8:11–14). The distinction between one city and the next is taken up in the theory of the remnant (4:7–8; cf. 5:3). In the end the gardens and vineyards are restored (4:9; cf. 9:14).

138 The addition (5:3) begins (5:3aA, *kî kōh ʾāmar ʾădōnāy yhwh*) and ends (5:3b, *lĕbêt yiśrāʾēl*) by distributing the words in the next statement in the original version (5:4a, *kî kōh ʾāmar yhwh lĕbêt yiśrāʾēl*).

139 The ending of the fourth part (5:8–9) is a hymnic element that relates it to the preceding part (cf. 4:13) and creates a long-range precedent for the day of Yahweh (cf. 5:18–20). It is inserted into the text by repeating the key word at the end of the original in a different context: compare 5:7a (*hahōpĕkîm lĕlaʿănâ mišpāṭ*), said of Israel's perversion, with 5:8a (*wĕhōpēk labbōqer ṣal-māwet*), said of Yahweh's cosmological control.

¹⁴⁰ The commentary (5:13–14) begins with a general but explicit reference to the timing (5:13, "At that time . . . [*bā'ēt hahî'*] . . . for it is an evil time [*kî 'ēt rā'â hî*]") of the punishment that Amos predicted (5:11). The gist of the commentary, however, is an exhortation that draws on the preceding canto (5:14; cf. 5:4–7) and creates an artificial link with it.

¹⁴¹ Amos 5:15 ("hate," "gate"); cf. 5:10. The flow of the edited version is eased by verbatim repetitions (5:15, *rā'* . . . *ṭôb*; cf. 5:14, *ṭôb* . . . *rā'*). The remnant (5:15, *šĕ'ērît yôsēp*) was suggested in the second part by limiting the downfall of the nation to physical destruction (cf. 3:15), and again in the preceding part by allowing for some survivors in the final battle (5:3).

¹⁴² The third part of the commentary (5:16–17) allows for survivors who will mourn for those who have died. It is attached artificially to the original text that follows by imitating one of its key words (5:16, *hô hô*; cf. 5:18 *hôy*), and it quotes one of the sayings of Amos in a contradictory sense (5:17b, *kî 'e'ĕbōr bĕqirbĕkā*; cf. 7:8b = 8:2b, *lō' 'ôsîp 'ôd 'ăbôr lô*).

¹⁴³ The commentary (5:25–27) repeats one word of the original (5:25, *ûminḥâ*; cf. 5:22, *ûminḥōtêkem*) and includes the list of sacrificial offerings under the single category of *zĕbāḥîm* (5:25; cf. 5:22 *'ōlôt . . . šelem mĕrî'êkem*). The wilderness period is the intermediate period between the exodus and the conquest (2:9–12; 9:7), or, in this passage, between the loss of the land and an eventual return from exile. The worship of the stars involved the making of images that had to be carried (5:26) and is opposed to the worship of Yahweh, whose name is the God of Hosts (5:27; cf. 4:13; 5:8–9).

¹⁴⁴ The commentary (6:8–11) has Yahweh—indicated by his titles, and by deictic personal pronouns (*'ānōkî*, 6:8) and pronominal suffixes (6:8, *bĕnapšô*)—reject "the pride of Jacob" (6:8, *'et gĕ'ôn ya'ăqōb*; cf. 8:7) which it identifies as the city (6:8, *'îr*) and its fortifications. The reference is to Zion, mentioned earlier (6:1), just as the concluding description of an enemy overrunning the country from Hamath to the brook of the Arabah (6:14) is a paraphrase of the opening geographical survey that went from Calneh and Hamath to Gath of the Philistines (6:2). This final description also has nothing to do with its original context and is attached to it by deictic pronouns and proper names (6:14).

¹⁴⁵ The third vision ends with the destruction of the high places of Isaac, the desolation of the sanctuaries in Israel, and the vindication of Yahweh against the house of Jeroboam (7:9). The story (7:10–17) begins with Amaziah's message to Jeroboam (7:10) and with an opposite-order paraphrase of the words of Amos (7:11, *baḥereb yāmût yārob'ām*; 7:9, *wĕqamtî 'al bêt yārob'ām bĕḥāreb*). The story also makes a point of mentioning the sanctuaries in Israel (7:13) and in the house of Isaac (7:16), and ends by applying to the house of Amaziah the message that was addressed at first to the house of Jeroboam (7:17; cf. 7:11).

¹⁴⁶ Amos began the conclusion of his prophecy by summarizing the injustices that he had condemned (8:4–6). The revision referred to them

specifically but in general as "all their deeds" (8:7). This use of a deictic connection signals, as usual, a comment that does not pertain to the actual context but to the ongoing argument of the second edition (cf. 4:13; 5:8–9, 25–27; 9:5–7). The conclusion ends with a final description of the day of Yahweh (8:9–10), and the revision added its remarks on the demise of prophecy by repeating and paraphrasing the same terms (8:11, "And now the days are coming . . ." [*hinnēh yāmîm bāʾîm*]; 8:13, "On that day . . ." [*bayyôm hahûʾ*]).

147 The conclusion follows on an editorial insertion and does not require any literary justification. The actual vision (9:1a) does not maintain the form of the original visions but is the occasion for a description of God's relentless pursuit of the sinners who worshiped in the sanctuary at Bethel. This relentless pursuit is possible because of Yahweh's transcendent control of the universe (9:5–7), as the revision has insisted from the beginning (4:13; 5:8–9). It is directed only against the sinful kingdom and not against the house of Jacob (9:8–10) and, therefore, when the sinners have been eliminated Zion will be restored and the exiles will return (9:11–15).

148 Prosody can vary from genre to genre, but genres can also share the same poetic form: a lament, for instance, and the rhetoric of a riddle are expressed in the same alternation of long and short lines (compare 3:3–6 and 5:2).

149 The clash consists in continuing nominal infinitival clauses with consecutive and disjunctive verbal clauses (1:9b, 11b; 2:4b) and suggests a deliberate conflation of original and editorial dictions. Balance is repetition without the symmetry or cadence of precise parallelism.

150 The alternation of long and short clauses is particularly evident at the beginning (2:6–8), and the narrative and catalog style is clearest at the end (2:13–16).

151 The balance is found in main (2:9b, 10, 11) and subordinate clauses (2:9a). The last stanza (2:11b–12) alternates long and short clauses.

152 For instance, there is a sequence of similar verbs in narrative consecution (1:4–5a, *wěšillaḥtî . . . wěšābartî . . . wěhikrattî*). The couplet at the end of the oracle against the Arameans is marked by strong alliteration, or alternating sequences of similar consonantal sounds (1:5b, *wěgālû ʿām ʾărām qîrâ / ʾāmar yhwh*). There is a similar alliteration in noting the crimes of the Philistines (1:6b, *ʿal haglôtām gālût šělēmâ lěhasgîr leʾědôm*), which the editor ignored in copying the text (1:9b, *ʿal hasgîrām gālût šělēmâ leʾědôm*). Other clauses have assonance and alliteration (e.g., 1:5a, 8a), or rhyme (e.g., 1:14 in -â; 2:13 in -â; 2:14–16 in -ô), or intricate patterns of sound (e.g., 2:16b, *ʿārôm yānûs bayyôm hahûʾ*). There is some of the same in the second edition, but it is usually associated with repetitive and balanced lines (1:11b; 2:9a, 11).

153 In Amos lions are literal beasts (3:6; 5:19), but in the revised edition

they are meant metaphorically (1:2, 11b). In Amos trampling and traveling are meant literally in relation to the pilgrimage festivals (2:6–7), but in the revision they are moral and spiritual attitudes (2:4). In Amos the exodus is a fact (3:1); in the revision it is the introduction to a way of life (2:9–12). In Amos Israel is one family among many (3:2), but in the revision it stands out against a fairytale background (2:9). The usual balance and repetition of the second edition are at odds with the rare parallelism in Amos (1:5a, 8a, 14b).

[154] The catalog (4:6–11), like the original (4:4b), has consistent rhyme in *kem*, but it also, besides its refrain, repeats words and whole clauses, and narrates past events without any direct appeal to the reader. The conclusion (4:12) is totally repetitive. The final hymnic element (4:13) bears no resemblance to the original text.

[155] In the first stanza (5:15) the balance is marked by a series of rhyming imperatives, and the imbalance of the final line is due to its length and subordination. In the second stanza (5:16–17) the balance is achieved by repetition, and the odd lines are subordinate and unmatched.

[156] The commentary (5:25–27) has opening and closing statements, in the manner of Amos (5:25, 27; cf. 5:18, 20), around a stanza with the same insistent rhyme as the first original stanza (5:26; cf. 5:21–22).

[157] In the original version the rhyme is initial or final or a mixture of both (6:1–7, 12–13), with the pattern disintegrating, as usual, toward the end (cf. 6:6b–7a, 12b). The commentary has a poetic introduction and conclusion (6:8, 11) and a prosaic point (6:9–10) and summation (6:14).

[158] The listlike narrative (8:4–6) uses infinitival forms that give the stanzas consistency (*wĕlaš̌bît, lĕhaqṭîn, ûlĕhagdîl, ûlĕʿawwēt, liqnôt*). The repetition is from the end of one stanza (8:5, *wĕnašbîrâ . . . bār*) to the end of the next (8:6, *bar našbîr*). The consecutive narrative (8:9–10) has initial rhyme in the first stanza (8:9–10aA), with alliteration in several lines (8:9aBb) and assonance in several others (8:10aA). The second stanza has repetition in its first two lines (8:10aB) and initial rhyme in its last two lines (8:10b).

[159] The hymnic commentary (8:8) has a prosaic introduction (8:7). The narrative commentary (8:11–14) has short balanced lines and long unmatched statements. The conclusion juxtaposes rambling descriptive sections filled with balanced and subordinate clauses (9:1–4), hymnic sections marked by balance (9:5–6a) and the alternation of long and short lines (9:6b–7), prosaic sections bound by balanced clauses and literal repetition (9:8–10) or by narrative consecution (9:11–15).

[160] The object of the verb *lōʾ ʾăšîbennû* ("I will not repeal *it*") is defined gradually in the sequence of oracles and in the progress from canto to canto. It is a day of destruction of kingdoms and capital cities (1:3–5, 6–8), a day of battle and of divine manifestation in a storm (1:13–15; 2:1–3), a day of worship and of defeat by Yahweh (2:6–8, 13–16). The second canto depicts

the siege of the city, the breaching of its walls, the death of the people who worshiped at Bethel and Gilgal. The third canto identifies it as the day of Yahweh, a day to which the people in Zion mistakenly looked forward because they thought that, being faithful to their religious traditions, Yahweh was on their side. The last canto insists on the inevitability and finality of the day on which their pleasant celebrations in the temple will finally end and be replaced with bitter lamentation.

161 In the sequel's account the battle at Ramoth-gilead and the crisis that it created in the Davidic succession (2 Kings 9–12°) is separated from the Syro-Ephraimite war (2 Kings 16°), in which Ahaz submitted to Assyria and appealed to Tiglath-pileser III for help only by an account of Hazael's invasion of Philistia and Judah (2 Kgs 12:18–19) and by brief notices on other irregularities in the Davidic succession.

162 Reference to the Syro-Ephraimite war includes a literal quotation (1:5b, wĕgālû ʿam ʾărām qîrâ = 2 Kgs 16:9b, wayyaglêbā qîrâ) and a paraphrase of the capture of Damascus and of the execution of the king (1:5a; 2 Kgs 16:9b). The allusion to the earlier battle in Ramoth-gilead is the mention of Gilead and Hazael (1:3b–4a; cf. 2 Kgs 8:28). The sequel mentioned an earlier foray into Israel by Ben-hadad, who was king of the Arameans and who had his capital at Damascus, and Amos also refers obliquely to this text (1:4b–5a; cf. 1 Kgs 15:18).

163 The oracle against the Philistines (1:6–8) is composed largely of words and themes from the oracle against Damascus (1:3–5).

164 In the sequel Hazael's success in the battle of Gilead (2 Kings 9–12°) was followed immediately by his capture of Gath and his preparations for an attack on Jerusalem (2 Kgs 12:18–19). The capture of Gath is listed in the third canto (6:2b) along with the calamity that befell Joseph (6:6). Its active participation in sending whole population groups into exile (1:5b, 6b) made it a model of the exile awaiting Judah (6:7). Its loss explains Amos's reference to the remnant of the Philistines in this oracle (1:8b).

165 The expression "I will not repeal it" (lōʾ ʾăšîbennû) occurs in the oracles of Balaam where the object of the verb is the blessing that Yahweh decreed for Israel and would not repeal (Num 23:20; Andersen and Freedman, Amos, 233–34). The quotation maintains the same word order as the original but uses the term in a contradictory sense to refer to a decree of abandonment and defeat. The contradiction exactly reflects the day of Yahweh as the reversal of every normal expectation. The quotation is confirmed by numerous allusions to the oracles of Balaam in the oracles against Ammon and Moab and in subsequent cantos. Both the oracles refer to a battle cry that accompanies the defeat of the nations, and the same word is used in describing Yahweh's triumphant advance from Egypt (tĕrûʿâ, 1:14; 2:2; Num 23:21). The Balaam oracles refer repeatedly to the king and princes of Moab (Num 22:4b, 13, 14, 15, 21; 23:6, 17), and Amos mentions the king and princes of Ammon and the princes of Moab (1:15; 2:3). Both texts use the metaphor of the lion and its prey in describing Yahweh (3:3–6; Num 23:24; 24:8b–9); both mention that

Yahweh acts for or against his people in accordance with his word (3:6; Num 23:19, 23); both refer to the people as Jacob or the family of Israel (3:1, 12; 7:2, 5; Num 23:10, 21, 23; 24:5). The epic says that Yahweh does not swerve or repent (Num 23:19), but Amos says that he does (7:3, 6). Both texts, finally, suppose that there is a vantage point, at the top of mountains or in the visions of the prophets, from which history can be surveyed (3:9; 7:1–9; 8:1–2; Num 22:41; 23:14, 28; 24:2–4).

166 The description of the extension of Ammon's borders (1:13, *lĕmaʿan harḥîb ʾet gĕbûlām*) uses the terminology of a promise to Israel in the covenant at Sinai (Exod 34:24) and in Transjordan (Deut 12:20). Ammon's intrusion into Gilead was the reason for the war in the time of Saul (1 Samuel 11°). In the battle of Rabbah the walls of the city figure prominently (1:14, *ḥômat rabbâ*; cf. 2 Sam 11:20, 21b, 24).

167 The crimes that Amos described are arranged systematically in the Elohist code. Selling the innocent for money (2:6bA) is listed as bribery that subverts the cause of the innocent (Exod 23:8), and selling the poor for a pair of shoes (2:6bB) is included as preventing justice in the poor person's suit (Exod 23:6). Crushing the poor (2:7aA) and denying recourse to the oppressed (2:7aB) are included in the code as prejudice against the poor (Exod 23:3) and as oppression and plain perversion of justice (Exod 23:2). The violation of a female servant by a man and his father (2:7) is included in the law that prevents a man from sexually abusing a female servant when he has given his son legal right to her (Exod 21:9). The use of garments taken in pledge is proscribed in the code (2:8a; Exod 22:25), and fines may be included in the prescriptions against interest (2:8b; Exod 22:24).

168 Amos describes Israel's inability to stand or flee and save itself and introduces the description with the image of a laden and ponderous cart (2:13–16). Isaiah, similarly, used the image of the people in Jerusalem tugging at their cartloads of sin (Isa 5:18) and described Jerusalem's final battle in terms of horses and riders and swift foot soldiers fleeing fast before their pursuers (Isa 30:15–17). The descriptions are general, although Amos includes more details, but they agree in describing the defeat on some specific day in the foreseeable future (2:16, *bayyôm hahûʾ*; Isa 30:8, *lĕyôm ʾaḥărôn*).

169 The Deuteronomist refers to Jeroboam II as Jeroboam son of Joash (1:1b; 2 Kgs 14:23, 27) to distinguish him from Jeroboam I son of Nebat, in whose sinful footsteps he followed (2 Kgs 14:24). The synchronism with Uzziah (1:1b; 2 Kgs 15:1) is peculiar to the History. In the sequel the king's name is Azariah (2 Kgs 14:21; 15:7); the History uses the same name but prefers the name Uzziah (2 Kgs 15:13, 30, 32, 34).

170 Amos 6:14b = 2 Kgs 14:25, in a contradictory sense.

171 The mourning of the pasturelands and the wilting of the headlands of Carmel reflect the lamentation liturgy in Joel, in which the land mourns (Joel 1:10), the animals groan and are dismayed, the pastures are devoured, and the well-watered land wilts (Joel 1:20). This use of Joel is especially apt since his

prophecy is an elaboration of Amos's image of the day of Yahweh. The use is confirmed by a requotation of the motto itself in the revision of the book of Joel (Joel 4:16a = Amos 1:1bB + 2a). The motto's reference to shepherds (1:2b, *nĕʾôt hārōʿîm*; cf. Joel 1:20, *nĕʾôt hammidbār*) reflects the editor's portrayal of Amos (7:15a) and a theme of the original prophecy (cf. 1:1a; 3:12).

172 The History mentions a treaty between Solomon and Hiram of Tyre (*bĕrît*, 1:9; 1 Kgs 5:26) under whose terms Hiram refers to Solomon as his brother (*ʾāḥîm*; cf. *ʾāḥî*, 1 Kgs 9:13; Andersen and Freedman, *Amos*, 261).

173 It is only in the epic (Exod 34:6–7) and in its literary reflexes (e.g., Nah 1:2–8) that a covenant is characterized by mercy (*rḥm*) and the restraint of anger (*ʾap*), and the editor's description of Edom eradicating mercy and nurturing anger forever reveals the violation of a covenant bond (1:11b). Jacob and Esau or Edom traditionally were brothers, and Edom's enduring anger at Jacob, reliance on the sword, and pursuit of Jacob with armed men are attested for the most ancient times (1:11; cf. Gen 27:40, 44–45; 32:7; 33:1). In the Historian's version of these early times two of the kings of Edom came from Bozrah and from Teman (1:12; cf. Gen 36:33–34). The violation of their bond of brotherhood is attested first at the time of the Babylonian capture of Jerusalem and is described and condemned in Obadiah (Obad 10, 12), where one of the punishments for this crime is the slaughter of the men of Teman (Obad 9). Obadiah recommended itself as a source for the revision of Amos since it had borrowed significant themes from the original version.

174 With one exception (2:4b, *ʿal moʾŏsām ʾet tôrat yhwh* = Jer 6:19bB, *wĕtôrātî wayyimʾăsû bāh*) the charges against Judah do not refer to specific texts but sum up prophetic and Deuteronomistic criticisms of Judah and Jerusalem.

175 The contemporary framework is supplied at the very beginning of the book by situating Amos in the distant past (1:1b) and by quoting what he said at that time (1:2, *wayyōʾmer*).

176 The comparison begins with the fact that the Amorites were annihilated (2:9, *šmd*; cf. Deut 7:23; 12:30; 31:4; Josh 11:14, 20). The Deuteronomist supposed that Israel was led astray by the example of the aboriginal nations (Deut 12:29–31; Josh 23:12–13), but to explain the apostasy of Ahab and Manasseh he appealed in particular to the example of the Amorites, whom Yahweh had driven out before Israel (2:9; cf. 1 Kgs 21:26; 2 Kgs 21:11). The native peoples were considered to have been giants (e.g., Deut 9:2), but the editor combines this idea with another allusion to Israel's infidelity by describing the wreck of the Amorites in terms that Ezekiel used to describe the ruin of Zedekiah (Ezek 17:1–18°).

177 The history typically includes the exodus, forty years in the wilderness, and the occupation of the land (2:10; Deut 29:1–8). The revised version quotes Amos's text on the exodus (2:10 = 3:1b) but completes it with the stylized recital (2:10b).

178 Prophecy originated in the days of the nazirites Samson and Samuel (2:11a; cf. Judg 13:5, 7; 16:17; 1 Sam 1:11b; 9:9) and continued through a continuous line of servants of Yahweh (3:7; cf. 2 Kgs 17:13–14), whom the people ignored or tried to silence (2:11b–12; 7:10–17).

179 A certain insistence on the fact that Yahweh is speaking (3:1a) is consistent with the covenant's emphasis on the same point (Exod 34:27; Deut 1:1a; 5:4). Reference to the punishment of the guilty includes its two main words (3:2b, *pqd*, *ʿāwōn*; cf. Exod 34:7). This quotation from the epic covenant is confirmed by an allusion to the same text at the end of the riddle: the covenant spoke of the wonders that Yahweh would do (*ʿśh*, Exod 34:10 [three times]), but Amos contradicts it by speaking of the evil that he does to the city (*ʿśh*, 3:6).

180 Amos's expression *ḥāmās wāśōd* (3:10b) is applied to Jerusalem by Jeremiah (Jer 6:7) and is quoted in the opposite word order by Habakkuk (Hab 1:3). It is also found in the book of Jeremiah (Jer 20:8) and in the revision of the book of Ezekiel (Ezek 45:9).

181 Compare 3:9b (*měhûmōt rabbôt*) and Deut 7:23 (*wěhāmām měhûmâ gědōlâ ʿad hiśśamědām*).

182 Amos points out that oppression lurked in the heart of the city (3:9, *waʿăśûqîm běqirbāh*) and that the people did not know how to accept reproof (3:10a, *wělōʾ yāděʿû ʿăśôt někōḥâ*). Isaiah had pointed out that the people rejected his words of reproof (Isa 30:10, *někōḥôt*) and persisted in oppression (Isa 30:12, *ʿōśeq*) and that this would be the crime (Isa 30:13, *ʿāwōn*; cf. Amos 3:2) that would suddenly be their undoing.

183 The first oracle (Isa 5:26–29) describes the enemy as a lioness and her cubs roaring (Isa 5:29, *śāʾag*), seizing their prey (Isa 5:29, *ṭerep*), and dragging it away so that it cannot be rescued (Isa 5:29, *nṣl*). The second (Isa 10:5–7, 13–14) mentions the sack of the city (Isa 10:6, *wělābōz baz*) and describes the Assyrian king as a bull who brings rulers down from their thrones (Isa 10:13, *wěʾôrîd*). Amos used the metaphor of the lion to expound his riddle (3:4, 12, *śāʾag*, *ṭerep*, *kěpîr*, *ʾărî*, *nṣl*) and borrowed Isaiah's words to picture the dethroning of the king and the sack of the city (3:11b, *wěhôrîd . . . wěnābōzzû*). Dependence on Isaiah explains the use of vivid imagery by someone as direct and down-to-earth as Amos.

184 Amos 3:7; cf. 2 Kgs 9:7; 17:13, 23; 21:10; 24:2. The editor also has a special interest in the altar at Bethel (3:14b; 9:1) and describes the encounter between Amos and Amaziah (7:10–17) in terms of the Deuteronomistic story (1 Kings 13) in which the altar of Bethel figured so prominently (1 Kgs 13:1–5). Interest in the destruction of houses includes, apparently, an oblique reference to the ivory house that Ahab built (3:15b; cf. 1 Kgs 22:39).

185 Compare 4:1–3 and Isa 5:1–2, 4–5, 11–12, 18–19.

186 The irony consists in inviting the people to Bethel, which was anathema

to the proponents of centralization, and to Gilgal, which violated the principle of a single place of worship, in order to be unfaithful to Yahweh by celebrating the festivals that the proponents of centralization prescribed. There is a pilgrimage to the central sanctuary (4:3a, *b*'; Deut 12:26) and a series of wrong-headed rituals: the offering of sacrifice in the morning (4:4b), corresponding to the Passover sacrifice that the sequel prescribed was to be offered at night before returning home in the morning (Deut 16:1, 7); tithes (4:4; Deut 12:17; 14:22) on the third day; burnt offerings in thanksgiving with leaven, as the ritual of Passover proscribed (4:5a; Deut 16:3); proclamation (4:5; Deut 5:1) of freewill offerings (4:5; Deut 12:17). The whole notion of pilgrimage is condemned in the third canto (5:21–22; Deut 12:13–14).

187 The prayer of Solomon (1 Kgs 8:12–61) expresses the belief, shared by the editor of the book of Amos, that the Name of Yahweh was in the temple but that Yahweh himself was universal and transcendent (4:13; 5:8–9; 1 Kgs 8:12, 27–30). In the prayer of Solomon each plague is an occasion to repent (*šwb*), and in each case the editor protests that the people did not repent (4:6–11). The editor supposes, as the Deuteronomist affirms elsewhere (1 Kgs 17:13), that repentance was the subject of the prophets' exhortations, to which in fact the people refused to listen (2:12). In referring to the calamities mentioned in the prayer of Solomon the editor lists them in a different order, combines them with other texts and materials, and attributes them to the agency of Yahweh rather than to happenstance or the agency of others.

188 The literal connection is with covenant promises (4:6, *ḥōser leḥem*; cf. Deut 8:9, *'ereṣ . . . lō' teḥsar kol bāh*) and curses (Deut 28:48, 57, *ḥōser kol*). However, the prayer of Solomon also mentions famine (1 Kgs 8:37, *rā'āb kî yihyeh bā'āreṣ*) and toward the end of the book the editor refers explicitly to this text (Amos 8:11, *wĕhišlaḥtî rā'āb bā'āreṣ*); in the prayer, besides, famine is joined with other plagues to which the editor refers later in the list (1 Kgs 8:37; compare 4:9). The reference to cities and places (4:6a, *'ārêkem . . . mĕqômôtêkem*) spreads the blame beyond the national shrines that Amos mentioned to individual cities and their sanctuaries (*mĕqômôt*; cf. Deut 12:2).

189 The connection with the prayer of Solomon consists in the lack of rain and the refusal to pray or repent (4:7; 1 Kgs 8:35–36). During the drought in the time of Elijah and Ahab (1 Kings 17–18) there was neither rain nor showers (4:7, *mṭr, gšm*; cf. 1 Kgs 17:1, 7, 14; 18:1, 41, 44, 45). The connection with Jeremiah's description consists in the withholding of the rain in order to provoke the people to repentance (4:7, 8b; cf. Jer 3:1, 3, 22).

190 Amos 5:6–7: "Lest the house of Joseph burst into flames / that will consume — and, because of Bethel, will not flicker — / those who make the law a bitter solution / and fling justice to the ground."

191 The epic lists violations of the covenant under the headings *'āwōn, peša'*, and *ḥaṭṭā'â* (Exod 34:7), and Isaiah uses the same terms (Isa 1:4, 18; 5:18; 30:13). Amos used the first term in the second canto (3:2, *'āwōnôtêkem*), the second term in the first and second cantos (*pš'*, 1:3, 6, 13; 2:6; 4:4), the last two terms in the third canto (5:12). In one of its descriptions of the land that

Israel is about to occupy the sequel mentions in particular the houses that they had not built and the vineyards that they had not planted (Deut 6:11), and Amos describes the frustration of building houses and not living in them or planting vineyards and not drinking their wine (5:11). His version is taken up in the Deuteronomistic curses in the book of the law (Deut 28:30, 39). Court proceedings at the city gate are described in the sequel's story of the revolt of Absalom (2 Sam 15:1–6) but with more atmosphere and less detail than Amos evokes.

192 The day of Yahweh (5:18–20) is taken up in Zephaniah, Joel, and Obadiah. The comparison with the fate of other nations (6:1–2) was copied by the Deuteronomist (2 Kgs 18:33–35; 19:11–13) and by III Isaiah (Isa 10:8–11). The last strophe (6:12–13) contains a proverb or riddle, its application, and its interpretation. The saying mixes martial and agricultural images: "Do horses run on rock / is it plowed with oxen?" (6:12a). The application draws on the agricultural image to describe the produce of this rocky and untillable land: "You have made justice bitter weed and the fruit of righteousness wormwood" (6:12b). The interpretation unravels the relationship between war and agriculture by comparing the men to the proverbial bulls and associating their disdain for justice with their nonsensical belief that they would not be defeated: "who take pleasure in nonsense / who say 'Is it not because of our strength that we have horns!' " (6:13). The editorial comment describes their defeat (6:14) in the words of a prophecy that was fulfilled during the reign of Jeroboam II (2 Kgs 14:25).

193 Defeat is modeled on the invasion announced by Jeremiah (6:14a = Jer 5:15a). The destruction of the houses in the city at the command of Yahweh (6:11) reflects the destruction of the houses of Jerusalem (2 Kgs 25:9). And its abandonment according to the word of Yahweh (2 Kgs 24:3, 20).

194 The text (Amos 5:13b, *kî 'ēt rā'â hî'* = Mic 2:3bB) originally referred to conditions in Jerusalem but was applied to the situation in Samaria.

195 The worship of astral deities (Amos 5:26–27) was common in Jerusalem according to the Deuteronomist and the book of Jeremiah (2 Kings 23; Jeremiah 7; 44) and is excluded by the book of Deuteronomy (Deut 4:19; 17:3). The image of the people lugging their Gods into a foreign land with them (Amos 5:25–26) is fitting revenge for worshiping foreign Gods (Deut 4:28; 28:36) but also reflects Hosea's ridicule of the God of Bethel being carted off into exile in Assyria (Hos 10:6).

196 The seasons are marked by representative crops or events. The sequence from (ingathering and) *lqṣ́* to *qāyiṣ́* (or *qāṣîr*, the harvesting of fruit crops) is known from the Gezer calendar. It is assumed, partly on the basis of the derivative description in Joel (Joel 1–2, esp. 1:19–20; 2:3–5) that the fire that devoured the fields and the underground sources of water describes the dry season (7:4; cf. Joel 2:23). In the third vision, assuming that the word *'ănāk* has several meanings (e.g., "tin, or lead" [< Akk. *annaku*] and "anklet(?)" [< Akk. *annuku*]) like *qāyiṣ́/qēṣ́* in the matching vision, there may be

a reference to the season (tin as a component of the brazen sky, Deut 28:23) and to some homophonous disaster (e.g., exile in fetters) that befell the city. In Joel the locust plague (7:1; Joel 1:4) was followed by the fierce heat of summer (7:3; Joel 2:3–5), by an attack against the city (7:7; Joel 2:6–9) and by the fall harvest (8:1–2; Joel 2:22–25). In the last vision the songs of the temple cease and are turned into lamentation (8:2–3a, 9–10), but Joel, on the contrary, sees the lamentation in Zion turned into joy (Joel 2:15–17, 21–23).

197 The same pattern is followed in the closing triptych in Hosea. Micah and Jeremiah, similarly, finish their prophecies with the story of early Israel.

198 In Amos and in the epic the visions begin with Yahweh showing something to the prophet (7:1, 4, 7; 8:1; Num 23:3). In both the people are usually referred to as Jacob and Israel (7:2, 5, 8; Num 23:10, 21, 23; 24:5), but they are also called "my people Israel" (7:8; 8:2) or simply "a people" (Num 23:9, 24).

199 The allusions to the epic account of creation consist in the vision of Yahweh forming (yôṣēr, 7:1; cf. Gen 2:7, 8) locusts and the reference to the grass (ʿēśeb hāʾāreṣ, 7:2; cf. Gen 2:5) coming up as the groundwater rose in the beginning (ʿālôt, 7:1; cf. Gen 2:6). The allusions to the story of Isaac and Jacob are the repeated saying that Jacob is small or young (7:2, 5, kî qāṭôn hûʾ), as he was when he stole the blessing from Esau (Gen 27:15, 42), and the unexpected reference to the high places of Isaac (7:9, bāmôt yiśḥāq) to balance the reference to the sanctuaries of Israel (7:9).

200 According to the epic (Exod 19:20; 34:6–7) Yahweh descended onto Mount Sinai, summoned Moses to the top of the mountain, and passed by in front of him (Exod 34:6, wayyaʿăbōr yhwh ʿal pānāyw). According to the sequel (Deut 5:4, 23a, 24a, 25a) Yahweh spoke to the people out of the fire, and the people were afraid that the fire would consume them (Deut 5:25a, kî toʾkĕlēnû hāʾēš haggĕdôlâ hazzōʾt). Similarly, the sequel declared that Yahweh would go before the people as a devouring fire (Deut 9:3) to destroy the nations who inhabited the land. In Amos, on the contrary, the fire devours Jacob's allotted land (7:4) and Yahweh declares that he will never pass by his people Israel again (7:8; 8:2, lōʾ ʾôsîp ʿôd ʿăbôr lô). In the last vision, the festivities that belonged to the observance of the covenant come to an end.

201 The repentance of Yahweh (7:3, 6, niḥam yhwh ʿal zōʾt), in the light of its possible sources, has an ominous ring. The word was used in the epic to express Yahweh's regret that he had made man and woman (Gen 6:6–7) and in the Balaam oracles to affirm that Yahweh would not change his mind about bestowing a blessing on Jacob and Israel (Num 23:19). According to the visions Yahweh wavers at first, in the early years of Jacob, at the beginning of the harvest season, but toward the end of the season decides to abandon his people Israel.

202 Amos used the terms Israel and Jacob as inclusive of the whole nation. The editor distinguished between Israel and Judah and saw in the condemnation of Israel a punishment of the sinful kingdom (cf. 9:8–10) and in the

repentance of Yahweh a hope for the house of Jacob (cf. 9:8b). The cosmic significance of Amos's visions is expressed in the editorial response of the elements to the list of crimes that he condemned (cf. 8:7–8).

203 The story of the encounter between Amos and Amaziah is like the Deuteronomistic legend (1 Kings 13) in supposing the Judean origin of the prophet (7:12; 1 Kgs 13:1), in pitting him against the king (7:10–11, 13; 1 Kgs 13:4–9), in referring to his refusal to eat bread at Bethel (7:12; 1 Kgs 13:7–9), and in condemning the priesthood at Bethel (7:17; 1 Kgs 13:2). Other elements of the encounter are borrowed from Amos (e.g., 7:11 = 7:9b + 5:5b; 7:14, cf. 1:1), from Micah (7:16bB, 17aB; cf. Mic 2:5–6) or from the Deuteronomist (e.g., 7:15a = 2 Sam 7:8).

204 The illustration (8:11–14) contains cross-references to the earlier catalog of calamities (cf. 4:6, 8, 10), to the lament over the house of Israel (cf. 5:2), and to the exhortations to seek Yahweh (cf. 5:4, 6, 14). It supposes, with the Historian, that Israelite territory extended from Dan to Beersheba (8:14a) and is interested in including Beersheba in order to accommodate the original reference to Isaac (Isaac, 7:9, 16; Beersheba, 5:5; 8:14; cf. Gen 26).

205 The vision (9:1–4) resembles Amos's third vision in having Yahweh standing (cf. 7:7), but otherwise it reveals the editor's interest in the altar and temple at Bethel and in Yahweh's universal dominion. The commentary on the vision has a further affirmation of this dominion (9:5–7) and stresses that punishment is restricted to the sinners of the sinful kingdom, but to them wherever they are, even in exile (9:8–10). This allows for the exemption of elements of the house of Jacob (9:8b), which is interpreted to mean Judah and Jerusalem (9:11–15). The fallen booth of David (9:11a) with its breached walls (9:11b) recalls Isaiah's designation of Zion as a booth in a field (Isa 1:8) and his image of Yahweh's destruction of the wall around the vineyard (Isa 5:5; cf. Isa 5:6–7 [II Isaiah], where the metaphor is applied to Judah and Jerusalem); the planting of the people in the land so that they will not be disturbed ever again (9:15) reflects the Song of the Vineyard (Isa 5:1–2) and a promise to David recorded in the Deuteronomistic History (cf. 2 Sam 7:10); the restoration of the land that the editor envisages is just the opposite of the destruction that Amos described (9:14; cf. 5:11).

206 An earlier version of this chapter has already appeared as "The Composition of Hosea" in *HAR* 11 (1987) 331–53 and is used with permission of the publisher.

207 See figure 6a. Stanzas are on separate lines; strophes are separated by horizontal lines. Narrative order, represented graphically as A-A', B-B', and so on consists in strophes that are partially repetitive but contribute to a continuous story. Descriptive order, represented as A-B, A'-B', and so on consists in sets of overlapping strophes that view the same matter from different or successively more comprehensive points of view. Explanatory order, represented as A-B-[C]-B'-A', is a way of gathering and interpreting evidence, first listing the facts in a logical or rhetorical order, then reviewing them to draw a conclusion.

208 War is treated in 1:5, 7; 2:2, 20b; government is the subject of 1:1; 2:1–2; 3:1–5.

209 The editor added stanzas (1:1, 5, 7) to change the strophic structure and also appended another strophe (2:1–2). The original narrative order (A = 1:2–4; A′ = 1:6, 8–9) became an explanatory structure (A = 1:1–2; B = 1:3–5; B′ = 1:6–7; A′ = 1:8–9; 2:1–2). The editor, in other words, is not telling a story or creating a dramatic effect but introducing arguments that will be developed through the rest of the book.

210 The editor added 2:3 ("Say to your brothers 'My people' and to your sisters 'Pitied' "). This repeats words from Hosea's text, but it contradicts his statements (cf. 1:6, "Unpitied," and 1:9, "Not my people") and clouds the point that he was making.

211 Hosea spoke of betrothal (2:20a, 21–22) and reconciliation (2:23–25). The editor added a remark (2:20b, "The bow, as well as the sword and war, I will break in the land, and I will let them lie down in safety") that spoiled the balance between the two strophes. Two other strophes, one about another marriage (A′ = 3:1–3), the other about national reconciliation (B′ = 3:4–5), match Hosea's composition but completely change its point.

212 Both strophes (2:20a, 21–22; 2:23–25) begin with the expression "On that day . . ." (bayyôm hahû').

213 The second wedding (3:1–5) replaces the first (1:2–4). It begins like the first ("Yahweh said to Hosea / to me" (1:2b; 3:1a) refers to it ("Go and take a wife . . ." / "Go again and love a wife . . ." 1:2b; 3:1a), follows the same formal pattern (command, reason, execution, explanation) and imitates it (1:9b, wĕ'ānōkî lō' 'ehyeh lākem / 3:3b, wĕgam 'ānî 'ēlāyik).

214 The introductory summary (4:1–2aAb, 3) sets the tone for the triptych and connects it to the preceding narrative by using or paraphrasing some of its key words. The remaining triptychs have the same sort of rubric, but they are slightly less noticeable; and the first evidently was composed as a model for the rest.

215 Cf. 1:2a (tĕḥillat ðibber yhwh) and 4:1a (šimʿû ðĕbar yhwh).

216 Cf. 2:4a (rîbû bĕ'immĕkem rîbû) and 4:1b (kî rîb layhwh ʿim yôšĕbê hā'āreṣ).

217 Cf. 2:21–22 (bĕḥeseð . . . be'ĕmûnâ . . . wĕyāðaʿat) and 4:1b (kî 'ên 'ĕmet wĕ'ên ḥeseð wĕ'ên ðaʿat . . .).

218 Cf. 2:20 (ʿim ḥayyat haśśāðeh wĕʿim ʿôp haššāmayim wĕremeś hā'āðāmâ) and 4:3 (bĕḥayyat haśśāðeh ûbĕʿôp haššāmayim wĕgam ðĕgê hayyām yē'āsēpû).

219 Cf. 1:4 (ðĕmê yizrĕʿe'l) and 4:2 (wĕðāmîm bĕðāmîm nāgāʿû).

220 At the beginning of the triptych there is a prophetic summons to hear

the word of Yahweh (4:1), and at the end there is another reference to the prophets and to the things that Yahweh said (6:5). In the beginning, similarly, the people are charged with ignorance and ill will (4:1), and at the end knowledge and good will are required (6:6).

221 All the references to the priests correct Hosea's text. All of them are abrupt or puzzling and distort the original flow (4:2aB, 4–5, 6b, 9, 11, 13b–15; 5:1–2, 5, 8–10). The last strophe (6:7–11) compares their activities to the treachery of murderers and brigands. It is an elaboration of the opening statement that murders abound (4:2aB), but it is totally extraneous to the drift of the triptych.

222 The pattern is: A = 4:1, 2aAb, 3; A' = 4:6a, 7–8, 10; B = 4:12–13a; B' = 4:16–19. The strophes develop the same themes and are connected by literal repetitions. The first accentuates the lack of knowledge (4:1b, *wĕ'ên da'at*). The second notes that the people are perishing for lack of knowledge (4:6a, *mibbĕlî hadda'at*) because they have abandoned Yahweh for another God (4:10, *znh*). The third says that they worship in shady groves because the wind of infidelity (4:12, *rûaḥ zĕnûnîm*) has led them astray, and the fourth describes this wind wrapping them in its wings (4:19, *ṣārar rûaḥ 'ôtāh biknāpêhā*).

223 The tableau (A = 5:3–4; A' = 5:6–7) shares with the first tableau the themes of knowledge and of Israel's association with animals. The second strophe develops the first: for instance, the first has the theme of Israel's infidelity, and the second strophe mentions their illegitimate children; the first mentions return to Yahweh, and the second describes it as a pilgrimage.

224 The pattern is: A = 5:11–14a; B = 5:14b–6:3; A' = 6:4–6. The strophes contribute to the development of the same themes and are linked by literal repetitions: the first and last refer to the *mišpāṭ* of Ephraim (5:11a; 6:5b); the first and second are linked by repetition of the pronoun "I" (5:14a, 14b); the second and third are linked by knowledge (*yd'*, 6:3, 6) and by the image of rain clouds in the morning.

225 The editor recognized the original pattern (A-A'-B-B'), added strophes (4:4–6°, 14–15) to match and correct the first (4:1–3°) and last (4:16–19) and then changed the rest (4:9; 4:11, 13b) to agree with each other. The new pattern is an expansion of the same (A-A'-B-B'-C-C') but with a different content and meaning.

226 Hosea criticized the people for taking oaths they did not keep (4:2aA, *'ālōh wĕkaḥēš*). The editor added that they committed murder, theft, and adultery (4:2aB), and included illustrations of each (4:13b–15; 6:7–11; 7:1b).

227 The strophe (4:4–6) is built around one line from Hosea (4:6a, "My people are perishing for want of knowledge") and blames the priesthood for not teaching the people. Its first stanza (4:4–5) is a jumble of allusions to the first triptych and to the present context and tries to convert Hosea's case against the people into Yahweh's case against the priests: both of Hosea's texts

mention a lawsuit (*rîb*, 2:4; 4:1), but the editor explains that the suit is not being brought by a husband against his wife (4:4a, "But let not a husband complain / let not a man protest") but by God against the priesthood, that the people are the case against the priest (4:4b, *wĕ'ammĕkā kimrîbê kōhēn*), that both the priest and the prophet will stumble (4:5a), and that the mother of the priest will perish (4:5b).

228 Hosea's strophe (4:6a, 7–8, 10) illustrates the immediate effects of ignorance among the people. The additional stanza (4:9) is an artificial attempt to include the priest (4:9a, "It will be like people like priest") and to make the priest alone responsible for their ignorance (4:9b, "I will requite him for his ways / I will do to him as he has done").

229 A line (4:11) was added to Hosea's first stanza (4:12) to make the dullness of the priests (4:11, *yiqqaḥ lēb*) the effect of their participation in the frolics of the unfaithful wives (4:11, *zĕnût wĕyayin wĕtîrôš*; cf. *znh*, 2:4, 6–7; *tîrôš*, 2:10, 11; in place of wine the first triptych mentions strong drink [2:7, *šiqqûyāy*], the vine [2:14a, *gapnāh*], vineyards [2:17, *kĕrāmêhā*], and grapes [3:1, *'ănābîm*]). Two lines (4:13b) were added to the end of Hosea's second stanza (4:13a) to link the sophistication of the priest's daughters and daughters-in-law with the rites that were celebrated in shady groves.

230 The first stanza (4:14) implicates the priest and his family in religious excesses but also reintroduces the people in order to make a transition to the final strophe (4:16–19). In Hosea's text the people were Israel (4:16) or the children of Israel (4:1), but in the second stanza the editor thinks of them as the kingdoms of Israel and Judah (4:15a) and warns them to stay away from the shrines, where supposedly the bad priests officiated.

231 The first stanza (5:1a) summons the priests, the northern kingdom, and the royal house to judgment. The second stanza (5:1b–2) accuses them of wrongs done at Mizpah and Tabor.

232 The alarm, as usual, refers to specific places and alludes to ancient or typical events (5:8–10). This shift from Ephraim to Israel and Judah and all the tribes seemed more sensible after the editor had added a prior stanza mentioning the three of them together (5:5).

233 In its edited version (5:1–10) the tableau begins and ends the same way with a formal invocation, a list of places, and an allusion to historical events. The position and formality of the additions make them seem to be the real point of the tableau and obscure both the flow of Hosea's material and its connection with the preceding tableau.

234 The additional strophe (6:7–11) corresponds concretely to Hosea's general account of a pilgrimage (5:14b–6:3), but it interprets repentance (*šwb*, 5:15a; 6:1a) as a return (*šwb*, 6:11) from exile. Its addition changes the original explanatory scheme (A-B-A') into a descriptive pattern (A-B-A'-B').

235 The crimes that kept Israel and Ephraim from turning to God (5:4,

ma'alĕlêhem) are the crimes that final overtook them (7:2b, *ma'alĕlêhem*). The people knew that Yahweh could heal them (*rp'*, 6:1), but every time he was about to heal them (*rp'*, 7:1) he discovered their insincerity.

236 When Hosea mentions the duplicity of the people (7:1a), the second edition adds a reference to thieves who enter a house and brigands who rob in the open (7:1b, *gnb*, *gdd*). Robbery was one of the general accusations against the priests in the preceding triptych (4:2, *gnb*), and the addition at the end of that triptych compared the priests to brigands on the road to Shechem (6:9a, "Like brigands [*gĕdûdîm*] lying in wait for someone / a gang of priests / murdering on the road to Shechem . . ."). The metaphor of the mad cook (7:3–7) continues the ambush theme in the same passage (7:6a, *bĕ'orbām*; cf. 6:9a). The metaphor was suggested by Hosea's comparison of Ephraim to a half-baked cake (7:8), but it deals with the kings, princes, and judges of the people, whom Hosea did not even mention.

237 The pattern is: A = 7:1a, 2; B = 7:8–9, 11–12; C = 7:13–14; C' = 8:1–3; B' = 8:7–9; A' = 8:11–13abA.

238 The editor added stanzas to strophes (7:1b, 10; 8:4, 10, 14) and whole strophes (7:3–7; 7:15–16; 8:5–6). These enlarged the argumentative pattern (A-B-C-C'-B'-A') but changed all except one (7:13–14) of its elements. Although the pattern remains the same (A-B-C-D-E-D'-C'-B'-A'), the substance does not correspond to the original.

239 Other remarks were added (7:10; 8:4b, 10) to link the commentary with the ongoing interpretation of the book (cf. 2:2; 3:2–4; 5:5).

240 The pattern (A-B-C-A'-B'-C') is an extension of the simpler descriptive form (A-B-A'-B'). The second part (A'-B'-C') is a transposition of the first and consists in a metaphorical transformation of its imaginative themes, based on the first triptych, in which Israel was the land and the people were the children that it bore for Yahweh. The links between the two parts are literal or figurative. In the first strophe (A = 9:1–3) wine fails and the wine vats are empty, and in the corresponding strophe (A' = 9:10a, 11–12) Israel is compared to grapes in the wilderness and threatened with the loss of her children. In the second strophe (B = 9:4–6) and its match (B' = 9:13–14), the day of Yahweh is a day of mourning for their children. The third (C = 9:7–8) and sixth (C' = 9:16–17) strophes feature the personal intervention of the prophet (9:7b–8, 14, 17).

241 The first insertion (9:9) separates the two parts of the description with an unexplained reference to general malfeasance at Gibeah. The second (9:10b) traces Israel's predicament to apostasy at Baal-peor. The third (9:15) refers to some event at Gilgal involving the royal house.

242 The descriptive strophic pattern (A = 10:1–2; B = 10:4–5; A' = 10:6, 8aBb; B' = 10:11–12) allows the same fact, event, image, or metaphor to be appreciated from different points of view.

243 The second edition expanded the descriptive pattern (A-B-[C]-A'-B'-[C']), but its similarity to the original is purely formal and superficial. The stanzas (10:3; 10:7–8aA) and strophes (10:9–10; 10:13–15) that were added in this edition repeat and vary the familiar argument that the people were undone by their kings, who introduced alien worship and indulged in wars.

244 Healing is a theme of the second and third triptychs (11:3, *rp*'; cf. 6:1; 7:1a). Sacrifice and altars are significant issues in the third triptych (11:2, *zbḥ*; cf. 8:11, 13; 9:4; 10:1, 8) and along with foreign alliances are the symptoms of Israel's wrongs (11:2, *qr*' + *ḥlk*; cf. 7:11–12).

245 Each of the stories is told in a separate tableau, and each is marked by the affirmation that Yahweh is their God from the land of Egypt (11:1b; 12:10; 13:4).

246 The cross-references are to the earlier part of the third triptych: the attack on their cities (11:6) was forecast (8:14); the appeal to a useless God was condemned in connection with their reliance on Egypt (11:7, *'el 'al*; cf. 7:16, *lō' 'āl*).

247 In the narrative pattern (A-A'), one strophe (11:4–5) simply retraces and advances the other (11:1–3).

248 The historical reason (11:6–7) is Israel's defeat in battle. The affirmation that Yahweh is God and not a man (11:9, *'îš*) is an implicit repudiation of Hosea's metaphor in which Yahweh is the husband (*'îš*) of Israel, and an explicit refutation of Hosea's description of Yahweh as a parent teaching Ephraim how to walk, taking the child in his arms, and treating him as a human person would (cf. 11:4). The same point is made in the final strophe (11:10–11) that portrays Yahweh's invincible transcendence in the traditional image of a lion stalking the world.

249 The strophes are arranged in an explanatory order (A-B-B'-A') that accounts for some of their density and lack of sequence. The first strophe (12:1–3) deals with Ephraim (12:1a) and Judah (12:1b) and again with Ephraim (12:2) and Judah (12:3): Ephraim is associated with the house of Israel (12:1a) and Judah with Jacob (12:3). The second strophe continues the story and maintains the contrast between Jacob, who met and overcame God (12:4–5) and Ephraim, who encountered Canaan and became wealthy by wrongdoing (12:8–9). The third reflects on the second: it implicitly compares Yahweh (12:10, "But *I* am Yahweh your God"), who spoke through the prophets (12:11, *wĕdibbartî*), with the God of Bethel, or the Messenger of God (12:4b–5a, "God" [*'ĕlōhîm*], "God the Messenger" [*'el mal'āk*]; 12:5b, "Bethel" [*bêt 'ēl*]), who spoke to Jacob (12:5, *wĕšām yĕdabbēr 'immānû*). It also contrasts Canaan (12:8) and the land of Egypt (12:10). The fourth strophe (12:13–15) returns to the first (cf. 12:3, *kĕma 'ălālāyw yāšîb lô*, and 12:15, *wĕḥerpātô yāšîb lô 'ădōnāyw*) and unravels the skein: Jacob, the allegorical Judah, and Israel are protected by the prophets (12:13–14), but Ephraim is rejected in return for his rebellion (12:15).

250 The first comment (12:6) agrees in general with Hosea's point that it is Yahweh and not Bethel who is the God of Israel (cf. 12:10). But it refers to Yahweh as the God of Hosts rather than as their God from the land of Egypt, and it holds out hope for Ephraim if it will give up its oppression and do what is right (12:7, 8). The second comment contrasts this hope in Yahweh with the altars and sacrifices that were founded at Gilead and Gilgal (12:12).

251 The revision (13:2aB, 9–11, 15; 14:1–10) expanded Hosea's descriptive pattern (A-B-A'-B') first by inserting a strophe with an alternative interpretation (13:9–11 = B'), and then by continuing and expanding the pattern to correct and complement Hosea's finale. In Hosea's text Ephraim worshiped calves (A = 13:1–2aAb) and, like a calf, was eaten by a lion (A' = 13:5–8); or, alternatively, he was like wispy smoke (B = 13:3–4) and now lingers wraithlike in Sheol (B' = 13:12–14). In the edited text, the fact that Ephraim ignored Yahweh his savior (B = 13:3–4) is balanced by his reliance on useless kings to save him (B' = 13:9–11); or, alternatively, the fact that he is a silly son (13:12–14) is balanced by the fact that he is just one son among many who deserved punishment (13:15–14:1). Hosea spoke of Ephraim's guilt (13:1, *'šm*) and compared his death to smoke, dust, dew, or a cloud dispersing (13:1–3°), and the editor speaks of Samaria's guilt (14:1, *'šm*) and of a destructive wind rising from the desert (13:15). Hosea said that Ephraim forgot his God (13:4), and the editor describes a repentance ritual in which the people profess that Yahweh is their God (14:2–4). The editor speaks at first of Yahweh's anger (13:9–11) and then of his anger abating (14:5–8). Hosea said that Ephraim was an unwise child (13:13), but the editor concludes that the wise will understand why the text had to be changed and why the changes are right (14:9–10).

252 The sequence of interlocutors and topics corresponds to the sequence of strophes (2:4–5; 2:6–7; 2:8–9; 2:10–11; 2:12–15; 2:16–19°).

253 See 1:2 ("The beginning of Yahweh's discourse with Hosea"); 2:4 (" . . . she is not my wife . . ."); and 2:20a ("On that day I will make a covenant . . .").

254 The first stanza (1:2) is Yahweh's complaint about the infidelity of his wife: it repeats that Yahweh spoke to Hosea, that Yahweh's wife was unfaithful and had children through her infidelity, and that she was truly unfaithful. The remaining stanzas record the birth of Gomer's children and share the same formulas: their repetitiveness consists in naming the children and in explaining the meaning of the names.

255 Some stanzas have a single rhyme throughout: the second stanza (2:5), for instance, is composed of five clauses that begin and end in the same sort of /a/ sound (-*â*, -*bā*, -*ā'*). Some stanzas have two competing rhymes: the eighth stanza (2:11), for instance, mixes rhymes in /i/ and /o/. Some have three consecutive rhymes: the fourth stanza (2:7b) has rhymes in /a/, in /ay/ and /i/. The use of rhyme is so pervasive (e.g., 2:12–13) that its absence in some clauses creates a special effect: the seventh stanza (2:10), for instance, has

double rhymes in its first, second, and fourth clauses, but alliteration without rhyme in the third and fifth.

256 The fourth stanza (2:25), for instance, mixes rhymes in /a/ and /i/, but ends with a blank and anomalous line. Repetition is of words (2:23–24) or of grammatical forms (2:20a, 21–22).

257 Catchword (1:1, 5, 7; 2:1, 3) consists in repeating one or more words of the original text in a different order or an opposite context. Cross-reference (2:1, 17aB, 20b; 3:1–5) consists in obvious, intrusive, and inconsequential references to the edited text.

258 The editorial title of the book (1:1) is modeled on the original heading (1:2). The use of a catchword inserts it into the context, but its content contradicts the thrust of Hosea's words. In Hosea's version the plot begins with "In the beginning Yahweh spoke to Hosea" (1:2), but the edited version is introduced as "The word of Yahweh . . ." in a particular time (1:1).

259 The references to war (1:5, 7; 2:20b) are artificially linked to the contexts that they paraphrase (2:20a) or contradict (1:3–4, 6). Together with the editor's comments on government (1:1; 2:1–3; 3:1–5) they constitute a continuous prosaic counterpoint to Hosea's drama.

260 The prediction (2:1–2, 3) interrupts the drama, refers to the words of Hosea as sayings from the distant past (2:1; cf. 1:9), and repeals the original verdict against the people (2:2b–3 = the opposite of 1:3–4, 6, 8–9).

261 The villain in the valley of Achor was Achan son of Karmi (krmy, "Vintager"), and there may be, as M. Fishbane pointed out (Biblical Interpretation in Ancient Israel [Oxford: Clarendon Press, 1985] 361), a subtle connection between the comment (2:17aB) and the original context that mentioned vineyards (2:17aA, kĕrāmêhā).

262 The marriage (3:1–5) is only a pretext for concluding the editorial themes of war and government. It was fitted into the general context of the first triptych by plagiarizing the text of the first marriage (cf. 1:2, 9).

263 Cf. 1:4 ("In a little while I will punish the house of Jehu for the blood shed at Jezreel") and 1:5 ("On that day I will break the bow of Israel in the valley of Jezreel").

264 The exemption (1:7) is a separate sentence, distinguished from the preceding sentence (1:6) by a change in sequence (from wayyiqtol, the consecutive form of qtl, to the yiqtol sequence) and by a disjunctive use of waw ("But [wĕ-] to the house of Judah I will be merciful" [wĕ'et bêt yĕhûdâ 'ărahēm]); see F. I. Andersen and D. N. Freedman, Hosea (AB 24; Garden City, N.Y.: Doubleday, 1980) 188–97. The finality of Yahweh's statement to Hosea ("I will never again be merciful to the house of Israel . . . ," 1:6) prompted the editor to assure Judah of Yahweh's continued mercy (1:7) and to predict a reversal of the judgment on Israel (2:1–3).

²⁶⁵ Into Hosea's "I will give her there the vineyards that were hers . . . and there she will respond as in the days of her youth," the editor inserted "and give [i.e., make] the valley of Achor a door of hope."

²⁶⁶ The title of the book (1:1) repeats the expression "in the days of . . . ," and the first decree of restoration (2:1–2) repeats its verbs (*wĕhāyâ, yēʾāmēr*). There is some rhyme (1:7; 2:1b, 2aB, 3) but it is neither intricate nor sustained.

²⁶⁷ There is some subordination (1:1; 2:1), but compound phrases and clauses are the editor's characteristic choice. There are lists of kings (1:1), of weapons (1:7; 2:20b), of symbols (3:3–4), and of devotion (3:5). The people are numbered and counted (2:1); what is said to the brothers is matched by what is said to the sisters (2:3); Hosea was supposed to love a wife who was loved by somebody else (3:1); and he bought a wife for fifteen shekels and for a homer of barley and a letech of barley (3:3).

²⁶⁸ Assonance (2:1a; 3:1b, 3a, 4a) and alliteration (1:5, 7bB; 2:2b, 17aB), like rhyme, generally are not sustained throughout an entire stanza.

²⁶⁹ Hosea, for instance, uses consecutive verbal clauses, and the editor regularly follows suit (1:5, 7; 2:1, 2, 20b; 3:5).

²⁷⁰ Hosea announces the lawsuit (4:1, *rîb*), lays the charge (4:1–2aAb), and presents the earth and its creatures as evidence or as witnesses (4:3).

²⁷¹ The characters are distinguished by person and number. The first person singular passages are spoken by Yahweh and define his relationship to Israel, addressed in the second or third person plural, and to Ephraim, addressed in the second or third person singular. Hosea speaks the parts that refer to Yahweh in the third person singular. The people speak in the first person plural.

²⁷² The first stanza (5:3) combines soliloquy and direct address to Ephraim. In the first strophe Yahweh also soliloquizes (5:3), and Hosea reflects on what Yahweh has said (5:4). In the second strophe (5:6–7) Hosea continues his own musings.

²⁷³ The speeches can be combined with narrative or description. In the first strophe (5:11–14a) the first stanza describes Ephraim's problems (5:11) and quotes Yahweh's reflections (5:12); the second stanza describes how Ephraim relies on Assyria (5:13a); the third stanza explains to Ephraim that Assyria is no solution (5:13b) and ends with Yahweh's musings (5:14a). In the second strophe (5:14b–6:3) the first stanza is a soliloquy in which Yahweh proposes a solution (5:14b–15), and the next two stanzas are Ephraim's reflection on what they plan to do (6:1–2, 3). In the last strophe Yahweh speaks to Ephraim (6:4), reflects on the prophetic tradition with the audience (6:5a), and appeals once again to Ephraim (6:5b–6).

²⁷⁴ The additions are mostly in the first person singular (4:4–5, 6b, 9, 14)

or are addressed to the people in the second person plural (4:13b, 14), and hence are attributed to Yahweh. In one stanza about the priest (4:9) the editor maintains the rhetorical mood of the original (cf. 4:7–8). The mixture of person and number in the editor's concluding stanza (4:15) and its reference to Yahweh in the third person suggest that it is spoken by Hosea.

275 The proclamations (5:1a, 8), like the proclamation at the beginning of the triptych (4:1), introduce the prophet as the messenger of the word of God. The editor does not allow for any dramatic or hermeneutic interplay between Yahweh and Hosea but has both speak to the people and at most juxtaposes their words. The editorial aside (5:5) fits into the musings of the prophet (5:4, 6–7) but comments on the context rather than furthering it.

276 Repetition is rare (cf. 4:1, 16). Rhyme is general, but it usually does not involve different kinds and is not maintained throughout a stanza (cf., however, 4:13a; 5:3; etc.).

277 In the second stanza (4:3), for instance, the first two lines share the same or similar sounds (*te'ĕbal* / *wĕ'umlal*), but the third has a different sort of assonance (*bĕḥayyat haśśādeh* . . .) and the last is marked by alliteration (*wĕgam dĕgê* . . .). Toward the end of the first tableau a stanza (4:16) opens with striking assonance and alliteration (*kî kĕpārâ sōrērâ sārar yiśrā'ēl*), continues with a less stiking alliteration (*'attâ yir'ēm yhwh*), and ends with a unique staccato line (*kĕkebeś bammerḥāb*).

278 Asyndetic clauses are juxtaposed without *waw* or any other conjunction (4:1; 4:6a, 7–8; 4:10; 4:16; 4:17–19; 5:6b–7; 5:11–12; 5:14b–15; 6:1–2; 6:3–4; 6:5). In some stanzas consecution continues to predominate (4:12; 5:4; 5:6a; 5:13a; 5:13b), and in others it is combined with asyndesis (4:13; 5:3). Asyndesis creates a more marked pause between clauses and gives stanzas a more measured staccato rhythm.

279 Most of the stanzas in the second edition are composed of consecutive clauses (4:4–5; 4:9; 4:14; 4:15; 5:1; 5:5). The use of compound clauses is most evident in the lists or catalogs (4:11; 4:15; 5:8; 6:7). Subordination is used to construct intricate or logical arguments (4:6b; 4:13b; 4:14; 5:1a; 5:1b; 6:9) and not, as in Hosea's text, to add different facets to a description.

280 The best example of imitation is the proclamation at the end of the second tableau composed largely of asyndetic clauses (5:8–10), although even here the editor cannot resist including a catalog of places (5:8). Another clause, similarly, imitates the asyndesis of its surroundings (4:12) but is betrayed by its odd conjunction of bad habits (4:11, "Infidelity and wine and alcohol weaken the will"). This particular clause hardly fits its context, but the jagged style is deliberate and is observable even in passages composed in their entirety by the editor. An adjacent stanza (4:14), for instance, has four lines that detail the perversions of the men and women of the Priestly families, and a fifth line that belongs in the editor's argument but does not fit very well in the stanza (4:14b, "And a people without insight fades away"). It is likely, therefore, that the abrupt and difficult style adopted by the editor was meant

to emphasize the new argument that was being developed but that was at best marginal to the original dramatic thrust of the prophecy.

[281] When Hosea announces that the day of retribution has arrived (9:7a), there is an outcry from the people (9:7b) to which Hosea responds by defending his role (9:8). As Yahweh gradually reveals the extent of the calamity, Hosea intervenes twice to express his approval (9:14, 17).

[282] See Andersen and Freedman, *Hosea*, 496; M. O'Connor, "The Pseudo-Sorites in Hebrew Verse," in *Perspectives on Language and Text: Essays and Poems in Honor of Francis I. Andersen's Sixtieth Birthday July 28, 1985*, ed. E. W. Conrad and E. G. Newing (Winona Lake, Ind.: Eisenbrauns, 1987) 239–53. Examples include 7:8–9; 7:11–12; 8:7; 8:11–12; 9:4; 9:5–6; 9:7b–8; 10:12. The same style is imitated in the revised version: 7:3–7; 7:15–16; 8:6; 10:13.

[283] It follows Hosea in its reliance on pronominal subjects in verbal clauses (7:6, 15; 8:4, 6, 13bB; 9:10) and in its use of pronominal suffixes to mark the progress of an argument (7:3–7; 8:4) or as a substitute for consecutive sequence (8:6; 9:10b, 15; 10:3, 15); its excesses are sometimes confusing (7:5; 8:5, 14).

[284] Lines: 7:1b; 8:13bB; 9:10b; stanzas: 7:10; 8:4; 8:10; 8:14; 9:9; 9:15; 10:3; 10:7–8aA; strophes: 7:3–7; 7:15–16; 8:5–6; 10:9–10; 10:13–15.

[285] Cf. 7:2 and 7:3 (*rāʿātām*).

[286] Cf. 8:2–3 and 8:5 (*ydʿ, znh*).

[287] Cf. 8:8–9 (*hitnû*) and 8:10 (*gam kî yitnû*).

[288] Cf. 9:7a and 9:9 (*pqd*).

[289] Cf. 10:11–12 and 10:13 (*ḥrš, qṣr*).

[290] The addition in 7:1b refers to 4:2aB and 6:9.

[291] The addition in 7:10 is constructed with reference to 5:4, 5, 6.

[292] Cf. 7:16 (*qešet*) and 1:5, 7; 2:20b.

[293] Cf. 8:6 and 8:14 (*ʿāśâ*).

[294] Cf. 9:15 (*rāʿātām*), 10:3 (*melek, hammelek*), and 7:3–7.

[295] The opening monologue (7:1a, 2) is interrupted by a comment (7:1b, "A thief tries to get in / a brigand robs outside") that exemplifies the notions of evil and deceit that were just mentioned (7:1a), but hardly illustrates the real evil and deceit perpetrated by Samaria. The metaphor of the mad baker (7:3–7) ends with a divine complaint, but it seems to be spoken by the author

(cf. 7:5, "On the day of our king . . ."). An editorial cross-reference (7:10) breaks up the second monologue. The tableau ends, however, with another divine monologue (7:15–16).

296 Hosea opens the first strophe with an alarm (8:1a) that introduces Yahweh's quotation and rejection of the prayer of the people (8:1b, 2–3). In this prayer the people complain that God has abandoned them (8:3a, zānaḥ yiśrāʾēl ṭôb), but the editor added another monologue-cum-speech, in which Yahweh explained that he had abandoned the calf of Samaria (8:5, zānaḥ ʿeglēk šōmĕrôn). In the second strophe Hosea describes the exile of the North, and the editor has Yahweh talk about their return from exile (8:10). In the last strophe Hosea describes the rituals surrounding their appeal for help, and the editor added another divine soliloquy, in which Yahweh rejected their kings, their cults, and their reliance on military might (8:14).

297 The corrections are references to the historical causes of the fall of Israel. They are added after Hosea's argument with the people (9:9), and in Yahweh's conversation (9:10b, 15) with him.

298 All the additions have to do with kings and war (10:3, 7–8aA, 9–10, 13–15). The first two conform to the monologue style, and the last fits more or less into Hosea's appeal; but Yahweh's direct address to Israel (10:9–10) breaks the dramatic pattern and conflicts with the following lament.

299 The commentaries (11:6–11; 13:15–14:10) conclude the editor's argument and contain numerous references to earlier passages in the book. Their most important effect is to deny once and for all the human and natural analogies that Hosea devised. The final sentence (14:10; see Andersen and Freedman, Hosea, 647–48) reflects on the meaning of the book and gives advice on how to read it.

300 See Hos 1:4 and 2 Kings 9° (see fig. 3). In the Deuteronomistic version, by contrast, the alliance brought Judah into contact with the dreaded house of Ahab, and Jehu was considered an inspired leader designated by God to combat the cult of Baal (2 Kings 9–10).

301 In Hosea's version foreign alliances are the obverse of their worship; they undermine it and display its insincerity (5:11, 13; 7:11–12; 12:1–3).

302 The name Jezreel means etymologically "May God plant" or "God has planted," and at the end of the first tableau, when Yahweh plants Jezreel in the land, Jezreel declares "My God" (2:24–25). However, the negative interpretation of Jehu's coup is suggested again at the beginning of the second triptych, when bloodshed (4:2, ∂āmîm; cf. 1:4) makes the real world wilt.

303 Cf. Hos 1:6 ("Call her name lōʾ ruḥāmâ, because I will not have any more pity [lōʾ . . . ʾăraḥēm] on the house of Israel, or ever forgive them [kî nāśōʾ ʾeśśāʾ lāhem]) and Exod 34:6–7 (ʾēl raḥûm . . . nōśēʾ ʿāwōn . . .).

304 Cf. Exod 34:6–7 (rḥm, ḥ∂∂, ʾmt) and Hos 2:21–22, 25; 4:1; 6:4–6.

305 Cf. Exod 34:7 (*'āwōn, peša', ḥaṭṭā'â*) and Hos 4:7–8; 7:1a, 13; 8:11, 13; 13:12–13.

306 Cf. Exod 34:6 (*pqd*) and Hos 8:13; 9:7; 13:3.

307 Cf. 1:8–9; Exod 3:9–14; Exod 34:6. Hosea contradicts the Elohist contention that Israel is the people of God (1:9 *lō' 'ammî;* cf. Exod 3:10, *'ammî*) but he also quotes the correlative Elohist prohibition against using the name of any other God (2:18–19, "I will take the names of the Baals off her lips, and they will no longer invoke their names"; cf. Exod 23:13, in opposite order, "You shall not invoke the name of another God, and it shall not be heard on your lips").

308 Cf. 2:20a (*krt bryt*) and Exod 34:10, 27.

309 Cf. 2:21 (*lĕ'ôlām*) and Gen 9:16 (*bĕrît 'ôlām*).

310 The Priestly writer (Gen 9:10) has "birds, cattle . . ." but Hosea (2:20) has "cattle, birds . . ." Hosea 2:20a (*ḥayyat haśśādeh . . . 'ôp haššāmayim . . . remeś hā'ădāmâ*) uses the words of the epic (Gen 2:19aA, *ḥayyat haśśādeh . . . 'ôp haššāmayim*) rather than the terminology of the Priestly writer (Gen 9:9–10, *'ôp . . . bĕhēmâ . . . ḥayyat hā'āreṣ;* cf. Gen 1:26).

311 Cf. 4:3b (*dĕgê hayyām*) and Gen 1:26 (*dĕgat hayyām*).

312 Cf. 1:2 (*tĕḥillat dibber yhwh*) and Gen 1:1 (*bĕrē'šît bārā' 'ĕlōhîm*). In both texts (2:23–25; Gen 1:1–12) the order of creation is heaven, earth, and seed.

313 Cf. 2:5b (*kammidbār . . . wahămittîhā baṣṣāmā'*) and Num 16:13 (*lahămîtēnû bammidbār;* cf. Exod 16:3; Num 20:4). Compare also 2:7b (*laḥmî ûmêmay . . . wĕšiqqûyāy*) and Exod 16:3 (*leḥem*), Num 20:5 (*mayim*), and Num 20:8 (*mêmāyw . . . wĕhišqîtā*).

314 Cf. 2:17 (*wĕnātattî lāh 'et kĕrāmêhā miššām*) and Num 16:14 (*'ap lō' . . . titten lānû . . . kerem*).

315 Cf. Deut 6:11; 11:14; 12:17; 14:22, 25–26; 2 Kgs 18:31–32.

316 Hosea (8:13, *bāśār* + *'kl;* and 9:1, *śmḥ, dgn, trš*) quotes the decree in an opposite order (Deut 12:17–18°, *dgn, trš, śmḥ;* Deut 12:20, *'kl* + *bāśār*).

317 Cf. 1:5 (*qešet*) and 2 Kgs 9:24 (*wĕyēhû' millē' yādô baqqešet*); also Hos 1:5 (*'ēmeq yizrĕ'e'l*) and Josh 17:16; Judg 6:33 (*'ēmeq yizrĕ'e'l*).

318 The editor refers to the return from exile in terms of the exodus from Egypt (2:2aB, *wĕ'ālû min hā'āreṣ* = Exod 1:10bB, *wĕ'ālâ min hā'āreṣ*). In the same passage Pharaoh worries that Israel is becoming too numerous (Exod 1:9b–10a), but the editor uses the Deuteronomistic cliché "like the sand of the sea" (Gen 22:17; 32:13; etc.) to express the fulfillment of the promise to the patriarchs.

319 Cf. 1:1 and 2 Kings 15–16; Hos 2:17aB and Joshua 7.

320 Cf. 2:2 (*qbṣ* + *bĕnê yiśrāʾēl*) and Ezek 37:21–22 (*bĕnê yiśrāʾēl* + *qbṣ*). The book of Ezekiel sees the reunification under one king (Ezek 37:22, *melek ʾeḥād*), but the editor, being leery of kings, uses the word "Head" and the Deuteronomistic installation formula (2:2, *wĕśāmû lāhem rōʾš ʾeḥād*; cf. Deut 17:14, 15, *śym mlk ʿl*; 1 Sam 8:5, *śîmâ lānû melek*). The quotation is confirmed at the end of the third tableau when the editor alludes to the book of Ezekiel again and mentions specifically that this leader is the Davidic king (3:5; cf. Ezek 37:24–25).

321 Hosea is commanded to love a woman who is an adulteress and loved by his neighbor (3:1a, *ʾiššâ ʾăhūbat rēaʿ ûmĕnāʾāpet*). The decalogue prohibits adultery and coveting a neighbor's wife (Deut 5:18 + 21 (*wĕlōʾ tinʾāp . . . wĕlōʾ taḥmōd ʾēšet rēʿekā*), as well as murder and theft (4:2aB, *wĕrāṣoaḥ wĕgānōb wĕnāʾōp*; cf. Deut 5:17–19, *rṣḥ, nʾp, gnb*). The basic prohibition of the decalogue is the worship of other Gods (Deut 5:7, *ʾelōhîm ʾăḥērîm*), but the editor quotes it in a typically Deuteronomistic form (3:1bB, *wĕhēm pônîm ʾel ʾĕlōhîm ʾăḥērîm* = Deut 31:18, 20).

322 Cf. 3:2–5 and Deut 4:27–30. The texts describe the same situation and use the same key words (*bqš, bĕʾaḥărît hayyāmîm, šwb*).

323 Cf. 5:11b (*hālak ʾaḥărê ṣaw*) and Isa 28:13 (*ṣāw lāṣāw ṣāw lāṣāw . . . lĕmaʿan yēlĕkû*). Isaiah confronted the lies of the people (Isa 28:15, 17, *šqr, kzb*) with justice and judgment (Isa 28:17, *mišpāṭ*), and Hosea sees Ephraim weighed down by judgment (5:11, *mišpāṭ*) for its lies. The lies that Isaiah condemned were the equivalent of their compact with Death and Sheol (Isa 28:15, 18), and Hosea's prophecy ends with Ephraim languishing in Death and Sheol for his lies (12:1, 2; 13:14).

324 Cf. 4:1a, *šimʿû dĕbar yhwh* = Isa 28:14.

325 Hosea indirectly argues with the people about his mission (9:7–8) and once pleads directly with them to turn to Yahweh (10:12) but otherwise engages in monologues or conversations with Yahweh. The editor is also reticent but addresses the people more often (4:15; 5:1, 8; 10:13–15; 14:2–3).

326 According to Isaiah, the people did not want to hear that Yahweh was a place of refuge and respite for them (Isa 28:12, *zōʾt hammĕnûḥâ hannîḥû lĕʿāyēp wĕzōʾt hammargēʿâ*) and would be swept away in the Assyrian storm. The last stanza in this tableau seems to say that Ephraim has taken refuge in idols (4:17, *ḥābûr ʿăṣabbîm ʾeprāyim hannaḥ lô*, "Under the spell of idols, Ephraim has found refuge for himself") that will be carried away in the wind.

327 Hos 4:10b (*kî ʾet yhwh ʿāzĕbû*) and Isa 1:4b (*ʿāzĕbû ʾet yhwh*).

328 Hos 5:7 (*kî bānîm zārîm yālādû*) and Isa 1:4 (*bānîm . . . nāzōrû ʾāḥôr*).

329 Hos 2:22; 4:1; 6:3; 7:9; 8:2; see also 11:3 and Isa 1:3; 5:19.

330 Hos 4:7 (*ḥaṭṭa't 'ammî yŏ'kēlû wĕ'el 'ăwōnām yiśĕ'û napšô*, "My people fed on sin and opened their mouths to guilt") and Isa 1:4 (*ḥṭ'*, *'wn*; cf. Isa 5:18).

331 Hos 5:13–14a, 6:1 (*ḥolyô, māzôr, yak wĕyaḥbĕšēnû*) and Isa 1:5–6 (*tukkû, ḥŏlî, lŏ' zōrû, lŏ' ḥubbāšû*).

332 Hos 8:7 (*zārîm yiblā'ûhû*) and Isa 1:7 (*zārîm 'ōkĕlîm 'ōtāh*).

333 Hosea describes Yahweh as a lion to Ephraim (5:14, *kî 'ānōkî kaššaḥal lĕ'eprayim wĕkakkĕpîr lĕbêt yĕhûdâ . . . wĕ'ên maṣṣîl*) as Isaiah had described the Assyrian invaders (Isa 5:29, *šĕ'āgâ lô kallābî' wiš'ag kakkĕpîrîm . . . wĕ'ên maṣṣîl*). Hosea returns to the image at the end of his work and includes a pun that relates the animal images of Yahweh and Assyria (13:7, *wā'ĕhî lāhem kĕmô šāḥal kĕnāmēr 'al derek 'ašûr*, "I was like a lion to them, like a leopard lurking by the road" [= *'ašûr*] or possibly, as a pun, "on the road to Assyria" [= *'ᵃaššûr*]).

334 Hos 4:5 (*kšl*) and Isa 28:13.

335 However, in condemning the princes of Judah (5:10), the editor combines references to Deuteronomy and Ezekiel: those who remove a boundary marker are cursed (5:10a, *kĕmassîgê gĕbûl*; cf. Deut 19:14; 27:17); a favorite expression in Ezekiel is "to pour out my wrath" (*špk ḥmh*, Ezek 7:8; 9:8; 14:19; 20:8, 13, 21, 33, 34; 22:22; 36:18), but the editor combined it with the similar Deuteronomistic expression "pour out the blood like water" (*špk dam kammayim*, Deut 12:16, 24; 15:23) and arrived at the saying "On them I will pour my wrath like water" (5:10b, *'ălêhem 'ešpôk kammayim 'ebrātî*).

336 The literal quotation is "Do not go to Gilgal," which reverses the order of the text in Amos (Hos 4:15b, *wĕ'al tābō'û haggilgāl* = Amos 5:5, *wĕhaggilgāl lō' tābō'û*). The quotation is confirmed by the command not to go up to Beth-awen (Hos 4:15, *wĕ'al ta'ălû bêt 'āwen*), which paraphrases the same text in Amos (Amos 5:5, *ûbêt 'ēl yihyeh lĕ'āwen*). The command not to swear by the life of Yahweh (Hos 4:15, *wĕ'al tiššābĕ'û ḥay yhwh*) paraphrases the prohibition in the book of Amos against going to Beersheba (Amos 5:5), where such an oath was customary (Amos 8:14, *ḥê 'ĕlōhêkā dān wĕḥê derek bĕ'ēr šāba'*). The editor also knew Amos's formula for the destruction of a capital city (Hos 8:14b, *wĕšillaḥtî 'ēš bĕ'ārāyw wĕ'ākĕlâ 'armĕnōtêhâ*; cf. Amos 1:4, 7, 14; 2:2) and the references in the book of Amos to the sanctuaries of Jacob (Hos 5:5a, *wĕ'ānâ gĕ'ôn yiśrā'ēl bĕpānāyw*; cf. Amos 6:8; 8:7, *gĕ'ôn ya'ăqōb*).

337 Hos 5:1, 8; Judges 19–21; and 1 Samuel 8–15. Tabor figures in the story of Gideon, who might have been king and who led Israel into the trap of his idolatry (Judg 8:18).

338 Both texts mention the road to Shechem (6:9; Judg 21:19) and an ambush (6:9; Judg 21:20–21). The lewd behavior attributed to the priests (6:9, *ki zimmâ 'āśû*) may refer to the rape described in the source text.

339 Hos 6:8 (*gilʿād qiryat pōʿălê ʾāwen*) and Judg 21:8–15; 1 Samuel 11.

340 Hos 5:8 (*ʾaḥărêkā binyāmîn* = Judg 5:14) and Judges 19–21.

341 Hos 6:7 (*ʿāběrû běrît*) and Josh 3:16 (*ʿāběrû*).

342 In Hos 9:10bA (*wayyinnāzĕrû labbōšet*) the author of the book refers to a text of Isaiah (Isa 1:4b, *nāzōrû ʾāḥôr*) in the language of Ezekiel (Ezek 14:5, 7, *nāzōrû, wěyinnāzēr*) to confirm its earlier quotation from the same text (9:9 = Isa 1:4a). The revision constantly refers to typical Deuteronomistic texts and formulations. The monarchy was established in opposition to Yahweh (8:4; cf. 1 Sam 8:22); the proper function of a king is to judge (7:7; 1 Sam 8:20); the end of the monarchy consists in cutting off succession (8:4, *yikkārēt*; cf. 1 Kgs 2:4; 8:25); Jeroboam's high place at Bethel became the sin of Israel (10:7–8aA, 10; 1 Kgs 12:30; 2 Kgs 17:4, 9); kingship is traced to Gibeah and Gilgal (9:9, 15; 10:9; cf. 1 Samuel 11); Baal-peor was an original sin (9:10b; Num 25:1–5); the calves of Samaria are a curse (8:6 = Deut 27:15).

343 The quotations are odd in their context (7:9aA = Isa 1:7bA; 7:12b = Isa 28:9a, 19b), confirmed by allusions (7:9aB, 9bB = Isa 1:3bA; 7:13 = Isa 28:15, 17), and supported by allusions in the revised version to the same texts (7:5b = Isa 28:14a; 7:16aB = Isa 28:11).

344 Hosea (10:4, *ûpāraḥ kārōʾš mišpāṭ*) quotes Amos in an opposite sense (Amos 6:12, *kî hăpaktem lěrōʾš mišpāṭ*). Both passages (10:4–5; Amos 6:12–13) condemn those who pretend to worship Yahweh and rely on alliances and military might, and both criticize those who just say words (10:4, *dibběrû děbārîm*) or who rejoice in non-words (Amos 6:13, *lōʾ dābār*). There is a variant expression in Amos (Amos 5:7a, *haḥōpěkîm lělaʿănâ mišpāṭ*), which occurs in his criticism of worship in Bethel (Amos 5:4–7). Hosea coined the name Beth-awen from this passage (10:5; cf. Amos 5:5) and quoted from the same passage a joke that Amos had made on the name Gilgal (10:5, *yāgîlû . . . kî gālâ*; Amos 5:5, *kî haggilgāl gālōh yigleh*).

345 Hos 9:5b (*yôm ḥag yhwh*), Amos 5:18, 20, 21 (*yôm yhwh . . . ḥaggêkem*) and Amos 8:9–10 (*yôm . . . ḥaggêkem*).

346 Hos 10:1 (*kěrōb lěpiryô hirbâ lammizběḥôt kěṭôb lěʾarṣô hêṭîbû maṣṣēbôt*) and Gen 35:11, 12, 14 (*pěrēh ûrěbēh . . . wěʾet hāʾāreṣ . . . lěkā ʾettěnennâ . . . maṣṣēbâ*). In the Elohist version Jacob built an altar at Bethel (Gen 35:6).

347 Hos 12:5 (*bêt ʾēl . . . wěšām yědabbēr ʿimmānû*) and Gen 35:15 (*ʾăšer dibber ʾittô šām . . . bêt ʾēl*). In the Elohist version of the same story, which was also available to Hosea, Jacob called the place "The God Bethel" (Gen 35:7, *ʾēl bêt ʾēl*).

348 For instance, 5:11 = Amos 4:1; 12:8 = Amos 8:5; 11:4 = Isa 5:18.

349 The Jacob story was composed by the author of the epic (= J), then

revised by the Priestly writer (= P) and the Elohist (= E). Hosea takes the story as a condemnation of Jacob rather than in its original laudatory sense and deliberately combines the sources, most notably when he has Jacob wrestle both with God, as the epic had it, and with the angel, whom the Elohist featured. The text and its sources are 12:4a = Gen 25:23 + 26 (P); 12:4b = Gen 32:29 (J); 12:5aA = Gen 32:29 (J) + Gen 32:2 and Gen 33:10 (E); 12:5aB = Gen 33:4 (J); 12:5bA = Gen 35:7 (E); 12:5bB = Gen 35:15 (P); 12:13a = Gen 27:43 (J) + Gen 28:2, 5 (P); 12:13bA = Gen 29:18 + Gen 30:31 (J); 12:14 = Exod 32:1, 23 (E).

[350] The references to Admah and Zeboim are from a speech in Deuteronomy (Hos 11:8–9; Deut 29:22–23). Yahweh's roar and the resulting terror are taken from Amos in a contradictory sense (Hos 11:10–11; Amos 3:6, 8). The references to Gilead and Gilgal are taken from the Deuteronomistic version of the story of Jacob and Laban (Hos 12:12; Gen 31:43–54). A comment on the calves of Samaria is taken from a curse in Deuteronomy (Hos 13:2aB; Deut 27:15). The institution of the monarchy is condemned with a quotation from the Deuteronomistic version (Hos 13:9–10; 1 Sam 8:6aB).

The Reformation

*U*nder the impetus of prophecy the Priestly writer and the Elohist set about revising the historical documents that were the foundation of Israelite faith. With these revisions in hand Micah and Jeremiah urged specific reforms in Judah and Jerusalem and extended the menacing oracles of their precedessors beyond the time of divine discipline to repentance and forgiveness and national reunification.

The Priestly document rewrote the epic as history, exalted its God, humbled its heroes, demystified their myths, and set the foundations of Israel in real and continuous time. It replaced the covenant that the sequel supposed with the creation of an ordered world, and it identified the place that supposedly Yahweh had chosen with a movable shrine invested with the glory of God. Annual pilgrimages to Jerusalem were abandoned, and the nationalism that they fostered was disassembled in natural and familial celebrations. Creatures were separate and clearly distinguished from God. The world was international and secular. Israel was not an ideal but a conglomerate of tribes descended from Jacob, heirs of the promise to Abraham, devoted to a transcendent and manifest God.

The Elohist rewrote the histories from a northern point of view. It eliminated the human and demonic features of the epic's Yahweh and embraced a God of concomitance and consolation. It traced the temple at Bethel to the time of Jacob and the cult of the golden calves to the inspiration of Aaron. It gave precedence to Joseph among his brothers and to Ephraim and Manasseh among the tribes. But above all it responded to the prophetic critique of contemporary Israelite society by incorporating a codified law into the revelation of the past. The God who provided for Israel, who promised to be with the people and give them gradual control of their land, now watched over the law to assure its observance.

Micah redid the earlier prophecies in the light of these historical insights. He magnified the prophetic threat to Judah and Jerusalem but based it less on the lesson to be learned from the history of Samaria than on the evident evils of the city. The problem was the self-satisfaction of those who believed that God was with them and was bound by local tradition. The charge was contempt for fundamental justice. The accused were the prophets, priests, and leaders who were supposed to administer the law. The plaintiffs were the people. But, with the law in place and tended by an attentive transcendent God, there was also a solution to the problem, and Micah could end his prophecy with the prayer and repentance of the city and its hope for a favorable verdict.

Jeremiah recomposed the prophets and historians in a drama of Israel and Judah. He reviewed the sins and punishment of the northern kingdom and portrayed the people repentant and willing to return to Yahweh. He retraced the prophetic threat to Judah and Jerusalem to their common disavowal of justice but issued a plea for lamentation and repentance. He saw, at the propitious moment, that tears welled up for Zion and that Judah had learned its lesson. At the end of the drama, in answer to their prayers, the remnant of Israel is saved; Jacob returns to Zion; Rachel and her children are reunited; and lament gives way to jubilation.

These literary claims were romanticized by the Deuteronomist in the ill-fated reform of Josiah. This Historian, in agreement with the prophets, showed once and for all in the story of the perfect Davidide who promulgated the law and renewed the covenant that the covenant did not work without the law and could not overcome the history of sin. But, in evident disagreement with the expectations of the prophet, the Deuteronomist also recounted the ignominious death of Josiah and the dismal inadequacy of his partial repentance and reform. In the event, if not in fact, the prophets were wrong and history was held in abeyance.

The Priestly Document (fig. 7)

The Priestly document is composed of ten genealogies.[1] These are records or brief historical accounts that are strung along a temporal,

F I G U R E   7

The Priestly Document (Pg)

Genealogies

	I		V		IX
Gen	1:1–2	Gen	11:10–11	Gen	36:1–3
	1:3–5a		11:12–13		36:4–5
	1:5b–10a		11:14–26		36:6–8
	1:10b–12a				37:1
	1:12b–16		VI		
	1:17–21abA	Gen	11:27–28		X
	1:21bB–25a		11:31–32	Gen	37:2aA
	1:25b–27		12:4b–5abA		46:6–7
	1:28–31a		16:1, 3, 15–16		47:27–31
	1:31b–2:3		17:1–2		49:33b
	2:4a		17:3–8		50:12–13
			17:9–14		
	II		17:15–18	Exod	1:1–4, 5b
Gen	5:1–24		17:19–21		1:6–7, 13–14
	5:25–29abA,		17:22–23		2:23aBb–25
	30–32		17:24–27		6:2–9
			21:1b, 2b, 4–5		6:10–12
	III		23:1–15		7:1–7
Gen	6:9–12		23:16–18		7:8–13
	6:13–22		23:19–20		7:19–20, 21b–
	7:11, 13–14		25:7–10		22
	7:15–16a				8:1–3, 9b–11
	7:18		VII		8:12–13
	7:19–21	Gen	25:12–16		8:14–15
	7:24; 8:1a		25:17		9:8–12
	8:1b–2				11:9–10
	8:3–4		VIII		12:1–6, 8–11
	8:5	Gen	25:19–23		12:28
	8:13a, 14–18		25:24–26		12:40–41
	8:19		25:27–30		12:42
	9:1, 9–17		25:31–34		14:1–4a
	9:28–29		28:1–4		14:4b, 8a, 9aBb
			28:5		14:10bB, 15–18
	IV		35:9–10abA		14:21–22
Gen	10:1		35:10bB–12		14:23, 25b–27a,
	10:2–5		35:13–15, 27		28
	10:6–7, 20		35:28–29		14:29
	10:22–23, 31–32				15:20–21
					15:22–25a, 27;
					16:1

continued

FIGURE 7 (cont)

	Genealogies				
	X (*Cont*)	Exod	36:12	Num	14:1a, 2–3
Exod	16:2–3, 6–7, 9–		36:13–15		14:26–27
	12		36:16–17		14:28–32
	16:13–15, 35a		36:18–19		14:36–38
	17:1abA; 19:1a,		36:20–22		20:1aBb, 2–5
	2a		36:23–24		20:7–8
	24:15–17		36:25–26		20:9–12
	24:18; 25:1–5, 8		36:27–28		20:13
	26:1–30; 29:43,		36:29a		20:22–25
	45–46		36:29b–30		20:27, 28aBb–
	31:13–14		36:31–32		29
	31:15–17		36:33		22:1; 27:12–13
	31:18; 35:1–3		36:34a		27:15–17
	35:4–7		36:34b–35		27:18–21
	35:20–22		36:36–38		27:22–23
	35:23–29		40:16–19	Deut	1:3
	36:2–3		40:35b–37		32:48–50, 51b–
	36:4–7				52
	36:8–9	Num	10:11–12;		34:1aAGb–5
	36:10		12:16b; 13:3		34:7–8
	36:11		13:21a, 26a, 32,		34:9
			33b		

Figure 7. Paragraphs are on separate lines.

calendrical, or generational line.[2] They all have the same formal introduction[3] and are composed either of formulas, verbatim repetition, incidents in recurring patterns, or stylized address.[4] They usually precede or envelop episodes or incidents in the epic and rarely are woven into its text.[5] They can be read in sequence with the epic, but, since they are both preemptive and redundant and further marked off from the original by their style and diction, they can also be read as a complete, independent, and consecutive history of Israel.

The first three genealogies enclose the episodes of creation and the flood and move man and woman from the epic past into legendary historical time. Creation took a week and set the cosmic clock in the orderly succession of days, weeks, months, and years. Man and woman were blessed, but so were the birds and the fish. They were given dominion over the other creatures, but they had the same sort of food to eat. Adam never had a chance to be immortal and in fact lived less than a full millennium and fewer years than Methuselah or Noah.[6] Noah was not, as the epic had suggested, an offspring of the Gods but one of the sons of Lamech in the line of Adam. The flood was not a weapon in a theogonic struggle, as the epic had insinuated, but God's response to specific crimes. It was not the end of the world but a datable event that lasted about a year and had no effect whatever on the order that was established in creation and reconfirmed in the covenant with Noah.

The epic material that these genealogies enclose seems naïve and fanciful by comparison. Yahweh who walked in his garden and fussed over its trees and worried that people could be like him and live forever is replaced by a God who works efficiently and without emotion and with better or more predictable results. In the process, of course, the rustic charm and clever conversations that pervade the epic are lost in the clipped cadences of command and execution. Every mythic detail, in fact, has its rational analogue. The resemblance between God and the man and woman that he made is only in appearance but not in ability or potential. The animals were not made as companions of man, but man and woman were made to govern the animals. Trees do not give knowledge or life but produce fruit to feed people. Gods did not marry mortal women but mortals like Noah walked with God or like Enoch lived for a relatively short time and were taken away by God. It was not just Noah and his family that survived the flood and disappeared in immemorial time; it was the world and time itself and the orderly succession of generations that were assured. It was still possible, perhaps pleasant, to read the epic, but it was no longer really required.

The fourth, fifth, sixth, and seventh genealogies envelop the third episode and give Abraham a firm foundation in historical and geographical fact. According to the epic, Abraham's migration to Canaan was part of the primordial dispersion of the nations. In the Priestly version, on the other hand, the nations were descendants of the sons of Noah, and each had its own land, language, and organization. Abraham, in this scheme, was a descendant of Shem from Ur of the Chaldeans. He was born 292 years after the flood, moved to Canaan with Sarah when he was seventy-five, became the father of Ishmael when he was eighty-six and the father of Isaac when he was one hundred. According to the epic, the birth of Isaac took place after a visitation from Yahweh, but in the Priestly version it was in fulfillment of Yahweh's promise to Abraham. The epic heroes do not die; but in the Priestly document Sarah died in Hebron when she was 127 years old; Abraham died when he was 175 years old; and they were both buried in Mamre in the field of Machpelah which he had purchased from Ephron the Hittite. In the epic Abraham was a hero from the distant past, but in the Priestly document he is the progenitor of nations and of the kingdoms of Israel.

The final genealogies are related to the history of Jacob and Israel. The genealogy of Isaac records Isaac's marriage with Rebekah, an Aramean from Paddan, the momentous birth of Jacob and Esau, Jacob's journey to Paddan-aram and his encounter with God at Bethel on his return to Canaan. It envelops the epic version and eliminates the family feuds and Jacob's mysterious encounter with the God of Canaan. The genealogy of Esau removes him from Jacob, as Lot was separated from Abraham, and gives the land of Canaan to Jacob. The genealogy of Jacob envelops and ignores the epic story of Joseph and attributes the journey from Canaan to Egypt to the initiative of the patriarch. The story of Israel coincides with the career of Moses and ends with the death of all the principals and the prospect of settlement in the land.

The Priestly document celebrated the holiness of God and, as an alternative to the prophecies and histories, provided a cool and nonpartisan interpretation of his dealings with Israel and the world. God is involved in creation by words and deeds but not by obligation or descent. God made the world, spoke to Israel's ancestors, and left physical signs and memorials of his active transcendence. Israel is not related to God by antiquity or by ritual or by any local, political, or historical bond of necessity but is implicated in the real world and is supposed to respond freely by obedience and recollection. The issues that divided the Priestly writer's contemporaries—issues of orthodox belief and practice—were simply subsumed in a wholly rational and sensible attachment to ordinary life.

The Priestly alternative was inspired by the theories, texts, and practices of late Assyrian times. Its principal sources, apart from the epic, whose steps it dogged, and from the sequel to the epic, whose ideas it disparaged, were the literary, scholarly, and professional texts they read and adapted. Its mannerisms are derived from the varieties of discourse that it imitated. Its interpretation draws on Isaiah's sense of divine indignation and is parallel or partly tangential to Amos's perception of time and fate. The alternative that the Priestly document offered was the first step in reconciliation and reform.

The first genealogy mimics and replaces the epic story of the Garden of Eden. It begins and ends with a quotation from the epic, maintains its combination of narration, divine command, and soliloquy, and supplies the standard story of creation, which the epic mentioned but omitted.[7] This story, derived from the *Enuma elish*, corrects the general thrust of the epic that it derived from the stories of Gilgamesh and Atrahasis by establishing a physical limit between God and the world and a temporal boundary between the creation of the world and its regular continuance.[8] The same source, denuded of its myth and ritual and distilled as science and mechanics, is adapted again in the description of the exodus and the construction of the tabernacle.[9]

The replacement of the epic account of creation is clinched by continuing with a genealogy that skips the epic and refers to the end of the preceding Priestly version.[10] This genealogy of the antediluvian ancestors of Noah has analogies in Sumerian, Assyrian, and Babylonian lists and is especially notable for its acquaintance with Babylonian mathematics.[11] But the genealogy also includes asides on Enoch and Noah that indicate familiarity with the legends of Gilgamesh and Atrahasis and allow the Priestly writer to preempt the reasons the epic gave for the flood by alluding to the orthodox Mesopotamian interpretation (Gen 5:24, 29).[12]

The third genealogy surrounds the epic story of Noah with a completely symmetrical calendrical reckoning.[13] It begins by repeating the end of the preceding genealogy in order to bracket and marginalize the story of the Titans that opened the epic version of the flood. It ends with a reference to the same text to complete the history of Noah. The difference between the two matching segments is that the Priestly writer alluded to Amos and commented on the epic in the first part but had no source for the second.[14] Next in the encompassing account of the flood are matching segments that anticipate and conclude the covenant with Noah. The difference between them, similarly, is that the writer quoted Amos's saying that the end had come and referred to the Mesopotamian story of the flood to describe the construction of the ark, but had no literary sources for the composition of the covenant.[15] The center of the story is a description of the flood that elaborates the epic text.[16] Around this pivot are sections with parallels in the Babylonian version that describe Noah and creation boarding and disembarking from the ark (Gen 7:11, 13–16a and 8:1–5, 13a, 14). The revision adheres to the canonical Akkadian version of the flood, and its effect is the conviction that, although the end had come as Amos said, nothing really occurred to alter the structure of the world or the order of creation.

The fourth genealogy is a geography of the world. It is partly a commentary on the next epic episode concerning the distinction of nations and languages[17] and partly a transition between the flood story and the life of Abraham.[18] Its source was not literary but scholarly and resembled a political and economic map of the Mediterranean world.[19]

The fifth genealogy completes and complements the fourth. Together they isolate the epic version of the Tower of Babel and eliminate the sense of mystery and antiquity that it conveyed to the story of Abraham.[20]

The sixth genealogy circumscribes the life of Abraham and embraces a mixture of genres. Its outline, as usual, is provided by opening and closing genealogical entries and by intermediate chronological links that put the story on a firm historical footing.[21] The first narrative fragment supplies information that the epic supposed but did not narrate—that Abraham had a wife named Sarah—and information that seems to contradict the epic's intention—that Abraham also had a family before Isaac was born and that he acquired his wealth in Haran rather than with the blessing of Yahweh in Canaan.[22] The story of Hagar and Ishmael combines both chronology and genealogy with elements of a birth narrative and, by making Abraham the father of many nations, ruins the epic's impression of a natural bond between Yahweh and the children of Abraham.[23] The covenant with Abraham preempts the epic narrative of the visitation of Sarah but imitates it in combining narrative and dialogue with its own legal and historical interests.[24] The account of Abraham's negotiations with the Hittites situates him in a particular historical and geographical context and corrects the epic impression that he was alone in the land, but it follows the pattern of mixed genres by framing a contractual agreement in a genealogical death notice (Genesis 23).[25] The life of Abraham, with these additions, becomes encased in a packet of legitimating documents that make him accessible to the reader as the ancestor of Israel in an enveloping cosmopolitan world.[26]

The eighth genealogy is composed of four incidents.[27] Apart from the opening formula and the notice of Isaac's death,[28] they contain little genealogical and chronological information and are modeled instead on the narrative style of the epic, with action, motivation, and dialogue. The first two incidents are alternatives to the epic account of Jacob's wiliness and explain from two different perspectives how Jacob acquired primogeniture. The third and fourth incidents are alternatives to the epic account of Jacob's sojourn in the East and explain how he came to be Israel and the heir to the promise to Abraham. The first incident has no parallel in the epic but, in a narrative adaptation of the formula for consulting God, attributes Rebekah's pregnancy and the precedence of Jacob to supplication and oracular response. The second incident redoes the epic story in which Jacob acquired the blessing of the firstborn by outwitting Esau and preparing game for Isaac, but it omits Isaac and contains a clever reversal in which Jacob acquires the right of the firstborn by preparing his own staple food for Esau. The third incident combines epic and Priestly material. It omits the epic conflict between Jacob and Esau and in place of the blessing of Isaac gives Jacob the blessing of creation and the hope of the covenant with Abraham. The fourth incident omits the epic fight with God, transmits the covenant to Israel and, in disagreement with Amos and the sequel to the epic, legitimates the sanctuary at Bethel and the separate kingdoms of Israel and Judah.[29]

The ninth genealogy combines a list of the descendants of Edom with a narrative of the separation of Jacob and Esau. The first is original to the Priestly writer.[30] The second reworks an earlier narrative in the epic and marks the fulfillment of the promise to Abraham.[31]

The genealogy of Jacob and Israel is by far the most complex and expresses more clearly the Priestly convictions that underlay its presentation of primeval and patriarchal history. At issue in most cases are theories and practices propounded by the epic and the sequel, but the writer also creates a new popular constitution that had serious repercussions in the development of prophecy and historiography.

The genealogy has three main sections. The first goes from Israel's descent into Egypt to the exodus and comes to a close with a quotation from the Song of Miriam.[32] The second covers the journey from the Sea to Sinai and ends when the tabernacle is prepared and poised for the journey through the wilderness (Exod 15:22–40:37*).[33] The third section is the story of the wilderness wanderings, and it ends with the deletion of the wilderness generation and all its leaders (Num 10:11–Deut 34:9*).[34]

The first section disputes the epic's legitimation of Moses and the sequel's instructions on the celebration of Passover[35] in a dramatic presentation of the effects of prophecy on history. It combines genealogy, commentary, narrative, discourse, and measured description in the framework of a lamentation liturgy that takes the reader from the cries of the people through the attentiveness of God to his victory over the Egyptians and its memorialization at Passover and in a final song of praise.[36] The second section disputes the epic covenant with Yahweh and in its place describes the glory of Yahweh that resides with a dedicated people willing to work and observe the sabbath. It is composed as a diptych of command and execution,[37] as the terrestrial tabernacle takes the form of its model in heaven. The third section disputes the epic interpretation of rebellion in the wilderness and oversees the annihilation of the ancient and formative society and the rise of a new generation freed from its sinful tradition. It is composed as an itinerary marked by a series of prophetic disputations.[38]

In the first section of the epic recounted the birth of Moses, his encounters with Yahweh, and the victory over the Egyptians at the

Sea, which led the people to believe in him and Yahweh. In the Priestly version the emphasis shifts to Yahweh, and the victory is assimilated to the primordial victory of creation.[39] Moses, far from being honored and successful, is sidelined and redundant. He is not, as he was in the epic, the subject of marvelous meetings with Yahweh that ultimately lead him into the magic of the covenant on Sinai, but he is simply allowed into the unfolding promise to Abraham, Isaac, and Jacob.[40] He is as God to Pharaoh, and Aaron is his prophet, but Pharaoh pays no attention to him.[41] Moses and prophecy have no effect on the course of events, and, as Miriam the prophet recognized, God alone gets glory in redoing the mysteries of creation for the sake of his covenant with the fathers.[42]

The second section develops the same theme of prophecy and history succumbing before the natural order governed by Yahweh. In the epic version Israel went directly from the Sea to Mount Sinai, where Yahweh made a covenant with Moses and the people. In the Priestly version the authority of Moses and Aaron is undermined by the people's need for food and drink, while the work of creation continues to be revealed in the construction of the tabernacle and the celebration of the sabbath.[43]

The journey through the desert to Mount Sinai has allusions backward to the crossing of the sea and to the time before that in Egypt and references forward to the wilderness wanderings and settlement in a habitable land.[44] It reveals the true temper of the people and, along with particular features of the tabernacle, contains implicit criticisms of the centralized place of worship proposed by the sequel.[45] The design of the tabernacle itself and the observance of the sabbath that is associated with it continue the criticism and are also presented as explicit substitutes for the epic covenant revealed on Sinai.[46] What is revealed on Sinai according to the Priestly version is the holiness of Yahweh that is manifested in creation and in the glory filling the tabernacle and that redounds to the holiness of the people who observe the sabbath.[47] The section ends as it began with the tabernacle ready to continue the journey from Mount Sinai to the land promised to the fathers.

The final section recounts this journey and the elimination of aboriginal Israel, which rebelled against its prophets and priests and refused to affirm the holiness of Yahweh. In the first scene the people travel from Sinai to the southern border of the land, but when the scouts report that the land devours its inhabitants they refuse to go any farther and are left to die in the desert. This is a correction of the epic account in which the people did not believe that Yahweh could defeat the inhabitants but were saved by the intercession of Moses and his appeal to the terms of the covenant (Numbers 13–14).[48] The same epic text is a source of the second scene, in which Moses and Aaron become implicated in the rebellion of the people, refuse to believe, deny the holiness of Yahweh, and are condemned to die in the wilderness (Num 20:1aBb, 2–5, 7–13).[49] The final scenes redo elements of the epic and the sequel and leave the next generation of Israel in the hands of Joshua, who is filled with the spirit of wisdom and assisted by Eleazar the priest.[50]

CONCLUSION

The Priestly document was composed as an alternative to the epic and the sequel. It not only commented on them, but rewrote them in an independent work that was designed to suit, surround, and circumvent them.

Its sources were mainly the epic and sequel themselves. In the earlier and later genealogies it relied on their Akkadian sources to correct their partial interpretations and develop a cosmological antidote to history. In the beginning, as well, it used a famous text from Amos to suggest that his words had come true in an earlier irrelevant time, and in the end it drew on Isaiah's appreciation of the holiness of God to divorce worship from political activity and ceaseless service.[51] Throughout it employed genres taken from religious and legal practice to fill out its scheme of natural descendancy, which it used to supplant historical sequence and the prophetic manipulation of events.

In place of the covenant cherished by the epic and its sequel and in place of an historically engaged Yahweh favored by the prophets, the Priestly writer presented God who created and managed the world. He spoke to Noah and Moses, revealed himself to Abraham and Jacob, met Moses in the cloud of his glory, to promise or require human and physical things that natural signs could recall. The people who died in the wilderness were those who argued about food and drink because they associated them with Egypt or some ideal land rather than with the God who could bring water out of the rock and make food from the dew. The people who led them were nobody, did nothing but speak or point to his deeds, and in the end were completely dispensable. The people who would worship him observed the sabbath, stopped what they were doing to observe what he had done, in a covenant like the covenant with Noah and the covenant with Abraham, designed to last forever.

The Priestly document gave Israel a brand new chance. There was no longer room for regional and religious factionalism, and the local bias and partisan positions of the epic and the sequel became strictly taboo. Everyone who could see a rainbow, claim to be a true descendant of Abraham, and keep the sabbath was an heir to the promise. The promise, essentially, was that life would go on forever.

The Elohist (fig. 8)

The Elohist retold the epic stories to prove a theory of divine providence. Its material consists in legends of the epic heroes, which were inserted into the epic version to disrupt its flow and draw attention to the theological significance of its stories. The legends are discontinuous, composed of incidental segments fitted into the epic at appropriate spots, and suppose their epic context. But each segment is also linked to the last, and their interpretation of the epic is both retrospective and anticipatory, referring to the immediate and the circumambient context, as well as progressive and cumulative from incident to incident and from legend to legend.

The Elohist also supposes the Priestly document, corrects its secular outlook, and elaborates on some of its scenes. Its material is sometimes linked to the Priestly text but is arranged so as not to disrupt it or diminish its overarching design on the epic.

STRUCTURE AND ORGANIZATION

The legends are distinguished from each other both by the intervening epic material with its changing perspective and by the consistency of their own argument. The incidents are linked to their epic or Priestly context by editorial artifice and to one another by logical, grammatical, and literary links.

The Legend of Abraham

The legend has four incidents that illustrate the providence of God in the succession from Abraham to Isaac. They break the epic sequence between the promise to Sarah and the birth of her child and pad the episodic connection between the birth of Isaac and his early career in Gerar.[52]

The first incident is linked to the preceding epic text by a deictic iteration: Abraham, in the epic version, went to the place *where* he had stood with Yahweh, and in the Elohist version he went *from there* to the Negeb.[53] The next three incidents are arranged in continuous sequence,

FIGURE 8

The Elohist (E)

Legends

GENESIS

I. Abraham

A	B	C	D
20:1aAb–3	21:6	21:22–23	22:1–2
20:8, 10–11	21:7	21:24, 27, 34	22:3
20:14–15	21:8–10		22:4–5
20:16	21:11–13		22:6–8a
	21:14–16a		22:8b–12
	21:16b–21		22:13–14, 19

II. Jacob

A	B	C
28:10–12	31:4–7	35:1
28:17–18,	31:8–9	35:2–3
20–22	31:10–13	35:4–5a, 6aAb
	31:14–16	35:7
	31:19a, 20–25	
	31:26–27, 29	
	31:36b, 38–39a	
	31:39b–40	
	31:41	
	31:42	
	31:51–53a	
	31:53b–32:2a	
	32:2b–3, 8–9	
	32:14b–22	
	32:23aA°b, 24b;	
	33:3	
	33:8–11, 18a	

III. Joseph

A	B	C	D
37:2aBb, 3b	39:6b–9	42:6, 8–9a	48:1–2, 8–9
37:5–8	39:10	42:18b, 21–23	48:10–11
37:9–11	39:11–15	45:4–13	48:12–16
37:19–20	39:16–18	45:14–15	48:17–21
37:21–24	39:19–20	46:1–4	50:1–6
37:28aAb, 29a	40:1–3	46:5	50:7–8
37:29b–30	40:4–5		50:14–18
37:31–33	40:6		50:19–21

continued

FIGURE 8 (*cont*)

		Legends	
A	B	C	D
37:34–36	40:7–10		50:22–24
	40:11–15		50:25–26
	40:16–19		
	40:20–23		
	41:1–7		
	41:8–13		
	41:14–16		
	41:17–21a		
	41:21b–24		
	41:25–32		
	41:33–40		
	41:41–43		
	41:44–49		
	41:50–54		

EXODUS

IV. Moses

A	B	C	D
3:1, 4b–6	13:17	18:1a, 2a, 3–5, 12	24:13–14
3:9–10	13:18–19	18:13–14	32:1–6
3:11	14:5b, 7	18:15–16	32:15–16
3:12	14:8b, 10abA,	18:17–20	32:17–19a, 21a,
3:13	19a, 25a	18:21–23	22–25
3:14		18:24–27	34:29aBb–31
4:18a		19:3a, 14a,	34:32a, 33
4:18b		16aBb–17, 18bB–19	
		20:1	
		21:2–11	
		21:12–27	
		21:28–37	
		22:1–8	
		22:20–26	
		22:27–30	
		23:1–5	
		23:6–9	
		23:10–13	
		23:14–16	
		23:20–22	
		23:27, 29–31	

Figure 8. Letters indicate incidents. Paragraphs are on separate lines.

but the first is linked to the epic and Priestly stories of the birth of Isaac by a pun on the child's name.[54]

The incidents are linked to one another in an alternating and a sequential pattern. The first incident ends when Abimelech dismisses Sarah from his harem saying that the money he paid to Abraham will close his eyes to the situation and vindicate her, but the second begins with Sarah protesting on the contrary that the birth of her son Isaac has made her a laughing stock.[55] The third incident is attached to the second, but grammatically it is linked to the first incident and in fact continues its story of Abraham and Abimelech.[56] The fourth incident is dated after the third but is linked by both grammar and theme to the second.[57]

The entire legend is devoted to the trials and tribulations of Abraham and deals with the single issue of the role of divine providence in designating his legitimate heir. In the first incident Abraham travels to Gerar, where the legitimacy of Isaac is threatened by Abimelech's dalliance with Sarah until God intervenes in a dream. In the second incident Ishmael is sent away, but the angel of God intervenes from heaven. In the third Abimelech reflects on God's enduring providence to Abraham. In the last the angel intervenes again to save Isaac, and Abraham moves on to Beersheba.

The Legend of Jacob

The second main part of the Elohist version is the legend of Jacob. It starts where the first left off with Jacob moving on to Haran from Beersheba (Gen 22:19; 28:10). It begins with his vow at Bethel, retells the epic story to show that God was with Jacob and protected him on his journey, and it ends with the fulfillment of his vow at Bethel.[58]

The first incident is linked to the adjoining Priestly text by minimal verbatim repetition.[59] The second is linked to the epic text preceding it by a paraphrase of its concluding clauses and is attached to the first incident by a literal reprise.[60] The last is a continuation of the Elohist text before it and is not tied to any earlier text.[61]

The legend was fitted in between the parts of the Priestly genealogy of Isaac and complements its mechanical transfer of the covenant to Jacob with stories of continuous divine care.[62] It straddles the epic narrative of Jacob and Laban and separates it from the story of Isaac in the first part of the episode.[63] But it also obstructs the flow of the narrative by adding an account of Jacob's escape from Laban and by interweaving an alternative interpretation of his encounter with Esau. The escape is a block of material linked to the epic by verbatim repetition.[64] The new interpretation of the encounter with Esau was added discretely to the various stages of the original with the help of deictic and repetitive sutures.[65]

The Legend of Joseph

The legend of Joseph has four main incidents. In the first he is a dreamer and his brothers sell him into slavery in Egypt. In the second he is put in prison, but by interpreting the dreams of fellow inmates and of the Pharaoh he is able to predict the famine that overtook the world and provide sufficient stores for its duration. In the third his brothers come to buy grain, and he makes himself known to them, explains his presence in Egypt as an act of divine providence, and summons Israel to Egypt until the famine is past. In the last incident Israel blesses Ephraim and Manasseh, dies and is buried in Canaan, and Joseph gives a final prospective and résumé of the workings of divine providence.

The first incident latches on to the epic text in four separate places. The first place is at the beginning. The epic began with the fact that the brothers hated Joseph because he was his father's favorite. The Elohist adds that Joseph was only seventeen, that he was a shepherd with his brothers and tattled on them, and that his father made him a long flowing robe. All of this is important for the story that the Elohist is going to tell, and it is fitted into the epic by brusque deictic manipulation of its text.[66] The second segment is the dream sequence. It finds a place in the epic by repeating part of it in a different sense but follows just as easily on the previous Elohist addition as it does on the contiguous epic text.[67] The third segment recounts the brothers' decision to kill Joseph, Reuben's intervention, and the compromise plan to smear his tunic in blood and pretend that he had been killed. It presupposes the original narrative, in which the brothers see Joseph approaching and decide to kill him but are persuaded by Judah to sell him to itinerant Ishmaelites on their way to Egypt. It is fitted into the original by using a deictic expression to indicate that Joseph was approaching.[68] The last part is wrapped around the end of the epic text and ends the way the next epic text begins.[69] The brothers' plan to leave Joseph in a pit and pretend that he was killed by a wild animal was modified at the last minute to suit the epic story, and so the Elohist version ends with Joseph sold to Midianites on their way to Egypt and with Israel grieving for his dead son.[70]

The second incident is all of a piece and fits in between the epic statements that Joseph was put in charge of palace food supplies and that his brothers came to Egypt to buy food during the great famine.[71] It is attached to the original by verbatim repetitions at both ends of the insertion and explains how, with the help of God, there happened to be grain in Egypt when the famine had affected the whole world.[72]

The third incident is the recognition scene and is composed as the fulfillment of the dream sequence in the first segment. It starts by reminding the reader that Joseph was the prefect of the land when his brothers came and bowed down before him and, lest the reference to Joseph's second dream be missed, says that this reminded Joseph of his dream. The reminder and reference are put into the epic text with deictics and simple repetition (Gen 42:6, 8–9a).[73] Before the recognition scene the Elohist inserted another allusion to the first segment and in particular to Reuben's attempt to save Joseph. It is affixed to the surrounding epic text by deictics and allows the brothers to rehearse their evil deeds and accept their present predicament as the fulfillment of Reuben's worried prediction (Gen 42:18b, 21–23; cf. 37:19–24, 29–30).[74] In the recognition scene itself, joined to the parallel epic text by verbatim repetition,[75] Joseph reviews the whole story up to this point to prove that providence has been at work in every incident and predicts the rest of the story to show how it will continue. The incident ends with Israel traveling to Egypt in accordance with Joseph's instructions in the preceding segment but also in literal agreement with the epic text around it and in anticipation of the Priestly text to follow (Gen 46:1–5; cf. 45:9–13).[76] On his journey God speaks to him at Beersheba, assures him of protection in Egypt, and predicts the events to be recounted in the next incident.

The last incident fits around the Priestly record of the provisions for Jacob's burial and the account of his death. The first part follows immediately on Jacob's instructions to Joseph concerning his burial in the family plot in Canaan. It is linked to the Priestly text by a deictic temporal reference and records, in the guise of Jacob's blessing on Ephraim and Manasseh, all the benefits of divine providence to the patriarch (Gen 48:1–2, 8–21).[77] The second part follows immediately on the death of Jacob, is tied to it by a pun and literal repetition, and describes the funeral cortege that took Jacob to his tomb in Canaan (Gen 50:1–8).[78] The last part continues the second without any basis in the epic or Priestly sources and is essentially a summary and anticipation of the Elohist text.[79]

The four incidents make a complete story that depends at every point on the epic and Priestly versions but still conveys a continuous univocal interpretation of what they wrote. Each of the incidents is finished in itself, and all are linked together in a staggered literary structure.

The first incident is a rounded dramatic whole revolving on the tunic that Israel made for Joseph and that his brothers tore off him and brought back to their father. At the very end of the incident Jacob proclaims that he will go down to Sheol weeping for his son, and the equivalent occurs at the end of the third incident when Israel goes down to Egypt to see his son and die there.[80] In the second incident Joseph is promoted from keeper of his master's house to ruler of Egypt, and from being accused of indecency with Potiphar's wife to marriage with Asenath, the daughter of a homophonous Potiphera (39:6b–20; 41:45, 50–52). This incident begins with Joseph being bought in Egypt just as the first incident ended with his being sold in Egypt, and it ends with Joseph's age when he entered into Pharaoh's service to match the reference to his age at the beginning of the story.[81] The next incident continues with the story of the famine begun in the second but reflects and fulfills the prophetic themes of the first incident. The last incident is linked to the second by its attention to Ephraim and Manasseh, but it also continues the story of Jacob in Egypt that was begun in the third and ends with a résumé and interpretation of the entire legend of Joseph.

The Legend of Moses

The legend of Moses is composed of unequal parts that correct their epic counterparts and divert attention from the idea of a covenant with Yahweh to the ideal of a law-abiding people attended by God and his messengers. The parts preempt the epic texts to which they are attached, separate them from each other in the episode, and enclose them in an alternative view of Israel's lot in life.

The first part surrounds the story of the burning bush with the story of Moses and Jethro (Exod 3:1 and 4:18). It encloses the epic version in which Yahweh says that he has come down to save the people from Egypt and bring them to the good land with a variant of the same in which God identifies himself as the God of the Patriarchs and promises to be with them (Exod 3:4b, 6a, 9–14). The new text is attached discretely to the original by the usual deictic and repetitive devices and, besides commenting on the epic text, prepares for its own sequel in the fourth part.[82]

The second part preempts the epic version of a sensational escape from Egypt with the story of an armed band of people that at first was allowed to leave and eventually with the help of the angel of God

defeated the pursuing Egyptian forces. Its elements are added piecemeal to the combined epic and Priestly text, and the victory that it
describes is what prompts Jethro to come and meet Moses in the next
part.[83]

The third part is related to the second[84] but is out of all proportion
to the others. It anticipates and corrects the epic version of Yahweh's
theophany on Sinai and the revelation of the covenant by instituting
law courts and introducing the revelation of the law. Its opening scene
is attached by anticipation to the following epic text to explain that
Moses went to the top of the mountain of God to bring difficult legal
cases before the divine tribunal.[85] The second segment is distributed in
the original to lighten the epic's insistence on Moses and faith and to
include the people in the theophany at the mountain (Exod 19:3a, 14a,
16aBb–17 & 18bB–19).[86] The third segment corresponds to the first
and contains the law that God revealed to Moses and to the people at
this time. It includes traditional case law, decisions of the divine
tribunal, legal procedures, the requirements of reverence for the law-
giver and of obedience to his legitimate representative, and the reason
for observing the law. It is presented as an alternative to the covenant
and is fitted into the original by preempting the covenant formula.[87]

The last part of the legend of Moses surrounds the epic covenant
with the tradition of the law. In agreement with the Priestly document
Moses ascends the mountain and receives the written version of the
law composed and inscribed by God himself. In disagreement with the
epic and its sequel, his sojourn on the mountain diminished his authority over the people, who chose the golden calf to lead them in his
absence. It corresponds to the first part where Moses first met God,
and it brings the legend to an end with the apotheosis of Moses
manifested in his radiance and evident in his silence.[88]

The four legends, though separate and attached to the texts they
interpret, combine to produce an intricate commentary on the epic and
Priestly traditions. In the first the scene is the Negeb, between Gerar
and Beersheba, and the issue is the survival of Abraham's legitimate
progeny in the face of exile and death. The second legend anticipates
the exodus in a journey from Bethel to Haran and back, and the issue
is the extent and detailed working of divine providence. The third
legend has explicit links with the first, including Jacob's worship of the
God of Isaac at Beersheba, and begins to resolve the issue of life and
death by associating it with the transformations of divine concomitance
from generation to generation. The last legend finally identifies God as
the God whose presence and constant care are revealed in the fulfillment of the law. The commentary is fairly plain and unobtrusive but

gathers force as it goes and ends well before the end of the history with all the clues to its unfolding.

SOURCES AND INTERPRETATION

Apart from legal precedents the Elohist did not quote any literary sources other than the epic and its congeners. Its main inspiration was the Priestly genealogies that had separated God from the pettiness of political factions and from the arrogance of historical fact. It responded to prophetic criticisms of the legal system by including the law and legislation that protected the courts and guided due process. It disagreed with Amos's sense of divine fate and with his negative assessment of Bethel, but it took up his appeal for justice and a positive approach to Joseph. It agreed with Isaiah's concern for holiness but had no sympathy for Judah and Jerusalem and little interest in their worldliness and self-importance. It was essentially a theological commentary written in the sophisticated narrative style of the epic and its sequel but with the conceptual clarity of the Priestly writer and the earnestness of the prophets.

Two parts of the legend of Abraham were composed as variants of epic incidents, one as an elaboration of a Priestly text, and one as a satire on the sequel's rules for the dedication of male children at the central sanctuary. Each part follows the text and the style of its source or reference, and each is matched by an analogous noncontiguous part that completes its interpretation.

The story of Abraham and Abimelech is broken into two parts but follows the epic story of Isaac and Abimelech.[89] It differs mainly in substituting the direct intervention of God for the epic's notion of ongoing blessing from Yahweh, in being explicit about Sarah's marriage to Abimelech, and in changing the plot from the amazing effects of Isaac's duplicity to the question of the paternity of Sarah's children.[90] It follows the narrative form of the epic, with monologue, dialogue, and consecutive storytelling, but differs from the epic in its background and choice of precise legal language.[91]

The interlocking story of Abraham and Sarah and their children is composed of two complementary incidents. The first depends on the Priestly account of the covenant with Abraham (Gen 16:1, 3, 15–16; 17:1–27)[92] and narratively expresses the premises on which the subsequent testing of Abraham depends. Abraham objects when Sarah tries to expel Hagar and Ishmael, but God intervenes to urge him to do as Sarah tells him because, even though it seems wrong to him, this in effect is what the covenant requires. At the last moment, when the child is about to expire from thirst in the wilderness, the angel of God calls to Hagar to assure her that the covenant concerning Ishmael will also be fulfilled, and God himself shows her where to find water. The second incident supposes the themes of the first but transposes them into a polemic against the sequel's cramped ideology of Passover and centralization.[93] Since it is explicitly a test, it is meant to prove something and it is evident from the start that what is commanded is not meant to be done. What is commanded, in fact, is a narrative version of the sequel's law of centralization. According to this law holocausts were to be offered in the place that Yahweh chose in one of the tribes; in the narrative Abraham is supposed to go to the place that God says, on one of the mountains that God says, and offer his son as a holocaust (Deut 12:13–14).[94] The difference is that God intervenes to abrogate the sequel's law of centralization and declares that what is really required is the fear of God.[95] The polemic is marked especially by the use of the name Yahweh at the crucial point of abrogation. As in the first incident, there are two manifestations of God. In one an angel calls from heaven, but it is the angel of Yahweh and not the angel of God. In the other Abraham calls the place "Yahweh will see" and, in a remarkable aside, the Elohist substitutes this expression of trust in divine providence for the law requiring all males to present themselves before Yahweh in the place that he would choose.[96]

This denigration of local Judean practice agrees perfectly with Elohist efforts to universalize the ways of God with Israel in the following legend of Jacob. The place at which Abraham was tested is contrasted with the place where Jacob saw the angels of God on a stairway to heaven. The inane offering of a child on a mountain is replaced by a better vow to worship God and offer him the tithe of all his gifts. The conditions of the vow are God's presence and solicitude, and the narrative of their fulfillment undoes all the details of the epic account.

The first and last scenes in the legend are indebted to the Priestly record of Jacob's encounter with God at Bethel and have very little directly to do with the epic account of Jacob's wrestling match with God. The elements that are not derivative are either typical of the Elohist interpretation or proleptic to its commentary on the episode.

From the Priestly version the Elohist took the description of Bethel as a sanctuary with memorial stones that were venerated with ritual anointing and libations (Gen 35:13–15).[97] From the epic account it assumed that Jacob fled from his brother and spent the night at the shrine.[98] What is typical of the Elohist is that God reveals himself in dreams and that the proper response to his presence is fear (Gen 28:12,

17).[99] As an introduction to the story that is about to be told, the first scene lists the ways in which divine providence will be manifested.[100] To refute the sequel to the epic and to confirm the abrogation of its law of centralization Jacob offers sacrifice and worships Yahweh at Bethel.[101]

The gist of this framing vow and its accomplishment is the legitimation of Bethel as a place of worship, or at least the neutralization of the criticisms of the place in prophecy and history. Amos advised against going to Bethel and scoffed at its liturgies and the offering of tithes. The sequel considered it the origin of the downfall of the North. The Elohist, however, considered it a national shrine that memorialized God's care for Jacob in exile and, by retelling the story of the patriarch and rewriting the origin of the golden calf, removed the stigma from its rituals and offered reconciliation to the North.

The framed account of Jacob's sojourn in Haran and return to the land of his birth follows the epic version step by step in order to correct it and bring it into line with Elohist ideas on the revelation of the law and divine providence. The account begins when Jacob summons Rachel and Leah and tells them the story that the epic just recounted about Jacob's cleverness in getting the better part of Laban's flock.[102] The main difference between the two versions is that God intervenes at every key point in the Elohist story to take care of Jacob and ensure both that justice is done and that the conditions of his vow are fulfilled.[103] The next part of the story recounts his homeward journey but interrupts it to retell the story of his servitude in Haran. The main story has no parallel in the epic and is told, against the background of the Aramean wars in Gilead, to describe the equitable settlement of Laban's dispute with Jacob and to illustrate how God fulfilled the conditions of Jacob's vow by taking care of him on his journey (Gen 31:19a, 20–27, 29; and 31:51–32:2a).[104] The retelling of the tale of his servitude has the same interest in law and providence and corrects the epic account by exonerating Jacob from all wrong (Gen 31:36b, 38–42).[105] The last part of the story is a massive assault on the story of Jacob's wrestling match; it substitutes Jacob's protection by the angels and his meeting with Esau for the epic version of his victory over God and man.[106]

The legend makes Jacob the model of Israel in exile. In the epic Jacob did bold and marvelous things to become Israel. In the Elohist version he feared God, observed the law, and was guided by the angels of God. In prophecy and history the exile hinged on worship at Bethel. In the Elohist version servitude in Haran was a phase in Jacob's life governed by the overarching providence of the God of Bethel. The

legend does not rewrite history but tries to dispel its bias and understand it with sympathy and compassion and from God's point of view.

The legend of Joseph is tangential to the epic version but elaborates
on the myth of Adonis that underlay it and interprets it in terms of
divine providence and concomitance. Its parts are staggered, as in the
legend of Abraham, so that the mythic themes of the first are developed
in the third and the theology of the second part continues in the fourth.

The elements of the myth of Adonis,[107] although disassembled and
transposed into narrative, are unmistakable and distinguish the Elohist
from its epic source. The epic episode of Joseph had some elements of
the myth and was applicable to the exile and return of the northern
kingdom, but it was conceived of and presented as a phase in the
history of Israel's origins. In the Elohist interpretation of the story,
historical imagination is overtaken by the metaphorical and theological
potential of the legend.[108]

The Elohist story begins with the statement that Joseph was only
seventeen years old and a shepherd (Gen 37:2aBb). He was beautiful,
like Adonis, and spurned the love that was offered him (39:6b–20). He
was killed, they said, by a wild animal, and went down into a waterless
pit or down into Egypt or, as his father said, down into Sheol or, as the
narrative has it, into prison (37:19–24, 28aAb–36). His death was
accompanied by a great famine that spread across the face of the earth,
but he, as the narrative has it, became the ruler of Egypt and supplied
his father and brothers with grain (40:1–41:59; 42:6); or, as Joseph
himself explains, he went down to Egypt before them in order to give
them life (45:4–13). In the recognition scene that ends the myth and
its ritual explanation, Joseph finally identifies himself to his brothers
as a father to the Pharaoh, the lord (ʾāḏôn) of his household, the ruler
of Egypt, the one whom God has made the lord (ʾāḏôn) of the land of
Egypt (45:8–9).[109]

The theological explanation of the myth and ritual occurs in the
history of God's dealings with Joseph.[110] Joseph is a dreamer and,
through the spirit of God that has been given to him, an interpreter of
dreams.[111] His own dreams come true when he becomes the ruler of
Egypt and his family does obeisance to him.[112] The Pharaoh's dreams
come true in times of plenty and of drought (Gen 41:1–32, 50–54).
The legend happens in his own life when he marries an alias or rival of
the woman who tormented him and in the time of plenty becomes the
father of two sons:[113] the elder was called Manasseh because God made
him forget all his travails; the younger was called Ephraim because
God made him fruitful in the land of his affliction (41:50–52). God
gave him the children, and Jacob blessed them with the blessing of the

God who guided him, with the blessing of the angel who saved him from every evil (48:1–2, 8–21). Before he died Jacob assured Joseph that God would be with him and bring him to the land of his fathers (48:21). When Jacob died, the brothers feared retaliation for the crimes of their youth, but Joseph explained the sequence of events as the fulfillment of God's plan (50:14–21). In this version everything is attributed to God, and the final unveiling of the myth and ritual occurs at the very end of the story when Joseph utters the subtle disclaimer "Fear not, am I a substitute for God?" (50:19).

The Elohist adaptation of the myth and ritual has historical implications. Precedence is given to Reuben and not to Judah (Gen 37:22, 29; 42:22). Of the two children of Joseph, Ephraim is to have preeminence (48:8–20). There is no reference to the "sons of Israel," and when Jacob dies Joseph takes his place among the brothers as the patriarch who lives to see the children of Ephraim and Manasseh to the third generation (50:22–24). Before he dies he predicts the exodus (50:25–26). This is, historically, the exodus from Egypt, which is to be recounted in the following legend of Moses, but in the Elohist perspective it is also the return of a remnant, a people implicitly identified as the children of Ephraim and Manasseh.[114] As the myth had both ritual and theological validity, so the history has metaphorical and prophetic propriety.

The legend of Moses is a much more careful commentary on the epic. It has the Elohist's usual interest in theology and ritual or liturgical phenomena and defines exactly how providence works in the life of the nation. It systematically removes the basis of the epic covenant by leaving in immediate jeopardy the possession of the land that it promised and supposed. It accepts the capture of the North as a consequence of the worship of the golden calf, not because the God or its rituals were obscene, but because the calf was made to replace the law and angelic leadership revealed on Horeb. The commentary is piecemeal but forceful and continuous and cumulative in its effect.

The first scene is a conflation of ideas drawn from the epic, the sequel, and the Priestly document. As in the sequel, the encounter with God takes place on Mount Horeb, but in distinction to the sequel it is the God of the fathers and not Yahweh who speaks; the meeting is a form of worship and not a preliminary to a pact; and Moses does not look at him face to face. (Exod 3:1, 4b–6; cf. Deut 5:2–4, 6).[115] As in the Priestly version, God is identified as the God of the fathers and sends Moses to Pharaoh to bring the people out of Egypt. But, in distinction to the Priestly document, God is with Moses, does not send Aaron with him, and promises a sign that will be enacted on the mountain of God and not in the presence of (Exod 3:6, 9–12; cf. 6:2–3, 10–12; 7:1, 3).[116] The next part of the scene combines Moses' mission to the people of Israel, as prescribed by the Priestly document, with an implicit rejection of the name "Yahweh" as it was revealed in the epic.[117] The scene ends with Moses returning to Egypt to see, in the mystique of the legend of Joseph, whether his brothers were still alive (Exod 4:18).[118]

The second scene is an explicit variant to the epic and Priestly accounts of Yahweh's victory at the Sea. The epic and the Elohist agree on the route that Israel took out of Egypt, but all three differ on the order of march. In the epic the people went in stages, and Yahweh went before them in the pillar of cloud and fire (Exod 13:20–22). In the Elohist's version, as in the Priestly record, they went up as an army prepared for battle, but the Elohist says that it was God, not Moses and Aaron, who led them and that they were not tempted to return to Egypt (Exod 13:17–19; cf. 16:3; Num 14:2–4; 16:13–14).[119] The victory itself is very schematic in the Elohist version and consists in a land battle fought by the angel of God without any of the mythical and ritual precedents of the other writers (Exod 14:5b, 7, 8b, 10abA, 19a, 25a).

The third scene is set at Horeb and continues in the factual and unadorned narrative mode of the second. It codifies the law that was promulgated at Horeb and establishes the institutions of its transmission and enforcement. It has a few parallels with the other versions but was designed on the basis of common law as an alternative to the prescriptions of the epic and the sequel.

The scene opens with the arrival of Jethro, the celebration of the exodus, and the institution of the courts (Exod 18:1a, 2a, 3–5, 12–27). The inclusion of Zipporah and her children supposes and quotes from the epic text.[120] Their celebration of the mighty acts that God performed on behalf of Moses and his people has circumstantial affinities with the Song of Miriam and the celebration of Passover.[121] The institution of the courts, however, is peculiar to the Elohist and reveals its usual interest in the formalities and details of the law. Moses was the chief magistrate, and when the people had a question or a quarrel they would stand before him while he inquired of God and gave the verdict or instructions. The lower courts dealt with lesser matters on the local level and were organized in a military hierarchy. This judicial reform, Jethro and the Elohist conclude, will ensure the authority of Moses and bring the people to their place in peace (Exod 18:23).[122]

The journey to this place is mentioned again at the end of the scene in a passage that preempts the epic covenant concerning the land

(Exod 23:20–22, 27, 29–31). The passage begins with the assurance, emulating the terms of Jacob's vow at Bethel, that the angel of God will go before them and guard them on the way and bring them to the place prepared for them (Exod 23:20; cf. Gen 28:20). If they obey, the angel will be an enemy to their enemies, but if they do not their disobedience will not be forgiven.[123] The place prepared for them is in a land whose borders resemble those described in the sequel but, unlike the sequel's version, in a land that will not be occupied all at once but, because the people are too few, gradually over the years (Exod 23:29–31).[124] The promise of the land, in this version, also differs from the epic covenant in granting to a lesser Israel a land no longer occupied by aboriginal nations but by an unnamed people and other enemies.[125]

Enclosed between the institution of the courts and the exhortation to obedience is the promulgation of the law on Horeb. It has two main parts that illustrate the Elohist penchant for formality and detailed organization (Exod 21:2–22:8; 22:20–23:16).[126] The first part is composed of traditional case law concerning persons and their possessions and concludes with cases to be tried by ordeal before God (Exod 21:2–22:8).[127] The second part contains five pieces of legislation that are at variance with laws in the sequel and are directed against the social and religious wrongs that Isaiah and Amos decried.[128] The first section legislates the care of aliens, widows, and orphans and responds directly to Amos's condemnation of those who afforded their religious festivals by gouging the poor and helpless.[129] The second section responds obliquely to this prophetic critique by listing regular religious obligations and carefully omitting the sequel's ideology of covenant and centralization and the excesses that they entailed (Exod 22:27–30).[130] The third section formulates the rules of due process and has parallels in Isaiah and Amos.[131] The fourth section completes the first by relating the fallow year and the sabbath to the care of the poor and the helpless (Exod 23:10–13).[132] The last section completes the second by decreeing the fulfillment of ordinary religious obligations at festivals celebrated apart from the central sanctuary.[133] The law, in the Elohist's perspective, was inspired by the prophets and became the basic document of the reform.[134]

The last scene in the legend of Moses is a final appeal for tolerance and reconciliation with the North. It mimics the Priestly version[135] and corrects the epic,[136] but it is devoted mainly to demolishing the sequel's insistence on the prerogatives of the city of David by retelling the story of the golden calf. In the sequel's version Jeroboam made two calves, one at Dan and one at Bethel, so that Israel would no longer worship in Jerusalem or show allegiance to the house of David. This, in its opinion, was a violation of the covenant and disobedience to the commands of Moses and the reason that Samaria fell to the Assyrians.[137] In the Elohist version, however, there was only one calf, made by Aaron at the instigation of the people to go before them and lead them into the land. It was not a rebellion against Moses, therefore, but against the angel of God, who was supposed to lead and defend them.[138] It was not a revolt against God but was in fact an emblem of Yahweh.[139] When Moses saw it and found out why it had been made he realized that the people were willful and with their calf had become the laughingstock of their enemies, but he did not try to stop them (Exod 32:15–19a, 21a, 22–25).[140] The golden calf in the Elohist's view symbolized lack of trust in providence and was the reason that Samaria fell, but the calf was not the crime that the sequel made it and defeat was not the end of Israel. At the end of the legend the matter is past and forgotten, as the Elohist returns to the original scene of Moses coming down from the mountain, radiant with the law in his hand, and speaking in turn to Aaron, the military commanders, and the people (Exod 34:29aBb–32a, 33).[141]

CONCLUSION

The Elohist redid the epic with the sequel and the Priestly document in mind. It added almost nothing to the history but was able to view it all in its furthest extension as an illustration of benignity and providence. It took strife from the stories, set up courts to settle disputes, was polemical but subtle and kind. In everything that happened and had been told it found what had been foretold and a dimension that needed retelling.

Its principal contribution was in laying the groundwork of a reasonable national existence. Its characters acted openly and honorably and expected the same. Their difficulties could be negotiated. The things that happened to them followed formal or ritual patterns that could be described and explained. Their lives could be seen from different perspectives, but the guiding perspective was providence. The law, and the rules that made it work, revealed to Moses at the acme of Israel's history, was the paradigm of providence, its principal ingredient and perfectly reasonable manifestation.

The law's inspiration was the prophets. They had criticized the histories and castigated their contemporaries for believing in God and doing nothing about it. The law, as the Elohist wrote it, was something that could be done.

Micah (fig. 9)

The fourth great prophet was Micah. He knew the epic and its sequel, their Priestly revision and their Elohist interpretation. His chief inspiration was the prophecy of Isaiah, and he quoted from it, emulated its form and style, and insisted on the truth and imminence of its predictions. He shared Amos's interest in the law and repeated some of his specific charges and condemnations. He agreed with Amos and Hosea in despising pretentious prayer and sacrifice, and he developed Hosea's notion of a divine lawsuit and his peculiar sense of a prophet's personal involvement in the history of the nation.

All of his instincts were confirmed by a later author who redid his prophecy on the basis of the same works in either their original or their contemporary versions. This writer knew II Isaiah's version of Isaiah's prophecy, quoted from it, and added elaborate commentaries on the quotations.[142] The new edition was familiar with Amos's descriptions of war and with Hosea's vivid depictions of religion in the North. It knew the Deuteronomistic version of the history of Israel and took it for granted. It often relied on images and phraseology that Jeremiah used to develop Micah's original artistry and insight. Its author wrote all the things that Micah might have written if he had lived to see his words come true.

STRUCTURE AND ORGANIZATION

Micah's prophecy is composed of four dramatic discourses, each comprising two complementary parts or scenes, each with a variety of interlocutory and descriptive vignettes. The second edition altered the structure of the work by adding a discourse in the middle and another at the end. They are juxtaposed rather than woven into the original text, but their point is anticipated in a break that the editor inserted between the two scenes of the second discourse.

The First Discourse

The first discourse is a dramatic enactment of Yahweh's legal proceedings against Judah. The first scene sets the stage, presents the main characters, and introduces the plot. The second scene narrates the action and describes the reaction of the defendant. The discourse is poetic and measured in stanzas and strophes (fig 9).[143]

The first strophe in the opening scene introduces Micah as the herald of Yahweh and portrays Yahweh's entrance on the scene by

FIGURE 9

Micah

Micah				*Book of Micah*		
FIRST DISCOURSE				**FIRST DISCOURSE**		
	Part One					
A		1:1aA		A		1:1aBb
	1	1:2			1	
	2	1:3–4			2	
B	1	1:5		B	1	
	2	1:6–7			2	
C	1	1:8		C	1	
	2	1:9			2	
	Part Two					
A	1	1:10		A	1	
	2	1:11–12			2	
B	1	1:13		B	1	
	2	1:14			2	
C	1	1:15		C	1	
	2	1:16			2	
SECOND DISCOURSE				**SECOND DISCOURSE**		
	Part One					
A	1	2:1		A	1	
	2	2:2			2	
	3	2:3			3	
B	1	2:4aA		B	1	
	2	2:4aBb–5			2	
C	1	2:6		C	1	
	2	2:7			2	
	3	2:8–9			3	
D	1	2:10		D	1	
	2	2:11			2	
				E	1	2:12
					2	2:13

continued

FIGURE 9 (*cont*)

	Micah			Book of Micah	
	Part Two				
A	1	3:1–2	A	1	
	2	3:3		2	
B	1	3:4	B	1	
	2	3:5		2	
C	1	3:6	C	1	
	2	3:7		2	
	3	3:8		3	
D	1	3:9–10	D	1	
	2	3:11		2	
	3	3:12		3	

THIRD DISCOURSE

A	1	4:1–2a
	2	4:2b–3abA
B	1	4:3bB–4
	2	4:5
C	1	4:6–7a
	2	4:7b
D	1	4:8
	2	4:9
E	1	4:10
	2	4:11–12
E'	1	4:13
	2	4:14
D'	1	5:1
	2	5:2–3
C'	1	5:4
	2	5:5
B'	1	5:6
	2	5:7–8
A'	1	5:9–11
	2	5:12–14

continued

F I G U R E   9   (*cont*)

Micah			*Book of Micah*	
THIRD DISCOURSE			**FOURTH DISCOURSE**	
Part One				
A	1	6:1	A	1
	2	6:2		2
B	1	6:3–4	B	1
	2	6:5		2
C	1	6:6	C	1
	2	6:7		2
	3	6:8		
Part Two				
A	1	6:9	A	1
	2	6:10–11		2
	3	6:12		
B	1	6:13	B	1
	2	6:14		2
C	1	6:15	C	1
	2	6:16		2
FOURTH DISCOURSE			**FIFTH DISCOURSE**	
Part One				
A	1	7:1	A	1
	2	7:2		2
B	1	7:3	B	1
	2	7:4		2
Part Two				
C	1	7:5–6	C	1
	2	7:7		2
D	1	7:8	D	1
	2	7:9		2

continued

FIGURE 9 (*cont*)

Micah	Book of Micah		
	SIXTH DISCOURSE		
	A	1	7:10a
		2	7:10b
	B	1	7:11–12
		2	7:13
	C	1	7:14a
		2	7:14b–15
	B	1	7:16
		2	7:17
	A	1	7:18a
		2	7:18b–19a
		3	7:19b–20

Figure 9. Letters indicate strophes. Numbers denote stanzas.

describing the effects of his presence. In the second strophe Yahweh introduces the plot by stating the charge against Israel and Judah and by recalling the sentence passed on Samaria. Micah responds to Yahweh's statement in the third strophe with wailing and lamentation, and his cries reveal that the same sentence of complete destruction has been passed on Jerusalem.

The second scene describes this impending doom. The first strophe begins the description with the advance of a conquering army that has been sent by Yahweh against Jerusalem. There is a pause at Lachish in the second strophe to relate the invasion of Judah to their emulation of the northern kingdom. The scene ends with the approach of the enemy, the departure of the glory of God to Adullam, and sorrow and lamentation for the children who have been taken into exile.

The two scenes have the same structure and conform exactly to each other. Each begins with the advent of the forces of Yahweh; each blames Judah for persisting in the sins of Israel, and each ends with grief and lamentation. But the first scene merely insinuates the fate of Judah, while the second describes it in greater detail by retracing the steps of the first in opposite order.

The last strophe in the first scene describes Micah barefoot and naked and howling because destruction has reached the gates of Jerusalem. The first strophe in the second scene reports that this destructive force is an invasion that cannot be withstood,[144] and describes the nakedness and lamentations of the cities on the route of the enemy's advance.[145] Similarly, the second strophe in each scene affirms the analogy of Israel and Judah, blames their destruction on rebellion and sin, implicates the kings of Israel, and alludes to the ruin and abandonment of cities.[146] Similarly, the opening strophe in the first scene and the last strophe in the second scene portray Yahweh's movement away from his temple and the dissolution of places along the path of his advance.

The first scene is mainly interlocutory. After the title (1:1aA) Micah summons the whole world to witness the theophany of Yahweh and proceeds with a description of its effects on the structure of the world. In the second strophe Yahweh soliloquizes on the fault of Samaria and Jerusalem and proceeds with a description of Samaria's ruin. In the third strophe Micah begins to mourn and finishes in the same way with another vivid description.

The second scene, by contrast, is not attributed to any particular personage in the drama. It is presumably Micah's part, but it has the characteristics of a choral interlude,[147] reflecting on the action described in the first scene and drawing the appropriate moral. It sees the advent of Yahweh in judgment as the advance of an army sent to punish, and it limits the cosmic and international effects of his theophany to a few places with witty and instructive names.[148] It recognizes the common guilt of Israel and Judah, but it replaces the first scene's survey of Samaria's physical destruction with the poignant vision of Zion's separation from Yahweh.[149] It agrees with the first scene in its presentiment of evil at the gates of Jerusalem, but it replaces the prophet's lavish grief with the bereavement and unutterable sorrow of Zion.

The Second Discourse

The second discourse in Micah's version is composed in the same way of counterbalancing and complementary scenes. The first scene is a debate between Micah and the people of Jerusalem and is filled with dialogue and quoted direct discourse. The second scene is a monologue and soliloquy in which Micah draws out the implications of the debate.

The first scene opens with Micah railing against local injustice and predicting swift retribution from Yahweh.[150] In the second strophe the scene shifts to the people with a parody of their imminent desolation and a quotation of their disconsolate complaint. Abruptly, in the next strophe, the people tell him to be quiet; he insists that he is right; and they accuse him of undermining the confidence of the city. In the last strophe he repeats the message that he has for them and reflects on their preference for lies.[151]

The second scene identifies Micah's interlocutors, gives details of the accusations against them, defends his own position, and announces the destruction of Jerusalem. It opens with Micah's formal accusation against the leaders and rulers who are supposed to uphold justice in the city but who in fact steal the skin off their people's bones. The second strophe continues with a charge against the prophets who mislead the people, and against the priests who devour the people whom the rulers have flayed. In the third strophe Micah separates himself from the prophets and mantics, claiming the authority of Yahweh for what he says, and predicting that they will be confounded and receive no answer from God. Finally, he returns to the leaders and the rulers, lumping them indiscriminately with the priests and the prophets and ridiculing their naïve expectation that Yahweh would be with them even though they neglected the duties of their office, and he announces the destruction of Zion and Jerusalem.

The two scenes, as in the first discourse, have the same structure and complement each other exactly. The first strophe in each scene inveighs against those who in general indulge in evil and in particular steal from the poor.[152] In each scene the second strophe turns to the punishment of the culprits and records their useless appeals for help.[153] The third strophe in each gives the conflicting claims of Micah and the other prophets and allows Micah to defend himself against the clichés of local tradition and common sense. The last strophe in each scene contradicts traditional beliefs on the presence of God and the inviolability of Zion and with more or less clarity announces the ruin of the city.

The second scene, however, does not just repeat the first but elaborates and explains it. The culprits are not, as it seems at first, just any powerful and unscrupulous group but the kings and princes of the royal house. Those who bewail their exclusion from the community of worship are not merely nameless miscreants but those who used to officiate at the sacrifices and prophesy for their share of the food. The dispute about what Yahweh might be expected to do and who is empowered to declare it is settled by contrasting the utter helplessness of visionaries and diviners with the overwhelming confidence that Micah has in speaking the truth. Wrangling over the privileged position of Jerusalem is settled curtly by arguing that traditional faith is superstitious belief.

In this discourse Micah is the plaintiff or prosecutor, and each scene defends his right to represent Yahweh. The first scene presents the accusation and the sentence to be imposed but allows the accused to state their case and defend themselves. The protagonist is Micah. The antagonists are defined only by their crimes and their inevitable retribution. The scene shifts rapidly and almost imperceptibly from one speaker to the next. The second scene, by contrast, is the prosecutor's summation and the final verdict in the case. Their defense is summarized and rejected, but otherwise Micah is the sole agent against time and tradition.

The Third Discourse

The third discourse in the original version has the same dramatic structure. The principal actors are Yahweh and Micah and the citizens of Jerusalem. In both scenes Yahweh takes his case to the people.

The first scene opens, as the very first discourse began (6:1–2 and 1:2–4), with Micah introducing Yahweh as the plaintiff in the case before the cosmic court. In the second strophe Yahweh appeals to the people to consider what he did for them at the critical points in their history so that they might recognize that he is entirely blameless in the case.[154] They respond, in the third strophe, by wondering with what sort of sacrifice or offering they might approach Yahweh, but Micah interjects that Yahweh has told them that what he wants is justice, fidelity, and submissiveness.

The second scene is complementary and, like the second scene in the first discourse, is played before the city. In the first strophe Micah introduces Yahweh as the plaintiff and lists his complaints against the residents and pilgrims in Jerusalem (6:1–2 and 6:9–12).[155] In the second strophe Yahweh appeals to the people to consider that what he is doing now is meant to punish them for their sins.[156] In the last strophe the chorus makes it clear that they have not done what Yahweh wanted and that his punishment has deprived them of the things they thought of offering in sacrifice.[157]

The first scene is filled with dramatic dialogue. Micah is the herald who announces the entrance of Yahweh. Yahweh urges the people to present their case, and Micah summons the mountains and the pillars beneath the earth to hear Yahweh's case against them. Yahweh speaks to the people in measured cadences of the exodus and the conquest. They respond with silly musings on festivals and forms of worship until Micah interrupts them with ridicule and stentorian warnings.

The second scene reflects on the first with a carefully reasoned judgment rendered by Yahweh. Micah hears the voice of Yahweh calling to the city and, before the judgment begins, remarks to Yahweh that the city would do well to pay attention.[158] The summation expresses Yahweh's indignation at those who would dishonor him and turn the temple and its treasuries into a den of iniquity by offering him the fruit of their unjust gain.[159] The sentence deprives them of the produce they meant to offer and of the wealth they amassed and reduces them to bare necessity. The trial concludes by tracing the origin of their wrongdoing to the shameful influence of Omri and Ahab.

The Fourth Discourse

The last discourse in the original version is a lamentation in response to the judgment that Yahweh rendered. It is composed as a soliloquy, in the first person singular, in which the city in the person of the prophet reflects on the charges laid against it and on the sentence that has been passed and comes to express its dissatisfaction with the leaders and its confidence in Yahweh. Since this concluding discourse also mirrors the second discourse, it actually records the desired effect of Micah's prophecy and confirms his triumph over the prophets, priests, and kings who kept misleading the people.

The first scene continues in the mood of the judgment. In the first strophe the city, deprived of its produce, compares itself to the land when the summer harvest is over and the vintage is finished and there is no fresh produce to eat (7:1). As this produce was offered to Yahweh instead of the justice and fidelity that he wanted, the city also describes its desolation in terms of the injustice, infidelity, and insidiousness of its population (6:8 and 7:2). The second strophe develops this theme with specific reference to the officials who were castigated in the second discourse, and in particular those who pervert the course of justice.[160] The scene ends with a warning to them that the day of punishment announced by the prophets has arrived.[161]

The second scene matches the first and draws the appropriate conclusions. In the first strophe the city concludes that no one can be trusted and therefore looks to Yahweh for help and asks her God to hear her. In the second the city confesses her sin, accepts her punishment and looks forward to a retrial and acquittal. The scene ends with the city proclaiming the justice of Yahweh that the preceding discourse asked her people to admit.[162]

The matching structure that is evident in the individual discourses is a feature of the entire composition. The first discourse announces Yahweh's theophany and his arrival, in the guise of an enemy army, at the gates of the city. The second recounts the prophet's quarrel with the city, parodies its pretended sorrow, and predicts its defeat. The third is Yahweh's trial of the city upon his arrival, and the fourth, in the person of the prophet, records its real repentance. This descriptive and dramatic development establishes the veracity of Micah's mission and proves Yahweh's case against the city in a remarkable example of prophecy and its instant fulfillment.

The Editorial Discourses

The editor of his work obviously recognized its structure and organization by separating the scenes in the first discourse, prying apart the prophecy and its fulfillment, and appending a different interpretation to each. These editorial discourses are attached artificially to the original and substitute a narrative and logical arrangement for its dramatic development.

The break in the first discourse (2:12–13) is a single strophe composed of two stanzas. It is fitted into the text graphically by repeating at the beginning of the first stanza and at the end of the second stanza the key opening words of the stanza that it displaced.[163] It is also woven into the context by converting the original imagery of the people as sacrificial animals skinned and eaten by their leaders into the image of the remnant of Israel as Yahweh's flock (2:12; cf. 3:2–3). Despite these references, however, the strophe not only interrupts but also contradicts its context. The first stanza refers specifically to the following context but has nothing to do with it and in place of its dismembering of the sacrifice has the assembling of the entire flock.[164] The second stanza refers to the preceding context but, instead of describing troops entering the city, speaks of its inhabitants breaking through the wall and pouring out of the city.[165] The crisscross pattern of references corresponds to the logic of the argument, in which the expectation of an eventual return from exile precedes and alleviates a vivid description of going into exile.

The first complete discourse added by the editor, the third in the book, is linked to the original context by the same sort of inconsequential repetition.[166] It is not separated into scenes but is composed of linked and overlapping strophes that narrate a sequence of events in inverse chronological order from the distant future to the recent past, and then develop the argument by going over the events in true but opposite order. This combination of narrative and argumentative patterns distinguishes the discourse from the racy presentation of the original.[167]

The first strophe is situated at the end of time, when all the nations will assemble peaceably in Jerusalem to learn the law of Yahweh. The second overlaps it with reflections on peace and the law and assembly before God.[168] The third strophe resumes some of the language and themes of the first two but also goes on to describe the gathering of the dispersed remnant of Israel in some future but less distant time.[169] The fourth agrees with it in picturing the remnant as a flock of sheep preceded by a ruler and with Yahweh as their king.[170] The fifth is linked explicitly to the preceding pairs, but it returns to the present time when Zion is under siege and about to go into exile.[171] The sixth is like it but also looks beyond the siege and the exile to the defeat of the besieging forces and the restoration of Zion.[172] The seventh strophe returns to the topic of the fourth, quotes extensively from it, looks forward to the restoration, and identifies the ruler of the flock as a shepherd from Bethlehem of Judah.[173] The eighth is its complement but also continues the theme of the sixth in describing the defeat of Assyria and Baby-lon.[174] The ninth moves toward the distant future described in the second and explains the position that the remnant of Jacob will hold in the assembly of the nations.[175] The final strophe ends where the first began but incorporates the intervening negative attitude toward the nations that opposed Israel (5:9–14).

The second discourse added by the editor, the last discourse in the book, has the same artificial relationship to its context, follows the pattern of the earlier additions in combining logical and narrative modes, and links narrative elements in a regressive chronological order.[176] The center of the discourse is an appeal to Yahweh in the present time to shepherd his flock as he did in the paradigmatic past.[177] Around it are two strophes that describe the fear and dishevelment of the nations as Zion is rebuilt and the world assembles awestruck before Yahweh (7:11–13, 16–17). Framing the whole discourse are two strophes that detail the disarray and defeat of the nations who thought God had abandoned Zion and the amazement of Zion at the generosity and forgiveness of God.

The editorial additions are obvious and contrary and give the prophecy a new climax and significance. But they are in total agreement with the general thrust of Micah's prophecy. He devised a dramatic presentation in which Jerusalem heard the traditional warnings of imminent destruction for its unjust and evil ways but for once listened and lamented and hoped for better days. In the editor's perspective the destruction had taken place, and the hope of those who returned was to live under the government of God, who would put an end forever to the nations that threatened them.

SOURCES AND INTERPRETATION

Micah modeled his work on the prophecies of Isaiah, Amos, and Hosea. They are his main inspiration, and he shares many of their ideas, supposes their arguments, and quotes some of their sayings. But he also knew the prose sources and could summarize episodes in the epic, or appeal to incidents and remarks in the sequel, or allude to elements in the Priestly and Elohist versions of the history. The originality of his work and his contribution to this developing literary tradition was the compromise he made between the demands of prophecy and the realities of history.

These sources are crucial for an understanding of Micah's prophecy. He supposes that they are known and establishes his own meaning in relation to them. His references combine a few words from one source with allusions to another comparable source and with some characteristic commentary of his own. His prophecy is not a real record of contemporary events but a subtle blend of tradition and expectation.

Micah's First Discourse

The influence of Isaiah is particularly evident in the structure and themes of the first two discourses. The allusions and citations are clear and are corroborated by complementary sources and by personal comment.

The references to Isaiah in the first discourse follow the order of his text. Both Micah and Isaiah begin with a herald's summons and with an indictment of the people for their sins and their rebellion (cf. 1:2a, 5 and Isa 1:2, 4). Both compare the consequences of Jerusalem's sin to wounds.[178] Isaiah sees that Assyria is the instrument of Yahweh's wrath, and Micah draws a parallel between the theophany of Yahweh and the advance of an enemy army.[179] Both describe the route of the enemy advance against Jerusalem through towns with vaguely familiar names and homophonous attributes (cf. 1:10–16 and Isa 10:28–32). Micah also alludes to Isaiah's Song of the Vineyard to describe the ruin of Samaria but without regard for the sequence of Isaiah's text (cf. 1:6 and Isa 5:1–2).

The second discourse corresponds in general to the second part of Isaiah's prophecy but without following its sequence. It quotes a saying of Isaiah in an opposite sense.[180] Like Isaiah, Micah records the opposition of the inhabitants of Jerusalem to the hard sayings of the prophets (cf. 2:6–9 and Isa 30:8–14), and like him he argues that prophecy will come to an end (cf. 3:4–8 and Isa 29:9–14). Both ridicule a traditional faith and reliance on Yahweh by a people that persists in injustice and oppression (cf. 3:9–12 and Isa 28:14–19; 30:12). Once more Micah refers to the Song of the Vineyard without concern for the sequence of the original text (cf. 2:1 and Isa 5:11–12).

The references in the first discourse are literal and eclectic and clearly marked by their dissonance or redundancy. They are mainly in the first scene but are interpreted in the second scene through the overlapping of one scene with the other. The herald's summons in the first strophe quotes two words from the introduction to Isaiah's prophecy,[181] combines the quotation with texts and themes taken from Amos,[182] and marks the quotations with a discordant third-person suffix in direct address.[183] In the second strophe the first stanza is an indictment of Israel and Judah, and the second is a picture of the ruin of Samaria. Both quote from the same text of Isaiah, but the first stanza also quotes from the sequel to the epic,[184] and the second also alludes to Isaiah's Song of the Vineyard and mixes the reference with quotations from Hosea.[185] Technically the allusion is fitting since the song ended with the vineyard in ruins, but literally it clashes with its context, in which Samaria is a ruin in a field, by also describing the city as vines planted in a vineyard.[186] In the third strophe Micah portrays the wounding of Samaria that has come to Judah and now lurks at the gates of Jerusalem. The image is odd and the grammar is all askew, but both features mark it as a quotation from the same passages in Isaiah where Samaria has been destroyed, Judah has been invaded, and the Assyrians are at the gates of Jerusalem.[187]

The discordances are bold and mark the critical points in Micah's interpretation of the tradition. All of the oddities in the first scene point to his sources and to their explanation in this scene and the next. The summons to the world is explained immediately as the physical effect of Yahweh's theophany. The ungrammatical summons to all the people is not to all the people of the world, in whom Micah shows no interest[188] but, as the next strophe explains, to the people of Israel and Judah, or Jacob.[189] The references to Jerusalem and Samaria in the second strophe point to the destruction not just of the cities but of their places and forms of worship.[190] The irregular grammar of the third strophe indicates that Yahweh, who left his temple in the first strophe, is now at the gates of Jerusalem.[191] The first strophe in the second scene with its odd expressions and impossible grammar turns this ritual theophany into a traditional and typical attack on Jerusalem.[192] The second strophe explains the association of Jerusalem and Samaria in the matching strophe of the first scene. In the end Yahweh leaves the city as the enemy approaches, and the city is left to bewail its inhabitants, who have been sent into exile. It becomes clear as the discourse progresses and reflects on itself that Micah is referring to things that are supposed to be known and is dramatizing the tradition as a contemporary fact. The only new fact, figured but not recorded, is the lament of the prophet and the city, but even it was predicted by Amos.[193]

Micah's Second Discourse

The first part of the second discourse alludes to Isaiah, Amos, Hosea, and the Elohist. The allusions are quaint and filled out with forensic argumentation and clever prattle. In the second scene, with little reference to sources, and in the extended image of a city that treats its people like sacrificial victims, the realities of the situation are clearly presented.

The first and second strophes are closely linked by literal and thematic repetitions and define the issues that are discussed in the rest of the discourse.[194] The first strophe declares the tit for tat of Yahweh's evil designs on those who devise evil.[195] The evil that they do is their greedy acquisition of hereditary land, and in retribution they will have to submit to the yoke. The punishment does not exactly fit the crime, but the following strophe, deriding their situation in a sarcastic lament, explains that as a result of their submission to the yoke their property will be parceled out among those who do not share their beliefs. It becomes clear as the discourse develops that the villains are the prophets, priests, and rulers and that their erroneous belief was that Yahweh would stay in the city no matter what they did.

The argument acquires complexity and conviction from its clever allusions. The image of those who stay up late to devise evil plans and then get up early to execute them is an adaptation of Isaiah's picture of those who got up early and stayed up late to drink at their festivals but failed to notice that Yahweh was actually doing (Mic 2:1; Isa 5:11–12). The tit-for-tat process by which Yahweh devises evil against the *family* of evildoers has its precedent in Amos's declaration to the *family* of Israel that evil would come upon the city from Yahweh.[196] The description of servitude as submission to the yoke recalls a saying in Hosea about Judah and Ephraim who were yoked and forced to plow and harrow the land.[197] Their lament is filled with puns and combines worry about the property they lost with allusions to abandonment by Yahweh and brittle comments on their exclusion from the community.[198]

In the third and fourth strophes Micah and the people debate his theory of retaliation and their belief that Yahweh would not abandon the city. They begin where he left off, telling him not to say that Yahweh will withdraw from them to their shame.[199] He defends his position and attacks theirs by quoting from Hosea's description of the fall of Samaria and adapting his definition of retribution as sowing the wind and reaping the whirlwind.[200] They reply, in the words of the sequel, by contrasting the capture of Samaria with Jerusalem's survival in the time of Hezekiah because it trusted in Yahweh,[201] and they accuse Micah, in his own words, of trying to deprive the people of the glory of Yahweh.[202] In the fourth strophe he repeats, in the words of Isaiah,[203] his warning that Yahweh would abandon the city and ends, alluding to Isaiah's conflict with false prophets, by ridiculing them for refusing to listen to the prophets.[204]

The second scene, after Micah has disposed of objections to his prophecy, continues with his accusations and predictions. It opens with a contrast between himself and the prophet of lies who opposed him.[205] It is addressed to Judah, in the style of Amos and Hosea, under the names Jacob and Israel (Mic 3:1; cf. Amos 7:1-9; Hos 10:11; 12:3-5, 13), but it is directed only to the leaders and rulers. The accusation is expressed abstractly at first, in terms familiar from Amos and Hosea,[206] and again in the sacrificial terms proper to the imagery that Micah develops. The prediction concerns the prophets who are condemned, in words taken from Amos, to endure the effects of the day of Yahweh.[207] The discourse ends with the departure of Yahweh, on whose presence they depended, and with the temple overrun with trees and shrubs.[208]

Micah's Third Discourse

This repudiation of beliefs fostered by the epic and its sequel, is balanced in the third discourse by the practice that is to take its place. It is not unexpected, then, that Micah should depend in this section on an interpretation and a correction of the narrative sources.

The first strophe resets the drama in the manner of the first discourse with Yahweh's appearance in judgment. The scene is set in the cosmic court. The world is summoned as witness in his case against his people, as Hosea would have said, and in his dispute with Israel, as Isaiah proclaimed.[209]

The second strophe begins Yahweh's lawsuit against his people by establishing the justice of his claim. It appeals to the people to consider what Yahweh has done for them and to admit that he is justified in rebuking them. The appeal itself contains some traditional elements, such as the fact that Yahweh acts on their behalf and their obligation to recall his benefits,[210] but most of it is peculiar to the forensic situation or typical of Micah's punning style.[211] The actual review of what he has done for them, however, summarizes the story of the exodus according to all the narrative sources[212] and amalgamates the epic and the sequel's account of the conquest.[213]

In the third strophe the people respond to this statement of claim by musing on their ritual obligations to Yahweh until Micah intervenes to tell them of their legal obligations. They think of offerings required by legislation in the epic, the sequel, and the Elohist.[214] He replies, in terms taken from the sequel, with the simple obligation of fidelity to the law and humble submission to God, which Hosea and the Priestly writer propounded.[215]

The fourth strophe rephrases the theme of the third by outlining the relationship between worship and social injustice. In it Yahweh addresses the city and those who have gathered there in solemn assembly.[216] The specific injustices of which they stand accused are cited from texts of Amos.[217] The general accusations of lies and malice reflect oracles of Isaiah, Amos, and Hosea, as well as the reason given for the flood in the Priestly genealogy of Noah.[218]

The fifth strophe brings as evidence of their guilt the fact that Yahweh has already punished them, and the sixth strophe warns them that the punishment will continue unless they change their ways. The fact of their punishment is derived from a text of Isaiah that described the effects of the Assyrian invasion in the time of Hezekiah.[219] Its form is a reversal of the benefits of the covenant described in the sequel, combined with the reversals of war that Amos reserved for the day of Yahweh.[220] The continuation of their punishment is described in terms taken from Isaiah and the prophets, and their wicked ways, in the words of Hosea and the Elohist law code, are customs that they borrowed from Omri and Ahab.[221] The accused, as the oscillation in person and number suggest, are the city, the tribe of Judah, and the pilgrims to Jerusalem, who were summoned to listen in the fourth strophe.[222]

Micah's Fourth Discourse

In the fourth discourse the city responds to the judgment of God with sorrow and hope. It is composed as a personal lament that reenacts the city's tribulation and searches out its causes before turning to God with trust and satisfaction.

The first scene contains the city's complaint. The first stanza describes the city's sorrow in terms of the punishment that has been exacted; the city bewails, perhaps with a nod to Amos's vision of the end, the end of summer and the absence of the firstfruits that could satisfy her soul.[223] In the second stanza the city perceives her desolation in terms of the accusations that have been made against her in the second and third discourses. In the second discourse Micah told those who flayed and devoured the people that anyone who walked on the path of justice would profit from his words. In the third discourse he said that what God wanted from them was fidelity to the law. Now the city weeps because the faithful have perished, the upright are gone, and the people are hunted and trapped and devoted like sacrificial victims to God.[224] In the second strophe the city turns to the cause of its troubles. As is usual in laments the cause is not just personal but can be located in a third party, whose evil is manifest and whose excommunication becomes a sign that the cause has been extirpated and that the tribulation will not last. The city finds the cause to be her leaders—the prophets, priests, princes, and judges whom Micah confronted in his second discourse and the people who got rich by lying and who were singled out in the third discourse.[225] The city rids herself of them, in the second stanza of this strophe, by invoking on them the day of Yahweh as Hosea described it in his argument with the prophets who opposed him (Mic 7:4; cf. 6:8; 7:2; Hos 9:7–8).

In the second scene the city, in the person of the prophet, puts her trust in Yahweh and looks forward to acquittal in the case against her. In the first strophe the city argues that no one else can be trusted, and the prophet takes the watch to wait for Yahweh's return.[226] In the second strophe, with allusions to Amos, the city professes her guilt, accepts her punishment, and finally admits that Yahweh was right.[227]

In the sequence of his discourses Micah synthesized the divergent viewpoints expressed in the historical and prophetic works of his time. He was not describing something new or really pressing but urged the people to take their traditions seriously. He tried to convince them by weakening their resistance and by, for the first time, offering them a real alternative to the way of life and beliefs that he criticized. The prophets before him had criticized the leaders and called for justice. He had at his disposal a law, designed for the people, that would work.

The Editorial Discourses

The editor who produced the book knew Micah's sources, the writings that he influenced, and prophets who arose after the reform had failed. This author also knew the histories and the orthodox version composed by the Deuteronomistic Historian and the revisionism it effected, and rewrote the original prophecy to suit a system of government that they proposed. Micah not only criticized the leaders of Jerusalem, but he held out hope for the survival of the city and dramatized how it would work. The editor of his book shared all his expectations in a later, less sanguine time.

The Break   The methodical break between the two parts of the first discourse combines, in argumentative rather than chronological order, a vision of Israel's return from exile with the scene of the initial departure from Jerusalem. Both are concatenations of references to familiar prophetic texts.

The vision of the return is expressed in words spoken by Yahweh without prophetic mediation. His promise to gather all of Jacob and collect the remnant of Israel like a flock in its fold combines a reference to Zephaniah with an allusion to Ezekiel and a quotation from the beginning of the book of Hosea.[228] The combination differs from Hosea and Ezekiel in omitting for the time being any mention of the shepherd and in supposing that Yahweh is at the head of his people.[229] The vision clearly breaks the original context, in which Micah is arguing with his opponents, but Yahweh's final and incongruous promise that the flock will be bursting with men is addressed to women and seems to suppose and settle their earlier dispute about the women and children.[230]

The departure into exile is modeled on the famous story of Zedekiah's attempted escape from the city when the Babylonians breached the wall of Jerusalem.[231] Its description, however, is an amalgam of references to this text, to texts concerning siege and exile, and to the story of David's humiliating exit from Jerusalem during the revolt of Absalom.[232] The scene, in this sense, agrees well with the original context of Micah's quarrels with the leaders of Jerusalem and subtly introduces the editor's amazing reticence toward the Davidic monarchy.

The First Editorial Discourse   The first editorial discourse describes the restoration of Judah and Jerusalem. Its contradiction of the original context in which the ruin of the city was just predicted is supported by quotations from Jeremiah, II Isaiah, and the book of Zephaniah and by the historical interpretation of the Deuteronomist. It does not necessarily agree with these sources and may modify them as it goes, but it relies on their alternative interpretations to smooth out its differences with Micah.

The first three strophes quote and correct a passage from II Isaiah in which Zion is pictured as the center of the restoration world (Mic 4:1–5 = Isa 2:1–5). The quotation is marked as usual by a change in context and word order.[233] The correction is made by relying on other authenticating texts. II Isaiah concluded the portrait of a world at peace gathered around Zion with the exhortation to Jacob to walk in the light of the Lord. The editor substituted a different conclusion, which made a clear distinction between Israel and the other nations of the world. First, the expected time of peace is reserved for Israel by likening it to the Deuteronomist's idyllic view of the reign of Solomon and to the wonderful era of the new covenant described in the book of Ezekiel.[234] Second, and contrary to the universalist tendencies of II Isaiah, the editor relegates the nations to the worship of their Gods and restricts the worship of Yahweh to Israel.[235] The changes introduce items fundamental to a theocratic state and are justified by quoting an authenticating clause from Isaiah.[236]

The next two strophes develop this interpretation (Mic 4:6–7, 8–9). The first stanza combines a reference to the fall of Jerusalem as Micah predicted it with an allusion to the book of Ezekiel that assures the return of the exiles.[237] The second stanza identifies these people as the remnant who will inherit the promise to Abraham and live in Zion under the direct rule of Yahweh.[238] The third stanza confirms the restoration of Jerusalem as a royal city, and the fourth, in a pastiche of quotations from Jeremiah and II Isaiah, proclaims Yahweh king.[239]

The pivot of the discourse in the next two strophes is the opening quotation from II Isaiah, and the editor continues to correct it by insisting on the conflict between Israel and the nations (Mic 4:10–12, 13–14). The first stanza views the fall of Jerusalem and exile in Babylon in the light of texts from Jeremiah and the Deuteronomistic History.[240] The second stanza considers these events from the perspective of the invaders and, in complete disagreement with the quotation from II Isaiah, sees Yahweh ready to thresh the warring nations who once gathered as enemies against Zion.[241] The third stanza, in a conflation of images and ideas from Hosea and the Deuteronomistic History, continues the image and describes Zion as the animal threshing the nations.[242] The second strophe ends as the first began and in a concatenation of references to Jeremiah and II Isaiah describes Jerusalem under siege.[243]

The next two strophes describe the return from exile and the role of the Davidic dynasty in the organization of the restored community (Mic 5:1–3, 4–5), and quote from II Isaiah, the Deuteronomist, and the revised version of Hosea. The first stanza relies on the History for the fact that David was from Bethlehem of Ephrathah, for the formula of humble acceptance of an office, and for the theory that the Davidic dynasty was foreseen by Jacob and Balaam.[244] The second lessens the impact of this reference to the dynastic promise by restricting its scope and by assigning its fulfillment to an indeterminate time on the basis of a novel interpretation of texts in Hosea, II Isaiah, and the History.[245] The third and fourth stanzas, relying in part on the same texts, further obscure the effect of the promise by distributing the dynastic inheritance among David and his brothers.[246] It becomes clear, as the discourse progresses, that the editor began with a quotation from II Isaiah only to update and correct it.

The final strophes rely on the same sources and others but omit any reference to II Isaiah. The first strophe sums up the ambivalent position of Israel among the nations—on the one hand as a source of blessing, on the other as an avenger of the wrongs that were done to it.[247] The second strophe views the same matter from Yahweh's perspective—in one stanza stripping Judah of all its national resources, in the other taking vengeance on the northern kingdom and the nations who worshiped other Gods.[248]

The Concluding Editorial Discourse   The concluding discourse fills out the final expectation of Micah's lament with details on the restored community. It resumes the editor's thesis that Yahweh alone is king and that the other nations, including the North, are punished rightly for what they did to Judah and Jerusalem.

The first two strophes, relying mainly on images from Isaiah, contrast the rebuilding of Jerusalem and the devastation of the world.[249] The last two, relying on the attributes of Yahweh expressed in the epic covenant, draw a similar contrast between the mercy that he extends to Jacob and the terror that he inspires among the nations.[250] The central strophe, relying on both of these sources, invokes Yahweh as the shepherd of his people in a land that includes Gilead and Bashan but pointedly omits the North.[251]

CONCLUSION

The editor of the book of Micah left his text alone and, in reorganizing it, tried to imitate its wit and density and erratic grammar. The issue for the editor, clearly, was not what Micah said but contemporary wrangling over the reconstruction of the people of God. The main adversary was II Isaiah, and therefore Micah, following faithfully in the line of Isaiah himself, was an excellent authority in the debate.

Micah polished his predecessors' arguments in a dramatic presentation of radical change. His work is structured like the prophecy of Isaiah. His message is borrowed from Amos. His part in the drama is modeled on Hosea's. His objection is to the vain confidence inspired by the epic and the sequel. His fulcrum was the law code published by the

Elohist. His irenic attitude was learned from the Priestly writer. He took the tradition and gave the people a chance.

Jeremiah (figs. 10–12)

Jeremiah went beyond the confessions of Zion in Micah to describe the return of the North and the reunion of Judah and Israel. His prophecy, like Micah's, is written in dramatic discourses or acts each of which is composed of countervailing scenes. His sources are the prophets and historians who preceded him, but his principal inspiration was the love story of God and the nation that Hosea recorded.

The problem with his prophecy was that it was open to easy misinterpretation and did not seem to be true. His prediction, especially, that Israel and Judah would be reunited was not fulfilled in his own time and had to be salvaged by II Isaiah. The editor of his work was at pains to prove that he was a true prophet and a real impetus in the history of the nation.

The editor did not attempt to save Jeremiah's meaning with patchwork commentary but created an entirely new work that could situate his prophecy in proper perspective. This work was composed on the analogy of an archive, or library of official documents, sorted according to subject and arranged in logical and chronological order. The archive incorporated Jeremiah's act and scenes, filed them along with other documents and notations related to his career, itemized the individual entries, supplied indices to the whole archive, and sorted the material generically into sections containing mainly dramatic presentation, biography, history, and prophetic oracles. The additional material concerned the personal and public life of Jeremiah, the events that touched him and the things that he said, their place in the prophetic tradition and in his particular prophetic mission, the effects of his message, and his gradual metamorphosis as Moses. The details are authentic, but the chronological arrangement is fictitious and allowed the editor, in the capacity of archivist, to make the last dramatic act, in which Israel and Judah are reunited, very late and peripheral in Jeremiah's career.

The complete new work was as much a history as a prophecy. It recorded the prophecy of Jeremiah, explained it, and narrated its fulfillment in events that had been recorded and analyzed by the Deuteronomistic Historian. It used the History's jargon and stereotypes, but it was composed as an alternative to the theory of the law and benevolent destiny that the History unveiled. In its place the author of the book of Jeremiah developed a theory of history governed by the word of God and by willingness to hear and understand it.

THE JEREMIAH ARCHIVE

Jeremiah, on the analogy of archives and of the separate sections, books, scrolls, or tablets they contained, was composed of separate parts and books and columns arranged in paragraphs or in stanzas and strophes. It is organized spatially, one column after the other, one book beside the next, all the parts in a row, on the model of the physical arrangement of a library or an archive.[252] The lack of immediate or intrinsic relationship between any of the elements—between stanzas, strophes, columns, books, and parts—is supplied by tabs, tags, markers, and similar signs that rationalize their contiguity, indicate their connection with noncontiguous elements, and mark their place in the whole collection. The apparent temporal distribution of these elements, as if they were an assemblage of records, documents, and marginal notes from disparate times, is a product of the system that the archive used to classify and reconcile historical and biographical interpretations.

The archival procedure itself is insinuated in the text in scattered comments on its contents and composition. Its contents are defined and circumscribed so that there is a clear boundary between the archive itself and a codicil identifying its indebtedness to the Deuteronomistic History.[253] Within this cover or literary binding the text also mentions "books" that Jeremiah composed for the archive or for some other purpose, and it uses the same term to refer to the different sorts of writings that it contains, such as oracles concerning Israel, Judah, Babylon, and the nations; a letter; a contract or a chronologically defined and annotated collection of sayings.[254] The archive describes what the original book of Jeremiah contained, its approximate length, how it was transcribed from dictation, written in columns, read, rewritten, and revised (Jer 36:2, 4, 8, 10, 11, 17–18, 23, 32; 45:1). At the end it adds colophons to identify the writer and his sources and the date and destination of the completed work (45:1–5).[255]

Archives

Archives were collections of public records and historical documents relative to specific persons and events.[256] They belonged to individuals or families, to a single reign, or a limited succession of kings.[257] They had either immediate usefulness or antiquarian interest and could include documents on practical matters as well as items of scientific, historical, and literary importance.[258]

Archives were locally defined, sorted, and cataloged. They were contained in rooms, on shelves, or in baskets, boxes, bags, and jars; and different types of materials were located in different places.[259] They could be filed according to their dockets, labels, or tags, and cataloged according to their size, shape, format, and genre.[260] Some documents, such as accounts, were probably kept in chronological order. In some cases they were exposed on shelves lying on their right sides and facing the reader so that their contents were clear from the top of the first column and their date from the inscription on their left edge.[261] In other cases the tablets had summarizing dockets[262] or were stored in jars with inscriptions that identified the author of the tablets and cataloged their contents.[263]

Archives tended to be homogeneous but sometimes contained anomalous elements that pertained less to the archive than to the archivist. The archive of Rapi'anu at Ugarit contained personal material including a conjuration against loss of eyesight, legal documents and financial accounts, as well as professional texts such as a bilingual pantheon list, polyglot vocabularies, a table of weights and measures, and copies of royal correspondence.[264] An archive from Nippur contained documents of family members and their agents, but the nine latest tablets do not mention the family and seem to have belonged to the individual who took over their business.[265] The Hermopolis papyri contained seven written in the same hand, sealed with the same seal, sent by members of the same family from the same place, as well as an eighth with none of these features, which shared only the same destination.[266]

All of these characteristics apply to the Jeremiah archive. It is chronologically limited: ostensibly it covers five reigns, but in fact it is concerned with a few fixed dates in only three of them.[267] It is locally contained under the rubric "The words of Jeremiah" (1:1; 51:64b). It is sorted and cataloged. It is distributed in parts arranged chronologically in historical and biographical sequence. The parts are composed of individual books that are carefully distinguished from one another and artificially linked. These are made up of separate columns that are self-contained and formally connected to each other. The columns are composed of paragraphs and strophes that are literarily distinct and paired in sequence or antithesis. The archive is not homogeneous but contains other things besides the dramatic composition that Jeremiah wrote, including a record of his speeches, an anthology of prayers and oracles attributed to him, excerpts from his life, a chronicle of the last days of Judah and Jerusalem, a codicil, and the incessant complaints of the archivist. Its organization as an archive reflects the writer's interest in the arrangement and verification of the documents from this critical period and the evidence for their authenticity.

Parts (fig. 10)

The archive is divided into three chronologically sequential and overlapping parts. Each part covers the history of Judah and Jerusalem during the reigns of Jehoiakim and Zedekiah. The three parts together cover the history from the thirteenth year of Josiah past the exile of Jeconiah to the capture of the city in the eleventh year of Zedekiah and the dispersal of the remaining Judeans among the nations. The sequence of the parts produces a narrative consistency with a temporal flow that allows the words of Jeremiah to be fixed on a chronological continuum and with reference to specific events. The overlapping and backtracking of the parts allows the editor and archivist to interpret the words of Jeremiah and fix them in the life and times of the prophet. In the archive as a whole, biography and history mesh but never quite coincide.

The first part covers the period between the early years of Josiah and the end of the reign of Zedekiah, from the birth and vocation of Jeremiah to his confrontation with each of the kings in turn.[268] It ends as it began with visions and a reference to the end of Zedekiah's

FIGURE 10

Jeremiah: The Arrangement of Parts and Books

Part						
	A — B		A' — B'		A" — B"	
I	Book 1	Book 2	Book 3	Book 4	Book 5	Book 6
	1–6	7–10	11–13	14–17	18–20	21–24
	.	.	.	.	.	.
	.	.	.	.	.	.
II	Book 7	Book 8	Book 9	Book 10	Book 11	Book 12
	25–29	30–31	32–33	34:1–7	34:8–22	35–39
	.	.	.	.	.	.
	.	.	.	.	.	.
III	Book 13	Book 14	Book 15	Book 16	Book 17	Book 18
	40–43	44–45	46	47–49:33	49:34–51:64	52

reign,[269] with a quotation from the initial commissioning of Jeremiah (see 1:10 and 24:6), and in anticipation of the following parts.[270]

The second part covers the period between the first year of Jehoiakim and the end of the reign of Zedekiah but also refers to the time after the prophet's call early in the reign of Josiah (chaps. 25–39).[271] It begins with the critical fourth year of Jehoiakim, moves to the new covenant in the future and back to the old in a desperate present, and ends in the same crucial year with history repeating itself.[272]

The third part covers the period after the fall of Jerusalem but also refers to the fourth year of Jehoiakim, when the prophecy of Jeremiah was written and rejected. It begins with an original history of the times and ends with the Deuteronomistic version (chaps. 40–43, 52), and fills the interval between them with oracles on Judah and the nations among whom it was dispersed.[273]

Each part is composed of six books arranged in a staggered progression so that alternating books correspond and also match from part to part. In the first part, the first, third, and fifth books situate oracles in the biographical context of Jeremiah's mission and the popular resentment and prophetic reproof that it inspired; the second, fourth, and sixth books feature his historic struggles against the kings and the cult. The second part has the same distribution, but each book also continues the topic or focus of the corresponding book in the first part. The pattern continues in the third part with cumulative references to the first and second parts.

In the first part, for instance, the first book begins with the vocation of the prophet and his mission to Judah, Jerusalem, and the nations of the world and is interspersed with diatribes against the prophets, priests, and kings who opposed him. The first book in the second part begins by clarifying his message to the nations and identifying by name specific prophets who opposed him. The first book in the third part, similarly, deals with the Judeans who live among the nations and describes a situation in which the people sought an oracle from Jeremiah and deliberately rejected it (chaps. 1–6, 25–29, 40–43).

In each part the third and fifth books continue the basic themes of the first, and each part responds to the last. The third book in the first part mentions, for instance, opposition from the people of his hometown of Anathoth, and the fifth develops the theme of repentance, lists his complaints, and ends with a curse on the day of his birth, which was ominous or auspicious in the first. In the second part, similarly, the third book brings him back to Anathoth and the fifth illustrates their refusal to repent. In the third part, finally, the third book develops a subsidiary theme from the matching book of the second part, and the fifth book deals with Babylon, to which the people were sent in exile in corresponding books of the first and second parts.[274]

The second book in the first part begins in its turn with Jeremiah's diatribe against the temple and the kings and with the special command to Jeremiah not to intercede for the people. In the fourth book intercession is replaced by lamentation, and in the sixth the kings are condemned one by one. In the second part the matching books either add detailed condemnation of the kings or predict a new era endowed with a humble monarch and a purified priesthood. In the third part the matching books elaborate on the ritual crimes mentioned at the start and bring the Gods, kings, and cults of the nations to an end.[275]

The careful separation of the parts is matched by the artful connections between them. The first book in the first part begins the biographical version and anticipates the scope of the entire archive. The second part begins with a reference to it and redoes the beginning of the historical version at the beginning of the second book in the first part. The second part also starts with a survey of the nations dealt with in the third part, and the third part begins with a literal repetition from the conclusion of the second part. The archive ends with the Deuteronomistic version of the events that were outlined at the very beginning.[276]

The three parts of the archive situate Jeremiah's prophecy in the last years of the monarchy. The biography marks time. The history strings out his words in a chronological continuum from their utterance to their fulfillment. Together they allow words and times to be related, repeated, and evaluated from a prophetic and historical point of view. These years were critical for the theory proposed by the Deuteronomistic Historian, and the archival model allows the editor to include all the information and ideas that were needed to refute it.

Books

The books are of unequal length. The first seventeen are separated from each other by headings, dates, and dockets, and the last is distinguished as a quotation from the History and as extraneous to the words of the prophet. They are the immediate intelligible context for the material they contain and illustrate most clearly the principles of caption and cross-reference that make the archive work.

The headings indicate that the books contain the words of Jeremiah. The standard form occurs with minor variations, but it usually specifies that the words originated with Yahweh. It resembles but is easily differentiated from other formulas that indicate the archive's preoccupation with incidental occurrences of the word of God. The heading also has a syntactically peculiar variant that distinguishes it as an artificial marker rather than a literal introduction to the following speech.[277]

The dates are according to reigns or regnal years (1:1–3; 25:1–3; 32:1; 35:1; 49:34), situate books in relation to past events (46:1; 47:1), or suggest that books be read in relation to future events (30:1–3). The dockets consist of a few words or clauses or whole sentences that allow the books to be sorted and arranged without being read. They are either jejune, suggesting the gist of the book, or more comprehensive, indicating its interpretation, but in either case they must be read in conjunction with the first column to grasp the actual contents of the book.[278]

The most jejune docket is at the top of the fourth book (14:1).[279] It indicates that the book is concerned with different forms of deprivation. This category is developed in the first column to include specific examples of deprivation ranging from drought to abandonment and complete devastation, and these in turn are elaborated in the rest of the book. The docket in the fifth book is the command to Jeremiah to go down to the potter's house and hear what Yahweh has to say: different types of pottery and the words of Yahweh that they occasion are the gist of the book.[280]

The comprehensive dockets are plainer indications of the thrust of the book but still depend on the detailed development in the first column to indicate its contents. The docket in the first book (1:1–3) makes it clear that what follows pertains to the fall of Jerusalem, but it is only the first column (1:1–19) that relates this to the career of Jeremiah, to the Babylonian invasion, and to the government's opposition to his words. In the second book the docket has to do with the temple and worship (7:1–2), but the first column makes it clear that the book has to do with the end of prayer and of the worship of Yahweh, and with Judah's wrongful assimilation to the nations that worship other Gods (7:1–34). In the third book the docket stands out as grammatically incongruous, but it highlights the covenant with Judah and Jerusalem (11:1–2):[281] the first column goes on to say that the covenant is finished (11:1–23), and the rest of the book describes the implications of saying such a thing. Thus, in all the books the docket is just a clue to the contents, easy to remember, a handy reference, a place to start, but hardly the whole story.

The books in each part are linked to each other in pairs. The links are literal and sometimes tenuous, but they signal both the separation and sequence of the books and their narrative and discursive development.

In the first part the links are bold and obvious. The first two books are linked by joining the end of the first to the beginning of the second. The most obvious join is the repetition of a whole strophe in each (6:13–15 = 8:10–12); the most cumbersome is the clause introducing the oracles in the second book, whose antecedent is not what immediately precedes but the commissioning of Jeremiah at the end of the first book.[282] The second pair is connected by similar but less incongruous types of repetition: both contain variations on nonintercession; on destruction by plague, famine, and the sword; and on commandments given to the fathers that they did not obey.[283] The third pair is linked by a repetition of the name "Pashhur," referring to two different persons associated with the establishment in Jerusalem.[284]

In the second part the first two books are connected by a key word that underscores their interest in the return from exile and its chronology.[285] The fourth book repeats the introduction to the third but in a historical rather than a biographical mode.[286] The fifth, in a biographical mood, ends with the lifting of the siege of Jerusalem, and the sixth begins historically with the time when the siege began.[287]

The last part has similar literal links between its books. The first and second are consecutive perspectives on the Judeans who migrated to Egypt (43:8–13 and 44:1–6). The third and fourth begin with a nod to the Pharaoh (46:1–2 and 47:1). The fifth and sixth start at the beginning of the reign of Zedekiah (49:34 and 52:1).

The organization of the archive in books is evident from their tags and their contents. Within each part books are linked serially and, within and between parts, are related in staggered progression. These are not just idle clues but *caveat lector*s on how the archive is to be read and understood.

Columns (fig. 11)

Columns are the equivalent of pages, entries, or tablets in the archive.[288] They usually correspond to individual chapters in the Hebrew Bible and are of different lengths,[289] with different components and genres. They are arranged, as the books are, on the analogy of tablets belonging to a series, by catchwords, catchlines, and colophons. In effect this means that in any book columns can be either (a) self-contained, ending as they began, and connected to each other by some form of repetition or cross-reference; (b) linked to one another by top-to-top or bottom-to-top connections;[290] or (c) bound by some combination of

FIGURE 11

The Jeremiah Archive

Part I					

BOOK 1 (Jeremiah 1–6)

Col. 1	Col. 2	Col. 3	Col. 4	Col. 5	Col. 6
1:1–3	2:1–3	3:1	4:1–4	5:1–3	6:1–3a
1:4–8	2:4–6	3:2–3	4:5–6	5:4–6	6:3b–6
1:9–10	2:7–8	3:4–5	4:7–8	5:7–9	6:7–9
1:11–16	2:9–13	3:6–10	4:9–12	5:10–12	6:10–12
1:17	2:14–17	3:11–13	4:13–14	5:13–14	6:13–15
1:18–19	2:18–20	3:14–16	4:15–17	5:15–17	6:16–17
	2:21–22	3:17–18	4:18–19	5:18–19	6:18–21
	2:23–25	3:19–20	4:20–22	5:20–24	6:22–23
	2:26–27	3:21–22	4:23–26	5:25–28	6:24–26
	2:28–30	3:23–25	4:27–28	5:29–31	6:27–30
	2:31–32		4:29		
	2:33–37		4:30–31		

BOOK 2 (Jeremiah 7–10)

Col. 1	Col. 2	Col. 3	Col. 4
7:1–2	8:1–3	9:1–2	10:1–4
7:3–4	8:4–5	9:3–5	10:5
7:5–7	8:6–7	9:6–8	10:6–7
7:8–10	8:8–9	9:9–10	10:8–9
7:11–12	8:10–12	9:11–15	10:10–11
7:13–15	8:13–15	9:16–19	10:12–13
7:16–19	8:16–19a	9:20–21	10:14–16
7:20	8:19b–23	9:22–25	10:17–20
7:21–26			10:21–22
7:27–28			10:23–25
7:29–31			
7:32–34			

BOOK 3 (Jeremiah 11–13)

Col. 1	Col. 2	Col. 3
11:1–5a	12:1–2	13:1–5
11:5b–8	12:3–4	13:6–7
11:9–12	12:5–6	13:8–11
11:13	12:7–9	13:12–14

continued

FIGURE 11 (*cont*)

Col. 1	Col. 2	Col. 3
11:14	12:10–13	13:15–17
11:15–17	12:14–17	13:18–20
11:18–20		13:21–23
11:21–23		13:24–27

BOOK 4 (Jeremiah 14–17)

Col. 1	Col. 2	Col. 3	Col. 4
14:1–6	15:1–2	16:1–4	17:1–4
14:7–9	15:3–4	16:5–8	17:5–8
14:10–12	15:5–6	16:9	17:9–11
14:13–16	15:7–9	16:10–13	17:12–18
14:17–18	15:10–11	16:14–15	17:19–20
14:19–22	15:12–14	16:16–18	17:21–23
	15:15–16	16:19–20	17:24–26
	15:17–21	16:21	17:27

BOOK 5 (Jeremiah 18–20)

Col. 1	Col. 2	Col. 3
18:1–4	19:1–5	20:1–2
18:5–6	19:6–9	20:3–6
18:7–10	19:10–13	20:7–10
18:11–12	19:14–15	20:11–13
18:13–18		20:14–15
18:19–23		20:16–18

BOOK 6 (Jeremiah 21–24)

Col. 1	Col. 2	Col. 3	Col. 4
21:1–2	22:1–2	23:1–4	24:1
21:3–6	22:3–4	23:5–8	24:2
21:7	22:5	23:9–10	24:3
21:8–10	22:6–9	23:11–12	24:4–7
21:11–12	22:10–12	23:13–15	24:8
21:13–14	22:13–17	23:16–18	24:9–10
	22:18–19	23:10–20	
	22:20–23	23:21–22	
	22:24–27	23:23–24	
	22:28–30	23:25–27	
		23:28–29	
		23:30–32	
		23:33–36	
		23:37–40	

continued

FIGURE 11 *(cont)*

Part II

BOOK 7 (Jeremiah 25–29)

Col. 1	Col. 2	Col. 3	Col. 4	Col. 5
25:1–3	26:1–7	27:1–7	28:1–4	29:1–3
25:4–7	26:8–15	27:8	28:5–9	29:4–7
25:8–11	26:16–19	27:9–10	28:10–11	29:8–11
25:12–14	26:20–24	27:11	28:12–14	29:12–14
25:15–16		27:12–15	28:15	29:15–19
25:17–26		27:16–17	28:16–17	29:20–23
25:27		27:18		29:24–28
25:28–29		27:19–22		29:29–32
25:30–33				
25:34–38				

BOOK 8 (Jeremiah 30–31)

Col. 1	Col. 2
30:1–3	31:1–3
30:4–7	31:4–6
30:8–9	31:7–9
30:10–11	31:10–14
30:12–15	31:15–17
30:16–17	31:18–20
30:18–21aA	31:21–22
30:21aBb–24	31:23–26
	31:27–30
	31:31–34
	31:35–37
	31:38–40

BOOK 9 (Jeremiah 32–33)

Col. 1	Col. 2
32:1–5	33:1–3
32:6–15	33:4–9
32:16–25	33:10–11
32:26–35	33:12–13
32:36–41	33:14–16
32:42–44	33:17–18
	33:19–22
	33:23–26

continued

F I G U R E 1 1 *(cont)*

BOOK 10 (Jeremiah 34:1–7)

Col. 1

34:1
34:2–3

34:4–5
34:6–7

BOOK 11 (Jeremiah 34:8–22)

Col. 1

34:8–11
34:12–20

34:21
34:22

BOOK 12 (Jeremiah 35–39)

Col. 1	Col. 2	Col. 3	Col. 4
35:1–10	36:1–3	37:1–3	39:1–3
35:11–15	36:4–8	37:4–8	39:4–6a
35:16–17	36:9–15	37:9–10	39:6b–7
35:18–19	36:16–20a	37:11–15	39:8–10a
	36:20b–22	37:16–17	39:10b–14
	36:23–25	37:18–21a	39:15–18
	36:26–31	37:21b–38:23	
	36:32	38:24–28	

Part III

BOOK 13 (Jeremiah 40–43)

Col. 1	Col. 2	Col. 3	Col. 4
40:1–4	41:1–3	42:1–4	43:1–7
40:5–8	41:4–6a	42:5–6	43:8–13
40:9–10	41:6b	42:7–12	
40:11–12	41:7	42:13–16	
40:13–14	41:8–9	42:17–18	
40:15–16	41:10–12	42:19–22	
	41:13–14		
	41:15–18		

continued

FIGURE 11 (*cont*)

BOOK 14 (Jeremiah 44–45)

Col. 1	Col. 2
44:1–6	45:1–3
44:7–10	45:4–5
44:11–14	
44:15–19	
44:20–23	
44:24–27	
44:28	
44:29–30	

BOOK 15 (Jeremiah 46:1–28)

Col. 1
46:1–2
46:3–6
46:7–9
46:10–12
46:13–14
46:15–16
46:17–19
46:20–24
46:25–26
46:27–28

BOOK 16 (Jeremiah 47:1–49:33)

Col. 1	Col. 2	Col. 3	Col. 4	Col. 5	Col. 6
47:1–4	48:1–2	49:1–2	49:7–8	49:23–24	49:28–30
47:5–7	48:3–5	49:3–6	49:9–10	49:25–27	49:31–33
	48:6–8		49:11–13		
	48:9–13		49:14–16		
	48:14–17		49:17–19		
	48:18–20		49:20–22		
	48:21–26				
	48:27–30				
	48:31–33				
	48:34–35				
	48:36–38				
	48:39–41				
	48:42–44				
	48:45–47				

continued

FIGURE 11 (*cont*)

BOOK 17 (Jeremiah 49:34–51:64)

Col. 1	Col. 2	Col. 3
49:34–38	50:1–3	51:1–2
49:39	50:4–7	51:3–5
	50:8–10	51:6–7
	50:11–13	51:8–9
	50:14–16	51:10–11
	50:17–20	51:12–14
	50:21–23	51:15–16
	50:24–25	51:17–19
	50:26–28	51:20–24
	50:29–32	51:25–26
	50:33–34	51:27–28
	50:35–40	51:29–33
	50:41–43	51:34–35
	50:44–46	51:36–40
		51:41–43
		51:44–45
		51:46–48
		51:49–53
		51:54–56
		51:57–58
		51:59–60
		51:61–64

BOOK 18 (Jer 52)

Col. 1

52:1–3
52:4–8

52:9–11a
52:11b

52:12–23
52:24–27

52:28–30
52:31–34

Figure 11. Strophes or paragraphs are on separate lines. Pairs are grouped together.

the two methods.[291] This use of columns is disruptive and a further complicating factor in the continuous reading of the archive, but, like the other types of repetition and cross-reference, it serves to sort, arrange, and systematize the material.

The top-to-top organization of columns in a book is clear and slightly exaggerated in the first book (chaps. 1–6). The first column begins, after the docket, with the formula "Now the word of Yahweh came to me, saying. . . ." The second column begins the same way, and the third repeats its last element—"saying . . ." (1:4; 2:1; 3:1). The third column also rings the changes on the term "return," and the same term is taken up in an obvious summary and transition at the top of the fourth column (3:1 and 4:1). The fourth column also introduces the oath formula "as Yahweh lives," which recurs at the beginning of the fifth (4:2 and 5:2).[292] The fifth column is self-enclosed, repeating at its end the elements with which it began,[293] and the sixth begins by repeating the key words that follow the summary and transition in the fourth column (6:1–4:5–6). The whole book is even more tightly knit by variations on the system: the bottom of the first column sets Jeremiah up as a city within a city, and the bottom of the sixth column takes up some of the image's key terms;[294] the top of the second column uses two key terms that are repeated in opposite order at the bottom of the third.[295]

A similar organization of columns is found in the fifth, seventh, ninth, twelfth, fourteenth, and sixteenth books. In the fifth book the first column begins with Jeremiah's going down to the potter's house to proclaim his message; the second begins with his buying a jug, needlessly adds the same key term, and ends with his breaking the jug, explaining its significance, and repeating his message in the temple; the third column begins like the bottom of the second with the priest who is in charge of the temple overhearing the message that Jeremiah repeated.[296] In the seventh book all of the columns begin with a date and with the words that Jeremiah heard or wrote. The first three tags are very similar, the fourth less so, at the last just barely the same; and clearly the reader is supposed to catch on to the archival system.[297] The ninth book opens with Jeremiah receiving the word of God in prison, and the second column begins by saying that he was still there when God spoke again (32:1; 33:1). In the twelfth book every column begins with a date and a reference to the word of Yahweh (35:1; 36:1; 37:1; 39:1), and the division into columns is clarified by making the first three self-contained. The first begins and ends with a reference to the house of the Rechabites; the second begins and ends with the writing of a scroll; the third begins by saying that Jeremiah was not yet in prison and ends by saying that he was in prison and stayed there until Jerusalem was captured; the last column recounts the capture of Jerusalem.[298] The fourteenth book has two columns that begin in almost the same way, the first with the formula that distinguishes books, the second with an introduction constructed on the same model.[299] The sixteenth book has the oracles against the nations, and all the columns begin in the same way with the name of the nation concerned (47:1; 48:1; 49:1; 49:7; 49:23; 49:28).

The bottom-to-top organization of columns in a book is used in the second, third, eighth, and thirteenth books. As usual, the first instances in the archive or in any particular book are the clearest, and the user of the archive obviously is expected to get used to the system. The second book has four columns. The first column ends with the people being buried in the cemetery until there are *no more places*, or left out in the open for the birds and the beasts, and the second begins with them being taken out of their graves and left in the open, or harried in all the *remaining places* where they might have been driven (7:32–34; 8:1–3). The second column ends with an interjection, and the third begins the same way.[300] The third ends with a reference to the nations, and the last begins and ends the same way.[301] The third book has three columns and is arranged so that everything that is said at the end of the first is repeated at the beginning of the second,[302] and so that the formula used at the top of the first column and the bottom of the second is repeated at the top of the third.[303] The eighth book has two columns, one ending and the other beginning with the covenant formula (30:22; 31:1).[304] The thirteenth book has four columns, the second beginning as the first ends (40:15–16; 41:1), the top of the third like the bottom of the second (41:15–18; 42:1), the top of the fourth like the end of the third (42:19–22; 43:1). The system is used in sorting poetry and prose, in simple narratives, and in more complicated arguments; it eases the sequence and interrelations of the text by marking its stops and starts.

The self-contained organization of columns with internal cross-references from one to the other is used in the fourth, sixth, tenth, eleventh, fifteenth, and seventeenth books. The fourth book has four columns. The first is a lament whose high points are marked by repetitions of the same words,[305] and whose stages are marked by a reference to nonintercession. The second condemns the people who resisted Jeremiah, and it is attached to the first by another reference to nonintercession.[306] The third begins and ends on the note of fathers and sons and is linked to the second by its reference to the word of God (16:1–4 and 16:19–21; 15:1 and 16:1). The fourth column breaks the pattern, with its top related to the bottom of the third,[307] its bottom tied to the top of the first,[308] and with an internal quotation from the second (17:3–4 = 15:13–14). In the sixth book the first column begins with a mention of the king and ends with a reference to the house of the king (21:1–2, 11–14). The second begins and ends with a reference to the king who sits on the throne of David but also mentions the house of the king (22:1, 2, 30). The third is about the prophets, but its top is linked to the bottom of the second by the mention of David (22:30; 23:5–6).[309] The fourth begins and ends with a reference to the kings and princes and is linked to the first by its mention of Nebuchadnezzar.[310] The tenth book contains one short column that begins and ends in exactly the same way (34:1–2a = 34:6–7a). The eleventh book also has one column that refers to the release of the people in a literal and a figurative sense, and the fifteenth is like it in being constructed around two battles in which the Egyptians were defeated.[311] The last book has a column that begins and ends with the mention of Elam, another that begins and ends with a reference to the land of the Chaldaeans, a third that is clearly marked off as an oracle against Babylon, and a last that is cleverly attached to the bottom of the third column by its reference to Zedekiah.[312]

The use of columns does not make the archive any easier to read. It was a way of incorporating, organizing, and synthesizing the original text composed by Jeremiah along with the editor's interpretation and the evidence for it in an ongoing historical and prophetic tradition. It allows the archive to be used and understood, in its entirety, without deletion or compromise, by paying attention to the order and interrelations of its elements.

Paragraphs, Strophes, and Stanzas (fig. 11)

Columns are composed of prose paragraphs or poetic strophes arranged in pairs.[313] The columns, especially in the first part, are not always arranged in a continuous sequence, either logical or narrative or descriptive, and it often happens that the pairs of paragraphs and strophes do not match or that incongruous breaks occur between them. The archival arrangement, in effect, extends beyond parts, books, and columns to the basic literary components of stanzas, strophes, and paragraphs, so that everything is subsumed under the historical and biographical principles of archival composition.

The archive is sorted and arranged from the front and accumulates as it goes. The first column in the first book is a biographical introduction, and every other column that is added to the book is referred to it.

The first column in the second book, similarly, is a historical introduction, and every other column in the book is related both to it and to the oracles in the first book. In the rest of the first part of the archive every book has formulaic or substantial references to these introductions, as well as quotations from the intervening prophetic oracles in the first two books, and cumulative cross-references to the preceding books. The second part is introduced with a resumption of the first, and all its books and columns are referred to this resumption or to the critical columns at the beginning and the end of the first part. The third part, similarly, refers to the first and second and brings the archive to a resumptive and conclusive close. All of the references are disruptive, but they constitute a cumulative index that sorts and arranges the material as it is added to the archive. The references are more numerous and critical at the beginning and gradually diminish as the archive takes shape.

The first column in the first book introduces the principal points to be developed in the archive and gives them a focus in the biography of the prophet. The first column in the second book includes these points in a summary of the argument that will be illustrated in successive books of the archive and situates the prophet and his message in a historical context. Constant cross-reference to these texts and to the developing context allows the editor to call up the original sayings of Jeremiah, imitate them in new genres and historical situations, integrate them into the prophetic tradition, and interpret them in relation to the closure of historical traditions achieved in the Deuteronomistic History.

The biographical bias predominates in the first book. As outlined in the first column, this consists of opposition to Jeremiah, a priest and a prophet to the nations, by the city and officials he was trying to dissuade from their idolatry. It crops up in all the subsequent columns as lines inserted in stanzas or as stanzas added to strophes or as whole strophes intruded into an otherwise continuous and coherent text. The cross-references to the column are either literal quotations, or variations on its ideas expressed in formulas or shorthand notes, or combinations of these and heterogeneous themes taken from the prophets and the Deuteronomistic History.

The historical and argumentative bias predominates in the second book. As outlined in the first column, the explanation for the inexorable doom that confronted Judah and Jerusalem was that they worshiped other Gods and refused to heed the warnings of the prophets (chap. 7). The historical argument crops up here and there in the second column (8:1-3, 10-12, 17), fills up most of the third column, and dominates the whole book. It is an elaboration of the themes that were introduced at the beginning of the archive and restates the biographical bias of the first book. It argues that, although Yahweh is God of Israel and of the whole world (10:1–16) and Jeremiah is a prophet to the nations, he cannot intercede with God for his own nation (7:16), and all that is left for him or for them is wailing and lamentation (9:6–8, 13–25). Elements of the argument are taken up in blunt and obvious ways through all the books of the first part.

In each book the columns are kept separate, and each deals with a particular subject. Their contents are either homogeneous and have literal links and some sort of logical, chronological, or narrative sequence from paragraph to paragraph or from strophe to strophe, or they are contrary or incongruous and have their links or sequence supplied by cross-reference to the historical and biographical paradigms and to the sayings in the first two books. The references are verbal or generic, sometimes intrusive and obvious, sometimes subtle or curious, but they mark the progress of the text and the peculiar place of every item in the archive.

The third book, for instance, deals with the abrogation of the covenant and fits into the archive as an expansion of the key columns in the first two books. Its first column begins with homogeneous pairs of paragraphs outlining the consistent violation of the covenant first in Israel and then in Judah and Jerusalem.[314] The argument is taken from the preface to the second book and is filled with verbatim repetitions from that column, but it is also attached to the first book by literal quotations and further expanded by references to Micah and the Deuteronomistic History.[315] The next pair of paragraphs does not follow on them but simply takes up other elements of the standard argument outlined at the beginning of the second book: Jeremiah is told again not to intercede for the people; intercession is replaced by a lament on the fate of the city; the lament fits by referring back to the reason for their punishment that was given in the standard argument.[316] The next pair does not follow on them but supposes their link to the very first column in the archive: a lament recalls its theme of public opposition to Jeremiah, and the response to the lament refers explicitly to the people of Anathoth who opposed him (11:18–20, 21–23). The second column has a series of poetic pairs linked by concatenation to this complaint, but it ends with a pair of paragraphs that have nothing to do with them and instead return to the biographical argument of the first book.[317] The third column pairs a paragraph on the metaphor of the loincloth with an incongruous paragraph on the symbol of wineskins (13:8–11, 12–14). The first is in the biographical mode, has an odd allusion to the opening biographical column, and also refers to the standard historical argument.[318] The second paragraph takes up its reference to the royal houses of Israel and Judah and extends its biographical bias with another condemnation of the prophets, priests, and kings (13:12–14). The rest of the column follows by concatenation, with the standard uses of lamentation and with a paraphrase of a saying from the original poetic narrative (13:17; cf. 8:23).

Paragraphs and strophes are the basic form of meaning in literary texts. They are always paired in the archive, and the unevenness of the pairing accounts for most of the obscurities in the text. When there is a logical, chronological, or narrative connection between the pairs the text reads smoothly. When there is not, the text is to be read in conjunction with the ideas and the material gathered at the beginning of the archive. It is all carefully marked and everything is fitted skillfully in place.

The Editorial Process (fig. 12)

The archive keeps revolving on itself to include commentary on a poem composed by Jeremiah and to distribute its components over historical and biographical time. Most of the poem is in the first two books, and most of the archival cross-references are to the columns that introduce and explain them. The end of the original poem predicts Israel's return from exile, but the archive concealed it in the second part, after the fate of Judah and Jerusalem had been sealed, where it could better suit the facts. Jeremiah, as it turned out, was right, and the archive was arranged both to prove this historical point and to demonstrate Jeremiah's integrity and personal distance from the conservative opposition prophets who vainly prophesied peace.

The poem was incorporated into the archive by the usual method of repetition and cross-reference. The repetitions are literal or deictic or formulaic. The cross-references are to the evolving archival system. The poem is carefully preserved but is split by the system, broken by ready comments, and overwhelmed by interpretation. The poem was written to be performed. The archive was meant to be consulted in conjunction with the Deuteronomistic History, which it disputed, and to be studied and understood with regard to the prophet and the prophetic tradition it defended.

Book 1 (fig. 12)   The poem begins in the second column and can be picked out and distinguished as the consecutive and dramatic narrative that is devoid of archival manners and ideologies. The column begins

FIGURE 12

Jeremiah

Jeremiah			*The Jeremiah Archive*		
			BOOK 1		
			Column 1		
				1	1:1–3
				2	1:4–8
				3	1:9–10
				4	1:11–16
				5	1:17
				6	1:18–19
			Column 2		
			A	1	2:1–2
Act I — Scene 1				2	2:3
A	1	2:4	B	1	
	2	2:5–6		2	
			C	1	2:7
				2	2:8
B	1	2:9	D	1	
	2	2:10–11		2	
	3	2:12–13		3	
C	1	2:14	E	1	
	2	2:15		2	
	3	2:16–17		3	
D	1	2:18	F	1	
	2	219a		2	2:19b
	3	2:20		3	
E	1	2:21	G	1	
	2	2:22		2	
F	1	2:23	H	1	
	2	2:24		2	
	3	2:25		3	
			I	1	2:26–27aA
				2	2:27aBb
			J	1	2:28
				2	2:29–30
G	1	2:31aBb	K	1	2:31aA
	2	2:32		2	
H	1	2:33	L	1	2:34
	2	2:35		2	
	3	2:36–37		3	

continued

F I G U R E   1 2   (*cont*)

Jeremiah				*The Jeremiah Archive*		
Act I — Scene 2				**Column 3**		
A	1	3:1a		A	1	
	2	3:1b			2	
B	1	3:2a		B	1	
	2	3:2b–3			2	
C	1	3:4–5a		C	1	
	2	3:5b			2	
				D	1	3:6–8
					2	3:9–10
				E	1	3:11–12
					2	3:13
				F	1	3:14–15
					2	3:16
				G	1	3:17
					2	3:18
D	1	3:19a		H	1	
	2	3:19b–20			2	
E	1	3:21		I	1	
	2	3:22			2	
F	1	3:23		J	1	
	2	3:24			2	
					3	3:25
Act II — Scene 1				**Column 4**		
				A	1	4:1–2
					2	4:3–4
A	1	4:5		B	1	
	2	4:6			2	
B	1	4:7		C	1	
	2	4:8			2	
				D	1	4:9
					2	4:10
					3	4:11–12
C	1	4:13		E	1	
	2	4:14			2	
D	1	4:15–16a		F	1	
	2	4:16b–17			2	
E	1	4:18		G	1	
	2	4:19			2	

continued

FIGURE 12 (*cont*)

Jeremiah			The Jeremiah Archive		
Act II—Scene 1			**Column 4**		
F	1	4:20	H	1	
	2	4:21–22aA		2	
	3	4:22aBb		3	
G	1	4:23	I	1	
	2	4:24		2	
	3	4:25		3	
				4	4:26
H	1	4:27	J	1	
	2	4:28		2	
I	1	4:29a	K	1	
	2	4:29b		2	
J	1	4:30a	1	1	
	2	4:30b–31aA		2	
	3	4:31aBb		3	
Act II—Scene 2			**Column 5**		
A	1	5:1	A	1	5:2
	2	5:3		2	
B	1	5:4	B	1	
	2	5:5		2	
	3	5:6		3	
			C	1	5:7
				2	5:8–9
C	1	5:10	D	1	
	2	5:11–12		2	
			E	1	5:13
				2	5:14
D	1	5:15–16	F	1	
	2	5:17		2	
			G	1	5:18
				2	5:19
E	1	5:20–21	H	1	
	2	5:22		2	
	3	5:23–24		3	
F	1	5:25–26	I	1	
	2	5:27–28		2	
			J	1	5:29
				2	5:30–31

continued

FIGURE 12 (*cont*)

Jeremiah			*The Jeremiah Archive*		
Act III — Scene 1			**Column 6**		
A	1	6:1	A	1	
	2	6:2–3a		2	
B	1	6:3b–4a	B	1	
	2	6:4b–5		2	
				3	6:6
C	1	6:7	C	1	
	2	6:8		2	
				3	6:9
D	1	6:10	D	1	
	2	6:11–12		2	
			E	1	6:13–14
				2	6:15
E	1	6:16	F	1	
	2	6:17		2	
F	1	6:18–19	G	1	
	2	6:20		2	
	3	6:21		3	
G	1	6:22	H	1	
	2	6:23		2	
H	1	6:24	I	1	
	2	6:25		2	
	3	6:26		3	
			J	1	6:27–28
				2	6:29–30
			BOOK 2		
			Column 1		
				1	7:1–4
				2	7:5–10
				3	7:11–15
				4	7:16–20
				5	7:21–28
				6	7:29–34
			Column 2		
Act III — Scene 2			A	1	8:1–2
				2	8:3
A	1	8:4°	B	1	8:4°
	2	8:5		2	

continued

FIGURE 12 *(cont)*

Jeremiah			The Jeremiah Archive		
Act III — Scene 2			**Column 2**		
B	1	8:6	C	1	
	2	8:7		2	
C	1	8:8	D	1	
	2	8:9		2	
			E	1	8:10
				2	8:11
				3	8:12
D	1	8:13	F	1	
	2	8:14a		2	
	3	8:14b–15		3	
E	1	8:16	G	1	
				2	8:17
	2	8:18–19a		3	
F	1	8:19b–21a	H	1	
	2	8:21b–22		2	
	3	8:23		3	
Act IV — Scene 1			**Column 3**		
A	1	9:1	A	1	
	2	9:2		2	
B	1	9:3–4a	B	1	
	2	9:4b–5		2	
			C	1	9:6
				2	9:7
				3	9:8
C	1	9:9	D	1	
	2	9:10		2	
D	1	9:11	E	1	
	2	9:12		2	9:13
				3	9:14–15
			F	1	9:16–17
				2	9:18
				3	9:19
			G	1	9:20
				2	9:21
			H	1	9:22–23
				2	9:24–25

continued

FIGURE 12 (*cont*)

Jeremiah			*The Jeremiah Archive*		
Act IV—Scene 1			Column 4		
			A	1	10:1–2
				2	10:3–4
			B	1	10:5a
				2	10:5b
			C	1	10:6–7a
				2	10:7b
			D	1	10:8–9a
				2	10:9aBb
			E	1	10:10
				2	10:11
			F	1	10:12
				2	10:13
			G	1	10:14–15
Act IV—Scene 2				2	10:16
A	1	10:17–18	H	1	
	2	10:19–20		2	
B	1	10:22	I	1	10:21
				2	
			J	1	10:23
	2	10:24–25		2	
			BOOK 8		
			Column 1		
			A	1	30:1–2
Act V—Scene 1				2	30:3
			B	1	30:4
A	1	30:5–6		2	
	2	30:7		3	
			C	1	30:8
				2	30:8b–9
B	1	30:10	D	1	
	2	30:11		2	
C	1	30:12–13	E	1	
	2	30:14		2	
	3	30:15			
D	1	30:16	F	1	
	2	30:17		2	

continued

FIGURE 12 (*cont*)

Jeremiah			The Jeremiah Archive		
Act V — Scene 1			Column 1		
			G	1	30:18–20a
				2	30:20b–21aA
			H	1	30:21aBb–22
				2	30:23–24
Act V — Scene 2			Column 2		
			A	1	31:1
A	1	31:2		2	
	2	31:3		3	
B	1	31:4–5a	B	1	
	2	31:5b–6		2	
C	1	31:7	C	1	
	2	31:8		2	
	3	31:9		3	
			D	1	31:10–11
				2	31:12
				3	31:13–14
D	1	31:15	E	1	
	2	31:16–17		2	
E	1	31:18	F	1	
	2	31:19		2	
	3	31:20		3	
F	1	31:21	G	1	
	2	31:22		2	
			H	1	31:23
				2	31:24–25
				3	31:26
			I	1	31:27–28
				2	31:29–30
			J	1	31:31–32
				2	31:33–34
			K	1	31:35
				2	31:36
				3	31:37
			L	1	31:38–39
				2	31:40

Figure 12. Letters indicate strophes. Numbers denote stanzas.

with a strophe that links the poem to the archival framework: it is composed of archival formulas and with terminology taken from the first column but summarizes the poem and alludes to the text of Jeremiah that it incorporates.[319] The poem begins with the ingratitude of the generation that experienced the exodus and the wilderness wanderings, but the archive adds a strophe to reflect on the defilement of the land by the prophets, priests, and kings. It is linked to the preceding strophe by the repetition of a word and a clause, and anticipates a key word in the following strophe but uses it in an archival sense.[320] Jeremiah described the vicissitudes of those who abandoned Yahweh, but the archive used deictics and formulas to identify Yahweh as the Lord of Hosts and the God of the nations.[321] The poem describes a people's restless pursuit of Baal and the good life: the archive, in strophes that imitate their context, interprets it as the worship of idols by the prophets, priests, and kings.[322] Jeremiah treats Israel like a worldly woman, but, through deictics and repetitions, the archive makes her a murderess and much like her kings.[323] The poem resisted conceptualization and was genuinely hard to understand and appreciate without the staging and illusions it required. The editor made it clearer and more complex and totally dependent on the archival system of labeled and cumulative interpretation.

The third column tells of Yahweh's divorce from the land and of her desolation until Yahweh and their children are reunited in the land. The archive intervened between the divorce and the reunion to refer the whole matter to Judah's infidelity, exile, and return, and appended a stanza at the end of the column to leave Israel weltering in its guilt. The middle part stands out as a mainly prose commentary that paraphrases its source.[324] The concluding stanza contradicts the happy ending and is fitted in by the repetition of a couple of words.[325]

The fourth column dramatizes an attack on Jerusalem. The editor prefixed a strophe, attached to the original text by its address to Judah and Jerusalem, that flags the column and puts conditions on the reunion that Jeremiah described in the third column.[326] Another strophe, attached to the text by a deictic formula, describes the convulsions of the city leaders when the prophets of peace are proved wrong.[327] A separate stanza, added to Jeremiah's portrayal of the invasion's cosmic symbolism, extends the destruction to the outlying regions of Judah.[328] All of the additions take the attack literally rather than dramatically and blend the text into the archive's historical perspective.

The fifth column gives the reasons for the threatened invasion, but its dramatic sweep was interrupted frequently to include the reasons that the editor thought appropriate. Two lines added to the first stanza, by repeating one of its words and anticipating the first word of the next stanza, tag the column and introduce the archival themes of idolatry and false prophecy.[329] The themes are developed in an adjacent strophe, added by deictics, that makes the city's guilt unpardonable and its punishment inevitable,[330] and in a later strophe that pits Jeremiah against the prophets.[331] Idolatry is mentioned again as the reason the city was captured and its population sent into exile,[332] and the column ends with another condemnation of the prophets whose lies brought the land to ruin.[333]

The sixth column calls on Jerusalem to respond to divine discipline, but the editor inserted comments to seal its fate. There are matching stanzas added by deictics and formulaics to two contiguous strophes that describe the siege of the city and the decimation of its inhabitants.[334] Another strophe shifts the blame to the prophets and priests who lied to the people and who will be punished along with them.[335] The column ends, in terms initially published in the introductory paradigm, with Jeremiah established as an impregnable city within the city that is about to be destroyed because of its evil.[336]

All of the editor's remarks are purple patches on their contexts, sensibly fitted in but ideologically out of place. They break up the dramatic flow of the text, and some replace symbols or metaphors that the drama developed into commonplace images and ideas. They all contribute to the portrait of Jeremiah standing alone against the city and its leaders, a prophet to the nations, an emissary of the Lord of Hosts.

Book 2 The poem continues in the second column of Book Two with the confusion, anxiety, and sorrow that overwhelm the city. The column was arranged in the archive by tying it to the intrusive historical paradigm in the preceding column and by forging links with the emended last column in the first book, with which it originally belonged.[337] The historical themes of the second book are suggested in one stanza that, by allusion to the bronze serpent of Mosaic times, insinuates that no charm or intercession can avert the city's doom.[338] In Jeremiah's version the drama is moving to its denouement, but in the archival version the history of Judah and Jerusalem is moving to its inevitable climax.

The third column portrays Yahweh leaving Jerusalem in tears because the city has not wanted to listen to him, but in the archival version Yahweh leaves the tears to professional mourners and refuses to relent. The first strophe is inserted by deictics and literal repetition and interprets Yahweh's abandonment of the city in terms of the

punishment that was decided from the start in the archive.[339] Two
stanzas and three strophes are appended at the end of the column to
comment on the original text and confirm the punishment described in
the historical paradigm.[340]

The last column finally has the city beg for mercy. It is headed in
the archival version by a didactic poem on worship of God and rejection
of idols. Jeremiah's text is interrupted twice with cross-references to
the poem that persist in condemning the kings who were responsible
for the worship of idols. Jeremiah's version ended on a note of strength
and anticipation, but in the archival version it is clear that nothing has
changed.[341]

Book 8   The first column in the eighth book, act V, scene 1 in the
original poem, is addressed to Jacob and Israel and undoes the pain of
the northern kingdom's defeat and exile. The second column looks
forward to the return from exile and envisages Ephraim's reunion with
Judah as the reunion of Rachel and her children. The archive made
the columns a separate book concerning the restoration of Israel and
Judah in the indefinite future. The heading, date, and docket identify
the book as a covenant document like the covenant that was narrated
in the epic and promulgated in the sequel.[342] Another strophe, linked
to the original poem by catchword repetition, includes the Davidic king
in the restored covenant community.[343] Two others, attached the same
way to the original text, associate the royal ruler with the restored line
of Levi.[344] Another strophe, imitating its source, interprets the return
of the remnant of Israel as the return of Jacob.[345] The book concludes
with a series of strophes that undo the dire predictions of the paradigmatic columns and describe the end of the exile and the inauguration
of a new covenant.[346]

The archive was arranged to give Jeremiah his proper place in
history and in the prophetic traditions of Israel. It saved his works but
annotated them and distributed them over time until their predictions
were fulfilled. What compelled the archivist is detailed in the history,
dramatized in the poem that Jeremiah wrote, and gone over with
excruciating detail as both history and prophecy are dissected and
analyzed in the incessant array of the archive.

JEREMIAH (FIG. 12)

Jeremiah composed his poem in five parts or acts each with two
matching sections or scenes.[347] The scenes contain strophes linked in
pairs. The strophes are constructed of stanzas filled with discourse and

dialogue and snippets of narration. The whole poem dramatizes the return of the North to Yahweh in Zion and their final reunion with a reformed and humbled Judah.

The drama presents the history of Israel in prophetic form. In the first act Yahweh speaks to Israel as a woman and wife who has abandoned him and cannot come back but whose children are persuaded at last to return to him. The climax of the story occurs in the fifth act, when the remnant of Israel who have been disciplined and forgiven return to Samaria and are reunited with their mother in Zion. The middle acts apply the lesson of Israel to Judah and Jerusalem. In the second act invaders come from the north because Judah thinks it can do what Israel did and still survive. In the third act the siege of Jerusalem is seen through the terror and turmoil within its walls, and Yahweh is reduced to tears. In the fourth act Yahweh is about to leave Jerusalem when finally the city is sorry, admits its mistakes, accepts its punishment, and begs for remission. The story ends with Jacob and Israel, Rachel and Ephraim rejoicing in the presence of Yahweh in Zion.

The sources of the poem are literary and historical. The land as Yahweh's wife and the people as their children, Ephraim as the favorite child, and the not-quite-perfect assimilation of Jacob to Israel were themes developed by Hosea. The enemy coming against the land and laying siege to the city was described by Isaiah as an event of historical import and achieved prominence in Micah's lament. The causes of the calamity and the reasons for it all had been set out in the prophets. The principles on which faith and hope were based—the permanence of world order, the presence of Yahweh in Zion, the possibility of adherence to the law—were detailed in the epic and the sequel and their Priestly and Elohistic revisions. The expected reform in which this hope would occur was encouraged by Isaiah and Amos and outlined in the dialogues of Micah and in the reunion of God and the land and his people in the play by Hosea. The poem was original for all that and, because it was not dictated by contemporary events, was left open to endless speculation.

Act I (Jeremiah 2-3)

After an introduction by the prophet, Yahweh speaks to Jacob and Israel. In the first strophe he wonders aloud why their parents would distance themselves from him after their journey together through the wilderness. In the second strophe Yahweh exclaims to the heavens and earth that such a thing has never happened before anywhere in the world and then begins court proceedings against the children of such parents. The exodus and the wilderness wanderings are a common historical and prophetic topic, but the contrast between the wilderness and the land, the trial involving parents and their children, the abandonment of Yahweh to go after other Gods, and being brought to court for doing such things are themes created and embellished by Hosea.[348]

The third and fourth strophes are addressed in the masculine singular to Israel as an individual and in the feminine singular to the land of Israel as the bride of Yahweh. The third strophe combines a soliloquy about Israel and an address to the land in which, with words and images taken from Isaiah, Yahweh describes an enemy invasion and attributes it to their abandonment of him. The fourth is addressed to the land and, in words taken from Hosea, recalls the rites and the foreign alliances that made them helpless before their invaders. Both strophes are attached to the first two strophes by literal links.[349]

The fifth and sixth strophes also combine references to Isaiah and Hosea. The fifth alludes to Isaiah's image of Israel as a vineyard and to the offer that Yahweh once made to cleanse Israel from its sins. The sixth attributes her uncleanness, in the words of Hosea, to her brute worship of Baal and her lovers. Both leave aside for a moment the image of the enemy attack to concentrate again on its causes.[350]

The last two strophes return to the attack and bring the scene to a close. The seventh resumes the contrast between the wilderness and the land that occurred at the beginning of the discourse and the theme of Yahweh's marriage with the land that the dialogue developed. The last sums up the infidelities of the land and leaves her without resources against the enemy attack. Both continue allusions to the prophets, and both are dominated by the image of a journey, which has pervaded the whole scene.[351]

The second scene is a genial reworking of the divorce and reconciliation of Yahweh and the land of Israel that Hosea once portrayed. The first two strophes are monologue and dialogue and express Yahweh's legal concern that a divorced woman cannot return to her husband without defiling the land.[352] The next two strophes, therefore, abandon the image of Yahweh's engagement to the land and replace it with the metaphor of parenting: he says what he had hoped for and quotes the response he expected from the land and sadly recalls her former infidelity.[353] In the last two strophes Yahweh calls his children home, and they answer in sorrow and confusion that they will come back to him.[354] The scene supposes the entire flow of Hosea's work and, replacing the marriage bond with the bond between parents and their children, resolves the dilemma of Israel's persistent unfaithfulness in the fantastic role that she sought as Yahweh's wife and the mother of his children. The land of Israel has been lost, but its people will be saved in Judah and Jerusalem.

Act II (Jeremiah 4-5)

The second act revolves around Judah and Jerusalem and, in reliance on Isaiah, Amos, Hosea, and Micah, describes an invasion and the stunning victories of the enemy and the various reactions of Yahweh, the prophet, and the people in the city. In the first part war, rumors of war, and scenes of devastation predominate. The second scene searches out of the causes of the war and settles on ignorance, failure to observe the law, and unwillingness to learn the lessons of history. The first scene mingles the words of Yahweh and the cries of the city with the report of a herald who announces the invasion and summons the city to repentance. In the second scene Yahweh and the prophet declaim, and the city is silent. The act follows the movement of the enemy approaching the city and the inhabitants retreating within its walls to contrast the blindness of the people with the clear-sightedness of their herald and watchman.

The first two strophes in the opening scene combine the herald's call to retreat to Zion and the fortified cities of Judah with the report of an enemy advancing and the summons to lament and do penance to avert the anger of Yahweh. The call and the summons paraphrase Micah's lament over the evil that Yahweh was bringing against Jerusalem.[355] The report describes the enemy as a lion and a destroyer of nations and is indebted to Isaiah's vision of the Assyrian empire roaming the world for its prey.[356]

The third and fourth strophes vary the war report and renew the herald's call. The report compares the horses and chariots of the advancing army to a storm and is joined in the third strophe with the worried reaction of the populace and with an appeal for reform. The herald's call announces that the enemy is nearer and is combined in the fourth strophe with Yahweh's reasons for the invasion. The third strophe supposes familiarity with the text of Micah, and both the third and the fourth allude to Isaiah's vision of the Assyrian armies of Sennacherib.[357]

The fifth and sixth strophes combine the cries of the besieged and abandoned city, composed by Jeremiah, and Yahweh's comments on the reasons for its predicament, quoted from Isaiah and Micah.[358] In the seventh and eighth strophes the herald sees the crumbling of a world order that the Priestly writer described, but Yahweh interjects, with reference to Hosea and the oracles of Balaam, that destruction is decreed but will not be complete.[359] In the final strophes of the first scene Jeremiah sees the city deserted and Zion left alone to her sorrow and pain.

The second scene engages Yahweh and Jeremiah his herald in conversation. In the first strophe Jeremiah is told to search Jerusalem for someone who observes the law, and he responds that they have learned nothing from the lessons they have been taught and no one has repented. In the second strophe he looks beyond the simple folk to the high and mighty and realizes that they are all doomed because their crimes are many and no one knows the law. In the third strophe Yahweh remarks that he has summoned the destroyers because Judah is no better than the house of Israel and imagines that it can act with impunity because Yahweh is supposed to be on their side. In the fourth strophe he identifies the invaders and describes what they will do to the land and the fortified cities. In the fifth he tells Jeremiah to ask Jacob and Judah why they are unwilling to fear him and why they are unable to see that they have upset the order of the created world. In the end Yahweh answers his own question by describing the city filled with evil and unwilling to observe the law.

The scene is constructed with the connivance of prophetic and historical precedents. From Isaiah it borrowed the image of wounds that were inflicted to teach a lesson and the perception of the Assyrians as a people with unintelligible speech.[360] From Amos it took the image of Yahweh as a lion ready to devour Israel for its crimes.[361] From Hosea it took the specifics of their crimes and the fact that they would not repent.[362] From Micah it borrowed the expression of their confidence in the presence of God.[363] From the Elohist it took the definition of the law and some of its basic prescriptions.[364]

The second act follows the same pattern as the first and has many literal links with it. In both acts the first scene explores the situation and the second attempts to resolve it. In both the drama is conveyed along a line of march or a journey — in the first along the route from Egypt through the wilderness with the people at first distancing themselves from Yahweh and then approaching from afar, in the second with the invaders marching from afar through the land and up to the walls of Jerusalem and with the people huddled in the city while Yahweh and Jeremiah look for some way to pardon and protect them. In the first act Israel could not cleanse itself of its worship of Baal, and in the second act Jerusalem is told to cleanse itself of the evil that lurks within it (4:14; 2:22). In the second act the city bewails the invasion and siege, but God blames it on the evil that the city did, as in the first act the invasion of Israel and the ridicule it endured from Egypt were blamed on Israel's abandonment of Yahweh.[365] In both acts the heavens are appalled by the deeds of the people (4:23, 28; and 2:12). In both the culprit is a woman who adorns herself for her husband or her lovers (4:30; and 2:32). In the first act northern Israel is like a highbrowed woman who feels no shame and cannot return to her husband or like a spoiled child who leaves and comes back to its parents, and in the second act Judah and Jerusalem are stony-faced and refuse to return.[366] In both acts the people of Israel have broken their yokes and snapped their bonds and are generally unmaleable (5:5 and 2:20; 5:11 and 3:20). In both they are devoured by their enemies (5:17 and 3:24).

Act III (Jeremiah 6; 8)

The scenes in the third act are linked separately to those in the second to portray the siege of Jerusalem in all its horror and the bitter sorrow of Yahweh that the city would not listen to his words and his law. The reality of war that the act represents is not new but was eked out of the prophetic tradition in Isaiah, Amos, Hosea, and Micah. But the perception of Yahweh's passion for his people led the editor to include it in a separate book, where the anger and sorrow of God could be filtered through its normal cosmic and community repercussions.[367]

The first scene is linked to the opening scene in the second act by repeating and paraphrasing its introductory stanzas, which herald the invasion and siege of the city.[368] The vision of the siege in the first two strophes interweaves description and dialogue and is indebted mainly to Micah. The herald is summoned to announce that Yahweh is bringing evil against the city. Yahweh speaks to her, in the person of the prophet and in the words of Hosea and Micah, as the darling daughter of Zion doomed to die. The herald describes her as a pasture where the enemies pitch their tents and quotes a saying from Isaiah and Micah as they prepare to attack.[369] The third strophe begins with Yahweh's soliloquy on the evil of Jerusalem and ends with his plea to the city to reform: it is cleverly composed in the mood of the poem, but the soliloquy in particular is filled with citations from the prophets.[370] In the fourth strophe Jeremiah reflects on the fact that no one listened to Yahweh's plea and, in the style of Micah, declares himself ready to do battle with words (Jer 6:10–12).[371] In the fifth strophe Yahweh speaks to the people again begging them to observe the law that the Elohist codified and thereby enjoy the peace that Isaiah proclaimed and, with a nod to what Jeremiah just said, reminds them that the prophets are the watchmen that he has appointed.[372] In the sixth strophe he turns to the nations of the world to be his witnesses that evil is coming upon his people because, instead of listening to him and observing the law, they have offered him incense and sacrifice. The argument is original, but its elements are familiar from the prophets and the words are taken from Isaiah and Amos and Micah.[373] In the seventh strophe, in words and images taken from Isaiah, Yahweh returns to a description of the siege, and in the last strophe, in the language of the prophetic tradition, the city cries out in terror and the prophet calls for lamentation and penance.[374]

The second scene begins like the corresponding scene in the second act as Yahweh muses on his people's frenzy and despair and refusal to return to him.[375] In the first strophe he reflects on contrary statements made by Amos and Micah—in his lament over Israel Amos said that Israel had fallen and would not rise, but in his prayer for Jerusalem Micah said that Israel had fallen and would rise again—and on the ambiguity of Israel's return and Judah's refusal to return.[376] In the second strophe, with reference to Isaiah, he observes that the city cries out in terror but not in sorrow and that it turns to battle instead of returning to observance of the law.[377] In the third strophe he quotes their reasoning and protests that they have rejected the word of God: they say that they know what they are doing and that they know the law, but, with an allusion to the recent Priestly and Elohist revisions of the epic and its sequel, they protest that scribes have turned it into a lie.[378] In the fourth strophe he uses images from Isaiah and the metaphor of harvesting to describe their lack of response, but he goes on to quote their confession of sin and words of despair and their decision to gather in their fortified cities and fight to the finish.[379] In the fifth and sixth strophes, as at the end of the second act, the herald announces the approach of the enemy, and the mingled voices of Yahweh and Zion ring out the changes on terror, sorrow, pain, and disappointment now that the harvest is past. It becomes clear at the end of the scene that the people do not accept the law and the proposed reforms because they believe that Yahweh their king is with them and will be manifested in a marvelous victory over their enemies.[380]

Act IV (Jeremiah 9–10)

In the fourth act Yahweh, in the person of the prophet, sees the impending ruin of the city and bemoans the fate of his people, and they, threatened with destruction and exile, finally transcend their self-pity and express true submission to the law. The first scene is set outside the city, in the wilderness and in the hill country, where Yahweh went to weep for his people.[381] The second scene portrays Jerusalem under siege and Judah destroyed and the people about to be cast into exile. The first scene ends with the prophet inquiring who might understand the drama of the ruined land or explain the words of Yahweh, and with Yahweh responding that it is because they have neglected the law and refused to walk in its ways. The second ends with the sound of thunder from the North and with Judah and Jerusalem begging Yahweh to teach them a lesson in the law.[382]

Act V (Jeremiah 30–31)

The last act resolves all the issues raised in the drama and brings all its themes to a close. In the first scene Jacob and Zion are taught their lesson and are assured of salvation. In the second scene a remnant of Israel returns from exile in the north country and joins with Rachel and Jacob in the worship of Yahweh in Zion. At last Yahweh is reunited with the daughter of Israel and with Ephraim their beloved child.[383]

The first scene has four strophes composed to conclude the drama of Judah and Jerusalem. The first concerns Jacob, and the second is addressed to him. The last two are spoken to a woman who in the end is identified as Zion. Each of the strophes is composed of words and images that are familiar from the preceding acts but are strung together and filled with reversals to convey a sense of quiet resolution.

The first strophe uses the familiar metaphor of the pains of childbirth to describe the anguish that Jacob has suffered in the preceding acts. Many of the words are taken from the same context, but the trials that he has endured are associated with the day of Yahweh that turned out, in Jeremiah's estimation, not to be the total end that Amos predicted.[384] In the second strophe Yahweh announces to Jacob and Israel in exile that his salvation is at hand. The strophe retrieves from the first act the image of Jacob as the servant of Yahweh, from the second act the image of invaders from afar and the notion of immense but incomplete ruin, and from the fourth act the longing to learn the lessons of the law and to be freed from foreign domination, and combines them all with allusions to Isaiah, Amos, and the epic.[385] In the third strophe, in an intricate interlacing of texts from earlier acts, Yahweh explains to Zion that he has caused her pain because of her sins and that no one else can heal her,[386] and in the last strophe he announces that he will heal her.[387]

The second scene reconsiders the fate of northern Israel, dramatized in the first act, in the light of the reform of Judah that has just been portrayed. In the first strophe there is the mixture of masculine and feminine that was typical of the first act, and in the remaining strophes Israel is alternately male and female. In the first strophe also, in language reminiscent of Hosea, Yahweh announces that the people who survived the sword found grace in the wilderness and that Israel is coming back to the place of his rest, and Israel confesses that Yahweh appeared to her in that distant place and professed his everlasting love for her.[388] In the second strophe Yahweh speaks to the young woman Israel and, in the language of the Song of the Vineyard, tells her that Samaria will be rebuilt but will worship in Zion.[389] In the third strophe the people are summoned to be happy for Jacob and to pray for the salvation of Israel, and in reply Yahweh reports that a remnant is returning from the north country and that his son Ephraim is coming home.[390] In the fourth strophe Rachel is found weeping for her children, as she was bidden at the end of act four, but Yahweh consoles her and rewards her tears with the return of her children.[391] The fifth strophe, in metaphors composed by Hosea, portrays Ephraim's return and repentance and confirms Yahweh's compassion toward his favorite child.[392] In the last strophe Yahweh summons his bride, the young woman Israel, and invites her to settle in the land and embrace Jacob.[393]

CONCLUSION

Jeremiah reconciled prophetic and historiographic traditions in a dramatic display of the nation's apostasy and repentance. He was influenced especially by the vigorous sensuality of Hosea's presentation, by the rhythmic measures of Micah's lament, and by the kindly persuasion of the Elohist's revelation of the law. The evidence that he assembled was the events described and imagined by the prophets. The principles that he supposed were those that the historians presented as they demonstrated the presence of God in the world and the history of Israel. What had happened once to the North could happen again to Judah and Jerusalem until Yahweh, in the person of the prophet, took part in the living drama that moved from their vanity and abandonment to their recognition and reform.

The editor of Jeremiah's prophecy gave historical and biographical substance to an essentially dramatic and imaginative work. It was not possible to correct the drama or eliminate the dream, but it was possible to illustrate it with reference to real events in the history of the nation and to scenes in the troubled career of a prophet like Jeremiah. The biography continues to be dramatic and imaginary. The history, when the reform that Jeremiah hoped for failed, showed his opponents that his prophecy was true. The evidence is all collected in the hodgepodge of an archive in his name.[394]

Conclusion

The movement toward reform was gradual and slow and required the cooperation of prophets, priests, and scribes. It originated really in Hosea, who became involved in the history of his people and tried to imagine how they could survive. Its philosophic platform was the Priestly work that separated God from familial ties with his people. Its theological basis was the Elohist idea of constant enveloping providence. Its practical source was the prophecy of Micah, who resumed the prophetic tradition and showed that the Elohist code was a reason for lamentation and change and a reliable motive for hope. Its immediate cause and reflection were Jeremiah's vivid dramatization of the whole process of vain defection, humble submission to the law, and total reprieve in the loving presence of God.

The problem, of course, was the pressure of events. But the lesson was well learned, and when Judah and Jerusalem fell they could look to the bold precedent and rise again to the occasion.

NOTES

[1] On genealogy as history, see C. W. Fornara, *The Nature of History in Ancient Greece and Rome* (Berkeley: University of California Press, 1983) 4–12. The genealogies, as indicated in fig. 7, are composed of smaller segments or paragraphs that are distinguished from one another grammatically and syntactically and are linked to each other in cumulative order.

[2] Some genealogies list a sequence of generations with little or no comment (nos. II, IV, V, VII). Others include alternative versions of the epic episodes (nos. III, VI, VIII, X) with more (no. VI) or less (nos. III, VIII, X) genealogical information. Some follow the calendar (I, III, X). Others keep track of time (II, III, V, X).

[3] The introductions include some deictic element and the word "generations." The usual form is *(wĕ)ʾēlleh tôlĕdôt* . . . + the name of the person from whom the generations are descended. The first introduction (2:4a) comes after the creation of the world—for which there was no progenitor—and before the beginning of the epic account. A variant form (Gen 5:1, *zeh sēper tôlĕdôt ʾādām*) separates the history of the world from the account of creation where it began.

The Priestly version hurries through the early history to arrive at the genealogy of Jacob and Israel (X), which takes up most of its time.

[4] The Priestly passages stand out from the context by their artificiality and formality. The severest instance of verbatim repetition occurs in the account of the tabernacle (Exodus 25–31°, 35–40°) where a set of instructions is carried out, despite a different emphasis and a partly opposite order, almost to the letter. Stylized address is most evident in Abraham's dealings with the Hittites (Genesis 23). Formulas abound in the account of creation (Gen 1:1–2:3). Repetitive patterns govern the story of the plagues (Exodus 1–15°).

[5] The Priestly writer did not edit the epic text but wrote around it, and the Priestly text, consequently, usually consists of extended blocks of material. Where it exists in smaller pieces affixed to the epic text (e.g., Gen 12:4b–5abA; 21:1b, 2b; 37:2aA) it makes consecutive sense with it, but even in these cases it can be read sensibly with the surrounding Priestly material and without reference to the epic.

[6] See J. Skinner, *A Critical and Exegetical Commentary on the Book of Genesis* (ICC; Edinburgh: T. & T. Clark, 1930) 130–39.

[7] The Priestly version marks its quotation of the epic by reversing its word order: in P God created the heavens and the earth (Gen 1:1, . . . *ʾĕlōhîm ʾet haššāmayim wĕʾet hāʾāreṣ*; Gen 2:4a, *ʾēlleh tôlĕḏôt haššāmayim wĕhāʾāreṣ bĕhibbārĕʾām*) and then rested from his labors of creation and construction (Gen 2:4a, *ʾăšer bārāʾ ʾĕlōhîm laʿăśôt*). The epic just mentioned that Yahweh God constructed the earth and the heavens (Gen 2:4b, *bĕyôm ʿăśôt yhwh ʾĕlōhîm ʾereṣ wĕšāmayim*) but did not pursue the story. The epic narrates Yahweh's actions, quotes his commands to the man and his conversation with the man and the woman, and ends with a soliloquy in which God decides to remove the man and the woman from the garden (Gen 3:22–23). The Priestly writer, similarly, has a creation account composed of actions and words and ends with a soliloquy in which God—again in the first person plural—decides to make man and woman (Gen 1:26).

[8] See E. A. Speiser, *Genesis* (AB 1; Garden City, N.Y.: Doubleday, 1964) 9–13; C. Westermann, *Genesis* (BKAT 1/1; Neukirchen-Vluyn: Neukirchener Verlag, 1974) 1:24–65. In the epic the divine aspirations of men and women are expressed in the episodes of creation and the flood and linger in a diminished form in the stories of Abraham's encounter with the travelers and of Jacob's encounter with God at the border of Canaan. In the Priestly version the end of creation is marked by the sabbath, and history becomes a record of human generation.

[9] Cf. Exodus 14°; 25–40°; F. M. Cross, "The Priestly Tabernacle in the Light of Recent Research," in *Temples and High Places in Biblical Times: Proceedings of the Colloquium in Honor of the Centennial of Hebrew Union College— Jewish Institute of Religion, 14–16 March 1977*, ed. A. Biran (Jerusalem: Nelson Glueck School of Biblical Archaeology, 1981) 169–80. The Priestly writer is interested in the story's scientific implications, its perception of cause-and-

effect, its cosmology, astrology, and so forth, and not in its pertinence to the cult of Marduk.

[10] The beginning of the second genealogy (Gen 5:1–2) repeats the end of the first genealogy (Gen 1:1 and 2:3, *br*ʾ, *ʿśh*; Gen 1:26–28, in the likeness of God, male and female, blessing). It also uses some of the epic terminology (Gen 5:1, *bĕyôm*; cf. 2:4b; Gen 5:2b, *wayyiqrāʾ ʾet šĕmām ʾāḏām*; cf. 2:7) but does not refer to the epic story.

[11] See R. S. Hess, "The Genealogies of Genesis 1–11 and Comparative Literature," *Bib* 70 (1989) 241-54; D. W. Young, "A Mathematical Approach to Certain Dynastic Spans in the Sumerian King List," *JNES* 47 (1988) 123–29; idem, "On the Application of Numbers from Babylonian Mathematics to Biblical Life Spans and Epochs," *ZAW* 100 (1988) 331–61; idem, "The Influence of Babylonian Algebra on Longevity among the Antediluvians," *ZAW* 102 (1990) 321–35.

[12] See Westermann, *Genesis* 1:484–88. Enoch, like Atrahasis, lives far away with the Gods. Noah's name is explained by the Priestly writer with allusions to the story of the flood. The meaning "this one will bring us relief from our work and from the labor of our hands" supposes that people were made to toil for the Gods. This is neither the epic (Genesis 2–3) nor the Priestly interpretation (Genesis 1) of the reasons for creation and the flood, but it is the understanding of their Mesopotamian sources from which the epic derived the idea that labor was a result of expulsion from the garden (Gen 3:24) and that the noise that workmen made was a reason for the confusion of tongues (Genesis 11). The Priestly interpretation of the name Noah, therefore, precedes the story of the sons of God and the daughters of Man and insinuates the more orthodox reason for the flood. This attempt to anticipate and correct the epic is confirmed by the expression "will bring us relief" (Gen 5:29, *yĕnaḥamēnû*), which, besides being a striking and unexpected etiology of Noah's name, plays on the expression that the epic used to explain Yahweh's decision to bring about the flood (Gen 6:6, *yinnāḥem*; cf. 6:7, *niḥamtî*).

[13] See F. H. Cryer, "The Interrelationships of Gen 5,32; 11,10–11 and the Chronology of the Flood," *Bib* 66 (1985) 241–61.

[14] The matching segments are Gen 6:9–12 and 9:28–29. The first repeats the last sentence of the preceding genealogy (6:10, "And Noah became the father of three children, Shem, Ham and Japhet" = Gen 5:32b), and the reasons that it gives for the flood correspond to reasons found in Amos (Gen 6:11b, 13, *ḥāmās*; cf. Amos 3:10; 6:3) and in Isaiah (Gen 6:11–12, 13 *šḥt* [four times]; cf. Isa. 1:4, *bānîm mašḥîtîm*). The first segment comments on the epic version in which Yahweh saw that people were bad and regretted that he had made them (Gen 6:5–8) by extending violence and corruption from people to the world and by eliminating God's change of mind.

[15] The matching segments are Gen 6:13–22 and 9:1, 9–17. The building of the ark is supposed in the epic but is recounted in the Priestly version (Gen 6:14–16) as it was in *Atrahasis* (3.1–2) and in *Gilgamesh* (II. 50–95). The

quotation from Amos (8:2, bāʾ haqqēṣ ʾel ʿammî) repeats his words in the opposite order (Gen 6:13, qēṣ kol bāśār bāʾ lĕpānay) and in a universal rather than national context.

16 The Priestly text (Gen 7:18, 19–21, 24) fills out the laconic epic text (Gen 7:17, 23aAb°) by changing the duration of the flood and, in preparation for the ark's anchorage on Ararat, by portraying its elevation above the mountains.

17 The genealogy shares with the following episode an interest in the differences between languages (cf. Gen 10:5, 20, 31 and 11:1, 7) and in the reasons for the geographical distribution of the nations (cf. Gen 10:5, 32). The epic attributes both to the intervention of Yahweh, while the Priestly writer describes them as matters of fact.

18 The next genealogy begins, as this one ends, with Shem (cf. Gen 10:22–23, 31 and 11:10) and concludes with Abraham.

19 The genealogy contains a list of countries grouped according to place and dependency rather than according to ethnic or racial ties. The descendants of Japhet, for instance, are Mediterranean countries linked by trade and commerce. The African nations are around the Red Sea and include Egypt and its province of Canaan. The Mesopotamian countries are gathered on either side of the river. The list was corrected (compare, e.g., 10:7 and 10:28–29) and completed (Gen 10:8–19, 21, 24–30) by the Deuteronomist from a historical and ethnographic perspective to include places and nations mentioned in the story of Abraham and later on in the History. The result is a strange mixture of worlds: see B. Oded, "The Table of Nations (Genesis 10)—A Socio-cultural Approach," ZAW 98 (1986) 14–31.

20 In the fourth genealogy (Genesis 10°) two subsidiary lines of relationship were listed in the territories of Japhet and Ham, but only one in the line of Shem: the Cimmerians and Ionians in the Japhet group (Gen 10:2–5), the congeners of Cush and Ramah in the Ham group (Gen 10:6–7, 20), but only the children of Aram in the line of Shem (Gen 10:22–23). The fifth genealogy repeats and develops the end of the fourth (Gen 11:10–13; cf. 10:22) and adds the missing second line of descendants that issued in Abraham.

21 The framework (Gen 11:27–28, 31–32; 12:4b–5abA; 25:7–10) spans the life and death of Abraham and includes chronological data and information that sets and concludes the scene. Each of the narrative incidents in the genealogy is dated according to the age of Abraham or Sarah (12:4b; 16:3, 16; 17:1, 24; 21:5; 23:1; 25:7).

22 The fragment (Gen 12:4b–5abA) is sewn into its context by initial (12:4b, wĕʾabrām = 12:4a) and final repetition (12:5bA ʾarṣâ kĕnaʿan = 12:5bB) of the original but stands out from its context by its repetitive patterns and listlike cadence. In the epic the birth of Isaac is a miracle, but according to the Priestly document Abraham had numerous descendants and

the birth of Isaac was extraordinary only because it was sanctioned by the covenant with Abraham. In the sequence of the epic narrative, similarly, Abraham seems to have acquired his wealth in Canaan (Gen 13:2) as a result of the blessing that he received when he left home (Gen 12:2a), but in the Priestly version it occurred without divine intervention in Haran.

[23] The story (Gen 16:1, 3, 15–16), apart from the genealogy (16:16) and chronology (16:3aB), resembles the story of the birth of Jacob and Esau (Gen 25:19–26).

[24] See Genesis 17 and 18. The Priestly version includes a series of divine speeches (17:1–2, 3–8, 9–14, 15–16, 19–22), but it also attributes to Abraham the confusion that Sarah felt (cf. 17:17 and 18:12) and lets him engage in conversation with God as Abraham did with the three men at Mamre (cf. 17:18; 18:3–8).

[25] See Westermann, *Genesis* 2: 452–61.

[26] The seventh genealogy emphasizes this fact by listing the nations that trace their ancestry through Ishmael to Abraham.

[27] The incidents are Gen 25:19–26; 25:27–34; 28:1–5; 35:9–15, 27–29.

[28] There is the usual framework (Gen 25:19; 35:27–29), but only the first incident has chronological significance (25:20, 26b).

[29] According to the blessing, Israel is to become a nation and a group of nations (Gen 35:11aB, *gôy ûqĕhal gôyim yihyeh mimmekā*), and kings will be descended from him (35:11b, *ûmĕlākîm mēhălāṣêkā yēṣēʾû*). The former is unprecedented, but the latter resembles and repeats in opposite order the dynastic promise to David (2 Sam 7:12, "I will confirm your offspring after you, your descendant [*ʾăšer yēṣēʾ mimmēʿêkā*], and I will establish his kingship" [*wahăkînōtî ʾet mamlaktô*]). The narrative also insists on the sanctuary (Gen 35:13, 15, *māqôm*) at Bethel, in contravention of the orthodox belief that there should be only the sanctuary that Yahweh chose (Deut 12:13–14), and describes the rituals that Jacob performed despite the warnings of Amos to stay away from the place (Amos 4:4–5; 5:4–7).

[30] Original but not peculiar, since it is corrected and enlarged by the Deuteronomistic Historian (cf. Gen 28:6–9; 36:9–43).

[31] The separation of Jacob and Esau (Gen 36:6–8; 37:1) is modeled on and quotes from the epic account of the separation of Abraham and Lot (Genesis 13°). In the transmission of the covenant to Israel, Jacob acquired title to the land of Canaan (Gen 35:12), and in this genealogy he assumes possession of it (Gen 37:1).

[32] The section begins at the start of the genealogy (Gen 37:2aA). The ending (Exod 15:20–21) is not formally marked. This song belongs in the

Priestly text but was separated from it by the Deuteronomistic insertion of the Song of the Sea (Exod 15:1–18). The insertion, however, made by repeating the Priestly text that originally preceded the song (Exod 15:19 = Exod 14:28–29, with opposite word order).

33 The beginning of the section (Exod 15:22, *wayyassaʿ mōšeh ʾet yiśrāʾēl miyyam sûp*) is unusual since the Priestly writer generally refers to the people of Israel (*běnê yiśrāʾēl*) and to the sea (*yām*) rather than the Reed Sea (*yam sûp*). The end of the section (Exod 40:35b–37) views the journey through the wilderness as completed and describes the conditions under which the people and the tabernacle traveled.

34 The beginning (Num 10:11–12) repeats key elements from the end of the second section (Exod 40:36). The end of the section is marked by the vision of the people settled in the land (Deut 34:1–4°).

35 The Priestly regulation of Passover (Exod 12:1–6, 8–11) differs from the sequel's legislation (Deut 16:1–2a, 3aA, 7) in almost every detail. In P it was inaugurated in Egypt (12:1), but across the Jordan in the sequel (cf. Deut 1:1a). In P it is dated to the month and the day (12:2–3a), but in the sequel to the month (16:1). In P the animal to be slaughtered is a one-year-old male lamb without blemish (12:3b–5), but in the sequel it is a lamb or a calf (16:2a; cf. Deut 15:19–20). In P it must not be boiled, but the sequel requires it to be boiled (Exod 12:9; Deut 16:7). In P it is a family occasion (12:3–4, 8–11), but in the sequel it is to be celebrated in the central sanctuary (16:7). The points of agreement between the two rules (e.g., that it is a memorial, an evening celebration, without leaven) make the differences all the more emphatic.

36 The section was organized on the model of a lamentation liturgy and represents a literary transformation of (i) the critical situation confronting the people (Exod 1:6–7, 13–14), (ii) the lament, including their cry for help and the reason that God listened to it (Exod 2:23aBb–25), (iii) the answer to their prayer (Exod 6:2–9), (iv) salvation from the critical situation (Exodus 7–9°, 11°, 14°), (v) praise of God (Exod 15:20–21), and (vi) the inauguration of the liturgical tradition (Exod 12:1–6, 8–11, 28). The section contains genealogical lists and notices (Exod 1:1–4, 5b; 7:7; 12:40–42), commentary on the epic (Exod 1:6–7, 13–14 [on 1:8–12]; 2:23aBb–25 [on 3:7]; 6:2–9 [on 3:8]; 14° [on 14°]), narrative (1:6–7, 13–14; 2:23aBb–25; 14°), legal and legislative discourse (6:2–9; 7:1–6; 12:1–6, 8–11), and repetitive formulaic description (7:8–13; 7:19–20, 21b–22; 8:1–3, 9b–11; 8:12–15; 9:8–12; 11:9–10).

37 The link between the two parts is the command to observe the sabbath (Exod 31:13–18) that Moses immediately relays to the people (Exod 35:1–3).

38 The disputations involve the people (Numbers 13–14°; 20:1aBb, 2–5, 7–13), Aaron (Num 20:22–25, 27, 28°–29), and Moses (Num 27:12–13, 15–23). The itinerary leads from Mount Sinai (Num 10:11–12) to Mount Nebo (Deut 34:1–9°). The genealogy ends with the death of Moses (Deut 34:5–9) and with a partial enumeration of the tribes (Deut 34:1–4°) that reflects the

list of tribes given at the beginning of the genealogy (Gen 46:6–7; Exod 1:1–4).

[39] The plagues have to do with portents on land and sea and in the sky, affect humans and animals, and are initiated by the magical creation of sea serpents (*tannîn*, Exod 7:9, 10, 12; cf. Gen 1:21). The Deuteronomistic Historian added other plagues that affected the Pharaoh's court, estates, and servants, but noted the cosmological significance of the Priestly plagues by replacing the primordial process of separation (*bdl*, Gen 1:4, 6, 7, 14, 18) with a process of differentiation between Israel and Egypt (*plh*, Exod 8:18; 9:4; 11:7). The Priestly version of the crossing of the Sea on dry ground is a historical transposition of the story in the *Enuma elish* in which Marduk split the sea and from the two parts established the order of the heavens and the earth. In the Babylonian version the Sea, the dragon Tiamat, was slain, but in the Priestly transposition it is the Egyptians who are killed in the Sea. The original was a cosmology dedicated to the glory of Marduk; the transposition is a history dedicated to the glory of Yahweh. In the original it was the world that was established; in the Priestly version it is Israel that is established as Yahweh's people (Exod 6:7).

[40] The people do not listen to Moses (Exod 6:9, 12), and at the crucial moment of escape from Egypt he is rebuked for not having them in tow (Exod 14:10bB, 15). The covenant with the patriarchs is fulfilled when the people increase and multiply in Egypt (Exod 1:7; cf. Gen 17:2–6). It is the reason that Yahweh listened to the cry of the people (Exod 2:23aBb–25), and the reason that he saved them from Egypt (Exod 6:2–5). In the epic Yahweh revealed his name as the preamble to covenant (Exod 34:6), but in the Priestly version when he reveals his name he identifies himself as the God who made a covenant with the patriarchs (Exod 6:2–3).

[41] As God-and-prophet, Moses and Aaron perform cosmological tricks that lead the Pharaoh's magicians to recognize the hand of God (Exod 8:15). Pharaoh himself is not convinced, however, because God intends to perform the ultimate cosmological trick (cf. Exod 11:9–10) that will bring him recognition and glory.

[42] The splitting of the sea is the last of the portents and leads to the glorification of Yahweh (*kbd*, Exod 14:4, 17) and to the recognition (*yd*') that Yahweh is God ('*ănî yhwh*, Exod 6:2, 6, 7, 8; 7:5; 14:4, 18). The revelation of Yahweh's name (Exod 6:2–3, etc.) corresponds to the revelation of the names of Marduk in the *Enuma elish*. The Song of Miriam, similarly, occurs after the splitting of the Sea and the appearance of dry land (cf. Genesis 1) and has the same relative position in the story as the praise of Marduk has in the *Enuma elish*. The building of the tabernacle (Exodus 35–36) is like the building of a shrine for Marduk. The Song of Moses (Exod 15:1–18) elaborates on the Song of Miriam and also has many affinities with the Babylonian story, notably the consternation and defeat of the allies of the Sea, the defeat of the Sea as an act of creation, and the building of a temple for the victorious God.

[43] The undermining is most evident in the story of the manna when Moses

and Aaron observe that Yahweh will hear their criticism and add "And who
are we that you criticize us" (Exod 16:7b). The sabbath commandment is
given to Moses, is repeated immediately to the people (Exod 31:13–17; 35:1–
3), and leaves traces throughout the narrative, for example, the glory of
Yahweh covered the mountain for six days before Yahweh summoned Moses
on the seventh (Exod 24:15–16), and the people stopped bringing materials
(*mĕlaʾkâ*) for the sanctuary because they had brought enough (Exod 36:1–7).

44 The people camp by the water at Elim (Exod 15:27, *wayyaḥănû šām ʿal
hammāyim*) as they did by the Sea at Baal-zephon (Exod 14:2, *nikḥô taḥănû ʿal
hayyām*). They arrived in the wilderness of Sin a month and a half after the
exodus (Exod 16:1), and when they say that they wish they had died in Egypt
Moses and Aaron reply that they will realize that Yahweh has brought them
out of Egypt (Exod 16:3, 6). The quails that come along in the evening are
the last of the meat that they ate in Egypt (Exod 16:6b, 12a, 13), and the
manna that was there in the morning they ate until they came to settle in the
land (Exod 16:6b, 12a, 13b, 35a). The contrast between eating meat at night
(*bên hāʿarbāyim*, Exod 12:6; 16:12) and manna in the morning (*bōqer*, Exod
12:10; 16:12) corresponds to Passover, which is to be eaten at night and not
left until the morning.

45 A corollary of centralization was the desacralization of the slaughter of
animals and the eating of meat (Deut 12:20 ". . . And if you say 'I want to eat
meat [ʾkl + bāśār]' because you like to eat meat [ʾkl + bāśār], you can eat all
the meat you want [ʾkl + bāśār]."). In the story of the manna and the quails
the Priestly writer considers the desire for meat a criticism of Yahweh and a
denial of their liberation from Egypt (Exod 16:3, *bāśār*, 12 ʾkl + *bāśār*). The
law of centralization prescribed that collections and freewill offerings be
brought to the place that Yahweh chose (Deut 12:17, *wĕnidbōtĕkā ûtĕrûmat
yādĕkā*), but the Priestly writer prescribed that they be brought for the
construction of the tabernacle (*ndb*, Exod 25:2; 35:5, 21, 22, 29; 36:3; *tĕrûmâ*,
Exod 25:2, 3; 35:5, 21, 24; 36:3, 6).

46 The epic covenant is defined as the words that Yahweh spoke on Sinai
(Exod 34:27, *haddĕbārîm hāʾēlleh*) and instructed Moses to inscribe on tablets
(Exod 34:27–28a), and the sequel refers to it in the same terms (Deut 1:1a,
ʾēlleh haddĕbārîm). The Priestly version, after prescribing the sabbath, notes
that Yahweh himself wrote down the words that he spoke to Moses (Exod
31:18) and has Moses present the sabbath and the design of the tabernacle as
the words that Yahweh commanded them to perform (Exod 35:1b, ʾēlleh
haddĕbārîm . . .). The sabbath is an eternal covenant (Exod 31:13, 16) and the
Priestly alternative to the epic covenant concerning the land.

47 The glory of Yahweh came from the desert (Exod 16:10) and appeared
in the cloud that covered Mount Sinai (Exod 24:15–16). On Sinai Yahweh
reveals the plan of the sanctuary (Exod 25:8, *miqdāš*) where he will dwell
among the people, and when it is finished the cloud settles on it and the glory
of Yahweh fills it (Exod 40:35b–36). In a cramped and obvious synthesis of
the Priestly writer's ideas Yahweh reveals himself and his holiness in his

sanctuary (Exod 29:43, *wĕniqdaš bikbōdî*), and the sabbath, because it is holy, makes the people holy (Exod 31:13–15; cf. Gen 2:3).

[48] The idea that the land devours its inhabitants (Num 13:32, *hā'āreṣ . . . 'ereṣ 'ōkelet yôšĕbêhā hî'*) is taken from the epic text, in which the earth opens its mouth and swallows the scouts who discouraged the people (Num 16:32, *wattiptaḥ hā'āreṣ 'et pîhā wattibla' 'ōtām*).

[49] Moses does not do exactly as he is told because he does not believe what he is told. He takes his staff as commanded but uses it to hit the rock (compare Num 20:8 and Num 20:9–10a, 11). He does not speak to the rock as he was told because he does not believe that water will come of it (Num 20:10b, 12a). The holiness of Yahweh, in this text (Num 20:12), consists in Israel's recognition that Yahweh can do as he says with the natural order.

[50] Moses' view of the tribes settled in the promised land (Num 27:12–13; Deut 32:48–50, 51b–52; 34:1–5) puts him in the position that the epic assigned to Balaam (Numbers 22–24°). The succession of Joshua (Num 27:15–23) differs from the version in the sequel by associating him with Eleazar the priest (cf. Deuteronomy 31°). The Priestly text is fitted with repetitions (cf. Num 27:12–13 and Deut 32:48–50, 51b–52) so that it can envelop the first part of the sequel (i.e., Deuteronomy 1–31°) as it enveloped epic texts that it meant to circumvent.

[51] Isaiah referred to Yahweh as "the Holy One of Israel" in contexts of divine activity (*'āśâ*, Isa 5:12, 18) and popular rest (Isa 30:15, *nwḥ*, *šqṭ*). The Priestly writer shared his disdain for the covenant that ordained political activity and regular worship and presented Yahweh as the God who made the world and rested and who expected people to observe the same rhythm.

[52] The epic episode ends with the promise to Sarah (Genesis 18–19°) and the birth of Isaac (Genesis 21°), and the next episode begins with Isaac a mature person in Gerar (Genesis 26°). The Elohist text straddles the central part (Genesis 20°; 21–22°).

[53] Cf. Gen 19:27b (*šām*) and Gen 20:1aA (*miššām*). The location is equally important in the Deuteronomistic version (Gen 18:22b).

[54] The epic says that Abraham called his son Isaac (Gen 21:3, *yiṣḥāq*) because Sarah laughed (Gen 18:12 [*tiṣḥaq*], 13, 15). In the Priestly version the name (Gen 21:4–5) is traced to the fact that Abraham laughed (Gen 17:17, *yiṣḥāq*). In both cases they laugh because they are too old to have children. But in the Elohist version Sarah protests that God has made a laughing stock of her (Gen 21:6, *ṣḥq*, *yiṣḥaq*) because Abraham is too old — implying that it is Abimelech (Genesis 20°) and not Abraham who is the father of the child. This is the first of the trials and tribulations that might have prevented Isaac from being the legitimate heir of Abraham if God had not provided.

[55] In both texts there is a contrast between the effect on Abraham and the

effect on Sarah. In the first (Gen 20:16) the money Abraham received is Sarah's vindication because it is a "covering of the eyes" (kĕsût 'ênayim) for Abraham. But in the second (21:6–7), Sarah feels that she is not vindicated and doubts whether Abraham or anyone else is blind to the affair.

56 The first and third incidents are about Abraham and Abimelech, and the second and fourth are about Abraham and his children. The chronological link is "Now . . . at that time" (Gen 21:22). The grammatical link is the expression "Now it happened" (wayhî) + a temporal phrase or clause (bā'ēt hahî, "at that time" + the narrative continuation of the story (wayyiqtol or qātal), which expresses sequence, not with the immediately preceding paragraph but with the penultimate narrative segment.

57 The fourth begins with "Now it happened (wayhî) + temporal phrase ("after these things") + narrative sequence ([qātal] wĕhā'ĕlōhîm nissâ 'et 'abrāhām). In it God requires the sacrifice of his son Isaac, as in the second Sarah required that he get rid of his other son, Ishmael. In both there is an *ex machina* happy ending.

58 The beginning and end of the story take place at Bethel and are remarkably similar (Gen 28:10–22°; 35:1–7°). The story itself (Genesis 31–33°) is a variant of the epic.

59 The Priestly text ends with Isaac sending Jacob and Jacob going to Paddan-aram (Gen 28:5, wayyišlaḥ . . . wayyēlek), and the Elohist version begins with one word from the text (Gen 28:10, wayyēlek). The quotation is minimal but, like any quotation, is put into an opposite context. In the P version Jacob went to Paddan-aram, but in the Elohist version he went to Haran. The same text, moreover, was quoted in the Deuteronomistic Historian to validate an insertion (Gen 28:6–9) about Esau. The insertion begins with Isaac sending Jacob (Gen 28:6, wĕsillaḥ) and ends with Esau going (Gen 28:9, wayyēlek).

60 Jacob's speech to his wives begins (Gen 31:4–5), like the epic text just before it (Gen 31:1–3), by noting that it made little difference that Laban's attitude toward Jacob had changed (31:2, 5) because God/Yahweh was/would be with Jacob (31:3, 5). The incident is joined to the first by repeating elements of Jacob's vow and by referring explicitly to his meeting with God at Bethel (Gen 31:5b, 7b, 13a; cf. Gen 28:20b, 22).

61 At the end of the second incident Jacob arrives safely at Shechem (Gen 33:18aA [safety being an element of his vow, Gen 28:21]), and in the beginning of the third incident he leaves Shechem for Bethel.

62 The Elohist text (Gen °28:10–35:7°) fits inside the Priestly text (Gen 28:1–5; 35:9–15). Besides being artificially linked to the first part of the Priestly text, the Elohist version ends in anticipation of the concluding Priestly apparition to Jacob at Bethel (cf. Gen 35:7 [E] and 35:9, 13–15 [P]).

63 The epic episode (Genesis °26–33°) begins with Isaac (Genesis °26–

27°). The Priestly writer took account of it by anticipation (Genesis 25°), and the Elohist had nothing to add. The Elohist straddled the epic text (Genesis °29–33°) by including the story of Jacob and Laban under the rubric of Jacob's vow at Bethel (Genesis 28°; 35°).

^{64} The block (Gen 31:4–19a, 20–27, 29, 36b, 38–42, 51–54; 32:1–2a) was modified by the Deuteronomistic Historian but fits into the epic text: at the beginning by literal repetition; at the end by substituting the messengers of God for the messengers that the epic sends to Esau (Gen 32:2, *mal'ăkê 'ĕlōhîm* = 32:4, *mal'ākîm*).

^{65} The first part of the Elohist interpretation (Gen 32:8–9) is joined to the preceding epic text (Gen 32:7) by deictics, namely, the proper name "Jacob" and two reflexive pronouns—"to himself," "with him" (Gen 32:8, *ya'ăqōb, lô, 'ittô*). It has to do with dividing his property into two camps and is constructed by cross-reference as a continuation of the preceding Elohist text (Gen 32:2–3), in which Jacob calls the messengers of God and the place where he met them "Two Camps" (*maḥănāyim*). The second part (Gen 32:14b–22 [32:10–13 is a Deuteronomistic addition]) was attached to the epic by repeating at its end the clause to which it was affixed at the beginning (32:22b, *wĕḥû' lān ballaylâ hahû' bammaḥăneh* = 32:14a, *wayyālen šām ballaylâ hahû'*). The third part (Gen 32:23a°b, 24b) introduces the epic account of Jacob's encounter with the man and God (Gen 32:25b–26aA, 27–30, 32a) to recount that Jacob and his possessions crossed (32:23, 24 *'ābar*) the fords of the Jabbok. It is a continuation and resumption of the contiguous Elohist text (32:23a°, *wayyaqom ballaylâ hû'*; cf. 32:22b). The fourth part (Gen 33:3) is affixed to the epic by a deictic personal pronoun ("and *he* [33:3 *wĕhû'*] went in front of them." Although it is attached to the epic text, it continues the Elohist text, which, read with or apart from the epic sequence, insists that Jacob crossed the fords of the Jabbok without encountering God (Gen 32:23° + 24° + 33:3). The fifth part (Gen 33:8–11) is attached to the epic by anticipating the first word of the epic text that it displaced (33:8, *wayyō'mer* = 33:12). The last addition duplicates the conclusion of the epic account (Gen 33:17a and 18aA).

^{66} The Elohist text (Gen 37:2aB, "*Joseph*, a lad of seventeen, was a shepherd with his brothers") is an abrupt beginning after the Priestly introduction ("These are the generations of Jacob," Gen 37:2aA) but no more abrupt than the epic text that it anticipates ("And Israel loved *Joseph* more than all his sons"). The statement that his father made him a special tunic fits against the epic text by repeating its last word (37:3b, *wĕ'āśâ lô* = 37:3a *lô*).

^{67} The story of Joseph's dreams (Gen 37:5–11) notes that his brothers hated him still more for dreaming (37:5aBb, *wayyaggēd lĕ' eḥāyw wayyôsīpû 'ôd śĕnō' 'ōtô*), which repeats the preceding epic words (Gen 37:4, *'eḥāyw wayyiśnĕ'û 'ōtô*) and reinforces the repetition with a deictic ("still," *'ôd*) and a pun (*yôsīpu* for "Joseph," *yôsēp*). The Elohist (Gen 37:2aBb, 3b, 5) predominates in the rewritten text (Gen 37:2aBb–5) and makes sense by itself without the epic text that it incorporates.

^{68} The Elohist version (Gen 37:19–24) breaks up the epic version (37:12–

18, 25–27, 28aB) and begins by referring to the point at which it intrudes. The epic says they saw Joseph from a distance, before he drew near (37:18), and the Elohist has them say "Look (*hinnēh*), there (*hallāzēh*), the dreamer is coming" (Gen 37:19).

69 Gen 37:28aAb–36 ends with the Midianites selling Joseph to Potiphar, Pharaoh's chief butler, precisely as the epic goes on to recount that Potiphar bought him from the Ishmaelites (Gen 39:1), the quotation being marked by the usual reversal.

70 Reuben is exonerated twice: first in saving Joseph from death and second by not being implicated in his sale to Egypt. However, he does cooperate in pretending that Joseph has been killed by a wild animal, a vital theme in the Elohist story.

71 The epic skipped from Joseph's rise to power in Egypt (Gen 39:1–6a) to his jurisdiction over the food supplies (Gen 42:1–4) and focused entirely on Joseph and his family. The Elohist was also interested in how the people of Egypt received their food allotments so that the famine, because of divine providence, did not affect the land.

72 At the beginning Joseph explains to Potiphar's wife that her husband has complete confidence in him (Gen 39:7) in the words that the epic used to describe Joseph's rise to power (Gen 39:5, 6). At the end the Elohist announces the seven years of famine (Gen 41:54) in the words that the epic used to introduce the same topic (Gen 41:56a).

73 The epic paragraph ended with the brothers coming to Egypt to buy grain (Gen 42:3, *lišbōr*). The Elohist reference to Joseph's authority begins with his name and another deictic (42:6, *wěyôsēp hû'*) and continues with another deictic and the fact that he was the one who sold the grain (Gen 42:6, *hû' hammašbîr*). The obeisance of the brothers is what he predicted in his dreams (Gen 42:6; cf. Gen 37:7, 9, 10). The reference to this fulfillment of his dreams (Gen 42:8–9a) is sewn into the epic text (Gen 42:7, 9b) by repeating, in opposite word order, that he recognized his brothers (Gen 42:7, *yôsēp 'et 'ehāyw wayyakkirēm*; 42:8, *wayyakkēr yôsēp 'et 'ehāyw*).

74 The Elohist interrupts Joseph's speech to his brothers with the protest that he is a God-fearing person. The text is introduced with the deictic accusative marker *'et* and ends with the deictic personal pronoun "I" (Gen 42:18b, *'et hā'ĕlōhîm 'ānî yārē'*). The brothers' discussion ends with another clause introduced by another deictic pronoun (Gen 42:23, "And *they* . . ." [*wěhēm*]), which leads into the original epic clause that follows (Gen 42:24).

75 Gen 45:4–15 is added to Gen 45:1–3 by repeating the end of the epic version (Gen 45:3, "And Joseph said to his brothers 'I am Joseph' ") at the beginning of the Elohist version (Gen 45:4, "And Joseph said to his brothers '. . . I am Joseph your brother' ").

76 The text begins (46:1) like the epic text before it (45:28) and ends with

Jacob and his family traveling in the wagons that, in the epic version, Pharaoh sent to fetch them (Gen 46:5; cf. Gen 45:19, 21). The text also begins and ends (Gen 46:1, 5b) in exact anticipation of the Priestly text that follows (Gen 46:6).

77 It follows naturally on the Priestly statement that Jacob was about to die (Gen 47:29) with the text of his deathbed blessing. The Deuteronomist included a biography of Jacob based on the Priestly account (48:3–7) and on its own story of the rape of Dinah at Shechem (48:22).

78 The Elohist account of Jacob's deathbed blessing, before the Deuteronomistic variant was added (Gen 48:22–49:32), immediately preceded the Priestly record of his death (49:33). The story of his burial in Canaan, similarly, follows right on the Priestly text and is joined to it by a pun on the name Joseph (49:33, *wayye'ĕsōp, wayyē'āsēp*; 50:1, *yôsēp*) and by repeated deictic pronouns (50:1).

79 Gen 50:14–21 reviews the story, with the brothers doing obeisance to Joseph as he predicted in his dreams and with Joseph expounding the Elohist theory of divine providence. Gen 50:22–26 predicts the exodus and requires that Joseph's bones be carried out of Egypt, and both are related later (Exod 13:19).

80 At the beginning of the incident Jacob makes the tunic (Gen 37:3b); in the middle the brothers strip it off Joseph (37:23); and at the end Jacob recognizes it (37:31–33) and tears his own garments. When this theme is finished Jacob mourns his son and makes his pronouncement (37:34–35), and the end of the third incident takes up its main point about going down to Egypt to his son and the subsidiary theme that the other sons are no consolation to him (cf. Gen 46:1–5). Jacob does not die in this incident, but his death is insinuated when God tells him that Joseph will close his eyes.

81 Compare Gen 37:36 and 39:1; 37:2 and 41:46.

82 The opening sentence (3:1) emphasizes the name Moses (*ûmōšeh*), which, as a deictic, attaches it to the first epic sentence (3:2, *'ēlāyw*). The next clauses (3:4b–6) intervene between elements of the epic text (Exod 3:4a, 7) by anticipating the first word of the continuing clause (*wayyō'mer*, 3:4b [twice], 5, 6a, 7a). The beginning of the main body of the Elohist reinterpretation (Exod 3:9–14) repeats the beginning of the preceding epic text in an opposite order (3:9 = 3:7). God tells Moses that his name is not Yahweh but is "I am with you" (Exod 3:12, 14) and that they will worship God on the mountain (Exod 3:12). Both elements refer to events that are related to the final incident: the first anticipates and corrects the epic revelation of the name Yahweh (Exod 34:6–7), and the second refers to the time that Moses and Joshua spent on the mountain (Exod 24:13–14; 32°; 34°).

83 The preceding text, before the Deuteronomistic additions (Exod 12:43–13:16), was the Priestly version of an armed exodus (12:40–42). The Elohist

text (13:17–19) is attached to it by repeating its formulaic expression (12:41; 13:17, *wyhy* + temporal clause + narrative clause (*qtl* or *wayyiqtol*). Since this formula indicates a reference not to the text preceding it but to an anterior text, the Elohist quotes from this text (11:9–10). The quotation, as usual, differs from the source: it said that Pharaoh did not send them out of Egypt (11:10b), but the Elohist says that he did (13:17; cf. 3:10). In the account of the exodus the Elohist added remarks that, taking the Priestly version literally, suggested a victory on dry land. The first remark (14:5b) corrects the epic account of an escape (14:5a) to agree with the Elohist idea of expulsion. The new text repeats the last word of the epic verse (*hā'ām*, 14:5a, 5b). The second is inserted by repeating one word (14:7, *wayyiqqah*; cf. 14:6, *lāqah*) and helps to correct the impression left by the epic that few troops followed Israel and that Pharaoh alone rode in a chariot. The third is attached to the adjacent Priestly text by repetition (14:8b and 14:8a, *ûbĕnê yiśrā'ēl*). The fourth is inserted into the surrounding Priestly text (Exod 14:9aBb, 10bB) by repeating some of each part (Exod 14:10abA). It leads into the fifth remark, in which the angel of God (14:19a), rather than the pillar of cloud of the epic version (14:19b), moves from the vanguard to the rearguard. The last remark describes how the angel stopped the Egyptians by twisting their chariot wheels: it (14:25a) is added to the preceding mention of Egypt with the help of deictic pronominal suffixes.

84 The text begins (Exod 18:1a) with a reference to the exodus—as the Deuteronomist is quick to endorse (18:1b)—but with reference to its epic formulation (Exod 14:31) rather than to any particular Elohist text.

85 As the epic traced the origin of the covenant relationship with Yahweh to the land of Midian (Exodus 2°–3°), so the Elohist attributed to Jethro the priest of Midian the idea of separate jurisdiction in the lower courts and the right of final appeal to Moses and God (Exod 18:1–27°). The first paragraph reproduces the circumstances described in the following epic text: Jethro comes to the wilderness where Moses was camped at the mountain of God (Exod 18:5), as in the epic text the people came to the wilderness and camped at the foot of the mountain (Exod 19:1b, 2b).

86 These texts are inserted with minimal repetition of the epic text: Exod 19:3a (*ûmōšeh 'ālâ 'el hā'ĕlōhîm*) anticipates the next epic clause in the opposite order (19:9a, *wayyō'mer yhwh 'el mōšeh*); 19:14a uses a word (*hā'ām*) from the next epic clause (19:14b); the Elohist text (19:16aBb–17) and the epic (19:16aA, 20) mention the mountain (*hāhār*).

87 The law is introduced (Exod 20:1, "And God spoke all these words" ['*et kol haddĕbārîm hā'ēlleh*]) in the terms that the epic used to define the covenant (Exod 34:27, '*et haddĕbārîm hā'ēlleh*). It includes case law (21:2–37; 22:1–8), laws with divine sanctions (22:20–30), rules of due process (23:1–9), ritual laws (23:10–16), and the assurance that those who obey the law eventually will take possession of the land (23:20–22, 27, 29–31).

88 The Elohist text (Exod 24:13–14 + 32:1–6, 15–19a, 21a, 22–25; 34:29aBb–32a, 33) encloses the Priestly (24:15–18 + °25:1–31:18°) and epic

(chap. 34°) versions of events. It differs from the Priestly version in associating Joshua with the revelation of the law and in involving Aaron and Hur in its transmission and interpretation. It is attached to the Priestly text by literal repetition at the beginning (Exod 24:13b = 24:15a), and at the end (cf. 31:18 and 32:1, 15). It differs from the epic and the sequel in attributing the inscribing of the tablets to God, in minimizing the role of Moses, and in deleting the connection between the law that was revealed on the mountain and the ritual practices of the people: it is linked to the end of the epic text by literal opposite-order repetition (34:29aBb = 34:28bA). It was interrupted by Deuteronomistic additions (32:7–14, 19b–20, 21b, 26–35) inserted by deictics and repetition: the first begins by summarizing the preceding text; the second anticipates a later statement (32:19b, cf. 22a); the third is linked by deixis (32:21b); the last begins like the sentence before it (32:26).

[89] The Elohist (Gen 20:1–16° + 21:22–34°) generally follows the order of the epic text (Genesis 26°).

[90] A sign or effect of God's action is fear (Gen 20:8, 11): it distinguishes the Elohist's awesome God from the epic's familiar Yahweh (cf. Gen 28:17; Exod 3:6a). The problem of the paternity of Isaac matches the problem of the maternity of Ishmael and, as the staggered structure of the legend indicates, both contribute to the Elohist theme that the true child of Abraham is designated and ordained by God.

[91] Some elements — God, instead of Yahweh, the fear of God, and dreams — are recurrent. Others, such as the populist attitude evident in Abimelech's concern for the people around him and for the whole country (Gen 20:8; 21:23), surface more clearly in later legends. The narrative supposes that events occur according to logic, legal principles, and standard form. Abimelech observes proper form by sending for Sarah and taking her as his wife (Gen 20:2 *šlḥ* + *lqḥ*). When God appears in a dream to Abimelech he says that Abimelech is deserving of death but not without detailing the charge. In reply to Abimelech's question how he could say that his wife was his sister, Abraham first states the principle ("because there is no fear of God in this place") and then the immediate motive ("and they would have killed me because of my wife," Gen 20:11). In the epic the answer, without any explicit reference to the principles of behavior, was that they would have killed Isaac because his wife was pretty (Gen 26:7). In trying to make amends Abimelech distinguishes between the wrong to Abraham and the slight to Sarah, and between the friction he caused in their marriage and the scandal he caused among her friends (Gen 20:15–16). In making a pact with Abraham, Abimelech outlines the form and content of the treaty before Abraham accedes to it (Gen 21:23; cf. 26:28–31).

[92] The Elohist quotes from this text (e.g., Gen 21:18b = Gen 17:20bB) and depends on it for the story of Hagar and Ishmael.

[93] Passover was a festival inaugurated by the sequel as part of its centralization program. The Priestly writer did not oppose the festival but redefined its theory and practice. The Elohist does not include it among the prescribed

festivals (Exod 23:14–16) but, as the Deuteronomistic Historian did later (Deut 16:3°–6, 8), replaces it with Massot. The reason for this reticence may be the festival's original connection with the offering, or sacrifice, of children, a connection that it still retains in the Deuteronomistic story of its institution (Exodus 11–12°).

94 The testing of Abraham insists on the fact that it is a holocaust ('ōlâ, Gen 22:2, 3, 6–8) at the place that God will indicate (māqôm, Gen 22:3, 4, 9) on one of the mountains that he will designate ('al 'aḥaḏ hehārîm, Gen 22:2). The precise terms and the vagueness of the instructions are exactly what is found in the original legislation.

95 Amos's rejection of holocausts in favor of justice (Amos 5:22) is a possible inspiration of the Elohist text that, in turn, is reflected in Micah's polemic against holocausts and the offering of firstborn children (Mic 6:6–7).

96 The expression "Yahweh will see" (Gen 22:14a, yhwh yir'eh) corresponds to Abraham's answer to Isaac's question about the sacrificial victim, "God will provide" (Gen 22:8, 'ĕlōhîm yir'eh). The aside "On the mountain of Yahweh he will present himself" (Gen 22:14b, bĕhar yhwh yērā'eh) corresponds to the rule "Three times a year all of your males shall present themselves before Yahweh your God in the place he will choose" (yērā'eh . . . 'et pĕnê yhwh 'ĕlōkêkā bammāqôm, Deut 16:16aA). The rule was introduced in the epic (Exod 34:24) but was not mentioned by the Priestly writer and was discarded by the Elohist (Exod 23:14–16). The Deuteronomist added it to the Elohist legislation (Exod 23:17) to harmonize it with the view expressed in Deuteronomy.

97 Libations are omitted in the Elohist account.

98 The Elohist agreed with the epic against the Priestly version that Jacob fled to Haran (Gen 35:1 = Gen 24:43; cf. Gen 28:5). The nocturnal ritual resembles the earlier epic encounter with God when Jacob spent the night at the Jabbok (Gen 32:14a, 22b).

99 Dream sequences reveal the plot of the legend in which they occur and differ in this way from divine or angelic speeches that affect only their own context.

100 Jacob vows to make Bethel a temple of God if God is with him, protects him on his journey, provides him with food and clothing, and brings him home safely. All of these conditions are fulfilled explicitly in the narrative of his journey to Haran and back.

101 The first scene (Gen 28:10–12, 17–18, 20–21a, 22) describes the place as strewn with monoliths where the angels of God ascended and descended from heaven. The rites include incubation, vows (cf. Deut 12:17), tithes (cf. Deut 12:17; 14:22; Amos 4:4), and anointing of the monoliths. The closing scene (Gen 35:1–5a, 6aAb) adds rituals that are also associated with events on Mount Horeb/Sinai and that ultimately undermine the ideology of the epic

and its sequel. Before going to Bethel the people change their garments (Gen 35:2), as on Sinai the people were instructed to wash their garments before the theophany on the third day (Exod 19:10b, 14b). They donate their earrings as freewill offerings (cf. Amos 4:5), as they did for the construction of the golden calf (Exod 32:3) or the tabernacle (Exod 35:22). They build an altar, in contravention of the sequel's law of worship in the central sanctuary (35:7; cf. Deut 12:13–14; 2 Kgs 18:22). In fulfillment of Jacob's vow that Yahweh would be his God, and in disagreement with the sequel's contention that Yahweh should be worshiped only in Jerusalem, they remove their amulets and bury their jewelry (Gen 28:21b; 35:4).

[102] The passage (Gen 31:4–16) is set apart as a conversation between Jacob and his wives: they are summoned at the beginning (31:4); he tells them the story (31:5–13); and they approve of his plan to return home with their father's flock (31:14–16). It quotes from the epic (31:5a = 31:2; 31:6 = 30:29; 31:13 = 31:3), alludes to its account of Jacob's marriages (31:14–16; cf. 29:16–30°), and refers to the preceding segment in the epic where Jacob outwits Laban with a trick of animal husbandry (31:7, 8, 10; cf. 30:28, 35, 39).

[103] Jacob is the main character and sole agent in the epic account, but in the Elohist version Jacob is the narrator and God is the agent, directly or in dreams, and with specific reference to the vision at Bethel and to the conditions of Jacob's vow (Gen 31:5b, 7b, 9, 10a, 11–13, 16). In the epic account Jacob cheated Laban out of his flock, but in the Elohist version God takes it from Laban because it rightfully belongs to Rachel and Leah as their dowry (31:14–16).

[104] The condition that God protect him on his journey (Gen 28:20) is fulfilled in God's admonition of Laban (31:24, 29) and in the determining of the boundary lines between Aram and Israel (31:51–54). Their confrontation in Gilead, and the identification of Laban as "the Aramean," replay the Aramean wars that the sequel treated as the beginning of the end of Israel. Laban's complaint that he was robbed of the opportunity of sending his daughters away in style (Gen 31:20, 26–28) is adjudicated in the pact that they made and sealed with a banquet (Gen 31:51–54) and in their fond farewells (32:1–2a).

[105] Jacob argues his innocence (31:36b) by insisting that he was a faithful shepherd who did not steal any of the flock but on the contrary paid for all its losses. The fact that he now owns most of Laban's flock he attributes to God, who took care of him and paid him for his services and advised Laban of the propriety of what he had done (31:42).

[106] Gen 32:2b–3, 8–9, 14b–22, 23a°b, 24b; 33:3, 8–11, 18a. The entire story hinges on his meeting with Esau, which the story describes as seeing the face of God (33:10, *pĕnê ʾĕlōhîm*) in contrast to the epic, which described Jacob's encounter with the man at Penuel (Gen 32:32a, *pĕnûʾēl*).

[107] See W. Burkert, *Structure and History in Greek Mythology and Ritual*

(Berkeley: University of California Press, 1979) 99–122. Adonis is known in Phoenician sources from Byblos (ibid., 193 n. 15), in a tenth-century inscription from Byblos (*l'dn wlb'lt gbl*), and in an inscription on an ivory coast casket from Ur which reads: *'rn . [z]n . mgn . 'mtb'l . bt . pt's . 'mt . '[dnn] . mtt . l'štrt . 'dty . tbrky . bymy . 'dnn . [b]' . bn . ys'd* = "This casket Amatba'al, daughter of Patisis, devotee of Adonis, gave as a gift to Astarte her mistress. May she bless her! In the days of Adonis, he himself had reclined within it." See P. Bordreuil, "Une inscription champlevée des environs de Byblos," *Semitica* 27 (1977) 23–27; M. G. Amadasi Guzzo, "Two Phoenician Inscriptions Carved in Ivory: Again the Ur Box and the Sarepta Plaque," *Bib* 59 (1990) 58–66.

108 The Deuteronomistic story of Tamar and Judah (Genesis 38), which so glaringly disrupts the story of Joseph, is another adaptation of the myth of Adonis.

109 In this context (45:4–15) it is clear that the title "Lord" (*Ādôn*) was given to Joseph because he overcame death and gave life to his people (45:5, 7). In the story as a whole it is clear that life and death are functions of the cycles—in this case, seven-year cycles—of fertility and drought, and more specifically of the cycles that affect the grain harvest. Joseph's death occurs symbolically at the hands of his brothers but dramatically at the hands of the woman whose love was spurned. Life coincides with his marriage to the woman's surrogate. Elements of the myth and ritual are distilled in the legend of Demeter and Persephone/Kore and are reflected in the story of David told in the book of *Ruth*: see G. R. H. Wright, "The Mother-Maid at Bethelehem," *ZAW* 98 (1986) 56–72.

110 The second and fourth parts of the legend of Joseph (Genesis 39°–41°, 48°–50°) where this occurs also contain elements or reflections of the myth, such as the seduction scene (chap. 39) and reference to the three-day interval embedded in the cycle of life and death (chap. 40), but they are explicitly an interpretation of the myth and ritual. This is evident when Joseph attributes the interpretation of dreams to God (Gen 40:8; 41:16, 38), since the dreams themselves are the form of the myth. The existence of parallel interpretations, myth and ritual vying with theology and history, is also clear in Joseph's words to his brothers, "You plotted evil against me but God planned it as good" (Gen 50:20).

111 Compare Gen 37:5–11 and 40:1–41:40, esp. 41:38.

112 Compare Gen 37:5–11 and 41:43; 42:6, 8–9a.

113 One woman is the wife of Potiphar, the captain of the guard (Gen 37:36; 39:6b–20); the other is the daughter of Potiphera, a priest (41:45, 50–52).

114 In the recognition scene Joseph explains that he was sent to install a "remnant" in the land, or to keep a large number of "survivors" alive (45:7).

In his final speech he adds that God meant to keep a numerous people alive (50:20). Since the story in general and the context of this last saying in particular distinguish between the house of Jacob (Joseph and his brothers, Gen 50:14–21, 24) and the house of Joseph (Joseph and his children, Gen 50:22–23), the "remnant" and "survivors" might refer to Ephraim and Manasseh, and the "numerous people" to Israel. In effect, Joseph predicts the exodus of Israel from Egypt (50:24–25) and the return of Ephraim and Manasseh to the land.

[115] The beginning of the passage (Exod 3:1a) has affinities with the preceding epic text (Exod 2:15, 16, 18), but the Elohist calls the priest of Midian Jethro instead of Reuel. It also anticipates the later epic text in which Moses meets Yahweh at the mountain in the wilderness of Sinai (Exod 3:1b; cf. 19:1b, 2b).

[116] The passage begins as a variant of the epic text (3:9, 10b = 3:7, 8).

[117] Exod 3:13, the mission to the people and their question on the identity of God, is like Exod 6:6. The name that God proposes (3:14a, *'ehyeh 'ăšer 'ehyeh*, 14b, *'ehyeh*) agrees with his preceding statement that he will be with Moses (Exod 3:12, *kî 'ehyeh 'immāk*) but also parodies the later revelation on Mount Sinai in which Yahweh presented himself and proclaimed his own name (Exod 34:6, *yhwh . . . yhwh yhwh*). This exclusion of the name is consistent with the Elohist's use of the name only in connection with a polemic against the theory of centralization (Genesis 22; 28; Exodus 32). Its exclusion, however, prompted the Deuteronomistic Historian to add a compromise and corrective (Exod 3:15): "And God also said to Moses 'Tell the people of Israel that Yahweh [= the epic name], the God of your fathers [= the Elohist version], the God of Abraham, Isaac and Jacob [= Priestly version] sent me to you [= Priestly and Elohist versions]—this is my name for ever [= the epic name], and this is how I am to be remembered from generation to generation' [= the Elohist and Priestly versions]." The name of God, in the Elohist version, is an expression of divine providence and is quoted in this sense by Hosea (Hos 1:9).

[118] The exodus, in line with the myth and ritual of Adonis, is Israel's return from Egypt, or Sheol, to the land of their fathers. Transporting the bones of Joseph maintains the symbolism (Gen 50:24–25; Exod 13:19).

[119] The exodus, in this view, is a fulfillment of Joseph's prediction, a continuation of the providence he symbolized, and a passage from death to life (Exod 13:19 = Gen 50:24–25).

[120] Moses' marriage with Zipporah and the name of their first child are recounted earlier in the epic (Exod 18:2a, 3 = 2:21b–22). The name of the second child and its interpretation (18:4, Eliezer "because the God of my father was my help and saved me from the sword of Pharaoh") supposes the epic episode in which Moses murdered an Egyptian and had to escape from Egypt to avoid being killed by the Pharaoh (Exod 2:15).

121 The celebration (Exod 18:1a, 12) frames the arrival (18:2a,3–5) and implicitly includes Zipporah and the children. It takes place at the mountain (18:5) where there was a sanctuary (Exod 3:5) and includes sacrifices and holocausts—in the manner of the sequel, which prescribed the offering of holocausts and of the Passover sacrifice at the central sanctuary (Deut 12:13–14; 16:1–2a). It celebrates what God did for Moses and for his people in terms that recall and modify the epic version (18:1a; cf. 14:31).

122 The delegation of judicial authority to military personnel (Exod 18:21, 24) is consistent with the Elohist's view of Israel leaving Egypt as an army (13:17–19).

123 Exod 23:21, *lōʾ yiśśāʾ lĕpišʿăkem*. The threat has a parallel in the epic covenant (Exod 34:7, *nōśēʾ ʿāwōn wāpešaʿ wĕḥaṭṭāʾâ*), but unlike the epic does not extend to the third and fourth generations. The command to obey the angel is accompanied by a prohibition of rebellion (Exod 23:21, *ʾal tammēr bô*) that alludes to the rebellion of Moses and Aaron in the Priestly version (Num 20:24; 27:14).

124 Cf. Deut 11:24; Josh 1:4; 11:23aAb.

125 The Elohist version distinguishes between the journey to the place (Exod 23:20–22) and the occupation of the land (23:27, 29–31). The occupation includes two phases, one directed against the people who live in the land and who will be driven out slowly by God (Exod 23:27a, 29–30), the other against the enemies of Israel whom they themselves will drive out (Exod 23:27b, 31b). The gradual occupation is due to the small number of Israelites, who are too few to occupy it completely (Exod 23:30). This is not quite consistent with the Elohist idea that Israel was a numerous people (Gen 50:20), but it does fit with the complementary idea of a remnant (Gen 45:7). The boundaries of the land to be occupied by Israel extend from Egypt to Assyria and implicitly define the enemies against whom they must struggle.

126 The Deuteronomistic Historian added constructive and harmonizing legislation to the end of each section (Exod 22:9–19; 23:17–19).

127 There is a section on slaves (21:1–11), on slaves and citizens (21:12–27), on domestic animals (21:28–37), and on property (22:1–8). The sections are connected to one another by the repetition of words or topics. The fourth is connected to the third by contiguous cases of theft involving oxen or sheep. The third is linked to the second by nearly contiguous cases of harm done to a man or a woman (21:22–25, 28). The intervening reference to slaves at the end of the second section (21:26–27) corresponds to similar cases in the first section, and the second section begins like the end of the first with a case concerning a man (21:7, 12). Each of the sections, except the third, has an appeal to God (21:6, 12; 22:7–8). This section, curiously enough, often mentions the "owner" (*baʿal*, 21:28, 29[twice], 34[twice], 36) of the property or the "master" (*ʾādôn*) of the slave. Since these words can also be names or titles of other Gods, it might have been inappropriate to mention God in the same breath (cf. Exod 23:13b).

[128] The five sections are arranged in a descriptive order (A = Exod 22:20–26; B = 22:27–30; C = 23:1–9; A' = 23:10–13; B' = 23:14–16). The focus (C) concerns due process. The concluding sections (A', B') give the ritual equivalent of the laws in the sections they match (A, B).

[129] The first section (Exod 22:20–26) is clearly an Elohist composition: the expression "For you were aliens in the land of Egypt" is like the etiological explanation of the name Gershom (Exod 2:22; 18:3); the statement that God hears the cry of the afflicted (22:22, 26) is like the introduction to God's address to Moses on Horeb (Exod 3:9). In common with Amos's opening and closing critiques (Amos 2:6–8; 8:4–6) it mentions taking garments in pledge (22:25; Amos 2:8) and mistreating the poor for money (22:24; Amos 2:6, 7; 8:6). In the sequel concern for widows and orphans and aliens is an attribute of Yahweh (Deut 10:18), but in the populist perspective of this version, although it remains a divine prerogative, it is expected of everyone (Exod 22:20–22).

[130] The prohibition against cursing God or a leader (22:27) corresponds to the command not to take the name of God in vain (Deut 5:11, *lōʾ tiśśāʾ ʾet šēm yhwh ʾĕlōhêkā laššāwʾ*), although the sequel's precise language is saved for the law against false delation (Exod 23:1, *lōʾ tiśśāʾ šemaʿ šāwʾ*). The offering of produce (Exod 22:28a) replaces tithes (Deut 14:22). The offering of firstborn children and animals (Exod 22:28b) has parallels in the epic (Exod 34:19) and in the sequel (Deut 15:19–20). The prohibition against eating prey (Exod 22:30) was taken up by the Deuteronomist (Deut 14:21) but is a limitation of the sequel's declaration that meat could be eaten (Deut 12:20). The legislation, however, differs from its sources in omitting both centralization and the schedule they imposed.

[131] The passage (Exod 23:1–9) also has specific links to other sections in the legislation. The ox and the ass (23:4) were the subject of legislation in the first part (Exod 21:28–37; 22:3) and are mentioned again in the law of the sabbath (Exod 23:12). Solicitude for the alien was legislated at the beginning of the second part and also is mentioned again in the sabbath law (Exod 23:9; cf. Exod 22:20; 23:12). In the first paragraph (Exod 23:1–5) the witness who does violence (Exod 23:1, *ʿēd ḥāmās*) recalls Amos's warning about sitting on the judgment seat of violence (Amos 6:3, *šebet ḥāmās*). Perverting justice (Exod 23:2, *nāṭâ*) and being partial in judgment against the poor (Exod 23:3, *dāl*) are an interpretation of Amos's condemnation of those who oppress the poor and pervert the way of the helpless (Amos 2:7, *dallîm . . . yaṭṭû*). The second paragraph (Exod 23:6–9) has affinities with Isaiah's condemnation of lies and appeal for justice and fair judgment (Exod 23:6–8, *mišpāṭ, ṣdq, šqr*; cf. Isa 28:15–17).

[132] The fallow year is supposed to supply food for the poor (23:11, *ʾebyônê ʿammekā*) and for the wild animals. It is composed in line with Amos's criticisms in order to correct the sequel's legislation of tithes (Deut 14:22, 25–26). Tithes were annual and affected the product of seed sown in the field (Deut 14:22, *kol tĕbûʾat zarʿekā hayyōṣēʾ haśśādeh šānâ šānâ*), but the Elohist legislation allowed sowing and reaping for only six years at a stretch (Exod

23:10 *šēš šānîm tizraʿ ʾet ʾarṣěkā wěʾāsaptā ʾet těbûʾātāh*). Tithes could be exchanged for money that was to be spent feasting at the central sanctuary (Deut 14:25–26), but Amos declared an end to the feasting and condemned those who cheated at the grain market and bought the poor for a bit of money (Amos 9:3a, 4–6). The sabbath is supposed to benefit slaves and animals and aliens (Exod 23:12): Amos in the same passage condemns those who chafe at the day of rest (Amos 8:5, *haššabbat*) because they want to arrest (Amos 8:4, *lašbît*) the poor and helpless.

[133] Exod 23:14–16 is formulated in opposition to the sequel's version of the three annual festivals at the central sanctuary. The law begins (23:14) the way the sequel's legislation ends (Deut 16:16) but omits its reference to the sanctuary and does not limit the obligation to males. It replaces Passover with Massot (Exod 23:15 = Deut 16:1) and tithes with the harvest festivals (Exod 23:16 = Deut 14:22) and makes the presentation of the firstborn casual (Exod 22:28) rather than an occasion at the central sanctuary (Deut 15:19–20).

[134] The Deuteronomist incorporated it into Deuteronomy, called it the Book of the Law or the Book of the Covenant and described the effect it had on the reform of Josiah.

[135] Moses climbed the mountain (Exod 24:13–14) as the Priestly version prescribed (Exod 24:15–18), but in the Elohist version Joshua goes with him and the cloud dissipates. In both versions the tablets were inscribed by God (Exod 31:18; 32:16bA), but in the Elohist version they were also made by God (Exod 32:16a). In the Priestly version they were made of stone (Exod 31:18), but in the Elohist version the material is not specified but they are inscribed on both sides like writing boards.

[136] It is God who writes the law (Exod 34:29aBb), not Moses who writes the covenant on the tablets (34:28abA). In the epic Moses continues to lead the people, but in the Elohist version his role ends at Horeb and the angel of God goes with the people.

[137] Deut 5:27; 12:14; 1 Kgs 12:25–29; 2 Kgs 18:12.

[138] The people ask Aaron to make them a God to go before them (Exod 32:1) despite the fact that God had sent his angel before them (Exod 23:20). The angel was to be an enemy to their enemies, but the calf is a rebellion against the angel and a delight to their enemies (Exod 23:20–22; 32:25).

[139] The calf is identified as Yahweh (Exod 32:4–5; cf. Deut 5:6), and the rituals associated with it are like the celebrations that the sequel prescribed for the worship of Yahweh (Exod 32:5–6; cf. Deut 12:18; 14:26). The identification is part of the continuing polemic against the sequel's law of centralization. Like the calf the law does not have Mosaic authorization, and, as history makes plain, it encourages beliefs and practices that have contrary and calamitous results.

140 Aaron and Moses make similar-sounding excuses for the people, Aaron explaining that they were anxious (Exod 32:22bB, *kî běrā' hû'*), Moses thinking that Aaron let them grow impatient (Exod 32:25aB, *kî pārūa' hû'*). In the Deuteronomistic version the golden calves not only were a violation of the covenant but were the sin of Jeroboam that led to the collapse of both kingdoms (1 Kgs 12:30–33); the Elohist version was changed to suit that interpretation. The tablets are broken (32:19b), to be replaced by the tablets of the decalogue (Exodus 34). The calf is sinful and has to be destroyed (Exod 32:20, 21b). The fault of the Aaronide priesthood is expiated by the Levites (Exod 32:26–29). The people are not abandoned (Exod 32:7–14), but the sinners among them are punished (32:30–35). The question of leadership, now that the calf is gone, becomes a pressing issue (Exodus 33).

141 The beginning of the passage returns to the earlier point in the story of the golden calf where Moses came down from the mountain with the tablets in his hand (Exod 32:15–16). The reprise makes the calf an isolated incident that does not prevent the story from having a happy ending.

142 Mic 4:1–5 = Isa 2:1–5: the commentary on this text (Mic 4:6–14) was mimicked by III Isaiah's commentary (Isa 2:6–22) on the original version in II Isaiah (Isa 2:1–5). Compare also Mic 5:4–5 and Isa 9:1–5; 10:24–27.

143 In fig. 9 stanzas are marked by numerals, strophes by letters.

144 Both strophes describe trouble arriving at the gates of Jerusalem (1:9, *nāga' 'ad ša'ar 'ammî 'ad yĕrûšālāyim*; 1:12, *kî yārad rā' mē'ēt yhwh lĕša'ar yĕrûšālāyim*). The people on the route of the enemy advance either do not march forth to war (1:11bA) or give way before the onslaught (1:11bB).

145 Both strophes mention mourning (*spd*, 1:8, 11) and nakedness (1:8, *'ārôm*; 1:11, *'eryâ*), weeping (1:10, *bkh*) or wailing (1:8, *yll*), and walking barefoot (1:8) or rolling in the dust (1:10).

146 The first scene focuses on the fall of Israel (1:5–7) and the second on the threat to Judah (1:13–14).

147 The choral quality is especially noticeable in the frequent change of address. The first stanza mixes plural imperatives (1:10a, *běgat 'al taggîdû / bākô 'al tibkû*) with a second person feminine singular imperative (1:10b, *hitpallaši[t]î*)—all for the sake of the pun on Gath of the Philistines. The second stanza addresses the town Saphir in the feminine singular imperative but with a masculine plural pronoun (1:11a, *'ibrî lākem*), and refers to Zaanan in the third person singular feminine but to its inhabitants in the second masculine plural (1:11b). Direct address to Lachish (1:13abB) is interrupted by an aside in which Lachish is referred to in the third person (1:13bA).

148 The theophany takes place before all the nations (1:2aA) and the whole world (1:2aB), but the chorus speaks to cities and towns whose names fit into the message in alliterative, assonantal, and rhyming patterns.

149 Lachish is presented as the symbol of Zion's sin (1:13) and Moreshet Gath as the sign of her divorce (1:14, *šillûḥîm*).

150 The first and second stanzas (2:1–2) are a monologue in which Micah inveighs against the tireless and remorseless guilt of his audience. The third begins as an address by Micah (2:3aA) but quotes another address in which Yahweh speaks first to Micah (2:3aB, "Behold, I have planned evil against this family") and then to the people (2:3b, "from which you will not free your neck or walk upright, for it is an evil time").

151 Change of speaker is marked either explicitly (2:4aA, 6a), or by a change in person, number, and mood of the verbs.

152 The first strophe (2:1–3) is directed against those who do evil (2:1, *poʿălê rāʿ*) and steal property (2:2, *gzl*). The second (3:1–3) mentions those who love evil (3:2, *ʾōhăbê rāʿâ*) and steal skin off the bones (3:2, *gzl*).

153 The first (2:4–5) quotes the appeal, and the second (3:4–5) says that Yahweh will not hear it.

154 The strophe (6:3–5) reviews the exodus and the conquest and ends with the statement "so that you might know that Yahweh is right" (*ṣiḏqôt yhwh*).

155 The strophes are linked by their summons (*šimʿû*, 6:1, 2, 9). The first concerns the people of Israel. The second is addressed to the city, to the tribe in which it is situated and who are the basis of its population, and to the pilgrims gathered in the temple (6:9, *ûmî yěʿāḏāh*).

156 The middle strophe in the first scene (6:3–5) contains a pun: "How have I bored you (6:3, *helʾētîkā*), I bore you out of Egypt (6:4, *heʿělîtîkā*)." The corresponding strophe in the second scene (6:13–14) continues the pun (6:13, *heḥělêtî*, "I made you sick").

157 In the first scene Micah tells them that they could not please Yahweh with a thousand sacrifices or with ten thousand rivers of oil (6:7), and in the corresponding strophe of the second scene they are told that they will crush the olives and not produce any oil at all (6:15). The strophe (6:15–16) begins as a continuation of the preceding strophe in the second person singular masculine (6:15). Its second stanza, however, mixes active and passive verbs and, like the second scene in the first discourse, repeatedly changes the person of the verbs and has the effect of many people speaking at once to a varied audience.

158 Literally, that "it would be wise to fear your name" (6:9).

159 The text (6:10–11) is composed of two rhetorical questions. In the second Yahweh asks, "Can I be innocent with iniquitous scales / with a bag of false weights!" (6:11, *haʾezkeh běmōʾzěnê rešaʿ / ûběkîs ʾabnê mirmâ*). The first

question explains what he means by referring to the temple and its treasuries, where these stolen goods are offered to defile him: "Moreover, is it a temple of iniquity / with crooked treasuries / and a small ephah worthy of a curse!" (6:10, *ʿôd haʾiš bêt rāšāʿ* / *ʾoṣĕrôt rešaʿ* / *wĕʾēpat rāzôn zĕʿûmâ*). Attempts to emend the text do not improve it. As it stands it explains why, as the corresponding second scene in the first discourse states, the glory of Yahweh leaves the city.

160 The second scene in the second discourse opens with an address to the leaders, who are supposed to know the workings of the law (3:1, *mišpāṭ*) but love evil and hate what is good (3:2, *śōnĕʾê ṭôb wĕʾōhăbê rāʿâ*). The second strophe in the last discourse, similarly, mentions those who do well at evil (7:3, *ʿal hārāʿ kappayim lĕhêṭîb*), the governor who should see that justice is done but looks for a bribe (7:3, *haśśar šōʾēl wĕhaśśōpēṭ baśśillûm*), and the people for whom decency is a thornbush and goodness is a brier (7:4, *ṭôbām kĕḥēdeq* / *yāšār mimmĕsûkâ*).

161 The prophets (7:4b, *yôm mĕṣappêkā* / *pĕquddātĕkā bāʾâ*) are Amos, who announced the day of Yahweh (Amos 5:18, *yôm*), and Hosea, the watchman, who announced the day of punishment (Hos 9:7–8, *bāʾû yĕmê happĕquddâ* . . . *ṣopeh ʾeprayim ʿim ʾĕlōhāy nābîʾ*).

162 Cf. 7:9 (*bĕṣidqātô*) and 6:5 (*ṣidqôt yhwh*).

163 The text that was displaced mentions the heads of Jacob (3:1, *rāʾšê yaʿăqōb*) and the rulers of Israel (3:1, *yiśrāʾēl*). The new material begins with Jacob and Israel (2:12, *yaʿăqōb* . . . *yiśrāʾēl*) and ends with Yahweh at the head of his people (2:13, *bĕrōʾšām*).

164 The first stanza begins "I will collect all of *you*, Jacob" (2:12), in a context that otherwise refers to Jacob in the third person singular or plural, to anticipate the original direct address to Jacob (3:1, "Listen now, you heads of Jacob"), and the anticipation is clearly marked by the deictic pronominal suffix (2:12, "all of you" [*kullāk*]).

165 The stanza describes people going out through the gate (2:13, *šaʿar*). The preceding context talked of the enemy lurking at the gate (*šaʿar*, 1:9, 12).

166 The original (3:9–12) and the beginning of the editor's discourse (4:1–3) share numerous terms ("house of Jacob," "Zion and Jerusalem," "judge," "teach," and "temple mount") but in a different order and with an opposite meaning.

167 The argumentative pattern (fig. 9: A–E, E′–A′) assembles the data and then analyzes it. The narrative pattern links strophes so that a minor theme or subtopic of one becomes the major interest of the next, and unresolved issues in each are taken up in the following pair.

168 The two strophes (4:1–3abA, 3bB–5) share lexical items (people, nations, walk, speak, Yahweh, God) and deal with the same topics.

169 The strophe (4:6–7) refers to some indefinite time that corresponds roughly to the end of time (4:6, *bayyôm hahû*'; cf. 4:1, *bĕ'aḥărît hayyāmîm*) and uses vocabulary from the first (4:7, *gôy, har ṣiyyôn*; cf. 4:1–2) and second strophes (4:7, *mē'attâ wĕ'ad 'ôlām*; cf. 4:5, *lĕ'ôlām wā'ed*). The gathering of the remnant under the kingship of Yahweh was announced in the break between the scenes of the first discourse (2:12–13).

170 The strophes (4:6–7, 8–9) share words and ideas (notably that Yahweh is their king), a pun (4:6b, *hărē'ôtî*, and 4:9a, *tārî'î rēa'*), and the image of a shepherd and flock traveling toward Zion or Jerusalem.

171 The most explicit link is with the fourth strophe (4:10, *bat ṣiyyôn kayyôlēdâ*; cf. 4:8a, *bat ṣiyyon* + 4:9b, *kayyôlēdâ*). The link with the first pair of overlapping strophes is the image of nations gathering in or against Zion and the quotation of their words (cf. 4:11 and 4:2).

172 This strophe (4:13–14), like the preceding, is addressed to the "Daughter of Zion" and follows the same pattern: imperative, followed by a reason for the command (introduced by "because") in the same stanza, and by another stanza introduced by "Now . . .".

173 Both strophes (4:8–9 and 5:1–3) refer to the ancient dominion of Judah, to the pregnant woman who is about to give birth, and to the ruler as Yahweh's lieutenant. They are also connected by puns: between the tower where his authority resides (4:8, *migdal*) and the extent of his authority (5:3, *yigdal*); between the counsel of the ruler (4:9, *yô'ăṣēk*) and his origin (5:1, *môṣa'ôtāyw*).

174 The seventh (5:1–3) and eighth (5:4–5) strophes are connected by their interest in shepherds. The eighth also develops the point that was made in the sixth (4:13–14) about the defeat of the besieging armies.

175 The strophe (5:6–8) contrasts Zion's opposite attitudes to the nations who did or did not hurt her and who will or will not submit to Yahweh.

176 The discourse begins with the two words (7:10a, *wĕtēre' 'ōyabtî*; cf. 7:10b, *'ênay tir'ênnâ*) that began and ended the preceding strophe in the original (7:8, *'ōyabtî*; 7:9, *'er'eh*).

177 The prayer (7:14–15) is addressed to God in the present time and concerns both the past and the future.

178 Cf. 1:9 (*makkôtêhā*) and Isa 1:6 (*makkâ*).

179 The first scene (1:2–9) describes the theophany of Yahweh and its results, and the second scene complements it in the route of the invading forces (1:10–16). Cf. Isa 10:5.

180 Cf. 2:10aB (*kî lō' zō't hammĕnûḥâ*) and Isa 28:12 (*'ăšer 'āmar 'ălêhem zō't hammĕnûḥâ*).

[181] Cf. Mic 1:2 (*šimʿû*, *ʾereṣ*) and Isa 1:2. The quotation is confirmed by later allusions to the same text of Isaiah. Micah's text is put into the mouth of the prophet Micaiah by the Deuteronomist (1 Kgs 22:28).

[182] Mic 1:2b, *ʾădōnāy yhwh*; cf. Amos 1:8; 3:11; 4:2, 5; 7:1, 2, 4–6). Mic 1:2b, *ʾădōnāy mēhêkal qodšô*; cf. Isa 1:4 (*qĕdôš*) and Amos 4:2 (*nišbaʿ ʾădōnāy yhwh bĕqodšô*).

[183] Mic 1:2, *šimʿû ʿammîm kullām.*

[184] The first stanza (1:5) refers to rebellion and sin (*bĕpešaʿ*, *bĕḥaṭṭôʾt*) as does Isaiah (Isa 1:2, 4) and Amos after him (Amos 5:12). It refers to the North as Israel and—in agreement with Amos (7:2, 5) and Hosea (10:11; 12:3)—to the South as Judah or Jacob. The idea that the sin of Judah or Jacob is Samaria (1:5b) is rephrased in the third discourse as Jerusalem's adherence to the theory and practice established by Omri and Ahab (6:16). The quotation from the sequel (1:5bB, "And what are the high places of Judah if not Jerusalem?" [*ûmî bāmôt yĕhûdâ hălôʾ yĕrûšālāyim*]) refers critically to the centralization of worship under Hezekiah (2 Kgs 18:22, *bāmôtāyw*, *yĕhûdâ*, *yĕrûšālāyim*). The quotation stands out by its peculiarities—e.g., that Jerusalem is not one but plural high places—and it is confirmed in the corresponding strophe of the second scene, which refers to the capture of Lachish in the same encounter with the Assyrians (1:13; cf. 2 Kgs 18:17; 19:8b). The quotation is appropriate since both Isaiah and the sequel are dealing with the same Assyrian invasion in 701 B.C.E.

[185] Mic 1:7, *yiššārĕpû bāʾēš . . . šĕmāmâ* (cf. Isa 1:7, *šĕmāmâ . . . śĕrûpôt ʾēš*); *wĕkol pĕsîlêhā* (cf. Hos 11:2, *pĕsîlîm*); *wĕkol ʾetnannêhā* (cf. Hos 2:14; 9:1); *wĕkol ʿăṣabbêhā* (cf. Hos 4:7; 13:2); *zônâ* (cf. Hos 1:2; 2:7; 4:12); *yāšûbû* (cf. Hos 2:9, 11; 6:1).

[186] The quotation is also marked by reversing Isaiah's word order (Isa 5:1–2, *kerem . . . wayyiṭṭāʿēhû*; Mic 1:6, *lĕmaṭṭāʿê kārem*).

[187] The expression "For grievous is her wounds / for it has come to Judah" combines a singular adjective and verb with a plural noun (1:9, *kî ʾănûšâ makkôtêhā / kî bāʾâ ʿad yĕhûdâ*). The next verb (1:9b, *nāgaʿ*), unlike the other verb and adjective, is masculine. The quotation is from Isaiah's first description of the Assyrian invasion (Isa 1:5, 6, *ʿal meh tukkû ʿôd . . . makkâ ṭĕrîyyâ*). The fact that the wounding "came" corresponds to his second description of the advance of the Assyrian army (Isa 5:26, *yābôʾ*; Isa 10:28, *bāʾ*), and the fact that it came to the gates of Jerusalem corresponds to his third (Isa 10:32).

[188] The editor is concerned with separating Israel from the peoples (*ʿammîm*, 4:1, 3, 5, 13; 5:7). Micah refers only to "my/his people" (*ʿammî*/*ʿammô*, 1:9; 2:8–9; 3:3, 5; 6:2–3), or "this people" (*hāʿām hazzeh*, 2:11).

[189] Items that are not explained immediately are taken up in the following stanzas and strophes. In this interlocking scheme "you people, all of them"

(1:2) is explained in the second strophe as Jacob and Israel. In fact, when Israel has been dealt with in the first discourse, Micah turns to Jacob in the second (2:7; 3:1, 9).

190 The undercurrent of ritual and liturgical interest that is evident in the theophany, in the list of cultic paraphernalia, and in the lament form, surfaces in the last two discourses, which dismiss the usual but corrupt forms of worship to rely on simple devotion.

191 The subject of the masculine verb (1:9bB, *nāgaʿ*), in Micah's interlocking scheme, is Yahweh ("he has reached the gates"), who, according to the first strophe, had left his shrine and was striding across the earth (1:3–4).

192 The reversal is marked by use of the same words: as Yahweh went out from his shrine (1:3, *yōṣēʾ*), so the people were afraid to go out of their cities (1:11, *lōʾ yāṣēʾâ*); as Yahweh came down and strode across the earth (1:3, *yārad*), so evil has come down (1:12, *yārad*) from Yahweh to the gates of Jerusalem. The mention of Gath in the first stanza (1:10–11a, *bĕgat . . . hitpallaš[t]î*) supposes what Amos said about Gath as a model of the destruction awaiting Zion (Amos 6:2, *ʿibrû . . . ûrĕdû gat pĕlištîm*). The names are plausible place-names but are chosen to suit the literary context (e.g., 1:11b, *ṣaʾănān* seems to fit etymologically with its verb *yāṣēʾâ*; 1:10, *bêt lĕʿaprâ* has to roll in the dust [*ʿāpār*]) or as purely descriptive references to Jerusalem and its environs (1:11b, *bêt hāʾēṣel*, "nearby town"; 1:12a *mārôt*, "rebellious").

193 Amos described the anguish of the day of Yahweh as mourning for an only child (Amos 8:10–11), and Micah, without specific reference to Amos, describes his mourning (1:9) and the anguish of the city when its children are taken into exile (1:16).

194 The two strophes (2:1–3, 4–5) are related as indictment and sentence. Both mention fields (2:2, *śādôt*; 2:4b, *śādēnû*), and the second plays with the word (2:4a, *śādôd nĕšaddûnû*). The image is important since at the end of the discourse Micah announces that Zion will be plowed like a field (3:12, *śādeh*). The first uses the verb *mwš* transitively (2:3b, "From which they will not remove their necks"), and the second uses it intransitively (2:4b, "How he *has removed* from me!").

195 The encompassing stanzas (2:1, 3) deal with retribution and balance each other. The middle stanza (2:2) explains what evil they have done, and it is balanced and developed in the second strophe (2:4–5).

196 Mic 2:3, "this family," *hammišpāḥâ hazzōʾt*; cf. Amos 3:1, "the family [*hammišpāḥâ*] I brought out of Egypt." Mic 2:3, *hinĕnî ḥōšēb . . . rāʿâ*; cf. Amos 3:6, *ʾim tihyeh rāʿâ bĕʿîr wayhwh lōʾ ʿāśâ*. The reversal of fortunes is emphasized by saying that the family of Jacob will not escape the threatened servitude (Mic 2:3b, *wĕlōʾ tēlĕkû rômâ*) as the family of Israel once escaped from servitude in Egypt (Exod 14:8b, *ûbĕnê yiśrāʾēl yōṣĕʾîm bĕyād rāmâ*).

197 The texts have one word in common (2:3, *ṣawwĕʾ rōtêkem*; Hos 10:11,

ṣawwāʾrāh), but Micah refers to the same passage again: cf. Hos 10:11b, "I will hitch up Ephraim / make Judah plow / have Jacob harrow" (*ʾarkîb ʾeprayim / yaḥărôš yĕhûdâ / yĕśaddēd lô yaʿăqōb*); Mic 3:12, "Zion is a field to be plowed" (*ṣiyyôn śādeh tēḥārēš*); and Mic 2:4, "we are utterly ruined" (*šādôd nĕšaddūnû*).

198 The sarcasm is explicit (2:4aA, "On that day he will taunt you and lament a lamented lament," *wĕnāhâ nĕhî nihyâ*). The taunt, recited by Yahweh (2:4, "He said . . . ," *ʾāmar*), alludes to a text in Hosea, later quoted by Jeremiah (Jer 2:11), according to which the people were ruined because Yahweh exchanged their glory for shame (2:4, *ḥēleq ʿammî yāmîr*; cf. Hos 4:6a, 7, *niḏmû ʿammî . . . kĕbôdām bĕqālôn ʾāmîr*) and contradicts an epic text in which the pillar of cloud and fire that marked Yahweh's presence did not remove from them (2:4, *ʾêk yāmîš lî*; cf. Exod 13:22, *lōʾ yāmîš*).

199 The clause *lōʾ yiṣṣag kĕlimmôt* (2:6bB) means literally "he will not withdraw in shame," or something similar. It therefore corresponds exactly to the scene of the departure of Yahweh's glory (1:15) and is an appropriate response by his opponents to Micah's allusion to Hosea's statement that Yahweh had changed the glory of his people into shame (2:4).

200 Micah refers to a saying that his adversaries are supposed to know (2:7a, "Has it not been said . . . ?" *heʾāmûr bêt yaʿăqōb*). The saying and its application (2:7a, "Has Yahweh reaped the wind [*hăqāṣar rûaḥ yhwh*]? If these things are what he intends to do, will not my words do good to the upright person") are made up from a saying in Hosea (8:7, "They have sown the wind and reaped the whirlwind," *kî rûaḥ yizrāʿû wĕsûpātâ yiqṣōrû*).

201 Since Micah is quoting their drivel (2:6, *nṭp*), the passage (Mic 2:8) might read: "Just yesterday (*ʾetmûl*) he raised up my people as an enemy against (*mimmûl*) Salmah, but you strip away the pride of those who march confidently (*beṭaḥ*) as they return from battle." In response to Micah's insistence that Yahweh is bringing evil on the people, they recall how Yahweh recently helped them withstand Shalmaneser (*šalmâ* ("cloak") juxtaposed to *ʾeder* ("pride") as a pun on *šalmanʾeser*). Each thinks the other is speaking drivel (2:6). They accuse him of stripping away the people's confidence, as he later accuses them of stripping away their skin (3:3). In the sequel's account Shalmaneser's capture of Samaria for failing to worship in Jerusalem is the backdrop of Jerusalem's survival because it trusted in Yahweh (2 Kgs 18:19–22 *bṭḥ*). The people's argument also juxtaposes the two events.

202 When the people quote Micah's words (1:15b–16) the quotation is marked by bad grammar: "the women of my people you (plural) drive out of her pleasant home" (2:9a, *nĕšê ʿammî tĕgārēšûn mibbêt taʿănūgêhā*). They, speaking as prophets and mouthing the words of God (2:6), say that he has stripped away the pride of "my" people and taken "my" honor from her children forever (2:8–9). He said her precious children were going into exile (1:16b); the glory of Israel was going to Adullam (1:15b); and their glory was leaving them to their shame (2:4, 6).

203 He tells them to leave the city because it is unclean (2:10b, *baʿăbûr*
ṭāmēʾâ) and corrupt (2:10b, *ḥbl*; cf. 2:5) and contradicts Isaiah's statement
that Jerusalem was a haven and a place of rest (Mic 2:10a, *kî lōʾ zōʾt hammĕnûḥâ*
= Isa 28:12, *zōʾt hammĕnûḥâ*).

204 The prophet who is swayed by any breeze (2:11a, *lû ʾîš hōlēk rûaḥ*) is
the opposite of the person who stays on the straight road (2:7b, *hayyāšār hōlēk*)
and profits from Micah's words. The one who adds lies to deception (2:11)
recalls Isaiah's words about those who would not listen to Yahweh, saying
"this is a place to rest," but trusted in lies and deception (Isa 28:15b). The
prophet who prophesies about liquor and wine (2:11) is like the people who,
Isaiah said, would be confounded not with liquor and wine but by their
prophets (Isa 29:9–10).

205 It begins "but I said" (3:1, *wāʾōmar*) in contrast to the drivel of the false
prophet (2:11) and as a continuation of Micah's words at the end of the first
scene (2:10).

206 Mic 3:1b, *mišpāṭ*; cf. Amos 5:7, 24; Hos 2:21; 10:4.

207 The prophets will call out to Yahweh and, not receiving an answer, will
shut their mouths (3:4, 7). The same judgment is expressed figuratively as a
night without vision and a day without light (3:6aAbB; cf. Amos 5:18–20),
when it becomes dark and the sun sets on the prophets (3:6aBbA, *wĕḥāšĕkâ*
. . . *ûbāʾâ haššemeš*; cf. Amos 8:9, *wĕhēbēʾtî haššemeš . . . wĕhaḥăšaktî*).

208 The belief that Yahweh was in the midst of the people (3:11) and
protected them from their enemies was expressed by the author of the sequel
(Deut 6:15; 7:21; Josh 3:5). Their reliance on the presence of Yahweh
(3:11b), which Micah disputes, was illustrated in the sequel's version of the
marvelous resistance of Jerusalem to the invasion of Sennacherib (2 Kgs
18:21–22).

209 The lawsuit theme (6:2, *šimʿû . . . ʾet rîb yhwh*) was introduced by Hosea
(Hos 4:1, *šimʿû . . . kî rîb layhwh . . .*). In Isaiah, Yahweh challenges the people
to dispute what he says (Isa 1:18, *lĕkû nāʾ wĕniwwākĕḥâ*; cf. Mic 6:2, *wĕʿim
yiśrāʾēl yitwakkāḥ*).

210 The first stanza begins "My people what have I done to you?" (6:3a)
and recalls the epic's covenant ceremony, in which the people are witnesses to
what Yahweh does (Exod 34:10). The second stanza begins "My people
remember" (6:5a) and is reminiscent of the sequel's theme of remembering
what Yahweh has done for them (cf. Deut 7:18).

211 The forensic situation is represented by the questions (6:3, 5, *meh, mâ*)
and answers (6:3, *ʿāneh bî*). The pun is on "I bore you" in the sense of carrying
or being tiresome (6:3–4, *helʾētîkā* and *heʿĕlītîkā*).

212 The review begins (6:4a, *kî heʿĕlītîkā mēʾereṣ miṣrayim* / *ûmibbêt ʿăbādîm*

pĕdîtîkā) with a quotation from the sequel's introduction to the covenant on Horeb (Deut 5:6b) but replaces its verb (Deut 5:6b, *hôṣ̌ē'tîkā*) with the verb that the epic used (Exod 3:8, *ʿlh*). It ends with a quotation from the Elohist (Mic 6:4b, "I sent before you," *wāʾešlaḥ lĕpānêkā*; Exod 23:20, "Behold I am sending an angel before you," *hinnēh ʾānōkî šōlēaḥ malʾāk lĕpānêkā*, cf. Exod 23:27) but replaces the Elohist's angel with Moses, Aaron, and Miriam, whom the Priestly writer touted as their leaders in the wilderness (Exod 7:1; 15:20; Num 20:1, 7–13).

213 The reference to the Balaam oracles (6:5a; cf. Numbers °22–24°), the epic version of Israel's settlement in the land, is combined incongruously ("My people, remember what Balak the king of Moab planned / and what Balaam the son of Beor answered him / from Shittim to Gilgal") with the sequel's version of the conquest, which began across the Jordan at Shittim and was directed from the camp at Gilgal (6:5b; cf. Josh 2:1; 3:1; 9:6a; 10:6, 9).

214 The proposal to come before Yahweh to offer holocausts or yearling calves (6:6) reflects legislation in the sequel (Deut 12:13–14; 15:19–20). The offering of firstborn children (6:7b) was legislated in the epic covenant (Exod 34:19), but Micah uses the language of the Elohist version (6:7b, *haʾettēn bĕkôrî pišʿî*; Exod 22:28b, *bĕkor bānêkā titten lî*). Offering them for the sins and offenses of their parents, however, is more in line with the epic and the sequel, which extended culpability from one generation to the next (6:7b; Exod 34:7; Deut 5:9–10).

215 The form of Micah's intervention (6:8) is borrowed from a speech by Moses in the sequel (Deut 10:12). Its content, as he says explicitly, is taken from available sources (6:8a, "He has told you Adam [*ʾāḏām*] what is good"). One of the sources, as "Adam" suggests, is the Priestly version of the pre-flood era, when Enoch and Noah walked with God and received his special favor (6:8b; cf. Gen 5:22; 6:9). The sources of the demand for fidelity to the law (Mic 6:8bA *kî ʾim ʿăśôt mišpāṭ wĕʾahăbat ḥeṣed*) are passages in the sequel and Hosea concerning fidelity to the covenant (Deut 5:10, *ʿōśeh ḥeṣed laʾălāpîm lĕʾōhăbay* . . . ; Deut 10:18, *ʿōśeh mišpāṭ* . . . *wĕʾōhēb*; Hos 2:21; 6:4–5).

216 The assembly (Mic 6:9, *ûmî yĕʿāḏāh*; cf. *mô̌ēd*, Hos 2:13; 9:5; 12:10) may have been for the celebration of Passover in the month Abib (Deut 16:1), which the Elohist called Massot and assigned to the *mô̌ēd* of that month (Exod 23:15).

217 The storehouses of guilt (Mic 6:10aB, *ʾōṣ̌ĕrôt rešaʿ*), in light of the later charge of malice (6:12aA, *ḥāmāṣ*), recall Amos's view of Samaria as a city that stored up malice and violence (Amos 3:10, *hāʾōṣ̌ĕrîm ḥāmāṣ wāšōd*). The use of undersized measures and false scales (Mic 6:10b–11) is modeled on Amos's accusation (Amos 8:5), and both became the basis for Deuteronomistic legislation concerning weights and measures (Deut 25:13–16). The defiling of the temple (Mic 6:10a, 11a, *hăʾiš bêt rāšāʿ* . . . *hăʾezkeh*) supposes that, as Amos said, the festivals were financed by the unconscionable profit they produced for individuals and institutions.

218 The charge that the rich people at the festival are full of malice (6:12, *ʾăšer ʿăšîrêhā mālěʾû ḥāmās*) resembles God's charge that the world was full of malice (Gen 6:11, 13, *kî mālěʾâ hāʾāreṣ ḥāmās*). The accusation that the inhabitants of the city are liars (Mic 6:12) resembles Isaiah's accusation of those who relied on the covenant (Isa 28:15) and Hosea's complaint against Samaria (Hos 7:1, 13).

219 The expression (Mic 6:13) "And indeed I have made you sick (*heḥĕlêtî*), I have struck you (*hakkôtekā*), I have devastated you (*hašmēm*), for your sins (*ḥaṭṭoʾtekā*)" is a quotation from the first scene in Isaiah, where Yahweh sees the sickness (Isa 1:5, *ḥŏlî*), wounds (Isa 1:5, 6, *tukkû, makkâ*) and devastation (Isa 1:7, *šĕmāmâ*) of the land because of its sins (Isa 1:4, 18 *ḥṭʾ*).

220 The futility of eating and not being satisfied (6:14a) is the opposite of eating and being satisfied, which the sequel assumed was characteristic of life in the good land (Deuteronomy 8), and which Hosea saw as the reason for the downfall of Ephraim (Hos 13:6). Their attempted escape (Mic 6:14b) contains a pun on Yahweh's removal from the temple (6:14b, *wĕtassēg*; cf. 2:6, *lŏʾ yissag*), but their failure to escape (6:14b, *wĕlŏʾ taplîṭ waʾăšer tĕpallēṭ laḥereb ʾettēn*) recalls Amos's insistence on the same point in his oracle against Israel (Amos 2:14–15, *lŏʾ yĕmallēṭ* [three times]).

221 Apart from its futility, planting and not harvesting (6:15a) frustrates the cycle of worship (cf. Exod 23:16), as crushing olives and not having the oil (6:15b; cf. 6:7) or the lack of liquor and wine (6:15b; cf. Isa 5:11–12; Deut 14:22, 26; Hos 2:7, 10–11) make plain. Devastation and dishonor (Mic 6:16b, *šammâ, ḥerpâ*) were portrayed in Isaiah and Hosea as effects of defeat (Isa 1:7; 30:5; Hos 12:15). The customs of Omri and Ahab (Mic 6:16a, *ḥuqqôt . . . maʿăśeh*) are negative alternatives to the customs initiated by Moses (Exod 18:20, *ʾet haḥuqqîm . . . wĕʾet hammaʿăśeh ʾăšer yaʿăśûn*). The counsels of Omri and Ahab (Mic 6:16a, *bĕmōʿăṣôtām*) refer to senseless worship of the calf at Bethel (cf. Hos 10:6).

222 The addressee is mostly second person singular masculine (6:13–15, 16bA), but occasionally second person plural (6:16aBbB), once third person singular feminine (6:16bA), and once impersonal (6:16aA). The original summons was addressed to the city and the tribe and the pilgrims (6:9, *ʿîr, maṭṭeh, ûmî yĕʿādāh*). The villains are referred to as her rich people and citizens (6:12).

223 Part of the punishment described in the third discourse was the failure of the crops and the consequent frustration of the cycle of worship (6:14a, 15). The first stanza in the lament compares the pain of the city to the desolation of the land (7:1a) and to the frustration of its firstfruits (7:1b). In the first comparison the expression *kĕʾospê qayiṣ* (7:1aA) recalls Amos's vision of a basket of summer fruit (Amos 8:2a, *qayiṣ*), which presaged the end (Amos 8:2b, *qēṣ*) of the nation on the terrible day of Yahweh.

224 The expression (7:2a) *ʾābad ḥāsîd min hāʾāreṣ / wĕyāšār bāʾādām ʾayin* seems to be a deliberate reference to 2:7b ("Would not my words do good *ʿim*

ḥayyăšār ḥōlēk?") and to 6:8 ("He has told you *ʾāδām* what is good, . . . loving *ḥeseδ* . . ."). The second part of the stanza (7:2b) uses images of hunting and trapping but also adds the word *ḥērem* ("net" or "*ex-voto*"), suggesting the sacrificial imagery of the second discourse.

225 The first stanza in the second strophe lists the people who do well at doing evil (7:3aA) and who conspire to do it together (7:3b), the prince in taking what he wants, the judge in taking bribes, rich people in saying what suits their greed (cf. 6:12).

226 Faith (7:5, *ʾal taʾămînû*) and trust (7:5, *ʾal tibṭĕḥû*) in Yahweh are attitudes that the epic and the sequel encouraged, and Micah has no quarrel with them on that point. The argument supposes what was said in the first scene about the city being bereft of anyone faithful to the law (7:2) and by elimination (7:5b–6 eliminates spouse, children, relatives) arrives at hoping in God (7:7). Micah is a prophet and a watchman (7:7, *ṣpḥ*), as Hosea was (Mic 7:4, *ṣpḥ*; Hos 9:7–8), and the dramatic argument supposes that Yahweh has left the city as planned (cf. 1:15; 2:4–6).

227 The references to Amos are in the play between light and darkness (Mic 7:8b, 9b; cf. Amos 5:18–20) and in the expression "Although I fell, I am standing" (Mic 7:8a, *kî nāpaltî qāmtî*), which is the opposite of his dirge over Israel, who fell and did not get up (Amos 5:2, *nāpĕlâ lōʾ tôsîp qûm*). In the third discourse Yahweh urged the people to accept that he was right (Mic 6:5, *lĕmaʿan daʿat ṣiδqôt yhwh*), and at the very end of the drama the city does (7:9, *ʾerʾeh bĕṣiδqātô*).

228 The quotation from Zephaniah (Mic 2:12, *ʾāsōp ʾeʾĕsōp yaʿăqōb kullāk*; Zeph 1:2, *ʾāsōp ʾāsēp kol*) contradicts its originally ominous intent. The quotation from the book of Hosea is itself a quotation from the book of Ezekiel, and Micah's editor seems to know both versions: the gathering of Judah and Israel as one is from Hosea (Mic 2:12, *qbṣ . . . yḥδ*; cf. Hos 2:2, *wĕniqbĕṣû . . . yaḥδāw*); their gathering as one flock is from Ezekiel (Ezek 34:12–13; 37:22–24). It is also the book of Ezekiel that uses "gather" and "collect" to describe the return from exile (Mic 2:12, *ʾsp, qbṣ*; cf. Ezek 11:17, *qbṣ, ʾsp*).

229 The book of Hosea, in the same passage, adds that Israel and Judah will *place* one head over them (Hos 2:2a, *wĕsāmû lāhem rōʾš ʾeḥāδ*). The editor of Micah, on the other hand, talks about them being *placed* together (Mic 2:12, *yaḥaδ ʾăsîmennû*) but rather pointedly puts Yahweh at their head (2:13, *wayhwh bĕrōʾšām*). Both the book of Hosea and the book of Ezekiel envision a restoration of the Davidic dynasty. However, the editor of Zephaniah supposes that Yahweh himself will be king, and the editor of Micah is also very discreet about the successor to David.

230 The vision ends "You / they [feminine plural] will be bursting with men" (2:12, *tĕhîmenâ mēʾāδām*). The use of the word *ʾāδām* to express "man" is odd if the text is actually referring to the women (1:16 = 2:9), but it fits perfectly with the opening quotation from Zephaniah whose text used the

same word (Zeph 1:3, 'ăsēp 'ādām). The combination of the symbolism of the flock and its interpretation in the same stanza had a precedent in the book of Ezekiel (Ezek 36:37–38, ṣō'n 'ādām).

231 The story is told in 2 Kgs 25:4–7, at least three times in the book of Jeremiah (32:4; 39:2–7; 52:7–11), and once in the book of Ezekiel (12:1–17).

232 The first clause (2:13, 'ālâ happōrēṣ lipnêhem) resembles Nahum's description of the siege of Nineveh (Nah 2:2, 'ālâ mēpîṣ 'al pānayik). The word "breach" (prṣ) was used by Isaiah to describe the collapse of the walls of Samaria (Isa 5:5) and by Amos to describe the women of Samaria rushing headlong into exile (Amos 4:3, ûpěrāṣîm tēṣe'nâ 'iššâ negdāh). Breaching of the wall and exit through the gate are recounted in the story of Zedekiah (Mic 2:13, ša'ar wayyēṣě'û bô; cf. Jer 52:7, wayyēṣě'û . . . derek ša'ar bên haḥōmōtāyim). The allusions to the flight of David are the repeated uses of the verb "pass" and contradictory opinions on whether the king went first (2:12, 'br; cf. 2 Sam 15:16–23).

233 The text of II Isaiah is quoted almost verbatim at first (4:1–3 = Isa 2:2–4), but the editor omits the superscription in Isa 2:1 and reverses some of the elements: cf. Mic 4:1, yihyeh . . . nākôn, and Isa 2:2, nākôn yihyeh; Mic 4:2–3, 'ammîm . . . gôyim, and Isa 2:2–3, gôyim . . . 'ammîm.

234 The saying wěyāšěbû 'îš taḥat gapnô wětaḥat tě'ēnātô wě'ên maḥărîd (Mic 4:4a) combines 1 Kgs 5:5 (wayyēšēb yěhûdâ wěyiśrā'ēl lābeṭaḥ 'îš taḥat gapnô wětaḥat tě'ēnātô) and Ezek 34:28 (wěyāšěbû lābeṭaḥ wě'ên maḥărîd).

235 Traces of II Isaiah's conclusion (Isa 2:5, "House of Jacob come and let us walk in the light of Yahweh") are preserved in the new conclusion (Mic 4:5), "For every nation will walk, each in the name of its God, but we will walk in the name of Yahweh our God forever and ever."

236 The expression kî pî yhwh ṣěbā'ôt dibbēr (Mic 4:4b) concludes a stanza in which the sword is banished. It has a parallel in Isa 1:18 (cf. Isa 40:5), where the people have the option of listening or of being devoured by the sword.

237 The beginning of the allusion to Ezekiel (Mic 4:6aA, 'ōsěpâ haṣṣōlē'â wěhanniddāḥâ 'ăqabbēṣâ; Ezek 34:13, 16, wěqibbaṣtîm . . . wě'et hanniddāḥat 'āšîb) substitutes the verb that was quoted from Zephaniah in the editorial break (Mic 4:6aA, 'ōsěpâ; cf. 2:12, 'āsōp 'e'ěsōp = Zeph 1:2). The last clause in the stanza (4:6b, "And those to whom I did evil") recalls Micah's statements that Yahweh had planned evil against those who did evil and that it was lurking at the gates of Jerusalem (1:12; 2:3).

238 The Deuteronomist includes the promises that Abraham would become a great nation (Mic 4:7, gôy 'āṣûm; Gen 18:18; Deut 9:14). The restoration of Zion as a royal city and Yahweh's kingship over the remnant "now and

forever" (4:7b, 8b, *mē'attâ wĕ'aḏ 'ôlām . . . mamleket*) replaces II Isaiah's oracle on the restoration of the Davidic monarchy (Isa 9:6, *mamlaktô . . . mē'attâ wĕ'aḏ 'ôlām*).

239 From Jeremiah it takes the image of Zion as a woman in labor (Mic 4:9, *kî heḥĕzîqēk ḥîl kayyôlēḏâ*; cf. Jer 6:24, *ṣārâ heḥĕzîqatnû / ḥîl kayyôlēḏâ*) and the quotation of one of her cries (Mic 4:9, *hămelek 'ên bāk*; cf. Jer 8:19, *hayhwh 'ên bĕṣiyyôn / 'im malkāh 'ên bāh*). From II Isaiah it takes the word "your counselor" to refer to the king (Mic 4:8b, 9b, *bārî'ṣônâ . . . 'im yô'ăṣēk 'ābāḏ*; cf. Isa 1:26, *wĕ'āšîbâ šōpĕṭayik kĕbārî'ṣônâ / wĕyô'ăṣayik kĕbattĕḥillâ*).

240 The first part of the stanza (4:10, "Writhe and yell . . . like a woman in labor, for now you must leave the city, pitch your tent in the field . . .") paraphrases the text of Jeremiah quoted in the preceding strophe (Jer 6:24–26, "Anguish has overwhelmed me, writhing like a woman in labor. Do not go out into the field . . ."). The last part (4:10) is like the consultation before David returned to Jerusalem after the revolt of Absalom (2 Sam 19:10): the allusion reinforces the editor's replacement of the Davidic king with a theocratic state under the kingship of Yahweh.

241 The stanza (4:11–12) repeats key words from the initial quotation (Mic 4:11, *'ālayik gôyim rabbîm ha'ōmĕrîm*; cf. 4:1–2, *'ālayw . . . gôyîm rabbîm wĕ'āmĕrû*). It also diverts Yahweh's decision to do evil away from Jerusalem and against the nations (4:12; cf. 2:3). The motivation of the attackers (4:11b, "she is defiled," *teḥĕnāp*) is a quotation from Jeremiah (Jer 3:1–2).

242 The description of Zion as a heifer threshing (4:13aA) supposes the image that Hosea created of Ephraim (Hos 10:11). The title "Lord of all the earth" and the dedication to him of the spoils of war are elements of the theory of the conquest devised by the Deuteronomist (cf. Josh 3:11, 13; 6:18–19).

243 Mic 4:14aA, *'attâ titgōḏĕḏî bat gĕḏûḏ*; cf. Jer 5:7, *ûbêt zônâ yitgōḏāḏû*. Mic 4:14aB, *māṣôr*; cf. Jer 10:17. Mic 4:14bA, *baššēbeṭ yakkû 'al halléḥî*; cf. Isa 10:24, *'al tîrā' . . . mē'aššûr baššēbeṭ yakkĕkâ*. Mic 4:14b, *'et šōpēṭ yiśrā'ēl*; cf. Isa 1:26.

244 It quotes in opposite order from the sequel's story of David and Goliath (5:1, *wĕ'attâ bêt leḥem 'eprātâ*; 1 Sam 17:12, *ben 'îš 'eprātî hazzeh mibbêt leḥem*); cf. Gen 35:16–21; 1 Sam 16:1, 18. The note that Ephrathah is the least among the clans of Judah (5:1a) resembles the polite disclaimers by Gideon (Judg 6:15) and Saul (1 Sam 9:21) that they had the least claim to the authority that was being offered them. The reference to the Davidic dynasty quotes from the original and from the Deuteronomistic version of the covenant with David (Mic 5:1, *mimmĕkā lî yēṣē'*; cf. 2 Sam 7:12, *'ăšer yēṣē' mimmē'êkā*; Mic 5:1, *lihyôt môšēl bĕyiśrā'ēl*; cf. 2 Sam 7:8b, *lihyôt nāgîḏ 'al 'ammî yiśrā'ēl*). The origin of the dynasty in the distant past (5:1b) refers to the Deuteronomistic oracles of Jacob and Balaam (Gen 49:10; Num 24:17).

245 The beginning of the stanza (Mic 5:2a, *lākēn yittĕnēm 'aḏ 'ēt yôlēḏâ*

yālāðâ) seems to combine allusions to Zion (cf. 4:9–10, *kayyôlēðâ*) with the Immanuel oracle in II Isaiah (Isa 7:14, *hāʿalmâ hārâ wĕyōleðet bēn*; Isa 9:5, *kî yeleð yullað lānû / ben nittan lānû*). The birth of the child is delayed, on the basis of a text in Hosea, until "the rest of his brothers return to the children of Israel" (5:2b; cf. Hos 2:2–3 and 3:5). His brothers are literally the seven brothers of David (1 Sam 16:10–11) and historically the remnant of Israel. The last part of the stanza refers back to the beginning of the discourse and subordinates the child to God and to his brothers (5:3; cf. 4:4, 5).

246 The theme of the strophe (5:4–5) is announced at the beginning of its first stanza (Mic 5:4, *wĕhāyâ zeh šālôm*, "And he will be peace") in reference to one of the names of the king in the Immanuel oracle (Isa 9:5, *śar šālôm*). The mention of seven or eight shepherds (5:4b), although it could be just a formulaic usage, should refer in the context of these strophes to the seven brothers of David, David himself being the eighth (1 Sam 16:10–11). The balance between "shepherds" and "leaders of men" was established in the editorial break in the balance between sheep and men (cf. 2:12). The reference to "coming into our land" and "trampling on our defenses" (5:4a, 5b) is an interpretation of Micah's texts where the arrival of the enemy is described in terms of Yahweh trampling on the earth (1:3) and of evil coming to the gates of Jerusalem (1:9).

247 The first stanza (5:6) weaves themes of the second edition into a quotation from the Song of Moses (5:6aB; cf. Deut 32:2). The second stanza (5:7–8) describes Jacob among the nations in terms that Isaiah used to describe Assyria's aggression against Judah (5:7; cf. Isa 5:29; 10:28–29).

248 As the early part of the discourse referred to the peace that marked the reign of Solomon (Mic 4:4a = 1 Kgs 5:5), so the first stanza at the end of the discourse refers to his military power, which ultimately was Judah's undoing (Mic 5:9 = 1 Kgs 5:6). This is combined with a reference to Jeremiah and the ruin of fortified cities (Mic 5:10; cf. Jer 4:5; 8:14), and with another reference to legislation in the Deuteronomistic History (Mic 5:11; cf. Deut 18:10). In the second stanza (5:12–14) there are references to the Deuteronomistic diatribes against cult objects (Mic 5:12; cf. 2 Kgs 17:10–12; 21:3–8; 23:4–14) and a quotation from an oracle against Edom in the book of Ezekiel (Mic 5:14; cf. Ezek 25:14).

249 Mic 7:10, 11, *lĕmirmās . . . gĕðērāyik*; cf. Isa 5:5, *gĕðērô wĕhāyâ lĕmirmās*. This image of a vineyard turned into pasture is filled out with fixed sayings about the things that Yahweh does to his enemies: covering with shame (7:10a; Obad 10), trampling like mud in the streets (2 Sam 22:43 = Ps 18:43), and dissolving world order (7:13a; Jer 4:27).

250 The editor considers them to be attributes of Yahweh, who made a covenant with Abraham (7:16–20; cf. Exod 34:6–7).

251 The wonders that Yahweh did during the exodus from Egypt (7:15) were mentioned in the epic (Exod 34:10). The plea that Yahweh shepherd his people with his staff (Mic 7:14a, *šibṭekā*) recalls Isaiah's saying that Assyria

was the staff of his anger against his people (Isa 10:5). The fact that the people live alone (Mic 7:14, *šokĕnê lĕbādād*) is a quotation from the epic when Balaam saw Israel living alone (Num 23:9, *lĕbādād yiškôn*) and not reckoning itself among the nations. The fact that they live alone in a forest in the center of meadowland (Mic 7:14a, *ya'ar bĕtôk karmel*) refers to Micah's prediction that Zion would become a high place overrun with trees (3:12, *ya'ar*) and to a description of Israel as meadowland in the book of Jeremiah (Jer 2:7, *'el 'ereṣ hakkarmel*).

252 There is more information on library acquisitions and catalogs than there is on the physical arrangement and use of libraries: see S. Parpola, "Assyrian Library Records," *JNES* 42 (1983) 1–30. The editor of Jeremiah, whose work was designed to replace the Deuteronomistic History's version of the last days of Judah, used the archival model to include records, opinions, and material of historical and biographical character that could be consulted to settle the debate. There are semblances of narrative continuity, but they are filled with iterations, interpretations, retrospects and digressions that harp on specific immutable moments and on a few salient features of the prophet.

253 The archive begins and ends identifying itself as the words of Jeremiah (*ϑibrê yirmĕyāhû*, 1:1; 51:64b). The codicil (52:1–34) is the conclusion of the books of Kings (= 2 Kgs 24:18–25:30), about which there was no question. The archivist's dispute was with the reasoning that led to it.

254 Cf. Jer 25:13; 29:1, 25, 29; 30:2; 32:10, 11, 12, 14, 16, 44; 36:32; 51:60, 63.

255 See H. Hunger, *Babylonische und assyrische Kolophone* (Alter Orient und Altes Testament 2; Neukirchen-Vluyn: Neukirchener Verlag, 1968); J. R. Lundbom, "Baruch, Seraiah, and Expanded Colophons in the Book of Jeremiah," *JSOT* 36 (1986) 89–114; R. D. Patterson, "Of Bookends, Hinges, and Hooks: Literary Clues to the Arrangement of Jeremiah's Prophecies," *Westminster Theological Journal* 51 (1989) 109–31; A. Rofé, "The Arrangement of the Book of Jeremiah," *ZAW* 101 (1989) 390–98. This colophon resembles the cuneiform examples in naming the scribe (45:1, Baruch), his patron (45:1, Jeremiah), the source of his text (45:1, the word of Jeremiah by dictation), its date (45:1, the fourth year of Jehoiakim), its purpose (45:4–5a, impending doom), and in quoting the scribe's invocation of his God (45:3, Baruch's lament), and his devout expectation (cf. 45:5, the response to his lament). The oracles against the nations (chaps. 46–51) are separated from the codicil by another colophon (51:59–64a; cf. Lundbom, "Baruch," 101–4) and by the closing of the archive (51:64b).

256 E. Posener, *Archives in the Ancient World* (Cambridge, Mass.: Harvard University Press, 1972); K. R. Veenhof, ed., *Cuneiform Archives and Libraries* (Leiden: Nederlands Historisch-Archaeologisch Instituut te Istanbul, 1986).

257 Middle Assyrian archives can belong to a year, a lifetime, or a career in the service of one or more kings. There are royal archives from the Neo-Assyrian period covering the entire reign of Sargon or the succession from

Sennacherib to Esarhaddon and Assurbanipal (see J. N. Postgate, "Administrative Archives from the City of Assur in the Middle Assyrian Period," and S. Parpola, "The Royal Archives of Nineveh," in *Cuneiform Archives and Libraries*, ed. Veenhof, 168–83, 223–40). The best-known personal and family archives are from Nippur and Elephantine (see R. Zadok, "Archives from Nippur in the first Millennium B.C.," in *Cuneiform Archives and Libraries*, ed. Veenhof, 278–88; B. Porten, *Archives from Elephantine: The Life of an Ancient Jewish Military Colony* [Berkeley: University of California Press, 1968]).

258 See K. R. Veenhof, "Cuneiform Archives: An Introduction," in *Cuneiform Archives and Libraries*, ed. Veenhof, 1–35.

259 See W. H. Van Soldt, "The Palace Archives at Ugarit," in *Cuneiform Archives and Libraries*, ed. Veenhof, 196–204; O. Pedersén, "The Libraries in the City of Assur," in *Keilschriftliche Literaturen: Ausgewählte Vorträge der XXXII. Rencontre Assyriologique Internationale, Münster, 8.-12.7.1985*, ed. K. Hecker and W. Sommerfeld (Berlin: Dietrich Reimer, 1986) 143–47.

260 See W. G. Lambert, "A Late Assyrian Catalogue of Literary and Scholarly Texts," in *Cuneiform Studies in Honor of Samuel Noah Kramer*, ed. B. L. Eichler (Neukirchen-Vluyn: Neukirchener Verlag, 1976) 313–18; S. Parpola, "Assyrian Library Records," *JNES* 42 (1983) 1–30.

261 See A. Archi, "Position of the Tablets of Ebla," *Or* 57 (1988) 67–69, pls. I–III. A Neo-Babylonian archive from Sippar contained tablets aligned in the same way and kept in niches constructed in the walls of a small storeroom (*Iraq* 49 [1987] 248–49).

262 M. W. Stolper, *Entrepreneurs and Empire: The Murasu Archive, the Murasu Firm, and Persian Rule in Babylonia* (Leiden: Nederlands Historisch-Archaeologisch Instituut te Istanbul, 1985).

263 See Postgate, "Administrative Archives," 170.

264 See J. Nougayrol, *Ugaritica V* (Paris: Imprimerie Nationale, 1968) 41–251.

265 See Stolper, *Entrepreneurs and Empire*, 23–24.

266 See B. Porten and J. C. Greenfield, "The Aramaic Papyri from Hermopolis," *ZAW* 80 (1968) 216–31; J. Naveh, "The Paleography of the Hermopolis Papyri," *Israel Oriental Studies* 1 (1971) 120–22; B. Porten, *Textbook of Aramaic Documents from Ancient Egypt, 1: Letters* (Winona Lake, Ind.: Eisenbrauns, 1986) 9–23.

267 Jehoahaz (Shallum, 22:11) and Jehoiachin (Coniah, Jeconiah, 22:24; 24:1; 37:1) are mentioned, but the archive revolves around the thirteenth year of Josiah (1:2; 25:3), the first, fourth, and fifth years of Jehoiakim (1:3; 22:18; 25:1; 26:1; 27:1; 35:1; 36:1, 9; 37:1; 46:2), and the first, fourth, and

ninth to eleventh years of Zedekiah (1:3; 21:1; 24:8; 27:3; 28:1; 32:1; 34:2, 8; 37:1; 38:5; 39:1, 2; 49:34; 51:59; 52:1, 4, 5). The time after the fall of Jerusalem shows how Jeremiah's condemnation of everyone who was left in Judah and Jerusalem worked, and it is included under the rubric of the fourth year of Jehoiakim (45:1).

268 The full range of events is anticipated at the beginning (1:1–3). It starts in the reign of Josiah (1:2; 3:6), ends with the reign of Zedekiah (chaps. 21–24), and contains a retrospective to the reigns of the intervening kings (22:1–30).

269 There are similar visions in 1:11–19 and 24:1–10. In the introduction there is a reference to the end of Zedekiah's reign that in the conclusion coincides with the end of the nation (1:3, *'aḏ tōm*; 24:10, *'aḏ tummām*).

270 The reference to the remnant left in the land (24:8) is a link to the second part (chaps. 25–39), which is concerned mainly with this postdeportation period. The reference to those who live in Egypt and to those who are scattered among the nations (24:8–9) introduces the major theme of the third part (chaps. 40–52).

271 Frequent reference to Josiah (25:1; 26:1; 27:1; 36:1; 37:1) keeps attention on Jeremiah's call in the thirteenth year of his reign (25:3).

272 The first five and the last five chapters (25–29; 35–39) cover the reigns of Jehoiakim and Zedekiah and reflect one another in many ways, including reference to the fourth year of the king who rejected the words of Jeremiah (25:1; 36:1). The middle chapters move ahead seventy years (25:12; 29:10) to the mystical time of the new covenant (chaps. 30–31) and back through real time to the reign of Zedekiah (chaps. 32–34).

273 There are oracles concerning Judah and Egypt (chaps. 44–45) and concerning Egypt and Nebuchadnezzar (chap. 46), both focusing on the fourth year of Jehoiakim (45:1; 46:2), on the nations and Nebuchadnezzar (47:1–49:33), and on Nebuchadnezzar and Babylon (49:34–51:64).

274 Jeremiah 11–13 (cf. 11:21–23); 18–20 (compare 20:14–18 and 1:5); 32–33 (cf. 32:6–15); 34:8–22, 46 (compare 46:2, 10 and 13:1–11 on the symbolism of the Euphrates); 49:34–51:64.

275 Compare chaps. 7–10; 14–17; 21–24 with 30–31; 34:1–7; 35–39 and with 44–45; 47:1–49:33; 52.

276 Jer 1:1–3 contains biographical and historical information and summarizes the point of the book and the time that it covers. Jer 25:3 refers to 1:2 and by implication situates the words recorded in chaps. 1–24 between the thirteenth year of Josiah and the fourth year of Jehoiakim. Jeremiah 26 redoes chap. 7 in a biographical mode. Jer 25:13 mentions Jeremiah's oracles against the nations as a separate book that he wrote, and 25:17–26 gives a list

of the nations that are mentioned in the third part. Jer 40:1–6 repeats 39:11–14. Chapter 52 is the story suggested in 1:3 and interpreted in the rest of the archive.

277 The standard formula contains a subordinate relative clause (*haddābār 'ăšer hāyâ 'el yirmĕyāhû [mē'ēt yhwh] [lē'mōr]*) and occurs in 7:1; 11:1; 18:1; 21:1; 25:1; 30:1; 32:1; 34:1; 34:8; 35:1; 40:1; 44:1; without *mē'ēt yhwh* in 25:1 and 44:1, without *lē'mōr* in 40:1. The peculiar variant has no antecedent to the relative clause and clearly supposes the standard form without which it would be bizarre (*'ăšer hāyâ dĕbar yhwh ['el yirmĕyāhû] [hannābî']*): it occurs in 1:2; 14:1; 46:1; 47:1; 49:34; without *hannābî'* in 14:1; without *yirmĕyāhû hannābî'* in 1:2. The other expressions belong to the archive's system of shorthand and jargon, which it injected into the text, in endless variations, combinations, and accumulations, in order to relate individual elements to the beginning of the archive and to the ongoing development of the argument: *wayhî dĕbar yhwh 'ēlay / 'el yirmĕyāhû / hannābî' / lē'mōr* (passim); date + *hāyâ haddābār hazzeh mē'ēt yhwh lē'mōr* (26:1; 27:10); *haddābār 'ăšer dibbēr yirmĕyāhû hannābî' 'el bārûk* (45:1). The use of the headings was pointed out by R. E. Caldwell, "Formulaic and Literary Structure in Jer 1:1–19 (M.A. thesis, University of Toronto, 1985).

278 The dockets are 1:1–3; 7:1–2; 11:1–2; 14:1; 18:1–2; 21:1–2; 25:1–3; 30:1–3; 32:1–5; 34:1; 34:8–11; 35:1–2; 40:1–4; 44:1; 46:1–2; 47:1; 49:34.

279 *'al dibrê habbaṣṣārôt* introduces chaps. 14–17.

280 The docket (18:2, *qûm wĕyāradtā bêt hayyôṣēr*) introduces chaps. 18–20. It is taken up in a redundant statement at the top of the second column (19:1, *baqbuq yôṣēr hāreś*), and this statement is taken up toward the end of the column (19:10) and leads into the next column.

281 The plural imperative (11:2, *šim'û 'et dibrê habbĕrît hazzō't*) is not addressed to Jeremiah but anticipates what he is supposed to say to Judah and Jerusalem (11:6) and leads from there to the fact that they did not listen and that Yahweh did not listen to them, and so on.

282 The introduction (8:4, *wĕ'āmartā 'ălêhem*) hangs in the air in its immediate context but follows naturally on the ending of the first book (6:27–28).

283 The pair includes chaps. 11–13 and 14–17. On nonintercession, cf. 11:14–17 and 14:11–12; on the agents of destruction, cf. 11:18–23; 12:1–13; and 14:13–16; 15:1–4; on the disobedience of the fathers, cf. 11:1–13 and 14:17–22; 16:1–8.

284 The first Pashhur (20:1–6) is integral to the argument of the fifth book, but the second (21:1) is totally tangential. A similar join occurs between the end of the fourth book, which forbids work on the sabbath (17:19–27, *'ăśâ mĕlā'kâ*) and the beginning of the fifth, where Jeremiah encounters a potter working on his wheel (18:3, *'ōśeh mĕlā'kâ*).

285 Cf. *šāb šĕbût*, 29:14; 30:3, 18; 31:23.

286 The introduction to the third book (32:1–5) quotes the oracle that prompted Zedekiah to imprison Jeremiah, but the oracle is not delivered until the fourth (34:1–7). In this part of the archive, chronology is fluid and vague. Books in the biographical system (chaps. 25–29; 32–33; 34:8–22) follow each other in chronological order but mesh with the books in the historical system, which do not (chaps. 30–31; 34:1–7; 35–39). The first book moves from the fourth year of Jehoiakim (25:1) to his first (26:1; 27:1), to the first year of Zedekiah (27:3; 28:1) and back to some indeterminate time after the exile of Jehoiachin (29:2). In the last book (chaps. 35–39), which belongs to the historical system but redoes the same period, events are recorded in chronological order from the beginning of Jehoiakim's reign to the end of the reign of Zedekiah. The flux suits the editor's attempt to redate the last part of Jeremiah's prophecy to a time when it could still seem reasonable and true.

287 Cf. 34:21 (*hā'ōlîm*) and 35:11 (*ba'ălôt*).

288 A column is a unit of writing and might be a page, a leaf, or a sheet of wood or papyrus (A. R. Millard, "An Assessment of the Evidence for Writing in Ancient Israel," in *Biblical Archaeology Today: Proceedings of the International Congress on Biblical Archaeology, Jerusalem, April 1984*, ed. A. Biran (Jerusalem: Israel Exploration Society, 1985) 301–12, esp. 307.

289 Uniformity apparently was not a characteristic of literary works, libraries, or archives. The Ugaritic Baal cycle, for instance, comprises six tablets written by the same scribe and distinguished by his handwriting, but they are all of different colors and sizes and textures—the largest more than three times the size of the smallest—with four, six, or eight columns and an irregular number of lines (see A. Herdner, *Corpus des Tablettes en cunéiformes alphabétiques* [Paris, 1963] 1, 5, 12–13, 21, 31, 37).

290 The top and bottom of columns are not their opening or closing words but their first and last strophes or paragraphs.

291 In literary texts that extend over a series of tablets, the tablets are joined by anticipating at the end of one the first line or a few words from the first lines of the next (Hunger, *Babylonische und assyrische Kolophone*, 1–2).

292 *hay yhwh*.

293 Cf. 5:2 (*lšqr*) and 5:31 (*bšqr*); 5:9 = 5:29.

294 Jer 1:18, *barzel, nĕḥōšet* = 6:28.

295 Jer 2:1, *n'rm, 'kl*; cf. 3:24–25.

296 The first and second columns are linked by key words: 18:1–6 (*bêt hayyôṣēr* [twice], *hayyôṣēr* [three times]); 19:1 (*baqbuq yôṣēr ḥāreś*); 19:10–11

(*baqbuq . . . yôṣēr . . . tōpet*); 19:14–15 (*tōpet*). The last column is linked to the second by a key word (19:14; 20:1, *bêt yhwh*) and by a deictic reference (20:1, "Pashhur heard . . . Jeremiah prophesying *these things . . .*").

297 Cf. 25:1; 26:1; 27:1 [LXX omits]; 28:1; 29:1. The top of the fourth column (28:1) refers explicitly to the top of the third (27:1). The text makes better archival than historical sense.

298 Jer 35:1 and 35:18–19; 36:1–3 and 36:32; 37:4 and 38:28; cf. 38:28 and 39:1–3.

299 Cf. 44:1 (*haddābār 'ăšer hāyâ 'el yirměyāhû 'el kol hayyěhûdîm . . .*) and 45:1 (*haddābār 'ăšer dibbēr yirměyāhû hannābî' 'el bārûk ben nēriyyâ*).

300 Cf. 8:23 (*mî yittēn*) and 9:1 (*mî yittěnēnî*).

301 The key word is *gôyim* (9:24–25; 10:2, 24–25).

302 The key words are *špṭ, ṣdq, rîb, yd', r'h* (11:18–20; 12:1–3).

303 Cf. 11:3; 12:14; 13:1 (*koh 'āmar yhwh*).

304 The intervening text (30:23–24) repeats 23:19–20 and is part of the archival system by which the second part is filled with references to the first.

305 Jer 14:7–8, 20–22 (*'wn, ḥṭ', miqwēh* [in two different senses]).

306 The expression *hā'ām hazzeh* is repeated at the beginning and the end of the column (15:1–4, 19–21). Jeremiah is prevented from interceding for the people in 14:11–16 and 15:1–4.

307 Cf. 16:19–21; 17:1–4 (fathers and sons).

308 Cf. 14:2; 17:19–27 (*šě'ārêhā*).

309 The intervening material (23:1–4) is a résumé of the condemnation of the kings. It has links with the bottom of the first column: 23:2b (*hiněnî pōqēd 'ălêkem 'et rōa' ma'alělêkem ně'ūm yhwh*) = 21:14a (cf. 23:2, 4 and 21:12b [*pqd*]); 21:13b (*mî yēḥat 'ālênû*) and 23:4b (*lō' yēḥattû*). Its main links are to the last column (cf. 23:1–4 and 24:5–6, 10).

310 Cf. 21:1–2 and 24:1 (two invasions of Nebuchadnezzar); 24:1 and 24:8 (kings and princes).

311 Cf. 34:8, 17 (*děrôr*); 46:1–12 refers to Nebuchadnezzar's defeat of the Egyptians at Carchemish, and 46:13–28 refers to the invasion of Egypt by Nebuchadnezzar.

312 Cf. 49:34 and 49:39; 50:1 and 50:45; 51:1 and 51:59–64; 52:1–34 and 51:59–64.

313 On figure 11 paragraphs and strophes are on successive lines and their pairing is indicated by single spacing within a pair and by double spacing between pairs.

314 Jer 11:1–8 (Israel), 9–13 (Judah and Jerusalem).

315 The paraphrase revolves around 7:22–26. The quotations from the first part occur at the beginning (11:2b = 4:3–4) and at the end (11:12, 13 = 2:28). The references to Micah (11:11a, 11b) combine two related texts (Mic 2:3; 3:4). The expression "to comfirm the oath . . . to your fathers" (11:5) is borrowed from the Deuteronomistic version of the promise to Abraham (Gen 26:3).

316 Jer 11:14a = 7:16; 11:15aA (*bĕbêtî*), cf. 7:2, 10–11; 11:17aA (*nṭᶜ*) = 1:10; 11:17b = 7:9.

317 Jer 12:14–15, 16–17, cf. 1:10; Jer 12:14, cf. 2:7; Jer 12:16; cf. 4:2 and 5:2.

318 Jer 13:3, *wayhî dĕbar yhwh ᵓēlay šēnît lᵉᵓmōr* = 1:13aA. Jer 13:10; cf. 7:6, 9, 24.

319 The formulas occur at the beginning and end of the strophe (2:1–2aA, 3bB). References to the original text include the journey through the wilderness (2:2bA = 2:6b), the time of their youth (2:2aB; cf. 3:24), and being devoured (2:3b; cf. 3:24). The summary of the poem is derived less from the poem itself than from its source in Hosea (cf. Hos 2:16, 17; 8:7; 9:4, 10). The combination of an address to a woman (Jer 2:2) with talk about a man (2:3) reflects the end of Jeremiah's poem, where this alternation of gender dramatizes the reunion of Rachel and Jacob and their children (cf. chaps. °30–31°). Terminology like that of the first column includes *nᶜr, qdš, rᶜh, bwᵓ* (cf. 1:5–6, 15–16).

320 The strophe (2:7–8) begins with a deictic (2:7aA, *ᵓetkem*) referring to the beginning of the preceding strophe (2:5, *ᵓabôtêkem*) and repeats the word *ᵓ ereṣ* that occurs at the end of the preceding strophe (cf. 2:7 and 2:6b). The second stanza (2:8) starts with an expression from the preceding strophe (2:8aA = 2:6aA) and closes with a word (2:8bB, *yôᶜīlû*) from the original (2:11b, *yôᶜîl*) but uses it in a forensic sense (*hlk ᵓaḥărê*).

321 The text (Jer 2:19b) clashes with its context (2:19a) by referring to Yahweh in the first person rather than the third person singular. It is inserted by means of deictic pronominal suffixes and by the formula *nᵉᵓūm*. The significance of the name *yhwh ṣĕbāᵓôt* is explained in the poem at the end of the second book (10:1–16).

322 The strophes (2:26–30) are inserted via deictics (2:26b) and by quoting, as the context does, what the culprits say (*ᵓmr*, 2:27; cf. 2:25, 31). The intrusion of the strophes required a transition to the original text, and this is

effected by other deictic expressions (2:31aA, *baddôr ʾattem rěʾû děbar yhwh*): the first expression is normal (*baddôr*; cf. 7:29), and the second (*ʾattem*) fits the original text into the plural context of the intrusive strophes (2:29–30), but together they are boldly out of place. The last expression ("See the word of Yahweh") is just as striking and suggests that the transition was made to be noticed. The strophes contain numerous allusions to the introductory column and anticipations of the original text that follows (e.g., 2:30, *mûsār lōʾ lāqāḥû* = 5:3; 2:30b *kěʾaryeh mašḥît* = 4:7a).

323 The archive added 2:34 by repeating a word (*gam*; cf. 2:33b) and by forging a deictic transition to the original continuation of the poem (2:34, *kî ʿal kol ʾēlleh*). The transition is forced and emphasizes the addition.

324 Jer 3:6–18 takes material from the preceding (3:1–5) and following (3:19–24) text and rephrases it in technical or familiar terms taken from Hosea, Ezekiel, and the Deuteronomistic History. It is linked to the preceding especially by reference to what Israel did (*ʿśh*, 3:5, 6, 7).

325 In the poem the children respond to Yahweh and admit they have done wrong in going after Baal (3:22–24). The last stanza repeats three of their words (3:25, "shame," "youth," and "fathers"; cf. 3:24) and concludes the column on the note of continuing guilt.

326 The strophe (4:1–4) is mainly an archival reference linking this column to the preceding and following columns. Its first stanza (4:1–2) is directed to Israel and, by reference to Hosea (cf. Hos 2:4; 7:13; 9:3, 17), summarizes the conditions under which it might return to Yahweh. The second is addressed to the South and, by reference to Amos (Jer 4:4b; cf. Amos 5:6), Hosea (Jer 4:3; cf. Hos 10:8, 12), and the Deuteronomist (Jer 4:4a; cf. Deut 10:16), sets out the conditions of its survival.

327 The strophe (4:9–12) is attached by the formula "It will happen on that day, says Yahweh . . . ," which refers to the whole preceding context rather than to anything in particular.

328 The stanza (4:26) begins like the others ("I looked . . . , and behold . . ."). It refers to an addition in the second column (cf. 2:7) and uses key terms from the first column (*wěkol ʿārāyw nittěṣû*; cf. 1:10 [*ntṣ*], 15 [*kol ʿārê yěhûdâ*]).

329 The lines (5:2) begin with the conjunction that began the preceding clauses (*wěʾim*; cf. 5:1) and with the name Yahweh, which begins the second stanza in Jeremiah's version (5:3).

330 The strophe (5:7–9) begins with a deictic that refers to the general context (5:7, *ʾê lāzōʾt*) and with words from the beginning of the column (5:7, *ʾeslaḥ lāk . . . wayyiššāběʿû*; cf. 5:1, 2).

331 The strophe (5:13–14) was added by loading it with deictics (5:13,

"And *the* prophets have become wind, and *the* word is not in them, *thus* it will be done to them. . . . Since *you* say *this* word . . . *I* . . . and *this* people . . .") in imitation of the preceding stanza (5:11–12). The second stanza also ends on the note (5:14b, *hinĕnî*) that begins the next strophe (5:15a, *hinĕnî*).

332 The strophe (5:18–19) is inserted with indefinite deictics that refer vaguely to the context ("And even in those days, says Yahweh, . . . and if you say 'Why has Yahweh our God done all these things to us?' . . .").

333 The strophe (5:29–31) begins with the refrain "For all *these* things should I not punish, says Yahweh, against a nation *such as this*, should I not avenge myself?" The deictics fit it into the context.

334 The first stanza (6:6) is attached to a strophe (6:3b–5) that describes besiegers launching attacks against the city: it is introduced by a deictic formula ("For thus says Yahweh of Hosts"), supposes the Deuteronomistic laws of siege warfare (6:6a, *kirĕtû 'ēṣâ*; cf. Deut 20:19–20), and concludes with deictics and a paraphrase of the refrain (6:6b, "*This is the city* that has to be punished, *all of it*, oppression inside *it*"; cf. 5:9, 29; 9:8). The second stanza (6:9) is introduced by the same deictic formula and contains a pun on the following text (6:9a, *'ôlēl yĕ'ôlĕlû*; cf. 6:11, *'ôlāl*).

335 The strophe (6:13–15) is attached to the text by repetition (6:13a, *kî* = 6:12b) and deictic pronominal suffixes (6:13a, "From the least *of them* to the greatest *of them*, each one *of them* . . . each one *of them* . . ."). The strophe is composed almost entirely of variations on familiar themes: Jeremiah has just talked about the great and the small (6:13a; cf. 5:4–5); prophets and priests have been singled out from the beginning (6:13b; cf. 1:18; 2:8); the opposition prophets promised peace (6:14, cf. 4:10); Jeremiah had announced a crushing defeat (*šeber*, 4:6; 6:14); shame and humiliation and punishment belong to his opponents (6:15; cf. 2:26; 3:25; 5:9, 29; 6:6). The rest of the material is borrowed from Isaiah and Hosea.

336 The text (6:27–30) owes a lot to Isaiah (Jer 6:28aAb; cf. Isa 1:4; 30:8) and to the original text of Jeremiah (6:28aB, *holĕkê rākîl*; cf. 9:3, *rākîl yahălōk*) but is constructed as an archival marker relating the end of Book I to its beginning (1:18). Thus "An assayer I have made you (*nĕtattîkā*) of my people—a fortified city" (6:27a) corresponds to the paradigm's "And I, today, have made you a fortified city . . . to the people of the land" (1:18, *nĕtattîkā . . . lĕ'îr mibṣār*). Similarly, "All of them . . . go around slandering—bronze and iron" (6:28) refers to the same text in which the fortified city is defended by walls of bronze and buttressed by an iron pillar (1:18). The two parentheses—a fortified city, bronze and iron—do not quite fit their separate contexts, but they belong together and fit the column into the perspective of the archive.

337 The column begins with a general deictic and formulaic link to the paradigm (8:1, "At that time, says Yahweh . . ."), and its opening paragraphs (8:1–3) simply continue the discussion initiated in the paradigm (7:1–34). The next clause (8:4, "And say to them") does not follow on these paragraphs but bypasses the paradigm and continues where the preceding book left off

(cf. 6:27–30). A whole strophe is repeated (8:10–12 = 6:13–15) to emphasize the continuity with the preceding book.

338 The sending of serpents to bite them (8:17, *kî binĕnî mĕšallēaḥ bākem nĕḥāšîm . . . wĕniššĕkû ʾetkem*) is a quotation from an incident in the wilderness recounted by the Deuteronomist (Num 21:4–9, *wayšallaḥ yhwh bāʿām ʾet hannĕḥāšîm . . . wayĕnaššĕkû ʾet hāʿām*). The people ask Moses to intercede (Num 21:7), as Jeremiah is prevented from doing (7:16), and Moses makes them the bronze serpent to charm the snakes, as this text excludes charms against the serpents.

339 The strophe (9:6–8) has three stanzas: the first (9:6) has deictic pronominal suffixes referring to the preceding context and a cross-reference to the end of the first book (9:6aB, *binĕnî ṣôrĕpām ûbĕḥantîm*; cf. 6:27b, 29b); the second (9:7) quotes from the preceding context (*lĕšônām mirmâ ðibbēr* = 9:4b–5; *ʾet rēʿēhû yĕðabbēr* = 9:3–4a; in 9:2 their tongue is a bow, in 9:7 it is an arrow); the third is the refrain that began in the first book (9:8 = 5:9, 29).

340 The whole passage (9:13–25) is affixed to the original by repeating its last word (9:13, *wayyēlĕkû* = 9:12, *wĕlōʾ hālĕkû bāh*). It is filled with quotations from columns 1–3 and has references to the preceding book (9:20b; cf. 6:11) and to later parts (9:25; cf. 25:24; 49:32).

341 The poem (10:1–16) follows on an editorial insertion (9:13–25) and needs no further editorial justification. It is tied to the end of the preceding column by their common reference to the nations (9:25; 10:2). The additions (10:21, 23) are stanzas that redivide an original strophe (10:22, 24–25) and separate it from its antecedent. Both contain allusions to the poem's condemnation of those who worship idols (cf. 10:5, 14). The first takes up themes from the beginning of the first book (10:21; cf. 2:8; 3:15).

342 The heading (30:1) marks the beginning of the book. The date (30:3a, "Behold the days are coming . . .") links the book to the interval predicted in the preceding column (29:10 = 25:12). The docket (30:2b, "Write all the words I have spoken to you in a book") has archival significance (cf. 36:2a) and resembles the instructions that Moses received after the covenant ceremony on Sinai (Exod 34:27). The transition from this paragraph to the original text of Jeremiah's poem (30:4, *wĕʾelleh haddĕbārîm ʾăšer ðibber yhwh ʾel yiśrāʾēl wĕʾel yĕhûðâ*) recalls the words of the covenant in the epic and in the sequel's account (*ʾelleh haddĕbārîm*, Exod 34:27; Deut 1:1a). The transition, formal and artificial, is the only connection between the text and the label that situates it in the archive.

343 Jeremiah says that Jacob will be saved from the great day of Yahweh (30:7a, *hôy kî gāðôl hayyôm hahûʾ . . . ûmimmennâ yiwwāšēaʿ*), and the archive introduces the new era as beginning from that predestined day (30:8, *wĕhāyâ bayyôm hahûʾ*).

344 The strophes (30:18–24) are introduced with the same formula (30:18,

koh 'āmar yhwh) that began the material they were designed to interpret (30:12a, *kî koh 'āmar yhwh*), and they begin with the formula that resumes the archive's point (30:18, *hinĕnî šāb šĕbût*; cf. 30:3). The strophes are constructed from Deuteronomistic notions. Although the apostate city is supposed to remain a tell forever (Deut 13:17), Jerusalem will be rebuilt on its tell (30:18b). Although Jacob comprised few people, he became a great people (30:19; Deut 26:5). His ruler will be chosen from among his people (30:21; Deut 17:15). Only the Levites chosen by Yahweh can approach and draw near (30:21; cf. Num 18:3, 7, 22).

345 The strophe (31:10–14) begins like the strophe that it interprets (cf. 31:7–9).

346 The first of these strophes (31:23–26) begins with formulas that refer to the beginning of the book (cf. 30:1–4) and ends with the insinuation that what it says about the time to come, that is, its interpretation of what Jeremiah had to say, is a dream or came to the writer when asleep (31:26). The second strophe (31:27–30) resumes the opening paradigm in a positive sense (cf. 1:10). The third strophe (31:31–34) replaces the covenant that the third book repudiated (cf. chaps. 11–13). The fourth (31:35–37) takes back the earlier warnings (cf. 5:22). In the last the city is rebuilt and all the threats are withdrawn (31:38–40).

347 On figure 12 acts and scenes are indicated as such. Strophes are marked by letters (A, B, C . . .). Stanzas are numbered (1, 2, 3 . . .).

348 The strophes (2:4–6, 9–13) contain numerous quotations and allusions to Hosea. (The quotations are marked by the formula *nĕ'um yhwh* [see Caldwell; "Formulaic and Literary Structure"], but the allusions are embedded in complete texts and are not emphasized.) The idea of leaving Yahweh and going after vanity and becoming vain (2:5b) is based on Hosea's description of Israel leaving Yahweh to go after her lovers (Hos 2:7). The contrast between the wilderness and the land (2:6b) was expressed in many ways in Hosea, including by the image of turning the land into a wilderness (cf. Jer 2:6b, *bammidbar . . . bĕ'ereṣ ṣiyyâ*; Hos 2:5b, *wĕśamtîhā kammidbār wĕšattîhā kĕ'ereṣ ṣiyyâ*). The case against the parents and the children is a retrial (Jer 2:9, *lākēn 'ōd 'ārîb 'ittĕkem nĕ'um yhwh wĕ'et bĕnê bĕnêkem 'ārîb*) and supposes the trial that Hosea described involving the land of Israel and her children (Hos 2:4, 6, *rîbû bĕ'immĕkem rîbû . . . wĕ'et bānêhā lō' 'ărāḥēm*; cf. Hos 4:1). The charge of changing Gods and leaving Yahweh for somebody else was also expressed in Hosea (2:10b–11, 13b; cf. Hos 4:7, 10).

349 The speaker is Yahweh, who, in the mood of the soliloquy, also refers to himself in the third person (2:17, 19a). The distinction between slaves and dependents (2:14a) may owe something to the Priestly rules of circumcision (cf. Gen 17:12, 13, 23, 27). The description of the invasion (2:14b, 15abA) repeats words and expressions from Isaiah's description of the invasion of Sennacherib (cf. Isa 1:7; 5:29; 10:5–6). The last stanza in the third strophe (2:16–17), "Now the people of Memphis and Daphne shake their heads at you and say 'Didn't this happen to you because you abandoned Yahweh your

God at the time he was leading you on the way?' ") refers to the first strophe's image of the wilderness wanderings (2:6b) and to the second strophe's charge of abandoning Yahweh (2:13b). The fourth strophe is constructed from references to Hosea: the first stanza condemns Israel's alliances with Egypt and Assyria (2:18; cf. Hos 5:11; 7:11); the second explains that the invasion is a lesson for having abandoned Yahweh (2:19a; cf. Hos 4:10); and the third lists their ritual wrongs (2:20; cf. Hos 4:13, 18; 10:11).

350 The first strophe (2:21–22) combines the unlikely images of a vine gone wild and of stains that will not wash out. The first is based on a quotation from Isaiah's Song of the Vineyard (Jer 2:21, *nĕṭaʿtîk śōrēq* = Isa 5:2), and the second combines an allusion to an earlier text in Isaiah (2:22; cf. Isa 1:18–20) with a quotation from Hosea (Jer 2:22b, *niktām ʿăwōnēk lĕpānāy*; cf. Hos 7:1, 2, *ʿāwōn . . . neged pānāy bāyû*): the quotation is marked by the formula "Says the Lord Yahweh" (2:22b). The second strophe is filled with quotations from Hosea: Jer 2:23 (*lōʾ niṭmēʾtî*), cf. Hos 5:3 (*niṭmāʾ yiśrāʾēl*); Jer 2:23 (*ʾaḥărê habbĕʿālîm lōʾ hālaktî*), cf. Hos 2:6, 15 (*ʾēlĕkâ ʾaḥărê mĕʾahăbay . . . habbĕʿālîm*); Jer 2:24 (*pereh limmud midbār*), cf. Hos 8:9 (*pereʾ bôdēd lô*); Jer 2:24b (*mĕbaqšêhā . . . bĕḥodšāh yimṣāʾûnĕhā*), cf. Hos 2:9, 13 (*ûbiqšātam wĕlōʾ timṣāʾ . . . ḥodšāh*); Jer 2:25 (*miṣṣimʾâ*), cf. Hos 2:5 (*baṣṣāmāʾ*); Jer 2:25 ("Because I have loved strangers and after them I will go"), cf. Hos 2:7; 5:7 ("I will go after my lovers"; "They have given birth to the children of strangers"). The image of Israel as an animal in heat (2:23b–24a) is a transposition of Hosea's image of Israel as a beautiful unbroken heifer (Hos 4:16; 10:11).

351 The first stanza (2:31aBb) is the reverse of the first strophe (2:4–6). Instead of being led by Yahweh through the wilderness and a land of shadows, the people think of him as a desert and a land of deep darkness. There they left him without a word, and here they have a reason for not returning. The second stanza (2:32) also refers indirectly to the same strophe. It combines a statement on the husband-and-wife relationship between Yahweh and the land with a reference to the people forgetting Yahweh from time immemorial (2:32b, *wĕʿammî šĕkēḥûnî yāmîm ʾên mispār*), which the first strophe defined as the time of the exodus and wilderness wanderings. In Hosea Yahweh's wife forgets him (Hos 2:15), and he woos her by taking her back to time immemorial in the wilderness (Hos 2:17). The second strophe (2:33, 35–37) refers again to Israel going after her lovers (2:33; cf. Hos 2:7) and includes an allusion to Isaiah's statement that Judah would be ashamed of its useless alliances with Egypt (2:11b, 36; cf. Isa 30:5).

352 The first strophe (3:1) is filled with allusions to Hosea (cf. Hos 1:2; 2:4, 7–9) and is the literary basis of legislation in Deut 24:1–4. See J. D. Martin, "The Forensic Background to Jeremiah 3:1," *VT* 19 (1969) 82–92; T. R. Hobbs, "Jeremiah 3:1–5 and Deuteronomy 24:1–4," *ZAW* 84 (1974) 23–29; R. Westbrook, "The Prohibition on Restoration of Marriage in Deuteronomy 24:1–4," in *Studies in Bible 1986*, ed. S. Japhet (Scripta Hierosolymitana 31; Jerusalem: Magnes, 1986) 386–405. The second strophe (3:2–3) sums up the same themes, has one other allusion to Hosea (Jer 3:3a; cf. Hos 6:3), and relates this scene to the first scene (3:2; cf. 2:23).

353 In a similar vein Hosea left the metaphor of marriage (Hosea 1–2°) for the metaphor of Yahweh as loving parent (Hosea 11–13°). The third strophe (Jer 3:4–5) alludes to the latter text (3:4b, *'allûp nĕ'ûray 'attâ*; cf. Hos 11:1, *kî na'ar yiśrā'ēl*). The fourth strophe (3:19–20) continues the metaphor of parenting, in which the bond between Yahweh and Israel might be renewed, but returns to the metaphor of marriage, and a text from Hosea, to describe the country's infidelity (3:20; cf. Hos 5:7).

354 The fifth strophe (3:21–22) resembles Hosea's picture of the people returning so that Yahweh might heal them (cf. Hos 6:1–3). The sixth strophe describes Israel's past in terms taken from Hosea: as they return the children admit that the mountains and hills were a delusion (3:23a; cf. 2:20b) just as Hosea thought they were (Hos 4:13a). They also admit that their sins, their dedication to Baal, have deprived them of their wealth and so make amends for Jacob, who thought that his wealth was secure and that his sin would not be discovered (3:24a; cf. Hos 12:9b; 13:1); part of this wealth was their sheep and cattle and their sons and daughters whom they lost in their worship of Baal (3:24b; cf. Hos 5:6–7; 9:12–14, 16–17).

355 The announcement that Yahweh is bringing evil from the north (4:6b, *kî rā'â 'ānōkî mēbî' miṣṣāpôn wĕšeber gādôl*) and the call to wail and weep (4:8a, *sipdû wĕhêlîlû*) suppose Micah's argument with the people who thought that Jerusalem was exempt from evil (Mic 3:11, *lō' tābô' 'ālênu rā'â*; cf. Mic 1:8, 12; 2:2) and his call for lamentation (Mic 1:8, *'al zō't 'espĕdâ wĕ'êlîlâ*).

356 The vision of the land and its cities in ruins (4:7b) is like Isaiah's description of the land in ruins and its cities burned to the ground (Isa 1:7). The combination of the metaphor of a lion and the nonmetaphorical epithet "destroyer of nations" (4:7a) suggests Isaiah's two descriptions of the Assyrian advance, one in which they are like lions (Isa 5:29), the other in which they misunderstand their role as instruments of Yahweh and set out to destroy the world (Isa 10:7).

357 Isaiah (Isa 5:26, 28b) saw the army in the distance coming quickly, their horses' hooves like flint, their chariot wheels like the wind. Jeremiah sees the army coming from a distant country rising like a cloud, its chariots like the wind, its horses quicker than eagles (4:13a, 16a). Isaiah saw Zion besieged (Isa 1:8, *kĕ'îr nĕṣûrâ*), and Jeremiah refers to the invading army as besiegers (4:16a, *nōṣĕrîm*). Both blame the invasion on rebellion (*mrh*, 4:17b; Isa 1:20; 30:9). Micah criticizes the people who spend the night plotting evil (Mic 2:1, *hôy hōšĕbê 'āwen ûpō'ālê rā' 'al miškĕbôtām*), and Jeremiah tells Jerusalem to cleanse itself of the evil plots that spend the night in it (4:14, *rā'â . . . 'ad mātay tālîn bĕqirbēk mahšĕbôt 'ônēk*). Micah ridiculed the lament of the people (Mic 2:4, *šādôd nĕšaddûnû*) and Jeremiah quoted it (4:13b, *'ôy lānû kî šuddādĕnû*).

358 Much of the description (4:18–19, 20–22) is a natural development of what precedes in the scene: the city speaks and therefore refers to its walls (4:19), to the turmoil in its heart (4:19; cf. 4:14), to the sound of the trumpet (4:19; cf. 4:5) and the shouts of the troops (4:19; cf. 4:16b), to the destruction

that Yahweh brings (4:20; cf. 4:6) and the devastation it dreads (4:20; cf. 4:13), and to the speed of the advancing enemy (4:20; cf. 4:13). From Micah Yahweh's comments take the notion of evil lurking at the gates (Jer 4:18b; cf. Mic 1:9b, 12b) because of their evil deeds (4:18a; cf. Mic 3:4). From Isaiah he takes the fact that his people do not know and are children without insight (Jer 4:22, ʿammî / ʾôtî lōʾ yādāʿû / bānîm . . . wĕlōʾ nĕbônîm hēmmâ; cf. Isa. 1:2–3, bānîm . . . yiśrāʾēl lōʾ yādaʿ ʿammî lōʾ hitbonān).

359 The description (4:23–25) undoes the creation account (Gen 1:2–3, 20–26), but some elements of the description and of the comment on it suppose an acquaintance with Hosea: the fact that the earth grieves (Jer 4:28, ʿal zōʾt teʾĕbal hāʾāreṣ; cf. Hos 4:3, ʿal kēn teʾĕbal hāʾāreṣ); the inclusion of the mountains and hills (4:25; cf. Hos 4:13a); the specific mention of the birds of the heavens that have strayed (Jer 4:25b, wĕkol ʿôp haššāmayim nādādû; cf. Hos 4:3; 7:12–13, kĕʿôp haššāmayim ʾôrîdēm . . . kî nādĕdû mimmennî). The references to the Balaam oracles (Jer 4:28b, ʿal kî dibbartî zammōtî wĕlōʾ nihamtî wĕlōʾ ʾāšûb mimmennâ) confirm Yahweh's determination to do what he promised (Num 23:19–20, lōʾ . . . yitnehām . . . dibbēr . . . wĕlōʾ ʾăšîbennâ).

360 Isaiah and Hosea described divine discipline as beatings and wounds that would not heal (Isa 1:5–6, nkh, ḥlh) without Yahweh's care (Hos 5:13; 6:1), and Jeremiah notes that Yahweh beat them but they were not even wounded (5:3, hikkîtâ ʾōtām wĕlōʾ ḥālû). In Isaiah's vision the Assyrians were an instrument of instruction, and he described Yahweh speaking to his people in this foreign language that seemed to them like gibberish because they refused to hear his own words (Isa 28:11–12, ûbĕlāšôn ʾaḥeret yĕdabbēr ʾel hāʿām hazzeh . . . wĕlōʾ ʾābû šemōaʿ). Jeremiah described the invaders as a nation with a language so strange that the people would not be able to make out the words they said (5:15b, gôy lōʾ tēdaʿ lĕšōnô wĕlōʾ tišmaʿ māh yĕdabbēr).

361 Cf. Jer 5:6a (ʾaryēh miyyaʿar . . . yiṭṭārēp) and Amos 3:4 (hăyišʾag ʾaryēh bayyaʿar wĕṭerep ʾēn lô); 5:6b (kî rabbû pišʿêhem ʿāṣĕmû mĕšûbôtêhem) and Amos 5:12a (kî yādaʿtî rabbîm pišʿêkem waʿăṣûmîm ḥaṭṭōʾ têkem).

362 Hosea condemned the recalcitrance (Jer 5:11, bgd; cf. Hos 5:7) and lies (Jer 5:12 kḥš; cf. Hos 4:2; 10:13; 12:1) of the people. He also described Israel as a child that God raised and tried to teach and who sinned and refused to repent (Jer 5:3b, mēʾănû lāšûb = Hos 11:5).

363 According to Jerusalem, the lies that they told about Yahweh included "That is not what he is, no evil will come upon us" (5:12). In Micah's dispute with the people he notes that they refuse to believe that Yahweh does such things (Mic 2:6–7) or that evil will come upon them (Mic 3:11).

364 The text twice defines the law as the way of Yahweh, the judgment of their God (5:4b, 5a, derek yhwh mišpaṭ ʾĕlōhêhem). The Elohist has Moses sitting in judgment over the people (Exod 18:13, 16, špṭ), delivering the decrees and instructions of God (Exod 18:16, 20, ʾet ḥuqqê hāʾĕlōhîm wĕʾet tôrōtāyw) and making known to the people the way they should walk (Exod 18:20, ʾet hadderek). Allusions to this conception of the law are found in the eternal

decree that the sea cannot transgress (Jer 5:22, *ḥoq ʿôlām wĕlōʾ yaʿabrenhû*) and in the weeks decreed for the harvest (5:24, *šĕbuʿôt ḥuqqôt qāṣîr*). References to specific laws include not doing justice to the orphan (5:28a; cf. Exod 22:21) and the poor (5:28b = Exod 23:6) and transgressing the decrees with evil words (5:28a; cf. Exod 23:2a, 7a).

365 Cf. Jer. 4:18 (*ðarkēk ûmaʿălālayik ʿāśôh ʾelleh lāk / zōʾt rāʿātēk kî mār*) and 2:17 (*hălōʾ zōʾt taʿăśeh lāk / ʿozbēk ʾet yhwh ʾĕlōhayik*) and 2:19a (*kî raʿ wāmār ʿozbēk ʿet yhwh ʾĕlōhayik*).

366 Cf. Jer 5:3 (*ḥizzĕqû pĕnêhem missela mēʾănû lāšûb* and 3:3b (*ûmēṣaḥ ʾiššâ zônâ hāyâ lāk mēʾant hikkālēm*) and 3:22 (*šûbû bānîm šôbābîm*).

367 The archival additions and rearrangements were designed to squelch any sympathy for Zion. The introductory column (chap. 7) portrays the city as inveterately sinful, the prophet as totally unsympathetic, and Yahweh as completely intransigent. The final column (chap. 10) made Yahweh universal and transcendent and so far removed from the drama of life that professional mourners had to take up the slack (chap. 9).

368 The first stanza in act III (6:1) takes up the form and content of the first strophe in act II (4:5–6). The differences are in act III's references to specific places with real and symbolic significance. Tekoa (6:1a) is Amos's hometown (Amos 1:1), and his message is a foundation of the scene. Beth-haccherem is a possible allusion to Isaiah's image of Israel as the vineyard (*kerem*) of God (Isa 5:1–2), and the scene owes much to his vision. Jerusalem belonged to Benjamin, and the withdrawal of the tribe (cf. Mic 6:9) leaves the city and Judah alone.

369 The evil that comes from the north (6:1) is a development of the notion introduced by Micah (Mic 1:9, 12; 2:3; 3:11). The direct address to Zion (6:2, "Pasture and Darling [*mēʿunnāgâ*], you are perishing [*ðāmîtî*], Daughter of Zion") combines Micah's description of the darling children of Jerusalem (Mic 1:16; 2:9, *taʿănûgayik*), Isaiah's image of the precious vineyard being turned back into pasture (cf. Isa 5:4–5), and Hosea's expression of the ruin of Israel (Hos 4:6a, *niðmû ʿammî*). The shouts that are attributed to the besiegers include, perhaps, "Let each one shake his fist" (Jer 6:3b, *rāʿû ʾiš ʾet yāðô* [root: *yrʿ*; cf. 2:16], an allusion to the scene depicted by Isaiah (Isa 10:32, "This very day . . . he will shake his fist at . . . the daughter of Zion"); "make holy war against her" (6:4, *qaddĕšû ʿālêhā milḥāmâ* = Mic 3:5, *wĕqiððĕšû ʿālāyw milḥāmâ*]).

370 The beginning of the first stanza (6:7a) returns to the early image of a water reservoir (2:13b), and the notion of divine disgust (6:8a, *pen tēqaʿ napšî mimmēk*) plays on the name Tekoa and on the besiegers who pitch their tents (6:1, 3, *tqʿ*). The evil in the city was deplored by Micah (6:7a; cf. 2:1). Physical harm and violence were decried by Amos (Jer 6:7b, *hāmās wāšōð yiššāmaʿ bāh*; cf. Amos 3:10, *hāʾōṣĕrîm hāmās wāšōð*). Stripes and wounds were described by Isaiah (Jer 6:7b, *hŏlî ûmakkâ*, = Isa 1:5–6), and the sight of Israel's sin was denounced by Hosea (Jer 6:7b *ʿal pānāy tāmîð*; cf. Hos 7:2,

neqeḏ pānāy hāyū). The threat of total destruction restates a fact envisaged by Isaiah (Jer 6:8b, *šĕmāmâ*; cf. Isa 1:7).

371 As Micah protested that he was full of the power and the spirit of God (Mic 3:8, *wĕʾûlām ʾānōkî mālēʾtî . . .*), so Jeremiah protests that he is full of the wrath of God (6:11, *wĕʾet ḥămat yhwh mālēʾtî*). Micah complained about those who did evil to acquire houses and fields and portrayed Yahweh devising evil against his whole family including, as his adversaries said, the women and children (Mic 2:2–3, 9); Jeremiah says that he will pour his wrath on husbands and wives, women and children and their parents, and that they will lose their houses and fields (6:11–12).

372 In the Elohist version of the codification of the law, Moses made known to the people the path they should follow (Exod 18:20, *ʾet hadderek yēlĕkû bāh*), and in Jeremiah they are asked to look for this traditional way and walk in it (6:16, *ʾê zeh ḏerek haṭṭôb ûlĕkû bāh*). According to Isaiah the words that the people would not listen to included "This is your respite" (Isa 28:12, *wĕzōʾt hammargēʿâ*), and Yahweh notes that the people refused to walk in the way and find respite (Jer 6:16, *margôaʿ*). Hosea was the first to refer to the prophets, specifically himself, as God's watchmen (Jer 6:17, *ṣōpîm*; Hos 9:8, *ṣōpeh ʾeprayim ʿim ʾĕlōhay nābîʾ*).

373 The invocation (6:18–19, *lākēn šimʿû haggôyim ûḏĕʿî ʿēḏâ ʾet ʾăšer bām šimʿî hāʾāreṣ*, "Therefore, let the nations hear, let the assembly know with those who are among them") reproduces Micah's invocations to the world and to those who assembled in the city for the festivals (Mic 1:2, *šimʿû ʿammîm . . . ʾereṣ*; Mic 6:1–2, *šimʿû . . . šimʿû*; Mic 6:9, *šimʿû maṭṭeh ûmî yĕʿāḏāh*). The idea that the evil that Yahweh is bringing on them is retribution for the evil that they planned is adapted from Micah (6:19; cf. Mic 2:1–3). The equation of the words of Yahweh with the law that instructs them (Jer 6:19b, *dĕbāray . . . tôrātî*) is original to Jeremiah but has good precedents in Isaiah (30:9), Hosea (8:1, 12), and the Elohist (Exod 18:16, 20). The contrast between the law and false worship (6:20) was established by Amos (5:21–24), Hosea (8:11–13), and Micah (6:6–8). It was Isaiah who first mentioned the stumbling blocks that would be Jerusalem's undoing (6:21; cf. Isa 28:13b).

374 Both Isaiah and Jeremiah describe a nation coming from afar (6:22; Isa 5:26), and both describe their roar (*nhm*, 6:23a; Isa 5:29 [Isa 5:30 was added by III Isaiah on the basis of Jer 6:23a]). The prophet's call for reform combines elements from Micah (6:26a, "roll in the dust"; cf. Mic 1:10), Amos (6:26, "mourn for an only child"; cf. Amos 8:10) and Hosea (6:26, "bitter lamentation"; cf. Hos 12:15). Isaiah announced the coming onslaught and said that it would be sheer terror to understand the message (Isa 28:9, 19, *hābîn šĕmûʿâ*), and Jeremiah describes the terror when the city hears the message (6:24a, *šāmaʿnû ʾet šomʿô*).

375 Cf. Jer 8:5 (*heḥĕzîqû battarmît mēʾănû lāšûb*) and 5:3b (*ḥizzĕqû pĕnêhem missalaʿ māʾănû lāšûb*); 8:7b (*wĕʿammî lōʾ yāḏĕʿû ʾet mišpaṭ yhwh*) and 5:4b (*kî lōʾ yāḏĕʿû ḏerek yhwh mišpaṭ ʾĕlōhêhem*).

376 Cf. Jer 8:4 (*hayippĕlû wĕlōʾ yāqûmû*) and Amos 5:2 (*nāpĕlâ lōʾ tôsîp qûm bĕtûlat yiśrāʾēl*) and Mic 7:8 (*kî nāpaltî qamtî*). The strophe has numerous parallels with the second scene in the first act (cf. 8:5 and 3:3b, 22a), and its expression "Has he turned away and will he not return" (8:4b, *ʾim yāšûb wĕlōʾ yāšûb*) refers to Israel as the model of Judah's defection (3:19, *ûmēʾaḥăray lōʾ tāšûbî*; cf. 31:19) and repentance (3:22, *šûbû bānîm šobābîm*).

377 The image of a horse "overflowing" or "flooding" or "running in flood" (8:6b, *šō ṭēp*) into battle is an oblique reference to Isaiah's image of the scourge overrunning the country (Isa 28:15, 18, *šôṭ šôṭēp kî yaʿăbōr*; cf. Isa 28:19, *ʿbr*). The image seems to be maintained in the fourth strophe, where Yahweh decides to abandon his unproductive vineyards and orchards to those who overrun them (8:13, "I well give to them those who will overrun them" [*wāʾettēn lāhem yaʿabērûm*]). The comparison between birds or animals who know and the people of Yahweh who do not know (8:7) was made first by Isaiah (Isa 1:2–3) and Hosea (Hos 7:11–12).

378 The first stanza expresses the people's position (8:8, "How can you say: 'We are wise and the law of Yahweh is with us but now the lying pen of the scribes has been working on lies' "), and the second stanza expresses the prophet's retort (8:9, "The wise are ashamed, they are dismayed and trapped, now that they have rejected the word of Yahweh what wisdom do they have?"). The law of Yahweh (8:8, *tôrat yhwh*) is known from Isaiah (28:9, *tôrat yhwh*), Hosea (8:1, 12), and the Elohist (Exod 18:16, 20) and always with reference to writing (cf. Isa 28:8; Hos 8:12; Exod 32:15–16). The people's objection that scribes distorted it counters the Priestly and Elohist insistence that Yahweh wrote it (Exod 31:18; 32:15–16).

379 The last three strophes in this scene describe the end of the harvest seasons (8:13, 20) and have precedents in Amos (8:1–2) and Micah (7:1). The specific notation that there are no grapes on the vine, however, may be an allusion to the Song of the Vineyard, where the poor harvest intimated the destruction of the country (8:13b; cf. Isa 5:4). The failure of the harvest is contrasted with the regrouping of the troops in fortified cities (*ʾsp*, 8;13, 14).

380 In Micah's argument with the people they expressed the conviction that Yahweh was in their midst (Mic 3:11, *hălōʾ yhwh bĕqirbēnû*) and that no evil would befall them, and he replied that Zion would be ruined. In Jeremiah's dramatization of Yahweh's dispute with the people they begin to wonder whether Yahweh is in Zion (8:19). Yahweh's victory over the enemies of his people takes place in battle and is represented in the healing of their wounds (8:22). His victory over his enemies, such as the idols that they worshiped (8:19b), takes place in the fertility of the land (8:20). The images of war and harvesting, consequently, are interwoven.

381 The first strophes stress, as Hosea did, that the people lie and do not know Yahweh (9:2, 4; cf. Hos 4:1b–2aA; 7:1). The warning to beware of the people (9:3–4a) is modeled on Micah's lament (cf. Mic 7:2, 5–7). The final address to Jeremiah at the end of the second strophe (9:5, "You are living in the midst of deceit") sets him apart from the people and anticipates the

question that he will ask in the fourth strophe (9:11, "Who is wise enough to understand this, or to explain what the mouth of Yahweh has spoken to him, about why the land is ruined, barren as a wilderness with no travelers?").

382 The whole fourth act has numerous literary overtones from the earlier parts of the drama (e.g., 9:9, cf. 4:24–25; 9:11, cf. 2:6, 15) and especially from the third act (e.g., 9:10b = 6:8b; 9;12, cf. 6:16, 19; 10:19, cf. 6:7). The final plea, therefore, to be disciplined according to the law (10:24a, *yassĕrēnî yhwh ʾak bĕmišpāṭ*) should be understood in relation to similar texts in the preceding acts (5:1, 4, 5, 28; 8:7b).

383 See N. Lohfink, "Der junge Jeremia als Propagandist und Poet. Zum Grundstock von Jer 30–31," in *Le livre de Jérémie: Le prophète et son milieu, les oracles et leur transmission*, ed. P.-M. Bogaert (BETL 54; Louvain: Peeters, 1981) 351–68; idem, "Die Gotteswortverschachtelung in Jer 30–31," in *Künder des Wortes: Beiträge zur Theologie der Propheten; Josef Schreiner zum 60. Geburtstag*, ed. L. Ruppert, P. Weimar, and E. Zenger (Würzburg: Echter Verlag, 1982) 105–19; U. Schröter, "Jeremias Botschaft für das Nordreich, zu N. Lohfinks Überlegungen zum Grundbestand von Jeremia 30–31," *VT* 35 (1985) 312–29.

384 The principal images are taken from the beginning of the third act (30:6–7, *yādāyw, kayyôlēdâ, ṣārâ*; cf. 6:24, *rāpû yādênû / ṣārâ heḥĕzîqatnû / ḥîl kayyôlēdâ*) as are some of the words (30:6, *šaʾălû nāʾ ûrěʾû*; cf. 6:16, *ûrěʾû ûšaʾălû*). The hope of salvation was expressed at the end of the same act (30:7b, *ûmimmennâ yiwwāšēaʿ*; cf. 8:20, *waʾănaḥnû lôʾ nôšaʿnû*). The editor and archivist recognized the references and quoted from the same act (30:5b, *wěʾên šālôm* = 6:14b; 8:11b). The image of Jacob giving birth is identified, suddenly and by juxtaposition, as the day of Yahweh (30:7a, *hôy kî gādôl hayyôm hahûʾ mēʾayin kāmōhû*) by reference to the two texts where Amos described it (Amos 5:18, *hôy . . . yôm yhwh*; 8:9, *wěhāyâ bayyôm hahûʾ*).

385 Cf. Jer 30:10 (*ʿabdî yaʿăqōb*) and 2:14, 20 (*haʿebed yiśrāʾēl . . . wattôʾměrî lôʾ ʾeʿĕbōd*); cf. 30:10 (*mērāḥôq*) and 4:16; 5:15; 8:19; cf. 30:11 (*ʿśh kālâ*) and 4:27; 5:10; cf. 30:11b (*wěyissartîkā lammišpāṭ*) and 10:24; cf. 30:11b (*běkol haggôyim*) and 10:25. The expression "return and be quiet" (30:10b, *wěšāb . . . wěšāqaṭ*) is taken from Isaiah where it is advice from Yahweh that Jerusalem refused to heed (Isa 30:15). The expression "at ease" (30:10b, *wěšaʾănan*) is taken from Amos, where it was used in a pejorative sense of the people of Zion (Amos 6:1). The expression "and I will not leave you unpunished" (30:11b, *wěnaqqeh lôʾ ʾănaqqekā*) is quoted from the beginning of the epic covenant (Exod 34:7).

386 The first stanza (30:12–13) includes references to the blows and wounds that Zion has suffered (cf. 6:7; 10:19), to the fact that she is alone, no one takes up her cause (cf. 5:28), and there is no healing (cf. 8:22) and combines them with a reference to Hosea (cf. Hos 5:13), where a similar situation was described. The second stanza (30:14) has a more exact quotation of the text of Amos that was used in the second act (30:14b = 15b = 5:6 = Amos 5:12) and combines it with a reference to Micah (30:12, 14b, 15 [*ʾānûš*

+ *makkâ*] = Mic 1:9). The last stanza (30:15) repeats the same references but combines them with a quotation from the epic description of slavery in Egypt (30:15a, *mah tizʿaq ʿal šibrēk / ʾānûš makʾōbēk*; cf. Exod 3:7, *wĕʾet ṣaʿāqātām šāmaʿtî . . . kî yādaʿtî ʾet makʾōbāyw*]).

387 The first stanza (30:16) combines reversals or earlier texts (30:16a, cf. 3:24; 5:17; 30:10a) with an allusion to Isaiah (30:16b; cf. Isa 10:5). The second stanza (30:17) refers to a text in the third act (30:17a: cf. 8:22) and includes an allusion to a text from the sequel to the epic (30:17b, *dōrēš ʾên lāh*; cf. Deut 11:12, *ʾereṣ ʾăšer yhwh ʾĕlōhêkā dōrēš ʾōtāh*).

388 The strophe (31:2-3) recalls the beginning of the first act, where Yahweh led the people through the desert until they went far away from him (2:4-6), and it also has echoes from the third act, where Yahweh pleaded with the people to walk in the path that would lead to their peace but they refused (31:2, *hālôk lĕhargîʿô*; 6:16, *ʾê zeh derek haṭṭob ûlĕkû bāh ûmiṣĕʾû margôaʿ lĕnapšĕkem*). The image of a people finding grace in the wilderness and being loved with an everlasting love was inspired by Hosea's depiction of Yahweh taking the land back to the wilderness to woo her (Hos 2:16-25°). Israel's statement "From afar Yahweh appeared to me" (31:3a) introduces the words that he said at that time (31:3b, "I have loved you with an everlasting love, and so I have drawn you [*mĕšaktîk*] with fidelity"), and the whole stanza is constructed from references to Hosea: Yahweh promises to marry the land forever and with fidelity (Hos 2:21); Yahweh recalls how he loved Israel and drew it [*ʾemšĕkēm*] with bonds of love (Hos 11:4).

389 The first stanza (31:4-5a) uses imagery from the second act (31:4bA; cf. 4:30) and Isaiah's metaphor of the vineyard (31:5a; cf. Isa 5:1-2). The second stanza (31:5b-6) supposes, in line with the thinking of the sequel, that Yahweh is to be worshiped in Zion.

390 The first stanza (31:7) is composed of a call to rejoicing for Jacob, of a summons to raise a cry for Israel (31:7aB; cf. Amos 6:1), and of a quotation of the cry they raised (31:7bB, "Save your people, Yahweh, the remnant of Israel"). The second stanza depicts the remnant as a flock of sheep returning (31:8). The third fulfills Yahweh's longing to be able to call Israel his children (31:9; cf. 3:19; Hos 11:1; 13:12-13).

391 The strophe (31:15-17) attributes to Rachel the tears that Yahweh shed (31:15aA, cf. 9:9; 31:16aB, cf. 8:23) and the sorrow of Jerusalem for the children she has lost (31:15aBb = 10:20b).

392 The first stanza (31:18) alludes to Hosea's descriptions of Ephraim as an unbroken calf (31:18a, *kĕʿēgel lōʾ lummād*; cf. Hos 10:11, *ʾeprayim ʿeglâ melummadâ*) and wandering aimlessly in exile (31:18aA, *ʾeprayim mitnôdēd*; cf. Hos 9:16-17, *ʾeprayim . . . nōdĕdîm baggôyim*) and has him admit that he learned his lesson (31:18aB; cf. 10:24). The second stanza (31:19) alludes to the first act and Israel's turning away from Yahweh (31:19aA, *šûbî*, cf. 3:19 *ûmēʾaḥăray lōʾ tāšûbî*; 3:22, *šûbû bānîm šôbābîm / ʾerpâ mĕšûbōtêkem*) and to Hosea's description of Ephraim's inglorious end (31:19b, *kî nāśāʾtî ḥerpat nĕʾûrāy*; cf. Hos

12:15–13:1, *wĕḥerpātô yāšîb lô ʾădōnāyw . . . nāśāʾ hûʾ bĕyiśrāʾēl*). The third stanza (31:20) describes Ephraim as Yahweh's son (31:20a; cf. Hos 13:13) and extends to him the mercy that Hosea promised (31:20b; cf. Hos 2:25).

393 The strophe (31:21–22) is allusive (e.g., 31:21, *tamrûrîm*; cf. Hos 12:15) and suggests a return to Zion (31:21, *ṣiyyûnîm*) and to the cities of Judah (31:21; cf. 4:7, etc.). The final clause (31:22b, *nĕqēbâ tĕsôbēb gāber*) sums up the changing roles of men and women explored in this last act— notably, Israel as Yahweh's wife or son—and refers specifically to the first strophe, where Jacob was a man in travail (30:6–7).

394 The editor's appreciation of the imaginative quality of Jeremiah's work is particularly evident at the end of the play. In the last scene of the last act Yahweh appears to Israel in exile, and she reports the vision and the love for her that he professed (31:3, "From far away Yahweh appeared to me"). At the end of the scene the editor added a blessing (31:23–25) and, as if the vision were a dream, concludes "At this I awoke and I saw, and my sleep had been consoling to me" (31:26).

CHAPTER 4

Decline and Fall

*D*espite the optimism of Jeremiah and his mentors, it soon became
evident that the reform would have no long-range effect on the future
of Judah and Jerusalem. Nahum knew Jeremiah's work but did not
agree with his tempering of the tradition, and described the onrush of
the divine storm that would be the undoing of the city. Habakkuk
recalled and reconfirmed the vision of Isaiah and knew that it would
be accomplished by the Chaldeans. Zephaniah went back to the day of
Yahweh envisaged by Amos and saw that the end of the world was at
hand. Ezekiel wrote when the worst was over to describe how and why
the people had died and the conditions of their rising again. For some
the reform had failed; for others it made no difference; for all there
was a prophetic fate and doom and historical predestination unrolling
in their own time before their very eyes.

The writings of the postreformation prophets were different from
their predecessors. They took the reconciliation of history and prophecy for granted and appealed to one as to the other for precedents.
They assumed the resolution of basic inhumaneness and irreligion in
the common acceptance of the principles of law and the practices of
justice. They wrote poetry that had almost no prophetic affectations
but was rooted in rituals and songs, or, as in the case of Ezekiel, they
wrote mainly prose and turned prophecy back into history. Clearly
something had happened in the reform, and just as clearly it was not
enough.

Nahum (fig. 13)

Nahum's vision was composed of a hymn, a ballad, and an ode.[1] The hymn extols Yahweh as the lord of the created world who storms against his enemies but protects those who trust in him (1:2–8).[2] The ballad illustrates the effect of this storm in the natural phenomena accompanying the fall of Nineveh (2:2–11).[3] The ode is addressed to another beautiful and prosperous city—Jerusalem as it turns out—whose wealth and charms cannot save her from the coming storm (3:1–4, 8–11).[4] The three poems are separate and self-contained, but they are linked together to compose a cycle that satisfies the single metaphor of Yahweh's dominion as it is manifested in the maintenance and disruption of the natural order.

The vision was understood by a later writer as an elegy on Nineveh with words of consolation for Judah and Jerusalem. In this version the title was changed to indicate that the vision of Nahum was concerned only with Nineveh.[5] The hymn was expanded to include derisive remarks about Nineveh, kind words for Jerusalem, and a threat against the king of Assyria and his allies, whom the editor identified as the enemies of Yahweh who conspired against him.[6] The ballad was fitted between a preface that announced good news to Judah and Jerusalem and a postscript that pronounced the end of the enemy empire.[7] The ode was emended to identify the other unnamed city with Nineveh,[8] and the elegy came to an end with a flourish of taunts against the city, the empire, and the king of Assyria (3:12–19).

The three poems are inclusive, complete, and related to each other by repetition, implication, and transformation. In Nahum's version the poems were constructed with reference to the epic in its original and its Priestly editions and in dependence on the texts of Isaiah, Amos, Hosea, Micah, and Jeremiah. In the revised anti-Assyrian version there are references to later editions of the same works, but the editor's peculiar perspective was influenced by the ideology of the Deuteronomistic Historian.

THE HYMN (FIG. 13)

The hymn composed by Nahum has two strophes. The first strophe has three stanzas and portrays the theophany of Yahweh. The second strophe also has three stanzas and describes the response of the world and of history to his dreadful appearance. Together they set the mood of the poem, and the relation between them determines its structure.

The theophany begins by identifying the attributes of Yahweh as

FIGURE 13

Nahum

	Nahum				*The Book of Nahum*		
I	*Hymn*			I	*Against Nineveh*		
			1:1b				1:1a
	A	1	1:2		A	1	
		2	1:3a			2	
		3	1:3b–4a			3	
	B	1	1:4b–5		B	1	
		2	1:6			2	
		3	1:7–8			3	
					C	1	1:9–10
						2	1:11
					D	1	1:12–13
						2	1:14
II	*Ballad*			II	*Against Nineveh*		
					A	1	2:1
	A	1	2:2			2	
						3	2:3
		2	2:4			4	
	B	1	2:5		B	1	
		2	2:6abA			2	
	C	1	2:6bB–8a		C	1	
		2	2:8b–9bA			2	
	D	1	2:9bB–10		D	1	
		2	2:11			2	
					E	1	2:12–13
						2	2:14
III	*Ode*			III	*Against Nineveh*		
	A	1	3:1		A	1	
		2	3:2–3			2	
	B	1	3:4		B	1	
						2	3:5–6
					C	1	3:7
		2	3:8–9			2	
	C	1	3:10		D	1	
		2	3:11			2	
					E	1	3:12–13
						2	3:14–15a
					F	1	3:15b–16
						2	3:17
					G	1	3:18
						2	3:19

Figure 13. Letters indicate strophes. Numbers denote stanzas.

they apply to his enemies and as they affect his friends; it concludes
with the appearance of Yahweh in a thunderstorm that upheaves the
Sea and reveals its dry foundations.[9] The epithets and attributes of
Yahweh that Nahum lists are those that were revealed in the epic
covenant when Yahweh appeared on Mount Sinai.[10] The thunderstorm
that occurred at that time was also a vehicle of Yahweh's apparition on
the day of battle described by Amos, and his victory over the Sea had
been dramatized in the Priestly account of the exodus from Egypt.[11]
The theophany is original to Nahum, but all its elements are familiar
from history and prophecy.

The response to the theophany takes place in the reactions of the
cosmic mountains in the North and along the mountains, hills, and
cultivated and inhabited land as the storm approaches. The response is
expressed in the outcry of the inhabitants who see the world crumbling
under the fire of Yahweh's wrath, and in the assurance given by the
prophet that the storm will affect the enemies of Yahweh but will
bypass those who trust in his goodness and protection.[12] The cosmic
and local repercussions that Nahum describes have imaginative precedents in prophetic descriptions of the advance of divine or foreign
armies.[13] The outcry concerns the anger and rage of Yahweh that Isaiah
and Jeremiah described, and Nahum's reassurance is founded on their
perceptions of the sort of destruction that Yahweh had in mind.[14]

The hymn is mostly descriptive and saves for the end its equivalent
of the direct invocation of Yahweh, which usually opens a hymn, and
its confession of Yahweh's goodness, with which hymns generally
conclude. Its stanzas are characterized by repetition of the same words
or by redundant balancing of synonyms and by the alternation of short
lines with and without a strong caesura. The first stanza says three
times that Yahweh takes vengeance on his enemies, and a fourth time
paraphrases the same statement.[15] The second stanza says, repeating
the verb, that Yahweh will not relent.[16] The third stanza says twice,
with some variation, that Yahweh travels in the storm and overcomes
the cosmic waters.[17] The fourth is composed of three sets of parallel
repetitive lines that have no caesura.[18] The fifth has two pairs of
rhyming parallel lines.[19] The last has two very long lines with a strong
caesura and two short parallel lines.[20] This constant bifurcation of the
poem is suited to its strophic construction and to the alternatives that
it offers to the friends and enemies of Yahweh.

The editorial modification of the hymn consisted in adding two
other strophes to identify the friends and enemies of Yahweh. The first
strophe identifies the enemies and is attached to the original poem by
literal repetition and deictics.[21] The second strophe has little reference

to the original, but it distinguishes the people of Judah from their enemies and from their fate.[22]

The first strophe is composed of two stanzas. The opening stanza compares Yahweh's rage to a fire and those who conspired against him to a pile of brush that it will consume. The second stanza points out that the conspiracy began in Nineveh when some reprobate set out to conspire against Yahweh. The two are related by their reference to those who plot evil against Yahweh and are distinguished from the original text by their prosaic syntax, their cluttering of images and ideas, and their use of innuendo. The lines have no caesura, and the stanzas are composed of clauses bound by consecution and subordination.[23] The first stanza, in an effort to modify the original text by appealing to authoritative sources, mixes up images of brush and tangled thorns and drunks who stumble in a jumble of alliterative clauses that constantly change the person and number of its address.[24] Both stanzas are overt condemnations of Nineveh and the king of Assyria[25] but, in the spirit of revenge and retribution that the editor embraced,[26] also allude to sources that originally were critical of Israel, Judah, and Jerusalem.[27] The strophe is woven from Nahum's text but barely follows it and gives it a completely different scope and direction.

The second strophe has a stanza addressed to Judah and Jerusalem and another stanza condemning the king of Assyria. The first stanza is a prophetic oracle that combines a reference to II Isaiah on the defeat of Assyria with a reference to the book of Jeremiah on the end of the Babylonian exile, and, typically, it is composed of subordinate and consecutive clauses and amasses odd and inconsistent imagery.[28] The second stanza proclaims Yahweh's victory over the king of Assyria in the language of II Isaiah and the Deuteronomistic Historian and, characteristically, accuses the king of crimes that the tradition originally imputed to Judah and Jerusalem.[29] The whole strophe is constructed on the pattern of the first and gives ritual and political substance to the retribution that it announced.

THE BALLAD (FIG. 13)

Nahum's ballad of the fall of Nineveh was composed of four strophes of two stanzas each. The first strophe describes the enemy advancing to lay siege to the city and their preparations for assault as seen from the city wall.[30] The second strophe describes the confusion in the city as chariots race through the streets and defenders hurry to man the walls.[31] The third strophe records the ramming and breaching of the walls, the panic in the palace, the capture of the city Goddess, and the wailing of her attendants as Nineveh's defenses collapse.[32] The fourth strophe describes the desertion and looting of the city and the terror that overtook the garrison.[33]

Nahum's work has the usual signature. The lines are taut, either brief and unbroken or slightly longer with a caesura, separated by pause, paired and balanced, and fitted in stanzas with cadences suited to the image they convey. In the first stanza siege is laid and rallying cries are heard, and most of the lines have two words and are marked by strong alliteration and assonance. In the second stanza most lines have three words, and the awesome array of the besieging army is noted in ponderous, neatly ordered lines. The third stanza expresses the commotion in the city in onomatopoetic lines linked by rhyme. In the fourth stanza the defenders hurry silently to their positions in three lines with the same construction and a rhythm that conveys their movement. In the fifth stanza the ramming of the walls and the rape of the Goddess are suggested in lines with two alliterative words, and the opening of the city and dithering of the palace are put in lines with three words and the same pattern of sounds. The sixth stanza has long lines with long words that rhyme and slow the cadence to suit the wailing of the ladies-in-waiting. In the seventh stanza the flight of the defenders and the eagerness of the despoilers are suggested by repetition and rhyme and a strong caesura. In the last stanza the cadence slows again to portray the city in ruins and the languor and despair of the garrison.

In its original version the ballad continues in the vein of the theophany. Nineveh must confront the force that has come up to scatter her armies, just as the enemies of Yahweh must face the raging storm of his anger.[34] Lookouts are appointed to watch the road as Yahweh travels a road through the storm.[35] The attackers are encouraged to be strong as Yahweh is strong.[36] Yahweh's rage was like flashing fire, and the besieger's chariots are clothed in fire.[37] The day the besiegers are drawn up in array is the day of adversity, when Yahweh is a good defense.[38] As at Yahweh's advance the mountains trembled and the branches on Lebanon withered, so the cypresses quiver before the assault on the city.[39] Yahweh is present in the storm and the chariots dart like lightning (1:3b and 2:5b). As Yahweh's appearance dried up the rivers and made the mountains tremble, so in the siege of Nineveh the enemy breaks through the river gates and the palace trembles.[40] No one can stand before the anger of Yahweh, and no one in Nineveh stands and fights.[41] The literal links between the ballad and the hymn make it clear that the force arrayed against Nineveh was Yahweh and the siege was under his command.[42]

The editor enclosed Nahum's ballad in a pseudo-prophetical frame-work with secondary links to the embellished hymn. At the beginning, two stanzas were added to the first strophe to turn the siege of Nineveh into good news for Judah and Jacob. The first is a continuation of the edited hymn and repeats key terms from the original and from the revision.[43] The second develops the first and is intruded into the strophe by deictics but without any relationship to the original.[44] At the end two other stanzas in a separate strophe were fitted in by deictics and by the vaguest repetition of the original and secondary contexts.[45] Without these additions the ballad is just that and is seriously lacking in the standard clichés of prophecy.

The additions display the usual grammatical and stylistic features of the revised text. The lines are long and bear no resemblance to the pithy poetic expressions of the original. The clauses are joined by consecution or subordination, and none has the abrupt asyndetic quality of the ballad.[46] Wherever possible there is a clutter of contrary images. In the first stanzas Judah is invited to reinaugurate its festivals because the temple has been restored, but the reason is complemented by two others that clash with it—namely, because plunderers plun-dered them and ruined their vines.[47] In the concluding stanzas Assyria is compared to a lion gathering prey for its cubs, but the image is mixed with references to Assyrian political and military might, which give it some connection with the original text. The density of expression is indicative of the editor's effort to maintain the original and simulta-neously modify it by incorporating other sources.

There are no Judean literary sources for the ballad, but the revised version tempers Nahum's stark originality with traditional themes from the prophets and the Deuteronomistic History. The first stanza begins with a quotation from II Isaiah, which incidentally confirms that Yahweh was the commander of the forces against Nineveh and an-nounces his victorious return to Jerusalem.[48] The second stanza com-bines references to updated versions of Amos and Hosea that refer to the temple as the pride of Jacob and Israel[49] with references to passages in Jeremiah and Ezekiel in which Israel is a grapevine gleaned by invaders.[50] The comparison between Assyria and a lion on the prowl was original to Isaiah and was taken up by Jeremiah, but in the edited book of Ezekiel it was developed into an allegory on the last kings of Judah, which the revision of Nahum applied to the king of Assyria.[51] The final statement in the last strophe is that the voice of the Assyrian messengers would not be heard again: it is a reference to an oracle that the Deuteronomistic Historian attributed to Isaiah concerning the messengers that the king of Assyria sent to defy Yahweh in the time of

Hezekiah.[52] All of these references shift attention away from the capture of Nineveh by forces under Yahweh's command, as the original ballad sang of it, to Yahweh's personal victory over the king of Assyria and his triumphant return with the exiles.

THE ODE (FIG. 13)

Nahum's ode was composed in three strophes of two stanzas each. In the first strophe one stanza is addressed to an unnamed city that is filled with bloodshed, lies, and rapine, and the other is a description of the horses and chariots that careen through its streets strewn with corpses. In the second strophe the first stanza describes the unnamed city as a worldly, sophisticated woman who charmed the nations, and the second is addressed to her and compares her to Thebes in all her splendor. In the third strophe one stanza describes the sack of Thebes and the other warns the charming woman that she too will be stunned and appalled and will look for protection from the enemy.

Nahum implies that the city is Jerusalem, but the revised version identifies the city as Nineveh by adding intrusive stanzas in the second strophe and at the end of the ode. The intrusive stanzas, suited to their context by deictics and repetition, copy those at the end of the ballad and treat the worldly woman with the bitterest contempt.[53] The added strophes, also fitted in by deictics and repetition, continue the ridicule and emphasize the identification. The first strophe addresses the woman but repeats details from the siege of Nineveh that the ballad recounted.[54] The second describes the recall of her envoys, which was mentioned at the end of the edited ballad.[55] The third comes back to the beginning of the ballad to describe the humiliation of the king of Assyria and the end of the empire.[56]

In Nahum's version the ode continues the theme of the hymn and the ballad. The unnamed city is like Nineveh, whose walls, barricades, streets, squares, palaces, and wealth were described in the ballad. The battle scenes in the ode and the ballad have chariots racing, troops running to their positions, the glint and glimmer of their weapons (3:2–3 and 2:4–5). The hymn portrays Yahweh drying up the rivers and the Sea; the ballad situates Nineveh by a river and remarks on her endless treasures; and the ode situates Thebes by the Sea and refers to her endless resources.[57] The hymn says that Yahweh is good protection on the day of adversity; the ballad mentions the day that he has appointed; and the ode refers to the unnamed city's need for protection.[58] In the hymn Yahweh appears in a storm; in the ballad the besieging army encircles Nineveh like a storm; in the ode the horses and chariots are like thunder and lightning in the city (1:3b; 2:4–5; 3:2–3). The theme is developed and transformed, but it is singular and consistent throughout the poem.

The revised version continued to relate the ode to the ballad and to the hymn, not in order to develop the original theme of the divine storm from which Yahweh himself is the only protection, but in order to insist on the identification of the unnamed city with Nineveh. The ballad saw the river gates open, and this version of the ode has the cowardly citizens opening the gates of Nineveh to the enemy. The ballad portrayed women weeping for Nineveh and compared the city to a cistern whose waters are running away, and the ode in its revised form says that Nineveh's defenders are women. Both have the same sort of prophetic oracle with the same introduction. Both refer to the Assyrian military campaigns that terrorized the world. Altogether the development of the theme is halted in the interest of making a point.

The identification of the unnamed city with Jerusalem in Nahum's version is by allusion and implication. The apostrophe to the city of blood that begins the ode was used later by Ezekiel explicitly against Jerusalem, but ultimately it is derived from Micah's condemnation of those who tried to build Zion on blood.[59] The city that is filled with falsehood resembles Zion, which Isaiah said trusted in lies, or is like Jerusalem, where Jeremiah found no one who told the truth.[60] The image of the city as a courtesan enticing and charming the nations was developed later by Ezekiel and was applied by him directly to Jerusalem, but it was original with Micah and derived ultimately from Hosea's portrayal of Israel's and Judah's insistence on abandoning Yahweh for status among world powers.[61] The description of incapacitating terror as drunkenness began with Isaiah, who used it to describe the reaction of the people of Jerusalem when they realized that Yahweh was against them.[62] The references to Jerusalem are subtle and insinuated, and it is only when it is too late to object that the reader who has been amused by the fall of Nineveh senses that Jerusalem must seek protection from the divine storm blowing from the North.

Nahum attributed the fall of Nineveh to the power of the wrath of Yahweh and drew the lesson that had been obvious to all the prophets. The editor of his poem, however, was more concerned with punishing the Assyrians and their successors for what they had done to Judah and Jerusalem. This version did not have any other information on the fall of Nineveh or the collapse of the Mesopotamian empires but relied on the principle of retribution to suggest that what they had done would be done to them. Most of its description, consequently, simply applies to Assyria a hodgepodge of texts that dealt originally with

Judah and Jerusalem. In this way the revision is a subtle reversal of the original, where, except for tradition and insinuation, the unnamed city might just as well have been Nineveh.

In the book of Jeremiah one of the threats against Jerusalem for trusting in lies is to have her skirt pulled over her head to show her nakedness and shame.[63] In Hosea Yahweh takes away the clothing of the unfaithful land and reveals her lewd and useless habits.[64] In Ezekiel Yahweh appeals to the people to throw away the things that pollute their eyes.[65] In II Isaiah it is Yahweh who consoles Jerusalem because she has been destroyed and there is no one to comfort her.[66] From such literary precedents the editor constructed a dense and allusive threat against Nineveh according to which Yahweh will "reveal" her skirt over her head, show her nakedness and shame to the nations, throw her pollution over her, lay bare her lewdness, reveal her habits, and let her be destroyed with no one to console or comfort her. The threat is oddly phrased, a composite of cruel, self-satisfied, stereotyped humiliations of women, and redundant after Nahum's description of the fall of Nineveh, but it does satisfy the need for revenge and retribution.

In Jeremiah invaders about to attack Jerusalem are compared to shepherds with their flocks against which fortified cities provide no line of defense.[67] In Isaiah one of the qualities of the Assyrian invaders is that they do not sleep.[68] In Amos and Joel the day of battle is like a plague of locusts.[69] In oracles against Babylon in the book of Jeremiah, her citizens are as numerous as locusts and her troops lose courage and become like women.[70] In Isaiah, Micah, and Jeremiah the effect of invasion is a wound that will not heal.[71] In Ezekiel death by the sword is accompanied by the clapping of hands.[72] In a legend recounted by the Deuteronomist, the prophet Micaiah saw Israel scattered on the mountains like sheep without a shepherd.[73] In Ezekiel one of the causes of the fall of Tyre was its abundant trade.[74] The writer who revised Nahum did not need any further knowledge of the fall of Nineveh but could simply use these references to invasion and the disaster that befell great cities as a model for the capture of Nineveh and the end of the Assyrian empire. The fortified cities of Assyria fall; the inhabitants of Nineveh are women; its troops are like locusts; its trade is abundant; its shepherds sleep; its people are scattered on the mountains with no one to gather them; there is no cure for its wounds; and all who hear of its fall will clap their hands.

Nahum keeps to the sharp staccato juxtaposition of lines and insists on lines with strong caesuras as the ode clips along to its awful conclusion. The revised version imitates his clipped expression and his alternation of long and short lines but also maintains its own prosaic manner and persists in its conjunction of images. The first stanza in the appendix, for instance, compares the fortified cities to ripe fruit, likens its militia to women, and has the gates of the city both opened and burned; it is filled with long lines with subordinate clauses but with no caesura. The second stanza describes the preparations for a siege but has the inhabitants of the city devoured both by a fire and by locusts. The editor all in all was very busy in providing proof that Nahum's poem really did portray a divine storm that put an end to Mesopotamian hegemony.

CONCLUSION

The two versions of the superscription indicate the two different perspectives of the book. Nahum had a vision that he unfolded in a poem with three parts. Each part describes a scene; each has a different mood; all together they portray a storm sweeping across the land, striking Nineveh, Thebes, and the city that wooed them both. The revision thought it should be good news for Judah and Jerusalem about Nineveh and the enemies of Yahweh. It added a rider to each part and made the odd little antecedent changes that let them fit.

Nahum is indebted to historical and prophetic tradition and is perfectly consistent in his reliance on them. His reference to the manifestation of Yahweh at the Sea and on Sinai follows the sequence of the epic narrative, where one is sequential on the other, and its complete dramatic fulfillment. His pursuit of the manifestation of Yahweh beyond Sinai and the Sea to Bashan, Carmel, and Lebanon follows the course of history and tradition beyond the exodus and wilderness into the land of Israel, whose boundaries were the river Jordan, the Sea, and the mountains to the north. His insistence on the anger of Yahweh recognizes the force of the epic covenant but agrees with the criticisms of its naïveté and one-sidedness that began with Isaiah and the lessons of history. His view of Yahweh as a warrior leading his forces into battle has its precedents in prophecy and covenant and is filled out from his acquaintance with a military economy and the records of war. His attitude to Jerusalem depends on the prophets before him and on a kind of pride in its power tempered by dismay at its reliance on arms. His work is traditional and original and proper to a time when, with less faith in weapons and alliances and more confidence in God, the city might have survived.

The revision supposes that the country had been overrun, that worship had ceased, and that the invader had been vanquished. There is some hope but less optimism and not much interest in preserving the past. What is crucial is that Yahweh has turned his anger away from Judah and Jerusalem to the people who deserve it—to Nineveh, for example, and the king of Assyria. To make this point the revision simply describes them and their fate in terms that once were used about Israel, Judah, and Jerusalem.

It is the revision that makes Nahum look like a prophet and puts him in the familiar prophetic mold. Nahum himself was a prophet of the old school, educated, clever with words, involved, entertaining. The author of the book was a pedant, smart, keen on words and ideas, careful to buttress a different opinion with a mass of authorities. What is different is what it omits. All the blame is shifted to the king of Assyria and his capital. There is no mention at all of Judah's or Jerusalem's guilt, of the things that its kings, princes, prophets, or people did wrong. The book of Nahum came after the Deuteronomistic History, knew its historical and theological theories, and obviously did not agree with them at all or pay them any mind.

Habakkuk (fig. 14)

Habakkuk composed his prophecy as a psalm of lamentation. The situation of distress that he sees is the vision of invasion that Isaiah presented. His prayer is that he should not have to see the vision fulfilled. The answer to his prayer is that the vision is taking its course and will not fail to occur. In reply Habakkuk recalls the terrible battles in which Yahweh gained victory for his people and in the midst of certain defeat still looks for salvation from God.[75]

The editor of the prophecy gave it a bipartite structure composed of a complaint and a diatribe against vanity and made the final recollection a separate psalm.[76] Habakkuk's text was liturgical, but the editor adorned it with sapiential musings.[77] The original was concerned with world affairs and their cosmic repercussions, but the revised version lapses into tirades against injustice that reflect domestic issues and purely local interests.[78] Habakkuk's prayer had the formal characteristics, continuity, and dramatic development typical of lamentations,[79] but the commentary is punctual and repetitive and has all the logical features of argumentation.[80] Habakkuk was engaged in the prophetic tradition and relied on prophetic and historical sources to give substance to his vision, but his editor was a philosopher and a theologian who used contemporary versions of the same works to provide proofs for a different interpretation.[81]

FIGURE 14

Habakkuk

The Vision of Habakkuk				The Book of Habakkuk			
		Introduction				*Introduction*	
I	A	1	1:1	I	A	1	
		Complaint				*First Complaint*	
		2	1:2–3aA			2	
						3	1:3aBb–4
	B	1	1:5		B	1	
		2	1:6			2	
						3	1:7
		3	1:8abA		C	1	
		4	1:8bB–9			2	
		5	1:10			3	1:10–11
		Confession of Trust & Petition				*Second Complaint*	
	C	1	1:12a		D	1	
		2	1:12b–13a			2	
						3	1:13b
					E	1	1:14–15a
						2	1:15b–16
						3	1:17
		Assurance of Being Heard				*Invectives*	
	D	1	2:1	II	A	1	
		2	2:2			2	
		3	2:3			3	
					B	1	2:4–5abA
						2	2:5bB–6a
					C	1	2:6b–7
						2	2:8
					D	1	2:9
						2	2:10–11
					E	1	2:12
						2	2:13–14
					F	1	2:15
						2	2:16
						3	2:17
					G	1	2:18
						2	2:19–20
						Psalm	
				III			3:1

continued

F I G U R E   1 4 (*cont*)

The Vision of Habakkuk				*The Book of Habakkuk*		
		Hymn				
II	A	1	3:2	A	1	
		2	3:3		2	
		3	3:4		3	
	B	1	3:5–6aA	B	1	
		2	3:6aBb–7		2	
	C	1	3:8	C	1	
		2	3:9		2	
	D	1	3:10–11a	D	1	
		2	3:11b–12		2	
				E	1	3:13aBb–14aA
					2	3:14aBb
	E	1	3:13aA, 15–16aA	F	1	
		2	3:16aBb–17aA		2	
	F	1	3:17aBb	G	1	
		2	3:18–19a		2	
						3:19b

Figure 14. Letters indicate strophes. Numbers denote stanzas.

STRUCTURE

The original text was a lament composed of an introduction, a complaint, a confession of trust and a petition, an assurance of being heard with hope for the future, and a concluding hymn and commitment to continuing devotion. The editor changed the confession of trust and petition into a duplicate complaint, made the assurance of being heard a response to the first complaint, added long and involved reflections to resolve the duplicate complaint, and turned the hymn and concluding commitment into a psalm with its own superscription and colophon and the barest connection to the preceding parts.

Habakkuk's introduction is the heading to the book, and it defines the theme of the lament as vision and prophecy.[82] The complaint has the standard triadic structure involving God, the petitioner, and the cause of the distress in an invocation of Yahweh and a vision of invasion.[83] The petition contains a prayer for life, trust in Yahweh's eternity, holiness and justice, and the suggestion that the vision is inconsistent with these attributes and ought to be annulled (Hab 1:12–13a).[84] The assurance of being heard includes Yahweh's reply to the prayer and the terrible certainty that the vision will be accomplished (2:1–3). The hymn that Habakkuk recites in response to this answer includes his hope for the future and determination to worship God in happier times.[85] The entire lament proceeds in stages from the presentation of a problem to its resolution, from not being heard to being answered, from the vision of defeat to the vision of restoration, and from not being saved to rejoicing in the hope of salvation.

The commentary changed the lament into a treatise on justice and divine retribution. This was achieved by repeated application of the principles of prolepsis and resumption, and the result was a book composed of multiple iterations.

The complaint's questioning invocation of Yahweh was altered by the addition of declarative comments on the law and the miscarriage of justice (1:3aBb–4). This addition states the commentary's theme, and its basic elements are applied to the Chaldeans in the remainder of the complaint and at critical points in the rest of the book. Its reference to violence and injustice is illustrated by the Chaldean policy of mass deportation, which becomes the topic of a later invective (1:3aBb; 1:9b; 2:5–6a). The plight of the innocent is blamed on the arrogance of the Chaldeans and is resolved in the dictum for which the book is famous (1:4b, 1:7b; 2:4). The ineffectiveness of the law is shown by the crimes and impunity of the Chaldeans, but this is finally rectified by the violent destruction of the guilty (1:4a; 1:11; 3:13aBb–14).

The petition was changed into a duplicate complaint by inserting another invocation of Yahweh in the questioning style of the original and by adding the parable of the fisherman to complement the first description of the enemy.[86] The invocation resumes the theme of innocence and guilt from the additions made to the opening invocation.[87] The parable of the fisherman resumes and elaborates on the issues that were mentioned in the original description of the enemy. The policy of mass deportation becomes the Chaldeans catching fish.[88] The propitiation of their Gods is described specifically as burning incense to their nets.[89] The pride of the Chaldeans is illustrated in their merciless killing of whole nations without regard for their own lowly place in the order of creation (1:7b and 1:14, 17). These changes replace the thematic movement of the lament with a concentration on issues, substitute simple iteration for dramatic sequence, and reduce the original vision of the Chaldeans sweeping across the land to subtle reflection on justice and divine retribution.

The second part incorporates the original assurance of being heard and the actual response that Habakkuk received into a detailed solution of the problems discussed in the first chapter. The specific problem discussed in the duplicate invocations of Yahweh is the inadequacy of normal legal procedures for the vindication of the innocent and the punishment of the guilty.[90] This problem is solved by the dictum that the book appends to Yahweh's confirmation of the vision: the innocent survive by believing in the vision, while the presumption of the guilty is no defense against it (2:4). The dictum is ambiguous and enigmatic, but it is explained in the following series of invectives, which illustrates the inevitability of divine retribution for violation of the law (2:5–20). But this series also responds to the issues that were raised in the first two complaints about the enemy invasion by describing the punishment appropriate to each crime. Mass deportation is countered by defeat and complete devastation (1:9b, 15 and 2:5–8). Arrogance is overcome by the manifestation of God's glory and the ultimate futility of human endeavor (1:7, 14, 17 and 2:9–14). Impunity dissolves before simple vengeance and total contempt for the idols that made their insolence seem plausible (1:11, 16 and 2:15–20). The second part, consequently, loses its connection with the lament and becomes another iteration of the editorial argument announced at the beginning of the book.

The third chapter is separated from the rest of the book by a superscription and a colophon and is generally peripheral to its argument. But the review of Yahweh's exploits in the hymn was emended to agree with the rest of the treatise by redirecting them from the salvation of the people to the institution of good government and the destruction of the guilty. When the commentary suppressed the dramatic sequence between lament and praise this final iteration became the only link between the hymn and the rest of the book.[91]

ORGANIZATION

The changes in the text are stanzas added to the ends of edited strophes or strophes inserted at turning points in the lament to constitute separate parts. They take up most of the complaint and almost half the poem and, being made by the usual process of repetition and cross-reference, are embedded and not always apparent.

In the first strophe Habakkuk protested against the evident doom that he was forced to observe and report. The editor added another stanza on the totally different matter of the courts and the application of the law by including a throwaway line that fitted it into the strophe. The line repeats what Habakkuk said about cruelty and uses a deictic pronominal suffix to replace his vision with the editor's sense of stubborn opposition. It fits by purportedly explaining what Habakkuk meant, although in fact it interrupts what Habakkuk was saying and is dense and itself needs explanation.[92]

In the second strophe, spoken to Habakkuk, Yahweh explains that he is doing the unbelievable by encouraging the Chaldeans to march to distant lands and take possession of territory that they did not settle.

The editor added that the Chaldeans were proud and a law to themselves. The addition was made by a deictic pronoun and pronominal suffixes that tied it to Habakkuk's description of the Chaldeans in the preceding stanza. Habakkuk referred to them as a gruesome and impetuous nation, and the editor added that they were awesome and frightening. Habakkuk portrays them setting out to conquer the world, and the editor saw their pride and their peculiar sense of justice going before them.[93]

In the third strophe, still the second in Habakkuk's version, Yahweh goes on to describe exactly how the Chaldeans went about world conquest quickly, methodically, and without hindrance. The editor compared them to a wind that blows across the land and is gone leaving nothing behind but the guilt they incurred from the Gods that they worshiped. This is said in two lines added to Habakkuk's last stanza by deictic particles and pronouns.[94] It has little to do with the preceding context but contrasts with the invocation of the true God in the next stanza and anticipates one of the invectives.[95]

In Habakkuk's version of the next strophe there is a two-line stanza with his petition and a four-line stanza expressing the basis of his trust and reasons that might motivate Yahweh to annul the vision (1:12a, 12b–13a). The editor added a different motivation in another two-line stanza at the end of the strophe. It fits in by repeating one word from Habakkuk's text, by using another word that anticipates the parable of the fisherman, and by continued cross-reference to the argument about innocence and guilt.[96] The parable of the fisherman follows without any editorial apology and with only the slightest reference to the context.[97]

Habakkuk's fourth strophe represents him as a prophet and watchman waiting for the word of Yahweh in reply to his complaint and records Yahweh's answer that the vision was certain even if the time of its occurrence was unknown (2:1, 2, 3). To this the editor appended a strophe to introduce his invectives and to identify them as allegories on the Chaldean invaders. The strophe begins, however, with the dictum on innocence and vindication that sums up the spirit of the edited version and attaches the strophe to Habakkuk's text.[98] The invectives follow and are fitted in by literal and thematic cross-references to the developing argument.

At the end of the hymn Habakkuk reflects on the significance of the ancient and primordial victories of Yahweh against Egypt and the Sea in two strophes, one expressing his astonishment and trepidation, the other his desolation and total confidence in his God.[99] The editor interrupted at the very beginning of the first strophe to identify these victories as total destruction of the guilty Chaldeans and all their allies. The addition is made by deictics and by the repetition of one word from the original.[100] It is a clever interpretation of the hymn but, like most of the editor's comments, obscure and not quite germane to the context.

LANGUAGE

The text of Habakkuk and the editor's commentary are distinguished from each other especially by their language. The language of the lament is physical and sensory—the language of vision, audition, action, and emotion. The language of the editor is imaginative and abstract. The imaginative language defines specific legal problems and occurs in logical discourse and in argumentation. The abstract language is mostly forensic.

The beginning and ending of Habakkuk's first strophe stress the language of vision, and the middle lines are filled with sound and audition.[101] The commentary, by contrast, is weighted with forensic language[102] and interjects imaginative elements to moot the miscarriage of justice.[103] The first strophe is thematic in both versions, and its principal terms recur in every important position.

The second and third strophes in the lament begin and end with the basic language of vision.[104] The stanzas describing Babylonian resurgence combine speech and action with motion, emotion, and stasis.[105] The stanzas portraying the advance of the Babylonian armies are filled with verbs of motion, expressions of fear, and the language of action and audition.[106] The commentary intrudes with forensic terms, with abstract designations of the typical enemy, and with vivid images of invasion and captivity.[107]

The fourth strophe in the lament collects all the language of vision, speech, motion, and stasis,[108] and the commentary adds a few forensic or abstract terms.[109] The invectives have some technical legal language but mainly abound in images and clever allusions (2:5–20). The policy of mass deportation is compared to the insatiable appetite of Death and Sheol and to the accumulation of vast debts. The futility of human endeavor is illustrated by the construction of a house from a faulty design or the building of a city on a mound of crime and bloodshed. The illusion of impunity is dispelled by evoking the image of a common cup or the sorry plight of an artisan before the idol he himself made.

The hymn deploys all the typical language of the lament. The first strophe describes the theophany of Yahweh by combining action, audition, emotion, and motion before stopping in an aura of mystery.[110] The second strophe describes the effect of Yahweh's appearance on the world and its inhabitants in the language of motion, stasis, vision, and emotion.[111] The third strophe describes his victory over the cosmos in word, in deed, and with emotion.[112] The fourth strophe portrays the vanquished cosmos in the language of vision, speech, motion, stasis, and emotion.[113] In the fifth strophe Habakkuk reflects on what Yahweh has done for his people and is filled with emotion.[114] In the last strophe he sees the world in ruins but still rejoices in the victories of Yahweh.[115] The commentary adds its usual forensic touch, some abstract words and detailed images of total destruction (3:13aBb–14).

The commentary uses abstract forensic language in the proleptic and resumptive texts that it imposes on the lament and uses descriptive and technical legal language in the passages it constructs to elaborate its own point of view. All its comments are marked by the discursive logic appropriate to a treatise rather than by the drama or anticipation of a prophecy nudged from inspired despair to triumphant exultation.

The issue in the commentary is injustice and the uselessness of recourse to the law, and it is argued logically and in great detail by describing the process that leads to the miscarriage of justice. The syntax is involved and precise: when a case is brought to court a counterclaim is sworn, with the result that the law is impugned and justice does not prevail, because the guilty manage to circumvent the innocent and thereby succeed in perverting justice.[116] Similarly, the parable of the fisherman portrays the crime of the Chaldeans in a concatenation of image, inference, and argument. They capture people like catching fish, and consequently are content, and therefore sacrifice to their nets because they provide good food; but surely this cannot continue because it was Yahweh and not their God who made people creatures like the fish that they catch (1:14–17).

The invectives are a special instance of simple logic and literary sensibility (2:5–20). They deal with specific crimes like assault, violence, murder, robbery, usury, fraud, and idolatry. Their complaint is against the arrogant, the presumptuous, the vain, the deceitful, the insolent, the haughty, and the proud who manage to evade justice. They develop the case for retribution by combining images of restitution, retaliation, and revenge with arguments derived from proverbial sayings, riddles, and literary allusions. The images are all derived from literary traditions; the logic is always arcane; but together they prove that justice does prevail.

STYLE

The lament is composed of balanced stanzas with short lines. The lines usually have only three main elements—generally a verb and a choice of subject, object, or adverbial modifier. The stanzas are marked by rhyme and regular cadence, their lines by internal rhyme, assonance, and alliteration. The commentary rarely adjusts to its original context and usually has prosaic lines of four or more elements and stanzas that feature simple repetition or parallelism in place of balance and regular cadence.[117]

In the first strophe of the lament the first stanza has two lines with constant alliteration. The second stanza has six lines that are alternately long and short in the manner of a lament, and with alliteration in the first, assonance in the third, rhyme between the second and fourth and between the fifth and sixth. But the commentary is quite different. The lines are longer and of the same length; there is no rhyme, little alliteration, extensive repetition of conjunctions and of whole sentences, and a simple repetitive cadence produced by the pairing of lines.

In the second and third strophes of the lament the stanzas have lines that rhyme at the beginning or at the end or from the end of one to the beginning of the next. The cadence of the first stanza is decided by reduplication and constant caesuras (1:5).[118] In the second stanza the measure is marked by rhyme, reduplication, and alliteration (1:6).[119] In the third stanza there is rhyme at the beginning and ends of lines (1:8abA).[120] In the fourth there is rhyme and a unique onomatopoetic depiction of galloping horses (1:9a).[121] In the fifth all the lines are joined by a concatenation of rhyme. In the third strophe the first stanza is almost blank but has some reverse rhyme between lines.[122] At the end there are lines that rhyme and lines with intricate assonance and alliteration.[123]

The commentary changed the structure and organization of the strophes, and none of its additions is completely consistent with the original context. The stanza that it added on the arrogance of the Chaldeans has the reduplication of the preceding stanza and the rhyme of the next, but one of its lines is too long.[124] The lines that allude to regular campaigns against the nations miss the concatenated rhyme of the original lines and are too long or too short and unbalanced.[125] The stanza added to the third strophe follows the same pattern of long and short lines and, though it imitates the original carefully, stands clearly apart from it.[126]

The fourth strophe has three stanzas, each with a different cadence and arrangement of lines to suit its topic. The first stanza has Habakkuk waiting on the rampart for an answer to his prayer; it has three consecutive lines with the same opening rhyme where he waits for Yahweh's arrival, and two lines with the same closing rhyme where he waits for him to speak (2:1).[127] The second stanza reports Yahweh's command to record the vision for every one to read: it encloses staccato commands between narrative and alliterative interpretation (2:2).[128] The third stanza contrasts the certainty of the vision with its apparent delay in four lines with assonance and alliteration and a strong caesura (2:3). The lines that the editor wrote to affix the invectives to it imitate its alliteration but follow the usual mannerisms of being excessively long or improperly short in their context (2:4).

The hymn displays the same range of poetic features. The few lines added by the commentator mostly imitate its style and are remarkable only for their difficulty and density of expression.

The commentary obviously tried to conform to the style of the original, and its divergences from the cadence and sentence structure of the lament seem to be deliberate. When it develops the opening invocation into a theory of jurisprudence it begins by imitating the three-element cadence of the lament but, instead of following with the expected two-element line, it adds a line with four elements and a pause in the middle (1:3aBb–4). When it persists in its argument against arrogance and injustice it is careful to imitate the surrounding rhyme, but it ignores the structure of the original stanzas (1:7). When it relates annual Babylonian campaigns to a fixation with their Gods, on the other hand, its additions stand out and signal the onrush of the argument (1:11). This procedure allows the editor to respect the integrity of the original and still make a distinction between the perennial significance of the lament and its immediate relevance.

SOURCES

The lament quotes from Isaiah, the Priestly writer, Micah, Jeremiah, and Nahum and seems to be familiar with sayings of Amos and Hosea. Its quotations are interpretations rather than literal renditions and suppose knowledge of complete texts rather than simple reminiscence or general acquaintance with tradition. The texts that it knows and interprets all contribute to the gradual transformation of Isaiah's vision. The commentary quotes from the same sources and from the standard Deuteronomistic edition of the Pentateuch. Its quotations contribute to the theme of justice and divine retribution. They are literal renditions or amassed in a single context from different sources. They suggest considerable learning, a concern for logical argument, and a serious interest in justifying the radical reinterpretation of the lament.

The first strophe combines vision and unanswered prayer and has a precedent in Micah's declaration that when the enemy attack came prayers would be unanswered and visions would cease.[129] Micah also drew a parallel between the appearance of Yahweh and the onslaught of the enemy and punctuated each with lament. His work may have inspired the balance in Habakkuk's lament between the advance of the Chaldeans and the cosmic manifestation of Yahweh (cf. Habakkuk 1° and 3° with Mic 1:2–9 and 1:10–16). It was also Micah, and Jeremiah, both of them relying on Amos, who saw violence as the symptom of corruption in the city.[130]

The commentary changed the invocation of Yahweh into a disquisition on justice and neglect of the law by combining two quotations from the confessions of Jeremiah with an allusion to Micah and a reference to Deuteronomy. One of the confessions portrayed Jeremiah's career as a protest against violence and destruction, and the commentary used the expression to modify Habakkuk's complaint about violence.[131] The other described Jeremiah as a man engaged in dispute and litigation, and the commentary quoted him to give Habakkuk's complaint a drift in the same direction.[132] Then the editor combined the late prophetic image of the law issuing from the tribunal in Zion[133] with the Deuteronomistic idea that the written law is the basis of judicial decisions and the criterion of guilt and innocence[134] to conclude that any failure of justice essentially undermined the law.

In Habakkuk's second strophe the command to look at the nations and notice what Yahweh is doing is a paraphrase of Isaiah's exasperation at the people who did not notice what Yahweh was doing.[135] Habakkuk's vision of an impetuous nation marching to the ends of the earth is an extension of Isaiah's vision of a nation coming quickly from the ends of the earth.[136] Incredulity, stupidity, and sheer stupefaction are the responses to the vision that Isaiah predicted.[137] The vision that did not transpire in Isaiah's time but was recorded for a later day is the vision that Yahweh assures Habakkuk has occurred in his days.[138] The Chaldeans come quickly from a distant land like the Assyrians in the vision of Isaiah.[139] They are like leopards or like wolves in the evening, as Jeremiah described them, and they come to attack Judah's fortified cities as he warned.[140]

In the third strophe Habakkuk confesses that Yahweh is a Holy God, as Isaiah insisted, and his prayer to escape death may allude to the covenant with Death that Isaiah described in his vision.[141] In attempting to dissuade Yahweh from accomplishing the vision of Isaiah,

Habakkuk naturally enough appeals to the firm foundation of law and justice that Isaiah had proposed as Zion's alternative to the covenant with Death.[142] In Micah's version of the vision Yahweh plotted and was about to execute evil against the city, but Habakkuk protests that Yahweh's holiness excludes an evil or unjust solution.[143]

The commentary on these strophes was taken from Isaiah, Jeremiah, Job, and the Priestly account of creation. It refers to the conquest of Jerusalem by quoting the Isaian description of Assyria overflowing its banks like the Euphrates and rushing into Judah.[144] It describes the invasion as a swallowing whole of an innocent people, as Jeremiah's oracle against Babylon described Nebuchadnezzar's capture of Judah and Jerusalem.[145] It refers to the fearsomeness and haughtiness of the Chaldeans, who strutted across the earth in the power of their Gods in terms that Job used to describe God or Leviathan.[146] It objects to the success of the Chaldeans and their Gods by evoking Yahweh's decision to create human beings in the menial order of fish and creeping things.[147] The effect of the commentary is the sense that the lack of justice leaves something radically wrong with the world.

In the fourth strophe the scene with Habakkuk on the parapet watching for the word of Yahweh owes something to Nahum's picture of the siege of Nineveh and to Hosea's and Jeremiah's portrayal of prophets as watchmen.[148] His assurance of being heard is based, perhaps, on Isaiah's invitation to reasonable discussion,[149] but Yahweh's response certainly is taken from Isaiah's instructions to write his vision on a tablet and inscribe it in a book because it is due to arrive suddenly and unexpectedly.[150] This vision of invasion and sudden destruction was described by Amos as the end of the world and time, and Yahweh's response seems to allude to his pronouncement.[151] In Amos the end is called the day of Yahweh, but in Hosea it is called the appointed day. Yahweh's response includes a separate allusion to this interpretation.[152]

The commentary inserted an aphorism to interpret the response and added a series of invectives to interpret it.[153] The introduction to the series paraphrases Isaiah's invective against those who drink wine at their festivals and ignore what Yahweh is doing and quotes a comment by III Isaiah in the same place that defines the punishment of such people as exile into the gullet of Sheol.[154] The series itself is a tissue of allusions to epic, legal and prophetic sources.

The first invective contains an allusion to the law in Deuteronomy governing loans and the year of release,[155] a quotation from Isaiah explaining Yahweh's summons to the Assyrian invaders,[156] and a saying with a concatenation of references to interrelated pentateuchal texts. There is an allusion to the murder of Abel and to the retribution that it engendered, a reference to the corruption of the world and God's retaliation with the flood, and an allusion to the fate of Sodom and Gomorrah, whose crimes cried out for vengeance.[157]

The second invective describes the futility of amassing the rewards of evil by combining a reference to Isaiah that describes the crime with allusions to Obadiah and Jeremiah that describe the punishment. Isaiah observed how the Assyrians cut off many nations and destroyed their nests, and the invective is directed against the Chaldeans for cutting off many nations.[158] In an oracle of Obadiah taken up in the book of Jeremiah Yahweh says that he will pull down the nest that the Edomites made high from the ground, and the invective applies the same image to divine retribution against the Chaldeans.[159] In a tirade against the prophets and priests the book of Jeremiah traces their doom to their shameless amassing of lies, and the invective scoffs at the attempt to avoid evil by shamelessly amassing it.[160]

The third invective simply juxtaposes three quotations from the books of Isaiah, Jeremiah, and Micah.[161] The fourth invective combines an allusion to the curse of Canaan with two other images of retribution,[162] with the cup of wrath described in the book of Jeremiah, and with the revenge of the beast of Lebanon suggested by the Deuteronomist and described in the epic of *Gilgamesh*.[163] The fifth invective combines quotations from diatribes against idols in III Isaiah with a reference to the Deuteronomistic repudiation of images and an allusion to the introductory appeal to Yahweh in the book of Micah.[164]

Habakkuk's hymn to the victories of Yahweh follows the epic account of Marduk's victory over Tiamat but adds cross-references to the Priestly version of the same story.[165] In this version, Yahweh's battle with the Sea took place on a journey that led from Egypt to Qadesh in the wilderness of Paran (Num 10:12; 12:16b; 13:26a; 20:1). The victory, as in the *Enuma elish*, was accomplished by a storm that split the Sea, divided it into two parts and turned it into dry ground, but in the Priestly version it was a victory over the Egyptians and not simply a defeat of the Sea.[166]

The hymn also refers indirectly to images of destruction in Isaiah and Jeremiah. In Isaiah, the Assyrian invasion manifested Yahweh's anger, fury, and rage against his people, and the hymn describes Yahweh's victory over the Sea and the nations in the same terms.[167] Jeremiah compared the invasion of Judah to the collapse of the created order, and the hymn shares some of its special features. In both there is an emphasis on seeing; in both all the cosmic elements are in disarray, and in both the ruin of nations is marked by the collapse of tents and pavilions.[168]

The commentary added a reference to Micah, an allusion to the book of Isaiah, and a theme from the *Enuma elish*. In Micah punishment is decreed against the house of the guilty and the storehouses of guilt, and the commentary similarly specifies the punishment of the guilty house.[169] In a composite of texts from Isaiah the Assyrian torrent rushing into Judah reached up to the neck, but Yahweh established a firm foundation against it; and in the commentary the principle of retribution prescribed that the guilty be punished from their foundations up to their necks.[170] The *Enuma elish* describes the destruction of Tiamat and then turns to the defeat of her allies, and the commentary in the same spirit records the destruction of the guilty and then turns to the defeat of their allies, who stormed with them against the innocent (3:13b–14).[171]

The ending of the hymn is indebted to Micah and Nahum. Nahum's hymn depicted the advent of Yahweh's anger, fury, and rage and claimed that Yahweh was the best defense on the day of its arrival, and Habakkuk expressed a similar confidence in Yahweh on the impending day of distress.[172] Habakkuk, like Micah, saw imminent doom in the desolation that followed the harvest and, like Micah, could still rejoice in the God of his salvation.[173]

CONCLUSION

The lament and the commentary interpret the same literary and historical traditions but belong to different stages in their development. The lament explained that the resurgence of Babylon fulfilled all of Isaiah's expectations, and the commentary moved that the destruction of Babylon fulfilled all the conditions of the law. The difference between the two was not just the passage of time or the succession of events, but the development of literary and historical traditions that can be traced through the sources they used and reconstructed from the meaning they convey.

The lament was resigned to the crushing defeat that prophecy determined because it trusted in the God that faith and history empowered. The commentary was not reconciled to defeat, because it undermined the foundations of the restored community. The law was supposed to determine guilt and innocence, but the commentary saw that the law, as it had been promulgated by the Deuteronomist, could neither enforce the punishment of the guilty nor guarantee the vindication of the innocent. The theory of divine retribution that the commentary developed made the law completely effective and universally valid by ensuring the inevitability of punishment for every affront to the law. But it also meant, against the monolithic theory of sin and guilt proposed by the Deuteronomist, that those who had suffered unjustly in the Babylonian captivity were finally vindicated by the decline of the Babylonian empire.

Zephaniah (fig. 15)

Zephaniah composed his prophecy as a poetic oration in three parts. His gruesome forecast of the end of the world was revised after the fact in a prosaic and turgid version that redefined the calamity to suit the humble and defiant attitude of those who had survived.[174]

The first part of the oration presents the major premise and confronts the audience in an imaginative but traditional manner with the prophet's premonition of universal destruction. The new edition limited its effects to Judah and Jerusalem and, with even greater specificity, to certain quarters and classes of the city. The second part of the oration presents the minor premise, where the prophet exhorts his audience with the examples of catastrophe that overtook Canaan and Assyria, the Philistine cities and Nineveh. The edited version was unmoved by this destruction of traditional enemies and was satisfied to assign their territory to survivors of the calamity in Judah. The third part of the oration draws the conclusion for those who had learned nothing from the theory of the day of Yahweh or from its application to the important people and nations of the world and who would have to learn its lesson directly from the dreaded day itself. The revised speech blamed the occurrence of the day of Yahweh on certain evil elements in the city and assured the rest of the population that when the evil was purged they would join with the returning exiles to worship Yahweh in Zion.

STRUCTURE AND ORGANIZATION (FIG. 15)

Each part of the speech is composed in balanced stanzas and strophes that give it individuality, symmetry, and thematic development. The editor's arguments were added at the beginning of the first part, in the middle of the second part, and at the end of the third part.[175]

The Exordium (Zephaniah 1)

The first part, or exordium, was composed originally of three strophes with two stanzas each. Its coherence is clear in the symmetry of the strophes, with the first describing the end of the world in general, the

FIGURE 15

Zephaniah

	Zephaniah				The Book of Zephaniah		
			Exordium				
I	A	1	1:1a		A *	1	1:1b
		2	1:2–3aA			2	1:3aB
						3	1:[3b], 4–6
					B	1	1:7
						2	1:8
						3	1:9
					C	1	1:10
						2	1:11
					D	1	1:12
						2	1:13
	B	1	1:14		E	1	
		2	1:15–16			2	
	C	1	1:17		F	1	
		2	1:18			2	
			Exhortation				
II	A	1	2:1–2	II	A	1	
		2	2:3			2	
	B	1	2:4		B	1	
		2	2:5–6			2	2:5–7
					C	1	2:8
						2	2:9a
					D	1	2:9b–10
						2	2:11
	C	1	2:12–13		E	1	
		2	2:14			2	
	D	1	2:15a		F	1	
		2	2:15b			2	
			Valediction				
III	A	1	3:1–2	III	A	1	
		2	3:3–4			2	
		3	3:5			3	
	B	1	3:6–7		B	1	
		2	3:8			2	
					C	1	3:9–10
						2	3:11–12
						3	3:13

continued

FIGURE   15 (*cont*)

Zephaniah	The Book of Zephaniah		
	D	1	3:14
		2	3:15
	E	1	3:16–17
		2	3:18
	F	1	3:19
		2	3:20

Figure 15. Letters indicate strophes. Numbers denote stanzas.

second attributing it specifically to the arrival of the day of Yahweh, and the third detailing the connection between the day and the destruction of the world.[176] In the revised version the first strophe was expanded, and three other strophes were inserted to delay the original denouement and to assign the day of Yahweh a purifying function in Judah and Jerusalem. The symmetry in this edition is equally impressive. The first and last strophes still correspond in their description of humanity's extirpation, but the sin of humanity that Zephaniah spoke of in general has now been defined as the worship of Baal and of the hosts of heaven in Jerusalem (1:1–6 and 1:17–18). The second strophe in the new edition redirects the cosmic calamity to the palace and the temple, but it also quotes a line from Zephaniah's second strophe, now the second to last strophe in the declamation, for which it was designed as an explanatory complement.[177] The two strophes in the middle of this part of the revised speech agree, similarly, in referring to wealthy inhabitants of the city whose wealth will not help them survive the day of Yahweh (1:10–11 and 1:12–13). The results are totally different in each version, but the technical features are the same and they allow the editor to incorporate, match, absorb, and interpret the original while completely obstructing its drift.

The first strophe in Zephaniah's version finds its thematic harmony in insistence on the word and sayings of Yahweh and on their significance for individuals and for people in general.[178] The introduction gets its cohesion from repeating words and syllables and from its oblique reference to pertinent attributes of Yahweh (1:1a).[179] The second stanza also repeats words and expressions and deploys the traditional pun relating earth and earthlings.[180] In such an atmosphere of iteration only three elements stand out as unrepeated and they, interestingly enough, recur in the first, second, and third parts of the speech.[181]

The second strophe in Zephaniah's version is composed of two stanzas portraying the rapid, audible, and oppressive approach of the dreadful day of Yahweh. The first stanza revolves on itself with repeated words and expressions and consonantal sequences and sums up the fearsomeness of the situation in the terrible roar of Yahweh's battle cry.[182] The second stanza describes the anxiety, despair, and darkness as the trumpets and battle cries signal that the dreadful day of Yahweh is advancing past the fortified towns to the ramparts of the city. The strophe defines the day as a day of defeat in battle and builds through repetition to an auditory and visual crescendo.[183]

The third strophe in Zephaniah's speech draws conclusions from descriptions in the second. There the day of Yahweh was a day of anxiety and darkness, and here Yahweh says that he will cause anxiety and make people walk as if they were blind. There Yahweh was a warrior, and here he spills their blood and tramples their dead bodies. Both strophes say that it is a day of wrath. In the first he strides through the land; in the second he puts an end to its inhabitants. In the first it is all-encompassing; in the second it puts an end to everything. The strophe does not repeat itself but repeats what precedes and brings the cosmic day of Yahweh to the doorsteps of Jerusalem.[184]

The editorial segments and strophes are attached to the original in the usual manner and imitate some of its repetitive features but add others as well to cement their thematic and topical coherence. The addition to the introduction repeats one of its words and cleverly pretends that Hezekiah, whom Zephaniah listed as his great-grand-father, was the king by that name and therefore the great-grandfather of Josiah, to whose reign it then assigns Zephaniah.[185] It is important as a thematic introduction to this part of the speech, where the kings and princes of Judah are singled out for opprobrium (1:5, 8–9). The stanza that was added to the first strophe was fitted into its context by repeating one word and the mood of the original before proceeding with the cultic crimes that have to be purged from the city by the day of Yahweh. It imitates the stanza to which it was attached by repeating some words and expressions and by constructing long lines, but it differs from the original in its grammar, syntax, and prosody.[186] The first additional strophe begins by repeating the first clause of the original strophe, which it displaced, and, in deference to the sounds of the day of Yahweh that that strophe contains, enjoins silence in the presence of Yahweh.[187] But it goes on in the same mood as the intrusive stanza and, besides some of the lexical repetitiveness of the original, has the repetitiveness of parallelism and alliteration.[188] The second and third intrusive strophes refer obliquely to the day of Yahweh and directly to each other and continue with alliteration and parallelism unlike the original and with an odd intermixture of regular, short, and uncontrolled lines.[189] As in the original, they make the day of Yahweh audible, visible, and sensible but restrict it to the streets of Jerusalem.

The Exhortation (Zephaniah 2)

The second part of the speech was composed originally of four strophes, each with two complementary stanzas. Unlike the first part of the speech where Yahweh and Zephaniah communed, it is addressed directly to the audience or, intermittently, to the nations whose example they cite. The theme of each strophe and the topic of each stanza are marked as usual by repetition or an allied form of emphasis.

The first strophe is marked by puns and by repetition of words, expressions, and whole clauses. The first stanza pleads with a nation that has no redeeming qualities to pull itself together before fate takes shape, before time is up, before the day of Yahweh is upon them. It repeats the same verb twice, the same clause twice, and the same conjunction three times and is related to the last stanza in the exordium by a pun on money and value.[190] The second stanza has a similar repeated exhortation to the people to seek Yahweh in justice and good faith if they want to be hidden from the day of Yahweh and has an inverse relation to the end of the exordium, where, it seemed, nobody on earth would escape the day of Yahweh's wrath.[191] The strophe altogether makes it clear that time is running out for the audience and that only a grasp of fundamental justice would suffice to save them.

The second strophe supplies the motivation for the appeal and has to do entirely with the example of the Philistine cities. The first stanza mentions four cities of the Pentapolis — Gath, as usual, is missing — and coheres in its metaphorical description of them as divorced, bereaved, barren, or abandoned women.[192] The next stanza develops the theme concretely from a masculine perspective and contains, in remarkable contrast to the first stanza, direct discourse to the Philistines spoken in long alliterative periods with pauses, breaks, and caesuras. It develops the theme of the strophe by leaving Canaan and the land of Philistia a pastureland without any inhabitants.[193]

The third strophe in Zephaniah's exhortation turns abruptly north in words of Yahweh and the prophet to Assyria and Nineveh. The first stanza refers to their ancient origins in Cush, to their identity as the enemy from the North, to their historical renown as Assyria and Nineveh, and to their ultimate destiny as barren wilderness. The second stanza develops the last image by describing Nineveh, and in particular its royal palace, in ruins. The stanzas have specific topics, the first describing Yahweh's furious activity in Assyria and Nineveh, the second calmly surveying its results, but they develop the single theme of total eradication of a people by Yahweh on the great and dreaded day.[194]

The fourth strophe in the original exhortation is an apostrophe to Nineveh, the once magnificent city that has now become a ruin. The first stanza describes the city as a woman, proud and secure, who thought only of herself. The second stands back and takes the wayfarers' view as they gasp and fidget at the sight of wild animals prowling in her ruins. The whole strophe is phrased in brief lines related by alliteration and rhyme that express at once haughtiness and bewilderment.

In Zephaniah's version the strophes are paired and the pairs are related to produce a narrative flow and development. The first two strophes are related logically so that the example of the Philistines is meant to support the opening exhortation to reflect and seek refuge in Yahweh. The second pair traces the history of Nineveh from early Cushite beginnings to sorry decline and continues the first pair through both literal and thematic enjambment. In both pairs of strophes the capital cities are women, and in both the decline of the empire is pictured as urban deterioration into pastureland, but Philistia comprised a coterie of women whose territory was taken over by shepherds and their flocks, while Nineveh was a dowager whose land was left to wild animals. In both pairs the population is traced through its distant ancestry — Assyria from Cush, the Philistines from Crete and Canaan — and in both they are utterly destroyed. The word of Yahweh was flung against the Philistines by Zephaniah, and it was Yahweh himself who spoke against Assyria, but in both the word was annihilation. There is a sort of sympathy for the Philistine cities, and the glory of Nineveh, its utter desolation, and the shock that its collapse created are felt in great detail.

The revised edition of the exhortation simply added two more strophes with the same sort of replication. They came between the original pairs, broke their continuity, and were affixed to the exhortation by the usual artificial and contrary repetition.

Zephaniah ended his example of the Philistine cities with a long concatenated line in which the seacoast gradually was turned into well-watered meadows for shepherds and folds for flocks. The new material is affixed by mentioning the seacoast again and by describing the remnant of Israel as the flock that will pasture in the meadows and lie down in the folds. The stanza was sewn into the fabric of the original exhortation — it even sees Israel settled on the seacoast on the evening of the day that Philistia fell at noon — but the adaptation is merely literal and the ideas and images have nothing to do with the original meaning or method of the text.[195]

The two strophes that were added imitate the original in their direct address of Yahweh to the nations, but, apart from one line that is modeled on the long concatenated link line and their concluding lines, which come back to the story of the Philistines, they have nothing to do with the original.[196] Like the original, however, they are composed of matching stanzas and blend in the development of common themes. The first strophe has stanzas on the crime and appropriate punishment of Moab and Ammon spoken under oath by Yahweh the Lord of Hosts.[197] The second strophe assigns their lands to the remnant of the people of Israel and refers again to the crimes of the nations and to the humiliation of their Gods before Yahweh the Lord of Hosts.[198] The two strophes together treat Zephaniah's lesson and exhortation as if they were a series, by the editor's time standard in prophetic literature, of oracles against the nations.

The Valediction (Zephaniah 3)

The last part of the speech, its conclusion or valediction, had two strophes addressed to Jerusalem but was adorned with four others, partly with the same address, that summed up the editor's argument. In Zephaniah's version the strophes match and draw the hard lesson to be learned from the history of God and the nations of the world. In the new version the strophes are also paired, but the lesson is easy and consoling.

The first strophe develops the images and issues of the exhortation.[199] It is an apostrophe to Jerusalem, not by name but in the guise of a proud and insolent city like Nineveh.[200] The first stanza is addressed to the city as a woman like Nineveh who was sure of herself and who, like the Philistine women, was an outcast and frightened, but who despite the prophet's exhortation had never learned her lesson or sought refuge in Yahweh.[201] The second stanza accuses her judges, prophets, priests, and princes of acting recklessly and continues the time scheme that the exhortation started with the abandonment of Ashdod at noon by tracing their lack of restraint from evening through the night to daybreak.[202] The third stanza begins at first light with the just judgment of Yahweh, who does not tolerate such shameful behavior, and it is the logical consequence and thematic reversal of Zephaniah's exhortation to seek Yahweh and just judgment.[203] The whole strophe in effect is a transformation of the preceding part, which draws the imaginative lesson to be learned from the examples in the exhortation.

The second strophe refers to this lesson and also reverts to the images and ideas of the exordium to conclude the oration. Its two stanzas are direct discourse to the city and its inhabitants. In the first Yahweh explains what he has done to Philistia and to Nineveh and protests that despite all his efforts to educate them they learned nothing and persisted in their perversion. Its terms are taken from the exordium and exhortation; its imagery is the daily time scheme developed in the previous strophe.[204] The second stanza summons up the image of the day of Yahweh, when he will put an end to the world and render judgment on the nations. The language is from the exordium and the exhortation, and the imagery is of the end of time.[205]

The editorial version is linked to the original by literal and deictic repetitions and, in the manner of Zephaniah himself, by frequent allusions to its text.[206] The first strophe changes the terrible day of Yahweh into an awesome day when a purified people will invoke the name of Yahweh and the dispersed will come from afar to worship him, and when the arrogant will have been removed and the city will be filled with humble and submissive servants of Yahweh (3:9–10, 11–12, 13). The stanzas develop the same theme and are linked by literal repetition, but the first is partly an editorial join and the second and third by repetition reverse the negative thoughts and images that were expressed by Zephaniah.[207] The next strophe rephrases its main points, ostensibly to inject the sound of happy laughter in Zion, but in fact to correct, deny, or update the dire warnings of Zephaniah.[208] The third strophe is connected to the first by its reference to the day, and to the second by its invocation of Zion, but it changes the import of the original prophecy by limiting the purpose of the day of Yahweh to the elimination of suffering caused by the reproach of her enemies.[209] The last strophe has two stanzas interrelated by their interest in the future magnificence of Zion as compared with the shame that she suffered, and it brings to a close the editor's argument on the reunion of the exiles with the purified remnant of Judah.[210]

The oration has three distinct parts. Each part is composed in steps and stages to create a single comprehensible impression. None supposes what follows, but each is linked to what precedes in an imaginative and rhetorically rounded antithesis and synthesis. The three parts combined were the last words to be spoken before the day took place and prophecy turned into history.

The revised edition recognized the parts, the steps, and the stages and intervened at crucial points to turn history back into prophecy.

The day of Yahweh and the end of the world, in the editor's view, were meant for those in Judah and Jerusalem who followed foreign customs and dedicated themselves to Baal. It put an end to other nations and left room for the faithful and those who returned from exile to settle in peaceful surroundings. When judgment day was past and the people were purified, Zion would resound with the happy cries of those who came from beyond the rivers of Cush to be united in the worship of Yahweh. The day had been predicted, but its apparent fulfillment was not satisfying and its meaning still lay in the future.

LANGUAGE AND STYLE

The two editions of the speech are distinguished by their lexicons, their grammatical and syntactic preferences, their tone and viewpoint, their rhetoric, and their means of persuasion. The distinctions are sometimes blurred by imitation, but they are perceptible and impressive in their cumulative effect.

The lexicons overlap in editorializing but otherwise tend in different directions. Zephaniah chose words, images, and ideas that personified the relations between Yahweh as a force in the physical universe and the nations, cities, and creatures that depended on his pleasure from day to day. The author who revised his work was interested in Yahweh as an object of veneration, in classes of people and categories of worshipers. The lexicons overlap mainly in their references to the day of Yahweh and to the city and the country as a whole.

Zephaniah's principal images have to do with the natural order and with light and darkness as phases in a single day. The exordium signals the end of the created world and divides its elements among earth, sky, and water, distinguished by the light called "day," and inhabited by birds, fish, and humans. The end of creation is interpreted as a harvest, and the world is seen as featureless except for the sights and sounds of war and the fortifications that dot the landscape. The exhortation maintains the image of the eschatological harvest, with its references to gathering straw and blowing chaff, and it develops the images of war with specific reference to the Philistine cities and Assyria. The Philistine cities are personified as women who have been divorced, widowed, abandoned, or deprived of children. The Philistines themselves are identified as a people from distant Crete who settled along the coast of Canaan and whose urban civilization will be replaced by pastureland. The Assyrians are deemed casualties of war, and their capital, Nineveh, is recognized as a proud woman who will become a wilderness, her buildings a bird sanctuary or inhabited by barbarians and wild beasts.

The valediction maintains this last image in its perception of Jerusalem as a woman whose husband left her or as a town whose leaders are roaring lions and ravenous wolves. It returns to the initial conception of a single day to describe the evil that transpires between the evening and the morning, to compare the judgment of Yahweh to the unfailing light of dawn, and to conjure up a whole populace rising early to do wrong. The oration ends with a final appeal to watch for the fire of divine jealousy and wrath ready to harvest the nations and consume the world.

The revised version turns away from the created order to Judah, Jerusalem, and the temple, where Baal and the hosts of heaven were worshiped. The day ceases to be a natural time and becomes a liturgical calendar, with sacrifices offered by the nobility who have taken on foreign, and specifically Philistine, habits, with lamentations performed by the merchants and their Canaanite counterparts, and with hard times for the people who encouraged or participated in their ritual practices. Despite the day, there will be survivors, who will settle in the land abandoned by their neighbors; the distant nations and their humiliated Gods will bow down to Yahweh; and the purified remnant will serve God simply and unaffectedly in Zion.

Zephaniah has a preference for short asyndetic lines. The revised version enjoyed long ornamental periods with consecution and subordination and a plethora of modifiers. Zephaniah uses few adjectives and adverbs and likes simple sets of statements. The revised version liked adjectives, adverbs, long words, and a pileup of ideas, sayings, and images.[211]

Zephaniah varies his tone from part to part but maintains the same viewpoint. He is an observer of the world who sees the regularity of nature and natural sequences as ominous, a symbol of necessity and fate. The writer of the book is a defender of the faith who sees political power and wealth as the nemesis of the people. Zephaniah exhorts and cajoles. The editor condemns and derides. Zephaniah appeals to facts and evidence to persuade. The writer of his book resorts to cliché and name-calling. The original is always clear; the words always make sense; the images that they suggest are the substance of his thought. The author of his book likes allusion and innuendo and writes as if a clutter of conflicting material was the source of sure and certain ideas.

SOURCES AND INTERPRETATION

Zephaniah wrote his oration for people who knew the epic, Amos, the Priestly writer, Jeremiah, Nahum, and Habakkuk. The author of the

revised version depended mainly on the completed versions of Isaiah,
Jeremiah, Ezekiel, and the Deuteronomistic History. In Zephaniah's
prophecy a grasp of his sources is critical to his meaning and premonition. In the edited version the sources give substance to a few basic but
simple ideas that are intelligible without them.

From the Priestly writer Zephaniah took the theory and the
hierarchy of creation, and from the epic he took the sense that God
was passionately involved in its unfolding. From Jeremiah he gathered
that history and time coincided and that the end of the nation was the
end of the world. From Amos he borrowed the image of the day of
Yahweh as a day of defeat in battle. From Nahum and Habakkuk he
took the realization that it was time to take refuge in Yahweh. From all
these he wrote an oration explaining to the people that if they missed
the lesson of literature and history they would not have another chance.
His premonition was all the more impressive when it turned out to be
right.

The exordium begins with a reversal of creation in a cosmic harvest
decreed by Yahweh. The harvest was suggested by Jeremiah in his
dramatic warnings to Judah and Jerusalem.[212] The hierarchy of creation and the creatures that live in it was proposed in the Priestly
cosmology,[213] and it was complemented in the story of the deluge by
the Priestly promise that world order would not be destroyed and that
people would never again be cut off by a flood.[214] The scouring of
humans off the face of the earth was the reasoning behind the epic
story of the flood.[215] The vision of the world in chaos without living
creatures was Jeremiah's analogy of an invasion of Judah led and
instigated by God.[216] In Zephaniah's oration one source is laid against
the other to create the novel impression that the world truly will return
to its original state before time, place, people, and political history
began.

The body of the exordium is an appeal to the day of Yahweh as
Amos and others had described it. The expression itself and its
association with storms, darkness, warriors, and the sounds of war
were literary contributions by Amos.[217] The rapid approach of the day
can be seen in Isaiah's vision of an enemy invasion.[218] Its association
with clouds and the awful anxiety it produced were described by
Nahum.[219] Its connection with the wrath of Yahweh and the invasion of
a bitter foe was suggested in the vision of Habakkuk.[220] Images of the
day of Yahweh and the end of the world were available in the sources,
but they became immediate and critical as Zephaniah summoned the
people to attend to the gathering decline of culture and civilization.

The seriousness of Zephaniah's insight is evident at the end of the exordium, when the two images are explicitly combined. In Jeremiah's presentation chaos was imminent but limited and meant as a lesson. In Nahum's version it would be total but limited to the enemies of Yahweh. In Zephaniah's speech, however, the end is imminent, unlimited, and universal, and no device or human resource can stop it.[221]

The exhortation begins with a contrast between the barren and abandoned women of Philistia and the fertile decree of Yahweh that is about to give birth to the day of his wrath.[222] The cities of Philistia that he mentions were included among Amos's oracles against the nations.[223] His urgent appeals to seek Yahweh and his judgment and to search for simplicity and justice are audible repercussions from the prophecies of Amos, Hosea, and Jeremiah.[224] The feeling that justice might afford a hiding place from the anger of Yahweh recalls Isaiah's description of the people in Jerusalem hiding in lies instead of taking a stand on justice.[225] Almost everything in the exhortation is traditional and familiar, except the extreme urgency and excitement of his speech and the presentiment that he had from the decimation of Canaan and the cosmopolitan Philistine cities.

The end of Zephaniah's exhortation is mostly original but has elements from typical descriptions of the ruin of Jerusalem. He demonstrates nice genealogical skills in tracing the origins of Assyria to Cush but records the capture of Nineveh in terms that Jeremiah used to project the ruin of Jerusalem.[226] He proves his rhetorical genius in describing the desolation of the palace of Nineveh but is careful to refer to the Priestly story of creation to suggest its return to a primitive state of nature.[227] He talks of Nineveh in terms that might just as well apply to Jerusalem and in effect displays the day of Yahweh as the end of the known urban civilization.[228]

The conclusion of his speech includes criticisms that date at least to the time of Isaiah, but they differ from those of most of predecessors in being directed against specific ranks of local government.[229] He describes the princes and judges in terms that Jeremiah and Habakkuk used to describe the enemy from the North.[230] He attributes to the prophets the treachery that Hosea and Jeremiah thought was characteristic of the court.[231] He blames the priests for defiling the cult and, as Micah, Jeremiah, and Habakkuk implied, for doing violence to the law.[232] He envisages Yahweh as the source of law and justice, whose judgment, as Hosea saw, is as sure as the first light of the sun.[233] In effect, the day of Yahweh is the day of Yahweh's judgment on the world and all its kingdoms.

The speech is impressive in its simplicity and fidelity to tradition. The warning of the prophets had produced a sort of reform, at least as

Jeremiah dramatized it, that had no real or lasting effect. Zephaniah simply saw Yahweh taking the law into his own hands.

The editor of his work was glad to see an end to the culture and civilization that Zephaniah wanted to save. In the exordium the new edition included all the classes of society that had to be eliminated along with their beliefs and worldly ways. In the exhortation it snapped at the Transjordanian nations who adapted to the shifting sands of imperial designs and seemed to threaten Judah's meager survival. In the last part it extolled the virtues of the pathetic remnant that submitted to the government of God in Zion. In the place of culture and civilization it put humility and unadorned worship of Yahweh.

The beliefs and practices that it opposed among the higher classes of Jerusalem society were those that the Deuteronomist in particular had seen as occasions of sin and causes of the fall of Jerusalem.[234] The worship of Baal and the hosts of heaven was one of the crimes of Manasseh that Josiah unsuccessfully expiated,[235] and in the book of Jeremiah it is given as one of the reasons for the Babylonian capture of the city (Zeph 1:5a and Jer 8:2; 19:13; 32:29). The editor, in anticipation of the theocracy that will be proposed at the end of the oration, associated this public worship of Baal with liturgies in honor of the kings[236] and with popular disloyalty to Yahweh, which might merit total annihilation.[237] The editor's perception of the day of Yahweh as a day inaugurating acceptable sacrifice is the other side of the coin and is indebted both to royal rituals and to the reflections of the editors of Isaiah and the book of Jeremiah.[238] The rebuke to those who skipped over the threshold of the temple and who filled the house of their divine overlord with violence and with fraud combines a quotation from the Deuteronomistic etiology of Philistine worship with an allusion to Micah's repudiation of the wealthy who defiled the temple in Jerusalem.[239] The lamentation of the merchants in the commercial district is represented in terms of the siege of Jerusalem as seen by Micah and Jeremiah.[240] The frustration of their plans is seen in Amos's image of building houses and planting vineyards that they will not inhabit or enjoy.[241] The day of Yahweh, in this version, does not have to do with torques in the structure of the civilized world but with willful deviation on the part of a few from the right worship of Yahweh.

The editor's exhortation inspired the audience with visions of Moab and Ammon in ruins and with the defiant sense that even the most distant nations would bow down in submission to Yahweh. There is some evidence that Moab and Ammon took advantage of Judah when it was defeated by the Babylonians (Zeph 2:8–10 and Ezekiel 25); but the way they behaved is modeled on the Deuteronomist's perception of the Assyrian challenge to Yahweh (Zeph 2:8 and 2 Kgs 19:6, 22), and retaliation is phrased in the Deuteronomistic cliché about Sodom and Gomorrah (Zeph 2:9 and Genesis 19; Deut 29:22; 32:32). The submission of the farthest reaches of the Mediterranean world to Yahweh is based on Zephaniah's geography, on Priestly terminology, and on the wishful thinking of the time.[242]

The editorial conclusion to the speech speaks of the return of the exiles and of the eschatological reform of the cult. The first strophe, in reliance on late historical and prophetic texts,[243] describes the return of the diaspora and the formation of a humble and pious community of worship. The second strophe matches it with the happiness of the community gathered, in the words of Jeremiah, around Yahweh their king.[244] The third strophe, in a reversal of the war games in Nahum, sees Yahweh relaxed in Zion's midst.[245] The last strophe complements it with the image, borrowed from the revision of Micah, of the tiny remnant from Babylon nestled in security and self-satisfaction under the comforting watch of Yahweh their shepherd.[246]

CONCLUSION

Zephaniah gave new life to the prophecy of Amos, after the euphoria of the reformation period had tried to temper its bitter thrust. His speech is addressed to the city and its inhabitants and encourages them to act responsibly in the hope that Yahweh might relent and not execute his judgment against them. He has given up on the political and religious leaders and has little hope that the city, no matter how superb, can survive when imperial and commercial empires have disappeared. His confidence was founded on the law that Yahweh had taken into his own hands and by whose principles he was now bound. The old order was going, and nothing was left but to submit to the divine judgments and to the fate that decreed creation's destiny.

The editor envisaged a new order under the direct governance of God. Zephaniah maintained his equanimity by putting his faith in the created order. The editor put the community's confidence in the liturgical order where the remnant, freed from wrongdoers and from the example of the nations, could serve Yahweh in unison and without pretension. Zephaniah believed in the old order the way the prophets and historians had constructed and perceived it. His editor thought he was right about seeking refuge in Yahweh but was not interested in thinking about the world, time, the cycles of culture, and civilization. It was humbling enough just to be alive.

Ezekiel (fig. 16)

Ezekiel composed his prophecy in Babylon as a chronicle of events surrounding the siege of Jerusalem and the ensuing revival of Israel. It begins at the end, with the vision that occasioned and authorized the chronicle, and it ends slightly earlier, with the vision of a new beginning that made sense of the intervening prophecies of doom. The chronology was problematic for those who lived in Jerusalem and had never heard any of his prophecies, and the chronicle was annotated to explain that, despite his original prophetic authorization, Ezekiel had been obliged to keep silent until after the fall of Jerusalem.[247]

The Ezekiel chronicle in its original Babylonian form is distinguished from its Jerusalem update by its perspective, its interests, its organization, and by the things that it supposes and expects. The annotations stand out by their insistence, their reduplication, and their verbosity as they endeavor to reduce the magic of the original to a more concrete and manageable scale.[248]

STRUCTURE AND ORGANIZATION

The original chronicle was composed of ten books, dealing alternately with the fate of Jerusalem and the house of Israel. The books, in turn, were composed of columns, containing visions, imaginary discourses, literary fiction, dramatization, and historical allusions. The columns, analogously, were composed of paragraphs or strophes containing riddles, allegories, symbols, metaphors, images, and their interpretations. The Jerusalem version maintained this distinction of books, columns, and components, but its many annotations interrupted their narrative sequence and required complementary notes and interjections to reestablish their continuity (fig. 16).[249]

The distinction of books, columns, and their components is marked by repetition.[250] Columns are distinguished by the way they begin and end and by internal topical connections between them. Books are configurations of columns that are joined formally to one another and separated in substance and function from their surroundings. The distinctions are relative, since repetition both binds and separates, and the books, columns, and components are cyclic movements in a continuous chronicle.

Books (fig. 16)

Books are distinguished by the way they begin and end, by the conjunction or concatenation of their columns, by the issues they treat,

F I G U R E   1 6

Ezekiel

BOOK ONE (Ezekiel 1–3)

Col. 1	Col. 2	Col. 3
1:1	1:28b; 2:1–3	3:1–7
1:[2–3a}	2:[4–5]	3:8–9
1:[3b]–6[7–8]	2:6[7]	3:10–11
1:[9]	2:8	3:12a[12b–13]
1:10[11aA]11aBb[12]	2:9–10	3:[14a]14b–15aA[Bb]
1:[13–14]		3:[16–17]
1:[15–16]		3:[18–19]
1:[17–18]		3:[20–21]
1:[19–21]		3:22–24
1:22–23		3:[25–27]
1:[24a]		
1:[24b]25a		
1:[25b–]26		
1:27–28a		

BOOK TWO (Ezekiel 4–7)

Col. 1	Col. 2	Col. 3	Col. 4
4:1–2	5:1–2	6:1–5	7:1–4
4:3abA[3bB]	5:[3–4]	6:6–7	7:5–7
4:[4–5a]	5:5–6	6:[8–10]	7:8–9
4:[5b–6]	5:[7–10]	6:11	7:[10–11]
4:[7–8]	5:11–12	6:12–13	7:[12–13]
4:9a[9b]10–11[12]	5:13	6:[14]	7:[14–16]
4:[13–15]	5:14–15		7:[17–19]
4:16–17	5:16–17		7:[20–22]
			7:[23–24]
			7:[25–27]

BOOK THREE (Ezekiel 8–11)

Col. 1	Col. 2	Col. 3	Col. 4
8:1–2	9:1–2a	[10:1–3]	11:1a[1b]2–4
8:3–4	9:[2b–3]4	[10:4–5]	11:5–7a[7b]8[9–10]
8:5–10,11°	9:5–6a	[10:6–9]	11:[11–12]
8:12–14	9:6b–7	[10:10–14]	11:[13]
8:15–16	9:[8]9–10	[10:15–17]	11:[14–21]
8:17–18	9:11	[10:18–19]	11:[22]23–25
		[10:20]	
		[10:21–22]	

continued

FIGURE 16 (*cont*)

BOOK FOUR (Ezekiel 12–15)

Col. 1	Col. 2	Col. 3	Col. 4
12:1–3	13:1–3	14:1–3	[15:1–5]
12:4–5[6]	13:4–6	14:4–5	[15:6–8]
12:7a[7b]8–10a[10b]	13:7–8	14:6–8	
12:[11a]11b	13:9	14:9[10]11	
12:[12–16]	13:10–12	14:[12–14]	
12:[17–20]	13:13–16	14:[15–16]	
12:21–25	13:[17–18a]	14:[17–20]	
12:26–28	13:[18b–19]	14:[21–23]	
	13:[20–21]		
	13:[22–23]		

BOOK FIVE (Ezekiel 16–19)

Col. 1	Col. 2	Col. 3	Col. 4
16:1–4	17:1–5	18:1–4	[19:1–9]
16:5–6	17:6a	18:5–9	[19:10–14]
16:7–11	17:6b–8	18:10–13	
16:12	17:9–10	18:14–18	
16:13–14	17:11–13bA[13bB–14]15	18:[19–20]	
16:15–16	17:16–18	18:[21–23]	
16:17–19	17:[19–21]	18:[24]	
16:20–22	17:[22–24]	18:[25–28]	
16:23–26		18:[29–30a]	
16:27–29		18:[30b–32]	
16:30–31			
16:32–34			
16:35–41			
16:42–43a[43b]			
16:[44–47]			
16:[48–51]			
16:[52]			
16:[53–55]			
16:[56–58]			
16:[59–63]			

BOOK SIX (Ezekiel 20–23)

Col. 1	Col. 2	Col. 3	Col. 4
20:1–3	21:[1–5]	[22:1–5]	23:1–4
20:4–6	21:6–8	[22:6–8]	23:5–10
20:7–9	21:[9–10]	[22:9–11]	23:11–15
20:10–12	21:11–12	[22:12]	23:16–21
20:13–14	21:13–15a	[22:13]	23:22–27
20:15–16	21:[15b–16]	[22:14–16]	23:28–29

continued

FIGURE 16 (*cont*)

BOOK SIX (Ezekiel 20-23)

Col. 1	Col. 2	Col. 3	Col. 4
20:17–20	21:[17–18]	[22:17–22]	23:[30–35]
20:21–22	21:[19–22]	[22:23–25]	23:[36–39]
20:23–26	21:[23–25]	[22:26]	23:[40–44]
20:27–28[29]	21:[26–28]	[22:27–28]	23:[45–49]
20:30–31	21:[29]	[22:29–31]	
20:[32–38]	21:[30–32]		
20:[39–44]	21:[33–34]		
	21:[35–37]		

BOOK SEVEN (Ezekiel 24-28)

Col. 1	Col. 2	Col. 3	Col. 4	Col. 5
24:1–5	[25:1–5]	26:1–6	27:1–25	28:1–10
24:6–8	[25:6–7]	26:7–14	27:26–27	28:11–19
24:9–12	[25:8–11]	26:15–18	27:28–32	28:[20–24]
24:13–14	[25:12–14]	26:19–21	27:33–36	28:[25–26]
24:[15–17]	[25:15–17]			
24:[18–24]				
24:[25–27]				

BOOK EIGHT (Ezekiel 29-33)

Col. 1	Col. 2	Col. 3	Col. 4	Col. 5
29:1–6a	[30:1–3]	31:1–4[5]6–9	32:[1–2]	[33:1–6]
29:6b–9a	[30:4–5]	31:10–13[14]	32:[3–6]	[33:7–9]
29:[9b–12]	[30:6–9]	31:15–18	32:[7–10]	[33:10–11]
29:[13–16]	[30:10–12]		32:[11–16]	[33:12–20]
29:[17–18]	[30:13–17]		32:17–21	[33:21–26]
29:[19–21]	[30:18–19]		32:22–23	[33:27–29]
	[30:20–21]		32:24–25	[33:30–31]
	[30:22–26]		32:26–28	[33:32–33]
			32:[29–30]	
			32:[31–32]	

BOOK NINE (Ezekiel 34-39)

Col. 1	Col. 2	Col. 3	Col. 4	Col. 5	Col. 6
34:1–2	[35:1–4]	36:1–2	37:1–2	[38:1–6]	[39:1–7]
34:3	[35:5–9]	36:3–4	37:3–6	[38:7–9]	[39:8–10]
34:4–5	[35:10–13]	36:5°–6	37:7–8	[38:10–13]	[39:11–13]
34:6	[35:14–15]	36:7–10	37:9	[38:14–16]	[39:14–16]
34:7–10		36:11–12	37:10–11	[38:17–20]	[39:17–24]
34:11–14[–16]		36:13–15	37:12–14	[38:21–23]	[39:25–29]
34:[17–19]		36:[16–21]	[37:15–17]		

continued

FIGURE 16 (*cont*)

BOOK NINE (Ezekiel 34-39)

Col. 1	Col. 2	Col. 3	Col. 4	Col. 5	Col. 6
34:[20–24]		36:[22–23]	[37:18–19]		
34:[25–27]		36:[24–25]	[37:20–23]		
34:[28–31]		36:[26–28]	[37:24–28]		
		36:[29–31]			
		36:[32]			
		36:[33–36]			
		36:[37–38]			

BOOK TEN (Ezekiel 40–48)

Col. 1	Col. 2	Col. 3
40:1–3	43:1–3	47:1–2
40:4–5bA	43:4–5	47:3–5
40:5bB–7	43:[6–9]	47:6–9
40:8–10	43:[10–12]	47:10–12
40:11–12	43:[13–17]	47:[13–14]
40:13–16	43:[18–27]	47:[15–16]
40:17–18	[44:1–3]	47:[17–20]
40:19–23a	[44:4–8]	47:[21–23]
40:23b–27a	[44:9–14]	[48:1–8]
40:27b–31	[44:15–16]	[48:9–10]
40:32–34	[44:17–19]	[48:11–13]
40:35–37[38]	[44:20–22]	[48:14–15]
40:[39–44]	[44:23–27]	[48:16]
40:[45–46]	[44:28–31]	[48:17]
40:[47]	[45:1–3]	[48:18]
40:[48–50]	[45:4–5]	[48:19–20]
41:1–2a	[45:6–7]	[48:21]
41:2b–3	[45:8]	[48:22]
41:4–6a	[45:9–12]	[48:23–28]
41:6b–7	[45:13–15]	[48:29]
41:8–12	[45:16–17]	[48:30–34]
41:13–14	[45:18–20]	[48:35]
41:[15–22a]	[45:21–25]	
41:[22b–26]	[46:1–3]	
[42:1–6]	[46:4–7]	
[42:7–12]	[46:8–10]	
[42:13–14]	[46:11–12]	
[42:15–20]	[46:13–15]	
	[46:16–17]	
	[46:18]	
	[46:19–20]	
	[46:21–24]	

Figure 16. Strophes and paragraphs are on separate lines. Brackets indicate the work of the editor.

by their different dates and circumstances, and by their alternating interest in Jerusalem and Israel. The revised version sometimes exaggerated their distinction and forged their editorial connection.

The first book is the vision that persuaded Ezekiel to write his prophetic chronicle (chaps. 1–3). In the first column he sees the vision and hears a voice; in the second column the voice speaks to him and tells him what to say; and in the third column he is taken into exile to say it.[251] The boundaries of the book are marked by verbatim repetitions. The book begins and ends with Ezekiel in exile by the river Chebar (1:1aB = 3:15a). After the vision and again in exile he is sustained in spirit (2:2a = 3:24a). At the end of the book he sees once more the vision of the glory of God that he saw at the beginning (3:23 = 1:1aBbA, 28a).

The Jerusalem version identified Ezekiel as a priest and prophet, made his vision inaugural by redating it to the fifth year of the exile of Jehoiachin, revised it to include traditional iconography and paraphernalia from the Solomonic temple, and introduced notions of prophecy and divine justice that become crucial as the chronicle progresses.[252] These changes are critical, substantial, and proleptic and overload the original context with so much extraneous material that the revision found it necessary to fake a secondary clarifying link to the following book (3:25–27).[253]

In both versions the first book is programmatic. In the first version it introduces the characters and the viewpoint of the chronicle. In the second version it introduces the principal images and ideas that will be developed bit by bit as the story progresses. In both there is startling material that recommends further reading.

In the original, or Babylonian, version God appears in amazing splendor in the likeness of a human person.[254] In what follows this is the God who abandons Jerusalem and settles on a mountain east of the city, where he remains until another temple is built (8:1–4; 11:23–25; 40:1–3; 43:1–3). The narrator, known by the name Ezekiel only in the later Jerusalem version (1:3; 24:24), is identified as a human person like God:[255] his character is universal, sustained throughout the chronicle, and derived from the story of creation that underlies the chronicle and is alluded to from time to time in metaphors and ditties of death and resurrection.[256] This person receives a message from God for the people of Israel written in a scroll filled with lamentation, meditation, and mourning (2:1–3, 6, 8–10). He is told to swallow the scroll and, since the house of Israel was unwilling to hear it, is taken away to tell it to the people in exile (3:1–12a, 14b–15aA, 22–24). By this conceit the scroll is identified with the following books that are unrolled in exile far from the land that devoured its people and that is strewn with their dead bodies (36:1–15) but in full view of the true homeland, where the house of Israel will be envisaged at the end of the prophecy as another creation living around the temple inhabited by the glory of God (37:1–14; 43:1–3).

In the Jerusalem version God is envisioned as enthroned upon the cherubim in a vehicle that moves from place to place through the skies. The original vision is changed just enough to indicate locomotion (1:7–9, 11*, 12–21, 24, 25b), but the real meaning of the vision is explained in the third book (9:3; 10:1–22; 11:22) and the proper setting for such a contraption is described in the revised plans for the temple (41:15–26). In this edited version Ezekiel is intruded into the chronicle and is given a human biography and a clearly defined role. He is identified as a priest, and later interest in diet and the Priestly accoutrements of the temple emphasizes this affiliation.[257] He is called a prophet (2:4–5 = 33:33), and the point is made by describing him as one of the ancient mummers whose bizarre behavior (4:4–8, 9b) had symbolic value,[258] and by attributing his silence to divine constraint.[259] He is called a watchman, and his attempt to rehabilitate the guilty is confirmed by the fact that a few people in Jerusalem did survive[260] and, correlatively, by the argument that it was only those who were misled by their prophets or persisted in their guilt who did not escape.[261]

The second book (chaps. 4–7) turns from the house of Israel to the fate of Jerusalem and its broader geographical significance. The book coheres because its four columns treat the same issue using the same terms. Because of its obscenities,[262] and to satisfy the anger of Yahweh that cannot be appeased,[263] Jerusalem, the mountain of Israel,[264] will be besieged and will be devastated by the sword, by famine, and by plague.[265] There is a sequence of images and some variation in the repetitions as the catastrophe builds up from siege and famine in the first column, to death by the sword, famine, and disease in the second column, which spreads from the city into its environs in the third column, and finally results in the total destruction of Israel and the whole world.

The revised version does nothing to change the structure of the book, but it interjects its own ideas and adds material that relates it to the surrounding books. The ideas have to do with just punishment and the survival of a remnant,[266] with a radical distinction between Israel and Judah (4:4–8), and with a correlative enumeration of those who deserved to die (6:14; 7:20–27). The links with the surrounding books occur in the first and last columns. The first column supposes the binding of Ezekiel, his role as prophetic intercessor, and his Priestly status, which were introduced in the preceding book.[267] The last column alludes to the defiling of the temple, which is the issue in the following book.[268] The additions obscure the single-mindedness of Ezekiel's book and its relative isolation from its environs, but nothing is done to disturb the relation of one column to the next.

The third book (chaps. 8–11) contains Ezekiel's vision of Jerusalem being decimated and abandoned by the glory of Yahweh. The date at the beginning separates this book from the preceding and relates it instead to the first book, where the system of dating began (8:1 and 1:1). This relationship is confirmed by the description of the glory of God at the beginning and end of both books,[269] by the vision that both books situate in the North (1:4 and 8:5), and by their common interest in Ezekiel's residence.[270] The boundaries of the book are marked by the presence of the glory of God in Jerusalem at the beginning and by its departure from the city at the end. The internal consistency of the book is derived from its tour of the temple precinct (8:5–18; 9:1–2a; 11:1a), where the sight of the obscenities[271] committed by the entire city, and in particular by its elders (8:11; 9:6), leads to the merciless defilement of the temple and to the final abandonment of the city.[272]

The Jerusalem version clearly recognized the connection between this book and the first and used the occasion to insert an interpretation of the amazing vehicle that Ezekiel had seen by the river Chebar (9:3; 10:1–2; 11:22). The insertion disrupted the simple sequence of the columns, and this was corrected by adding similar references in the first and last columns to two different men with the same name (Jaazaniah, 8:11aA; 11:1b). This artificial link became the occasion for further musings on the remnant that were anticipated by an interjection early in the book (9:8; 11:13). This concern for the remnant is continued at the end of the book, where the conflicting claims of the exiles and of those left in Jerusalem are resolved in favor of the exiles and, by implication, of those few in Jerusalem who might not have gone after the disgusting and obscene desires of their heart (11:14–16, 17–20, 21). This discussion, in turn, relates this book to the beginning of the next, where exile is a special issue. All in all, the revision tried to maintain the structure of the original and at the same time construct an argument that developed coherently from book to book.

The fourth book (chaps. 12–15) is distinguished by its boundaries and its internal consistency.[273] All of its columns are concerned with the fulfillment of prophecy. The first column deals figuratively and explicitly with the enactment of oracles and the accomplishment of visions.[274] The second berates the prophets who mislead the people by

lying about their visions (13:1–16). The third blames the people who
are set in their ways and inquire of the prophets, who mislead them by
providing the answers their inquiry provokes (14:1–9, 11). The book
is separated from the preceding book and related to earlier books in
the chronicle. It ignores the temple in Jerusalem, which occupied the
preceding book, and turns to Israel, the land of Israel, and the house
of Israel, which were the focus of the first and second books.[275] It is
related to the first book by repeated use of one of its peculiar designations of the house of Israel,[276] and to the second or penultimate book
by its use of mime,[277] its aversion to idols,[278] and its assurance that the
day of Yahweh had arrived.[279]

The revised version recognized the structure and connections of the
original and added its own arguments and emphases. It is concerned,
as usual, with justifying the punishment inflicted on Jerusalem by
limiting it to the guilty and exempting an innocent remnant,[280] and by
including among the guilty especially the kings and their immediate
associates.[281] It recognizes the connection between this and the penultimate book and adds a whole series of cross-references to punishment
by the sword, famine, and disease that it described.[282] In Ezekiel's
version the histories of Israel and Jerusalem coincide, and he moves
deliberately, in successive books, from one to the other. The revision,
on the contrary, assures the coherence of its argument by creating a
continuity and development from book to book. It relates this book to
the preceding book by recalling that divine punishment was a response
to violence,[283] and by referring to the metaphor of a branch fueling the
fire of divine anger, which occurs in the same context.[284] It anticipates
the argument of the following book by heaping scorn on the kings and
by alluding to the upcoming debate on individual guilt and innocence
(14:12–23 and 18:1–32).

The fifth book (chaps. 16–19) returns to Jerusalem to consider its
relations with Yahweh and the nations. The boundaries of the book are
marked by references to parents and their children: in the first column
Jerusalem is called the abandoned Canaanite child of an Amorite father
and a Hittite mother; in the last column the guilt or innocence of the
child is distinguished from the guilt or innocence of its parents (16:3
and 18:1–8). The coherence of the book depends on its repetition of
ideas and images. Each column deals with growing up and the choices
that it involves. The first describes the young girl who became Yahweh's
darling and grew up to be a woman of the world (16:1–43a). The
second describes the sprout that grew wild and withered (17:1–13abA,
15–18). The third describes the typical boy who either grows up to be
like his father or goes his own way (18:1–18). Each column, besides,

deals with the process of growing up as a matter of life or death: the girl almost died but Yahweh kept her alive; the sprout is the king who died in Babylon; the innocent father or son will live but the guilty will die.[285] All of the columns also deal with Jerusalem's foreign relations. The first two columns contrast the city's covenants with Yahweh and with the nations,[286] and among these nations include Egypt, Assyria and Babylon, Canaan, and the Philistines.[287] The second column says that the king of Babylon will take away the lives of many people, but the third column makes it clear that people's lives belong to Yahweh and will be taken away according to actual rather than imputed guilt or innocence.[288] The entire book traces Jerusalem's history to its origins to explain that its fault is its own.

The revised version followed its regular pattern by trying to clarify Ezekiel's ideas and include them in a comprehensive argument that could be developed from book to book. Another story was added to the first column to prove that Jerusalem deserved to be punished but nevertheless would survive and enter into a new covenant with Yahweh (16:44–63). Another interpretation was added to the second column to prove that, although the king deserved to die, some would survive and be incorporated into a new kingdom (17:19–24). Other clauses were added to the rules of guilt and innocence to allow for the possibility of repentance and survival (18:19–32). Another column was added to redirect some of Yahweh's fury from Jerusalem, the faithless woman, to the woman who was mother to the faithless kings (19:1–14). The book maintains its own coherence but is also attached more surely to the surrounding argument: Ezekiel referred again to the obscenities committed in Jerusalem,[289] and the additions to the first column stress this connection with the third book.[290] The fate of the king in the second column is described in terms taken from the fourth book (17:19–21 and 12:13–16). The possibility of repentance and survival takes up the argument that was introduced in the first book (18:21–32 and 3:16–21). The lament for the leaders is supposedly part of the scroll that Ezekiel consumed,[291] but it also anticipates topics discussed in the next book (22:6–13).

The sixth book (chaps. 20–23) continues the alternating scheme by turning away from the possible origins of Jerusalem's crimes to the true story of Israel's guilt. Its boundaries are marked by the date at the beginning of the book and by the concern of the first and last columns to trace responsibility for the nation's crimes to its connections with Egypt.[292] The coherence of the book depends on its argument from history—the history of Israel in general and the records of Samaria and Jerusalem in particular—proving that the nation as a whole was wrong and that both the innocent and the guilty deserved to die.[293]

This argument caused enormous difficulty for the Jerusalem version, which insisted from the beginning that a remnant would survive and that only the guilty would be punished. It modified the chronicle in the usual way by adding its ideas at the end of columns and by fabricating connections between the columns and with the surrounding books. The first column in the Babylonian version traced the history of Israel from the exodus to the settlement in the land to prove its inveterate evil. The Jerusalem version adds a postscript on a new exodus from exile during which Yahweh will scrutinize the nation and sift out the wrongdoers before bringing the rest into the land to worship him (20:29, 32–38). In the original version Yahweh's response to this inveterate evil was to draw his sword and strike indiscriminately throughout the land (21:6–8, 11–15a). In the Jerusalem version there is an attempt to interpret this as an allegory, to consider the sword a form of divine discipline, to take it away from God and put it in the hands of the king of Babylon, and to limit its critical effect to the princes of Judah and the Ammonites (21:1–5, 9–10, 15b–37). The matter was of such importance to this version that another column was added to prove the guilt of the princes and their associates and insist that the sword was used to test or refine the rest (22:1–31). In the Babylonian version the next column justified the verdict against both the innocent and the guilty by tracing the history of evil down to most recent events in Samaria and the city. The Jerusalem version added a postscript to insist on their guilt, and also to point out that there were some innocent people who deplored the evil of the city and who consequently were excluded from its fate (23:30–49). The whole argument of the revised version gains force from deliberate connections with its antecedents in the preceding book and with its sequel in the next book.[294] The Babylonian chronicle is sketchy and episodic and gets its strength from the breadth of its vision. The Jerusalem version had to bridge the gaps between the episodes to ensure the logic and persuasiveness of its argument.

The seventh book (chaps. 24–28) continues the alternating pattern by returning to the siege and capture of Jerusalem. The siege is mentioned explicitly, but the actual destruction of the city is evoked in the allegory of a sacrificial caldron, or alluded to in the gloating of Tyre, or exemplified in descriptions of the military, commercial, and mythical collapse of the Tyrian empire.[295] The book is distinguished by its dates and by its interest in great cities that are besieged and taken by the king of Babylon. Its boundaries are marked by reuse of the images of gravel and bare rock and by repeated use of the image of death as being consumed by fire and water.[296] In this book the Jerusalem of history disappears, and Ezekiel does not mention it again.

The Jerusalem version joins this book with the next as a series of oracles against the nations of the world. The series begins with the siege of Jerusalem and ends with its fall (24:1–14; 33:21–22), and its boundaries are marked by reflections on Ezekiel's prophetic office and the reasons for his silence until it was too late (24:15–27; 33:1–20). In this book the Jerusalem edition added postscripts to the first and last columns and inserted another column to fill in the details. From its perspective the distinction between Judah and Israel takes on special importance, and the different nations are vituperated for what they did to each separately; Moab, Edom, and Ammon for what they did to Judah; and Sidon for what it did to Israel.[297]

The eighth book (chaps. 29–33) turns to Israel's reliance on Egypt. It is distinguished by the dates that occur in every column and that overlap with the dates cited in the seventh book.[298] It gets its internal consistency from a description of the gradual banishment of Egypt from the land of the living into the recesses of Sheol. The description continues the reversal of the myth of creation, which began in the preceding story of Tyre and, like it, is an allegory of Israel's destruction and descent into the realm of the dead.

The Jerusalem version, as usual, elaborates on the links between this book and those around it in order to develop its own argument. The first column emphasizes the allegory by drawing an exact parallel between the dispersal and restoration of Egypt and Israel (29:9b–21). The second column continues in the same vein and applies to Egypt all the language and imagery that has been used to describe the crimes of Israel and its fate (30:1–26). The fourth column has a lament for the Pharaoh like the lament for the kings of Judah (32:1–16; cf. 19:1–14) and lists among the nations languishing with Egypt in Sheol the archetypical enemies of Israel and Judah.[299] The last column draws the logical conclusion that Jerusalem has fallen, but it uses the occasion to stress that only the guilty died and to reflect on the fact that the allegorical mode used by Ezekiel would not have been comprehensible prior to the events he interpreted (33:1–20, 21–22, 23–33).

The ninth book (chaps. 34–39) describes the return of the exiles, the restoration of the land, and the return to life of those who had died at the hand of Yahweh.[300] It is circumscribed and finds its internal consistency in the primary agency of Yahweh and in concomitant prophetic enunciations. In the first column, while Ezekiel is prophesying, the shepherds of Israel are repudiated and Yahweh himself becomes the shepherd of his people. In the second column, as Ezekiel prophesies, Yahweh puts an end to the ridicule that the nations heaped on the mountains of Israel for purportedly devouring the people who lived there. In the third column, while Ezekiel is prophesying, the bones of those who died are brought back to life by the spirit of Yahweh.

The Jerusalem version develops these metaphors into a practical program of restoration by adding postscripts to the three original columns, by matching the column on the return of the exiles to the land with another condemning Edom for wanting to take over the land, and by appending two columns to interpret the vision of the valley of bones. The postscript to the shepherd prophecy allows for a discrimination between worthy and unworthy sheep and envisages a shepherd in the line of David administering a new covenant between God and the people (34:15–31). The postscript to the prophecy concerning the mountains of Israel interprets this as the vindication of Yahweh's holiness in a holy and purified people of God (36:16–38). The postscript to the vision of the valley of bones develops this into the reunion of an ideal Israel and Judah under David in accordance with the promise to Jacob (37:15–28). The additional columns deal with the submission of the nations and liken the valley of bones to the land strewn with the dead bodies of the invading nations (chaps. 38–39).

The tenth book (chaps. 40–48) describes the return of the glory of God to the temple. Its boundaries are marked by the measurements that take place at the beginning and the end of the book (40:1–37; 47:1–12), and it acquires internal consistency in its progression from a circuit of the temple to the advent of the glory of God and the revival of all the land centered on the temple.[301] The Jerusalem version tried to give substance to the vision by describing a structured society centered on the temple, with priests, a code to which princes and Levites would be subject, and an ordered assembly of the tribes in a duly apportioned land (chaps. 40–42; 43–46; 47–48).

There is a calendrical and metaphorical movement from book to book in Ezekiel's version of the chronicle. The first date is the latest and intimates that what follows is a history of prophecy, or of his prophecy in retrospect, rather than a record of live reportage. The story, as he remarks at the start, takes place in Babylon, so that distance in time is matched by distance in space, and everything that seems to be immediately applicable to the real course of contemporary events in Jerusalem turns out to be a metaphor of things past. What transpires from book to book is either animated conversation with God, disputation with neighbors in exile, or sorrowful reflection on what has come to pass, but it is all subsumed in a latent and compelling vision that gradually superimposes itself on what has already happened.

The distinction of books reflects the discrete phases in this gradual unveiling. A sort of climax is reached in the fifth and sixth books (chaps. 16–18 and 20–23), where the history of wrongdoing leads first to the perception of an individual guilt that is based on individual responsibility, and then to the correlative realization that the corrective to national guilt is universal retaliation (chaps. 18 and 21). At this point Ezekiel's chronicle loses interest in manifest history and turns instead to the upheaval and general restructuring of world order that it reveals. Chaos and a return to the primal point of creation are represented by an imaginary destruction of the Mediterranean world ruled by Tyre, and by the fictional descent of Egypt and the Near East into the underworld. The restructuring centers on Israel to the exclusion of other nations and revolves around the immediacy and creativity of God. Other leaders are excluded; the land is restored; those who died are brought back to life; the glory of God returns to its place; and the temple becomes the center of the habitable world. From this focus and perspective the books preceding the climax clearly lead up to it. The first book depicts Yahweh enthroned above the storm brewing in the North. The second book portrays the siege and destruction of Jerusalem as total annihilation sweeping across the mountains of Israel to the four corners of the world. The third book sees Yahweh as the instigator of universal doom, and the fourth makes it inevitable by identifying it with the day of Yahweh announced by the prophets.

This was all very puzzling and disconcerting to the author of the Jerusalem version. The world had not come to an end. Some people in Jerusalem were innocent and had not been punished. The exiles came back, but the dead did not return to life. The temple would be the old temple under a new regime, with government in the hands of the Zadokite priests and of kings in the line of David. This version, therefore, maintained the distinction of books but fitted them into a cumulative argument that minimized the mystery. The opening vision, in this version, took place at the beginning of Ezekiel's career and consisted of a hodgepodge of ritual and iconographic elements that someone from Jerusalem or living in Babylon would associate with the manifestation of Yahweh and the authorization of a prophet. Ezekiel, consequently, really was a prophet, but he did bizarre things because he was under divine constraint not to speak until Jerusalem had fallen. He interceded for the people, and his worst criticism was reserved for the kings and prophets who misled them. Jerusalem did wrong, in this version, and the kings got what they deserved; but the innocent were spared and repentance was always possible. This principle of retributive justice had always been operative in the history of Israel, and recent events were no exception. It would also be evident in Yahweh's treatment of the other nations and would govern the restoration of Israel and the punishment of all the nations that conspired against it. Justice such as this was a manifestation of the holiness of God truly worshiped in the holy community centered in the temple. The Jerusalem version, in effect, found that Ezekiel was less puzzling when his prophecies could be tied to institutions that needed reform but nevertheless actually existed.

Columns (fig. 16)

Books are composed of separate columns or chapters that are distinguished by their subject matter and linked to one another by verbal repetition. The repetitions are usually at the top or at the bottom of the columns, sometimes in the middle, and occur in regular configurations: (1) a column ends as it began, or begins again in the middle, and is connected to other columns by medial repetition; (2) the bottom of one column anticipates what is said at the top of the next; (3) the top of a column repeats elements from the top of the preceding column. Books generally follow a particular pattern, but various combinations occur. The revised version usually made its additions at the end of columns, either by repeating what had just been said, or by anticipating what was about to be said, or more often by starting again with what had been said at the top of the column.

In the first book the columns deal with different but related subjects and are linked by top to bottom repetition. The first column describes the vision by the river Chebar. The second column records what was said in the vision and begins with key terms from the bottom of the first column.[302] The third column begins the way the second column ends, with a command to eat the message on the scroll (2:8–9 and 3:1–3), and goes on to explain why the message was sent to the exiles. Most of the revisions are implanted in the columns, but there is a final addition at the end of the third column that begins like the top of the first column in the next book.[303]

In the second book the first two columns are joined top-to-top by their introductory words and their reference to the siege of Jerusalem,[304] bottom-to-bottom by their repetition of the same expression,[305] and bottom-to-top by their use of the same word in different contexts.[306] The first column threatens famine;[307] the second column adds the threat of the sword and pestilence; and the third column begins with a standard prophetic formula and refers to famine, the sword, and pestilence.[308] The fourth column begins with the same prophetic formula and is linked to the third by top-to-top repetition.[309] The revisions are mostly inside the columns, but the additions in the last column were affixed by repeating what had just been said in the original version and anticipate the theme of the next column.[310]

In the third book the first and second columns are joined bottom to top,[311] the second and third are joined bottom to top,[312] and the first and fourth are linked both top-to-top[313] and top-to-bottom (8:2–4 and 11:23–24). The revisions are made inside the columns or by adding a column, and all of the comments refer back to the first book.

In the fourth book all the columns are joined top-to-top by repetition of the standard prophetic formula.[314] The first also starts again in the middle with the same formula (12:21), but it ends as it began with the same key expression.[315] The bottom of this column and the top of the second column are linked by their common interest in vision and prophecy (12:26–28 and 13:1–6). The second and third columns are connected by their interest in prophecy, and the third ends as it began.[316] The revisions in the Jerusalem version consist mainly of additions at the end of columns and at the end of the book. The addition at the end of the second column starts again in imitation of the top of the column (13:1–3a and 13:17–18a). The text added at the end of the third column begins with the formula that was used at the top of the column (14:2 and 14:12). The column added at the end of the book begins with the same formula and mimics the medial split of the earlier columns by beginning again in the middle with what was said at the top (15:2 and 15:6a).

The columns in the fifth book are linked top-to-top and are either self-contained or reduplicated. The first column is the story of Yahweh and his bride, and it ends as it began with the woman named and forlorn (16:7, 39). The Jerusalem version added another story and tacked it on by repeating elements from the beginning of the first version (16:3 and 16:44b, 45b). The second column is the riddle of the eagle and the vine. It begins with the same formula as the first column and is reduplicated by starting again in the middle with the same formula to explain the riddle.[317] The application of the riddle in the Jerusalem version is tacked on by repeating key elements from the end of the column.[318] The third column opens with the same formula as the other columns and ends as it began with a contrast between the guilt of the father and the innocence of his son.[319] The revised version developed the argument and suited its new material to the context by beginning as the first version began and ended (18:19 and 18:5, 18).

The last column has a rubric at the top and the bottom and is attached to the book by beginning like the first column.[320]

The sixth book has four columns joined top-to-top by repetition of the same prophetic formula.[321] The first column interprets the history of Israel, and it begins and ends with the same expression.[322] It is emended in the revised version to include future events, and the new text is affixed by rephrasing what was said at the end of the original.[323] The second column is all about the sword that Yahweh drew to strike the land. The Jerusalem version made its additions at the end of the column and fitted them in by repeating the prophetic formula and by putting the sword into the hands of the king of Babylon.[324] The third column, added to describe the guilty parties in Jerusalem, begins with an expression from the first, and each of its elements is introduced by the standard prophetic formula.[325] The last column is the story of Jerusalem and Samaria. The second edition has a different version of the story, and its text pivots on the use of one word from the end of the original.[326]

There is a top-to-top connection between the columns in the seventh book[327] that is bolstered by similar links at the bottom of the columns. At the bottom of the first column a reference to the desecration of the sanctuary anticipates a related accusation against the Ammonites at the top of the second column.[328] The bottom of the third column anticipates the bottom of the fourth, and the last phrase in the fourth is repeated at the bottom of the fifth.[329] The revised version added comments at the bottom of the first and fifth columns by repeating the prophetic formula used in the original top-to-top connection (24:15; 28:20; and 24:1).

The eighth book links its columns at the top by repeating the prophetic formula and combining it with serial chronological references.[330] The columns, besides, are mostly broken in the middle and start again with the same combination of formula and chronology.[331] The revised version used this scheme to add columns to the book and to append commentaries to the columns,[332] but it also used the other types of repetition to insert or affix its material. In the first column it inserts material on the exile and restoration of Egypt by repeating things from the top of the column.[333] In the fourth column it affixes its references to Edom and Sidon by repeating the prior context.[334]

In the ninth book all the columns are linked at the top by the command to prophesy,[335] combined either with the standard prophetic formula or with a significant part of it.[336] Three columns were added in the Jerusalem edition, and material was appended to the bottom of the others. The first column described Yahweh as the shepherd of his people, and the Jerusalem version gave the metaphor a political interpretation by interposing the office of the Davidic king. The addition begins by repeating the end of the original.[337] In the third column, the second in Ezekiel's version, the land of Israel that was despised by the nations comes back to life, but the Jerusalem version shunned this naïve belief in regeneration and concentrated instead on the reasons for the contemptuous attitude of the nations. It has the prophetic formula used at the beginning of the other columns and it ends with what was said at the end of the original version.[338] The fourth column described the dead bodies of the slain coming back to life. The Jerusalem version found this belief in resurrection preposterous and thought instead in terms of the reunification of Israel and Judah. Its text was added by using the same prophetic formula and by making the original return of the dead to the land a reference to the return of Israel from exile (37:21 and 37:12).

The tenth book has three columns that are set off by their references to the visions at the beginning of the chronicle and to one another.[339] The revised version filled out the columns with instructions on the reorganization of worship.

Columns are to books as tales are to a romantic cycle, or episodes to a narrative, scenes to a dramatic act, circumstances to events, or oracular evidence to interpretation in a prophetic chronicle. They are literary expressions of things that were thought or said about some particular occasion, or descriptions of a complicated situation, or reflections on what happened and what matters in life and death. They are distinct from one another but are combined with other columns in the same book, and both their sequence and their distribution are literary features. These features are usually formal rather than substantial and sometimes are completely artificial. They are obvious and make columns, like chapters on a printed page, easy stages in the composition and comprehension of the book.

Paragraphs and Strophes

The Jerusalem edition of the chronicle observed and changed the structure of the original either by inserting paragraphs or strophes into columns or, more usually, by adding them at the end of columns. In either case the change often was anticipated by some proleptic modification. An inserted paragraph, especially if it conflicted with its context, became less obtrusive by adding sentences to earlier or later paragraphs to modify the context. The appended paragraphs, similarly, when they corrected rather than simply interpreted the original column, made more acceptable sense if the original was prepared to receive them. In both cases the modification was included by repeating and mimicking its context. Altogether the changes combine to illustrate the drift from a language common to Ezekiel and his reader into a jargon or impersonal parlance peculiar to the editor's milieu.

In the first book most of the changes in the Jerusalem version are introduced into the columns rather than added at the end. In the first column an approaching and progressively clearer vision of God is obscured by undue concentration on the vehicle that supports it. The vehicle is described in great detail (1:13–21), but the description is integrated into the original column by giving a different cast to the living creatures that propel it.[340] In the second column this version was anxious to note that the people in exile were just as perverse as the people in the land, and it integrated its intrusive remarks by repeating part of them in the immediately following context (2:4–5; 2:7). In the third column, where Ezekiel was taken up into the vision, the Jerusalem version modified three paragraphs to accommodate him on the vehicle that was supposed to transport him into exile (3:12b–13, 14a, 15aBb).

The changes in the first column follow the original text paragraph by paragraph.[341] The first paragraph in the Babylonian version set the stage for the vision in a series of consecutive verbal clauses that situated the narrator by the river Chebar in the thirtieth year.[342] Another paragraph was added to it in the Jerusalem version to change the date, name the narrator, and identify him both as a priest and as an ordinary prophet inspired not by visions but by the word of God (1:2–3a).[343] It differs from the original by combining a nominal sequence with non-consecutive past narrative, but it is fitted in by deictics and is adapted to the original context by repeating phrases and key words from the first paragraph.[344] The next paragraph, in the original version, describes the approaching storm cloud, the animals that were revealed by the flashes of lightning, and the firmament above their heads.[345] It is composed of a consecutive verbal clause and nominal phrases, and the Jerusalem version added more of each to distribute it over eight paragraphs that reduced the vision to a glimpse of a cultic contraption. The animals that Ezekiel saw had faces and wings, but the editor added hands and feet in a series of nominal clauses marked by deictic pronominal suffixes and by a concluding repetition of the last phrase in Ezekiel's text.[346] Their legs and wings made them apt for locomotion, but, in view of the fact that they were attached to a wheeled vehicle and moved under the impulse of the spirit, the editor added another paragraph to make them motionless. This continues the editorial addition and is linked to it by literal repetition, but it also leads back into

the original version and repeats part of it.[347] The original version went
on to describe the wings and faces of the animals, but the Jerusalem
version, to insist that the creatures had locomotion without individual
movement, added another reference to their faces and their wings. This
made the animals exceedingly strange and ruined Ezekiel's text but, by
constant cross-reference, made the edited text look original.[348] Once
the fact of locomotion had been established, the Jerusalem version
could add paragraphs that repeated the prior context and also explained exactly how the animals were moved from place to place and
how they made the loud noise that Ezekiel heard.[349] All in all, the vision
that in Ezekiel's mind made sense of prophecy and history became, in
the editor's view, the inauguration and ritual authorization of his
unusual prophetic career.

In the second column the Babylonian chronicle has four paragraphs
detailing Ezekiel's mission to an unresponsive people. Since it is the
prelude to his mission to the exiles, the Jerusalem version took the
occasion to make it clear that there were also unresponsive people
among the exiles, that is, not those who went with Jehoiachin but the
people taken into exile at the time of the fall of Jerusalem, the
"children" of the first exiles.[350] The clarification consists in adding a
paragraph, most of which is made up of words from the immediate or
distant context,[351] that breaks up the original sequence of paragraphs.
It is blended into the overall context by adding a sentence to the
following paragraph that repeats the basic accusation in the terms of
rebellion that Ezekiel himself used.[352]

In the third column there is an appendage on the silencing of
Ezekiel that seems to contradict his reasons for being in exile.[353] It is
blended into the column, however, by a proleptic change that tries to
fit it into his prophetic calling (3:16–21). This modification, in turn, is
woven into the text by changing the end of the preceding paragraph
and then beginning the prolepsis in imitation of it. In Ezekiel's version
the spirit lifted him, but in the revised version he is carried on the
wheeled vehicle that the editor imagined in the first column.[354] In his
version he went and lived with the exiles, and in the Jerusalem version
he did exactly the same thing again,[355] but stayed only seven days
before Yahweh revealed to him the responsibilities of a prophet. The
reference to seven days is repeated at the start of the proleptic paragraph in which he receives this revelation,[356] and the appendage in
effect releases him from his responsibility as a prophet to the exiles. It
is all cleverly done and terribly profound, but none of it has very much
to do with the point that Ezekiel was making or with how he expressed
it. He described his involvement in an encompassing vision, but the

Jerusalem version described him as a typical functionary. He is the prophetic narrator and historical protagonist, but the new version makes him the passive recipient of a familiar message.

The emergence of a different parlance is clear in the second book, where the revision imitates the original but, nevertheless, wants its changes known and makes them evident without being too conspicuous. The changes are sentences added to a paragraph (4:9b, 12), or paragraphs added to balance other paragraphs in a column,[357] or a series of paragraphs added to the end of a column (7:10–27).

In its Babylonian version the first column was a mime depicting the famine that occurred during the siege of Jerusalem. In the Jerusalem version attention shifts away from the city to the prophet who performed the mime in order to depict him as a priest who bore the guilt of the people. This is done by adding two matching paragraphs in which Ezekiel performs a rite of atonement,[358] another paragraph to relate this rite of atonement to the famine (4:7–8 and 4:9–12), and a penultimate paragraph to balance famine and exile (4:13–15 and 4:16–17). The original opens with two grammatically identical paragraphs composed of a series of consecutive imperatives. The rite of atonement is described in two paragraphs, intruded as usual through deictics, that begin the same way but end in an indicative sequence.[359] They ruin the continuity of the mime and require the insertion of another paragraph to reintroduce the topic of the siege. The next paragraph, therefore, is resumptive and mentions the siege twice, but it also relates the atonement ritual to the established fact that Ezekiel was a prophet who had been forbidden to help the people make amends.[360] The following paragraph was changed by relating the days of atonement that the editor inserted to the duration of the famine that Ezekiel had described, and by insinuating through the rules of ritual purity that Ezekiel really was a priest.[361] The last intrusive paragraph imitates the last paragraph in the original both in grammatical construction and in content, but it develops the editor's interest in Ezekiel's Priestly status and also adds extraneous material on the exile.[362] All the changes are woven into the original by respecting its expression and, smoothly or brusquely, diverging from it.

A concomitant feature of grammatically and syntactically correct composition is the symmetry and balance of paragraphs. Paragraphs do not occur in isolation or simply in series but in literal conjunction with other matching or parallel paragraphs. The revision was bound, therefore, to account for any changes that it made either by making corresponding changes in matching texts or by composing a text to match.

In the second column, for instance, Ezekiel begins with a ceremonial shaving in which the razor represents the sword and what is done to the hair symbolizes what will happen to the inhabitants of the city. This paragraph is balanced by another about the city and the reasons for striking it with the sword (5:1–2, 5–6). The revised version adds a paragraph that prolongs the ritual and matches the first but also allows for a few survivors in the city. It has the same pattern of imperative clauses as the first, but it distinguishes itself from the original by using synonyms instead of the same words.[363] The addition of this paragraph ruined the original symmetry and had to be corrected by adding another paragraph to correspond to it and balance the second paragraph in Ezekiel's version. This paragraph also follows the grammatical pattern of the original and uses many of the same words but goes its own way in allowing for a few survivors in the city.[364]

The same sort of compensatory composition is evident in the third column. In Ezekiel's version there are two paragraphs that describe the pall cast on the mountains of Israel and two others that relate it to the devastation symbolized in the ceremony of the sword.[365] The Jerusalem version, as usual, was anxious to allow for a few survivors who escaped into exile and, having inserted a paragraph that made the point,[366] ended the column with a matching paragraph that alluded to the attempted escape of Zedekiah and his entourage, which ended ignominiously in their summons to Riblah.[367]

There is a slight variation on this method of composition in the fourth column. In the original Babylonian version there are three paragraphs announcing the end of Israel and of the whole world. The first leads into the second by its reference to the end, and the third resumes the first by its reference to pitiless punishment.[368] According to the Jerusalem version the end was a punishment for the guilt of specific classes of society and was compatible with the survival of a remnant. This is explained in a series of alternating paragraphs that was added to the end of the column.[369] But to make this pattern harmonize with the rest of the column the new edition had to add another paragraph that gave the same structure to the original. This paragraph was composed to balance the second, to which it has literal links, but it added the notion of guilt and an allusion to the monarchy that led in to the themes of the appended paragraphs.[370]

The rule of compensatory composition is strictly observed, and intrusive elements that have no immediate match are either proleptic or resumptive of other contexts. In the third book, for instance, the Jerusalem version inserted a whole column to give a rational interpretation of the inaugural vision (10:1–22), but otherwise was content to add sentences to paragraphs and a few explanatory paragraphs. In the first column the vision of the seventy elders is interrupted by a parenthesis calling one of them, Jaazaniah, by name. It fits in by repeating its context[371] but is intrusive and is not explained in the rest of the column. In the last column, however, there is the same sort of parenthesis mentioning another Jaazaniah and a person called Pelatiah. In this column the parenthesis is clearly proleptic, and now the point of both parentheses is explained.[372] When Pelatiah is struck dead Ezekiel wonders aloud whether anyone will survive (the name Pelatiah denotes survival). Since Jaazaniah did not die there is an implicit answer to his question, and the chronicle's belief in a remnant is reconfirmed.

This use of prolepsis and resumption maintains the symmetry of the text and allows the revision greater scope in insinuating its own ideas. In the second column of the third book, for instance, there is an unexpected reference to the cherub over which the glory of God had hovered. It fits into the context by literal repetition, but it hardly belongs and is just proleptic to the next column, where the reference is explained.[373] In the last column, similarly, there is a proleptic reference to survival and judgment that will be developed in what follows, as well as a resumptive reference to the cherubim who were described in the preceding column.[374]

Composition in sentences and paragraphs, reliance on prolepsis and resumption, and the compensatory balancing of paragraphs account for the basic order and progression of the text and for the intricate arrangement of text and commentary. They produce a carefully segmented text that is filled with striking inconsequences and puzzling irregularities but sorts itself out as it goes.

The fourth book has to do with the appreciation of visions. In the first column the fact that the people have eyes to see but do not see is emphasized by the need to explain simple things to them by mimicry and visible signs.[375] In Ezekiel's version the point is made by describing the action to be performed and then explaining the meaning of its performance.[376] In the revised version, on the other hand, the action becomes an explicitly prophetic activity, and its application is limited to the king. This change is made by adding another sentence to the first paragraph and by repeating the same material in several ways in the second paragraph.[377] The additions are grammatically and syntactically correct but deliberately abrupt and clumsy to signal a radical reinterpretation.[378] There is no room for this in the original paragraphs, and so two other paragraphs are added to explain that some of those who went into exile with Zedekiah will be spared while those who died in the destruction of Jerusalem deserved their fate.[379] Once this explanation became part of the book it was possible to interpret the other columns accordingly. The second column dealt with the prophets who misled the people, but a series of symmetrical paragraphs was appended to insist that some of these people were innocent.[380] The third column described how people could be misled by a prophet, but the revised version insisted on individual responsibility and added a series of paragraphs to prove it.[381] The fourth column, finally, was added to deal more comprehensively with the fate of Zedekiah and with the future of the monarchy.[382]

In the fifth book the editorial procedure follows the pattern of the fourth, with additions at the end of columns and with an extra column to sum up the editor's argument. The first column is the story of the mistress of Jerusalem who was ruined by the anger of her Lord. The editor, with the usual sutures, added a different version of the story that argued issues of innocence and guilt and ended with reconciliation.[383] The second column is the story of the last kings of Judah, and the editor, with a view to the eventual restoration of the Davidic monarchy, emphasizes the crimes and punishment of Zedekiah and looks forward to his successor.[384] The third column argues about guilt and innocence and individual limits of responsibility, and the editor added comments on repentance and recidivism.[385] The last column treats the mistress of Jerusalem as the mother of the last kings of Judah and argues the collective guilt and responsibility of the monarchy (19:1–14).

The method of composition and revision is obvious in those books where the columns were not modified but merely reduplicated or complemented. Most of the later books in the chronicle fall into this category. A partial and notable exception is the sixth book, where conflicting notions of divine justice result in an intricate and farfetched text (chaps. 20–23). In the second column of the Babylonian version Yahweh draws his sword against the innocent and the guilty and makes it clear that no one will escape.[386] The Jerusalem version tried to correct this apparent injustice by inserting comments that made the text difficult to understand without recourse to related texts. It began with an introductory paragraph that copied the first paragraph in the original but gave it vague and veiled references (21:1–5 and 21:6–8). Ezekiel looked toward Jerusalem and prophesied against the sanctuary and the land, but the Jerusalem version has him look southward and prophesy against the forest of the Negeb.[387] In Ezekiel's version Yahweh had raised the sword against the city, but the revision has him send fire against the trees in the forest (21:8 and 21:3). Ezekiel sighed and groaned about the killing, but in this version everyone from North to South gets burned and all flesh sees that Yahweh has set the fire (21:11–12 and 21:3–5). The punishment is mitigated since the fire is sent to purge rather than consume,[388] but the symbolism of the forest and the trees and the geography of North and South still have to be explained. The explanation is delayed, however, and in its place the Jerusalem edition interpolates another paragraph in which, admitting that the innocent and the guilty have been killed, Yahweh is made to draw his sword not against the city and the land but against all flesh from North to South.[389] Then this version explains the symbolism by adding an allusive and contorted reference to the trees and to the staff that supplants them.[390] This addition does not fit its context but is a clever and completely artificial cross-reference to other contexts where the staff is understood to belong to a ruler or to a shepherd who sorts the sheep and where the trees are interpreted as kings.[391] The reference is confirmed immediately in a matching paragraph that identifies the trees with the leaders, the fire with testing, and the staff with the staff of the new covenant (21:17–18; cf. 20:37). At the end of the column there are other paragraphs that bring all the loose ends together. God's justice is preserved by taking the sword out of Yahweh's hand and putting it in the hands of the king of Babylon. Hidden crimes are imputed to those who had been thought innocent. The guilt of the present leaders of Israel is affirmed, and innocence is reserved for the ruler who is to come. The people of the North are the Babylonians; the people of the South are the Ammonites, and it is against them that both the fire and the sword are directed.[392] Ezekiel's text was clear but unacceptable. It was changed by interlacing it with images and confusing it with ideas that made sense in the Jerusalem version and were part of its developing argument.[393]

In the seventh book Ezekiel apotheosized the siege and fall of Jerusalem as the decline of the Mediterranean world, but his editor made him an ideal prophet implicated in the affairs of his people and dead set against the nations who opposed them.[394] In the eighth book Ezekiel portrayed the demise of Jerusalem as the undoing of creation by imagining Egypt as the crown of creation now languishing in Sheol. His editor, on the contrary, thought of Egypt as a country captured by Nebuchadnezzar, as Jerusalem was, but as a country that would survive, like Jerusalem, as a shadow of its former self.[395] In the ninth book Ezekiel saw Israel come back to life, but his editor explained the phenomenon as a political and religious revival.[396] In the last book Yahweh returned to the city, and the editor made sure that the proper institutions were in place to welcome and worship him.[397]

LANGUAGE AND STYLE

The language and style of each version are appropriate to its purpose. Ezekiel had a vision to explain, and every part of the chronicle he composed is marked by the polarization of word and image. At the sentence level his work is balanced and cadenced, composed of short measured clauses in pairs or parallelism, with duplicate expressions, and a strong caesura. At the paragraph level it is a patterned discourse composed alternately of vivid description and pithy explanation. At the column level it is a juxtaposition of related perspectives on different aspects of the vision. At the book level it is a narrative unfolding of phases in the cycle of life and death.

At every level the Jerusalem version copied Ezekiel but was more studied and prosaic. It had to explain why the vision was so late in arriving and how it could possibly apply to real expectations. At the sentence level it tends to be wordy, redundant, and repetitive, to substitute subordination for matching and logical disruption for caesura or pause. At the paragraph level it combines image and word, mixes metaphors, and injects mumbo jumbo or obscure images that it gradually unravels. At the column level it is discursive. At the book level it tends to harangue and homogenize. It often imitates the original and is not always easy to detect, but it was in its interest to make its viewpoint known and it did with considerable bravado and panache.

Ezekiel's language and style are peculiar but well in line with the prophetic tradition. The earlier prophets wrote poems that could be recited, declaimed, or dramatized and that demanded accompaniment, attention, or audience participation. The poems were written in various styles, but they were all composed of individual pieces with distinctive figures, moods, and meanings. Ezekiel kept to this tradition of direct discourse but, in the manner of historians, wrote prose. His speeches, consequently, have the traditional rhythm and tempo of poetic discourse, the contemporary logic and flair of occasional oratory, and the standard continuity of historical narrative. They are assembled in books where one style relieves and complements the other. The books are aligned in a dramatic presentation of the mysterious cycles of life and death. His texts can be read individually, in series, or in sequence and do not ever demand response as much as admiration and assent.

His commentator was a parvenu prophet, a priest perhaps, schooled in the law, with more sense of decorum than of history. The speeches were touched up and became long-winded. They were taken out of their historical setting and put into a prophetic framework and a system of theological reasoning. The novelty of the work was attributed to the idiosyncrasy of the prophet. The absence of predictive elements, of warning and intercession, was explained by his physical incapacity. The mysteries he revealed were ridiculed and reduced to familiar concepts, concrete events, ordinary institutions, and normal expectations. His worldly and historical bias was corrected with eschatological and apocalyptic imaginings. The things that he ignored or neglected to say were supplied by theories of divine justice and holiness. His words were repeated; his language was imitated; his style was copied; but everything was changed to suit the commentator's situation, the standard interpretation, the orthodox point of view.

SOURCES AND INTERPRETATIONS

Ezekiel wrote a literary work. It was not a commentary on current events and was not meant for oral delivery. It was a vision of the future that was based as much on what had been written as on what had happened. He knew the earlier prophecies and paraphrased the histories. He knew things they did not and was familiar with literary forms and motifs they did not use. He was popular with later authors, especially with II Isaiah and the writer who revised Jeremiah, but his vision became of marginal interest when his work was revised.

His commentator had the same sources, some in their second editions, but worked in an orthodox milieu created by the recent writings of the Deuteronomistic Historian. The new edition of his work signaled the close of the prophetic tradition; but it was an important source for Leviticus, and it became the model of legal procedure in the Chronicler's school.

Ezekiel's visions in the first book are in the cosmological tradition of the Priestly writer and in the literary tradition of Isaiah of Jerusalem. They were revised in Jerusalem to conform to notions of prophecy and revelation current in the Deuteronomistic History, II Isaiah, and the book of Jeremiah.

The first vision resembles the Priestly account of creation and borrows images from its description of Yahweh's manifestation to Moses on Mount Sinai. The wind from the North is like the wind hovering over the primal waters.[398] The cloud and the fire that accompany the appearance of the glory of Yahweh also accompanied the manifestation of the glory of Yahweh on Mount Sinai.[399] In the vision and in the Priestly account the firmament is the boundary of creation;[400] the distinction between Adam and the animals is its climax;[401] and the similarity between God and Adam is its point.[402] In both the rainbow is the symbol of creation and the sign that the created order will not be disturbed.[403] The vision of Ezekiel is totally different from the Priestly account, but it shares the same world and transcends its expectations.[404]

The second vision is of a book or open scroll inscribed on both sides.[405] It resembles the book Isaiah wrote, except that Isaiah's was sealed,[406] and like it Ezekiel's scroll concerned a rebellious nation,[407] children who resisted Yahweh,[408] people who could not understand the language or grasp its message[409] and who refused to listen.[410] This refusal to listen became a theme of prophecy, and Ezekiel uses an expression that Jeremiah coined to describe the blank incomprehension of his audience[411] and, like the prophets and historians before him, resolved the problem by writing down his words. In the third vision, consequently, he is transported to the alluvial plain where foreign languages and the problem of incomprehension began.

The Jerusalem edition changed the vision to correspond to the manifestation of Yahweh in the temple, put it at the start of Ezekiel's prophetic career, and modified his message to make him conform to the typical prophet charged with proclaiming the law. The basic change consisted in turning attention away from the vision of the glory of God to the visionary and the mechanics of his vision. Like Jeremiah he is considered a priest (Ezek 1:3; Jer 1:1) and is appointed a prophet[412] through an inaugural vision that is dated according to the system used in the Deuteronomistic History.[413] Like Moses, he must explain to the people the things he has heard from God (Ezek 3:17; Exod 18:20). As in II Isaiah, his vision occurs in the temple and displays elements of temple decor (cf. Isaiah 6). The animals turn out to be cherubim like those in the temple[414] or like those on the ark of the covenant above which Yahweh is enthroned.[415] They are immobile and attached to a four-sided vehicle with wheels resembling the bronze stands in the Solomonic temple that moved on wheels like chariot wheels and were decorated with lions, oxen, and cherubim.[416] Since they do not move and cannot fly, they, like Isaiah's seraphim, have hands to pick up the burning coals that lie between them and that make them seem to flash and dart.[417] The display is the thing, and the fact that the glory of God appeared like Adam is pretty well lost in the paraphernalia that proclaim his holiness.

The design of the second book is influenced by Ezekiel's reliance on earlier prophetic works. The siege of Jerusalem with which it begins was predicted by Isaiah, imagined by Jeremiah, and visualized by Nahum and Habakkuk.[418] Ezekiel describes its different stages, but it is literary, imaginary, and symbolic of the opposition between prophet and people. The city is a picture on a brick, a miniature of the cities that primeval exiles had to build with bricks.[419] Ezekiel looks squarely at it as he did at the people who refused to listen (4:3 and 3:7–9), but the siege is just the opposite of what Yahweh intended for the city that he placed at the center of the world. The mountains that surround the city represent Israel,[420] where, as Hosea and Jeremiah described it, the people had innumerable altars on every high hill, on every mountaintop, under every green tree, and under every leafy oak.[421] The image of corpses strewn across the mountains before the idols they worshiped is adapted from the Priestly writer on the destruction of the generation that refused the land (Ezek 6:5; Num 14:29, 32). Amos was the first to declare that the end had come,[422] but it was the Priestly writer who first gave it the universal application that it has in Ezekiel.[423] Ezekiel also describes the end of the world in terms of the day of Yahweh, as Zephaniah saw it,[424] or in terms of the approaching evil that Micah and Jeremiah saw,[425] or as the bad times described by Micah.[426] The references are reflections on history and its prophetic interpretations. Ezekiel was a prophet to people who had not listened to the prophets. He did not speak to them but composed a literary and historical work and addressed it to those who knew it was true.

The Jerusalem version tried to make Ezekiel a little less aloof, and by other quotations from the prophets and the law it engaged him in the affairs of the city and the fate of its inhabitants. It involved Ezekiel himself in the siege[427] and made him share the guilt of Israel and Judah for the duration of the exile. The length of Israel's exile seems to be computed from the time of the division of the kingdom of David,[428] and the time of Judah's exile is fixed according to the reckoning in the book of Jeremiah and by analogy with the wilderness wanderings.[429] In this way the Jerusalem edition made Ezekiel a priest in the line of Aaron[430] whose duty it was to atone for the sins of the people,[431] and therefore he naturally protests that he cannot eat the food that was forbidden to priests.[432] After this expiatory rite has been performed, the revision is confident that a few will be spared, and it justifies its correction of the original prophecy by using expressions from the Deuteronomistic History and the book of Jeremiah.[433] Instead of a blanket condemnation of the city, consequently, it has Ezekiel single out the culpable and allow for some escapees. The merchant class is cited, and the day of Yahweh that confronts them is described in the words of Ezekiel and in terms taken from Habakkuk.[434] The survivors escape from a destruction described by Jeremiah.[435] The panic overtaking the merchant class is described in terms of the day of Yahweh as it was portrayed by Amos and Zephaniah.[436] The capture of the city is suggested by alluding to Isaiah.[437] The crimes of the city are compared to the crimes that brought on the great flood,[438] and the awfulness of defeat is noted by reference to Isaiah and the book of Jeremiah.[439] All these changes make Ezekiel conform to living institutions by turning him into a prophet and a priest, and diminish the originality of his message by bringing him into line with prophetic and legal tradition.

In the third book Ezekiel associates the vision that he saw at the river Chebar with the temple in Jerusalem and refers to the same complex of prophetic and cosmological texts that was cited in the first book. The image of jealousy at the gate of the temple alludes to the jealousy of Yahweh, which excludes the worship of all other Gods. This was expressed originally in the epic account of the Sinai covenant and in Nahum was combined with the vision of Yahweh subduing the primordial powers.[440] Its concomitants are the wrath of Yahweh and the punishment of the recalcitrant, and both are verified in the aftermath of the temple vision.[441] The cycle of unacceptable worship that Ezekiel witnesses corresponds to the order of creation. The creeping things and cattle depicted on the walls are the creatures that the creation account lists along with animals and Adam.[442] It is in the darkness that the elders say that Yahweh has abandoned the earth and does not see them, in connection with this abandonment that the women weep for Tammuz, and in contrast with this that the men worship the sun (Ezek 8:12–16; Gen 1:1, 14–18). The whole cycle is summed up in the terms that the Priestly writer used to justify the flood and the end of the world. Yahweh knows what is in the minds of the people as he understood the intentions of the primeval heroes, and those who are exempted from death are marked on the forehead, as Cain was in later tradition.[443]

The Jerusalem edition treated his flight of cosmological fancy as it did the first by adapting it to historical reality and the actual figuration of the temple. Specific people are mentioned (8:11; 11:1b, 13). The scribe is associated with a cherub, the cherub with an altar, the altar with fire, the fire with the other cherubim and the vehicle of Yahweh's apparition (9:2b–3; 10:1–22). There is an allusion to the flight of Zedekiah and to the judgment passed on him at Riblah beyond the borders of Israel (Ezek 11:9–12; Jer 52:9). There is talk of the exiles and a reference to the remnant of the house of Israel, for whom, as II Isaiah once said, Yahweh had become a temple for a time.[444]

In the fourth book Ezekiel builds his text on quotations and allusions to Isaiah, Jeremiah, Micah, Nahum, and Habakkuk. The Jerusalem edition, on the other hand, tends to repeat itself and earlier texts from the original version.

In the first column the mood is set by quotations from Jeremiah[445] and Isaiah[446] to which the text keeps referring.[447] The dramatization of the exile ends with a quotation from Nahum in which the destruction of Thebes was presented as a warning to Jerusalem.[448] To this the Jerusalem edition reacts by referring once again to the flight and capture of Zedekiah and to the preservation of a remnant in terms that are familiar from the earlier books.[449] The corollary of the city's willful blindness and deafness is its unwillingness to accept the fulfillment of visions and the word of Yahweh. Ezekiel's response to its proverbial indifference consists of allusions to Isaiah, Micah, and Habakkuk that insist that visions will happen and the word will come true.[450]

In the second column the tone is set by a reference to Isaiah and quotations from Amos. In his song of the vineyard Isaiah alluded to the fall of Israel in terms of the breaching of its wall and drew the lesson for Jerusalem in the image of a sudden storm and a wall that suddenly collapses. Ezekiel applies the images to the prophets who would not build up the wall or stand in the breach and compares them to a wall that suddenly collapses after a heavy storm.[451] Amos referred to this sudden and unexpected turn of events as the day of Yahweh or the day of war, and Ezekiel combines the two expressions in excoriation of the prophets.[452] Micah combined all the images in his description of Yahweh's battle against Samaria, which leveled its walls right down to their foundations, and Ezekiel reinforces his description with an allusion to this version as well.[453] The Jerusalem edition was satisfied with repeating its theory of justification with a few words from the original and references to related texts (13:17–23; cf. 3:16–21; 18:1–32).

In the third column Ezekiel's main inspiration is still Isaiah. The stumbling block of the people's iniquity is the inverse of the stumbling block that Yahweh put in front of the people, and their idolatry reflects their estrangement from him as Isaiah described it.[454] The Jerusalem version, on the other hand, continues to recapitulate materials from the preceding books[455] and persists in leaving a few survivors after the city has been destroyed.

In the fourth column the Jerusalem edition anticipates the later allegory of the vine (15:1–8 and 17:1–18), refers to an earlier statement by Ezekiel,[456] begins its own peculiar interest in the symbolism of wood, trees, and forests,[457] and continues to be intrigued by the prospect of judgment by fire.[458] The vine, as in the allegory woven by Ezekiel, refers to the kings of Judah, but its particular interpretation in this column is derived from II Isaiah. In an oracle on the capture of Jerusalem, II Isaiah blames the ambassadors who negotiated with the king of Assyria in the time of Hezekiah and compares Eliakim in particular to a peg on whom the whole house of David hangs. The Jerusalem version, in the same way, traces the fall of the city to its kings and compares them to a piece of vine that is useless as a peg and suitable only for burning.[459] Another variation on this theme is woven into the lamentation on the leaders that this version appended to the original allegory on the vine.[460]

In the fifth book Ezekiel depends especially on Hosea, Jeremiah, and the Elohist law code. The marriage of Yahweh with the land of Israel was described by Hosea and applied by Jeremiah to the relationship between Yahweh and Jerusalem, and Ezekiel knows both versions. The birth and adolescence of the girl are peculiar to his treatment of the subject, but the elements and order of her infidelity are taken from his predecessors. Her headstrong independence is called prostitution.[461] She made male statues and gave them the bread, oil, and incense that Yahweh had given her.[462] She took her children and sacrificed them to her lovers and forgot the days of her youthful romance.[463] Her independence took her to Egypt and Assyria and still she was not satisfied.[464] Instead of receiving money she paid her lovers.[465] Consequently, she will be stripped before her lovers,[466] for whom she sat and waited like an Arab in the wilderness,[467] and will be put to death for enraging her God.

The connection between this tale of unrequited love and the other traditional conception of Israel as a vine was established in a text of Jeremiah that combined references to Hosea and to Isaiah's Song of the Vineyard.[468] Ezekiel used the connection to move from the story of Jerusalem's infidelity to the tale of the vassal who became unfaithful like a grapevine growing wild.[469] The suzerain in his story, however, is not Yahweh but the king of Assyria, portrayed in traditional terms as an eagle on expedition to the cedar forests. Naturally enough, the Jerusalem edition took the parable of the vineyard back toward its original sense and interpreted the vassal's infidelity as Israel's rejection of its covenant with Yahweh.[470]

The third column combines this metaphor of the vineyard with the stipulation of the epic covenant that the sins of the vassal would be punished to the third and fourth generations. Ezekiel's dispute with the epic convention is centered on the proverbial saying that parents ate sour grapes and their children's teeth were set on edge and is based on the alternative to the epic's covenant ideology in the Elohist law code. The basic concern is for justice and innocence.[471] The list of sins begins with those that were illustrated in Israel's infidelity: worship of idols on the mountains[472] and defiling another man's wife or oneself by importunate demands on a woman.[473] The other prescriptions and prohibitions are expressed in the usual pairs and doublings that Ezekiel likes, but they correspond to items in the Elohist Book of the Covenant

(Ezek 18:7–8a; Exod 22:24–26). It is only the basic principle affirmed by Ezekiel, along with the possibility of repentance, that interests the Jerusalem edition, and consequently its version begins with a para-phrase of Ezekiel's dictum expressed in terms borrowed from the Deuteronomistic History (Ezek 18:20; Deut 24:16; 25:1).

The sixth book has a similar dependence on historical and prophetic sources. The first column is a summary of the history of Israel taken from pentateuchal sources and Jeremiah, and it is revised in the Jerusalem edition with clichés and quotations from the Deuteronomistic History. The second column is indebted to Isaiah, Micah, and Jeremiah, and the Jerusalem edition revised it with reference to the same texts and the Deuteronomistic History. The third column was added in the revised version and is mainly a rehash of preceding books combined with a paraphrase of texts from Jeremiah and Zephaniah. The last column, like the first column in the preceding book, is based on a reading of Hosea and Jeremiah.

The historical summary in the first column begins with the situation described in the Elohist version, when the people come to inquire of Moses and he presides over them as judge.[474] The first paragraph quotes from the Priestly preamble to the exodus and combines it with narrative elements from Numbers and Jeremiah: Yahweh made himself known to them in Egypt, declared that he was Yahweh their God, and took an oath to the seed of the house of Jacob to bring them out of the land of Egypt to the land that he reconnoitered for them, a land flowing with milk and honey, the most beautiful land in the world.[475] The second paragraph projects into that period the negative responses of a later time described by Isaiah and Jeremiah. Although Yahweh was their God, they rebelled against him,[476] refused to listen to him,[477] and defiled themselves with idols.[478] He would have destroyed them but did not because of his name, which he had revealed to them and because of what the nations might think.[479] The third paragraph continues with the story of the exodus as told by the epic, the sequel, the Elohist, and the Priestly writer. Yahweh brought the people out of Egypt into the wilderness, where he gave them the laws and the statutes, which bring life, and the sabbath, which was a sign for them.[480] The fourth paragraph continues the story but has the same sort of retrojection and creates the same kind of negative hiatus as the second paragraph. The people rebelled in the wilderness, and Yahweh was about to pour out his fury on them but acted for the sake of his name.[481] The fifth paragraph is the story of rebellion in the wilderness tempered with gentler allusions to Jeremiah.[482] The sixth and seventh paragraphs retell the story, alluding to Jeremiah and the epic, and add to the traditional story another rebellion in the wilderness by the children of the exodus generation.[483] The eighth paragraph claims that one of the prescriptions of the covenant on Sinai—the law requiring the dedication of firstborn males to Yahweh—was mean and wrong,[484] and retrojects into the wilderness period a later threat of exile. The ninth paragraph brings the narrative up to date by recounting, on the basis of texts from Hosea and Jeremiah,[485] how their fathers entered the land and sacrificed under all the leafy trees on every high hill. The tenth paragraph addresses the present generation, and the narrative ends with the unwillingness of Yahweh to be consulted by them.

The revised version goes over some of the same ground and brings the story to a happy conclusion. Its first paragraph is made up of a hodgepodge of material written in Ezekiel's pairing style that combines some of his expressions with stereotypes drawn from the Deuteronomistic History and other works. It begins with a quotation from Samuel in which the people say that they want a king so that they can be like the other nations and pairs it with a term from Priestly geography.[486] Since the literary context of their request is the exile, being like the nations is qualified further, in terms taken from Deuteronomy's view of the exile, as worship of idols of wood and stone.[487] The return from exile is introduced by an expostulation that combines a cliché from the Deuteronomistic History with an expression used by Ezekiel in the preceding narrative.[488] Both phrases are used again in the immediate sequel, where they are combined with a variation on the exodus formula, some editorial phraseology on return from exile, material from Ezekiel, and language that belongs to the exodus and covenant traditions.[489] Some of this is repeated again in the next paragraph, where the editor anticipates proper worship in Jerusalem and repeats ideas and expressions that are familiar from earlier books and that crop up throughout the edited text.[490]

The second column begins the chant of the sword with an allusion to Micah.[491] The chant itself is an original composition, but the reaction to the sword is described in terms taken from similar contexts in Isaiah, Jeremiah, and Nahum.[492] The revision uses the same expression from Micah and adds allusions to Micah's description of the temple ruins and to Huldah's oracle against Jerusalem in the Deuteronomistic History.[493] The remainder of the column in this version deals with the Babylonian invasion and the plight of the wicked kings.

The third column is constructed from earlier texts[494] and by paraphrasing the prophets. Jerusalem is referred to in terms that were coined by Nahum and used by Ezekiel in the next book.[495] The crimes of the kings include those that Ezekiel mentioned (22:10b–11; cf. 18:6;

20:43), one that is under a curse in Deuteronomy, and one that is condemned by Isaiah, Amos, and Jeremiah.[496] The cleansing of Jerusalem is compared to burning rust from metal and, although it anticipates an image developed by Ezekiel in the next book, its formulation depends on other examples in II Isaiah and the edited book of Jeremiah.[497] The irresponsibility of the priests, prophets, and kings is a paraphrase of Zephaniah combined with excerpts from the Deuteronomist and related texts.[498]

The seventh book returns to the cosmological perspective of the early chapters of Genesis and works it out in historical terms and with reference to earlier prophetic works. The revised version, as usual, sees a connection between the cosmology and the physical structure of the temple and adds historical events related to its destruction.

The first column describes the siege of Jerusalem in terms reminiscent of Micah.[499] The similitude of the sacrificial pot into which the pieces and bones of the people are put recalls Micah's description of what the prophets did to the city (Ezek 24:3–5; Mic 3:2–3). The logic of the similitude led Micah to call Jerusalem a city built on blood, and Ezekiel uses the same image but in terms that Nahum used to express it (Ezek 24:6; Mic 3:10; Nah 3:1). The siege was parodied in another Mican similitude, which apportioned the city to the besiegers and left no part for the assembly of Yahweh, and Ezekiel interrupted his own description of the siege to refer to it.[500] The cosmological significance of this sacrificial imagery is suggested in the book's final parody of the king of Tyre, who was thrown out of Eden and consumed by fire for defiling his sanctuary (28:14–18). The revised edition made a literal connection with the temple in Jerusalem defiled by Yahweh and added a few paragraphs that diverted attention from Adam to the personal life of Ezekiel and the suasive function of prophecy (24:15–17, 21). It then added the second column, condemning the Ammonites and others for their complacency in the defiling of the temple and for their complicity in the fall of Jerusalem and thereby submerged the symbolism in fact and historical interpretation (25:1–17).

The third column draws an exact parallel between the fall of Jerusalem and the destruction of Tyre and then compares it to the destruction of the world in the great flood (26:1–14; cf. 26:19b; Gen 7:11, 19). This is developed in the fourth column, where the nations of the world, many of them from the world map drawn by the Priestly writer, are listed and assemble to bewail the sinking of the Tyrian fleet (27:1–36; cf. Gen 10:1–7, 20, 22–23, 31–32). The fifth column then retells the history of Tyre as the story of creation and attributes to its king the divine aspirations of Adam (28:1–19). The Jerusalem version, naturally enough, replaced this myth of Tyre with an interpretation of the actual history of Sidon (28:20–26).

In the eighth book Ezekiel uses the same traditional story to structure his remarks on Egypt and represent the descent of Israel into the underworld. The Jerusalem version, again, was anxious to replace this ritual and imaginative viewpoint with facts and historical speculation.

The first column refers to the Pharaoh in the derogatory terms that were used by the king of Assyria during the siege of Jerusalem but also describes him as the primordial sea creature created by God.[501] The Jerusalem version lessens the impact of the creation myth by citing Egypt's geographical boundaries, by subjecting it to a historical timetable, and by limiting it to a clearly definable historical destiny (29:9b–12, 13–21; 30:1–26). In his second column Ezekiel compares the Pharaoh to a cedar of Lebanon, which no tree in the garden of God could match, and describes how it will be cut down and descend to Sheol. The Jerusalem version compares him to the primordial sea creature, which the creator can catch in a net like any fish and cast up on the riverbank to die (31:1–8; 32:1–16). In his third column Ezekiel envisions Egypt and Assyria and their allies languishing in Sheol, and the revised version recounts the causes and circumstances of the fall of Jerusalem (32:17–28; 33:1–33).

In the ninth book Ezekiel devotes a column to the ascendancy of Yahweh, another to the renewal of the land, and a third to the resurrection of Israel. The Jerusalem version imagines instead a government headed by a descendant of David, retaliation against Edom, the return of the exiles, the rebuilding of the city, the reunification of Israel and Judah under a new covenant, and the humiliation of all world powers. In Ezekiel's version the book is a recapitulation of earlier themes surrounding the fall of Jerusalem, the desolation of the mountains of Israel, and the sacrificial offering of the people of Israel to Yahweh. In the revised version, the book draws the conclusions to the arguments on bad kings and the preservation of a remnant. Neither displays new sources, and the revised version as usual depends on earlier books for its basic structure and expression.

The last book describes the restored community. In Ezekiel's version it is centered on the temple and consists in a new creation. In the revised version, the temple is endowed with a priesthood and a liturgy and becomes the literal focus of a new community that is composed of the twelve tribes of Israel settled in the land, according to the ideal pattern envisioned by the Deuteronomistic Historian.[502]

In the first column Ezekiel returns in a vision to the land of Israel.

He is brought to a high mountain that has a structure like a city on its summit. This is the temple, and Ezekiel is led through it step by step from gate to gate and courtyard to courtyard until he reaches the holy of holies and grasps its full extent. The revised version simply points out other features that pertain to sacrifice and the residence of the priests. In the second column Ezekiel describes how the glory of God returned and filled the temple, but the revised version organizes the civil and the religious administration of the city and institutes its festal calendar. In the third column, Ezekiel situates the temple at the center of a new Garden of Eden, well-watered with a life-giving stream, with every tree bearing edible fruit and healing leaves. The revised edition situates the temple at the center of the land of Israel and gives the city the name "Yahweh is there."

CONCLUSION

Ezekiel states clearly at the beginning of his prophecy that his work was inspired by a vision that occurred late in the exile and that allowed him to understand the sequence of events leading beyond the fall of Jerusalem to the restoration of Israel. He wrote about these events in chronological sequence, as history, and in direct discourse, as prophecy, in a rhythmical, cadenced prose that was suitable to his chronicle but made it resemble the poetic works of the earlier prophets. His work, however, was not purely traditional but was influenced by ritual and speculation. He was familiar with all the earlier works and used them freely and frankly, but his own prophecy dealt with the more fundamental issues of life and death and the real or imaginary relationships between natural and divine cycles. He set himself out from the beginning as a son of Adam who had seen what seemed to be the glory of God in the likeness of Adam (Book One). He ends up in a city that has no name but has all the characteristics of Eden and that is centered on a mountain inhabited by the glory of God (Book Ten). He starts in exile, where he imagines the siege and capture of Jerusalem and understands it as the end of the world (Book Two). He comes to realize that the land will flourish again and that life will follow on death and sees the dead bodies of the slain rise out of their graves (Book Nine). He begins with the desecration of the temple, the departure of the glory of God, and the sorry flight of the king (Books Three and Four). He sees in the end, in the image of Egypt and Tyre, that the glory of Adam has departed and the kings lie limp in Sheol (Books Seven and Eight). He knows that life and death are individual, in the instance of the lover, the king, the innocent son, but he comes to a resolution when he realizes that the whole nation must die to be brought back to life (Books Five and Six).

Ezekiel was not a naïve dreamer, and what he wrote was not random reflection. Others were saying some of the same things and some would almost agree, and many were saying the opposite. The book of Jeremiah reacts viciously against prophets such as Ezekiel in Babylon who thought that the temple was about to be restored. The Deuteronomistic Historian adopted his ideas on individual guilt, but could not accept their application to individual cities and nations and could only explain the fall of Jerusalem by appealing to an inexorable fate unleashed by the crimes of Manasseh. The restoration of the Davidic dynasty seemed certain for a while, but Ezekiel would have none of it. He lived in a cosmopolitan world where the national interests of Judah and Jerusalem seemed petty. He did not talk about traditional things like covenant, prayer, and sacrifice, but he thought about peripheral traditions like the death and resurrection of God and imagined a world where they applied not to kings or Gods but to a nation in the image of God.

This was pretty heady stuff and far too late to do much good for those who had not died and who had to adjust to a simpler and more traditional life. There was not much point talking about the resurrection or pretending that Jerusalem was the center of some new creation, and so there was no reason to talk about some vision in the sky and no point pretending that the whole world would be destroyed. It made a lot more sense to situate Ezekiel's vision in the temple (Book One) and to admit from the beginning that some would survive (Book Two), because then it would be possible to start making plans for restructuring the country (Book Nine) and restoring the cult (Book Ten). It was important from the Jerusalem point of view, consequently, to be precise about whose fault it was that the city was captured (Book Four) and who was to blame for destroying it (Book Seven), and it simply did not do to attribute it to avenging angels (Book Three), to imagine it as a descent into Sheol (Book Eight), or to think that people could not have repented (Book Five) and that Yahweh was indiscriminate in his judgment (Book Six).

Ezekiel was nobody's fool, except in the eyes of the new establishment in Jerusalem. They put him among the prophets and gave him a few biographical references to ruin his mystique. They made his visions weird, his behavior bizarre, and his words unintelligible when there was no other easy way to diminish their impact. They put in conflicting viewpoints so that it would seem, despite what he said explicitly, that he was active in Judah and Jerusalem and not just seeing things in

Babylon. He represented the exiles' point of view that the old order was finished and a new world was beginning. His editor represented the point of view of the Jerusalem establishment that nothing basically had changed and that a new regime with new rules would be just fine. From his point of view the old Israel was all bad and the new Israel would not be centered on Jerusalem. From their point of view some of the exiles were good and would be brought back to a better land organized around a restored and purified cult. He worked with worldly ideas of creation and with universal belief in natural cycles. They relied on the Torah and the recent demonstration by the Deuteronomistic Historian that the world was historical and that history conformed to the law. He had a vision. They had an agenda.

Conclusion

The postreformation prophets were in touch with a different reality. Their classical predecessors lived in a world formed by historical theory where Israel and Judah emerged from the mass of nations into a splendid individuality set against the background of their relationship with God. The new generation was stuck with realized prophecy and the historical fact that Israel was just an ideal and Judah an abandoned tract.

Isaiah dealt with the constraints of history by elevating Yahweh above them. Amos saw history and time converging on an independent catastrophic course. Hosea abandoned history for the realms of natural, physical, legal, and political relationships. For Micah history was a script from which Yahweh extricated himself to pass judgment on Jerusalem. Jeremiah redid history as a drama in which Yahweh achieved distinct personality as the protagonist.

But those who followed did not have the luxury of research and the ease of speculation. Nahum began with traditional diction but left historical theory for contemporary events that demanded immediate action and left no room for deliberation. Habakkuk had recourse to prayer and discovered that history and prophecy were incommensurable with the realities of destiny and certain defeat. Zephaniah saw the whole known world being swept away and creation reverting to indiscriminate origins. Ezekiel described the chaos and tried to imagine the new creation.

For a brief period Judah had flourished in the world of wealth and political power. The historians made the world neat and intelligible. The prophets kept unearthing the surds of its nonconformity with tradition. As the world and Judah fell apart it was time to find an immutable place to stand. For the prophets of the postreformation period this turned out to be, very much as it was in the beginning, a physical world governed by an aloof and personal God and transcendent creator. What Judah would be in such a world might be imagined but was still to be seen.

NOTES

[1] For an analogous division and a different analysis, see H. Schulz, *Das Buch Nahum: Eine redaktionskritische Untersuchung* (BZAW 129; Berlin: Walter de Gruyter, 1973).

[2] The hymn is sometimes identified as a psalm and ascribed to a later writer (see B. Renaud, "La composition du livre de Nahum: ("*ZAW* 99 Une proposition," [1987] 198–219). The psalm, in turn, is often analyzed as an acrostic and is rewritten to suit the form (D. L. Christensen, "The Acrostic of Nahum Reconsidered," *ZAW* 87 [1975] 17–30; idem, "The Acrostic of Nahum Once Again: A Prosodic Analysis of Nahum 1,1–10," *ZAW* 99 [1987] 409–15; K. Seybold, "Vormasoretische Randnotizen in Nahum 1," *ZAW* 101 [1989] 71–85).

[3] The ballad tells a simple story in short manageable stanzas. It begins in 2:2 and ends at 2:11 (W. Rudolph, *Mica-Nahum-Habakkuk-Zephania* [Kommentar zum Alten Testament 13/3; Gütersloh: Gerd Mohn, 1975] 165, 172). J. Jeremias explains how 2:3 fits into the context, but he is almost alone in including it in the song (*Kultprophetie und Gerichtsverkündigung in der späten Königszeit Israels* [WMANT 35; Neukirchen-Vluyn: Neukirchener Verlag, 1970] 25–28).

[4] The ode is a rhetorically sophisticated poem addressed to a particular but unnamed city. Its ebb and flow are described by Rudolph (*Nahum*, 174–87), and its typical language and universal appeal are noted by C. A. Keller ("Die theologische Bewältigung der geschichtlichen Wirklichkeit in der Prophetie Nahums," *VT* 22 [1972] 399–419).

[5] The original superscription (1:1b, "Book of the vision of Nahum from Elqosh" [*sēper ḥāzôn naḥûm hā'elqōšî*]) relates Nahum's work to the prophecy of Isaiah, which was also entitled a vision (Isa 1:1a, "The vision of Isaiah the son of Amos" [*ḥāzôn yěša'yāhû ben 'āmôṣ*]) and inscribed in a book (Isa 30:8, *sēper*). The title in the revised version (1:1a, "Elegy over Nineveh" [*maśśā' nîněwēh*]) is appropriate to the book as it now stands (see J. M. P. Smith, *A Critical and Exegetical Commentary on Nahum* [ICC; Edinburgh: T. & T. Clark, 1911] 284–87).

[6] Taunts against Nineveh (1:9–10) and words of consolation for Jerusalem (1:12–13) both conclude with threats against the king of Assyria (1:11, 14).

7 The preface is added in pieces (2:1, 3) and distorts the beginning of the ballad. The postscript (2:12–14) takes the form of a prophetic taunt totally out of tune with the ballad.

8 The identification takes place in a prophetic taunt (3:5–7 [question + declaration]) that reverses the pattern of the first (2:12–14 [declaration + question]).

9 The strophe is composed of two four-line stanzas encircling a two-line stanza (1:2, 3a, 3b–4a). The four-line stanzas express a combination or contrast: the first has two lines defining Yahweh as jealous, vengeful, and full of rage (1:2a), but the other two lines direct these passions against his enemies and adversaries (1:2b). The second has two lines describing his apparition in the storm (1:3b) and two others describing its effect on the rivers and the Sea (1:4a). The two-line stanza is transitional between them and expresses a similar contrast between Yahweh's reluctance to be angry with his friends and his insistence on punishing his foes (1:3a).

10 The epic covenant began with a theophany in which Yahweh declared his names and attributes (Exod 34:6–7). The significance of the declaration is evident in the epic story of rebellion in the wilderness, where it is Moses' reason to believe that Yahweh might relent (Num 14:17–18). Nahum reproduces its emphasis by repeating the name Yahweh five times (1:2–3a; cf. Exod 34:6 [three times]) and by citing one of his epithets (1:2a, ᵓēl qannô² = Exod 34:14bB). He also quotes the distinction that the covenant declaration makes between Yahweh's tolerance (1:3a, yhwh ᵓerek ᵓappayim ûgĕdôl kōaḥ = Exod 34:6b; Num 14:17a + 18aA, yigdal nā² kōaḥ ᵓădōnāy . . . yhwh ᵓerek ᵓappayim) and his determination (1:3a, wĕnaqqēh lōᵓ yĕnaqqeh yhwh = Exod 34:7b; Num 14:18b). His text differs from the epic declaration mainly in putting more emphasis on the anger of Yahweh (1:2; cf. Exod 34:6b–7aA) and in including among his names not only Yahweh and El but also Baal (1:2).

11 Nahum describes the cloud at Yahweh's feet (1:3b), and the cloud is a feature of the Priestly version of the theophany on Sinai (Exod 24:15–18) and in the Elohist version is combined with thunder and lightning (Exod 19:16aBb). In Amos the day of Yahweh, a day of expected jubilation, becomes a day of decisive defeat in battle, and this is described as a storm (Amos 1:14b, bitrûᶜâ bĕyôm milḥāmâ / bĕsaᶜar bĕyôm sûpâ), and both Amos and Nahum predict that no one will be able to withstand it (Nah 1:6, mî yaᶜămôd; Amos 2:15, lōᵓ yaᶜămōd). Victory over the Sea in a storm was ascribed first to Baal and Marduk and was adapted by the Priestly writer in the stories of creation and the exodus. Nahum is careful to note that Baal is an epithet of Yahweh (1:2a) and uses key terms from the Priestly version of the exodus (1:4a, yām, ybš, ḥrb; cf. Exod 14:21–22, yām, ḥrb, ybš) to describe his victory over the Sea.

12 The strophe is composed of a six-line stanza (1:4b–5) and two four-line stanzas (1:6, 7–8). The six-line stanza is narrative and describes events in chronological and dramatic sequence—that is, a storm that comes from the mountain ranges in the North, down through the topographically varied hill country, to the flat lands, which are distinguished only by their habitations.

The four-line stanzas are marked by contrast: the first has a question about who might withstand Yahweh's anger (1:6a) and an answer describing what it does to the topography (1:6b); the second has a contrast between Yahweh's friends (1:7) and his enemies (1:8).

[13] Jeremiah, like Nahum, saw the mountains quaking and the hills writhing (1:5a; cf. Jer 4:24) and the inhabited world returning to chaos (1:4b, 5b; cf. Jer 4:23, 25). Micah described the effect of Yahweh's theophany like a fire on the mountains (1:6b; cf. Mic 1:4), and Hosea described the desolation of the world when Yahweh came in judgment against it (1:4b, 5b, *'umlal . . . wĕkol yōšĕbê bāh*; cf. Hos 4:3aA, *'al kēn te'ĕbal hā'āreṣ / wĕ' umlal kol yôšēb bāh*).

[14] Isaiah, like Nahum, described war as an expression of Yahweh's anger and rage (Nah 1:6a, *za'am, 'ap*; Isa 10:5, *'ap, za'am*). Jeremiah spoke of Yahweh's wrath that might be poured out on Jerusalem or on the nations (*ḥēmâ*, Jer 6:11; 10:25). Isaiah referred to invasion as a flood of overwhelming the land (Isa 28:15b, 18b, *šôṭ šôṭēp kî ya'ăbōr*), and Nahum uses the same expression (1:8aA, *ûbĕšeṭep 'ōbēr*; 3:2, *qôl šôṭ*). Isaiah criticized the leaders of Jerusalem for rejecting Yahweh, taking refuge in Egypt, and trusting in its protection (Isa 30:2b, *lā'ôz bĕmā'ôz par'ōh / wĕlaḥsôt bĕṣēl miṣrāyim*), and Nahum points out that it is Yahweh who is a refuge and who knows those who trust in him in a time of trouble (1:7, *mā'ôz, ḥōsê bô*). Jeremiah tempered Amos's notion of the end by saying that Yahweh would not bring Judah and Jerusalem to a complete end (*kālâ lō' ya'ăśeh*, Jer 4:27; 5:10; 30:11), but Nahum says that Yahweh will bring his adversaries to a complete end (1:8, *kālâ ya'ăśeh*).

[15] The only items not repeated in the stanza (1:2) are that Yahweh is a jealous El and a wrathful Baal. The first two lines are compound and have a caesura marked by "and" ("A jealous God / and vengeful is Yahweh // vengeful is Yahweh / and a Master of wrath"). The last two lines are simple and have no caesura ("Vengeful is Yahweh to his enemies // surly is he to his foes").

[16] The stanza (1:3a) repeats the word *yhwh* and the root *nqh* (*wĕnaqqēh lō' yĕnaqqeh*). The first line has a caesura marked by "and," but the second is simple and has no caesura ("Yahweh is slow to anger / and great in power // and Yahweh does not relent").

[17] The first line is compound and the third is complex and both have a caesura, while the second and fourth are simple statements (1:3b–4a, "In the wind / and in the storm is his way // and a cloud is the dust at his feet // rebuking the Sea / so that it dries // he evaporates all the rivers").

[18] The parallel lines repeat synonyms to express nature's awe in the presence of Yahweh (1:4b–5): "Withered Bashan and Carmel // the bloom of Lebanon withered // the mountains quaked before him // the hills shuddered // and the earth surrendered before him // the world and all its inhabitants."

[19] The first line has a caesura (1:6aA, *lipnê za'mô mî ya'ămôd*); the second is partly repetitive and maintains the rhyme in /o/ (1:6aB, *ûmî yāqûm baḥărôn*

'appô); the third begins with the same rhyme (1:6bA, ḥămātô nittĕkâ kā'ĕš); and the last is parallel to it (1:6bB, wĕḥaṣṣurm̂ nittĕṣû mimmennû).

²⁰ Nah 1:7–8: "Yahweh is good / a defense on the day of battle // knowing who trusts him // when the flood sweeps through / he puts an end to his opponents // chasing his enemies into the dark."

²¹ The first strophe (1:9–11) repeats the name "Yahweh" from the preceding stanza (cf. 1:7a) and uses the deictic personal pronoun (1:9, "he" [hû']) to refer to him. It repeats the expression "put an end to" and the word "adversity" from the preceding stanza (1:9a, kālâ hû' 'ōšeh = 1:8a, kālâ ya'ăšeh mĕqômāh; 1:9b, ṣārâ = 1:7a) and the expression "withstand" from the stanza before that (1:9b, lō' tāqûm; cf. 1:6a, mî yāqûm).

²² The original referred to a flood passing through the land (1:8, 'ōbēr), and the second strophe refers to the enemy passing away (1:12, wĕ'ābār).

²³ Instead of caesura these stanzas use apostrophe or apposition that produces almost the same effect (1:9a, kālâ hû' 'ōšeh; 1:11b, yō'ēṣ bĕliyyā'al).

²⁴ The point of the first stanza, plotting against Yahweh, is introduced in the second person plural (1:9aA). The connection with the preceding text is expressed in the third person singular masculine (1:9aB) and feminine (1:9b). The conclusion is in the third person plural (1:10) in clauses filled with assonance and alliteration.

²⁵ In the revised version Nineveh is referred to in the second person singular feminine, the king of Assyria in the second person singular masculine, and the Assyrians as typical enemies in the second or third person plural.

²⁶ Yahweh's vengeance was announced by Nahum (1:2), but the editor develops it into a scheme of retribution against Assyria for what it did to Judah and Jerusalem.

²⁷ The allusions are marked, as in Deuteronomy and Micah, by the changes in person and number. Conspiring (1:9a, mah tĕḥaššĕbûn) or plotting evil against Yahweh (1:11a, ḥōšēb 'al yhwh rā'â) were crimes that the book of Hosea imputed to the leaders of Israel (Hos 7:15b, wĕ'ēlay yĕḥaššĕbû rā'). The strange combination of being entangled in thorns (1:10aA, kî 'ad sîrîm sĕbukîm) and being drunk in their drunkenness (1:10aB, ûkĕsob'ām sĕbû'îm) recalls two separate texts of Hosea condemning Ephraim's devotion to idols (Hos 2:8, hinĕnî šāk 'et darkēk bassîrîm; 4:18, sār sob'ām). The Assyrian king's devotion to idols surfaces explicitly in the next strophe (Nah 1:14). The notion of the Assyrian enemy making plans against Yahweh (1:11b, yō'ēṣ) and not succeeding (1:9b, lō' tāqûm) recalls the text of II Isaiah where essentially the same thing was said (Isa 8:10, 'uṣû 'ēṣâ wĕtupār dabbĕrû dābār wĕlō' yāqûm; cf. Isa 7:7 lō' tāqûm). As Nahum relied on the Priestly version of the crossing of the Sea, so the editor adopted the image of divine wrath devouring the enemy like chaff (1:10b, 'ukkĕlû kĕqaš yābēš mālē') from the Deuteronomistic Song of the Sea (Exod 15:7b, tĕšallaḥ ḥărōnĕkā yō'kĕlēmô kaqqaš).

28 The image of mighty enemies (1:12, *rabbîm* [plural]) passing through or away (1:12, *'ābār* [singular]) is taken from II Isaiah's description of Assyria as a mighty torrent (Isa 8:7a, "The mighty waters of the River . . ." [*'et mê hannāhār . . . harabbîm*]) that flooded Judah and flowed through the land (Isa 8:8a, *'ābar* [singular]), an image created originally by Isaiah (Isa 28:15, 18–19). It is combined with an obscure image of Assyria as a flock of sacrificial animals who will be shorn (Nah 1:12, *šĕlēmîm . . . wĕkēn nāgozzû*). The destruction of Assyria signals the end of Judah's affliction (1:12, *wĕ'innitik lō' 'ă'annēk 'ôd*; cf. Deut 8:2–5) and this is expressed as the breaking of the Assyrian bonds on Judah (cf. Jer 5:5; 27:2; 28:10).

29 The stanza (1:14) blends an accusation and elements of a curse. The curse concerns the lack of offspring and memorial and proper burial that II Isaiah recited in his taunt against the king of Babylon (Isa 14:19–21). The accusation is implicit and is essentially the worship of images and idols of which Israel was said to be guilty (*pesel ûmassēkâ*; cf. Deut 27:15; Judg 17:3, 4; 18:14).

30 The first stanza (2:2) describes the arrival of the enemy, their building of a rampart, the appointment of lookouts, and mutual words of encouragement. The second (2:4) describes the spectacle of the besieging army with its troops in array and its chariots glistening in the sun.

31 The first stanza (2:5), like the second stanza in the preceding strophe (2:4), describes the glint of chariots. The second stanza (2:6abA), like the first in the preceding strophe, (2:2) describes the posting of troops.

32 In the first stanza (2:6bB–8a) the mantelet is set up (2:6bB, *wĕhukan hassōkēk*); the gates are opened (2:7a, *ša'ărê hannĕhārôt niptāḥû*); the palace shakes and shudders (2:7b–8°, *wĕhahêkāl nāmôg wĕhussab*); and the idol of its Goddess Ishtar is removed (2:8a, *gullĕtâ hō'ălātâ*). In the second stanza (2:8b–9bA) Ishtar's ladies-in-waiting accompany her into exile moaning like doves (2:8bA, *wĕ'amhōtêhā mĕnahăgôt kĕqôl yônîm*), beating their breasts (2:8bB, *mĕtōpĕpôt 'al libĕbêhen*), and Nineveh is like a reservoir (2:9a, *wĕnînĕwēh kibrēkat mayim*), like the waters of the reservoir that are escaping (2:9bA, *mîmê hî' wĕhēmmâ nāsîm*). See H. W. F. Saggs, "Nahum and the Fall of Nineveh," *Journal of Theological Studies* 20 (1969) 220–25.

33 In the first stanza (2:9bB–10) the deserters are encouraged to take a stand but do not turn back to their positions (2:9bB, *'imdû 'ămōdû wĕ'ên mapneh*), and the attackers are urged to loot and plunder (2:10). In the second stanza (2:11) Nineveh is completely discombobulated, and her few defenders are seized with terror.

34 Cf. Nah 2:2a (*'ālâ mēpîs 'al pānayik*) and 1:6aA (*lipnê za'mô mî ya'ămōd*).

35 Cf. Nah 2:2b (*sappēh derek*) and 1:3b (*bĕsûpâ ûbis'ārâ darkô*).

36 Cf. Nah 2:2b (*'ammēs kōaḥ mĕ'ōd*) and 1:3a (*ûgĕdol kōaḥ*).

37 Cf. Nah 1:6b (*ḥāmātô nittĕkâ kā'ēš*) and 2:4a (*bĕ'ēš pĕlādôt hārekeb*).

38 Cf. Nah 2:4a (*bĕyôm hăkînô*) and 1:7a (*bĕyôm ṣārâ*).

39 Cf. Nah 1:4b (*ûpĕraḥ lĕbānôn 'umlāl*) and 2:4b (*wĕhabbĕrōšîm horʿālû*). The latter text is usually considered nonsensical in the context of preparations for battle and is either rewritten ("the chargers" [*happārāšîm*]) or understood to refer figuratively to troops in battle array.

40 Cf. Nah 1:4a, 5a (*hannĕhārôt, hitmōgāgû*) and 2:7 (*hannĕhārôt, nāmôg*).

41 Cf. Nah 1:6a (*mî yaʿămōd*) and 2:9b (*ʿimdû ʿămōdû*).

42 The role of Yahweh as disperser and scatterer of the nations (2:4, *mēpîṣ*) was established in the epic story of the Tower of Babel (Gen 11:4, 9).

43 Since the stanza (2:1) continues the editing, it is not marked at the beginning as editorial but only contains cross-references to the editor's argument. The first part (2:1a) is essentially a quotation from II Isaiah, but its reference to the proclamation of peace from the mountaintops (2:1aA, *hinnēh ʿal hehārîm*) is a nice contrast to the quaking of the mountains before the anger of Yahweh (1:5, *hārîm rāʿăšû mimmennû*). The second part repeats the point that the editor made: cf. 2:1b (*kî lōʾ yôsîp ʿôd laʿăbor bāk bĕliyyaʿal*) and 1:9–10 (*lōʾ . . . kî*), 1:11b (*bĕliyyāʿal*), 1:12 (*wĕʿābar*); also 2:1b (*kulloh nikrāt*) and 1:9 (*kālâ hûʾ ʿōśeh*), 1:14 (*ʾakrît*).

44 The first stanza announces the end of Assyrian domination, and the second (2:3) announces the restoration of Jacob. It is fitted in by repeating the prior context (2:3, *kî*; cf. 2:1, *kî*) and by deictic reference to the adjacent context (2:3: the proper name "Yahweh" is deictic and specifies the *mēpîṣ* [2:2] of the original ballad).

45 Both stanzas (2:12–13, 14) are attached to the ballad by deictics (2:12a, *ʾayyeh . . . hûʾ*; 2:14, *hinĕnî ʾēlayik*) but only the second has any relationship to the original (2:14, *rikbāh*; cf. 2:4a, 5a, *hārekeb*) or the edited context (2:14b, *wĕhikrattî . . . wĕlōʾ yiššāmaʿ ʿôd*; cf. 1:14, *lōʾ yizzāraʿ . . . ʿôd . . . ʾakrît*). The topic of the lion's prey, on the other hand, anticipates an original statement in the ode (*ṭrp*, 2:13, 14; cf. 3:1) and makes it logical to suppose that the city addressed there by the editor is also Nineveh, rather than Jerusalem as Nahum insinuated.

46 In the ballad *waw* ("and") is rare at the beginning of lines and is used mainly for contrasting parts of a stanza, except in the last stanza, where it indicates a sequence of developing terror. In the revised version *waw* indicating sequence is most common.

47 The first part of the stanza (2:3a) fits with the summons to restore the rituals in the temple (2:1a), but the second part combines repetitions from the original (2:3b, *kî bĕqāqûm bōqĕqîm*; cf. 2:11, *bûqâ ûmĕbûqâ ûmĕbullāqâ*) with the contrary image of a vineyard (2:3b).

⁴⁸ The new context of the quotation (2:1aA = Isa 52:7a, *mah nāʾwû ʿal hehārîm raglê mĕbaśśēr maśmîaʿ śālôm*) resembles its original Isaian context in describing the return of Yahweh as seen and announced by a watchman on the wall (cf. Nah 2:2–3 and Isa 52:8).

⁴⁹ Cf. Nah 2:3 (*ʾet gĕʾôn yaʿăqōb kigʾôn yiśrāʾēl*) and Amos 6:8 and 8:7 ([*ʾet*] *gĕʾôn yaʿăqōb*) and Hos 5:5 and 7:10 (*gĕʾôn yiśrāʾēl*). These contexts suggest that *gāʾôn* is a pejorative reference to the temple as a place in which the people take pride instead of submitting to the glory of Yahweh that dwells in it. A similar expression with this meaning is used often in the revised edition of Ezekiel (*gāʾôn* + *ʿz*, Ezek 7:20, 24; 24:21; 33:28).

⁵⁰ Cf. Nah 2:3b (*ûzĕmōrêhem śihētû*); Jer 5:10 (*ʿălû bĕśārôtêhā wĕśahētû*; cf. also Jer 6:9; 8:13), and Ezek 15:2 (*hazzĕmôrâ*).

⁵¹ Cf. Nah 2:12–13; Isa 5:29; Jer 4:7 and 5:6; and especially Ezek 19: 2–3.

⁵² Cf. Nah 2:14b (*qôl malʾākēk*) and 2 Kgs 19:22–23.

⁵³ The stanzas (3:5–6, 7; cf. 2:12–13, 14) are introduced by the deictic expressions *hinĕnî ʾēlayik / nĕʾum yhwh ṣĕbāʾôt* (3:5aA), and the first refers to the nations that are mentioned in the preceding original stanza (*gôyim*, 3:4b, 5b).

⁵⁴ The strophe (3:12–15a) is attached to the last stanza of the ode (3:11) by deictic pronominal suffixes (3:12–15a, "your"). The ballad said that the inhabitants were fleeing Nineveh and, relying on a pun, the editor relates the unnamed city to Nineveh by saying that its inhabitants were women (cf. 2:9, *wĕhēmmâ nāsîm*; and 3:13, *ʿammēk nāśîm*). Both the ballad and the ode refer to the opening of the gates (2:7a; 3:13a), and both mention the siege and fire (*mĕṣurâ / māṣôr*, 2:2; 3:14; *ʾēś*, 2:4; 3:15).

⁵⁵ The strophe (3:15b–17) is attached artificially to the preceding strophe by repeating one word (3:15a, 15b, *kayyeleq*). The envoys who were mentioned at the end of the edited ballad (2:14b, *malʾākēk*) are identified in this strophe as merchants, garrison commanders, and diplomats (3:16–17).

⁵⁶ The strophe (3:18–19) continues the list of officials begun in the preceding strophe to include the ambassadors and the king himself. The dispersal of the people on the mountains is a pun on the beginning of the edited ballad, where the herald on the top of the mountains announces that the scatterer has come up against Nineveh (cf. 3:18b, *nāpōśû ʿammĕkā ʿal hehārîm*; and 2:1–2, . . . *ʿal hehārîm . . . mēpîṣ*). The final exclamation, "For on whom has your evil not trespassed" (3:19b, *ʿābĕrâ*), recalls the assurance given in the same text that the reprobate would never again trespass against Judah (2:1b, *laʿăbôr*).

⁵⁷ Cf. Nah 1:4; 2:7a, 10; 3:8, 9. The literary quality of the connection is clear since Thebes was not by the Sea.

58 Cf. Nah 1:7a (*lĕmāʿoz bĕyôm ṣārâ*); 2:4a (*bĕyôm hăkînô*); and 3:11b (*māʿôz mĕʾôyēb*).

59 Cf. 3:1a (*hôy ʿîr dāmîm*); Ezek 24:6, 9 (*ʾôy ʿîr haddāmîm*); Mic 3:10 (*bōneh ṣiyyôn bĕdāmîm*); Mic 7:2 (*kullām lĕdāmîm yeʾĕrōbû*); cf. also Hos 4:2.

60 Cf. Nah 3:1b (*kullāh kaḥaš*); Isa 28:15, 17 (*kāzāb, šeqer*); Jer 5:12 (*kiḥăšû bayhwh*); Jer 9:1–5; Hos 4:2; 9:2.

61 Cf. Nah 3:4 (*mērōb zĕnûnê zônâ . . . hammōkeret gôyim biznûnêhā*); Hos 1:2; 2:4, 6; 4:12; 5:4; Mic 1:7; Ezek 16:1–43; 23:1–29.

62 Cf. Nah 3:11 (*tiškĕrî*) and Isa 29:9 (*šākĕrû*).

63 Cf. Nah 3:5–6 (*wĕgillêtî šûlayik ʿal pānāyik / wĕhārʾêtî . . . mamlākôt qĕlônēk / wĕhišlaktî ʿālayik šiqqūṣîm*) and Jer 13:26–27 (*wĕgam ʾănî ḥāśaptî šûlayik ʿal pānāyik / wĕnirʾâ qĕlônēk . . . rāʾîtî šiqqûṣāyik*).

64 Cf. Nah 3:6 (*wĕnibbaltîk wĕśamtîk kĕrōʾî*) and Hos 2:12, 14 (*wĕʿattâ ʾăgalleh ʾet nablūtāh . . . wĕśamtîm lĕyaʿar*).

65 Cf. Nah 3:6a (*wĕhišlaktî ʿālayik šiqqūṣîm*) and Ezek 20:7 (*ʾîš šiqqûṣê ʿênāyw hašlîkû*).

66 Cf. Nah 3:7 (*šoddĕdâ nînĕwēh mî yānûd lāh / mēʾayin ʾăbaqqēš mĕnaḥămîm lāk*) and Isa 51:19 (*mî yānûd lāk / haššōd . . . / mî ʾănaḥămēk*).

67 Cf. Nah 3:12, 14, 18; Jer 6:3 (*ʾēlêhā yābōʾû rōʿîm wĕʾedrêhem*); and Jer 8:14 (*ʿārê hammibṣār*).

68 Cf. Nah 3:18 (*ʾayyām nāmû*) and Isa 5:27 (*lōʾ yānûm*).

69 Cf. Nah 3:15–17 (*yeleq, ʾarbeh, gōbay*); Amos 7:1 (*gōbay*); Joel 1:4 (*ʾarbeh, yeleq*).

70 Cf. Nah 3:13, 15–17 (*ʿammēk nāšîm, kayyeleq*) and Jer 51:14 (*kayyeleq*); 51:30 (*hāyû lĕnāšîm*).

71 Cf. Nah 3:19a (*ʾên kēhâ lĕšibrekā / naḥlâ makkāteka*) and Isa 1:6; Mic 1:9; Jer 10:19; 30:12 (*ʾānûš lĕšibrēk naḥlâ makkātēk*).

72 Cf. Nah 3:19b (*tāqĕʿû kap*) and Ezek 6:11; 21:19, 22 (*nkh kap*).

73 Cf. Nah 3:18b (*nāpōšû ʿammĕkā ʿal hehārîm wĕʾên mĕqabbēṣ*) and 1 Kgs 22:17 (*nĕpōṣîm ʾel hehārîm kaṣṣōʾn ʾăšer ʾên lāhem rōʿeh*).

74 Cf. Nah 3:16a (*hirbêt rōkĕlayik*) and Ezek 28:16 (*bĕrōb rĕkullātĕkā*).

75 An earlier form of this chapter appeared as "The Vision of Habakkuk,"

CBQ 48 (1986) 617–36, and is used with permission of the Catholic Biblical Association of America.

[76] The editor has managed to convince most commentators that the psalm does not belong to the prophecy but is a much older, or even ancient, liturgical text (see T. Hiebert, *God of My Victory: The Ancient Hymn in Habakkuk 3* [HSM 38]; Atlanta: Scholars Press, 1986).

[77] See C. A. Keller, "Die Eigenart der Prophetie Habakuks," *ZAW* 85 (1973) 156–67; Jeremias, *Kultprophetie*, 55–110.

[78] See E. Otto, "Die Stellung der Wehe-Worte in der Verkündigung des Propheten Habakuk," *ZAW* 89 (1977) 73–107.

[79] The form and development of laments are described by C. Westermann, *Praise and Lament in the Psalms* (Atlanta: John Knox, 1981) 64–81.

[80] See, e.g., J. G. Janzen, "Habakkuk 2:2–4 in the Light of Recent Philological Advances," *HTR* 73 (1980) 53–78.

[81] See Rudolph, *Micha-Nahum-Habakkuk-Zephania*, 193–251; J. G. Janzen, "Eschatological Symbol and Existence in Habakkuk," *CBQ* 44 (1982) 394–414.

[82] Hab 1:1 "The fate (*hammaśśāʾ*) that Habakkuk the prophet (*hăbaqquq hannābîʾ*) foresaw (*ʾăšer ḥāzâ*)."

[83] The invocation involves the petitioner and God (1:2–3aA), and the vision describes the third-party cause of the distress (1:5–6, 8–10).

[84] The prayer for life (1:12a, *lōʾ nāmût*) is sometimes taken as a pious, but to orthodox thought unthinkable, hope that Yahweh would not die (*°lōʾ tāmût*). This would make the prayer the literal and logical match of the statement that God is eternal (1:12a, *miqqedem*) but would ignore the thematic movement of the psalm in which the petitioner's hope for life is inspired by the eternity of God (cf. 3:2) (see C. McCarthy, *The Tiqqune Sopherim and Other Theological Corrections in the Massoretic Text of the Old Testament* [Göttingen: Vandenhoeck & Ruprecht, 1981] 105–11).

[85] The hymn (3:3–12) begins with hope (3:2) and ends with a contrast between the present desperate situation (3:13aA, 15–17aA) and the time of salvation (3:17aBb–19a).

[86] Cf. Hab 1:13b (*lammâ*) and 1:3aA (*lammâ*). The parable of the fisherman (1:14–17) illustrates how the guilty swallow the innocent (1:13b).

[87] Cf. Hab 1:13b (*rāšāʿ ṣaddîq*) and 1:4b (*rāšāʿ . . . ṣaddîq*).

[88] Cf. Hab 1:9 (*ʾsp*) and 1:15 (*ʾsp*).

89 Cf. Hab 1:11 (*wĕʾāšēm zû kōḥô lēʾlōhô*) and 1:16 (*ʿal kēn yĕzabbēaḥ lĕḥermô wîqaṭṭēr lĕmikmartô*).

90 In their revised form these invocations (1:2–4, 12–13) note that the law does not work and there is no justice because the guilty always manage to circumvent the innocent.

91 The superscription (3:1) and colophon (3:19b) indicate the hymn's general irrelevance to the editor's argument. The inclusion of Yahweh's Anointed (3:13aB) suggests the restoration of the rule of law and the exclusion of the guilty from the purview of the restored community (3:13b–14).

92 The line (1:3aB, *wĕšōd wĕḥāmās lĕnegdî*) is a contrived link. It continues the first-person discourse of the original (1:2–3aA) by including its pronominal suffix (*lĕnegdî*; cf. 1:3aA, *tarʾēnî*), and repeats one of the words in the original (cf. 1:2b, *ḥāmās*). But it is not really related to its own stanza, which continues with a third-person description, and it has nothing to do with the vision or with the cruelty that Habakkuk described.

93 The deictic pronoun occurs in the first line of the intrusive stanza (1:7a, *ʾāyōm wĕnôrāʾ hûʾ*) and relates it to the first two lines in the previous stanza (1:6), where Habakkuk gives his impression of the Chaldean character. The pronominal suffixes occur in the second line (1:7b, *mimmennû mišpāṭô ûśĕʾētô yēṣēʾ*) and relate the expression (*yēṣēʾ*) of the Chaldean's evil characteristics to their forced marches, which Habakkuk described (1:6b, *haḥôlēk*).

94 Habakkuk describes the Chaldeans as scoffing at kings and scornful of governors as they made fun of fortifications and piled up earth and captured them (1:10). The editor refers vaguely to that situation (1:11, *ʾāz*), adds his own interpretation of Chaldean world conquest (1:11a, *ḥālap rûaḥ wayyaʿăbōr wĕʾāšēm*), and ends with a flurry of deictics—a demonstrative and two pronominal suffixes—that identify the wind with the Chaldeans Habakkuk described (1:11b, *zû kōḥô lēʾlōhô*).

95 Cf. Hab 1:11b (*lēʾlōhô*) and 1:12a (*ʾĕlōhay*) and 2:18–20 (*ʾĕlîlîm*).

96 The new stanza (1:13b) repeats *tabbîṭ* (cf. 1:13a, *wĕhabbîṭ*), uses the word "swallow" (1:13b, *bĕballaʿ*) to allude to the fisherman's contentment with his catch, and continues the topic of guilt (*ršʿ*) and innocence (*ṣdq*); cf. 1:4.

97 The main connections are *kullōh* and *wĕyaʾaśĕpēhû* (1:15a), which recall the same words earlier in Habakkuk's text (1:9, *kullōh*, *wayyeʾĕsop*); constant use of the suffix *-ô* (1:14–17 [eight times]) relates the new strophe to the preceding strophes (cf. 1:11, 12b).

98 The dictum (2:4) does not seem particularly apt in its own stanza (2:4–5bA) or in the whole strophe (2:4–6a) but is crucial for the editor's argument and essential to smooth the transition to the invectives: the links with the original are a deictic pronominal suffix ("Vainglory has no defense *against*

it . . .") and repeated patterns of sound (cf. 2:4, *hinnēh ʿuppĕlâ lōʾ yāšĕrâ napšô bô / wĕṣaddîq beʾĕmûnātô yiḥyeh*; and 2:3b, . . . *ḥakkēh lô / kî bōʾ yābōʾ lōʾ yĕʾaḥēr*).

[99] The two strophes (3:13aA, 15–17aA; and 3:17aB–19a) each have two stanzas and the same pattern of reverence and dismay.

[100] Habakkuk says that Yahweh went out to save his people (3:13aA, *yāṣāʾtā lĕyēšaʿ ʿammĕkā*). The editor, by adding a parallel line and the deictic particle *ʾet*, says that Yahweh went out to save "*your* Anointed One" (3:13aB, *lĕyēšaʿ ʾet mĕšîḥekā*). Habakkuk sees Yahweh in his chariot battling with the Sea, and the editor describes how Yahweh split this traditional enemy and its allies from their guggle to their zatch.

[101] Hab 1:1, 3aA: see, perceive, look (*ḥzh, rʾh, nbṭ*); Hab 1:2: call, hear, cry (*šwʿ, šmʿ, zʿq*).

[102] Hab 1:3aBb–4: lawsuit, contention, law, justice, guilty, innocent (*rîb, mādôn, tôrâ, mišpāṭ, rāšāʿ, ṣaddîq*).

[103] The law grows numb (1:4aA, *tāpûg tôrâ*). The guilty circumvent (1:4b, *maktîr*) the innocent. Justice does not proceed (1:4a, *lōʾ yēṣēʾ*) to a proper conclusion but issues crookedly (1:4b, *mĕʿuqqāl*).

[104] Hab 1:5, 12b–13a: perceive, look (*rʾh, nbṭ*).

[105] Hab 1:5–6. Speech: count, mumble (*spr, mr*). Action: do, occupy (*pʿl, yrš*). Motion: rise, move quickly, walk (*qwm, nmhr, hlk*). Emotion: be astounded (*tmh*). Stasis: believe (*ʾmn*).

[106] Hab 1:8–10. Motion: be fast, be alert, cavort, come, fly, precede (*qll, ḥdd, pwš, bwʾ, ʿwp, qdm*). Emotion: awe (*mgmt*). Action: pile, capture (*ṣbr, lkd*). Audition: ridicule, laugh (*qls, šḥq*).

[107] Hab 1:7, 11, 13b. Forensic: justice, guilty, innocent (*mišpāṭ, rāšāʿ, ṣaddîq*). Abstract: dignity, treachery (*šĕʾēt, bōgĕdîm*). Images: invaders as a wind (1:11) or as devourers (1:13b).

[108] Hab 2:1–3. Vision: watch, perceive, see (*ṣph, rʾh, ḥzh*). Speech: speak, answer, reply, say, call, breathe, lie (*dbr, šwb, ʿnh, ʾmr, qrʾ, pwḥ, kzb*). Motion: run, come (*rwṣ, bwʾ*).

[109] Hab 2:4. Forensic: justify, innocent (*yšr, ṣdq*). Abstract: vanity, truth (*ʿuppĕlâ, ʾĕmûnâ*).

[110] Hab 3:2–4. Action: do, cover, fill (*pʿl, ksh, mlʾ*). Audition: hear (*šmʿ*). Emotion: pity, be anxious (*rḥm, rgz*). Motion: come (*bwʾ*). The last stanza (3:4) lacks all of these and describes the brightness emanating from Yahweh's hiding place.

111 Hab 3:5–7. Motion: walk, march, shake, scatter, succumb (*hlk*, *yṣ'*, *ntr*, *pṣṣ*, *šwḥ*). Stasis: stand ('*md*). Vision: see (*r'h*). Emotion: be anxious (*rgz*).

112 Hab 3:8–9. Word: utterance ('*ōmer*). Deed: ride, split (*rkb*, *bq'*). Emotion: anger, wrath, rage (*ḥrh*, '*ap*, '*ebrâ*).

113 Hab 3:10–12. Vision: see (*r'h*). Emotion: trembling, fury (*ḥyl*, *z'm*). Speech: shout (*ntn qôl*). Motion: go by, lift up, tread, trample, walk ('*br*, *nś'*, *ṣ'd*, *dwš*, *hlk*). Stasis: stand ('*md*).

114 Hab 3:13aA, 15–17aA. Action: march, stride (*yṣ'*, *drk*). Audition: hear (*šm'*). Emotion: be anxious, quiver, sag, expect (*rgz*, *ṣll* [+ *śĕpātay*], *bw'* [+ *rqb*], *nwḥ*).

115 Hab 3:17aBb–19a. Action: do, cut off, place ('*śh*, *gzr*, *śym*). Motion: stride (*drk*). Stasis: fail (*kḥš*). Emotion: exult, be glad ('*lz*, *gyl*).

116 The argument (1:3aBb–4) is constructed of consecutive and subordinate clauses and is more like prose than poetry.

117 See R. D. Haak, " 'Poetry' in Habakkuk 1:1–2:4?" *JAOS* 108 (1988) 437–44.

118 The first line has *rĕ'û* . . . *wĕhabbîṭû*; the second has *wĕhittammĕhû tĕmāhû*; the third has *pō'al pō'ēl*; and the last has *lō'* . . . *kî*.

119 The first line is alliterative, assonantal, and has internal rhyme (*kî hinĕnî mēqîm 'et hakkaśdîm*). The middle lines have alliteration in /h/, /m/, /r/ (*haggôy hammar wĕhannimhār / hahôlēk lĕmerḥăbê 'ereṣ*). The fourth line has alliteration in /l/ and /š/ (*lāreśet miškānôt lō' lô*). The most obvious reduplication is the final *lō' lô*.

120 The opening rhyme is in *-û*. The end rhyme is in *-ayw* (*wĕqallû minnĕmērîm sûsāyw / wĕhaddû mizzĕ'ēbê 'ereb / ûpāšû pārāšāyw / ûpārāšāyw mērāḥôq yābō'û*).

121 "Awe at their presence precedes them" (*mĕgammat pĕnêhem qādîmâ*).

122 The two lines (1:12a) contrast the eternity of God and the fragility of the suppliant and have parts of words that rhyme (*HĂLÔ' 'attâ miQQEDem yhwh / 'ĔLŌhay QĔDōšî LŌ' nāmût*).

123 The rhyme is at the beginning of the stanza (1:12b, *śamtô* . . . *yĕsadtô*), and the assonance and alliteration are in the last two lines (1:13a, *ṭĕhor 'ênayim mērĕ'ôt rā' / wĕhabbîṭ 'el 'āmāl lō' tûkāl*).

124 The stanza (1:7) begins with double epithets like the preceding stanza ('*āyōm wĕnôrā'*; cf. 1:6a, *hammar wĕhannimhār*) and has two deictics with the *-û* rhyme of the next stanza (*hû' / mimmennû*; cf. 1:8 *wĕqallû*, etc.). Its second line

has a rhyme like that of the last line in the preceding stanza (1:6b, *lōʾ lô*) and intricate alliteration, and its clumsiness derides the haughtiness it describes (1:7b, *mimmennû mišpāṭô ûśᵉʾētô yēṣēʾ*).

¹²⁵ Hab 1:11, "Then the wind changes and he passes by and is covered with guilt / whose strength is his God's (*ʾāz ḥālap rûaḥ wayyaʿăbōr wᵉʾāšēm / zû kōḥô lᵉʾlōhô*); cf. 1:10, "He scoffs at kings / leaders are a laugh to him / he laughs at every walled town / builds up walls of earth and takes it" (*wᵉhûʾ bammᵉlākîm yitqallās / wᵉrōzᵉnîm miśḥāq lô / hûʾ lᵉkol mibṣār yiśḥāq / wayyiṣbōr ʿāpār wayyilkᵉdāh*).

¹²⁶ Habakkuk's confession of trust (1:12b–13a) has two lines with three elements (1:12b) and two lines with four or five (1:13a). The added stanza (1:13b) has the same pattern in a line with three elements followed by a line with five. In Habakkuk's version the longer lines have a caesura created by the intricate alliteration, but in the revised version, despite alliteration, there is no caesura.

¹²⁷ The opening rhyme (in *-ā*) is established in the first line (2:1aA, *ʿal mišmartî ʾeʿĕmōdâ*) and continues in the next two. The last two lines begin with the same word (*mah, ûmâ*) and end in the same rhyme (in *-î* [also announced in the first line]). Each of the five lines, besides, has the same vowels at the beginning (a, e, or i) and at the end (a, e, or i, *and* o).

¹²⁸ The first and fourth lines are long and alliterative, and the second and third are short and plain.

¹²⁹ Cf. Hab 1:2 (*ʾezʿaq ʾēlêkā ḥāmās wᵉlōʾ tôšîaʿ*) and Mic 3:4 (*ʾāz yizʿăqû ʾel yhwh wᵉlōʾ yaʿăneh ʾôtām*). Micah also says that the opponents of the word of God will see the sun set on prophecy and will go through a night without vision (cf. 1:1 and Mic 3:6).

¹³⁰ Cf. Hab 1:2, 9 (*ḥāmās*); Mic 6:12; and Jer 6:7 = Amos 3:10 (*ḥāmās wāšōd*).

¹³¹ Cf. Hab 1:3aB (*wᵉšōd wᵉḥāmās lᵉnegdî*) and Jer 20:8 (*ʾezʿāq / ḥāmās wāšōd ʾeqrāʾ*).

¹³² Cf. Hab 1:3b (*wayhî rîb ûmādôn yiśśāʾ*) and Jer 15:10 (*ʾîš rîb wᵉʾîš mādôn*).

¹³³ Cf. Hab 1:4 (*tôrâ / yēṣēʾ mišpāṭ*) and Mic 4:2 = Isa 2:3 (*tēṣēʾ tôrâ*); cf. Isa 42:1 (*mišpāṭ laggôyim yôṣîʾ*).

¹³⁴ Cf. 1:4 (*tôrâ, mišpāṭ*) and Deut 17:11 (*hattôrâ, hammišpāṭ*); 1:4 (*rš°, ṣdq*) and Deut 25:1 (*ṣdq, rš°*).

¹³⁵ Cf. Hab 1:5 (*rᵉʾû baggôyim wᵉhabbîṭû . . . kî pōʿal pōʿēl bîmêkem*) and Isa 5:12b (*wᵉʾēt pōʿal yhwh lōʾ yabbîṭû / ûmaʿăśeh yādāyw lōʾ rāʾû*).

136 Cf. Hab 1:6 (*haggôy . . . hannimhār / hahôlēk lĕmerḥābê ʾereṣ*) and Isa 5:26 (*laggôyim mērāḥôq . . . miqṣēh hāʾāreṣ . . . mĕhērâ qal yābôʾ*).

137 Cf. Hab 1:5 (*wĕhittammĕhû tĕmāhû . . . lōʾ taʾămînû kî yĕʤuppār*); Isa 28:16b (*hammaʾămîn lōʾ yāḥîʤ*); Isa 29:9a (*hitmahmĕhû ûtĕmāhû*); and Isa 30:8 (*bôʾ kotbāh . . . ʿal ʤēper*).

138 Cf. Hab 1:5 (*bîmêkem*) and Isa 30:8b (*ûtĕhî lĕyôm ʾaḥărôn*).

139 Cf. Hab 1:8 (*wĕqallû . . . mērāḥôq yābôʾû*) and Isa 5:26ʹ (*mērāḥôq . . . qal yābôʾ*).

140 Cf. Hab 1:8 (*minnĕmērîm . . . mizzĕʾēbê ʿereb*) and Jer 5:6 (*zĕʾēb ʿărābôt . . . nāmēr*); cf. 1:10 (*mibṣār*) and Jer 5:17 (*mibṣār*).

141 Cf. Hab 1:12a (*ʾĕlōhê qĕdōʤî*) and Isa 5:19; 30:11, 12, 15. Both references to death (1:12a [*lōʾ nāmût*] and Isa 28:15 [*kāratnû bĕrît ʾet māwet*]) are quoted speech in the first person plural.

142 Cf. Hab 1:12b (*yhwh lĕmiʤpāṭ ʤamtô / wĕṣûr lĕhôkîaḥ yĕʤadtô*) and Isa 28:16–17 (*hinĕnî yiʤʤad bĕṣiyyôn ʾāben . . . wĕʤamtî miʤpāṭ lĕqāw*).

143 Cf. Hab 1:13a (*rāʿ*) and Mic 1:12; 2:3; 3:11; Jer 4:6.

144 Cf. Hab 1:11a (*ʾāz ḥālap rûaḥ wayyaʿăbōr wĕʾaʤēm*) and Isa 8:8a (*wĕḥālap bîhûdâ ʤāṭap wĕʿabar*).

145 Cf. Hab 1:13b (*blʿ*) and Jer 51:34 (*blʿ*).

146 Cf. Hab 1:7 (*ʾāyōm wĕnôrāʾ hûʾ / . . . ûʤĕʾētô*) and Job 41:17 (*miʤʤētô yāgûrû*); cf. also Job 13:11; 31:23.

147 Cf. Hab 1:14 (*wattaʿăʤeh ʾādām kidgê hayyām / kĕremeʤ . . .*) and Gen 1:26 (*naʿăʤeh ʾādām . . . bidgat hayyām . . . ûbĕkol hāremeʤ*).

148 Cf. Hab 2:1 (*ʿal miʤmartî ʾeʿĕmōdâ / waʾetyaṣṣĕbâ ʿal māṣôr / waʾăṣappeh lirʾôt*) and Nah 2:2 (*nāṣôr mĕṣūrâ / ṣappēh derek*) and Jer 6:16–17 (*ʿimdû. . . . ṣōpîm*); cf. Hos 9:8.

149 Cf. Hab 2:1 (*ûmâ ʾāʤîb ʿal tôkaḥtî*) and Isa 1:18 (*lĕkû nāʾ wĕniwwakĕḥâ yōʾmar yhwh*).

150 Cf. Hab 2:2–3 (*kĕtôb ḥāzôn ûbāʾēr ʿal halluḥôt . . . kî bôʾ yābôʾ*) and Isa 30:8, 13 (*kotbāh ʿal lûaḥ ʾittām wĕʿal ʤēper ḥuqqāh. . . . pitʾōm lĕpetaʿ yābôʾ*). See D. T. Tsumura, "Hab 2:2 in the Light of Akkadian Legal Practice," *ZAW* 94 (1982) 294–95.

151 Cf. Hab 2:3 (*wĕyāpēaḥ laqqēṣ. . . . kî bôʾ yābôʾ*) and Amos 8:2 (*bāʾ haqqēṣ*).

152 Cf. Hab 2:3 (*kî ʿōd ḥāzôn lammôʿēd*) and Hos 9:5; 12:10 (*yôm môʿēd*).

Hosea's expression is repeated in Lam 2:22, where it is combined with other language from the standard description of the day of Yahweh in Amos 5:18–20.

153 See J. M. Scott, "A New Approach to Habakkuk II 4–5a," *VT* 35 (1985) 330–40.

154 Cf. Hab 2:5 (*wĕ²ap kî hayyayin bôgēd / geber yāhîr wĕlō² yinweh*) and Isa 5:11–12 (*yayin*) and Isa 5:22 (*hôy gibbôrîm lištôt yayin*). The editor's reference to this complex of texts is assured by the exact quotation from III Isaiah (Hab 2:5b, *²ăšer hirḥîb kiš²ôl napšô / wĕhû² kammāwet wĕlō² yiśbāʿ*; cf. Isa 5:14, *lākēn hirḥîbâ šĕ²ôl napšāh*).

155 Cf. Hab 2:6 (*ʿabṭîṭ*) and Deut 15:6, 8 (*ʿbṭ*).

156 Cf. Hab 2:8a (*šallôtā . . . yĕšallûkā*) and Isa 10:6 (*lišlōl šālāl*).

157 Cf. Hab 2:8b (*middĕmê ²ādām waḥămās ²ereṣ / qiryâ wĕkol yōšĕbê bāh*) and Gen 4:10 (*qôl dĕmê ²āḥîkā*); Gen 9:6 (*šōpēk dam hā²ādām bā²ādām dāmô yiššāpēk*); Gen 6:11, 13 (*timmālē² hā²āreṣ ḥāmās*); Gen 19:24–25, *ʿal sĕdōm wĕʿal ʿămōrâ . . . ²et heʿārîm hā²ēl . . . wĕ²ēt kol yōšĕbê heʿārîm*). Yahweh rained down fire and brimstone on Sodom and Gomorrah because the clamor of their sins had come up to him (Gen 18:20–21; 19:24b).

158 Cf. Hab 2:10 (*qĕṣôt ʿammîm rabbîm*); Isa 10:7 (*ûlĕhakrît gôyim lō² mĕʿāṭ*); and Isa 10:14 (*wattimṣā² kaqqēn yādî lĕḥêl hāʿammîm*).

159 Cf. Hab 2:9 (*lāśûm bammārôm qinnô*); Obad 4 (*²im bên kôkābîm śîm qinnekā miššām ²ôrîdĕkā*); and Jer 49:16 (*mārôm . . . / kî tagbîah kannešer qinnekā / miššam ²ôrîdĕkā*).

160 Cf. Hab 2:9a (*hôy bōṣēaʿ beṣaʿ rāʿ lĕbêtô*) and Jer 6:13 (*bôṣēaʿ beṣaʿ*).

161 Cf. Hab 2:12–14 and Isa 11:9; Jer 51:58; Mic 3:10.

162 Cf. Hab 2:15 and Gen 9:20–27. See A. Catastini, "Reminiscenze noachiche in 1QpHab," *Annali dell'Istituto Orientale di Napoli* 44 (1984) 483–89.

163 Cf. Hab 2:16 and Jer 25:15–28; 51:7; cf. Hab 2:17 and 2 Kgs 19:21–28 (= Isa 37:22–29). See J. Gray, *I & II Kings: A Commentary* (OTL; Philadelphia: Westminster, 1970) 690.

164 Cf. Hab 2:18–19 and Isa 2:20; 44:9–10; Cf. Hab 2:18a (*môreh šāqer*) and Isa 9:14 (*môreh šeqer*); cf. 2:19a; Deut 4:28; and Deut 7:25; cf. 2:20 and Mic 1:2b.

165 The hymn contains elements that are proper to the epic, such as Yahweh's aura (3:4; *Enuma elish* IV, 58), retinue (3:5; *Enuma elish*, IV, 50–60), armament (3:9; *Enuma elish* IV, 33–48) and procession (3:15; *Enuma elish* IV,

141–46) as well as the frenzy, defeat, and trampling of Tiamat (3:10–12; *Enuma eliš* IV, 87–104); see W. A. Irwin, "The Mythological Background of Habakkuk, Chapter 3," *JNES* 15 (1956) 47–50.

166 Exod 14:21–23; *Enuma eliš* IV, 95–102, 130–40. The two traditions of Marduk's victory are reflected in the hymn's question (3:8, "Was Yahweh angry at the rivers / was your rage at the rivers / your wrath against the Sea / that you rode on your horses / the chariot of your salvation?"), which uses the language of Exodus 14 (Hab 3:8a *yām, sûs, merkābâ, yĕšûʿâ*) to ponder the theme of the epic (*nĕhārîm // yām*).

167 Cf. Hab 3:8, 12 (*ʾap, ʿebrâ, zaʿam*) and Isa 10:5–6 (*ʾap, zaʿam, ʿebrâ*).

168 Cf. Hab 3:7 (*rāʾîtî*) and Jer 4:23–25; cf. Hab 3:7 (*ʾohŏlîm, yĕrîʿôt*) and Jer 4:20.

169 Cf. Hab 3:13b (*bêt rāšāʿ*) and Mic 6:10 (*bêt rāšāʿ ʾōṣĕrôt rešaʿ*).

170 Cf. Hab 3:13b (*ʿārôt yĕsôd ʿad ṣawwaʾr*); Isa 8:8 (*ʿad ṣawwaʾr yaggîaʿ*); and Isa 28:16 (*yissad . . . mûsad mûssād*).

171 See F. J. Stephens, "The Babylonian Dragon Myth in Habakkuk 3," *JBL* 43 (1924) 290–93.

172 Cf. Hab 3:8, 12 (*ʾap, ʿebrâ, zaʿam*) and Nah 1:7 (*zaʿam, ʾap, ḥēmâ*); also Hab 3:16b (*lĕyôm ṣārâ*) and Nah 1:7 (*bĕyôm ṣārâ*).

173 Cf. Hab 3:17 and Mic 7:1; also 3:18 (*waʾănî . . . ʾāgîlâ bēʾlōhê yišʿî*) and Mic 7:7 (*waʾănî . . . ʾôḥîlâ lēʾlōhê yišʿî*). The final assurance in Habakkuk (3:19a, *wĕʿal bāmôtay yadrīkēnî*) resembles the beginning of Yahweh's theophany in Micah (Mic 1:3b, *wĕdārak ʿal bomŏtê ʾereṣ*).

174 All of the critical problems are recognized and treated, if not satisfactorily resolved, in K. Seybold, *Satirische Prophetie: Studien zum Buch Zefanja* (SBS 120; Stuttgart: Katholisches Bibelwerk, 1985).

175 The strophic, stanzaic, and tripartite organization of the original, combined with the editorial rearrangement of the speech's structure, has misled some to suppose that the prophecy is a collection of pieces and fragments (e.g., Seybold, *Satirische Prophetie*).

176 The first (1:1a, 2–3aAb) and third strophes (1:17–18) agree in their use of the first person singular and in their premonition that humanity will disappear from the face of the earth. They are different in the extent of the cosmic upheaval they envision, the first seeing it as inclusive of land, sea, and sky, and the third concentrating on people in the inhabited world. The first and second (1:14–16) agree in their emphasis on Yahweh's intervention, but the second is transitional, including cosmological features like the first strophe (1:15b, darkness and cloud) and political features like the third strophe (1:16,

cities and battlements). The second and third agree in their references to the day of Yahweh.

177 The correspondence of 1:7–9 and 1:14–16 is emphasized by the line that they share (1:7b, 14a, [kî] qārôb yôm yhwh) and by the repeated reference to the day of Yahweh in the new strophe (1:8, [bĕyôm], 9 [bayyôm hāhûʾ]).

178 There is a reference to the word of Yahweh (1:1a, ðebar) and to the fact that he has spoken (1:2, nĕʾum yhwh) and, in the names Zephaniah and Amariah, to Yahweh speaking and concealing. The word of Yahweh to Zephaniah and the list of Zephaniah's individual ancestors (1:1a) make a startling contrast with the insistence that Yahweh is going to wipe people off the face of the earth.

179 The word ben ("son") is repeated four times. The syllable yâ occurs six times. The names Gedaliah and Hezekiah signify the strength and power of Yahweh.

180 Most of the stanza (1:2–3aAb) is repetitive (ʾsp [four times], ʾāðām . . . mēʿal pĕnê hāʾăðāmâ [twice], nĕʾum yhwh [twice]) or paired (ʾāðām ûbĕhēmâ, ʿôp haššāmāyim ûðĕgê hayyām).

181 The name of Zephaniah's father (1:1a, kûšî) is the name that he uses to refer generically to the Assyrians in the second part of his speech (2:12; cf. 3:10). The word kōl (1:2, "all") recurs at the end of the first speech (1:18, kol [twice], kālâ). The expression wĕhikrattî (1:3b, "I will cut off") is important at the end of the speech (3:6–7).

182 The stanza (1:14) repeats qārôb ("near") and yôm yhwh ("the day of Yahweh"). The alliteration (mahēr mĕʾōð . . . mar) covers the speed and the sound of the approaching day. The next-to-last line refers to the awful sound of the day (qôl . . . mar) and the last line defines it as the roar of a hero (ṣōrēaḥ šām gibbôr) who in the context is evidently Yahweh the Warrior.

183 The second stanza (1:15–16) has eight lines linked by repetition of words (especially yôm, "day") and rhyme and interlinear alliteration.

184 The second strophe (1:14–16) is written in a distinctive staccato manner that corresponds to the encroachment of the great and ineluctable day and, especially in the edited version where other strophes have preempted it (cf. 1:7–13), sometimes seems to be separate and independent (see Seybold, *Satirische Prophetie*, 39–42). However, it can just as easily be seen as a pivot between the general announcement of destruction and its specific elaboration, and it is repeated and transformed in the final strophe (1:17–18).

185 The addition (1:1b) follows the pattern of the original in giving the name of the king (yōʾšiyyāhû) and of his father (ben ʾāmôn) and, by implication, of his grandfather (1:1a, ḥizqiyyâ).

186 The stanza (1:[3b]–6) was formed by adding a line that ended the

preceding stanza (1:3aB [*wĕhammakšēlôt ʾet hārĕšāʿîm*] ends the stanza 1:2–3aA) and by including two original lines in the new stanza (1:3b, *wĕhikrattî ʾet hāʾādām mēʿal pĕnê hāʾădāmâ / nĕʾum yhwh*). With this accomplished it continued in the first person of the original (1:4a, *wĕnāṭîtî yādî*) and repeated its preposition (*ʿal, wĕʿal*) and then repeated its introductory verb (1:4b, *wĕhikrattî*). The new version constantly repeats the object marker (*ʾet, wĕʾet*), the name Yahweh, and the words "worship" and "swear," and all of its lines are wordier and more prosaic than the original. It differs grammatically in having mostly nominal clauses, syntactically in having lines connected by *waw*, and prosodically in its use of parallelism and rhyme.

187 Cf. Zeph 1:7bA (*kî qārôb yôm yhwh*) and 1:14aA (*qārôb yôm yhwh haggādôl*): without the intrusive materials (1:4–6, 7–13) this line (1:14aA) was next in Zephaniah's composition. The injunction to silence (1:7a, *has mippĕnê ʾădōnāy yhwh*) supposes similar injunctions in the book of Amos relative to the day of Yahweh (cf. Amos 5:13; 6:10) but also contrasts with the sounds of the day of Yahweh (1:14b, 16a).

188 The lexical repetitiveness is mostly of particles (1:7, *kî*) and prepositions (1:8–9, *ʿal, wĕʿal*) but also includes one verb (1:8–9, *ûpāqadtî*) that continues the first person speech and mood of the preceding stanza (cf. 1:4). Each stanza has parallelism (1:7, 8, 9). Alliteration is drawn out through long clauses (1:8b, *wĕʿal kol hallōbĕšîm malbûš nokrî*; 1:9b, *hamĕmalʾîm bêt ʾădōnêhem ḥāmās ûmirmâ*).

189 In 1:11, for instance, all the lines match, and the last has a nice alliteration that sounds like the tinkle of silver (1:11bB, *nikrĕtû kol nĕṭîlê kāsep*). In 1:12b, on the other hand, the lines are lazy, unmatched, and prosaic to reflect the indolence that they describe (*ûpāqadtî ʿal hāʾănāšîm haqqōpĕʾîm ʿal šimrêhem / hāʾōmĕrîm bilbābām / lōʾ yêṭîb yhwh wĕlōʾ yārēaʿ*). The variety, clearly, is not due to lack of artistry or skill.

190 The stanza (2:1–2) repeats the verb *qšš* in the intransitive sense of "pull yourselves together" (2:1a, *hitqôšĕšû*) and in the transitive sense of "gather" (2:1a, *wāqôššû*), which would be apt, for instance, in the gathering of chaff (2:2, *mōṣ*). The nation is called "not sought after, desirable" or—if the word is taken as a denominative of *kesep* ("silver")—"not redeemable" (2:1b, *lōʾ niksāp*). In either case the expression reflects the previous stanza's statement that their silver would not redeem them (1:18a, *gam kaspām . . . lōʾ yûkal lĕhaṣṣîlām*). The conjunction *bĕṭerem* is repeated three times, and the last two clauses (2:2b) are almost exactly the same. The middle line (2:2a, *bĕṭerem ledet ḥōq kĕmōṣ ʿabar yôm*) seems to refer to the divine decree (*ḥōq*) coming to fruition (*ledet*) or, equivalently, to the day (*yôm*) that has been decreed blowing past like chaff (*kĕmōṣ ʿābar*).

191 The topic of the stanza is indicated by the repeated verb "seek" (2:3, *baqqĕšû*) and the repeated word "submission" (*ʿnw*). The reference to the "submissive people of the world / land" (2:3a, *kol ʿanwê hāʾāreṣ*) contrasts with the exordium's sense that the whole world was finished (1:18, *kol [. . .] hāʾāreṣ*).

192 See L. Zalcman, "Ambiguity and Assonance at Zephaniah 2:4," *VT* 36 (1986) 365–71; R. Gordis, "A Rising Tide of Misery: A Note on a Note on Zephaniah 2:4," *VT* 37 (1987) 487–90.

193 The stanza (2:5) supposes that the audience knows that the Pentapolis is located near the coast (2:5a), in Canaan and the land of the Philistines (2:5bA). The last line (2:6) illustrates the divisive alliteration and repeated breaks of the composition (*wĕhāyĕtâ ḥebel ḥayyām / nĕwōt kĕrōt rōʿîm / wĕgidrōt ṣōʾn*).

194 The stanzas (2:12–13, 14) also have a similar clipped construction, where individual lines are separated by their special alliterative or blank features.

195 The new stanza (2:7) begins like the end of the old but makes "seacoast" masculine rather than feminine (cf. 2:6, *wĕhāyĕtâ ḥebel ḥayyām*, and 2:7, *wĕhāyâ ḥebel*). The preceding stanza in the original said that Ashdod would be abandoned at noon (2:4), and the new stanza says that the flock of the remnant of Israel will lie down in the houses of Ashkelon in the evening (2:7b). The anomaly is that the original is referring to Philistia and is using it as an example in an exhortation, while the new material refers to Israel as the exemplar in an outburst of assurance. The original is creative: its last line, for instance, is interesting both visually and audibly and includes a pun on the Cretan origin of the Philistines (2:6, *kĕrōt*). By contrast, the new material is doctrinaire and filled with clichés ("remnant," "house of Judah," "visit," "bring back the captives").

196 The first strophe is spoken by Yahweh (2:8–9a). In the second strophe the first stanza (2:9b–10) is spoken by Yahweh and the second is a summary by the prophet (2:11). The last line of the first strophe (2:9aB, *mimšaq ḥārûl / ûmikrēh melaḥ / ûšĕmāmâ ʿad ʿôlām*) imitates the alliteration and internal breaks of the last line in the preceding strophe by Zephaniah (2:6). The last two lines of the last strophe describe the Mediterranean islands bowing down to Yahweh where they are (2:11b, *wĕyištaḥăwû lô ʾîš mimmĕqômô / kōl ʾiyyê haggôyim*) and so return to the topic of Zephaniah's last stanza, which mentioned the people of Crete (2:5a, *gôy kĕrētîm*; 2:6, *kĕrōt*).

197 The first stanza (2:8) has two pairs of parallel lines that match each other exactly and repeat the same word (*ḥrp*, 2:8a, 8b). The second stanza (2:9a) is joined to it logically as a conclusion (2:9a, *lākēn*), literally by reference to Moab and Ammon, and formally by identifying the speaker of the first stanza as Yahweh the Lord of Hosts the God of Israel. Together they develop the notion, introduced in the stanza that was added to Zephaniah's strophe (2:7), that Israel will take over the land of the neighboring states when Yahweh has destroyed them.

198 The first stanza (2:9b–10) refers to the first stanza of the preceding strophe (2:8) and repeats the gist of two of its lines (cf. 2:10b, *kî ḥērĕpû wayyagdîlû ʿal ʿam yhwh ṣĕbāʾôt*, and 2:8b, *ʾăšer ḥērĕpû ʾet ʿammi / wayyagdîlû ʿal gĕbûlām*). It also repeats the title "Yahweh of Hosts" from the second stanza in

that strophe (2:10; cf. 2:9a) and comes back to the notion of remnant that was introduced in the earlier intrusive stanza (2:9b; cf. 2:7). The second stanza (2:11) is a summary of the intrusive material and a transition back to the original text, but it also draws out of the intervening material the implication that by defeating the nations Yahweh has overcome their Gods, an idea that relates it to the additions in the first part of the speech about the foreign religious practices in Jerusalem.

199 The three stanzas (3:1-2, 3-4, 5) are linked by literal (qrb, yhwh) and deictic repetitions (the pronominal suffixes in the second and third stanzas refer to the feminine singular city addressed in the first stanza). The second stanza explains how the city is oppressive (yônâ) by describing the habits of her officials, and the third contrasts her refusal to be near Yahweh with the fact that he is near her.

200 The end of the exhortation (2:15) has the same form as the beginning of the apostrophe to Jerusalem (3:1-5). Both places are simply referred to as "City," Nineveh a city living in confidence (2:15, lābeṭaḥ), Jerusalem a city that did not put its confidence in Yahweh (3:2, lōʾ bāṭāḥâ).

201 The expression nigʾālâ refers to the defiling (gʾl II) or to the rejection (gʾl I) of Jerusalem. The defiling (3:1a, nigʾālâ) of Jerusalem would remove her from the holy things (3:4, qōdeš) and separate her from Yahweh—whom in fact she refused to approach (3:2, qrb)—and leave her like the divorced, abandoned, and rejected Philistine women. The rejection of Jerusalem (3:1a, nigʾālâ) would refer to her being unwanted or an outcast from a previous marriage.

202 Cf. Zeph 2:4 (baṣṣohŏrayim) and 3:3b (ʿereb . . . bōqer). The reference to lions and wolves that prey at night and leave no bones to chew in the morning (3:3b, lōʾ gārĕmû labbōqer) is the thematic opposite of the Philistine cities, which have become pastures and sheepfolds (2:5-6).

203 Cf. Zeph 3:5 (ṣaddîq . . . mišpāṭô) and 2:3 (mišpāṭô . . . ṣedeq). The exhortation is addressed to the humble people (2:3a, kol ʿanwê hāʾāreṣ) and to those who seek humility (2:3b, baqqĕšû ʿănāwâ) and contrasts with the incrimination of the city leaders (3:3-4), who do no such thing (3:5).

204 Cf. Zeph 3:6a, 7a (hikrattî, yikkārēt) and 1:3b (wĕhikrattî); cf. 3:6b (mēʾên yôšēb) and 2:5 (mēʾên yôšēb); 3:6a (mibbĕlî ʿōbēr) and 2:15b (kōl ʿōbēr). The sequence in the previous strophe from evening, to morning, to first light (3:3-5) is resumed in the statement that the inhabitants of the city persist in, that is, get up early to do (3:7, hiškîmû), perverse and corrupt things.

205 Cf. Zeph 3:8 (lĕyôm) and 1:14-16, 18; 2:2-3; also 3:8b (mišpāṭî) and 2:3 (mišpāṭô) and 3:5 (mišpāṭô); also 3:8b (leʾĕsōp) and 1:2-3 (ʾsp); also 3:8b (ḥărôn ʾappî) and 2:2 (ḥărôn ʾap); also 3:8b (kî bĕʾēš qinʾātî tēʾākēl kol hāʾāreṣ) = 1:18a. The day of Yahweh is announced in the exordium; time ticks away in the exhortation and the conclusion; and at the end, time is up and the day is at hand.

206 The additions (3:9–20) begin with a literal repetition (3:9a, *kî* = 3:8bB, *kî*), a deictic temporal reference (3:9a, *'āz*) that is soon taken up as an explicit reference to the day (3:11, *bayyôm hahû'*; cf. 3:8, *lĕyôm*), and a pun (3:9, *'ehpōk 'el 'ammîm*; cf. 3:8b, *le'ĕsōp gôyim . . . lišpōk 'ălêhem*).

207 The first stanzas are joined by direct and oblique references to the day of Yahweh (3:9a, 11a) and by their interest in the name of Yahweh (3:9b, 12b, *bĕšēm yhwh*). The second and third are linked by their reference to the remnant (3:12a, *wĕhiš'artî*, and 3:13a, *šĕ'ērît*). The first includes the exiles by referring, as Zephaniah did, to Cush (2:12; 3:10). The second and third are filled with references to strophes in which Zephaniah exhorted and condemned the city: 3:11 (*lō' tēbôšî*), cf. 3:5 (*bōšet*); 3:11 (*'ălîlōtayik*), cf. 3:7b (*'ălîlôtām*); 3:11b, 12a (*qirbēk*), cf. 3:3a, 5a (*qirbāh*); 3:11b (*'allîzê*), cf. 2:15a (*hā'allîzâ*); 3:11b (*bĕhar qodšî*), cf. 3:4b (*qōdeš*); 3:12a (*'am 'ānî*), cf. 2:3 (*kol 'anwê hā'āreṣ, 'ănāwâ*); 3:13 (*lō' ya'ăśû 'awlâ*), cf. 3:5b (*wĕlō' yôdēa' 'awwāl bōšet*). The strophe ends with a cross-reference to the editor's earlier description of the resettlement of the remnant (3:13b, *kî hēmmâ yir'û wĕrābĕṣû wĕ'ên maḥărîd* = 2:7, *yir'ûn . . . yirbāṣûn*).

208 The first stanza (3:14) is addressed to Zion, and the second (3:15) is attached to it by deictic pronominal suffixes referring to Zion. Now that the proudly exultant have been removed (3:11, *'āsîr . . . 'allîzê ga'ăwātēk*) and the meek have been restored (3:12), Zion is told to exult (3:14b, *wĕālĕzî*). Zephaniah mentioned the judgment of Yahweh (3:8b, *mišpāṭî*), but the editor says that the judgment has been overturned (3:15a, *hēsîr yhwh mišpāṭayik*). Zephaniah saw Yahweh in Jerusalem giving judgment (3:5, *bĕqirbāh*), but the editor sees Yahweh in Zion as the king of Israel (3:15b, *bĕqirbēk*). Jerusalem used to be afraid (3:1, *mor'â*) but will not have to fear (3:15b, *lō' tîrĕ'î rā' 'ôd*). The day of Yahweh was a day of battle cries (1:16, *tĕrû'â*), but now Israel is invited to cry out in joy (3:14a, *hārî'û yiśrā'ēl*). It was directed against lofty battlements (1:16, *happinnôt*), but now it is the enemy who are embattled (3:15a, *pinnâ 'ōyĕbēk*).

209 The beginning of the first stanza mentions the day (3:16a; cf. 3:9a, 11a) and, like the preceding strophe, calls on Zion not to be afraid (3:16, *'al tîrā'î / ṣiyyôn . . .* ; cf. 3:14, 15, *bat ṣiyyôn . . . lō' tîrĕ'î*). Zephaniah says that Yahweh pronounced judgment (3:5b) and would rise up as a witness against the city (3:8a), and the editor says that in his love for the city Yahweh will keep quiet (3:17b). Zephaniah says that the day of Yahweh would gather the nations and the whole world (*'sp*, 1:2–3; 3:8b), but the editor says that Yahweh has gathered those who grieved in Zion and has gathered her burden of shame (3:18a, *nûgê mimmô'ēd 'āsaptî / mimmēk hāyû / maś'ēt 'ālêhā ḥerpâ*).

210 The stanzas (3:19, 20) share the expressions *bā'ēt hahî', lithillâ ûlĕšēm*, and *qbṣ*. The first stanza refers to all those who troubled Zion rather than, as the previous strophe had done, just to those who were members of the community (3:18) and takes up the image of the remnant as a flock (3:19b; cf. 2:7). The second stanza also resembles the revision of the exhortation in referring to the return of the captives (*šāb šĕbût*, 2:7b; 3:20b).

211 Most of the differences are apparent in a comparison of the edited (1:7–13) and original (1:14–18) descriptions of the day of Yahweh. The styles and moods of each writer differ from part to part, and the best comparisons are between contiguous materials.

212 The expression "I will gather a harvest . . ." (1:2–3, *ʾāsōp ʾāsēp . . . ʾāsēp . . . ʾāsēp*) is modeled on Jeremiah's complaint that when Yahweh went to harvest his people (Jer 8:13, *ʾāsōp ʾăsîpēm*) he found that they had produced nothing for him. The same text of Jeremiah is a source for later statements in the exordium. In response to the disappointing harvest the people take refuge in their fortified cities, where they expect to die because they have sinned against Yahweh (Jer 8:14, *beʾāsĕpû wĕnābôʾ ʾel ʿārê hammibṣār . . . kî hātāʾnû layhwh*) just as Zephaniah sees the day of Yahweh descending on the fortified cities because the people have sinned against Yahweh (1:16b, 17a, *ʿal heʿārîm habbĕṣūrôt . . . kî layhwh hātāʾû*).

213 Cf. Zeph 1:3a (*ʾādām ûbĕhēmâ . . . ʿôp haššāmayim ûdĕgê hayyām*) and Gen 1:26 (*ʾādām . . . dĕgat hayyām . . . ʿôp haššāmayim . . . bĕhēmâ*).

214 Cf. Zeph 1:3b (*wĕhikrattî*); 3:7 (*wĕlōʾ yikkārēt mĕʿônāh*); and Gen 9:11 (*lōʾ yikkārēt*).

215 Cf. Zeph 1:2 (*kōl mēʿal pĕnê hāʾădāmâ*); 1:3b (*wĕhikrattî ʾet hāʾādām mēʿal pĕnê hāʾădāmâ*); Gen 6:7 (*ʾemḥeh ʾet hāʾādām . . . mēʿal pĕnê hāʾădāmâ*); and Gen 7:23 (*wayyimaḥ ʾet kol hayqûm ʾăšer ʿal pĕnê hāʾădāmâ*).

216 Cf. Zeph 1:3a (*ʾāsēp ʾādām . . . ʾāsēp ʿôp haššāmayim*) and Jer 4:25 (*rāʾîtî wĕhinnēh ʾên hāʾādām / wĕkol ʿôp haššāmayim nādādû*).

217 Cf. Zeph 1:14 (*yôm yhwh*) and Amos 5:18, 20 (*yôm yhwh*); Zeph 1:15 (*yôm hōšek waʾăpēlâ*) and Amos 5:20 (*hălōʾ hōšek yôm yhwh wĕlōʾ ʾôr wĕʾāpēl wĕlōʾ nōgah lô*); Zeph 1:15b, 16a (*yôm šōʾâ ûmĕšōʾâ . . . yôm šōpār ûtĕrûʿâ*) and Amos 2:2b (*ûmēt bĕšāʾôn môʾāb bitrûʿâ bĕqôl šōpār*); Zeph 1:14 (*gibbôr*) and Amos 2:16 (*gibbôr*).

218 Cf. Zeph 1:14 (*māhēr*) and Isa 5:26 (*wĕhinnēh mĕhērâ qal yābôʾ*).

219 Cf. Zeph 1:15 (*yôm ṣārâ*) and Nah 1:7 (*bĕyôm ṣārâ*); Zeph 1:15 (*yôm ʿānān*) and Nah 1:3 (*wĕʿānān ʾăbaq raglāyw*).

220 Cf. Zeph 1:14 (*ûmahēr . . . mar*) and Hab 1:6 (*haggôy hammar wĕhannimhār*); Zeph 1:15a (*yôm ʿebrâ*) and Hab 3:8 (*ʿebrātēk*).

221 Cf. Zeph 1:18b (*kî kālâ . . . yaʿăšeh*); Jer 4:27 (*wĕkālâ lōʾ ʾeʿĕšeh*; also Jer 5:10); and Nah 1:8 (*kālâ yaʿăšeh mĕqômāh*); cf. Zeph 1:18a (*bĕʾēš qinʾātô*) and Nah 1:2 (*ʾēl qannôʾ . . . yhwh*); cf. Zeph 1:17a, 18b (*wahăṣērōtî lāʾādām. . . . ʾēt kol yōšĕbê hāʾāreṣ*) and Jer 10:18 (*hinĕnî qôlēaʿ ʾet yôšĕbê hāʾāreṣ . . . wahaṣērôti lāhem*).

222 The expression "before destiny is in labor, before the day goes by like

chaff" (2:2a, *bĕṭerem lĕdet ḥōq / kĕmōṣ ʿābar yôm*) is in contrast especially with Ekron, which is called barren (2:4b). It follows from the general conception of the forces of life and death as female, whether personified and deified or not, while the forces of havoc and control are male.

223 The cities (2:4, Gaza, Ashkelon, Ashdod, and Ekron) are not in the same order as in the oracle (Amos 1:6–8, Gaza, Ashdod, Ashkelon, and Ekron), nor does Amos treat them as women, titular Goddesses, and mothers of their people.

224 It is especially Amos among the prophets who was concerned with the downtrodden (Zeph 2:3, *kol ʿanwê hāʾāreṣ*; cf. Amos 2:7, *wĕderek ʿānāwîm yaṭṭû*) and who protested against contempt for the law and justice (2:3, *mišpāṭô . . . ṣedeq*; cf. Amos 5:7, *mišpāṭ / ûṣĕdāqâ*; also Amos 6:12; cf. Isa 28:16; Hos 2:21). Both he and Hosea objected to those who either did not seek Yahweh (Hos 5:6, 15, *bqš*) or looked for him in liturgical observances (Amos 5:4–5, *ðrš*) instead of in justice and observance of the law. It was Jeremiah and Nahum who saw the anger of Yahweh like a pall over the city (Zeph 2:2, *ḥărôn ʾap yhwh*; cf. Jer 4:8, 26; Nah 1:6).

225 Cf. Zeph 2:3 (*mišpāṭô . . . / . . . ṣedeq . . . / ʾûlay tissātĕrû bĕyôm ʾap yhwh*) and Isa 28:15–17 (*nistarnû . . . mišpāṭ . . . ṣĕdāqâ*).

226 Yahweh stretches out his hand for destruction (Zeph 2:13, *wĕyēṭ yādô*) as in Jeremiah Yahweh stretched out his hand over the inhabitants of the land (Jer 6:12, *kî ʾatteh ʾet yādî ʿal yōšĕbê hāʾāreṣ*). Destruction takes place *in* the North (2:13, *ʿal ṣāpôn*), as Jeremiah described destruction coming *from* the North (Jer 4:6; 6:1, 22; 10:22). Jeremiah predicted that Jerusalem would be devastated (*šammâ / šĕmāmâ*, Jer 4:7; 6:8; 9:10; 10:22) without inhabitant or wayfarer (*yôšēb, ʿobēr*, Jer 4:7; 6:8; 9:9, 10), that is, like a desert where there is neither inhabitant nor wayfarer (Jer 2:6, *bammidbār . . . bĕʾereṣ ṣiyyâ . . . bĕʾereṣ lōʾ ʿābar bāh ʾîš wĕlōʾ yāšab ʾādām šām*). Zephaniah, similarly, describes Nineveh as a desolation, barren like a desert (Zeph 2:13b, *lišmāmâ / ṣiyyâ kammidbār*).

227 The image of flocks taking shelter in the ruins (2:14) was used in the description of the Philistine cities (2:6), but he adds "every animal of a nation" (2:14, *kol ḥaytô gôy*) in imitation of the Priestly account of the creation of animals (Gen 1:24, "and the animals of the world" [*wĕḥaytô ʾereṣ*]) prior to the creation of people. He adds the image of birds nesting on the pillars and chirping in the windows, on the bare sills stripped of their cedar (Zeph 2:14b, *qôl yĕšôrēr baḥallôn / ḥoreb bassap / kî ʾarzâ ʿērâ*).

228 Self-confidence (Zeph 2:15a, *hayyôšebet lābeṭaḥ*) was an annoying characteristic of Samaria (Amos 6:1, *habbōṭĕḥîm bĕhar šōmĕrôn*). A ruin that would make passersby gasp (Zeph 2:15b, *kōl ʿōbēr ʿālêhā yišrōq*) is what Micah predicted for Jerusalem (Mic 6:16, *lĕmaʿan tittî ʾōtĕkā lĕšammâ wĕyōšĕbêhā lišrēqâ*).

229 Isaiah condemned Jerusalem for not listening and not trusting in

Yahweh (Zeph 3:2, *lōʾ šāmĕʿâ . . . lōʾ bāṭāḥâ*; cf. Isa 28:12; 30:15). It was Jeremiah who criticized them for not listening (Jer 5:21) and not learning their lesson (Zeph 3:2, *lōʾ lāqĕḥâ mûsār*; cf. Jer 5:3, *mēʾănû qaḥat mûsār*).

230 Cf. Zeph 3:3 (*ʾărāyôt šōʾăgîm . . . zĕʾēbê ʿereb*) and Jer 5:6 (*ʾaryēh . . . zĕʾēb ʿărābôt*) and Hab 1:8 (*zĕʾēbê ʿereb*).

231 Cf. Zeph 3:4a (*nĕbîʾêhā . . . ʾanšê bōgĕdôt*) and Hos 5:7; Jer 3:20; 5:11.

232 Cf. Zeph 3:4b (*ḥāmĕsû tôrâ*) and Mic 6:12; Jer 8:8; Hab 1:2.

233 Cf. Zeph 3:5b (*babbōqer babbōqer mišpāṭô yittēn / lāʾôr lōʾ neʿdār*) and Hos 6:3, 5 (*kĕšaḥar nākôn môṣāʾô . . . ûmišpāṭĕkā ʾôr yēṣēʾ*).

234 On the Deuteronomistic affinities of the second edition, see J. Scharbert, "Zefanja und die Reform des Joschija," in *Künder des Wortes: Beiträge zur Theologie der Propheten: Josef Schreiner zum 60. Geburtstag*, ed. L. Ruppert, P. Weimar, and E. Zenger (Würzburg: Echter Verlag, 1982) 237–53; Seybold, *Satirische Prophetie*, 83–93.

235 The worship of the hosts of heaven, in the Deuteronomistic scheme of historical emergence, was cited by Moses at Horeb as a sufficient reason for the exile (Deut 4:19; cf. 17:3) and then surfaced in the reign of Manasseh as one of its actual causes (2 Kgs 21:3). The fact that Josiah tried to suppress it (2 Kgs 23:4) and the witness of later writers that the worship of the hosts of heaven continued to the end, explain, as many have noted, the editor's expression "the remnant of Baal" (1:4).

236 The condemnation of those who worship the hosts of heaven on the rooftops (1:5a) is matched by a repudiation of those who take an oath in the name of Yahweh and take an oath in the name of their king (1:5b). In this specific context, with its allusions to the Deuteronomistic evaluations of Manasseh and Josiah and to the latter's deposing of idolatrous priests whom the kings of Judah had ordained for service at the royal shrines (Zeph 1:4bB, *ʾet šēm hakkĕmārîm ʿim hakkōhănîm*; cf. 2 Kgs 23:5, 8, *ʾet hakkĕmārîm . . . babbāmôt . . . ʾet hakkōhănîm*), it seems that taking an oath by their kings (1:5bB) had to do with services for the dead kings at their royal mortuary shrines. Some such services are described in the book of Jeremiah (e.g., Jer 22:18–19).

237 The image of Yahweh stretching out his hand to do harm (Zeph 1:4, *wĕnaṭîtî yādî ʿal yĕhûdâ / wĕʿal kol yôšĕbê yĕrûšālayim*) has a parallel in Jeremiah (Jer 6:12b, *kî ʾaṭṭeh ʾet yādî ʿal yōšĕbê hāʾāreṣ*) and anticipates a statement in Zephaniah's speech (cf. Zeph 2:13a *wĕyēṭ yādô ʿal ṣāpôn*). Similarly, the fact that they did not seek or search out Yahweh (Zeph 1:6b, *waʾăšer lōʾ biqšû ʾet yhwh wĕlōʾ dĕrāšūhû*) anticipates Zephaniah's urgent plea (Zeph 2:3, *baqqĕšû* [three times]) and, with the expression "this place" (Zeph 1:4b, *hammāqôm hazzeh*), reveals the editor's interest in right worship at the place of Yahweh's choice (cf. Deut 12:4; etc.). The expression "turn back [away from Yahweh]"

(Zeph 1:6a, *wĕʾet hannĕsôgîm mēʾaḥărê yhwh*) had a literal (2 Sam 1:22; Jer 38:22; 46:5) and a metaphorical meaning (Isa 59:13, 14; Ps 35:4; 40:15 = 70:3; 129:5) at the time that the editor was writing.

238 Cf. Zeph 1:7bB (*kî hēkîn yhwh zebaḥ / hiqdîš qĕrûʾāyw*); 1 Sam 9:12, 22 (*zebaḥ . . . qĕrûʾîm*); and 1 Kgs 1:9–10, 49 (*wayyizbaḥ ʾădōniyyāhû . . . wayyiqrāʾ . . . haqqĕrûʾîm*).

239 Cf. Zeph 1:9a (*ûpāqadtî ʿal kol haddôlēg ʿal hammiptān*) and 1 Sam 5:5 (*ʿal miptan dāgôn bĕʾašdôd*); cf. also Zeph 1:9b (*hamĕmalʾîm bêt ʾădōnêhem ḥāmās ûmirmâ*) and Mic 6:10, 12 (*bêt rāšāʿ ʾōšĕrôt rešaʿ . . . ʾăšer ʿăšîrêhā mālĕʾû ḥāmās . . . ûlĕšônām rĕmiyyâ bĕpîhem*).

240 Cf. Zeph 1:10–11 (*ṣĕʿāqâ miššaʿar . . . wîlālâ . . . wĕšeber gādôl . . . kî nidmâ*); Mic 1:8–9 (*ʾêlîlâ . . . kî bāʾâ . . . ʿad šaʿar*) and Jer 4:6, 8 (*šeber gādôl . . . hêlîlû*).

241 Cf. Zeph 1:13b (*ûbānû battîm wĕlōʾ yēšēbû / wĕnāṭĕʿû kĕrāmîm wĕlōʾ yištû ʾet yênām*) and Amos 5:11 (*battê gāzît bĕnitem wĕlōʾ tēšbû bām / karmê ḥemed nĕṭaʿtem wĕlōʾ tištû ʾet yênām*). The image became indigenous to treaty curses (cf. Deut 28:30, 39).

242 The expression *ʾiyyê haggôyim* is borrowed from the Priestly table of nations (Gen 10:5) but supposes Zephaniah's interest in the Aegean origin of the Philistines (2:5). The perception of the islands cowering in fear before Yahweh, as distinguished from II Isaiah's sense that they would welcome the majesty of Yahweh, is consistent with the view of III Isaiah (cf. Isa 24:15; 40:15; 59:18; 60:9; 66:19).

243 The reference to the people worshiping Yahweh with pure lips (Zeph 3:9a, *ʿammîm šāpâ bĕrûrâ*) is the antithesis of II Isaiah's objection that he lived among a people with unclean lips (Isa 6:5, *ûbĕtôk ʿam ṭĕmēʾ śĕpātāyim ʾānōkî yôšēb*). The image of them serving Yahweh "on one shoulder" (Zeph 3:9b, *šekem ʾeḥād*) is taken from the blessing of Jacob on Ephraim in exile in Egypt, where Jacob assigns to him "one shoulder" over his brothers (Gen 48:22, *šekem ʾeḥād*). The saying that the diaspora will bring gifts to Yahweh from beyond the rivers of Cush refers to the Mesopotamian Cush that Zephaniah mentioned (2:12) but in the words of II Isaiah's oracle on this land of Cush (cf. Zeph 3:10 [*mēʿēber lĕnahărê kûš . . . yôbîlûn minḥātî*] and Isa 18:1, 7 [*mēʿēber lĕnahărê kûš. . . . yûbal šay layhwh ṣĕbāʾôt*]). The removal from the midst of the city of those who exult in their pride (Zeph 3:11b, *ʿallîzê gaʾăwātēk*) refers to a text of III Isaiah on the day of Yahweh according to which Yahweh assembled troops who exulted in their pride (Isa 13:3, *ʿallîzê gaʾăwātî*). The fact that the remnant of Israel will not speak lies (Zeph 3:13, *wĕlōʾ yĕdabbĕrû kāzāb*) is the opposite of what Hosea found when Yahweh tried to save Israel (Hos 7:13, *wĕhēmmâ dibbĕrû ʿālay kĕzābîm*).

244 Cf. Zeph 3:15b (*melek yiśrāʾēl yhwh bĕqirbēk*) and Jer 8:19 (*hayhwh ʾên bĕṣiyyôn / ʾim malkāh ʾên bāh*).

245 The difficult expression concerning the source of Zion's troubles and shame (3:18, *mimmēk hāyû*) seems to reflect and adapt the statement by Nahum's editor that the reprobate who plotted evil against Yahweh came out of Nineveh (Nah 1:11, *mimmēk yāṣā'*).

246 Cf. Zeph 3:19b (*wĕhôša 'tî 'et haṣṣōlē'â / wĕhanniđđāḥâ 'ăqabbēṣ*) and Mic 4:6 (*'ōsĕpâ haṣṣōlē'â / wĕhanniđđāḥâ 'ăqabbēṣâ*).

247 The introductory (1:1) and concluding visions (40:1–3) are dated in the thirtieth and twenty-fifth years respectively of Ezekiel's exile in Babylon, which, in the second edition, coincided with the exile of Jehoiachin. The intervening material is dated just before and after the fall of Jerusalem. The capture and sack of the city are not noted, and instead Ezekiel recites poetic oracles describing a comparable siege and capture of Tyre in the eleventh year (26:1) and oracles concerning the complicity of Egypt and its eventual descent into the underworld in the tenth, eleventh, and twelfth years of his exile (29:1; 31:1; 31:1; 32:17). The annotations in the Jerusalem version of the chronicle antedate Ezekiel's calling to the fifth year of the exile of Jehoiachin (1:2–3), put the fall of the city in the twelfth year of the exile, give it critical importance in Ezekiel's prophetic career (33:21), and transfer Egypt's connivance and punishment out of the realm of analogy and myth into the order of datable historical events (29:17; 30:20; 32:1).

248 All of the critical issues are dealt with by W. Zimmerli, *Ezechiel* (BKAT 13/1–2; Neukirchen-Vluyn: Neukirchener Verlag, 1969); Eng. trans. *Ezekiel* I, trans. R. E. Clements (Philadelphia: Fortress, 1979); *Ezekiel* II, trans. J. D. Martin (Philadelphia: Fortress, 1983). Traditional, philological, and literary matters are discussed by M. Greenberg, *Ezekiel 1–20* (AB 22; Garden City, N.Y.: Doubleday, 1983).

249 On figure 16 the additions in the editorial, or Jerusalem, version are included in square brackets. Asterisks mark verses whose parts, not indicated by the major Massoretic accents, are shared by both versions.

250 Ezekiel's work is like the book of Jeremiah but lacks its archival elements, notably its systematic indexing of materials with reference to introductory tables of contents that summarize its biographical and historical argument, its system of constant cross-referencing by cumulative formulaic expressions, and its system of conspicuous labeling used to sort and file disparate nonnarrative information.

251 The columns, in Ezekiel's text, are (1) 1:1, 4–6, 10, 11aBb, 22–23, 25a, 26–28a; (2) 1:28b; 2:1–3, 6, 8–10; (3) 3:1–12a, 14b–15aA, 22–24. The rest is editorial and was written into the text by the usual devices of repetition and cross-reference. In this book, since it sets the tone and agenda for all that follows, the editorial additions are crucial and obvious.

252 There are chronological and biographical items (1:2–3), ritual and architectural elements (1:7–9, 11aA, 12–21, 24, 25b; 3:12b–13), and theolog-

ical categories relative to the admonitory role of a prophet (2:4–5; 3:16–21, 26–27).

253 The link is literal and artificial (3:25, *hinnēh nātěnû ʿālêkā ʿăbôtîm* = 4:8, *wěhinnēh natattî ʿālêkā ʿăbôtîm*) but underlines pseudo-biographical material on the intercessory role of prophets, in particular of prophets with Priestly obligations such as Ezekiel has in the edited Jerusalem version.

254 Ezek 1:26bB (*děmût kěmarʾeh ʾāḏām*).

255 As Yahweh appears in the likeness of a human person, or Adam, (*ʾāḏām*), so the prophet is addressed here (2:1) and henceforward as a human person, or descendant of Adam (*ben ʾāḏām*).

256 Cf. 28:2, *ʾāḏām wělōʾ ʾēl*; 29:8, *ʾāḏām ûběhēmâ*; 31:1–4, 6–13, 15–18; 36:10–14.

257 Ezek 1:3; 4:12–15; 40:38–47; 42:1–20; 43:13–17; 44:1–31.

258 Cf. *ʾôt* (4:3bB); *môpēt* (12:6; 24:24, 27).

259 Ezek 3:25–27; 14:12–23; 24:25–27; 33:21–22.

260 Ezek 3:16–21; 5:3–4, 7–10; 6:8–10; 9:8; 11:13; 14:12–23; 17:19–24; 24:25–27.

261 Ezek 7:10–13, 16, 20–27; 13:17–23; 16:44–63; 18:19–32; 20:32–44; 21:1–5, 9–10, 15, 17–18; 22:6–13; 23:30–49; 33:1–20; 34:17–31.

262 Cf. *tôʿēbôt*, 5:11; 6:11; 7:3–4, 8–9.

263 Ezek 5:11, 13, 15; 6:12; 7:4, 8, 9.

264 Ezek 6:1–6, 12–13; 7:7.

265 Ezek 4:1–3, 9a, 10–11, 16–17; 5:2, 12, 17; 6:3, 11–12.

266 Ezek 5:3–4, 7–10; 6:8–10; 7:14–19.

267 Cf. Ezek 4:8 and 3:25; 4:4–7, 9b and 2:4–5 and 3:16–21; 4:12–15 and 1:3.

268 Cf. Ezek 7:19b, 20–27 and 8:1–18.

269 Compare Ezek 1:1, 4–6, 10, 11aB, 22–23, 25a, 26–28a and 3:22–24 with Ezek 8:1–4 and 11:23–25.

270 Cf. Ezek 3:24bB (*bōʾ hissāgēr bětôk bêtekā*) and 8:1 (*ʾănî yôšēb běbêtî*).

[271] Cf. *tôʿēbôt*, 8:6, 9, 13, 15, 17; 9:4.

[272] Cf. 8:18; 9:5, 7, 10; 11:6, 7a.

[273] See S. Talmon and M. Fishbane, "The Structuring of Biblical Books: Studies in the Book of Ezekiel," *ASTI* 10 (1975–76) 129–53.

[274] Figuratively, 12:1–5, 7a, 8–10a, 11b. Explicitly, 12:21–28.

[275] Elements of Israel are mentioned in Ezek 6:2 and in 12:23; 13:2, 4, 16; 14:1. The land of Israel is mentioned in Ezek 7:2 and in 12:22; 13:9. The house of Israel is mentioned in Ezek 3:1, 4, 7; 6:11 and in 12:24, 27; 13:5, 9; 14:4–7, 11.

[276] Cf. *bêt hammerî*, Ezek 2:6, 8; 3:9; 12:2–3, 25.

[277] Cf. Ezek 4:1–3; 5:1–2; and 12:1–5.

[278] Cf. *gillûlîm*, Ezek 6:4–6, 13; 14:3–7.

[279] Cf. Ezek 7:1–9; 12:21–28; 13:5.

[280] Cf. Ezek 12:16; 13:17–23; 14:10, 12–23.

[281] Cf. Ezek 12:6, 7b, 10b–11a, 12–16; 15:1–8.

[282] Cf. Ezek 12:17–20; 14:12–23; and 4:1–5:17.

[283] Cf. *ḥāmās*, Ezek 7:11, 23; 8:17; 12:19.

[284] Cf. *zĕmôrâ*, 8:17; 15:2.

[285] Ezek 16:6; 17:16; 18:4, 9, 13, 17.

[286] Cf. 16:8; 17:13, 16, 18.

[287] Egypt (Ezek 16:26; 17:15); Assyria and Babylon (Ezek 16:28, 29; 17:12, 16); Canaan and the Philistines (Ezek 16:3, 27, 29; 17:4).

[288] Cf. Ezek 17:17 (*nĕpāšôt rabbôt*) and 18:4 (*bēn kol hannĕpāšôt lî hēnnâ*).

[289] Cf. *tôʿēbôt*, Ezek 16:22, 36 and 8:6, 9, 13, 15, 17; 9:4.

[290] Cf. *tôʿēbôt*, Ezek 16:43b, 47, 51, 52, 58.

[291] Cf. *qînâ*, Ezek 2:10; 19:1, 14.

[292] Egypt is mentioned throughout chap. 20 and in 23:3, 8, 27.

²⁹³ The critical statement (21:8, "I will cut off from you the innocent and the guilty" [*wĕhikrattî mimmēk ṣaddîq wĕrāšā'*]) supposes the earlier argument about guilt and innocence (18:1–18) and the intervening proof of inveterate evil (20:1–28, 30–31) and will be verified in the individual sinful histories of Samaria and Jerusalem (23:1–29).

²⁹⁴ There are references, for instance, to the worship of idols, which was condemned in the preceding book (cf. 18:6, 15 and 20:39), and to the princes of Israel, who were lamented there (cf. 19:1 and 22:6). The additions also tend to diminish the harshness of Ezekiel's statements by distributing guilt and punishment among the nations, who are the topic of the next book (cf. 20:32–38; 21:23–37; 22:16; 23:30–35).

²⁹⁵ Ezek 24:1–14; 26:1–21; 27:1–36; 28:1–19.

²⁹⁶ There are dates in the first and second columns of the original (24:1; 26:1), images of gravel and rock in the first and second (24:7–8; 26:4), images of death by fire and water in the first and fourth (24:3–14; 28:1–19), and similar laments in the second and third (26:15–18; 27:28–36).

²⁹⁷ Cf. Ezek 25:1–17 concerning Judah, and Ezek 28:20–26 concerning Israel.

²⁹⁸ See Ezek 29:1; 31:1; 32:17; compare 24:1; 26:1.

²⁹⁹ Ezek 32:29–30; cf. 25:1–17; 28:20–26.

³⁰⁰ Ezek 34:1–14; 36:1–15; 37:1–14.

³⁰¹ Ezek 40:1–37; 43:1–5; 47:1–12.

³⁰² Cf. Ezek 1:28b (*qôl, 'er'eh*) and 1:25, 27.

³⁰³ The addition (3:25–27) begins like the section that it displaced (3:25, *wĕ'attâ ben 'āðām* = 4:1).

³⁰⁴ Cf. Ezek 4:1a; 5:1a (*wĕ'attâ ben 'āðām qah lĕkā*); Ezek 4:2; 5:2, (*māṣôr*).

³⁰⁵ Cf. Ezek 4:16 and 5:16 (*šbr mth lhm*).

³⁰⁶ Cf. 4:16; 5:1, *mišqāl*.

³⁰⁷ The first column is also self-enclosed by its mention of Jerusalem at the beginning and the end (4:1, 16).

³⁰⁸ Cf. 6:11–12 (*bahereb bārā'āb ûbaddeber*) and 5:12 (*baddeber . . . bārā'āb . . . bahereb*); cf. 5:16–17.

³⁰⁹ Cf. 6:1 and 7:1 (*wayhî ðĕbar yhwh 'ēlay lē'mor ben 'āðām*).

310 Cf. 7:10–12 (*bāʾâ, haṣṣĕpîrâ, mēhem / mēhămônām / mēhĕmēhem, bāʾ hāʿēt*) and the original in 7:5–7 (*bāʾâ, haṣṣĕpîrâ, bāʾ hāʿēt, mĕhûmâ*). The second- and third-to-last paragraphs in the addition mention the defiling of the temple by obscene images (7:20–22, 23–24) and anticipate the first column of the next book (8:1–18).

311 Ezek 8:18, *qrʾ bʾzn ql gdl* = 9:1.

312 Ezek 9:11, *hāʾîš lĕbūš habbaddîm* = 10:2.

313 Cf. 8:3b (*wattiśśāʾ ʾōtî rûaḥ . . . wattābēʾ ʾōtî . . . ʾel petaḥ šaʿar happĕnîmît*) and 11:1 (*wattiśśāʾ ʾōtî rûaḥ wattābēʾ ʾōtî ʾel šaʿar . . . haqqadmônî*).

314 Cf. 12:1; 13:1; 14:2; 15:1 (*wayhî dĕbar yhwh ʾēlay lēʾmor ben ʾādām*).

315 Ezek 12:2 = 12:25, *bêt hammerî*.

316 Ezek 14:3, 7 (*drš*).

317 Ezek 16:1 = 17:1 = 17:11.

318 The two new paragraphs (17:19–21, 22–24) are added by repeating the beginning of the last original paragraph (17:19a = 17:16a).

319 Ezek 18:1 = 17:1; cf. 18:2 and 18:18.

320 Ezek 19:1a = 19:14b. Like the first column in the book, it begins with a reference to the city's mother (19:2a, *ʾimmĕkā*; 16:3b, *ʾimmēk*).

321 Ezek 20:2 = 21:1 = 22:1 = 23:1.

322 Ezek 20:3b, *ḥay ʾānî ʾim ʾiddārēš lākem nĕʾum ʾădōnāy yhwh* = 20:31b.

323 The new text (20:29, 32–44) repeats two segments of the original: 20:34a, cf. 20:23b; 20:39a, cf. 20:31a.

324 Ezek 21:23 = 21:1; 21:24, cf. 21:19–22.

325 Ezek 22:1–2 = 20:4. The formula is in 22:1, 17, 23.

326 Ezek 23:30 (*ʿšh*) = 23:29 (*ʿšh*).

327 Ezek 24:1 = 25:1 = 26:1 = 27:1 = 28:1.

328 Cf. 24:21 (*hinĕnî mĕḥallēl ʾet miqdāšî*) and 25:3b (*yaʿan ʾomrēk heʾāḥ ʾel miqdāšî kî niḥāl*).

329 Cf. 26:15–21 and 27:28–36; cf. 27:36 (*wĕʾênēk ʿad ʿôlām*) and 28:19 (*wĕʾênĕkā ʿad ʿôlām*).

330 Cf. 29:1; 30:1; 31:1; 32:1; 33:1.

331 Cf. 29:17; 30:20; 32:17; 33:21; cf. 31:15.

332 The columns are 30:1–26; 33:1–33. The additions are 29:9b–21; 32:1–16, 29–32.

333 Cf. 29:9b (*yẹʾōr lî waʾănî ʿăśîtî*) and 29:3b (*lî yẹʾōrî waʾănî ʿăśîtînî*).

334 Ezek 32:29 = 32:26 + 28.

335 Cf. 34:2; 35:2; 36:1; 37:4; 38:3; 39:1.

336 Cf. 34:1; 35:1; 36:1; 37:3; 38:1; 39:1.

337 Cf. 34:15 (*ʾănî ʾerʿeh ṣōʾnî*) and 34:11 + 14 (*ṣōʾnî + ʾerʿeh*).

338 Cf. 36:16 and 34:1; also 36:38 and 34:14.

339 Ezek 40:1–3; 43:1–5; 47:1–2.

340 Ezek 1:2–3, 7–9, 11aA, 12, 24, 25b.

341 The changes are made by deixis, which tends to be obvious or even rude and ridiculous, and by repetition, which tends to blend in with the original (see D. I. Block, "Text and Emotion: A Study in the 'Corruptions' in Ezekiel's Inaugural Vision [Ezekiel 1:4–28]," *CBQ* 50 (1988) 418–42). The editing is more startling in the first book, where the point of the revision is made; but the ruined vision is explained in the third book, and its new interpretation becomes clear as the argument develops.

342 The paragraph (1:1) ends with a paratactic imperfect (*wāʾerʾeh*) distinct from the consecutive form of the same verb that begins the second paragraph (1:4 *wāʾēreʾ*).

343 In Ezekiel's version he sees visions (1:1), but in the revised version he receives the word of Yahweh (1:3a). The same correction is made in the next paragraph, where Ezekiel says what he saw (1:4), and the revised version says that the hand of God was on him (1:3b).

344 The day is repeated from the original (1:2a, *baḥămiśśâ laḥōdeś* = 1:1a), but the year is changed by a combination of deixis (demonstrative pronoun and definite article) and by repetition (1:2b, *hîʾ haśśānâ haḥămîśît*; cf. 1:1a). The new paragraph also refers, like the original, to exile by the river Chebar (1:2b, 3a; cf. 1:1a). The elements that are not repeated from the original have to do with institutions and functions and foreign nations—kings, prophets, priests, Chaldeans—all of which are especially important to the editor of the Jerusalem version.

345 Ezek 1:4–6, 10, 11°, 22–23.

346 The original ascribed human features to the animals (1:5). The addition
(1:7–8) begins by describing more human features and has deictic pronouns
that refer back to the creatures as Ezekiel described them (*"Their* legs were a
straight leg, and *their* feet . . ."). The addition ends repeating the end of the
text to which it was attached: 1:8b, *ûpĕnêhem wĕkanpêhem lĕ'arba'tām*; cf. 1:6,
wĕ'arbā'â pānîm lĕ'eḥāt wĕ'arba' kĕnāpayim lĕ'aḥat lāhem).

347 This paragraph (1:9) is distinguished from the preceding nominal
sequence by its verbal clauses. It repeats the last phrase of the addition (1:8b
= 1:9a) both literally (*kanpêhem* = 1:8b) and obliquely (*'el 'ēber pānāyw*; cf.
1:8b *pĕnêhem*). The oblique usage also anticipates the next feature in the
original text (1:9b, *pānāyw*; cf. 1:10, *ûdĕmût pĕnêhem*).

348 Ezekiel described the animals' faces (1:10, *ûdĕmût pĕnêhem*) and wings
(1:11aBb, *wĕkanpêhem*). The editor added one word "their faces" (1:11aA,
ûpĕnêhem) before the description of the wings. The text as edited (1:11a,
ûpĕnêhem wĕkanpêhem, "their faces and their wings") repeats an earlier addition
(1:8b) and absorbs Ezekiel's description into the perspective of the revision.
The word is added by the deictic pronominal suffix and by repeating the key
word of the original (1:10, *ûpĕnê*). It is an anacolouthon (as the Massoretic
accent might indicate, see Greenberg, *Ezekiel 1–20*, 45) that leads into the next
addition (1:11aA, 12, "And their faces . . . each went in the direction of his
face . . .") and frames Ezekiel's description of their wings (1:11aBb), which
had been reinterpreted in the preceding addition to exclude movement (1:9).
In order to reaffirm that the creatures were motionless but still traveled from
place to place in any direction, the latter addition (1:12) repeats what was
said earlier (1:9b) and adds that they moved under the impulse of the spirit
(1:12bA). This text is inserted by repetition of the original (1:12a, *wĕ'iš*; cf.
1:11b, *lĕ'iš*). In Ezekiel's vision the animals, controverting the Priestly account
of creation (Genesis 1), are intermediate between God, whose glory appears
in the likeness of Adam, and Ezekiel, who is presented as a son of Adam. In
the Jerusalem version, which was revolted by the implications of such a vision,
they are not animals but immobile representations of outlandish creatures
fixed to a movable throne.

349 See figure 16. In the third paragraph in the original version (1:25a,
26–28a) Ezekiel heard a voice from above the firmament (1:25a); in the next
paragraph he heard it speaking to him (1:28b). In the revised version this
voice becomes the sound of the creatures' wings (1:24a; cf. 43:2bA): the
insertion is made by repeating the preceding and following original contexts
(1:24a, *wā'ešma' 'et qôl kanpêhem kĕqôl . . . kĕqôl . . . qôl . . . kĕqôl*; cf. 1:23,
kanpêhem; 1:25a, *qôl*; 1:28b, *wā'ešma' qôl mĕdabbēr*. The change is marked and
insisted on by repeating that their wings drooped when they were still (1:24b
= 1:25b, *bĕ'omdām tĕrappênâ kanpêhen*). The additions are made by deictics
(the pronominal suffixes) and by repetition and are typical of the editor's
efforts to be obvious in changing the text when it mattered most.

350 Ezekiel referred to the people of Israel and their fathers (2:3), and the
editor referred to them and their children (2:4–5). These children, literal or
metaphorical, are of concern to the editor (cf. 5:10; 14:16, 18, 22) and

ultimately are identified as the people left behind in Jerusalem by the first exiles (24:21, 25), that is, people doomed to die in the destruction of the city or, in the case of a few, allowed to escape into exile.

351 The addition (2:4–5) is made by deictics and by literal repetition. The reference to the children is emphatic (2:4aA *wĕhabbānîm*) and is taken up in a resumptive pronominal suffix (2:4aB, *ʾălêhem*). Ezekiel's mission to the children still left in Jerusalem at this time (1:2–3a: in the fifth year of the exile of Jehoiachin) is confirmed by repeating his original commission to Israel (2:4aB, *ʾănî šôlēaḥ ʾôtĕkā ʾălêhem* = 2:3a, *šôlēaḥ ʾănî ʾôtĕkā ʾel bĕnê yiśrāʾēl*). The addition ends with the editor's note that Ezekiel was a prophet (2:5b), but the rest is taken from his original missions to Israel (2:5aB, *kî bêt mĕrî hēmmâ* = 2:6bB) and to the exiles (2:4b–5aA = 3:11).

352 An addition (2:7) in the third paragraph (2:6) repeats the point of the insertion (cf. 2:4b) but in the words of Ezekiel to the exiles (3:11). It is added by literal repetition of a deictic expression (2:7b, *kî mĕrî hēmmâ* = 2:6bB, *kî bêt mĕrî hēmmâ*).

353 The appendage (3:25–27) is affixed by a deictic formula (3:25, *wĕʾattâ ben ʾādām*) that anticipates the original sequel in Ezekiel's version (4:1, *wĕʾattâ ben ʾādām*).

354 The editorial insertion (3:12b–14a) begins with a deictic (i.e., an expletive with a proper name) that completely spoils the original sequence (3:12b, "Blessed be the glory of Yahweh from its place" [*bārûk kĕbôd yhwh mimmĕqômô*]). This refers to Ezekiel's vision of the glory of God in the first column and to his vision in the third book of the glory of God leaving the city and tries to situate the vision in the temple in Jerusalem (*mimmĕqômô*) and to associate the sound that Ezekiel heard with the clatter of the wheeled contraption (3:13, *qôl* [3 times]; cf. 1:24, *qôl* [5 times]). The insertion is made by repeating at the end, in opposite order, the text to which it was affixed (3:13b–14a, *wĕqôl raʿaš gādôl wĕrûaḥ nĕśāʾatnî wattiqqāḥēnî* = 3:12a, *wattiśśāʾēnî rûaḥ wāʾešmaʿ ʾaḥăray qôl raʿaš gādôl*).

355 The addition (3:15aBb, *hēmmâ yôšĕbîm šām wāʾēšēb šām šibʿat yāmîm mašmîm bĕtôkām*) is intruded by a deictic pronoun, a deictic adverb repeated twice (*šām*), and by a literal reduplication of the original (3:14b–15aA, *hayyōšĕbîm ʾel nĕhar kĕbār wāʾēšēb*).

356 Cf. 3:16a (*wayhî miqṣēh šibʿat yāmîm*) and 3:15b (*šibʿat yāmîm*).

357 Ezek 4:3bB–5a, 5b–6, 7–8, 13–15; 5:3–4, 7–10; 6:8–10, 14.

358 Ezek 4:4–5a, 5b–6; see Greenberg, *Ezekiel 1–20*, 98–128, esp. 104, 125.

359 The insertion is facilitated by an addition to the end of Ezekiel's second paragraph (4:3bB, *ʾôt hîʾ lĕbêt yiśrāʾēl*) that has the usual deictic accoutrements

and makes a transition between the symbol that Ezekiel developed and the interpretation that the editor gave it. The interpretation itself (4:4–6) also begins with a common deictic formula (4:4, *wĕ'attâ*).

360 The paragraph (4:7–8) has the same pattern of modal and indicative verbs that was used in the preceding editorial paragraphs (4:4–5a, 5b–6). It begins and ends with a reference to the siege as Ezekiel described it (4:7 [*mĕṣôr yĕrûšālāyim*], cf. 4:1b–2a [*yĕrûšālāyim . . . māṣôr*]; 4:8 [*yĕmê mĕṣûrekā*], cf. 4:3b [*wĕhāyĕtâ bammāṣôr wĕṣartā 'ālêhā*]). In between it refers to the fact that Ezekiel is a prophet (4:7a) and alludes to the fact that he is being prevented from fulfilling his prophetic office (4:8a; cf. 3:25).

361 The rite of atonement was clearly marked as an editorial addition (4:4–6), and the change in the description of the famine is just as clearly marked by cross-reference to it (4:9b, *mispar hayyāmîm . . .* , = 4:4b, 5a). It fits into its context by ending with the verb that began the original that it displaced (4:9b, *tōʾkălennû*; cf. 4:10a, *ûmaʾăkālĕkā 'ăšer tōʾkălennû*). The idea that Ezekiel might have to eat unclean food (4:12) is inserted through deictics (4:12a, *tōʾkălennâ*; 4:12b, *wĕhîʾ . . . tĕʿûgenâ*). These deictics refer to the food that Ezekiel mentioned (4:10–11, masculine) but turn it into baked goods (4:12, feminine), and the change in gender may also be an editorial marker. In the first column Ezekiel used both genders to refer to the animals (feminine) that had human features (masculine), and the editor copied but also reversed the genders (cf. 1:5 and 1:13; 1:11 and 1:9; also 1:23 and 1:24; see Block, "Text and Emotion," 420 nn. 8–10).

362 Ezekiel talked about the famine in Jerusalem (4:16–17), but the revision dealt with the diet of the exiles (4:13–15). Both segments begin the same way (*wayyōʾmer* + concern for food), but the editor is as interested in pseudo-biographical elements as in the historical status of the exiles.

363 The new paragraph (5:3–4) uses "burn" and "fire" (*śrp* and *'ēš*) for Ezekiel's "consume" and "blaze" (*bʿr* and *'ûr*, 5:1–2).

364 The new paragraph (5:7–10) begins by repeating the end of the original paragraph (cf. 5:7 and 5:6). It anticipates and replaces the homogeneous punishment that Ezekiel described (5:11–12) with an odd and unheard-of punishment—the opposite of a Deuteronomistic covenant curse (cf. 5:8–10a and Deut 28:53; see Greenberg, *Ezekiel 1–20*, 113–14)—that marks the paragraph as an editorial addition and emphasizes the editor's point that some will be saved (5:10b).

365 Ezek 6:1–5, 6–7, 11, 12–13.

366 The paragraph (6:8–10) comments on the preceding paragraphs in the original (6:1–5, 6–7) and is attached to the second of these by an initial deictic clause and by a final repetition. The deictic clause is odd and disruptive (6:8–9, *wĕhôtartî bihyôt lākem pĕlîṭê ḥereb baggôyîm . . . wĕzākĕrû pĕlîṭêkem . . .* , "And I will leave—when you are [*bihyôt lākem*]—survivors of the sword among the

nations . . . and your survivors will remember . . .") because it resumes and mimics the original (cf. 6:13aB, . . . *biḥyôt ḥalĕlêhem bĕtôk gillûlêhem* . . . , "And you will know, when their dead are [*biḥyôt*] among their idols . . ."; see Greenberg, *Ezekiel 1–20*, 133–34). The final repetition is unexceptional (6:10, *wĕyādĕʿû kî ʾānî yhwh* . . . ; cf. 6:7b, *wîdaʿtem kî ʾānî yhwh*).

367 The paragraph was added via deictics (6:14aA, *wĕnāṭîtî ʾet yādî ʿālêhem*, "I will raise *my* hand against *them*") and pseudo-repetition (cf. 6:13b, *nātēnû šām*, and 6:14aB, *wĕnātattî* . . . *šĕmāmâ ûmĕšammâ*; see Greenberg, *Ezekiel 1–20*, 137). The expression "from the wilderness to Diblah" (6:14aB, *mimmidbar diblātâ*) seems to allude to the flight of Zedekiah to the plains of Jericho, where he was captured and brought to Riblah (2 Kgs 25:4–6; Jer 39:4–5; 52:7–9). In the first column of the fourth book the editor refers to the present text and to records of the event to recall that Zedekiah was blinded and taken to Babylon (12:7b, 10*, 11a, 12, 13–16, 17–20).

368 The paragraphs are arranged in an explanatory pattern in which the first (A = 7:1–4) makes a point, the second explains it (B = 7:5–7), and the third draws the conclusion (A' = 7:8–9). A and B are related by reference to the end (*qēṣ*, 7:2, 6), and A and A' are related by literal repetition (7:4 = 7:9).

369 The paragraphs are arranged in a descriptive pattern in which a situation is described, evaluated, redescribed, and reevaluated, etc.: A (= 7:12–13)–B (= 7:14–16)–A (= 7:17–19)–B (= 7:20–22)–A (= 7:23–24)–B (= 7:25–27).

370 The new paragraph (7:10–11) begins with literal quotations from the second (7:10, *hinnēh hayyôm hinnēh bāʾâ* . . . *haṣṣĕpîrâ* = 7:6b–7a). The first four paragraphs, therefore, now correspond in the descriptive pattern (A-B-A-B) that continues through the rest of the additional paragraphs. The notion of guilt (7:11, *rešaʿ*) is taken up literally (7:21a, *ršʿ*), in the question of responsibility (*ʿāwôn*, 7:13b, 16b, 19b), in the image of evildoers (7:24, *rāʿê gôyim*), and in the notion of judgment (*špṭ*, 7:23, 27). The allusion to the monarchy is anticipatory (7:10–11, *ṣāṣ hammaṭṭeh* . . . *lĕmaṭṭeh rešaʿ*; cf. 19:12, 14, *maṭṭeh*).

371 The parenthesis (8:11a*, *wĕyaʾăzanyāhû ben šāpān ʿōmēd bĕtôkām*) breaks up and partially repeats the context (8:11aA, *wĕšibʿîm ʾîš mizziqnê bêt yiśrāʾēl* [. . .] *ʿōmĕdîm lipnêhem*); see Zimmerli, *Ezekiel I*, 220, 241.

372 The parenthesis (11:1b, *wāʾerʾeh bĕtôkām ʾet yaʾăzanyâ ben ʿazzur wĕʾet pĕlaṭyāhû ben bĕnāyāhû śārê hāʿām*) is marked by deictics (a pronominal suffix, the object marker *ʾet*, proper names, and the definite article). The explanation takes place in a question about survivors (11:13), which repeats a question inserted into the second column (9:8) and is immediately answered in favor of a remnant of purified exiles (11:14–21). The question and answer are prepared by changing Ezekiel's text to allow for escapees from the destruction of Jerusalem who will undergo God's judgment outside the country (11:7b, 9–10).

373 The addition (9:2b–3) is fitted in surreptitiously but ends repeating the text to which it was attached (9:3b, "And he called to the man dressed in linen who had the writing case on his belt" = 9:2a, "And there was a man among them dressed in linen with a writing case on his belt"). The point of the addition is to note the presence of the bronze altar and a cherub from the Solomonic temple (1 Kgs 6:23–28; 8:64; 2 Kgs 16:14).

374 The references to survival and judgment (11:7b, 9–10, 11–12) are intruded by deictic pronouns and pronominal suffixes and by repetition of the original context (e.g., see 11:7a, "They are the flesh and it is the caldron" and 11:11a, "This will not be a caldron for you, but you will be in it like flesh").

375 Mimicry and visible signs are emphasized by the expression "in their sight" (lĕʿênêhem, 12:3a, 3b, 4a, 4b).

376 Ezek 12:1–5 and 12:7a, 8–10a, 11b.

377 The added sentence (12:6) reveals the editor's interest in the biography of the prophet by saying that Ezekiel himself is a portent to the house of Israel. The main points of the revision are repeated in the revision of the third and fourth paragraphs (12:7b, 10b, 11a).

378 The additional sentence (12:6) is affixed to the original paragraph by repeating its key word (lĕʿênêhem) and its command to exit through the hole in the wall (12:6, tôṣîʾ; cf. 12:5b, wĕhôṣēʾtā bô). Similar instructions are inserted into the third paragraph, and the same key word also functions as a deictic indicator (12:7b, lĕʿênêhem). This cross-reference to the edited text makes it seem original. The new mime is interpreted as the attempted flight of the king (12:10b—the passage is inserted by a whole series of deictics [pronouns, definite articles, proper names] that makes it particularly unwieldy; see Greenberg, Ezekiel 1–20, 211–12). After this interruption the fourth paragraph has to begin with a resumptive statement referring to what preceded its insertion (12:11a, "Say, . . ." [ʾĕmor ʾănî môpetĕkem]; cf. 12:10a, "Thus says . . ." [kōh ʾāmar ʾădōnāy yhwh]).

379 The first paragraph (12:12–16) is added by deictics (12:12, wĕhannāśîʾ . . . hûʾ), and its first part (12:12) consists entirely of cross-reference to the preceding edited text: the editorial procedure is strained and obvious (see Greenberg, Ezekiel 1–20, 211–16). The second paragraph (12:17–20) follows on it and consists mostly of cross-references to famine and the desolation of the land described in the second book.

380 The paragraphs (13:17–18a, 18b–19, 20–21, 22–23) correct and reduplicate the original. They were added via the deictic formula "And you, son of Man" (12:17) and by repeating at the beginning of the editorial addition the beginning of the original text (cf. 12:17–18a and 12:1–3). The original referred to the prophets. The addition refers to the prophetesses and illustrates the editor's custom of marking some abrupt changes in the text by a change of gender (see n. 361 above).

381 Ezekiel's last paragraph in this column (14:9, 11) explained how false prophets were deceived and how they would be punished. The editor insisted on the personal guilt of such prophets and of those who relied on them (14:10) and inserted the remark by using a deictic suffix and the definite article to refer to the original context (14:10, "They will bear *their* guilt, as the guilt of *the* inquirer, so the guilt of *the* prophet"). The additional paragraphs (14:12–14, 15–16, 17–20, 21–23) develop this point and are added to the text by reduplicating it, by beginning again as the column began (cf. 14:12 and 14:2), by repeating the preceding context (14:13aB, *wěnāṭîtî yāḏî 'ālêhā* = 14:9b, *wěnāṭîtî 'et yāḏî 'ālāyw*), and by cross-referencing the penultimate book (cf. 14:13 and 4:16; 5:16; 6:14).

382 The column (15:1–8) begins like the other columns in the book (*wayhî ḏěbar yhwh 'ēlay lē'mor ben 'āḏām*, 12:1; 13:1–2; 14:2–3; 15:1).

383 Ezekiel's story of divine wife-beating ended as it began with the forlorn female naked and abandoned and God's rage spent (16:43a). The editor began again with deictics that defended Yahweh's actions (16:43b, *wěgam 'ănî bě' ḏarkēk*) and recalled how the story began (16:45b = 16:3b). This version ends with a covenant (16:62) as the first story began (16:8).

384 The concluding paragraphs (17:19–21, 22–24) were added with deictics (17:19a, *lākēn kōh 'āmar 'ăḏōnāy yhwh*) and with literal repetition of the last part of Ezekiel's text (cf. 17:19 and 17:16a). The point of the addition was prepared by changing the second-to-last paragraph of the original to include a reference to the humiliation of the city and its monarchs (17:13bB–14; cf. 17:22–24). This insertion begins with a deictic (17:13, *wě'et*) and with a sort of pun on the last word of the original (17:13bB, *'êlê*; cf. 17:13bA, *'ālâ*), and it ends paraphrasing the text to which it was affixed (cf. 17:14b and 17:13aBbA).

385 The additional paragraphs (18:19–20, 21–23, 24, 25–28, 29–30a, 30b–32) were grafted onto the original by starting again where the original began (18:19aA, "But you will say . . ." [*wa'ămartem*]; cf. 18:2, "What are you doing making up this proverb . . ." [*māh lākem 'attem . . .*]; 18:20a = 18:4), by repeating the statements at the end of the original (18:19a = 18:18; 18:19b = 18:17), and by summarizing its point (18:20b; cf. Exod 34:7; Deut 24:16; 25:1). See Greenberg, *Ezekiel 1–20*, 334–47.

386 The drawing of the sword (21:6–8 and 21:13–15a) and its effects (21:11–12) are described in interlocking paragraphs.

387 In Ezekiel's version he addresses the holy place and the land of Israel (21:6–7), and in the editor's version he addresses the South and the forests in the fields of the Negeb (21:1–2). Apart from these specifics there are no differences in the texts.

388 Ezek 21:4 (*bǐ'artîhā*); cf. Deut 13:6; 17:7, 12; 19:19; 21:21; 22:21, 22, 24; 24:7.

389 The admission (21:9a, *ya'an 'ăšer hikrattî mimmēk ṣaddîq wĕrāšā'*) is merely a rhetorical link with Ezekiel's text (21:8b, *wĕhikrattî mimmēk ṣaddîq wĕrāšā'*). The substance of the editorial addition (21:9b–10) turns Yahweh's sword away from indiscriminate destruction in Jerusalem to the officials and nations who deserve to be punished.

390 The addition begins with a clause (21:15b, "Or let us rejoice in the staff, my son, that supplants every tree" [*'ô nāśîś šēbeṭ bĕnî mo'eset kol 'ēṣ*]) that many consider corrupt (see Zimmerli, *Ezekiel* I, 426–28). It is fitted into the context by repeating after it (21:16) a version of what preceded it (21:14–15a), which manages to take the sword out of Yahweh's hand and put it into the hand of the slayer (21:16b, *bĕyad hôrēg*), who turns out to be Nebuchadnezzar (21:26–28).

391 Cf. *šēbeṭ* in 19:14; 20:37; the image of trees as kings in 15:2, 3, 6; 17:24; cf. 31:8.

392 Ezek 21:23–25, 26–28, 29, 30–32, 33–34, 35–37.

393 The argument of the book is developed in additions to the end of the first (20:32–44) and last columns (23:30–49) that prove the justice of God in the careful assignment of guilt and innocence, and by the addition of the third column (22:1–31), which traces the guilt of Jerusalem to the monarchy. The additions are made, as usual, by deictic and literal repetition.

394 The additions are made at the ends of columns (24:15–27; 28:20–26) and in an additional column (25:1–17). Their links with the original are purely formal (the additions begin the way the original columns began [cf. 24:15 and 24:1; 28:20 and 28:1]). Their contents are filled with cross-references to the editor's argument and give a concrete historical sense to Ezekiel's bold imaginings.

395 Most of the additions are made at the beginning (32:1–16) and ends of columns (29:9b–21; 32:29–32) and in separate columns (30:1–26; 33:1–33). In the first column the additions begin and end like the beginning and end of the original (cf. 29:9b and 29:3b; 29:21b and 29:9a). The notes added to the third column (31:5, 14) repeat their immediate context and refer to the diminished grandeur of the nation. The beginning of the fourth column copies the beginning of the third (cf. 32:1 and 31:1) and the text that it displaced (cf. 32:17). The additions to the end of the fourth column mention Edom and Sidon, which the editor included (cf. 25:12–14; 28:20–26), and are affixed by deictics and repetition.

396 In the first column Ezekiel's sanguine vision of Yahweh assuming the role of shepherd of his flock is countered by the practical problems of distinguishing between the sheep and the goats (34:15–31). The text is added by deictics and repetition (cf. 34:15, *'ănî 'er 'eh ṣō'nî*, and 34:14, *'er 'eh 'ōtām*). In the third column the land is restored, but the editor thought of the renovation of the people (36:16–38). The addition is made with the deictic

"Son of Man" (36:17) in imitation of the beginning of the column. The editor also used a deictic suffix to include a cross-reference to Edom (36:5, "And against Edom, all of *it*" [*wĕ⁽al ʾĕdôm kullāh*]; cf. 35:1–15). In the fourth column the people are brought back to life, but the editor thinks instead of the restoration of Israel and Judah under David (37:15–28). The addition is introduced by the deictic formula "And *you*, son of man . . ."

397 The additions in the first column concerning the sacrificial system (40:38–50; 41:15–26; 42:1–20) are made by repeating elements of their immediate context. In the second column the additions (43:6–46:24) are linked to the original mention of the temple (43:5, *habbayit*; cf. 43:6, 10–12). In the third column the additions (47:13–48:35) are made via a pun on the words "stream" (*nahal*) and "inherit" (*nāhal*); cf. 47:6–12 and 47:13–14.

398 Cf. Ezek 1:4 (*rûah śĕᶜārâ . . . wĕʾēś mitlaqqahat*) and Gen 1:2 (*rûah ʾĕlōhîm mĕrahepet*). According to Jeremiah, the enemy from the North comes as clouds and a gathering storm (Ezek 1:4a; cf. Jer 4:13).

399 Cf. Ezek 1:28a (*ᶜānān . . . hûʾ marʾēh dĕmût kĕbôd yhwh*) and Exod 24:15–18, esp. 17 (*ûmarʾēh kĕbôd yhwh*).

400 *rāqîaᶜ*, 1:22, 25a, 26; Gen 1:6–8.

401 Cf. Ezek 1:5 (*dĕmût ʾarbaᶜ hayyôt wĕzeh marʾēhen dĕmût ʾādām lāhennâ*) and Gen 1:25–26 (*wayya ᶜaś ʾĕlōhîm ʾet hayyat hāʾāreṣ . . . wayyōʾmer ʾĕlōhîm naᶜăśeh ʾādām bĕṣalmēnû kidmûtēnû*).

402 In Ezekiel the glory of Yahweh appears in a human likeness (1:26, 28a, *dĕmût kĕmarʾēh ʾādām . . . hûʾ marʾēh dĕmût dĕbôd yhwh*), and in the Priestly account of creation humans are made in the likeness of God (cf. Gen 1:26–28, *bĕṣalmēnû kidmûtēnû*; 5:1, *ʾādām / kidmût ʾĕlōhîm*).

403 Cf. 1:28a (*haqqeśet ʾăśer yihyeh bĕᶜānān*) and Gen 9;13, 14, 16 (*haqqeśet bĕᶜānān*).

404 The vision shares the epic suppositions that the distinction between people and God was a gradual, geographical, and historical development (Genesis 2–3) and that Yahweh was manifested in fire and cloud (Exod 13:21–22; 14:19b, 24).

405 Ezek 2:9 (*mĕgillat śēper*); 3:1–3 (*mĕgillâ*); 2:10 (*wĕhîʾ kĕtûbâ pānîm wĕʾāhôr*). The book was handed to Ezekiel by Yahweh and was inscribed on both sides, as were the tablets on Sinai according to the Elohist (Exod 32:15–16).

406 Cf. Isa 29:11–12 (*hassēper [hehātûm]*); Isa 30:8 (*ᶜattâ bôʾ kotbāh . . . ᶜal śēper*).

407 Cf. Ezek 2:6, 8 (*bêt mĕrî*); Isa 30:9 (*kî ᶜam mĕrî hûʾ*); cf. Isa 1:20.

^{408} Cf. Ezek 2:3 (*hēmmâ waʾăbôtām pāšĕʿû bî*) and Isa 1:2 (*bānîm . . . wĕhēm pāšĕʿû bî*).

^{409} Cf. Ezek 3:4b–5 (*wĕdibbartā bidbāray ʿălêhem kî lōʾ ʾel ʿam ʿimqê šāpâ wĕkibdê lāšôn ʾattâ šālûaḥ*) and Isa 28:11 (*kî bĕlaʿăgê šāpâ ûbĕlāšôn ʾaḥeret yĕdabbēr ʾel hāʿām hazzeh*).

^{410} Cf. Ezek 3:7 (*lōʾ yōʾbû lišmōaʿ*) and Isa 28:12 (*wĕlōʾ ʾābû šĕmôaʿ*).

^{411} Cf. Ezek 3:8–9 (*pānêkā ḥăzāqîm . . . kĕšāmîr ḥāzāq miṣṣōr*) and Jer 5:3 (*ḥizzĕqû pĕnêhem misselaʿ*).

^{412} Cf. Ezek 2:4–5; 3:17 (*ṣopeh nĕtattîkā*) and Jer 1:5 (*nābîʾ nĕtattîkā*).

^{413} Cf. Ezek 1:3 and Jer 1:11, 13; 1:2b and 2 Kgs 25:27; Jer 52:31.

^{414} Cf. Ezek 1:9; 10:1–22; 1 Kgs 6:27.

^{415} Cf. 1 Sam 4:4; 2 Sam 6:3; 1 Kgs 8:6–10.

^{416} Cf. Ezek 1:12–21 and 1 Kgs 7:27–37.

^{417} Cf. Ezek 1:7–8, 13–14; 10:2, 6–8; and Isa 6:6.

^{418} Cf. Ezek 4:2–3; 5:2; and Isa 29:3; Jer 10:17; Nah 2:2; Hab 2:1.

^{419} Cf. Ezek 4:1 and Exod 1:13–14; also Gen 11:3 and Exodus 5.

^{420} Ezek 6:1–7, 11–13; cf. 34:13, 14; 36:1, 4, 8.

^{421} Ezek 6:13a, *sĕbîbôt mizbĕḥôtêhem*, cf. Hos 8:11; 10:1; Ezek 6:13b, *ʾel kol gibʿâ rāmâ* = Jer 2:20, *ʿal kol gibʿâ gĕbōhâ*; Ezek 6:13b, *bĕkōl rāʾšê hehārîm* = Hos 4:13, *ʿal rāʾšê hehārîm yĕzabbēḥû*; Ezek 6:13b, *wĕtaḥat kol ʿēṣ raʾănān* = Jer 2:20; Ezek 6:13b, *wĕtaḥat kol ʾēlâ ʿăbuttâ* = Hos 4:13, *taḥat ʾallôn wĕlibneh wĕʾēlâ kî ṭôb ṣillāh*.

^{422} Cf. Ezek 7:2, 3, 6 (*bāʾ haqqēṣ, qēṣ bāʾ*) and Amos 8:2 (*bāʾ haqqēṣ ʾel ʿammî yiśrāʾēl*).

^{423} Cf. Ezek 7:2b (*bāʾ haqqēṣ ʿal ʾarbaʿat kanpôt hāʾāreṣ*) and Gen 6:13 (*qēṣ kol bāśār bāʾ lĕpānay*).

^{424} Cf. Ezek 7:7 (*qārôb hayyôm*) and Zeph 1:14 (*qārôb yôm yhwh haggādôl*); cf. Amos 5:18, 20.

^{425} Cf. Ezek 7:5 (*rāʿâ hinnēh bāʾâ*) and Mic 1:12; 3:11; Jer 4:6; 5:12; 6:1.

^{426} Cf. Ezek 7:7 (*bāʾ hāʿēt*) and Mic 2:3.

427 Cf. Ezek 4:8, ". . . the days of your siege . . ." (*yĕmê mĕṣûrĕkā*).

428 The editor looks forward to the reunion of Israel and Judah under David (37:15–28). The 390 years of Israel's exile (4:5, 9b) are approximately the length of time from the secession of Israel under Jeroboam I to the exile in the reign of Zedekiah. Combined with the forty years of Judah's exile (4:6), they equal the total of 430 years that, according to the Priestly writer, Israel spent in Egypt (Exod 12:40). Some such speculation and allusion may account for the numbers (see Greenberg, *Ezekiel 1–20*, 104–6).

429 The thirty years of the exile of Jehoiachin (1:1) and the forty years of the exile of Judah (4:6) amount, literarily, to the seventy years of exile predicted in the book of Jeremiah (Jer 25:11). The forty years of Judah's exile are also literary and correspond exactly to the forty years in the wilderness (4:4b + 5a + 6b [*lĕmispar yāmîm . . . tiśśā' 'et 'ăwōnām . . . 'arbā'îm yôm yôm laśśānâ yôm laśśānâ*] = Num 14:34 [*bĕmispar hayyāmîm . . . 'arbā'îm yôm yôm laśśānâ yôm laśśānâ tiśĕ'û 'et 'awōnōtêkem*]).

430 Cf. Ezek 4:14b (*ûnĕbēlâ ûṭĕrēpâ lō' 'ākaltî*) and 44:31 (*kol nĕbēlâ ûṭĕrēpâ . . . lō' yō'kĕlû hakkōhănîm*).

431 Cf. Exod 28:38; see Greenberg, *Ezekiel 1–20*, 104.

432 The dietary law (4:14) has antecedents in the law codes (Exod 22:30; Deut 14:21), but it was the editor's formulation that was taken up in the later revision of the Pentateuch (cf. Ezek 4:14 and Lev 22:8).

433 Compare Ezek 5:3 (*mĕ'aṭ bĕmispār*) and 6:8 (*bihyôt lākem pĕlîṭê ḥereb baggôyim*) with Deut 4:27 (*wĕniš'artem mĕtê mispār baggôyim*); Deut 26:5 (*bimtê mĕ'āṭ*); and Jer 44:28 (*ûpĕlîṭê ḥereb yĕšûbûn min 'ereṣ miṣrāyim 'ereṣ yĕhûdâ mĕtê mispār*).

434 Ezek 7:12–13; cf. 7:12aA and 7:7b; 7:13bA (*kî ḥāzôn . . . lō' yāšûb*) and Hab 2:3 (*kî 'ôd ḥāzôn lammô'ēd . . . lō' yĕkazzēb*).

435 Cf. Ezek 7:14a (*tāqĕ'û battāqôa'*) and Jer 6:1 (*ûbitqôa' tiqĕ'û šôpār*); cf. 7:15 (*ḥereb baḥûṣ . . . baśśādeh baḥereb*) and Jer 5:12; 6:25.

436 Cf. 7:18–19; Amos 8:10; Zeph 1:18.

437 Cf. Ezek 7:21a (*lābaz . . . lĕšālāl*) and Isa 10:6 (*lišlōl šālāl wĕlābōz bāz*).

438 Cf. Ezek 7:23bB (*wĕhā'îr māl'â ḥāmās*) and Gen 6:11, 13 (*kî māl'â hā'āreṣ ḥāmās*).

439 Cf. Ezek 7:26a (*ûšĕmû'â 'el šĕmû'â tihyeh*) and Isa 28:9, 19 (*wĕ'et mî yābîn šĕmû'â . . . wĕhāyâ raq zĕwā'â hābîn šĕmû'â*); Ezek 7:26b = Jer 18:18.

440 Cf. Ezek 8:5 (*sēmel haqqin'â hazzeh*) and Exod 34:14 (*kî yhwh qannā' šĕmô 'ēl qannā' hû'*); Nah 1:2.

441 Cf. Ezek 8:17–18; 9:1 and Exod 34:6–7; Nah 1:6.

442 Cf. Ezek 8:10 (*remeś ûbĕhēmâ*) and Gen 1:25 (*wĕʾet habbĕhēmâ . . . wĕʾet kol remeś*).

443 Cf. Ezek 8:17b (*kî mālĕʾû ʾet hāʾāreṣ ḥāmās*) and Gen 6:11, 13 (*kî mālĕʾâ hāʾāreṣ ḥāmās*); Ezek 9:4 and Gen 4:15; Ezek 11:5 and Gen 6:5.

444 Cf. Ezek 11:16b(*wāʾehî lāhem lĕmiqdāś mĕʿaṭ*) and Isa 8:14 (*wĕhāyâ lĕmiqdāś . . . liśnê bāttê yiśrāʾēl*).

445 Ezek 12:2b, *ʾăśer ʿênayim lāhem lirʾôt wĕlōʾ rāʾû / ʾoznayim lāhem liśmōaʿ wĕlōʾ śāmĕʿû* = Jer 5:21b.

446 Ezek 12:2b, *kî bêt mĕrî hēm* = Isa 30:9.

447 Cf. *lĕʿênêhem* (12:4, 5); *bêt mĕrî* (12:9).

448 Cf. Ezek 12:11b (*baggôlâ baśśĕbî yēlēkû*) and Nah 3:10 (*gam hîʾ laggōlâ hālĕkâ baśśĕbî*).

449 Cf. 12:6, 7b, 10b–11a, 12–16 and 5:3, 10, 12; 11:9–12, 16.

450 Cf. Ezek 12:24 (*ḥāzôn, ḥālāq*) and Isa 30:10; Ezek 12:22b, 24 and Mic 3:6–7; Ezek 12:22–23 and Hab 2:3; Ezek 12:25 (*bîmêkem*) and Hab 1:5 (*bîmêkem*).

451 Compare Ezek 13:5 (*lōʾ ʿălîtem bappĕrāṣôt wattigdĕrû gādēr ʿal bêt yiśrāʾēl*) and 13:11, 13 (*geśem śôṭēp*) with Isa 5:5 (*pāroṣ gĕdērô*) and Isa 28:15, 18 (*śôṭ śôṭēp*) and Isa 30:13–14 (*kĕpereṣ nōpēl*).

452 Cf. Ezek 13:5 (*bammilḥāmâ bĕyôm yhwh*) and Amos 1:14 (*bĕyôm milḥāmâ*) and Amos 5:18–20 (*yôm yhwh*).

453 Cf. Ezek 13:14 (*wĕniglâ yĕsōdô*) and Mic 1:6 (*wîsōdêhā ʾăgalleh*).

454 Cf. Ezek 14:3, 4, 7 (*mikśôl ʿăwōnām*) and Isa 28:13 (*wĕkāśĕlû ʾāḥôr*); Ezek 14:5 (*ʾăśer nāzōrû mĕʿālay*); 14:7 (*wĕyinnāzēr mĕʾaḥăray*); and Isa 1:4 (*nāzōrû ʾāḥôr*).

455 Cf. Ezek 14:13, 15 and 4:16; 5:16–17; 6:14; cf. 14:17, 19, 21 and 5:17; cf. 14:23 and 6:10.

456 Ezek 15:2 (*hazzĕmôrâ*) = 8:17.

457 Ezek 15:2, 3, 6; 17:24; 21:3, 15; 34:27; 36:30; 37:16, 19, 20; 39:10; 41:16, 22, 25.

458 Ezek 5:4; 10:2, 6, 7; 15:4–7; 19:12, 14; 21:3, 36, 37; 22:20, 21, 31; 23:47; 30:8, 14, 16; 38:19, 22; 39:6, 10.

459 Cf. 15:3b (*'im yiqḥû mimmennû yātēd litlôt ʿālāyw kol kĕlî*) and Isa 22:23–24 (*ûtĕqaʿtîw yātēd . . . wĕtālû ʿālāyw . . . kol kĕlê haqqāṭān . . . kol kĕlê hannĕbālîm*).

460 Ezek 19:12, 14.

461 Ezek 16:15–16; Hos 1:2; Jer 2:20.

462 Ezek 16:17–19; Hos 2:7, 10, 15.

463 Ezek 16:20–22; Hos 2:17; 4:17–19.

464 Ezek 16:23–29; Hos 4:10; 9:3; 11:5; Jer 2:36.

465 Ezek 16:30–34; Hos 2:14; 8:9; 9:1; Mic 1:7.

466 Ezek 16:36; Hos 2:12.

467 Ezek 16:37; Jer 3:2.

468 Cf. Jer 2:20; Hos 4:13; cf. also Jer 2:21 (*wĕʾānokî nĕṭaʿtîk śorēq*) and Isa 5:2 (*wayyiṭṭāʿēhû śorēq*).

469 Ezek 17:1–13abA, 15–18.

470 Ezek 17:13bB–14, 19–24.

471 Cf. 18:5, 8b (*ṣaddîq . . . mišpāṭ ûṣĕdāqâ*) and Exod 23:6–8 (*mišpāṭ . . . ṣaddîq . . . ṣaddîqîm*).

472 Cf. 18:6a and 6:1–7; 14:1–9, 11; 16:36.

473 Ezek 18:6b; cf. 16:32.

474 Cf. Ezek 20:1 (*bāʾû ʾănāšîm . . . lidrōš ʾet yhwh*) and Exod 18:15 (*kî yābōʾ ʾēlay hāʿām lidrōš ʾĕlōhîm*); cf. Ezek 20:4 (*hătišpōṭ ʾōtām hătišpōṭ ben ʾādām*) and Exod 18:13 (*wayyēšeb mōšeh lišpōṭ ʾet hāʿām*).

475 Cf. Ezek 20:5a (*ydʿ*) and Exod 6:3; Ezek 20:5b and Exod 6:2, 6, 7; Ezek 20:5a and Exod 6:8 (cf. Gen 46:7); Ezek 20:6 and Exod 6:6 (cf. Exod 3:10–12); Ezek 20:6b and Num 13:2, 17, 25, 32; Ezek 20:6b and Exod 3:8a; Ezek 20:6b (*ṣĕbî hîʾ lĕkol hāʾărāṣôt*) = Jer 3:19.

476 Cf. Ezek 20:8a (*wayyamrû bî*) and Exod 23:21 (*ʾal tammēr bô*).

477 Ezek 20:8a = Isa 1:19–20.

478 The "idols of Egypt" (Ezek 20:7a) are the golden calf that was made with jewelry brought from Egypt (Exod 32:1–6).

479 Cf. Ezek 20:9a; Exod 6:3; Num 14:13–19.

480 Cf. Ezek 20:10a and Exod 12:42; Ezek 20:10b and Exod 13:18, 20; Ezek 20:11a and Exod 18:13–27; Ezek 20:11b and Deut 8:1; Ezek 20:12 and Exod 31:13.

481 Cf. Ezek 20:13 (*wayyamrû bî*) and Num 20:10 (*mōrîm*); Ezek 20:14a and Num 14:18. It is Nahum (1:2–3, 6–8) and Habakkuk (3:8) who associate fury and rage with Yahweh's manifestation on Sinai: cf. Ezek 20:13b (*wā'ōmar lišpōk ḥāmātî 'ălêhem bammiḏbār lĕkallōtām*) and Nah 1:6, 8 (*ḥāmātô nittĕkâ kā'ēš . . . kālâ ya'ăśeh mĕqômāh*).

482 Cf. Ezek 20:15–16 and Num 14:21, 23; Jer 3:19.

483 Cf. Ezek 20:17b (*wĕlō' 'ăśîtî 'ōtām kālâ bammiḏbār*) and Jer 4:27 (*wĕkālâ lō' 'e'ĕśeh*; cf. Jer 5:10). Ezekiel's account of the rebellion and punishment of the children of the exodus generation (20:18–20) supposes the contribution that this generation made to the golden calf (Exod 32:2) and the connection that Jeremiah saw between the parents and their children (Jer 2:4–6, 9–13).

484 Ezek 20:25–26 = Exod 34:19.

485 Ezek 20:27–28; cf. Hos 4:13; Jer 2:4–6, 20.

486 Cf. Ezek 20:32b, 33b (*nihyeh kaggôyim . . . 'ănî . . . 'emlôk 'ălêkem*) and 1 Sam 8:19–20 (. . . *kî 'im melek yihyeh 'ālênû wĕhāyînû . . . kĕkol haggôyim*). The expression "like the nations" is paired with a similar expression from the table of nations: cf. Ezek 20:32b (*kĕmišpĕḥôt hā'ărāṣôt*) and Gen 10:31 (*lĕmišpĕḥōtām . . . bĕ'arṣōtām lĕgôyêhem*).

487 Cf. Ezek 20:32 ("To worship wood and stone" [*lĕšārēt 'ēṣ wā'āben*]) and Deut 4:28 ("And there you will serve Gods made with human hands, wood and stone . . ." [*wa'ăbaḏtem . . . 'ēṣ wā'eben*]).

488 Ezek 20:33b ("With a firm hand and an outstretched arm" [*bĕyaḏ ḥăzāqâ ûbizrôa' nĕṭûyâ*]) = Deut 4:34; Ezek 20:33b ("and in a flash of anger" [*ûbĕḥēmâ šĕpûkâ*]) = Ezek 20:8, 13, 21.

489 Cf. Ezek 20:34, 35 (*wĕhôṣē'tî 'etkem . . . wĕhēbē'tî 'etkem*) and Deut 5:6 (*'ăšer hôṣē'tîkā*) and Deut 6:10 (*kî yĕbî'ăkā*). Cf. Ezek 20:34 and 11:17; 20:35 and 20:4 (*špṭ*); 20:38 (*'ereṣ mĕgûrêhem*) and Exod 6:4; 20:35 (*pānîm 'el pānîm*) and Deut 5:4.

490 Ezek 20:39–44; cf. 20:40a and 17:23; 20:40b and 45:1, 13, etc.; 20:41 and 6:13.

491 Cf. Ezek 21:7 (*haṭṭēp*) and Mic 2:6, 11.

492 Cf. Ezek 21:12 and Isa 28:19; Jer 6:24; 10:22; Nah 2:10.

493 Cf. Ezek 21:2 (*haṭṭēp*) and Mic 2:6, 11. Micah's prediction that Jerusalem would become a ploughed field and a wooded height (Mic 3:12, *śādeh . . . yaʿar*) allowed the editor to shift attention from Jerusalem by referring to the woods in the fields of the Negeb (Ezek 21:2–3, *yaʿar haśśādeh negeb*). Huldah's oracle compares Yahweh's wrath to a fire and says that it will rage against the city and will not be put out (2 Kgs 22:17, *wěniṣṣětâ ḥāmātî bammāqôm hazzeh wělōʾ tikbeh*). The editor applies the image to symbolic woods (Ezek 21:3b, *hiněnî maṣṣît běkā ʾēš . . . lōʾ tikbeh*).

494 E.g., Ezek 22:2 (*hătiśpōṭ hătiśpōṭ*) = 20:4.

495 Ezek 22:1 (*ʿîr haddāmîm*) = 24:6 = Nah 3:1a; cf. Mic 3:10.

496 Ezek 22:12a = Deut 27:25; cf. 22:12 (*ōšeq*) and Isa 30:12; Amos 3:9; Jer 6:6.

497 Cf. Ezek 22:17–22 and 24:6–14; Isa 1:22, 25; Jer 6:27–30.

498 Cf. Ezek 22:23–31 and Zeph 3:1–8; Ezek 22:26 and Lev 10:10.

499 The date for the beginning of the siege is also noted in the Deuteronomistic History (Ezek 24:1 = 2 Kgs 25:1).

500 Cf. Ezek 24:3 (*māšāl*) and Mic 2:4; Ezek 24:6 (*lōʾ nāpal ʿālêhā gôrāl*) and Mic 2:5 (*lākēn lōʾ yihyeh lěkā mašlîk ḥebel běgôrāl biqhal yhwh*).

501 Cf. Ezek 29:6–7a (*mišʿenet qāneh*) and 2 Kgs 18:21 (*mišʿenet haqqāneh*); cf. also Ezek 29:3 (*hattannîn haggādôl*) and Gen 1:21 (*ʾet hattannînīm haggědôlîm*).

502 Cf. Ezek 47:13–48:35 and Numbers 34; Joshua 13–19, esp. Joshua 19.

CHAPTER 5

The Deuteronomistic History

*T*he Deuteronomistic History was written after the fall of Jerusalem to situate the catastrophe in a systematic history of the world. It incorporated all the earlier histories and clever surrogates of the prophets in a learned and persuasive synthesis that fully explained the past and laid a dogmatic foundation for the future. It completely transcended the Judean bias of earlier writings, gave precedence to the northern kingdom, and described the emergence and enduring structures of an ideal Israel. It had access to libraries, administrative records, detailed scholarly information, informal sources, ribald stories, and the relative wisdom of the ages ensconced in lives and living institutions that forever underlay and outlived the political, religious, and commercial establishments. It was written to suit the works that it incorporated or the topic that it treated or the mood that it meant to engender and is filled with elegance and humor and fits of genius and frustration. The world of the Bible is the world it created.

The History immediately became a compendium of knowledge, a *vade mecum* of moral authority, the standard of diligence, the norm of orthodox interpretation. There was cavil and resentment, some alienation and a measure of downright disagreement, but no apathy or indifference to its publication. Writers rushed to revise the literature, and the Deuteronomistic History acquired the force of ancient tradition. When all had been said and done, its authority was inviolate and secure.[1]

Measured against its sources and origins and against the retorts and the major revisions that it inspired, the History, remarkable for its perspective, diversity, and scope, is one among a multitude of interpretations. It has been treated, however, from ancient times as a true account, as factual information, as the transmission of reliable and once contemporary records and, like the epic and the sequel that it enveloped, as the sure basis of belief. This devoted adherence suits the persuasive manner of its composition without doing justice to the levels of attention that the History required. The Deuteronomistic interpretation, however historical or true, was part Torah, part paradigm, a partial projection of the future on the past, a decided model of discipline, hope, and universal expectation.

The History begins at the beginning, in Genesis, and ends in 2 Kings with the exile. It knows the epic in its original, Priestly, and Elohist editions, and follows the historical scheme devised by the sequel to the epic. It includes annotations and comments on these texts, adds complementary or supplementary material, and develops a meticulous, exhaustive, and overarching interpretation. Its interests include legend, folklore and stories, law, prophecy and poetry, women, war and politics, architecture, administration, and organized religion. Its focus is on geography, ethnography, etiology, genealogy, and theology. Its perspective is atemporal and transcendent and casts a negative shadow on the eras and persons it pursues. Its method is scientific and marked by masses of data, conflicting evidence, logical argument, explanatory principles, and the assignment of causes and their consequences. Its enduring achievement was its proof that Yahweh was supreme, universal, and transcendent in fixing on Israel among all the nations of the world. The proof was the law that set Israel apart or, if ignored, doomed it to be like the others and that, being gradually revealed from the beginning, in the end was a verified and acceptable fact.

The History is large and complex but the product of a single time, place, and person. The time is sometime after the exile and Ezekiel, to which it refers, and before Job, Obadiah, Joel, and the revisionist prophets who refer to it. The place is Judah and Jerusalem, where the sources were located, where it was then possible to be impartial and uncompromising, where the existence of enclaves beyond the borders of Judah in the land allotted to the Transjordanian tribes would be problematic, where the exiles received no sympathy, where God who dwelt in heaven and filled the universe was not anymore. The person was educated, a familiar of the higher echelons of government and society, an individual who stepped forward in the text in typical speeches and poetic résumés, a character of great acumen, independence, aloofness, and personal abnegation for whom nothing really mattered but telling the truth and telling it well.

Structure and Organization (fig. 17)

The History is organized in books, the books in parts and chapters, the chapters in sentences and paragraphs. Considered in its literal expanse, it is a huge jigsaw puzzle in which every space is determined by the borders and by the contraction of the developing whole and in which every piece fits by convergence and in relation to every other. Considered in its historical depth and intensity, it is a scroll that unrolls from the front in which everything that is written refers to what follows and to what has been said in the past. The History is like any other that informs and moves and requires participation and response.

The books all deal with distinct chronological eras; with different geographical domains, political regimes, and social structures; and with religious behavior and stages in the revelation and implementation of the law. They are distinguished by the gradual development of personality in their main characters, by variations in material interests and genres and by the increasing intrusion of the Historian as the History comes to a close. They are linked literarily by hinges, pivots, and repetitions between books, and by a cumulative and cyclic movement from one book to the next in the series.

GENESIS

The first book in the History narrates the Mesopotamian and Egyptian origins of the children of Israel. It closes with the deathbed blessing that they received from their father and with a preview of the story as it continues in the second book. It takes place between primordial time and the death of Joseph in the era of the patriarchs Abraham, Isaac, and Jacob. It presents these men as shepherds, and their life story follows the route of the flocks and herds that they pastured. They lived on the verge of kingdoms, and their women, though troubled by barrenness and often beset by knaves and fools, were the motive of their actions, the source of their endurance, and the ordinary occasion of their contact with God and with the powers of the world. God was named Yahweh, and appeared, spoke, and traveled with the patriarchs and their wives and children, and enjoyed the epithets of all the familiar, local, and cosmic forces. They were a great family that stood out against an opaque and undifferentiated background as they slowly separated and distinguished themselves from the nations among whom they moved. They sacrificed to the God who appeared to them and worshiped the God who was present to them by submission to an unwritten law that was known even to their neighbors and that

FIGURE 17

The Deuteronomistic History

BOOK ONE: GENESIS

Part

I	A	[1:1–2:4a]
	B	2:7b, 10–15, 19aBb–20a, 23b–24
	C	3:14–21, 24
	D	4:1–26
II	A	5:29bB
	B	6:3–4aA, 7aB
	C	7:1b–3, 5–6, 8–9, 12, 16b, 22, 23°
	D	8:7, 13b, 20–22
	E	9:2–8, 18–27
III	A	10:8–19, 21, 24–30
	B	11:2–3, 8a, 9a, 29–30
	C	12:2b, 3b, 6b–7, 8b, 10–20
	D	13:1, 3–4, 6b, 7b, 10b, 13–17, 18b
	E	14:1–24
IV	A	15:1–21
	B	16:2, 4–14
	C	[17:1–27]
	D	18:1a, 17–33
	E	19:1aA, 9aB, 11, 15–23, 24b, 26, 29–38
	F	20:1aB, 4–7, 9, 12–13, 17–18
	G	21:25–26, 28–33
	H	22:15–18, 20–24
	I	[23:1–20]
	J	24:1–67
V	A	25:1–6, 11, 18
	B	26:1aB, 2–6, 10, 15, 18–25, 32–35
	C	27:36a, 45–46
	D	28:6–9, 13–16, 19
	E	29:24, 29, 31–35
	F	30:1–24
	G	31:17–18, 19b, 28, 30–36a, 37, 43–50
	H	32:10–13, 23a°, 24a, 25a, 26aBb, 31, 32b–33
	I	33:1b–2, 5–7, 17b, 18b–20
	J	34:1–31
	K	35:5b, 6aB, 8, 16–26
VI	A	36:9–43
	B	37:2aB
	C	38:1–30
	D	39:21–23
	E	[40:1–23]
	F	41:55, 56b

continued

FIGURE 17 *(cont)*

	G	42:25–28, 35, 37
	H	43:12, 14a, 15aB, 17–23a, 29b, 32–34a
	I	44:1–17
	J	45:21b–24
VII	A	46:8–27, 34b
	B	47:7–26
	C	48:3–7, 22
	D	49:1–33a
	E	50:9–11

BOOK TWO: EXODUS

Part

I	A	1:5a, 12b, 15–21
	B	2:6bB, 7aB, 13–14
	C	3:15–22
	D	4:1–17, 20b–23, 26b–31
	E	5:1–23
II	A	6:1, 13–30
	B	7:14–18, 21a, 23–29
	C	8:4–9a, 16–28
	D	9:1–7, 13–35
	E	10:1–29
	F	11:1–8
	G	12:7, 12–27, 29–36, 39, 43–51
III	A	13:1–16
	B	14:11–14
	C	15:1–19, 25b–26
	D	16:4–5, 8, 16–34, 35b–36
	E	17:1bB–16
	F	18:1b, 2b, 6–11
	G	19:3b–8, 9b, 10aA, 12–13, 15b, 18abA, 21–25
	H	20:2–26
	I	21:1
	J	22:9–19
	K	23:17–19, 23–26, 28, 32–33
	L	24:1–12
IV	A	25:6–7, 9–40
	B	26:31–37
	C	27:1–21
	D	28:1–43
	E	29:1–42, 44
	F	30:1–38
	G	31:1–12
V	A	32:7–14, 19b–20, 21b, 26–35
	B	33:1–23
	C	34:1–5, 8–9, 13, 15–18, 20a, 23, 25–26, 28bB–29aA, 32b, 34–35

continued

F I G U R E   1 7   *(cont)*

VI	A	35:8–19, 30–35
	B	36:1
	C	37:1–29
	D	38:1–31
	E	39:1–43
	F	40:1–15, 20–35a, 38

BOOK THREE: LEVITICUS and NUMBERS

Leviticus

Part

I	A	8:1–36
	B	9:1–24
	C	10:1–20
	D	11:1–45

Numbers

II	A	1:1–54
	B	2:1–33
	C	3:1–51
	D	4:1–49
	E	5:1–31
	F	6:1–27
	G	7:1–89
	H	8:1–26
	I	9:1–23
	J	10:1–10, 13–28, 33b–36
III	A	11:1–35
	B	12:1–16a
	C	13:2b, 4–16, 21b, 22b, 24, 25b, 26b, 29, 33a
	D	14:1b, 4–10, 11bB, 19b, 22, 25, 33–35, 39–45
	E	15:1–41
	F	16:1–11, 15–24, 25b–27a, 32b, 33b, 35
	G	17:1–28
	H	18:1–32
	I	19:1–22
IV	A	20:1aA, 6, 16aB, 26, 28aA
	B	21:1–20, 24bB, 25–35
	C	22:2–4a, 7a, 21aB, 22–35
	D	[23:1–30]
	E	24:7, 14–24
	F	25:1–19
V	A	26:1–65
	B	27:1–11, 14
	C	28:1–31
	D	29:1–39

continued

FIGURE 17 (*cont*)

	E	30:1–17
	F	31:1–54
VI	A	32:1–42
	B	33:1–56
	C	34:1–29
	D	35:1–34
	E	36:1–13

BOOK FOUR: DEUTERONOMY

Part

I	A	1:1b–2, 4–5, 9–18, 19*, 31, 35aB, 37–46
	B	2:1–37
	C	3:1–29
II	A	4:1–49
	B	5:1aBb, 5, 8, 12–22, 23aBb, 24b, 26, 28–33
	C	6:1–3, 14b, 15b, 16–25
	D	7:2bA, 3–16, 19–20, 22, 25–26
	E	8:2–6, 11b, 15–16, 18b–20
	F	9:4–29
	G	10:1–11, 13, 15–16, 19, 21–22
	H	11:1–7, 16–17, 26–32
III	A	12:1–12, 15–16, 18aB, 19, 21–25, 27–31
	B	13:1–19
	C	14:1–3, 6–10, 13–21, 23–24, 27–29
	D	15:1–18, 21–23
	E	16:2b, 3aBb–6, 8–15, 16aB, 17–22
	F	17:1–20
	G	18:1–22
IV	A	19:1–21
	B	20:1–20
	C	21:1–23
	D	22:1–29
	E	23:1–26
	F	24:1–22
	G	25:1–19
V	A	26:1–19
	B	27:1–26
	C	28:1–69
	D	29:1b–8, 9b–10, 12, 15–28
	E	30:1–20
VI	A	31:2b, 3b–5, 7–30
	B	32:1–47, 51a
	C	33:1–29
	D	34:1aB, 6, 10–12

continued

FIGURE 17 *(cont)*

BOOK FIVE: JOSHUA

Part

I	A	1:2bD, 6–18
	B	2:9b–11, 17–21, 24b
	C	3:1aB, 2–4, 6–10a, 11–16a, 17
	D	4:1–24
	E	5:1–15
	F	6:1aB, 4aAb, 5aA, 6, 7b–9, 10aA, 11–13, 15b, 16aB, 17–19, 20b–21, 23aBb–24, 25aB, 26–27
	G	7:1–26
	H	8:2aB, 5b, 6aB, 8, 9aBb, 10b, 11b–13, 17, 19b–20, 21aB, 22–35
II	A	9:6b–7, 9bB–10, 14, 15b–27
	B	10:1°, 10b–43
	C	11:4, 6b, 8b–22, 23aB
III	A	12:1–24
	B	13:1–33
	C	14:1–15
	D	15:1–63
	E	16:1–10
	F	17:1–18
	G	18:1–28
	H	19:1–51
	I	20:1–9
	J	21:1–45
	K	22:1–34
	L	23:1–16
	M	24:1–33

BOOK SIX: JUDGES

Part

I	A	1:1–36
	B	2:1–23
	C	3:1–31
	D	4:1–24
	E	5:1–31
II	A	6:1–40
	B	7:1–25
	C	8:1–35
	D	9:1–57
III	A	10:1–18
	B	11:1–40
	C	12:1–15
IV	A	13:1–25
	B	14:1–20

continued

FIGURE 17 *(cont)*

	C	15:1–20
	D	16:1–31
V	A	17:1–13
	B	18:1–31
	C	19:1–30
	D	20:1–48
	E	21:1–25

BOOK SEVEN: SAMUEL

1 Samuel

Part

I	A	1:3b, 9aBb–10, 11bB–18a, 20bB, 23aB, 24aB, 25–28
	B	2:1–36
	C	3:1–21
	D	4:1–22
	E	5:1–12
	F	6:1–21
	G	7:1–17
II	A	8:1–22
	B	9:2aBb, 6aB, 7–9, 15–17, 20b–21, 22b–24a, 27
	C	10:1–9, 10aBb–13, 17–27
	D	11:6, 8, 12aBb, 13, 14b, 15aB
	E	12:1–25
	F	13:1–23
	G	14:1–51
	H	15:1–35
III	A	16:1–23
	B	17:1aBb, 4aBb–7a, 10, 12b, 13aAb, 14–16, 18a, 23aB, 25aB, 26–31, 34–36, 38–39, 42–48, 50, 52–54
	C	18:1, 3–4, 6–19, 21–27a, 28–30
	D	19:1–24
	E	20:1–42
	F	21:1–16
	G	22:1–23
	H	23:1–28
	I	24:1–23
	J	25:1–44
	K	26:1–25
	L	27:1–12
	M	28:1–25
	N	29:1–11
	O	30:1–31
	P	31:1b, 4a, 7–13

continued

FIGURE 17 (*cont*)

2 Samuel

IV	A	1:1–27
	B	2:1–32
	C	3:1–39
	D	4:1–12
	E	5:1bB, 2b–3a, 5, 6bB, 8–25
	F	6:1–23
	G	7:1–3, 5b–11, 13, 14b, 15b, 16b, 17aB, 18–29
	H	8:1–18
	I	9:1–13
	J	10:1–19
	K	11:4–13, 21a, 27aBb
	L	12:1–24a, 26–31
V	A	13:2aB, 12aBb–13, 16–18, 19aB, 21–22, 30–39
	B	14:1–33
	C	15:8, 11–12a, 14–16, 18b–37
	D	16:1–23
	E	17:1–29
	F	18:6b–7, 17aB, 18
	G	19:6bB, 9bB, 10–43
VI	A	20:1–26
	B	21:1–22
	C	22:1–51
	D	23:1–39
	E	24:1–25

BOOK EIGHT: KINGS

1 Kings

Part

I	A	1:1b–4, 6, 11–31, 35b–37, 41bA, 45b–48, 50–53
	B	2:1–9, 11b–46a
	C	3:1–28
	D	4:1–20
	E	5:1–32
	F	6:1–38
	G	7:1–51
	H	8:1–66
	I	9:1–28
	J	10:1–29
	K	11:1–25, 27–39

continued

F I G U R E 1 7 (*cont*)

II	A	12:2–3a, 5, 12, 15, 16aB, 18a, 21–24, 30–33
	B	13:1–34
	C	14:1–20, 21b–24, 26b–28
	D	15:1, 3–6, 9, 11–16, 25–34
	E	16:1–34
III	A	17:1–24
	B	18:1–46
	C	19:1–21
	D	20:1–43
	E	21:1–29
	F	22:1–41, 43–44, 47, 52–54

2 Kings

IV	A	1:1–18
	B	2:1–25
	C	3:1–27
	D	4:1–44
	E	5:1–27
	F	6:1–33
	G	7:1–20
	H	8:1–16, 18–19, 22b, 25, 27
V	A	9:1–13, 14b–15, 21bB, 22bB, 25–26, 29–37
	B	10:1–36
	C	11:4b–11, 15–16, 17aBb, 18
	D	12:2aA, 3–17
	E	13:1–25
VI	A	14:1, 3–4, 6–17, 21aB, 22–29
	B	15:1, 3–4, 8–32, 34–35, 37
	C	16:1, 2b–4, 6, 10–19
	D	17:1–41
	E	18:1, 3–4, 6, 8, 9aB, 10aAbA, 14–16, 17bB, 32b–35, 37
	F	19:1–7, 9b–35
	G	20:1–21
VII	A	21:1–26
	B	22:1–20
	C	23:1–37
	D	24:1–20
	E	25:1–30

Figure 17. Letters indicate separate sections and correspond to chapters in the printed Bible.

Abraham, by believing, observed in an exemplary manner. Their history was engineered by promise, blessing, and covenant and it ended with the blessing of Jacob and the deathbed promise by Joseph that their sojourn in Egypt would end.

The individual parts in the first book, like the book itself, are distinguished by clear beginnings and by conclusions that both end the part and link it by anticipation to the next. Each part deals with a separate time, place, person, and sequence of events. The beginnings generally coincide with the beginnings of the Priestly genealogies. The endings are genealogical lists and the stories that they inspired.

The first part is the Deuteronomistic interpretation of the stories of creation. It begins in the beginning and ends with an alternate explanation of the origin of sin in the world and with an alternative to the Priestly genealogy of Adam, which occurs at the beginning of the second part (Gen 4:1–15 and 4:16–26). It includes a geography of the Garden of Eden (2:10–15), etiologies of marriage and of the worship of Yahweh (2:23–24; 4:25–26), a theology of labor and oppression (3:14–21), and editorial sutures that reduce the Adam of the epic to the creature of the Priestly version.[2] The epic removed people from the realm of the Gods. The Priestly writer separated God from the world and time. By dint of redundant records and comments the Deuteronomist began the history of the inhabited world, its institutions, professions and practices, and began to insinuate the ominous subplot of sin and the wrath of God that would gradually overwhelm the world and time.

The second part covers the original and edited versions of the flood. It begins with the Priestly genealogical notice and ends with the curse of Canaan, which anticipates the genealogies and geographies of the following part.[3] The intervening material that the Deuteronomist added is mainly editorial, smoothing out the differences between the epic and its Priestly interpretation, and etiological, explaining the origin of viticulture, limited life spans, and sacrificial rituals.[4] But it also illustrates the Deuteronomist's interest in including data that conflict with the texts commented on and that indicate independent research into the original sources.[5]

The third part is the story of the call of Abraham and his immediate unquestioning obedience to the word of Yahweh. It begins with a revised version of the Priestly genealogy and map of the world,[6] and it ends with an alternate version of the destruction of Sodom and Gomorrah, which the epic recounted in the following part.[7] It situates Abraham in Canaan between the great powers of Egypt and Mesopotamia[8] and illustrates in particular the Historian's ability to write literary adaptations of lists and typical sources[9] and to combine genealogy and geographical detail with historical and theological theory.[10]

The fourth part outlines the theory and practice of the promise to Abraham. It is introduced by a prophecy that links it to the preceding part, and it closes with the search for a wife for Isaac, which anticipates the following part.[11] The story told in this part is fully rounded at the finish, when the servant who was sent and found Rebekah recounts its salient points.[12] The Deuteronomistic materials, with their usual historical and theological bias, are all subordinated to the validation of the prophecy and promise. The prophecy combines covenant rituals and a vision of future history that is recounted in the following books.[13] The story of Sarah and Hagar retells the Elohist version and confirms the vision of Abraham.[14] The intercession of Abraham for the people of Sodom and Gomorrah repeats part of the vision and emphasizes the initial impression that Abraham was a just man.[15] The survival of Lot and his daughters proves the power of the patriarch's intercession.[16] The conflict with the king of Gerar proves that he is a prophet, and the settlement of the conflict gives him access to the southern part of the promised land (Gen 20:7, 17–18; 21:28–33). The averted sacrifice of Isaac is an occasion to renew the promise and to allude to the collateral ancestry of Rebekah (22:14b–18, 20–24). The narrative ends with the promise transferred to Isaac and Rebekah and the next generation.

The fifth part is the story of Jacob and his children. It begins with genealogical and chronological lists and the Priestly genealogies of Isaac and Ishmael,[17] and it ends with other lists and in anticipation of the genealogies of Esau and Jacob in the next part (35:16–26; cf. 36:1–37:1). The explicit point of the story is the fulfillment of the promise to Abraham in the birth of the sons of Israel. The point is made repeatedly by deploying different genres to express the political, social, theological, and religious import of the story. As soon as possible at the beginning of the cycle Isaac is made a surrogate of an exemplary Abraham who observed the law and assured the permanence of the promise, and at every crucial point in the story the paradigm is repeated.[18] The birth of Jacob's children is recounted as part of a typical conflict between rival wives and gains historical credibility in the etiologies of their names.[19] Their independence from their Aramean forebears is assured in the treaty between Jacob and Laban concerning the right of inheritance of their mothers and their own control over Transjordan.[20] Their right to the land promised to Abraham is settled concretely, as his was, by purchasing part of it, and is suggested symbolically by the rite of circumcision, which assured their foothold in the land and proved to be Shechem's undoing (33:19; 34:1–31). The climax of the story, then, is reached at Shechem where Jacob worshiped El, the God of Israel, and acquired uncontested access to the land (33:20; 35:5b).

The sixth part is the story of Joseph. It begins with the genealogies of Esau and Jacob and ends with the revelation to Jacob at Beersheba, which previews the events recounted in the next part (36:1–43; 46:1–7). The Deuteronomistic material consists of genealogies and lists, a story inspired by genealogical and legal interests, and a sinister subplot to the story of Joseph that culminated in his purchase of the land of Egypt for the Pharaoh and the subsequent enslavement of the people.[21]

The last part is the story of Israel in Egypt. It begins with the genealogy of the sons of Israel and ends in anticipation of events recounted in the book of Exodus. Apart from information of ethnographic interest, the Deuteronomistic material consists of genealogies and a prophecy spun from a genealogical list.[22]

The Deuteronomistic edition of the book of Genesis adapts the myths and legends of the earlier versions to the history of Israel conceived from the beginning as a confederation of tribes. Each part is transformed by snippets of information and stories that situate the recounted past in the present perspective of the narrator. All the parts converge on the prophecy and promise to Abraham and diverge again to exemplify their immediate and long-range fulfillment. Around this pivot, the earlier and later parts correspond, the third and fifth bringing one of the patriarchs from the East to the land of Canaan, the second and sixth telling of a distant ancestor who saved their lives in a time of natural disaster, the first and last contrasting Abel and Israel, who were shepherds, with Cain and the Egyptians, who tilled the land. The whole book, in an ongoing history, comes at once to a satisfying close.

EXODUS

The book of Exodus contains the history of Israel at Sinai. It refers back to the patriarchal age and ahead to the time in the wilderness but deals in detail with the law and the covenant and with cultic and ritual arrangements. It begins with a list of the sons of Israel and with an explicit reference to the story of Joseph told in the first book, and it ends with preparations for the ordination of Aaron, which is recounted in the beginning of the third book.

In the epic version Exodus began the story of Moses with his marvelous adventures in Midian, Yahweh's extraordinary victory over the Egyptians at the Sea, and the signing of the covenant on Sinai. In the Priestly version it described the manifestation of the glory of God first in the signs and wonders performed against the Egyptians and then really and permanently in the tabernacle that presaged Israel's possession of the land. In the Elohist version it located the presence and providence of God in observance of the law and fidelity to the guidance of an angel. In the History it was a separate book that established the prophetic, admonitory, and intercessory role of Moses in the humiliation of Egypt, the revelation of the law on Mount Sinai, and the construction and accoutrement of the tent of meeting.

The first part recounts the call of Moses and the resistance that he met from the Egyptians and his own people. It begins with a list of the children of Israel in the generation after Joseph and, in contrast to the freedom and prestige enjoyed by the sons of Jacob, with an account of their condition as state slaves in the construction of store cities (Exodus 1; cf. Genesis 46–50). It ends on a construction site describing how Israel had adapted to slavery and resented the interference of Moses (Exodus 5). Throughout the Deuteronomist gave the original versions a historical cast by including material of genealogical, ethnographic, theological, political, and practical interest. Some of this conflicts with the earlier sources, but most of it is just an interpretation and a rewriting of their material. The History identifies the people as Hebrews, gives details of Hebrew midwifery, and traces the origins of their families.[23] It describes the organization of work gangs, the political role of Moses and Aaron, and the making of bricks (chap. 5). It tries to reconcile the Elohist and epic versions of revelation to Moses in Midian by explaining that the Elohist God of the fathers is really Yahweh the God of Abraham, Isaac, and Jacob (3:15). It relates in great detail how God commissioned Moses as prophet and wonder-worker and gave him an authority tempered only by his reliance on Aaron and the levitical order (4:1–17, 27–31). Throughout it borrows material from the next part,[24] and it ends in anticipation of the plagues (4:18 and chaps. 6–12) and of the Pharaoh's eventual willingness to comply with the exodus.

The second part is the story of the plagues. In the Priestly version the signs and wonders manifested God's judgment on Egypt and brought Yahweh recognition and glory. In the Deuteronomistic version they are plagues that confirm the prophetic authority of Moses, humiliate and destroy the Egyptians, set the Israelites apart as a nation, and make it evident that Yahweh is God. They begin with a summary and restatement of the first part, and they end with the celebration of Passover and a preview of the exodus, which is recounted in the next part (chaps. 6–12).

The third part covers the exodus from Egypt to Sinai (chaps. 13–24). It begins with rituals that memorialize the events narrated in the preceding part, and it ends with other rituals that anticipate the events of the next part.[25] The Deuteronomistic materials are all related to law, liturgy, and the awful unworthiness of the people. At the moment of the exodus the people rebel, but Moses assures them that Yahweh will fight for them; and when he has defeated the Egyptians they together sing the praises of their God (14:11–14; 15:1–18). They rebel again, despite Yahweh's warning, but in the end fulfill the law in the celebration of the sabbath.[26] They rebel once more, but again Yahweh fights for them and Jethro blesses Yahweh and confesses that he is God (chap. 17; 18:6–11). At Sinai they are called a holy nation and a kingdom of priests, but they cannot approach the holy mountain.[27] They receive the Ten Commandments from God who is in heaven and are warned not to worship other Gods or profane the worship of Yahweh (chap. 20).[28] The fidelity that God requires is essentially the exclusion of every other visible God, and in the end Moses reads them his ritual and liturgical version of the covenant, and they, as the twelve tribes of Israel, seal it with the blood of the sacrifice.[29]

The fourth part is the revelation of the model of the tent of meeting on Mount Sinai (chaps. 25–31). In the Priestly version this was the tabernacle where Yahweh would dwell in the midst of his people, but in the Deuteronomistic version it is a movable shrine—fully accoutred with the ark of the covenant, altars, and the regalia of the priests—where Moses alone encountered God. The part begins as the preceding part ended with Moses ascending the mountain of God to receive the tables of the law,[30] and it ends when God has finished speaking to him and gives him the tablets of stone (31:12–18).

The fifth part recounts the rebellion of the people at the mountain of God (chaps. 32–34). It includes the epic version of the covenant and the Elohist version of the defection of the North in a stalwart defense of the decalogue and the peculiar authority of Moses in interpreting the revealed law. It begins, in reference to the beginning of the preceding part, with the people concerned about the length of time that Moses has spent on the mountain, and it ends, in reference to the conclusion of the same part, when Moses comes down from the mountain with the tablets in his hands. The opening story of Aaron and the golden calf is modified to suit the Deuteronomist's perception of prophetic intervention against the calves and cult inaugurated by Jeroboam I.[31] The epic version of the covenant is changed to make it a renewal ceremony for the decalogue (34:1–5, 15–18, 28bB). The intervening debate on the presence of God among the people focuses on the tent of meeting, designed in the preceding part and about to be built in the next, where Moses meets God before relaying to the people his interpretation of the law (chap. 33).[32]

The last part is the actual construction and dedication of the tent of meeting. It is related to the end of the penultimate part by its promulgation of the sabbath law, and ends with cultic installations that are required for the rituals at the beginning of the next book (chaps. 35–40).

The Deuteronomist gave the antecedent writings historical and practical actuality. The tale of Moses' birth and miraculous escape is tempered by the story of brave women who kept the Hebrew children from the Pharaoh. The plagues culminate in the death of the firstborn, for which there were compensatory rituals in Israel. The escape from Egypt is related to ritual and prophecy and to historical conflicts with Moabites, Edomites, Amalekites, Philistines, and Canaanites. The Priestly tabernacle begins to look like the temple of Solomon; rebellions in the wilderness resemble the defection of the northern kingdom; the covenant is the mnemonic decalogue; and the presence of God takes place in observance of the Mosaic law. Everything that was written was true but was written for Israel's instruction.

LEVITICUS 8–11 AND NUMBERS

The third book describes Israel's tribal constitution and religious administration in the wilderness, at Sinai, on their way to the promised land. It begins with the ordination of Aaron according to the instructions that were given in the preceding book and ends in Transjordan, in the plains of Moab by the Jordan at Jericho, where the next book begins. Everything in between is designed to illustrate that Israel exists as an ordered assembly of tribes gathered in the worship of Yahweh.

The first part supposes the construction and dedication of the tent of meeting that was described at the end of the second book and fulfills the commands that Moses received at that time concerning the ordination of Aaron and his sons (Lev 8:1–4; Exod 40:12–15). It contains diverse descriptive and prescriptive material in four exotically linked chapters that give substance, duration, and actuality to the ancient rite (chaps. 8; 9; 10; 11:1–45). The first chapter describes the ordination and ends with Aaron and his sons waiting seven days at the door of the tent of meeting until the ritual is complete. The second chapter begins on the eighth day, describes the rite of atonement that was suggested at the end of the first chapter, and ends when fire came out from Yahweh and consumed their burnt offerings. The third chapter begins with this fire, prescribes elements of the priestly regime, and ends with a discussion between Moses and Aaron on the eating of the sin offering. The last chapter follows suit by describing what may and may not be eaten. The whole part ends, as the next part begins, with a reminiscence of the exodus from Egypt (Lev 11:45; Num 1:1).

The second part begins on the first day of the second month in the second year after the exodus from Egypt, and it ends on the twentieth of the same month, with the people setting out from Sinai.[33] The chapters are arranged concentrically to correspond to the disposition of the wilderness camp that they describe. The first chapter begins on the outer perimeter of the camp with a census of tribal members old enough to go to war, and the last chapter has them setting out in battle array. The second chapter arranges the tribes around the tent of meeting ready to set out, and the second to last chapter explains that the appearance of the tent of meeting determined whether or not they set out. The third and fourth chapters converge on the tent of meeting to list the Levites and their duties in transporting the tent, and the seventh and eighth continue with their tasks when the tent has been pitched. The fifth and sixth chapters move to the center of the camp to list the obligations and privileges of the priests. The whole part leads into the next, which begins and ends with the respective roles of Moses and Aaron at the tent of meeting.

The third part focuses on Israel's rebellion in the wilderness and refusal to take the promised land but surrounds it with other incidents of wrongdoing and complaint that interfered with the proper administration of the camp. The chapters imitate the preceding concentric arrangement, which reflects the imagined organization of the camp. The middle chapter takes place at the altar in the center of the camp and looks ahead to ritual errors in the land and backward to a ritual misdemeanor that occurred in the wilderness. This prospect and retrospect are enclosed by the epic and Priestly narrative of a popular uprising against Moses, which the Deuteronomist embellished with annotations proving that only the guilty were punished. The story of this uprising in turn is enclosed by chapters that deal with complaints against Moses and Aaron. The complete account is enclosed by two other chapters that describe Aaron's presumption and atonement in the vicinity of the tent of meeting, and then by two others that are concerned with guilt and rebellion and the boundaries of the camp. The arrangement of the Deuteronomistic material, therefore, reflects the organization of the camp from its periphery to the central place of sacrifice, but it is also an idealistic reinterpretation of the original history of popular rebellion that it contains.[34]

The fourth part is the history of the vaunted conquest of Transjordan. It begins and ends with incidents in the tent of meeting and is linked both to the preceding story of rebellion and to the following account of a census (Numbers 20–25).[35] The Deuteronomistic material, apart from editorial remarks, consists of historical, geographical, and legendary supplements to the original epic and Priestly narratives.[36] The first and second chapters were a natural pair, containing the Priestly narrative of the rebellion at Meribah, the epic version of Edom's resistance to an invasion by Israel, the death of Aaron for his part in the rebellion, and the epic account of the defeat of the Amorites in an Israelite invasion.[37] The Historian left the first chapter alone but added supplements to both sources in the second chapter: the failed invasion of Edom was matched by total defeat of the Canaanites in Arad (21:1–3); the rebellion at Meribah was the model for a similar rebellion at the borders of Edom;[38] and the defeat of Sihon, king of the Amorites, was the occasion to include other victories in the same vicinity that were attested by legend and popular songs (Num 21:10–20, 25–35). The second and third chapters contained the epic version of Balaam's oracles, to which the Deuteronomist added the legend of Balaam's ass to denigrate and domesticate the purported prophet from the East.[39] The fourth chapter concluded Balaam's oracles, but the Historian added other prophetic oracles like them[40] and a repudiation of the Gods that Balaam supposedly had worshiped (Numbers 25; cf. 31:16). The conquest becomes, in this version, more scientifically based, morally justified, and scarred with undermining serious sin.

The fifth part establishes legal and religious guidelines for the inheritance of the tribes. It begins with a census of the military capabilities of the tribes after their decimation by plague at Baal-peor, and it ends with troops being sent from each tribe to take vengeance on Midian for the affair at Baal-peor. In between it deals with the rights of women to inherit property or to dispose of their inheritance and with the obligation of all to make regular offerings to Yahweh. The entire part, except for the Priestly censure of Moses, is composed of lists, legislation, and allusions to the earlier parts.[41]

The last part summarizes the wilderness era and anticipates the conquest to be recounted in the book of Joshua. It begins and ends with the inheritance of the Transjordanian tribes, follows the itinerary from Egypt to Jericho in the plains of Moab, traces the borders of the land, and lists the names of the men who will oversee its distribution to the Cisjordanian tribes. It has links with the earlier parts and ends with a summary statement binding it to the following book.[42]

The artificial construction of the third book corresponds exactly to its ideal and utopian interpretation. Parts contain disparate materials but align and link them chapter by chapter. The parts themselves follow the concentric pattern the Historian prefers and, though mightily different, unravel and rewind the interpretation. The whole book is a mine of minute information gathered under the glaring light of historical and theological theory.

DEUTERONOMY

The fourth book is the law of Moses. It was composed as a continuation of the history but in the form of a covenant that Yahweh made with Israel in the land of Moab. It incorporates the first part of the sequel to the epic, combines it with an update of the law promulgated in the Elohist's version of the epic, and differs in manner and intensity according to its dependence on or independence of each.

The concentric construction that the Deuteronomist favors is perfectly obvious in the organization of its parts. The first part, linked to the preceding book by evident overtures, redoes the historical background of the covenant by recounting in great detail how the tribes assembled in Transjordan for the conquest of Canaan.[43] The last part, supposing the promulgation of the law that has intervened, continues directly on the first with Moses' final instructions and prophecies prior to the crossing of the Jordan and the conquest of the land.[44] The second part, built on the sequel's preamble to the covenant, introduces the decalogue as the basis of revelation, gives examples of obedience as well as paradigms of defection from the law, urges obedience with a promise of blessing or threat of curse, and previews the history of sin from Sinai to the exile. The second to last part, incorporating the sequel's oath of the covenant, describes the ceremony of Israel's acceptance of the law, defines the law as a matter of life and death, seals the law with an elaborate list of traditional and historical curses, makes provision for the law and the curses to be transported and implanted in the land, and foresees the tragic results of the land's contempt for the decalogue.[45] The third part, concentrating on the sequel's law of centralization, appeals to ritual and religious legislation as a bulwark against defection from the decalogue by neglecting its exhortations and worshiping other Gods.[46] The fourth part redoes elements of the Elohist code to give historical substance to the prescriptive laws of the decalogue.[47] The concentric construction allows the Deuteronomist to include the law and its attendant prophecies under the aegis of history; to argue that the covenant and the decalogue are one; to mark the coincidence of history, law, and prophecy; and to make the nation's choices a predictable matter of life and death.

The first part illustrates the Deuteronomist's interest in scientific history. The sequel's spy narrative is interrupted to recall that, as the Elohist told the story, the judicial system that was still in force had been established by Moses at Horeb. Then the narrative is expanded, as it was in Numbers, to argue that the rebellion in the wilderness was a sin and that, as their failure to capture the hill country indicates, one of the results of sin is abandonment on the day of battle. As a consequence, Israel was forced to take a circuitous route through Transjordan, and, even though the route has already been traveled in Numbers, it becomes an occasion to include other interesting ethnographic, administrative, and theological information. Moab and Ammon are supposedly the descendants of Lot, as the Deuteronomist recounted in Genesis, but they are also the offspring of giants who once inhabited the land. The sinful generation dies to the man and to the day, as Yahweh threatened, but the defeat of Sihon, king of Heshbon, immediately illustrates for the following generation the effective principles of holy war. The defeat of Og remains more or less a mystery, but it follows the pattern of the defeat of Sihon and is a chance to include the geography of the Amorites and Canaanites and to mention a wonderful relic of Og that proves that he was the last of the giants and was soundly defeated. Then the historical evidence is summarized, repointed, and redirected to the future by reviewing the inheritance of the Transjordanian tribes, their appointment as the vanguard of the armies invading Canaan under the leadership of Joshua, and the exclusion of Moses from the promised land for the sin of the people. This is not really news but scientific history probing the origin and causes of things and their paradigmatic effect on what follows.

History is atemporal, with a remote past, an urgent present, and a timeless structure, governed by God, generated by words like prophecy and ideas like law, which together determine the form and substance of the future. In the second part of Deuteronomy such a theory of history is established and illustrated in the preamble to the covenant and the witness to the law.

The first chapter in the second part is linked to the end of the preceding part but actually returns to the beginning of that part to explain the significance of the revelation at Horeb.[48] The essential point is that they saw nothing but only heard Yahweh's voice, and that if they do not listen to that voice they will worship in a foreign land dumb Gods whom they can see but do not know (4:15–24, 25–31). What they have to do is observe the covenant, that is, the Ten Commandments, because it is the acme of creation and the rationale of a history that can be traced from the beginning to their own times (4:9–14, 32–40). This covenant is a source of life and wisdom and sets them apart from the nations, not just theoretically but also physically, as cities of refuge are set apart to save the lives of those whom the law would spare.[49] It is this law, finally, that was given to them by Moses after the conquest of Transjordan and that will let them live in the land that Yahweh has given them (4:1–2, 44–49). The chapter as a whole identifies the law with the decalogue and the covenant and makes it the hinge on which past and future history turn.

The intermediate chapters in the second part delve into the law and the ravages of time. The second chapter includes the decalogue and describes Moses as the recipient of the revelation of the unwritten law. It is tied, like the first, to the beginning of the first part and describes once again what is supposed to have really happened at Horeb.[50] It is also linked by literal repetition to the beginning of the next chapter,[51] where the revelation of the decalogue is presented as the crucial difference between the times of rebellion during the preceding generation and the next generation's potential obedience and enjoyment of the good life in the land (6:16–19, 20–25). But the fifth and sixth chapters go over the same ground again and narrate a different version of the same story (8:1–20 and 9:1–10:11). The sixth chapter returns to Horeb to tell how the people did not listen but made images of visible Gods, and the fifth situates the decalogue between the wilderness, where they were tested, and the coming temptations of the land. All of the chapters correspond and together depict the decalogue as the narrow defile of Israel's historical destiny.

The pivotal chapter in this part separates Israel from the nations of the world and is constructed from the sequel's warning not to make treaties with the inhabitants of the land. The focus of the chapter is the observance of the law. It is motivated by a survey of history from the fathers through the exodus to now, and it is bolstered by blessings like those on the fathers and by curses like those against Egypt. The warning itself lies on the periphery of the chapter, but it is developed into a threat of contamination from the elements of the nations and their Gods who were left in the land.[52]

The last chapter corresponds to the first and brings the second part to a sound conclusion.[53] As Yahweh set his heart on their ancestors, so they are to love him who is God of all Gods and their Lord. As Yahweh's supremacy was demonstrated in events from creation to the present, so his suzerainty is manifested in events from the exodus to his present creative care for the land. As the worship of other Gods would end in the exile, so neglect of Yahweh's commands would end in the loss of the land. As Yahweh was near to them when they called, so he is finally the subject of their praise. The law would ruin those who ignore it, but its observance is ever at hand.

The third part begins like the end of the second and ends, as the second part began, with references to Moses and Horeb.[54] The chapters have the concentric arrangement preferred by the Deuteronomist and are related by their substantial agreement on the importance of the law and of worship at the central sanctuary as a bulwark against the worship of other Gods. The first chapter deals with the law of centralization and the elimination of foreign cults, and the last chapter deals with the rights of the Levites at the central sanctuary, the authority of Moses, and the suppression of alien prophetic practices (12:1–31 and 18:1–22). The second chapter deals with cases of sedition in which a prophet, or townspeople, or another city might be drawn to the worship of other Gods. The second to last deals with similar issues and with the authority of the courts and the king with respect to the law of Moses, and the two are related by their insistence on purging the evil from the people of God (13:1–19 and 17:1–20). The third chapter includes dietary laws and the laws of the annual and triennial tithes; the third to last chapter legislates the annual festivals, and the two correspond in their concern for the poor and the unfortunate who are unable to participate in the celebrations (14:1–29 and 16:1–22). The fourth chapter follows arithmetically on the third with the law of release in the seventh year, and leads into the fifth with the law of firstborn lambs and calves that could be offered as Passover sacrifices (15:1–23). The law is enormously compacted and, issuing from the mouth of the prophet Moses, gives a simple and foreseeable focus to history as it is enacted in the annual and repeatable life of the people.

The fourth part begins with the levitical cities mentioned at the end of the first part, ends with the tranquil possession of the land promised at the beginning of the second part,[55] and legislates the individual basis of the community described in the third part. The laws deal with particular cases in the categories of murder and death, marriage and adultery, theft and oppression, local courts and false witness, and the alienation of persons and property. They are grouped in chapters related concentrically and by the same sort of literal links that account for the order and arrangement of the laws. The first and last chapters deal, under different headings, with accidental death and deliberate murder, with inheritance, with witnesses, and with decisions by the local courts and elders.[56] The second contains the laws of war, and the second to last deals with property and monetary matters, but they are connected by their concern for newlyweds, their property, and actions that might defile the land.[57] The third and the third to last chapters deal with different matters but are both concerned with the treatment of foreigners and slaves.[58] The middle chapter deals with the different situations that arise in the city or in the country and thereby makes the transition between the first three chapters, which deal with towns and their environs, and the last three chapters, which have to do predominantly with the land. The laws deal with disparate situations, but their arrangement is formal, artificial, and argumentative and reflects exactly, in a different genre, the effort of reflection and synthesis that constantly went into the composition of the Deuteronomistic History.

The fifth part is the ceremony ratifying the law (chaps. 26–30).[59] It was written around the sequel's covenant oath and surrounds it with ominous curses that make the ineffectiveness of the covenant a foregone conclusion. The first chapter makes the ceremony an oath of obedience to the law and the culmination of a story that began with their fathers in Egypt. The second chapter prescribes that the law should be transported physically into the land, inscribed in stone, and enforced by ritual blessings and curses. The third chapter lists the blessings and curses attendant on the law, which range from Israel's preeminence among the peoples to its ruin and dispersal among the nations. The fourth chapter repeats the ceremony in its original form as a covenant oath but situates it in a story that extends from the exodus and the wilderness, past the impending conquest, to the ultimate devastation of the land. The last chapter returns to the law as a matter of life and death but sees it now written in a book and inscribed in the minds and hearts of the people.

The last part contains the epilogue to the story of Moses, a prophetic survey of Israel's common history and destiny, and the blessing of Moses on the individual tribes (chaps. 31–34). The first chapter has Moses' farewell as it was recounted by the sequel but fills it out with links to the book of Joshua, with provisions for regular reading of the law, and with Moses' presentiment that the law would not be observed. The second chapter contains the Song of Moses and part of the Priestly conclusion to the life of Moses. The third chapter is the Blessing of Moses on the tribes conceived as an antidote to the dreadful fate of the nation as a whole. The last chapter contains the Priestly vision of the tribes settled in the promised land, the succession of Joshua, and the decalogue epitaph on the prophetic career of Moses.

Deuteronomy recapitulates the history recounted in the books of the Pentateuch and subsumes it under law and prophecy. The law, present by presentiment and insinuation from the beginning, becomes formally and officially the force and moving structure of history as it has been and as it will perpetuate itself. The law of Moses underlies and informs the rest of the Deuteronomist's work and is the substance of the Historian's prophetic speeches and summaries, but it will remain latent until it is rediscovered by Josiah, too late to help Judah and Jerusalem, just in time for Israel, as history is about to begin again in Babylon, in Egypt, and in the promised land.

JOSHUA

The fifth book subsumes the sequel's story of the conquest in a theory of tribal settlement in the land. It is tied to the book of Deuteronomy by the succession of Joshua and is linked to the book of Judges by the notice of his death.[60] As the conquest illustrated the effectiveness of the covenant, so the allotment of the land is an extension of the workings of the law and the teachings of Moses.

The book is divided into three parts. In the first part the people cross the Jordan, learn the lessons of war, and establish the law in the land. In the second part they do battle with the kings and the original inhabitants of the land and take all of it under control. In the third part much of the land remains out of control but is allotted to the individual tribes by Joshua and in accordance with instructions given by Moses. Each of the parts is complete in itself and is attached to the others by summaries.

In the original version of the first part Joshua succeeded Moses, sent scouts to reconnoiter the land, led the people across the Jordan, and achieved exemplary victories at Jericho and Ai (chaps. 1–8*). In the Deuteronomist's version everything takes place much more methodically. In the first chapter Joshua not only succeeds Moses but assumes responsibility for carrying out his instructions and becomes the agent of a conquest that is totally contingent on the observance of the law. In the second chapter Rahab takes time out to relate the looming conquest to Yahweh's victories over Egypt and in Transjordan, and the spies hang around to explain that her escape will take place in accordance with precepts of the law. In the third and fourth chapters the sequel's auspicious crossing of the Jordan is transformed into a triumphal procession in which the ark of the covenant and the law gain a foothold in the land. In the fifth chapter the era of disobedience in the wilderness finally comes to an end in the renewed rite of circumcision and the celebration of Passover. In the sixth chapter the capture of Jericho becomes a ritual victory performed by the ark of the covenant containing the tablets of the law. In the seventh the march of conquest is impeded by violation of the law, and in the eighth, when the guilty have been destroyed, the law is inscribed in the land. All of the chapters are joined by literal or logical links and together locate the law in one of the turning points of history.

In the second part the occupation of the land recounted by the sequel took place quickly by diplomacy and conquest and centered on the capture of Jerusalem.[61] In the Deuteronomist's version it was limited to certain areas, took a long time, and illustrated the effectiveness of the laws of war (Joshua 9–11).[62]

The third part is a Deuteronomistic composition that exposes the conquest as consistent with the national consciousness of the author of the sequel but incompatible with Israel's origins and tribal constitution. The first chapter summarizes the victories recorded in the second part, and the last chapter includes such a summary in an overview of Israel's history from Abraham to the present (chaps. 12; 24; cf. 24:11–13). The second and the second to last chapters contain speeches by Joshua in his old age which outline Israel's option of obeying the law and gradually taking possession of the land, or of worshiping other Gods and suddenly losing it (chaps. 13; 23). The intervening chapters distribute the land and set aside levitical cities and cities of refuge among the tribes but maintain the same strict, logical, interlocking order that gives the History its meaning and incontrovertible force.[63]

The book of Joshua functions as a corrective to the sequel's confidence in the covenant and as an immediate verification of the authority of Moses in promulgating the law. The correction is by diffusion and drift, on the one hand emphasizing the killing that went on in the conquest, on the other noting that many of the enemy were not defeated and that Joshua's particular role was to draw the boundaries of the tribes. The verification is direct and consists in showing that the law was effective if obeyed and destructive if it was not observed, or indirect and consists in witnessing the fulfillment of Moses' commands and promises under his successor and alter ego Joshua. The book of Joshua, in this way, begins the proof of the theory of history that was outlined in the book of Deuteronomy.

JUDGES

The book of Judges creates another era and interval between the arrival in the land and the amalgamation of the tribes under the monarchy, which the author of the sequel narrated. It supposes the relative failure of the invasion relayed by the Deuteronomist in

Joshua,[64] but it also assembles quantities of disparate and sometimes conflicting materials relative to tribal struggles for the land that do not suppose the sequel's theory of the conquest and ultimately make it seem peripheral or redundant. The interval that it creates is character-ized by heroic inspiration and common degradation and represents the seedy side of the ideal assembly described in the book of Numbers and a general refraction of the rebellions it witnessed in the wilderness.

The book has five parts filled with inconsistencies and tensions. The parts span lengthy periods of war and peace but in the overall construction of the book the incidents that they narrate take place in the single generation after Joshua, during the lifetime of Phinehas, son of Eleazar and grandson of Aaron.[65] Each part, besides, is composed of two unequal sets of chapters that view the same place, period, person, or sequence of events from different perspectives. Each part, furthermore, supposedly fulfills the ritual paradigm of danger and distress, divine intervention, heroic deliverance, and the dull defection of the people, but the paradigm is forced on unmalleable material with another or neutral meaning. Each part, again, contains a glimpse of tribal feuds and local disorganization, but together they form a concen-tric circle of pervasive guilt from which there seems to be no respite. The book by indirection illustrates the Deuteronomistic Historian's determination to gather all the available evidence, no matter how irregular, irrational, or inconsequent, and subsume it in an overriding theory of history that in the long run would account for it.

The first part has five chapters, three with particulars of the theory of history and two others that partly illustrate the theory with a repeated example.[66] The theory is presented for its own sake and does not quite match the material: the career of the judge is recounted in legendary detail; the sin of the people is typical and affirmed without adequate illustration; and the evidence is plentiful but unaffected by the theory it is meant to support. The whole part is filled with information on incidents or events that are interpreted differently in the other books,[67] and in the end it becomes clear that the most important point of the part is the theory of history it represents.[68]

The second part is the story of Gideon. With the paradigm of the judges firmly in place the Deuteronomist can elaborate on its various parts. The sin of the people, as declared by an anonymous prophet, is identified as their violation of the decalogue in the worship of Baal and Asherah or the Amorite Gods. The inspiration of the judge is not as peremptory as the first part suggested but turns out to be a solemn and orchestrated affair modeled on the mission of Moses. The inevitable defection of the people is not as stupid and willful as it seemed in the paradigm but is traced to the priestly pretensions or ritual crimes of the judge who once saved them. The story of Gideon is complete in itself, but, in the manner of history, it is immediately complemented by the barely related story of Abimelech illustrating in another time and place the perennial problems of kingship.

In the third part the cycle of sin, oppression, lament, and salvation is peripheral to the legend of Jephthah and only obliquely relevant to the history of the judges who preceded and followed him.[69] He was a tribal hero whose inspired leadership and ability to recite the history of Israel in defense of its legal title to the land[70] made him, in the Historian's eyes, a model judge, who could salvage the careers of undistinguished and all-but-unremembered local chiefs. In the fourth part the legend of Samson the judge illustrates the prevailing historical theory, but it is combined with the story of Samson the nazirite, which has proleptic and paradigmatic force.[71] The fifth part, similarly, combines a section on the migration of Dan with a section on the tribal assemblies in Bethel and Mizpah but uses this evidence for the history of the tribes to foreshadow the rise and the decline of the monarchy in Israel (chaps. 17–18; 19–21).

The historical theory, it is evident, is a way of organizing and rationalizing material on the prehistory of the tribes and of important places and localities in the land without attempting to synthesize it or remove its discrepancies. All of the tribes are mentioned in turn or together. All of the holy and profane places that were important in the patriarchal history or that will be in the history of the prophets and kings are situated politically or at least mentioned in passing. War in this heroic age is a way of life, and all the traditional or perennial enemies pass in review. The period of the judges is portrayed as a distant primitive time, but all the institutions of civilized society are present in nuce and about to appear on the historical scene. It is a transitional period whose pieces are part of the past or programmatic for the future, and the theory absorbs them but does not attempt to reduce or resolve them.

SAMUEL

The seventh book, Samuel, is the history of the monarchy from Samuel and Saul to its high point in the reign of David. It has six parts, each characterized by narrative, enclosure, and allusion to the preceding books, and each with its theoretical point put in speeches, summaries, and asides by one of the main characters or the narrator. In it the period of the judges comes to a close and, in accordance with the program begun in the book of Exodus, the ark and the tent of meeting arrive in Jerusalem; the priestly and prophetic underpinnings of the monarchy are established; the tribes of Joseph and Judah are united; and the whole land at last is secure in the hands of David.

The first part concludes the period of the judges with the careers of Eli and Samuel. The first chapter, incorporating the sequel's story of the dedication of Samuel at Shiloh, and the last, describing his function as judge at other sanctuaries in the North, enclose another story about the family of Eli, the ark of the covenant, and the hereditary priesthood at Shiloh. This story, which includes Samuel in his other roles of prophet and priest par excellence, predicts the end of this priestly line, which traced its ancestry to Moses. It naturally comes to a close with the death of Eli and his sons, when the ark before which they served leaves Shiloh and, after a circuitous route through the cities of Philistia, arrives in the South and is taken in charge by the Levites. The enveloping story is tied especially to the book of Judges, but the story of Eli and the peregrinations of the ark has significant links backward to the book of Exodus and forward to other parts of Samuel and Kings.[72] The critical comments that situate both stories in the ongoing history are made in the Song of Hannah and in the predictions of prophets and priests.[73]

The second part is the story of Saul and the beginning of Israelite kingship. It is told in two sections, one introduced by the Deuteronomistic critique of the monarchy and culminating in the coronation of Saul at Gilgal (1 Samuel 8–11), the other introduced by a summary of the history of the monarchy and culminating in his reprobation at Gilgal (chaps. 12–15).[74] Each section encloses a variant account that does not quite agree with the enveloping interpretation. The first section incorporates the sequel's story of Saul's chance meeting with Samuel as well as the Deuteronomistic comments that allude to his priestly and prophetic status and make him king by divine decree.[75] The second section encloses a chronicle of his reign and a mostly positive evaluation of his actions.[76] Both sections refer to earlier books, and each has an editorial aside in which the narrator and commentator collide.[77] The entire part assembles information and opinions on a particular period in the history of Israel and relates them to the theory and the ongoing interpretation of history proposed by the Deuteronomist.

The third part is the story of David's rise to power. It uses the elements of the original story of Saul's heroic stand against the Philistines as a framework for a much different story about his conflict with David.[78] In this story the historical point is made by reduplicating some of the incidents and by dotting the others with conversations that analyze and preview the plot.[79] When all is said and done the Deuteronomist leaves it open to question, since it makes no difference to the immanent and unfolding plan of history,[80] whether David was a brigand, or a traitor, or loyal to Saul and a victim of his madness.[81]

The fourth part continues the third[82] with the story of David's accession to the throne. It includes the sequel's story of the amazing origins of the Davidic dynasty in a chronicle of the military and political schemes surrounding its foundation. It focuses on the dynastic promise but combines it with the story of the ark, changes it into a promise of Yahweh's fidelity to his people, and makes the Davidic king the lieutenant and vassal of the God of Israel (2 Samuel 6–7). In this revised version the inauguration of the Davidic dynasty is a turning point in the history of Israel, the goal of the exodus and the fulfillment of the promise of the land, but the Deuteronomist, as usual, is careful to surround the theory with the elements of its interpretation. Chapters 5 and 8, which surround this center of interest, describe in a more mundane manner the wars and diplomacy that established the kingdom of Israel in David's hands.[83] Chapters 4 and 9 deal with Ishbosheth and Mephibosheth and the mysterious circumstances surrounding the decline of the house of Saul.[84] Chapters 2 and 3 deal with the wars between the house of Saul and the house of David, and Chapters 10 and 11 chronicle the wars that brought all the land under David's control.[85] The first chapter protests David's innocence in the matter of Saul's death, but the last insists on his guilt in the affair of Uriah the Hittite. All together they reflect the Deuteronomistic theory that history mirrors or parodies and finally reveals a timeless divine plan.[86]

The fifth part is the story of the revolt of Absalom and the growing ascendancy of Judah over Israel. The plot was determined by the sequel's version of the revolt, but in the Deuteronomistic account it is adorned with the subplot of the repudiation of the descendants of Saul.[87] The historical point of the story and its place in the development of the Deuteronomist's interpretation is strung along the themes of knowledge, the wise counselor, and the prevenient wisdom of God. It was bad advice that got Amnon into trouble. It was shrewd and patient plotting that let Absalom take revenge. It was Joab who planned Absalom's return from Geshur, a wise woman from Tekoa who was instrumental in altering the course of events, and David in his incomparable wisdom and knowledge and discernment who did it. Absalom conspired against David, stole the hearts of the people, and relied on the advice of Ahithophel. David prayed that Yahweh would undermine Ahithophel's advice but, leaving nothing to chance, left spies and a contrary counselor in Jerusalem. Although the advice that Ahithophel gave was good and like consulting the oracle of God, God overturned it to bring evil on Absalom and the counsel of Hushai prevailed. Wisdom, in the Historian's view, may be unpredictable, but history proceeds according to plan.

The last part reaffirms this point in uncovering some of the hidden forces of history. Its focus is the psalm that David sang when Yahweh saved him from the hand of Saul and all his enemies, and the surrounding chapters illustrate what this might mean. The first chapter (chap. 20), in continuation of the preceding part, tells about the revolt of Sheba and the traditional wisdom of a woman of Abel, whose counsel saved the day; an appendix to the chapter lists the officials in David's court. The second chapter (chap. 21) traces the famine that plagued the land to a crime that Saul committed against the Gibeonites and that is expiated by the execution of his children; an appendix to the chapter lists battles against the Philistine giants and, in a typical Deuteronomistic concern for historical accuracy, records an alternate version of the battle of David and Goliath. The third chapter (chap. 22) is a stylized review of David's career that attributes his success to the concomitant care of Yahweh. The fourth chapter (chap. 23) rephrases this point in terms of the covenant that Yahweh made with the house of David; an appendix lists the names of David's warriors and other battles with the Philistines that were won with the help of God. The last chapter (chap. 24) is the story of David's foolishness in taking a census, the choice that he had in determining the destiny of the nation, and the plague that was averted by prayer and sacrifice. Each of the surrounding chapters deals with human effects on history and contrasts with the center, which sees history as an effect of divine law.[88]

The book of Samuel is filled with information and opinions on the final settlement of the land by the conquests in the time of David. The information is carefully sorted and arranged, and the opinions or traditions are left without reconciliation. The obvious and overriding emphasis of the book is on the Historian's interpretation. This is set out fairly clearly in conversations and more systematically in speeches and develops perceptibly from part to part. In sum and by severe reduction it consists in the conviction that history takes place in accordance with the word of Yahweh in its spoken and written form and every effort is made to bring this word to light.

KINGS

The last book recounts the aftermath of David's reign. It has seven parts with information on the kingdoms of Israel and Judah from the founding of the temple in the time of Solomon to the destruction of the temple in the reign of Zedekiah. The theoretical framework for the historical information is supplied by a regular succession of prophets and the establishment of a prophetic tradition.

The first part contains the annals of the reign of Solomon. It is connected loosely to the end of the preceding book and more explicitly to its earlier parts. The narrative thread magnifies Solomon in the manner of famous potentates but, as usual in the History, contains the materials for its own undoing.[89] The first two chapters contain the conspiracy of Adonijah, the coronation of Solomon, David's final instructions, and the administrative purge that established the kingdom in Solomon's hands. The last two chapters (chaps. 10–11) contain the queen of Sheba's congratulations, a list of the dignitaries and tribute that Solomon received, the fact that he did not heed David's instructions but worshiped other Gods, conspiracies in Edom, Aram, and Israel, and the prophetic division of his kingdom.[90] Chapters 3 and 4 mention his marriage to the Pharaoh's daughter, note that the temple had not been built, and describe his inaugural vision at Gibeon and the wisdom and providence with which he governed all Israel. Chapters 8 and 9 mention the Pharaoh's daughter, explain the labor gangs recruited for the construction of the temple and public buildings, and include portents and ominous warnings in his prayers at the dedication of the temple and in his second vision at Gibeon. The other chapters are paired in the same way and cover the construction of the temple, the palace, and the administrative offices of the kingdom. All together the chapters present Solomon as the climax and apogee of the kingdom and the ambiguous symbol of its gradual decline.

The second part (1 Kings 12–16) is the chronicle of the kingdom from the revolt of Jeroboam to the accession of Omri and Ahab. It is tied to the first part as a fulfillment of the oracle of Ahijah and is linked to the next in anticipation of the annals of Ahab.[91] It refers back to Joshua's curse against Jericho and forward to the fall of Samaria and the reign of Josiah and interprets political and religious events as repercussions of the sin of Jeroboam and as fulfillments of consistent prophetic condemnation.[93] The part ends as it began, with Ahab surpassing Jeroboam as an exemplar of ongoing evil.[93]

The third part (1 Kings 17–22) mixes the annals of Ahab with the legends of Elijah the Tishbite. The first three chapters present Elijah as a true prophet, a prophet of the true God, succeeded by Elisha and reliving the precedents set by Moses.[94] The last three chapters are their mirror image and depict the workings of prophecy in the wars and private affairs of Ahab and a typical king of Israel.[95] In the first chapters the true prophets are persecuted but still prevail, and in the latter chapters the prophets, true or false, are sent by Yahweh to criticize or to encourage and to bring good or evil on the king. In the opening chapters the prophets of Baal are executed, but in the closing chapters the king who violated the law of Yahweh repents and the true prophecy against him is delayed to a later generation while the evil word of the lying prophets takes immediate effect. All together the part reflects the Deuteronomist's interest in presenting all the evidence for the issue at hand and allows that the witness of prophecy, on which the structure and direction of history depend, is ambiguous when it is not checked by the prophetic tradition and the criterion of obedience to the law.[96]

The fourth part (2 Kings 1–8), related to both sections of the third and transitional to the fifth, demonstrates in the career of Elisha that Yahweh is God and manipulates the destiny of nations.[97] The first two chapters[98] conclude the career of Elijah by recounting the wonders that Yahweh performed against the Baal of Ekron and by describing the transmission of the prophetic spirit to Elisha in the symbolism of the succession from Moses to Joshua.[99] The next two chapters illustrate the power of the prophetic tradition in the miracles of Elijah that Elisha repeats and in the victory that he, unlike the lying prophets, can perform (2 Kings 3–4; cf. 1 Kings 17; 22). The third pair is ostensibly about the Aramean wars but is actually about the hidden force and universal dominion of Yahweh that is manifested in the miracles that his prophets perform.[100] The fourth pair (2 Kgs 6:24–8:29) is about the wars with Ben-hadad of Damascus but concludes with the anointing of Hazael and a vision of Aramean domination, which will be described in the next part. The fantastic framework for the historical narratives dissolves at the end as the part returns to the chronicles of the kings.[101] But throughout it has proved that the secret things that Yahweh does among the nations are revealed to his servants the prophets.

The fifth part (2 Kings 9–13) is the history of the Aramean wars.[102] It incorporates the sequel's narrative of the revolt of Jehu and the critical period in Judean history when Athaliah threatened the succession of the Davidic dynasty, but it tells a different story of cleansing and renewal in both kingdoms. The first chapter (chap. 9), in its original version, recounted Jehu's assassination of the kings of Israel and Judah that put an end to the alliance between the two kingdoms and led to no end of trouble. In its revised version it recounts an important military coup during the Aramean wars and the beginning of the purge of the house of Ahab, which had been announced by

Elijah and seconded by Elisha.[103] The last chapter (chap. 13) supposes that the purge is complete, records the death of Elisha and Hazael, and puts an end to Aramean domination; but it strikes an ominous chord for the future by balancing Yahweh's fidelity to the covenant with Abraham against Israel's persistence in the sin of Jeroboam.[104] The second chapter (chap. 10) tells of Jehu's purge of the prophets and cult of Baal during the Aramean wars. The fourth (chap. 12) is like it in describing Jehoiada's restoration of the temple in Jerusalem.[105] The middle chapter (chap. 11) is the sequel's account of the rescue and coronation of Jehoash with editorial comments by the Deuteronomist that integrate it into the religious perspective of the part. Throughout the chapters cleansing and renovation are crisscrossed by oppression and the sins of the past in a grim duel resolved at the end of the History when the reform of Josiah was unable to overcome the effect of the sin of Manasseh.

The sixth part (2 Kings 14–20) is the story of the decline and fall of the North and of the respite granted to Judah. It has seven chapters, three on the Assyrian invasions of the North, one on the Deuteronomistic explanation of history, and three on the Assyrian and Babylonian invasions of the South. It is a history of conspiracy within the kingdoms and of war without, the North laboring under the sin of Jeroboam, the South except for Ahaz blessed with good kings, both temporarily reprieved, both destined to be destroyed. The evidence on enemy aggression is plentiful. The theory of sin and perdition prevails.[106]

The last part (2 Kings 21–25) is the history of the dying days of Judah and Jerusalem. It begins with the sin of Manasseh, moves to repairs to the temple, focuses on the reform of Josiah, returns to the sin of Manasseh, and ends with the ruin of the temple.[107] The wages of sin are death, and the Deuteronomistic theory of history wins the day. The book of the law that underlay and determined the forces of history surfaces at last; the covenant that framed and motivated the law is observed; but no remedy can be found for its perennial neglect. All of the evidence is there, the politics and the shame of it all, but it is only history and the law that endure.[108] What it proves is all that Judah had to hear, that the God of Israel is God and his word is law.

The seven parts in this book are aligned in an explanatory and argumentative pattern that assembles the evidence, comes to a climax, and then reviews the evidence in inverse order in light of the accumulated insight. The first part is about the glorious reign of Solomon and the building of the temple, but it ends with Solomon's defection and Yahweh's warning to him at Gibeon that worshiping other Gods as he did would lead to the destruction of the temple. The last part focuses

on the pious reign of Josiah and his attempt to undo the sins of
Solomon and Manasseh and ends with the pillage and destruction of
the temple. The second part is about the division of the Davidic
kingdom and the typical sin of Jeroboam, which was condemned by
the prophets from generation to generation, and the second-to-last part
attributes the fall of the northern kingdom and the impending exile of
Judah to the typical sin of Jeroboam and to persistent neglect of the
warnings of the prophets. The third part is about Elijah and Ahab and
the worship of Baal, and the third-to-last part is about Elisha and Jehu
and the purge of the house of Ahab and the cult of Baal. The argument
formulated in the middle part is that Yahweh is God, as the law attests,
and is active through the succession of prophets in the creation and
destruction of kingdoms. The ruin of his own people is the ultimate
proof of the truth and power of his word.

CONCLUSION

The eight books in the Deuteronomistic History trace the eras of the
world from creation and the beginning of life in a garden somewhere
between Egypt and Mesopotamia to the dispersal of Israel and Judah
in Egypt, Assyria, and Babylon. The conclusion for those who read
and understood the history was not the end but the beginning. The
past was ruined by sin and disobedience to the law, but history
remained the form of the future.

The Deuteronomist wrote for the people's instruction. There was
much that they knew and believed but also a lot of research, interpretation, theory, and programs for the future. The History was comprehensive, accurate, and demanding, but it allowed Israel to situate itself
in the world and to extricate itself from the nations where it was
dispersed.

Language and Style

The Deuteronomist incorporated the earlier histories into a history of
the world. In editing, commenting on, and interpreting their texts the
Historian imitated their language and style, generally preserving their
individuality, sometimes assimilating one to the other. In composing
original texts these archaizing tendencies were maintained and gave the
Deuteronomistic material the appearance of diversity, complexity, and
antiquity beyond the range and capabilities of an individual author.
The histories and their imitations, furthermore, are distributed from

book to book so that the language and style of the History vary from era to era. The history of the world, in effect, seems to benefit from the wisdom of the ages.

The principal genres of the Deuteronomist are history, law, and prophecy. Each appears in various forms, and each is sometimes combined with one or both of the others. All are subordinated to the historiographic and educational aims of the writer.

Prophecy includes forms derived from or appropriate to the activities of individuals and institutions that were associated or contrasted with traditional Mosaic prophecy.[109] Among these the most important are visions and dreams; rites of fertility and war; magic, charms, and divination; and necromancy, oracles, sayings, and taunt songs. They are woven or spun into stories and legends, historical incidents, and legal wranglings. They occur in every era from the patriarchs to the kings and, being characterized by retrospects, interpretations of the present, and predictions, fill the History with the sense of accumulation and living tradition.

Law includes various types of legislation, codification, and related forms of argumentation. It is represented in stories made up from legal precedents, in laws formulated on the basis of earlier stories,[110] and in historical narratives consisting mostly of sequential commands and their detailed execution. It comprises ritual, civil, religious, political, and administrative kinds and is promulgated and enforced, in the Deuteronomist's perspective, by prophets, priests, and kings. It is a reflection of the order of the world and, being present from the start, gives the History its logical cohesion.

History comprises all the narrative and descriptive forms that situate events on a consecutive or chronological continuum. There is the epic manner of episodes and incidents in the life of a hero, or the Priestly interest in genealogies and lists and analytical chronologies, or the Elohist's liking for lessons, or the sequel's reliance on speeches, persuasion, and fantasy. The Deuteronomist kept them all and added political, administrative, and scribal genres such as annals, chronicles, covenants, and catalogs, as well as the personal, biographical, and dramatic genres introduced by the prophets. The forms are often mixed, and every book or part of the History is characterized by its clever combination of kinds.

The Deuteronomist's language is predominantly imaginative and abstract. The abstraction is evident in a predilection for models and types of persons and circumstances and for situations, scenes, or statements that can be repeated from time to time with little variation. It is also expressed in summaries of chapters, parts, or books; in résumés and introductions that are unraveled as the narrative proceeds; and in parentheses, interruptions, and asides that mark the point or the pertinence of the material. The imagination is evident in favorite images, themes, and motifs and especially in monologues, speeches, and conversations that combine vivid depiction and astute observation. It is mostly visual and auditory and is especially defined in the description of natural circumstances, military matters, and personal— either antagonistic or amorous—relations.

The language and style of the Deuteronomist are determined by a search for historical accuracy, detail, and depth. Everything is seen from as many angles as possible, related to other similar or dissimilar things, and traced to its causes. Everyone is given a chance to be good or bad, strong or weak or inadequate, human or divine but imperfect. The fine line between the reconstruction of history and its fabrication is always maintained by including a different version, the opposite evidence, and the unassimilated facts. The force of imagination is constrained by the clarity and logic of ideas and argument. The official or traditional position is often set against its contemporary interest or interpretation; the vulgar and the arcane collide; the world and its true meaning are not ever reconciled. The Deuteronomistic History, it appears, is the past as it was and as it might be envisaged.

THE PROPHETIC PERSPECTIVE

Genesis

In Genesis the prophetic mode begins among the legends of creation. Prophecy was already present as incantation, vision, and incubation in the epic cycles of Abraham, Isaac, and Jacob;[111] as apparition in the Priestly document (Genesis 17; 35:9–15); and as angelic mediation and the interpretation of dreams in the Elohist story of Joseph (37:5–11; 40:1–41:45).[112] But it was extended by the Deuteronomist to the earliest times and was emphasized in all parts of the book. In the account of creation Yahweh God, in the style of a soothsayer or sorcerer, utters a curse against the snake, the woman, and the man, and its effects are felt immediately in the antagonisms of Cain and Abel and Lamech.[113] In the following story of the flood a spell is cast upon the Nephilim, and a curse is hurled at Canaan to situate the story on the historical course defined by the Deuteronomist.[114] In the beginning of the Abraham cycle, in the cultic context of offerings and tithes, Melchizedek pronounces a blessing on Abraham that interrupts the story of his war with the kings of the East but integrates it into the rest of the cycle.[115] The next part begins with Abraham's prophetic vision, situated in a ritual and magical context, which both preempts the Priestly covenant with Abraham and anticipates and interprets all the subsequent history of Israel.[116] This vision systematized, as elements of the covenant with Abraham, the Deuteronomistic promises of descendants and possession of the land, and these are renewed throughout the histories of Isaac and Jacob to keep their stories in line with the prophecy.[117] In the story of Joseph the hero's abilities are extended beyond the interpretation of dreams to include divination and the detection of crimes in a subplot that gives economic and historical substance to the largely mythical or ritual dimensions of the epic and Elohist narratives (44:1–17). At the end of the book Jacob blesses his children with invocations that recall incidents recounted earlier in the book or with charms that provide for the future (chap. 49). The prophetic mode, throughout the book, assimilates one incident to another, relates members of the family of Abraham, Isaac, and Jacob to each other, anticipates the course of events, and makes history the outcome and effigy of their fateful deeds and decisions.

Exodus

The book of Exodus begins to create the image of the Mosaic prophet — not quite distinguishable from the Levites, disdainful of monarchical authority, a spokesperson for the people, advocate of justice and the law, the immediate representative of God, in touch with magic and the mysteries of life and death. In each part the prophet is predominant, elements of prophecy abound, and prophetic forms and conventions give shape to the text.

The first part is built on the epic and Elohist apparitions of God to Moses but ignores their Midianite setting and follows the Priestly writer in supposing that Moses is in Egypt.[118] It takes their relatively simple narrative of oppression, petition, and promised salvation and expands it into a formal confirmation of Moses' prophetic commission. At first Moses is designated the emissary of Yahweh, as the sources already explained, but he is sent to the elders of Israel as the Historian's theory of local government required, rather than to Pharaoh or directly to the people as the tradition maintained. Moses objects that he will be unable to convince the Pharaoh, but Yahweh patiently explains to him the Deuteronomistic theory of the prophetic word. He objects again that the people will not believe him, but he is endowed with magical powers, immediately modeled in paradigmatic examples,[119] which ultimately persuade them to believe. His objective as wizard and prophet is to bring the people to their place of worship in the wilderness, but the last chapter shows him unsuccessful in his dealings with the Egyptian court and resented by his own people; the completion of the project is left to the later parts. The Deuteronomist added political and social realism to the sources but essentially repeated and rephrased them to show that prophets have a place in popular government and that the word of God they speak has immediate power and permanent effect.

In the second part the book of Priestly signs and wonders is subsumed in demonstrations of prophetic power culminating in the celebration of Passover but also associated, as the Deuteronomist warns, with the death or dedication of firstborn sons.[120] In the Priestly version the plagues take place in commands that are obeyed by Moses and that become progressively more difficult and eventually impossible for the Egyptian magicians to imitate.[121] In the Deuteronomistic version the plagues are preceded by prophetic warnings and followed by repentance and prophetic intercession, until Pharaoh finally refuses to accede to the cultic schedule that Moses announced and the firstborn children of the Egyptians are executed.[122] History, in this version, is governed by prophecy and is recapitulated in the Passover festival, which reflects and reenacts it. The dark side of prophecy is magic and is associated with the sacrifice of children.

In the third part legislation and the revelation of the decalogue predominate, but Moses continues to perform magic and mantic functions that give the law its prophetic dimension. In the Priestly version Miriam the prophet sang the Song of the Sea, but in the Deuteronomistic version it is sung by Moses and, in true Mosaic fashion, it recapitulates the past and predicts the course of history, not just for their own sakes but to prove that Yahweh is God and king of the world.[123] In the Priestly version Yahweh responds directly to the complaints of the people by producing the manna, but in the Deuteronomistic version the prophetic authority of Moses is maintained by a miracle at Horeb and by a marvelous and representative victory over Amalek.[124] In the Priestly version Moses ascends into a cloud concealing the glory of God, but in the Deuteronomistic version he performs an exorcism and reads from the Book of the Covenant before he and the elders of Israel see God in his habitation in heaven.[125] The indications are slight but persistent that as law originated in prophecy so prophecy is checked by the law.[126]

In the fourth and sixth parts attention is paid to the tent of meeting, where Moses received his instructions from God, and in the fifth part his role as prophet is situated among alternative theories of government.

In effect, the law becomes the structure and direction of history through prophetic proclamation.[127]

Leviticus 8–11 and Numbers

In the third book, Leviticus 8–11 and Numbers, the Historian explores expressions of prophecy and the prophetic tradition and makes a clear distinction between prophets and priests. Most of the book is given over to administrative rules and regulations, but the central part, incorporating the narrative of rebellion in the wilderness, is introduced by two models of Mosaic authority. The first instance is a variant of the earlier Priestly account of the manna and is also composed of a paradigm and elaboration. The paradigm (Num 11:1–3) presents a typical scene of popular disgruntlement and divine exasperation, in which Moses mediates between God and the people and resolves the ugly situation. The following account of the manna uses the same form but is more elaborate (Num 11:4–35). There is the usual public outcry, a drastic reaction by Yahweh, and an attempt at reconciliation by Moses; but Moses is taxed beyond his patience and appeals to Yahweh for help in governing the people. In response Yahweh chooses seventy elders to assist him, inspires them with the spirit that has been given to Moses, and makes them prophets for a moment and no longer. In typically Deuteronomistic fashion, just when the lesson of government seems clear, prophecy flares up in the camp, under the influence of Yahweh's spirit—but not at the tent of meeting or through the mediation of Moses. The discrepancy is explained in the next incident when Aaron and Miriam pretend to be prophets and Yahweh appears at the tent of meeting to explain the difference between ordinary prophets, who have visions and dreams, and Moses, to whom the word of Yahweh is entrusted (Numbers 12). The scene is programmatic, and the rest of the part defines the hierarchy of spiritual government with the subjection of the Levites to Aaron and the submission of Aaron to Moses.

Deuteronomy, Joshua, and Judges

Deuteronomy, therefore, presents Moses as the prophet who proclaims the law and outlaws variant forms of prophecy that do not conform to its demands.[128] Joshua makes its hero a replica of Moses, entrusted with the law, endowed with visions and magical powers, and responsible for the history of the people.[129] Judges fits history into a scheme of sin and salvation that is manipulated at key points by angelic or prophetic messengers who rehearse the lessons of the Deuteronomic law.[130]

Samuel

In Samuel it is prophets of the Deuteronomic school versed in the law who have a grasp of history and who are instrumental in its development. In the first half of the book the prophet Samuel is deputed to inaugurate the monarchy under Saul and, when this turns out to be a mistake, to anoint David the viceroy of Yahweh in Israel. Each prophecy takes place and is confirmed both by signs and wonders and in a meticulous narrative. The first step toward kingship is the termination of the era of the judges. This takes place in an anonymous prophecy to Eli about the end of his line and the rise of a priestly family in the reign of David (1 Sam 2:27–36). The prophecy is confirmed both immediately and gradually as the story progresses. In the following story Eli and his sons die and the people are delivered from their enemies, not by a judge but in a prophetic liturgy at Mizpah (1 Samuel 4; 7). In the narrative of David's rise to power, Abiathar at first seems to be the obvious choice to fulfill the prophecy, but he begins to share the priesthood with Zadok and in the end it is the deposition of Abiathar and the choice of Zadok that fulfills the prophecy to Eli.[131] The next step is the choice of Saul and his gradual elimination, one taking place in a prophecy that is confirmed by signs and wonders, the other in a prophecy that the narrative unravels.[132] The last step is the choice of David. It begins with his anointing and prophetic designation, immediately confirmed by his victory over Goliath and Saul's affliction by an evil spirit; climaxes in the oracle of Nathan, to which all of the intervening narrative constantly alludes; and culminates in the predicted accession of Solomon.[133] The prophets decry violations of ritual and religious laws, but they all understand history; and history unfolds in accordance with their words.[134]

Kings

In Kings, history is under the cloud of disobedience to the Deuteronomic law, and the prophets intervene to criticize and to condemn. The reign of Solomon fulfills the promise to David, and unmediated visions confirm that his kingdom and the temple are founded on observance of the law. But when he violates the law by worshiping other Gods, it is the prophet Ahijah who announces the division of the kingdom. (1 Kings 1–11; esp. chaps. 3; 9; 11). Ahijah, another prophet from Judah, and Jehu all conspire against the northern kingdom for the persistent sin of Jeroboam (1 Kings 12–16). Elijah and Elisha work wonders for the people in Israel and in Phoenicia but announce judgment against kings and dynasties who fail to observe the decalogue (1 Kings 17–22;

2 Kings 1–13). Elisha, Micaiah, and anonymous prophets sometimes help and sometimes hinder the kings in their wars, but all together illustrate the power and unpredictability of the word of God in world affairs (1 Kings 17–22; 2 Kings 1–8). When a king observes the law it is reported,[135] but sin and prophetic condemnation traverse the noblest reigns. Hezekiah received some support from Isaiah but is considered somehow responsible for the exile (2 Kings 18–20). Josiah did his best but could not even save himself (2 Kgs 22:18–20; 23:28–30), and the history of Israel comes to the dreadful end that all the prophets predicted (2 Kings 17; 24:2–4, 20).

Prophecy had chthonic, demonic, and eccentric aspects, and the Deuteronomist was not uncritical in projecting it onto the course of history. It was a literary fact and a force that the Historian had to consider in presenting an exhaustive and accurate account of legislative reform and political disaster. Prophecy begins as a primitive resonance with ritual and vital cycles. It assumes an archetypal quality as the word that takes effect. It becomes a literary fixture that organizes the theological significance of otherwise neutral, plain, or inexplicable historical series. Like the prophets themselves it is against the government, opposed to the priesthood, and set on the law; but it is an ambiguous witness, unruly, unflattering, and ultimately right.

THE LEGAL SYSTEM

The Deuteronomist regularly alludes to laws, customs, and precedents, to their origins, the reasons for observing them, and the effects of ignoring them. The History attempts to persuade with moralizing stories, debates, and arguments that combine evidence, principles of interpretation, and motives for action or belief. A law can be largely a survey of history, and history can be little more than a concatenation of commands and their execution. The laws are formulated differently for different times, but by the end of the life of Moses the law is codified and conceptualized, written, latent, abstract, a totality summarized in the decalogue or in its shorthand exclusion of any God but Yahweh.

Genesis

The Deuteronomistic History supposes that the law was present in its totality from the start. It refers to the law and to crimes that contravene it; it mentions precedents, customs, and decrees; and it relates stories and anecdotes that suppose the various types of law and legal procedures and the principles of fundamental justice. In the epic Yahweh

made woman a companion and an equal of man, but in the Deuteronomistic version the man and woman get married (Gen 2:23b–24). In
the epic, the man and woman eat the fruit of the forbidden tree and
risk becoming like God, but the Historian's version dwells on the
effects of disobedience (3:14–19). In the story of Cain and Abel there
are two related judicial procedures. In the first Cain is disappointed
that his offering was not accepted; Yahweh questions him and in his
decision explains that Cain's options are to do good and be accepted
by Yahweh or not to do good and become a prey to sin (4:1–7). In the
second instance, Cain murders Abel; Yahweh makes inquiries to be
certain of his guilt, passes judgment, and mitigates the sentence when
Cain persuades him it is too severe (4:8–15). In the epic the sons of
God marry the daughters of men and their offspring are the heroes of
old, but in the Deuteronomistic version Yahweh intervenes with a
decree reducing them to human dimensions (6:3–4aA). In the Deuteronomistic flood story Noah can distinguish between clean and unclean
animals, and the subplot of acceptable sacrifice proceeds through a
series of commands and their accomplishment (7:16–3, 5–6, 8–9, 12,
22, 23*; 8:7, 20–22). The covenant with Noah and creation is changed
by a decree that allows living things to be eaten, but the rule that they
cannot be eaten with their blood is supported by arguing that the blood
is life and by appealing to the example of Cain and Abel (9:2–6). The
narrative link between the genealogy of Noah, the etiology of wine,
and the history of the world is the legend that Canaan sinned against
some unwritten law and was cursed (9:18–27). Abraham offered tithes
to Melchizedek and was familiar with the rules governing the distribution of the spoils of battle (14:20–24).[136] Because he believed, Abraham
is considered a just man, is credited with obedience and with observance of Yahweh's precepts, commands, statutes and law, and is
expected to tell his children to keep to the way of Yahweh by doing
what is right and just (15:6; 18:19; 26:2–5). In the story of Sarah and
Hagar, Sarah feels that Abraham has been cruel to her and summons
Yahweh to judge between them (16:1–5). In the same story Sarah feels
no compunction for her mistreatment of her slave but the angelic
messenger who meets Hagar makes sure that the law has been observed
before giving her orders to return and providing reasonable motives
for her to obey them.[137] When Yahweh plans to destroy Sodom and
Gomorrah Abraham is amazed that the judge of the whole world would
think of punishing the innocent along with the guilty and carries out a
reasoned defense of the principles of law (18:22–23). Abraham requires
a conditional oath of his servant before sending him to Mesopotamia to
find a wife for Isaac (chap. 24). Jacob and Laban make a covenant

and invoke God as witness and guarantor of their agreement (31:43–50). In the story of Dinah and Shechem the topic constantly shifts from the legal questions surrounding the rape of Dinah to the constitutional problems involved in Shechem's proposal of marriage, while the whole plot turns on the law of circumcision.[138] The story of Judah and Tamar, similarly, revolves around the law of levirate marriage and ends in a mock trial in which Tamar is vindicated (chap. 38; cf. Deut 25:5–10). There are additions to the story of Joseph that have to do with issues of innocence and guilt and with the development of customs and legal institutions in Egypt (42:25–28; 43:18, 23; 44:1–17; 47:13–26). In every instance, no matter what the predominant genre or narrative interest, the Deuteronomist demonstrates familiarity with some law and legal procedure and writes as if their formality and reasonableness were inherent in the structure of history.

Exodus

The book of Exodus is devoted to disputes and negotiations, to ritual, administrative, and constitutional law, and to commands and their literal fulfillment. These texts are attached mainly to Priestly and Elohist elements of the same sort but are clearly distinguished, despite their imitative and archaizing tendencies, by the topics, themes, sequences, and method of argumentation that they pursue.

The pattern of command and fulfillment-of-the-command is so well established as a narrative technique, notably in the design and construction of the tent of meeting, that any departure from the norm has to be explained or counterbalanced. In the story of the Hebrew midwives, for example, Pharaoh orders them to kill the male children but allows the female children to survive. They do *not* obey because they fear God, and God rewards them by giving them children of their own. The broken command-and-fulfillment pattern is compensated for by the Pharaoh's inquiry why they refused to kill the children, and this in turn allows the Deuteronomist to introduce the principal theme of the book concerning Yahweh's promises to the patriarchs and Israel's growing distinctiveness and separation from Egypt (Exod 1:15–21).

This theme is pursued most vigorously in the Deuteronomistic version of the plagues, which are also characterized by their use and modification of the command-and-fulfillment pattern. In the plague of flies, for instance, Moses is sent to Pharaoh with orders to let the people go and serve Yahweh, and the entire plot hinges on Pharaoh's disobedience (8:16–28). The orders include a warning about failure to obey, and Pharaoh's disobedience is implicit in the ensuing plague of flies. The plague afflicts only the Egyptians, however, and this discrimination proves to Pharaoh that Yahweh is responsible. In subsequent negotiations with Moses he agrees to let the people sacrifice to Yahweh, but he will not let them go. When Moses insists that they must go into the wilderness to sacrifice to Yahweh, Pharaoh relents, Moses intercedes, and the plague is lifted. In the end, of course, Pharaoh hardens his heart and the pattern begins again, but in the meantime the Deuteronomist has been able to develop the argument to which the History constantly returns that Yahweh is known as God by the things that he does in the history of his people.

The role of Moses as legislator and interpreter of the law is insinuated from the beginning. In the epic version Moses fled to Midian because he had killed an Egyptian, and Pharaoh meant to kill him. In the Deuteronomistic version Moses becomes involved in an identical quarrel but is given a chance to moralize and to be identified not only as a reputed murderer but as a potential judge and administrator (2:13–14).[139]

The authority of Moses is expressed as the willingness of the people to believe in him. In the epic version this happens after Yahweh's victory over the Egyptians at the Sea (14:30–31). In the Historian's version belief is a result of the plagues that Moses and Aaron produce, but, in typically Deuteronomistic fashion, it is put into a preface and paradigm of the plagues rather than into the narrative of their actual occurrence.[140]

With this authority in hand Moses is able to reformulate the laws of Passover. The Passover ritual was legislated by the Priestly writer as the conclusion and memorial of the exodus from Egypt, but in the Deuteronomist's version it is associated with the feast of Unleavened Bread, integrated into the narrative of the plagues, and elaborated for celebration in the promised land. In the Priestly version the festival is dated and the ritual is described in every detail (12:1–6, 8–11, 40–42). In the Deuteronomist's version other details concerning the sprinkling of blood are inserted into the text and then interpreted.[141] The interpretation relates the ritual to the death of the Egyptian firstborn, but it also makes this final plague Yahweh's vindication against the Gods of Egypt. With these changes made, the Deuteronomist returns to the ritual to describe the feast of Unleavened Bread: the rules are stated; the historical reasons for the festival are given; and the rules are reformulated to associate Unleavened Bread with Passover (12:14–20). Then the modified and interpreted law of Passover is repeated to the elders, explained with reference to the final plague, and is actually obeyed by the people (12:21–28). This typical pattern is followed by the final plague, by a resumptive reference to the humiliation of the Egyptians, and by an elaboration of the laws of Passover for celebration in the land.[142] The law, in true Deuteronomistic fashion, is neither isolated nor authoritarian but a reasonable and persuasive demand integral to the process of history.[143]

The Historian's patient and exacting method of formulating and interpreting the law is evident in the planning of the Sinai pericope. As it was found in the combined epic, Priestly, and Elohist version, this consisted of the crossing of the Sea and the journey to the mountain of God, a theophany at the mountain, the revelation of the law and of the plan of the tabernacle, and the confirmation of the authority of Moses in the covenant that Yahweh made with him and with the people of Israel. In its latest Deuteronomistic version it was divided into three different parts dealing with the law (chaps. 13–24), the tent of meeting (chaps. 25–31), and the decalogue (chaps. 32–34).

In the first part Moses assumes priestly, administrative, and legislative roles. The victory at the Sea is preceded by the laws and rites that commemorate it (13:1–6). Its ritual significance is pointed in a dispute between Moses and the people in which they express their willingness to serve the Egyptians and he, in the guise of a Deuteronomic priest, encourages them to stand firm and witness Yahweh's victory over their enemies (14:11–14).[144] The liturgical status of the victory is also evident in the song that Moses and the people sing and in a subsequent dispute, whose resolution is marked by the observance of the sabbath (chaps. 15; 16). The theological point of the victory is stressed in another dispute and in a more positive manner, when news of the victory at the Sea persuades Jethro to believe that Yahweh is greater than all the Gods (chap. 17; 18:6–11). It is, on the basis of this historical exploit, disputed, reiterated and rationalized, that the Historian expects obedience to Yahweh and observance of the covenant (19:3b–8). In typically Deuteronomistic style the detailed law is preceded by the paradigmatic revelation of the decalogue and by reflection on its form, its significance, and its observance (19:21–25; 20:2–26). In the same way, the revelation of the law is resumed by reading it and accepting it (24:1–11; cf. Deut 31:9–13). The first part of the pericope ends as it began with sacrifice and celebration.

In the second part Moses receives detailed instructions on the design and accoutrement of the tent of meeting, and everything that is commanded is executed exactly in the corresponding last part of the book.[145] This idea of revealing the plan of the place where Yahweh spoke to Moses before going through all the same steps again to construct it corresponds to the Deuteronomist's frequent device of

presenting a model, paradigm, or prediction of the facts before mar-
shaling the concrete legal or historical evidence for their interpretation.

In the third part the Deuteronomist replaces the covenant with the
decalogue and the promise to the patriarchs and sets out once and for
all the basis of the authority of Moses. The promise to the patriarchs is
introduced in the argument that Moses mounts against Yahweh's
proposed annihilation of the people who made the golden calf (32:11–
14). The decalogue is introduced, against all the epic's evidence, as a
substitute for the covenant (34:28bB; cf. Deut 4:13). The issue of the
authority of Moses is established in formal negotiations that he has
with Yahweh (chap. 33). These negotiations are managed, as commonly
happens, by breaking the pattern of command and accomplishment in
which they occur. The command is to lead the people to the land
promised to the patriarchs, but in giving it Yahweh says he will not
travel with them and, naturally enough, the people are grieved and
Moses does not comply (33:1–6). In compensation for the break in the
pattern of command and obedience, the argument is interrupted to
note that Moses has regular access to Yahweh in the tent of meeting,
which does travel with them (33:7–11). The argument then begins
again at the beginning and establishes, by redoing epic and Priestly
views of his familiarity with God, that Moses is the sole and authentic
leader of the people. The authority of Moses in matters of law is
confirmed, in effect, in dispute with the historical sources and in a
model of jurisprudence and legal wrangling.[146]

Throughout the book of Exodus the Deuteronomistic additions and
interpretations are obvious from their interest in the law and its
reasonable entry into the affairs of the nation. The law, however, is not
only the unitary and abstract structure of history but also particular
decisive motives and patterns of moral and ritual behavior. In every
instance, by command, discussion, arbitration, and analysis, the law is
defended and takes effect. Its results are evident in the growing
authority of Moses and in the gradual separation of Israel from its
international environment.

Leviticus and Numbers

The early parts of these books are dominated by pseudo-narrative
written in the style of command and fulfillment. The latter parts, aside
from lists, contain consultation and debate pertaining to refinements in
the law. In the central parts laws are formulated as conclusions and
comments on the sources.

The first part describes the ordination of Aaron and his sons in a series of commands issued by Yahweh, relayed by Moses, and executed by the priests. In the first chapter Yahweh gives the full range of commands, and the Deuteronomist notes in advance that Moses obeyed them before in fact they are carried out one by one.[147] In the second chapter the system is the same but more intricate. Moses issues orders to Aaron and his sons and includes instructions that they are to relay to the people. The people obey their instructions first. Then Moses refers to the orders that he has given as commands from Yahweh and says that the glory of God will appear to them when the commands have been observed. The commands are observed by Aaron and his sons in the order in which they were given, and the glory of God in fact appears to all the people. The third chapter is mainly a commentary on the second, but the system of command and obedience is observed so rigorously that when something is done that has not been commanded disaster ensues.[148] The last chapter, containing the dietary laws, is a list of edible and inedible living things: the food is not eaten, and therefore obedience to the command is replaced with a motive for its observance (Lev 11:1–45).

In the second part the entire history of Israel's early days in the wilderness is framed in similar but more complicated sets of command and perfect compliance. In the first chapter there is a command to take a census of the tribes; but before it is carried out there is a model census in which assistants from each tribe are assigned to help Moses, and after it is carried out there is a conclusion to that effect and a rider explaining why the tribe of Levi was not included (Num 1:1–3, 4–16, 17–43, 44–46, 47–54). In chap. 2, on the arrangement of the tribes around the tent of meeting, there is the same system of command, exception to the command, and concluding record that the command was obeyed. In chap. 3 there is a command, a statement that the command was obeyed, and then the actual execution of the command; but the sequence is introduced by a summary of the preceding part and by commands that will be obeyed later in this part and the next.[149] In chap. 4 the command contains the information the chapter means to convey, and the execution of the command is noted in detail for each of its parts (4:1–33, 34–49). In chap. 5 the trial by ordeal of a woman accused of adultery is not carried out, but it concludes with a résumé and restatement of the rules to be observed (Num 5:11–31). Similarly, the rules of restitution are too general to be complied with at once, but the pattern of command and obedience that is meant to govern them is exemplified in the model case that introduces them (Num 5:1–4, 5–10). All the remaining chapters follow the simple pattern of command and execution and sometimes mark the completion of the pattern with

some unrelated instance of authority and observance of the law.[150] By
the end of the part, when Israel is about to break camp and set out for
the promised land, it is perfectly clear that everything is supposed to
take place in accordance with the words of Yahweh to Moses. It is not
surprising, but just as awful nonetheless, when many things do not.

In the third part the rebellions in the wilderness are an occasion to
formulate laws that reflect and counteract them. In the middle chapter,
when a whole generation has been excluded from the land for refusing
to believe that Yahweh could give it to them, the Deuteronomist
introduces legislation to be observed in the land, makes provisions for
the atonement of unintentional sins, condemns high-handed and willful
crimes, decrees that the violation of the sabbath is deserving of death,
and authorizes tassels on the corners of their cloaks to remind them of
the law they are to observe (Numbers 15). After the rebellion, in
which, according to the Deuteronomist, the Levite Korah was involved,
Moses makes the Levites servants of Aaron in the tent of meeting and
holds Aaron responsible for the wrongdoing of the priests (Numbers
18). The story of the rebellion concludes with rituals for purifying the
people and rules for maintaining the cleanliness of the camp (Numbers
19).

In the fourth part the story of Israel's wars and settlement in
Transjordan is punctuated by incidents of sin and punishment. In one
they rebel against the authority of Moses and are bitten by snakes. In
the other a popular uprising and general defection from the covenant
are illustrated in one particularly sordid case attributed to the influence
of Balaam. It becomes apparent as the History proceeds that the law is
plagued by a parallel history of sin (Num 21:4-9; 25:1-8; 31:16).

The fifth and sixth parts are devoted to rituals, rules, and regulations and to tying up loose ends of the history before the law and the
covenant are systematized. Each has a segment on the inheritance of
the daughters of Zelophehad that illustrates how the law developed, in
the mind of the Deuteronomist, and how the authority of Yahweh was
always presumed for reasonable rules (Num 27:1-10; 36:1-13).

Deuteronomy

In the symmetrical construction of Deuteronomy the various parts
correspond in their use and interpretation of the law. In the first and
last parts attention is given to legal traditions and institutions. In the
second and second-to-last parts the law and the principles of the law
are argued and defended. In the central parts of the book legislative
acts are related to past and future events as they are recorded in the

History. Each part is slightly different, and all together give a rounded impression of the Deuteronomistic conception of law.

In the first part, where Moses set about explaining the law, the law refers to the following book of Deuteronomy, and the explanation consists in a survey of written history covering the events from Sinai to Beth-peor. Similarly, the establishment of the courts responsible for the preservation and application of the law consists of a recapitulation of the judicial system that was inaugurated at Sinai before the law was revealed and of the prophetic tradition that was initiated in the wilderness when the people fussed and rebelled (cf. Deut 1:9–18; Exodus 18; and Numbers 11). The law, from this perspective, is a synthesis of the past and a paradigm of the future.

In the last part, where Moses wrote the law, the law refers to the book of Deuteronomy, which it concludes and which has been designed to be read, taught, and put into practice. But instead the law is committed to the ark of the covenant, and Moses sings a prophetic song that interprets the history of its neglect (Deut 31:9–13, 24–29). The law, from this perspective, is the motive of history, the image of the hidden destiny of the people, and the opposite of the evil that befalls them (see Deut 29:28).

In the second part Moses teaches the law, and every chapter points to some principles and to the conclusions to be drawn from them. The lessons are usually learned from the example of history as the Deuteronomist wrote and explained it.

In the first chapter, for instance, a few easy lessons prepare the people for the final argument. The first lesson is that the law gives life, and the proof is that they are alive and those who abused the law at Baal-peor are dead (4:1–4).[151] Another lesson is that they are not to make images of God because they saw nothing when Yahweh spoke to them at Horeb except the fire of a jealous God (4:15–24). The main argument is that Yahweh alone is God, and the proof is a survey of history from creation to the present (4:32–40).

The point of the second chapter is that the law revealed at Horeb was the decalogue, while the rest of the law was confided to Moses. The argument consists in repeating and paraphrasing the Exodus account of what happened at Horeb. The conclusion is that the people have agreed in principle to learn and observe the law that Moses is about to teach them (chap. 5).

In the third chapter the lesson is taught in the form of a question and answer (6:20–25). In the fourth the argument proceeds from the premise that Yahweh chose the people, through a proof drawn from the history of their salvation, to the logical conclusion that Yahweh is

God and must be obeyed (7:6–11). In the fifth chapter a consideration of the story of the manna in the wilderness leads to the conclusion that Yahweh wants them to learn that obedience is life (8:2–6). In the sixth chapter a review of their history as it has been interpreted in the preceding books teaches them that the land is given in fulfillment of the promise to the patriarchs and not because they are obedient (chap. 9). In the seventh chapter the priority of the decalogue that is preserved in the ark of the covenant is proved by the exclusive vocation of the Levites who care for it (chap. 10). In the last chapter the argument concludes with the choice that they have to make between life or death.

In the corresponding second-to-last part the same choice is repeatedly argued and illustrated. In the first chapter this is done by formalizing the agreement between themselves and Yahweh that he will be their God and they will obey his commandments (chap. 26; esp. 26:16–19). In the second chapter it is illustrated in the blessings and the curses divided among the tribes situated on Ebal and Gerizim, and in the third it is obvious in the contrast between the blessings they received and the curses that have afflicted them (chaps. 27; 28). In the fourth chapter it is demonstrated in the destruction of the land because they disobeyed the covenant (chap. 29). In the last chapter the necessity of choice is argued from the constant and ever-present possibility of obeying the law and living (chap. 30).

In the third part the law in general is organized around the future choice of a central place of worship as a hedge against apostasy. In the first two chapters the point of centralization is made and illustrated by its opposite. The central chapters systematize the customs and festivals of the central sanctuary that distinguish Israel from the other nations and devote it to Yahweh. The final chapters organize the institutions of the law's transmission and interpretation. The law, in effect, is reduced to its first and basic commandment and is understood to project a society structured in its own image — one law, one sanctuary, one God, and one people (chaps. 12–18).

The fourth part rephrases the laws and customs recorded in earlier episodes of the History in the light of the principles established in the preceding parts of the book. The first chapter, for instance, rewrites the instructions in the book of Numbers concerning cities of refuge to correspond to general principles of the law and to the specific judicial system that was established in the previous part (chap. 19).[152] The second chapter outlines the theory pursued in the wars of conquest in Joshua but is also based on principles that were formulated in the decalogue and on precedents established in the book of Exodus.[153] In the third chapter some of the laws are illustrated in Joshua; some reflect situations that are described in Genesis; and some are extrapo-lated from principles set forth earlier in the book of Deuteronomy.[154] The fourth chapter assembles legislation related to laws in Exodus and governed by precedents in Deuteronomy;[155] the fifth chapter is tran-scribed from situations described in Numbers;[156] the sixth is based on Exodus and Numbers;[157] and the last refers to incidents narrated in Genesis and Exodus.[158] But all reflect the interpretation of the law that was presented in the beginning of the book. The total procedure has the remarkable effect of making the book of the law the climax of a historical and living tradition.

Joshua–Kings

Once the law has been promulgated and inserted into the history and destiny of Israel, its principles and effects are simply presumed or recalled as occasion requires. When the book of the law is written or, according to the Deuteronomistic conceit, discovered early in the reign of King Josiah, its truth and interpretation are certain.

In Joshua the conquest of the land is a reenactment of the crossing of the Sea and the covenant on Sinai (Josh 4:20–24).[159] The book of the law is confided to Joshua and his principal role as the successor of Moses is to observe the law that Moses entrusted to him (Josh 1:6–9). The decalogue and the book of the law enter the land with the ark of the covenant, and a copy of the law is inscribed on stelae set up at Ebal (chaps. 3–4; 8:30–35).[160] Everything that Joshua does is done in obedience to the commands of Moses and in fulfillment of the promises that Yahweh made to Israel. At the end of the book Joshua exhorts the people to observe everything that is written in the law of Moses, and they adhere to its basic stipulations by choosing Yahweh and rejecting the Gods of the nations (chaps. 23–24).

In Judges the law is a counterpoint to the narrative of the settlement in the land. The reason for Israel's constant struggle to survive in the land is that the covenant that Yahweh commanded them had not been obeyed (Judg 2:1–4). The individual heroes who saved them are called judges, rather than tribal leaders, and are precursors of the kings. The judgment against the people is persistent and apparently gratuitous, and their wrongdoing is generally unrelated to the narrative at hand. The law is not in evidence or explicit except by its rejection that, as the law itself warned, consisted in worshiping the wrong Gods in the wrong places in essentially wrong times.

In Samuel the presence of the law is apparent in the crimes of individuals. The ark of the covenant finds its way from Shiloh to

Jerusalem, but the decalogue and the book of the law belonging with it are not mentioned. Samuel exercises the office of judge in a public ceremony of repentance for the worship of other Gods, but from the beginning of the kingdom the History mentions only the crimes of its antagonists. Saul is a model of disobedience to the commands of Yahweh and represents in his own person the fault that all the prophets condemned.[161] Doeg the Edomite was wrong in applying the ban to the priestly city of Nob (1 Sam 22:19; cf. Deut 20:10–18). David protests his innocence of crimes committed against the house of Saul but eventually is condemned for his part in the affair of Uriah the Hittite (2 Sam 3:31–39; 4:1–12; 12:1–23; 1 Kgs 15:5). The sin that he committed in taking a census of his kingdom is the only crime in Samuel that, like the sins of the kings after him, is imputed to the people and expiated by their punishment (2 Samuel 24).

In Kings, beginning with David's valediction, the law starts to reappear and take effect in the history of the nation. David exhorts Solomon to observe the law; Yahweh makes promises to him that are contingent on his obedience to the law; and his kingdom is divided because he worshiped other Gods. Jeroboam inaugurated the worship of calves at Bethel and Dan and brought a sin on the North that burdened all succeeding generations. The sin of Ahab bedeviled his house in the next generation. Most of the kings followed in the sin of Jeroboam, and even the best did not remove the high places as the law required. Hezekiah was an exception and Josiah fulfilled the law, but the nation was left to bear the scourge of the sins of Ahab and Jeroboam, imitated by Manasseh, and in the end felt the full force of the law.

The law, for the Deuteronomist, was a book and a way of life. It could be read. It had to be learned. It had simple principles and evident proofs. It was present from the beginning and became apparent at every turn in the history of the people. It was the form and substance of some incidents, the contrary and critique of whole eras, a system of wisdom, love, and justice that people appropriated but that had a life of its own. It developed over time and resumed in many ways the origin and destiny of the people.

THE HISTORICAL AGENDA

Although there is a moral to the History, history itself is the thing. The Deuteronomist clearly meant to write a convincing and entertaining account of the past that would allow the future to be different, better, and unpredictable. Everything pertinent is examined or included in a variety and commingling of literary genres. Things are repeated, or apparently contradicted, or put into opposite perspectives as the Historian completes the task of acknowledgment, understanding, and interpretation. All in all, what history is the History tries to teach.

History is continuous from beginning to end. Where the epic dealt in episodes, the Deuteronomist tried to bridge the gaps with information or the illusion of chronological sequence. When the Priestly writer provided regimens or lists, the Historian related them to the world and time. If the Elohist was satisfied to write legends and lessons, the Historian smoothed them into a narrative tract. The sequel might delay with ideology or compress temporal sequence to make a point, but the Deuteronomist supplied the story and tradition that ideas could not suppress. In each era time was of the essence and was marked by incidents and accidents and the structured sequence of events.

The continuity is convoluted and complex to allow for the inclusion of selected evidence and interpretation and informed but residual data. Book follows on book and part on part, but each is also relatively complete and related to others. Each part has chapters and information not all of the same genre or intention. A story is interrupted to make its point, to refer it to another, to include subplots and causes and principles of interpretation. A narrative can be simple and consecutive or an assemblage of analogous vignettes. Eras have their appropriate mannerisms and identifying styles and unrelated or unintegrated clues to their contribution to the history. Traditions are rarely unitary but are often distributed over time, place, and institution. The continuity is reasonable and arguable, distinct in discourse, description, and narration, but present and purposeful and meant to be grasped.

Genesis

A typical medley and sequence of materials is found in the two parts of Genesis that interpret the history of Abraham. One part liberates him from his Egyptian and Mesopotamian ties; the other establishes him as resident and heir in the promised land of Canaan. In both the Deuteronomist adds data, evidence, and interpretations to the sources to situate the distant origins of Israel in the history of the civilized world (Genesis 10–14; 15–24).

The first chapter contains the genealogy of the children of Noah, which the Priestly writer used to introduce continuity and duration between the episodes of the flood and the abandoned Tower of Babel. The Deuteronomist corrected it to produce a more accurate historical map of the world and to establish the Hebrew ancestry of Abraham.

Assyria occurred in the Priestly list, but it is now given a chronological, geographical, and cultural context with respect to Sumer and Akkad. Its principal cities are listed, along with Babylon and Uruk, and its military power and antiquity are suggested in its derivation from Nimrod, who was both a mighty warrior and a hunter of ancient repute (10:8–12). Egypt, similarly, is taken out of its African isolation and related to Mediterranean culture and the world of the Philistines (10:13–14). Canaan is identified by listing some of its cities, by associating it with population groups that Israel would have to displace, and by mentioning some border and compass points, such as Gerar, Sodom, and Gomorrah, which contrive to situate it in the following narratives (10:15–19). The Priestly writer had traced Abraham's ancestry to Eber, but the Deuteronomist made a special point of relating it to the story of the Tower of Babel and of including a segmented genealogy that brought him into contact with other people and places mentioned in the History (10:21, 24–30; cf. 11:16–17). By dint of research into chronology, culture, ethnography, etiology, and geography the Deuteronomist absorbed the tripartite world that the Priestly writer knew into a world of international relationships.

In the second chapter the epic episode is modified to relate it to this historical context. In one sentence the Deuteronomist situates the episode of the tower in the time of migrations from the east, where the story of creation took place, to the land of Sumer, where Babylon, Uruk, and Akkad were located (11:2).[162] In another the tower takes on historical proportions in a description of its construction from bricks and how they were made (11:3).[163] In another the tower is said to have been in Babylon, and the proof of its location is that it was in Babylon that people began to babble in incomprehensible tongues (11:8a, 9a). The final modifications are to the Priestly genealogy that concludes the chapter, but these relate it to the story of Abraham and Sarah, which is told in the following part (11:29–30).[164] The melange of genres, information, and indices is a reflection of reasoned interpretation in a continuous account of the past.

The third and fourth chapters retrieve the genealogy of Egypt and Canaan as a framework for the itinerary of Abraham. The map of the world in which these people and countries appeared is reflected in the Historian's statement that all the families of the world would find their blessings in Abraham.[165] Abraham's arrival at Shechem is marked by the observation that he built an altar there, although the area still belonged to the Canaanites, and the narrative is punctuated again by a similar etiology of the worship of Yahweh in the vicinity of Bethel and Ai (12:6b–7, 8b). The genealogical and historical connection between

Canaan and Egypt is confirmed in a typical Canaanite famine and
Abraham's symbolic sojourn in Egypt (12:10–20; 13:7b, 10b). The
itinerary concludes with proleptic and resumptive cross-references to
the Deuteronomistic story of Sodom and Gomorrah and to the world
rivers in the Garden of Eden (13:10b).[166] In the epic and Priestly
versions Abraham wandered and settled at will. In the Deuteronomist's
view Canaan was an inhabited and age-old province of Egypt, and the
wanderings of Abraham represented a critical phase in the relations
between the old and the new, the East and the West.

This critical phase is described by the fifth chapter in an anecdote
that makes Abraham an ally of Sodom and Gomorrah in the struggle
with the kings of the East (chap. 14). It pits Abraham against his
Mesopotamian origins and, symbolically, lets him vanquish the nations
that conquered Israel and Judah and took them into exile; but it has
an artificial literary construction and studied links with the surrounding
material and illustrates the Deuteronomistic History's determination to
present all the contrary evidence and to include all the material for its
own critique. The antagonists are kings of countries that were listed in
the opening historical geography. The situation of subjugation, rebellion, and repeated retaliation is attested in the time of the kings. The
anecdote's protagonists are the people of Sodom, who become the
subject of the following part. The victims are the natives of Canaan,
who were ousted by Moab, Edom, Ammon, and Israel in the later
times of national consciousness. Abraham is a Hebrew settled by the
oaks of Mamre, as the earlier texts confirm, but he leads loyal bands of
fighters like the heroes of the time of the judges. Among his subjects
are house-born slaves that the law of circumcision takes into account.
Among his exploits are forays beyond Damascus in the land of the
Aramean foe. He is blessed by Melchizedek, priest of Salem, as Yahweh
proclaimed at the start. He pays tithes as the law commanded and
brings blessings on his friends as the History thought. The chapter, in
effect, summarizes the point of the part by portraying Abraham's
privileged place in the history of Israel and the world (chap. 14).[167]

The historicity of this bold presentation is presumed and verified in
the following central part. The first chapter is the covenant that Yahweh
made with Abraham for his role in world affairs (chap. 15). In the last
his messenger reports his settlement and success in Canaan to his
relatives in the land of his birth. In the meantime he and his heirs gain
unhindered rights to the land. Every chapter is literarily distinct, and
in each the historical interpretation is based on reasonable evidence
and fact. The first chapter is a vision and prophecy of Abraham, whose
veracity is established by a preview of the subsequent history of Israel

and by a geography of the promised land. The second is a dramatic dispute and inquisition supported by the etiologies of Ishmael and Beer-lahai-roi and by the historical assumptions of the Priestly covenant with Abraham (chaps. 16; 17). The fourth has an inquiry into the justice of God that is seconded by Abraham's commission to teach the law to his descendants (chap. 18). In the fifth the fact that Lot escaped the destruction of Sodom and Gomorrah is based on the etiologies of Zoar and the pillar of salt and is verified in the genealogies of Moab and Ammon (chap. 19). The sixth is a legend of Abraham's prophetic powers that is grounded in historical reality by reference to his genealogy and journeys (chap. 20, esp. 20:12–13).[168] The seventh is a variant of the second supported by the etiologies of Beersheba and the cult of El Olam (chap. 21). The eighth is the legend of Abraham's binding of Isaac, which is confirmed by the concluding catalog of the descendants of Abraham's brother Nahor (chap. 22, esp. 22:20–24).[169] The last is the story of Rebekah, whose typical pastoral setting gains specificity from a geographical reference, a traditional saying, and a summary of this and the preceding part (chap. 24, esp. 24:60, 62).

The epic and Elohist stories of Abraham tried to maintain the illusion of his individuality. The Priestly writer situated him in the real world and related his life more explicitly to the written history of the nation. The Deuteronomist put him into the history of the world and armed him with marvelous adventures but made him more typical or official or representative and abstract. The etiologies and similar historical asides place him in remote antiquity but as purveyor of the promise, or in his official role as prophet, upholder of the law, founder of cults, and champion of the oppressed, he is a timeless personification of the history of his people. One side restrains the other, the drift to theory being checked by evidence and facts and the rule of principles or reason resting in imagination.

Exodus

Particular parts of the History in which speculation and reflection predominate are balanced by parts that transcribe the passage of time and the manipulation of concrete detail. In the book of Exodus the plan of the tabernacle and the tent of meeting is offset by the business of their construction, which lasts for almost a year. The rest of the time, represented in the part that intervenes, is taken up with the transcription of the law and the covenant and with Deuteronomistic reflections on the principles of theocratic government (chaps. 32–34).

The first chapter in this part contains the Elohist story of the revolt of Aaron and the people against the authority of Moses in the episode of the golden calf. In its original form it was a dispassionate analysis of the secession of the northern kingdom that, by abutting the epic formulation of the attributes of God, implied that the North was subject both to the rigors and to the mercy of Yahweh.[170] The Deuteronomistic version was less tolerant of the rebellion and was particularly harsh toward the irregular priesthood of the northern shrines, but what distinguishes it most clearly from its source is its backward and forward linking of the episode to the overall thrust of the History.

Its analysis proceeds in the Historian's usual manner, at one point interrupting the original narrative sequence to insert an argument, at another enclosing the narrative as emended in a stylized juridical framework.[171] The argument is taken from the epic narrative of rebellion in the wilderness but differs from it by interpreting the calf as a violation of the law that impels God to anger, from which the people can be saved only by appealing to his covenant with their fathers (32:7–14; cf. Num 14:11–25). The juridical framework is a trial by ordeal in which the people are forced to drink water mixed with the dust of the calf and in which, being guilty, they are struck down by a plague (32:20, 35).[172] The emendations consist of two different conclusions to the story. One is an etiology of the levitical order, which is thoroughly intrusive in the context but will be explained bit by bit as the History progresses.[173] The other implicates the people in the sin of the golden calf and is an occasion to commence the discussion of the immediacy of the government of God (32:30–35). The etiology gives the incident historical depth. The argument situates it in an ongoing sequence of events.

The second chapter deals with the question of government. The argument develops, as often happens in the History, according to a system of intrusion and interruption. The first paragraph, a synthesis of epic and Elohist texts, sets the agenda by proposing that the people travel to the land without Yahweh.[174] The second responds to the proposal with a lament of the people and a ritual rejection of other Gods (33:4–6). The third paragraph is intrusive. It describes the protocol at the tent of meeting and the location of the tent in the desert encampment (33:7–11), although the tent exists only in the model that was revealed on Sinai in the previous part and will not be constructed until later in the next part, and the camp will not be organized until the tribes are mustered in the following book. The intrusion, therefore, supplies the argument with its historical reference and credibility by situating it in a chronological continuum and relating it to concrete realities. The fourth paragraph returns to the agenda of the first

paragraph when Moses repeats his commission but corrects the impression that the people are his people and insists that they are distinct
from other nations only because Yahweh goes with them (33:12–17).
The last paragraph anticipates his encounter with Yahweh in the next
epic incident and retrieves the point of the intrusion by stating that
Yahweh speaks to Moses face to face as a friend but that he cannot be
seen (33:18–23). In effect, theocratic government works through the
agency of the word and of prophets like Moses and not through the
immediacy of God's glory or presence.

The last chapter integrates the epic covenant and the end of the
Elohist version into the History's theory of government. The first
paragraph relates it to the story of the golden calf and to the original
theophany on Sinai (34:1–3).[175] The second paragraph includes the
manifestation of Yahweh in a continuation of the theocratic perspective
(34:4–9).[176] The covenant itself is emended to make it conform to legal
and historical precedents,[177] and the conclusion of the covenant resumes
the Deuteronomist's argument on prophecy and the operations of a
theocratic government.[178]

The sources had action, drama, and elements of sequence. The
Deuteronomist integrated theory and argument into the action and
extended the sequence over many dimensions. By stopping and starting
the story it was possible to make it part of a whole and ongoing history.

Leviticus 8–11 and Numbers

The fourth part of this book is a history of the conquest of Transjordan.
It incorporates the Priestly rebellion at Meribah and the epic highlights
on Israel's contacts with Moab, Edom, and Ammon into a disjointed
and densely argued interpretation of the wars of Yahweh and Israel's
place among the nations.

In the first chapter the Deuteronomist makes a few changes that
relate the epic and Priestly materials to the earlier views expressed in
the History. When the people complain that there is no water, Yahweh
does not intervene until, as protocol would have it, Moses and Aaron
convene at the tent of meeting (Num 20:6).[179] When Moses recites the
story of the exodus, the Deuteronomist, in the spirit of the recent
debate on government and leadership, adds that the angel of Yahweh
brought them out of Egypt (Num 20:16aB).[180] When Aaron, for his
part in the rebellion, has to die and Eleazar has been appointed to take
his place, the Deuteronomist naturally has to deprive him of his priestly
garments and hand them down to his successor (Num 20:26, 28aA).[181]
The chapter combined disparate materials and was already complex,

but the Deuteronomist included it in a much broader system of reference.

The second chapter incorporates the epic narrative account of the defeat of Sihon, king of the Amorites. In the original version this was the counterpoint to Israel's meeting with Edom and the immediate antecedent of the oracles of Balaam, but in the Deuteronomist's version it is an occasion to develop the Priestly itinerary and to include a record of the important battles that were fought in Transjordan.

Before coming to the tale of Balaam, the Deuteronomist takes up and corrects the epic account of Israel's war with Sihon, king of the Amorites. In this version there is one battle at Jahaz, and victory gives Israel possession of all the land of the Amorites. The first correction, supported by a few lines from a song, is that Sihon was not king of the Amorites but the Amorite king of Heshbon (Num 21:25–30).[182] The following corrections are other battle accounts, modeled on the defeat of Sihon, which account for the occupation of the rest of the land of the Amorites (Num 21:31–35).[183]

The third chapter begins the Balaam cycle and was changed in anticipation of the materials that would be added at the end. The disparagement of Balaam in the story of his ass's encounter with the angel expresses the Deuteronomist's views on the uncertainty of vision and prophecy apart from wisdom and the law, but it is also in line with the Historian's condemnation of Balaam for provoking the sin of Baal-peor (22:21aB, 22–35; cf. chap. 25; 31:16). The inclusion of Midianites among the ambassadors who were sent to him anticipates the same story but also provides a historical context for more detailed accounts of the Midianite wars (22:2–4a, 7a; 31:1–54; Judges 6–8). The oracles were unchanged, but the conclusion of the cycle in the fourth chapter was rewritten to include allusions to the battles and wars of conquest fought by David and his successors in the southern and eastern parts of the country (24:7, 14–24).[184]

The last chapter allows the Deuteronomist to round out the part before proceeding with other issues in the Transjordanian history of Israel. The first incident recapitulates the theme of rebellion: it takes place where the sequel's conquest narrative began, but it is a model of the nonconquest and unfortunate coexistence with indigenous people that the Deuteronomist will describe in the book of Judges (Num 25:1–5).[185] The second incident concludes the story of Eleazar's ordination and reemphasizes the importance of the tent of meeting in defining the exclusiveness of the preconquest community (25:6–13; cf. 20:22–29). The last incident summarizes the evidence for the first two and creates a link to the next part (25:14–18).

The density and disjointedness of the part are a product of research and scrupulous interpretation. The epic said that Israel could not enter the land by way of Edom and brought the people to the border of the land in Moab. The Priestly writer brought the story of Moses and Aaron to a close and added details to the epic itinerary. The Deuteronomist was not satisfied with any of this and integrated their interpretations into a History with antique roots and a distant destination. Everything is documented either by quoting sources or by referring to other texts where the topic is discussed. Stories are not told just for their own sake but to contribute to a continuous and developing interpretation, and they can be broken, backtracked, and anticipated. The quotations are obvious and partly artificial, the cross-references are clear but sometimes quaint or allusive. The community in Transjordan was not just a horde of invaders but a people looking for their place in the history of the world.

Deuteronomy

The historical framework of the book of Deuteronomy is an interpretation of the antecedents and effects of the law.[186] It illustrates, in a paradigmatic way, the History's interest in reviewing, refining, synthesizing, and repointing the drift of its interpretation.

The first chapter includes the sequel's version of rebellion in the wilderness in an incipient itinerary. The sequel situated the words of Moses beyond the Jordan, but the Deuteronomist locates them more specifically in the wilderness and in relation to particular places on the route that Israel took from Egypt (Deut 1:1b–2, 5).[187] Similarly, where the sequel mentioned the journey from Egypt or from Horeb, the Deuteronomist adds references to the wilderness itinerary and to the impossibility of traveling directly through the territory of the Canaanites (1:19, 31, 37–46). Typically, before Moses gets a chance to speak, the Deuteronomist anticipates the wars with Sihon and Og at the end of the journey,[189] and as soon as Moses begins to speak interrupts him to repeat and embellish the story of the constitution of the courts that took place earlier in the journey.[189]

The second and third chapters begin again at Horeb and review the journey through the wilderness to Transjordan. The first stage takes up the epic encounter with Edom but adds some chronological and geographical detail and, omitting the ominous rebellions that were associated with this part of the journey in Numbers, begins the etiology and argument of the law (2:1–8a).[190] The second stage elaborates on the journey to the border of Moab, alludes to the rebellions in Numbers by putting an end to the contentious wilderness generation, and includes learned asides that revive and expand ethnographic issues in Abraham's war with the coalition of eastern kings (2:8b–15).[191] The third stage explains why the Ammonites, merely alluded to in the Numbers account, were not attacked but also includes important information that supplements the history of Abraham (2:16–25).[192] The theory of holy war that began to intrude in the third stage becomes predominant in the next stage in retelling the story of Sihon king of Heshbon and summarizing the claims of the Transjordanian tribes (2:26–37).[193] The fifth stage is the battle with Og, retold as it was in Numbers but expanded with geographical, etiological, and ethnographic details (3:1–7, 8–11).[194] At the end of the journey there is a summary of the Deuteronomistic distribution of land in Transjordan, a reprise of the Priestly writer's appointment of Joshua as the successor of Moses for the conquest, and an allusion to the crimes of Beth-peor, which would ultimately undo his efforts (3:12–29).[195]

This retelling of history allows for the accumulation of data, an elaboration of the historical evidence, a synthesis of texts and viewpoints, and a repointing of interpretation in the direction of the law. It is with this understanding of the past that Moses can set about explaining how the observance of the law will affect the future. When his explanation is done there is a sense of impending blessing and curse that becomes the subject of still another recapitulation and refinement before the account of the conquest can proceed.

In the last part of Deuteronomy the argumentative style of the History is evident in the constant interruption of narrative and theme to introduce the crucial evidence. The death of Moses is announced in the first chapter but delayed until he finishes another address. In this he recites the words of his unhappy song, but he also intones a blessing on Israel. In each chapter history advances mainly by deferral and indirection.

In the first chapter paragraphs on the appointment of Joshua alternate with paragraphs on the transcription and interpretation of the law. In the first paragraph Moses announces his death and names Joshua as his successor, but not before he has epitomized the review of history proposed at the beginning of the book and the laws of war included in the code (31:1–8).[196] In the second paragraph the law is transcribed in a book and confided to the priests who carry the ark of the covenant, with provisions for its septennial reading (31:9–13). In the third paragraph, the Deuteronomist returns to the fact that Moses must die and be succeeded by Joshua, but not without retrieving from Exodus and Numbers the institutions and ideologies of the tent of meeting (31:14–15).[197] In the fourth paragraph the Song of Moses is dictated, written, and taught in anticipation of the law and the covenant being broken.[198] In the fifth paragraph Joshua is commissioned for the conquest, and in the sixth the Book of the Law, like the song that now accompanies it, is presented to the priests as a witness against the people (31:23, 24–29). One point of this alternation, as the book of Joshua will explain, is that the land can be conquered by Joshua and occupied by Israel only in accordance with the law (see Josh 1:6–9; 8:30–35).

The Song of Moses in the second chapter is composed of an analogous interweaving of historical summaries and theological themes. The song is introduced, in line with its interpretation in the previous chapter, as a lesson to the ungrateful children of God (32:1–7). The following strophes summarize, in the metaphors and elevated cadences of poetry, the history of the people recounted and intimated up to this point by the Deuteronomistic History or its sources (32:8–12, 13–14, 15–17). The next strophes return to the theme of Yahweh as parent who disciplines, with uncontrolled cosmic forces, the thoughtless and forgetful children who abandoned him to go after other Gods (32:18–21, 22–25). The fourth group of strophes displays this divine discipline in the history of the people by referring to texts or to typical historical occurrences (32:26–36).[199] The final strophes return to the intervention of Yahweh, less as parent to his children than as God and avenger of their historical enemies (32:37–43). The main difference between the song and its prior interpretation is its dependence on the prophets—in its thematic strophes on the older prophetic conceptions of God, and in its historical sections on their interpretations of the history of the people.[200] The chapter ends with an exhortation on its use and with the reminder, ominous in its allusion to the refusal of the land by an earlier generation, that it is an interpretation of the law that is to be observed in the land (32:44–47).[201]

The third chapter follows the pattern of deferral only in its use of sequential hymnic elements at the beginning and the end of the poem, with their continuity broken by the individual blessings on the tribes that intervene (32:2–5, 6–25, 26–29). The hymnic elements recapitulate and synthesize the manifestation of Yahweh on Sinai, the revelation of the law and the covenant, and the promised conquest of the land as these were recorded in various texts of Exodus and Numbers.[202] Some of the intervening oracles allude to the blessings in Genesis, some to events in the wilderness, but most are laconic references to the settlement of the tribes that will be described more accurately in the later allotment of the land.[203]

The book of Deuteronomy is the high point of the History, and its synthesis of history, law, and prophecy is presumed in all the following books. The book ends, therefore, with an epitome of the life of Moses and a nostalgic intimation of decline (34:10–12).

Joshua

The book of Joshua juxtaposes two views of the taking of the land, one military, the other administrative; and each of its parts evinces some aspect of this polar method of interpretation. The first part, in particular, includes paradigms of the conquest in a binary scheme that allows each battle to be seen from both a legal and a historical point of view.

The first two chapters ostensibly describe preparations for the battle of Jericho. In the sequel's version this involved the investiture of Joshua and the mission of the spies (Josh 1:1–5; 2:1–9a, 12–16, 22–24a). In the Deuteronomist's version both elements are reduplicated. Joshua is not only named the successor of Moses for the conquest; he is also appointed in place of Moses to apportion the land in accordance with the law and the commands of Moses (1:6–9).[204] The role of the spies is diminished by making other preparations, not for the attack on Jericho but for the crossing of the Jordan (1:10–11, 12–18). The Deuteronomist announces in advance that the whole account is to be understood partly as a narrative of past events and partly as a reenactment of the exodus and the strategy rehearsed by Moses in Transjordan.[205]

Chapters 3 and 4 recount the crossing of the Jordan as a matter of fact and as a procession that involved the wilderness camp and was dominated by the ark of the covenant. The procession follows a measured ritual pattern that is plotted in one chapter and interpreted in the next using the systems of envelopment and intrusion, prolepsis and resumption, and command and execution, which the Historian regularly deploys in arguments and explanations. The ceremony marks the end of rebellion in the wilderness and the beginning of domination by the law, and so the new era begins like the old with the crossing of the river and the Sea.

In the first paragraph Joshua's address to the people is interrupted by preparations in the camp and a harangue by the officers about following the ark of the covenant carried by the Levites. The harangue alludes to the organization of levitical cities prescribed in Numbers and treats following the ark like following the law (3:1, 2–4, 5).[206] The second paragraph records instructions for the priests but is interrupted by Yahweh to assure Joshua that he would have authority like that of

Moses in the allotment of the land (3:6–8). In the third paragraph
Joshua, in the words of the sequel and of the History, previews both
the crossing and the conquest, but interrupts himself to designate a
representative of each tribe for an indeterminate task. In the sequel's
words the conquest is the culmination of the covenant; from the
perspective of the History the crossing proves to the people that
Yahweh is among them and encourages them to obey (3:9–13).[207] The
fourth paragraph describes the journey to the Jordan but stops to
synchronize the crossing with harvest time and to let the whole nation
pass by on dry ground (3:14–17). The fifth paragraph tells how the
representatives of the tribes transported stones out of the Jordan to
Gilgal and back into the Jordan to mark the footsteps of the priests,
but it stops to explain their meaning for succeeding generations
(4:1–9). The sixth paragraph records that all the commands of Yahweh,
Moses, and Joshua were obeyed in the liturgical crossing and implau-
sibly pauses to note that the priests, who stood in the Jordan with the
ark until the people finished crossing, went ahead of the people as the
officers had instructed (4:10–13). The seventh paragraph confirms the
authority of Joshua and brings the people to Gilgal but stops to remove
the ark from the Jordan and conclude the crossing (4:14–19). The last
paragraph explains that the crossing of the Jordan is a reenactment of
the crossing of the Sea and a motive for obedience to Yahweh (4:20–
24).

Chapters 5 and 6 describe the battle of Jericho, the sixth as a siege
with ritual embellishments, the fifth as the rites and spectacles that
preceded its celebration (chaps. 5–6).[208] In the sequel's estimation the
conquest was a marvelous corroboration of the covenant and could be
proved by the ruins at Jericho and Ai. In the Historian's perspective
the conquest was piecemeal and not quite complete until the time of
David and not half as important as legal title to the land. Its ritual
appropriation began with the rite of circumcision, which made the
children of the wilderness generation heirs of the promise and owners
of the land (5:1–9). It was celebrated at the feast of Passover, observed
in accordance with the law, which put an end to the wilderness era
with its manna and its rebellions (5:10–12). It was confirmed by
Joshua's vision at Jericho of the commander of Yahweh's army of
conquest and by the holiness of the land that it revealed (5:13–15). It
was illustrated in the battle of Jericho, which was conducted in
accordance with the law and was won on an exemplary sabbath by the
priests and the ark of the covenant (chap. 6).

In chaps. 7 and 8 two battles for Ai prove the power and intransi-
gence of the law in Israel's appropriation of the land. The first battle

begins, as the Deuteronomist likes to do, with a summary of its significance. Achan did not observe the law of the ban, and defeat was certain. The sin is purged by supplication, purification, and the execution of the culprit and his family, but not before Yahweh makes it perfectly clear that observance of the law is the prerequisite of victory (chap. 7). The second battle is won; the ban and the other commandments are observed; and the law is committed to writing in the land (chap. 8).

The Deuteronomist did not adduce any new evidence for the conquest but concentrated on the form it had taken in the sequel. The original spoke of the wonders that Yahweh would perform and presented Jericho and Ai as principal examples. The Deuteronomist enlarged on the wonders with rituals that symbolized or reenacted the words and deeds of Yahweh. The conquest became more certain in their performance, and Israel's title to the land became clear.

Judges

The book of Judges is fitted with an artificial ideology and an unassimilated chronological scheme but derives its continuity and sequence mainly from its interlocking of personal, tribal, and local legends. The system is set forth clearly and pedagogically in the first part.

Chapter 1 is a table of contents of the tribes and their holdings and the cities where they lived in symbiosis with the inhabitants of the land (Judges 1). It introduces, or retrieves from Joshua, items of importance for the first part[209] and expresses, in annalistic terms, the themes of strife and coexistence to be traced throughout the book. In the jagged manner of the book, it does not mesh with the form or content of the following parts but suggests their point or counterpoint or context in the developing history of the nation.[210] It improves the discrete analysis of the evidence given in Joshua by redistributing the tribes among the houses of Judah and Joseph[211] anticipating, as the last part of the book does more explicitly, the foundation of the kingdom.

Chapter 2 restates the annalistic themes in terms of the motive force of the law and outlines the pattern that each part will follow. The opening paragraph explains the evidence presented in the first chapter by attributing nonconquest and coexistence to violation of the covenant (2:1–5). The second paragraph returns to the end of Joshua and to the beginning of Judges to explain that this violation occurred after the death of Joshua and his generation (2:6–10). The third paragraph explains in greater detail the means and effects of violating the covenant (2:11–14). The chapter ends by retrieving the example of lamentation from the first paragraph to describe the pattern of violation, lamentation, and salvation that will give the following anecdotes, accounts, and legends their continuity and sequence (2:15–23; cf. 2:4–5). The restatement of themes in this chapter is a juridical interpretation, argued reasonably,[212] that the Deuteronomist prefixed without further ado the ambiguous or recalcitrant evidence of the stories to be told.

Chapter 3 is another illustrative introduction to the part and to the book. It begins by summarizing the point of the second chapter—that coexistence with the inhabitants of the land would be a test of Israel's obedience to the law—and adds the analogous conception that coexistence would test their skill in war (3:1–6). This point is illustrated immediately in the abstract and inspired example of Othniel's defeat of the doubly wicked king of the land-of-the-two-rivers.[213] This image of the triumph of good over evil is filled out with gory details in the story of Ehud's revolt against the domination of Moab and the traditional spite of Amalek (3:12–30). The chapter ends with the pithy example of Shamgar, which omits the theme of testing in the law to concentrate on his warlike skills (3:31). The illustrations, particularly the prime example of Othniel, present the prophetic interpretation of history in which the judges are inspired to give instruction in the law and save the people from their sins.[214]

Chapters 4 and 5 reinterpret the defeat of the Canaanites that the book of Joshua recounted as Joshua's victory over Jabin of Hazor and his allies. The narrative is included in the continuous chronological sequence of Judges and is supposed to be understood in the context of its annalistic, juridical, and prophetic introductions.[215] The reinterpretation consists mainly in assigning the leadership of the Canaanite coalition to Sisera and in removing the battle from Hazor and the time of Joshua. The evidence of this reinterpretation is the Song of Deborah, which it quotes.[216]

The book of Judges is informative, instructive, and rigorous in its presentation of evidence and historical interpretation. In the first part a single battle that the sequel assigned to Joshua and the symbolic past surges onto a historical scene concretized by annalistic, legal, and legendary attributes. In the following parts its model is applied to regions, localities, personalities and types that contributed to the ongoing history. The book takes shape as entertainment, but its seriousness is pointed and becomes the basis of the history of David and the kingdom he represents.

Samuel

In the books of Samuel the Deuteronomist had to save the sequel's proposition that Saul and David were the spontaneous choices of the people and still construct a critical analysis of the origins and functions of kingship in Israel and Judah. The first part traces the origins of kingship *tout court* to the Philistine crisis, which the anarchy of the era of the judges could not resolve. The second part allows the people to insist on a king but attributes the choice of Saul to prophetic instinct and his rejection to the requirements of the law. The third part describes, in the ragged career of David, the gradual emergence of a separate Judean state and a shift in the balance of power to the South. The fourth part explains how David came to be king of all Israel and fought to establish its boundaries. The fifth describes the local and regional resentment of his rule and the amazing grace of his office. The last part eliminates all his opponents and lists the legendary basis and divine legitimation of his government.

The analysis, as the first part might illustrate, takes the form of consecutive narrative dotted with deliberative discourse. The narrative often is interrupted to organize the evidence or to include a subplot. The discourse explains the steps and the place of the narrative in the continuous development of the History. In the first part an effect of the system is the incorporation of an episode in the sequel's life of Samuel into a critical history of the era and institution of the judges.

The first chapter narrates a typical pilgrimage to Shiloh by Hannah and Elkanah and the vow and birth of a child that made one year different from the rest. The Deuteronomist interrupted and expanded the narrative to include three subplots that surface and merge as the part develops. The first parenthesis introduces the sons of Eli: he assumes a dominant role in the expanded narrative, and they become the issue of the following chapters (1 Sam 1:3b, 9aBb, 12–18a, 25, 26). The second subplot is an emendation of Hannah's vow that identifies Samuel as a prophet and nazirite as he will appear in his later dealings with Eli (1 Sam 1:10, 11bB, 12–18, 23aB, 24aB, 25). The third subplot subtly intrudes into the etiology of Samuel's name and makes him a surrogate of Saul and the monarchy.[217] The Deuteronomist's discourse, and especially Hannah's vow and conversation with Eli, relate Samuel to Samson and Hannah to the frivolous festivals held at Shiloh in the time of the judges.[218]

The beginning of the second chapter is the Song of Hannah. It breaks into the account of Elkanah's journey from Shiloh to Ramah,[219] but it also emphasizes the royal motifs of the emended narrative and echoes the theme of divine transcendence that will thread the narrative of Eli and his sons (1 Sam 2:6, 8a, 10b). Although it refers to specific events related in this part and in the later career of Samuel,[220] its official function in the History is to install Yahweh in the narrative as creator, judge, and true God.[221]

The remainder of this chapter and the third fill in the biographical blanks in Samuel's growth from childhood to maturity with the parallel story of Eli and his sons. One topic interrupts the other, and both are pointed by oracles and interpretation. The framework of the Song of Hannah ended with Samuel as a young boy at Shiloh. The next section describes the sinful things that the sons of Eli did in diverting to their own use the sacrifices that were offered as tribute to Yahweh (1 Sam 2:12–17). The third section returns to Samuel, who is still a boy but is growing up and is clothed in the garments and insignia of a priest, and gives the narrative of Hannah and Elkanah a happy ending.[222] The fourth section returns to the sins of the sons of Eli and to the realization that prayer and intercession cannot save them because Yahweh is determined to kill them.[223] The fifth section breaks the narrative flow again to note that Samuel was getting older (1 Sam 2:26). The sixth section is an oracle of an anonymous prophet who predicts the death of Eli's sons and the extermination of his priestly line and the rise of a priestly house in the service of Yahweh's anointed (1 Sam 2:27–36). In the seventh section the scene shifts again to Samuel to repeat that he was an attendant of Yahweh's under the supervision of Eli but, in anticipation of coming events, to note as well that the word of God was rare in those days (1 Sam 3:1). In the eighth section it is Eli who recognizes that God is speaking to Samuel; in the ninth it is Samuel to whom Yahweh reveals that the house of Eli is doomed; in the tenth Eli asks Samuel for a full report of his vision, and in the last Samuel has grown to maturity and has been established as the prophet of Yahweh (1 Sam 3:2–9, 10–14, 15–18, 19–21).

The next four chapters are paired in the same way but are included under the auspices of Samuel. Chapter 4 begins with the notation that the word of Samuel touched all Israel and, with chap. 5, it contrasts the end of the Shilonite priesthood who attended the ark with the autonomy, power, and permanence of the ark as it devastated the Philistine cities. Chapter 6 describes the rituals and ceremonies surrounding the return of the ark to Judah and contrasts with chap. 7, where the word of Samuel goes out to all Israel from the shrines at Bethel, Gilgal, Mizpah, and his hometown of Ramah. This inclusion (cf. 1 Sam 4:1a and 7:3–11)[224] allows the Deuteronomist to find and analyze evidence on the transition from the amphictyonic era of tribal preeminence to the critical era of statehood.

In the fourth chapter narrative alternates with speeches that explain it. It begins with the account of Israel's defeat at Ebenezer, which the elders correctly attribute to Yahweh and seek to remedy by calling on the help of the ark of the covenant. In the second segment another victory of the Philistines is pointed by their realization that in fighting against the ark they were fighting against the almighty God, who overcame the Egyptians with plagues. The third segment reports the loss of the ark and the death of the sons of Eli and marks the end of the house of Eli; the fourth reflects on these facts in the birth and naming of Ichabod. In the fifth chapter there is a ritual degradation of the God Dagon of Ashdod and an admission by the Philistines that the presence of the ark signifies the presence and power of God. The narrative is of disastrous wars with the Philistines, but the explanation is that the glory of Yahweh has departed from Israel into exile.

In chaps. 6 and 7 the ark and the glory of God return to Judah, while Samuel is left in the North to fulfill the amphictyonic offices of prophet, priest, and judge. The sixth chapter describes how the ark of Yahweh, who brought Israel out of Egypt, came to be venerated in the land of Judah.[225] The seventh chapter describes the continuing struggle of judges in the North to undo the inveterate worship of other Gods (1 Sam 7:3–17). The two chapters together explain, in the interplay of action and interpretive discourse, the institutional decay that required the inauguration of kingship.

The narrative presentation of history is deceptively clear. The gradual decline of the house of Eli is paralleled by Samuel's growing preeminence. The ineffectiveness of the northern tribes against Philistine infiltration is matched by the departure of the glory of God to Judah and the South. The concentration in Samuel of the roles of judge, prophet, priest, and surrogate king foreshadows the tragic conflict they created in the person of Saul and their gradual definition in the Davidic dynasty. The circumambulations of the ark reflect the ebb and flow of history from Egypt to the tranquil possession of the land. The individual stories are clear but incomplete, and each phase corrects the last.

Kings

The problem in the book of Kings was to weigh the obvious advances of the monarchy against the reasons for its demise. The sequel was entirely positive about the Davidic dynasty and candid about its kings and ignored the northern kingdom except to say that it reneged on the covenant. The Deuteronomist was concerned with greater Israel and knew that the South had been subverted by sin and kept one kingdom balanced against the other. The problem was resolved by recreating their idyllic origin and then tracing the complex relations that contributed to their gradual decline.

The first part of the book is a model of the kingdom and of the forces, at first benign but increasingly ferocious, that tore it apart. It covers the reign of Solomon, the kingdom he created, and the flaws it contained in a concatenation of literary genres that reflects its historical complexity. It mixes fact and fantasy and from time to time compares Solomon in his kingdom to Adam in the garden of Eden.

The first two chapters are a narrative of the succession of Solomon written from the opposite perspectives of inaugurating a new era and renouncing the past. In them the sequel had told of Adonijah's attempted coup that was foiled when David abdicated in favor of Solomon, the son whom Yahweh loved and had designated as his successor,[226] but in rewriting the chapters the Deuteronomist reveals the secular origins of the kingdom. In the first chapter the Historian follows the intrigue, like the intrigue in the Garden of Eden, that led to David's designation of Solomon as heir to the throne and king of the separate states of Israel and Judah.[227] In the second chapter, in a series of speeches and inquisitions, the Deuteronomist notes that the kingdom depends on obedience to the law (1 Kgs 2:1–4)[228] but also reveals that Solomon's hold on the kingdom was secured by banishing or killing the officials and princes in David's court who might oppose him.[229] In this view, piety is banished and the kingdom is created as a worldly power separate from God.

Chapters 3 and 4 describe the wisdom of Solomon and the wise decisions that produced satisfaction and contentment in his kingdom. The third begins with a proleptic reference to the building of the temple and the royal palace but is devoted to Solomon's first vision at Gibeon.[230] In this dream Solomon asks for the ability to judge and distinguish between good and evil (1 Kgs 3:9),[231] and Yahweh, delighted with the request, also gives him wealth and honor and long life. His wisdom becomes immediately apparent in the judgment that he renders, but his wealth and fame accumulate as the part progresses. The fourth chapter lists the officials of his court and the deputies who supplied the royal household from the provinces. Although the chapter ends on the note that Israel and Judah were satisfied and content, both lists contain the seeds of the kingdom's undoing, one by including the official in charge of forced labor, the other by noting that most of the provisions were supplied by tribal centers in the North.[232]

Chapter 5 has two complementary sections. The first section ascribes to him an empire extending from the Euphrates to Egypt and, in alternating paragraphs that allude to the Garden of Eden, refers to the extent of his dominion and the wealth of his provisions.[233] It ends with an ode to his wisdom manifested in his proverbs and songs and, in the guise of Adam, to his vast knowledge of trees, animals, fish, beasts, and birds (1 Kgs 5:1–14; cf. Gen 2:19–20). The second section describes his alliance with Hiram of Tyre, the very model of the primordial king,[234] and the agreement that gave Solomon timber and precious stones for the temple in return for the palace provisions that he supplied (1 Kgs 5:15–32; cf. Ezek 28:13).

Chapters 6 and 7 describe the construction of the temple and of the royal palace. The temple is an extension of the desert tent of meeting; its utensils and appointments have a cosmological significance; and the entire account is modeled on the account of the construction of the desert shrine. Their link with the story of the Garden of Eden is the cherubim who once guarded the tree of life and now protect the ark of the covenant. The emerging image of the idyllic kingdom gathered around the worship of God, as the wilderness community surrounded the tent of meeting, is fraught with the recollection of the broken idylls of the past.

Chapters 8 and 9 combine incompatible views of the temple and palaces that Solomon built. In the eighth chapter the temple is a summation of history and creation, and the focus of the dreadful things that will befall the kingdom. In the ninth his building operations presage his glorious reign in the eternal dynasty of David, or they symbolize the ugly effects of mingling with the nations and coexisting with the people who were left in the land. The kingdom, from this perspective, is the pinnacle of perfection and the cause of its own undoing.

Chapters 10 and 11 illustrate the enigma in the contrasting stories of the queen of Sheba, who was astonished at his magnificence, and the queens from other lands, who stole away his heart. In the tenth chapter he is, in the manner of the king of Tyre, the merchant king of the world (1 Kings 9; cf. Ezekiel 27). In the eleventh chapter he is surrounded by enemies within and without and bereft of all but the rump of his empire.

The overt history of Solomon's reign is filled with facts and analyses presented in different genres. The implied history is fraught with images and symbols and expressed in the contrast and comparison of its chapters. The kingdom is a new creation where Israel and Judah might have lived forever if their kings had listened to the words of the law. When it ended they would begin again with the promises to Abraham, with his faith and his exemplary obedience.

CONCLUSION

The genres adopted by the Deuteronomist were a synthesis of late Judean literary traditions. Law, prophecy, and history, the issues they confronted, the topics and themes they conveyed, the forms they took, the practices they involved, the varied ways of life they supposed, were all brought together and embellished in a comprehensive history of Israel and the world. The History became all of these things—a record of the past, instruction for the present, a view of the future. In a way, when the History was done there was not much to be said that was not already written.

Sources and Interpretation

The Deuteronomist was familiar with the histories and the writings of the prophets and with the sources they used and the laws and legal traditions they supported. The History includes them, alludes to them, imitates and paraphrases them, or uses them as models and sometimes evokes them and their authors in poetic or dramatic presentations. It has other sources, mentions some of them by name, quotes them when it can, reconstructs them when necessary, and changes them to suit the interpretation they receive.

The sources, comments, and interpretations are abstracted, synthesized, and reworked under an overarching theory of destiny and divine predestination. Everything has its reason, its match, and its opposite. Actions have motives, patterns, and effects. People are moved by good or evil, intelligence or guile; nations are in conflict or aligned; the world assumes chronological and logical sequence and direction. God is removed from it, located by prayer and sacrifice, represented by prophets, priests, kings, and the wisdom manifested in the law, implicated in the covenant, present by words and by the deeds that they effect. History is all of these together, diverse and unsystematic, partly planned, partly inevitable, partly predictable, but entirely by design.

The histories are incorporated, used as the basis of other stories, and expanded in other interpretations. The prophets are quoted in direct discourse or in poetic passages and are a source of historical interpretation rather than a mine of warnings and exhortations. In recapitulating the tradition the Deuteronomistic History became the acme of late Judean literature.

GENESIS

The Deuteronomistic additions and corrections to the epic consisted mainly of genealogical, geographical, and political comments that began to outline the tribal constitution of Israel and situate its growth in continuous time and in relation to known nations, places, and institutions. The Historian's changes to the Priestly version were principally ritual or ethnographic annotations. The Elohist text was most often modified by the insertion of theological comments relative to prophecy and the promise traditions. The changes sometimes were pointed by using insights and imagery from prophetic texts.

In the first part the Garden of Eden was relocated in the real world. The relationship between man and woman is bracketed by the familiar institution of marriage. Children are born and take up the usual pastoral or agricultural occupations. Strife is common. Violence is a way of life. Animal husbandry and the festivals of Pan begin. Bronze and iron tools are invented. The garden, by a feat of surreal geography, becomes the center of the known world. In the wealth of detail and research a few elements are borrowed from the imagination of the prophets. The river that flowed out of Eden and watered the garden is like the river that Ezekiel saw flowing out of the temple in the recreation of Israel (Gen 2:10–14; Ezek 47:1–12). Woman and man are prevented from fulfilling their divine aspirations by the cherubim who guarded the way to the tree of life as, in Ezekiel's Garden of Eden, a cherub was stationed to protect the life of the king of Tyre (Gen 3:24; Ezek 28:14). For their disobedience the land will be overrun by thorns and thistles, as Hosea described the ruins of the altar of Bethel, where similar crimes prevailed (Gen 3:18; Hos 10:8). With these subtle devices the primordial past was contemporized and assumed a familiar ring.

In the second part the flood story is given moral and ritual resonance through allusions to the literatures of the world. The heroes of the epic version are historicized by being identified as the Nephilim, but their limited life spans reflect the Hesiodic and common image of deteriorating ages of the world (Gen 6:1–4).[235] The end of the flood, as its Mesopotamian models suggested, was marked by sacrifice, but in the Deuteronomistic version it was offered in accordance with well-defined ritual prescriptions.[236] The age after the flood, as the example of Canaan makes clear, was the last and the worst of all, and since there was no prophetic justification for this understanding, a blessing and curse took its place (Gen 9:18–27).

In the third part the idea that all the nations of the world would find their blessing in Abraham was supported by bringing him into genealogical or geographical contact with them. Some of the material was taken from maps, some from lists of names, and some was reconstructed from epic texts and episodes.[237] His amazing war with the kings of the East was transposed from a Mesopotamian tradition of astrological and political speculation and confirmed by the omen of El Elyon.[238]

In the fourth part, where Abraham emerges as a prophet, the Deuteronomist mostly imitates or plagiarizes historical sources but also deals with prophetic traditions and texts. Abraham's inaugural prophetic vision is an abstract of Priestly, Elohist, and sequel texts, but his faith and justification fulfill the requirements set out by the epic and Isaiah.[239] The prophetic mood continues in Hagar's meeting with the angel, but the story is copied from a following Elohist incident (Genesis 16; cf. chap. 21).[240] In the narrative of Abraham's meeting with the three men the Deuteronomist presents him as a prophet who intercedes for the people, in the name of justice, when God reveals to him what he is about to do to Sodom and Gomorrah. In the Deuteronomist's view what happened to these places was meant as a lesson to Jerusalem and, not surprisingly, the intercession of Abraham is based on texts that Jeremiah and Ezekiel wrote for the city (cf. Deut 29:22–27). Ezekiel, seeing that the crimes of Jerusalem were the culmination of a tradition of sin, proclaimed that the innocent and the guilty in Jerusalem would be punished, but Abraham protested to Yahweh that this would be unthinkable.[241] Jeremiah, seeing that evil loomed from the North, went through Jerusalem trying to find even one person who would justify saving the city, and Abraham carried out the same sort of search in his persistent questions to Yahweh.[242] In the conclusion of the story of Sodom and Gomorrah Lot becomes involved in an incestuous relationship with his daughters in a story modeled on the curse of Canaan (Gen 19:29–38; cf. 9:18–27). The Elohist story of Sarah and Abraham at the court of Abimelech in Gerar was altered to conform to the story of Sodom and Gomorrah and to articulate the patriarch's prophetic and intercessory powers (chap. 20),[243] but in agreement with Hosea and Jeremiah it also associates prophecy and the healing power of God.[244] The Elohist story of Hagar is expanded by borrowing from the epic account of Isaac (21:25–26, 28–33; cf. chap. 26). The adventures of Abraham's servant who went to Mesopotamia to find Isaac a wife are taken from the adventures of Moses and Jacob (chap. 24).[245] Among the many new things the Historian had to say there were many that had been said before.

In the fifth part the Deuteronomist was exercised chiefly by the genealogies of Abraham and his descendants. The first chapter disposes of his non-Israelite descendants with lists (25:1–4), itineraries (25:11, 18), and customs (25:5–6). The second chapter copies texts to remake Isaac in his religious image, and the third and fourth are homologations of his rights to the promise (chaps. 26; 27; 28). The fifth and sixth chapters, by etymology and clever allusion, introduce the amphictyonic twelve-tribe system of his descendants (29:31–30:24).[246] The seventh chapter belittles the rites of ancestral Gods; the eighth and ninth domesticate the numinous origins of Israel; the tenth undermines the Historian's heroes with the usual indulgence in sex and violence; and the last completes the tawdry genealogical frame (chaps. 31–35).

In the sixth and seventh parts the Deuteronomist added genealogical lists and tales and ethnographic notes to give the myth and ritual of Adonis some acceptable historical color. The sources are mostly those at hand, revised to suit contemporary or ideological issues. The story of Tamar has a genealogical basis and repeats traditional elements from the story of Rebekah, but it is constructed in illustration of the law (chap. 38).[247] The subplot of payment and surreptitious return of their money, which trapped the brothers every time they went to Egypt to buy grain from Joseph, concludes with the possibility of their enslavement and with the Egyptians actually selling themselves and their land in slavery to the Pharaoh. It is a concrete historical touch in an otherwise ethereal plot, but it also illustrates what the Historian thought was an inevitable evil of the monarchy.[248] The final blessing of Jacob takes some of its material from the preceding stories but mainly reinforces the ideology of the twelve-tribe league (chap. 49).[249]

EXODUS

The pattern of Deuteronomistic commentary on the sources remains the same. The epic is corrected in the historical and legal mode that it assumes. The Priestly document is copied and corrected with ritual and liturgical elements. The Elohist text is outfitted with theological comments. Prophecy predominates but references to prophetic texts are rare.

In the first part the revision simply repeats parts of the epic text and fills them with political and ethnographic details on midwifery, the management of disputes, and state slavery.[250] The Elohist interpretation of the name of God is corrected (3:15; cf. 3:14; 34:6). The Priestly text of the next part is anticipated in a discussion of prophecy. The effect of the revision is to begin the biography of Moses and to present his prophetic credentials in the adverse but concrete conditions of Egypt.

In the second part the Deuteronomist duplicated the Priestly plagues to recount the ritual humiliation of Egypt. In their original version the plagues represented the undoing of creation, beginning with a sea monster, proceeding with plagues against the waters, the earth, man and beast, and the heavens, and concluding with the destruction of the Egyptian army in a reenactment of the drama of creation.[251] The Deuteronomist emphasized this connection in duplicate plagues and added others to continue the analogy,[252] but in the plagues of hail, locusts, darkness, and the death of the firstborn the Deuteronomist may also have been indebted to Ezekiel's vision of the creator and to Amos's account of the day of Yahweh.[253] The form of the plagues reflects the sequence of lamentation liturgies[254] and, as creation consisted in the separation of elements, effects Israel's separation from Egypt.[255]

In the third part of Exodus the Deuteronomist drew on texts from other parts of the sources and commentaries to insinuate and draw attention to the practical significance of the decalogue and particularly of its opening commandment. The festivals of Massot and the dedication of the firstborn are expansions on later epic and Elohist texts[256] and are notable for their insistence on the opening affirmation of the decalogue that Yahweh who brought Israel out of Egypt is God (13:3, 8–9, 14–16). The nation's fear and unwillingness to proceed when they saw the Egyptians at the Sea implicitly disputes this affirmation and may reflect Ezekiel's contention that the people worshiped other Gods in Egypt (Exod 14:11–14; cf. Ezek 20:6–8). The Song of the Sea reflects on their miraculous passage and is punctuated by frequent confessions that Yahweh who overcame the Egyptians is God and has become the King of Israel.[257] The story of the manna was revised to inculcate the law of the sabbath (chap. 16). Rebellion at Horeb anticipates a Priestly rebellion in the wilderness, and its lesson, that Yahweh is among his people, is confirmed by a battle with Amalek, which looks like the later battle at Ai.[258] The Elohist appointment of the courts is interrupted to let Moses recount the exodus and permit Jethro to draw the conclusion that Yahweh is greater than all the Gods (18:6–11). The preamble to the covenant recalls the exodus and sets Israel apart as a holy nation (19:3b–8). At Sinai it is principally the decalogue that is revealed, and other additions merely reinforce its prescriptions (20:2–26).[259] At the end Moses and the leaders of Israel see a vision, like Ezekiel's, but of the God of Israel without any distracting appearance.[260]

The plan and construction of the tent of meeting are adapted from the Priestly portrait of the tabernacle and elaborated with diverse elements of the Solomonic and restoration temples. In the Priestly version the tabernacle was a pavilion where Yahweh, fresh from his cosmic victory at the Sea, would dwell among his people.[261] In the

Deuteronomistic version the tent of meeting was a movable shrine, built on a heavenly model and in imitation of the temple of Solomon,[262] its priests accoutred like the king of Tyre in Ezekiel's Garden of Eden,[263], where all due rites and rituals might be performed. It is an ideal place, an amphictyonic shrine, where the tribes of Israel would congregate around their God to do battle with their common foe.[264]

LEVITICUS 8–11 AND NUMBERS

The exterior parts of this concentrically designed book list the officers and outline the organization of the Israelite tribes, while the central parts describe the hierarchical structure and the wars of the amphictyony. The amphictyonic ideal had its roots in the epic and Priestly genealogies of Israel and in the seeming catholicity and concord of the Davidic and Solomonic empires as the sequel and the Deuteronomist understood them. It allowed the Historian to correct the genealogical model of Israel's origins, to revise the nationalist model of invasion and conquest, to explain the alliances and dissolutions that produced the divided monarchy, to synthesize local and regional material on wars and warfare, law, authority, kingship, theocracy, cult places and the covenant, and to be indifferent to the collapse of the kingdoms and the decline of national states.[265]

The first part defines the amphictyony as a community of tribes assembled in camp and gathered before Yahweh at the tent of meeting. Aaron is anointed, attired, garlanded, purified, and sanctified as the keeper and officiant of the tent, and he and his sons are awarded their priestly allowances. The community is said to comprise the children of Israel, governed by elders, and is designated a holy people to whom Yahweh their God, who brought them out of Egypt, revealed his holiness and his glory. It is a nearly perfect community but troubled from the start with rivalry and disputes (Lev 8:1–11:45).[266]

The second part describes the organization and function of the amphictyony. The first two chapters take note of the tribes, their representatives in the assembly, their designated leaders, their military commanders, their battle array at cardinal points around the tent of meeting, and their order of march (Numbers 1–2). The last two chapters provide a cultic calendar for the assembly, making Passover its principal festival, describing the irregular ritual of pitching and breaking camp and the rubrics for the liturgical and military use of trumpets, and recording the date of the first order of march and the usual circumstances of the procession of the ark (Numbers 9–10). The third and fourth chapters dedicate the Levites, in place of firstborn children from each of the twelve tribes, to the service of God at the tent of meeting (Numbers 3–4). The seventh and eighth chapters install the Levites in their service of the altar and list the contributions of the individual tribal representatives to the altar in money and in kind (Numbers 7–8). The central chapters decree the obligations of members of the assembly in the maintenance of the physical and spiritual purity of the holy encampment. Within the religious and political order of the camp that the Historian proposes, Aaron is appointed to pronounce the blessing imparted by Yahweh; Moses is set apart to hear, like Ezekiel and the Delphic oracle, the voice of Yahweh speaking to him from above the mercy seat over the ark in the tent of meeting; and the ark personifies the dynamic presence of Yahweh.[267]

The image of the amphictyony as an armed camp is supposed and sustained in the third part, which records its first defeats and describes its developing hierarchical system. In the first chapter a divine fire consumes the outer edge of the camp; the rabble complains about the manna they have to eat; members of the militia receive the prophetic spirit generally reserved for the elders; and plague decimates the people.[268] In the second chapter (Numbers 12) Miriam and Aaron pretend to share the prophetic authority of Moses, but Yahweh appears at the tent of meeting and Miriam is struck with leprosy and must remain outside the camp. In the third and fourth chapters (Numbers 13–14) the scouts who reconnoiter the land are representatives of the twelve tribes; their refusal to enter the land is supported by a popular movement to choose another leader and return to Egypt; and their belated and wrongheaded attack on the Canaanites fails because neither the ark, nor Moses, nor God was with them. The fifth chapter (Numbers 15) opportunely stops to consider rules to be observed when eventually the land is taken, as well as the system of oracular inquiry that Moses followed in making such rules in the wilderness. The sixth and seventh chapters (Numbers 16–17), with marvels and magic, reaffirm the sole authority of Moses and the preeminence of Aaron among the priests. The last two chapters (Numbers 18–19) delimit the authority and functions of the Levites and rites of purification for the camp contaminated as it has been by the dead bodies of the slain. This image of an armed assembly, centered on the ark when camp is pitched and following it at a distance when camp is broken, allows the Historian to describe the interlocking levels of authority and obedience in a mutable but permanent theocratic state.

This theocratic state is the subject of the fourth part (Numbers 20–25), in which Moses and Aaron disappear from the scene and Yahweh takes direct charge of the destiny of his people. Both are condemned for the sin of Meribah; Aaron dies; and Moses is not present for the wars with the Amorites and Moab. His place is taken by the mantic Balaam, who sees and speaks as Yahweh directs, and by God himself, who brought the people out of Egypt and is among them as their king. At the end of the part Moses reappears in preparation for his farewell, and the priest Phinehas reinstates the service of the tent of meeting that had been jeopardized by the cult of foreign Gods.

The fifth part (Numbers 26–31) reviews the troops mustered at the borders of Canaan, prepares the vanguard for the attack, and establishes the rules of holy war.[269] The image of the camp fades into the reality of the land in decrees and oracular decisions by Moses concerning the rights of women to acquire or alienate property. The assembly acquires permanence and cohesion in the daily, weekly, monthly, and yearly festivals that it is to observe. The definition of the tribal confederacy is assured by the appointment of Joshua as the successor of Moses for the battles to come.

The last part (Numbers 32–36) reviews the history of the camp and its route from Egypt to Transjordan. The amphictyonic ideal is reaffirmed in the establishment of levitical cities and cities of refuge to assure the sanctity of God's land. The boundaries of the land are determined, and the tribal leaders who will help Joshua and Eleazar in its apportionment are named. The ideal will be tested in the time of the judges but not until its constitution has been promulgated by Moses.

The amphictyony defines Israel as a holy assembly of tribes gathered around a place of worship that is also the instrument of their salvation and separation from the nations. It is an image and idea for which the evidence is assembled and analyzed as the History progresses, but in the meantime it is the theory around which the wilderness era is constructed. It is not asserted or meant as a fact but is presented as the model in which past and future can be understood as contemporary and continuous.

DEUTERONOMY

The History's dominant theories and lines of interpretation are systematized in the book of Deuteronomy. Much of the text is transposed from the earlier books, but there is also an attempt to incorporate specifying insights from the prophets.

The first part preserves the concept of the tribal league as the context of the law. It is mostly a brute repetition of texts from Exodus and Numbers that, through combination, compression, and slight modification, rewrites history as a preface to the law and the covenant.

The judicial system is reestablished, this time on a tribal basis, and the camp gets rid of the generation that rebelled in the wilderness before hearing Moses' interpretation of the law (Deut 1:13–15; 2:14–15).

The last part corresponds to it but also rewrites history as prophecy. The law is confided to the priests who carry the ark of the covenant, and it becomes an instrument of the conquest (chap. 31). In the covenant ceremony the law is read; Yahweh becomes king in the tribal assembly; and Moses proclaims the individual exploits and blessings of the tribes (31:9–13; 33:1–5). But history and the warnings that have accumulated around it in earlier parts of this book are rewritten in the Song of Moses, with the help of classical prophetic texts, as a poetic preview of the history yet to be recorded.

The song begins, as the vision of Isaiah began, with an invocation of heaven and earth. The first strophe presents Moses as a skilled orator but agrees with the prophetic texts in portraying Yahweh as a God of honesty, uprightness, judgment, and justice.[270] The second strophe introduces the theme of the poem, taken from the same text of Isaiah, by insisting that the people of Israel are spoiled children who refuse to recognize Yahweh as their parent.[271]

The first section of the poem reviews the history of Israel from Egypt to the occupation of the land and is influenced by the critical viewpoint of the prophets. The first strophe, beginning with the Priestly map of the world, describes Yahweh's choice of Israel in Egypt and their journey through the wilderness with allusions to the negative aspects of these themes in Hosea, Micah, and Jeremiah.[272] The second strophe depicts their entry into a land such as the sequel described, but it also includes allusions to their points of rebellion in the wilderness.[273] The third strophe, in images drawn from the sequel, Hosea, Jeremiah, and Ezekiel, sees them succumbing to the temptations of the land and the worship of other Gods (32:15–17).[274] The review of history, in this way, looks beyond the story that has been told thus far to include the future condemnations by the prophets.

The second section describes Yahweh's initial response to the crimes of his people. The first strophe, in retaliation for the crime that the people committed in choosing another God and in dependence on Isaiah, pictures Yahweh choosing another people instead of his own (32:18–21).[275] The second strophe, in reliance on texts of Amos and Jeremiah, becomes more specific in describing the pain this would entail for the people who have been rejected (32:22).[276] This response, being simple retribution, turns out to be hardly what Yahweh had in mind.

The third section is a soliloquy and reflection on the first response.

In the first stanza Yahweh reflects on the motive of divine self-interest to which Moses appealed in asking him to forgive his people in the wilderness (32:26–27).[277] In the second stanza he explores the theme of ignorance that Isaiah, Hosea, and Jeremiah developed and cites as an example the people's incomprehension of the defeat that Isaiah had predicted (32:28–30).[278] In the third stanza he turns to the nations that might have replaced his own and, in the stereotypes of Isaiah and the Pentateuch, sees them as a vineyard producing the wine of Sodom and Gomorrah (32:31–33). In the fourth stanza, in a crasis of images from the prophets, Yahweh turns against these nations (32:34–35),[279] and in the fifth stanza he takes up the cause of his people (32:36).

The poem ends with Yahweh's victory over the other Gods and vengeance on his enemies. The Gods to whom they sacrificed are as useless as Jerusalem's covenant with Death and Sheol, criticized by Isaiah, because it is Yahweh who governs life and death or, in Hosea's words, who hurts and heals and cannot be resisted (Deut 32:37–39).[280] The sharpened sword that Ezekiel saw flashing against Jerusalem will now devour the flesh of their adversaries, as Yahweh, in the words of Nahum, takes vengeance on his enemies (Deut 32:40–43).[281]

The poem is an original composition that summarizes events in the wilderness and anticipates the stories to be told in the book of Judges. It reflects the Deuteronomist's special interests and is included as their source and compendium, but it also gives force and actuality to the prophecy of Moses by intertwining it with words and images from the prophetic tradition.

The second part of Deuteronomy introduces and explains the decalogue and in particular its prohibition of images of the Gods and its insistence on obedience and total dedication to Yahweh. The second-to-last part interprets the decalogue as the basis of the covenant and illustrates its importance in the blessings and curses that attend it. The first part is mostly an elaboration of the sequel by cross-referencing preceding Pentateuchal texts, but both it and its match are tempered by quotations and allusions to the prophetic tradition.

The exhortation at the beginning of the second part excludes images of created things to represent Yahweh who created them and so relies on the account of creation in Genesis, but its argument is constructed by agreeing and taking issue with Ezekiel. The basic point of the argument is that the people heard the sound of words at Horeb but did not see anything and therefore should not make statues or images of anything, of man or woman, of animals or birds or creeping things or fish. In his opening vision, on the contrary, Ezekiel not only heard a voice but he keeps insisting that he saw, and he describes living beings with the features of humans and animals and birds and the glory of Yahweh in the apparent likeness of a human form.[282] In his vision of the temple in Jerusalem, however, it is precisely the worship of an invidious statue and images of animals and creeping things and prostration before the Sun that, as the Deuteronomist warns, led to the destruction of the city and exile.[283] The visions are not incompatible in the development of Ezekiel's prophecy, but the Deuteronomist was eager to distinguish them and keep the people away from the entrapments of the prophet's vivid imagination.

In the corresponding second-to-last part the covenant is made on the decalogue, the people agreeing to observe the law, Yahweh agreeing to be their God and promising, when they have been taken into exile for their disobedience, to steal them from the distant heavens (chaps. 26; 30).[284] There is a ceremony to be celebrated by the tribes when they come into the land, with twelve curses to match their number, and a warning to families, clans, and tribes not to forsake the covenant and worship other Gods (chaps. 27; 29). There are some curses copied from Assyrian prototypes and some with evident bases in texts of the law and the prophets.[285] The threat, for instance, of a nation whom they have not known devouring the fruit of their land and of their labors and leaving them crushed and oppressed is taken from Hosea's picture of Ephraim oppressed, crushed, and unknowingly devoured by aliens.[286] Similarly, the warning that they would have to return to Egypt, although Yahweh promised them they would not, is taken intentionally from Hosea's warning that they would not return to Egypt but would die in Assyria (Deut 28:68).[287] In the same way, the threat of invasion and defeat by a distant nation whose language they cannot comprehend is essentially an amalgam of sayings from Isaiah and Jeremiah (Deut 28:49–53).[288] In the Deuteronomist's view the penalty for breaking their covenant with Yahweh is entirely a matter of tradition.

In the third part the Deuteronomist sets out the legislation that distinguishes Israel from its environment, and in the fourth part, which corresponds to it, legislates its own particularity. The opening section draws on traditions of Israel's independence that Isaiah and Hosea transmitted,[289] as the legislation in its parallel part sometimes supposes traditions elaborated in Isaiah, Jeremiah, and Ezekiel.[290] The brunt of the Deuteronomist's argument is borne by the regional and international resources tapped first by the Elohist but its particular cachet is a product of local prophetic intervention.

Deuteronomy is a special book, a mine of information and of legal reasoning and tradition, a prospectus of upright behavior. Its special force is its reliance on the insight and teaching of Moses and in this regard it was forever indebted to the prophets.

JOSHUA

The three parts of Joshua have individual and distinctive sources. The first part, revolving on the sequel's account, is based on pentateuchal sources. The second part, built on original narratives of covenant and conquest, elaborates the amphictyonic theory of holy war. The last part, composed by the Deuteronomist, is a geography and genealogy of the tribes seeded with federalist ideology. The sources do not exist as such but only in the image that they received from the astute analytical formulation of the Historian.

The first part expands the sequel's narrative of fantastic victories against Jericho and Ai into a ritual conquest of Canaan by the tribal league performed according to the pattern laid down in the Pentateuch. The Transjordanian tribes, who otherwise would be excluded from the holy land, are reconfirmed as the vanguard of the invading forces (Josh 1:12–18; cf. Numbers 32; Joshua 22). The inhabitants of the land dutifully assume the attitude prescribed in the Song of the Sea (2:9–10; cf. Exod 15:15–16). The ark of the covenant sets out ahead of the people as it did during their wilderness wanderings (3:3–4; cf. Num 10:33b–36). The Jordan, like the Sea, stops flowing so that the people can cross on dry ground (3:16–17; 4:21–24; cf. Exod 14:29). The manna ceases as had been predicted (5:12; cf. Exod 16:35), and Passover is celebrated at the time prescribed (5:10–11; cf. Exod 12:18). The priests sound the usual blasts of the trumpet, and the walls of Jericho come tumbling down (Joshua 6; cf. Num 10:1–10). Joshua builds an altar and writes out a copy of the law exactly as Moses required (8:30–35; cf. Deut 27:1–8). The only misstep in the ritual, awkward and ominous, is the crime of Achan, but it is quickly corrected by magic in the full assembly of the tribes (chap. 7).

The second part enacts the laws of holy war and notably the ban that Achan failed to enforce. In the sequel's version Joshua made a peace treaty with the Gibeonites, but the Historian shifts the blame from him by having the leaders of the assembly take the oath to let them live (9:14, 15b). The assembly complains as usual, but for a change they are right and the leaders, in accordance with a special provision of the covenant, make the Gibeonites slaves of the assembly and hewers of wood and drawers of water at the altar of Yahweh (9:16–27; cf. Deut 29:10). In the sequel's version Joshua defeated a coalition of southern kings by coming upon them suddenly and taking advantage of the panic that Yahweh inspired among them. In the Historian's version the battle was one among many over cities in the South, all of which exemplified the ferocity of the ban, and it was won when Joshua, as the book of Yashar records, made the sun and the moon stand still in the valley of Aijalon (10:10b–43). In the sequel's version Joshua defeated a northern coalition led by the king of Hazor and so took all the land as Yahweh had promised Moses. In the revised version the victory was achieved according to the laws of war, but there were many other battles to be fought before the inhabitants of the land could be put under the ban and exterminated (11:4, 6, 8b–22).

The third part reviews the conquest from the point of view of the individual tribes and their amphictyonic assembly. There are tribal allotments at Gilgal and at Shiloh, where the heads of the tribes gathered around Joshua at the entrance to the tent of meeting (14:6; 18:1; 19:51). There are cities of refuge to offset the insistence on family and tribal loyalties and maintain the holiness of the land. The levitical cities are set up like amphictyonic sanctuary cities, with sacred areas designated outside their walls (Joshua 21; cf. Num 35:1–8). The Transjordanian tribes are well aware that they live outside the holy land and, when it appears that they have violated the law of the central sanctuary of the league, all the other tribes gather at Shiloh to do battle with them (chap. 22). At the end of the book all the tribes, along with the elders, heads, judges, and officers of the league, assemble at Shechem to take an oath of allegiance to God and the law (chap. 24).

JUDGES

The narrative sources of the book of Judges are dotted with the tokens of their Deuteronomistic inspiration. The legends and folktales do not fit into their form but still have no integrity or coherence apart from the historical lessons they were designed to teach. Each part takes a closer look at the uneasy federation of originally politically or geographically distinct tribes with their individual, clan, and regional differences. Together they present the problem that the monarchy and national states would try to resolve.

In the first part the sources are marked by paradigms and by frameworks. The imaginary judgeship of Othniel, whose real story is well known, is recounted completely in clichés which reappear in the story of Ehud to set apart the original legend. Similarly, the history of Deborah and Barak, with its framework elements and some typical Deuteronomist storytelling features, emphasizes by the recurrence of these items in the duplicate Song of Deborah what parts of the song are original. As usual, the opening clues are especially clear but become more subtle or absent as the book progresses.

The legend of Ehud tells of his bold exploits in freeing his people from the power of the king of Moab (Judg 3:12–30).[291] It is the historical theory, not the legend, that makes him an appointee of Yahweh's and a pan-Israelite hero, that assigns him to a time of national apostasy, that aligns Ammon and Amalek on the side of the king, and that ends with full-scale war and a massive victory over the Moabites.[292] The legend itself, full of irony and puns that make it memorable, was satisfied to recount the clever and degrading revenge taken by common people on the pompous foreign king who oppressed them. It was the Deuteronomist who gave it a context and rationale and made it the stuff of history.[293]

The story of Deborah and Barak is essentially a correction of the sequel's version of victory over the Canaanite coalition in the North (Judges 4–5; cf. Joshua 11). The evidence for this correction was the Song of Deborah, once perhaps the Song of Jael, which the Deuteronomist first paraphrases and then cites in an appropriately convincing version. The original song can be reconstructed by undoing the editorial process that brought it into the History[294] and by observing what parts of the History crept into the recording of the song.[295] The song tells of Yahweh's stunning victory over the Canaanites and Jael's winning ways with Sisera.[296] In the prose version the prophet Deborah domesticates an unknown Jael, and Barak brings the tale into the purview of history. They are not the same story, as the Deuteronomist is careful to observe, but they are literarily and historically inseparable.[297]

In the second part the method of marking sources is more complicated. In the story of Gideon the account of his exploits against Midian is combined with tales of a losing battle with the cult of Baal. In the story of Abimelech the narrative of the king alternates with interpretations of his reign by his enemies. One is the model for the other, and both combine to create an allegory of would be dynasts, usurpers, and kings.

The combination of a legendary source and its historical interpretation in the Gideon narrative is marked by using the alternative name Jerubbaal for the hero and by duplicating every aspect of his story. The story is presented in outline at the beginning, where the Midianite menace that is supposed in the source is traced by the narrator to Israel's evil ways, and by a prophet more specifically to their worship of Amorite Gods.[298] The story is elaborated, in a scene resembling the installation of Moses as prophet, when Yahweh chooses Gideon to defend Israel against Midian and his first act, as Jerubbaal, is to remove the Gods of the Amorites, Baal and his Asherah, whose worship the unnamed prophet condemned (6:11–24, 25–32). The model is repeated again when, in response to the menace, Gideon is possessed by the spirit and summons the neighboring tribes to arms but requires further signs of his prophetic appointment (6:33–35, 36–40). This tension between inspiration and effective leadership is developed when, as Jerubbaal, Gideon defeats Midian and executes their princes, and when again as Gideon he kills their kings, makes an idol of their ornaments, and is offered the throne of Israel and dynastic succession (7:1–25; 8:1–35). The historical interpretation is developed from a straightforward legend of a hero who with a few brave troops thwarted Midianite incursions. It keeps suggesting its use of the legendary source, without ever exactly identifying it, by moving from the simpler to the more complex, from a blunt statement of apostasy and its prophetic condemnation, to the dramatic appointment of Gideon as Jerubbaal, who removed the altar of Baal, to Gideon who mustered Israel and was confirmed in his quasi-prophetic office, to the legendary victory by Gideon and its allegorical interpretation. The legend, in effect, maintained its force by being completely subsumed in the history.

The story of Abimelech is linked to the story of Jerubbaal and has a similar reduplicating pattern. In the opening section Abimelech, illegitimate son of Jerubbaal, usurps the throne that Gideon rejected. In the second section Jotham, Gideon's youngest son, interprets this evil deed by reciting the fable of the trees and the shrubs and explaining its application to Abimelech. In the third section the troubles of the usurper are attributed to God, and in the fourth they are explained as the work of the troublemaker Gaal and the God of the covenant in Shechem. In the fifth section, where fire leaps out of the brush to burn the tower of Shechem, the fable seems to work in Abimelech's favor, but in the last section Jotham's interpretation is vindicated. Gideon was a warrior, not a judge, who could have been king. Abimelech, as his name suggests, is the king of Israel that Gideon might have been, in a town that was known, as tradition attests, for its treachery in the making and breaking of kings.

The third part is constructed to suggest that it, like the whole book, was composed by adding recollections of rivalry and war to a chronicle of local leaders. The list of judges includes Jephthah and notes about each one, more or less in the manner of the kings: his genealogy or his male and female descendants, his tribe or hometown, the length of his rule, and the place of his burial. In Jephthah's case each of these items is elaborated in historical or cultic legends that give his war with the Ammonites a paradigmatic place in the History. He was the illegitimate son of Gilead. He was an outcast, lived for a while in Tob, but had no hometown and was buried "in the cities of Gilead." In place of a hometown it is noted that he held office at Mizpah and in proof of this point the Historian includes the letter that he sent from there to the Ammonites justifying, by summarizing the narratives in Numbers, Israel's title to Amorite, not Ammonite, territory in Transjordan. He had one daughter who is included in the story, on the pretext of fulfilling his vow, by reciting the origins of the rites of Adonis. His victory has some geographical interest but is noted perfunctorily and mainly as an opportunity to recall the ancient and ridiculous animosity between Ephraim and Gilead. The sources of Jephthah's story, apart from those included in the earlier books of the History, are practical knowledge of grammar, geography, and girls.[299]

The fourth part was constructed to counterbalance the second and illustrate the unobstructed outcome of pure charisma. Samson, like Gideon, had a special calling, and like him had a legendary role that did not quite mesh with its historical interpretation. Gideon, the warrior who won a name for himself by defeating the marauding Midianites, resisted kingship but could not overcome the tug of his religious roots. Samson, the Danite legend who represented the early relations between Israel and Judah and the Mediterranean world, was a renegade hero tragically undone by his nazirite calling.[300]

The sources of his story are set apart in the narrative by regular reference to his vocation. The hero's divine origin is insinuated in a clever combination of folktale elements familiar from the cycles of Abraham and Jacob and from the more recent example of Gideon (chap. 13).[301] His unlucky marriage is the occasion of brilliant feats of valor against the Philistines that were copied in part from the legends of Hercules and punctuated by reference to his vocation and his Israelite heritage.[302] The heroic feats associated with his dalliance in Gaza and in Sorek with Delilah were inspired in part by the same legends and are interrupted, as the first were, by references to his nazirite calling (16:1–31; see 16:17, 20, 22). They end with a prayer and the humiliation of Dagon, which set Samson's romance apart as the source of the Historian's interpretation (15:18–19; 16:20–31).

The last part of Judges is transitional and is composed on the model of earlier and later narrative accounts. Its specific function in the History is to explain the migration of the tribe of Dan, the minority position of Benjamin in the tribal league, and the relative importance of the amphictyonic shrines at Bethel and Dan. Their overall interpretive function is to describe the cohesion and cooperation of the tribal league, with Judah in a position of preeminence, before the monarchy and its cults became the ruination of the people.

The first section describes the inauguration of the cult at Dan under the direction of a levitical priesthood descended from Moses. It is derived, literarily, from circumambient stories, is cast in the mold of the exodus and conquest, and distinguishes its sources as uniquely nonrepetitive.[303] The second section is modeled on it, refers backward and forward to familiar themes, and presents the dark side of Saul's inauguration of the monarchy by telling terrible stories about the people and places with whom he was associated.[304]

It is apparent in Judges that the ratio of information to sources and interpretation is slight. The fact that Hazor was not defeated by all Israel under Joshua but by a few volunteers from the North is told and retold in poetry and in prose. Midianite incursions are the stuff of the legend of Gideon, which itself is a pretext for reflections on religion and politics. Jephthah is a chance to discuss boundaries in Transjordan and to give Gilead a prominent place in the history of Israel. The history of Dan and the Philistines barely shines through the legends of Samson. The legends of Bethel are mostly a reflection of evil intention in a variety of times. What is of interest, of course, is that each of the elements is indelibly marked and clearly related to the rest.

SAMUEL

The Historian's main source in Samuel is the sequel's story of the foundation and confirmation of the Davidic dynasty despite the many setbacks and vicissitudes that threatened it. This was subdivided and elaborated by the Historian in separate stories of Samuel, Saul, and David, each with its own peculiar information and sources.

The story of Samuel includes the sequel's account of his birth and dedication at Shiloh in a final episode of the period of the judges that describes a turn in the tide of Philistine supremacy, the transition of power from Israel to Judah, and the alignment of prophets, priests, judges, and kings in an all-Israel regime. The first chapter is expanded in the archaic style of the original by dramatizing the ritual dedication of the nazirite (1 Samuel 1; cf. Num 6:1–5). Chapter 2 includes a psalm that might have been used on such an occasion; illustrates the Deuteronomist's usual interest in sacrificial ritual, priestly paraphernalia, and the customs of the tent of meeting; and continues to explain the rivalry between the priestly houses in Israel.[305] Chapter 3 illustrates the prophetic function of dreams and introduces Samuel as the authentic successor of Moses in the line of prophets and servants of Yahweh. Chapter 4 puts an end to the authority of the house of Eli and, in reliance on words of Hosea and of themes from Micah and Ezekiel, describes the removal from Israel of the ark and the power it symbolized.[306] Chapters 5 and 6 continue this digression by describing, with reference to Exodus and Numbers, the progress of the ark to the territory of Judah and the devastation that it left in its wake.[307] The last chapter (chap. 7) unites in the person of Samuel all the powers of prophet, priest, and judge that will be transmitted, with disastrous results, to Saul.[308]

The story of Saul is the sequel's version punctuated and framed by the theory of kingship, enlarged with annalistic and legendary materials and interwoven with a subplot on kingship and the cult. The theory is the Deuteronomist's and is stated with reference to earlier parts of the History.[309] The annalistic material concerns his wars with the Philistines and is fitted out with Deuteronomistic summaries and information.[310] The legendary material concerns the heroic exploits of Jonathan, but it is worked into a Deuteronomistic lesson on the law and worship.[311] The subplot, in which Saul is tricked into sacrificing at Gilgal and so is deprived of his kingdom, is an artificial allusion to Amos's diatribes against the cult at Bethel and Gilgal.[312] The wealth of information and variety of material are evidence of considerable research and compositional skills, but all likewise contribute to the Historian's single-minded interpretation.

The first part of the history of David incorporates the sequel's narrative of Saul's wars, his choice of David as his commander in chief, and his death. In the Historian's version (1 Samuel 16–31) Saul's dementia and growing aversion to David; his son Jonathan's perfidious alliance with David; the collusion of Samuel, priests, and prophetic types in David's rise to power; the attraction of the disaffected to his cause; and his desperate enlistment with the Philistines are all subordinated to an itinerary that brings David into contact with the farthest reaches of Judean territory and into favor with its leaders.[313] The history is recounted in fits and starts according to the plan set out at the beginning. In the first chapter Saul is rejected and David is anointed; the spirit comes on David and leaves Saul; and David is called into the service of the king to soothe his troubled mind. This is the whole story in outline, but it has internal conflicts—the David who is anointed is a young shepherd, while the David who is taken into Saul's service is a famous warrior—and conflicts with the story of their meeting in the second chapter. And so the history goes, with one chapter presenting clues to the next, the next not quite fulfilling its promise, the next beginning over again, one adding to the plot, the other interpreting it. This jagged method was used to correct the sequel and to organize and interpret the material in the historical record.[314]

The second part of the story of David confirms his kingship in Judah, over the North, and in all Israel (2 Samuel 1–12). It includes from the sequel the narrative of his anointing and installation in his capital, the oracle of Nathan, and the birth of Solomon that was its fulfillment. It adds from the Deuteronomist's research and learning lists, prayers, and laments; details of battles and of peaceful negotiations; information on the boundaries and internal organization of the kingdom; and an illustration of the monarch's merely human status. David is presented as the conqueror of the Near Eastern world who, by putting an end to Aramean aggression, gave Israel access to the vaunted boundary of the promised land at the river Euphrates (2 Samuel 8–12).[315]

The fifth part of the book is the story of Absalom's role in the revolt of the North. It is built on the sequel's account with the help of material related to the protocol and conversations of the court. The rape of Tamar is changed to include, besides her fear and outrage, her technical protests and the reticence of the king, which give the conversation legal coloring.[316] The woman of Tekoa persuades David to let Absalom return in a speech tempered with allusions to the law and to the legends of creation (2 Samuel 14).[317] The king's flight from Jerusalem begins with a procession of the ark across the brook Kidron, reenacting in the opposite direction the procession of the ark across the Jordan (2 Samuel 15; esp. 15:23–29).[318] The route is peopled with friends and adversaries, and the city is filled with plots, as the king makes his humble pilgrimage to the storied centers of the kingdom before returning in triumph to Jerusalem.[319] In the sequel's version David never left Jerusalem but waited at the city gate until news of the death of Absalom reached him. In the Deuteronomist's version, where every word and gesture conspires to take attention away from Absalom, there is a ritual exile and humiliation of the king in which by complete submission to God he comes to realize that he is indeed the king of Israel.[320]

The last part is an appendix with information and syntheses to be integrated into the preceding and following texts. The care that the Historian has taken to correct the sequel by asserting David's separate authority in Israel and in Judah and diminishing the reality and effects of Absalom's revolt is justified now by recording another revolt, more stylized but otherwise quite like it, that was led in reality by Sheba (2 Samuel 20).[321] The extermination of the house of Saul, which was denied or qualified in earlier parts, is admitted in the second chapter but is justified by reference to the covenant and to the curse of infertility that attended it (2 Sam 21:1–14).[322] The mistake that the sequel made in supposing that David had defeated a Philistine champion in single combat is corrected by assigning the victory, along with others like it, to the men in his entourage (2 Sam 21:15–22). The thanksgiving that was omitted when David returned to Jerusalem is expressed in a psalm resuming the same ritual themes of humiliation and magnification of the king (2 Samuel 22).[323] Instead of the standard Deuteronomistic evaluation of the king and concluding remarks, David sings his own eulogy, summarizing the perfection of his reign and the stability of his dynasty (2 Sam 23:1–7).[324] In anticipation of the sequel's list of those who sided with Solomon in Adonijah's attempted coup, the Historian returns to David's early days and gives a complete anecdotal list of the heroes who fought by his side (2 Sam 23:8–39; cf. 1 Kgs 1:8). To reaffirm David's control of the kingdoms of Israel and Judah a census is devised, but to signal the endurance of his dynasty and the power of repentance the resulting plague, described with the panoply of Ezekiel's vision of the destruction of Jerusalem, is not allowed to touch his capital city (2 Samuel 24).[325] The material is not well integrated into the flowing narratives that surround it, but it is a well-marked and vital pivot in the history.

KINGS

The sources of the book of Kings are regularly identified. The unmarked sources are the texts and persons of the prophets and writers who preceded the Historian and whose work the History was meant to supplant.

The first part is based on the sequel, on hearsay, on the Priestly ideology of the tabernacle as the Historian understood it, and on the image of world empire conjured by Ezekiel in his marvelous poetic diatribes against Tyre. The sequel sees peaceful transition of power; the Deuteronomist sees intrigue and violence and an accommodating legacy from David. Ezekiel admired and took exception to the wisdom, wealth, and world renown of the Tyrian empire, but the Deuteronomist used it as the model of an empire that stretched from sea to sea supported by vamps and magnates of every ilk. The Historian was aware of every nuance; the sources were satisfied with images and innuendo.[326] It is a wonder that the Solomonic empire was nearly perfect but no wonder that it was doomed from the start.[327]

In the second part the sequel recounted Judah's resistance to Israel with the help of Aramean allies, while the History told of the rot and intrigue that was gnawing away at the North. The division of the kingdom, as the sequel saw it, was due to Judah's miscalculation, but in the Historian's view it was the outcome of ignorant and willful repression. Prophets naturally opposed it, a prophet like Amos spoke out against it, but the sin of Jeroboam prevailed.[328]

In the third part the sequel mentioned that Jehoshaphat made peace with the king of Israel and referred specifically to his dealings with Ahaziah the son of Ahab (1 Kgs 22:42, 45–46, 48–51). The Deuteronomist knew that Jehoshaphat and Ahab were contemporaries, that Ahaziah died prematurely, and that Jehoshaphat made an alliance with Ahaziah's brother and successor Jehoram (1 Kgs 22:41, 52; 2 Kgs 3:1). In writing about Ahab, therefore, there were two perspectives to be reconciled. On the one hand, Ahab, by marrying Jezebel of Sidon and introducing the cult of Baal into Israel, was the worst of all kings after Jeroboam, and this aspect of his reign is brought out in his confrontations with Elijah (1 Kings 16–19; 21). On the other hand, Ahab kept the Arameans in check and, when he had repented, was joined in one of these ventures by Jehoshaphat, and this aspect of his reign is recorded under the auspices of Micaiah and the sons of the prophets (1 Kings 20; 22).[329] Elijah is portrayed as a prophet in the image of Moses. Micaiah and his associates imitate the bizarre behavior of Ezekiel,[330] but Micaiah's prophecy, as his last words show, was that of his namesake Micah.[331]

The fourth part continues with the legends of the prophets and the wars against the Arameans. It is the mirror image of the third and allows the Deuteronomist to digest information without putting it in chronological order or historical perspective and so conceive a crasis of historical events. The legends stand out as unlikely but instructive and indicate that the information is to be understood apart from its actual context. The record is a collection of vignettes about various times and a synthesis of prophecy and history.[332]

The fifth part interprets the revolt of Jehu, a critical situation for the Davidic dynasty in the sequel's exposition, as a time of religious revival in the North and the South. In the North it consisted in exterminating Baal, and the Aramean raids that devastated the whole country during the same period receive only incidental notice. In the South the reform consisted in renovating the temple and removing vestiges of the cult of Baal, and Israel's victories over the Arameans are mentioned only in passing or as an afterthought. The revivals are paradigmatic and, as a final note on the kindness and mercy of Yahweh, are preludes to the collapse of the kingdoms that no reform was able to forestall.[333]

The sixth part is the history of Assyrian invasions ending in the fall of Samaria, the siege of Jerusalem, and a premonition of the Babylonian exile. It is composed of short notices from the Chronicles of the kings, with reference to the history of Israel outlined in the earlier books, and with sporadic quotations from the prophets.[334] The explanation of the fall of Samaria appeals to the prophetic tradition and suggests its sources with quotes from Jeremiah and Micah (2 Kings 17).[335] The revised speech of the Rabshaqeh paraphrases the argument from recorded history that Amos was the first to use.[336] Hezekiah's appeal to Isaiah takes expressions from Hosea and Zephaniah.[337] Isaiah's oracle against Assyria has some of his diction but mixes his words with images from Jeremiah and Ezekiel (2 Kgs 19:21–28).[338] His cure of Hezekiah revolves around a ritual that Hosea described (2 Kgs 20:5, 8; cf. Hos 6:2). At such a critical juncture, when the sequel thought that everything was all right, the Historian could appeal to the prophets to prove that it was not.

The last part goes from the sin of Manasseh to the fall of the city and is mostly a resumption of the Historian's themes. In the critical matter of Josiah's exemption from the fate of the city, however, the prophetess Huldah intervenes with sayings that are already familiar from the writings of Jeremiah (2 Kgs 22:14–20).[339]

CONCLUSION

Judean writers of the exilic years rallied around the History, stood off from it, or scurried to bring the literature into line with its teachings. There were some poets and geniuses, but many were just talented hacks impressed, perturbed, or even overwhelmed by the truth and beauty of what they read. It was not to be ignored and fairly soon there was nothing left to be said.

The History summarized and synthesized the gist and thrust and potential of the earlier writings. The historians had wanted to reconstruct the past for their own time. The Historian imbibed their spirit and reconstructed the past from the beginning of the world and for all time. The prophets resisted innovation, pleaded for the truths and values of *les temps perdus*, mimed and sang and dramatized their visions, and promoted the cause of customary law and traditional justice with vivid appeals to the void left by their absence. The Deuteronomist elevated law to the plan, design, and structure of history and bolstered it from the beginning, in the primitive and variegated forms appropriate to each time, with the cumulative and analytical movement of prophecy.

The History was a compendium of truth and knowledge, a *vade mecum* of the soul, that satisfied the need to move forward without risking a loss of the past.

The History recorded, interpreted, and persuaded. Everything was explained, related to the evidence, aligned with its apparent opposite, and proved. The simplest sign of reasonableness was the sequence of command and performance. More compelling was the word or vision of a prophet, especially from the distant past, that once occurred or was just now about to happen. More complicated were the arguments about God and human behavior and the reasoned exposition of the law. The most amazing was how the History kept confirming itself, rotating on its own axis, swelling with its accumulated theory and verification, until even the fall of the kingdoms and the abandonment of the people seem to be irrefutable proof that Yahweh was God, the beginning and the end of history.

NOTES

[1] The Deuteronomistic History, extending from Genesis to 2 Kings, was not edited or revised. The Chronicler, however, redid the History in a separate work (1–2 Chronicles) and completed the Pentateuch by adding communitarian laws (Leviticus 1–7; 11:46–47; 12:1–27:34) to the Deuteronomist's priestly and ritual precepts (Lev 8:1–11:45). The addition of these laws, including what is called the Holiness Code (H = Leviticus 17–26) and a supplement (Ps) to the work of the Priestly writer (P), separated the first part of the third book of the History (Lev 8:1–11:45) from the rest (Numbers 1–36) and incorporated it into Leviticus. The History originally contained eight books (fig. 17) arranged in an explanatory order (A-B-C-D-D'-C'-B'-A'). The addition of Leviticus made Deuteronomy pivotal in the History and the last book of the Pentateuch and so established the traditional distinction between the law and the Former Prophets.

[2] Gen 2:7b assimilates the epic version (Gen 2:7a) to the Priestly version of creation (Gen 1:24, 30). Adam's assignment of names to the animals (Gen 2:19aBb–20a) illustrates human dominion (cf. Gen 1:28), and clothing made of skins supposes a similar hierarchy (Gen 3:21).

[3] The boundaries of the part are marked by Gen 5:1 and 9:18–27. The curse of Canaan (9:18–27) anticipates elements of the map of the world in Gen 10:1–32. It also illustrates the Deuteronomist's ability to turn a genealogy into a ribald or disquieting story and, in its theme of unlawful unions, corresponds to the earlier story of the union of the sons of the Gods and the daughters of men (Gen 6:1–4).

⁴ The editorial material includes 5:29bB, which links the flood with the Deuteronomistic notion that the ground was cursed (Gen 3:17b); 6:7aB and 7:23°, which assimilate the epic list of flood victims to the standard Priestly list of creatures (Gen 7:21); 7:5–6, which assimilate the epic to the Priestly version of who survived the flood; 7:12, which combines the epic and Priestly versions of the origin of the flood waters; and 7:22, which adds an epic touch to the Priestly version of the effect of the flood. The etiologies are life span (6:3–4aA); viticulture (9:20–21); and sacrifice (7:1b–3, 8–9; 8:20–22; 9:2–8).

⁵ The conflicting data concern the distinction between clean and unclean animals and the command to take on board seven pairs of the former and one pair of the latter. The independent research is illustrated by including, as the Mesopotamian flood story did, a raven among the birds that Noah sent to reconnoiter the land. The Deuteronomist also intrudes on the narrative by identifying the Titans with the Nephilim and by noting that all this happened long ago (6:4).

⁶ The Deuteronomist overrides the divisions created by the Priestly genealogies by writing connective links between them: the map of the world in Genealogy IV (fig. 7) is changed to include Eber (Gen 10:21, 24–30), who was listed in Genealogy V (Gen 11:16–17). The connection between the genealogy of Shem (Genealogy V) and the genealogy of Terah (Genealogy VI) is made by repeating bits of each (Gen 10:29–30).

⁷ Genesis 10 and 14. The story of Sodom and Gomorrah is also anticipated in Gen 10:19; 13:10b, 13.

⁸ The map of the world is changed to include Assyria and Babylonia (Gen 10:8–12), Egypt and the Mediterranean (10:13–14), Canaan (10:15–19), and the Hebrews (10:24–30). In what follows Abraham the Hebrew (Gen 14:13) leaves Babylon (Gen 11:2–3, 8a, 9a), arrives in Canaan, goes down to Egypt (Gen 12:8b–20), and defeats the kings of Mesopotamia (Genesis 14).

⁹ The changes to the map of the world (Genesis 10) and the story of the rout of the Mesopotamian coalition (Genesis 14) are narratives spun out of lists. Abraham's descent into Egypt (Gen 12:10–20) is a rehash of the epic and Elohist stories of the patriarch and his beautiful wife (cf. Genesis 20; 26) combined with the typical pattern of descent into and exodus out of Egypt.

¹⁰ Abraham's presence among the nations of the world is allowed because he is the source of their blessing (Gen 12:2b, 3b). Their genealogies and geographical boundaries are listed; Abraham's are supplied by the promise of the land, an heir, and a multitude of descendants (Gen 13:14–17). The historical theory treats history as past and paradigmatic. Its bent is indicated by the narrator's intrusion on the narrative, particularly in notices about chronological antiquity (Gen 12:6b; 13:7b, 10b) and first-time or exemplary events (Gen 10:8–9, 10; 12:7, 8b; 13:3; 14:17–24).

¹¹ The prophecy (Genesis 15) begins with a general deictic reference to

the preceding part (15:1, "After these things . . .") and with a specific reference to the reward he will have for not accepting anything from the sack of the Mesopotamian camp (15:1–2; cf. 14:16, 17–24). It also includes a number of details from the preceding part: the fact that Abraham is childless (15:2; cf. 11:30), his association with Damascus (15:2; cf. 14:15), the promise of a multitude of descendants (15:5; cf. 13:14–17), the exodus from Ur of the Chaldees to the land of Canaan (15:7; cf. 11:31; 12:5; 13:15). The concluding narrative (Genesis 24) includes, among other things, a blessing on Rebekah (24:60) that is fulfilled in a spectacular fashion in the next part (Gen 25:19–26).

12 The concluding story (Genesis 24) is spun out of the genealogy of Nahor included earlier in the part (Gen 22:20–24). It remarks that Abraham was old and had received every blessing just as the prophecy predicted (Gen 15:15), and it repeats the gist of the covenant (24:7 = 15:18). The servant also retells the important parts of the story that was recounted bit by bit in the whole part (cf. 24:34–41).

13 The rituals are associated with the covenant (Gen 15:7–11, 17–21), and the history is presented as prophecy (Gen 15:1–6, 12–16).

14 Cf. Genesis 16 and 21:8–21. The exclusion of Hagar and Ishmael is like the exclusion of Eliezer of Damascus and confirms the promise that Abraham's own son would be his heir (cf. Gen 15:2–4).

15 The promise is rephrased in terms taken from the Priestly covenant with Abraham (Gen 18:16–18; cf. chap. 17). Abraham's role as a teacher of justice (Gen 18:19) tends to confirm that he himself was considered just (Gen 15:6).

16 The survival of Lot and his daughters is attributed to Lot's attitude, God's compassion, and the intercession of Abraham (Gen 19:9, 16, 29). The birth of Moab and Ammon from their incestuous union illustrates the perversity of the nations (Gen 19:29–38).

17 Abraham's marriage with Keturah (Gen 25:1) follows not on the preceding story of Isaac and Rebekah but on the marriage of Abraham and Hagar (Gen 16:3). The list of nations descended from their union (Gen 25:1–6) includes variants to the Priestly table of nations (cf. Gen 10:7). The next paragraph (Gen 25:7–10), by the Priestly writer, relates this part backward to the story of the purchase of Mach-pelah (chap. 23), but at the end of the paragraph the Deuteronomist added a reference to Beer-lahai-roi, which once again ties this part to the story of Abraham and Hagar (Gen 25:11; cf. 16:14; 24:62). The fifth part properly begins with the genealogy of Ishmael (25:12–17), but here too the Deuteronomist added a peculiar link with the earlier material (Gen 25:18a; cf. 2:10–14; 20:1aB) and specifically with the story of Hagar (25:18b = 16:12b).

18 Isaac relives incidents in the life of Abraham (Gen 26:1aB, 2–6, 10, 15, 18–25, 32–33) and Jacob is heir to the promise to Abraham and Isaac (28:13–15; 32:10–13).

19 The story of the birth of the children is spun out of the genealogy that listed them according to the principal wives of Jacob and their maids: Gen 29:24, 29, 31–35; 30:1–24; 32:23; 33:1b–2, 5–7; 35:16–26. There are etiologies for all the names except Dinah's (Gen 30:21), but she is the victim in the story of Shechem (Genesis 34) and her name is vindicated when Simeon and Levi execute judgment on the inhabitants of the city for the crime Shechem committed in raping her.

20 Gen 31:17–18, 19b, 28, 30–36a, 37, 43–50.

21 There are genealogies of Edom, Esau, and Seir (Gen 36:9–43), allusions to the genealogy of the children of Israel (Gen 37:2aB), and the story of Judah and Tamar constructed from items of family law, genealogy, and the myth of Adonis and Myrrha. Apart from editorial elements that smooth out the relationships among the sources (Gen 39:21–23; 43:14a), and a reference to Egyptian customs (Gen 43:32–34a), most of the material is devoted to the money that the brothers paid for the grain and that was returned to them surreptitiously in order that they might be accused of theft and threatened with slavery (Gen 42:25–28, 35, 37; 43:12, 15aB, 17–23a; 44:1–17; 45:21b–24). This subplot is resolved with Joseph's father and brothers settled as clients of the court and the rest of Egypt indebted to the Pharaoh (41:55, 56b; 47:7–26).

22 The ethnographic material concerns Egyptian customs and institutions (Gen 46:34b; 47:7–26; 50:9–11). The genealogical material includes the list of the sons of Israel (Gen 46:8–27), the substitution of Ephraim and Manasseh for Joseph (Gen 48:3–7, 22), and the list of tribes in the blessing of Jacob (Genesis 49). The blessing is introduced as a prophecy (Gen 49:1) and, like typical prophecy, is expressed in poetic form.

23 Exod 1:15–21; 2:6bB, 7aB, 13–14; 3:15–22; 5:1–23.

24 Cf. Exod 3:18–20 and 7–11; 3:21–22 and 11:2; 4:1–5 and 7:8–13.

25 The introductory rituals (Exod 13:3–10, 11–16) reflect their historical interpretations (4:21–23; 11:1–9; 12:1–36). The concluding rituals (24:1–8, 9–11) preempt the epic covenant (34:6–7, 10).

26 Exod 15:25b–26; 16:4–5, 8, 16–34, 35b–36.

27 Exod 19:3b–8, 12–13, 15b, 21–25.

28 The ideology of the decalogue inspired the addition of the laws in Exod 22:9–19. Although the antecedent context suggests that the decalogue was proclaimed on the mountain, the Deuteronomist makes it clear that it was proclaimed from heaven (Exod 20:22; cf. 24:9–11).

29 Exod 23:17–19, 23–26, 28, 32–33; 24:1–11.

30 Exod 24:12 [Deuteronomistic], 13–14 [Elohist], 15–18 [Priestly] repro-

duce the framework to the covenant ceremony in Exod 24:1-2, 9-11, which the Deuteronomist wrote in anticipation of them.

[31] The intercession of Moses (Exod 32:7-14) is like the epic intercession of Moses (Num 14:13-19) but undermines the epic covenant by appealing to the covenant with Abraham. The sin that Aaron brought on the people and the ordination of the Levites (Exod 32:19b-20, 21b, 26-29) correspond to the sin of Jeroboam and his institution of an illegitimate priesthood (1 Kgs 12:30-33).

[32] The issue is broached in the preceding story (Exod 32:30-35) and continued in the ceremony renewing the publication of the decalogue (Exod 34:8-9, 34-35).

[33] The opening date (Num 1:1) relates this part to the end of the second book, when the tent of meeting was assembled for the first time (Exod 40:2, 17). The concluding date (Num 10:11) is the last in the lifetime of the exodus generation, which perishes, in the third part, for refusing to take the land. The fourth part begins again forty years later (Num 14:33-35) in the first month (Num 20:1aA).

[34] The center is Numbers 15. The surrounding chapters are paired (Numbers 14 and 16; 13 and 17; 12 and 18; 11 and 19).

[35] In the Priestly version rebellions take place at Qadesh in the wilderness of Paran (Num 13:26; 20:1aB). In the Deuteronomistic version Qadesh and the rebellions are relocated in the wilderness of Zin (Num 13:21b; 20:1aA; 27:14; 33:36; Deut 32:51a). In the rebellion at Meribah Moses and Aaron turn to the tent of meeting, and in the rebellion at Baal-peor Phinehas kills the couple who desecrated the tent of meeting (Num 20:6; 25:6). The decimation of the camp by a plague (chap. 25) is the occasion for the new census at the beginning of the next part (chap. 26).

[36] The editorial material consists of a link to the preceding part's interest in the tent of meeting (Num 20:6), references to the Elohist's guardian Angel (Num 20:16aB) and to the ordination of Aaron (Num 20:26, 28aA), and the inclusion of Midian among the allies of Moab (Num 22:2-4a, 7a; cf. 25:6, 14-16).

[37] Num 20:2-13, 14-21, 22-25, 27, 28aBb, 29; 21:21-24.

[38] The rebellion (Num 21:4-9) is a long-range etiology of a cult object in the temple at Jerusalem (cf. 2 Kgs 18:4).

[39] Num 22:22-35; cf. Num 31:16; Deut 23:5-6; Josh 13:22.

[40] These oracles (Num 24:14-24) are obscure, genealogically based allusions to nations in the Deuteronomist's purview: cf. Num 24:17 (Sheth), 24:21-22 (Cain, Kenites), and Genesis 4; cf. Num 24:22-24 (Asshur, Eber,

Kittim) and Genesis 10; cf. Num 24:18 (Edom, Seir) and Genesis 36; cf. Num 24:20 (Amalek) and Exod 17:8–16; Deut 25:17–19; 1 Samuel 15.

[41] The central chapters (chaps. 28–29) list the feasts and festivals in calendrical order. The surrounding chapters (chaps. 27; 30) explain the rights of women in their fathers' or husbands' households with respect to movable and immovable property. The enclosing chapters (chaps. 26; 31) deal with the muster of the troops and are connected explicitly (26:1; 31:1–20) to the preceding part. The battle narrative (chap. 31) illustrates the Deuteronomistic rules of war (Deuteronomy 7; 20; Joshua 6) and becomes an occasion to legislate the division of spoils (Num 31:25–31).

[42] The last part centers on the future acquisition of the land (Numbers 34). The first and last chapters consider various aspects of the Transjordanian tribes' rights of inheritance (chaps. 32; 36). The intervening chapters (chaps. 33; 35) deal with unmatched matters but are linked artificially by literal repetitions (cf. Num 33:54 and 35:8).

[43] The beginning of Deuteronomy (1:1) is linked to the end of Numbers (36:13). The next sentences (Deut 1:2, 4) refer to the roundabout journey that brought the Israelites, according to the Deuteronomist, from Sinai to Qadesh (Num 20:1), Edom (Num 20:14–21), and the kingdoms of Sihon and Og (Num 21:25–35).

[44] The narrative continuity between the two parts is basic to the standard theory of the Deuteronomistic History (M. Noth, *Überlieferungsgeschichtliche Studien: Die sammelnden und bearbeitenden Geschichtswerke im Alten Testament* (Halle an der Saale: Max Niemeyer, 1943) according to which the substance of Deuteronomy—the parts within the historical framework—was derived from a tradition with a distinct origin and development.

[45] The correspondence between the second (Deuteronomy 4–11) and the second to last part (Deuteronomy 26–30) is marked in many ways. Some of the more obvious are that both describe a ceremony of blessing and curse that is to take place on Ebal and Gerizim (Deut 11:26–32; 27:1–8), that both describe the people actually present at the covenant ceremony (Deut 5:1–5; 29:1–14), and that both assume that the exile was retribution for worshiping false Gods (Deut 4:25; 28:36–37).

[46] The decalogue (Deut 5:6–21) includes reasoned commands and prohibitions (5:6–15) and blunt self-evident prohibitions (5:16–21). The first part, concerning the prohibition of other Gods, observance of the sabbath, and respect for parents, is elaborated in the first part of the laws (chaps. 12–18), where centralization is interpreted as a bulwark against false Gods, the sabbath is extended in principle to the year of manumission and in practice to the celebration of the festivals, and the celebrations are a family affair requiring the harshest measures against any of its recalcitrant members. The second part is elaborated in the second part of the laws (chaps. 19–25), which deals in particular with the categories of murder, theft, adultery, and the like.

47 A list of correspondences between Exodus 21–23 and the laws in Deuteronomy can be found in S. R. Driver, *Deuteronomy* (ICC; Edinburgh: T. & T. Clark, 1895) iv–vii.

48 The first part ends at Beth-peor (Deut 3:29), and the first chapter in the second part recalls what happened there (4:3). This chapter returns to Horeb, to the time indicated at the beginning of the first part (1:6). It ends with a summary of the Transjordanian battles, which were noted there proleptically and then narrated in the first part (i.e., Deut 4:44–49 = 1:4 + 2:26–3:11). The list of cities of refuge just before that summary (4:41–43) elaborates material in Numbers and resituates Moses and the people where they have to be, in Transjordan in the inheritance of the Transjordanian tribes (cf. Numbers 35).

49 In the literary logic of the chapter, constructed in the preferred concentric pattern, the opening praise of wisdom and life corresponds to the concluding regulation of the cities of refuge designed to protect the life of the unwitting manslayer (Deut 4:3–8, 41–43).

50 The new beginning of the chapter (Deut 5:1aBb) is a link to the beginning and end of the preceding chapter (4:1, 45). The original text (5:1aA, 2–3) returns to the scene at Horeb described at the beginning of the first part (1:6).

51 Deut 5:32–34 = 6:1–3, in reverse order; see N. Lohfink, *Das Hauptgebot: Eine Untersuchung literarischer Einleitungsfragen zu Dtn 5–11* (Rome: Biblical Institute Press, 1963) 150–51.

52 The center of the chapter is an argument for observance of the law (Deut 7:6–16). The periphery (Deut 7:1–5, 17–26) contains the sequel's theory of an exclusive covenant and the Historian's emendations excluding the worship of other Gods.

53 Many elements of this last chapter (10:12–11:32) are taken from earlier chapters in the same part: it begins with the words of the first chapter ("And now Israel . . ." 4:1; 10:12); it repeats the summary of the law (10:20 = 6:13; 11:18–21 = 6:4–9); and it has the same assurance of invincibility (11:25 = 7:24).

54 The beginning of the third part (12:1–18:22) repeats the final sentences of the second part (12:1 = 11:31–32) and alludes to the point of its final paragraph (cf. 12:2–3 and 11:29–30). The third part ends insisting on the exclusive authority of Moses in interpreting the law, as was stated at the beginning of the first Horeb account (cf. Deut 18:18–22 and 4:1–2), and with a quotation from the second account of events at Horeb (Deut 18:16–17 = 5:23–29).

55 The cities of refuge are mentioned in Deut 19:1–10 and 4:41–43. Israel's finding rest from their enemies on all sides is mentioned in Deut 25:17–19 and

12:9–10, and the enlarging of their borders is mentioned in Deut 12:20 and 19:9. The part also begins and ends (Deut 19:1–3; 25:17–19) with references to the defeat of enemies, possession of the land that Yahweh has given them as an inheritance, and the roads they travel.

56 The laws in the first chapter are relatively homogeneous and are related by the repetition of key words. The first section introduces cases of manslaughter (Deut 19:1–3, *rōṣēaḥ*). The second section assigns three cites of refuge for the person guilty of involuntary manslaughter (19:4–7, *rōṣēaḥ*). The third section (19:8–10) allows for three more cities when Yahweh has enlarged their boundaries so that innocent blood will not be shed by the blood-avenger. The fourth section (Deut 19:11–13) hands the willful murderer who attacks his neighbor over to the blood-avenger to allay the guilt of innocent blood, and it removes all pity. The fifth section (19:14) deals with the traditional boundaries between neighbors. The last section (19:15–21) deals with the malicious witness who attacks his brother and removes all pity. In the last chapter the laws are much less homogeneous, and the literal links seem more artificial. The first and second sections (25:1–3, 4) are related by the negative (*lōʾ*). The third and fourth (25:5–10, 11–12) are connected by the similarity in the situations (*kî . . . yaḥdāw*). The fifth and sixth share one word (25:13–16, 17–19, *ʿāśâ*) and are related to the second pair by the expression "blot out the name/the memory" (25:6, 19, *mḥh*).

57 In the second chapter the first two sections are continuous and connected by speeches of the priests and officers (Deut 20:1–4, 5–9). The other two sections deal with the siege of a city (20:10–18, 19–20), and the two pairs are related by their use of the same introductory expression (20:2, 10, "When you draw near [to a city] to do battle . . ."). Most of the pairs in the second to last chapter have the same sort of formal literal connection (Deut 24:1–4, 5 [*kî yiqqaḥ*], 6, 7 [*nepeš*], 14–15, 16 [*ḥṭʾ*], 17–18, 19–22 [slavery in Egypt]). Two, however, seem to be related by their reference to a common source: the law concerning leprosy mentions Miriam and refers to an incident in the book of Numbers (Deut 24:8–9; cf. Num 12:1–15), and the law that matches it (Deut 24:10–13) has to do with loans and seems totally unrelated but uses an expression from the same story (Deut 24:12, *ʾim ʾîš ʿānî hûʾ* = Num 12:3, *wĕhāʾîš mōšeh ʿānāw mĕʾōd*). The two chapters are connected especially by the laws exempting a newly engaged or married man from military service (24:5; cf. 20:5, 7).

58 In the third chapter the first section deals with murder and the second deals with marriage to a captive of war (21:1–9, 10–14), but at the end the first changes from the impersonal to second person singular address (21:9, "And you . . ." [*wĕʾattâ*]) to prepare for a similar address in the second section (21:10). The next sections (21:15–17, 18–21) are connected by their interest in wives and children, but are also related to the opening sections by their use of the purge formula (21:9, 21). A final section on the death penalty (21:22) rounds out the chapter and in its concern that the land not be defiled relates the chapter to its mate, which is concerned with the holiness of the camp. In this corresponding chapter two sections deal with the assembly (23:1–6, 7–9), two with the camp (23:10–11, 12–15), and two with vows (23:16–21, 22–25).

59 The chapters are arranged in a descriptive pattern: A = 26; B = 27; C = 28; A' = 29; B' = 30.

60 The beginning of the book (Josh 1:1–9) is linked to the succession of Joshua and the promulgation of the law as these were presented in the enveloping chapters of the last part of Deuteronomy (cf. Deuteronomy 31, 34). The last part of the book (Josh 24:19–30)—excluding literary links to the Pentateuch (Josh 24:32) and to the latter part of the book of Judges (Josh 24:33; cf. Judg 20:28)—is repeated at the beginning of the book of Judges (cf. Judg 2:6–10). Judges 1, besides, restates the point of the last part of Joshua that much of the land was not conquered. It is usual, as these examples indicate, to separate the linking repetitive texts with intrusive material which thereby appears original and independent.

61 Each of the three chapters (Joshua 9; 10; 11) begins the same way (*wayhî kišmōaʿ* . . .). The first and second (Josh 9:1–3; 10:1) refer to the destruction of Jericho and Ai in the first part.

62 The basic law required the extermination of the indigenous population (*ḥrm*, Deut 20:17), and it was observed in every instance. The battles also illustrated perfect obedience to particular commands concerning the destruction of the Canaanite chariotry (Josh 11:6, 9) and the role of the Gibeonites in the new society (9:15b–27; cf. Deut 29:10).

63 The third chapter (Joshua 14) has to do with a promise that Moses made to Caleb and to the Transjordanian tribes concerning their inheritance of the land, and the third to last has to do with the Transjordanian tribes' obedience to the command of Moses and their access to the promised land (chap. 22). The fourth chapter concerns the inheritance of Judah (chap. 15) and the fourth to last chapter assigns the levitical cities, notably in Judah (chap. 21). The fifth chapter distributes the inheritance of Joseph—that is, Ephraim and Manasseh—and the corresponding chapter has to do with the cities of refuge, particularly those in Ephraim and Manasseh (chaps. 16–17; 20). The middle chapters (chaps. 18; 19) distribute territory to the other tribes.

64 Judges 1–3 suppose the tribal apportionment of the land and the proposition put forward in Joshua that some of the indigenous inhabitants were left in the land.

65 See B. Organ, "Judges 17–21 and the Composition of the Book of Judges" (Ph.D. thesis, University of Toronto, 1987). The periods of oppression and peace given in the narratives and the length of time the other judges held office amount to 389 years. But the book as such also purports to recount the failings of the generation after Joshua (Judg 2:10) and in fact its latest events are dated to the tenure of Moses' grandson Jonathan at Dan (18:30) and to the installation of Aaron's grandson Phinehas at Bethel in the same generation (20:28). The calendrical reckoning accounts for the time from the exodus to the building of the Solomonic temple (1 Kgs 6:1) and allows the Historian to refer ahead to the fall of the northern kingdom (Judg 18:30) or

backward to the defeat of Sihon three centuries before Jephthah (Judg 11:26). The generational reckoning belongs to the system of eras and historical development and allows the Deuteronomist to refer to the period of the judges as the time before the monarchy (17:6; 18:1; 19:1; 21:25). The lack of exact correspondence between the two systems is consistent with the Deuteronomist's theory that history is a sequence of disparate and irrational, or unimportant but interesting, events governed by an intrinsic and overriding plan of universal significance.

66 The theory is presented in Judges 1–3, the examples in Judges 4–5.

67 The joint venture of Judah and Simeon supposes their tribal allotment (Judg 1:1–7; cf. Josh 19:1–9). Judah's capture of Hebron was attributed to Caleb (Judg 1:10–11, 20; cf. Josh 15:13–15), and Othniel's exploits have already been recounted (Judg 1:12–15; cf. Josh 15:16–19). The capture of Bethel corrects earlier versions suggesting it was in Israel's hands (Judg 1:22–26; cf. Gen 28:19; 35:6). The war with Jabin of Hazor took place in the time of Joshua (cf. Judges 4–5 and Joshua 11).

68 The example of Othniel is an empty paradigm (Judg 3:7–11). There are duplicate accounts of the defeat of Jabin of Hazor, but one treats it as a parade example of the cycle of sin, oppression, and salvation (Judges 4) and the other retells it in a song that has hardly a trace of the dominant theory.

69 The part is arranged symmetrically with lists of judges at the beginning and the end (10:1–5; 12:8–15) enclosing the pattern of apostasy, defeat, lament, and salvation (10:6–16; 12:7), which in turn envelopes the history of Ammonite incursions (10:17–18; 12:1–6) and the legend of Jephthah (11:1–40).

70 Ammonite claims to land beyond the Jordan are rejected by appealing to the evidence of history as it was interpreted in the latter part of Numbers (Judg 11:12–28).

71 The legend of Samson is divided into two unequal parts (13:1–15:20; 16:1–31) distinguished by formulas (13:1; 15:20; 16:31) and by their different assessments of Samson's wisdom and success.

72 Samuel's stint at Mizpah (1 Samuel 7) is recounted like the stories in Judges (cf. Judges 10–11). The house of Eli is traced to Moses, and the reference supposes familiarity with his adoption into the Pharaoh's household recounted in the book of Exodus (1 Sam 2:27; cf. Exodus 2–4). The women who served at the tent of meeting are mentioned in the same book (1 Sam 2:22; Exod 38:8). The plagues that beset the Philistines are related explicitly to the plagues in Egypt (1 Sam 4:8; 6:6). The etiology of Samuel's name anticipates the story of Saul (1 Sam 1:20, 27–28). The song of Hannah anticipates the history of the monarchy (1 Sam 2:10).

73 The Song of Hannah, besides referring to her own situation, marks the

transition between the period of the judges and the era of the monarchy (1 Sam 2:1–10). An anonymous prophet recounts in advance what transpires in the story of Eli and in later episodes, and his prophecy is fulfilled only in the time of Solomon (1 Sam 2:27–36; 1 Kgs 2:26–27). The Philistines, their priests and their prophets, explain the power of the ark (1 Sam 4:7–8; 6:1–9).

74 The two sections together have the pattern A-B-C-D-A'-B'-C'-D'. The A's and D's are the framework: the A's (chaps. 8 and 12) are Deuteronomistic speeches and summaries; the D's (chaps. 11 and 15) pertain to Saul's coronation and dethronement at Gilgal. The B's and C's are the enclosed evidence for the ongoing interpretation: the B's (chaps. 9 and 13) are the meetings between Saul and Samuel and have many points in common, such as Saul's purported priestly status and temporary royal destiny; the C's (chaps. 10 and 14) put Saul in situations over which he has no control.

75 The enclosed story (1 Sam 9:1–10:16) includes a rider that relates it to the introductory evaluation (1 Sam 10:17–27; cf. 1 Samuel 8). Saul's priestly status is suggested by reserving a priestly portion for him (1 Sam 9:24; see P. Kyle McCarter, Jr., *I Samuel* [AB 8; Garden City, N.Y.: Doubleday, 1980] 180). His prophetic status is noted in the proverb "Is Saul also among the prophets?" (1 Sam 10:12). Other comments reveal the Deuteronomist's thesis that Israel was not to have kings like the nations but kings who were lieutenants or viceroys of Yahweh (*nāgîd*; cf. 1 Sam 9:15–17).

76 The chronicle (chaps. 13–14) also includes a proleptic reference to his repudiation (13:13–14; cf. chap. 15).

77 The elders' appeal for a king (1 Sam 8:5) was allowed by legislation in Deuteronomy (Deut 17:14). Saul is appointed in response to a situation like that of the people in Egypt, and he acts like a judge in saving them (1 Sam 9:16; cf. Exod 3:7; Judg 2:18). The fragility of his position is intimated by the fact that the first sign of his appointment takes place at Rachel's tomb, which, as the writer repeated in Genesis, is on the way to Bethlehem (1 Sam 10:2; cf. Gen 35:20; 48:7). Yahweh refers to his earlier exploits in Egypt and in the land in terms familiar from the book of Judges (1 Sam 10:18; cf. Exod 3:9; Judg 2:18; 6:9). Saul's dismemberment of his oxen as a warning to the tribes to assemble was adapted in the story of the Levite and his concubine in the book of Judges (1 Sam 11:7; Judg 19:29–30). The testimony that Samuel gives concerning his innocence corresponds to issues in the Elohist law (1 Sam 12:3; cf. Exod 22:8, 9; 23:8–9), and his summary of Israelite history is taken from Exodus and Judges (cf. 1 Sam 12:6–12 and Exodus 3–4; Judges 3–11). Agag received honorable mention in Numbers (cf. 1 Samuel 15; Num 24:7), and the vendetta against Amalek is a constant of the Deuteronomistic History (cf. Num 24:20; Deut 25:17–19). The editorial asides have to do with inquiry and the etiology of prophecy (1 Sam 9:16; 14:18b).

78 Saul's Philistine wars (chaps. 17°–18°; 31°) are taken up in a narrative that compares him unfavorably with David in their dealings with Michal and Jonathan (chaps. 18–20), with the house of Eli (chaps. 21–23), with each other (chaps. 24–26) and with the Philistines (chaps. 27–31).

[79] The most important of the reduplicated incidents are those in which David does not use an opportunity to kill Saul and Saul acknowledges that David will be king (1 Samuel 24; 26). The analyses focus on the growing popularity of David and the evil spirit that drives Saul mad, and the previews mark David's progress to the throne. Some of these have been considered by T. Veijola, *Die ewige Dynastie: David und die Entstehung seiner Dynastie nach der deuteronomistischen Darstellung* (Helsinki: Suomalainen Tiedeakatemia, 1975).

[80] The Deuteronomist's idea of history is indicated in the organization of the narrative. The plot—the rejection of Saul and the anointing of David as king—is declared at the start (1 Sam 16:1–13). Similarly, the theme—the spirit of Yahweh that overwhelmed David from that day forward and the evil spirit that tormented Saul—is presented clearly at the beginning in a scene that preempts the original meeting between Saul and David (1 Sam 16:14–23; cf. 17:55–58). The rest of the narrative shows how the plan evolved. The declared plot is an obvious overriding interpretation of evidence that could be interpreted differently.

[81] This part anticipates the next and has fewer connections with the preceding books. Some of these are the similarity between the victory song of the Israelite women and the song of Miriam and her companions (1 Sam 18:6–7; cf. Exod 15:20–21); the requirement of ritual purity in order to share in the bread of presence (1 Sam 21:3–6; cf. Exod 19:15b; 25:30); and ephod and Urim as priestly articles (1 Sam 23:6, 9; 28:6; cf. Exod 28:4–14).

[82] This part (2 Samuel 1–12) is linked to the third by retelling the story of the battle of Gilboa, in which Saul and his sons were killed (cf. 1 Samuel 31 and 2 Samuel 1). The retelling has a different version of his death (cf. 1 Sam 31:3–5 and 2 Sam 1:6–10) and, by adding David's lament for Saul and Jonathan, suggests that David had no pretensions to the throne, despite the ambiguous evidence assembled in the preceding story of his rise to power.

[83] These two chapters (2 Samuel 5 and 8) are alike in numerous ways: chap. 5 begins with David being made king over all Israel, and chap. 8 ends with the government in his control (2 Sam 5:1–5; 8:15–18); in chap. 5 David receives emissaries from Hiram of Tyre, and in chap. 8 he receives an embassy from the king of Hamath (2 Sam 5:11–12; 8:9–10); in both he defeated the Philistines (2 Sam 5:17–25; 8:1), and both mention his growing renown (2 Sam 5:10; 8:13–14). Chapter 5 describes his capture of Zion (2 Sam 5:6–10), which is crucial in all that follows, and chap. 8 summarizes the victories that are described in detail in the following chapters (2 Sam 8:3–8, 11–14; cf. chaps. 10–11).

[84] The decline of the house of Saul is in accordance with the decree of Yahweh (1 Samuel 16; 2 Sam 7:15) but the two chapters (2 Samuel 4 and 9) supply the historical details. The first deals with Ishbosheth (chap. 4) but mentions Mephibosheth, who is the topic of chap. 9 (2 Sam 4:4).

[85] The chapters (2 Samuel 2–3; 9–10) are related in various ways, notably

in the predominance of Joab and in the opposite attitudes of David to the deaths of Abner and Uriah.

86 The relationship between the sequence of historical events and the goal they are meant to attain is most explicit in the dynastic oracle in which Yahweh reviews events from Egypt onward, explains their import, and anticipates their course for eternity (2 Sam 7:4–17).

87 The seven chapters in this part (2 Samuel 13–19) are arranged concentrically (A-B-C-D-C'-B'-A'). The climax of the story is David's solemn procession out of Jerusalem and meeting with the representatives of the house of Saul (chap. 16 = D): the story naturally ends with the procession back to the city and another meeting with the representatives (chap. 19 = A'). However, the story, as the concentric arrangement indicates, is not only told but interpreted. The first and last chapters are the beginning and the end of the revolt and share David's lament for Absalom (A–A'; chaps. 13; 19). The second and second-to-last chapters (B–B'; chaps. 14; 18) are the story of Absalom and Joab and share, rather artificially, a reference to Absalom's hair (literally, "head"; 2 Sam 14:25–26; 18:9–10, 14–15) and, strangely, a reference to his children and his childlessness (2 Sam 14:27; 18:18). The third and third-to-last chapters (C–C'; chap. 15; 17) share the battle of wits between Ahithophel and Hushai.

88 The five chapters in the part are arranged concentrically (2 Samuel 20–24 = A-B-C-B'-A'). They do not have a narrative plot but tie together loose ends in the story of David and prepare for the following story of Solomon. The psalm at the center (chap. 22) describes Yahweh's intervention in cosmological (22:1–20) and international (22:32–51) terms but itself centers on the law and its observance. In the next part the effect of the law on the right order of history is made explicit in David's parting advice to Solomon (1 Kgs 2:1–4).

89 The chapters (1 Kings 1; 2; 3; 4; 5:1–14; 5:15–32; 6; 7; 8; 9; 10; 11) follow in narrative sequence, that is, in pairs, with links from chapter to chapter and from pair to pair. The point of the narrative—bluntly, that God will keep his word, beneficent if Solomon observes the law, disastrous if he does not—is made in conversations, addresses, divine discourse and prophecies, and it gives the grandeur of the kingdom a hollow ring.

90 The narrative sequence and contrast between the two sets of chapters (1 Kings 1–2; 10–11) is exemplified in the statements that the kingdom was established in the hands of Solomon (1 Kgs 2:46) and then torn out of his hands (1 Kgs 11:31).

91 The part is spent on the sin of Jeroboam, who revolted against Solomon at the end of the first part (1 Kings 11), and on the crimes of Ahab, whose story is told in the next part (1 Kings 17–22).

92 The prophecy against the altar at Bethel refers to Josiah and the things

that he actually does (1 Kings 13; 2 Kgs 23:15–20). Ahijah refers to the exile of the North (1 Kgs 14:15). The narrator refers to the accomplishment of Joshua's curse (1 Kgs 16:34 = Josh 6:26).

93 The materials in the chapters (1 Kings 12–16) are of diverse sorts but are held together by literal and structural repetition. The structure pivots on the oracle of Ahijah (chap. 14) and lets the Deuteronomist include information on the conflicts between Israel and Judah in a general interpretation of the rise (chaps. 12–13) and decline (chaps. 15–16) of the house of Jeroboam. The most obvious literal repetitions are the constant condemnations of the sin of Jeroboam (1 Kgs 12:30–33; 13:1–10, 33–34; 14:1–20, 21–24; 15:3, 26, 29–30, 34; 16:1–7, 12–13, 19, 25–26, 29–33).

94 Each of these chapters (1 Kings 17; 18; 19) makes a point of affirming (1 Kgs 17:24; 18:36–37; 19:10, 14) and of proving by miraculous means that Elijah is a true prophet of the true God. Of the commands that he receives to anoint Hazael and Jehu kings and Elisha as his successor (1 Kgs 19:15–18) Elijah executes the last (1 Kgs 19:19–21), and the others are carried out by Elisha in the next two parts (2 Kings 1–8; 9–13).

95 The first and last of these chapters concern the wars of the king (chaps. 20; 22), and the middle chapter is Elijah's dispute with Ahab in the matter of Naboth's vineyard. The first section has a similar structure, with chapters on Elijah as a prophet in the line of Moses (chaps. 17; 19) surrounding a chapter on his dispute with the prophets of Baal (chap. 18).

96 The importance of the prophetic tradition is implied by casting Elijah as another Moses, by assuring the succession of Elisha, by having Elijah perform miracles that Elisha will copy, by assigning tasks to one that are performed by the other, and by illustrating the alternative in the example of Micaiah ben Imlah. The importance of the law—in principle the decalogue—is shown in Elijah's disputes (1 Kings 18; 21), which prove that Yahweh is God and will punish transgression from generation to generation.

97 The first two chapters (2 Kings 1–2) continue the career of Elijah from the first section (1 Kings 17–19) but are literally linked to the end of the second section in continuing the chronicle of the reign of Ahaziah (2 Kings 1; cf. 1 Kgs 22:51–53). The third chapter continues the story of the military alliance between Israel and Judah (2 Kings 3; cf. 1 Kings 22). In the fourth Elisha repeats the miracles performed by Elijah (cf. 2 Kings 4 and 1 Kings 17). The last four chapters deal with the Aramean wars and end at Ramoth-gilead (2 Kgs 8:28–29). The next part begins with the revolt of Jehu at that time and is linked to them by verbatim repetition (2 Kgs 9:14–15).

98 The pairing of the eight chapters in this part (2 Kings 1–8) is indicated by their introductory references to other pairs. The first pair (chaps 1–2) begins with a statement that does not introduce them but anticipates the narrative in the first chapter of the second pair (2 Kgs 1:1, "After the death of Ahab Moab rebelled against Israel" = 2 Kgs 3:5). This narrative, in turn, has nothing much to do with the first pair but is a continuation of the story in the

preceding part (2 Kings 3; cf. 1 Kings 22). Similarly, the third pair (2 Kgs 5:1–6:23) begins with a reference not to the preceding pair but to the Syrian victory over Ahab recounted in the same story in the preceding part (2 Kgs 5:1; cf. 1 Kings 22). The first chapter in the fourth part (2 Kgs 6:24–8:29) begins by referring back to these wars with Ben-hadad (2 Kgs 6:24; cf. 1 Kings 20), and the second chapter begins by referring back to the second pair (2 Kgs 8:1; cf. 2 Kings 4).

99 Both Elijah and Elisha are able to cross the Jordan on dry ground (2 Kgs 2:8, 13–14), as Moses parted the Sea and Joshua divided the Jordan. The first chapter says explicitly that Yahweh and not Baal is God (2 Kgs 1:3–4, 6, 16) and, since it is only God who gives life and takes it away (2 Kgs 5:7), proves the point by killing Ahaziah and his messengers. On this basis the second chapter turns to the prophets of this God and proves their authority in the wonders they work.

100 The first chapter (2 Kings 5) recounts the healing of Naaman and has him declare, "Now I know that there is no God in all the world except in Israel" (5:15). Elisha, appropriately, is called "the man of God" (5:8, 14, 15), and the king of Israel declares that only God could work such a miracle (5:7). The second chapter (2 Kgs 6:1–23) reveals that Yahweh's armies fight for Elisha and Israel. The forces are hidden; the eyes of his servant have to be opened; the eyes of the Arameans are closed; and the vision is granted by God.

101 The anointing of Hazael (2 Kgs 8:7–15) takes place in fulfillment of a command of Yahweh to Elijah (1 Kgs 19:15). His succession to the throne of Damascus (2 Kgs 8:15) makes an easy transition to the succession of Jehoram in Judah and from there to the chronicles of the kings (2 Kgs 8:16–29).

102 The part begins with the anointing of Jehu (2 Kgs 9:1–10) and harks back to Yahweh's command to Elijah in the penultimate part (1 Kgs 19:16). It covers the reign of Hazael and ends when Elisha and Hazael die (2 Kgs 13:20, 24). It is related to the next part by the continuation there of the chronicle of the reign of Jehoash (2 Kings 14).

103 The chapter was anticipated in the third part by Elijah's condemnation of Ahab and Jezebel for the crimes committed against Naboth (cf. 1 Kgs 21:17–24 and 2 Kgs 9:7–10, 21–22, 25–26, 30–37).

104 The chapter begins with the pattern of sin, punishment, repentance, salvation, and repeated apostasy that was established in the book of Judges (2 Kgs 13:1–6). It ends with a reflection on Yahweh's fidelity to his promises (2 Kgs 13:22–23a), with an editorial aside on his constancy (13:23b), and with some further examples of his salvation (13:24–25).

105 Both chapters contain continuous narratives on different but related religious themes and end with annalistic accounts of the activity of Hazael.

106 The focus of this part is the Deuteronomistic explanation of the fall of

the city of Samaria (2 Kgs 17:1–23) and of the continued apostasy of the Assyrian province with the same name (2 Kgs 17:24–41). The other six chapters are aligned in a repetitive pattern (A-B-C-X-A'-B'-C') to balance the affairs of North and South. The connection between the matching chapters is sometimes slight and artificial: the first and fourth (A, A' = chaps. 14; 18) share a reference to Lachish and to the temporary respite effected by Jeroboam and Hezekiah. The second and fifth (B, B' = chaps. 15; 19) record the Assyrian invasion. The third and last (C, C' = chaps. 16; 20) share the formulas for the reign of Hezekiah.

[107] The five chapters in this part are aligned in the repetitive pattern of the preceding part (A = 21, B = 22, C = 23, A' = 24, B' = 25) and contrast two opposite and, apart from the theory of history they support, exclusive situations.

[108] According to the covenant, as the sequel and like-minded writings understood it, no evil should have come on Jerusalem. According to the law, to the covenant as the Deuteronomistic Historian understood it, evil was inevitable. The covenant could be broken. The law was unassailable and ready to be observed. The political and military struggles of the time are mentioned, and the tragic death of Josiah is recorded. All the evidence is there; some other explanation might be available, but nothing else makes sense of history's whole trajectory.

[109] The most complete lists of prophetic and pseudo-prophetic roles are in Deut 13:2–6 and 18:9–22.

[110] See C. M. Carmichael, *The Laws of Deuteronomy* (Ithaca, N.Y.: Cornell University Press, 1974); idem, *Women, Law and the Genesis Traditions* (Edinburgh: Edinburgh University Press, 1979); idem, *Law and Narrative in the Bible: The Evidence of the Deuteronomic Laws and the Decalogue* (Ithaca, N.Y.: Cornell University Press, 1985).

[111] The incantations are expressed as invocations of blessing and curse (Gen 12:2a, 3a; 27:27–29, 39–40); the vision (so-called in the Deuteronomistic version, Gen 18:1a) revolves around a meal and includes a birth oracle (Gen 18:1b–15); the incubation takes place in Jacob's tussle with God (Genesis 32°). They are all vestiges and transformations rather than actual and explicit prophetic forms.

[112] Jacob's vision at Bethel also takes place in an incubation ritual (Gen 28:10–12, 17–18, 20–21a), and the angelic messengers respond to lamentation and sacrifice (Gen 21:15–21; 22:11–13).

[113] The curses or spells (Gen 3:14–19; see E. A. Speiser, *Genesis* [AB 1], Garden City: Doubleday, 1964, 24) are written in stanzas in the manner of poetry. The connection between them and the story of Cain and Abel (Gen 4:1–16) is marked by a quotation (Gen 4:7b = Gen 3:16b) and by the curse on Cain that extends the curse on the land (Gen 4:11–12; cf. Gen 3:17). The

curses have an etiological ring, and are dispelled in part by the sacrifices offered by Noah (Gen 8:21–22) and in part by the blessings on Abraham, Isaac, and Jacob.

114 Both (Gen 6:3–4aA; 9:18–27) occur in etiologies. The first spell consists in taking away from people the spirit of Yahweh with which they had been endowed. The curse on Canaan bestows a blessing on Shem and prepares for the transferal of the land of Canaan to Abraham.

115 The first half of the story (Gen 14:1–16) situates Abraham in the history and geography of the world as they were described at the beginning of this part (chap. 10), gives historical substance to the otherwise ethereal or mythical cities of Sodom and Gomorrah, and illustrates the Deuteronomistic dictum that the nations of the world would bless themselves in Abraham (cf. Gen 12:2b, 3b). The interruption in the second half of the story (Gen 14:17–[18–20]–24) is typical of the Deuteronomist's style and relates the story to the epic blessing on Abraham (Gen 12:1–2a, 3a).

116 In this incident (Genesis 15), modeled to some extent on the covenant with David (2 Samuel 7), Abraham is priest and prophet and paragon of observance of the law. It combines the vision with a sacrificial ritual and, in a manner typical of the Deuteronomist, interrupts one to deal with the other (Gen 15:1–6, 7–11, 12–16, 17–21). The historical survey includes the sojourn in Egypt as a model of the exile. Abraham's prophetic role as intercessor is explicit in the Deuteronomist's version of Abraham and Abimelech (Gen 20:4–7, 17–18).

117 Before the prophecy (Genesis 15) the promises are associated with sacrificial rituals (12:7, 8b) and with visions (Gen 13:13–17). After the prophecy the promises are concatenated and cross-referenced to the covenant (18:17–19; 22:15–18; 26:2–6; 28:13–15; 32:10–13).

118 The Deuteronomistic material in chaps. 3–4 interprets the epic and Elohist materials in the same chapters and anticipates the Priestly version as it appears in chaps. 6–7. Items that are not commentaries on their context (e.g., 3:21–22; 4:21–23) are proleptic to developments in the following part (see chaps. 11–12).

119 The signs that Moses performs (Exod 4:1–9) are taken from the Priestly signs and wonders (Exodus 7°) or anticipate the plight of the prophet Miriam (Numbers 12). They are simple and illustrate the structure of the Deuteronomistic plagues (Exodus 7–12°), which themselves are more complicated and adapt the form to prophetic purposes.

120 In Deut 18:10–11 (cf. Deut 12:30–31) and 2 Kgs 21:6 the various types of prophecy that the Deuteronomist illustrates in the history but formally condemns in the laws are associated with the offering of firstborn sons.

121 The signs and wonders contain a command to Moses and Aaron (Exod

7:8–9, 19; 8:1, 12; 9:8–9), their execution of the command (7:10, 20; 8:2, 13; 9:10), the Egyptian magicians' attempt to produce the same results (7:11–12, 22; 8:3, 14; 9:11), and the hardening of Pharaoh's heart (7:13, 22; 8:11, 15; 9:12). The last sign and wonder is the crossing of the Sea (chap. 14°), in which Pharaoh is destroyed and Yahweh is glorified.

122 In the Deuteronomistic version the plagues consist of prophetic judgment and prophetic intercession. The judgment includes Yahweh's commissioning of Moses as his messenger, the message concerning worship in the wilderness introduced by the formula "Thus says Yahweh," the punishment that will befall him if the Pharaoh does not let the people go, and the plague that is sent in judgment (Exod 7:14–18, 20–21, 23–24; 7:25–29; 8:16–20; 9:1–7a; 9:13–26; 10:1–15; 10:21–23; 11:1–8 + 12:29–30). The intercession includes the repentance of Pharaoh, renewed demands by Moses, the intervention of Moses, and the final hardening of the Pharaoh's heart (Exod 7:23; 8:4–11; 8:21–28; 9:7b; 9:27–35; 10:16–20; 10:24–29; 12:31–32).

123 The Song of Miriam (Exod 15:21) is sung in praise of Yahweh's victory at the Sea. The Song of Moses (Exod 15:1–19) draws from this victory (15:4–10) the conclusion that Yahweh alone is the God of Israel (15:1–3, 11–12) and that, having defeated his enemies (15:13–16), he will be enthroned in his temple as king of his people (15:17–18).

124 The miracle at Horeb (Exod 17:1–7) is modeled on the Priestly story of Meribah (Num 20:2–5, 7–13). The victory over Amalek (Exod 17:8–16) is modeled on Joshua's victory at Ai (Joshua 8; Joshua is actually mentioned in Exod 17:9, 10, 13) and becomes a paradigm for later oracles, laws, and historical narratives (Num 24:20; Deut 25:17–19; 1 Samuel 15).

125 Before the revelation of the law the people accept Moses as the prophet of God (Exod 20:18–20). In the closing ceremony (Exod 24:1–11) the sacrificial rituals performed by Moses and his assistants (24:3–8) are preliminary to the encounter with God that circumscribes them (24:1–2, 9–11). Similar rituals are mentioned but not described in the epic account of Balaam's prophetic meetings with God (Numbers 22–24).

126 The rules governing the relationship between law and prophecy that are formulated by the Deuteronomist (Deut 13:2–6; 18:15–22) are suggested obliquely and imaginatively in the connection that the Deuteronomist makes between medicinal wonderworking that the Priestly writer described (Exod 15:23–25a) and healthy observance of the law (Exod 15:25b–26).

127 It is typical of the Deuteronomist to disrupt the connection between related narrative elements (Exodus 32; 34) with a dogmatic reflection on both (Exodus 33). In this reflection (see esp. Exod 33:7–11), and in references to it (cf. Exod 25:22; 34:34–35), it is clear that the principal prophetic function is to proclaim the law and that this ability, rather than any other device, is the basis of authority and government.

128 The Mosaic prophet is distinguished from local and unreliable sorts

(Deut 13:2–6; 18:9–22; 34:10–12). Moses' parting words are expressed in a song (chap. 32) that surveys Israel's history and options and that differs from the hymns and laments of the later prophets only in its total adherence to Deuteronomistic doctrine, and in a blessing describing the charmed existence of the tribes.

[129] Joshua has a vision of the armies of Yahweh (Josh 5:13–15), utters a curse on Jericho that takes effect in the time of Ahab (Josh 6:26; 1 Kgs 16:34), works a miracle at Gibeon (Josh 10:12–14), issues an ominous warning (chap. 23), and reviews the history of Israel, as the Deuteronomist saw it, from Mesopotamian origins to the land of Canaan (chap. 24).

[130] Cf. Judg 2:1–5 and Deuteronomy 7; Judg 6:7–10 and Joshua 24; Judg 10:6–16 and Deut 32:15–16, 21, 37–38 and Joshua 24.

[131] The promise of a priestly house is modeled on the promise to David (cf. 1 Sam 2:35; 2 Sam 7:16) and keeps pace with the story of David's rise to power (cf. 1 Sam 4:19–22; 1 Sam 21–23; 2 Sam 8:17; 15:24–29, 32–37; 1 Kings 1–2).

[132] The choice of Saul is framed by historical summaries and speculation (1 Samuel 8; 12). It is decided by prophecy (chap. 9), is accompanied by prophecy, signs, and wonders (10:1–16), and happens again by lot (10:17–27) and prophetic designation (chap. 11). The link between his choice and his dismissal is in the fulfillment of the sign of sacrifice at Gilgal (10:8), which, by Saul's neglect, turns out to be a sign of his repudiation (chaps. 13; 15).

[133] After David's anointing by Samuel the spirit leaves Saul and is transferred to him (1 Samuel 16). The rest of the story of Saul, ending with his attempt at necromancy (chap. 28), illustrates the effects of his abandonment. In typically Deuteronomistic fashion the choice of David is secret and is revealed only as history unfolds and mainly in speeches of the principal characters that anticipate the oracle of Nathan (2 Samuel 7). The remainder of the history, up to the accession of Solomon (1 Kings 1–2), is governed by this oracle.

[134] The anonymous prophet and Samuel intervene against the house of Eli because his sons abused their priestly privileges (1 Samuel 2–3). Samuel conducted a ceremony of expiation at Mizpah because the people had worshiped other Gods (1 Samuel 7). Saul is rejected for sacrificing at Gilgal and for not devoting Agag to God (1 Samuel 13; 15). David is chosen in connection with the building of the temple (2 Samuel 7). Gad intervenes when David neglects to collect the offerings required at census time (2 Samuel 24; cf. Exod 30:11–16; see P. Kyle McCarter, Jr., *II Samuel* [AB 9; Garden City, N.Y.: Doubleday, 1984] 512–18).

[135] Apart from noting in general whether kings comply with the rule of centralization, the Deuteronomist also notes observance of a particular law (2 Kgs 14:6). The singularity of the deed merely emphasizes the general neglect of the law.

136 Cf. Num 31:25–31; 1 Sam 30:21–25.

137 The affliction of Hagar the Egyptian and her flight from her mistress is modeled on Israel's affliction in Egypt and their flight from the Pharaoh. Sarah was mean to her but did not break any law (cf. Exod 21:7–11; Deut 21:10–14). The angel knew that female slaves, unlike male slaves who escaped from their masters, had to submit to their owners (Gen 16:6–9; cf. Deut 23:16–17).

138 Rape and proposed marriage alternate (Gen 34:1–2, 3–4, 5–7, 8–12, 13–17, 18–24, 25–36). The rape is unacceptable (34:7, 31), but there are legal remedies, which Shechem is willing to pursue (Deut 22:28–29). The problem is that the legal solution, marriage, is a violation of the covenant, which prohibits intermarriage and mingling with the nations (cf. Gen 34:9; Deut 7:3).

139 There is a judge (2:14, *śar wĕśōpēṭ*; cf. Exod 18:21–26) and a guilty party (2:13b, *rāśāʿ*). The quarrel is like a formal inquiry and is based on the distinction between murder and manslaughter (2:13bB, 14aB; cf. Exod 21:12–15; Deut 19:4–13).

140 All of the plagues are anticipated in the commissioning of Moses (chap. 4). At the beginning of the account Moses raises the question of the people's faith in him (4:1), and at the end the words and signs convince them and they believe (4:31). To prevent the plagues from being redundant the Deuteronomist included an account of slave labor in Egypt (chap. 5), in which negotiations with Pharaoh are unsuccessful and the people appeal to Yahweh to judge (5:21, *špṭ*). This judgment, of course, turns out to be the plagues (7:4, *mišpāṭîm*).

141 The insertion (12:7) is made via deictics ("*the* blood . . . where they eat *it* [the lamb; cf. 12:5–6] in *them* [the houses, cf. 12:3–4]"). The interpretation (12:12–13) is added by a deictic ("*that* night," 12:12), by repetition (12:13, *ûpasaḥtî*; cf. 12:11, *pesaḥ*) and by cross-reference to the insertion and to the preceding announcement of the final plague (chap. 11).

142 Exod 12:29–32, 33–36 [cf. 3:21–22], 43–50. The final formulation of the laws of Passover (12:43–49) concerns the resident aliens, who were mentioned earlier in the legislation of the feast of Unleavened Bread (12:19).

143 The law of Passover is reformulated at the beginning of the third part (chap. 13) in anticipation of the law regulating the dedication of firstborn male children, which in turn is rewritten to agree with the reformulation (34:19–20). The repetition of the law marks the transition from one part (chaps. 6–12) to the next (chaps. 13–24).

144 In their willingness to serve the Egyptians the people undermine the purpose of the exodus, which was to serve Yahweh in the wilderness (cf. 8:16; 9:1, 13; 10:3). The encouragement that Moses gives them is modeled on the address that the priest is supposed to make before battle (Deut 20:3–4).

145 Cf. chaps. 25–31° and 35–40°. Moses is shown a model of the tent (*tabnît*, Exod 25:9, 40) before seeing to its construction.

146 The command (33:1–3) is an amalgam of epic, Priestly, and Elohist texts (cf. 3:7–8; 6:2–9; 23:20–22). The response of the people (33:4–6) is taken from an Elohist text (Gen 35:1–4; cf. Josh 24:23–26). The argument disputes the epic notion that Moses is a surrogate of the people (Exod 33:13; cf. 34:10, 27; Num 14:12) and the epic and Priestly versions of his access to God (Exod 33:17–23; cf. 24:15–18; 34:6).

147 The commands (Lev 8:1–3) are obeyed (Lev 8:4a), beginning with the last (Lev 8:4b = 8:3) and then in the order in which they were given. In each case it is noted that the command was executed as Yahweh directed (Lev 8:9, 13, 17, 21, 29, 36).

148 Nadab and Abihu do what they have not been commanded and are consumed by fire from Yahweh, and the break in the usual pattern occasions an explanation by Moses (Lev 10:1–3). This event leads into a sequence of commands by Moses that are immediately obeyed (Lev 10:4–7), and into a series of addenda to the rituals listed in the preceding chapter (Lev 10:8–11, cf. 9:22–24; Lev 10:12–15, cf. 9:4–5; Lev 10:16–20, cf. 9:6–7).

149 The beginning of the chapter (Num 3:1–4) refers to Lev 10:1–7, and the instructions concerning the Levites (Num 3:5–10, 11–13) are taken up in Num 8:5–19 and chap. 18.

150 Chapter 6 regulates vows and ends with a résumé and reconfirmation of the rules (Num 6:1–21). With the essential pattern maintained, the priestly blessing concludes the chapter (Num 6:22–27). The list of offerings is complete in chap. 7 (Num 7:1–88), and the chapter ends with a description of Moses' meetings with Yahweh (Num 7:89). Chapter 9 has amendments to the laws of Passover (Num 9:1–14) but ends with a description of how the people pitched camp only at the command of Moses and Yahweh (Num 9:15–23). Chapter 10 establishes the rituals for breaking camp, but it ends with a ritual paradigm in which the ark responds to the commands of Moses to remain or set out (Num 10:33b–36).

151 In the epic Peor is a mountain site from which Balaam can see the encampments of Israel stretching into the distant future (Num 23:28). In the History the place acquires sinister overtones, like Balaam himself, and is known either as Beth-peor (Deut 3:29; 4:46; 34:6; Josh 13:20) or, after the God who was worshiped at the site, Baal-peor (Num 25:3, 5; Deut 4:3).

152 Cf. Exod 21:12–27; Numbers 35. Compare 19:1 and 6:10–11; 19:3 and 12:9 and 14:24; 19:8 and 12:20; 19:9 and 6:5; 19:17–18; and 13:15 and 17:8–13.

153 The general situation of siege (Deut 20:10–20) and war with a superior army (Deut 20:1–9) is illustrated in the battles at Jericho, Gibeon, and Hazor

(Joshua 6; 9–11). The exemption of troops from military service (Deut 20:5–9) supposes the property rights defended in the decalogue (Deut 5:21) and original descriptions of the land (Deut 6:10–11; 8:7–10). Encouragement (Deut 20:3–4) is modeled on Moses' exhortation at the Sea (Exod 14:11–14). The annihilation of the indigenous peoples of Canaan was required by the covenant (Exod 23:20–33; 34:11–16).

154 The first law, concerning the corpse of a murdered person, is an extrapolation from the law concerning cities of refuge and also supposes the judicial system established in the preceding parts (cf. Deut 21:1–9 and 10:6–9; 17:9–13). The law concerning the woman taken captive in war (Deut 21:10–14) and the law on the right of primogeniture (Deut 21:15–17) could reflect the problems involved in the dismissal of Hagar and in the disinheritance of Reuben (cf. Genesis 16; 35:22; 49:3–4). The law on the disposal of the body of a person who has been hanged (Deut 21:22–23) will be illustrated in Joshua's treatment of the king of Ai (Josh 8:29).

155 Cf. Deut 22:1–4 and Exod 22:8; 23:4–5; cf. Deut 22:12 and Exod 22:26 + Num 15:37–41. The precedents are either explicit (Deut 22:26; cf. Deut 19:11) or suggested by the use of formulas (Deut 22:5b, 7b, 21b, 22b, 24b). Some aspects of the true or false accusation of prostitution are illustrated in the stories of the two Tamars (cf. Deut 22:13–21; Genesis 38; and 2 Samuel 13).

156 The laws concerning the camp and the assembly of Yahweh (Deut 23:1–15) suppose the descriptions given in Numbers, and the wars of conquest recorded in the latter part of that book are summarized in the laws excluding Ammonites and Moabites from the assembly (Deut 23:4–7). The rules regarding the admission of Edomites and Egyptians refer to familiar stories at the beginning of the History (Deut 23:8–9).

157 For example, cf. Deut 24:8–9 and Numbers 12; Deut 24:10–13 and Exod 22:24–26. The law of individual guilt and responsibility is obeyed by Amaziah (2 Kgs 14:6).

158 The levirate law in particular is anticipated in the story of Tamar (Genesis 38), and the condemnation of Amalek was decreed by Moses in the wilderness (Exodus 17).

159 Both the conquest and the covenant on Sinai (Exod 24:3–8; Joshua 3–5, 8:30–35) are memorialized by writing the law, erecting twelve stelae in honor of the tribes, and offering sacrifice.

160 A replica of the altar constructed at this time (8:30–35) is a symbol for the Transjordanian tribes of their inclusion in the conquest of the promised land (chap. 22).

161 Saul's sin consists in not obeying the commandments (1 Sam 13:13; 15:11), as the prophets interpreted them (1 Sam 15:22–23; cf. Deut 18:9–

22), and specifically in contravening the laws of war (cf. Deut 20:10–18; 25:17–19).

162 Cf. Gen 2:8, 14; 3:24; 4:16; 10:10.

163 Cf. Exod 1:14; 5:4–21.

164 Cf. Gen 20:12; 22:20–24; 24:1–67.

165 Gen 12:2b, 3b, *mišpĕḥôt*; cf. Gen 10:5, 20, 31, 32.

166 Cf. Gen 2:10; 19:15–23.

167 Some of its material is from the earlier chapters (chaps. 10–13), some from the next part (esp. chap. 17), some from the history of Transjordan (chaps. 2–3), and some is modeled on records of invasion, subjugation, rebellion, and punishment (e.g., 2 Kings 24–25). The chapter is full of asides and parentheses (Gen 14:2, 3, 7, 8, 10, 13, 18, 24) that relate it to its context and, in the archaizing mode of the Deuteronomist, make it look like an annotated source.

168 Cf. Gen 11:29–30; 12:1–3.

169 The catalog was anticipated in additions to the genealogy of Abraham (Gen 11:29–30).

170 The Elohist version ended (Exod 32:25) with the realization that betraying the guidance of the Angel would be calamitous. The epic text that immediately followed it (Exod 34:6–7) declared Yahweh to be a merciful and gracious God, apt to punish but still forgiving.

171 The argument (Exod 32:7–14) interrupts the sequence and removes the dramatic tension by making Moses aware of the calf before he sees it. The framework (32:19b–20, 35) surrounds the original conclusion of the story (32:21a, 22–25) and its Deuteronomistic commentary and interpretation (32:21b, 26–34).

172 Since apostasy is like infidelity (Exod 34:14–16) the people undergo the ordeal forced on a woman accused of adultery by a jealous husband (Num 5:11–31). Judgment by plague is from the narrative of rebellion in the wilderness (Num 14:12, 37).

173 The incident (Exod 32:26–29) takes place at the gate of the camp that has not yet been either designed or put into operation and concerns the Levites, who are known only from genealogies but will be associated with Aaron in the following book. The incident is recalled in Deut 33:8–11 and has a historical analogue in the Deuteronomistic critique of the reform of Jeroboam (1 Kgs 12:30–33).

174 The paragraph has Moses appointed to lead the people out of the land

(33:1, 3), but it is interrupted to include the Elohist angel as their guide and champion (33:2).

[175] Cf. Exod 19:11–13, 21–25; 32:19b.

[176] The first sentence brings Moses back up the mountain where he had gone at first (Exod 34:4–5; cf. 19:20; 24:12–18). The concluding sentence refers to the preceding discussion of divine leadership (Exod 34:8–9; cf. 33:1–6).

[177] The emended stipulations (Exod 34:11–26) include many from the revised Elohist version (23:12–33). The festivals are regulated according to earlier Deuteronomistic legislation (cf. 34:18–20 and chaps. 12–13). The exclusion of intermarriage (34:15–16) has precedents in the stories of Shechem (Genesis 34) and Baal-peor (Numbers 25). The prohibition of images (Exod 34:13, 17) becomes critical in the theory of centralization (Deut 12:3).

[178] In the Elohist conclusion Moses finishes speaking to the people and covers his face. In the Deuteronomist's version (Exod 34:32b, 34–35) it is presumed that Moses is stationed at the tent of meeting (cf. Exod 33:7–11).

[179] Cf. Exod 25:22; 33:7–11; Numbers 18.

[180] Cf. Exod 32:34; 33:2.

[181] Cf. Exod 28:1–29:9; Lev 8:5–9; Num 19:7.

[182] The epic seems to include the Ammonites in the occupied territory (Num 21:24bA). The Deuteronomist immediately added a note to exclude them (21:24bB) and composed new texts to dispel the confusion (Deut 2:16–25; Judg 11:12–28).

[183] The battle of Jazer (21:31–32; cf. 32:1) uses the phraseology of the war with Sihon (cf. 21:24b–25). The defeat of Og (21:33–35) is compared to the defeat of Sihon and fulfills the requirements of the ban (cf. Deut 3:1–7; 20:16–18).

[184] Cf. 1 Samuel 15; 27; 30; 2 Samuel 8–10.

[185] Cf. Josh 2:1; 3:1. The incident refers to the judges of Israel, and the angelic warning in Judg 2:1–5 seems to allude to it.

[186] The framework (Deuteronomy 1–3; 31–34) follows the Deuteronomist's practice of interrupting a major line of argument with a minor one or, analogously, of collecting all the evidence before drawing a conclusion. The method is exaggerated in Deuteronomy, where there are two subsidiary systems (chaps. 4–11 and 26–30; chaps. 12–18 and 19–25) so that the book, in effect, is composed of interlocking frameworks.

[187] Some of the places mentioned (Suph, Paran, Hazerot, Horeb, Kadesh-

barnea) are stations on the journey (cf. Exod 15:22; 17:6; Num 12:16; 20:1; 33:17–18), but the others are additional map references that are not found in the earlier versions of the journey. Similarly, the time it takes to travel from Horeb to Kadesh and the name Barnea have not been mentioned before but give this repetition of the earlier material a measure of historical verisimilitude.

188 The prolepsis (1:4) is a typically Deuteronomistic preview and with the resumption (2:26–3:11) constitutes another of the book's characteristic frameworks.

189 The story (Deut 1:9–18) combines elements of the Elohist version (Exodus 18) with allusions to the earlier Deuteronomistic version (Numbers 11).

190 Cf. Numbers 20; 24:18.

191 Cf. Num 21:4–9, 10–15; Gen 14:5–6.

192 Cf. Num 21:24; Gen 10:14; 14:5–7.

193 Cf. Num 21:21–30; 32:1–42; Deut 20:3–4, 10–18.

194 Cf. Num 21:33–35.

195 Cf. Numbers 25; 27; 32.

196 The final sentences (31:7–8) apply to Joshua the encouragement that the sequel offered to the people (31:1–2a, 3a, 6). The rest of the text is an epitome of earlier texts (cf. Deut 31:2b and 3:25–26; 31:3 and 3:21–22, 28; 31:4 and 1:4 and 2:26–3:11; 31:5 and 20:1–20).

197 Cf. Exod 33:7–11; Num 2:17; 9:15–23; 10:11–28; 11:1–35; 12:1–15; etc.

198 Deut 31:16–22 is composed mainly of allusions to chap. 32.

199 Cf. Exod 32:11–14; Num 14:13–25; Deut 29:22.

200 A clue to this dependence on the prophets is presented at the beginning of the poem: the appeal to listen and hear the words that are spoken repeats the opening of Isaiah, partly in opposite order (Deut 32:1; Isa 1:2a, 20b); the theme of the people as children who have gone astray (Deut 32:5, *šiḥēt lô lōʾ bānāyw mûmām*) is taken from the same text of Isaiah and with a similar reversion of word order (Isa 1:4, *bānîm mašḥîtîm*). It is this use of prophetic sources that gives the song its elevation and relative distance from the nasty historical realities that it condemns.

201 Joshua joins in singing the song (cf. 31:30), and the allusion to the rebellions in the wilderness consists in using the name that he had when he

was one of the scouts who was sent to reconnoiter the land (cf. Deut 32:44 [Hosea bin Nun] and Num 13:16 ["And Moses called Hosea bin Nun Joshua"]). Much of the song is based on the work of the prophet Hosea, and the name might also contain a reference to this fact.

202 Deut 33:2–5 mentions Sinai, alludes to the wilderness wanderings, and ends with the present assembly in the plains of Moab. Deut 33:26–29 continues from this time and place to Israel's secure possession of the land.

203 For example, cf. Deut 33:12 (*ktp*) and Josh 18:12–19.

204 In the sequel Joshua is encouraged to take the land that Yahweh is giving Israel in accordance with the covenant (Josh 1:3). In the revised version he is encouraged to partition the land promised to the patriarchs and to meditate on the book of the law.

205 The Transjordanian vanguard, as the text itself notes, was planned by Moses (Josh 1:12–18; Numbers 32). The analogy of the exodus and the wilderness campaigns is established explicitly in words put into the mouth of Rahab (Josh 2:9b–11, 24b; cf. Exodus 15; Numbers 21), and implicitly in the orders that the officers give to the camp. The people prepare provisions they did not have time to prepare when they left Egypt (Josh 1:10; Exod 12:39). They are told, as they were at Sinai, to be ready for the third day (Josh 1:11; Exod 19:11, 15–16).

206 Cf. Num 35:5. The exhortation to follow the ark in order to know the way (Josh 3:3–4) uses the language of worship and of obedience to the law. It marks the crossing as the end of the era of rebellion in the wilderness and the beginning of obedience to the law in the land.

207 Cf. Exod 17:7; 33:3, 5; 34:9.

208 In the sequel's version the battle of Jericho is magic but nevertheless a military affair. In the Deuteronomist's version it is conducted by the priests.

209 It reintroduces Othniel, who later becomes a model judge (Judg 1:10–15; 3:7–11); the Kenites, who are crucial for its interpretation of the defeat of the Canaanites (1:16; 4:11, 17–22; 5:24); the towns Megiddo and Taanach in Manasseh, where this battle was fought (1:27; 5:19); and the town of Bet 'Anat in Naphtali, the home of Shamgar, who was a judge before Barak from the same tribe (1:33; 3:31; 4:6).

210 The annalistic style is represented in its standardized reportage interspersed with more detailed narrative accounts. The reportage varies in the two sections of the chapter dealing with the house of Judah and the house of Joseph. The anecdotes explain the relationship of Judah and Simeon (Judg 1:3–7), Judah and Caleb (1:12–15), Judah and the Kenites (1:16), Joseph and Bethel (1:22–26), and the migration of the tribe of Dan (1:34–36).

211 The section on the house of Judah (Judg 1:1–21) is divided into six

paragraphs: the first and last give two different views of the capture of Jerusalem (1:1–9, 21); the second and the second to last give the local and national opinion on the defeat of the sons of Anak (1:10–13, 20); the third and fourth have anecdotes about irregular settlement patterns by contemporaries and relatives of Moses (1:14–15, 16–19). The section on the house of Joseph (1:22–36) is composed of pairs of paragraphs that are mutually explanatory (1:22–23, 24–26, 27, 28–29, 30, 31–32, 33–35, 36).

212 The argument is stated at the beginning (Judg 2:1–5). It does not have a context and seems to hang in the air, but the proof is presented in the second paragraph (2:6–10), the evidence in the third (2:11–14), and the conclusion in the fourth (2:15–23). The part is constructed similarly and is a similar abrupt but comprehensive introduction to the whole book.

213 The example (Judg 3:7–11) assembles all the clichés and technical terms to be used in a story of a judge. The name of the king is distorted to represent Cush, the ancestor of Assyria and Babylonia (cf. Gen 10:8–12), from Mesopotamia (Aram Naharaim; cf. Gen 24:10; Deut 23:5), as doubly evil (*riš'ātayim*, Judg 3:8 [twice], 10 [twice]). Othniel's escapade, in effect, redoes the victory of Abraham over the kings of the East (Genesis 14).

214 The Othniel paradigm is repeated in the example of Samuel at Mizpah (1 Samuel 7), where the fusion of prophecy and judgment is more evident.

215 The two chapters are bound by framework texts (Judg 4:1–2; 5:31) that fit them into the chronological and juridical context of the book. The relevance of the prophetic viewpoint is suggested by identifying Deborah as a prophet and judge (Judg 4:4; 5:12). The annalistic context is preserved by the catalog of tribes who went with Deborah and Barak (4:6, 10; 5:12–18) and especially by the reference to the Kenites, who were mentioned in the annalistic introduction (1:16; 4:11, 17–22; 5:24).

216 The Deuteronomist corrected the sequel's story of Joshua and Jabin (Josh 11:1–3, 5–6a, 7–8a) by including chariots (11:4, 6b, 9) and by making the defeat of Hazor a separate battle (11:10–15). These chapters repeat both points (4:3, 7, 13–16, 23–24; 5:28).

217 The name "Samuel" is explained as if it were derived from the root of the name Saul. The intrusion becomes less and less subtle and finally uses the form "Saul" (1 Sam 1:20bB, 27, 28a).

218 Samson was also a nazirite (cf. 1 Sam 1:11 and Judg 13:5) and, like Samuel, renowned for his trouncing of the Philistines. Eli's supposition that Hannah was drunk (1 Sam 1:12–18) is based on the preceding tale of the vintage festivals held at Shiloh (Judg 21:19–22).

219 The narrative sequence that the Song of Hannah (1 Sam 2:1–10) interrupts took Elkanah from Shiloh (1 Sam 1:28b) to Ramah (1 Sam 2:11).

220 The song's statement that Yahweh thunders against his enemies (1 Sam

2:10a) is verified in the ritual victory over the Philistines at Mizpah (1 Sam 7:10). The statement that Yahweh brings down to Sheol and brings back up is verified when Samuel is summoned by the witch of Endor (1 Samuel 28).

[221] The first strophe (1 Sam 2:1–2) places Yahweh above the other Gods; the second (2:3–5) resumes his role in the story of Hannah; and the third (2:6–10) describes his cosmological and political functions.

[222] In this section (1 Sam 2:18–21) Hannah and Elkanah continue their annual pilgrimages to Shiloh and bring Samuel new clothing. Each year Eli blesses them and Hannah has five more children, an observation that gives more precise chronological significance to the statement that Samuel was growing up with Yahweh (2:21b).

[223] The exclusion of intercession (1 Sam 2:22–25) alludes to the prophetic role of Samuel, as the later exclusion of sacrifice (1 Sam 3:14) supposes his office as priest.

[224] The inclusion is also marked by duplicate battles at Ebenezer (1 Sam 4:1b; 7:12).

[225] The chapter (1 Sam 6:1–7:2) ends with the ark installed in Judah, attended by the Levites and an interim priesthood, and with the house of Israel lamenting its loss.

[226] 2 Sam 12:24b–25; 1 Kgs 1:1a, 5–10, 31–35a, 38–41abB, 42–45a, 49.

[227] In the sequel Solomon was anointed king of Israel (1 Kgs 1:34). In the Deuteronomist's version the intrigue, which makes the choice of Solomon more political than providential, surrounds his accession to the throne of David, and he is appointed ruler of Israel and Judah (1 Kgs 1:35). This politicizing of his destiny is balanced by invoking on him the blessings of Yahweh, the God of David and of Israel (1 Kgs 1:35b–37, 47–48). The intrigue, like that in the Garden of Eden is instigated by a shrewd male, becomes effective through the cooperation of a determined mother and is a matter of life and death. The symbolism of the garden was prepared by the Deuteronomist, who named one of the rivers that flowed from the garden after the river in Jerusalem where Solomon was anointed (Gihon, Gen 2:13; 1 Kgs 1:33, 38).

[228] The story of the Garden of Eden, similarly, revolves around the command not to eat the fruit of the tree of knowledge of good and evil.

[229] The symbolism of the garden is suggested by the banishment of Abiathar, who deserved death but was spared because of his proximity to God and the king (1 Kgs 2:26–27; cf. Gen 3:22–24).

[230] The prolepsis contains a sinister insistence on the fact that Solomon and the people used to offer sacrifice at the high places (1 Kgs 3:1–2, 3).

231 Cf. Gen 2:9, 16–17; 3:1–7. Solomon's claim that he is a child without military skills—literally, "who does not know coming and going"—reinforces the allusion to the tree of knowledge of good and evil.

232 The analogy of this chapter with the Garden of Eden, if it exists, would be in the institution of forced labor (1 Kgs 4:6; Gen 2:15) and the provision of food and drink (Gen 2:17; 3:3, 17; 1 Kgs 4:20).

233 This alternating pattern (1 Kgs 5:1 [cf. Gen 2:10–13]; 5:2–3; 5:4 [rɔb; cf. Gen 1:26]; 5:5; 5:6; 5:7–8; 5:9–11; 5:12–14) is characteristic of the Deuteronomist's argumentative style.

234 The qualities and achievements that rate Solomon a kingdom like the Garden of Eden are those which Ezekiel attributed to the king of Tyre in Eden (cf. Ezek 28:1–19).

235 See V. Fritz, "Weltalter und Lebenszeit: Mythische Elemente in der Geschichtsschreibung Israels und bei Hesiod," *ZTK* 87 (1990) 145–62; A. Draffkorn Kilmer, "The Mesopotamian Counterparts of the Biblical *Nepilim*," in *Perspectives on Language and Text: Essays and Poems in Honor of Francis I. Andersen's Sixtieth Birthday July 28, 1985*, ed. E. W. Conrad and E. G. Newing (Winona Lake, Ind.: Eisenbrauns, 1987) 39–43.

236 The sacrifice that Noah offered (Gen 8:20–22) was prepared by maintaining the distinction between clean and unclean animals and was followed by the prohibition of eating the blood (Gen 9:2–7).

237 The existence of such maps is evident in a text like Ezekiel 27, on which elements of this part may depend (cf. Gen 10:15, 18 and Ezek 27:8). The map, however, could be condensed or scrambled in the interests of interpretation (cf. Gen 10:19). Abraham's trip to Egypt (Gen 12:10–20) is modeled on Isaac's sojourn in Gerar (Genesis 26). His vision of the promised land (Gen 13:14–17) combines elements of the Balaam cycle with the final incident in the life of Moses (Numbers 27; Deuteronomy 34).

238 The text (Genesis 14) is a mixture of fact and fantasy presented in a compressed and pseudo-cryptic form (obvious in the names of kings and places, e.g., ". . . the king of Sumer, . . . the king of Elam, . . . the king of Nations, Bad the king of Sodom, Evil the king of Gomorrah. . . ."). It is a narrative transposition into past tense of the genre of political omen texts known from Assyria and Babylonia, and it ends with a good omen for Abraham. See M. C. Astour, "Political and Cosmic Symbolism in Genesis 14 and in its Babylonian Sources," in *Biblical Motifs: Origins and Transformations*, ed. A. Altmann (Cambridge, Mass.: Harvard University Press, 1966) 65–112.

239 The expression "I am Yahweh who brought you out of Ur of the Chaldaeans" combines the sequel's profession "I am Yahweh your God who brought you out of the land of Egypt" (Deut 5:6) with the Priestly table of Abraham's origins (Gen 11:31). Problems of inheritance are discussed in the

Priestly covenant with Abraham (cf. Gen 15:3 and Gen 17:18). The history of the people (Gen 15:12–16) is that recounted in Genesis and Exodus. The boundaries of the land (Gen 15:18) are modeled on those described by the sequel (Josh 1:4) and the Elohist (Exod 23:31), and the list of indigenous inhabitants is an expansion of the epic's list (Gen 15:19; cf. Exod 34:11). Faith in Yahweh was required by the epic, by Isaiah, and by the sequel (Exod 14:31b; Num 24:11b; Deut 1:32; Isa 28:16), but it is Isaiah who makes the link between faith and justice (Isa 28:17). The vision of Abraham, not surprisingly, is a compendium of the history of Israel.

240 The Deuteronomistic text initiates discussion of whether it is possible to see God and live (Gen 16:13–14), which becomes crucial in later discussions of prophecy.

241 The quotation (Gen 18:23, "Would you really wipe out the innocent with the guilty?" [*ṣaddîq ʿim rāšāʿ*]) has the same word order but questions and implicitly contradicts the original statement (Ezek 21:8, "I will draw my sword from its sheath and cut down the innocent and the guilty" [*ṣaddîq wěrāšāʿ*]).

242 Abraham's repeated questioning (Gen 18:22–33) represents literarily Jeremiah's search in the city (Jer 5:1, 3–5).

243 Abimelech's question (Gen 20:4, "Will you kill an innocent people?") rephrases Abraham's question (Gen 18:23). It is a Deuteronomistic idea that prophets are intercessors (Gen 20:4–7, 17–18). Parts of the story are taken from the Elohist original (dreams: Gen 20:6 = 20:3) and parts from earlier Deuteronomistic texts (cf. Gen 20:12–13 and 11:29–30; Gen 20:18 and 16:2). The idea that the sin of the king or leader is the sin of the people (Gen 20:3–4, 9) is expressed in the story of the golden calf (Exod 32:35) and is the leitmotif of the book of Kings. The location of the scene between Havilah and Shur draws on Deuteronomistic historical geography (Gen 25:18; 1 Sam 15:7).

244 Gen 20:17; cf. Exod 15:26; Hos 5:13; 6:1; 7:1; 11:3; Jer 3:22; 8:22; 30:13, 17.

245 Cf. Gen 29:1–30; 31:1–54; 47:29–31; Exod 2:15–22.

246 The first two children, for instance, are named according to the norms of the loved and hated wives (Gen 29:31–33; cf. Deut 21:15–17). All of the children are born into the rivalry and strife that characterize their history.

247 Cf. Gen 38:27–30 and 25:24–26.

248 State slavery is taken for granted by the sequel (1 Sam 17:25). The Deuteronomist warned against it (Deut 17:16; 1 Sam 8:10–18; 12:3–5).

249 Judah, for instance, fulfills one of the dreams of Joseph (cf. 49:8 and 37:9–11).

250 Compare Exod 1:15–21 and 1:22; 2:13–14 and 2:11–12; 3:15–22 and 3:1–14; 5:1–21 and 1:11.

251 Exod 7:8–13 (*tannîn*; cf. Gen 1:21), 7:19–20, 21b–22, 24 (waters; cf. Gen 1:9–10); 8:1–3, 9b–11 (earth); 8:12–15 (human and beast); 9:8–12 (heaven); 14° (separation of water and dry land); see Z. Zevit, "The Priestly Redaction and Interpretation of the Plague Narrative in Exodus," *JQR* 66 (1976) 193–211.

252 The Deuteronomist revised two of the Priestly plagues (redoing Exod 7:19–20, 21b–22 in Exod 7:14–18, 21a, 23–24; and redoing Exod 8:1–3, 9b–11 in Exod 7:25–29 + 8:4–9a), added others to match the Priestly plagues (Exod 8:16–28 [flies] parallels Exod 8:12–15 [gnats]; Exod 9:1–7 [plague] matches 9:8–12 [boils]), and appended four others in the same system of pairing (Exod 9:13–35; 10:1–20; 10:21–29; 11:1–8 + 12:29–32). These emphasize the ruin of world order and add further references to heaven, the sun, light and darkness, and human offspring, which are features of the Priestly creation account.

253 The eighth plague (Exod 9:13–35) usually mentions hail (9:18, 22, 25, 26, 28, 29) but sometimes mentions thunder (*qōlōt*, 9:23, 28) and twice mentions fire (9:23, 24), once describing it in terms that Ezekiel used in the description of the storm he saw gathering in the North (Exod 9:24, *wĕʾēš mitlaqqaḥat* = Ezek 1:4). His vision occurred in exile, by the river Chebar near Tel Abib, and could be appropriated for Israel in slavery in Egypt. The plague of darkness (Exod 10:21–29) draws on themes of creation but also suits the description of the day of Yahweh in Amos (Amos 5:18, 20). In detailing the effects of this day Amos refers to plagues of locusts (Amos 7:1–3), to judgment by fire (7:4–6), and to bewailing the death of little children (7:2, 5; 8:9–10). Both sets of texts imply a similar reversal of creation.

254 The plagues usually include announcement of the plague, its significance for Israel, and the confession required of Egypt; the occurrence of the plague; Pharaoh's plea and tentative agreement, which becomes progressively more like a confession that Yahweh is God; intercession, remission, and recidivism. The same elements, though not necessarily in the same order, are found in lamentations composed for Israel (Judg 10:6–16; 1 Sam 7:5–11).

255 The Priestly creation story insists on separation (*bdl*, Gen 1:4, 6, 7, 14, 18) and the separation of kinds (Gen 1:11–12, 21, 24, 25) except in the instance of woman and man, who are made in the likeness of God. The Deuteronomist insists on the separation between Israel and Egypt, in different terms (Exod 8:22–23; 9:4, 6; 9:26; 10:23), and as part of the argument that Yahweh alone is God.

256 Exod 13:1, 11–16, cf. 34:19–20; 13:2–10, cf. 23:15.

257 The song is fitted between a matching introduction and conclusion (Exod 15:1, 20–21) and is composed of six strophes, each with two stanzas

(15:2, 3–4; 5, 6–7; 8–9, 10; 11, 12–13; 14–15a, 15b–16; 17, 18–19), that develop the theme proposed in the refrain (15:1b, 21b: "Horse and rider he hurled into the Sea"). It refocuses the preceding prose narrative (chap. 14), especially the Priestly version of the victory, and anticipates the following journey to the mountain of God, in particular the Priestly itinerary from the Sea to the sanctuary of God (cf. 15:17; 25:8) and illustrates the Historian's interest in adding ritual and liturgical flourishes to the Priestly text.

[258] Cf. Exod 17:1–7 and Num 20:2–13; Exod 17:8–13 and Josh 8:18–23.

[259] The updating of the laws (22:9–19) is an obvious revision of its context (cf. 22:8) but ends as usual with the exclusion of other Gods (22:19). The revision of the Elohist covenant (chap. 23) emphasizes the exclusive worship of Yahweh.

[260] Cf. Exod 24:9–11 and Ezek 1:26–28; cf. Ezek 28:13–14. For both writers there is a vision, like heaven in its clarity, of God seated or standing on sapphire. Ezekiel sees the glory of God as it were in human form and appearance (cf. Exod 24:15–18). The Deuteronomist insists that no image, form, or appearance was seen on the mountain (Deut 4:15–24), suggests that the vision took place in heaven (Exod 20:22; 24:10), and emphasizes that Moses and the others saw God as God of Israel (Exod 24:10, 11b). Ezekiel's vision took place amid cosmic phenomena. The vision of Moses had liturgical features (Exod 24:11b).

[261] In the Priestly version the wilderness stages (Exod 16:1–3, 6–7, 9–12; 17:1abA; 19:1a, 2a) mark the journey of Yahweh, who gained glory over the Egyptians (Exod 14:18), to Sinai where the tabernacle is built for his glory (Exod 29:43). This follows the Near Eastern pattern of the victorious God, a pattern adopted with greater fidelity and specificity by the Deuteronomist in the Song of the Sea, where the historical enemies are listed, the road to Israel is traced, and the enthronement of Yahweh is described.

[262] The tent, the tabernacle, and the temple correspond in many ways: in being built according to a design revealed by God (Exod 26:30, *mišpāṭ*; Exod 25:9, 40, *tabnît*); in their reliance on master craftsmen (Exod 35:30–35; 36:1–2; 1 Kgs 7:13–14); in the regalia of the ark (Exod 25:10–22; cf. 1 Kgs 6:23–28; 7:7; 8:4–11); in the construction of the table and lampstand (Exod 25:23–39; 1 Kgs 7:48–50), of the entranceways (Exod 26:31–37; cf. 1 Kgs 6:19–22, 33–36), and of the altar (Exod 27:1–8; 1 Kgs 7:40–43; 8:22, 54, 64).

[263] The stones in Aaron's breastplate and their gold settings correspond to the nine precious stones and gold in the Garden of Eden (Exod 28:15–27; 39:8–21; Ezek 28:13), but with three more stones in the Deuteronomist's list to correspond to the twelve tribes of Israel.

[264] The fifth part (chaps. 32–34) supposes this warlike assembly: in the Elohist version the shouting in the camp is understood at first as the sign of victory or defeat (Exod 32:17–18); in the Deuteronomistic version the Levites

assume their traditional role of ruthless warriors (Exod 32:26–29; cf. Genesis 34).

265 The amphictyony summarized the realities and possibilities of an originally diverse and politically fragmented society. It was, in the Deuteronomist's theory, a community of families, clans, and tribes, each with their proper organization, gathered to worship and defend the territory of one God that had been allotted to it, assisted in these goals by religious, political, and military officials, bound by regulations and obliged to contribute to the economic stability of the central shrine and its government. It was a synthetic and supple model for which the evidence varied from era to era. It was displayed at Sinai, legally constituted beyond the Jordan, incorporated in the allotment of the land, illustrated in the wars of the judges, realized under David and Solomon, coexisting with the monarchy and still viable when the North and the South had been captured.

266 The community (ʿēdâ, Lev 8:3–5; 9:5; 10:6) assembles (qhl, Lev 8:3–4) at the tent of meeting designed for it (ʾōhel môʿēd). It comprises the bĕnê yiśrāʾēl (Lev 9:3; 10:11; 11:2), represented by their elders (Lev 9:1), in a single people (ʿām, Lev 9:7, 22–24; 10:3). The raison d'être of the assembly is to express the holiness and glory of God manifested at the tent of meeting (Lev 9:6, 23–24; 10:3; 11:44–45). The rivalry is illustrated in the pretensions of Nadab and Abihu (Lev 10:1–7). The dispute involves Moses and Aaron (Lev 10:16–20). Both cases reveal the tensions that the Deuteronomist perceived between political and theocratic government.

267 The image of Moses entering the tent of meeting to speak to it (ʾittô) and hearing a voice speaking to him (wayyišmaʿ ʾet haqqôl middabbēr ʾēlāyw) from above the mercy seat and from between the cherubim that were over the ark of the testimony (Num 7:89) is reminiscent of Ezekiel, who entered into the vision of God and heard a voice speaking to him from above the firmament over the heads of the living creatures (Ezek 1:25, 28, wāʾešmaʿ qōl mĕdabbēr). This emphasizes the oracular qualities of the tent rather than any particular revelation of Yahweh (cf. Exod 25:22). In a similar way the ark, to the sound of Moses' voice, used to set out and return from battle (Num 10:35–36).

268 The rebellion is attributed to the people (ʿām, Num 11:1–3). Complaints about the manna are attributed to irregular elements of the army (Num 11:4, wĕhāʾsapsūp ʾăšer bĕqirbô), who are distinguished from the recruits (Num 11:26, bakkĕtūbîm; cf. Numbers 1). The unrestrained spirit of prophecy indicates a certain incongruity between the system of twelve tribes with its natural leaders and the amphictyonic ideal with its charismatic leaders.

269 Holy war is waged by God and requires the dedication of the spoils of battle to God.

270 The first stanza (Deut 32:1–2) quotes from Isaiah, and the second stanza (Deut 32:3–4) is an amalgam of allusions to him and his successors (cf. Deut 32:1 and Isa 1:2a, 20b; Deut 32:4 [tāmîm, mišpāṭ, ʾĕmūnâ, ʾên ʿāwel, ṣaddîq, yāšār] and Isa 28:16; Amos 5:24 [ṣedeq, mišpāṭ]; Jer 5:1 [mišpāṭ,

ʾĕmûnâ]; Mic 2:7; 7:2 [yāǰār]; and Zeph 3:5 [yhwh ṣaddîq bĕqirbāh / lōʾ yaʿăśeh ʿawlâ].

271 Deut 32:5–7; cf. Isa 1:3–4. Isaiah refers to Israel as children gone bad (Isa 1:4, bānîm maǰḥîtîm): the poem refers to them as having gone bad and being nonchildren because of it (Deut 32:5, ǰiḥēt lô lōʾ bānāyw mûmām), but also puts it in Deuteronomistic terms of being a "generation" (cf. Deut 1:35aB; 2:14) that is crooked and perverse. Isaiah said that even an ox knows its owner, but that Israel did not understand (Isa 1:3, qōnēhû . . . lōʾ hitbônān): the poem begs them to understand that Yahweh is their owner (Deut 32:6b, 7a, hălôʾ hûʾ ʾābîkā qānekā . . . bînû ǰĕnôt dōr wādôr), but also adds the Deuteronomistic views of creation, the succession of generations, and local government by elders (Deut 32:6–7).

272 Deut 32:8–9; cf. Gen 6:4; 10:32; 14:19; Isa 10:13; Deut 32:9 [kî ḥēleq yhwh ʿammô yaʿăqōb ḥebel naḥălātô]; cf. Mic 2:4–5 [ḥēleq ʿammî yāmîr . . . lākēn lōʾ yihyeh lĕkā maǰlîk ḥebel bĕgôrāl biqhal yhwh]; Deut 32:10–12, cf. Exod 19:3–6; Jer 2:6; Hos 13:4.

273 Deut 32:13–14; cf. Num 20:7, 10–11 and Deut 8:8–9 and their Deuteronomistic reflexes (Exod 17:6; Deut 8:15).

274 Cf. Deut 8:11, 12–14; Hos 13:6; Jer 5:27–28. The invidious images and provocative abominations that the people worshiped (Deut 32:16, yaqnîʾûhû bĕzārîm bĕtôʿēbōt yakʿîsûhû) are like the things that Ezekiel saw in the temple (Ezek 8:3, ǰēmel haqqinʾâ; 8:17, . . . ʾet hattôʿēbôt . . . wayyāǰûbû lĕhakʿîsēnî). The aliens who affronted Yahweh (Deut 32:16, zārîm) are the aliens whom Hosea saw devouring the people (Hos 5:7; 7:9; 8:7).

275 Cf. Isa 10:5–7, 13–14. The passage returns to the figure of filiation that began the poem (Deut 32:18–19; cf. 32:5–7) and says in a negative way (32:20bB, "children in whom there is no truth") what Isaiah said in a positive way (Isa 30:9, "children who lie"). Similarly, as Isaiah said that the children rejected Yahweh (Isa 1:4, nʾṣ), so the poem says that he has rejected them (Deut 32:19, nʾṣ); or, as their rejection of him tempted fate (Isa 1:4, nāzorû ʾāḥôr), so he will wait to see their fate (Deut 32:20, ʾaḥărîtām; cf. Num 23:10; Amos 8:10).

276 Cf. Amos 7:4–6; Deut 32:23–24; cf. Ezek 5:16–17; Hab 3:5, 9; Deut 32:25, cf. Jer 6:10–12, 25.

277 Cf. Exod 32:11–12; Num 14:15–16.

278 Cf. Isa 30:1, 17; Jer 8:8.

279 Cf. Isa 29:11; Nah 1:2; Zeph 1:14.

280 Cf. Isa 28:15, 17; Hos 5:14; 6:1; 13:4. Parts of the text were quoted in the book of Jeremiah (Jer 2:27–28).

281 Cf. Ezek 21:15, 20; Nah 1:2.

282 Cf. Deut 4:12 ("You heard the sound of words . . . just the sound, without seeing any shape") and Ezek 1:25–28 ("a voice . . . I saw . . . the likeness . . . the appearance . . . and when I saw it I prostrated myself and heard the voice speaking").

283 Deut 4:15–24; Ezek 8:3, 10, 13–17. The decalogue excludes images and likenesses (Deut 5:8, *pesel kol tĕmûnâ*), but the opening argument also excludes statues and symbols (Deut 4:16, [*semel / tabnît*]) and gives as the reason the fact that Yahweh is a jealous God (Deut 4:24, *ʾēl qannāʾ*). In his temple vision Ezekiel was shown such a statue provoking jealousy (Ezek 8:3, 5, *semel haqqinʾâ*) and symbols of animals and creeping things carved upon the wall (Ezek 8:10, *kol tabnît remeś ûbĕhēmâ*), which provoked Yahweh to anger (Ezek 8:17, *wayyāśūbû lĕhakʿisēnî*; cf. Deut 4:25, *lĕhakʿisô*).

284 The image of gathering the exiles from the far edge of heaven (Deut 30:4) is repeated in the assurance that the word of Yahweh that they are to observe is not in heaven, where only some hero might steal it, or across the sea in the isles of the blest, but in their hearts and on their lips (30:11–14).

285 See M. Weinfeld, "Traces of Assyrian Treaty Formulae in Deuteronomy," *Bib* 46 (1965) 417–27. The Assyrian curses sometimes are repeated and paraphrased with reference to the plagues in Egypt: for instance, the curse that the heavens be as brass and the earth as iron is taken from an Assyrian prototype in opposite order (Deut 28:23; see Weinfeld, "Traces," p. 417) and then explained by allusion to the plagues (Deut 28:24; cf. Exod 8:12; 9:9).

286 Cf. Deut 28:33 and Hos 5:11 + 7:9.

287 Cf. Hos 11:5. Hosea, like Isaiah and Jeremiah, notes among the crimes of the people the fact that they were in alliance with Egypt (Hos 9:6). The editor of his work, apparently on the basis of this Deuteronomistic curse, says that they will return to Egypt (Hos 8:13).

288 Cf. Isa 5:26–29; 28:11–13; Jer 5:15–17.

289 Compare Deut 12:2b, Hos 4:13 and Jer 2:20; Deut 12:3 and Hos 10:1–2; Deut 12:9 [*mĕnûḥâ*], Isa 28:12, Mic 2:10 and 1 Kgs 8:56.

290 Compare Deut 21:18–21, Isa 30:9, Hos 4:16 and Jer 5:23; Deut 24:1–4 and Jer 3:1–2 (which is corrected in Jer 3:6–8 to suit the Deuteronomist's view). Compare also Deut 24:16 and Ezek 18:5–18.

291 Since Judges presents the dark side of the story told in Joshua, it is not surprising that the stones that Joshua set up at Gilgal turn out to be idolatrous images (Josh 4:20; Judg 3:19, 26). They substantiate the purported apostasy of the people (Judg 3:12), reflect prophetic condemnations of the place (Amos 4:4; 5:5) and match, in the balanced structure of the book, the idol of the priests of Dan (Judg 17:3, 4; 18:18, 31).

292 The Ammonites and Amalekites (Judg 3:13) are antagonists in the time of Gideon and Jephthah (Judges 6; 11) and are prominent in the Deuteronomist's history of the early monarchy.

293 The historical evidence that the account adduces is part of a continuous string of references to Moab in the History starting with its origins (Genesis 19) and including such things as its wars in Transjordan (Numbers 21) and its revolt after the death of Ahab (2 Kings 3). All this evidence is included and interpreted differently in the Mesha inscription (see J. C. L. Gibson, *Textbook of Syrian Semitic Inscriptions, I: Hebrew and Moabite Inscriptions* [Oxford: Clarendon, 1971] 71–83).

294 The Song of Jael (Judg 5:6, 8, 10, 11aAB, 19–21a, 22, 23abA, 24aAb, 25–30) was converted into the Song of Deborah and the tribal league (Judg 5:1–5, 7, 9, 11aGb, 12–18, 21b, 23bB, 24aB, 31) by the usual method of repetition and cross-reference. The preface (Judg 5:1–2, 3, 4–5) followed on the Deuteronomist's text (Judges 4) and needed no justification. It turned the song into a hymn (cf. Exod 15:1–4; Deut 32:1), introduced a new cast and themes, and related the song to the continuous history of Israel. Comments were attached to both stanzas in the first strophe (Judg 5:6, 8). The first stanza mentions Jael and the cessation of travel (5:6), but by repeating "cessation" the Deuteronomist brought Deborah and the militia on the scene (5:6, *ḥādĕlû*; cf. 5:7, *ḥādĕlû . . . ḥādĕlû*). The second stanza describes the desperate situation in Israel (5:8), but by using a deictic subject ("*my* heart") and by repeating the name "Israel" and the new incipit ("volunteers among the people, bless Yahweh" = 5:2) the Deuteronomist managed to substitute tribal officials (5:9, "the commanders of Israel") for the contingents mentioned in the song. The second strophe (5:10–11aAB) describes the setting of the song at way stations, where travelers recounted the exploits of Yahweh. By repeating one word (5:11aG, *ṣidqôt*) the Deuteronomist suggests a settled way of life and includes a list of the tribes who were involved in the battle (5:11b–18). The third strophe narrates Yahweh's celestial and elemental victory (5:19–21a, 22), but the Deuteronomist used deictics to add a hymnic touch (5:21b). The fourth strophe begins the story of Jael's brave deeds, but the Deuteronomist kept the focus on the tribes by repetition (5:23bB, *lĕʿezrat*) and an appositional phrase (5:24aB). The rest of the song narrates the cunning and bravery of Jael (5:26–27) and the anguish of Sisera's mother (5:28–30). The Deuteronomist wrote an epilogue (5:31a, "*So, Yahweh, may all your enemies perish . . .*") and the rest of the standard framework (5:31b).

295 Deborah and Barak sing a song about themselves (Judg 5:1, 7, 12; cf. chap. 4). Jael becomes the wife of Heber the Kenite (5:24aB; cf. 1:16; 4:11). The song mentions Shamgar ben Anat (5:6), but the History is careful to mention him first (3:31).

296 The first strophe (Judg 5:6, 8) pictures Israel at peace, engaged in trade and commerce and totally unprepared for war. In the second strophe the war is over; Yahweh is victorious; and, in their usual round of activities, travelers gather to sing of his exploits (5:10–11aAB). The remaining strophes are the song that they sing: the third is the ballad of Taanach, where the

Canaanite kings were defeated by the stars and the river Kishon (5:19–21a, 22); the fourth and fifth tell how Jael killed Sisera when he tried to escape (5:24aAb, 25–27); the last emphasizes the enormity of his defeat by seeing it through his mother's eyes (5:28–30).

297 The most obvious difference between the two versions is their representation of Israel as organized in tribes, settled in towns, gathered as a worshiping community, an amphictyony armed and ready for war (Judges 4) or as caravaneers without any military resources whose champion was Yahweh (chap. 5°). The difference is emphasized by the Deuteronomist in changing the source to agree with its interpretation. The change gave the song the detail and concreteness of historical evidence.

298 The part is composed in the alternating pattern often used by the Deuteronomist: the usual apostasy and national crisis, with prophetic intervention (Judg 6:1–10); the appointment of Gideon as savior (6:11–24); extirpation of the apostate cult by Jerubbaal (6:25–32); the rallying of the tribes to confront the national crisis and confirmation of Gideon's appointment (6:33–40); the battle against the Midianites led by Jerubbaal (7:1–25); pursuit of the Midianites by Gideon (8:1–35); and the story of Abimelech, son of Jerubbaal (chap. 9). Various sections are also constructed in the same alternating pattern: in the pursuit of the Midianites there is emphasis on Succoth and Penuel (8:4–9), on Zebah and Zalmuna (8:10–12), Succoth and Penuel (8:13–17), and Zebah and Zalmuna (8:18–21). In the story of Abimelech the focus shifts from the king to his opponents (9:1–6, 7–21, 22–25, 26–45, 46–49, 50–57).

299 The war with Ammon has to do with disputed boundaries in Transjordan already discussed in Numbers (cf. Num 21:13–14, 25–35). The story of the animosity between Ephraim and Gilead revolves around regional differences in the pronunciation of sibilants (Judg 12:1–6). The rites of Adonis were celebrated by women every year (Judg 11:40, *tannôt*; cf. Judg 5:11) and had been historicized in the story of Joseph.

300 The Samson stories reflect the period when Dan was settled in the southern coastal region among the Philistines (Josh 19:40–46) before migrating to northern Israel (Josh 19:47–48; Judges 17–18). Appropriately enough they are constructed from legends that were indigenous to this region.

301 Cf. Genesis 16–18; 32:23–33; Numbers 6; Judges 6. Hercules, whose legends were a model for much of the Samson cycle, was the son of Zeus and the wife of Amphitryon, a modest woman whose husband was busy with other matters and whose marriage had not been consummated.

302 The introduction to the marriage (Judg 14:1–4) develops the theme of Israelite exclusiveness (cf. Genesis 24; 28:1–9) and the idea of Samson's calling, which are intrinsic not to the legend but to its interpretation. His first feat consists, like Hercules', in killing a lion. The second feat (Judg 15:1–17), reflecting an era of Philistine domination in Judah, is like the first but is also set apart as derivative by the same device (Judg 15:14, "The spirit of Yahweh

engulfed him . . ."). The conclusion (Judg 15:18–20) resembles the introduction (Judg 14:1–4), but it is a prose rendition of a typical prayer of petition.

303 The section begins like the sequel's stories of Samuel and Saul (cf. Judg 17:1 and 1 Sam 1:1; 9:1) and is linked to the story of Samson (cf. Judg 17:2 and 16:5). The making of the idol supposes the curse on those who do such things (Judg 17:2–5; cf. Deut 27:15), the example of Gideon (Judg 8:24–27) and the making of the golden calf (Exodus 32). The introduction of the Levite from Bethlehem is inspired by the introduction of David in the battle with Goliath (cf. Judg 17:7 and 1 Sam 17:12). The sending of scouts to reconnoiter the land is like the earlier versions of the spies sent to survey the land (Judges 18; cf. Numbers 13; Deuteronomy 1). The theft of Micah's teraphim was anticipated in Rachel's theft of Laban's teraphim (Judg 18:14–26; cf. Genesis 31). The capture of Laish is an elaboration of a notice in Joshua (Judg 18:27–29; cf. Josh 19:47).

304 This section (Judges 19–21) resembles the first especially in narrating the adventures of a Levite who journeyed from Bethlehem to the North. It repeats themes from the stories of Sodom and Gomorrah (cf. Judges 19 and Genesis 19), of Abraham and Isaac (Judges 19; Genesis 22), of Saul at Gibeah (Judg 19:29–30; cf. 1 Sam 11:5–7), of casting lots at Mizpah (Judg 20:1–11; cf. 1 Sam 10:17–27, and of ambush at Ai (Judges 20; cf. Joshua 8); see J. Unterman, "The Literary Influence of 'The Binding of Isaac' (Genesis 22) on 'The Outrage at Gibeah' (Judges 19)," *HAR* 4 (1980) 161–66.

305 The psalm (1 Sam 2:1–10) is suitable to its immediate and distant context: cf. 2:3 (*'al tarbû tĕdabbĕrû*) and 1:12 (*wĕhāyâ kî hirbĕtâ lĕhitpallēl*); 2:5 (the barren woman gives birth to seven children) and 1:6 and 2:21; 2:10 ("against him he thunders in the sky") and 7:10; 2:8, 10 (throne, anointed one) and 1 Samuel 10. It also has parallels in poetic compositions (1 Sam 2:2; cf. Exod 15:11; Deut 32:30; 2:6a; cf. Deut 32:39) and in Amos (1 Sam 2:8a; cf. Amos 2:7a; 8:4). Priestly activity around the sacrificial kettle was a topic of prophecy (1 Sam 2:12–17; cf. Mic 3:1–3; Ezek 24:1–14). The priests who traced their lineage to Moses were displaced by the line of Aaron (cf. Judg 18:30–31; 1 Sam 2:27–36).

306 Cf. 1 Sam 4:21–22 (*gālâ kābôd miyyiśrā'ēl* and Hos 10:5bB (*'al kĕbôdô kî gālâ mimmennû*); also Mic 1:15 and Ezek 11:23.

307 The story supposes, with the theory presented in Numbers, that the ark had numinous power (Num 10:33b–36). It also refers explicitly to the plagues in Egypt and makes the same point that they did about the transcendence of Yahweh. It has other plagues and, in the spirit of this part of Samuel, has the rituals by which such plagues were averted.

308 The chapter, in addition to its imitation of battles in the time of Joshua and the judges, has this part's interest in ritual. The ritual of drawing and pouring out water before Yahweh (1 Sam 7:6) is the basis of a legend about David (2 Sam 23:15–17).

309 The theory (1 Samuel 8; 9:15–17; 10:17–27; 12) supposes the law of kingship (Deut 17:14–20), the stories of the judges (1 Samuel 12), the example of the Pharaoh (Gen 47:13–26), and the idea that Yahweh is king (cf. Exod 15:18; Deut 33:5). It disapproves of kings but accepts the appointment of a viceroy (nāgîd) to govern all the people the way the judges were inspired to lead elements of the tribal league.

310 The annalistic material (1 Sam 13:2–7, 15b–18, 23) melds with the legendary material (1 Samuel 14) and includes nonnarrative elements (1 Sam 13:1, 19–22; 14:21–23, 47–51) that are important to the Deuteronomist's interpretation. Saul is made out to be like one of the judges (1 Sam 14:48) and, as in the time of Jael, the people have no weapons (1 Sam 13:19–22; cf. Judg 5:8b).

311 Jonathan's heroism (1 Sam 14:1–46) begins the process of his alienation from Saul. The story has the standard Deuteronomistic markings: the ark, supposedly in Judah, is present in the battle and causes enormous confusion in the enemy ranks (cf. Judg 7:22; 1 Sam 4:5–9); the people are supposed to abstain from food before the battle (cf. 1 Samuel 7); Saul instructs the people on the rules of sacrifice (1 Sam 14:31–35; cf. Gen 9:2–8; Deut 12:23–25); the priest in charge of the ark carries the Urim and Thummim (1 Sam 14:41; cf. Exod 28:30; Lev 8:8).

312 1 Sam 10:8; 13:8–15a; 15:1–35; cf. Amos 4:4–5; 5:4–5; 5:21–24. Saul was supposed to wait seven days until Samuel came to Gilgal and offered burnt offerings and peace offerings (1 Sam 10:8). It seems contrived that Samuel did not come to Gilgal on the seventh day and the statement to that effect (1 Sam 13:8, wĕlōʾ bāʾ šĕmûʾēl haggilgāl) merely reflects, in opposite word order, Amos's command not to come to Gilgal (Amos 5:5, wĕhaggilgāl lōʾ tābōʾû; the text is quoted by Hosea's editor in the inverted order used by the Deuteronomist but as a prohibition rather than a statement [Hos 4:15, wĕʾal tābōʾû haggilgāl]). The offering corresponds to the sacrifices that are rejected by Amos (1 Sam 10:8; 13:9, hāʿōlâ wĕhaššĕlāmîm; cf. Amos 5:22, ʿōlôt . . . wĕšelem mĕrîʾêkem), and the text of Amos's condemnation is approximated in Samuel's condemnation of Saul for preferring sacrifice to obedience (cf. 1 Sam 15:22–23; Amos 5:21–24 and 3:1 = 4:1 = 5:1 [šimʿû haddābār hazzeh]; also Isa 28:11–13; Jer 6:19). Amos disapproved of the sacrificial rituals at these shrines because they were symptoms and motives of injustice and oppression. His editor, like the editor of Hosea, agrees with the Deuteronomist in associating the rituals with unwanted kings (cf. Amos 7:10–17; Hos 10:10; 13:9–11).

313 Beginning with the story of Goliath (1 Sam 17:1, 54) David is located in various parts of the South (1 Sam 19:18; 20:1, 6; 21:2, 11; 22:1, 5; 23:1, 15, 24; 24:1; 25:1, 2; 26:3; 27:4, 6, 8–10; 30:1, 9–10). This part of the story ends with him sending gifts to the elders of Judah in all the places where he and his people had roamed (1 Sam 30:26–31).

314 The sequel described David as a young shepherd (1 Samuel 17°) who happened to be present when the Philistine champion hurled a challenge at

the ranks of Israel and whose stunning victory over the Philistine brought him into Saul's service. The Deuteronomist accepted this portrayal in the anointing scene (1 Sam 16:1–13) and for the most part in the story of single combat (1 Samuel 17) but actually thought of David as a professional warrior (1 Sam 16:14–23; 17:54; 18:7), although not the famous warrior who engaged in single combat with a Philistine giant. The correction of the sequel is gradual: the Historian first identifies the Philistine champion as a giant, and by name as "Goliath" (1 Sam 17:4aBb–7a), then at the end of the book registers disagreement with the episode and corrects the sequel by revealing that it was not David but a certain Elhanan of Bethlehem who killed Goliath, including at the same time some of the evidence that confused the author of the sequel (2 Sam 21:18–22). The sequel had told a good story about David, and the Deuteronomist, rather than spoil it, used it for what it was worth by adding geographical, military, political, and theological depth and precision (1 Samuel 17). The Deuteronomist's sense of history, however, required the inclusion of the contradictory evidence.

315 The triumphal tour of the Euphrates region (2 Sam 8:3) follows Aramean practice (see I. Eph'al and J. Naveh, "Hazael's Booty Inscriptions," *Israel Exploration Journal* 39 [1989] 192–200). Some of the information is meant as a corrective to the simplistic views expressed in the sequel: the idea that Saul was made king because of his victory over the Ammonites (1 Samuel 11) is opened to question by reviewing the evidence in the time of David (2 Sam 2:5–7; 10:1–14; 11–12); Saul's heroic death is interpreted as treachery (cf. 1 Samuel 31 and 2 Samuel 1).

316 See McCarter, *II Samuel*, 314–28.

317 Ibid., 335–52. It is possible that the Deuteronomist chooses a woman from Tekoa to lament for the dead as a subtle parody of Amos of Tekoa, who portrayed the desolation of the day of Yahweh as mourning for an only child (2 Sam 14:1–3; Amos 6:6; 8:3a, 10). Her pretended predicament, like the flight of Absalom to Geshur, is based on the laws of blood vengeance. The story that she tells is a clever allusion to the story of Cain and Abel. The wisdom that she ascribes to David (2 Sam 14:17, 20) makes him like the man in the Garden of Eden.

318 Cf. Joshua 3–4. Both texts have the same insistence on the ritual crossing ('*br*); both have the ark stop until the people have crossed; and both use some of the same expressions (e.g., "until the people / nation finished crossing," 2 Sam 15:24; Josh 3:17; 4:1). David sends the ark back into the city and proceeds across the Jordan (2 Sam 17:22).

319 See McCarter, *II Samuel*, 374–77.

320 At the beginning of his exodus David expresses the hope that Yahweh will bring him back (2 Sam 15:25), and at the end when Judah comes to Gilgal to bring the king back across the Jordan he expresses the conviction that he is now the king of Israel (2 Sam 19:23). The ritual humiliation of the king (2 Sam 15:23–16:14; 17:15–29), including the appointment of an impos-

tor (2 Sam 16:15–23; 17:1–14), and the subsequent magnification of the king (2 Samuel 19) are features of the Babylonian New Year festival. The battle account, described by the author of the sequel, was dotted by the Deuteronomist with another reminder of the ritual (2 Sam 18:18).

321 This revolt also anticipates the secession of Israel under Jeroboam (cf. 2 Sam 20:1 and 1 Kgs 12:16). The revolt of Absalom suited the sequel's interest in the family history of David. The Deuteronomist gave it symbolic value and included another version of the revolt, led by Sheba, that had good tribal, regional, and historical credentials.

322 The passage harks back to the death of Saul and provides the proper death and burial notice for the king (2 Sam 21:12–14) to complete the regnal formula begun shortly after his coronation at Gilgal (1 Sam 13:1).

323 The psalm (see McCarter, *II Samuel*, 452–75) has the archaizing, imaginative, abstract, and derivative qualities of a Deuteronomistic composition.

324 See McCarter, *II Samuel*, 476–86. The first strophe (23:1–3a) presents David as a prophet and seer, and the second (23:3b–7) describes his righteousness, the permanence of his dynasty, and the ruin of his enemies. Its archaizing, eclectic, and synthethic temper identifies it as a Deuteronomistic composition.

325 See McCarter, *II Samuel*, 502–18. The plague (24:13, *ðeber*) is one of three choices. The other two have already occurred: flight before his enemies during the revolt of Absalom (24:14; cf. 2 Sam 15–17); famine (*rā'āb*) when he had to expiate the crimes committed by Saul at Gibeon (2 Sam 21:1–14). The three choices are offered by the prophet Gad from the list of calamities proposed by Ezekiel (Ezek 5:12, plague, famine, sword). The specific form that the plague takes—a destroying (*maðḥît*) angel (24:16)—was also represented in Ezekiel's vision of the destruction of Jerusalem by the heavenly scribe or census taker and his associates (Ezek 9:1, 6). In Ezekiel's vision the three calamities began in the city, because the temple had been defiled, and then overtook the land, but in the Deuteronomist's view plague first strikes the land and the destruction of the city is averted by building an altar. In the History David assumes personal responsibility for the plague (24:10) and intercedes for the people, "the sheep" (2 Sam 24:17), but in Ezekiel all the shepherds were to blame and the sheep belonged to Yahweh (Ezek 34:1–14). David intercedes when he sees the angel striking the people (2 Sam 24:17), and Ezekiel's editor uses the same occasion to intercede for a remnant (Ezek 9:8). David's reluctance to invoke punishment on his dynasty is matched by this writer's provision for the future of the dynasty (Ezek 34:15–31).

326 Solomon is created in the image of the king of Tyre, and his temple, like the Priestly tabernacle, in the image of the world. Like the king of Tyre, Solomon is the child of creation—rich and wise, the votary of regions, tribes, and petty kingdoms, the goal of human aspiration. Like the island and citadel of Tyre, the Solomonic capital is the true omphalos and representation of the

created world. His people are at peace; slavery seems right; the kingdom is in contact with Egypt and Mesopotamia; distant lands bring him tribute; the love that makes him ruins him. Cf. 1 Kings 1–11; Ezekiel 26–28.

[327] Destiny is expressed by David (1 Kgs 2:1–4) and in visions (1 Kgs 3:3–14; 9:1–9). Solomon—proud, ruthless, opportunistic—is the image of the wise, wealthy, egocentric king of Tyre. The system of provisionment that he arranges is just slightly less magnificent than the world trade that sustains the Tyrian empire. His intrigue with the king of Tyre is exactly what Ezekiel was willing to accept. His oppression of his own people is what the prophets resented. The temple was surrounded by threats of death, but in Ezekiel it was a source of life. Solomon was the origin, ideal, and model of what a monarch might be but the reality, when it materialized, was disappointing and ephemeral.

[328] The story of the Judean prophet who went to Bethel (1 Kings 13) is a parody of Amos and was so understood by the editor of the book of Amos, who rewrote it as a tribute to the prophet (cf. Amos 7:10–17). Amos mentioned Jeroboam I, and the Deuteronomist made them contemporaries; but Amos's editor interpreted his words with reference to Jeroboam II. In the editor's version Amos is an honest prophet whose prophecy came true. The parody reflects the Deuteronomist's disagreement with Amos concerning centralization of sacrifice and worship.

[329] In his association with Jehoshaphat Ahab is not mentioned by name but is called "the king of Israel" (1 Kings 22). This keeps some sort of distance between the good king of Judah and the bad king of Israel, but, more important, it allows the Deuteronomist to correct the sequel by letting it appear that the sequel's reference to the alliance between Jehoshaphat and "the king of Israel" (1 Kgs 22:45) was actually an alliance with Ahab. The repentance of Ahab (1 Kgs 21:27–29) seems farfetched—it is juxtaposed to the statement that he was the worst king ever (1 Kgs 21:25–26)—but, besides explaining why calamity was avoided in his lifetime, it justifies Jehoshaphat's association with him.

[330] The form and content of Micaiah's prophecy (1 Kgs 22:13–23) draw on texts of Ezekiel. His opening statement to the king ("I saw all Israel scattered upon the mountains as sheep that have no shepherd," 1 Kgs 22:17) is like Ezekiel's condemnation of the kings ("My sheep strayed over all the mountains and every high hill, my sheep were scattered over the face of the earth, and there was no one to search for them or look for them," Ezek 34:6). His vision of God sitting on his throne attended by the host of heaven (1 Kgs 22:19) is like Ezekiel's vision of the glory of Yahweh on a throne above the living creatures who attended him (Ezek 1:26–28). A spirit enters Ezekiel (Ezek 2:2), and in opposing the prophets of peace he ridicules them for following their own spirit and telling lies (Ezek 13:3–7), and in the same vein Micaiah sees a lying spirit possessing the prophets (1 Kgs 22:22–23). These allusions make Micaiah a veiled criticism of Ezekiel, whose prophetic tastes and theory of history were hardly acceptable to the Deuteronomist.

331 The king of Israel complains that Micaiah prophesies evil against him and not good (1 Kgs 22:8, 18), as Micah in fact did (Mic 1:12; 2:3; 3:11; cf. 1 Kgs 22:23). Micaiah's last words have a separate introduction (1 Kgs 22:28b, "And he said: Hear you people, all of them" [*šimʿû ʿammîm kullām*]) and are a literal quotation of Micah's opening words (Mic 1:3, "Hear you people, all of them" [*šimʿû ʿammîm kullām*]). The appropriateness of the quotation supposes what follows in Micah, notably his association of Judah and Samaria (Mic 1:5–6), his description of defeat in battle (Mic 1:10–12), his words against the kings of Israel (Mic 1:12–13), his condemnation of people like Ahab (Mic 6:16), who deprive others of their property and inheritance (Mic 2:2; cf. 1 Kings 21), and his conflict with the prophets who had a lying spirit (cf. Mic 2:11 [*lû ʾiš hōlēk rûaḥ wāšeqer kizzēb*] and 1 Kgs 22:22 [*rûaḥ šeqer*]).

332 The siege of Samaria (2 Kgs 6:24–7:20), for instance, is composed of typical siege scenes such as famine (6:24–29; cf. Deut 28:52–57), the king in sackcloth (6:30; cf. 2 Kgs 19:1), alliance with Egypt (7:6; cf. 2 Kgs 17:4–5; 18:21), and the sudden lifting of the siege (7:3–15; cf. 2 Kgs 19:29–31, 35–36). Similarly, the war with Mesha of Moab ends suddenly when he sacrifices his son and Israel lifts the siege and returns to its land (2 Kgs 3:27; cf. 19:7, 36). The unexpected result of his sacrifice was that raging anger overtook Israel: the source of the raging anger is not noted, but child sacrifice was one of the crimes that Israel learned from the nations (Deut 12:31; 2 Kgs 17:17) and one of the crimes of Manasseh (2 Kgs 21:6) that enraged Yahweh and could not be expiated. The account agrees in many details—but not in their interpretation—with the Mesha inscription, according to which, curiously enough, it was not his son whom Mesha sacrificed but the sons and daughters of Israel.

333 The passage (2 Kgs 13:23) combines the Sinai ("Yahweh was kind and merciful to them") and patriarchal covenants ("He turned toward them because of his covenant with Abraham, Isaac and Jacob"). The statement that Yahweh was not willing to annihilate Israel and had not rejected them even now (2 Kgs 13:23) anticipates the fall of the northern kingdom and, by implication, suggests that the renovation of the temple, which is to be repeated in Josiah's time (2 Kgs 22:4–7; cf. 2 Kgs 12:10–17), is associated with the fall of the southern kingdom.

334 The Deuteronomistic text is economical. Reigns are recorded in brief. The cross-references to earlier texts are signaled by an explicit citation at the beginning (2 Kgs 14:6 = Deut 24:16 = Ezekiel 18°). The influence of the prophets is emphasized by calling Isaiah onto the scene (2 Kings 19–20).

335 Apostasy is put in the words of Jeremiah: 2 Kgs 17:10b ("on every high hill and under every green tree") = Jer 2:20b; 2 Kgs 17:15 ("they went after vanity and became vain") = Jer 2:5. The bad example that Judah got from Israel is expressed in terms taken from Micah (2 Kgs 17:19, "[they] followed the customs that Israel had devised" = Mic 6:16, "the clung to the customs of Omri . . . and followed their schemes").

336 Cf. 2 Kgs 18:32–35 and Amos 6:2. The Deuteronomistic text is taken up by III Isaiah (Isa 10:8–11) in interpreting the story as it was told by Isaiah (Isa 10:5–7, 13–14) and touched up later by II Isaiah (Isa 10:15–19, 24–27).

337 Cf. 2 Kgs 19:3 ("This is a day of distress, rebuke, and rejection, this day, for children have come to the breach and there is no strength to bear them") and Hos 13:13 ("the pangs of birth have come upon him, he is an unwise child, for at the moment he does not wait at the breach of children") and Zeph 1:15 ("A day of wrath is that day, a day of distress"); cf. also Nah 1:7; Hab 3:16.

338 Familiar from Isaiah are especially the title "Holy One of Israel" (2 Kgs 19:22; cf. Isa 1:4; 5:19; 30:15) and the derisive word that he used to describe Assyrian boasting (*l'g*, 2 Kgs 19:21; Isa 28:11). The image of the invader ascending the heights (2 Kgs 19:23) has a basis in Isaiah's description of Assyrian boasting (Isa 10:13–14) but is indebted especially to Ezekiel (cf. Ezek 17:3) and to *Gilgamesh*. The description of ruined cities (2 Kgs 19:25) takes up a theme from Jeremiah (cf. Jer 5:17; 8:14; 9:10; cf. Zeph 1:16).

339 In appealing to the prophet, Josiah notes that Yahweh's wrath has flared against the city because their ancestors did not listen to the words of the book or do what was written in it (2 Kgs 22:13). In reflecting on the fact that no one would listen to the word of Yahweh Jeremiah exclaims that he is full of the wrath of Yahweh and will pour it out on the city (Jer 6:10–11). Huldah's statement that Yahweh is bringing evil on the city (2 Kgs 22:16, 20) quotes words of Jeremiah's opening address to Judah (Jer 4:6) that he repeats when he reflects on the fact that the people have not listened to the words of Yahweh and have rejected his law (Jer 6:19). The Deuteronomistic reason for the fall of the city—that they abandoned Yahweh and offered incense to other Gods in order to provoke him (2 Kgs 22:17)—is taken up later by the editor of Jeremiah in the introduction to his work (Jer 1:16).

CHAPTER 6

Revision and Response

*A*fter the publication of the Deuteronomistic History, each of the prophetic works was brought up to date and into line with its thinking. All of the revisions used the Deuteronomist's language and ideas; some were opposed to the History's interpretation or simply reticent; others used it to reduce the prophetic work to the dimensions of a developing orthodoxy. All of the revisions were relatively extensive, and some of them, such as the revisions of Isaiah, Jeremiah, and Ezekiel, were major new works. Other writers such as Joel, Jonah, and Obadiah were without precedent and went their own way in opposition to the Deuteronomistic system. These eventually were broken and cast into the mold of conformity.

The Deuteronomistic system was not open to cavil or quibble or superficial retort. What evoked response from this generation of writers, apart from the genius and the amazing comprehension displayed by the History, were the basic theoretical issues that it raised and resolved. It was not just a record of the past, but a program for the future, and it made a difference to late sixth century society in Judah and Jerusalem.

The revisions and responses were written in the interests and from the perspective of local reconstruction. There was some concern for the return of the exiles and some dispute concerning the identity of the true remnant from which the new society would spring, but much was written to heal the wounds of Jerusalem and to justify Judah's unique restoration. In revising the prophetic works it was possible to include as prophecy contemporary issues as they might have been debated by the tradition.

The Responses

Three prophets responded to the Deuteronomist's contention that Jerusalem was captured because of a history of sin that was fully manifested in the reign of Manasseh. Joel wrote an elegant and ironic reply suggesting that the capture of the city was just a natural calamity in which no grand philosophical or theological principles were at stake. Obadiah avoided direct confrontation with the theory by describing the event and blaming Edom for being involved. Jonah scoffed at the Deuteronomistic idea that the city was destroyed because it did not listen to the prophets by noting that a typical prophet did not want repentance but simple retribution and by describing how even its wicked archrival did listen to such a prophet and escape. All three went to the heart of the Deuteronomistic philosophy that, given the standard cause, the necessary effect had to follow.

Each of these prophets was reprimanded by an editor who opted for the more traditional or specifically Deuteronomistic interpretation. Obadiah was paraphrased by the editor of Jeremiah into a typical oracle against the nations. Jonah was heard to recite a psalm that converted him to the orthodox point of view. Joel was made an advocate of old-fashioned retribution. Their charm and originality were hidden by the facade of a fixed and stereotypical prophetic tradition.

JOEL (FIG. 18)

The prophecy of Joel is an allegory on the Babylonian invasion and capture of Jerusalem. The invading forces that devastated the land are locusts that darkened the sky on the day of Yahweh and consumed the produce that should have been offered to Yahweh in the temple. Joel summons the people and the priests to a ritual of fasting and lamentation, and Yahweh responds to their prayer by restoring the crops and ridding the land of the locusts. The prophecy ends with the land at rest and with great celebration in Zion.

The devastation of Judah and the interruption of temple rituals were a natural disaster with a natural solution provided by Yahweh. There are no moral implications. The invasion and defeat were an evil brought upon the land by Yahweh, to whom the order of the universe

FIGURE 18

Joel

	Joel				*Book of Joel*			
I	A		1:1	I	A			
		1	1:2			1		
		2	1:3			2		
		3	1:4			3		
	B	1	1:5		B	1		
		2	1:6			2		
		3	1:7			3		
	C	1	1:8–10		C	1		
		2	1:11–12			2		
		3	1:13–15			3		
	D	1	1:16–17		D	1		
		2	1:18			2		
		3	1:19–20			3		
II	A	1	2:1–2aA	II	A	1		
		2	2:2aBb			2		
	B	1	2:3a		B	1		
		2	2:3b			2		
	C	1	2:4–5		C	1		
		2	2:6			2		
		3	2:7–8aA			3		
	D	1	2:8aBb–9		D	1		
		2	2:10–11			2		
	E	1	2:12–13		E	1		
		2	2:14			2		
	F	1	2:15–16		F	1		
		2	2:17			2		
	G	1	2:18–19a		G	1		
		2	2:19b–20			2		
	H	1	2:21–22		H	1		
		2	2:23–24			2		
		3	2:25–27			3		
				III	A	1	3:1	
						2	3:2–3	
					B	1	3:4	
						2	3:5	
				IV	A	1	4:1–3	
						2	4:4–6	
						3	4:7–8	
					B	1	4:9–10a	
						2	4:10b–11a	
						3	4:11b–13	
					C	1	4:14–15	
						2	4:16	
						3	4:17	
					D	1	4:18	
						2	4:19–21	

Figure 18. Letters indicate strophes. Numbers denote stanzas.

and the dependability of natural cycles are attributed. It is not a punishment for sin and has nothing to do with social or political wrongs. The rain, in this view, is its own justification, and the new crops will make up for the years of failure and prove that Yahweh is among his people (Joel 2:23–27).

The prophecy is indebted to Amos and Zephaniah for the notion and description of the day of Yahweh, to Jeremiah and Zephaniah for the perception of enemy invasion as a natural catastrophe, to Jeremiah and Nahum for a description of troops infiltrating the city, and to the Deuteronomistic History for the rituals of repentance in times of crisis. Its omission of public confession and moral criteria is a theological position taken in opposition to the same History, which claimed that the capture of Jerusalem and the fall of Judah were inevitable because of their history of sin and specifically because of the sin of Manasseh.

The prophecy, therefore, had to be revised to bring it into line with the History and lay the blame somewhere. The blame naturally enough was laid on Israel's neighbors. The solution is moral and religious: Yahweh is the dispenser of justice; those who call on his name survive; those who oppose him or his people suffer retribution. The inspiration is Ezekiel, the book of Amos, Micah, and Obadiah. The effect is the jettisoning of history in favor of some neutral future where right order will be restored.

Structure and Organization

The prophecy is composed of two matching columns that describe the catastrophe and the lamentation of the people (chap. 1) and then interpret the catastrope as the long-awaited day of Yahweh, from which Yahweh himself will deliver them (chap. 2). The revision of the prophecy added two columns of unequal length to correspond to the original reduplication. The first of these (chap. 3) rewrites the first column and gives the book a familiar prophetic cast by rehearsing the catastrophe as a future event from which a precious few in Zion and Jerusalem will escape. The second (chap. 4) redoes the second column and interprets the promised deliverance as a return from exile and retribution on their neighbors.

The columns are composed of stanzas and strophes. The stanzas are poetic sentences in different sequences and with different constructions. The strophes are formal and thematic units. The stanzas have between two and twelve lines and are combined in twos or threes to form a strophe. The strophes are all paired so that the prophecy advances and reflects on itself as it goes.

Column 1 (Joel 1)   The first strophe has three stanzas that begin the
story of an unprecedented plague of locusts (1:2, 3, 4). The second
strophe has three stanzas that make the story an allegory of invasion
against the land of Yahweh (1:5, 6, 7). The third strophe has three
stanzas that summon the land, those that till it, and the priests to wail
and lament before Yahweh, whose rituals have been interrupted by the
plague (1:8–10, 11–12, 13–15). The fourth strophe has three stanzas
that match it by describing the actual rites of wailing and lamentation
by the priests, the land — represented by the sheep and the cattle — and
those that till it — represented by the prophet (1:16–17, 18, 19–20).

The strophes are constructed in formal patterns determined by the
types of stanzas they contain. The types of stanzas are distinguished by
the number of lines that they contain and by their different functions
in the development of the discourse. The formal patterns admit only
one or two types of stanzas in a few regular arrangements.

Three-line stanzas mark a pause in the development of a discourse.
They are summaries and transitions, reflections on things that have
been said, or indications of new directions. One of these, after the call
to attention in the first column, makes it clear that the story is about a
unique and unprecedented event by insisting that it be told to their
children to the third and fourth generations (1:3).[1] Another introduces
the locusts that figure allegorically in the rest of the prophecy (1:4).
Their types and sequence are normal, and consequently it is not the
locusts that are unprecedented but the unique occurrence that they
symbolize. The effect of the pause created by these two stanzas
becomes clear at the start of the next strophe, where the opening call
to attention has to be repeated.[2]

Four-line stanzas are explanatory and contain some contrast, combination, or contradiction. The first of these in the column contains a
summons to the elders and the inhabitants of the land and a question
for them to consider. The two elements are simply juxtaposed since the
summons is to listen not to the question but to the story of the plague
that follows.[3] The second four-line stanza (1:5) combines another
summons with the issue to be discussed: the contrast or contradiction
consists in summoning drunkards and wine drinkers to learn that there
is no wine. The third (1:6a + 1:6b) combines a statement about
invading nations with a metaphor of lions to evoke their destructive-
ness. Both are odd and oddly paired, because the problem has been
defined as locusts and not an enemy and because lions, however
destructive, do not usually destroy vineyards and vintages. The fourth
(1:7a + 1:7b) talks in general terms about what the invading nation
has done to the vines and fig trees but combines this with a more

graphic version of stripping bark from the trees and squeezing the life from the vine. The last four-line stanza in the column (1:18a + 1:18b) describes the lamentation of the cattle and sheep and then adds the reason for each.

Six-line stanzas are narrative and trace an idea or event in logical and/or chronological order. The first of these (1:16–17) says that there is no food and therefore no happiness or rejoicing in the temple, and then follows the actual crisis from planting to the failure of the harvest. The second (1:19–20) is the prayer recited by the farmers, which begins by narrating how the pastures and fruit trees have been ruined and then illustrates the point by saying that the animals mourn too for lack of grass and water.

The basic types of stanzas range from three to six lines, and the others are multiples, variants, or combinations of the same. Eight-line stanzas, therefore, are variants of four-line stanzas and contain elaborated forms of contradiction, combination, or contrast. The first of these in the column combines an invitation of the land to mourning because the crops have failed with a list of the effects of this failure on temple service, the priests, and the countryside.[4] The second (1:11–12aA + 1:12aBb) combines the effect of the locust plague on farmers and vinegrowers with a list of its effects on the fruit trees that give pleasure to people. Twelve-line stanzas, in the same way, are variants of six-line stanzas. The only example in this column (1:13–15) simply narrates all the steps in a lamentation liturgy, from the preparations of the priests, to the summoning of the people to fasting and mourning, to the words of their wailing.

Column 2 (Joel 2)   The second column is composed of eight strophes in four matching pairs that narrate the lamentation of the people and the response of Yahweh. The first strophe has stanzas of four and six lines: the first stanza warns the people in Zion and the rest of the country that the day of Yahweh is approaching, and the second stanza portrays that day overshadowing the land like a great swarm of people.[5] The second strophe corresponds to the first by describing the gradual encroachment of the day. The first stanza (2:3a) has two lines and describes, from a cosmological perspective, the scene before and after its advance.[6] The second stanza (2:3b) has three lines and describes the same scene from an ecological point of view. The third strophe describes the approach of the hordes and the panic that they cause: the first stanza (2:4–5) has five lines describing the great swarm of people in cosmological and military terms; the second stanza (2:6) has two lines describing the panic in Zion; the third stanza (2:7–8aA) has five lines describing the relentless attack of the invading army.[7] The fourth strophe matches the third by repeating and continuing the description and drawing its implications: the first stanza portrays the advance of the army of locusts through the city and into the houses; the second stanza has ten lines likening the locusts to an army led by Yahweh and describing the meteorological effects of the plague.[8] The fifth strophe has two stanzas, in which the prophet addresses the people and then reflects on the point of the address: the first of these stanzas (2:12–13) has eight lines that explain the form and motivation of the lamentation ritual; the second (2:14) has three lines and reflects on the mercy of God, which motivated the lament.[9] The sixth strophe matches the fifth with the lamentation ritual and a motive for Yahweh to respond: the first stanza (2:15–16) narrates the preparations for the ritual, from the blowing of the trumpet and the proclamation of the fast, to the gradual assembly of all the people; the second stanza (2:17) summons the priests to intercede, and they provide Yahweh with a motive to intervene that matches the motive he gave them to perform the lament.[10] The seventh strophe is a report of Yahweh's response: the first stanza (2:18–19a) has six lines in which Yahweh relents and promises to supply the crops; the second stanza (2:19b-20) has eight lines explaining that the invading army will be expelled from the land, leaving behind the corpses of its troops. The eighth strophe matches it by letting Yahweh make the same points in a direct address to the country: the first stanza (2:21–22) has seven lines, in which Yahweh speaks to the land and the animals; in the second (2:23–24) he speaks to Zion; in the third (2:25–27) he promises to make up for the years that have been lost and to stay with his people for ever.

Column 3 (Joel 3)   The third column is by the author of the book of Joel. It is written in imitation of the original first column and has ideas from it and from the second column as well. It has four stanzas that are combined in two strophes of two stanzas each. Its most significant contribution to the prophecy is its implicit denial of Joel's welcome news and promises by setting the day of Yahweh and its resolution in some vague and distant future.

The first stanza (3:1) begins with the formulaic future,[11] which always represents the beginning of a text that is not related to the immediately preceding text but to the penultimate or some antecedent text. An indication that it is actually referring to the beginning of the first column is its use of some of the key terms from the first strophe in that column in opposite order and with opposite intent. It mentions the children and the elders in opposite order.[12] There they were told to listen to the story and tell it to each other, but here they are assured that they will be prophets and get the story straight from God (cf. 1:2–3 and 3:1).

The second stanza (3:2–3) continues the theme of the first stanza by repeating that Yahweh will pour out his spirit[13] not only on the elders and the children but on all the slaves as well. Its particular contribution to the theme consists in listing the prophetic signs of this impending future, signs in the sky and on the ground—blood, fire, and columns of smoke.

The third stanza begins with a reference to Joel's text in the second column and links it artificially to the preceding stanza by repeating the one word "blood" (3:4).[14] The darkening of the sun and the moon that this version reserves for the apocalyptic future was a feature of the great and terrible day of Yahweh as it was described in the second column (cf. 2:1b, 10b, 11b). As often happens in an edited text, the words are repeated in the same order but in an opposite sense: the point of the second column was that the day of Yahweh had come and gone, and the point of the third column is that it is still to come.

The fourth stanza begins with a variant of the formulaic future.[15] It too quotes from the second column in opposite word order and contradicts it. In the second column nothing escaped the day of Yahweh, whereas in this column the whole point is that on the future day of Yahweh some will flee or survive and some people in Zion and Jerusalem will escape.[16] The editor adverts to the contradiction and justifies it by appealing to a prior saying of Yahweh.[17]

Column 4 (Joel 4)   The fourth column follows on the third and gives another version of what will happen on the future day of Yahweh. It is composed of eleven stanzas grouped in four matching strophes. The first strophe has three stanzas, which describe the return of the people from exile and slavery and taunt the nations that were responsible (4:1–3, 4–6, 7–8). The second strophe has three stanzas, which respond to the first strophe by declaring war on the nations who took the people of Judah and Jerusalem into exile and slavery (4:9–10a, 10b–11a, 11b–13). The third strophe has three stanzas on the day of Yahweh: it is described in terms taken from the second column, but it no longer portends a dreadful war and certain defeat but the establishment of Yahweh's dominion in Jerusalem (4:14–15, 16, 17; cf. 4:15; 2:10b). The fourth strophe corresponds to it by describing the beneficial results of this dominion in ecological and political terms (4:18, 19–21).

The book of Joel is composed in parallel columns constructed from antiphonal stanzas and matching strophes. Joel's version was complete in two columns. The revision left it unchanged but added two matching columns as footnotes to give the prophecy a totally different direction.

Joel wrote sometime after the fall of Jerusalem and after the publication of the Deuteronomistic History but before Jonah and Obadiah and the revision of the book of Amos, who knew his work and quoted it. The editor of Joel's text wrote before III Isaiah, who quoted the completed work, but after II Isaiah and Obadiah and the revision of Amos, whose texts it quotes.

The two texts say more or less opposite things but also say them in different ways and for different reasons. The structure, the language and style, and the sources and their interpretation make it quite clear that there are two versions of the prophecy. The only reason for putting them together was that the second was a commentary on the first.

Language and Style

The prophecy of Joel is phrased as a lamentation liturgy. The first part contains four strophic movements. The first is the announcement of the locust plague, unheard of and unrepeatable. The second explains the problem: the plague is a nation invading God's land and destroying his crops. The third movement summons the land and the priests to lament because the crops have been ruined and there is nothing to offer to God in the temple. The fourth is the lament of the land and the animals, the priests and the people of the land, because the pastures are burned and the temple rituals are no more. The second part moves to Zion and Jerusalem and gives another view of the problem and the effect of the lament. It has eight strophic movements. The first sounds the alarm in Zion and announces the arrival of the day of Yahweh. The second describes the cosmological and mythological dimensions of that day. The third makes it a military event, with chariots and cavalry and relentless waves of warriors. The fourth ascribes the event to Yahweh and to his cosmic and corporeal armies. The fifth appeals to tradition to remind the people that even in such dire circumstances Yahweh remains merciful. The sixth, therefore, calls on the people and the priests to respond with prayer and fasting. The seventh declares that their supplications have been heard and that God will rid the land of the army of the plague. The last summons Zion, the land, and the animals to rejoice, since God will assure the crops and make up for the years of want.

The language and style of Joel's prophecy are suited to its form. The prophecy is directed to an audience whose response is vital to its fulfillment. Appeals and imperatives abound in the first part. The lines are short and staccato, except the few that refer to the cessation of worship in the temple and record words of worry and lament (1:8–9, 13aBb, 16–17aA, 19bB–20a). The lines are mostly separated by stops and intervals rather than glides[18] and often have strong caesuras marked by the same sort of internal interval or stop. The words in the first column are all taken from the realms of agriculture, viticulture, animal husbandry, and religious ritual. The second column is much more descriptive, and its language is the language of war. Urgency is indicated by asyndesis or by series of abrupt subordinate clauses.

The allegory is accompanied by sudden shifts in tone that indicate a shift in significance, referent, or perspective. In the first column these shifts are marked by changes in the patterns of assonance, alliteration, and rhyme. According to the allegory, the invading army is a swarm of locusts. When this is said for the first time the invasion is described in two lines filled with the same assonance and alliteration,[19] but the metaphor of the locusts is juxtaposed in two other lines, each with a different sort of assonance and alliteration.[20]

The shifts occur within stanzas and between stanzas in strophes. In the first strophe the second stanza continues the idea and the rhyme of the first, but the third stanza introduces the allegory of the locusts and, apart from its insistent repetition, is entirely different from the first two.[21] In the third strophe references to the liturgy are in slow, mournful, blank cadences, but references to the crops and the ruination of the land are filled with rhyme, alliteration, and assonance, the attribution of the ruin to the Lord of the fields being the most exemplary.[22] In the fourth strophe the first stanza deals with the destitution of the cult: its references to the rituals are in long ponderous lines, but its references to the failure of the crops and to the lack of offerings are contained in short snappy lines that rhyme.[23] The second stanza describes the lamentation of the animals and is marked by a different kind of alliteration, by rhyme, and by repetition (1:18). The third stanza is a prayer and, as a liturgical element, has long lines, a rather ponderous cadence, and more morphological, lexical, and literal repetition (1:19–20).[24]

In the second column the shifts are lexical and imaginative. In the first strophe the first stanza announces the arrival of the day of Yahweh in traditional words and imagery taken from Amos and Zephaniah. The second stanza abruptly identifies it as an invading nation and makes the day unique in the history of the world, and its main connection with the first stanza is another synonym for darkness (2:1–2aA and 2:2aBb). This stanza ends on a temporal note, and the first stanza in the next strophe uses the same expression in a spatial sense.[25] In the third strophe the invading nation is compared to horses, and the sound that it makes is compared to chariots; or, abruptly, by using the same word, to the sound of fire burning dry straw; or, more abruptly still, by using the same preposition, to an army arrayed for battle (2:4–5, 6, 7–8aA).[26] In the third and fourth strophes there is a detailed description of the enemy attacking the city, coming over the walls, climbing through the water conduits, infiltrating the city streets, and getting into the houses, but abruptly the description is broken off and replaced with a cosmological perspective, as the commander of the troops turns out to be Yahweh advancing with earthquakes, eclipses, thunder, and celestial signs as he leads his mighty army on the awaited dreaded day.[27] This description ends suddenly with Yahweh addressing the people in kindly terms, requiring repentance but assuring them of his mercy, and with the hope that Yahweh will relent and bless them (2:12–13, 14). Abruptly, but not unexpectedly, in the final strophes there is a summons to fasting and lament, divine outrage at what has happened, and a promise of happiness and perpetual security.

Joel's work is filled with dramatic sense as it moves from narrative, to interpellation, to descriptive interpretation, to familiar conversation. The prophecy is carried on the movement of a lamentation liturgy. The stages in the liturgy are parallel to a continuous narrative background detailing the reasons for their distress. The narrative is interrupted by invocations and sudden exclamations. The liturgy devolves into friendly conversation.

The revision of the prophecy reinterprets only the ending of the liturgy and the promises that are made. Essentially it says that the dark times that the people have experienced are not the day of Yahweh but a prelude to the day of Yahweh, when he will get even with the enemies of his people. In all of it Yahweh is the principal speaker; the conversational tone is replaced with bald rhetoric; interpellation is a formality; and the future narrative requires nothing of the audience.

In the third column poetic stanzas alternate with prosaic stanzas. The first stanza (3:1) opens formally and rather prosaically, but it is carried by repetition, alliteration, and rhyme. Rhyme matches the start and the finish; repetition matches the last two parallel lines; and alliteration crosses over from line to line.[28] The second stanza (3:2–3) is almost unadorned, its most obvious poetic features being a little end-to-end rhyme and the stop and caesuras in its last line.[29] Otherwise the lines are unbalanced and the cadence is prosaic, produced notably by the succession of modifiers between the opening construction and the verb. The third stanza is more poetic but is mostly adapted from a text of Joel. Even here the poetic cadence slips away as simple modification replaces rhythm and balance.[30] The fourth stanza has long lines distinguished by their individual assonance and alliteration, but subordination within and between lines gives the stanza a blank and deliberate mood.

The fourth column's prosaic elements are mainly consecution, subordination, and unnecessary repetition. These produce a flow of discourse different from the stop-and-go cadence of the lyric and elegiac poetry favored by Joel.

The first stanza (4:1–3), for instance, is filled with consecution, intricate subordination, and redundancy. The last feature is most obvious: the first line repeats "in those days" and "at that time"; the second fills out the standard expression "return the captives" with still another standard bifurcation "of Judah and Jerusalem." There is a little pun on the valley of "Yahweh-is-Judge" and the valley where Yahweh judges, but this judgment is exercised both for "my people" and for "my inheritance." This distinction, in turn, leads to further talk about the land and the people, and this again to more details on the youngsters who were sold and deported. The whole stanza flows and interlocks from beginning to end with a maze of ideas, images, and sounds, and the rhythm is quite different from the singing style of Joel.

The second stanza (4:4–6) has more asyndesis but continues with its emphatic use of redundancy and subordination. It pairs "Tyre and Sidon," asks them twice if they are trying to get even with God, uses two expressions for "quickly," pairs "silver and gold" and "sons of Judah and sons of Jerusalem," and uses pleonastic pronouns. The subordinate clauses are consecutive and constitute a full list of Phoenician crimes. The asyndesis and redundancy create an urgency and an insistence that are more appropriate to a speech than to the sort of dramatic representation characteristic of Joel.

In the third stanza (4:7–8), the lines are shorter and filled with rhyme, but the redundancy continues. Here, however, it exactly fits the idea of retribution and tit for tat that the stanza expresses. The fourth stanza (4:9–10a) is more poetic, but it is essentially an adaptation of the original (cf. 2:7–9, 15). The imperatives in the fifth stanza (4:10b–11a) are repetitive and unbalanced and characteristic of the deliberate cadence of the revision. The sixth stanza (4:11b–13) has a similar cadence with asyndesis, subordination, and redundant expressions. In the seventh stanza (4:14–15), again, the poetic form is indebted to Joel, and the contribution of the revision consists in blank repetition (cf. 1:15b; 2:10b).

The language and style are suited to the purpose of each. Joel based his argument on the normal expectations of prayer and wrote a poem composed of historical narrative and the dramatic sequence of a lamentation ritual. It extended naturally from a vivid description of the circumstances that produced the prayer to the circumstances that prevailed when the prayer was answered. The revision took the poem beyond prayer and history to the final consummation of Yahweh's rule. This version of the story does not move along a dramatic line but under the demands of logic and the need to bring matters to their necessary conclusion.

Sources and Interpretation

The two versions are distinguished by their structure and organization, their language and style, and by their sources and interpretation. In Joel's prophecy the allegory works because its different elements are known from other writings. In the revision the future works because prophecy had been normalized and given a peculiar cast.

Column 1 The first stanza begins with an expression coined by Isaiah, adopted by II Isaiah, imitated by III Isaiah, and adapted by the Deuteronomistic History and its clients.[31] Joel's reference to "all the inhabitants of the land" may be due to his familiarity with the History, where the expression is current[32] or, in view of later thematic developments in the prophecy, it might indicate his indebtedness to Zephaniah, who uses the same expression in announcing the day of Yahweh (cf. Zeph 1:18). The question whether such a thing had happened in their days or in the days of their fathers, in combination with the later affirmation that such a thing had never happened, resembles the Deuteronomist's call to consider the old days and the distant past and to ask their fathers and their elders (Joel 1:2b; 2:2b; cf. Deut 32:7). It is an odd question since, of course, it has happened in their days, and the expression is clearly dependent on a statement to this effect by Habakkuk that was sufficiently well known to be taken up almost literally by Ezekiel.[33] The first stanza, in other words, was not written inconsiderately but clearly indicates that Joel was familiar with tradition and with poetic and prophetic conventions.

The second stanza mentions four generations and in this respect resembles the traditional extent and duration of a family circle first invoked in the epic covenant.[34] This reference is all the more compelling since Joel quotes directly from the same text at the crucial turning point in his prophecy and carefully marks it as a quotation by the usual inversion of word order.[35]

Locust plagues became a topic of prophecy in the work of Amos. Although Amos mentions a different species of locusts, in his text, as in Joel's, locusts are associated with the day of Yahweh and with fire, and in both there is some hope that Yahweh might relent.[36] The Deuteronomistic History, however, mentions some of the same species, associates them with enemy invasions, and includes them among the occasions for prayer and lamentation[37] when the people turn again to God.[38] Joel is certainly familiar with one or the other or both, and any reader of his work with a literary background would immediately recognize the plague as an element in Israel's confrontation by God.

The fourth stanza mentions those who drink wine and has to be taken in conjunction with the sixth, which talks about the vineyard. The metaphor of the vineyard, of course, is taken from Isaiah, who went on to criticize those who drank its wine for not paying attention to what Yahweh was doing.[39] Joel, however, also combines the metaphor with a traditional description of the land as prosperous and fertile,[40] with a standard Deuteronomistic expression of Yahweh's impatience,[41] and with images of pruning the vine and ruining the vintage.

The fifth stanza describes the invaders as a great nation, without number. The first expression is familiar from the epic and the Deuteronomistic History, where it applies to Israel.[42] The second expression was used in the Deuteronomistic History to describe the invaders it had compared to innumerable locusts.[43] The metaphor of the enemy as a lion, with which this description of the invaders is combined, became a familiar topic of prophecy with Isaiah, Amos, Hosea, and Jeremiah.[44]

The seventh stanza beings with an address to the land and supposes, with Isaiah, Hosea, and Jeremiah, that the land was Yahweh's bride and that he was her husband (1:8–10).[45] It combines this metaphor with practical details on regular offerings prescribed in the History[46] and with the notion that the levitical priests were ministers of Yahweh.[47] The desolation of the land consists in the failure of the grain, the wine, and the oil, which are typical features of a fertile land, as well as offerings to be made to Yahweh and gifts belonging to the priests.[48]

The eighth stanza continues in the same vein with another reference to the traditional description of the fertile land that Yahweh gave to Israel, a land of wheat and barley, of vines, fig trees, and pomegranates (1:11b–12bA; Num 20:5; Deut 8:8). To this Joel adds apples (1:12b)[49] and other fruit trees,[50] references to the laborers who take care of them, and a summary statement on the absence of all joy.

The ninth stanza begins with an injunction that might have been taken from Jeremiah's announcement of impending invasion.[51] It is, as

quotations often are, in a different order and used in a different sense —
addressed in Jeremiah to Judah and Jerusalem, but in Joel to the
priests who minister to Yahweh. The call to sanctify a fast and summon
an assembly reverses the order found in the Deuteronomistic History,
where an assembly is sanctified and people are summoned to a fast.[52]
The address to the elders and the inhabitants of the land is consistent
with the opening summons, and the command to cry out is a regular
introduction to lamentations.[53] The stanza, consequently, describes the
wailing of the priests and the lamentation of the assembly in language
taken mainly from Jeremiah and the Deuteronomistic History.

The tenth stanza begins with an expression that was taken up in
the revision of the book of Ezekiel and ends with another that was
taken up by III Isaiah.[54] The last clause in the stanza is original to Joel
and suitable to the context prepared for it,[55] but the rest of the elements
are known from the Deuteronomistic History and the prophetic tradition. The exclamation "Alas" is used by the Historian and in later
prophetic texts to express sudden grief and pain.[56] The day of Yahweh
is a topic that was introduced by Amos and that was developed
especially by Zephaniah, in whose time the day was recognized as
near.[57] In Hosea and Habakkuk invasion and defeat were perceived as
obliteration.[58]

The eleventh stanza is mostly a free composition of Joel's, summarizing in lament form the things that were said earlier to describe the
circumstances of the lament. The fact that food offerings are scarce has
been mentioned (1:9a, 16), and therefore the particular expression that
Joel uses in this stanza — "food has been taken away before our very
eyes" — may reflect Isaiah's description of an enemy devouring the land
"before your very eyes."[59] Similarly, the absence of happiness and joy
may owe something to Hosea's portrayal of the sadness that accompanies the failure of crops.[60] The rest of the stanza is filled with *hapax
legomena* or with words used in an applied sense.

The twelfth stanza interprets the bleating and bellowing of the
animals as pleas directed to God. The idea was taken up by Jonah,
who observed that in Nineveh even the animals repented (Joel 1:18;
cf. Jonah 3:7–8; 4:11). The image is novel, but the language of lament
is unexceptional since confusion is a sign of desolation[61] and groaning
is a form of supplication.[62]

The thirteenth stanza repeats the fact that the animals beseech God
and that all the trees in the meadows are wilted (1:19b; cf. 1:12b). It
takes from Amos the fact that fire is associated with the day of Yahweh
but expresses it in words taken from Jeremiah and the Deuteronomistic
History.[63] Other elements of his expression are familiar from the

Psalms,[64] and part of the stanza was quoted by the editor of Amos to express the theme of that edition.[65]

It is clear, therefore, that Joel was familiar with earlier prophetic literature and with the Deuteronomistic History. This means, among other things, that Joel is not to be interpreted as a firsthand description of actual events, but can be taken as a literary work with other than reportorial interests.

Column 2 The second column repeats a lot of details from the first and continues its references to the Deuteronomistic History and the prophets. Both are reminders that Joel wrote an allegory and that prophecy and the History are integral to his meaning.

The first stanza begins with the command to blow the trumpet and sound the alarm in Zion. The source is Zephaniah's picture of the day of Yahweh,[66] although both expressions are most common in the Deuteronomistic History and in dependent texts,[67] and the blowing of the trumpet was the basis of one of Jeremiah's famous puns.[68] The stanza continues with a description of the day of Yahweh and further quotations from Amos and Zephaniah.[69] The trembling that the day inspires was noted by Habakkuk, and Joel seems to know his text.[70]

The second stanza uses an expression from the epic story of the exodus to describe the size of the invading army,[71] and the image of an enemy darkening the land from the Deuteronomistic version of the locust plague in the same story.[72] The end of the stanza restates what was said at the beginning of the poem about the unprecedented plague of locusts.[73]

The third stanza repeats what was said in the first column about the destructive fire (2:3a; 1:19–20), and the fourth matches it with literary allusions. The image of the land like the Garden of Eden before the plague struck and like a blasted wilderness after it had passed is taken, in an opposite sense, from II Isaiah, who described the restoration of Zion as turning the wilderness into Eden and the desert into the garden of God.[74] The references to the Deuteronomistic History are direct and indirect. In the story of the locust plague, to which the third stanza referred, the Deuteronomist said that the locusts left nothing in Egypt. Joel says essentially the same thing about Judah and Jerusalem, but he says it by using and contradicting the terms that the Historian used in another text to refer to the remnant in Zion.[75]

The fifth stanza turns abruptly from allusions to the locust plague to a description of troops attacking. The simile may be based on the actual similarity between the head of a locust and the head of a horse,[76] but the description seems to be indebted to the account of the fall of

Nineveh in Nahum. In both there is a reference to horses and riders, to the sound of clattering chariots, and to the flash of weapons.[77] The difference is that Joel repeats what he had said earlier about destruction by fire and about the size of the attacking forces, and adds a reference to Jeremiah's description of the invasion by the enemy from the North.[78]

The sixth stanza has a familiar reference to the agony of the people[79] and combines it with a quotation from Nahum's description of the anxiety that gripped Nineveh under attack by the Babylonians.[80] The seventh stanza describes the attackers in terms that Nahum used to describe the attackers of Nineveh but is otherwise a free composition by Joel.[81] The eighth includes a reference to the water conduit built by Hezekiah and introduces the image of an enemy crawling through the window, which was taken up in the book of Jeremiah.[82]

The ninth stanza reverts to the traditional imagery of the day of Yahweh as a day of darkness with no light but also relies on the text of Habakkuk for its expression.[83] The rest of the stanza is filled out with the cosmic repercussions of the day of Yahweh and depends on images and sayings in the Deuteronomistic History. The quaking of the earth and shimmering of the sky are mentioned in the Song of David,[84] and thunder is one of Yahweh's attributes in the same song.[85] The day of Yahweh is a "great" day according to Zephaniah, but "great and terrible" usually are epithets of Yahweh himself.[86] The fact that Yahweh has an army is most explicit in the Deuteronomistic History but is implicit in Nahum's description of the capture of Nineveh.[87] The stanza, in effect, combines the theory of the day of Yahweh, manifested in war and in the cosmic elements, with traditional images of Yahweh as the God of weather and storms. Later writers, like the editor of Joel and the author of Malachi, applied some of the text to the vague and dreary future lurking at the boundaries of time and history.[88]

The tenth stanza relies on the epic covenant at Sinai and the prayer of Solomon for its theory of repentance. It is the prayer of Solomon that mentions returning to God with all one's heart,[89] but the difference is that the Deuteronomistic History supposes that adversity is a punishment for sin (1 Kgs 8:46) and that returning to God requires divine forgiveness (1 Kgs 8:50), while Joel supposes that adversity is characteristic of natural cycles, and that the motive for returning to God is divine mercy and pity. The notion of return, therefore, is qualified in Joel's view by a quotation from the epic covenant where God himself affirmed his mercy and fidelity (Joel 2:13b = Exod 34:6). To this he adds that God might take pity and relent, an attitude that the Deuteronomist associated with Yahweh's fidelity to his promises rather than with change or weakness or a particular interest in prayer.[90] Since the stanza is filled with literal quotations, its omissions become especially significant: Joel agrees with the Deuteronomistic Historian that in times of adversity people should pray to Yahweh in the temple; he differs in thinking that Yahweh is actually there and that attention to the prayer of his people does not involve judgment on the worthiness or sinfulness of the suppliant.[91]

The eleventh stanza is the obverse of the tenth. It supposes that if the people have a change of heart Yahweh will change his mind: the idea is new and is taken up by Jonah as a basis of his argument (Joel 2:14; Jonah 3:9). The hope that Yahweh might leave a blessing behind him is the opposite of the image of Yahweh's army leaving a trail of devastation in its wake[92] and refutes the presumption of the Deuteronomistic Historian that such punishments as these are a curse for disobeying the law and the covenant (cf. Deut 28:38). The fact that this blessing involves offerings to be presented in the temple, similarly, is an implicit refutation of the Deuteronomistic idea that the temple was just the place of Yahweh's name and, since Yahweh dwelt in heaven, was expendable.

The twelfth stanza begins with repetitions from the beginning of this column and the end of the first (2:15–16; cf. 1:14a; 2:1). It adds to the list of those summoned to fasting and lamentation all those who are traditionally exempt—babies, children, and newlyweds—but who, beginning with Jeremiah, and then especially in the Deuteronomistic History, began to be included in the pain and the punishment.[93] These are the same, however, who are celebrated in the stories of love and success, and they belong appropriately in Joel's perspective of natural and recurrent cycles.[94]

The thirteenth stanza is addressed to the priests and continues the summons to lamentation. The first phrase is taken from Ezekiel's vision of people in the temple facing the east to worship the sun.[95] The text is taken in an opposite sense, and the reversal is appropriate since in Joel's vision of the day of Yahweh the sun has been darkened. The remainder of the stanza is based mainly on texts of Ezekiel and the Deuteronomistic History. The drift of the stanza reflects the stories of intercession for the people after their rebellion in the wilderness. In Ezekiel's version of the story Yahweh took pity on the people;[96] in the epic and Deuteronomistic versions Yahweh's motivation for not destroying the people is what the neighbors might think.[97] The expression reflects the language of the History and the prophets. It is the Deuteronomist who refers to Israel as the inheritance of Yahweh[98] and who includes among the proposed blessings on Israel its freedom from foreign domination.[99] It is Ezekiel who equates invasion and defeat with shame among the nations.[100] It is the Psalms and the later revision of Micah that record the taunt of the enemy "Where is your God?"[101]

The fourteenth stanza reverts to the covenant as recorded in the epic and like-minded historians and prophets. In a reversal of its usual implications Yahweh's jealousy is directed to the benefit of his land.[102] In a reversal of Ezekiel's constant threats of merciless punishment, Yahweh is kind to his people.[103] In agreement with the covenant as the sequel understood it, and in fulfillment of Hosea's expectations, Yahweh gives his people grain, wine, and oil to satiety.[104] The covenant was the basis of the nation's confidence, and the effect of their prayer shows that their confidence was not misplaced.

The fifteenth stanza turns from the fertility of the land to the retreat of the enemy and the end of the plague of locusts. The Northerner that Joel repudiates is the Assyrian, the typical and traditional enemy from the North.[105] Zephaniah saw the ruins of Nineveh as a desolation and a wasteland, and it is to such a land that the enemy will be driven,[106] heading east with its tail toward the border of Israel at the western sea,[107] driven to the distant sea as the locusts in Egypt were swept into the Reed Sea.[108] The stink of the dead is noted in the book of Amos and later in III Isaiah and is a characteristic feature of the first plague in Egypt.[109]

The sixteenth stanza is mostly a repeat, but in it joy and happiness bring a reversal of the elements of lamentation: the land and animals are not afraid; the pastures in the plains are fresh and green; the vines and fig trees and orchards are bearing fruit.[110] The seventeenth stanza is much the same, and references to Jeremiah and to the Deuteronomistic History make it clear that the covenant with life has been restored.[111] The eighteenth stanza is designed to bring the lamentation to a proper conclusion and to make it clear that the original order of creation and covenant has been restored.[112]

It is clear that Joel was familiar with historiographic and prophetic traditions and that his allegory depends on acceptance of them as the background to his work. Prophets at the end of the seventh century, before the fall of Jerusalem became inevitable, called for lamentation (e.g., Jeremiah) and wrote their prophecies as if they were prayers and lamentations (e.g., Nahum and Habakkuk). The Deuteronomistic History ended with Josiah carrying out just such a ceremony, with practical reforms, cleansing of the temple, and covenant renewal, but all to no avail because of the sin of Manasseh. Joel was in line with the prophets and historians who thought that Yahweh was involved in the physical life of the nation, and he wrote an allegory that took the

Deuteronomistic Historian to task for concocting a theory of history that excluded such immanence or involvement. The Babylonian invasion was not the end of the world, just a phase in the natural history of the people of Israel. Things happen apart from the sequence of sin, guilt, and punishment. The Deuteronomistic theory was universal, however, and difficult to combat, and most were ready to believe it. Such was the writer who took Joel's allegory and stretched it beyond the bounds of popular credibility to the arid and arcane reaches of apocalyptic speculation.

Column 3 The third column repeats significant pieces of the original prophecy in order to give the allegory a completely different thrust. Its interest is not in natural cycles but in supernatural justification of a spiritual way of life.

The first stanza has a sort of pun by which the spirit that Yahweh puts into all flesh becomes the spirit of prophecy that is expressed in traditional dreams and visions.[113] The effect of the pun is to justify the following modifications of Joel's prophecy. He had made no such claim. The pun works because it repeats parts of his text.

The second stanza elaborates the same point. The list of beneficiaries of the spirit is extended beyond those mentioned by Joel to include their male and female slaves: these were either their former captors or Hebrew slaves, and the bestowal of the spirit on them is the sign of liberation from captivity.[114] Since it is the spirit of prophecy that is bestowed, it is accompanied by signs (3:3; cf. Deut 13:1–5). To make any of this fit into Joel's perspective at all these signs have to be in the sky and on earth and have to include the great cosmic fire.[115] To adapt Joel to the revision's feeling for retaliation against the enemy the scenario has to include blood, and to suit it to the notion of Zion as the holy mountain and residence of God it has to include fire and smoke.[116] The total effect of the stanza is to deny Joel's prediction of immediate relief by projecting events into a foreboding future and by putting awesome destruction in the place of fertilizing rains.

The third stanza is essentially an adaptation of Joel's words (3:4; cf. 2:10, 11). The fourth is the same with the addition of words from Obadiah.[117] The stanzas flatly contradict what Joel said[118] and prepare for the reinterpretation of the day of Yahweh as a day of judgment when Yahweh purifies Zion and takes vengeance on his enemies.

Column 4 The fourth column explains how retribution works. It deals with the conflict between Joel and the Deuteronomistic Historian by denying their premises. Both of them thought that Yahweh was directly responsible for the fall of Judah and Jerusalem, but each thought of it differently. The author of the book of Joel, on the contrary, does not consider the part that Yahweh had in these events and instead blames Judah's neighboring nations for the dispersion of the people and the despoiling of the temple. In this view, there is no moral or theological problem: those who called on Yahweh were saved and will continue to live with him in Jerusalem; those who tried to harm them, on the other hand, will be brought to judgment.

The first stanza identifies the indefinite future as the time of return from exile in terms made familiar by the author of the book of Jeremiah.[119] It follows Zephaniah in reversing the expectations and using the expression "reassemble" to refer to other nations rather than to those who came back from exile.[120] It invents a valley of Jehoshaphat to accommodate the judgment of Yahweh. It uses the Deuteronomistic term "inheritance" for the people of Israel but blames their dispersion on the nations instead of attributing it, as is usual in prophecy, to the initiative of Yahweh.[121] It blames the dispossession of the people on these nations instead of considering it, as Micah did, an act of God (cf. Joel 4:2bB and Mic 2:4). It adds a quotation from Obadiah to justify its claims[122] and then makes it clear, with an allusion to Obadiah, that it is referring specifically to what the neighboring nations did rather than to the deportation by the Babylonians (Joel 4:3b–4; cf. Obad 19–20).

The second stanza identifies these nations and provides more information on what they did and where the people were dispersed. It describes the despoiling of the temple and the city in terms used by the Deuteronomist and the author of Lamentations.[123] The theme of retribution that it inaugurates continues in the third stanza, where the Judeans are described as retaliating for being sold into slavery to the West by selling these same nations into slavery to the East.

The fourth stanza supposes the images of war and solemn convocation in Joel's prophecy (cf. 4:9–10a; 1:4; 2:7) and quotes a saying from II Isaiah and the book of Micah in a contradictory sense to portray the ongoing cosmic battles.[124] The fifth stanza continues in the same vein, and the sixth also but with another contradiction of Joel's text (4:13; cf. 2:24). In these lines the people of Judah, who were the victims of foreign aggression, become the instruments of divine retribution in a war against the nations.

The seventh stanza simply quotes Joel on the day of Yahweh and identifies the invented valley of Jehoshaphat with the valley of divine decision.[125] The eighth stanza quotes the book of Amos to prove the editor's point about the day of Yahweh, adds another reference to what

Joel had said about the day, and paraphrases a saying of Nahum in a way reminiscent of the Psalms, of Jeremiah, and of III Isaiah.[126] The ninth stanza uses a favorite formula of the Priestly writer and Ezekiel, an expression that will be used by III Isaiah and others, a saying of Obadiahs, and an adaptation of a promise from the book of Jeremiah.[127] This mass of authorities confirms the author's application of Joel to the real problems of the restoration when the point of his allegory was no longer acceptable.

The tenth stanza takes up images from Ezekiel and the book of Amos.[128] The last stanza follows suit with sayings from the book of Ezekiel about Egypt and Edom,[129] from Obadiah and the Deuteronomistic History about Edom,[130] and from the beginning of Joel about Judah (4:20; cf. 1:2).

Joel's prophecy was a bit too fanciful, and its point a bit too trenchant, to be of much help in settling the problems of the restoration. To the perennial problem of who deserved to be the favorites of Yahweh—those who had gone into exile or those who suffered in Jerusalem—the editor answered pretty unequivocally that it was the people of Jerusalem who had been oppressed by the Phoenicians and Philistines who were now the nucleus of the holy restored community. To the question why any of this had happened there was the obvious answer that it was the fault of the nations around them. Others, like II Isaiah, were irenic toward the nations and some, like II Isaiah and the author of the book of Jeremiah, gave precedence to the exiles, but this editor had a simpler vision. What he shared with many others, such as III Isaiah, was the conviction that Yahweh was just and that people were to blame and the rest was speculation.

Conclusion

It is clear that Joel wrote sometime after the composition of Ezekiel, the Deuteronomistic History, and II Isaiah, but before the other prophecies were revised and before Jonah was written. The enemy has come and gone; the temple services have been interrupted; but there is a veiled allegorical hope that everything will return to normal. This is not the purpose of his prophecy, however, and the editor of his work does not take issue with it. The editor knew his work well and used bits and pieces of it to make another point. This edition also knew the prophecy of Obadiah, the books of Micah and Jeremiah, and the revised versions of Amos and Ezekiel, but preceded III Isaiah and was early enough to be quoted freely by him and Haggai and the like. This edition took issue with the idea that the capture of Jerusalem could be assimilated to a natural catastrophe and with the grave omission of moral culpability. It may not have agreed with the Deuteronomistic notion of a sinful history, but it did think in terms of a holy remnant who rightly survived to worship Yahweh in a better day and who had suffered at least as unjustly from their neighbors as the exiles had suffered at the hands of the Babylonians.

One of the people most influenced by Joel was Jonah. The most obvious point of contact between them is their witty idea that even the animals mourned or repented. Their basic point of agreement, however, was in opposing the arbitrariness of the Deuteronomistic History in assigning the fall of Jerusalem to sin or to the theory of sin. Jonah ridiculed the idea in a humorous story about innocent sailors who suffered at the hands of a bad prophet, and about bad people who repented and were saved despite him. Joel was even more subtle in composing an allegory in which the Babylonians were like bugs that overran the country but in time and with prayer died and disappeared.

The editor of the book made the allegory a typical prophecy with protagonists and antagonists and morality and theology. The things that Joel predicted had not quite come true, but they would, as they were meant to be, and at another time. Joel's argument with the Deuteronomistic Historian over the meaning of history was transcended by his editor in a time and according to a rigid convention where it did not really matter.

OBADIAH

The prophecy of Obadiah predicts that the people of Judah will get even with Edom for its part in the siege and capture of Jerusalem. It is mostly an original work but betrays knowledge of earlier narrative, poetic, and prophetic traditions. It was not revised, but a revised form of the prophecy was incorporated into the book of Jeremiah.

Structure and Organization (figs. 19, 19a)

The prophecy is composed of six matching strophes with two or three stanzas each. The first strophe[131] declares war against Edom for its grandiosity and arrogant behavior. The second (vv. 3aBb, 4) is like it in warning Edom that it will be humiliated despite its vaunted impregnability. The third strophe (vv. 5, 6–7, 8–9) describes Edom's desertion by its allies and its future annihilation. The fourth strophe (vv. 10–11) matches it by predicting Edom's eternal shame for its alliance with the Babylonians during the siege of Jerusalem. The fifth strophe (vv. 12, 13–15a, 15b–16) gives more details on what they contributed to the

FIGURE 19

Obadiah

	Obadiah		Book of Obadiah
		1a	
A	1	1b	Jeremiah 49:7, 14
	2	2–3aA	Jeremiah 49:15–16aA
B	1	3aBb	Jeremiah 49:16aB
	2	4	Jeremiah 49:16b
C	1	5	Jeremiah 49:9
	2	6–7	Jeremiah 49:10a
	3	8–9	Jeremiah 49:7
D	1	10	
	2	11	
E	1	12	
	2	13–15a	
	3	15b–16	Jeremiah 49:12
F	1	17–18	
	2	19	
	3	20–21	

Figure 19. Letters indicate strophes. Numbers denote stanzas.

siege and warns them that the same will be done to them. The last strophe (vv. 17–18, 19, 20–21) is like it in describing how those who survived in Zion will get even with Edom and its allies.

The revision quotes part of the text, in inverse order to indicate that the quotation is taken in a different sense, and includes it in a great series of oracles against the nations that express Israel's exclusiveness and Yahweh's universal dominion. It contains six strophes arranged in a descriptive order that relates what Yahweh is about to do, first from one perspective and then from another (Jer 49:7–22).[132] The first strophe announces, in terms proper to the book of Jeremiah, that the time has come to punish Edom (Jer 49:7 = Obad 1, 8). The second declares, in words taken from Obadiah, that the punishment will be complete, leaving nothing but widows and orphans (Jer 49:9–10a, 10b–11 = Obad 5, 6). The third points out, in language partly indebted to Obadiah, that the punishment is divine retribution for their treatment of people who did not deserve to suffer (Jer 49:12, 13 = Obad 15, 16). The fourth makes the same announcement in terms taken from Obadiah (Jer 49:14, 15–16aA, 16aBb–17 = Obad 1–4). The fifth describes the punishment in the more traditional language of

FIGURE 19A

Jeremiah 49:7–22 and Obadiah

		Jeremiah	
A	1	49:7	Obadiah 1, 8
	2	49:8	
B	1	49:9–10a	Obadiah 5, 6
	2	49:10b–11	
C	1	49:12	Obadiah 15, 16
	2	49:13	
A	1	49:14	Obadiah 1
	2	49:15–16aA	Obadiah 2, 3
	3	49:16aBb–17	Obadiah 3, 4
B	1	49:18	
	2	49:19	
C	1	49:20	
	2	49:21	
	3	49:22	

Figure 19a. Letters indicate strophes. Numbers denote stanzas.

the author of the book of Jeremiah (Jer 49:18, 19). The sixth points out in more detail how Yahweh will exact retribution of Edom (Jer 49:20, 21, 22).

In Obadiah's version stanzas are linked to each other in strophes by literal repetition, and strophes are matched with each other both by literal repetition and by thematic transformation. In effect the poem progresses in overlapping and interlocking steps, with everything said at least twice from different points of view, so that the character of Edom and its fortune are set out in a multidimensional mode.

The stanzas have between three and eight lines and are combined in regular patterns. Three-line stanzas tend to be declarative and unimaginative statements of fact with summary, transitional, or emphatic functions (vv. 2–3aA, 10, 12). Four-line stanzas are marked by contrasts or contradictions that explain both sides of an event or situation (vv. 1b, 3aBb, 4). Five-line stanzas are descriptive and combine some idea or image with its interpretation (vv. 11, 19). Six-line stanzas are marked by a logical or narrative flow or by a combination of the two in succession (vv. 5, 8–9, 13–15a, 15b–16). Eight-line stanzas are just multiples of four-line stanzas and have more complicated contrasts or contradictions (vv. 6–7, 17, 20). Only two types of stanzas are combined in a strophe, and only in specific arrangements that reflect the simplest patterns of speech.[133]

In the first strophe there are two stanzas linked by the repetition of the phrase "among the nations."[134] The first stanza has four lines referring to Edom indirectly in the third person: the first and fourth lines contain Yahweh's declaration of war against Edom, and in the second and third lines Israel and the nations answer that they have heard it.[135] The second stanza has three lines addressed directly to Edom that state the reason for Yahweh's declaration: Edom was the smallest and most contemptible of nations but suffered delusions of grandeur.[136]

The second strophe has two four-line stanzas joined by variations on the expression "bring down."[137] It is linked to the first strophe by its reference to the word of Yahweh and by the same combination of indirect and direct discourse.[138] The first stanza contrasts Edom's lofty perch, described in the first two lines, with its lofty dismissal of the possibility that it might be brought down to earth, quoted in the last two lines.[139] The second stanza has the same distribution of lines contrasting the heights of Edom's arrogance with the depths to which Yahweh will bring it.

The third strophe links its stanzas in rather artificial ways. The first and second stanzas share the exclamation "How!" and a glimpse of Edom's utter destruction. The second and third stanzas play with the "intelligence" that is missing in Edom and the "intelligibility" that is lacking in its foreign affairs (vv. 5, 6–7, 8–9).[140] The first stanza has six lines and gives two examples of the restraint that will be lacking in Yahweh's utter destruction of Edom: the first example is that thieves do not steal everything but pick and choose what they need; the second is that even grape pickers leave some bunches behind. The point of the comparison is made by the exclamation that imagines for a moment, in a sort of aside, that if the thieves were killers Edom would be finished.[141] The second stanza develops the exclamation by pointing out that Edom has been thoroughly ransacked and deceived by its alliances: its eight lines contain two contrasts, one between its political alliance and the pillage that resulted, the other between its military alliance and the wounds that resulted.[142] The last stanza has six lines, which narrate how Yahweh will put an end to Edom's scheming and belligerence. The lines are paired and proceed from Yahweh's initiative, to the frustration of Edom's schemes, to the defeat of its troops and total annihilation of its people.[143]

The fourth strophe is linked to the third by reference to a day in the future when Yahweh will intervene, a future day that contrasts with a specific day in the past when Edom intervened with Babylon against Jerusalem.[144] The first stanza has three lines stating that Edom will disappear in everlasting shame, its first line giving the reason and the next two declaring the result (v. 10). The second stanza has five lines, three describing the Babylonian siege of Jerusalem, the overwhelming of the garrison, the entry into the city, and the capture of the population, and two incriminating Edom.[145] The strophe develops the single theme of the violence that Edom did to Jacob—with details on what they did—and total but generic punishment for doing it.

In the fifth strophe the first two stanzas are linked by the repetition of imperatives and by references to the critical time, and the second and third are linked by their references to the nations (vv. 12, 13–15a, 15b–16).[146] The first stanza has three lines, which have verbatim links to the preceding strophe and restate the charge against Edom as gloating and boasting (v. 12).[147] The second stanza has six lines, which list in order all the things they should not have done on this day, because it turns out to have been the day of Yahweh, which affects all nations. Under gloating it lists walking into the city and watching the terrible things that were done; under boasting it includes disarming the troops, arresting fugitives, and handing over those who escaped (vv. 13–15a). The third stanza has six lines, which portray first in ideas and then in images how, on the day that has been determined, Yahweh will exact retribution from Edom for the crimes they have committed (vv. 15b–16).

The sixth strophe is related to the fifth by its mention of the mountain of Yahweh and by its reference to those who managed to escape (vv. 17–18, 19, 20–21).[148] Its stanzas are related to each other in any number of ways, most notably by repeated reference to the occupation of the land, Mount Zion, Yahweh, and Mount Esau.[149] Its first stanza has eight lines with the characteristic complementarity and contrast: there is a contrast in the first two and last two lines between the survivors in Zion and the lack of survivors in the house of Esau and complementarity in the middle four lines between Jacob and Joseph as fire and the house of Esau as chaff. The second stanza has five lines, four lines describing the occupation of the land from the Negeb to Samaria, the last adding a reference to Gilead and making it clear that by the land is meant the entire territory of the two kingdoms. The last stanza has eight lines, five describing the occupation of the land by the exiles, the last three dealing with the administration of this ancient territory by Yahweh and by the redeemers who will arise, as in days of yore, to be the judges of the people on Mount Zion.

Language and Style

The stanzas are distinguished by their grammar and syntax and prosody. The distinctiveness of Obadiah's language and style can be noted where the text is adopted, changed, and interpreted by the author of the book of Jeremiah.

The first stanza is distributed between two stanzas in the Jeremiah version, its first line occurring there in the first stanza, the middle two lines repeated, and the last paraphrased in a later stanza.[150] In Obadiah's version there is a contrast between Yahweh's proclamation and the response of the nations; there is use of alliteration and repetition of words; and statements are paired by patterns of sound. In the Jeremianic version there are formulas; repetition is avoided; and rigid parallelism replaces pairing and intricate balance. Obadiah has "Thus said my Lord Yahweh about Edom," but Jeremiah has "Concerning Edom: Thus says Yahweh Sebaot." Obadiah says "Arise and we will rise up against her in battle," but Jeremiah has "Gather together and go against her / and rise up in battle." Obadiah interrupts the proclamation with the response of those who heard it, but Jeremiah flattens it into the statement that they heard the proclamation.

The second stanza encloses an unmatched line between two alliterative lines that rhyme (vv. 2–3aA).[151] It coheres topically because it affirms Edom's pride ("The pride of your heart misled you") against the background of what it really was ("I made you the least of the nations") and what others thought of it ("you are thoroughly despised"). The stanza is rephrased in Jeremiah in two sets of parallel lines (Jer 49:15–16aA).

The third and fourth stanzas contrast Edom's loftiness with the depths of its coming degradation, and each correlates its contrasting parts by rhyming the middle lines.[152] The Jeremianic version omits a line or two from each stanza, combines the others, and adds three lines of explanation marked by Jeremianic cliché. Its most distinctive feature, and the evident reason for the omissions and combinations, is rigid parallelism (Jer 49:16aBb–17).

The fifth stanza is held together by repetition and rhyme and by parallelism between its disjunctive parts. The examples of the thieves and the vintagers are joined by parallelism, and the interpretive aside that disrupts the parallelism to reflect on nightstalkers and killers is fitted in as a rhyming couplet. The Jeremianic version preserves the parallelism by omitting the aside, reverses the order of the questions, turns the thieves into thieves in the night, and adds three lines of explanation paraphrasing the first lines of Obadiah's sixth stanza (Obad 5; Jer 49:9–10a).

The sixth stanza continues the image of robbery introduced in the fifth and links it with political and military treachery. All the lines except the first two and the last are joined by the same rhyme, often at the beginning and the end of the lines, and are distinguished from each other by their particular assonance and alliteration. Pairs of lines are also linked by parallelism, and therefore the imperfect parallelism in the last pair gives the final exclamation its peculiar force (Obad 6–7). The stanza is partly paraphrased but otherwise omitted in the revised version.

The seventh stanza introduces the theme of the day of Yahweh and announces the annihilation of Edom in ponderous, unadorned, and unbalanced lines. The Jeremianic version omits the theme and the stanza but uses some of its words in its opening imprecation against Edom (Obad 8–9; cf. Jer 49:7).

Although each of the remaining stanzas is different and has its own rhythm and cadence, they are all characterized by rhyme, alliteration, and assonance and by simple repetition rather than parallelism. The Jeremianic version is an adaptation and, both interpretively and prosodically, goes its own way.

Sources and Interpretation

Obadiah was familiar with the stories of the patriarchs, with Deuteronomistic legislation and historical interpretation, with the second edition of Isaiah, and with the unedited versions of some other prophecies. His familiarity with the literature is expressed in allusions and a few quotations in an otherwise original and genial work. His own work was quoted in the revision of Amos and Joel and was taken over by the editor of the book of Jeremiah.

The superscription is reminiscent of the heading of the books of Isaiah and Nahum.[153] This is consistent with references to these authors later in the prophecy and suggests the peculiar eclecticism of Obadiah's work.

The first stanza combines elements that are known from a wide range of prophetic texts. The introductory formula, marking what follows as prophecy, is familiar from Amos and especially from Ezekiel.[154] The second line has an expression that can suggest rumors or gossip but that usually refers to news from the battlefront and, in the style of Isaiah, Obadiah has the news originate with Yahweh.[155] The third line combines this military communiqué with a diplomatic report, again in the manner of Isaiah.[156] The last line quotes from the international conspiracy against Edom in the words of the war council that

Jeremiah described taking place outside the walls of Jerusalem.[157] These, except the reference to Jeremiah, are allusions rather than quotations, but they suggest that the first stanza, in a mood appropriate to the theme of retribution that will be developed, is an adaptation against Edom of sayings originally addressed to Judah and Jerusalem.

The second stanza supposes the stories of Jacob and Esau. Esau despised the right of the firstborn and so assumed the role of younger son, which properly belonged to Jacob.[158] In the original stories, as in Obadiah, this disinheritance of Esau is ascribed to Yahweh, entails Esau's subordination to Jacob in the divine scheme of things, and is a paradigm of the relationship between the two nations.[159] Obadiah paraphrased the story and attributed Edom's ambition and lack of perspective to vanity and stupidity.

The third stanza situates Edom in rocky fastnesses and compares it to a bird nesting on a cliff. The vanity attributed to Edom, thinking that because it was up high it could not be brought down, recalls in inverse order the boasts of the king of Babylon in II Isaiah's taunt.[160] The allusion is all the more striking since the fourth stanza, with reference to this same text of Isaiah, sees Edom aspiring to build its nest among the stars and Yahweh making sure that it is brought down to earth.[161]

The fifth stanza may have a slight allusion to the same text,[162] but it is essentially a concordance of legislative and prophetic references. In Joel the troops who infiltrate the city and get into the houses are compared to thieves.[163] In the legislation of the Book of the Covenant it is clearly supposed that the thieves come during the night;[164] in Jeremiah invaders are destroyers who are all the more terrifying when they attack at night;[165] and in II Isaiah just such a fate befalls Moab.[166] The law states that the vineyards are not to be picked clean, but the later book of Jeremiah saw just such a terrible thing happening to Judah and Jerusalem.[167] The stanza, therefore, combines these traditional images of enemy invasion—robbery and vintage—with standard but more technical references to assailants and assault in order to intimate that Edom would be completely annihilated.

The sixth stanza has no evident sources, but some of it is quoted against Zedekiah in a taunt composed for the book of Jeremiah.[168] The second-to-last line refers to the wound that will be inflicted on Edom by those for whom it is fighting, and there is a faint reminiscence of the wound that Yahweh inflicted on his own people when they thought they were fighting for him.[169]

The seventh stanza takes up the reference to Edom's borders from the preceding stanza and mentions places that are known primarily from the Deuteronomistic History. The mountain of Esau is Mount Seir, where Esau lived.[170] Teman is a city and region of Edom (Obad 9a).[171] Teman, however, is also the place of origin of one of Job's interlocutors, the one whom Yahweh singled out for his mistaken opinion, and Obadiah may be alluding to this literary tradition, as well as to more mundane interests, in affirming that the wise men of Edom will be destroyed (Obad 8b–9a).[172] The expression "a man will be cut off" generally refers to the end of dynastic succession, and its use in this stanza may be another allusion to the same Deuteronomistic texts on Edom and Esau and the earliest evidence for kingship.[173]

The eighth stanza is a resumptive transition. It refers again to the patriarchal traditions on the brotherhood of Jacob and Esau and to the termination of Edomite genealogical or dynastic succession. Its innovations are its incrimination of Esau for the violence done to Jacob and its sentencing of Esau to dismal confusion. The charge of violence derives ultimately from the Priestly writer's reason for the flood, but it was taken up by Micah, Habakkuk, and Ezekiel to explain why Jerusalem was destroyed.[174] Obadiah alludes to these texts in an opposite sense, consistent with his notion of divine retribution, to refer not to the crime of Jacob or Jerusalem but to the crimes committed against them. Confusion is the usual penalty for depending on unreliable resources. It is associated, in Obadiah's eyes, with plain dismay, and these are the penalty for Edom's uncircumspect alliance with the Babylonians in the siege of Jerusalem.[175]

The ninth stanza refers to successive stages in the siege and capture of Jerusalem—taking up a position in the siege, wiping out the garrison, entering through the gates, and taking the people captive—and accuses Edom of being no different from their Babylonian allies. The stages are recorded differently, and less sympathetically, in the Deuteronomistic History and later in the book of Jeremiah (Obad 11; cf. 2 Kgs 25:1–5; Jer 39:1–4). The casting of lots for the citizens of Jerusalem reflects familiarity with Nahum's allegorical account of the capture and destruction of Thebes.[176]

The tenth stanza is another transitional résumé that goes over some of the earlier material to point out the precise crime and predicament of the Edomites. The new material is its repeated reference to "the day" in its various manifestations. It is, in agreement with the evaluation of the prophets who wrote just before the fall of Jerusalem, the day of distress.[177] In agreement with the Deuteronomistic Historian's less sympathetic view, it is a day of destruction or, as the next stanza says, of calamity.[178] Or, in Obadiah's own words, it is the day of alienation.[179]

The eleventh stanza repeats some of the same material and identifies the day with the traditional day of Yahweh. There is a reference to Edomites entering the city with the Babylonians on the day foretold by Micah, Jeremiah, and Huldah.[180] There are references, but in different words, to the overtaking of the troops that fled from the city,[181] to the breach that was made in the wall (Obad 14; cf. 2 Kgs 25:5), and to the fettering of those who escaped death and were captured. All of this is associated, in words and ideas taken from Zephaniah, with the day of Yahweh, which is approaching for the world and all its inhabitants.[182]

The twelfth stanza expresses retribution in terms taken from II Isaiah concerning the cup of Yahweh's wrath, which was given to Jerusalem to drink but will be taken away and given to those who oppressed the city (Obad 15b–16; Isa 51:17–23).[183] It also alludes to a cognate text in which II Isaiah assures Jerusalem that all the nations who besieged and captured the city will be like a dream about eating and drinking that does not satisfy the dreamer's hunger and thirst (Obad 16; cf. Isa 29:5–8).

The thirteenth stanza gives more detailed information on this retaliation. The opening line quotes, from the Historian's account of the failure of the siege of Sennacherib, the assurance that a remnant would survive.[184] The image of Jacob and Joseph, the two kingdoms of Israel, as fire and flames devouring the straw of Esau reverses the damage that was done to Jerusalem according to Joel and is consistent with the text of II Isaiah cited in the preceding paragraph, in which Yahweh takes vengeance on his enemies with fire and devouring flames (Obad 18).[185]

The fourteenth stanza refers to the occupation of the land of Israel in accordance with Deuteronomistic geography. The Negeb, Shephelah, and mountains are regions of the land of Israel described in the History (Obad 19),[186] and the territory of the Philistines and of the Canaanites was reckoned as land belonging to Israel that Joshua had not been able to occupy (Obad 19–20; cf. Josh 13:1–7). The restoration will also include Ephraim, with its capital at Samaria, and Israel's Transjordanian possessions in Gilead.

The last stanza repeats some of the same material and looks back to the period of the judges for its administrative model. In this period, as the Deuteronomist described it, there was no king and Israel was governed by saviors who acted as judges in lieu of Yahweh, who was the legitimate king of Israel.[187]

Obadiah, in short, describes the role of the Edomites in the siege of Jerusalem and the retribution that would overtake them, in terms that were familiar to those who knew the Deuteronomistic History and the prophetic tradition. The point of the prophecy, however, is slightly more subtle than that and takes issue with the standard interpretation of the fall of Jerusalem incorporated into the History. Obadiah sees the fall of the city as a defeat that was due in part to the treachery of Israel's traditional friends but views it without any recrimination against the city for past or present faults. In the same vein, and with a similar distance from the History, Obadiah envisages the restoration of Israel and Judah and sees it as something that Yahweh determined to do to bring the patriarchal history to a fitting close. The prophet's contempt for the Edomites, whom the Deuteronomist took as natural rivals of Jacob, is merely symptomatic of Obadiah's disagreement with the History's rather jaundiced view of Jacob's chances.

The revision of his prophecy in the book of Jeremiah omits this positive perspective and treats his words as condemnations of Edom with little satisfaction for Judah and Jerusalem apart from the sense that Yahweh is in control of world history. The revision takes place by bringing the prophecy into line with the sources and opinions common to the book.

The first strophe is related to Obadiah (Jer 49:7, 8; cf. Obad 1b, 8) but uses the formulaic language that is typical of the book of Jeremiah and especially of its oracles against the nations. When Obadiah says that Yahweh will confound the wise men of Edom, this version combines two clichés from elsewhere in the book of Jeremiah. One is taken from the passage that defines the permanent function of prophets, priests, and wise men.[188] Another reflects the book's interest in the succession of generations from fathers to sons, expressed in the oracle against the Philistines as terror that prevents the fathers from turning back to help their sons.[189] Obadiah refers to the day of calamity that confronted Jerusalem, and this version refers in stereotypes to the calamity that Yahweh is bringing upon Edom,[190] and to the time that has been set for its punishment.[191] These changes stylize the oracle against Edom and obscure Obadiah's idea that Edom's involvement in the siege of Jerusalem was a serious miscalculation that put an end to its historic ties with Jacob.

The second strophe has one stanza paraphrasing Obadiah and one stanza fitting Obadiah's text into the perspective of the book of Jeremiah (Jer 49:9–10a [= Obad 5–6], 10b–11). The paraphrase attributes to Yahweh's doing the things that Obadiah attributed to Edom's allies: instead of ransacking Edom Yahweh lays it bare, and rather than searching through its treasures Yahweh uncovers its secret places, giving it no place to hide.[192] The homogenizing stanza describes the total destruction of Edom in terms of family and kin and entails stereotypical usage.[193]

The third strophe alludes to Obadiah's image of drinking from the cup of Yahweh's wrath, but it leaves out his references to Zion and rephrases the image to fit it into the book of Jeremiah's general theory of the oracles against the nations (Jer 49:12, 13; cf. Obad 15–16; Jeremiah 25). There is a specific mention of the cup of Yahweh's wrath, of not being able to avoid the punishment, and of all the terrible things that will happen to Edom, all of which are part of the general theory.[194] In order to omit the specific historical facts that Obadiah collected to implicate Edom and absolve Zion, and still retain Obadiah's theory of retribution, the book refers vaguely to the fact that, since some undeserving people had to drink the cup, Edom certainly will not be exempt (Jer 49:12aA). The effect, again, is to eliminate Edom's role in the siege of Jerusalem and make the sayings on Edom symbolic of Yahweh's universal dominion.

The fourth strophe redoes the opening of Obadiah's prophecy with a few typical variants (Jer 49:14, 15–16aA, 16aBb–17; cf. Obad 1–4). With its usual dependence on the language of the Deuteronomistic History, the book has the nations assemble before attacking Edom.[195] Similarly, it is not content to ridicule Edom's pride but makes it a derivative of their ignorant belief in idols.[196] Again, it ignores the niceties of retribution and describes the fate of Edom in formulas characteristic of the book.[197] In effect, retribution is ascribed to Yahweh without any basis in history or current events.

The fifth strophe proceeds in the same line by comparing the punishment of Edom to the overthrow of Sodom and Gomorrah, or by attributing it symbolically to a lion from the Jordan Valley. The first combines commonplaces in the book of Jeremiah concerning Sodom and Gomorrah and ghost towns without permanent residents or even squatters (Jer 49:18; cf. 23:14; 49:33; 50:40). The second was taken from prophetic traditions about Bethel[198] and was combined with typical images from the restoration period about the Jordan Valley, where Lot, the hero or villain of the story, once lived.[199]

The last strophe concludes with Edom's place in Yahweh's universal plan (Jer 49:20, 21, 22). The existence of such a plan, in conflict with the plans of others, is a staple of the book of Jeremiah.[200] The image of Yahweh as an eagle spreading its wings is known from the Deuteronomistic History, and the book of Jeremiah used it earlier to describe how Yahweh suddenly pounces on his enemies (Jer 49:22).[201] The terrible pangs of childbirth are often mentioned in the book, and the comparison between them and the fear that warriors feel before Yahweh has already been applied in the account of Yahweh's attack on Moab (Jer 49:22; cf. 48:40). The shouts of those under attack and the earthquakes that accompany Yahweh's battles are also standard in the book (Jer 49:21).[202]

The revision of Obadiah's prophecy fits it into the general pattern of Jeremianic oracles against the nations. It removes most of the connection between the prophecy and historical opinion and hurls Edom into the realm of the typical and the universal. It deletes, in the same motion, Obadiah's confrontation with the History and leaves his work as little more than a witty tirade against a mean and miserable people.

Conclusion

Obadiah belongs in the historical and prophetic traditions of Israel after Ezekiel, the Deuteronomistic History, II Isaiah, Joel, and Job but before the revisions of Amos, Joel, and Jeremiah. It belongs among the historical traditions because it interprets specific facts in the light of literary evidence and from the perspective of prior and subsequent events. It belongs late in the prophetic traditions because it relies on them for its perception of cause and effect. To those who had stood in the breach it gave a little hope that what had been written would really come true.

JONAH

The book of Jonah is a parody of prophecy and a scathing criticism of contemporary historiography. It was toned down and fitted into the prophetic canon by the addition of a psalm proclaiming Jonah's submission to Yahweh.

The original work was written in response to the fatalism of the Deuteronomistic History and the book of Jeremiah, in which the fall of Jerusalem was a necessary consequence either of sin or of the rejection of the prophets. Its story of Jonah's unwillingness to intercede and his preference for death, of his propensity for self-pity and his wariness of the mercy of God, ridicules the sorry fate of the prophet in the book of Jeremiah, who whined and refused to intercede or ever suggest that there was any real alternative to complete devastation. Its point that anyone, old salts, the king of Nineveh, or even the animals, can regret the evil they have done proves that God is not bound to punish and casts serious doubt on the Deuteronomistic claim that punishment for sin, or for the typical sin of Manasseh, was inevitable. The work is ironic, satirical, and indirect and uses the standard comparison between Nineveh and Jerusalem to make its point about prophecy, history, and the law.[203]

Structure and Organization (fig. 20)

The book of Jonah is written in paragraphs that match, reach a climax, and go on to a resolution. The climax is heightened and weakened in the revised version by the addition of a psalm for Jonah to recite in the belly of the whale.

The paragraphs are distinguished by the rules of grammar and syntax. The matching of paragraphs is marked by the repetition of key words, ideas, and images in each. The climax is reached when one part of the story ends and a second part begins the same way. The resolution

FIGURE 20

Jonah

	Jonah			*Book of Jonah*			
1	a	1:1–2	1	a			
	b	1:3		b			
2	a	1:4–5a	2	a			
	b	1:5b–6		b			
3	a	1:7a	3	a			
	b	1:7b–8		b			
4	a	1:9	4	a			
	b	1:10–11		b			
5	a	1:12	5	a			
	b	1:13–14		b			
6	a	1:15–2:1	6	a			
			7	A	1	2:2–3a°	
					2	2:3	
				B	1	2:4a	
					2	2:4b–5	
					3	2:6	
				A¹	1	2:7–8	
					2	2:9–10	
	b	2:11–3:2		b			
7	a	3:3	8	a			
	b	3:4		b			
8	a	3:5–7aA	9	a			
	b	3:7aBb–9		b			
9	a	3:10–4:2aA	10	a			
	b	4:2aB–3		b			
10	a	4:4–5	11	a			
	b	4:6a		b			
11	a	4:6b–7	12	a			
	b	4:8–11		b			

Figure 20. Numbers indicate pairs of paragraphs or strophes.

is achieved when all the pieces of both parts of the story become mutually explanatory. The psalm interprets what happened to Jonah in the first part of the story but interrupts and contradicts the point of the story in both parts.

The first and second paragraphs (Jonah 1:1–2, 3) are matched by their common references to Yahweh and the presence of Yahweh, to Jonah and the beginning of his journey.[204] They also are related by their mutual interest in cities and by the contrast between coming and going, going up and going down.[205]

The third and fourth paragraphs are matched by their various references to prayer and are related as well by their description of the ship, the hold, the crew, the captain, and the cargo.[206] The pair also duplicates the first pair in its choice of words. In the first Yahweh sends Jonah to a big city, and in the second he sends a big wind against the sea.[207] In the first pair Yahweh tells Jonah to get up and go and call out, and in the second pair the captain tells Jonah to get up and call out to his God.[208] In the first pair Jonah reacts to the situation by going down to Joppa and going down into a ship, and in the second pair he goes down into the hold and goes to sleep.[209]

The fifth and six paragraphs are matched by their reference to casting lots in order to find out why evil had befallen the crew.[210] They are also related by the discussions the sailors have among themselves and with Jonah.

The seventh and eighth paragraphs are matched by their mention of fear, of doing, and of the sea.[211] They are also related to each other by their witty contrast between devoted fear of Yahweh and running away from him in fear. The pair is further related to the preceding pair by giving more answers to the questions that were asked there: the sailors asked Jonah what he did for a living, where he came from, what country he lived in, and his nationality, and he answered only the last question by saying that he was a Hebrew (cf. Jonah 1:7–8, 9). In this pair there is an answer to the question where he came from, and it too is humorous since he is fleeing to Tarshish in a boat away from God in heaven, who made the sea and the dry land.

The ninth and tenth paragraphs (1:12, 13–14) are matched by their reference to the storm at sea.[212] They are also related by the contrast between Jonah's advice to throw him into the sea and their attempt to reach dry ground.

The eleventh and twelfth paragraphs (1:15–2:1; 2:11–3:2) are matched by their references to the whale. They are related to the preceding pair, where the sailors pick up Jonah and throw him into the sea as he suggested.[213] They also are related to the very beginning of the story, since Jonah again receives the same command he received then from Yahweh (3:1-2 = 1:2a).

The connection between the eleventh and twelfth paragraphs is broken by the prayer of Jonah, and the sequence between the two parts of the story is interrupted (2:2-10). The prayer is composed of three strophes that are related to each other in a concentric pattern that gives the prayer a beginning, a middle, and an end. The first strophe contains the introduction in prose and a stanza in the long line–short line cadence of laments, which recalls how Jonah prayed in his distress and received an answer to his prayer (2:2-3).[214] The second strophe has three stanzas: the first (2:4a) describes the distress as being cast into the primordial sea by Yahweh; the second (2:4b-5) interprets the distress as a temptation to despair that was resisted by looking in expectation toward the temple; the third stanza (2:6) resumes the first by returning to the original description of distress and repeating one of its key words. The third strophe has two stanzas: the first (2:7-8) repeats in more detail what was said in the first strophe about Yahweh's answer to prayer in a time of distress; the second stanza (2:9-10) compares Jonah to the sailors, who like him offer vows and sacrifices,[215] but it also contrasts the salvation that Yahweh provides with the uselessness of the idols that they purportedly worshiped (2:9-10).[216] The prayer, in this way, makes some attempt to end on the same note as the story had before its intrusion (cf. 2:7-10 and 1:15-2:1).

The thirteenth and fourteenth paragraphs are matched by their reference to Jonah and Nineveh and to the number of days it took to cross the city.[217] They are related to the first pair of paragraphs at the very beginning of the story by repeating many of its key points, such as that Nineveh was a great city[218] and that Jonah got up and went and made the announcement.[219] Since the story began over again after Jonah got back to dry ground, some of these repetitions also relate this pair of paragraphs to the preceding paragraph.[220]

The fifteenth paragraph describes how the people of Nineveh fasted and wore sackcloth and how the king followed suit, and the sixteenth is matched with it by making this repentance the result of a royal decree (3:5-7aA, 7aBb-9). This pair of paragraphs is related to the second pair at the beginning of the story (cf. 3:5-9 and 1:4-6) by repeating some of its words and themes, such as by mentioning the sailors before the captain and the people before the king, and by reporting how they lamented, cried out, and abandoned their possessions or their ways in the hope of not perishing.[221]

The seventeenth and eighteenth paragraphs are matched by their reference to Yahweh's relenting.[222] The pair is related to the third pair of paragraphs at the very beginning of the story by its mention of real or impending evil[223] and is also related to the preceding pair in this part of the story by its reference to repentance and relenting.[224]

The nineteenth and twentieth paragraphs are matched by their reference to Yahweh and Jonah and the shade (4:4–5, 6a). The pair is also related to the fourth pair in the first part of the story by telling how Jonah left the city just as he originally avoided the city by fleeing to Tarshish (cf. 1:9–11).

The twenty-first and twenty-second paragraphs are matched by their reference to the shade plant.[225] They are also related to the preceding pair by reference to this plant, by the question that Yahweh asks Jonah, and by their interest in the fate of the city.[226] They are related to the fifth pair of paragraphs in the first part by illustrating that Yahweh does what he pleases (1:14b and 4:11), and they bring the whole story to a close with a final mention of Nineveh as a great city.[227]

The repetitive patterns are typical of narrative structure. The pairing of paragraphs allows the story to advance by telling one thing at a time and relating it to what has been said. The linking of pairs in each part gives the story a didactic form by letting it reflect on itself. The rise to a climax and repetition from part to part make the story a lesson to be learned.

Language and Style

The repetitions are puns. Used in opposite or contradictory contexts they become ironic. Distributed from part to part they make the story of Jonah a parody of history and prophecy.

The first pair of paragraphs (1:1–2, 3) begins the puns. In one Jonah is told to get up and go to Nineveh, but in the next he gets up and flees to Tarshish. In one paragraph evil ascends into the presence of Yahweh, and in the other Jonah descends from the presence of Yahweh. It is not clear yet whether this is meant to be funny. The things that are not repeated are reserved for later retrieval. The word of Yahweh comes up again in the climax and in the second part, where it is contrasted with the word of Jonah.[228] Jonah's full name is not mentioned again, but its traditional pair becomes a topic of discussion in the psalm and in the story of Nineveh.[229] That Nineveh was a metropolis is crucial to the whole story.[230] The evil of Nineveh is what makes the story work, and it contrasts with the evil that Jonah causes, with the anger that he thinks is good, and with the evil that Yahweh threatened but kept himself from doing.[231]

The second pair of paragraphs is full of puns in silly or humorous contexts (1:4–6). Yahweh hurls a wind against the sea, and the sailors hurl their cargo into the sea. Jonah avoided the big city, but he found himself in a big storm with a big wind. Yahweh was responsible for the storm, but the sailors pray to their own gods and Jonah does not pray at all. The storm God lived in the recesses of Saphon, and Jonah tries to escape from him by going into the recesses of the *sĕpînâ*. Jonah was supposed to get up and go to Nineveh and speak the word of Yahweh, and the captain tells him to get up and speak to his God. The puns are visual and aural: the ship was bent on breaking;[232] Jonah was down and out;[233] the captain was his mate.[234] The story is not serious, and the joke is on Jonah.

The third pair is not so amusing (1:7–8). The captain could not persuade Jonah to pray, but when the crew found out that Jonah was to blame for the storm the captain has to question him. A prior question is "Why us? What have we done to anyone that this evil has come upon us?" But it never gets answered. It is a rhetorical question protesting that they are being punished for something they did not do. Combined with the denouement in the second part of the story, where Nineveh is not punished for things they did do, this protest puts the whole system of retribution seriously in doubt. The four questions that the captain addressed to Jonah concern the reason for his trip, the city and country from which he is traveling, and his nationality. Only the first and last are answered, the last immediately and directly, when Jonah replies that he is a Hebrew, the first indirectly and by repeating what the reader knows already. The answer to the other two questions depends on getting the point of the story.

The fourth pair (1:9–11) is clever because Jonah is afraid of God and the sailors fear God, and because Jonah tries to escape by sea from the maker of the sea. There is a parenthesis that refers the reader back to the beginning of the story, and the question that it interrupts and emphasizes pretty well expresses the theory of retribution that the story is ridiculing: "And they said to him, 'What is this you have done?'—for the crew knew that he was fleeing from Yahweh, because he had told them—and they said to him, 'What shall we do to you?'" (1:10–11; cf. 1:3). It is strange to think that prophets bring bad luck and that getting rid of the prophets spells relief, but so the story goes.

The fifth pair is witty and a little pathetic (1:12–14). The sailors found out that Jonah was responsible for the evil that had come upon them, but Jonah admits only that he was responsible for the storm. The sailors come around to his point of view when they ask Yahweh not to hold them responsible for the blood of an innocent man. The solution that Jonah offers is to jettison him along with the rest of the cargo. It is silly, but the sailors figure that it is what Yahweh wants and that it is better than dying because of him. It is quite a reversal of the traditional wisdom that opposition to the prophets and the shedding of their innocent blood were the main reasons for the dreadful doom of Israel and Judah.

The sixth pair is serious and ludicrous (1:15–2:1, 2:11–3:2). The funny part is being swallowed by a whale and thrown up on dry land. The serious part is that Yahweh gets his way with or without the prophets and that anybody, even the crew of a Tarshish ship, can worship him and be saved by him.

The seventh pair (3:3–4) is not particularly comical, except in the rest of the story where the words of the prophet turn out to be an ineffective cliché. The forty days before Nineveh is to be destroyed are like always or never. The destruction Jonah described is the overthrow that happened to Sodom and Gomorrah (3:4).[235] The funny part is the timetable: the city takes three days to walk across, but Jonah walks for just one day; the downfall of the city is set for forty days later, and of course does not happen.

The eighth pair is sort of silly (3:5–9). The prophetic cliché works and everybody in the big city of God believes in God and repents. Even the animals fast and wear sackcloth. The king of Nineveh arrives a little late and breathless on the scene, but he is the one who thinks that Yahweh might change his mind.

The ninth pair (3:10–4:3) is queer because the people turn from their evil; Yahweh repents of the evil he intended; and Jonah takes it as evil. Jonah becomes angry and blames Yahweh for being slow to anger. The city survives and Jonah wants to die. The sailors did not want to perish because of this man, and now he wants to perish because of the city.

The tenth pair (4:4–6a) is clever. Jonah builds himself a hut and sits in its shade to see what will happen in the city. Yahweh grows a plant to shade him and to save him from his evil anger. The city has been saved; Jonah leaves it for some lean-to; and Yahweh has to save him from that.

The eleventh pair (4:6b–11) is ridiculous because Jonah, who was mad when the city was saved, is madder when his lean-to collapses. It is serious because Yahweh tells him that they are interested in different things—not that Jonah is right or wrong, just that he does not represent Yahweh's point of view.

Yahweh's point of view is represented in the psalm. It has its own kind of irony when it turns the silly fish into a symbol with cosmic repercussions. The psalm is sort of peculiar too when it says that it is

Yahweh who threw him into the water, not the sailors, and when it attributes Jonah's distance from Yahweh not to his flight but to the storm. It is Yahweh's point of view, but not the point of view of the author of the book of Jonah.

Sources and Interpretation

The irony, parody, and puns take on a satirical cast by reference to the sources quoted and twisted in the story. It is strange that Jonah should recite a psalm in the belly of the whale, especially when it is a series of snippets from other well-known psalms. But the really strange thing about Jonah is that everything that happens to him happened before to somebody else with the opposite effect.

Jonah makes prophecy look foolish and makes history look like a lie. It is amazing that Nineveh was not destroyed when history says that it was. It is astounding that a city like Nineveh could repent and be saved when a city like Jerusalem could not be saved even when it repented. It is astonishing that prophets do harm to those around them and refuse to intercede for them. It is incredible that prophets are mistaken in their predictions and do not want the truth to be known. Jonah is a sign that prophecy is finished and that history lies in the telling.

The first paragraph sets the stage for the satire (1:1–2). Jonah ben 'Amittai was a prophet in the time of Jeroboam II and the only prophet highlighted in the Deuteronomistic History for having announced good news to a bad king chosen by God to save Israel because, no matter how bad, Yahweh had never planned on blotting out Israel for the sins of some king (2 Kgs 14:25–27). Nineveh was a great city according to the table of nations in Genesis[236] but it was odd of God to notice the evil it had done and send a prophet to warn it. There is a comparable divine awareness of evil in the story of the flood, in the variants of this story that were told about the Tower of Babel and about Sodom and Gomorrah, and in the still more distant variant told about Israel's affliction in Egypt; and in every case it is a function of Yahweh's interest in some particular person or people.[237] There is no analogue to Jonah's mission in the annals of the prophets except the vague similarity in Elijah's mission to the widow of Zarephath[238] and the general parallel in Elijah's career, which took place mostly outside of his own country. The paragraph is full of literary references and suggests that there is more than meets the eye and that the story is not yet saying quite what it means. Nineveh, after all, in the prophecies of Nahum and Zephaniah, was just a foil for Jerusalem, another great city, as Jeremiah called it.[239]

The second paragraph is ominous (1:3). The flight from Yahweh seems hazardous, but taking a ship to Tarshish is disastrous, as anyone who had read Ezekiel would know (Ezek 27:25–36).

The third paragraph (1:4–5a) describes a storm at sea whose elements would also have been familiar from Ezekiel's ballad of the good ship Tyre on a voyage to Tarshish. There is first the wind,[240] then the storm, and when the ship is about to founder[241] the sailors and the captain cry out and jettison the cargo that was the purpose of the voyage.[242] The difference is that, in Ezekiel's version the ship sank, and in this version the cry of the crew is heard and the storm abates. So nothing is quite as it should be.

The fourth paragraph (1:5b–6) puts Jonah in the hold with the cargo and points out that he was lost in reverie and did not pray. The only other prophet who did not intercede for those who asked him to pray was Jeremiah (Jer 7:16; 11:14).

The fifth and sixth paragraphs (1:7a, 7b–8) blame Jonah for the evil that has befallen the crew but without knowing why he is responsible. It is supposedly typical of prophets to prevent evil by helping people avoid evil. The only reason the crew is being punished, as they realize in the seventh and eighth paragraphs (:9, 10–11), is that Jonah fled from Yahweh instead of trying to persuade Nineveh to repent. The prophet is the cause of evil.

The ninth and tenth paragraphs (1:12, 13–14) insist on the fact that Jonah was responsible and that the crew was completely undeserving of the evil that had befallen them because of the prophet. They do everything they can to avoid throwing Jonah overboard. They expressly attempt to exonerate themselves from the charge of shedding innocent blood. This is an expression that was coined by the Deuteronomistic code, that Jeremiah used to ward off the threat against his own life, and that the Historian took as one of the unforgivable crimes of Manasseh.[243] You begin to wonder if Jonah is not another Jeremiah responsible for the evil that he announced, or if the prophet who brought evil on the people is really innocent.

The eleventh and twelfth paragraphs (1:15–2:1; 2:11–3:2) make it clear that throwing Jonah overboard was not susceptible to the charge of shedding innocent blood. The storm abates; the crew worships Yahweh; and Jonah is swallowed and thrown up by the whale. There is no morality involved. Jonah is not reprimanded. God has not changed. The original command is repeated. The prophet turns out to be peripheral to the plans of the God of heaven, who made the sea and the dry land.

The thirteenth and fourteenth paragraphs (3:3, 4) are a sort of parody on Elijah. When Elijah fled from Jezebel, he got up and went to Beersheba, and so Jonah got up and went to Nineveh.[244] Elijah went a day's journey into the wilderness, and so Jonah goes a day's walk into the city that it actually takes three days to cross (Jonah 3:4; 1 Kgs 19:4). Jonah threatens Nineveh with the fate of Sodom and Gomorrah (Jonah 3:4; Gen 19:25), a fate that was reserved for Jerusalem (cf. Deut 29:22; Isa 1:7; Amos 4:11), Edom (cf. Jer 49:18), and Babylon (cf. Isa 13:19; Jer 50:40), but the forty-day delay is like Elijah's forty-day trek to Horeb (Jonah 3:4; 1 Kgs 19:8). The parody makes Jonah the typical prophet, the summation of prophecy, with a message filled with clichés and meant for likelier places than Nineveh.

The fifteenth and sixteenth paragraphs (3:5–9) represent the totality of response ever required of Judah and Jerusalem by any of the prophets. Faith was what Isaiah required.[245] Fasting and sackcloth were what Joel advised (Jonah 3:5b; Joel 1:8, 13, 14; 2:12) with the same hope as the king of Nineveh, who mused, "Who knows whether [God] will turn and repent" (Jonah 3:9a = Joel 2:14a). The king wore sackcloth and sat in the dust as the prophet Jeremiah had suggested to Jerusalem (Jonah 3:6b; Jer 6:26). He exhorted his people to turn from their evil ways just as Jeremiah warned Jehoiakim and Jerusalem, but to no avail (Jonah 3:8bA; Jer 26:3; 36:3, 7).[246] He told them to stop their violence, as most of the prophets and writers had urged (Jonah 3:8bB).[247] The irony is that the king of Nineveh expects Yahweh to turn from his fierce anger, which is exactly what the Deuteronomistic Historian says that Yahweh did not do when Josiah and the people of Jerusalem repented (Jonah 3:9b; 2 Kgs 23:26).

The seventeenth and eighteenth paragraphs compact references to Elijah and the prophetic tradition (3:10–4:3). The real or intended repentance of God is mentioned in the prophets and the histories: it actually happens to Nineveh precisely as it did not happen to Jerusalem.[248] This reversal of expectations becomes especially obvious in Jonah's reaction. Jonah was angry that the people repented and Yahweh relented. He takes up the anger that Yahweh abandoned and assumes the evil that Yahweh rejected. He refused to intercede when the sailors were threatened with evil but prays now that evil has been avoided. Joel had based his expectation of forgiveness on the kindness and mercy of Yahweh, and this is just what Jonah resents about Yahweh (Jonah 4:2b; cf. Joel 2:13). Elijah was sick and tired of trying to convert the people and wanted to die, but Jonah wants to die because the people have been converted (cf. Jonah 4:3; 1 Kgs 19:4b). On every point Jonah turns out to be an antiprophet or, alternatively, the true picture of prophecy. As Jonah fled because he knew that Nineveh would listen and be saved, so prophets traditionally spoke only to those who would not listen and be saved. They were not very interested in the word of God, just self-serving and rather too keen on using it to explain the evil that befell the city. It was time to put an end to the tradition.

The twentieth and twenty-first paragraphs (4:4–6a) ridicule the stubbornness of Jonah. Yahweh questions his right to be angry, but Jonah does not even answer. He goes out and sits in the shade and waits for Yahweh to bring the threatened evil on the city. He builds the hut symbolic of the destruction of Jerusalem and life in the open,[249] but God who is in heaven and who made the sea and *terra firma* grows a plant. His hut is to nurture his anger. God's plant is to shelter him from that same evil anger.

The last paragraphs (4:6b–11) keep focusing on Jonah as an alter-Elijah and represent God's final answer to the pretensions of the prophetic and historiographic traditions. Jonah sits under the plant as Elijah sat under the juniper tree (Jonah 4:6b–7; 1 Kgs 19:4), and when the plant withers he asks to die as Elijah had begged (Jonah 4:8b; 1 Kgs 19:4b). Jonah has forgotten about the fate of the city and worries about his own. God is still interested in the city, as the God of heaven might be, because it is a big city full of people and animals that just such a God may have created.[250] The characteristic feature of these people, and the only one that God mentions, is their total ignorance. It is a lot better than anything that Jonah knows.

The psalm that the revision of the book has Jonah sing in the belly of the whale is filled with traditional wisdom. It is composed of stereotyped phrases and a concatenation of quotations from other psalms[251] and probably reflects the availability of the book of Psalms to its readers. It is a good commentary on the storm at sea in the first part and recognizes that description's dependence on Ezekiel's ballad of Tyre.[252] It deals with the theme of death implicit in the three days and three nights that Jonah spent in the belly of the whale and explicit in his desire for death rather than life. It describes death as a walled city at the foot of the mountains under the seas and so contrasts it with the great city where Jonah is sent. But it takes Yahweh out of heaven, out of his role as the God who made the sea and the dry land, the plants and the animals and people, and puts him in his holy temple. It contradicts the story of Jonah by putting a prayer in his mouth, a prayer of thanksgiving from the belly of the whale, and a prayer of petition during the storm, which Jonah says he never recited. It disagrees with the story that tried to show that prophetic and historiographic interpretations of the fall of Jerusalem were wrong and self-serving by appealing to the idolatry that these sources blamed for the fall of the city. It is odd and irregular, but the book of Jonah would not be prophecy without it.

Conclusion

The book of Jonah is a comedy deriding the pretensions of prophecy. It comes after the peak of prophecy and during the spate of revisions that tried to make the prophetic tradition conform to the theorems of the Deuteronomistic History. Its inspiration was Joel and Job and their determined resistance to fate and contrived necessity.

The comedy might have many points but one of them is that if Nineveh, the king, the potentates, the people big and small, and the animals, could repent and be saved at the word of a stubborn and unwilling prophet, then Jerusalem could have been saved. It was not and either the theory is wrong or nobody wanted it saved. It is not a question of sin and guilt but of punishment. God does it. God is merciful. God can change his mind. This is not the God of the revisionist prophetic and historiographic tradition, but the God of simple uneducated people. They do not know, therefore, that God is not supposed to do as he pleases but is supposed to act in accordance with the system of retribution that people like the Deuteronomist and the writer of the book of Jeremiah devised to explain what had actually happened. If Nineveh could repent and be saved, it is nonsense to suggest that the reform of Josiah did nothing. If Nineveh repented at a few words of Jonah, it is stupid to insist that Jerusalem did not listen to the compendium of prophecy in the archive of Jeremiah.

The seeds of Jonah's view are present in the prophets who came just before the fall of Jerusalem. They all situated fate in the theory of creation and saw the punishment of Jerusalem as a kind of reversal of creation. Jonah saw it the same way and simply left out the attributions of guilt and inevitable punishment. It was just as easy for him to suppose that God could change his mind when people repented as others found it to pretend that he could only be satisfied by expending his wrath.

The book of Jonah confronts the interpretations of the prophetic tradition as they developed after the fact during the exile. It does not deny guilt; it just does not make it the answer. Evil can befall the sailors, who have no guilt, or not befall guilty Nineveh. Guilt and evil are not correlative.

The Revisions

The revisions of the prophets produced a whole new body of literature. It was limited at times by editorial necessities and constraints, a little hackneyed at times by its involvement in disputation, but quite remarkable in its understanding and in its expression of the tradition.

II ISAIAH (FIG. 21)

Isaiah had been the fulcrum of prophetic tradition. His vision was unprecedented in declaring Yahweh's opposition to the Jerusalem understanding of the state. It was disconcerting, above all, in the certainty that he ascribed to it by recording it in writing for some later day. Every one of the prophets dealt with it, and when it actually occurred, II Isaiah went through it again in the light of these later works to glean from it some fragment of hope for the future.

The Deuteronomistic Historian, equally critical of the narrow Judean viewpoint, described this prophetic tradition as a continuous succession of servants of Yahweh who had urged the people to repent and avoid their otherwise inevitable doom and who had been mocked and even killed for their trouble. Inasmuch as repentance, on the Historian's terms, required absolute allegiance to Yahweh according to the standards set out in the law, the Deuteronomistic position was consistent and completely accurate. But it was not quite fair and gave little credence to the positive forces of history that had been manifested in reform and renovation and revealed by Isaiah in his vision of the rebuilding of Zion on a foundation of faith and according to the plan of justice. II Isaiah, to sift out the positive elements in the tradition, had to deal with the dark side of history revealed by the Deuteronomist.

II Isaiah rewrote Isaiah's prophecy in five parts. The first part rewrites Isaiah's vision of the Assyrians invading a deserving sinful kingdom as a vision of Assyria's defeat and the renewal of the Davidic kingdom. The second part depicts the fall of Babylon and the destruction of its dynasty and, in a series of oracles to cities and nations situated at the cardinal points, draws a schematic map of the world that will do homage to Yahweh and David in Zion. The third part rewrites Isaiah's vision of the siege and capture of Jerusalem to include the narrative of its miraculous escape in the time of Hezekiah and

FIGURE 21

II Isaiah

Part One

1:1	2:1–2a	6:1–2	7:1–3aAb	10:5–6	11:1–2
1:2	2:2b–4bA	6:3–4	7:4	10:7	11:3–4
1:3	2:4bB–5				
		6:5	7:5–6	10:13	11:5–6
1:4	3:13–14a	6:6–7	7:7–9	10:14	11:7–8
1:5–6	3:14b–15				
		6:8–10	7:10–14a	10:15	11:9
1:7abA	5:1a	6:11	7:14b–15	10:16–17	11:10
1:8	5:1b–2a			10:18–19	
	5:2b		8:1–4		12:1
1:16–17			8:5–8	10:24–25	12:2
1:18a	5:3			10:26	
1:18b–20	5:4		8:9–10	10:27	12:3–5
	5:5		8:11–15		12:6
1:21				10:28	
1:22–23aA	5:6		8:23°	10:29	
1:23aBb	5:7		9:1–3		
				10:30	
1:24–26a	5:8		9:4	10:31–32	
1:26b	5:9–10		9:5–6abA	10:33–34	
	5:11–12				
	5:13				
	5:18–19				
	5:20–23				
	5:24				
	5:26				
	5:27				
	5:28				
	5:29				

Part Two

14:1–2	15:1–2a	18:1–2	21:1–2abA	22:1–2	23:1
14:3	15:2b	18:3	21:2bB	22:3	23:2–3
14:4–6	15:3	18:4	21:3–4	22:4	23:4
14:7–8	15:4	18:5	21:5	22:5	23:5–6
14:9	15:5a	18:6	21:6–7	22:6–11	23:7
14:10–11	15:5b–6	18:7	21:8	22:12–13	23:8–9
14:12	16:1		21:9	22:14–16	23:10–11
14:13–14	16:2		21:10	22:17–19	23:12
14:15–17	16:3–4a			22:20–21	
14:18–19	16:4b–5			22:22–24	
14:20					
14:21					

continued

FIGURE 21 *(cont)*

Part Three

28:9–10	29:1	30:1–2	36:1–10	38:1–3	39:1–2
28:11–12	29:2–3	30:3–5	36:11–22	38:4–8	39:3–4
28:13	29:4				
		30:6abA	37:1–20	38:9–20	39:5–7
28:14	29:5–6	30:6bB	37:21–38	38:21–22	39:8
28:15	29:7	30:7			
28:16	29:8				
28:17–18		30:8			
28:19	29:9–10	30:9–11			
	29:11–12				
28:20	29:13–14	30:12–14			
28:21		30:15–17			
28:22	29:15				
	29:16				
28:23–26					
28:27–28	29:17				
28:29	29:18–19				
	29:20–21				
	29:22				
	29:23–24				

Part Four

40:1–2	41:1	42:1	43:1	45:1	47:1–2
40:3–5	41:2–3	42:2–4	43:2	45:2–3	47:3
40:6	41:4	42:5	43:3	45:4	47:4
40:7–8	41:5–6	42:6–7	43:4	45:5–6a	47:5
40:9–10	41:8–9	42:10	43:5–6	45:6b–7	47:6a
40:11	41:10	42:11–12	43:7–8	45:8	47:6b–7
	41:11–12	42:13	43:9	45:9–10	47:8
	41:13	42:14–16°	43:10–11	45:11	47:9
	41:14		43:12–13	45:12–13a	47:10a
	41:15–16		43:14–15	45:13b	47:10b–11
	41:17–18		43:16–17a		
	41:19–20		43:17b		
			43:18–19		
			43:20–21		

Part Five

49:1–3	50:1a	51:1	52:7	54:1	55:1
49:4	50:1b	51:2	52:8	54:2–3	55:2
49:5	50:2a	51:3	52:9	54:4	55:3

continued

FIGURE 21 (*cont*)

49:6	50:2b–3	51:4	52:10	54:5	55:4–5
49:7	50:4	51:5	52:11	54:6	55:6–7
49:8	50:5	51:6	52:12	54:7–8	55:8–9
49:9	50:6	51:7	52:13–14	54:9	55:10
49:10–11	50:7	51:8	52:15	54:10	55:11
49:12	50:8	51:9a	53:1–2a	54:11–12a	55:12
49:13	50:9	51:9b–10	53:2b–3	54:12b–13	55:13
49:14	50:10	51:11	53:4	54:14	
49:15	50:11	51:12	53:5	54:15	
49:16–17		51:13	53:6	54:16	
49:18		51:14	53:7	54:17	
49:19		51:15	53:8		
49:20		51:16	53:9		
49:21		51:17	53:10–11		
49:22–23aA		51:18	53:12		
49:23aBb		51:19			
49:24–26		51:20			
		51:21–22			
		51:23			

Figure 21. Stanzas are on separate lines. Strophes are separated by a space.

intimations of its reprieve at the end of the Babylonian exile. The fourth part describes the fall of Babylon, the glorious return of Yahweh and Jacob to Zion, and the submission of all the nations to Yahweh and his servant. The last part portrays the liberation of Zion, reunion with the returning exiles, the restoration of the Davidic regime, and the deliverance of the world.[253]

In the first part II Isaiah shows considerable familiarity with the Deuteronomistic History and quotes from it approvingly, but disagrees with it on its evaluation of the monarchy. In the early chapters II Isaiah agrees with Isaiah that the people have refused to listen (chaps. 1–6*) and with the Deuteronomistic notion that this refusal spells their doom. The difference is that II Isaiah looks to the monarchy—specifically to a king in the line of David and the image of Hezekiah—to institute justice and establish peace in the world (chaps. 7–12). In the third part, therefore, where Isaiah is very critical of the kings, II Isaiah quotes a revised version of the Deuteronomist's account of the reign of Hezekiah that omits his supposed capitulation to Sennacherib and makes him out to be the model of the once and future king.

II AMOS (FIGS. 5, 5A)

The writer who redid the prophecy of Amos mostly wrote footnotes to the original cantos to explain the reasons and the limits of the calamity that Amos described. The revision shows a remarkable comprehension of the Deuteronomistic History, relies on its syntheses, uses its language, agrees with much of what it had said, and is circumspect in its disagreements.

In the first canto, besides including the by-now-standard vituperation of Edom and Tyre, and attributing Judah's downfall to neglect of the written law,[254] the writer sums up the history of Israel as it was recorded in the Deuteronomistic History.[255] In the second canto, the writer shares the Deuteronomist's contempt for the altar at Bethel and is familiar with the prayer that Solomon recited at the dedication of the temple but describes Amos as a faithful prophet who pleaded with the people to repent.[256] In the third canto this writer begins to develop the theory of the remnant, which the Historian seems to have applied only to the situation in Judah, to include some part of the northern kingdom (Amos 5:14–15).[257] In the last canto the editor takes issue with the Deuteronomistic History over its characterization of Amos and its theory of sin. In telling the story of the prophet from Judah who went to Bethel, the Historian ridiculed Amos and limited his prophetic function to predicting the career of Josiah. In the editor's opinion Amos was a great prophet who confronted Jeroboam and fearlessly spoke the words of Yahweh and correctly predicted the end of the northern kingdom.[258] In the Historian's view both kingdoms were doomed because of the sins committed and inspired by their kings (e.g., 2 Kings 17; 21), but in the editor's opinion only the sinners were doomed and some from each kingdom survived to flourish under the restored kingdom of David (Amos 9).

II JEREMIAH

The book of Jeremiah is a replacement for the concluding part of the Deuteronomistic book of Kings.[259] It is written in imitation of the Historian's work—in prose where possible, with some of the old clichés and others like them—but it differs from the authoritative account on fundamental matters relating to sin and the covenant.[260]

The last part of Kings gives the impression that prophecy was almost nonexistent from the reign of Manasseh to the end of the kingdom, but the book of Jeremiah makes it abundantly clear that Jeremiah was very active from the time of Josiah until after the fall of Jerusalem and stood alone against a strong prophetic peace movement.[261] In this part the Deuteronomist argues that the kingdom was destroyed because of sin, specifically sin against the basic stipulation of the decalogue prohibiting the worship of other Gods, but focuses on the inevitable repercussions of the sin of Manasseh. The book of Jeremiah includes all this but goes on to show that the kingdom was destroyed because specific kings refused to listen to the words of Jeremiah—not just to standard prophetic calls for repentance, but to daring and offensive words urging them to surrender to the Babylonians.[262] One reason for the Historian's concentration on the sin of Manasseh was to prejudge Josiah's reform and prove that the covenant theory, which he was made to represent, had to give way to the law and the promises and predestination. The author of the book of Jeremiah did not agree and went so far as to base the future on a new covenant that was to embrace the law, wisdom, and every natural expectation (cf. Jer 31:31–34).

The reign of Manasseh was long, peaceful, and prosperous and filled with the historical and prophetic activity that made the reform of Josiah possible. The Deuteronomistic Historian did not have a good word to say about his reign and the author of Jeremiah was willing to skip it. It was making a fool out of Jeremiah and the reform that he fostered that prompted the editor of his work to write the unauthorized biography of Jeremiah and his unpublished interpretation of history.

II EZEKIEL (FIG. 16)

Ezekiel had written a prophetic history of the last days of Judah and Jerusalem, and his editor was anxious to bring it into line with familiar and acceptable traditions. The prophets, what they said and how they comported themselves, were the principal target of the revision, but the conformity of Ezekiel's vision to the Deuteronomistic interpretation of the past was an important clue to its orthodoxy.

In his visions Ezekiel saw the glory of Yahweh in something like human appearance, once in exile by the river Chebar, once in the temple in Jerusalem. His editor was scandalized by the vision and converted it into an inaugural prophetic commission, like II Isaiah's or Jeremiah's, in the picturesque and flamboyant setting of the Solomonic temple (Ezekiel 1–3; 8–11).[263] In his vision of the glory of Yahweh returning to the temple Ezekiel saw its basic structural features and its significance in the restoration of the land. His editor took the occasion to fill it with regulations and with replicas of its Solomonic functionaries and furniture and to reenact the restoration of the land according to the plan set out in the book of Joshua (Ezekiel 40–48).

The editor agrees with the History on most points. When Ezekiel prepares food for the siege, the editor has him protest his faithful observance of the dietary laws (Ezek 4:14).[264] When Ezekiel shaves his head and his beard to signify the end of Jerusalem, the editor agrees with the Deuteronomist that some will escape (Ezek 5:3–4, 7–10; 6:9).[265] In Ezekiel's version Yahweh summons executioners to destroy the city, but in the revised version they stand beside the bronze altar in the Solomonic temple to hear Yahweh's instructions (Ezek 9:2b–3).[266] When Ezekiel describes the breaching of the walls and the flight into exile, the editor interprets it as the attempted escape and capture of Zedekiah (Ezekiel 12).[267] Ezekiel explains why it is impossible to make inquiry of Yahweh for the people, and the revised version adds a scene derived from the Deuteronomistic story of Sodom and Gomorrah to affirm the justice of God in such circumstances (Ezek 14:10, 12–23).[268] The Deuteronomist was critical of kings and idealized monarchs who would be viceroys of Yahweh, and the editor of the book of Ezekiel is critical of kings and idealizes leaders who might be his adjutants.[269] Such agreement with the Deuteronomist allowed this edition to refurbish Ezekiel and gave legitimacy to its bold but significant contribution to the development of the law.[270]

II HOSEA

The editor of Hosea, like the editor of Ezekiel, relied wholeheartedly on the Deuteronomistic History to fit the original dazzling drama into the more familiar patterns of historical and prophetic tradition. Like the Deuteronomist, but without the same discrimination, the editor dealt with the categories of prophecy, law, and history.

Prophets and prophecy are represented in the genre and the content of the editor's additions. Hosea told of the birth of three children with ominous names, but the editor contradicted him with a salvation oracle indebted to the Deuteronomist for its terms and formulations (Hos 2:1–2, 3).[271] Hosea's concern for the nation's lack of knowledge of God is pointed in this edition by blaming the prophets (Hos 4:5). Hosea's portrayal of Ephraim's worship of Asherah at its hilltop shrines provokes the editor to utter a typical, in fact a borrowed, prophetic appeal to conversion (Hos 9:15).[272] Similar, more or less impassionate statements by Hosea provoke the same kind of sentimental reflection or appeal (Hos 5:5; 7:10). The concluding historical triptych, especially, is framed and dotted by impassioned pleas and assurances that give the book its final prophetic thrust (Hos 11:6–11; 12:6–7; 14:1–10).

The law is associated with the priests. The sterile symbolic marriage into which Hosea enters in this edition represents Israel's deprivation of priesthood, sacrifice, and the forbidden elements of ancestral religion before it is reunited under David in observance of the law (Hos 3:1–5).[273] In defining what he meant by the lack of knowledge of God, Hosea mentioned dishonesty and false oaths, but his editor ransacked the decalogue to add murder, stealing, and adultery to the list (Hos 4:2). Not surprisingly, therefore, the priests are accused of rejecting knowledge and forgetting the law, and their forgetfulness is illustrated in the murders, thefts, and adulteries that they and their families commit (Hos 4:4–5, 6b, 13b–14; 6:7–11; 7:1b).

History is associated with the kings and the bedevilment of worship. Most of the references are obscure or jarring in their contexts or explicable only by counterreference to associated passages. The odd intrusion of the valley of Achor refers to the ancient misuse of silver and gold, the very elements of idolatry, which were meant for the service of God (Hos 2:17).[274] The strange collusion between priests and kings at Mizpah and Tabor could refer to the monarchic temptations of Gideon and to Jephthah's thoughtless sacrifice of his daughter, or to any one of the times that Mizpah was at the center of kingship and conspiracy.[275] The references to Gibeah, Ramah, Bethel, and Benjamin are allusions to the story of the decimation of Benjamin, where the same towns and shrines figure prominently or in passing and in anticipation of the story of Saul.[276] The mention of insolent princes who will die by the sword in Egypt could allude to any one of the times that Judah was condemned for its Egyptian alliances.[277] Kingship was not a good idea and was the source or manifestation of idolatry, as the Deuteronomist often insisted.[278] The last reference is to the war in which Shalmaneser conquered Samaria and, with no good source in the History, marks the seriousness of the editor's historical intent (Hos 10:13–15; cf. 2 Kgs 18:9).

II MICAH

The editor of Micah demonstrates some literal familiarity with the Deuteronomistic History but very little interest in its presentation. It is mostly a crude basis for the second edition's resistance to the work of II Isaiah. As the original prophecy was deeply indebted to Isaiah, so the second edition tries to remain faithful to the early tradition and critical of the updating that it received from Isaiah's avid disciple. The History was helpful in providing some of the needed words, ideas, and images.

II JOEL

The editor of Joel, like many contemporaries, was influenced more by the language and individual concepts of the Deuteronomist than by the Historian's interpretation, system, or speculation. It is the final tribute to the History, perhaps, that it became the stuff of hard core apocalyptic.[279]

III ISAIAH (FIG. 22)

III Isaiah's main sources were Isaiah and II Isaiah. He used their phrasing and wrote variations on their themes and made their writings and research the basis of his own composition. He was familiar with the work of the other prophets and imitated the meditative mode of the Psalmists, but he was influenced especially by current philosophical speculation and by the historical theory of the book of Jeremiah. The Deuteronomistic History is of importance to III Isaiah only in responding to II Isaiah's use or misuse of the source.[280]

III Isaiah divided the first part of II Isaiah's commentary into two distinct sections, one dealing with the purification of Zion (chaps. 1–5), the other with the Syro-Ephraimite war and the return of the exiles from both kingdoms (chaps. 6–12).[281] II Isaiah looked forward to the exaltation of Zion and the restoration of the Davidic monarchy, but III Isaiah despised all forms of human arrogance and looked forward to a humble and purified existence under the dominion of Yahweh.

The first chapter (Isa 1:1–9)[282] was changed by the addition of a line to one of the stanzas and of a stanza in the third strophe composed by Isaiah. The line repeats two words used by Isaiah in the same stanza and includes a word that always refers to the destruction of Sodom and Gomorrah.[283] The stanza refers to the same story but also introduces the theory of the remnant by repeating one of the original words of Isaiah and drawing on several Deuteronomistic expressions for escape and survival.[284]

The second chapter (1:10–31)[285] continues the story and begins III Isaiah's critique of II Isaiah's defense of the Davidic monarchy by referring to the kings as leaders of Sodom and Gomorrah. Its repudiation of senseless sacrifice is based on texts of Amos and Hosea and the Deuteronomistic History, and its elimination of the sinners who are

FIGURE 22

III Isaiah

Part One

1:1	1:10	2:1–2a	3:1–3	4:2	5:1a
1:2	1:11	2:2b–4bA	3:4–5	4:3	5:1b–2a
1:3	1:12	2:4bB–5			5:2b
			3:6–7	4:4–5a	
1:4	1:13	2:6	3:8	4:5b–6	5:3
1:5–6	1:14	2:7–8			5:4
	1:15		3:9		5:5
1:7		2:9	3:10–12		
1:8	1:16–17	2:10			5:6
1:9	1:18a		3:13–14a		5:7
	1:18b–20	2:11	3:14b–15		
		2:12–16			5:8
	1:21		3:16–17		5:9–10
	1:22–23aA	2:17	3:18–23		
	1:23aBb	2:18–19			5:11–12
			3:24a		5:13
	1:24–26a	2:20–21	3:24b–4:1		
	1:26b	2:22			5:14
					5:15–17
	1:27–28				
	2:29–31				5:18–19
					5:20–23
					5:24
					5:25a
					5:25b
					5:26
					5:27
					5:28
					5:29
					5:30

Part Two

6:1–2	7:1–3	8:1–4	8:23°	10:1–2	11:1–2
6:3–4	7:4	8:5–8	9:1–3	10:3–4	11:3–4
6:5	7:5–6	8:9–10	9:4	10:5–6	11:5–6
6:6–7	7:7–9	8:11–15	9:5–6	10:7	11:7–8
6:8–10	7:10–14a	8:16–18	9:7–9	10:8–11	11:9
6:11	7:14b–16	8:19	9:10–11a	10:12	11:10
6:12	7:17	8:20–23°	9:11b		11:11–12

continued

FIGURE 2 2 *(cont)*

7:18–19	9:12–14	10:13	11:13
7:20	9:15–16a	10:14	11:14–15
	9:16b		11:16
7:21–22		10:15	
7:23–25	9:17–18	10:16–17	
	9:19–20a	10:18–19	
	9:20b		
		10:20	
		10:21–23	
		10:24–25	
		10:26	
		10:27	
		10:28	
		10:29	
		10:30	
		10:31–32	
		10:33–34	

Part Three

13:1	14:1–2	14:28–29	15:1–2a	17:1–3	18:1–2
13:2	14:3	14:30	15:2b	17:4–6	18:3
13:3					
	14:4–6	14:31	15:3	17:7–8	18:4
13:4–5	14:7–8	14:32	15:4	17:9	18:5
13:6–8					
	14:9		15:5a	17:10	18:6
13:9	14:10–11		15:5b–6	17:11	18:7
13:10					
	14:12		15:7–8	17:12–13	
13:11–12	14:13–14		15:9	17:14	
13:13					
	14:15–17		16:1		
13:14–16	14:18–19		16:2		
13:17–18					
	14:20		16:3–4a		
13:19	14:21		16:4b–5		
13:20–22	14:22–23				
			16:6–7		
	14:24		16:8		
	14:25				
	14:26–27		16:9–10		
			16:11–12		
			16:13		

continued

FIGURE 22 *(cont)*

Part Four

19:1–2	20:1–2a	21:1–2abA	21:11	22:1–2	23:1
19:3–4	20:2b–4	21:2bB	21:12	22:3	23:2–3
19:5–6aA	20:5	21:3–4	21:13–15	22:4	23:4
19:6aBb–7	20:6	21:5	21:16–17	22:5	23:5–6
19:8–10					
		21:6–7		22:6–11	23:7
19:11		21:8		22:12–13	23:8–9
19:12					
		21:9		22:14–16	23:10–11
19:13–14a		21:10		22:17–19	23:12
19:14b–15					
				22:20–21	23:13
19:16–17				22:22–25	23:14
19:18–20					
					23:15–16
19:21–22					23:17–18
19:23					
19:24–25					

Part Five

24:1–2	24:17–18	25:1–2	26:1	26:12	27:1
24:3	24:19–20	25:3–4	26:2–3	26:13	27:2–3
24:4	24:21–22a	25:5	26:4–5a	26:14	27:4–5
24:5–6	24:22b–23	25:6	26:5b–6	26:15–16	27:6
24:7–8		25:7	26:7	26:17–18a	27:7–8
24:9		25:8	26:8–9	26:18b–19a	27:9
24:10–12		25:9	26:10	26:19b	27:10
24:13		25:10–12	26:11	16:20	27:11
24:14–15					27:12
24:16					27:13

Part Six

28:1	29:1	30:1–2	30:18	31:1	32:1–2
28:2	29:2–3	30:3–5	30:19	31:2	32:3–4
	29:4				
28:3–4		30:6abA	30:20–21	31:3	32:5–6
28:5–6	29:5–6	30:6bB	30:22	31:4–5	32:7–8
	29:7	30:7			
28:7–8	29:8		30:23	31:6–7	32:9
28:9–10		30:8	30:24	31:8–9	32:10
28:11–12		30:9–11			

continued

FIGURE 22 (*cont*)

28:13	29:9-10		30:25	32:11-13a
	29:11-12	30:12-14	30:26	32:13b-14
28:14	29:13-14	30:15-17		
28:15			30:27	32:15-17
28:16	29:15		30:28	32:18-20
28:17-18	29:16			
28:19			30:29	
	29:17		30:30	
28:20	29:18-19			
28:21	29:20-21		30:31-32	
28:22			30:33	
	29:22			
28:23-26	29:23-24			
28:27-28				
28:29				

Part Seven

33:1	34:1	35:1-2aA	36:1-10	38:1-3	39:1-2
33:2	34:2-3a	35:2aBb	36:11-22	38:4-8	39:3-4
	34:3b-4				
33:3-4		35:3-4	37:1-20	38:9-20	39:5-7
33:5-6	34:5	35:5-7	37:21-38	38:21-22	39:8
	34:6a				
33:7		35:8-9			
33:8-9	34:6b-7	35:10			
	34:8-9				
33:10					
33:11-12	34:10				
	34:11-12				
33:13-14					
33:15-16	34:13-14				
	34:15				
33:17-18					
33:19	34:16				
	34:17				
33:20					
33:21-22					
33:23					
33:24					

Part Eight

40:1-2	41:1	42:1	43:1	44:1-2	45:1
40:3-5	41:2-3	42:2-4	43:2	44:3-4	45:2-3
40:6	41:4	42:5	43:3	44:5	45:4
40:7-8	41:5-6	42:6-7	43:4	44:6	45:5-6a
	41:7				

continued

F I G U R E   2 2 (*cont*)

40:9–10		42:8	43:5–6	44:7	45:6b–7
40:11	41:8–9	42:9	43:7–8	44:8	45:8
	41:10				
40:12		42:10	43:9	44:9	45:9–10
40:13–14	41:11–12	42:11–12	43:10–11	44:10–11	45:11
	41:13				
40:15		42:13	43:12–13	44:12	45:12–13a
40:16–17	41:14	42:14–16°	43:14–15	44:13	45:13b
	41:15–16				
40:18		42:16bB	43:16–17a	44:14	45:14a
40:19–20	41:17–18	42:17	43:17b	44:15	45:14b–15
	41:19–20				
40:21–23		42:18–20	43:18–19	44:16	45:16
40:24	41:21	42:21–22	43:20–21	44:17	45:17
	41:22–24				
40:25–26		42:23–24	43:22–24	44:18–19	45:18
40:27	41:25	42:25	43:25	44:20	45:19
	41:26				
40:28			43:26	44:21	45:20a
40:29–31	41:27–28a		43:27–28	44:22	45:20b
	41:28b–29				
				44:23–25a	45:21
				44:25b–28	45:22
					45:23
					45:24–25

Part Nine

46:1	47:1–2	48:1a	49:1–3	50:1a	51:1
46:2	47:3	48:1b–2	49:4	50:1b	51:2
46:3	47:4	48:3–4	49:5	50:2a	51:3
46:4	47:5	48:5	49:6	50:2b–3	51:4
46:5–7aA	47:6a	48:6	49:7	50:4	51:5
46:7aBb	47:6b–7	48:7–8a	49:8	50:5	51:6
46:8–11	47:8	48:8b–9	49:9	50:6	51:7
46:12–13	47:9	48:10–11	49:10–11	50:7	51:8
	47:10a	48:12	49:12	50:8	51:9a
	47:10b–11	48:13	49:13	50:9	51:9b–10
	47:12	48:14	49:14	50:10	51:11
	47:13	48:15–16	49:15	50:11	51:12
	47:14	48:17	49:16–17		51:13
	47:15	48:18–19	49:18		51:14

continued

F I G U R E   2 2 *(cont)*

48:20	49:19	51:15
48:21	49:20	51:16
	49:21	51:17
	49:22–23aA	51:18
	49:23aBb	51:19
	49:24–26	51:20
		51:21–22
		51:23

Part Ten

52:1	54:1	55:1	57:1	58:1	59:1–2
52:2	54:2–3	55:2	57:2–3	58:2	59:3
52:3	54:4	55:3	57:4	58:3	59:4
52:4	54:5	55:4–5	57:5	58:4	59:5
52:5	54:6	55:6–7	57:6	58:5	59:6
52:6	54:7–8	55:8–9	57:7	58:6	59:7
52:7	54:9	55:10	57:8–9	58:7	59:8
52:8	54:10	55:11	57:10	58:8	59:9
52:9	54:11–12a	55:12	57:11	58:9	59:10–11
52:10	54:12b–13	55:13	57:12–13	58:10	59:12
52:11	54:14	56:1	57:14	58:11	59:13–14a
52:12	54:15	56:2	57:15–16	58:12	59:14b–16
52:13–14	54:16	56:3	57:17–19a	58:13	59:17
52:15	54:17	56:4	57:19b–21	58:14	59:18
53:1–2a		56:5			59:19–20
53:2b–3		56:6			59:21
53:4		56:7			
53:5		56:8–9			
53:6		56:10a			
53:7		56:10b			
53:8		56:11			
53:9		56:12			
53:10–11					
53:12					

continued

FIGURE 22 *(cont)*

Part Eleven

60:1–2a	61:1	62:1	63:1	65:1–3	66:1
60:2b–3	61:2–3	62:2–3	63:2–3	65:4–5	66:2
60:4	61:4–5	62:4	63:4–5	65:6–7	66:3a
60:5–6	61:6–7	62:5	63:6	65:8	66:3b–4
60:7	61:8–9	62:6a	63:7	65:9	66:5
60:8–9	61:10–11	62:6b–7	63:8–9	65:10	66:6–7
60:10–11		62:8–9	63:10–13	65:11	66:8–9
60:12–13		62:10	63:14	65:12	66:10–11
60:14		62:11	63:15	65:13	66:12–13
60:15		62:12	63:16	65:14	66:14
60:16			63:17	65:15	66:15
60:17			63:18–19a	65:16	66:16–17
60:18			63:19b–64:1	65:17	66:18–19a
60:19			64:2–3	65:18	66:19b–20
60:20			64:4	65:19	66:21–22
60:21–22			64:5	65:20–21	66:23–24
			64:6	65:22	
			64:7–8	65:23	
			64:9–10	65:24	
			64:11	65:25	

Figure 22. Stanzas are on separate lines. Strophes are separated by a space.

guilty of such ritual offenses allows the remnant to be identified as those who are ritually pure.[286]

The third chapter (2:1–22) incorporates II Isaiah's ode to Zion into a massive diatribe against human initiative and pride that simply rejects everything the original praised. II Isaiah appealed to the house of Jacob to walk in the light of the Lord, but III Isaiah says that the Lord has rejected the house of Jacob. The exaltation of the mountain of Zion is countered by its actual leveling. The wonderful but indeterminate future that II Isaiah foretold becomes the dreaded day of Yahweh. The assembly of the nations thronging to Jerusalem to worship Yahweh is replaced by unwanted foreigners who fill the city. Pride is represented by Solomon, who amassed silver, gold, horses, and chariots and who was seduced, as the Historian imagined, by his foreign wives into worshiping other Gods. Pride goes before a fall, and the fall, as the Deuteronomist insisted, is caused by the worship of idols, which would not be forgiven but would lead to the rejection of the nation (2:1–22).[287]

The fourth and fifth chapters (3:1–4:1; 4:2–6) are based on II Isaiah's description of Yahweh's lawsuit against the nations and against the leaders of his own people. They disagree with II Isaiah's vision of the restoration of Zion by omitting the assembly of the nations and by making Zion the exclusive residence of a purified worshiping community (4:2–6; cf. 2:1–5). They anticipate and deride II Isaiah's expectation of a child who would be heir to the Davidic throne by describing the desperate straits of a city ruled by insolent children (3:1–5; cf. 7:10–15; 9:1–6abA; 11:1–10) and by ridiculing the idea that the ruined city would be governed by an upstart from Bethlehem.[288] They declare unclean the woman who might have given birth to this royal child and replace the vaunted Davidic kingdom with a holy remnant born of Yahweh and Zion (3:16–4:1; 4:2–6). The whole section is an elaborate portrayal of the destruction of Judah and Jerusalem that takes the Historian's theory of government to its logical conclusion by substituting a pathetic religious regime, framed by a theocracy, for II Isaiah's vision of a cosmopolitan capital governed by a son of David.[289]

The second section incorporates Isaiah's explanation of the Assyrian invasion and II Isaiah's argument for the restoration of the Davidic dynasty into a comprehensive restatement of III Isaiah's doctrine of the remnant. The issue is defined at the start by identifying the Davidic shoot from the stump of Jesse with the holy remnant (6:13; cf. 4:2–3; 10:33–11:10) and by including among the children of Isaiah one who is called "A Remnant Shall Return," a rival of the child Immanuel (7:3; 10:20–23). When II Isaiah tried to rewrite the history of the Syro-

Ephraimite war to correct the Deuteronomist and restore the sequel's version magnifying Hezekiah, III Isaiah rewrote the chapter to erase Immanuel and insist on his idea of a remnant (7:1–15).[290] When II Isaiah named another child "Quick-Plunder-Fast-Booty" to symbolize the ruin of Judah and ushered in Immanuel to signal the ephemeral success of the Assyrian invaders, III Isaiah insisted that he and his own children, including "A Remnant Shall Return," were the true symbols and, in overt disagreement with II Isaiah, warned against listening to mediums and wizards who would conjure the dead on behalf of the living.[291] When II Isaiah launched into praise of the child Immanuel, III Isaiah returned to II Isaiah's starting point and gave another version of the Syro-Ephraimite war that implicated both the leaders and the prophets — a veiled allusion to II Isaiah and the Davidides — in the final ruin of the country.[292] When II Isaiah suggested that the neo-Davidic king would be the scourge of the invading armies, III Isaiah disagreed by assigning the king's titulary to God and predicting that only a remnant would return to Yahweh.[293] When II Isaiah eulogized the successor of David and basked in the era of peace and justice that he would inaugurate, III Isaiah predicted the end of the feud that had erupted into the Syro-Ephraimite war and summoned the remnant of Israel and Judah from all the nations of the world where they had been dispersed (cf. 11:1–10 and 11–16). Their disagreement is played out against the background of the Deuteronomistic History, and each is capable of referring to it to suit the argument and the mood.

Conclusion

III Isaiah was a compendium of all prophecy and heralded the end of the prophetic tradition. After him musicians and orators — Nahum, Habakkuk, and Zephaniah — were entered on the rolls of the prophets, but after them the prophets were singers or politicians. Everyone knew the Deuteronomistic History, but no disagreement was sufficient to dislodge it and every reference enhanced its power and authority. What was left was the arduous but simpler task of reconstruction.

NOTES

[1] That the event is unprecedented is affirmed by questioning whether something that has never happened before could actually have happened in the recent past (1:2b). That it is also unique and will not happen again is affirmed by surveying the generations to come (1:3).

2 Cf. Joel 1:2 ("Hear this . . . and listen . . . ") and 1:5 ("Wake up . . . and wail . . . ").

3 Joel 1:2a (summons) + 2b (question).

4 The invocation and its reason (1:8, 10b) enclose the list of effects (1:9–10a).

5 The contrast in the four-line stanza is between the city and the country (2:1aA + 1aBb). The six-line stanza portrays the darkness moving across the land (2:2).

6 Two-line stanzas are variants of four-line stanzas. They contain an emphatic contrast and, in the manner of three-line stanzas, are exclamatory comments on their context.

7 Five-line stanzas are descriptive and combine images and their imaginative interpretation.

8 The seven-line stanza combines the image of troops advancing with the image of locusts swarming (2:8aBb–9). The ten-line stanza has five main clauses describing a violent thunderstorm instigated by Yahweh (2:10–11aA) and five subordinate clauses identifying it as the day of Yahweh when he advances with his army (2:11aBb).

9 In the first stanza the lament involves repentance, fasting, crying, mourning, sorrow, and conversion (2:12–13a), and the motive is the kindness and mercy of Yahweh (2:13b). The second stanza reflects on the results of Yahweh's forgiveness.

10 The priests persuade Yahweh to act by appealing, as Moses did (Exod 32:12; Num 14:15–16; Deut 9:28), to his world renown.

11 The formulaic future is *wĕhāyâ* + temporal phrase or clause (3:1, "afterwards" [*'aḥărê kēn*]) + *yqtl*. It has the same syntactic function as the formulaic perfect (*wayhî* + temporal phrase or clause + *qtl* / *wayyiqtol*).

12 Cf. Joel 3:1 (*bĕnêkem, ziqnêkem*) and 1:2, 3 (*hazzĕqēnîm, bĕnêkem*).

13 "I will pour out my spirit," 3:2bB = 3:1aA.

14 Apart from the word "blood" (3:3b, *ðām*; 3:4a, *lĕðām*), all the terms of this stanza are taken from the ninth stanza in the second column (2:10–11).

15 In late texts like this one (3:5) the temporal reference is implicit and is replaced by an explanatory clause.

16 Cf. Joel 2:3bB (*wĕgam pĕlêṭâ lōʾ hāyĕtâ lô*) and 3:5b (*kî . . . tihyeh pĕlêṭâ*).

17 Joel 3:5b, "Because . . . there will be survivors, *as Yahweh said*."

¹⁸ The separation between lines is marked by the way they begin. The separation is stronger, the cadence more clipped, when the lines begin with prepositions and conjunctions (= intervals) or with no introductory element (= stops) rather than with *waw* (= glides).

¹⁹ Joel 1:6a, *kî gôy ʿālâ ʿal ʾarṣî / ʿāṣûm wĕʾên mispār.*

²⁰ Joel 1:6b, *šinnāyw šinnê ʾaryēh / ûmĕtallĕʿôt lābîʾ lô.*

²¹ Cf. Joel 1:2b (*-kem / -kem*) and 1:3a (*-kem / -kem*). The third stanza (1:4) has neither alliteration nor assonance but repeats the same words two or more times.

²² In the first stanza (1:8–10) compare the liturgical cadences ("Lament like a young girl, girdled in sackcloth, over the boy of her girlhood / cut off are the cereal and drink offering from the house of Yahweh / the priests mourn, the attendants of Yahweh") and the descriptive cadences (1:10, "The field ruined / the land lamenting / for the grain is ruined / the wine gone / the oil depleted" [*šuddad śādeh / ʾābĕlâ ʾădāmâ / kî šuddad dāgān / hôbîš tîrôš / ʾumlal yiṣhār*]).

²³ Cf. Joel 1:16 ("Has there not been cut off from before our very eyes everything to eat / from the house of our God happiness and celebration) and 1:17 (" . . . the storehouses are empty / the granaries are bare / for the grain has failed").

²⁴ The first three lines repeat the prophet's prayer and have assonance and alliteration (1:19), *ʾēlêkā yhwh ʾeqrāʾ / kî ʾēš ʾākĕlâ nĕʾôt midbār / wĕlehābâ lihăṭâ kol ʿăṣê haśśādeh*). The last three lines translate the prayers of the animals and are blank (1:20, *gam bahămôt śādeh taʿărôg ʾēlêkā / kî yābĕšû ʾăpîqê māyim / wĕʾēš ʾākĕlâ nĕʾôt hammidbār*).

²⁵ Cf. Joel 2:2b (*wĕ ʾahărāyw* = "afterwards") and 2:3 (*wĕʾahărāyw* = "and behind it").

²⁶ In the first stanza the sudden shifts are manipulated by the first words in each line (*kĕ-, ûkĕ-, kĕqôl, kĕqôl, kĕʿām*). In the second stanza the shift takes place by using the same word in different forms and senses (2:6, *mippānāyw, pānîm*).

²⁷ Joel 2:7–8aA describes troops advancing relentlessly; 2:8aBb–9 suggests that these troops are grasshoppers; and 2:10–11 moves to the celestial and meteorological sphere.

²⁸ The opening is: "And afterwards I will pour out my spirit on all flesh." The more poetic part is bound by a rhyme from the beginning to the end (3:1aB, *wĕnibbĕʾû . . . ; 3:1bB, yirĕʾû*). The alliteration is carried by the morphology (*bĕnêkem ûbĕnôtêkem ziqnêkem . . . bahûrêkem*).

²⁹ The rhyme is minimal (3:2bB–3a, *ʾet rûḥî / wĕnātattî*).

30 Compare Joel 3:4 and 2:10; also 3:4 (*lipnê bô' yôm yhwh haggādôl wĕhannôrā'*) and 2:11 (*kî gādôl yôm yhwh / wĕnôrā' mĕ'ōd / ûmî yĕkîlennû*).

31 Joel 1:2, *šim'û . . . ha'ăzînû*; cf. Isa 1:2; 1:10; 28:23; Deut 32:1; Judg 5:3; Hos 5:1.

32 Joel 1:2, *kol yôšĕbê hā'āreṣ*; cf. Num 33:52, 55; Josh 2:9, 24; 7:9; 9:24; also the revised version of Jeremiah (Jer 1:14; 6:12; 13:13; 25:29, 30).

33 Cf. Joel 1:2b, *hehāyĕtâ zō't bîmêkem*; Hab 1:5bA (*kî pō'al pō'ēl bîmêkem / lō' ta'ămînû kî yĕsuppār*); Ezek 12:25 (*kî bîmêkem . . . 'ădabbēr dābār wa'ăśîtîw*). All of these are based on Isaiah's prediction that destruction was reserved for a later day (Isa 30:8).

34 Cf. Joel 1:2b–3 ("in your days . . . in the days of your fathers. . . . Tell your children . . . and their children . . . and the next generation") and Exod 34:7 ("Parents and children and their children to the third and fourth generation").

35 Cf. Joel 2:13b (*kî hannûn wĕrāḥûm hû' / 'erek 'appayim wĕrab ḥesed*) and Exod 34:6 (*'ēl rāḥûm wĕhannûn / 'erek 'appayim wĕrab ḥesed we'ĕmet*).

36 Locusts (Joel 1:4; Amos 7:1–3); the day of Yahweh (Joel 1:15; 2:1–2; Amos 5:18–20); fire (Joel 2:3, 5a; Amos 7:4–6); relenting (*nîham*, Joel 2:13–14; Amos 7:3, 6).

37 Cf. 1 Kgs 8:37–40; also Exod 10:4, 12–14, 19; Judg 6:5; 7:12.

38 Cf. Joel 2:13 (*šwb*) and 1 Kgs 8:33, 35; Amos 4:9.

39 Cf. Joel 1:5 (*šikkôrîm . . . kol šōtê yāyin*); 1:7 (*gapnî*); and Isa 5:1–2, 4–5, 11–12 (*yayin, šēkār*).

40 Joel 1:7a, *gepen, tĕ'ēnâ*; cf. Deut 8:8; 1 Kgs 5:5; 2 Kgs 18:31.

41 The idea of divine impatience (*qṣp*) is introduced in Deuteronomistic texts (Lev 10:6; Num 16:22; Deut 9:19) and is taken up in Isa 47:6; 57:16, 17; 64:8; Lam 5:22; Zech 1:2, 15.

42 "Great nation" (*gôy 'āṣûm*): Joel 1:6; Gen 18:18; Num 14:12; Deut 9:14; 26:5; cf. Exod 1:9.

43 "Without number" (*'ēn mispār*): Joel 1:6; Judg 6:5; 7:12.

44 Joel 1:6b; cf. Isa 5:29; Amos 3:4; Hos 5:14; Jer 5:6.

45 Compare Joel 1:6 ("my land" [*'arṣî*]) and 1:8 ("Wail [*'ĕlî*, feminine singular] like a young girl . . . for the husband of her youth") and Isa 5:1; Hos 2:3, 9, 17 (husband and wife, days of her youth); and Jer 3:1–5.

⁴⁶ Joel 1:9a (*minḥâ wānesek*); cf. Exod 29:40, 41; 30:9; Num 4:7; 6:17; 15:5, 7, 10; 28:7, 9; Ezek 45:17.

⁴⁷ "Minister" (*šrt*): Joel 1:9; Num 3:6; 8:26; Deut 18:7; "the priests, the ministers of Yahweh (*kōhănîm mĕšārĕtê yhwh*): Joel 1:9; Jer 33:21–22; Ezek 44:11, 19; 45:4, 5; 1 Chr 6:17; 16:4; 2 Chr 13:10; Ezra 8:17; Neh 10:37, 40.

⁴⁸ Joel 1:10 (*dāgān, tîrôš, yiṣhār*): cf. Num 18:12; Deut 12:17; 2 Kgs 18:32; Hos 2:10.

⁴⁹ Cf. Cant 2:3, 5; 7:9; 8:5.

⁵⁰ Joel 1:12b (*tāmār*); cf. Cant 7:8, 9; Joel 1:12 (*ʿăṣê haśśādeh*); cf. Ezek 17:24; 31:4, 5.

⁵¹ Cf. Joel 1:13aA (*ḥigrû wĕsipdû . . . hêlîlû*) and Jer 4:8 (*ḥigrû śaqqîm / sipdû wĕhêlîlû*).

⁵² Cf. Joel 1:14aA (*qaddĕšû ṣôm qirĕʾû ʿăṣārâ*) and 2 Kgs 10:20 (*qaddĕšû ʿăṣārâ*) and 1 Kgs 21:9, 12 (*qrʾ ṣôm*); cf. also Isa 58:5, 6; Jer 36:9; Jonah 3:5; 2 Chr 20:3; Ezra 8:21.

⁵³ Cf. Joel 1:14aB and 1:2 (*kol yôšĕbê hā ʾāreṣ*); cf. Joel 1:14b (*wĕzaʿăqû*); Hos 7:14; and 1 Sam 7:8–9.

⁵⁴ Cf. Joel 1:15abA (*ʾăhāh layyôm / kî qārôb yôm yhwh*) and Ezek 30:2b–3a (*hêlîlû hāh layyôm / kî qārôb yôm / wĕqārôb yôm layhwh*). Cf. Joel 1:13a, 15b (*hêlîlû . . . kî qārôb yôm yhwh / ûkĕšōd miššadday yābôʾ*) and Isa 13:6 (*hêlîlû kî qārôb yôm yhwh / kĕšōd miššadday yābôʾ*).

⁵⁵ Joel 1:15bB (*ûkĕšōd miššadday yābôʾ*); cf. Joel 1:10 (*šuddad śādeh . . . kî šuddad dāgān*).

⁵⁶ Joel 1:15a (*ʾăhāh*). The earliest occurrences of the word are in the Deuteronomistic History (Josh 7:7; Judg 6:22; 11:35; 2 Kgs 3:10; 6:5). It also occurs in the later revision of Jeremiah and Ezekiel (Jer 1:6; 4:10; 32:17; Ezek 4:14; 9:8; 11:13; 21:5).

⁵⁷ Cf. Joel 1:15b (*kî qārôb yôm yhwh*); Amos 5:18–20; and Zeph 1:14 (*qārôb yôm yhwh haggādôl / qārôb ûmahēr mĕʾōd*).

⁵⁸ Joel 1:15b (*ûkĕšōd*); cf. Hos 7:13; Hab 1:3.

⁵⁹ Cf. Joel 1:16a (*hălôʾ neged ʿênênû ʾōkel nikrāt*) and Isa 1:7 (*ʾadmatĕkem lĕnegdĕkem zārîm ʾokĕlîm ʾōtāh*).

⁶⁰ Cf. Joel 1:16b (*. . . nikrāt / mibbêt ʾĕlōhênû simḥâ wāgîl*) and Hos 9:1, 4 (*ʾal tiśmaḥ yiśrāʾēl / ʾel gîl kāʿammîm . . . bêt yhwh*).

⁶¹ Joel 1:18 (*nābōkû*); cf. Exod 14:3; Mic 7:4.

62 Joel 1:18 (neʾenḥâ); cf. Exod 2:23; Ezek 9:4; 21:11, 12; Lam 1:4, 8, 11, 21; Isa 24:7.

63 Joel 1:19b, 20b (ʾēš ʾākĕlâ nĕʾôt [ham]miδbār); cf. Amos 7:4 (hinnēh qōrēʾ lārîb bāʾēš . . . wattōʾkal ʾet tĕhôm rabbâ wĕʾākĕlâ ʾet haḥēleq); Jer 9:9, 23:10, and Ps 65:13 (nĕʾôt miδbār); Deut 32:22 (ʾēš . . . wattōʾkal . . . wattĕlahēṭ . . .).

64 E.g., lhṭ + lhbb, Ps 83:15; 106:18.

65 Cf. Joel 1:19bA, 20bB (ʾēš ʾākĕlâ nĕʾôt miδbār) and Amos 1:2b (wĕʾābĕlâ nĕʾôt hārōʿîm); also Jer 9:9.

66 Cf. Joel 2:1 (tiqĕʿû šôpār . . . wĕhārîʿû . . .) and Zeph 1:16 (yôm šôpār ûtĕrûʿâ); cf. Amos 2:2.

67 The expression tqʿ špr is found in Josh 6:4, 8, 9, 13, 16, 20; Judg 3:27; 6:34; 7:18–20, 22; 1 Sam 13:3; 2 Sam 2:28; 18:16; 1 Kgs 1:39; 2 Kgs 9:13. The alarm (rwʿ) is found, e.g., in Josh 6:5, 10, 16; cf. also Hos 5:8.

68 Jer 4:5 (tiqĕʿû šôpār); 6:1 (bitqôaʿ toiqĕʿû šôpār).

69 Cf. Joel 2:2aA (yôm ḥōšek waʾăpēlâ); Amos 5:20 (hălōʾ ḥōšek yôm yhwh . . . wĕʾāpēl . . .); Zeph 1:15 (yôm ḥōšek waʾăpēlâ).

70 Cf. Joel 2:1 (yirgĕzû kōl yōšĕbê hāʾāreṣ) and Hab 3:16 (šāmaʿtî wattirgaz biṭnî); cf. Joel 2:13b (raḥûm) and Hab 3:2 (bĕrōgez raḥēm tizkôr).

71 Joel 2:2aB (ʿam rab wĕʿāṣûm) = Exod 1:9b.

72 Joel 2:2aB ("like darkness creeping along the mountains"); cf. Exod 10:14–15 (". . . before there had not been locusts like them and afterwards there will not be [cf. Joel 1:2b–3], and they covered the eye of the earth and darkened the land . . . ").

73 Joel 2:2 = 1:2b; cf. Exod 10:14 (n. 72, above).

74 Cf. Joel 2:3b (kĕgan ʿēden hāʾāreṣ lĕpānāyw / wĕʾaḥărāyw miδbar šĕmāmâ) and Isa 51:3b (wayyāśem miδbārāh kĕʿēden / wĕʿarĕbātāh kĕgan yhwh).

75 Joel 2:3bB ("And indeed there is no survivor on it" [wĕgam pĕlēṭâ lōʾ hāyĕtâ lô]); cf. Exod 10:15 ("And nothing was left . . . "); 2 Kgs 19:31 ("For a remnant will come out of Jerusalem and survivors from mount Zion" [kî mîrûšālāyim tēṣēʾ šĕʾērît / ûpĕlêṭâ mēhar ṣiyyôn]).

76 See J. A. Bewer, Commentary on Joel (ICC; Edinburgh: T. & T. Clark, 1911) 98.

77 Cf. Joel 2:4–5 (sûsîm, pārāšîm, qôl markābôt . . . yĕraqqĕδûn, lahab) and Nah 3:2–3 (qôl, sûs, merkābâ mĕraqqēδâ, pārāš, lahab).

[78] Cf. Joel 2:5 (*ʾēš, ʿām ʿāṣûm ʿērûk milḥāmâ*) and 1:19–20; 2:2; cf. 2:5b (*kĕʿam ʿāṣûm ʿērûk milḥāmâ*) and Jer 6:23 (*wĕʿal sûsîm yirkābû / ʿārûk kĕʾîš milḥāmâ*).

[79] Joel 2:6a (*yāḥîlû*); cf. Jer 5:22; Hab 3:10.

[80] There is some inversion of word order: cf. Joel 2:6b (*kol pānîm qibbĕṣû pāʾrûr*) and Nah 2:11 (*ûpĕnê kullām qibbĕṣû pāʾrûr*).

[81] Cf. Joel 2:7 ("Like warriors they run / like men of war they climb the wall / each goes his own way") and Nah 2:6 ("He summons his mighty ones / they stumble as they go / they hurry to the wall").

[82] Joel 2:8b (*baššelaḥ*); cf. Isa 8:6 (*ʾet mê baššilōaḥ*); Joel 2:9 (*bĕʿad haḥallônîm yābōʾû kaggannāb*); cf. Jer 9:20 (*kî ʿālâ māwet bĕḥallônênû / bāʾ bĕʾarmĕnôtênû*).

[83] Cf. Joel 2:10b (*šemeš wĕyārēaḥ qādārû / wĕkôkābîm ʾāsĕpû noghām*); Amos 5:20b (*wĕlōʾ nōgah lô*); and Hab 3:11 (*šemeš yārēaḥ ʿāmad zĕbūlâ . . . lĕnōgah bĕraq ḥănîtekā*).

[84] Joel 2:10a (*rgz, rʿš*); cf. 2 Sam 22:8; Ps 18:8.

[85] Joel 2:11 (*wayhwh nātan qôlô*); cf. 2 Sam 22:14 (= Ps 18:14) and Amos 1:2 (= Joel 4:16).

[86] Joel 2:11b (*kî gādôl yôm yhwh / wĕnôrāʾ mĕʾōd*); cf. Zeph 1:14 (*yôm yhwh haggādôl*); Deut 10:17 (*hāʾēl haggādōl haggibbôr wĕhannôrāʾ*).

[87] Joel 2:11 (*kî rab mĕʾōd maḥănēhû*); cf. Josh 5:14; Nah 2:2, 4, 6.

[88] Joel 2:11 (*kî gādôl yôm yhwh wĕnôrāʾ mĕʾōd*) = Joel 3:4; Mal 3:23.

[89] Joel 2:12a (*šūbû ʿāday bĕkol lĕbabkem*) = 1 Kgs 8:48 (*wĕšābû ʾēlêkā bĕkol lĕbābām*).

[90] Joel 2:14a (*mî yôdēaʿ yāšûb wĕnîḥām*); cf. Exod 32:12 (*šûb mēḥărôn ʾappekā wĕhinnāḥēm ʿal hārāʿâ lĕʿammekā*); 1 Sam 15:29 (*lōʾ ʾādām hûʾ lĕhinnāḥēm*); also Jer 18:8; 26:3, 13, 19; 42:10.

[91] In the Deuteronomist's thinking Yahweh is in heaven; his Name is in the temple (1 Kings 8); and prayers are addressed to the temple when the people have sinned. In Joel's view Yahweh is among his people (Joel 2:27).

[92] Cf. Joel 2:14b (*wĕhišʾîr ʾaḥărāyw bĕrākâ*) and Joel 2:3 (*wĕʾaḥărāyw*).

[93] Joel 2:16; cf. Jer 6:11; Deut 20:7; 24:5; 32:25; 1 Sam 15:3; 22:19.

[94] Cf. Cant 4:8–12; 5:1; 8:1. In the book of Jeremiah (Jer 7:34; 16:9; 25:10; 33:11) the voices of the bride and bridegroom become the symbol of happiness.

[95] Cf. Joel 2:17aA (*bên hāʾûlām wĕlammizbēaḥ*) and Ezek 8:16 (*bên hāʾûlām ûbên hammizbēaḥ*).

[96] Cf. Joel 2:17b (*ḥûsâ yhwh ʿal ʿammekā*) and Ezek 20:17 (*wattaḥos ʿênî ʿălêhem*).

[97] Joel 2:17b; cf. Exod 32:12; Num 14:15–16; Deut 9:28.

[98] Joel 2:17 (*naḥălātĕkā*); cf. Deut 9:26.

[99] Joel 2:17 (*limsol bām gôyim*); cf. Deut 15:6 (*ûmāsaltā baggôyim rabbîm ûbĕkā lōʾ yimsōlû*).

[100] Joel 2:17 (*lĕḥerpâ . . . gôyim*); Ezek 5:14–15 (*wĕʾettenēk . . . lĕḥerpâ baggóyim . . . wĕhāyĕtâ ḥerpâ . . . laggôyim*).

[101] Joel 2:17b; cf. Mic 7:10; Pss 42:4, 11; 79:10.

[102] Joel 2:18a; cf. Exod 34:14; Nah 1:2.

[103] Joel 2:18b (*wayyaḥmōl ʿal ʿammô*); cf. Ezek 5:11; 7:4, 9; 8:18; 9:5, 10 (*lōʾ ʾeḥmōl*).

[104] Joel 2:19a; cf. Deut 8:10; 12:17; 2 Kgs 18:32; Hos 2:10; 13:6.

[105] Joel 2:20aA; cf. Jer 4:6; Zeph 2:13.

[106] Joel 2:20 (*ʾel ʾeres siyyâ ûsĕmāmâ*); cf. Zeph 2:13 (*sĕmāmâ / siyyâ*).

[107] Joel 2:20a; cf. Deut 11:24; Josh 1:4.

[108] Cf. Joel 2:20aB (*wĕsōpô ʾel hayyām hāʾaḥărôn*); Exod 10:19 (*wayyitqāʿēhû yāmmâ sûp*).

[109] Joel 2:20b; cf. Exod 7:18, 21; Isa 34:3; Amos 4:10.

[110] Joel 2:21–22; cf. 1:10, 12, 18.

[111] Cf. Joel 2:23–24; Deut 11:14–15; Jer 5:24.

[112] Cf. Joel 2:25–27; Exod 34:10; Num 14:14; Deut 5:6.

[113] Joel 3:1; cf. Gen 6:3; Ezek 37:14; 1 Sam 10:6, 10; Ezek 2:2.

[114] Joel 3:2a; cf. Isa 14:2; Jer 34:8–22.

[115] Compare 3:3a and 2:10; also 3:3b and 1:19, 20; 2:3, 5.

[116] Joel 3:3b; 4:21; cf. Exod 13:22; 14:24; 19:18; Isa 4:5; Cant 3:6.

117 Joel 3:5bA (*kî bĕhar ṣiyyôn ûbîrûšālāyim tihyeh pĕlêṭâ*); cf. Obad 17 (*ûbĕhar ṣiyyôn tihyeh pĕlêṭâ*).

118 Joel 2:3, *wĕgam pĕlêṭâ lōʾ hāyĕtâ lô*.

119 Joel 4:1–3; cf. 4:1 [*šāb šĕbût*] and Jer 30:3.

120 Joel 4:2 (*qbṣ*); cf. Zeph 3:8.

121 Joel 4:2b; cf., e.g., Jer 9:15; Ezek 4:13.

122 Cf. Joel 4:3a (*wĕʾel ʿammî yaddû gôrāl*) and Obad 11 (*wĕʿal yĕrûšālāyim yaddû gôrāl*).

123 Cf. Joel 4:5 and 2 Kgs 25:15; Lam 1:7, 10.

124 Joel 4:10a = Isa 2:4 = Mic 4:3; cf. 1 Sam 13:19–23.

125 Joel 4:14–15 = Joel 1:15; 2:6; cf. Joel 4:14b (*bĕʿēmeq hehārûṣ*) and Isa 10:22 (= III Isaiah).

126 Joel 4:16; cf. Amos 1:2a; Nah 1:7; Pss 46:2; 71:7; 73:28; Jer 17:17; Isa 4:6.

127 Joel 4:17; cf. Ezekiel (passim); Joel 4:17 (*wĕhāyĕtâ . . . qōdeš*), cf. Obad 17 (*wĕhāyâ qōdeš*); Joel 4:17 (*šōkēn bĕṣiyyôn*), cf. Isa 8:18; Ps 74:2; Zech 8:3; Joel 4:17bB (*wĕzārîm lōʾ yaʿabrû bāh ʿôd*), cf. Jer 30:8 (*wĕlōʾ yaʿabdû bô ʿôd zārîm*).

128 Joel 4:18; cf. Amos 9:13; Ezek 47:1–12.

129 Joel 4:19–21; cf. Ezek 29:12; 32:15; 35:3–4.

130 Joel 4:19b; cf. Obad 10; 2 Kgs 21:16; 24:4 (*šāpak . . . dām nāqî*).

131 After the superscription (Obad 1a) the first strophe is Obad 1b–3aA and is composed of two stanzas (vv. 1b, 2–3aA).

132 The descriptive order reduplicates itself: A = 49:7, 8; B = 49:9–10a, 10b–11; C = 49:12, 13; A' = 49:14, 15–16aA, 16aBb–17; B' = 49:18, 19; C' = 49:20, 21, 22. Quotations from Obadiah are found in 49:7 (Obad 1, 8); 49:9 (Obad 5); 49:10a (Obad 6); 49:12 (Obad 15, 16); 49:14 (Obad 1); 49:15–16aA (Obad 2, 3); 49:16aBb–17 (Obad 3, 4); cf. Figs. 19, 19a.

133 The patterns are narrative (A-A), descriptive (A-B, or A-B-B) and explanatory (A-B-A'). The first, fourth, and fifth strophes are descriptive (A-B[-B] : vv. 1b–3aA [4 lines + 3 lines], vv. 10–11 [3 lines + 5 lines], vv. 12–16 [3 lines + 6 lines + 6 lines]); the second is narrative (A-A: vv. 3aBb-4 [4 lines + 4 lines]), and the third and sixth are explanatory (A-B-A': vv. 5–9 [6 lines + 8 lines + 6 lines], vv. 17–21 [8 lines + 5 lines + 8 lines]).

134 Obad 1b, 2–3aA (*baggôyim*).

135 The stanza (v. 1b) contrasts the declaration and the answer that it envelops: "Thus said my lord Yahweh to Edom / —'We have heard the news from Yahweh / the report has been sent among the nations'— / 'Arise and let us rise against her in battle.'"

136 The stanza (vv. 2–3aA) is an unadorned indictment of Edom. Following the pattern of the first stanza, the outside lines are linked and enclose another remark: "Behold I made you the least of nations—you are most contemptible—the arrogance of your heart misled you."

137 Obad 3aBb (*mî yôrĭdēnî ʾāreṣ*), 4 (*miššam ʾôrîdĕkā*).

138 Obad 1b (*kōh ʾāmar . . . yhwh*), 4b (*nĕʾum yhwh*).

139 The contrast is marked by metathesis and rhyme in the middle lines (v. 3aBb, *mĕrôm šibtô* / *ʾōmēr bĕlibbô*).

140 Cf. Obad 5 (*ʾim šôdĕdê laylâ* / *ʾêk nidmêtâ*) and v. 6 (*ʾêk nehpĕśû ʿēśāw* / *nibʿû maṣpūnāyw*); cf. also *tĕbûnâ* in v. 7 ("It is incomprehensible") and in v. 8 ("I will annihilate wisdom in Edom / and comprehension in the mountain of Esau").

141 The stanza (Obad 5) combines two images and an aside: "If thieves came to you—or killers in the night, how you would be terminated!—would they not steal what they need, if grape pickers came to you, would they not leave gleanings?"

142 The whole stanza (Obad 6–7) is marked by the unexpected activities of allies, but seems to be in two parts: "How Esau has been ransacked / his hidden treasures exposed / to the border they send you / all the men of your alliance // they deceive you, outwit you / the men with whom you are at peace / your comrades in arms have wounded you in the back / there is no understanding it." In view of what follows, the image seems to be that Edom, as an ally of the Babylonians in the siege of Jerusalem, left itself open to attacks in its rear. The attackers are inspired by Yahweh and the ruin is complete.

143 The stanza (Obad 8–9) is the continuation of the first (v. 5). Its opening question, "On that day, says Yahweh, will I not destroy . . ." (*hălōʾ bayyôm hahûʾ . . .*), reproduces the questions about the thieves and the grape pickers (v. 5, *hălōʾ*). The middle stanza is left hanging but will be developed at length in what follows. The hanging pattern is typical of stanzas, strophes, and the entire composition.

144 Cf. Obad 11a (*bĕyôm . . . bĕyôm*) and v. 8a (*bayyôm hahûʾ*).

145 Obad 11: "For the day you took your stand / —the day aliens stopped

his forces / and strangers came through his gates / and rolled dice for Jerusalem— / you too were like one of them."

146 Cf. Obad 12 (*wĕʾal* [three times]) and vv. 13–15a (*ʾal* [twice], *wĕʾal* [three times]); cf. v. 12 (*bĕyôm* [three times] and vv. 13–15a (*bĕyôm* [four times], *yôm* [once]). Cf. vv. 15a (*kōl haggôyim*), 16 (*kōl haggôyim*).

147 Cf. "Your brother" (*ʾāḥîkā*, vv. 10a, 12a), "on the day" (*bĕyôm*, v. 11a [twice], 12 [four times]), "aliens" and "alienation" (v. 11b, *nokrîm*; v. 12a, *bĕyôm nokrô*).

148 Cf. Obad 16aA (*har qodšî*) and v. 17a (*har ṣiyyôn*); also v. 14a (*pĕlîṭāyw*) and 17a (*pĕlêṭâ*).

149 Cf. Obad 17b, 19a, 20b (*yrš*); 17a, 21aA (*har ṣiyyôn*); 18bB, 20b (*yhwh*); 19aA, 21aB (*har ʿēśāw*).

150 Obad 1b = Jer 49:7aA, 14 (i.e., the original stanza has been distributed in the A [Jer 49:7–8] and A′ [Jer 49:14–17] strophes of Jeremiah; see fig. 20a).

151 The first and third lines rhyme at the beginning (*qāṭōn / zēdôn*) and at the end (*nĕtattîkā / biśśîʾekā*), but each has a different pattern of alliteration. The middle line shares some of the sounds of the first and third and is made to suit them.

152 Obad 3aBb (*mĕrôm šibtô / ʾōmēr bĕlibbô*), 4 (*wĕʾim bên kôkābîm śîm qinnekā / miśśām ʾôrîdĕkā*).

153 Cf. Obad 1a (*ḥăzôn ʿōbadyâ*); Isa 1:1 (*ḥăzôn yĕšaʿyāhû ben ʾāmôṣ*); Nah 1:1b (*sēper ḥăzôn naḥûm hāʾelqōšî*).

154 Obad 1b (*kōh ʾāmar ʾădōnāy yhwh leʾĕdôm*); cf. Amos 3:11; 5:3; Ezek 2:4; 3:11; 7:2, 5.

155 The expression (Obad 1b, *šĕmûʿâ šāmaʿnû mēʾēt yhwh*) refers to rumors (e.g., 1 Kgs 10:7), gossip (e.g., 1 Sam 2:24), battle reports (Isa 28:9, 19; 37:7; Jer 6:24; 10:22; Ezek 7:26; 21:12).

156 Compare Obad 1b (*šlḥ + ṣîr*) and Isa 18:2; also Isa 57:9; Prov 13:17; 25:13.

157 Cf. Obad 1b (*qûmû wĕnāqûmâ ʿālêhā lammilḥāmâ*) and Jer 6:4a, 5a (*qaddĕšû ʿālêhā milḥāmâ / qûmû wĕnaʿăleh baṣṣohŏrāyim . . . qûmû wĕnaʿăleh ballāylâ*).

158 Cf. Obad 2b (*bāzûy ʾattâ mĕʾōd*) and Gen 25:34 (*wayyibez ʿēśāw ʾet habbĕkōrâ*); cf. Obad 2a (*qāṭōn*) and Gen 27:15, 42 (*qāṭān*).

159 Cf. Obad 2a (*hinnēh qāṭōn nĕtattîkā baggôyim*) and Gen 25:23 (*gôyim*).

[160] Cf. Obad 3 (*mĕrôm šibtô* / *'ōmēr bĕlibbô*) and Isa 14:13 (*wĕ'attâ 'āmartā bilbābĕkā* / . . . / *'ārîm kis'î*).

[161] Cf. Obad 4aB (*wĕ'im bên kôkābîm śîm qinnekā*) and Isa 14:13 (*mimma'al lĕkôkĕbê 'ēl 'ārîm kis'î*). This is a bit high even for an eagle and the Jeremianic version omits the reference (Jer 49:16). Cf. Obad 3b, 4b (*mî yôrîdēnî 'āreṣ* . . . *miśśām 'ôrîdĕkā*) and Isa 14:12, 15 (*nigda'tā lā'āreṣ* . . . *'ak 'el śĕ'ôl tûrād*).

[162] Cf. Obad 5 (*'êk nidmêtâ*) and Isa 14:12 (*'êk nāpaltā*).

[163] Cf. Obad 5aA (*'im gannābîm bā'û lāk*) and Joel 2:9 (*bĕ'ad hahallônîm yābō'û kaggannāb*).

[164] Cf. Obad 5aA ("If thieves . . . at night" [*'im gannābîm* . . . *laylâ*]) and Exod 22:1–2 ("If a thief is discovered by chance and is hit and dies, there is no bloodguilt attached to it; but if the sun has risen . . .").

[165] Cf. Obad 5aA (*śôdĕdê laylâ*) and Jer 4:13, 20, 30 (*śdd*) and Jer 6:5 (*laylâ* [this text is quoted in Obad 1b]).

[166] Cf. Obad 5aA (*'im śôdĕdê laylâ* / *'êk nidmêtâ*) and Isa 15:1 ("Ar is destroyed at night / Moab is ruined / Qir is destroyed at night / Moab is ruined" [*kî bēlêl śuddad 'ār* / *mō'āb nidmâ* / *kî bēlêl śuddad qîr* / *mō'āb nidmâ*]).

[167] Cf. Obad 5bB (*hălô' yaš'îrû 'ōlēlôt*) and Deut 24:21 (*kî tibṣōr karmĕkā lō' tĕ'ôlēl*). The book of Jeremiah combines both texts (Jer 6:9, *'ôlēl yĕ'ôlĕlû kaggepen śĕ'ērît yiśrā'ēl*).

[168] Cf. Obad 7aB ("Your allies / they deceived you and took advantage of you" [*biśśî'ûkā yākĕlû lĕkā* / *anśê śĕlōmekā*]) and Jer 38:21–22 ("Your allies / they fooled you and took advantage of you" [*hissîtûkā wĕyākĕlû lĕkā 'anśê śĕlōmekā* . . .]).

[169] Cf. Obad 7b ("Those you fight for will wound you for your trouble" [*lahmĕkā yāśîmû māzôr tahtêkā*]); Hos 5:13 ("When Judah saw its wound [*mĕzōrô*]); Jer 30:13 ("There is no one to judge your case, no healing for the wound [*lĕmāzôr*] . . . ").

[170] Obad 8, 9, 21 (*har 'ēśāw*); cf. Gen 36:8, 9; Deut 1:2; 2:1, 5; Josh 15:10; 24:4; Ezek 35:2, 3, 7, 15; 1 Chr 4:42; 2 Chr 20:10, 22, 23.

[171] Cf. Gen 36:11, 15, 34, 42; Amos 1:12; Ezek 25:13; Hab 3:3; 1 Chr 1:36, 53.

[172] Cf. Job 2:11; 4:1; 15:1; 22:1; 42:7, 9.

[173] Obad 9b (*lĕma'an yikkāret 'iš mēhar 'ēśāw miqqāṭel*); cf. 1 Kgs 2:4; 8:25; Jer 33:17, 18; 35:19; on dynastic succession in Edom, see Gen 36:31–39.

[174] Obad 10a (*mēhămās 'ăhîkā ya'ăqob*); cf. Gen 6:11, 13 (*hāmās*); Mic 6:12 (*hāmās*); Hab 1:2 (*hāmās*); Ezek 8:17; 12:19 (*hāmās*).

175 Obad 10a (*tĕkassĕkā bûšâ*); cf. Isa 30:5; Hos 2:7; 4:19; 10:6; Jer 2:36. Cf. Obad 9a (*ḥtt*) and Jer 8:9.

176 Obad 11b (*wĕʿal yĕrûšālayim yaddû gôrāl*); Nah 3:10 (*wĕʿal nikbaddêhā yaddû gôrāl*); cf. Mic 2:5.

177 Obad 12b (*bĕyôm ṣārâ*); cf. Nah 1:7; Hab 3:16; Zeph 1:15; also 2 Kgs 19:3 = Isa 37:3; and Jer 16:19.

178 Obad 12aB (*bĕyôm ʾobdām*); cf. *ʾbd*, Deut 4:26; 8:19–20; 11:17; 28:20, 22; 30:18; Josh 23:13, 16. Obad 13aA (*bĕyôm ʾêdām*), cf. Deut 32:35 (*kî qārôb yôm ʾêdām*); 2 Sam 22:19 (*bĕyôm ʾêdî*).

179 Obad 12aA (*bĕyôm nokrô*).

180 Obad 13a (*ʾal tābôʾ bĕšaʿar ʿammî bĕyôm ʾêdām / ʾal tēreʾ gam ʾattâ bĕrāʿātô bĕyôm ʾêdô*); cf. Mic 1:12 (*kî yārad rāʿ mēʾēt yhwh lĕšaʿar yĕrûšālāyim*); Jer 4:6 (*kî rāʿâ ʾānōkî mēbîʾ miṣṣāpôn*); 2 Kgs 22:16 (*hinĕnî mēbîʾ rāʿâ ʾel hammāqôm hazzeh*).

181 Obad 13b (*wĕʾal tišlaḥnâ bĕḥêlô bĕyôm ʾêdô*); cf. 2 Kgs 25:4–5.

182 Obad 15a (*kî qārôb yôm yhwh ʿal kol haggôyim*); cf. Zeph 1:14 (*qārôb yôm yhwh*); Zeph 3:8 (*gôyim . . . tēʾākēl kol hāʾāreṣ*).

183 Obadiah is explicit and emphatic about retribution (Obad 15b, "As you have done, it will be done to you / your retribution will come back on your head"). He also repeats the gist of Isaiah's address, first speaking to Jerusalem (Obad 16aA; cf. Isa 51:17), then to the nations (Obad 16aBb; cf. Isa 51:21–23).

184 Obad 17a (*ûbĕhar ṣiyyôn tihyeh pĕlêṭâ wĕhāyâ qōdeš*); cf. 2 Kgs 19:31 (*kî mîrûšālayim tēṣēʾ šĕʾērît ûpĕlêṭâ mēhar ṣiyyôn*). These texts are quoted in the revision of Joel (Joel 3:5) and in III Isaiah (Isa 4:3).

185 Cf. Joel 1:19; 2:3, 5; Isa 29:6b.

186 Cf. Deut 1:7; Josh 9:1; 10:40; 11:2, 16; 12:8; Judg 1:9.

187 Compare Obad 21a (*mošiʿîm*) and, for example, Judg 2:16; 3:9; also Obad 21a (*lišpōṭ*) and Judg 2:16; 3:10; Obad 21b (*wĕhāyĕtâ layhwh hammĕlûkâ*) and 1 Sam 8:7.

188 Cf. Jer 49:7 (*haʾên ʿôd ḥokmâ bĕtêmān / ʾābĕdâ ʿēṣâ mibbānîm*) and Jer 18:18 (*lōʾ tōʾbad . . . wĕʿēṣâ mēḥākām*); cf. also Ezek 7:26.

189 Cf. Jer 49:7bA + 8aA (*ʾābĕdâ ʿēṣâ mibbānîm . . . nūsû hopnû heʿmîqû lāšebet*) and Jer 47:3 (*lōʾ hipnû ʾābôt ʾel bānîm*).

190 Cf. Jer 49:8b (*kî ʾêd ʿēšāw hēbēʾtî ʿālāyw ʿēt pĕqadtîw*); 18:17 (*bĕyôm ʾêdām*);

46:21 (*kî yôm 'êdām bā' 'ălêhem 'ēt pěquddātām*); 48:16 (*qārôb 'êd mô'āb lābô'*); and 49:32 (*ābî' 'et 'êdām*).

191 Jer 49:8b (*'ēt + pqd*); cf. Jer 6:15 = 8:12; Jer 10:15 = 51:18; 46:21; 50:27, 31. The "season" (*'ēt*) is a variant of the "day" of Yahweh in Amos 5:13; Mic 2:3; Ezek 7:7, 12; 21:30, 34; 35:5; Jer 15:11; 50:27, 31.

192 Cf. Obad 6 (*ḥpś*) and Jer 49:10aA (*ḥśp*); cf. Obad 6 (*nib'û maṣpūnāyw*) and Jer 49:10aA (*gillêtî 'et mistārāyw*) and Jer 23:24 (*'im yissātēr 'îś bammistārîm . . .*).

193 Jer 49:10b–11. On *yātôm* and *'almānâ*, cf. Deut 10:18; 14:29; 16:11; 24:17, 19–21; 26:12, 13; 27:19; Jer 5:28; 7:6; 15:8; 22:3.

194 Compare Jer 49:12aA and 25:15–17, 27–29; also 49:12aBb and 25:29; also 49:13 and 25:9, 11, 18 (variants of the formulas occur in Jer 7:34; 22:5; 24:9; 27:17; 42:18; 44:2, 12, 22).

195 Cf. Jer 49:14b (*hitqabbēṣû*); Josh 9:2; 1 Sam 22:2; 2 Sam 2:25.

196 Cf. Jer 49:16aA (*tiplaṣtěkā*) and 1 Kgs 15:13.

197 Jer 49:17; cf. 1 Kgs 9:8; Jer 18:16; 19:8; 25:9, 18; 50:13; 51:37.

198 Jer 49:19; cf. 1 Kgs 13:24–25; 2 Kgs 17:25; Amos 3:4, 8; 5:19; Hos 5:14; cf. also the vassal treaties of Esarhaddon, lines 467–68, "May [Bethel and Ana]th-Bethel hand you over to the paws of [a man-eating] lion" S. Parpola and K. Watanabe, *Neo-Assyrian Treaties and Loyalty Oaths* [State Archives of Assyria 2; Helsinki: Helsinki University, 1988] p. 49).

199 Cf. Gen 13:10–11; Jer 12:5; 50:44; Zech 11:3.

200 Jer 49:20; cf. Jer 11:19; 18:11, 18; 29:11; 49:20 = 50:45; 49:30.

201 Cf. Exod 19:4; Deut 32:11; Jer 48:40.

202 Cf. Jer 8:16; 10:10; 25:36; 48:3, 5; 50:46.

203 J. S. Ackerman, "Satire and Symbolism in the Song of Jonah," in *Traditions in Transformation: Turning Points in Biblical Faith*, ed. B. Halpern and J. D. Levenson (Winona Lake, Ind.: Eisenbrauns, 1981) 213–46; D. L. Christensen, "The Song of Jonah: A Metrical Analysis," *JBL* 104 (1985) 217–31; F. M. Cross, "Studies in the Structure of Hebrew Verse: The Prosody of the Psalm of Jonah," in *The Quest for the Kingdom of God: Studies in Honor of George E. Mendenhall*, ed. H. B. Huffmon et al. (Winona Lake, Ind.: Eisenbrauns, 1983) 159–67; R. E. Friedman and B. Halpern, "Composition and Paronomasia in the Book of Jonah," *HAR* 4 (1980) 79–92; N. Lohfink, "Jona ging zur Stadt hinaus (Jon 4, 5)," *BZ* 5 (1961) 185–203; J. Magonet, *Form and Meaning: Studies in Literary Techniques in the Book of Jonah* (Bern: Herbert Lang, 1976).

204 Jonah 1:2b, *lĕpānāy*; 1:3, *millipnê*; 1:2a, *qûm*; 1:3, *wayyāqom*.

205 Jonah 1:2, Nineveh; 1:3, Tarshish; 1:2, *ʿālĕtâ*; 1:3, *wayyēreḍ*; 1:2, *hlk*; 1:3 *bwʾ*.

206 Jonah 1:4–5a, 5b–6; cf. 1:5a (*wayyizʿăqû ʾîš ʾel ʾĕlōhāyw*) and 1:6 (*qûm qĕrāʾ ʾel ʾĕlōhêkā*).

207 Cf. Jonah 1:2 (*hāʿîr haggĕḍôlâ*) and 1:4 (*rûaḥ gĕḍôlâ*).

208 Cf. Jonah 1:2 (*qûm lēk . . . ûqĕrāʾ*) and 1:6 (*qûm qĕrāʾ*).

209 Cf. Jonah 1:3 (*wayyēreḍ*) and 1:5 (*yāraḍ . . . wayyērāḍam*).

210 Jonah 1:7a, 7b–8 (*npl gôrāl[ôt]*).

211 Jonah 1:9, 10–11; cf. *yrʾ*, 1:9b, 10a; *ʿšh*, 1:9, 10–11; *hayyām*, 1:9, 11.

212 Jonah 1:12b (*kî bĕšellî hassaʿar haggāḍôl hazzeh ʿălêkem*); 1:13b (*kî hayyām hôlēk wĕsōʿēr ʿălêhem*).

213 Cf. Jonah 1:12a ("Pick me up and throw me into the sea") and 1:15a ("So they picked Jonah up and threw him into the sea").

214 It is typical of lament psalms that the crisis is over and has become an occasion for praise.

215 Cf. Jonah 1:16b and 2:10 (*nḍr, zbḥ*).

216 Although the sailors pray and worship Yahweh (Jonah 1:14, 16), they each had their own Gods (1:5).

217 Jonah 3:3, 4 (*mahălak*).

218 Cf. Jonah 1:2 and 3:3b (*ʿîr gĕḍôlâ*).

219 Cf. Jonah 1:2, 3aA and 3:3a, 4b (*qûm, hlk, qrʾ*).

220 Cf. Jonah 3:3 and 2:11–3:2 (*qûm, hlk, qrʾ, ḍbr yhwh*).

221 Cf. Jonah 1:5a and 3:7aA (*zʿq*); 1:6b and 3:8aA (*qrʾ*); 1:6b and 3:9b (*wĕlōʾ nōʾbēḍ*).

222 Jonah 3:10–4:2aA; 4:2aBb–3, *nḥm*.

223 Cf. Jonah 3:10–4:3 and 1:7–8: "evil" [*rāʿâ*] occurs in 1:7a, 8a; 3:10a, 10b; 4:1a, 2b.

224 Cf. Jonah 3:8, 10 (*šwb mḍrk hrʿh*); 3:9, 10 and 4:2 (*nḥm*).

225 Jonah 4:6b–7, 8–11 (*qîqāyôn*, 4:6b, 7, 9, 10).

226 Cf. Jonah 4:6a (*qîqāyôn*) and 4:6b, 7, 9, 10; also 4:4aB and 4:9aB ("Do you do well to be angry?"); and 4:5b and 4:11 ('*ir*).

227 Cf. Jonah 1:2a and 4:11a (*ninĕwēh hā'îr haggĕdôlâ*).

228 Cf. Jonah 1:1 and 3:1 (*dĕbar yhwh*); 3:3 (*kidbar yhwh*) and 4:2 (*dĕbārî*).

229 Jonah 1:1 *ben 'ămittay*. His name, from *'ĕmet* ("truth"), matches the "honesty" (*hesed*) that is an attribute of God . . . (2:9; 4:2). Beginning with the declaration in the Sinai covenant (Exod 34:6) the two words are conventionally paired.

230 Jonah 1:1; 3:2, 3; 4:11 ("Nineveh, the great city").

231 Nineveh is an evil city (Jonah 1:1), but the people repent of their evil (3:8, 10). Jonah causes evil (1:7, 8; 4:1) but thinks he is doing good (4:4, 9). Yahweh decides not to do the evil he intended (3:10; 4:2).

232 Jonah 1:4 (*hiššĕbâ lĕhiššābēr*).

233 Jonah 1:5b (*yārad . . . wayyērādam*).

234 Jonah 1:6a (*wayyiqrab . . . rab*).

235 The term "overthrow" (3:4b, *nehpāket*) usually refers to the overthrow of Sodom and Gomorrah (cf. Gen 19:25).

236 Gen 10:12 ("And Resen between Nineveh — that was the great city [*hî' hā'îr haggĕdôlâ* = the capital] — and Calah").

237 Cf. Gen 6:5, 13; 11:1–9; 18:21; Exod 2:23.

238 Cf. Jonah 1:1–2a (*wayhî dĕbar yhwh 'el yônâ . . . lē'mōr qûm lēk 'el ninĕwēh hā'îr haggĕdôlâ*) and 1 Kgs 17:8–9 (*wayhî dĕbar yhwh 'ēlāyw lē'mōr qûm lēk ṣārĕpatâ 'ăšer lĕṣîdôn*).

239 Nah 2:2, 4–11; 3:1–11; Zeph 2:12–15; 3:1–8; Jer 22:8 ("And many nations will pass by this city and they will say, one to another: 'Why did Yahweh do such a thing to this great city?' ").

240 Jonah 1:4aA; Ezek 27:26 (*rûah*).

241 Jonah 1:4b; Ezek 27:26 (*šbr*).

242 Jonah 1:5–6; Ezek 27:27–30 (*hammallāhîm, hahōbēl, zā'aq*).

243 Jonah 1:14 (*dām nāqî'*); cf. Deut 19:10; 21:8; 2 Kgs 21:16; 24:4; Jer 26:15.

244 Cf. Jonah 3:3 (*wayyāqom yônâ wayyēlēk*) and 1 Kgs 19:3 (*wayyāqom wayyēlēk*).

245 Jonah 3:5a, *wayya'ămînû*; cf. Isa 7:9b; 28:16.

246 Cf. also Jer 18:11; 23:14, 22; 25:5; 35:15.

247 Cf. Amos 3:10; 6:3; Gen 6:11, 13; Exod 23:1; Mic 6:12; Jer 6:7; Hab 1:2; Ezek 8:17.

248 Cf. Jonah 3:10 and 2 Kgs 23:26–27; cf. also Amos 7:3, 6; Joel 2:13; Jer 18:8; 26:3, 13, 19; 42:10; Exod 32:14; 2 Sam 24:16.

249 Jonah 4:5 (*sukkâ*); cf. Isa 1:8; Amos 9:11.

250 Jonah 4:11b (*'ādām . . . ûběhēmâ*). This resumes Joel's theme that even the animals were sorry (Jonah 3:8; cf. Joel 1:18; 2:22), but it also represents the totality of sensate creation.

251 Cf. Jonah 2:3 and Pss 107:28; 120:1; Jonah 2:4a and Ps 107:24; Jonah 2:4b = Ps 42:8b; Jonah 2:5a = Ps 31:23; Jonah 2:6a and Pss 18:5; 69:3; 107:26; 116:3; Jonah 2:7b and Ps 103:4; Jonah 2:8a = Ps 142:4.

252 Cf. Jonah 2:4a (*bilbab yammîm*) and Ezek 27:25 (*bělēb yammîm*).

253 See figure 21. Each part contains six subsections or columns, usually the equivalent of chapters in the printed Bible, which are composed either of matching paragraphs or of series of strophes and antistrophes each with two or three stanzas. Within each part the columns or subsections are arranged in a repetitive descriptive order (A-B-C-A'-B'-C'), more obvious in some parts than in others (e.g., Isaiah 14 [A] concerns Babylon; chaps. 15–16° [B] concern Moab and David; chap. 18 [C] concerns all the nations of the world, with a focus on the East; chap. 21 [A'] concerns Babylon; chap. 22 [B'] concerns David; chap. 23 [C'] concerns Tyre and the western nations). Revisions were made by adding stanzas to strophes (e.g., Isa 1:16–17 was added to Isaiah's 1:18–20), strophes to subsections (e.g., 5:6–7 and 5:8–10 were added to Isaiah's allegory of the vineyard), subsections to parts (e.g., 6:1–11), and whole parts (e.g., chaps. 14–23°). II Isaiah's style conforms to the commented text (in the first and third parts II Isaiah comments on Isaiah in Isaiah's poetic style and on the Deuteronomistic History in prose [chaps. 6–8; 36–39]) and is more regular and more lyrical in the passages that II Isaiah composed for the occasion (in II Isaiah's material, for instance, strophes usually are composed of two matching stanzas, while in commenting on Isaiah they often have three stanzas related to the original as much as to each other).

254 On *ḥuqqîm* and *tôrâ* (Amos 2:4), cf. Exod 18:20; also Gen 26:5 (*ḥuqqôt* and *tôrâ*).

255 The sequence described in Amos 2:9–12 (destruction of the mighty

Amorites, exodus, forty years in the wilderness, possession of the land of the Amorites, commissioning of nazirites and prophets) corresponds to the sequence of events described between Deuteronomy (chaps 1–2, an invasion of the land occupied by the Amorites, who are bigger and taller than the Israelites; cf. 3:11), Joshua (Rahab repeats the story of the exodus [chap. 2]; the exodus is reenacted [chaps. 3–4]; the forty years in the wilderness come to an end [chap. 5]; Israel takes possession of the Amorite lands [5:1; 9:1–2; 11:1–3]), Judges and Samuel (Samson as nazirite; Samuel as both nazirite and prophet).

256 Cf. Amos 3:13–15 and 1 Kings 13; Amos 4:6–11 and 1 Kings 8.

257 The concept of a remnant was devised first by the Elohist and Jeremiah and applied to the northern kingdom (Gen 45:7; 50:20; Jer 31:7). The Deuteronomist seems to restrict it to exiles from Judah and Jerusalem (Deut 4:27; 28:62; 2 Kgs 17:18; 19:29–31; 24:14; 25:22) and writes off the northern kingdom (2 Kgs 17:24–41).

258 Cf. 1 Kings 13 and Amos 2:9–12; 3:7–8; 4:6–11; 7:10–17; 8:11–14.

259 The book of Jeremiah ends by quoting its final chapter (Jeremiah 52 = 2 Kings 25), which it had already interpreted (Jeremiah 21–24; 25–29) and excerpted (Jeremiah 39). The book and the last part of Kings cover the same period (from Manasseh to Zedekiah), include many of the same people and events, and share basic theological ideas but go their own ways in interpreting the causes and effects of the fall.

260 The mixture of prose and poetry in the book of Jeremiah reflects its sources, the poetry original to Jeremiah or composed in imitation of his dramatic style to situate his words in real historical contexts, the prose imitating, elaborating, and often correcting the History.

261 The Deuteronomist admits that there were mediums and wizards and augurers and soothsayers (2 Kgs 21:6; 23:24) and suggests that prop] ets were killed by Manasseh (∂ām nāqî, 2 Kgs 21:16; 24:4) but among the prophets mentions only Huldah by name (2 Kgs 22:14–20). The book of Jeremiah rails against the prophets who proclaim peace and shows Jeremiah confronting such people and their royal patrons (e.g., Jeremiah 26; 28).

262 The book of Jeremiah even mentions the sin of Manasseh (Jer 15:4) but overwhelms his wrongdoing with the crimes of subsequent kings. The book considers, with Jeremiah, that the law is in place, but a symptom of its disagreement with the Deuteronomist on the significance of the law is its repudiation of the ark of the covenant, in which the tablets were contained (Jer 3:16). It is aware of the Historian's views of prophecy, and makes Jeremiah a prophet in the line of Moses (e.g., Jeremiah 1; 15) but removes him from the orthodox role of the prophet as intercessor.

263 Typical of the change is that Ezekiel saw a throne, like sapphire, and

above it the appearance of a human shape (Ezek 1:26), while the editor allows him to see only the throne (Ezek 10:1). In the rest the prophet is distracted by the panoply of the cherubim riding their celestial vehicles.

264 Cf. Deut 14:21; Lev 17:15.

265 Cf. 2 Kgs 19:31.

266 Cf. 1 Kgs 8:64; 2 Kgs 16:14–15.

267 Cf. 2 Kgs 25:4–7.

268 Cf. Gen 18:22–33. The same issue of God's justice is confronted in analyzing Ezekiel's theory of individual responsibility (Ezek 18:19–32).

269 In contrast to the Deuteronomistic term *nāgîd*, the editor of Ezekiel uses the term *nāśî*² (e.g., Ezek 37:24–25).

270 The revised version of Ezekiel is an important source for the supplement to the law in Leviticus 1–7; 12–27.

271 The promise of an innumerable multitude of descendants like the sand on the seashore was introduced by the Deuteronomist into the patriarchal histories (2:1; cf. Gen 22:17, etc.). The expression "the living God" (Hos 2:1) occurred first in the History (Josh 3:10; cf. 2 Kgs 19:16). The choice of a Davidic leader is expressed in terms used of the choice of a king (Hos 2:2; cf. Deut 17:14).

272 Cf. Amos 4:4–5; 5:4–6.

273 In the list of deprivations (Hos 3:4, ". . . without sacrifice or pillar, without ephod or teraphim") the first and third refer to the priestly ministry, and the second and fourth to articles of ancestral religion. The return to Yahweh and David is stated explicitly (Hos 3:5a). Observance of the law is noted by mentioning its basic stipulation and the blessing that results from it (Hos 3:5b, ". . . and they shall come in fear to Yahweh and to his goodness in the latter days").

274 Cf. Joshua 7; Deut 7:25–26.

275 Cf. Judg 8:18; 11:34. The reference is uncertain since the text (Hos 5:1–2) also expresses the contrast between the mountain (Tabor) and the plain (Mizpah) or the valley (Hos 5:2, *he῾mîqû*). The editor, however, refers elsewhere to texts that mention one of the places called Mizpah (cf. Hos 12:12 and Gen 31:47–49; Hos 5:8 and Judges 19–21 or 1 Samuel 8–10).

276 Hos 5:8–10; 9:9; 10:9; cf. Judges 19–21; 1 Samuel 8–15.

277 Hos 7:15–16 ("They turn, like a treacherous bow, to what does not

profit. Their princes, for the insolence they muttered, will die by the sword in Egypt"). The text seems to combine texts of Isaiah that mention the muttering of the Assyrians (Isa 28:11) and go on to condemn Jerusalem for its profitless alliances with Egypt (Isa 30:1–5); cf. Hos 8:13.

278 Hos 8:4–6, 10, 14; 9:10; 10:3, 7–8°, 9–10; cf. 1 Samuel 8; 1 Kings 12.

279 Among the items borrowed from the Deuteronomist are the division of prophets into speakers and dreamers (Joel 3:1; cf. Deut 13:2), the association of prophecy and signs (Joel 3:3; Deut 13:2), the promise of survivors in Jerusalem (Joel 3:5 = 2 Kgs 19:30–31), and the plundering of the temple (Joel 4:5; 2 Kgs 25:13–17).

280 III Isaiah sees humanity as an affront to God. His special contempt for women identifies him as a man.

281 III Isaiah returns to the Syro-Ephraimite war in an oracle against Damascus (chap. 17).

282 This is separated from the rest of the original text by a new introduction (Isa 1:10), which reproduces the first introduction (1:1). This new section (1:10–31) ends (1:27–31) with a summary of the first and second chapters.

283 Isa 1:7bB (ûšěmāmâ kěmahpēkat zārîm); cf. Isa 1:7abA. On the term mahpēkat, cf. Deut 29:22; Isa 13:19; Jer 49:18; 50:40; Amos 4:11.

284 Isa 1:9 (hôtîr) = Isa 1:8 (wěnôtěrâ); Isa 1:9 (śārîd), cf. the Deuteronomistic expression ś'r + śārîd, Num 21:35; Deut 2:34; 3:3; Josh 8:22; 10:28, 30, 33, 37, 39, 40; 11:8; Judg 5:13; 2 Kgs 10:11. The word "a few" (Isa 1:9, kim'āṭ) is redundant and alludes to the Deuteronomistic expression for the few who would be left in Jerusalem (Deut 28:62, wěniš'artem bimtê mě'āṭ).

285 This begins and ends like the first chapter (cf. 1:10 and 1:1; 1:28 and 1:2, 4).

286 Cf. Isa 1:11 (zibḥêkem . . . 'ōlôt) and 1 Sam 15:22 [Amos 5:22]; Isa 1:13 ('āwen wa'ǎṣārâ), cf. Amos 5:5 (bêt 'ēl yihyeh lě' āwen) + Amos 5:21b (wělō' 'ārîaḥ bě'aṣṣěrōtêkem); Isa 1:13 (ḥōdeš wěšabbat), cf. Amos 8:5; Isa 1:14 (ḥodšêkem ûmô'ǎdêkem), cf. Hos 2:13; Isa 1:15 (ûběpāriškem kappêkem 'a'lîm 'ênay mikkem), cf. 1 Kgs 8:22, 38, 54. The final strophe identifies those whom Isaiah called sinners (cf. Isa 1:28 and 1:2, 4) with those accused of ritual offenses and, as often in III Isaiah, gets rid of them in a conflagration.

287 Cf. Isa 2:5 and 2:6 (house of Jacob); 2:2 and 2:12–16 (exaltation and humiliation of Zion); 2:2 and 2:11, 12, 17, 20 (days to come and the day of Yahweh); 2:7 and 1 Kgs 10:14–29 (the aggrandizement of Solomon); 2:6, 8 and 1 Kgs 11:1–13 (foreigners and the worship of foreign Gods); 2:8b and 2 Kgs 22:17 (worship of idols); 2:9b and Josh 24:19 (apostasy as an unforgivable sin); 2:6 and 1 Sam 12:22, 25; 2 Kgs 21:14 (Yahweh's rejection of his people).

[288] Isa 3:6–8: "If someone pressed his brother, from the house of his own father [with these words]: 'You have a cloak, be our leader, and let this ruin be under your authority'—he would protest on that day, as follows: 'I will not be a quack,' and 'in my house there is no bread (*ûbĕbêtî ʾên leḥem*, = "Bethlehem") and there is no cloak. You will not make me leader of the people.' "

[289] The same themes are maintained in III Isaiah's version of the next chapter (5:1–30) and make a transition to the second part (cf. 5:14–17 and 2:9, 11, 17, 22 and 3:6–8; cf. 5:25 and 9:11, 16, 20; 10:4; cf. 5:30 and 8:22–23).

[290] In the sequel's version Ahaz's submission to Tiglath-pileser III was the immediate antecedent of the Assyrian invasions to which Samaria succumbed and from which Jerusalem was rescued by Hezekiah's devotion to the covenant with Yahweh (2 Kings 16°; 18°). In the Deuteronomist's version other causes were at work and Jerusalem also succumbed. III Isaiah (Isa 7:16–25) uses II Isaiah's words and images to portray a few survivors enjoying the provisions that II Isaiah intended for the successor of David (Isa 7:22; cf. 7:15), and also includes an allusion to a text in the Deuteronomistic History to focus on the humiliation of the Davidic dynasty (Isa 7:20; cf. 2 Sam 10:4).

[291] Cf. Isa 8:1–15 (II Isaiah) and 8:16–23 (III Isaiah). II Isaiah has witnesses attest to the veracity of his child's name (8:2) but III Isaiah calls attention to the witness of his teaching (8:16, 20). III Isaiah assumes that people should consult God and relies on a Deuteronomistic text to justify his repudiation of II Isaiah's prophecy that the Davidic dynasty would be restored—as if II Isaiah were a necromancer invoking the dead to help the living (Isa 8:19 = Deut 18:11), or as if he were a dreamer for whom there was no dawn (8:20), or as if he were misleading the people so that eventually they would curse both their king and their God (8:21–22).

[292] Cf. Isa 9:1–6abA (II Isaiah) and 9:6bB–20 (III Isaiah). The enemies of Rezin that Yahweh incites against Ephraim and Samaria are the Assyrians (Isa 9:10; 2 Kgs 16:7–9), but their adversaries also include, in agreement with the Deuteronomistic History, the Arameans and the Assyrians (Isa 9:11; cf. 2 Kgs 16:6) as well as the Philistines (Isa 9:11; cf. 2 Kgs 18:8).

[293] Cf. Isa 10:24–27 (II Isaiah) and 10:20–23 (III Isaiah). II Isaiah refers to the preceding text of Isaiah (cf. 10:5–6), to Judges (Isa 10:26 = Judg 7:25), and to related texts; III Isaiah refers to a text in the second part of Isaiah (cf. 28:15, 17) and to the titles that II Isaiah assigned to Immanuel (10:21; cf. 9:5).

CHAPTER 7

The Politics of the New Age

*T*he period of reconstruction was peaceful and serene. The war had been lost; the exiles who wanted had returned; the people were settled; the city was being rebuilt; and it was urgent that a normal situation prevail. The intellectual battles had been fought; the reasons were clear; practical decisions remained; the choices were evident; it was time for recrimination to stop. The literature of the period is of a piece with its time.

Prophecy and history were amalgamated in the writings of Haggai, Zechariah, the Chronicler, and Malachi. The prophets wrote prose and resolved contemporary problems. The Chronicler rewrote history as reportage, filled with interesting, newsworthy detail, and thought of the prophets as singers and included some of their songs. Haggai's interest was religious and centered on the city. Zechariah's interest was educational and focused on the attitude of the country to its own rebuilding. The Chronicler presented a placid review of history that began with creation but ignored the rest of the world to focus on the enormous accomplishments of the Davidic monarchy in Judah. Malachi's interest was ecumenical and centered on the significance of the temple in the ongoing history of the world. Besides these writers and thinkers there were the inevitable scribes whose ideas insinuated themselves into their works to reaffirm perennial principles of law or homologate the claims of the descendants of David and revive the ancient regime.

Haggai

Haggai composed his prophecy in imitation of the book of Jeremiah. It has precise dates for his oracles, in the manner of Ezekiel and the book of Jeremiah, but it follows the latter's convention in referring to the prophet in the third person. It insists, as its model does, on the prophetic character of its author[1] and on the divine authority of his words.[2] It differs from the book of Jeremiah in its favorable attitude to the temple and, even more notably, in recording the acceptance and total success of his prophecy. His work was mentioned by Zechariah (Zech 1:16–17; 8:9–13) and was revised, in conjunction with the revision of Zechariah, by a writer who was familiar with the royal and priestly perspectives of the Chronicler.[3]

STRUCTURE AND ORGANIZATION (FIG. 23)

Haggai's prophecy is arranged in two complementary parts. The first (1:1–15a) has to do with the building of the temple and with the dissatisfaction that resulted from its abandonment. The second (1:15b–2:9) compares this temple with the Solomonic temple and describes the brilliance that will accrue to it in the future as a focus of the world and its inhabitants. A third part was added in the revised version (2:10–23) and attributes the initial dissatisfaction of the people to their unworthiness but contrasts it with the greater blessings that will accrue to the people under Zerubbabel.

The prophecy is composed in prose and arranged in matching paragraphs, with the paragraphs organized so that each part rises to a crescendo and ends as it began. The revision follows this general pattern of denouement and inclusion but without matching paragraphs and with a merely formal correspondence between the beginning and the end of the part that it added.

Part I (Haggai 1:1–15a)

The first paragraph introduces the people and the problem involved in the prophecy (1:1–2). The prophecy is dated according to the regnal years of Darius and is addressed to the governor of Judah and the high priest, but it concerns the negative attitude of the people toward the rebuilding of the temple. Their resistance to the plan is based on their perception that the time is not right,[4] and the rest of the prophecy deals with the temple and resistance to it in terms of times and seasons.

FIGURE 2 3

Haggai

	Haggai				Book of Haggai		
I	A	1	1:1–2				
		2	1:3–4				
	B	1	1:5–6				
		2	1:7–8				
	C	1	1:9				
		2	1:10–11				
	D	1	1:12a				
		2	1:12b–13				
	E	1	1:14a				
		2	1:14b–15a				
II	A	1	1:15b–2:3				
		2	2:4				
	B	1	2:5				
		2	2:6–7				
	C	1	2:8				
		2	2:9				
				III	A	1	2:10–12a
						2	2:12b–13a
						3	2:13b
						4	2:14
					B	1	2:15
						2	2:16
						3	2:17
					C	1	2:18
						2	2:18°–19
					D	1	2:20–22
						2	2:23

Figure 23. Roman numerals distinguish parts. Letters and numbers indicate pairs of paragraphs.

The second paragraph (1:3–4) is matched with the first by its repetition of the formula of Haggai's prophetic authorization and by its sarcastic response to the objection of the people.[5] The response contrasts the finished houses in which they live with the house of Yahweh, stripped of its paneling.[6] It suggests that the rebuilding of the temple, about which the people felt no particular urgency, consisted in adding finishing touches, which ultimately took less than a month to complete (1:15a).

The third paragraph (1:5–6) contains a distinct message from

Yahweh to consider what they are doing, and specifically to reflect on their meager plantings, bad crops, and poor yields, such that there is not enough to eat or drink or wear or even keep a hired hand busy. The paragraph follows logically on the preceding,[7] but it paints a picture of hard times, which contrast with the opulence of their furnished homes.

The fourth paragraph (1:7–8) is linked to the third by its nearly identical introduction.[8] It appeals to their present predicament to persuade the people to go to Lebanon and get the wood needed to build the kind of house that Yahweh can appreciate (1:8).

The fifth paragraph (1:9) elaborates the preceding paragraphs and adds that their present predicament is a warning from Yahweh to get the temple finished. The bad crops mentioned in the fourth paragraph are reflected in the adage that they look for a lot but in fact look at a little.[9] They stayed at home, in the preceding paragraphs, and lacked purpose and direction, and now they turn first one way, then another, and run to their houses when things go wrong.[10] In the preceding paragraph God asked them to bring wood and build a house that he could be happy with, and now they bring things to their own homes only to have them blown away (1:8a). From the very beginning the problem was that the house of Yahweh was not finished, and this paragraph makes the point emphatically (1:9bB = 1:4b).

The sixth paragraph (1:10–11) matches it by making a connection between the bareness of the temple and the dryness of the land.[11] The suggestion in the preceding paragraph that Yahweh blew away their harvests is developed in this paragraph in terms of a cosmic conspiracy: heaven withholding the dew, the earth its produce, a drought stifling the land, the mountains, the grain, the wine, and the oil, everything that the ground or people or animals might produce, and everything that they did. This is the climax of the first part, and the contrast between the touted opulence of their homes and the visual ruination of their land becomes so stark and severe that it provokes them to action.

The seventh paragraph is the denouement (1:12a). In response to the terrible things that Haggai has said in the name of Yahweh, Zerubbabel, Joshua, and the people accept him as a prophet and pay attention to his message. The paragraph corresponds, in the structure of the part, to the first set of paragraphs, where the prophet confronts the leaders and people with the authority of the word of Yahweh.[12]

The eighth paragraph (1:12b–13) matches the seventh in its references to the people and to the mission of the prophet. It is complete in itself, progressing from the initial fear of the people to the standard oracle of consolation, "I am with you," and complements the preceding paragraph by marking the transition from acceptance of the message to veneration of its source.

The ninth paragraph (1:14a) summarizes the part by saying that Zerubbabel and the high priest and the people were inspired to act. It corresponds, in the structure of the part, to the third and fourth paragraphs, where they were all uninspired. The tenth paragraph (1:14b–15a), in the same structure, matches the fourth paragraph, where they were urged to build the house, and rounds out the part by recording the date at which they finished the work.[13]

The first part, then, has a clear narrative development from the address of Haggai to the effect of his intervention, and from a situation of distress to its resolution. The climax is reached when it becomes clear that the cause of the distress is Yahweh, and its reason the fact that the temple is unfinished. The plot proceeds in hyperbole, beginning with an odd conjunction of great national prosperity and lack of every basic necessity and ending with apparent cosmic catastrophe and lack of basic supernatural needs. This hyperbole indicates that the thread of the narrative is the belief that the cycle of the elements reflects the history of the Gods. The problem, as Haggai described it, was that the cycles became unmeshed, and the solution consisted in recognizing that having a family house and no crops is the reverse of the normal pattern, in which the building of the palace of the Gods is the beginning of fertility and life.

Part II (Haggai 1:15b–2:9)

The first paragraph (1:15b–2:3) duplicates the beginning of the prophecy with a date in the reign of Darius, a synchronism with the tenure of Zerubbabel and Joshua, a prophetic formula, a reference to the people, and an interest in the house of Yahweh. What is new is the comparison between the finished temple and the temple in its original splendor. With this, Haggai moves from times and seasons to historical time, from ritual patterns of distress and resolution, from religious patterns of victory over death, to historical traditions and their interpretation.

The second paragraph (2:4) matches the first by mentioning the same people and by connecting the present time when strength and obedience are required with an allusive past when they actually were documented. It is attached to the end of the preceding part by repeating the same oracle of consolation.[14]

In the third paragraph (2:5) the references to the past are explicit rather than allusive: the exhortation to obedience is an allusion to the original agreement to obey[15] the covenant[16] that Yahweh made with Israel[17] when they came out of Egypt[18] and Moses stood between them and God[19] because they were afraid.[20] The syntax is cramped and indicative of this crasis of allusions, but the paragraph conforms to Haggai's regular practice of combining and unraveling in one paragraph the gist of the things that were said in the preceding paragraphs.

The fourth paragraph (2:6–7) matches the third by insisting on the spoken word of God and by going along with it in explicating the things that were said in the second paragraph. There the triple command to be strong, which was addressed to Zerubbabel and Joshua and the people, and the assurance that Yahweh was with them were taken from the conclusion to the book of Deuteronomy, where Moses exhorted Joshua three times to lead the people against the nations and assured him that Yahweh was with him.[21] The same text also urged Joshua and the people not to be afraid, and Haggai has given the same exhortation to his audience.[22] This new paragraph explains that, as Yahweh went with Joshua to conquer the nations in those former times, so now Yahweh will shake the nations and gather their windfall into his temple (2:6).

The fifth paragraph (2:8) is connected to the preceding paragraph by its reference to the Lord of Hosts, but it makes an apparently unrelated statement about the silver and gold that belongs to Yahweh. In the context of the preceding paragraphs this would have to be an oblique reference to Joshua's rule that the silver and gold of the conquered nations belong to Yahweh (Hag 2:8; Josh 6:19; cf. Deut 7:25).

The sixth paragraph (2:9) resumes the part by concluding that the glory of the refinished temple will be greater than the glory of the first temple. It adds, under the direct authority of God, a promise of peace, which was repudiated in the book of Jeremiah as a saying of the false prophets.[23]

The second part, then, compares the finished temple to the temple that some of Haggai's contemporaries had seen in Jerusalem before the Babylonian invasion. Within this framework of former and later things it recalls the exodus, the covenant, and the conquest, and adapts them to the new situation. It redoes in historical terms the sequence of divine actions, not in terms of Yahweh's victory over the cosmic powers but in terms of Yahweh's victory as it affected the nation and as it was understood by the historians. The second part, in short, matches the first and goes over the same ground from a different perspective. The first part described what everyone believed about the world and God, but the second part went over the things that they knew about themselves and God.

Part III (Haggai 2:10–23)

The third part is not constructed of matching paragraphs but of matching sections composed of progressively fewer paragraphs. The first section (2:10–14) is a transition from the building of the temple to an account of its cultic accoutrements and is composed of four paragraphs describing Haggai's disputation with the priests. It is matched by the last section (2:20–23) in a formal manner by repeating some of its words and ideas, and in an artificial fashion by associating, but in opposite order and with another intent, Zerubbabel and the priests. The second section (2:15–17) has three paragraphs and refers to the curses of past times, and is matched by the third (2:18–19), with two paragraphs, that refers to a time of future blessing.

The first paragraph begins the same way as the first and second parts, with a date in the reign of Darius and a reference to Haggai's prophetic authority, but it omits their synchronism with Zerubbabel and Joshua and has nothing to say about the people or about finishing the temple. It supposes that the temple rituals have been restored, that the priestly courses have been confirmed, and that instruction in the law is a proper priestly function. Its references to wine, oil, meat, and bread are related inversely to the absence of all these things in the first part (2:10–12a; cf. 1:10–11), but its explicit legal viewpoint is alien to the ritual and historical perspectives of the earlier parts.

The second paragraph (2:12b–13a) is related to the first by literal repetition and logical sequence, the first dealing with dedicated goods, the second with contaminated goods. The third paragraph (2:13b) has a similar connection with the second, and the fourth (2:14) with the third. The four paragraphs together form a disputation whose argument leads away from the ritual and historical justification of the second temple to the inculcation of the cultic laws that had been codified recently in the Chronicler's supplement to the Priestly work.[24] It ends, therefore, excluding the people from the temple service[25] and setting the nation[26] apart from the priests who rule it.

The fifth paragraph (2:15) takes up an expression from the first part[27] but applies it to the consideration of past times rather than, as the first part did, to reflection on present behavior. These past times extend beyond the recent past of Haggai's time, when the house of Yahweh was finished, to the earlier times before the stonework was begun. Neither is there a reference to the house as such, but to the temple or its sanctuary where the people could not enter. The sixth paragraph (2:16) is attached to the fifth paragraph by a single preposition and mentions the features of those past times that the priests are to consider. They pretty well paraphrase what Haggai had said earlier about bad crops and poor yields (2:16 and 1:6aA, 9aA) but they have the familiar cadence of curses.

This cadence becomes explicit in the seventh paragraph (2:17) in a standard list of curses on the produce of the land.[28] The list has no particular connection with the preceding paragraph, which describes the depletion of granaries and wine vats, but it takes up a key term from the end of the first section that referred to the produce of the land that was offered in the temple.[29]

The eighth paragraph (2:18) begins the third section with the expression that opened the second section,[30] but it looks forward from the time after the laying of the foundations of the temple instead of backward to the time when it lay in ruins. It differs from Haggai's presentation by referring to the construction of the sanctuary instead of to the finishing of the temple,[31] by dating it in the ninth month instead of in the sixth (1:1, 15 and 2:18) and by being concerned about its practical use rather than its ritual and historical significance.

The ninth paragraph (2:18–19) is paired with it by its use of the same introductory expression and, in combination with it, is parallel to the second section. That section described (2:16) the disappointing crops, but this section says, amazingly enough, that from the very day of the foundation of the temple, even though the seed grain was still in the granary and the vineyards and fruit trees have not budded, they would enjoy the blessing of Yahweh. In contrast to Haggai, then, who saw a real connection between the finishing of the temple and the cycles of fertility, this version goes to marvelous lengths to dissociate them. In its view, crops have nothing to do with the building of temples but are just a blessing from God in return for right worship.

The last section catapults Zerubbabel from his governorship to succession in the line of David. The first paragraph repeats elements from the beginning of the part and from both parts of Haggai's version (2:20–21 and 1:1; 2:6; 2:10b). It is related exclusively to the foregoing reinterpretation, rather than to Haggai's work, by making this the second time that Yahweh spoke to Haggai, on the twenty-fourth day of the ninth month rather than in the sixth month (2:20; cf. 2:10). It refers to the nations, as Haggai does, but sees them as enemies to be defeated in battle rather than as admirers and sources of wealth to be applied to the temple (2:22; cf. 2:6–7). It agrees with the book of Jeremiah, against Haggai's contradictory opinion (2:9; Jer 14:13), that world wars will precede the restoration of Judah (Jer 14:13; 25:16) and that the defeat of the nations is a prelude to the restoration of the Davidic monarchy (Jeremiah 33; Ezekiel 37).

The last paragraph (2:23) is linked to it by its temporal reference and by its interest in Zerubbabel. It makes Zerubbabel a king in the line of David, the servant of Yahweh, the one he has chosen, the signet ring on his finger. It falls into line with the general expectation that the Davidic monarchy would be restored, and along with it a permanent priestly establishment, but it has nothing to do with Haggai's confidence in history and the natural order of the world.

LANGUAGE AND STYLE

The differences between the two versions in language and style are difficult to describe but can be seen quite easily in the passages where they overlap. The difficulties are partly due to the fact that the revision imitates the original and in those places where it disagrees marks its disagreement by deliberate complexification, and partly due to the different sources they use and the different traditions to which they belong.

In lexical choices, Haggai prefers concrete and active forms, and the author of his revision seems to like abstract, passive, and general terms. In the prophetic formula, for instance, Haggai likes the Deuteronomistic expression derived from diplomatic and courier service,[32] and the author of the book prefers the simple messenger form. The original gives Haggai an active part in the prophecy, and the other is stereotyped and often nothing but a notation in the text. In Haggai, in fact, the formula introduces speeches that are addressed directly to the audience, while in the revised version they introduce talks that Yahweh has with the prophet. Similarly, in describing the effects of the drought, Haggai uses active terms like "you sow, eat, drink, dress, and are not satisfied or slaked or warmed," while the reviser talks about things like "seed, meat, bread, food" in their pure or contaminated state. Or Haggai always addresses specific persons and groups, and the author of his book can talk about persons in general.[33] In the same way, Haggai talks about the first temple and the one they now see, and the other writer talks about some vague and indeterminate time before and after the foundations of the sanctuary were laid. In Haggai's view, both Zerubbabel and Joshua had a specific concrete task; in the other view Joshua is replaced by the priesthood and Zerubbabel becomes a symbol of the Davidic restoration. Again, when Haggai pictures Yahweh sifting the heavens and the earth for treasures for his temple, the second writer repeats the first part of the image but joins it with an incongruous, cliché-ridden victory over the international forces of evil.

In grammatical choices, Haggai uses the infinitive to indicate present punctual action of a typical sort, and the author of the revision expresses it in the subjunctive (cf. 1:6a, 9a and 2:12a). Or again, Haggai uses asyndesis or parataxis, where the revision uses consecution.

In syntactic choices, Haggai uses verbal clauses almost exclusively in main clauses, and nominal phrases and clauses to express subordination, but his editor likes subordinate verbal clauses. Haggai has some anacolouthon or ellipsis, but his reviser uses a great deal of it. Haggai avoids long consecutive series, but the author of his book enjoys them.

In prosodic choices, Haggai likes balance and contrast, and the author of the book likes asymmetrical clauses and paragraphs. Haggai likes pairs and triads of clauses with the same initial element and the same structure. He likes paragraphs with matching pairs of lines, or paragraphs that begin and end with long clauses bracketed around shorter clauses, or the alternation of paragraphs with longer and shorter lines. The author of the book, on the other hand, while maintaining some of this, prefers oddly structured paragraphs. For instance, the second paragraph (2:12b–13a) has three balanced consecutive clauses followed by a long clause filled with nouns and by another clause composed of one verb. The next paragraph (2:13b) has the opposite pattern with progressively shorter lines. The fourth paragraph is regular. The fifth has clauses that are related to each other, other than syntactically, only by the repetition of words (2:15). The sixth paragraph has balanced main clauses but upsets the balance of the potentially regular subordinate clauses by changing word order and clause type (2:16).[34] The seventh paragraph (2:17) begins with a very long clause and ends with progressively shorter clauses linked only by syntax and repetition. The eighth is almost regular but has a totally anomalous middle line.[35] Even where the syntax suggests regularity the paragraph disintegrates into a falling close (2:20–22).

In their literary choices, Haggai likes lists that evoke a total image, and the author of the book likes repetitions that clarify an idea. The drought is described in a list of the things that are wanting, or in sets of contrasts (1:6a, 9a). There is a catalog of creation at the time of the drought (1:10–11), and another when the temple is finished (2:6–7). The exhortation to finish the temple goes through all the steps of gathering the material, getting it finished, and dedicating it (1:8). It is not enough for Yahweh to inspire Zerubbabel; he inspires Joshua and the people as well, and encourages each one of them in turn (1:14;

2:4). The author of the book, on the other hand, can set up the case for the priests to decide with a complete list that has lots of repetition but that simply clarifies the case without going anywhere (2:11–12). Similarly, in a paragraph that has balance, there is an inventory and a literal repetition, but the product is an idea rather than an image, and the fact is marked emphatically by a final asymmetrical clause.[36] This interest in plain facts is clear in another paragraph, where the same expression is repeated three times in order to make no mistake about the date of the foundation of the sanctuary (2:18). Finally, when the revision takes over the image of Yahweh sifting through the nations, it immediately abandons it and repeats words about the destruction of kingdoms and their implements of war (2:20–22).

SOURCES AND INTERPRETATION

Haggai composed his prophecy on the basis of theories and schemes available in the Deuteronomistic History and in clear opposition to some of the beliefs it had engendered concerning the relative importance of the temple in the life of the people and in the history of the nation. The writer who revised his work disagreed with him and tried to bring his prophecy into line with the recent update of the Deuteronomistic History in the work of the Chronicler on the Pentateuch and the history of the monarchy.

Part I (Haggai 1:1–15a)

The first paragraph is composed mainly of formulas and formulaic expressions establishing the date and authority of the prophecy. Zechariah dates his prophecy accordingly to fix the purport of his visions (Zech 1:7; 7:1), but the practice began with Ezekiel and the book of Jeremiah. In Ezekiel the dates match his meaning by beginning with the last and revolving in a circle from the beginning to the end in imitation of the cycle of life and death and resurrection. In Jeremiah the dates verify his prophecies by situating their exact fulfillment in the chronology of the world governed by the Babylonian empire. This chronology was extended seventy years[37] to include the return of the exiles and the rebuilding of the city. However, the chronology did not include the return of the temple vessels (Jer 27:16–22; 28:1–17), or mention the temple, or refer to the return of the glory of God as Ezekiel envisaged it; and Haggai had to dispute popular interpretations of the chronology and prove to the people that it was time to finish the temple. Their argument that it was not time to finish the temple because it was not "the time of the coming" is probably a reference to the coming of the glory of Yahweh to the temple as Ezekiel described it since, when the temple has been finished, Haggai takes up this issue and contrasts the apparent glory of the first with the greater glory of the second temple.[38]

The terminology that Haggai uses to designate the officials of Judah was introduced into the literature by the sequel and by the Deuteronomist and was taken up by later writers in different senses. Governors[39] have local authority and are answerable to the king. In the sequel and in Ezekiel they are mentioned as officials in the Assyrian provincial system (2 Kgs 18:24; Ezek 23:6, 12, 23). In the History they are local Israelite or Arabian administrators (1 Kgs 10:15; 20:24). In the book of Jeremiah they are Babylonian officials (Jer 51:28, 57). In Malachi, Ezra, Nehemiah, and Esther they are part of the Persian satrapal system. High priests, similarly, are known from the History and from later literature. In the History they are associated either with the collection of money and temple repairs (2 Kgs 12:11; 22:4, 8; 23:4) or with the judicial process regulating cities of refuge (Num 35:25, 28, 32; Josh 20:6). In the revised version of Zechariah the high priest is a symbol of the coming messianic age (Zech 3:1, 8; 6:11). In Nehemiah he is titular head of the city (Neh 3:1, 20; 13:28). In Haggai, the governor and the high priest are always paired and together represent Judah and Jerusalem. The people they represent are the inhabitants of Jerusalem,[40] those who survived the Babylonian invasion,[41] or those who live in the country.[42] The officials, apart from their representative character, are featureless. Although their jurisdiction extends as far as Lebanon, their interest lies with those who frequent the city (cf. Hag 1:8).

The second paragraph contrasts two times and two buildings, the time for Yahweh's coming to the unfinished temple and the time for the people to live in furnished houses (1:3–4). The key words are taken from the book of Jeremiah and from the Deuteronomistic History. Woodwork was a feature of the first temple, and Haggai's complaint that the people lived in finished houses when Yahweh did not is a way of saying that the woodwork in the temple had to be finished.[43] The ruin in Yahweh's house could refer simply to its unfinished or abandoned state, as Zephaniah refers to the temple in Nineveh stripped of its woodwork (Hag 1:4b; cf. Zeph 2:14), or as Jeremiah describes the royal palace in Jerusalem.[44] The latter is the only exact parallel to Haggai's statement and would suggest that he is being sarcastic, describing the houses in the city in terms traditionally reserved for the temple, and the house of Yahweh, conversely, in terms the prophetic tradition reserved for urban blight.[45]

The third paragraph (1:5–6) is a narrative paraphrase of typical futility curses. The expression "set your mind to . . ." was used by the Deuteronomistic Historian.[46] "Your ways," which they are supposed to consider, has a negative connotation in prophetic literature.[47] One of the curses of the covenant was to plant a lot and harvest a little, and it is not much different from Haggai's remarks on planting a little, expecting a lot, and harvesting next to nothing (cf. Hag 1:6, 9; Deut 28:38). Hunger, thirst, and nakedness are covenant curses (Deut 28:48); eating and not being satisfied are the opposite of the covenant blessing;[48] and drinking without getting drunk is the frustration of another convention.[49] The list ends as it began with the hired hand's wages falling through a hole in his pocket (1:6b). Without saying as much, Haggai suggests to the people that their misfortune is their own doing.

The fourth paragraph (1:7–8), in the same vein, suggests what they can do to remedy the situation. The word "mountain" often refers to an entire region,[50] as distinguished from the plains or more arid regions. It also refers, particularly in the context of building the temple, to the mountains of Lebanon (Josh 13:6; 1 Kgs 5:29), and that is its likely reference in Haggai, where the entire prophecy leads up to a comparison between the two temples. It is usual for Yahweh to take pleasure in his people,[51] in the land (Ps 85:2), or in sacrifice,[52] but Haggai thinks of the temple as giving him pleasure. Yahweh usually acquires glory in war[53] or from the praise of the people (e.g., Ps 29:2; 96:8), or manifests his glory in the temple (Ezek 43:1–5; 1 Kgs 8:11), but Haggai thinks of the temple as giving glory to God.

The fifth paragraph (1:9) continues the image of "setting your minds to your ways" with words that denote movement. They go out to the fields looking for a large harvest, and finding nothing much they come back home and even that gets blown away. They run to their houses when Yahweh's house is bare. This commotion is in contrast to going up to the mountain and bringing back wood and building the temple so that Yahweh might come to his house and find pleasure and glory in it (cf. 1:2 and 1:8).

The sixth paragraph paraphrases covenant curses that reverse the order of creation (1:10–11). Haggai refers to the covenant curses in the Deuteronomistic History, which sealed heaven and earth so that there was no rain or produce (cf. Hag 1:10 and Deut 11:17; 28:23), and to the blessings of Jacob and Joseph, which promised them the dew of heaven.[54] He quotes from Hosea and the History the obvious fact that grain, wine, and oil were primary gifts of the land and that a drought was a curse.[55] He knows from the History and from Joel how this curse affected people and beasts,[56] destroyed everything that the land might produce,[57] and ruined every human effort.[58] The fact that he is referring to these texts is evident from the artificiality of his list, which includes seasonal produce and crops that are excluded in principle under the curse he describes.

The seventh paragraph (1:12a) notes that Haggai's argument convinced the leaders and the people. It uses the Deuteronomistic phrase for obedience,[59] pairs Yahweh and Haggai the way the historical traditions paired Yahweh and Moses,[60] and gives Haggai a mission comparable to his.[61] The remnant of the people who obeyed are those who survived the fall of Jerusalem, those who stayed in the city rather than those who went into exile.[62] From other sources it is known that the building of the temple was a project undertaken by those who returned from exile, including Zerubbabel the governor and Joshua the high priest. From Haggai it is clear that those who stayed in the city were less than enthusiastic about finishing the project until he convinced them that it was an important part of ordinary living.

The eighth paragraph (1:12b–13) insists on Haggai's mission. The people are afraid of Yahweh, presumably because they know that he has spoken to them, and they assume the attitude of the people of Israel in the time of Moses on Sinai or Horeb.[63] Haggai calls himself Yahweh's messenger[64] in the tradition of the angelic figures associated with Sinai and similar places of worship, where elements of the law were revealed. His role as messenger, like that of the messengers before him, includes calming their fear and giving them the assurance they need for their task.[65] This confirmation of Haggai's mission authorizes the dedication of the temple for which there is no other justification in tradition or the word of God.

The ninth paragraph (1:14a) then reconfirms his mission by having Yahweh directly inspire the leaders and the people to get to work. The expression he uses — "Yahweh roused their spirit" — is used in the book of Jeremiah and in Chronicles but depends on the common and familiar image of shaking off sleep, which the tradition applied to God and to famous people and even to places like Zion and Jerusalem.[66]

The tenth paragraph (1:14b–15a) notes that they actually did the work and completed it in a few weeks. God is called either Yahweh or Yahweh of Hosts in Haggai, but it is unusual to call the temple the "House of Yahweh of Hosts." The expression may allude to the shrine at Shiloh, whose destruction the book of Jeremiah took as an argument for not relying on the temple in Jerusalem (Hag 1:14b; cf. 1 Sam 1:3, 24; Jeremiah 7).

Part II (Haggai 2:1–9)

The first paragraph compares the finished temple unfavorably with the temple that could have been seen before the Babylonian invasion (1:15b–2:3).[67] The glory that he ascribes to the first temple is usually ascribed to Yahweh's presence in the temple, but Nahum, in the parody that he composed on Nineveh and Jerusalem, referred as Haggai does to the silver and gold and glory in the temple.[68]

The second paragraph contains words of encouragement for Zerubbabel, Joshua, and the people and matches the exhortation that Haggai gave the people in the first part before the temple was finished (2:4; cf. 1:12b–13). Haggai's words are marked as quotations by the prophetic formula that accompanies them and are taken, in fact, from similar words of encouragement given by Moses and by God to an earlier Joshua (2:4).[69] The exact formulation, combining a command with the encouragement, may reflect contemporary parlance or may imply, by alluding to the covenant ceremony at Sinai, that the critical point is acceptance of the authority of Haggai and obedience to Yahweh.[70] The latter is suggested by the references in the third paragraph to the exodus and the exhortation that Moses gave them at that time not to fear,[71] and to the mediation of Moses in the revelation of the law on Horeb.[72] Quotations and allusions such as these justify Haggai's insistence on the rebuilding of the temple, for which there was little prophetic, historical or legal precedent.[73]

The fourth paragraph (2:6–7) alludes to Ezekiel and some of the same texts. Nahum included precious instruments and objects, as Haggai does, among the distinguishing features of the temple.[74] Heaven and earth, sea and dry land describe the four corners of creation as seen from the opposite perspective from that visible in the drought.[75] The sifting of the nations for treasures to be dedicated to Yahweh marks the end of the seventy years of foreign domination as seen by III Isaiah.[76] Haggai's prediction that the temple would be filled with glory adapts Ezekiel's vision of the dedication of the temple and its application by the Deuteronomist to the realities of carpentry and actual construction.[77]

The next paragraph (2:8), therefore, is essentially a quote, as the prophetic formula indicates, from the law of the ban declared in Joshua.[78] The last paragraph dispels the people's doubt by assuring them that the new temple will be more glorious than the old and, ignoring the disputes recorded in the book of Jeremiah between the self-styled true and false prophets, proclaims an era of peace (Hag 2:9b; Jer 14:13). The book of Jeremiah had implied that the temple, with the ark and all its accoutrements, was a delusion on which Jerusalem had relied to its detriment. It was just such an attitude among the leaders and people that Haggai had to combat, and he marks his disagreement with the book of Jeremiah by quoting its saying in opposite order. Since Jeremiah, in the biography and history under his name, had assumed the character of Moses, it was at least politic of Haggai to claim Mosaic authority.

Part III (Haggai 2:10–23)

The first paragraph (2:10–12a) mimics the beginning of the first two parts but has a totally different thrust. The governor, the high priest, and the people are gone, and in their place are priests and a hypothetical suppliant. The temple has dropped out of sight or has become an encompassing context. The inquiry that is made of the priests in the whole first section has earlier precedents,[79] but the subject of the inquiry was canonized in the supplement to the Priestly document in its rules governing peace offerings.[80] The answer is simple enough, but the revision uses it as a legal precedent or ploy for disagreeing with Haggai and repudiating the work that the people had done and the offerings that they had brought to the temple.

The second section (2:15–17) explains this repudiation by the fact that the inner part of the temple had not been built.[81] It makes this the problem that Haggai confronted and so presents another version of the drought that he described (Hag 2:16–17; cf. 1:6, 11). What was lacking was the abundance that Joel predicted (Hag 2:16; cf. Joel 2:24). In its place was the sort of curse that the Deuteronomistic Historian considered typical, including destructive hailstorms like those that had ruined the crops in Egypt (Hag 2:17aA).[82] The third section refers to the time after the sanctuary had been built, an occasion supposedly coinciding with the finishing of the temple that Haggai described, and portrays it as a time of typical blessing (Hag 2:19; cf. Deut 8:8). This temporal coincidence, however, is a literary device that allows the new edition to copy the sequence of phases in Haggai's work without adopting his point of view. In effect, the revision disagrees with Haggai, talks about construction and not merely redecorating, dates this construction of the temple to the ninth month and not to the sixth, leaves out Haggai's ritual and historical interpretation, and puts a cultic and legal perspective in its place.

The last section (2:20–23) involves another reinterpretation of Haggai's work. In Haggai's perspective, Zerubbabel and Joshua were a counterbalance to the apathy of the people who had not left Jerusalem and who did not see any urgency in getting the temple finished, but in the perspective of his editor Zerubbabel was the successor of David and the restoration of the temple was a sign of his coming. The reinterpretation becomes completely obvious when the editor quotes Haggai's words (2:21b = 2:6bA) in a radically different context that substitutes the total submission of the nations for their generous cooperation (2:22).[83] The reinterpretation is not without authority but is based on Jeremiah and Ezekiel and on Deuteronomistic conceptions of the Davidic monarchy.[84]

CONCLUSION

Haggai made a significant contribution to prophetic and historical traditions by bringing their evidence to bear on the centrality of the temple in the restoration of Israel. In the style of Ezekiel and the author of the book of Jeremiah he wrote in prose and about himself in the third person. In the mood of Joel he related the presence of God to the tranquil possession of a productive land. In the style of the Deuteronomistic Historian he took bad crops as a curse and saw a parallel between natural cycles and historical process. He took issue with the mood of his time and with the speculation that might support it and looked forward to a happier time, when peaceful nations would convene in the place that Yahweh chose.

The vision did not last long without correction. The chronological speculation that Haggai disputed won out, and the foundation of the temple had to be redated. There was work still to be done and matters of ritual purity to settle. There was the promise to David to incorporate into the life of a community that had been split and separated by the exile. There was a different appreciation of tradition: Haggai, for instance, going with II Isaiah; his editor preferring the updated version in III Isaiah; or Haggai relying on the Deuteronomistic synthesis and his reviser using the programs developed by the Chronicler; or Haggai a kind of innovator and his successor aware of what Zechariah had contributed. What happened was a different vision—truer perhaps—more idealistic, and more satisfying in the long run.

Zechariah

Zechariah was composed before the second edition of Haggai and, along with Malachi, was responsible in part for the revision of that book. Zechariah itself was included in the second edition and was elaborated by the same editor in directions that had been merely insinuated into the prophecy of Haggai.

Zechariah is a partial corrective and supplement to Haggai. Haggai had related the construction and dedication of the temple to natural and historical cycles and had addressed the common sense of the people and the sense of tradition among the leaders. But Zechariah appeals to visionary cycles of peace, purification, and reconciliation and founds the temple on the mercy and initiative of God. The revision of Zechariah supposed the foundation and dedication of the temple and related it instead to the structure and function of the Judean state in a world run from the outside by aliens.

Haggai was in the line of Isaiah and the Deuteronomistic Historian and relied on a lyric sense to avoid the partisan positions of people like the author of the book of Jeremiah. Zechariah is obviously indebted to Amos and Ezekiel and uses make-believe to display the workings and repercussions of the here and now. The editor who redid Haggai and Zechariah was in the tradition of Isaiah and Jeremiah and constructed a stage and a drama to project into future times the traditional reasons for opposing the unspeakable intrusion of aliens into the affairs of Judah and its God.

STRUCTURE AND ORGANIZATION (FIGS. 24, 24A)

Zechariah composed his prophecy in six adventures arranged in pairs in a chiastic order. Each adventure, similarly, is composed of scenes that match and move to a narrative or descriptive or explanatory finish, and each scene is made up of paragraphs or strophes in pairs or triads. The editor expanded these six into eight adventures with insertions and additions that followed the original pattern of matching, and then composed a second part with six symbolic dramatizations that reflected and corrected the revised original (fig. 24a).

The prophecy and the revision are written as history and in prose. The prophecy deals with the past in two adventures, with the present in the next two, and with the future in the last two adventures. The revision deals with the interplay between the present and the future and, in its own contributions, pits Judah and Jerusalem against the world.

Part One (Zechariah 1–8)

The First Adventure (Zechariah 1:1–17)   The first adventure fixes the time of the prophecy and its temporal extent. The first two scenes (1:1–4, 5–6) relate the present to the past, the former prophets to

FIGURE 24

Zechariah

	Zechariah				The Book of Zechariah		
I	A	1	1:1–2	I	A	1	
		2	1:3			2	
		3	1:4			3	
	B	1	1:5		B	1	
		2	1:6			2	
	C	1	1:7–8		C	1	
		2	1:9			2	
	D	1	1:10		D	1	
		2	1:11			2	
	E	1	1:12		E	1	
		2	1:13			2	
		3	1:14–15			3	
	F	1	1:16		F	1	
		2	1:17			2	
II	A	1	2:1–2	II	A	1	
		2	2:3–4			2	
	B	1	2:5–6		B	1	
		2	2:7–9			2	
	C	1	2:10		C	1	
		2	2:11–13			2	
	D	1	2:14–16		D	1	
		2	2:17			2	
				III	A	1	3:1
						2	3:2
					B	1	3:3–4a
						2	3:4b
						3	3:5abA
					C	1	3:5bB–7
						2	3:8a
					D	1	3:8b–9
						2	3:10
III	A	1	4:1–2	IV	A	1	4:3
		2	4:4–6aA			2	4:4–6
					B	1	4:7
						2	4:8–9
					C	1	4:10a
			4:10b°			2	

continued

FIGURE 24 (*cont*)

	Zechariah				The Book of Zechariah		
					D	1	4:11
						2	4:12
						3	4:13–14
	B	1	5:1–2	V	A	1	
		2	5:3			2	
		3	5:4			3	
	C	1	5:5		B	1	
		2	5:6			2	
	D	1	5:7		C	1	
		2	5:8–9a			2	
		3	5:9b–11			3	
IV	A	1	6:1–3	VI	A	1	
		2	6:4–5			2	
	B	1	6:6–7a		B	1	
		2	6:7b–8			2	
					C	1	6:9–12
						2	6:13abA
					D	1	6:13bB–14
						2	6:15
V	A	1	7:1	VII	A	1	
		2	7:2–3			2	
	B	1	7:4–6		B	1	
		2	7:7			2	
	C	1	7:8–10		C	1	
		2	7:11–12a			2	
	D	1	7:12b–13		D	1	
		2	7:14			2	
VI	A	1	8:1–2	VIII	A	1	
		2	8:3			2	
	B	1	8:4–5		B	1	
		2	8:6			2	
	C	1	8:7–8		C	1	
		2	8:9–10			2	
	D	1	8:11–12		D	1	
		2	8:13a			2	
		3	8:13b–15			3	
	E	1	8:16–17		E	1	
		2	8:18–19			2	

continued

FIGURE 24 (*cont*)

Zechariah				The Book of Zechariah			
F	1	8:20–21		F	1		
	2	8:22			2		
	3	8:23			3		
				IX	A	1	9:1–2
						2	9:3–4
					B	1	9:5–7aA
						2	9:7aBb–8
					C	1	9:9–10
						2	9:11–12
					D	1	9:13–14
						2	9:15–17
				X	A	1	10:1–3
						2	10:4–7abA
					B	1	10:7bB–10
						2	10:11–12
				XI	A	1	11:1–3
						2	11:4–6
					B	1	11:7–8
						2	11:9–11
					C	1	11:12–14
						2	11:15–17
				XII	A	1	12:1–3
						2	12:4–5
					B	1	12:6–8
						2	12:9–14
				XIII	A	1	13:1–2
						2	13:3–5
					B	1	13:6–7abA
						2	13:7bB–9
				XIV	A	1	14:1–3
						2	14:4–5
					B	1	14:6–9a
						2	14:9b–11
					C	1	14:12–13
						2	14:14–15
					D	1	14:16–17
						2	14:18–21

Figure 24. Roman numerals refer to Adventures and Dramatizations. Letters indicate scenes. Numbers denote paragraphs.

FIGURE 24A

Zechariah: An Outline

Zechariah			The Book of Zechariah		
			PART ONE		
A	=	1:1–17	A	=	1:1–17
A	=	2:1–17	A	=	2:1–17
			B	=	3:1–10
B	=	4:1–6aA, 10b°	B	=	4:1–14
		5:1–11	B¹	=	5:1–11
B	=	6:1–8	B¹	=	6:1–15
A¹	=	7:1–14	A¹	=	7:1–14
A¹	=	8:1–23	A¹	=	8:1–23
			PART TWO		
			A	=	9:1–17
			A	=	10:1–12
			B	=	11:1–17
			B	=	12:1–14
			A¹	=	13:1–9
			A¹	=	14:1–21

Figure 24a. Letters indicate the pattern of composition.

Zechariah, the past time of Yahweh's anger to the present time manifesting its effects—their fathers' resistance and their own repentance. The next two scenes (1:7–9, 10–11) recount the vision of the horsemen who patrolled the earth and found it at peace, with one scene composing the vision and the other its interpretation. The last two scenes (1:12–15, 16–17) divert Yahweh's anger away from Jerusalem to the nations and announce the building of the temple and reconstruction of Jerusalem: the first scene queries Yahweh's mercy; the second declares that Yahweh in his mercy is about to return to Jerusalem. The prophecy is dated right after Haggai's story of the finishing of the temple but talks about the construction of the temple as an unfinished future event.[85]

The first scene is composed of three paragraphs. The first establishes the date of the document, its prophetic authority, and the residue of divine anger that Zechariah had to resolve (1:1–2). The second suggests the reason for Yahweh's anger by recalling his pleas for repentance (1:3). The third concludes the argument and returns to the point of the first by pleading with the people not to be like their fathers (1:4).

The second scene has two paragraphs. The first takes up the topic of their forefathers and the former prophets from the first scene (1:5), and the second matches it by having the people, unlike their fathers, repent (1:6).

The third scene (1:7–9) is dated three months later and deals with a different theme. Zechariah's prophetic inspiration is derived from a vision and its interpretation. The vision is of a rider on a red horse with other horses behind him. The angel who gives him his words promises to interpret the vision. The two paragraphs (1:7–8, 9) are distinguished by their grammar and syntax but are related to each other by theme, genre, and the logic of a question and its answer.

The fourth scene (1:10–11), responds to the third by interpreting the vision. Both of its paragraphs feature the rider on the red horse, and both explain that the horsemen who were sent to survey the earth found that it was free of strife.

The fifth scene (1:12–15) turns abruptly to another theme. The first paragraph introduces the temporal consideration that underlies the specific dates—the end of the seventy-year period predicted by the book of Jeremiah—and questions Yahweh's mercy toward Jerusalem (1:12). In the second Yahweh gives a favorable answer to the question (1:13). In the third the angel who asked God the question relays to Zechariah the generous answer he received (1:14–15).

The sixth scene (1:16–17) corresponds to it, declaring Yahweh's mercy toward Jerusalem and his favor toward Zion. The first paragraph takes up the topic of Yahweh's kindness mentioned in the middle paragraph in the preceding scene (1:16; cf. 1:13), and the second develops the theme of Yahweh's jealous regard for Zion and Jerusalem broached in its first and third paragraphs (1:17; cf. 1:12, 14–15).

The matching of the scenes means that there is a break after each pair: the first two scenes fit together, but the third goes in a different direction; the fourth goes with the third, but the fifth and sixth break with them and abruptly begin another topic. The coherence of the three pairs is marked formally and artfully but is not logically clear until the end of the adventure. The first pair has the people recognize the reason for Yahweh's rage and repent. The second pair points out that the whole world is at peace. The third pair draws the conclusion that the seventy years of foreign domination must be at an end and with it the time of Yahweh's rage against Jerusalem.

Within each scene the paragraphs match by literal and topical repetition. Between paired scenes the connection consists in thematic transformation. Literal repetition extends beyond words to phrases and clauses. Topical repetition is logical and literal. Thematic repetition is marked by variation in style, viewpoint, or attitude on particular issues. When a scene is composed of two paragraphs, both are taken up in the matching scene. When it is composed of three paragraphs, the middle topic becomes the main topic of the following scene. The matching and pairing correspond to the necessities of narrative, description, explanation, or argumentation.

The Second Adventure (Zechariah 2:1–17)   The first scene (2:1–4) is a vision of the horns that scattered the nation. The first paragraph describes the horns tossing Judah and Jerusalem (2:1–2), and the second is a vision of blacksmiths twisting the horns downward into a useless and unthreatening position (2:3–4). The paragraphs present two successive views of the same thing and are joined by literal repetition of a whole clause.[86]

The second scene is a vision of Jerusalem being measured and about to be inhabited (2:5–6, 7–9). The first paragraph describes Zechariah talking to someone who is setting out to measure the length and breadth of the city, and the second explains that the city will be unbounded by walls but distinguished by the glory and jealousy of God.

The third scene is a summons to the exiles to flee from the north and escape to Zion (2:10, 11–13). The first paragraph attributes the exile to Yahweh's control of the world, and the second rewards Zion with the resources of the world. The two are joined by the verbatim repetition of the summons and by the thematic relation between the north and Babylon or between the four winds of heaven and all the nations of the world.

The fourth scene announces Yahweh's return and residence in Zion. The first paragraph calls on Zion to rejoice because Yahweh has roused himself and many nations will come to him (2:14–16). The second paragraph warns the rest of the world to be wary because Yahweh has roused himself and resides in Jerusalem (2:17).

The four scenes are arranged in matching pairs, with a break between them. The first two scenes are visions of Jerusalem as it was in the past and as it will be soon. The second two scenes are visions of the confluence of Yahweh, the exiles, and the nations to Zion. The break is marked plainly by the change from reportage to direct address. Together they deal with the past seen from the vantage point of a new era.

The Third Adventure (Zechariah 3:1–10)   The first scene (3:1, 2) represents the trial of Joshua the high priest. The first paragraph describes the disposition of the court, and the second gives Yahweh's verdict. They are joined by their repeated references to the prosecutor and his case and are distinguished by their patterns of verbal and nominal clauses.[87]

The second scene (3:3–4a, 4b, 5abA) describes the solemn investiture of Joshua as high priest. In the first paragraph his old clothing is soiled; in the third his new clothing is clean; and in the middle paragraph the change is interpreted as taking away his guilt.

The third scene comprises two exhortations to Joshua. The first encourages him to walk in the ways of Yahweh by promising him preeminence among the priests (3:5bB–7). The other urges him and his confreres to pay attention to the exhortation because they have been designated as portents (3:8a).

The fourth scene explains that they portend the coming of Yahweh's servant from the line of David (3:8b–9, 10). The first paragraph explains that there will be a cornerstone with seven faces and an inscription that will remove the guilt of the land. The second is linked to it by a reference to the same indefinite future and describes the tranquility that will pervade the land.

The scenes are paired, as usual, with the problems of the priesthood dealt with in the first two, and the messianic age described in the last two. The break between the two is marked by the change in speakers: Yahweh and Zechariah speaking to Joshua's case in the first pair, the angel of Yahweh acting as a witness against him in the second pair.

The adventure stands out from the others by its tone and by its treatment of the characters as much as by the issues that it raises. Yahweh takes an active part in rebuking Satan and in the investiture of Joshua. Zechariah acts independently of the angel who inspires him. The angel harangues Joshua instead of pursuing the angelic mission of interpreting visions. Interest shifts from Judah, Jerusalem, and Israel to a few petty officials, an ideology and a grand scheme. The peace that has already been achieved at the end of the second adventure is now marred by strife and recrimination and dire warning. The difference that this makes will be evident in the next adventure, which is forced to conform to it.

The Fourth Adventure (Zechariah 4:1–14)   The first scene (4:1–3, 4–6) is Zechariah's vision of a candlestick and its interpretation. The vision is detailed, but the angel's explanation is tentative and truncated, and instead of explaining the details the angel simply declares its pertinence.

The second scene (4:7, 8–9) is related to the first by its interest in Zerubbabel. The first paragraph deals with him in terms of the cornerstone that was mentioned in the preceding adventure (4:7; cf. 3:9). The second relates this cornerstone to the building of the temple (4:8–9). Neither paragraph has anything to do with the vision presented in the first scene.

The third scene is bifurcated (4:10a, 10b). Its first paragraph relates to the second scene dealing with Zerubbabel and the cornerstone, and its second paragraph is the interpretation of the candlestick shown in the first scene. The connection between the paragraphs is neither literary nor logical but artificial and complicated. In Zechariah's version the seven-branched candlestick is interpreted in the second paragraph as the eyes of Yahweh that dart all over the face of the earth. In the revised version these seven eyes are the seven facets of the cornerstone described in the preceding adventure and associated with Zerubbabel's building operations mentioned in the preceding scene.[88] The editing is forced, but its effect is suitably eerie and visionary.

The fourth scene takes up the vision of the two olive trees that were added to the vision of the candlestick at the beginning of the adventure (4:11, 12, 13–14; cf. 4:3). The first question refers to the olive trees. The second question reformulates the question in order to inject a more elaborate description of the olive trees and their link with the candlestick. The last gives the not unexpected answer that the two olive trees are Joshua and Zerubbabel.

The scenes in Zechariah's version narrate a vision and its interpretation. In the edited version they are arranged in an interlocking descriptive order. The second scene in this version, although it is linked artificially to the first by its mention of Zerubbabel, introduces a totally different issue. The third scene responds to the first but in terms of the things that were said in the preceding adventure. The fourth is linked artificially to the third and brings the whole adventure to a close, but it mainly completes and corrects the second scene by associating Zerubbabel the artisan with Joshua the priest. The effect is puzzling but is suitable to the mystery being fashioned by the editor.

The Fifth Adventure (Zechariah 5:1–11) The first scene is a vision and its interpretation. The first paragraph is a vision of a flying scroll (5:1–2). The second says that the scroll contains a curse going through the world against liars and thieves (5:3). The third directs the scroll against these people and their houses (5:4).

The second scene is a vision of a basket and its meaning (5:5, 6). Its two paragraphs are distinguished by syntax and are linked by their interest in eyes.[89]

The third scene is a closer look at the basket (5:7, 8–9a, 9b–11). The first paragraph is a vision of a woman in the basket. The second is a vision of two women with the wind in their wings. The third has the winged women carrying the bad woman in the basket to the land of Shinar.

The third scene is related to the second by its interest in the basket, but it is also related to the first by contributing to the development of the same theme. In both the first and the third scenes there is a vision of something flying, and in both there is a reference to a house built by evil men and women. The second scene, by contrast, is related to the first scene in the preceding adventure because in both the interpretation concerns eyes that peruse the whole world.

It is evident, therefore, that these three scenes belong with the first scene in the preceding adventure. Together they describe how Yahweh, from his temple in Jerusalem, purifies the land and ships the evil that overtook it back to where it belongs in Mesopotamia. The link between them was broken by inserting the third adventure and by changing the fourth to correspond to it: both adventures, in their edited versions, deal with Joshua and Zerubbabel and the coming messianic age. The present adventure, therefore, originally part of the third adventure but editorially the fifth, is naturally matched in both editions with the next.

The Sixth Adventure (Zechariah 6:1–15)   The first scene is a vision of four chariots representing the four winds of heaven (6:1–3, 4–5). The second scene corresponds to it by describing the direction that the chariots take but with special concentration on the chariot that patrolled the North and thereby set Yahweh's spirit at rest (6:6–7a, 7b–8).

This adventure begins the prophecy's denouement. It is like the first, in which riders and four technicolor horses went out to patrol the world. It resembles the second, where Yahweh summons back to Jerusalem those who have been dispersed to the four winds and especially to the North. It is like the fifth, the third in Zechariah's version, in which eyes patrol and scour the earth and evil is taken back to its source. Together with the fifth it is about the present time, in which the land has been purified and prepared for the return of Yahweh.

The third scene (6:9–12, 13abA) is a political screed in which people who have returned from exile are designated to make a crown for the high priest Joshua as precursor of the offspring of David who is to build the temple. The first paragraph is his program, and the second matches it by repeating his role in the building of the temple and describing the honor and authority that will be his. The scene represents the usual break after paired scenes and has only implicit and tenuous connections with the preceding. Its real connections are with the subplot running through this part that, through the two anointings, relates the restoration of Zion to the problems of government and national sovereignty.

The fourth scene matches it by referring to the same people and the same issues (6:13bB–14, 15). The first paragraph states that the two anointed will be compatible, and the second includes people from distant places in the building of the temple but makes obedience the condition of its construction.

The Seventh Adventure (Zechariah 7:1–14) The first scene is a diary entry rather than a vision (7:1, 2–3). The first paragraph fixes the date to the day and the month, and the second paragraph makes inquiry of the priests and prophets in Bethel concerning the fasts that have taken place for so many years in the fifth month. The second (scene (7:4–6, 7) matches it with an answer that belittles the fasts that have taken place for seventy years in the fifth and seventh months and supports its criticism by quoting what the former prophets said when Jerusalem was still inhabited and prosperous.

The third scene (7:8–10, 11–12a) presents the alternative to fasting and notes that an earlier generation refused to take this advice from their prophets. The fourth scene (7:12b–13, 14) recalls the effects of their refusal, first the great anger of Yahweh, finally the destruction of the land and bitter languishing in exile.

The two pairs of scenes are narrative and consecutive and do not have the break that characterized the earlier adventures. They mark the transition from past to present to future time by noting the end of the seventy-year period and the beginning of a new time when, as once was the case, fasting will not be important.

The Eighth Adventure (Zechariah 8:1–23) The first scene (8:1–2, 3) has two related declarations of Yahweh. The first concerns his interest in Zion, and the second announces his return to Jerusalem. Both retrieve items from the beginning of the prophecy and make it clear that the happy conclusion is at hand (8:1–2 and 1:4; 8:3 and 1:15; 2:14).

The second scene has two other declarations by Yahweh. They are related to each other artificially by literal repetition and formally as factual statement and theoretical commentary. They are connected with the first two declarations by implication (8:4–5, 6; note 8:4aA = 8:6aA).

The third scene describes the return of the exiles and some of the conflict that it caused in Jerusalem. The first paragraph brings the people from the East and the West back to Jerusalem and lets them dwell there with Yahweh (8:7–8). The second paragraph refers to Haggai's mission and paraphrases his prophecy (8:9–10; cf. Hag 1:2, 6, 11; 2:4) and is addressed to the people in Judah and Jerusalem for whom things had not been going well, as he was careful to point out to them, because the temple had been begun but not finished.

The fourth scene is another thorough paraphrase of Haggai's prophecy (8:11–12, 13a, 13b–15). The first paragraph contrasts the times to come with the time of drought that Haggai described (8:11–12; cf. Hag 1:6, 10–12). The second paragraph tries to convince them of Yahweh's good will in the words that Haggai used to persuade them that they no longer lived under the curse and that a time of prosperity had begun (8:13a; cf. Hag 2:4–5). The difference is that Haggai thought of the temple as finished, while Zechariah thought that the restoration had just begun. It was Zechariah's point of view that allowed another writer to go back and correct Haggai before bringing Zechariah up to date.

The fifth scene is a final appeal for concord in the country that Yahweh has restored (8:16–17, 18–19). Its first stanza sets out the rules of common sense and good order that were set out at the start of the preceding matching adventure, and the second demonstrates the blessings that will accrue from their observance.[90]

The sixth scene resumes the theme of Zion as the center of a civilized universe (8:20–21, 22, 23; cf. chaps. 1–2). The first paragraph, building on the return of Yahweh to the city that was intimated at the beginning of the prophecy, portrays nations encouraging one another to assemble in his presence. The second paragraph confirms that the nations will come to entreat Yahweh, and the third portrays their open envy of a nation like Judah, which has God in its capital.

Part Two (Zechariah 9–14)

The First Dramatization (Zechariah 9:1–17) The first scene is composed of two strophes each with two stanzas (9:1–2, 3–4). The first strophe describes the borders of Israel to visualize the position of Israel among the nations. Its first stanza gives the word of Yahweh status among the tribes of Israel and among the northern coalition that was led by Damascus (9:1) and notes enigmatically that Yahweh has a human eye.[91] The second stanza points out that Tyre and Sidon, noted for their wisdom, border on Israel as well (9:2). The second strophe lets the eye of God roam over the destruction of Tyre: its first stanza pictures Tyre as a walled city where the dust was silver and the walls were gold, and the second explains that Yahweh took possession of it, destroyed its fleet, and burned it (9:3, 4).

The second scene is also composed of two strophes, each with two stanzas (9:5–7aA, 7aBb–8). It matches the first scene by describing the astonishment of Tyre's southern neighbors when she was destroyed, by promising that God will protect the borders of Israel, and by explaining what it meant by ascribing a human eye to Yahweh.[92] The first strophe begins with the reaction of the Philistine cities and then brings on them an even more humiliating defeat by Yahweh (9:5b–7aA). The second strophe (9:7aBb–8) begins by apportioning Philistine territory to Judah and ends with Yahweh encamped to protect his own land from invaders, because now he has seen the awful chaos and humiliation that invasion can bring.[93] The effect of the two scenes together is to locate Israel in its territory, bounded on the north by Damascus and the Hittites and on the west by the Phoenicians and Philistines, and centered on the inhabitation of God.

The third scene is also composed of two strophes, each with two stanzas, that describe the installation of Yahweh as king in Jerusalem and the return of the exiles (9:9–10, 11–12). The first stanza (9:9) calls on Zion to rejoice because her king has come back to her, humble and riding on an ass. The second (9:10) is its match and describes the peace that his kingdom brings when he puts an end to the armies of Ephraim and takes command of the land from sea to sea, from the Euphrates to the end of the world. The third stanza (9:11) describes the release of the captives in exile, and the fourth (9:12; cf. Isa 40:2) invites them back to Jerusalem to receive double for all that they have suffered.

The fourth scene also has two strophes, each with two stanzas, one strophe describing Yahweh's victory over the Greeks, the other describing his stalwart presence in Jerusalem and the happiness and prosperity of his people (9:13–14, 15–17). The first stanza (9:13) pictures Yahweh drawing Judah like a bow, fitting Ephraim like an arrow, shooting the people of Zion against the Greeks, and brandishing Zion herself as a sword. The second stanza (9:14) matches it by having Yahweh manifesting himself against the Greeks, like a storm from the south, with thunder and lightning his battle cry. The third stanza (9:15) reverses the picture and sees Yahweh as the protector of his people and them eating the slingstones of the enemy like bread, drinking the blood of the slain like wine, surfeited like a full bowl, like the edge of a bloodied altar. The fourth stanza (9:16–17) matches it by describing the beauty and the fertility of the land, the splendor of the people, the food that makes the boys strong, and the wine that makes the girls blush.

The entire dramatization develops themes of divine kingship that Zechariah had broached (cf. 1:10–17; 8:1–6) but includes them in the context of victory over the nations. The new era that was beginning in the prophecy of Zechariah is catapulted from a time of happiness and glory into an age of world supremacy.

The Second Dramatization (Zechariah 10:1–12) The first scene is composed of two strophes, each with three stanzas, all together a dense concatenation of established but incongruous images (10:1–3, 4–7abA).[94] The first strophe describes the people as a flock and exacts punishment of their shepherds, and the second strophe equips the flock for battle against its enemies. The first stanza takes up the image of fertility presented at the end of the previous dramatization and portrays Yahweh as the God of rain who makes the grass grow. The second stanza compares Yahweh to the wizards and diviners who cannot keep their promises but instead make the people wander like sheep without a shepherd. The third stanza develops this theme, declaring Yahweh's anger with the shepherds and care for his flock, and finally transforming the flock into a war horse. The second strophe elaborates on this theme in three stanzas. The first stanza lists what this flock, this war horse, this house of Judah will produce and includes from Isaiah such marvelous and random items as the cornerstone, the wall peg, armaments, and a leader. The second stanza develops this military theme by describing the flock as Yahweh's warriors battling for Judah and Joseph. The third stanza visualizes Ephraim returning to the land like a warrior, happy as can be, his children watching him and filled with joy. The future, in this view, is filled with bits and pieces of the past.

The second scene is composed of two strophes, each with two stanzas. The first strophe describes how Ephraim and his children will return from Egypt and Assyria, and the second describes this return as a victorious exodus (10:7bB–10, 11–12).[95] The first stanza resumes the theme of Ephraim's children, which was introduced at the very end of the preceding scene, and describes their joyful return and eventual prosperity. The second stanza explains that when Yahweh had dispersed them they remembered him in far-off lands and were brought back from Egypt and Assyria to Gilead and Lebanon. The third stanza describes this return as a new exodus through the sea of sorrow in a storm that buffets the sea with waves and dries up its bed, breaking the pride of Assyria, and bending the staff of Egypt.

The dramatization is dense and distorted by its inclusion of multiple ideas and images from Isaiah. The compactness is obvious at the boundaries between strophes where the inconsequence of the images and ideas is smoothed out a little bit by anticipating at the end of one the change that takes place at the beginning of the next. The first strophe ends with the sudden transformation of the flock into a war horse because the next strophe deals with Judah as the arm of Yahweh's military might. This strophe ends with a reference to children, who become the theme of the next strophe; the third strophe ends with an abrupt reference to Yahweh leading the people in anticipation of the story of the exodus, which follows in the last strophe. The enjambment, of course, is how the entire dramatization began, with a stanza on rain and fertility linking it to the end of the previous section, and is one of the devices that makes the drama intelligible and effective.

The Third Dramatization (Zechariah 11:1-17) The third dramatization traces the antecedents of the events described in the first two dramatizations. They dealt with models of Israel's oppression and release from captivity, and the third goes back to the earlier history of Israel and Judah to trace the reasons for their exile and the shape of their restoration.

The first scene is composed of two strophes, each with two stanzas. The first strophe (11:1-2, 3) is directed against the shepherds. Its first stanza, by referring to the cedars, cypresses, and oak trees, is a transition from the preceding dramatization, which foresaw the people settling in Gilead and Lebanon (11:1-2; cf. 10:10). The second stanza is connected to it by literal repetition but reintroduces the theme of the shepherds.[96] The second strophe interprets the first by identifying the sheep and the shepherds (11:4-6). The first stanza (11:4-5) tentatively appoints the prophet as the shepherd but goes on to identify the shepherds as aliens and the sheep as those people whose own shepherds do not care for them. The second stanza (11:6) initiates Yahweh's vendetta against the world by making all peoples subject to the whim of their kings and shepherds.

The second scene is composed of two strophes, each with two stanzas (11:7-8, 9-11). The first strophe is linked to the preceding scene by describing how the prophet became the shepherd of the people doomed to death, and the second strophe matches it by describing how he dealt with the alien shepherds and their flocks. The first stanza (11:7abA) has the prophet taking the two staffs of kindness and compatibility, and the second (11:7bB–8) portrays him tending his flock, killing three shepherds in one month, and arousing their hatred for him. In the third stanza (11:9) the prophet abandons his charge, and in the fourth (11:10–11) he breaks the staff of kindness to symbolize the end of the treaty that Yahweh had made with the nations.

The third scene is composed of two strophes, each with three stanzas (11:12–14, 15–17).[97] The first strophe describes how the shepherd asked for his wages and broke the staff of compatibility between Israel and Judah. The second describes how another worthless shepherd took his place.

The scenes are arranged in an explanatory order. The first scene has the elements; the second sorts them out; and the third identifies them. The dramatization projects the past into the future and is filled with symbolism and insinuations that can apply as well to the future of Persian domination as to the past of monarchic rule.

The Fourth Dramatization (Zechariah 12:1–14)   The fourth dramatization has two scenes, each with two strophes, each of them with two stanzas.[98] It matches the third dramatization by explaining what was meant by the shepherds and the sheep and by observing that while Judah will be preeminent among the nations of the world, and Jerusalem in Judah, the ruler in the line of David will not be preeminent in the land.

The first scene distinguishes Judah among the nations. The first stanza declares Yahweh the creator of the world and sets up Judah as a cup that will make the other nations reel. The second stanza makes Jerusalem a rock too heavy for the nations to lift. The second strophe is a match for it in the positive things that are done for Judah and Jerusalem. The third stanza describes what Yahweh will do to the war horses, and the fourth relays what the people of Judah will say about Jerusalem. The two strophes correspond exactly but develop quite different themes: the first indulging in the image of the cup, the second returning to the favorite theme of war and the man of war.

The second scene goes over the same ground, establishing the checks and balances between Judah and the nations, between Judah and Jerusalem, and between the leaders of Jerusalem and its citizens. The first stanza pits Judah against the nations and makes sure that Jerusalem will continue to be inhabited. The second stanza elevates the citizens of Jerusalem to the status of the Davidic kings under God, and the Davidic kings to the status of God. The third begins again with Yahweh threatening to destroy the nations that come against Jerusalem and giving to the house of David and the people of Jerusalem feelings of pity for the one whom they pierced. The fourth describes the order of precedence among the tribes and personages as they lament for this person in Jerusalem and throughout the land.

The Fifth Dramatization (Zechariah 13:1–9) The first scene has two strophes (13:1–2, 3–5): the first purifying the house of David and ridding the land of prophets, the second describing in more detail how prophecy will come to an end. The second scene also has two strophes (13:6–7abA, 7bB–9): the first identifying the person who was pierced as the shepherd who was appointed by God, the second sorting out a few of the people to be saved.

The Sixth Dramatization (Zechariah 14:1–21) The sixth dramatization has four scenes, each with two strophes, each of these composed of two stanzas. The first scene projects into the future the events that accompanied the fall of Jerusalem and symbolizes the rift that the exile caused in the splitting of the land north and south of Jerusalem (14:1–2, 3, 4a, 4b–5). The second scene (14:6–7, 8–9a, 9b–10, 11) predicts for this future a wonderful unity of time, space, and worship. The third scene (14:12, 13, 14, 15) turns from this precious remnant to the ruin that will befall all the rest of the world, and the fourth scene allows for a few survivors among these who will come up every year to worship in Jerusalem at the feast of Succoth (14:16, 17, 18–19, 20–21).

The dramatizations consist mainly in telling about the future the things that are known about the past. The symbolism is subtle or even arcane and allows the writer to reflect on present history in the duality of the known and the unknown.

The key players are Judah, Jerusalem, and the nations. Within Jerusalem there is a clear balance between the populace and the representative of the line of David, and among the latter it is Zerubbabel who is singled out as having suffered wrongly at the hands of the people and their leaders.

The symbolism is rich and varied. It is based on the ready bifurcation of time and event and is filled out by reference to many disparate texts. Among these the chief is III Isaiah, and it is this in particular that distinguishes the second edition from the work that Zechariah completed.

Language and Style

The main difference between the prophecy of Zechariah and the second edition of his work is that the original was written in prose and the revision, in imitation of III Isaiah, was composed in poetry. Within each mode, the writings differ in lexicon, the construction of strophes and paragraphs, their preference for narration or conglomeration, and genre. In general, Zechariah wrote in a clear, imaginative, and racy style, while the editor was fond of ponderous, contorted, and symbolic expression.

In each of his adventures Zechariah fills his narrative with conversation or dramatic dialogue. The second edition, on the other hand, is oratory filled with preciosity and with rhetorical flourishes.

In the first adventure (1:1–17), for instance, the first two scenes have Yahweh talking to Zechariah, giving him things to say, quoting what the earlier prophets said, talking directly to the people, and quoting the words of an earlier generation. There is an abrupt shift in the next two scenes: as in all the visions, the stage if set by announcing the word of Yahweh, but the live performance takes place between Zechariah and the messenger from Yahweh and around the characters they portray. In the last two scenes the messenger talks to Yahweh; Yahweh talks to the messenger; the messenger to Zechariah; and Zechariah to Judah and Jerusalem about the words of Yahweh.

This sort of performance and dramatic exchange is evident in all the visionary adventures but is varied in the last two, where the main characters are historical personages. In the second (2:1–17), for instance, there is a conversation between the messenger and Zechariah, between Zechariah and the man who wanted to measure Jerusalem, between the messenger and another messenger about Zechariah and the proclamations to be made to Jerusalem. In the fifth adventure (7:1–14), however, the action takes place between Jerusalem and Bethel and between Zechariah and the priests and prophets, and there is a speech by Zechariah about practices that have become traditional during the past seventy years, and another speech by Yahweh on the practices to replace them. In the last adventure (8:1–23), similarly, Yahweh ceases to be the setting or backdrop of the prophecy and comes forward to speak to Zechariah and the people in a series of remarks that sum up the point of everything that has preceded.

The different manner of the editor is evident, but slightly veiled, in the items added to these first adventures. The third adventure is modeled on those composed by Zechariah and has its dramatic features. It is a court scene. The court is crowded with Yahweh, Zechariah and the messenger, Joshua the high priest, his accuser, his friends, and spectators (3:1–10). The difference is that Yahweh and Zechariah enter directly into the proceedings, and the usually pithy messenger gives a long-winded speech. But in the fourth adventure (4:3, 6aBb, 7–10a,

11–14) there is no such drama and the narrative sequence of the vision and its interpretation is interrupted by speeches and asides. There is a quotation of what Yahweh said to Zerubbabel, an expostulation to the mountain, a separate word for Zechariah with its own apostrophe to the crowd, an interpretation left hanging, a question and a second clarifying version of the same question—anything to turn a dramatic narrative into a rhetorical feast. In the sixth adventure (chap. 6, esp. 6:9–15), there is vision and interpretation, but then the editor puts in another speech about cooperation between the high priest and the government.

The editor's oratorical skill becomes more evident in the further dramatizations, where there is no need to conform to the language or style of the original. The first of these (9:1–17) begins with a brilliant description of Israel surrounded by nations destined either to oblivion or destruction, turns to Zion in an impassioned plea, and ends in a divine soliloquy emblazoned with a commentating monologue by the prophet. The second (10:1–12) begins with the prophet addressing the reader in a speech that includes sayings of Yahweh and their interpretation, and bombast. It ends with a companion speech by Yahweh that vacillates between direct address and prophetic third-person references to Yahweh.

The third dramatization (11:1–17) begins with an apostrophe to Lebanon, moves abruptly to a divine command, then to a dramatic narrative that interprets its accomplishment, and finally to another speech and another apostrophe. It is a little like the original adventures of Zechariah, but it is filled with allusions and symbols and is artfully compacted. The last dramatizations also imitate the end of Zechariah's work by including speeches by Yahweh, but they are multiple and diverse and interlarded with comments by the editor.

The difference between the two versions in the genres they prefer is emphasized by their lexicons and expressions. The original prophecy delights in show and tell, in setting up an image or proposal and then unraveling it. The revised version likes to lump everything together with explanations few and far between. The original, for instance, links elements in pairs so that the same issue can be seen from two complementary points of view. The revised edition, by contrast, links opposites at all levels of its composition—in stanzas, strophes, and individual dramatizations.

SOURCES AND INTERPRETATIONS

Zechariah is familiar with the entire prophetic tradition, thinks of it as having come to an end, and insinuates himself into it by references to the threats and promises it made. His antecedents are Amos and Ezekiel, his principal sources include Haggai, Isaiah, Lamentations, and the book of Jeremiah. The new edition of his work knew the same material but was particularly interested in bringing his work into line with III Isaiah, with the latest version of the law and with the Chronicler's update of the Deuteronomistic History.

Zechariah 1:1–17

The first scene refers to the ancestors of Zechariah's audience and to their prophets. Its distinction between earlier and later prophets reflects the distinction that the last Isaiah made between earlier and later times.[99] Its idea that Yahweh was outraged in those earlier times can be traced remotely to the Deuteronomist and immediately to the later Isaiahs.[100] The prophetic call to conversion began with Hosea and became usual in Jeremiah.[101] Linking it with Yahweh's change of heart and return to his people was original to Joel and Jonah,[102] but linking it with Yahweh's return to Jerusalem is original to Zechariah (1:3; 8:3). Yahweh's return presupposes his absence, described by Ezekiel (11:23–25), but the linking of conversion and return was done for the context, and "return" replaces the simple expectation that Yahweh would "come back" to Jerusalem.[103] Zechariah's reference to the former prophets' appeal for conversion in fact summarizes the repeated exhortations in the book of Jeremiah,[104] and the people's refusal to listen was then their standard response.[105] The first scene, in short, makes sense in the prophetic tradition that can be traced through the books of Jeremiah and Isaiah to the Deuteronomistic History.

The second scene is based on some of the same sources. The notion that the words of the law might overtake those who neglected them is a reference to the Deuteronomistic History.[106] The fact that Yahweh does what he threatens to do was expressed in the book of Jeremiah concerning the fall of Babylon and in Lamentations concerning Jerusalem.[107] The repentance of the preceding generation is intimated by Joel,[108] and their willing obedience to the word of God was narrated by Haggai (Hag 1:12).

The third scene is original to Zechariah and states his adherence to the prophetic tradition. He uses the standard prophetic formulas and shares in prophetic visions, but he does not claim direct access to the word of Yahweh. Instead, the word of Yahweh is addressed to him indirectly by an angel.[109]

The fourth scene interprets the riders that he saw in the third scene. Their survey of the land now at rest resembles the survey done in the time of Joshua when all the land was at rest, or the more sinister survey done in the time of Job.[110] Their description of the land as inhabited and at rest is borrowed from the apocalyptic vision of the land in the fantasy of Gog in the book of Ezekiel.[111]

The fifth scene refers to the period of seventy years devised by the book of Jeremiah (Zech 1:12; cf. Jer 25:12; 29:10) and combines it with allusions to earlier prophecies. The jealousy and rage of Yahweh, as they affect his friends and his enemies, were described by Nahum.[112] Yahweh's jealous zeal for Zion and Jerusalem was mentioned by the Deuteronomistic Historian in a passage that was quoted by III Isaiah, Obadiah, and the editor of Joel.[113] His kind words for Jerusalem were reported by II Isaiah.[114] His virulence toward the complacent among his own people was noted long before by Amos and more recently by III Isaiah,[115] but his detestation of complacent enemies of his people was first noted by the Deuteronomistic Historian (2 Kgs 19:28).

The sixth scene has Yahweh return in mercy to Jerusalem and in the same spirit reverses some earlier statements of doom. The statement that his house will be built contradicts Haggai's worry about the slackness of the people.[116] The measuring tape that will be stretched over Jerusalem does away with the mean measure of Samaria that the Deuteronomistic Historian said would be stretched over the city because of the sins of Manasseh.[117] The choice of Jerusalem belongs to Deuteronomistic ideology (Zech 1:17b; cf. 2 Kgs 21:7) and pity for Zion is integral to the prophecy of II Isaiah.[118]

Zechariah 2:1–17

The first scene is the vision of the horns that dispersed Israel, Judah, and Jerusalem. The language of dispersal is original to Ezekiel.[119] The image of a bull tossing its horns is standard in the description of a powerful enemy (2:1–4);[120] horns of steel might indicate invincibility (2:1–4);[121] and turning them downward as the blacksmiths do in the vision nullifies their effect.

The second scene is indebted to Ezekiel's vision of the measurement of Jerusalem (Zech 2:5–4; cf. Ezekiel 40–42). In both cases there is a vision; in both cases there is a man with a measuring rod or tape in his hand; and in both cases the man measures the length and breadth of the emplacement (Zech 2:5–6; cf. Ezek 40:2–3; 41:13–14). The main difference is that in Ezekiel's plan there is a wall around the temple, but in Zechariah's vision Yahweh himself is the wall[122] although both agree that the glory of God resides within the walls (Zech 2:9b; Ezek 43:1–5).

The third scene describes the return of the exiles to Zion (2:10–13). The image of Yahweh shaking his fist at his enemies may be taken from II Isaiah (Zech 2:13; cf. Isa 19:6). Return to Zion from the north country was predicted by Jeremiah (Zech 2:10, 11; cf. Jer 31:6–7), and the final despoiling of the despoilers was expected by the authors of the books of Habakkuk and Ezekiel (Zech 2:12–13; cf. Ezek 39:10; Hab 2:8).

The fourth scene is filled with familiar language. Like II Isaiah it calls on Zion to rejoice (Zech 2:14; Isa 12:6; 54:1). The return of Yahweh to the city that it proclaims was described by Ezekiel and noted by Haggai (Zech 2:14; Ezek 43:1–5; Hag 1:2). The presence of Yahweh as a resident of the city is a local aspiration mentioned in the same text of Ezekiel.[123] Its declaration that many nations will depend on Yahweh adapts a saying that the book of Jeremiah attributed to the returning exiles.[124] The distribution of the land to Judah reflects the mission of Joshua and the climax of the book of Ezekiel (Zech 2:16a; cf. Joshua 13–19; Ezek 47:13–23). Its final exhortation to silence before Yahweh who has roused himself in his holy retreat is taken from the end of Habakkuk's spoof on the Babylonians and from the book of Jeremiah's elegy on Babylon and the nations.[125]

Zechariah 3:1–10

The first scene takes up material from the end of the preceding sections.[126] The figure of Satan coming forward to trip or entrap the careless is known from the Deuteronomistic History, from Job, from Psalms, and from Chronicles.[127] The comparison of a derisory person to a burning ember pulled from the fire is known from II Isaiah and the book of Amos.[128] The courtroom or audience scene was described by Job, and Joshua the high priest is known from Haggai. The combination of all these elements, however, is original to the author of the revision.

The second scene describes something like the investiture of the priests but supposes other late texts in Isaiah and Ezekiel on the removal of unit garments (Zech 3:3–5abA; cf. Exod 29:5–7; Lev 8:7–9). The book of Ezekiel, in one of its repudiations of the royal house, calls on the prince to remove his turban and his crown, and III Isaiah describes the degradation of the women in Zion as removal of their linen and headdress (Zech 3:4–5; cf. Ezek 21:31; Isa 3:22–23). The author of the revision described Joshua's unworthiness in similar terms but supposed that his clothing had been soiled in exile and that his investiture suited him to the service of the temple that was about to be completed.

In the third scene the angel of Yahweh bestows conditional and limited authority on Joshua. The conditions, expressed in familiar Deuteronomistic terms, are that he observe the law and ritual prescriptions.[129] The limitations are defined as authority over the temple precinct and access to the priestly chambers and subordination to the offspring of David (Zech 3:7-8a; cf. Ezek 42:4).

The fourth scene describes the political circumstances of his priestly authority. The leader is the offspring of David whose government in cooperation with the priests was predicted in the book of Jeremiah[130] and whose title "Servant" situates him in the company of Jacob, Moses, Joshua, and David. He is symbolized by the rock put before Joshua, which in turn is the rock predicted by Isaiah as the foundation of Zion and the temple.[131] The peace and prosperity in his time recall the days of Solomon described in the Deuteronomistic History or the messianic age foreseen in the book of Micah (Zech 3:10b; 1 Kgs 4:5; Mic 4:4).

Zechariah 4:1-13

The first scene is Zechariah's vision of candelabra, to which the editor has added a vision of olive trees and a saying about Zerubbabel. This saying alludes to II Isaiah's description of the shoot from the stump of Jesse endowed with the spirit of Yahweh and agrees with II Isaiah's portrayal of the messianic age as a time of peace without recourse to human strength or to military might.[132]

The second scene, added by the editor, makes Zerubbabel the architect and engineer of the temple (4:7-9).[133] The great mountain that it apostrophizes is like the high mountain of Zion described by Ezekiel and II Isaiah.[134] Although in the spirit of III Isaiah's disdain for everything proud or pretentious this mountain will be leveled, the leveling is described in words that II Isaiah used to describe the level route prepared for the exiles' return to Jerusalem.[135] The rock that was before Joshua in an earlier section, and that seemed to be synonymous with the leader that he preceded, now becomes the cornerstone of the new building,[136] and the city that once fell amidst shouting now shouts out its praise.[137] In a massive enjambment of images and ideas the editor manages to make Zerubbabel the architect of a city that Isaiah envisioned, that II Isaiah saw as the city of David, and that III Isaiah recognized as the humble capital of a glorious God.

The third scene combines, in the same compactness, two quite contrary images (4:10). The original Zecharian vision interpreted the seven-branched candelabra as the eyes of Yahweh that survey the world, an image with political implications that was introduced by the author of the sequel, and an idea that is developed in the prophecy as Yahweh's ability to recall the exiles and requite the kingdoms of Mesopotamia (4:10b).[138] In the edited version the eyes are facets of the cornerstone of the temple, and this interpretation is simply juxtaposed with the original. Its idea that those who might despise the day of small things will rejoice in this stone in the hand of Zerubbabel is an allusion to Haggai's suggestion that the second temple was nothing compared to the first, on the grounds presumably that the work was not finished in his time, as Haggai claimed, but only later when the sanctuary had been built by Zerubbabel (4:10a; cf. Hag 2:3, 9, 18).

The fourth scene takes up the imagery of the olive trees that was inserted into the vision (4:11–14). Compactness remains the signature of the writer: the prophet asks two questions in quick succession. The first question concerns the olive trees, but the second asks about the branches of the trees, identifies them as golden spouts, and explains that gold flows through them. The answer comes back to the image of the olive trees and explains that they are two sons of oil, Joshua and Zerubbabel, who stand before the Lord of the whole world. The imagery is impossible but in a few entangled words tells the whole story.

Zechariah 5:1–11

The first scene is a vision of a flying scroll. The image may allude to the scroll of Jeremiah, since the interpretation of the scroll refers to things that are said in his book. The flying scroll is called the curse that besets the world, and such a curse was invoked by the book of Jeremiah and taken up by III Isaiah.[139] The reason for the curse is theft and swearing, or lying oaths, and such were singled out by Hosea and then more systematically in the book of Jeremiah as reasons for the desolation of the land (Zech 5:3–4; cf. Hos 4:2; Jer 7:9).

The second scene is a pun that connects the flying scroll with a basket suspended in midair and then links this with the eyes of Yahweh that survey the world.[140] The third scene ties it all together by having the basket, Pandora's box of evil, and with it the curse, transported to Mesopotamia to build a house to replace the house that had collapsed under the weight of its own evil[141] — all of it an allegory, presumably, on the collapse of the Neo-Babylonian and the beginning of the Persian empire.

Zechariah 6:1–15

The first scene is a vision like the first, second, and third visions combined (6:1–5; cf. 1:7–9; 2:1–4, 10), and the second scene interprets it in the same way (6:6–8; cf. 2:10–13). The third and fourth scenes were added in the second edition to relate it to the intervening additions concerning the government of Joshua and Zerubbabel.

Zechariah 7:1–14

The first two scenes allude to things described in Joel (Zech 7:1–3, 4–7). The delegation from Bethel gives the scene an ominous cast. The inquiry of the priests in Jerusalem contains an allusion to the priests mentioned by Joel, and the question they are asked about lamentation recalls his exhortation to the priests to weep and lament (7:3; cf. Joel 1:5; 2:17). The inclusion of prophets, apart from its plausibility, may be an oblique reference to Joel himself. The fasts that Joel proclaimed are considered in Zechariah's text to have extended over the seventy years of the exile, and the contrast that Joel made between present fasts and future satisfaction are the things that this text belittles (7:4–7).[142] The negative tone of the two scenes is emphasized by referring to Jerusalem in past times in terms that the book of Ezekiel used to refer to Sodom and Gomorrah.[143]

The third and fourth scenes explain this negative tone by recalling the message of the former prophets and the lack of response that it received from their contemporaries (7:8–12a, 12b–14). The kindness, goodness, and mercy that these prophets advocated were the qualities attributed to Yahweh at Sinai.[144] Honest judgment and the care of widows, orphans, strangers, and the poor were inculcated in the law and the prophets, and according to the book of Jeremiah, it was precisely failure to observe this law that destroyed Jerusalem.[145] Micah pointed out that their evil schemes made Yahweh plot evil against them, and Zechariah urges them not to plot evil against one another (Zech 7:10b; cf. Mic 2:1–3). Refusal to listen was a problem from the beginning,[146] as was being rebellious,[147] shrugging off advice, blocking their ears,[148] having a heart of stone,[149] or, in general, rejecting a whole succession of prophets.[150] The result was, as the prophets had predicted, that Yahweh did not listen when they called to him[151] and that they were driven into countries that they had never heard of,[152] while their own precious country[153] became a ruin without inhabitant or wayfarer.[154]

Zechariah 8:1–23

The first scene takes up from the beginning of the prophecy the ideas of Yahweh's jealousy and return to Jerusalem (8:1–3)[155] and develops them with images of Jerusalem taken from II Isaiah and Jeremiah.[156] The second scene (8:4–6) embellishes these with a description of prosperity that resembles predictions in the book of Jeremiah that astonished even Jeremiah and that are quite the opposite of the wretched conditions that Jeremiah and III Isaiah saw.[157]

The third scene begins with the restoration of the people expressed in terms of return taken from II Isaiah and in terms of the covenant taken from the book of Jeremiah.[158] The rest of the scene is a paraphrase of the situation described by Haggai before the temple was finished. It uses the same terms of encouragement, refers to his words about the building of the temple, alludes to what he said about hired hands and about men and animals, and describes the residue of oppression and strife that Haggai had to counteract in order to get the temple built.[159]

The fourth scene continues the references to Haggai and elaborates on the benefits that accrue to the people from the building of the temple. It uses Haggai's expression "this remnant of a people."[160] He said that they had sowed few seeds and reaped little but in the end promises peace to Jerusalem, while Zechariah in this scene mentions seeds of peace (Zech 8:12; cf. Hag 1:6 + 2:9). He noted that the sky withheld the dew and the earth did not yield its produce, while Zechariah remarks on just the opposite (Zech 8:12a; cf. Hag 1:10). In Haggai all these things were the effect of a curse, and Zechariah, and the revision of Haggai in due course, refer to their opposite as a blessing that undid the curse (Zech 8:13a).[161] Haggai told the people not to be afraid, and Zechariah does the same (Zech 8:13b, 15b; cf. Hag 2:5). The main differences between them are that Haggai thought that the government was in charge of building the temple, and Zechariah attributed everything to Yahweh. Haggai, therefore, could think of it as being finished, but Zechariah thought of the finishing of the temple as something that Yahweh would do for the people and the whole land.

The fifth scene repeats the prescriptions of the law and the prophets that the preceding generations had not observed (8:16–19 = 7:8–12a), and the sixth paraphrases the expectation formulated by II Isaiah and the book of Micah that all nations would come to Jerusalem to worship Yahweh (Zech 8:20–22; cf. Isa 2:1–5; Mic 4:1–5). The prophecy ends with a paraphrase and critique of III Isaiah: III Isaiah had notable contempt for the nations and an exclusive view of Jerusalem, and had talked of a desolate time when seven women would beg one man to be their husband. Zechariah, like II Isaiah, had an inclusive view of Jerusalem and talked of a time when ten foreigners would beg one Jew to take them with him to Jerusalem (Zech 8:23; cf. Isa 4:1, 2–6).

Zechariah 9:1–17

The author of II Zechariah shared III Isaiah's xenophobia and resistance to foreign domination. This is reflected in the first two scenes (9:1–4, 5–8), which describe Yahweh's interest in keeping aliens out of his territory and in subduing nations at his borders. These scenes mention the northern coalition of Arameans and Neo-Hittites but concentrate on Israel's western border with Tyre and the Philistines. Ezekiel had admired the wealth and wisdom of Tyre and Sidon and had seen Tyre sinking in the seas, and Micah had envisaged Israel trampling on its enemies like mud in the streets; and all the images are combined in the first scene (Zech 9:2–4).[162] There were bonds of origin and enterprise that linked Canaanite Tyre and Sidon with the Philistines, and Zephaniah had seen them all destroyed and taken over by Judah. The second scene paraphrases the passage but in language culled from Amos and from a variety of sources (9:5–8; cf. Zeph 2:4–6; Amos 1:6–8). The scenes end with Yahweh encamped in his house to protect it from passersby so that no one would ever be able to bother it again.[163] It is a far cry from Zechariah's resolution of the same problem and presages a fascination with armies and war and utter devastation.

The third and fourth scenes illustrate this fascination (9:9–12, 13–17). The third is partly parallel to Zechariah's summons to rejoice, but its interests are mainly in the accoutrements of war that are to be disavowed. Zion is told to rejoice, but also to shout—as they do in battles (9:9; cf. 2:14–16). Zion's king is riding, but on an unwarlike donkey with its colt. The parade has no horses or chariots or bowmen but announces peace and universal dominion and the release of captives from the pit (9:11 = Jer 38:6) and double indemnity for all that Zion has suffered (Zech 9:12b).[164] The fourth scene, however, explains that this peace will be gained in a ferocious battle fought by Yahweh. Israel, Judah, and Jerusalem are weapons of war in the hands of Yahweh: Judah is a bow; Ephraim is a quiver of arrows; Zion is a hero's sword against the Greeks. A trumpet sounds; Yahweh's arrows are the lightning; his route is through the storm; he is a shield to his people; slingshots are treated like loaves of bread, gore like wine. This mighty fixation on war is all the more evident since the display ends with an allusion to the return to Zion described in the book of Jeremiah, a happy time witnessed by the nations, a time of feasting and song (Zech 9:17; cf. Jer 31:10–14).

Zechariah 10:1–12

The first scene deals with false prophets and bad leaders. The false prophets are those who cannot even predict the rain, and in the present context this has to refer to Haggai and Zechariah, who talked precisely about such things to describe a new era of peace (Zech 10:1–2; cf. 8:12; Hag 1:10–11). The bad leaders are proverbial, but in this case they are identified with the gangsters who ruled other nations of the world and are contrasted with the legitimate rulers who will arise in Judah.[165] These legitimate rulers, in the dense and compact style of the editor, are equipped with bows and turn out to be warriors who trample their enemies in the mud and put an end to war because Yahweh is with them and will answer them (10:4–6; cf. 7:13; 9:3). The passage was written by someone who had read the conclusion of Zechariah's prophecy and who thought that it would be better to include a native government in the new age that was dawning. The government is identified by allusions to passages in Isaiah that referred, or came to refer, to the family of David. The allusions are veiled and slightly seditious.

The second scene matches the first by describing the foreign lands from whose clutches Yahweh reclaims his people (10:7bB–12). It begins like the passage in the book of Jeremiah quoted at the end of the preceding dramatization[166] and includes, as did III Isaiah, Egypt and Assyria among the nations to which they had been dispersed (cf. Isa 11:11; 27:13). It ends with a new exodus and a reference to II Isaiah's promise of deliverance (Zech 10:11; cf. Isa 10:24–27).

Zechariah 11:1–17

The first scene opens with a reference to the decline of Egypt (11:1–6), likened as it was in Ezekiel to a great cedar cut down in the forest (11:1–2; cf. Ezek 31:3), and to the decline of Babylon, compared as it was in the book of Jeremiah to the panic of shepherds confronted by lions from the jungle of the Jordan (11:3; cf. Jer 12:5; 49:19; 50:44). The rest of the scene compares Judah to a flock sold to shepherds such as these who did not care about them — sold in fact by Yahweh.

The second scene takes up images of shepherding from the book of Ezekiel, but it changes the two sticks that represent the bond between

Joseph and Judah into two staffs a shepherd might use and break (11:7–11; Ezek 34:11–19; 37:15–23). The allusions are obscure, but the third scene conjures up still another bad shepherd and refers to the parallel passage in Ezekiel about the mean and incompetent shepherds who let Israel go astray (11:16; cf. Ezek 34:3–4), and the whole passage must refer to local rulers who let three foreign governments, and then a fourth, take charge of Yahweh's flock (11:8, 15). In the present context these would have to be Assyria (= Assyria and Babylonia), Egypt, and Persia, but the text is careful not to say.

Zechariah 12:1–14

The first scene (12:1–5) confirms the impression of politicking given in the preceding dramatization by declaring the vindication of the city of Jerusalem in the sight of Judah and the nations of the world. The cup of staggering that is given to the surrounding nations was borrowed from II Isaiah, where it is given to all those who made Jerusalem suffer and is like the cup that the book of Jeremiah passed to all the nations and then to Babylon (Zech 12:2; cf. Isa 51:21–23; Jer 25:8–29).

The second scene (12:6–14), in the spirit of III Isaiah, makes sure that Jerusalem does not magnify itself more than Judah, and makes certain that Judah and Jerusalem will be freed from the nations. It knows from the Deuteronomistic History that David was like the angel of the Lord (Zech 12:8b; cf. 2 Sam 14:17, 20) and from the Chronicler's history a list of important families in Jerusalem (Zech 12:11–13).[167] It contradicts the spirit of Zechariah's prophecy by eliminating the pilgrimage of the nations to Jerusalem and by replacing it with the threat that the nations pose for the city and with their eventual destruction (Zech 12:9; cf. 8:23).

Zechariah 13:1–9

The first scene (13:1–5) exalts the house of David and brings the prophetic tradition to a close. The exaltation is conditioned and refined and supposes that the house has been sinful and unclean. The prophetic tradition is rejected as wrong, improperly inspired and erroneous in its judgment (13:2–3). Elijah seems to be included, his cloak being compared to the hairy mantle of Esau's skin that allowed Jacob to mislead his father Isaac.[168] If so, the end of the book of Malachi clearly takes issue with it (Mal 3:23–24).

The second scene (13:6–9) plays again with the image of the shepherd. The opening question repeats the gist of the first scene, in which parents forbid their children to be prophets under pain of punishment or death (13:6; cf. 13:3). Attached to it is a similar threat against the shepherd that Yahweh has chosen—the leader from the house of David as the first scene made clear—and with it Yahweh's assurance that this will be a test that the shepherd and some of the people will survive (13:8b, 9).[169]

Zechariah 14:1-21

The first scene describes a future battle in which Jerusalem will be captured (14:1-5). Half its population will be sent into exile, and the other half will remain in the city. Yahweh will go out and fight against the nations and will stand on the mountain that faces the city (14:4a)[170] and it will split and move and "you" will flee when "my" God comes, and the holy ones with "thee." This clearly projects into the future things that have already happened. Among these past things the most obvious are the fall of Jerusalem and the exile. Less obvious, and indicated by allusions to Ezekiel, is the return of the glory of God to Jerusalem—as announced at the beginning of the additions (Zech 9:1-17). It is projected into a future time on the analogy established by Zechariah. Haggai had seen the glory of Yahweh coming to Jerusalem as soon as the temple was repaired; Zechariah delayed the coming until the land could be settled and at peace; the book of Zechariah invented a time when Judah would be free from foreign domination in which to situate the same event.

The second scene describes the fulfillment of this hope in terms taken from Jeremiah and Ezekiel (14:6-11; cf. Jer 31:38; Ezekiel 47). The third scene then describes the terrible things that happen to those who fought against Jerusalem (14:12-15), and the last brings about the submission of the whole world to Yahweh the king and describes the annual trek to Jerusalem on the feast of Succoth (14:16-21).

The book of Zechariah knows the same traditional material as Zechariah but is anxious to bring the tradition to a resounding close. It also knows the Davidic perspective of the Chronicler's history and its spiritualization of the priestly and levitical vocations, and includes Joshua and Zerubbabel as their immediate representatives. It is more interested, however, in the creation of a state under God, and in linking the presence of God in the temple to his real authority over the land.

The ideas were potentially seditious, and veiling their real import led to their compactness and distortion. The theocracy was not compatible with Persian rule. The house of David was to be subject to Yahweh and totally exempt from the confusion caused by the lies and mistakes of meddling prophets—people presumably like Haggai and

Zechariah, who compromised their allegiance to an indigenous government by following the chronology of Persian rule in referring to Zerubbabel and the completion of the temple. The fulfillment of history and prophecy in some clear but distant time was filled with literary hazards. The author of the book was very careful to get it right, and so every reference is chiseled and fitted carefully into place; every future event reflects the evident past; nothing is said that has not already been said in the prophecy or the history that now has come to an end.

CONCLUSION

One of the more interesting things about Zechariah is his plainness and simplicity. He is like other late postexilic prophets in thinking that the past is over and done, unlike them, though, in remembering that it was not a good time and in thinking that the future would be quite different. Unlike Jonah and Joel, and even Haggai, he refers to the wrongs that were done and to the divine anger that ensued. He does not believe, as Haggai did, that it is enough to get the temple finished for the curse to be lifted and for Yahweh to return. The land has to be restored; the rifts in the community have to be repaired; wrongdoing and troublemakers have to be banished to Babylon; rituals have to be modified; the law and the prophets have to be heeded; and then it will be time—when Yahweh has returned—for the temple to be completed and dedicated.

The author who revised his work tried to bring Haggai into line with it. Zechariah knew his work and quoted it. This author changed it and quoted the changes. And then it was time to think about the real rifts and wrongdoings and a really new order of things without the mediation of the law and the prophets and with Yahweh in direct command.

FIGURE 25

The Chronicler

A	1 Chr 1–10	H	A'	2 Chr 10–12
B	11–12	2 Chr 1–9	B'	13–16
C	13–16		C'	17–20
D	17–20		D'	21–24
E	21–22		E'	25–28
F	23–27		F'	29–32
G	28–29		G'	33–36

Figure 25. Letters indicate parts.

The Chronicler (fig. 25)

The Chronicler rewrote the Deuteronomistic History from beginning (Genesis) to end (2 Kings) and finished the Pentateuch by adding a ritual and prescriptive supplement to the laws. This history, like the sequel to the epic, is devoted to the southern kingdom and mentions the North only when it impinges on the story to be told. The story is substantially the story of David and his line, the wars of conquest and expansion that he and his dynasty fought, the temple and cult that he inaugurated and that his son established, the periods of decline under less-worthy heirs, the revival of the cult under Hezekiah and Josiah, and the fulfillment of prophecy and history in the decree of Cyrus, which put an end to the exile and authorized the rebuilding of the temple. As in the History, there was a lesson to be learned, but it was relatively simple and straightforward, without disappointment or surprises.[171]

The Chronicler's history supposes that the Deuteronomistic version—its information, its interpretation, and its theories—is known, and excerpts and epitomizes it. It is not a narrative, therefore, but a factual report that groups and synthesizes—also supplements and sometimes corrects—the information in the History under new headings and theories and interpretations. In the History, law and prophecy were the substance of the sequence of events, but in the Chronicler's version they are not elements of human destiny but on the surface, in plain view, and provide simple explanations of past events. In the Historian's version they governed and rationalized the world, but in the Chronicler's version they sustain and prolong the promise to David. The History revolved around the law of Moses, and its basic argument was illustrated in the links between the exodus, the wilderness, and the conquest. But in Chronicles David assumes the stature and attributes of Moses, and history is woven in the basic pattern of war and peace and worship in the temple.[172] The Chronicler makes it evident that the Deuteronomistic History, for all its density and skill, is not a mirror of reality but one among many opinions and interpretations.

The climax of Chronicles is the building of the temple. The history begins with an intimation of its ending by mentioning the exile and listing those who returned, and it ends with the decree of Cyrus and the rebuilding of the temple and an intimation of a new beginning. Everything leads up to the temple and follows the same path again in tracing its declension.[173]

The first part (1 Chronicles 1–10)[174] hurries over the early history of Israel in genealogies gathered from various parts of the History and filled out from contemporary lists.[175] Its chapters are paired,[176] and the really important things are said twice—once in summary fashion and once in some detail. The first chapter has lists from the book of Genesis and includes Israel and Edom. The second is like it in listing the sons of Israel, but it is restricted to Judah and draws on genealogical information in the Pentateuch and the Former Prophets. David is included in the list and becomes the subject of the third chapter, which lists his children and the descendants of Solomon. The fourth chapter continues the Judean list but also includes Simeon and is related to the third chapter by recalling an incident from the reign of Hezekiah. The fifth chapter lists the Transjordanian tribes and some Levites and is held together by its historical references, either to what had happened to various tribal elements during the reigns of certain kings or to how the tribes and individuals fared until the exile (1 Chr 5:10, 17, 22, 26, 41).[177] The sixth is like it in listing the rest of the Levites. The seventh chapter lists the members of the other tribes, including Benjamin, and the eighth chapter continues with the genealogy of Benjamin. The ninth chapter concludes the genealogies and skips to the exile of Judah and to the return of Israel and Judah from exile, listing some of the tribal elements but concentrating on the priests and Levites, and ends with the genealogy of Gibeon. Among the descendants of Gibeon were Saul and his sons, and the tenth chapter repeats the Deuteronomist's account of their death on Mount Gilboa. Everything that the Deuteronomist thought was important about the founding of the nation or the establishment of the monarchy is simply omitted.

The second part is an account of David's reign in Hebron.[178] The first chapter combines the narrative of his anointing and of his capture of Zion, from the early part of Samuel, with the list of his heroes that the Deuteronomist left unassimilated at the end of the same book. The second chapter, backtracking to the time when Saul was still king, lists the warriors from the other tribes who deserted to David at Hebron. There is no trace of the negotiations to which the Deuteronomist attributed the union of the kingdoms and hardly a hint of David's treachery, which mad Saul suspected. David was simply God's choice, and his troops were like the army of God (1 Chr 12:19, 23).

The third part (1 Chronicles 15–16) covers David's early days in Jerusalem. The first chapter retrieves from the Deuteronomistic History the story of the ark's transferal to Jerusalem and acknowledges that much of the History has been omitted by referring to the years of the ark's neglect during the reign of Saul. The second chapter, again from the Deuteronomist, gets David settled in Jerusalem in a house provided by Hiram of Tyre. The third returns to the ark and describes the preparations for its transferal, including the instructions for the Levites and the tent that David pitched for it instead of the tent of meeting that Moses made (1 Chr 15:1; 16:1).[179] The last is the story of the actual transferal of the ark, with a quotation of the psalm that was sung on the occasion, but it ends like the second chapter with David at home.

The fourth part (1 Chronicles 17–20) is the oracle of Nathan and an account of the victorious battles for the kingdom that it inspired. The first chapter is the oracle, in most respects like the version in the History, but differing from it in several ways. It implies that David did well to pitch a tent for Yahweh and simply rebuffs his plan to build the temple. It omits the reference to crimes committed by his sons and their punishment and instead promises him God's lasting fidelity. It more emphatically associates his son with the building of the temple and dissociates him from the ideology of the kingdom by promising that his son will take his stand in Yahweh's house and in Yahweh's kingdom. The second chapter, also from the History, lists the victories that secured the kingdom in David's hands. The third and fourth chapters are records of David's Ammonite wars, omitting the affair of Uriah the Hittite, and of his heroic battles with the Philistines. The part has none of the drama of the original but is a fair résumé of the events surrounding the confirmation of David's kingship.[180]

The fifth part marks the transition between the end of the conquest and the beginning of the building of the temple (1 Chronicles 21–22). The first chapter is the story of the census and of the plague that was averted when David built an altar and offered sacrifices that were sanctified by fire from heaven. The second chapter makes the emplacement of the altar the locus of the temple, reviews the oracle that commissioned Solomon to build it, and describes the peace that David forged from victories over all his enemies to make the building possible. The Chronicler, as often is the case, has integrated into a different interpretation material that the Deuteronomist left unassimilated and pending.

The sixth part (1 Chronicles 23–27) continues David's preparations for the temple by assigning the Levites their tasks. The introduction lists four assignments—temple maintenance, government, gate keeping, and music—and each is covered in detail in the next chapters. The part has no parallel in the History and in fact contradicts or corrects the History by attributing the rules of the levitical and priestly orders to David rather than Moses.

The seventh part (1 Chronicles 28–29) is David's adieu. In the first chapter David explains that he could not build the temple because he was constantly engaged in war but that he had made all the necessary preparations and, like Moses at Sinai, he actually provides Solomon with detailed written plans for the temple revealed by Yahweh. The second chapter continues the analogy and, as they did for the construction of the tabernacle at Sinai, has the people present their donations for the temple. The part ends with the accession of Solomon, but without the conspiracy that surrounded it in the History, and with a reference to the prophetic sources that have been used.

The eighth part covers the reign of Solomon by reorganizing the material in the Deuteronomistic History (2 Chronicles 1–9). The first chapter contains his inaugural vision at Gibeon, the place of the tent of meeting where Moses used to meet God, and a note on the amazing wealth that he amassed in fulfillment of the promise he received at that time. The second chapter records his deals with Hiram of Tyre in preparation for the building of the temple and matches the first by confirming that Solomon had been granted the wisdom for which he prayed in his vision. The third and fourth chapters recount the building of the temple and the preparation of its furnishings, mostly in the words of the History, and the fifth describes the procession of the ark to the temple and records a psalm that was sung at the time. The sixth is the prayer of the king, with another quotation from the Psalms, and the seventh is the dedication of the temple, with the refrain from the psalm that was sung during the procession of the ark. The eighth, like the second in mentioning Solomon's dealings with Hiram of Tyre, concludes the account of Solomon's buildings and establishes the rituals and order of service to be observed in the temple. The last matches it but is also like the first in confirming the wealth and wisdom of Solomon that had been bequeathed to him in his vision in Gibeon. In the Chronicler's account Solomon, by his association with the temple, was the perfect king. Its omission of the sin that according to the Deuteronomist he was seduced to commit is consistent with the Chronicler's plan of redoing the text of the History without the constraint of its overriding theories and interpretations.

The ninth part (2 Chronicles 10–12) covers the succession of Rehoboam and the secession of the North.[181] It differs from the Deuteronomistic account in concentrating on Judean affairs, in being specific about the treatment of the priests and Levites in Israel, and in omitting its harping on the sin of Jeroboam. In the place of this original ineluctable sin that the Deuteronomist would see seeping into Judah from the North, the Chronicler records manageable sins committed by individual kings. The effect of these sins, starting with Rehoboam, was not some terrible curse but defeat in battle, subjection to aliens, and loss of some or all of the land.

The tenth part (2 Chronicles 13–16) develops this theory of holy war through the reigns of Abijah and Asa.[182] The first chapter records Abijah's victory over Jeroboam in a battle waged and won by Yahweh, the true God, who was worshiped in Jerusalem. The second describes the stunning victory that Yahweh and his army achieved against the Egyptians. The third chapter is like the first in describing the reform of worship in Jerusalem in the reign of Asa. The last is the opposite of the second, to which it refers in describing how Asa relied on an alliance with the Aramaeans instead of on Yahweh for victory over Israel.

The eleventh part covers the reign of Jehoshaphat (2 Chronicles 17–20).[183] It differs from the Deuteronomistic account in recording his fabulous victory over Moab, Edom, and Ammon but especially in attributing to him the judicial reforms that the History had ascribed to Moses (2 Chronicles 19; Deut 1:9–18; Exodus 18).

The twelfth part (2 Chronicles 21–24)[184] deals with the influence of the house of Ahab on Judah. The first two chapters recount the infidelity of Jehoram and Ahaziah. The last two record the accession of Joash, his repairs to the temple, and his apostasy late in life, which resulted in defeat by the Aramaeans and death at the hands of his servants. It differs from the Deuteronomistic account mainly in ignoring the cult of Baal and the purported reforms of Elisha and Jehu.[185]

The thirteenth part (2 Chronicles 25–28) covers the reigns of Amaziah, Uzziah, Jotham, and Ahaz. Apart from the Deuteronomistic material, each of the reigns is tarnished by false worship or ritual impropriety.[186]

The fourteenth part (2 Chronicles 29–32) is an account of the reign of Hezekiah that differs in most respects from the account in Kings.[187] The first chapter supposes the ritual misdemeanors mentioned in the preceding part and records the cleansing of the temple. The second chapter is an account of the Passover. It attributes to Hezekiah a ritual prescription that the Deuteronomist ascribed to Moses, omits the History's diatribe against the sin of Jeroboam, includes the northern kingdom in the festivities, and equates return to Yahweh and return from exile with worship of Yahweh in the temple in Jerusalem.[188] The third chapter is like the first in its concentration on the Levites and, although it refers to the Deuteronomistic festal calendar, describes the continuation of the king's cultic reforms in terms of the law of centralization promulgated by the sequel.[189] The fourth chapter, like the second in its reference to the Assyrians, is an account of the invasion of Sennacherib. It agrees with the sequel that the siege was not successful but does not share its lack of concern for the fate of Samaria.[190] It all but leaves Isaiah out of the picture and omits all reference to his charge that Judah did not believe in God and was saved by its reliance on Egypt. It does not attribute the lifting of the siege to faith and trust, however, but to an act of Yahweh, whose cult had been restored in Jerusalem.

The last part (2 Chronicles 33–36) covers the period from the reign of Manasseh to the end of the exile and the decree of Cyrus revealing his divine mission to build the temple in Jerusalem.[191] It differs from the Deuteronomistic History in exonerating Manasseh and foregoing its history of sin,[192] in attributing Josiah's reform to his devotion to the God of David rather than to his implementation of the law of Moses, and in gently reprimanding Josiah for fighting at Carchemish. It agrees instead with the book of Jeremiah that Judah fell because it did not listen to the prophets and would be restored at the end of seventy years.

CONCLUSION

The Chronicler is an interesting counterpoint to the Deuteronomistic History. Its intention, as is clear from the start, is to explain that the life of Israel revolves around the temple that the Davidic dynasty was chosen to build and maintain. It has no secrets and no hidden agenda, has no truck with fate, and leaves out, along with its narrative art and brilliance, all the sinister effects of the History. It is interested in Judah, irenic toward the North, and concerned for the restoration of Israel. It has no disputes with the prophets and none of the Historian's vehemence toward the kings.[193] It has more information, a plainer grasp of evidence, another interpretation, a different history.

Malachi (fig. 26)

The prophecy of Malachi was written after Zechariah and Chronicles and before the revision of Haggai and Zechariah. Its interest, like theirs, is in the temple, but it deals with a significant omission in their work. Haggai was concerned to have the temple finished and based his argument on meteorological phenomena and historical tradition. Zechariah was concerned to relate the finished temple to forgiveness and an age of national reconciliation. Malachi's interest was in ritual traditions and the actual management of the temple. He was eager to remove the

FIGURE 26

Malachi

		Malachi		*The Book of Malachi*
I	A	1	1:1–2a	
		2	1:2b–3	
	B	1	1:4	
		2	1:5	
	C	1	1:6	
		2	1:7	
		3	1:8	
	D	1	1:9	
		2	1:10	
	E	1	1:11	
		2	1:12	
	F	1	1:13	
		2	1:14	
II	A	1	2:1–2	
		2	2:3–4	
	B	1	2:5	
		2	2:6	
		3	2:7	
	C	1	2:8	
		2	2:9	
	D	1	2:10	
		2	2:11	
		3	2:12	
	E	1	2:13	
		2	2:14	
	F	1	2:15	
		2	2:16	
		3	2:17	
III	A	1	3:1	
		2	3:1	
	B	1	3:2	
		2	3:3–4	
	C	1	3:5	
		2	3:6–7aA	
	D	1	3:7aBb	
		2	3:8	
		3	3:9	

continued

FIGURE 26 (*cont*)

Malachi			The Book of Malachi		
E	1	3:10–12			
	2	3:13–15			
F	1	3:16			
	2	3:17–18			
	3	3:19			
			G	1	3:20–21aA
				2	3:21aBb
			H	1	3:22
				2	3:23–24

Figure 26. Roman numerals indicate columns. Letters and numbers denote matching pairs of paragraphs.

cult from the perennial pressure of natural cycles and insisted instead on the meaning of sacrifice and its relationship to the levitical vocation. He was intent on freeing the temple from its purely local and national significance and on establishing the international status of its God. His approach was rational and abstract and his detachment from the immediacy of natural and historical pressures influenced the revision of Haggai and Zechariah in its thrust toward speculation.

STRUCTURE AND ORGANIZATION (FIG. 26)

The prophecy is written in three columns, each composed of matching pairs of paragraphs, arranged in interlocking series. The first column (1:1–14) deals with sacrifice, the second (2:1–17) with the levitical covenant, and the last (3:1–19) with the new order of right worship. Paragraphs are linked in arguments, and arguments or pairs of paragraphs are matched in disputations. The prophecy was left unchanged except for a codicil (3:20–24) that situated Malachi's narrow priestly expectation in the current of the law and the prophets.

Column 1 (Malachi 1:1–14)

The first argument has a pair of paragraphs (1:1–2a, 2b–3) on the relationship between Yahweh and Israel. The first argues that Yahweh loves Israel, and the second develops the argument by contrasting Jacob and Esau and by reasoning from Yahweh's evident hatred for Esau to his love for Jacob. It is simple inference: if Jacob and Esau are opposites and Esau is hated, then Jacob must be loved.

The matching pair (1:4, 5) adds another argument to conclude the disputation. The first paragraph argues that if Edom tries to rebuild, Yahweh will destroy it, and from this concludes that Edom is an evil place that Yahweh will despise forever. The obvious implication is that Yahweh's love for Jacob is eternal, but the second paragraph lets Israel draw its own conclusions and marvel at Yahweh's international influence.

The next argument has three paragraphs dealing with Yahweh's international status (1:6, 7, 8). The first paragraph reasons that if children and slaves respect their masters, and Yahweh is their master, the priests should respect him instead of despising him. In the second the priests object that they do not despise him, and Yahweh retorts that they do by defiling his altar. The third paragraph concludes the argument by showing how they defile the altar of their great Master with gifts they would not dare to present to a provincial governor.

The matching pair of paragraphs (1:9, 10) concludes the disputation by insisting that Yahweh does not approve of them and is not pleased with their offerings. Both paragraphs emphasize his preeminent power by insisting on his title "Lord of Hosts."

The next argument begins with a pair of paragraphs that resume and reformulate the preceding argument (1:11, 12). The first takes up the issue of Yahweh's status as an international God by arguing that incense is burned to him and gifts are brought to him everywhere in the whole world. The second sums up the problem with the priests by repeating that their measly offerings profane his name and that they are alone in the whole world in defiling his table.

The disputation ends with a matching pair of paragraphs (1:13, 14). The first paragraph details their measly offerings—the lame, sickly, injured animals—and their impatience with criticism. The second insists on the enormity of the insult to Yahweh, who is not only their master but a mighty king feared throughout the world.

Column 2 (Malachi 2:1–17)

The argument begins with two paragraphs that outline the seriousness of the situation (2:1–2, 3–4). The first reminds the priests that sacrifices are subject to divine ordinances, whose neglect entails curses—the curses in fact that have come upon them. The second argues that these ordinances are implicit in the covenant with Levi and that the curses consequently will have an effect on their offspring.

The matching set of paragraphs (2:5, 6, 7) describes this covenant with Levi. The first paragraph (2:5) describes it as a covenant of life and peace whose basic conditions were that he fear Yahweh and have respect for his name. The second (2:6) includes among the stipulations of the covenant the obligation to teach, to give fair and just decisions, and to make sure that the general population does not incur guilt. The third (2:7) explains this by making the priest Yahweh's delegate, from whom the people are to seek knowledge and advice.

The argument continues with two paragraphs that point out how and where the priests went wrong (2:8, 9). First, they violated the levitical covenant in their conduct and by giving bad advice. Second, the fact that they are so despised and unimportant proves that they did not observe the stipulations of the covenant and in particular that they were partial in their decisions.

The next three paragraphs develop the complementary argument and conclude the disputation (2:10, 11, 12). The first argues that they have the same father and the same God but have been unfair to one another and have violated the covenant. The second extends the accusation to include Judah, Jerusalem, and Israel, and identifies their specific crime as marriage with the daughter of a foreign God. The third paragraph describes the culprits as "awakeners" and "answerers" who bring their gifts to Yahweh, and it decrees exclusion from the tents of Jacob as their punishment.

The argument continues with two paragraphs that explain the consequences of their crime (2:13, 14). They cover the altar with tears, crying and sobbing, without noticing whether God is pleased with their offerings. They wonder why this is wrong, and the answer is that they have been unfair to their wives, their companions, the women with whom they have made a covenant.

The next three paragraphs (2:15, 16, 17) are complementary and conclude the disputation. The first paragraph argues that Yahweh made them one, that this oneness shares some of his spirit and looks for divine offspring, and so they should care for their own spirits and be fair to the wives they married when they were young. The second concludes that Yahweh hates divorce, putting a cloak over violence, and that they should care for their own spirits and not be unfair. The last insists that their protests bore God—their claiming that the bad things they do are good and that Yahweh is pleased with them, and their doubt that Yahweh will do anything about it.

The argument concerns the decisions that the priests hand down, their lack of conformity with the levitical covenant, and the effect that they have on the general public. The specific instance concerns marriage and divorce, and the argument is that their decision was wrong. The first reason is that marriage made them one with a touch of the spirit and with offspring from God, while the other women that they take, the women to whom they become lord or "Baal," are daughters of a lesser God. The second is that Yahweh is worshiped with incense and pure gifts, while this lesser God requires awakeners and answerers who weep and sob and honor him with tears. The result is that all Judah, Jerusalem, and Israel are led astray because they have neglected the law and their levitical duties.

Column 3 (Malachi 3:1-19)

The first part of the argument (3:1) is that the judgment that they await (2:17) is on its way. The first paragraph announces the arrival of the angel who prepares the way for the Lord they are seeking (3:1): "Lord" (*ʾădōnāy*) is a title of Yahweh (1:6, 12, 14), but it may also evoke the name of Adonis, the lesser God whose daughters they married and for whom they wept and bathed the altar in tears. The second paragraph identifies the angel as the angel of the covenant and one in whom they delight (3:1).

The complementary argument (3:2, 3–4) makes it clear that the angel of the covenant comes in judgment. On the day of his arrival and manifestation the messenger himself will appear like fire and be like soap. He will purify the Levites so that their offerings and the offerings of Judah and Jerusalem will be as they were in the past.

The next part of the argument (3:5, 6–7aA) explains again what their crimes were and how Yahweh differs from the lesser God. They were guilty of incantations and adultery, of taking false oaths, of oppressing hired hands, widows, and the orphans, of disregarding the aliens, and of not fearing Yahweh. Yahweh does not change and neither do they, and this disregard of the law has been going on from time immemorial.

The complementary argument calls for their repentance (3:7aBb, 8, 9). The first paragraph links their repentance with Yahweh's change of heart, but typically they do not see what has to be changed. The second explains that in their tithes and their offerings they are slighting Yahweh, not something that a people should do to a God. The third explains that the whole nation is doing it and that therefore they are laboring under a curse.

The next part of the argument (3:10–12, 13–15) describes the lifting of the curse. The curse is essentially the curse of the dry season, the time that traditionally was set aside for the rites of Adonis, and the remedy is rain. Their response is that it is pointless to serve Yahweh and that it does not do any good to weep to Yahweh and that this sort of forgiveness shows that it is possible to slight God and get away with it.

The complementary part of the disputation (3:16, 17–18, 19) describes how those who feared Yahweh paid attention and were inscribed in the book, and announces the day of punishment for those who did not return. The day is the day of drought they meant to escape, and the day of the manifestation of God in fire and devastation that leaves neither root nor branch.

The Codicil (Malachi 3:20–24)

The codicil is composed of complementary arguments, each with two paragraphs, that continue where Malachi left off and add a few correctives. The first argument has two paragraphs (3:20–21aA, 21aBb) that describe the day as a day when the sun of justice will rise on those who fear Yahweh. It will heal them and they will go out and dance and trample on the wicked like dust beneath their feet. The second argument also has two paragraphs (3:22, 23–24) that identify those who fear God and the angel who will precede the day. Those who fear God are not those who observe the covenant with Levi but those who observe the law of Moses, the commandments given to all Israel on Horeb. The angel of the day is not a priest, as Malachi suggests, but the prophet Elijah.

The codicil recognizes the elements of the rites of Adonis that Malachi repudiated and uses them to better advantage. There will be healing for those who fear Yahweh, and dancing, and the manifestation of God in the sunrise. But it will be a time of innocence, a time of observance of the law of Moses, a time for the return of Elijah.

LANGUAGE AND STYLE

The most significant elements of language and style are related to the logical arrangement of Malachi's material. The text is an extended argument about ritual observances. It moves gradually from the more obvious cases where the offerings were blemished and the priests had excuses to the less obvious cases, where the priests misled the people and violated the covenant with Levi, to the possible resolutions of the problem. Each step is reasoned; everything follows by implication; everything comes to a resolution. Things are said, explained, and repeated as the basis for another explanation and repetition.

The manner is plain, but in such a text words are carefully chosen. Everything hinges on words; all the argument depends on the priests quibbling about the meaning or applicability of words; the drift of the argument is based on definitions and groupings of words. The care is sometimes painfully evident in choices and allusions that defy recognition.[194]

SOURCES AND INTERPRETATIONS

Malachi clearly knew Haggai, Zechariah, Obadiah, Jeremiah, Ezekiel, and the Deuteronomist. His work is a mixture of learning and observation. He knows history and law, is clear about what is right and wrong, and tries to sort out the merits of contemporary practices. He has little enough respect for local government and displays a keen interest in order and theocratic rule. His use of reason and abstraction to create the image of a better time was a real inspiration to the editor of Haggai and Zechariah.

Column 1

The language of the first argument is familiar from the prophets and the law. The idea that the word of Yahweh came through the mediation of Malachi is not new but had been used most recently by Haggai.[195] The massing of expressions in the heading to identify the work as prophecy was also used by the author of the book of Zechariah.[196] The love of God for his people became an acceptable literary expression with Hosea (Mal 1:2; cf. Hos 11:1, 4), but the contrast between love and hate is typical of covenant texts.[197] The brotherhood of Esau and Jacob was known from the earliest texts in Genesis, but it had become an issue recently in Obadiah and in the revision of the book of Amos (Mal 1:2; cf. Obad 10; Amos 1:11). That the mountains of Edom became a wasteland was mentioned in the book of Ezekiel,[198] and the conversion of a pleasant countryside into a pair of jackals was an image first used by Jeremiah.[199]

The second argument uses some of the same texts. Rebuilding of the ruins is a major theme in Haggai (Mal 1:4; cf. Hag 1:2, 4). The contrast between building and tearing down was a theme invented for the book of Jeremiah (Mal 1:4; cf. Jer 1:10). The notion that the authority of Yahweh extended beyond the borders of Israel, combined with the personal witness formula, was adopted from Malachi by the book of Zechariah (Mal 1:5; cf. Zech 9:1–8). The image of sweeping evil outside the borders of Israel into another country was already in the prophecy of Zechariah (Mal 1:4; cf. Zech 5:8–11).

The third argument is aware of the dedication of the temple according to Haggai and Zechariah and refers obliquely to it in its question about the glory of Yahweh (Mal 1:6–8; cf. Hag 2:3, 9; Zech

2:9). The singling out of the priests and the conviction that the priests were responsible for advice and instruction were drawn from a tradition represented in Chronicles and influenced the editor of Haggai (Mal 1:6; cf. 2 Chr 15:3; Hag 2:10–14). The prohibition against sacrificing lame or blind animals was contained in the Deuteronomistic code, but the inclusion of the sick and injured is proper to Malachi (Mal 1:8; cf. Deut 15:21; cf. also Mal 1:13). The mention of the governor is conceivably a reference to Zerubbabel, who is given that title by Haggai (Mal 1:8; cf. Hag 1:1; 2:2).

The fourth argument uses the expression "pay reverence to the presence of Yahweh" coined by Zechariah (Mal 1:9; cf. Zech 7:2). The closing of the doors of the temple probably has significance for the rituals that are described in the second column.

The fifth and sixth arguments stress the grandeur of Yahweh and the magnificence of his name. The pair "great and terrible" can be traced to the Deuteronomistic Historian, but references to the kingship of Yahweh and to his great and terrible name, though they are known from the History, are typically hymnic (Mal 1:11, 14; cf. Pss 96:10; 99:3; 111:9).

Column 2

The diffusion of blessing and curse in relation to the building or operation of the temple is familiar from Haggai and Zechariah (Mal 2:1–2; cf. Haggai 1; Zech 8:13). The reference to seed, in particular, is an allusion to the same texts (Mal 2:3; cf. Hag 1:6; Zech 8:12). The covenant with Levi combines the covenant of peace known to the Deuteronomistic Historian and to the book of Ezekiel with the covenant of life described in Deuteronomy.[200] Reverence is a Deuteronomistic topic, and the role of the priests in disseminating the law originated in the Deuteronomistic rules of government (Mal 2:5, 6; cf. Deut 6:13; 17:8–13). The law as the way and "turning from the way" as disobedience is a Deuteronomistic property, and being partial in judgment is condemned both in Deuteronomy and in the Elohist Book of the Covenant.

The fourth argument refers obliquely to the declaration that Yahweh is One and projects the idea onto the story of creation (Mal 2:10; cf. Deut 6:4). The same terminology recurs in the sixth argument (Mal 2:15; cf. Gen 2:7, 24), where the creation of man and woman from mud and the spirit of Yahweh and their union in marriage as one flesh are the point. The references to the rites of Adonis are obscure but include his awakening (2:12), rites of incantation and response,[201] weeping and tears (2:13), women as devotees of the God,[202] marriage of a lord or "Baal" (2:11) with the daughter of a foreign God (2:11), the expectation of divine progeny (2:15), the reference to the day of the God's manifestation (3:2), insistence that Yahweh is God, not a man, and does not change (3:6, 8), the fact that the problem that led to the wrong sort of worship was the dry season and that the resolution to the problem was rain, and the unwillingness of the people to abandon their sullen treks in search of the God (3:14).

Malachi confronts these syncretistic practices with the weight of the law and the covenant. The priesthood is to blame, but as sons of Levi they are essentially a symbol of a covenant that extends from generation to generation. The most interesting aspect of his resolution is that he does not expect it to work very well. Some will fear Yahweh and be inscribed in his book, but some will persist. Malachi seems to admit that his argument, which he has tried so hard to hone, is not entirely convincing. The inclusion of the alien God was obviously wrong, but the rites were not so obviously out of place, as the Song of Songs might attest, and Malachi simply made the covenant the test. The way he began was the way he ended—"I love you, says Yahweh"— a saying that might be questioned but could hardly be answered.

NOTES

[1] Hag 1:1b, 3, 12; 2:1 (*ḥaggay hannābî*); Hag 1:12 (*ka'ăšer šĕlāḥô yhwh 'ĕlōhêhem*); Hag 1:13 (*ḥaggay mal'ak yhwh bĕmal'ăkût yhwh*).

[2] Hag 1:1b, 3; 2:1 (*hāyâ dĕbar yhwh*); Hag 1:2, 5, 7, 8; 2:6, 7, 9 [*koh*] *'āmar yhwh* [*ṣĕbā'ôt*]; Hag 1:9, 13; 2:4, 8, 9 (*nĕ'um yhwh* [*ṣĕbā'ôt*]); Hag 1:12 (*bĕqôl yhwh 'ĕlōhêhem wĕ'al dibrê ḥaggay hannābî*).

[3] The same writer seems to have been responsible for Hag 2:10–23 and Zech 3:1–10; 4:6aBb–10a; 6:9–15; 9:1–14:21 and to have known the full extent of the Chronicler's work (1 and 2 Chronicles and the supplement to the law [P_s]).

[4] Hag 1:2b, *lō' 'et bō' 'et bêt yhwh lĕhibbānôt*.

[5] Hag 1:1b ("There was a word of Yahweh by the hand of Haggai the prophet") = 1:3. Their objection refers to the time (1:2, *'et*) and his reply quotes them (1:4, *'êt*).

[6] Hag 1:4b (*wĕhabbayit hazzeh ḥārēb*); cf. Zeph 2:14b, on the ruin of the temple in Nineveh (*qôl yĕšôrēr baḥallôn / ḥoreb bassap / kî 'arzâ 'êrâ*, "Hooting of an owl in the window / on the bare sill / stripped of its cedar").

7 Hag 1:5a, "Now, then . . ." (*wĕʾattâ*).

8 Hag 1:5 ("Thus Yahweh of Hosts has spoken") = 1:7 ("Now, then, thus Yahweh of Hosts has spoken").

9 Hag 1:9aA, *pānōh ʾel harbēh / wĕhinnēh limʿāṭ.*

10 Hag 1:5b, 7b ("Set your mind to where you are going" [*śîmû lĕbabkem ʿal ḏarkêkem*]). Cf. Hag 1:4a (*lāšebet bĕbāttêkem*) and 1:9b (*wĕʾattem rāṣîm ʾîš lĕbêtô*).

11 Cf. Hag 1:9bB, *ḥārēb* ("ruin") and 1:11aA *ḥōreb* ("drought").

12 Cf. Hag 1:1–2, 3–4. In the first part the sets of paragraphs are arranged so that the argument builds to a climax and becomes resolved (i.e., A-B-C-A'-B'). In this pattern the first and fourth sets of paragraphs correspond (i.e., A = 1:1–2, 3–4; A' = 1:12a, 12b–13).

13 The statement (Hag 1:14bA) that they went and did the work corresponds to the command (Hag 1:8) to go up to the mountain and get wood and build the house. Haggai began to exhort them on the first day of the sixth month (Hag 1:1), and they finished on the twenty-fourth of the same month (Hag 1:15a).

14 Hag 2:4 ("For I am with you") = Hag 1:13b.

15 Hag 2:4a (*waʿăśû*) = Deut 5:27 (*wĕšāmaʿnû wĕʾāśînû*) = 2 Kgs 18:12.

16 Hag 2:5aA (*haddābar*); cf. Deut 5:1, 4, 5.

17 Hag 2:5aA (*ʾăšer kārattî*); cf. Deut 5:2–3.

18 Hag 2:5aA; cf. Deut 4:45–46; 5:6.

19 Hag 2:5aB (*wĕrûḥî ʿōmedet bĕtôkĕkem*); cf. Deut 5:5 (*ʾānōkî ʿōmēḏ bên yhwh ûbênêkem bāʿēt hahîʾ*).

20 Hag 2:5b, *ʾal tîrāʾû*; cf. Deut 5:29; Exod 20:20, *ʾal tîrāʾû.*

21 Cf. Hag 2:4 (*ḥăzaq . . . waḥăzaq . . . waḥăzaq . . . kî ʾănî ʾittĕkem*) and Deut 31:1–8, 23 (*ḥizqû wĕʾimṣû . . . ḥăzaq wĕʾĕmāṣ . . . hûʾ yihyeh ʿimmĕkā . . . ḥăzaq wĕʾĕmāṣ*).

22 Cf. Hag 2:5b (*ʾal tîrāʾû*) and Deut 31:6, 8 (*ʾal tîrĕʾû; lōʾ tîrāʾ*).

23 Haggai's authority for the statement is expressed in the formula "Says Yahweh of Hosts" (Hag 2:9, *nĕʾum yhwh ṣĕbāʾôt*). Haggai's promise of peace (2:9b, "And in this place I will give peace . . ." [*ûbammāqôm hazzeh ʾettēn šālôm*]) agrees with the statement that is attributed to the lying prophets in

the book of Jeremiah and, to mark the quotation, it has the opposite word order (Jer 14:13b, "The prophets told them. . . . I will give you real peace in this place" [*kî šĕlôm ʾĕmet ʾettēn lākem bammāqôm hazzeh*]).

24 P_S = Leviticus 1–7; 12–27.

25 Hag 2:14aA, *hāʿām hazzeh*; cf. 1:2, 12, 13, 14; 2:2, 4.

26 Hag 2:14aA, *haggôy hazzeh*.

27 Hag 2:15, *šîmû nāʾ lĕbabkem*; cf. 1:5b, 7b.

28 Hag 2:17; cf. Deut 28:22; 1 Kgs 8:37; Amos 4:9.

29 Hag 2:17, *maʿăśeh yĕdêkem* = 2:14.

30 Hag 2:18, *šîmû nāʾ lĕbabkem* = 2:15.

31 Cf. Hag 1:8, 9, 14; 2:3, 7, 9 (*bayit* + *bnh*) and Hag 2:18 (*yussad hêkal yhwh*).

32 The expression *hāyâ* + *dbr* + *bĕyad* is used by the History and by later authors influenced by it: 1 Kgs 8:53, 56; 12:15; 14:18; 15:29; 16:12, 34; 17:16; 2 Kgs 9:36; 10:10; 14:25; 17:13; 21:10; 24:2; Isa 20:2; Hos 12:11; Jer 37:2; Ezek 38:17; Zech 7:7, 12; Mal 1:1. It derives from the practice of sending letters through messengers (1 Sam 11:7; 2 Sam 11:14; 2 Kgs 19:23).

33 The editor speaks to the priests as a class (Hag 2:11, 12b, 13b) and about general cases concerning individual men (Hag 2:12, *îš*) or specific persons (Hag 2:13, *nepeš*).

34 The main clauses are almost the same (*wĕhāyĕtâ ʿăśārâ . . . wĕhāyĕtâ ʿeśrîm*). The subordinate clauses have the same expression (*bāʾ ʾel*) but in different positions and with different predicates (*mihyôtām bāʾ ʾel ʿărēmat ʿeśrîm . . . bāʾ ʾel hayyeqeb laḥśōp ḥămiššîm pûrâ*).

35 Hag 2:18°–19: "Consider: is the seed still in the barn—have the vine and the fig tree and the pomegranate and olive tree not yielded—from now on I will bless you."

36 Hag 2:14: "And Haggai answered, and he said: 'Such is this people, and such is this nation before me—says Yahweh—and such is everything they do, and everything they offer—it is unclean."

37 Jer 25:12; 29:10–14; cf. Isa 7:8 (65 years); 23:15, 17 (70 years).

38 Hag 1:2b (*lōʾ ʿet bōʾ ʾet bêt yhwh lĕhibbānôt*); cf. Ezek 43:1–5 (after his vision of the temple: *wĕhinnēh kĕbôd ʾĕlōhê yiśrāʾēl bāʾ* [Ezek 43:2]). The Ezekiel passage influenced the Historian's version of the dedication of the Solomonic

temple (1 Kgs 8:11b, *kî mālēʾ kĕbôd yhwh ʾet bêt yhwh*; cf. Ezek 43:5b, *wĕhinnēh mālēʾ kĕbôd yhwh habbayit*). Zechariah knows Haggai's prophecy and agrees with it in putting the completion of the temple (a) at the end of the seventy years forecast by Jeremiah, and (b) after the return of Yahweh to Jerusalem (Zech 1:16). The clause *lōʾ ʿet bōʾ* would be an unusual way of expressing "The time has not come." It can mean "It is not the time . . ." (Gen 29:7, *lōʾ ʿēt*): the initial negative (*lōʾ*) introduces two complementary statements: "It is not (a) the time of the coming, (b) the time for the house of Yahweh to be built." The relation of this statement to the chronology in the book of Jeremiah was argued by C. L. Meyers and E. M. Meyers, *Haggai, Zechariah 1–8* (AB 25B; Garden City, N.Y.: Doubleday and Co., 1987) 20.

[39] *Peḥâ*, Hag 1:1, 14; 2:2.

[40] Hag 1:2, *hāʿām hazzeh*.

[41] Hag 1:12, 14; 2:2, *šĕʾērît hāʿām*.

[42] Hag 2:4, *ʿam hāʾāreṣ*.

[43] Hag 1:4aB, *sĕpûnîm*; cf. 1 Kgs 6:9, 15; 7:3, 7.

[44] Hag 1:4b, *wĕhabbayit hazzeh ḥārēb*; cf. Jer 22:5, *kî lĕḥorbâ yihyeh habbayit hazzeh*.

[45] The terms *ḥārēb, horeb, horbâ* often refer to the ruined or abandoned houses in Jerusalem or the cities of Judah: Isa 5:17; 44:26; 51:3; 52:9; 58:12; 61:4; Jer 25:9; 26:9; 27:17; 33:10; Ezek 5:14; 13:14; 33:24, 27; 36:4, 10; Lev 26:31, 33. They are not used specifically of the temple (e.g., Jer 26:9 ". . . this house will be like Shiloh, this city will be ruined . . .").

[46] Exod 9:21; Deut 32:46; 1 Sam 9:20; 2 Sam 18:3.

[47] Cf. Jer 7:3, 5; 18:11; Ezek 18:25, 29; 20:43, 44; 33:11; 36:31, 32; Lev 26:22.

[48] Hag 1:6; cf. Deut 6:11; 8:10, 12; 11:15; 14:29; 26:12; Isa 9:19; Amos 4:8; Hos 4:10; 13:6; Mic 6:14.

[49] Cf. Gen 9:21; 43:34; 2 Sam 11:13; 1 Kgs 16:9; 20:16; Cant 5:1.

[50] That is, *har* (e.g., Josh 10:6, 40; 11:16, 21; Jer 32:44; 33:13), as distinguished from the *šĕpēlâ* and the *negeb*.

[51] "Take pleasure" (*rṣh*), e.g. Isa 42:1; Jer 14:10; 2 Chr 10:7.

[52] E.g., Isa 56:7; Hos 8:13; Amos 5:22 = Mal 1:10; Jer 6:20; 14:12.

[53] E.g., Exod 14:4, 17, 18; Ezek 28:22; 39:13.

[54] Hag 1:10, *šāmayim miṭṭal*; cf. Gen 27:28, 39; Deut 33:13.

[55] Hag 1:11; cf. Deut 12:17; 28:22; Hos 2:10, 24.

[56] Hag 1:11b; cf. Deut 28:4, 11; 30:9; Joel 1:18, 20.

[57] Hag 1:11, *tôṣî' hā'ădāmâ* = Gen 1:12, 24, *tôṣî' hā'āreṣ*.

[58] Hag 1:11b, *yĕgîa' kappāyim* = Deut 28:33.

[59] Hag 1:12aA, *wayyišma'... bĕqôl yhwh 'ĕlōhêhem*; see H. W. Wolff, *Haggai* (BKAT 14/6; Neukirchen–Vluyn: Neukirchener Verlag, 1986) 33–34.

[60] Hag 1:12a, *wayyišma'... bĕqôl yhwh ... wĕ'al ðibrê ḥaggay*; cf. Exod 14:31, *wayya'ămînû bayhwh ûbĕmōšeh 'abdô*.

[61] Hag 1:12a, *ka'ăšer šĕlāhô yhwh 'ĕlōhêhem*; cf. Num 16:28–30, *yhwh šĕlāḥanî*; also Jer 25:17; 26:12, 15; 42:21.

[62] *šĕ'ērît hā'ām* [*hanniš'ār*], Hag 1:12; 2:2–3; cf. 2 Kgs 25:22; Isa 4:3; Jer 52:15; 2 Chr 34:21. In the book of Jeremiah the adjective *hanniš'ārîm* usually refers to elements who remained in the land (Jer 8:3; 21:7; 24:8; 38:4; 39:9; 40:6; 41:10) just as *šĕ'ērît* regularly refers to those in Judah who survived the first deportation (e.g., Jer 6:9; 24:8).

[63] Hag 1:12b ("And the people were afraid of Yahweh"); cf. Exod 20:18–21; Deut 5:23–29.

[64] Hag 1:13a, *wayyō'mer ḥaggay mal'ak yhwh bĕmal'ăkût yhwh lā'ām*; cf. Gen 28:10–22; Exod 23:20; Judg 6:11–14; 13:15–20.

[65] Hag 1:13b, *'ănî 'ittĕkem*; cf. Judg 6:12; Isa 43:5; Jer 1:8, 19; 30:11.

[66] Cf. Judg 5:12; Isa 41:2, 25; 42:13; 45:13; 51:9, 17; 52:1; Jer 51:1, 11; 1 Chr 5:26; 2 Chr 21:16; 36:22 = Ezra 1:1, 5.

[67] Haggai does not refer to the destruction of the temple but only to its need for repairs.

[68] Hag 2:3a, 7, 8, 9; cf. Nah 2:10, *bozzû kesep bozzû zāhāb ... kābōd mikkōl kĕlî ḥemðâ*.

[69] Cf. Deut 31:1–8, 23; Josh 1:6–9.

[70] Hag 2:4a (*ḥāzaq ... wa'ăśû*); cf. *wā'ăśû* in Deut 5:27 and 2 Kgs 18:12; cf. also 1 Chr 28:7, 10; 2 Chr 19:11; 25:8; Ezra 10:4.

[71] Hag 2:5aAb, *'ăšer kārattî 'ittĕkem bĕṣē'tĕkem mimmiṣrāyim ... 'al tîrā'û*. When the people came out of Egypt, they objected that Moses had brought

them out into the wilderness to die but he encouraged them with the same words (Exod 14:13, *'al tîrā'û*).

[72] Hag 2:5a, *haddābār . . . wĕrûḥî 'ōmedet bĕtôkĕkem*; cf. Deut 5:1–5, . . . *yhwh 'ĕlōhênû kārat 'immānû bĕrît bĕḥōreb . . . 'ānōkî 'ōmēd bên yhwh ûbênêkem bā'ēt hahî' lĕhaggîd lākem 'et dĕbar yhwh kî yĕrē'tem.* . . .

[73] III Isaiah associated the rebuilding of Jerusalem (Isa 44:28b, *wĕlē'mōr lîrûšālāyim tibbāneh*) and the cities of Judah (Isa 44:26, *ûlĕ'ārê yĕhûdâ tibbānênâ wĕḥārĕbôtêhā 'ăqômēm*), a theme borrowed from the book of Jeremiah (Jer 30:18; 31:38, *wĕnibnĕtâ [hā]'îr*), with laying the foundation of the temple (*wĕhêkāl tiwwāsēd*), a theme taken from Isaiah (Isa 28:16, *hinĕnî yissad bĕṣiyyôn 'āben . . . pinnat yiqrat mûsād mûssād*), and gave Cyrus the credit for decreeing (Isa 44:28b, *wĕlē'mōr*) that these projects be undertaken (Isa 44:28a; cf. 2 Chr 36:23). Haggai alluded to the prophecy (Hag 1:2–3, *lĕhibbānôt . . . ḥārēb*) and Zechariah, alluding to Haggai's version, quoted it in full (Zech 8:9, . . . *mippî hannĕbî'îm 'ăšer béyôm yussad bêt yhwh ṣĕbā'ôt hahêkāl lĕhibbānôt*).

[74] Hag 2:7aB, *ûbā'û ḥemdat kol haggôyim ûmillē'tî 'et habbayit hazzeh kābôd*; cf. Nah 2:10, *kābôd mikkōl kĕlî ḥemdâ.*

[75] Hag 2:6b; cf. 1:10–11; Gen 1:1, 9–10.

[76] Hag 2:7a; cf. Isa 23:17–18; 60:1–22.

[77] Hag 2:7b, *ûmillē'tî 'et habbayit hazzeh kābôd*; cf. Ezek 43:5, *wĕhinnēh mālē' kĕbôd yhwh habbāyit*; 1 Kgs 8:11, *kî mālē' kĕbôd yhwh 'et bêt yhwh.*

[78] The prophetic formula (*nĕ'um yhwh ṣĕbā'ôt*) often marks a quotation taken in the same sense from a distant context. Cf. Hag 2:8 (*lî hakkesep wĕlî hazzāhāb*) and Josh 6:19 (*wĕkōl kesep wĕzāhāb ûkĕlê nĕḥōšet ûbarzel qōdeš hû' layhwh / 'ôṣar yhwh yābô'*).

[79] Hag 2:10–14; cf. Deut 17:8–13; Jer 18:18; Ezek 7:26.

[80] Cf. Lev 7:15–18, 19–21; 21:1–4; Num 19:11–13. See Meyers and Meyers, *Haggai, Zechariah 1–8*, 55–56. These rules (Hag 2:11 *tôrâ* = Lev 7:11) are the only ones that allow for the saving and transporting of sacrificial meat by an individual and that deal with what becomes unclean by touching. Since the sacrifice is to be eaten with bread and with meal and oil, the question (Hag 2:12, *wĕ'el šemen wĕ'el kol ma'ăkāl*) gives away the answer. The Deuteronomistic conception of *tôrâ*, on the other hand, pertained to more difficult questions that were submitted to the adjudication of the priests in Jerusalem. The Deuteronomistic law on the defilement that comes from touching a dead body (Num 19:11–13) was included in this supplement (Lev 21:1–4; 22:4–6, [*wĕhannōgēa' bĕkol ṭĕmē' nepeš . . . nepeš 'ăšer tigga' bô wĕṭāmĕ'â . . . wĕlō' yō'kal baqqŏdāšîm . . .*]) and is referred to in these sacrificial regulations (Lev 7:19–21).

[81] Haggai's prophecy concerns the finishing or the refurbishing of the

house (*bayit*). The editor was concerned about the inner sanctuary, the *hêkāl* (2:15, 18; cf. Ezek 41:1, 4, 15, 20, 21, 23, 25; 42:8).

[82] Cf. Deut 28:22; 1 Kgs 8:37; Amos 4:9; Exodus 9–10.

[83] Cf. Isa 60:10–12; Jer 50:37; Zech 9:10.

[84] Cf. Hag 2:23 (*ḥôtām*) and Jer 22:24; Ezek 26:12; also Hag 2:23 (*bāḥar*) and 1 Sam 16:8, 9; 2 Sam 6:21; 1 Kgs 8:16.

[85] Zech 1:1 (the eighth month of the second year of Darius); Hag 2:1 (the end of the seventh month of the second year of Darius).

[86] Zech 2:2bB = 2:4bA ("These are the horns that scattered Judah" [*ʾēlleh haqqĕrānôt ʾăšer zērû ʾet yĕhûdâ*]).

[87] The scene is set in a series of nominal clauses (Zech 3:1), and the judgment is expressed in verbal and nominal clauses (3:2).

[88] That is, Zech 4:10b° continues 4:6aA and simply identifies the symbolism of the lamp, but Zech 4:10a continues the image of Zerubbabel the artisan (4:6aBb–9) and recalls that the cornerstone he is working with (4:7) has seven facets (3:9) or, in Zechariah's terms, seven eyes (4:10b).

[89] The first paragraph emphasizes that Zechariah is to lift up his eyes (5:5). The second paragraph (5:6) first identifies what he sees as a basket, but then associates it with the eyes of Yahweh that move over the face of the earth (5:6bB; cf. 4:10b).

[90] See Meyers and Meyers, *Haggai, Zechariah 1–8*, 425–45.

[91] Zech 9:1, *kî layhwh ʿên ʾādām / wĕkōl šibṭê yiśrāʾēl*.

[92] Cf. Zech 9:8b (*kî ʿattâ rāʾîtî bĕʿênāy*) and 9:1 (*kî layhwh ʿên ʾādām*).

[93] Zech 9:8, "For now I see with my own eyes!"

[94] The stanzas are 10:1, 2, 3, 4, 5, 6–7abA.

[95] The stanzas are 10:7bB–8, 9–10, 11, 12.

[96] Zech 11:3, *yll, ʾdr, šdd*; cf. 11:2.

[97] The stanzas are 11:12, 13, 14, 15–16, 17.

[98] The scenes are 12:1–5; 12:6–14. The strophes are 12:1–3, 4–5, 6–8, 9–14. The stanzas are 12:1–2, 3, 4, 5, 6–7, 8, 9–10, 11–14.

[99] Zech 1:4 ("the former prophets"); cf. Isa 41:22; 42:9; 48:3; 65:16, 17 ("former things").

100 Zech 1:2 (*q*$\dot{s}$*p*); cf. Num 16:22; Deut 9:7, 8, 19, 22; 29:27; Isa 47:6; 54:9; 57:16–17; 64:8.

101 Zech 1:3 (*šwb*); cf. Hos 5:4; 6:1; Jer 3:1, 22.

102 Zech 1:3 ("Return to me . . . and I will return to you"); cf. Joel 2:14; Jonah 3:9.

103 Zech 1:3 (*šwb*); cf. Zech 2:14 (*bw*ʾ = Ezek 43:1–5).

104 Zech 1:4a ("turn from your evil ways and from your evil deeds"); cf. Jer 7:3, 5; 17:10; 18:11; 23:22; 25:5; 26:13; 32:19; 35:15.

105 Zech 1:4b ("but they did not listen, and they did not pay attention to me"); cf. Jer 6:10, 17, 19; 7:26.

106 Zech 1:6a (*nśg*); cf. Deut 28:2, 15, 45.

107 Zech 1:6b (*zmm* . . . *ʿśh*); cf. Jer 51:12; Lam 2:17.

108 Zech 1:6b ("And they repented and said . . ."); cf. Joel 2:12–14, 18–27.

109 The myrtle trees among which the rider was standing (Zech 1:8a, 11a) are mentioned in II Isaiah as symbols of the new age (cf. Isa 41:19; 55:13).

110 Zech 1:10 (*lĕhithallēk bā*ʾ*āreṣ*), cf. Josh 18:8 (*wĕhithallĕkû bā*ʾ*āreṣ*); Zech 1:11 (*wĕhinnēh kol hā*ʾ*āreṣ yōšebet wĕšōqāṭet*), cf. Josh 11:23; 14:15 (*wĕhā*ʾ*āreṣ šāqĕṭâ*); cf. also Job 1:7; 2:2.

111 Zech 1:11 ("And behold all the land was settled and at rest" [*wĕhinnēh kol hā*ʾ*āreṣ yōšebet wĕšōqāṭet*]) + Zech 2:8b–9 ("Jerusalem will be settled as villages without walls [*pĕrāzôt tēšēb yĕrûšalayim*] . . . and I will be a wall of fire [*ḥômat* ʾ*ēš*] around her . . ."); cf. Ezek 38:11 "[Gog] will say: 'I will go up against a land of villages without walls [ʾ*ereṣ pĕrāzôt*], I will attack people who are at rest and settled securely, [*haššōqĕṭîm yōšĕbê lābeṭaḥ*], all of them living without walls [*bĕ*ʾ*ên ḥômâ*] . . .").

112 Zech 1:12, 14 (*rḥm, zʿm, qn*ʾ); cf. Nah 1:2, 6; Exod 34:6–7, 14.

113 Zech 1:14; cf. 2 Kgs 19:31; Isa 9:6; Obad 17; Joel 3:5.

114 Zech 1:13b, *dĕbārîm niḥumîm*; cf. Isa 40:1.

115 Zech 1:15, *ša*ʾ*ănannîm*; cf. Amos 6:1; Isa 32:9, 11, 18.

116 Zech 1:16, *bêtî yibbāneh bāh*; cf. Hag 1:2, *lō*ʾ . . . ʾ*et bêt yhwh lĕhibbānôt*.

117 Zech 1:16b, *wĕqāw yinnāṭeh ʿal yĕrûšalāyim*; cf. 2 Kgs 21:13, *wĕnāṭîtî ʿal yĕrûšalayim* ʾ*ēt qāw šōmĕrôn*.

118 Zech 1:17b, *wĕniḥam yhwh 'ôd 'et ṣiyyôn*; cf. Isa 51:3.

119 Zech 2:1–4 (*zrh*); cf. Ezek 5:10; 6:5, 8; 12:15; 20:23; 22:15; 29:12; 30:23; 36:19.

120 Cf. Deut 33:17; Hab 3:4; Ps 22:22.

121 Cf. 1 Kgs 22:11; Mic 4:13; Jer 28:13.

122 Ezek 40:5 ("And behold there was a wall all around the outside of the temple" [*wĕhinnēh ḥômâ miḥûṣ labbayit sābîb sābîb*]); cf. Zech 2:9 ("And I will be . . . a wall of fire around her" [*wa'ănî 'ehyeh lāh . . . ḥômat 'ēš sābîb*]).

123 Zech 2:14 (*škn*); cf. Ezek 43:7.

124 Zech 2:15, *wĕnilwû gôyim rabbîm 'el yhwh bayyôm hahû'*; cf. Jer 50:4–5, *bayyāmîm hahēmmâ . . . bō'û wĕnilwû 'el yhwh*.

125 Zech 2:17 ("Let all flesh be quiet before Yahweh, for he has roused himself in his holy retreat"); cf. Hab 2:20 ("Yahweh is in his holy temple, let the whole world be quiet before him"); Jer 25:30 (". . . and from his holy retreat he roars").

126 Zech 3:2, *habbōḥēr bîrûšālāyim* = 1:17b and 2:16b, *ûbāḥar 'ôd bîrûšālāyim*.

127 Zech 3:1–2, esp. 3:1b (*wĕhaśśāṭān 'ōmēd 'al yĕmînô lĕśiṭnô*); cf. 1 Sam 29:4; 2 Sam 19:23; 1 Kgs 5:18; 11:14, 23, 25; Job 1:7–9, 12; 2:1–7; Ps 109:6 (*wĕśāṭān ya'ămōd 'al yĕmînô*); 1 Chr 21:1 (*wayya'ămōd śāṭān 'al yiśrā'ēl*).

128 Zech 3:2b, *hălō' zeh 'ûd muṣṣāl mē'ēš*; cf. Isa 7:4; Amos 4:11, *kĕ'ûd muṣṣāl miśśĕrēpâ*.

129 Cf. Zech 3:7 (*hlk bdrk*) and 1 Kgs 2:3; Ezek 48:11; cf. Zech 3:7 (*šmr mšmrt*) and Num 18:4, 5, 8; Ezek 40:45–46.

130 Zech 3:8b (*ṣemaḥ*); cf. Jer 23:5; 33:17–22; Isa 4:2.

131 Zech 3:8b–9a ("For behold I am bringing my servant Branch / for behold the Rock" [*kî hinĕnî mēbî' . . . ṣemaḥ / kî hinnēh hā'eben . . .*]); cf. Isa 28:16 ("Behold I am laying a foundation in Zion, a Rock . . ." [*hinĕnî yissad bĕṣiyyôn 'āben*]); also Isa 8:14.

132 Zech 4:6aBb ("This is the word of Yahweh to Zerubbabel: 'Not with arms and not with strength but by my spirit' " [*lō' bĕḥayil wĕlō' bĕkōaḥ kî 'im bĕrûḥî*]); cf. Isa 11:2 (". . . and the spirit of Yahweh will rest upon him, a spirit of wisdom and understanding, a spirit of counsel and determination, a spirit of knowledge and the fear of Yahweh"); Isa 42:1, "Behold my servant . . . I have put my spirit upon him"); Isa 2:4.

133 See Meyers and Meyers, *Haggai, Zechariah 1–8*, 244–55.

134 Zech 4:7a, *mî 'attâ har haggādôl*; cf. Ezek 40:2 and Isa 2:2.

135 Although II Isaiah thought of the eschatological Zion as a lofty mountain (Isa 2:2), III Isaiah was determined that all such loftiness would be humbled and brought low (Isa 2:11–19). The leveling of the mountain (Zech 4:7a, *lĕmîšôr*) is like the leveling of hills and valleys for the journey home (Isa 40:4, *lĕmîšôr*). The same term, however, describes the just judgments of the messianic king (Isa 11:4, *bĕmîšôr*), and some such pun may be intended here.

136 Zech 4:7b, *wĕhôṣî' 'et hā'eben hārō'šâ*; cf. Zech 3:9; Isa 28:16.

137 Zech 4:7, *tĕšu'ôt ḥēn ḥēn lāh*; cf. Isa 22:2, *tĕšu'ôt mĕlē'â 'îr hômiyyâ qiryâ 'allîzâ*.

138 Cf. Deut 11:12; also Zech 9:1–17.

139 The scroll is mentioned in Jer 36:32. The curse (Zech 5:3, *'ālâ*) is mentioned in Jer 23:10; 29:18; 42:18; 44:12; Isa 24:6.

140 Zech 5:5–6; cf. 5:1, 2 ("flying scroll" [*mĕgillâ 'āpâ*] and 5:6 "basket" [*'êpâ*]).

141 Zech 5:4bB, *wĕkillattû wĕ'et 'ēṣāyw wĕ'et 'ăbānāyw*; cf. Hab 2:9–11.

142 Cf. Joel 1:5, 9, 13, 14; 2:12, 24, 26.

143 Zech 7:7, *yōšebet ûšĕlēwâ*; cf. Ezek 16:49; Jer 22:21.

144 Zech 7:9b, *ĕmet . . . wĕḥesed wĕraḥămîm*; cf. Exod 34:6–7; Hos 2:21; Jer 16:5.

145 Zech 7:9–12a; cf. Deut 10:17–18; 14:29; 16:11, 14, 18; 24:17, 19–21; 27:19; cf. Zech 7:9b–10a ("Make honest judgments, and be kind and merciful to one another, and do not oppress widows, orphans, aliens and the poor . . .") and Jer 7:5b–6a (". . . if you establish justice among one another, and do not oppress aliens, orphans and widows . . .").

146 Zech 7:11 (*m'n*); cf. Isa 1:20; Jer 13:10.

147 Zech 7:11 (*srr*); cf. Isa 1:23; 30:1; Jer 5:23; 6:28; Hos 4:16; 9:15.

148 Zech 7:11b; cf. Isa 6:10.

149 Zech 7:12; cf. Ezek 11:19.

150 Zech 7:12a; cf. 2 Kgs 17:13–14.

151 Zech 7:13; cf. Mic 3:4; Jer 11:14.

152 Zech 7:14; cf. Deut 4:28; 28:36.

153 Zech 7:14b; cf. Jer 3:19; 12:10.

154 Zech 7:14; cf. Jer 4:7; 6:8; 9:9–10.

155 Cf. Zech 1:14, 16; 2:14–15; Ezek 43:9.

156 Zech 8:3, ʿîr hāʾĕmet; cf. Isa 1:21, qiryâ neʾĕmānâ; Zech 8:3, har haqqōdeš = Jer 31:23.

157 Cf. Zech 8:4–5 and Jer 31:10–14; Zech 8:6 (yippālēʾ) and Jer 32:17, 27; Zech 8:4–5 (". . . old men and women will sit in the squares of Jerusalem once more, each with a cane because of their age, and the streets of the city will be filled with boys and girls . . .") and Jer 6:11 ("Therefore I am full of the wrath of Yahweh, I am tired of restraining it. Pour it out on the youngsters in the street, on the crowds of young men too; both husband and wife will be taken, old people and the aged . . ."); cf. Isa 3:1–4.

158 Zech 8:7–10; cf. Isa 43:3, 5; Jer 30:22; 31:1.

159 Cf. Zech 8:9 (hzq) and Hag 2:4; Zech 8:9b (mippî hannĕbîʾîm . . . bahêkāl lĕhibbānôt) and Hag 1:2; 2:18; Zech 8:10a and Hag 1:6b, 11bA; Zech 8:10b and Hag 1:3–6.

160 Zech 8:11a, liʾērît hāʿām hazzeh; cf. Hag 1:12, 14; 2:2.

161 Cf. Hag 2:19; Jer 26:6; 2 Kgs 22:19.

162 Cf. Ezek 27:26; 28:4, 20; Mic 7:10.

163 Cf. Zech 9:8 and Zech 7:14a; Isa 29:3; cf. also Zech 9:8 (ngś, "oppressor") and Exod 3:7; 5:6, 10, 13, 14 [= Egypt] and 2 Kgs 23:35 [= Egypt] and Isa 9:3; 14:2, 4 [= Babylon] and Isa 3:5, 12 [= internal strife].

164 Cf. Joel 2:25; Isa 40:2; 61:7.

165 Cf. Zech 10:3 (ʿattûdîm) and Isa 14:9. Cf. Zech 10:4 (pinnâ, yātēd, nôgēś) and Isa 28:16 (pinnâ [= Isaiah]) and Isa 22:23, 25 (yātēd [= II, III Isaiah]) and Isa 3:5, 12 (ngś [= III Isaiah]).

166 Zech 10:7bB–10 (qbṣ, pdh, mrḥq); cf. Jer 31:10–14; Zech 9:17.

167 Cf. 1 Chr 3:19 (šimʿî, brother of Zerubbabel).

168 Zech 13:4b (ʾadderet śēʿār); cf. Gen 25:25; 27:16, 22; 1 Kgs 19:13, 19; 2 Kgs 2:8, 13, 14.

169 Cf. Jer 6:27–29; Ezek 5:1–4.

170 Cf. Ezek 11:23; 40:2; 43:2.

171 See S. J. De Vries, *1 and 2 Chronicles* (The Forms of the Old Testament Literature 11; Grand Rapids: Eerdmans, 1989); D. N. Freedman, "The Chronicler's Purpose," *CBQ* 23 (1961) 436–42; B. Halpern, "Sacred History and Ideology: Chronicles' Thematic Structure — Indications of an Earlier Source," in *The Creation of Sacred Literature: Composition and Redaction of the Biblical Text*, ed. R. E. Friedman (Berkeley: University of California Press, 1981) 35–54; S. Japhet, "Conquest and Settlement in Chronicles," *JBL* 98 (1979) 205–18; W. Johnstone, "Guilt and Atonement: The Theme of 1 and 2 Chronicles," in *A Word in Season: Essays in Honour of William McKane*, ed. J. D. Martin and P. R. Davies (JSOTSS 42; Sheffield: JSOT Press, 1986) 113–38; J. D. Newsome, "Towards a New Understanding of the Chronicler and His Purposes," *JBL* 94 (1975) 201–17; M. Noth, *Überlieferungsgeschichtliche Studien* (2nd ed.; Tübingen: Max Niemeyer, 1957) 110–80; A. Spalinger, "The Concept of the Monarchy during the Saite Epoch — An Essay of Synthesis," *Or* 47 (1978) 12–36; H. G. M. Williamson, *I and II Chronicles* (New Century Bible; Grand Rapids: Eerdmans, 1982).

172 Since David is assimilated to Moses, the accession of Solomon is treated in terms of the succession of Joshua. See H. G. M. Williamson, "The Accession of Solomon in the Books of Chronicles," *VT* 26 (1976) 351–61; S. J. De Vries, "Moses and David as Cult Founders in Chronicles," *JBL* 107 (1988) 619–39.

173 The Davidic dynasty is remembered for its contributions to the temple. The Chronicler does not take sides in the debate, evident in II Zechariah, about the possible succession of Zerubbabel: he is listed among the descendants of David (1 Chr 3:19) but not among those who returned from exile (1 Chronicles 9). David's dynasty lives on less in its members than in the temple and worship that he founded.

174 The parts are distinguished by their topics and internal arrangement. The conclusion of one part contains a clue to the contents of the next. The first part, for instance, ends with the note that "the kingdom was turned over to David the son of Jesse" (10:14), and the second part (chaps. 11–12) concerns the beginning of his reign.

175 The line of David, for instance, is traced down to Zerubbabel and his children (1 Chr 3:1–19). It conforms to the interests and division of the book by listing the offspring of David (3:1–9; cf. 1 Chronicles) separately from Solomon and the continuation of his dynasty (3:10–19; cf. 2 Chronicles). The latter part of the list (3:20–24) seems to be an addition and would have to be if the Chronicler's history was composed after Haggai and Zechariah at the end of the sixth century. Without it the list of Solomon's descendants ends like the list of David's children (3:9, "And Tamar was their sister"; 3:19, "And Shelomith was their sister"); the summary and deictic statement at the end of the list of Zerubbabel's children (3:20, "five [in all]") does not include the two

sons of Zerubbabel mentioned in the original (3:19). The lists are not official but are the product of recollection and research. The Chronicler differs from Haggai and Ezra, for instance, in naming Pedaiah rather than Shealtiel the father of Zerubbabel (1 Chr 3:17–19); see Meyers and Meyers, *Haggai, Zechariah 1–8*, 9–14.

[176] Chapters coincide with chapters in the printed Bible. The fifth chapter, for instance, ends with one list of Levites, and the sixth contains another, each with a different purpose. The Septuagint and some translations put all the lists in the sixth chapter.

[177] The Chronicler corrects the Deuteronomistic History by naming Azariah, rather than Zadok, as the priest in the temple that Solomon built (1 Chr 5:36).

[178] The part (1 Chronicles 11–12) lists all those who came to Hebron to make David king (cf. 11:1; 12:39). It agrees with the sequel to the epic, which said that all the tribes came to Hebron to make him king, rather than with the Deuteronomist, who said that the elders came to Hebron to make him king (cf. 2 Sam 5:1–3).

[179] Later the Chronicler notes that David left Moses' tent of meeting at Gibeon (2 Chr 1:3–4).

[180] The Bathsheba affair was a story told by the sequel. In the Deuteronomist's version it became a vehicle for royal propaganda and was not taken seriously or at face value. In the Chronicler's version Solomon's mother is not Bathsheba but Bathshua (1 Chr 3:5) and the whole story, besides being a slur on the dynasty, is not pertinent to the Chronicler's non-narrative and undramatic record and evaluation of actual events.

[181] This part corresponds to the first part of the history (1 Chronicles 1–10) by undoing it, by taking the united kingdom away from David, and by forcing the Levites out of their land.

[182] This part corresponds to the second part (1 Chronicles 11–12) in its concentration on war and in describing the defection of troops from their rightful sovereign (cf. 2 Chr 13:6–7 and 1 Chronicles 12).

[183] This part is related to the third part (1 Chronicles 13–16) at least in quoting the refrain from the psalm that was sung there in its entirety (cf. 2 Chr 20:21 and 1 Chr 16).

[184] This part is like the fourth (1 Chronicles 17–20) by its interest in the temple (1 Chronicles 17; 2 Chronicles 24), in war, and in the submission and revolt of Edom (1 Chr 18:12; 2 Chr 21:8–10).

[185] Elijah appears, without personality, as a letter writer (2 Chr 21:12–15).

186 This part is like the fifth (1 Chronicles 21–22) in recording the sins of the kings.

187 This part matches the sixth part (1 Chronicles 23–27), notably in matters concerning the Levites (e.g., compare 2 Chr 29:25–26 and 1 Chr 25:1–8).

188 Cf. 2 Chr 30:2–3 and Num 9:10–11; also 2 Chr 30:8–9.

189 Cf. 2 Chr 31:3 and Numbers 28–29. The actual contributions to the sanctuary—tithes of grain, wine and oil, cattle and sheep and dedicated things, freewill and required offerings—are those listed in the sequel's, rather than in the Deuteronomist's, law of centralization (2 Chr 31:3, 5, 6, 10, 12, 14; cf. Deut 12:17, 26 [sequel] and 12:6, 11 [Deuteronomist]).

190 The Chronicler is favorable to the remnant of the North (2 Chr 30:6; 34:21) and includes Israelites among the first people to return (1 Chr 9:2).

191 This part is like the seventh (1 Chronicles 28–29) in its concentration on the dynasty, in the parallel it draws between Solomon and Cyrus as divinely designated architects of the temple, and in mentioning its prophetic sources.

192 The Chronicler supposes (2 Chr 33:18) that Manasseh paid attention to the prophets who composed their works during his reign.

193 The kings usually are portrayed as meek and mild servants of the people. Exceptions (e.g., Asa, 2 Chr 16:10) are carefully noted.

194 Malachi's use and rebuttal of the Priestly Blessing (Num 6:23–27; Mal 1:6–2:9) has been demonstrated by M. Fishbane, *Biblical Interpretation in Ancient Israel* (Oxford: Clarendon, 1985) 332–34.

195 Mal 1:1, *bĕyad*; cf. Hag 1:1.

196 Mal 1:1, *maśśā' dĕbar yahweh 'al / 'el yiśrā'ēl*; cf. Zech 9:1; 12:1.

197 Mal 1:2–3 (*'hb / śn'*); cf. Deut 5:10–11; 2 Sam 19:7.

198 Mal 1:3, *har / šĕmāmâ*; cf. Ezek 35:7, 12, 15.

199 Mal 1:3; cf. Jer 9:10; 10:22; 23:10; 49:33; 51:37.

200 Mal 2:5; cf. Num 25:12; Ezek 34:25; Deut 8:1; 30:15–20.

201 Mal 2:12 (*'ōneh*); 3:5 (*kśp*).

202 Mal 2:14 (*ḥbr*); cf. Hos 4:17.

Conclusion

*L*ate Judean literature was written to be read or performed. Its authors were poets, singers, orators, lawyers, priests, and scholars who tried to situate the Judah of their time in the flow and scheme of history. Its audience was those who gathered in the squares, at the gates, on the walls of the city, or who met and lingered at the threshing floors, mills, and watering holes scattered through the kingdom. It comprised occasional drama, epic recitation, tragedy and comedy, ballads and speeches, reports and commentaries, debates and disputations, traditional stories, the stuff of books and libraries and literary appreciation.

The literature was a novelty that coincided with the floruit of the kingdom. It began after the Assyrians were established in the West and about the time that Greek literature flourished. Its golden age was the period of Assyrian domination, from Hezekiah to Josiah, when peace was established and the principalities and kingdoms of the West were still prosperous. It was still vigorous and original in the exile during the Babylonian renaissance. With the advent of the Persians Judah gradually settled into being a poor, petty, and provincial enclave with a meager and self-serving literature to match. Whatever the real inspiration and causes, the coincidences are striking, and the literature of Judah kept pace with its engagement in the life and destiny of empires.

The histories were composed, perhaps, to celebrate the eras of the kingdom's prosperity. When Samaria fell and the Sidonian empire was crushed, wealth and influence drifted to the South, to Tyre and her sister kingdom Judah, whose founders, the Historian liked to think, were contemporaries and united by the political bonds of brotherhood and love. It was then, late in the eighth century, that the epic was composed, inspired by Homer and Hesiod, from the amazing literary treasures of ancient Assyria and Babylon and from the diverse recollections of regions and tribes, to narrate Israel's splendid emergence from the motley indistinction of the nations. When Jerusalem and Judah survived the insurrection of coastal neighbors at the end of the century a writer, a precursor of the Deuteronomist, wrote a sequel to the epic that magnified the kingdom's covenant with its God and gave dignity to its dalliance with Egypt and to its submission to an Assyrian suzerain. In the reign of Manasseh, much maligned for the cosmopolitan bias of his reign, the Priestly writer and the Elohist combined to give Judah a law and an incipient constitution. The Deuteronomistic Historian, in the first part of the sixth century, in an age of great libraries and literary revival, bereft of kings and patrons, citizen of a world expanding in commerce and colonization, abandoned local pride and regional interests to write a history of the universe where God was king.

The prophets were the foci of their native traditions in a blossoming culture and an international civilization that was stirring a simple agricultural and pastoral land into a gala and frenzy of urban delight. Isaiah, for all his wit and education, was dead-set against the government and the literati that it sponsored, and imagined Yahweh the God of the people building a better city on the ancient foundations of justice. Amos was glad to be a rancher from Tekoa and could hardly wait for the gloating city, with its luxury and pompous celebrations, to succumb before the God who made time and seasons and occasions and was about to annul them. Hosea celebrated love and the family and the orgies of a fertile land cavorting with its God and decried its waste on aliens and their alliances. The kingdom, it seemed to people like these, was thriving by tearing at its own roots.

Many agreed and the works of these prophets became standard references for the people. Micah was appalled that traditional values — things like honesty, decency, friendship, family, trust — were being squandered for political and commercial profit. In a play by Jeremiah the same theme recurs, but he thinks that it is the equivalent of giving up on history. Nahum saw a real parallel between Jerusalem and gorgeous, deadly Nineveh, the seductress of nations. Habakkuk stood on the wall and saw destruction coming. Zephaniah pictured it as the end of the world brought on by the palace, and prophets and priests who should have realized that, if Jerusalem became a metropolis like the capitals of Assyria and Egypt, it would have to share their inglorious fate.

In an amazing blend of copying, correction, and creation one literary figure followed on another to reflect the sentiments and fill the minds of a proud inquiring age. When the speeches were done, the songs sung, the plays finished, the recitals at an end, when the predictable had occurred and the impossible happened, it was time to reread their writings and see why most of their readers, or those that mattered, had missed their point. It was a time of narrow gaze, tortured thinking, and bitter consolation for some, of splendid aloofness for people like the Historian, of hauteur and wounded pride for the biographer of Jeremiah, or of laughter for the few who were unafraid. This too was a reflection of the times and was read into the tradition they cared for and copied and passed on to the generations to come.

In all of this they were not the dupes of a critical present, the slaves of a recorded past, or wizards molding the future but historians and prophets who tried to understand what happened and to convince their contemporaries that understanding mattered and was worth the trouble. The past was not available until it was created; the present was flat without it; and the future was certain but undefined, a blank and necessary blessing.

The epic was the first to create a past and a future. From myth, legend, folklore, hearsay, and opinion its writer wove the family history of Israel on its blessed journey to individuation and separation from the nations. It had a nod in all directions and a story for every taste. Israel, if you wanted, came from the North, from the cradle of civilization, or, if you preferred, came from the South, out of Egypt, or from the land of the Philistines to the West, or even by Moab, Edom, and Ammon to the East. It made more difference what it was and where it was going, how it came together in a covenant with Yahweh, and why it would journey forever in the company of its God.

All of this did matter to the Deuteronomist, however, who thought that facts were important and evidence had to be sifted, positions taken, and decisions made. The History opted for the theory of amphictyony, a model from the Mediterranean world that it admired, to explain the cohesion of diverse and incompatible people who made up Israel. It invented playgrounds in the desert where they could learn to live together. It went along with the earlier fantasy, neither illogical nor impossible, that the land had been taken in one brief and magnificent campaign under Joshua and the God of the covenant. It actually thought that the land had been assigned to the individual tribes rather than captured by the nation, and it found wonderful examples of local wisdom and heroic courage in the face of adversity that it could inflate and transform into a time of national struggle like its own when the country was overrun with wicked foreigners and mean neighbors. It knew, however, that it was David who first stabilized the nation, winning over the South with diplomacy and pluck, bringing the North together to shelter in his protection, providing a God and a religion to mastermind their fate. The beauty of the system was apparent in the reign of Solomon when the temple that he built became not only the focus of a people but the center of a world that stretched from the river to Egypt and from the river Jordan to the Sea. The value of the theory was clear when the kingdom was gone and nothing but the tribes and the focus remained.

The theory, like those before and after it, was constructed from the materials of the time, from the facts, the ideas and the aspirations. All the writers had their day, their adherents and commentators, the critical audience that cared, the disciples who imagined that their theories were somehow matters of fact worth registering, the people who knew differently and better and went on to concoct theories of their own. This ragged and determined development of late Judean literature, this *sic et non* of the equally inspired, might well be a lesson to us all in sifting the debris of time to reconstruct their history or recreate a world.

Bibliography

A Selection of Critical and Complementary Interpretations

Introduction

Barton, J.
  1986   *Oracles of God: Perceptions of Ancient Prophecy in Israel after the Exile.*
           London: Darton, Longman & Todd, 1986.

Blenkinsopp, J.
  1983   *A History of Prophecy in Israel: From the Settlement in the Land to the
           Hellenistic Period.* Philadelphia: Westminster Press, 1983.

Boorer, S.
  1989   "The Importance of a Diachronic Approach: The Case of Gene-
           sis–Kings." *CBQ* 52:195–208.

Cooper, J. S.
  1977   "Symmetry and Repetition in Akkadian Narrative." *JAOS* 97:508–
           12.

Cross, F. M.
  1973   *Canaanite Myth and Hebrew Epic: Essays in the History of the Religion
           of Israel.* Cambridge, Mass.: Harvard University Press.

  1983   "The Epic Traditions of Early Israel: Epic Narrative and the
           Reconstruction of Early Israelite Institutions." Pp. 23–39 in *The
           Poet and the Historian: Essays in Literary and Historical Biblical
           Criticism.* Ed. R. E. Friedman. HSS 26. Chico, Calif.: Scholars
           Press.

Cruikshank, J.
  1988   "Myth and Tradition as Narrative Framework: Oral Histories
           from Northern Canada." *International Journal of Oral History* 9:198–
           214.

Finet, A.
1986   "Allusions et réminiscences comme source d'information sur la diffusion de la littérature." Pp. 13–17 in *Keilschriftliche Literaturen*. Ed. K. Hecker and W. Sommerfeld. Berlin: Dietrich Reimer.

Fishbane, M.
1985   *Biblical Interpretation in Ancient Israel*. Oxford: Clarendon Press.

Fishelov, D.
1989   "The Prophet as Satirist." *Prooftexts* 9:195–211.

Foley, J. M.
1985   *Oral-Formulaic Theory and Research: An Introduction and Annotated Bibliography*. New York: Garland Publishing Inc.

Fornara, C. W.
1983   *The Nature of History in Ancient Greece and Rome*. Berkeley: University of California Press.

Freedman, D. N.
1962   "Pentateuch." Vol. 1, pp. 711–17 in *The Interpreter's Dictionary of the Bible: An Illustrated Encyclopedia*. 4 vols. Nashville: Abingdon.

Friedman, R. E., ed.
1981   *The Creation of Sacred Literature: Composition and Redaction of the Biblical Text*. University of California Publications: Near Eastern Studies 22. Berkeley: University of California Press.

1987   *Who Wrote the Bible?* New York: Summit Books.

Frye, N.
1982   *The Great Code: The Bible and Literature*. Toronto: Academic Press.

Geller, S. A.
1983   "Were the Prophets Poets?" *Prooftexts* 3:211–21.

Gentili, B.
1988   *Poetry and Its Public in Ancient Greece: From Homer to the Fifth Century*. Trans. A. T. Cole. Baltimore: Johns Hopkins University Press.

Goldstein, B. R., and A. Cooper
1990   "The Festivals of Israel and Judah and the Literary History of the Pentateuch." *JAOS* 110:19–31.

Greenspahn, F. E.
1989   "Why Prophecy Ceased." *JBL* 108:37–49.

Halpern, B.
1988   *The First Historians: The Hebrew Bible and History*. New York: Harper & Row.

Harris, W. V.
1989   *Ancient Literacy*. Cambridge, Mass.: Harvard University Press.

Havelock, E. A.
1982   *The Literate Revolution in Greece and Its Cultural Consequences*. Princeton: Princeton University Press.

Holladay, J. S., Jr.
1970   "Assyrian Statecraft and the Prophets of Israel." *HTR* 63:29–51.

Isserlin, B. S. J.
1984   "Israelite Architectural Planning and the Question of the Level of Secular Learning in Ancient Israel." *VT* 34:169–78.

Jacobsen, T.
1982   "Oral to Written." Pp. 129–37 in *Societies and Languages of the Ancient Near East: Studies in Honour of I. M. Diakanoff.* Warminster: Aris & Phillips.

Kirk, G. S.
1970   *Myth: Its Meaning and Functions in Ancient and Other Cultures.* Berkeley: University of California Press.

Lemaire, A.
1984   "Sagesse et écoles." *VT* 34:270–81.

Lord, A. B.
1987   "Characteristics of Orality." *Oral Traditions* 2:54–72.

McKenzie, S. L.
1985   *The Chronicler's Use of the Deuteronomistic History.* HSM 33. Atlanta: Scholars Press.

Millard, A. R.
1985   "An Assessment of the Evidence for Writing in Ancient Israel." Pp. 301–12 in *Biblical Archaeology Today: Proceedings of the International Congress on Biblical Archaeology, Jerusalem, April 1984.* Ed. A. Biran. Jerusalem: Israel Exploration Society.

Noth, M.
1943   *Überlieferungsgeschichtliche Studien: Die sammelnden und bearbeitenden Geschichtswerke im Alten Testament.* Halle an der Saale: Max Niemeyer.

1948   *Überlieferungsgeschichte des Pentateuch.* Stuttgart: W. Kohlhammer.

Parker, S. B.
1989   *The Pre-Biblical Narrative Tradition: Essays on the Ugaritic Poems of Keret and Aqhat.* Atlanta: Scholars Press.

Petersen, D. L.
1981   *The Roles of Israel's Prophets.* JSOTSS 17. Sheffield: University of Sheffield.

Porter, J. R.
1982   "The Origins of Prophecy in Israel." Pp. 12–31 in *Israel's Prophetic Tradition: Essays in Honour of Peter R. Ackroyd.* Ed. R. Coggins, A. Phillips, and M. Knibb. Cambridge: Cambridge University Press.

Rendtorff, R.
1976   *Das überlieferungsgeschichtliche Problem des Pentateuch.* BZAW 147. Berlin: Walter de Gruyter.

Ross, J. F.
1970   "Prophecy in Hamath, Israel, and Mari." *HTR* 63:1–28.

Savran, G. W.
1988   *Telling and Retelling: Quotation in Biblical Narrative.* Bloomington: Indiana University Press.

Shaver, J. R.
  1989   *Torah and the Chronicler's History Work*. Brown Judaic Studies 196.
          Atlanta: Scholars Press.

Shinan, A., and Y. Zakovitch
  1986   "Midrash on Scripture and Midrash within Scripture." Pp. 257–
          77 in *Studies in Bible 1986*. Ed. S. Japhet. Scripta Hierosolymitana
          31. Jerusalem: Magnes Press.

Silver, M.
  1983   *Prophets and Markets: The Political Economy of Ancient Israel*. The
          Hague: Kluwer-Nijhoff.

Sternberg, M.
  1985   *The Poetics of Biblical Narrative*. Bloomington: Indiana University
          Press.

Tadmor, H., and M. Weinfeld, eds.
  1983   *History, Historiography and Interpretation: Studies in Biblical and Cu-
          neiform Literatures*. Jerusalem: Magnes Press.

Van Seters, J.
  1983   *In Search of History: Historiography in the Ancient World and the Origins
          of Biblical History*. New Haven: Yale University Press.

Weinfeld, M.
  1977   "Ancient Near Eastern Patterns in Prophetic Literature." *VT*
          27:178–95.

Wellhausen, J.
  1927   *Prolegomena zur Geschichte Israels*. 6th ed. Berlin: Walter de Gruyter.

Wilson, R. R.
  1980   *Prophecy and Society in Ancient Israel*. Philadelphia: Fortress.

Chapter 1: The Foundations of Belief

Bloom, H.
  1990   *The Book of J*. New York: Grove Weidenfeld.

Campbell, A. F.
  1986   *Of Prophets and Kings: A Late Ninth-Century Document (1 Samuel 1–
          2 Kings 10)*. Catholic Biblical Quarterly Monograph Series 17.
          Washington, D.C.: Catholic Biblical Association of America.

Coats, G. W.
  1983   *Genesis, with an Introduction to Narrative Literature*. The Forms of the
          Old Testament Literature 1. Grand Rapids: Eerdmans.

Cohen, C.
  1979   "Neo-Assyrian Elements in the First Speech of the Biblical Rab-
          Šāqê." *Israel Oriental Studies* 9:32–48.

Coote, R. B., and D. R. Ord
  1989   *The Bible's First History: From Eden to the Court of David with the
          Yahwist*. Philadelphia: Fortress.

Friedman, R. E.
    1981   "From Egypt to Egypt: Dtr¹ and Dtr²." Pp. 167–92 in *Traditions in Transformation: Turning Points in Biblical Faith*. Ed. B. Halpern and J. D. Levenson. Winona Lake, Ind.: Eisenbrauns.

Gonçalves, F. J.
    1986   *L'expédition de Sennachérib en Palestine dans la littérature hébraïque ancienne*. Publications de l'Institut Orientaliste de Louvain 34. Louvain: Institut Orientaliste.

Grayson, A. K.
    1987   "Akkadian Treaties of the Seventh Century B.C." *JCS* 39:127–60.

Gunkel, H.
    1987   *The Folktale in the Old Testament*. Trans. M. D. Rutter. Sheffield: Almond Press.

Halbe, J.
    1975   *Das Privilegrecht Jahwes Ex 34, 10–26: Gestalt und Wesen, Herkunft und Wirken in vordeuteronomischer Zeit*. Göttingen: Vandenhoeck & Ruprecht.

Hallo, W. W.
    1990   "The Limits of Skepticism." *JAOS* 110:187–99.

Halpern, B.
    1981   "The Centralization Formula in Deuteronomy." *VT* 31:20–38.

Hecker, K.
    1974   *Untersuchungen zur akkadischen Epik*. Alter Orient und Altes Testament — Sonderreihe B. Neukirchen-Vluyn: Neukirchener Verlag.

Heidel, A.
    1963   *The Babylonian Genesis*. Chicago: University of Chicago Press.

Hendel, R. S.
    1987   *The Epic of the Patriarch: The Jacob Cycle and the Narrative Traditions of Canaan and Israel*. HSM 42. Atlanta: Scholars Press.

Irvin, D.
    1978   *Mytharion: The Comparison of Tales from the Old Testament and the Ancient Near East*. Alter Orient und Altes Testament 32. Neukirchen-Vluyn: Neukirchener Verlag.

Ishida, T.
    1977   *The Royal Dynasties in Ancient Israel: A Study on the Formation and Development of Royal-Dynastic Ideology*. BZAW 142. Berlin: Walter de Gruyter.

Jacobsen, T.
    1976   *The Treasures of Darkness: A History of Mesopotamian Religion*. New Haven: Yale University Press.

Kuhl, C.
    1952   "Die 'Wiederaufnahme'—ein literarkritisches Prinzip?" *ZAW* 64:1–11.

Lambert, W. G.
  1985   "Old Testament Mythology in its Ancient Near Eastern Context."
          Pp. 124–43 in *Congress Volume: Salamanca 1983*. Ed. J. A. Emerton.
          VTSup 36. Leiden: Brill.

Levine, B. A.
  1985   "The Balaam Inscription from Deir 'Alla: Historical Aspects." Pp.
          326–39 in *Biblical Archaeology Today: Proceedings of the International
          Congress on Biblical Archaeology, Jerusalem, April 1984*. Ed. A. Biran.
          Jerusalem: Israel Exploration Society.

Lohfink, N.
  1984   "Zur deuteronomischen Zentralisationsformel." *Bib* 65:297–329.

Moore, M. S.
  1990   *The Balaam Traditions: Their Character and Development*. SBL Disser-
          tation Series 113. Atlanta: Scholars Press.

Moran, W. L.
  1963   "The Ancient Near Eastern Background of the Love of God in
          Deuteronomy." *CBQ* 25:77–87.

Müller, H.-P.
  1985   "Das Motiv für die Sintflut: Die hermeneutische Funktion des
          Mythos und seiner Analyse." *ZAW* 97:295–316.

Nelson, R. D.
  1981   *The Double Redaction of the Deuteronomistic History*. JSOTSS 18.
          Sheffield: JSOT Press.

Newman, J. K.
  1986   *The Classical Epic Tradition*. Madison: University of Wisconsin
          Press.

Oinas, F. J., ed.
  1978   *Heroic Epic and Saga: An Introduction to the World's Great Folk Epics*.
          Bloomington: Indiana University Press.

Parpola, S.
  1970   *Letters from Assyrian Scholars to the Kings Esarhaddon and Assurbani-
          pal: Part I, Texts*. Alter Orient und Altes Testament 5/1. Neu-
          kirchen-Vluyn: Neukirchener Verlag.

  1981   "Assyrian Royal Inscriptions and Neo-Assyrian Letters." Pp. 117–
          41 in *Assyrian Royal Inscriptions: New Horizons in literary, ideological,
          and historical analysis. Papers of a Symposium held in Cetona (Siena),
          June 26–28, 1980*. Rome: Istituto per l'Oriente.

  1987   "Neo-Assyrian Treaties from the Royal Archives of Nineveh." *JCS*
          39:161–89.

Perlitt, L.
  1988   "Priesterschrift im Deuteronomium?" Supplement to *ZAW*
          100:65–88.

Redford, D. B.
  1985   "The Relations between Egypt and Israel from El-Amarna to the
          Babylonian Conquest." Pp. 192–205 in *Biblical Archaeology Today:
          Proceedings of the International Congress on Biblical Archaeology, Jeru-
          salem, April 1984.* Ed. A. Biran. Jerusalem: Israel Exploration
          Society.

Rendsburg, G. A.
  1986   *The Redaction of Genesis.* Winona Lake, Ind.: Eisenbrauns.

Ruppert, L.
  1985   "Die Aporie der gegenwärtigen Pentateuchdiskussion und die
          Josefserzählung der Genesis." *BZ* 29:31–48.

Ruprecht, E.
  1990   "Die ursprüngliche Komposition der Hiskia-Jesaja-Erzählungen
          und ihre Umstrukturierung durch den Verfasser des deuteronom-
          istischen Geschichtswerkes." *ZTK* 87:33–66.

Schmitt, H.-C.
  1980   *Die nichtpriesterliche Josephsgeschichte: Ein Beitrag zur neuesten Penta-
          teuchkritik.* BZAW 154. Berlin: Walter de Gruyter.

Skweres, D. E.
  1979   *Die Rückverweise im Buch Deuteronomium.* Analecta Biblica 79. Rome:
          Biblical Institute Press.

Tadmor, H.
  1983   "Autobiographical Apology in the Royal Assyrian Literature." Pp.
          36–57 in *History, Historiography and Interpretation: Studies in Biblical
          and Cuneiform Literatures.* Ed. H. Tadmor and M. Weinfeld. Jeru-
          salem: Magnes Press.

Thalmann, W.
  1984   *Conventions of Form and Thought in Early Greek Epic Poetry.* Baltimore:
          Johns Hopkins University Press.

Thompson, T. L.
  1987   *The Origin Tradition of Ancient Israel: I, The Literary Formation of
          Genesis and Exodus 1–23.* Sheffield: JSOT Press.

Tigay, J. H.
  1985   "The Evolution of the Pentateuchal Narratives in the Light of the
          Evolution of the Gilgamesh Epic." Pp. 21–52 in *Empirical Models
          for Biblical Criticism.* Ed. J. H. Tigay. Philadelphia: University of
          Pennsylvania Press.

Van Seters, J.
  1988   "The Primeval Histories of Greece and Israel Compared." *ZAW*
          100:1–22.

  1989   "The Creation of Man and the Creation of the King." *ZAW*
          101:333–42.

Vermeylen, J.
  1985   "Les sections narratives de Deut 5–11 et leur relation à Ex 19–
          34." Pp. 174–207 in *Das Deuteronomium: Entstehung, Gestalt und
          Botschaft.* Ed. N. Lohfink. BETL 68. Louvain: Peeters.

Wallace, H. N.
1985   *The Eden Narrative.* HSM 32. Atlanta: Scholars Press.

Weimar, P.
1977   *Untersuchungen zur Redaktionsgeschichte des Pentateuch.* BZAW 146. Berlin: Walter de Gruyter.

Weinfeld, M.
1976   "The Loyalty Oath in the Ancient Near East." *UF* 8:379–414.

1982   "The King as the Servant of the People: The Source of the Idea." *JJS* 33:189–93.

1983   "Zion and Jerusalem as Religious and Political Capital: Ideology and Utopia." Pp. 75–115 in *The Poet and the Historian: Essays in Literary and Historical Biblical Criticism.* Ed. R. E. Friedman. HSS 26. Chico, Calif.: Scholars Press.

Wenham, G. J.
1991   "Method in Pentateuchal Source Criticism." *VT* 41:84–109.

West, M. L.
1966   *Hesiod: Theogony.* Oxford: Clarendon Press.

1985   *The Hesiodic Catalogue of Women: Its Nature, Structure and Origins.* Oxford: Clarendon Press.

1988   "The Rise of the Greek Epic." *Journal of Hellenic Studies* 108:151–72.

Whybray, R. N.
1987   *The Making of the Pentateuch: A Methodological Study.* Sheffield: JSOT Press.

Chapter 2: The Prophetic Paradigms

Ackroyd, P. R.
1977   "Isaiah I–XII: Presentation of a Prophet." Pp. 16–48 in *Congress Volume: Göttingen 1977.* VTSup 29. Leiden: Brill.

Andersen, F. I., and D. N. Freedman
1980   *Hosea: A New Translation with Introduction and Commentary.* AB 24. New York: Doubleday.

1989   *Amos: A New Translation with Introduction and Commentary.* AB 24A. New York: Doubleday.

Beentjes, P. C.
1982   "Inverted Quotations in the Bible: A Neglected Stylistic Pattern." *Bib* 63:506–23.

Blenkinsopp, J.
1981   "Fragments of Ancient Exegesis in an Isaian Poem (Jes 2:6–22)." *ZAW* 93:51–62.

Brodie, L.
1979   "The Children and the Prince: The Structure, Nature and Date
            of Isaiah 6–12." *Biblical Theology Bulletin* 9:27–31.

Christensen, D. L.
1976   "The March of Conquest in Isaiah 10:27c–34." *VT* 26:385–99.

Clements, R. E.
1980a   *Isaiah 1–39*. New Century Bible Commentary. Grand Rapids:
            Eerdmans.

1980b   "The Prophecies of Isaiah and the Fall of Jerusalem in 587 B. C."
            VT 30:421–36.

1982   "The Unity of the Book of Isaiah." *Interpretation* 36:117–29.

1985   "Beyond Tradition-History: Deutero-Isaianic Development of
            First Isaiah's Themes." *JSOT* 31:95–113.

Crüsemann, F.
1971   "Kritik an Amos in deuteronomistischen Geschichtswerk: Erwäg-
            ungen zu 2. Könige 14:27." Pp. 57–63 in *Probleme biblischer
            Theologie: Gerhard von Rad zum 70. Geburtstag*. Ed. H. W. Wolff.
            Munich: Kaiser.

Dearman, J. A.
1988   *Property Rights in the Eighth Century Prophets*. SBL Dissertation
            Series 106. Atlanta: Scholars Press.

Dietrich, W.
1974   *Jesaja und die Politik*. Beiträge zur evangelischen Theologie 74.
            Munich: Kaiser.

Easterling, P. E., and B. M. W. Knox, eds.
1989   *Early Greek Poetry*. Cambridge History of Classical Literature 1/1.
            Cambridge: Cambridge University Press.

Evans, C. A.
1986   "On Isaiah's Use of Israel's Sacred Tradition." *BZ* 30:92–99.

Fohrer, G.
1961–62 "The Origin, Composition and Tradition of Isaiah I–XXXIX."
            Annual of Leeds University Oriental Society 3:3–38.

1962   "Jesaja 1 als Zusammenfassung der Verkündigung Jesajas." *ZAW*
            74:251-68.

Fox, M. V.
1980   "The Identification of Quotations in Biblical Literature." *ZAW*
            92:416–31.

Fritz, V.
1989   "Amosbuch, Amos-Schule und historischer Amos." Pp. 29–43 in
            *Prophet und Prophetenbuch: Festschrift für Otto Kaiser zum 65. Geburts-
            tag*. Ed. V. Fritz, K.-F. Pohlmann, and H.-C. Schmitt. Berlin:
            Walter de Gruyter.

Gitay, Y.
1983   "Reflections on the Study of the Prophetic Discourse: The Ques-
            tion of Isaiah I 2–20." *VT* 33:207–21.

Good, E. M.
1966   "The Composition of Hosea." *Svensk exegetisk årsbok* 31:21–63.

Graffy, A.
1979   "The Literary Genre of Isaiah 5,1–17." *Bib* 60:400–9.

Gunneweg, A. H. J.
1989   "Die Prophetenlegende I Reg 13—Missdeutung, Umdeutung, Bedeutung." Pp. 73–81 in *Prophet und Prophetenbuch: Festschrift für Otto Kaiser zum 65. Geburtstag*. Ed. V. Fritz, K.-F. Pohlmann, and H.-C. Schmitt. Berlin: Walter de Gruyter.

Herrington, C. J.
1985   *Poetry into Drama: Early Tragedy and the Greek Poetic Tradition*. Sather Classical Lectures 49. Berkeley: University of California Press.

Höffken, P.
1982   "Probleme in Jesaja 5,1–7." *ZTK* 79 (1982) 392–410.

1989   "Grundfragen von Jesaja 7,1–17 im Spiegel neuer Literatur." *BZ* 33:25–42.

Janzen, J. G.
1982   "Metaphor and Reality in Hosea 11." *Semeia* 24:7–44.

Jensen, J.
1973   *The Use of* torâ *by Isaiah: His Debate with the Wisdom Tradition*. Catholic Biblical Quarterly Monograph Series 3. Washington, D.C.: Catholic Biblical Association of America.

Jeremias, J.
1981   "Zur Eschatologie des Hoseabuches." Pp. 217–34 in *Die Botschaft und die Boten: Festschrift für Hans Walter Wolff zum 70. Geburtstag*. Ed. J. Jeremias and L. Perlitt. Neukirchen-Vluyn: Neukirchener Verlag.

1988   "Amos 3–6: Beobachtungen zur Entstehungsgeschichte eines Prophetenbuches." Supplement to *ZAW* 100:123–38.

1989   "Völkersprüche und Visionsberichte im Amosbuch." Pp. 82–97 in *Prophet und Prophetenbuch: Festschrift für Otto Kaiser zum 65. Geburtstag*. Ed. V. Fritz, K.-F. Pohlmann, and H.-C. Schmitt. Berlin: Walter de Gruyter.

Koch, K., et al.
1976   *Amos*. 3 vols. Alter Orient und Altes Testament 30. Neukirchen-Vluyn: Neukirchener Verlag.

Kugel, J. L.
1981   *The Idea of Biblical Poetry: Parallelism and Its History*. New Haven: Yale University Press.

Kutsch, E.
1982   " 'Wir wollen miteinander rechten.' Zur Form und Aussage von Jes 1,18–20." Pp. 23–33 in *Künder des Wortes: Beiträge zur Theologie der Propheten: Josef Schreiner zum 60. Geburtstag*. Würzburg: Echter Verlag.

L'Heureux, C. E.
1984   "The Redactional History of Isaiah 5.1–10.4." Pp. 99–119 in *In
         the Shelter of Elyon. Essays on Ancient Palestinian Life and Literature in
         Honor of G. W. Ahlström*. Ed. W. B. Barrick and J. R. Spencer.
         JSOTSS 32. Sheffield: JSOT Press.

McKenzie, S. L.
1986   "The Jacob Tradition in Hosea XII 4–5." *VT* 36:311–22.

Mittmann, S.
1989   " 'Wehe! Assur, Stab meines Zorns.' (Jes 10, 5–9. 13aß–15." Pp.
         111–32 in *Prophet und Prophetenbuch: Festschrift für Otto Kaiser zum
         65. Geburtstag*. Ed. V. Fritz, K.-F. Pohlmann, and H.-C. Schmitt.
         Berlin: Walter de Gruyter.

Müller, H.-P.
1974   "Glauben und Bleiben: Zur Denkschrift-Jesajas Kapital VI 1–
         VIII 18." Pp. 25–54 in *Studies in Prophecy*. VTSup 26. Leiden:
         Brill.

Neef, H.-D.
1987   *Die Heilstraditionen Israels in der Verkündigung des Propheten Hosea*.
         BZAW 169. Berlin: Walter de Gruyter.

Niditch, S.
1980   "The Composition of Isaiah 1." *Bib* 61:509–29.

Niehr, H.
1984   "Bedeutung und Funktion kanaanäischer Traditionselemente in
         der Sozialkritik Jesajas." *BZ* 28:69–81.

1986   "Zur Gattung von Jes 5,1–7." *BZ* 30:99–104.

Nielsen, K.
1979   "Das Bild des Gerichts (Rib-Pattern) in Jes. I–XII: Eine analyse
         der Beziehungen zwischen Bildsprache und dem Anliegen der
         Verkündigung." *VT* 29:309–24.

1986   "Isaiah 6:1–8:18* as Dramatic Writing." *Studia Theologica* 40:1–
         16.

Parpola, S.
1987   *The Correspondence of Sargon II: Part I, Letters from Assyria and the
         West*. State Archives of Assyria 1. Helsinki: Helsinki University.

Parunak, H. van D.
1981   "Oral Typesetting: Some Uses of Biblical Structure." *Bib* 62:153–
         68.

1983   "Transitional Techniques in the Bible." *JBL* 102:525–48.

Perlitt, L.
1989   "Jesaja und die Deuteronomisten." Pp. 133–49 in *Prophet und
         Prophetenbuch: Festschrift für Otto Kaiser zum 65. Geburtstag*. Ed. V.
         Fritz, K.-F. Pohlmann, and H.-C. Schmitt. Berlin: Walter de
         Gruyter.

Phillips, A.
1982   "Prophecy and Law." Pp. 217–32 in *Israel's Prophetic Tradition: Essays in Honour of Peter R. Ackroyd*. Ed. R. Coggins, A. Phillips, and M. Knibb. Cambridge: Cambridge University Press.

Rendtorff, R.
1984   "Zur Komposition des Buches Jesaja." *VT* 34:295–320.

Roberts, J. J. M.
1982   "Isaiah in Old Testament Theology." *Interpretation* 36:130–43.

1985a   "Isaiah and His Children." Pp. 193–203 in *Biblical and Related Studies Presented to Samuel Iwry*. Ed. A. Kort and S. Morschauser. Winona Lake, Ind.: Eisenbrauns.

1985b   "Isaiah 2 and the Prophet's Message to the North." *JQR* 75:290–308.

Roth, M. T.
1989   *Babylonian Marriage Agreements 7th–3rd Centuries B. C.* Alter Orient und Altes Testament 222. Neukirchen-Vluyn: Neukirchener Verlag.

Schmidt, W. H.
1965   "Die deuteronomistische Redaktion des Amosbuches: Zu den theologischen Unterschieden zwischen dem Prophetenwort und sein Sammler." *ZAW* 77:168–93.

Sweeney, M. A.
1988   *Isaiah 1–4 and the Post-Exilic Understanding of the Isaianic Tradition.* BZAW 171. Berlin: Walter de Gruyter.

Tsumura, D. T.
1983   "Literary Insertion (AXB Pattern) in Biblical Hebrew." *VT* 33:468–82.

Van Der Lugt, P.
1980   *Strofische Structuren in de Bijbels-Hebreeuwse Poëzie.* Kampen: J. H. Kok.

Van der Toorn, K.
1988   "Echoes of Judaean Necromancy in Isaiah 28,7–22." *ZAW* 100:199–217.

Veijola, T.
1985   "Des Klagegebet in Literatur und Leben der Exilsgeneration am Beispiel einiger Prosatexte." Pp. 286–307 in *Congress Volume: Salamanca 1983.* Ed. J. A. Emerton. VTSup 36. Leiden: Brill.

1989   "Die Propheten und das Alter des Sabbatgebots." Pp. 246–64 in *Prophet und Prophetenbuch: Festschrift für Otto Kaiser zum 65. Geburtstag.* Ed. V. Fritz, K.-F. Pohlmann, and H.-C. Schmitt. Berlin: Walter de Gruyter.

Vollmer, J.
1971   *Geschichtliche Rückblicke und Motive in der Prophetie des Amos, Hosea und Jesaja.* BZAW 119. Berlin: Walter de Gruyter.

Weinfeld, M.
1972   "The Worship of Molech and of the Queen of Heaven and its Background." *UF* 4:133–54.

1982   " 'Justice and Righteousness' in Ancient Israel against the Background of 'Social Reforms' in the Ancient Near East." Pp. 491–519 in *Mesopotamien und seine Nachbarn: Politische und kulturelle Wechselbeziehungen im Alten Vorderasien vom 4. bis 1. Jahrtausend v. Chr.* Ed. H.-J. Nissen and J. Renger. Berlin: Dietrich Reimer.

Weippert, H.
1985   "Amos: Seine Bilder und ihr Milieu." Pp. 1–19 in *Beiträge zur prophetischen Bildsprache in Israel und Assyrien.* Ed. H. Weippert, K. Seybold, and M. Weippert. Göttingen: Vandenhoeck & Ruprecht.

Weippert, M.
1981   "Assyrische Prophetien der Zeit Asarhaddons und Assurbanipals." Pp. 71–115 in *Assyrian Royal Inscriptions: New Horizons in literary, ideological, and historical Analysis. Papers of a Symposium held in Cetona (Siena) June 26–28, 1980.* Rome: Istituto per l'Oriente.

1985   "Das Bildsprache der neuassyrischen Prophetie." Pp. 55–93 in *Beiträge zur prophetischen Bildsprache in Israel und Assyrien.* Ed. H. Weippert, K. Seybold, and M. Weippert. Göttingen: Vandenhoeck & Ruprecht.

Werner, W.
1982   *Eschatologische Texte in Jesaja 1–39: Messias, heiliger Rest, Völker.* Forschung zur Bibel 46. Würzburg: Echter Verlag.

1985   "Vom Prophetenwort zur Prophetentheologie: Ein redaktionskritischer Versuch zu Jes 6,1–8,18." *BZ* 29:1–30.

Westbrook, R.
1990   "Adultery in Ancient Near Eastern Law." *RB* 97:542–80.

Westermann, C.
1966   *Das Buch Jesaja Kapital 40–66.* Das Alte Testament Deutsch 10. Göttingen: Vandenhoeck & Ruprecht.

Whitt, W. D.
1991   "The Jacob Traditions in Hosea and their Relation to Genesis." *ZAW* 103:18–43.

Wildberger, H.
1982   *Jesaja.* BKAT 10. Neukirchen-Vluyn: Neukirchener Verlag.

Willi-Plein, I.
1971   *Vorformen der Schriftexegese innerhalb des Alten Testaments: Untersuchung zum literarischen Werden der auf Amos, Hosea und Micha zurückgehenden Bücher im hebräischen Zwölfprophetenbuch.* BZAW 123. Berlin: Walter de Gruyter.

Willis, J. T.
1983   "On the Intepretation of Isaiah 1:18." *JSOT* 25:35–54.

1984   "The First Pericope in the Book of Isaiah." *VT* 34:63–77.

1986   "Lament Reversed—Isaiah 1,21ff." *ZAW* 98:236–48.

Wiseman, D. J.
 1955 "Assyrian Writing-Boards." *Iraq* 17:3–13.

Wolff, H. W.
 1965 *Dodekapropheton, 1: Hosea*. BKAT 14/1. 2nd ed. Neukirchen-Vluyn:
    Neukirchener Verlag.

 1969 *Dodekapropheton, 2: Joel und Amos*. BKAT 14/2. Neukirchen-Vluyn:
    Neukirchener Verlag.

Chapter 3: The Reformation

Ackroyd, P. R.
 1968 "Historians and Prophets." *Svensk exegetisk årsbok* 33:18–54.

Albertz, R.
 1982 "Jer 2–6 und die Frühzeitverkündigung Jeremias." *ZAW* 94:20–
    47.

Barré, L. M.
 1988 "The Riddle of the Flood Chronology." *JSOT* 41:3–20.

Brin, G.
 1989 "Micah 2,12–13: A Textual and Ideological Study." *ZAW*
    101:118–24.

Burke, D. E.
 1988 "Hope for Your Future: The Composition and Coherence of Jer
    30–33." Ph.D. thesis. Toronto School of Theology, University of
    Toronto.

Clifford, R. J.
 1984 "Cosmogonies in the Ugaritic Texts and in the Bible." *Or* 53:183–
    201.

Cloete, W. T. W.
 1989 *Versification and Syntax in Jeremiah 2–25: Syntactical Constraints in*
    Hebrew Colometry. SBL Dissertation Series 117. Atlanta: Scholars
    Press.

Coats, G. W.
 1980 "Strife without Reconciliation: A Narrative Theme in the Jacob
    Traditions." Pp. 82–106 in *Werden und Wirken des Alten Testaments:*
    Festschrift für Claus Westermann zum 70. Geburtstag. Ed. R. Albertz,
    H.-P. Müller, H. W. Wolff, and W. Zimmerli. Neukirchen-Vluyn:
    Neukirchener Verlag.

Cross, F. M.
 1981 "The Priestly Tabernacle in the Light of Recent Research." Pp.
    169–80 in *Temples and High Places in Biblical Times: Proceedings of the*
    Colloquium in Honor of the Centennial of Hebrew Union College—Jewish
    Institute of Religion, Jerusalem, 14–16 March 1977. Ed. A. Biran.
    Jerusalem: Nelson Glueck School of Biblical Archaeology.

Deissler, A.
  1982   "Das 'Echo' der Hosea-Verkündigung im Jeremiabuch." Pp. 61–
            75 in *Künder des Wortes: Beiträge zur Theologie der Propheten: Josef
            Schreiner zum 60. Geburtstag*. Würzburg: Echter Verlag.

Diamond, A. R. P.
  1990   "Jeremiah's Confessions in the LXX and MT: A Witness to
            Developing Canonical Function?" *VT* 40:33–50.

Dozeman, T. B.
  1989   *God on the Mountain: A Study of Redaction, Theology and Canon in
            Exodus 19–24*. SBL Monograph Series 37. Atlanta: Scholars Press.

Eissfeldt, O.
  1970   "Adonis und Adonaj." *Sitzungsberichte der Sächsischen Akademie der
            Wissenschaften zu Leipzig. Philologisch-historische Klasse, Band 115,
            Heft 4*. Berlin: Akademie Verlag.

Elliger, K.
  1952   "Sinn und Ursprung der priesterlichen Geschichtserzählung."
            ZTK 49:121–43.

Emerton, J. A.
  1988   "The Priestly Writer in Genesis." *Journal of Theological Studies*
            39:381–400.

Fontenrose, J.
  1981   *Orion: The Myth of the Hunter and the Huntress*. Berkeley, Calif.:
            University of California Press.

Fox, M. V.
  1974   "The Sign of the Covenant: Circumcision in the Light of the
            Priestly 'ot Etiologies." *RB* 81:557–96.

Freedman, D. N.
  1963   "The Law and the Prophets." Pp. 250–65 in *Congress Volume:
            Bonn, 1962*. VTSup 9. Leiden: Brill.

  1983   "Discourse on Prophetic Discourse." Pp. 141–58 in *The Quest for
            the Kingdom of God. Studies in Honor of George E. Mendenhall*. Ed.
            H. B. Huffmon, F. A. Spina, and A. R. W. Green. Winona Lake,
            Ind.: Eisenbrauns.

Friedman, R. E.
  1981   *The Exile and Biblical Narrative: The Formation of the Deuteronomistic
            and Priestly Works*. Chico, Calif.: Scholars Press.

Gross, W.
  1968   "Jakob, der Mann des Segens: Zu Traditionsgeschichte und
            Theologie der priesterschriftlichen Jakobsüberlieferungen." *Bib*
            49:321–44.

Hess, R. S.
  1989   "The Genealogies of Genesis 1–11 and Comparative Literature."
            Bib 70:241–54.

Hillers, D. R.
1984   *Micah: A Commentary on the Book of the Prophet Micah.* Hermeneia. Philadelphia: Fortress.

Hurowitz, V.
1985   "The Priestly Account of Building the Tabernacle." *JAOS* 105:21–30.

Hurvitz, A.
1988   "Dating the Priestly Source in Light of the Historical Study of Biblical Hebrew a Century after Wellhausen." Supplement to *ZAW* 100:88–100.

Jaroš, K.
1974   *Die Stellung des Elohisten zur kanaanäischen Religion.* Orbis Biblicus et Orientalis 4. Göttingen: Vandenhoeck & Ruprecht.

Jeremias, J.
1971   "Die Deutung der Gerichtsworte Michas in der Exilszeit." *ZAW* 83:330–54.

Kearney, P. J.
1977   "Creation and Liturgy: The P Redaction of Ex 25–40." *ZAW* 89:375–87.

Knohl, I.
1987   "The Priestly Torah Versus the Holiness School: Sabbath and the Festivals." *HUCA* 58:65–117.

Koch, K.
1987   "P—Kein Redaktor! Erinnerung an zwei Eckdaten der Quellenscheidung." *VT* 37:446–67.

Kutsch, E.
1974   " 'Ich will euer Gott sein:' *berit* in der Priesterschrift." *ZTK* 71:361–88.

Lescow, T.
1972   "Redaktionsgeschichtliche Analyse von Micha 1–5." *ZAW* 84:46–85.

Levine, B. A.
1983   "Late Language in the Priestly Source: Some Literary and Historical Observations." Pp. 69–82 in *Proceedings of the Eighth World Congress of Jewish Studies, Jerusalem, August 16–21, 1981: Bible Studies and Hebrew Language.* Jerusalem: World Union of Jewish Studies.

Lloyd, G. E. R.
1966   *Polarity and Analogy. Two Types of Argumentation in Early Greek Thought.* Cambridge: Cambridge University Press.

Lohfink, N.
1968   "Die priesterliche Abwertung der Tradition von der Offenbarung an Mose." *Bib* 49:1–8.

1970   "Die Ursünden in der priesterlichen Geschichtserzählung." Pp. 38–57 in *Die Zeit Jesu: Festschrift für Heinrich Schlier.* Ed. G. Bornkamm and K. Rahner. Freiburg: Herder.

1976   "Die Sabbatruhe und die Freizeit." *Stimmen der Zeit* 194:395–407.

1978   "Die Priesterschrift und die Geschichte." Pp. 189–229 in *Congress Volume: Göttingen 1977*. VTSup 29. Leiden: Brill.

Longacre, R. E.
1979   "The Discourse Structure of the Flood Narrative." *Journal of the American Academy of Religion* 47, Supplement B:89–133.

1989   *Joseph: A Story of Divine Providence: A Text Theoretical and Textlinguistic Analysis of Genesis 37 and 39–48*. Winona Lake, Ind.: Eisenbrauns.

McEvenue, S. E.
1971   *The Narrative Style of the Priestly Writer*. Analecta Biblica 50. Rome: Biblical Institute Press.

1974   "The Style of a Building Instruction." *Semitics* 4:1–9.

McKane, W.
1980   "Relations between Poetry and Prose in the Book of Jeremiah with Special Reference to Jeremiah III 6–11 and XII 14–17." Pp. 220–37 in *Congress Volume: Vienna 1980*. VTSup 32. Leiden: Brill.

Mays, J. L.
1976   *Micah: A Commentary*. OTL. Philadelphia: Westminster.

Mettinger, T. N. D.
1982   *The Dethronement of Sabaoth: Studies in the Shem and Kabod Theologies*. Lund: C. W. K. Gleerup.

Nicholson, E. W.
1970   *Preaching to the Exiles: A Study of the Prose Tradition in the Book of Jeremiah*. Oxford: Basil Blackwell.

Oded, B.
1986   "The Table of Nations (Genesis 10)—A Socio-cultural Approach." *ZAW* 98:14–31.

Oliva, M.
1968   "Interpretación teológica del culto en la perícopa del Sinai della historia sacerdotal." *Bib* 49:345–54.

1974   "Las revelaciónes a los patriarcas en la historia sacerdotal." *Bib* 55:1–14.

Paterson, R. M.
1984   "Reinterpretation in the Book of Jeremiah." *JSOT* 28:37–46.

Petersen, J. E.
1980   "Priestly Materials in Joshua 13–22: A Return to the Hexateuch?" *HAR* 4:131–46.

Renaud, B.
1977   *La Formation du livre de Michée: Tradition et actualisation*. Paris: J. Gabalda.

1981   "Jér 1: structure et théologie de la rédaction." Pp. 177–96 in *Le livre de Jérémie: Le prophète et son milieu, les oracles et leur transmission*. BETL 54. Ed. P.-M. Bogaert. Louvain: Peeters.

1990 "Les généalogies et la structure de l'histoire sacerdotale dans le livre de la Genèse." *RB* 97:5–30.

Rendsburg, G. A.
1980 "Late Biblical Hebrew and the Date of 'P'." *Journal of the Ancient Near Eastern Society of Columbia University* 12:65–80.

1990 "The Internal Consistency and Historical Reliability of the Biblical Genealogies." *VT* 40:185–206.

Richter, W.
1967 "Das Gelübde als theologische Rahmung der Jakobsüberlieferungen." *BZ* 11:21–52.

Rofé, A.
1989 "The Arrangement of the Book of Jeremiah." *ZAW* 101:390–98.

Saebø, M.
1981 "Priestertheologie und Priesterschrift: Zur Eigenart der priesterlichen Schicht im Pentateuch." Pp. 357–74 in *Congress Volume: Vienna 1980*. VTSup 32. Leiden: Brill.

Schüpphaus, J.
1975 "Volk Gottes und gesetz beim Elohisten." *Theologische Zeitschrift* 32:193–210.

Seitz, C. R.
1989 "The Prophet Moses and the Canonical Shape of Jeremiah." *ZAW* 101:3–27.

1990 "Mose als Prophet: Redaktionsthemen und Gesamtstruktur des Jeremiasbuches." *BZ* 34:234–45.

Shaw, C. S.
1987 "Micah 1:10–16 Reconsidered." *JBL* 106:223–29.

Stansell, G.
1988 *Micah and Isaiah: A Form and Tradition Historical Comparison*. SBL Dissertation Series 85. Atlanta: Scholars Press.

Thiel, W.
1973 *Die deuteronomistische Redaktion von Jeremia 1–25*. Neukirchen-Vluyn: Neukirchener Verlag.

1981 *Die deuteronomistische Redaktion von Jeremia 20–45*. Neukirchen-Vluyn: Neukirchener Verlag.

Tov, E.
1972 "L'incidence de la critique textuelle sur la critique littéraire dans de livre de Jérémie." *RB* 79:189–99.

1981 "Some Aspects of the Textual and Literary History of the Book of Jeremiah." Pp. 145–67 in *Le livre de Jérémie: Le prophète et son milieu, les oracles et leur transmission*. Ed. P.-M. Bogaert. BETL 54. Louvain: Peeters.

1985 "The Literary History of the Book of Jeremiah in the Light of its Textual History." Pp. 211–37 in *Empirical Models for Biblical Criticism*. Ed. J. H. Tigay. Philadelphia: University of Pennsylvania Press.

van der Woude, A. S.
  1969   "Micah in Dispute with the Pseudo-Prophets." *VT* 19:244–60.

Vieweger, D.
  1988   "Die Arbeit des jeremianischen Schülerkreises am Jeremiabuch
          und deren Rezeption in der literarischen Überlieferung der Pro-
          phetenschrift Ezechiels." *BZ* 32:15–34.

Vincent, J. M.
  1986   "Michas Gerichtswort gegen Zion (3,12) in seinem Kontext."
          ZTK 83:167–87.

Wallis, G.
  1971   "Die Sesshaftwerdung Alt-Israels und das Gottesdienstverständ-
          nis des Jahwisten im Lichte der elohistischen Kritik." *ZAW* 83:1–
          15.

Weimar, P.
  1974   "Die Toledot-Formel in der priesterschriftlichen Geschichtsdar-
          stellung." *BZ* 18:64–93.

  1988   "Gen 17 und die priesterschriftliche Abrahamsgeschichte." *ZAW*
          110:22–60.

Weinfeld, M.
  1976   "Jeremiah and the Spiritual Metamorphosis of Israel." *ZAW*
          88:17–56.

  1981   "Sabbath, Temple and the Enthronement of the Lord—The Prob-
          lem of the Sitz im Leben of Genesis 1:1–2:3." Pp. 501–12 in
          Mélanges bibliques et orientaux en l'honneur de M. Henri Cazelles. Alter
          Orient und Altes Testament 212. Ed. A. Caquot and M. Delcor.
          Neukirchen-Vluyn: Neukirchener Verlag.

Weippert, H.
  1973   *Die Prosareden des Jeremiabuches*. BZAW 132. Berlin: Walter de
          Gruyter.

Westbrook, R.
  1988   *Studies in Biblical and Cuneiform Law*. Paris: J. Gabalda.

Westermann, C.
  1970   "Die Herrlichkeit Gottes in der Priesterschrift." Pp. 227–49 in
          Wort—Gebot—Glaube: Walter Eichrodt zum 80. Geburtstag. Ed. H. J.
          Stoebe, J. J. Stamm, and E. Jenni. Zurich: Zwingli Verlag.

Willis, J. T.
  1969a   "The Structure of the Book of Micah." *Svensk exegetisk årsbok*
          34:5–42.

  1969b   "The Structure of Micah 3–5 and the Function of Micah 5:9–14."
          ZAW 81:191–214.

Wilson, R. R.
  1977   *Genealogy and History in the Biblical World*. New Haven: Yale Univer-
          sity Press.

Wimmer, J. F.
  1967   "Tradition Reinterpreted in Ex 6,2–7,7." *Augustinianum* 7:405–18.

Wolff, H. W.
1969   "Zur Thematik der elohistischen Fragmente im Pentateuch." *Evangelische Theologie* 27:59–72.

1982   *Dodekapropheton, 4: Micha.* BKAT 14/4. Neukirchen-Vluyn: Neukirchener Verlag.

Zevit, Z.
1982   "Converging Lines of Evidence Bearing on the Date of P." *ZAW* 94:481–511.

Chapter 4: Decline and Fall

Albright, W. F.
1950   "The Psalm of Habakkuk." Pp. 1–18 in *Studies in Old Testament Prophecy Presented to Professor Theodore H. Robinson.* Ed. H. H. Rowley. Edinburgh: T. & T. Clark.

Anderson, G. W.
1978   "The Idea of the Remnant in the Book of Zephaniah." *ASTI* 11:11–14.

Ball, I. J., Jr.
1987   "The Rhetorical Shape of Zephaniah." Pp. 155–65 in *Perspectives on Language and Text: Essays and Poems in Honor of Francis I. Andersen's Sixtieth Birthday, July 28, 1985.* Ed. E. W. Conrad and E. G. Newing. Winona Lake, Ind.: Eisenbrauns.

Baltzer, D.
1971   *Ezechiel und Deuterojesaja: Berührungen in der Heilserwartung der beiden grossen Exilspropheten.* BZAW 121. Berlin: Walter de Gruyter.

Barnett, R. D.
1969   "Ezekiel and Tyre." *Eretz-Israel* 9:6–13.

Brownlee, W. H.
1971   "The Composition of Habakkuk." Pp. 255–75 in *Hommages à André Dupont-Sommer.* Ed. A. Caquot and M. Philonenko. Paris: Adrien Maisonneuve.

Clements, R. E.
1982   "The Ezekiel Tradition: Prophecy in a Time of Crisis." Pp. 119–36 in *Israel's Prophetic Tradition: Essays in Honour of Peter R. Ackroyd.* Ed. R. Coggins, A. Phillips and M. Knibb. Cambridge: Cambridge University Press.

De Roche, M.
1980   "Zephaniah I 2–3: The 'Sweeping' of Creation." *VT* 30:104–9.

Eaton, J. H.
1964   "The Origin and Meaning of Habakkuk 3." *ZAW* 76:144–71.

Edler, R.
1984   *Das Kerygma des Propheten Zefanja.* Freiburger theologische Studien 126. Freiburg: Herder.

Gunneweg, A. H. J.
1986   "Habakuk und das Problem des leidenden *ṣdyq*." *ZAW* 98:400–15.

Haak, R. D.
1988   " 'Poetry' in Habakkuk 1:1–2:4?" *JAOS* 108:437–44.

Haran, M.
1979   "The Law Code of Ezekiel 40–48 and its Relation to the Priestly School." *HUCA* 50:45–71.

House, P. R.
1988   *Zephaniah: A Prophetic Drama.* Sheffield: Almond Press.

In der Smitten, W. T.
1977   "Habakkuk 2,4 als prophetische Definition des Gerechten." Pp. 291–300 in *Bausteine biblischer Theologie: Festgabe für G. Johannes Botterweck zum 60. Geburtstag dargebracht von seinen Schülern.* Bonner biblische Beiträge 50. Ed. H.-J. Fabry. Bonn: Peter Hanstein.

Jeremias, J.
1977   *Theophanie: Die Geschichte einer alttestamentlichen Gattung.* WMANT 10. 2nd. ed. Neukirchen-Vluyn: Neukirchener Verlag.

Jöcken, P.
1977   "War Habakuk ein Kultprophet?" Pp. 319–32 in *Bausteine biblischer Theologie: Festgabe für G. Johannes Botterweck zum 60. Geburtstag dargebracht von seinen Schülern.* Bonner biblische Beiträge 50. Ed. H.-J. Fabry. Bonn: Peter Hanstein.

Johnson, M. D.
1985   "The Paralysis of Torah in Habakkuk I 4." *VT* 35:257–66.

Kapelrud, A. S.
1975   *The Message of the Prophet Zephaniah. Morphology and Ideas.* Oslo: Universitetsforlaget.

Keel, O.
1977   *Jahwe-Visionen und Siegelkunst: Eine neue Deutung der Majestätsschilderungen in Jes 6, Ezek 1 und 10 und Sach 4.* Stuttgart: Katholisches Bibelwerk.

Keller, C. A.
1972   "Die theologische Bewältigung der geschichtlichen Wirklichkeit in der Prophetie Nahums." *VT* 22:399–419.

Krinetzki, G.
1977   *Zefanjastudien: Motiv- und Traditionskritik + Kompositions- und Redaktionskritik.* Frankfurt: Peter Lang.

Langohr, G.
1976   "Le livre de Sophonie et la critique d'authenticité." *ETL* 52:1–27.

Levenson, J. D.
1976   *Theology of the Program of Restoration of Ezekiel 40–48.* HSM 10. Missoula, Mont.: Scholars Press.

Lust, J., ed.
1986   *Ezekiel and his Book: Textual and Literary Criticism and their Interrelation.* BETL 74. Louvain: Peeters.

Margulis, B.
1970   "The Psalm of Habakkuk: A Reconstruction and Interpretation."
        ZAW 82:409–42.

O'Connor, M.
1980   *Hebrew Verse Structure*. Winona Lake, Ind.: Eisenbrauns.

Otto, E.
1977   "Die Stellung der Wehe-Worte in der Verkündigung des Prophe-
        ten Habakuk." *ZAW* 89:73–107.

1985   "Die Theologie des Buches Habakuk." *VT* 35:274–95.

Parunak, H. van D.
1978   *Structural Studies in Ezekiel*. Ann Arbor, Mich.: University Micro-
        films.

1980   "The Literary Architecture of Ezekiel's *marʾôt ʾĕlōhîm*." *JBL* 99:61–
        74.

Renaud, B.
1987   "La composition du livre de Nahum: Une proposition." *ZAW*
        99:198–219.

Schulz, H.
1973   *Das Buch Nahum: Eine redaktionskritische Untersuchung*. BZAW 129.
        Berlin: Walter de Gruyter.

Scott, J. M.
1985   "A New Approach to Habakkuk II 4–5a." *VT* 35:330–40.

Seybold, K.
1985   "Die Verwendung der Bildmotive in der Prophetie Zefanjas." Pp.
        30–54 in *Beiträge zur prophetischen Bildsprache in Israel und Assyrien*.
        Ed. H. Weippert, K. Seybold, and M. Weippert. Göttingen:
        Vandenhoeck & Ruprecht.

1989   "Vormasoretische Randnotizen in Nahum 1." *ZAW* 101:71–85.

Steck, O. H.
1990   "Zu Zef 3,9–10." *BZ* 34:90–95.

Sweeney, M. A.
1991   "Structure, Genre, and Intent in the Book of Habakkuk." *VT*
        41:63–83.

Tov, E.
1986   "Recensional Differences between the MT and LXX of Ezekiel."
        ETL 62:89–101.

Tsumura, D. T.
1982   "Hab 2:2 in the Light of Akkadian Legal Practice." *ZAW* 94:294–
        95.

1986   "Niphal with an Internal Object in Habakkuk 3:9a." *Journal of
        Semitic Studies* 31:11–16.

van Grol, H. W. M.
1988   "Classical Hebrew Metrics and Zephaniah 2–3." Pp. 186–206 in
        The Structural Analysis of Biblical and Canaanite Poetry. Ed. W. van
        der Meer and J. C. de Moor. JSOTSS 74. Sheffield: JSOT Press.

York, A. D.
  1977   "Ezekiel 1: Inaugural and Restoration Visions?" *VT* 27:82–98.

Zimmerli, W.
  1980   "Das Phänomen der 'Fortschreibung' im Buche Ezechiel." Pp. 174–91 in *Prophecy: Essays Presented to Georg Fohrer on his Sixty-Fifth Birthday, 6 September 1980*. Ed. J. A. Emerton. BZAW 150. Berlin: Walter de Gruyter.

Chapter 5: The Deuteronomistic History

Barr, J.
  1990   "Mythical Monarch Unmasked? Mysterious Doings of Debir King of Eglon." *JSOT* 48:55–68.

Boling, R. G.
  1975   *Judges: Introduction, Translation and Commentary*. AB 6A. Garden City, N.Y.: Doubleday.

Boling, R. G., and G. E. Wright
  1982   *Joshua: A New Translation with Notes and Commentary*. AB 6. Garden City, N.Y.: Doubleday.

Brettler, M.
  1989   "The Book of Judges: Literature as Politics." *JBL* 108:395–418.

Carmichael, C. M.
  1974   *The Laws of Deuteronomy*. Ithaca, N.Y.: Cornell University Press.

  1979   *Women, Law and the Genesis Traditions*. Edinburgh: Edinburgh University Press.

  1985   *Law and Narrative in the Bible: The Evidence of the Deuteronomic Laws and the Decalogue*. Ithaca, N.Y.: Cornell University Press.

Cogan, M., and H. Tadmor
  1988   *II Kings: A New Translation with Introduction and Commentary*. AB 11. Garden City, N.Y.: Doubleday.

Cohn, R. L.
  1985   "Convention and Creativity in the Book of Kings: The Case of the Dying Monarch." *CBQ* 47:603–16.

Dietrich, W.
  1972   *Prophetie und Geschichte: Eine redaktionsgeschichtliche Untersuchung zum deuteronomistischen Geschichtswerk*. Forschungen zur Religion und Literatur des Alten und Neuen Testaments 108. Göttingen: Vandenhoeck & Ruprecht.

  1977   "Josia und das Gesetzbuch (2 Reg. XXII)." *VT* 27:13–35.

  1987   *David, Saul und die Propheten: Das Verhältnis von Religion und Politik nach den prophetischen Überlieferungen vom frühesten Königtum in Israel*. Stuttgart: W. Kohlhammer.

Emerton, J. A.
1982 "The Origin of the Promises to the Patriarchs in the Older Sources of the Book of Genesis." *VT* 32:14–32.

Fokkelman, J. P.
1975 *Narrative Art in Genesis: Specimens of Stylistic and Structural Analysis.* Assen: Van Gorcum.

1981 *Narrative Art and Poetry in the Books of Samuel: A Full Interpretation Based on Stylistic and Structural Analyses, I: King David (II Sam 9–20 and I Kings 1–2.* Assen: Van Gorcum.

Freedman, D. N.
1972 "The Refrain in David's Lament over Saul and Jonathan." Vol. 1, pp. 115–26 in *Ex Orbe Religionum: Studia Geo Widengren Dedicata.* 2 vols. Ed. J. Bergman, K. Drynjeff, and H. Ringgren. Leiden: Brill.

1974 "Strophe and Meter in Exodus 15." Pp. 163–203 in *A Light unto my path: Old Testament Studies in Honor of Jacob M. Myers.* Ed. H. N. Bream, R. D. Heim, and C. A. Moore. Philadelphia: Temple University Press.

1976 "Divine Names and Titles in Early Hebrew Poetry." Pp. 55–107 in *Magnalia Dei—The Mighty Acts of God: Essays on the Bible and Archaeology in Memory of G. Ernest Wright.* Ed. F. M. Cross, W. E. Lemke, and P. D. Miller, Jr. Garden City, N.Y.: Doubleday.

1979 "Early Israelite Poetry and Historical Reconstructions." Pp. 85–96 in *Symposia Celebrating the Seventy-Fifth Anniversary of the Founding of the American Schools of Oriental Research (1900–1975).* Ed. F. M. Cross. Cambridge, Mass.: American Schools of Oriental Research.

García López, F.
1980 "Del 'Yahvista' al 'Deuteronomista': Estudio critico de Genesis 24." *RB* 87:242–73, 350–93, 514–59.

Gerbrandt, G. E.
1986 *Kingship According to the Deuteronomistic History.* SBL Dissertation Series 87. Atlanta: Scholars Press.

Greenspahn, F. E.
1986 "The Theology of the Framework of Judges." *VT* 36:385–96.

Gunn, D. M.
1974 "Narrative Patterns and Oral Tradition in Judges and Samuel." *VT* 24:286–317.

1976 "Traditional Composition in the 'Succession Narrative'." *VT* 26:214–29.

1980 *The Fate of King Saul: An Interpretation of a Biblical Story.* JSOTSS 14. Sheffield: JSOT Press.

Halpern, B.
1983a "The Resourceful Israelite Historian: The Song of Deborah and Israelite Historiography." *HTR* 76:379–401.

1983b   "Doctrine by Misadventure: Between the Israelite Source and the Biblical Historian." Pp. 41–73 in *The Poet and the Historian: Essays in Literary and Historical Biblical Criticism*. Ed. R. E. Friedman. HSS 26. Chico, Calif.: Scholars Press.

Hendel, R. S.
1989   "Sacrifice as a Cultural System: The Ritual Symbolism of Exodus 24,3–8." *ZAW* 101:366–90.

Hoffmann, H.-D.
1980   *Reform und Reformen: Untersuchungen zu einem Grundthema der deuteronomistischen Geschichtsschreibung*. Abhandlungen zur Theologie des Alten und Neuen Testaments 66. Zurich: Theologischer Verlag.

Jason, H.
1979   "The Story of David and Goliath: A Folk Epic?" *Bib* 60:36–70.

Jenkins, A. K.
1978   "A Great Name: Genesis 12:2 and the Editing of the Pentateuch." *JSOT* 10:41–57.

Kalluveettil, P.
1982   *Declaration and Covenant: A Comprehensive Review of Covenant Formulae from the Old Testament and the Ancient Near East*. Analecta Biblica 88. Rome: Biblical Institute Press.

Kenik, H. A.
1983   *Design for Kingship: The Deuteronomistic Narrative Technique in 1 Kings 3:4–15*. Chico, Calif.: Scholars Press.

Kloppenborg, J. S.
1981   "Joshua 22: The Priestly Editing of an Ancient Tradition." *Bib* 62:347–71.

Köppel, U.
1979   *Das deuteronomistische Geschichtswerk und seine Quellen: Die Absicht der deuteronomistischen Geschichtsdarstellung aufgrund des Vergleichs zwischen Num 21,21–35 und Dtn 2,26–3,3*. Bern: Peter Lang.

Labuschagne, C. J.
1982   "The Pattern of the Divine Speech Formulas in the Pentateuch." *VT* 32:268–96.

Langlamet, F.
1969   *Gilgal et les récits de la traversée du Jourdain*. Cahiers de la Revue Biblique 11. Paris: J. Gabalda.

Lemaire, A.
1986   "Vers l'histoire de la rédaction des Livres des Rois." *ZAW* 98:221–36.

Lemche, N. P.
1984   " 'Israel in the Period of the Judges' — The Tribal League in Recent Research." *Studia Theologica* 38:1–28.

Lohfink, N.
1963   *Das Hauptgebot: Eine Untersuchung literarischer Einleitungsfragen zu Dtn 5–11*. Analecta Biblica 20. Rome: Biblical Institute Press.

1978   "Die Gattung der 'historischen Kurzgeschichte' in den letzten Jahren von Juda und in der Zeit des babylonischen Exils." *ZAW* 90:319–47.

1983   "Die Schichten des Pentateuch und der Krieg." Pp. 51–110 in *Gewalt und Gewaltlosigkeit im Alten Testament.* Ed. N. Lohfink. Quaestiones Disputatae 96. Freiburg: Herder.

1985   "Zur neueren Diskussion über 2 Kön 22–23." Pp. 24–48 in *Das Deuteronomium: Entstehung, Gestalt und Botschaft.* Ed. N. Lohfink. BETL 68. Louvain: Peeters.

Long, B. O.
1984   *I Kings, with an Introduction to Historical Literature.* The Forms of the Old Testament Literature 9. Grand Rapids: Eerdmans.

1986   "Framing Repetitions in Biblical Historiography." Pp. 178–85 in *Proceedings of the Ninth World Congress of Jewish Studies, Division A: The Period of the Bible.* Jerusalem: World Union of Jewish Studies.

McCarthy, D. J.
1974   "The Wrath of Yahweh and the Structural Unity of the Deuteronomistic History." Pp. 99–110 in *Essays in Old Testament Ethics (J. Philip Hyatt In Memoriam).* Ed. J. L. Crenshaw and J. T. Willis. New York: KTAV.

McConville, J. G.
1989   "Narrative and Meaning in the Books of Kings." *Bib* 70:31–49.

Mayes, A. D. H.
1983   *The Story of Israel between Settlement and Exile: A Redactional Study of the Deuteronomistic History.* London: SCM.

Mullen, E. T., Jr.
1982   "The 'Minor Judges:' Some Literary and Historical Considerations." *CBQ* 44:185–201.

1984   "Judges 1:1–36: The Deuteronomistic Reintroduction of the Book of Judges." *HTR* 77:33–54.

Nelson, R. D.
1988   "The Anatomy of the Book of Kings." *JSOT* 40:39–48.

Nicholson, E. W.
1967   *Deuteronomy and Tradition.* Philadelphia: Fortress.

Perlitt, L.
1969   *Bundestheologie im Alten Testament.* WMANT 36. Neukirchen-Vluyn: Neukirchener Verlag.

Polzin, R.
1980   *Moses and the Deuteronomist: A Literary Study of the Deuteronomic History. Part One: Deuteronomy, Joshua, Judges.* New York: Seabury.

1989   *Samuel and the Deuteronomist: A Literary Study of the Deuteronomic History: 1 Samuel.* New York: Harper & Row.

Provan, I. W.
1988   *Hezekiah and the Books of Kings: A Contribution to the Debate about the Composition of the Deuteronomistic History.* BZAW 172. Berlin: Walter de Gruyter.

Rendtorff, R.
1980   "Genesis 15 im Rahmen der theologischen Bearbeitung der Vätergeschichten." Pp. 74–81 in *Werden und Wirken des Alten Testaments: Festschrift für Claus Westermann zum 70. Geburtstag.* Ed. R. Albertz, H.-P. Müller, H. W. Wolff, and W. Zimmerli. Neukirchen-Vluyn: Neukirchener Verlag.

1989   " 'Covenant' as a Structuring Concept in Genesis and Exodus." *JBL* 108:385–93.

Rose, M.
1981   *Deuteronomist und Jahwist: Untersuchungen zu den Berührungspunkten beiden Literaturwerke.* Zurich: Theologischer Verlag.

Sawyer, J. F. A.
1986   "Cain and Hephaestos: Possible Relics of Metalworking Traditions in Genesis 4." *Abr-Nahrain* 24:155-66.

Schmid, H. H.
1976   *Der sogenannte Jahwist: Beobachtungen und Fragen zur Pentateuchforschung.* Zurich: Theologischer Verlag.

Schmitt, H.-C.
1979   " 'Priesterliches' und 'prophetisches' Geschichtsverständnis in der Meerwundererzählung Ex 13,17–14,31: Beobachtungen zur Endredaktion des Pentateuch." Pp. 139–55 in *Textgemäss: Aufsätze und Beiträge zur Hermeneutik des Alten Testaments: Festschrift für Ernst Würthwein zum 70. Geburtstag.* Ed. A. H. J. Gunneweg and O. Kaiser. Göttingen: Vandenhoeck & Ruprecht.

1982   "Redaktion des Pentateuch im Geiste der Prophetie: Beobachtungen zur Bedeutung der 'Glaubens'-Thematik innerhalb der Theologie des Pentateuch." *VT* 32:170–89.

1989   "Tradition der Prophetenbücher in den Schichten der Plagenerzählung Ex 7,1–11,10." Pp. 196–216 in *Prophet und Prophetenbuch: Festschrift für Otto Kaiser zum 65. Geburtstag.* Ed. V. Fritz, K.-F. Pohlmann, and H.-C. Schmitt. Berlin: Walter de Gruyter.

Stager, L. E.
1988   "Archaeology, Ecology, and Social History: Background Themes to the Song of Deborah." Pp. 221–34 in *Congress Volume*: Jerusalem 1986. Ed. J. A. Emerton. VTSup 40. Leiden: Brill.

Talmon, S.
1978   "The Presentation of Synchroneity and Simultaneity in Biblical Narrative." Pp. 9–26 in *Studies in Hebrew Narrative Art Throughout the Ages.* Ed. J. Heinemann and S. Werses. Scripta Hierosolymitana 27. Jerusalem: Magnes Press, 1978.

Tov, E.
1986   "The Growth of the Book of Joshua in the Light of the Evidence
        of the LXX Translation." Pp. 321–39 in *Studies in Bible 1986*. Ed.
        S. Japhet. Scripta Hierosolymitana 31. Jerusalem· Magnes Press.

1987   "Some Sequence Differences between the MT and LXX and their
        Ramifications for the Literary Criticism of the Bible." *Journal of
        Northwest Semitic Languages* 13:151–60.

Van Seters, J.
1975   *Abraham in History and Tradition*. New Haven: Yale University
        Press.

1980   "The Religion of the Patriarchs in Genesis." *Bib* 61:220–33.

1984   "Joshua 24 and the Problem of Tradition in the Old Testament."
        Pp. 139–58 in *In the Shelter of Elyon: Essays on Ancient Palestinian
        Life and Literature in Honor of G. W. Ahlström*. Ed. W. B. Barrick
        and J. R. Spencer. JSOTSS 31. Sheffield: JSOT Press.

1986   "The Plagues of Egypt: Ancient Tradition or Literary Invention?"
        ZAW 98:31–39.

Veijola, T.
1975   *Die ewige Dynastie: David und die Entstehung seiner Dynastie nach der
        deuteronomistischen Darstellung*. Helsinki: Suomalainen Tiedeaka-
        temia.

1977   *Das Königtum in der Beurteilung der deuteronomistischen Historiographie:
        Eine redaktionsgeschichtliche Untersuchung*. Helsinki: Suomalainen
        Tiedeakatemia.

1982   *Verheissung in der Krise: Studien zur Literatur und Theologie der Exilszeit
        anhand des 89. Psalms*. Helsinki: Suomalainen Tiedeakatemia.

Vermeylen, J.
1985   "L'affaire du veau d'or (Ex 32–34): Une clé pour la 'question
        deutéronomiste'?" *ZAW* 97:1–23.

Vorländer, H.
1978   *Die Entstehungszeit des jehowistischen Geschichtswerkes*. Frankfurt: Pe-
        ter Lang.

Wallace, H. N.
1986   "The Oracles against the Israelite Dynasties in 1 and 2 Kings."
        Bib 67:21–40.

Weimar, P.
1976   "Die Jahwekriegserzählungen in Exodus 14, Josua 10, Richter 4
        und 1 Samuel 7." *Bib* 57:38–73.

Weinfeld, M.
1972   *Deuteronomy and the Deuteronomic School*. Oxford: Clarendon.

1983   "Divine Intervention in War in Ancient Israel and in the Ancient
        Near East." Pp. 121–47 in *History, Historiography and Interpretation:
        Studies in Biblical and Cuneiform Literatures*. Ed. H. Tadmor and M.
        Weinfeld. Jerusalem: Magnes Press.

1985   "The Emergence of the Deuteronomic Movement: The Historical
            Antecedents." Pp. 76–98 in *Das Deuteronomium: Entstehung, Gestalt
            und Botschaft*. Ed. N. Lohfink. BETL 68. Louvain: Peeters.

Zakovitch, Y.
    1983   "Story versus History." Pp. 47–60 in *Proceedings of the Eighth World
            Congress of Jewish Studies, Jerusalem, August 16–21, 1981: Bible Studies
            and Hebrew Language*. Jerusalem: World Union of Jewish Studies.

Chapter 6: Revision and Response

Ackerman, J. S.
    1981   "Satire and Symbolism in the Song of Jonah." Pp. 213–46 in
            Traditions in Transformation. Turning Points in Biblical Faith. Ed. B.
            Halpern and J. D. Levenson. Winona Lake, Ind.: Eisenbrauns.

Ahlström, G. W.
    1971   *Joel and the Temple Cult of Jerusalem*. VTSup 21. Leiden: Brill.

Carroll, R. P.
    1978   "Second Isaiah and the Failure of Prophecy." *Studia Theologica*
            32:119–31.

    1979   *When Prophecy Failed: Reactions and Responses to Failure in the Old
            Testament Prophetic Tradition*. London: SCM.

Childs, B. S.
    1978   "The Canonical Shape of the Book of Jonah." Pp. 122–28 in
            *Biblical and Near Eastern Studies: Essays in Honor of William Sanford
            LaSor*. Ed. G. A. Tuttle. Grand Rapids: Eerdmans.

Clements, R. E.
    1975   "The Purpose of the Book of Jonah." Pp. 16–28 in *Congress
            Volume: Edinburgh 1974*. VTSup 28. Leiden: Brill.

Clifford, R. J.
    1980   "The Function of Idol Passages in Second Isaiah." *CBQ* 42:450–
            64.

Coggins, R. J.
    1985   "Judgment between Brothers: A Commentary on the Book of
            Obadiah." Pp. 65–88 in *Israel among the Nations: A Commentary on
            the Books of Nahum and Obadiah and Esther*. Ed. R. J. Coggins and
            S. P. Re'emi. Grand Rapids: Eerdmans.

Cross, F. M.
    1983   "Studies in the Structure of Hebrew Verse: The Prosody of the
            Psalm of Jonah." Pp. 159–67 in *The Quest for the Kingdom of God:
            Studies in Honor of George E. Mendenhall*. Ed. H. B. Huffmon, F. A.
            Spina, and A. R. W. Green. Winona Lake, Ind.: Eisenbrauns.

Deist, F. E.
1988   "Parallels and Reinterpretation in the Book of Joel: A Theology of the Yom Yahweh?" Pp. 63–79 in *Text and Context: Old Testament and Semitic Studies for F. C. Fensham*. Ed. W. Claassen. JSOTSS 48. Sheffield: JSOT Press.

De Vries, S. J.
1988   "Moses and David as Cult Founders in Chronicles." *JBL* 107:619–39.

1989   *1 and 2 Chronicles*. The Forms of the Old Testament Literature 11. Grand Rapids: Eerdmans.

Dick, M. B.
1984   "A Syntactic Study of the Book of Obadiah." *Semitics* 9:1–29.

Feuillet, A.
1974   "Les sources du livre de Jonas." *RB* 54:161–84.

Freedman, D. N.
1987   "The Structure of Isaiah 40:1–11." Pp. 167–93 in Perspectives on Language and Text: Essays and Poems in Honor of Francis I. Andersen's Sixtieth Birthday, July 28, 1985. Ed. E. W. Conrad and E. G. Newing. Winona Lake, Ind.: Eisenbrauns.

Fretheim, T. E.
1978   "Jonah and Theodicy." *ZAW* 90:227–37.

Gitay, Y.
1980   "Deutero-Isaiah: Oral or Written?" *JBL* 99:185–97.

Halpern, B., and R. E. Friedman
1980   "Composition and Paronomasia in the Book of Jonah." *HAR* 4:79–92.

Hamborg, G. R.
1981   "Reasons for Judgement in the Oracles against the Nations of the Prophet Isaiah." *VT* 31:145–59.

Holbert, J. C.
1981   " 'Deliverance belongs to Yahweh!' Satire in the Book of Jonah." *JSOT* 21:59–81.

Kapelrud, A. S.
1982   "The Main Concern of Second Isaiah." *VT* 32:50–58.

Kraeling, E. G.
1971   "The Evolution of the Story of Jonah." Pp. 305–18 in *Hommages à André Dupont-Sommer*. Ed. A. Caquot and M. Philonenko. Paris: Adrien Maisonneuve.

Martin-Achard, R.
1980   "Esaïe 47 et la tradition prophétique sur Babylone." Pp. 83–105 in *Prophecy: Essays Presented to Georg Fohrer on his Sixty-Fifth Birthday, 6 September 1980*. Ed. J. A. Emerton. BZAW 150. Berlin: Walter de Gruyter.

Melugin, R. F.
1976   *The Formation of Isaiah 40–55*. BZAW 141. Berlin: Walter de Gruyter.

Merendino, R. P.
1981   *Der Erste und der Letzte: Eine Untersuchung von Jes 40–48*. VTSup 31. Leiden: Brill.

Mettinger, T. N. D.
1978   "Die Ebed-Jahwe Lieder: Ein fragwürdiges Axiom." *ASTI* 11:68–76.

Millar, W. R.
1976   *Isaiah 24–27 and the Origin of Apocalyptic*. HSM 11. Missoula, Mont.: Scholars Press.

Myers, J. M.
1962   "Some Considerations Bearing on the Date of Joel." *ZAW* 74:177–95.

Plöger, O.
1968   *Theocracy and Eschatology*. Trans. S. Rudman. Oxford: Basil Blackwell.

Porten, B.
1981   "Baalshamem and the Date of the Book of Jonah." Pp. 237–44 in *De la Torah au Messie: Études d'exégèse et d'herméneutique bibliques offertes à Henri Cazelles pour ses 25 années d'enseignement à l'Institut Catholique de Paris (Octobre 1979)*. Ed. M. Carrez, J. Doré, and P. Grelot. Paris: Desclée.

Prinsloo, W. S.
1985   *The Theology of the Book of Joel*. BZAW 163. Berlin: Walter de Gruyter.

Ratner, R. J.
1990   "Jonah, the Runaway Servant." *Maarav* 5–6:281–305.

Ringgren, H.
1977   "Zur Komposition von Jesaja 49-55." Pp. 371–76 in *Beiträge zur alttestamentlichen Theologie: Festschrift für Walther Zimmerli zum 70. Geburtstag*. Ed. H. Donner, R. Hanhart, and R. Smend. Göttingen: Vandenhoeck & Ruprecht.

Robinson, B. P.
1985   "Jonah's Qiqayon Plant." *ZAW* 97:390–403.

Robinson, R. B.
1988   "Levels of Naturalization in Obadiah." *JSOT* 40:83–97.

Rofé, A.
1985   "Isaiah 66:1–4: Judean Sects in the Persian Period as Viewed by Trito-Isaiah." Pp. 205–17 in *Biblical and Related Studies Presented to Samuel Iwry*. Ed. A. Kort and S. Morschauser. Winona Lake, Ind.: Eisenbrauns.

Schmitt, H.-C.
1979   "Prophetie und Schultheologie im Deuterojesajabuch: Beobach-
        tungen zur Redaktionsgeschichte von Jes 40–55°." *ZAW* 91:43–
        61.

Schoors, A.
1973   *I am God Your Saviour: A Form-Critical Study of the Main Genres in Is
        XL–LV*. VTSup 24. Leiden: Brill.

Sehmsdorf, E.
1972   "Studien zur Redaktionsgeschichte von Jesaja 56–66." *ZAW*
        84:517–76.

Snyman, S. D.
1989   "Cohesion in the Book of Obadiah." *ZAW* 101:59–71.

Stuhlmueller, C.
1980   "Deutero-Isaiah (Chaps. 40–55): Major Transitions in the Proph-
        et's Theology and in Contemporary Scholarship." *CBQ* 42:1–29.

Vanoni, G.
1978   *Das Buch Jona: Literar- und formkritische Untersuchung*. St. Ottilien:
        EOS Verlag.

Walsh, J. T.
1982   "Jonah 2:3–10: A Rhetorical Critical Study." *Bib* 63:219–29.

Watts, J. D. W.
1969   *Obadiah: A Critical Exegetical Commentary*. Grand Rapids: Eerd-
        mans.

Weimar, P.
1984   "Jon 2,1–11: Jonapsalm und Jonaerzählung." *BZ* 28:43–68.

Wolff, H. W.
1986   *Obadiah and Jonah: A Commentary*. Trans. M. Kohl. Minneapolis:
        Augsburg.

Chapter 7: The Politics of the New Age

Ackroyd, P. R.
1977   "The Chronicler as Exegete." *JSOT* 2:2–32.

1988   "Chronicles-Ezra-Nehemiah: The Concept of Unity." *ZAW*
        100:189–201.

Baker, D. W.
1979   "Division Markers and the Structure of Leviticus 1–7." Pp. 9–15
        in *Studia Biblica 1978, I: Papers on Old Testament and Related Themes*.
        Ed. E. A. Livingstone. JSOTSS 11. Sheffield: JSOT Press.

Begg, C. T.
1988a   "The Classical Prophets in the Chronistic History." *BZ* 32:
        100–7.

1988b   "Babylon and Judah in Chronicles." *ETL* 64:142–52.

Blenkinsopp, J.
1988   *Ezra-Nehemia: A Commentary*. OTL. Philadelphia: Westminster.

Braun, R. L.
1979   "Chronicles, Ezra, and Nehemiah: Theology and Literary History." Pp. 52–64 in *Studies in the Historical Books of the Old Testament*. Ed. J. A. Emerton. VTSup 30. Leiden: Brill.

Carroll, R. P.
1980   "Prophecy and Dissonance: A Theoretical Approach to the Prophetic Tradition." *ZAW* 92:108–19.

Cross, F. M.
1975   "A Reconstruction of the Judean Restoration." *JBL* 94:4–18.

Deboys, D. G.
1990   "History and Theology in the Chronicler's Portrayal of Abijah." *Bib* 71:48–62.

Dillard, R. B.
1984   "The Literary Structure of the Chronicler's Solomon Narrative." *JSOT* 30:85–93.

Eph'al, I.
1978   "The Western Minorities in Babylonia in the 6th–5th Centuries B.C.: Maintenance and Cohesion." *Or* 47:74–90.

Eskenazi, T. C.
1986   "The Chronicler and the Composition of 1 Esdras." *CBQ* 48:39–61.

1988   *In an Age of Prose: A Literary Approach to Ezra-Nehemiah*. SBL Monograph Series 36. Atlanta: Scholars Press.

Freedman, D. N.
1961   "The Chronicler's Purpose." *CBQ* 23:436–42.

Glazier-McDonald, B.
1987   *Malachi: The Divine Messenger*. SBL Dissertation Series 98. Atlanta: Scholars Press.

Halpern, B.
1974   "Sectionalism and the Schism." *JBL* 93:519–32.

1981   "Sacred History and Ideology: Chronicles' Thematic Structure — Indications of an Earlier Source." Pp. 35–54 in *The Creation of Sacred Literature: Composition and Redaction of the Biblical Text*. Ed. R. E. Friedman. Berkeley: University of California Press.

Handy, L. K.
1988   "Hezekiah's Unlikely Reform." *ZAW* 100:111–15.

Hanson, P. D.
1971   "Jewish Apocalyptic against its Near Eastern Environment." *RB* 78:31–58.

Hill, A. E.
1982   "Dating Second Zechariah: A Linguistic Reexamination." *HAR* 6:105–34.

Hillers, D. R.
  1972   *Lamentations: Introduction, Translation and Notes*. AB 7A. Garden City, N.Y.: Doubleday.

Houtman, C.
  1981   "Ezra and the Law: Observations on the Supposed Relation between Ezra and the Pentateuch." *OTS* 21:91–115.

Japhet, S.
  1968   "The Supposed Common Authorship of Chronicles and Ezra-Nehemiah Investigated Anew." *VT* 18:330–71.

  1979   "Conquest and Settlement in Chronicles." *JBL* 98:205–18.

  1982–83 "Sheshbazzar and Zerubbabel—Against the Background of the Historical and Religious Tendencies of Ezra-Nehemiah." *ZAW* 94:66–98; 95:218–29.

Johnstone, W.
  1986   "Guilt and Atonement: The Theme of 1 and 2 Chronicles." Pp. 113–38 in *A Word in Season: Essays in Honour of William McKane*. Ed. J. D. Martin and P. R. Davies. JSOTSS 42. Sheffield: JSOT Press.

Kugel, J. L.
  1987   "On Hidden Hatred and Open Reproach: Early Exegesis of Leviticus 19:17." *HTR* 80:43–61.

Lescow, T.
  1990   "Dialogische Strukturen in den Streitreden des Buches Maleachi." *ZAW* 102:194–212.

Lipiński, E.
  1970   "Recherches sur le livre de Zacharie." *VT* 20:25–55.

McCarthy, D. J.
  1982   "Covenant and Law in Chronicles-Nehemiah." *CBQ* 44:25–44.

McConville, J. G.
  1986   "Ezra-Nehemiah and the Fulfillment of Prophecy." *VT* 36:205–24.

McEvenue, S. E.
  1981   "The Political Structure in Judah from Cyrus to Nehemiah." *CBQ* 43:353–64.

McKenzie, S. L., and H. N. Wallace
  1983   "Covenant Themes in Malachi." *CBQ* 45:549–63.

Mason, R. A.
  1977   "The Purpose of the 'Editorial Framework' of the Book of Haggai." *VT* 27:413–21.

  1982   "The Prophets of the Restoration." Pp. 137–54 in *Israel's Prophetic Tradition: Essays in Honour of Peter R. Ackroyd*. Ed. R. Coggins, A. Phillips, and M. Knibb. Cambridge: Cambridge University Press.

  1984   "Some Echoes of the Preaching in the Second Temple? Tradition Elements in Zechariah 1–8." *ZAW* 96:221–35.

Mosis, R.
 1973 *Untersuchungen zur Theologie des chronistischen Geschichtswerkes*. Freiburg: Herder.

Myers, J. M.
 1965a *I Chronicles*. AB 12. Garden City, N.Y.: Doubleday.

 1965b *II Chronicles*. AB 13. Garden City, N.Y.: Doubleday.

 1965c *Ezra-Nehemiah*. AB 14. Garden City, N.Y.: Doubleday.

North, R.
 1972 "Prophecy to Apocalyptic via Zechariah." Pp. 47–71 in *Congress Volume: Uppsala 1971*. VTSup 22. Leiden: Brill.

Petersen, D. L.
 1977 *Late Israelite Prophecy: Studies in Deutero-Prophetic Literature and in Chronicles*. SBL Monograph Series 23. Missoula, Mont.: Scholars Press.

 1984 *Haggai and Zechariah 1–8: A Commentary*. OTL. Philadelphia: Westminster.

Rendtorff, R.
 1984 "Esra und das 'Gesetz.' " *ZAW* 96:165–84.

Rosenbaum, J.
 1979 "Hezekiah's Reform and the Deuteronomistic Tradition." *HTR* 72:23–44.

Saley, R. J.
 1978 "The Date of Nehemiah Reconsidered." Pp. 151–65 in *Biblical and Near Eastern Studies: Essays in Honor of William Sanford LaSor*. Ed. G. A. Tuttle. Grand Rapids: Eerdmans.

Spalinger, A.
 1978 "The Concept of the Monarchy during the Saite Epoch—An Essay of Synthesis." *Or* 47:12–36.

Sperling, S. D.
 1989 "Rethinking Covenant in Late Biblical Books." *Bib* 70:50–73.

Steck, O. H.
 1971 "Zu Haggai 1:2–11." *ZAW* 83:355–79.

Throntveit, M. A.
 1982 "Linguistic Analysis and the Question of Authorship in Chronicles, Ezra and Nehemiah." *VT* 32:201–16.

van der Woude, A. S.
 1986 "Malachi's Struggle for a Pure Community: Reflections on Malachi 2:10–16." Pp. 65–71 in *Tradition and Re-Interpretation in Jewish and Early Christian Literature*. Ed. J. W. Van Heuten, J. H. de Jonge, P. T. van Rooden, and J. W. Wesselius. Leiden: Brill.

 1988 "Zion as Primeval Stone in Zechariah 3 and 4." Pp. 237–48 in *Text and Context: Old Testament and Semitic Studies for F. C. Fensham*. Ed. W. Claassen. JSOTSS 48. Sheffield: JSOT Press.

Watson, W. G. E.
1972   "Archaic Elements in the Language of Chronicles." *Bib* 53:191–207.

Weinberg, J. P.
1989   "Der König im Weltbild des Chronisten." *VT* 39:415–37.

Welten, P.
1973   *Geschichte und Geschichtsdarstellung in den Chronikbüchern.* Neukirchen-Vluyn: Neukirchener Verlag.

Westermann, D. C.
1986   "Zur Erforschung und zum Verständnis der prophetischen Heilsworte." *ZAW* 98:1–13.

Whedbee, J. W.
1978   "A Question-Answer Schema in Haggai 1: The Form and Function of Haggai 1:9–11." Pp. 184–94 in *Biblical and Near Eastern Studies: Essays in Honor of William Sanford LaSor.* Ed. G. A. Tuttle. Grand Rapids: Eerdmans.

Willi, T.
1972   *Die Chronik als Auslegung: Untersuchungen zur literarischen Gestaltung der historischen Überlieferung Israels.* Forschungen zur Religion und Literatur des Alten und Neuen Testaments 106. Göttingen: Vandenhoeck & Ruprecht.

Williamson, H. G. M.
1977   *Israel in the Books of Chronicles.* Cambridge: Cambridge University Press.

1979a   "Sources and Redaction in the Chronicler's Genealogy of Judah." *JBL* 98:351–59.

1979b   "The Origins of the Twenty-Four Priestly Courses: A Study of 1 Chronicles XXIII–XXVII." Pp. 251–69 in *Studies in the Historical Books of the Old Testament.* Ed. J. A. Emerton. VTSup 30. Leiden: Brill.

1982   *I and II Chronicles.* New Century Bible. Grand Rapids: Eerdmans.

1985   *Ezra, Nehemia.* Word Biblical Commentary 16. Waco, Tex.: Word Books.

Wilson, R. R.
1982   "From Prophecy to Apocalyptic: Reflections on the Shape of Israelite Religion." Pp. 79–95 in *Anthropological Perspectives on Old Testament Prophecy.* Ed. R. C. Culley and T. W. Overholt. Semeia 21. Chico, Calif.: Scholars Press.

Wolff, H. W.
1986   *Dodekapropheton 6: Haggai.* BKAT 14/6. Neukirchen-Vluyn: Neukirchener Verlag.

Zalewski, S.
1989   "The Purpose of the Story of the Death of Saul in 1 Chronicles X." *VT* 39:449–67.

Index of Authors

Index of Subjects

Index of Biblical References

❧